Psychology

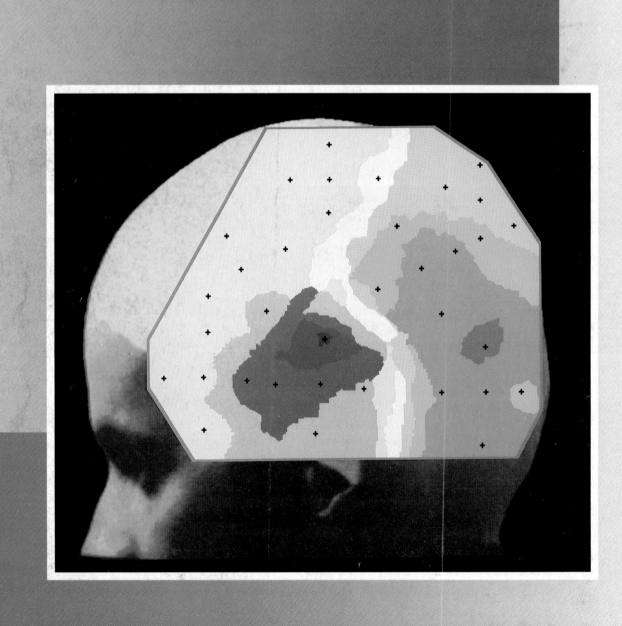

Psychology

An Introduction

Charles G. Morris
University of Michigan

Prentice Hall
Englewood Cliffs, New Jersey 07632

Seventh Edition

Library of Congress Cataloging-in-Publication Data

Morris, Charles G.
   Psychology: an introduction/Charles G. Morris.—7th ed.

      p.   cm.
   Includes bibliographical references.
   ISBN 0-13-732108-2
   1. Psychology.   I. Title.
BF121.M598   1990
150—dc20   89-38792
                                       CIP

Development editor: Leslie Carr
Editorial/production supervision: Marianne Peters
Interior design: Linda Conway and Christine Gehring-Wolf
Photo research: Anita Dickhuth
Photo editor: Lorinda Morris-Nantz
Interior art: Network Graphics
Manufacturing buyer: Ray Keating/Bob Anderson
Cover design: Bruce Kenselaar
Cover photo: Jackson Beatty
About the cover: This color MEG scan (or magnetoencephalograph) is a
composite produced by Jackson Beatty, Professor of Psychology at the
University of California, Los Angeles. The colored map of the MEG represents
the magnetic fields produced by the brain—in this case about one-tenth of a
second after being presented with a particular sound of human speech. Blue
indicates the strength of the field exiting the scalp; red, the intensity entering
the scalp; and white indicates zero or no magnetic field. Such maps give us
information from which the actual location of speech-related brain activity can
be estimated. MEG scans are discussed on page 51 of the text.

Chapter 12 opening photo: P. Giovanopoulos, *Mona Lisa* 1988, 72 × 54",
mixed/canvas. Photograph courtesy Louis K. Meisel Gallery, New York.

 © 1990, 1988, 1985, 1982, 1979, 1976, 1973 by Prentice-Hall, Inc.
A Division of Simon & Schuster
Englewood Cliffs, New Jersey 07632

Printed in the United States of America
10 9 8 7 6 5 4 3 2 1

ISBN 0-13-732108-2

Prentice-Hall International (UK) Limited, *London*
Prentice-Hall of Australia Pty. Limited, *Sydney*
Prentice-Hall Canada Inc., *Toronto*
Prentice-Hall Hispanoamericana, S.A., *Mexico*
Prentice-Hall of India Private Limited, *New Delhi*
Prentice-Hall of Japan, Inc., *Tokyo*
Simon & Schuster Asia Pte. Ltd., *Singapore*
Editora Prentice-Hall do Brasil, Ltda., *Rio de Janeiro*

Overview

Contents

Preface

Writing to teach, like teaching itself, is not so much a matter of presenting information as it is a matter of helping students *learn*—helping them to take information and transform it into something they can recall and refer to when the occasion demands: not just on a quiz or test but outside the course in the context of their own lives. In this edition of *Psychology: An Introduction*, a special effort has been made not only to ensure that students have the facts, terms, ideas, and research findings that form the basis of modern psychology, but also that material is presented in such a way that it can be learned and applied more effectively.

Starting with this edition, the process of learning has been integrated into both the text and the accompanying student Study Guide.

Integrating the Process of Learning into the Text

The structure of each chapter reflects the process of learning.

THINKING CRITICALLY. Each chapter begins with a series of questions called Thinking Critically, which is designed to engage student interest and curiosity and start the reader off on the process of learning. These questions get readers asking questions about the material *in advance of their reading the chapter*. That way, they are prepared to encounter the information of the chapter, but in a manner that is different from most other advance preparers—they are actually thinking questioningly or critically about the chapter material as they encounter it.

For example, in Chapter Five instead of asking students to consider, "What is shaping?" we ask, "How do you train a tiger to jump through a burning hoop?" Instead of asking them to consider the role of observation in learning, we ask them, "Why do so many children from abusive homes grow up to be abusive parents?"

The body of the chapter becomes the source of information used to answer the questions posed in Thinking Critically. As students read the chapter they are not just reading facts; they are actively gathering information that will enable them to answer the questions which open the chapter. For example, in the discussion of shaping in Chapter Five, students find the answer to the question, "How do you train a tiger to jump through a burning hoop?" as well as an additional example of how this learning principle was used to get a little boy to wear his glasses— a learned behavior that had a great impact on his enjoyment of school. These examples serve not only to link chapter content to the critical thinking questions, but also to transform abstract concepts, such as shaping, into a form that students can learn and use. Those using past editions of the text have indicated that this is one of its strongest features—the information is not just there, it's *accessible*.

Each Chapter Summary not only summarizes the key terms and concepts of the chapter, but also demonstrates how the content of the chapter answers the critical thinking questions posed at the start of the chapter. In the Chapter Summary, each of the critical thinking questions appears just before the concept or principle that provides the answer. The summary on shaping is preceded by the now-familiar question "How do you train a tiger to jump through a flaming hoop?" Returning to the critical thinking questions in this way helps integrate and reinforce the chapter and keeps the student engaged in the process of learning.

▤ Integrating the Process of Learning into the Study Guide

The completely new and quite remarkable Study Guide by Maria Lasaga of the University of Virginia offers a carefully crafted series of review and self-test exercises that build on each other. Students are first helped to master the factual material in each chapter. Once mastery has been achieved, the focus shifts to increasing comprehension of the chapter content and to applying that knowledge to new situations.

Each chapter in the Study Guide begins with a comprehensive list of Chapter Objectives that describes specifically what the student should be able to do after mastering the chapter content. Following the Chapter Objectives, student learning is strengthened through a series of multiple choice questions that progress from simple recognition of factual content to comprehension and deeper understanding of information and, finally, to application of chapter material to real-world situations.

Once the student has reached a minimal level of mastery of chapter content through the multiple choice questions, the process is repeated using fill-in-the-blank questions that require active recall of important information from the chapter as well as deeper comprehension of the material and increasing ability to apply the material to new situations.

Then, through a series of short-answer and essay questions, students are encouraged to further develop their comprehension of chapter content and to strengthen their ability to apply key concepts from the chapter to real-life situations with only minimal guidance.

The new Study Guide is an extraordinarily powerful learning tool that is, in my opinion, both unique and without equal. As such it is an important component in our attempt to make the Seventh Edition of *Psychology: An Introduction* an incomparable teaching and learning package. But there is more!

■ What Else Is New? New Coverage, Supplements, and a Means of Tying Together Some of the Threads That Run through the Introductory Course

Throughout the text there is a new, *ongoing* consideration of gender differences and similarities. In addition to describing what psychology has to say regarding some of the *common* principles underlying all behavior, I have put considerably greater emphasis in this edition on the ways in which people *differ* from one another. Are men really less emotional than women? Why are the prevalence rates for certain disorders higher for women than for men? Are women biologically superior to men in verbal ability? I ask students to consider these and other apparent gender differences thoughtfully and encourage them to look beyond their immediate reactions and consider the data that has thus far been gathered. Race and cultural differences, too, are discussed when data is available.

For students: A free workbook to help them learn the structures and functions of the nervous system. For many students, the biological basis for behavior is the most difficult aspect of the introductory course. With the assistance of Mark Kristal, a biological psychologist at the State University of New York at Buffalo, we created *A Guide to the Brain: A Graphic Workbook*. This booklet gives students a chance to quiz themselves visually on the structures and functions of the nervous system. As our understanding of the neurological bases of behavior has grown, discussions of the role of the brain and other structures of the nervous system have come to play a part in many chapters, making this a valuable reference for students throughout the course.

An Expanded Annotated Instructor's Edition with Cross-Chapter Connections. It is not surprising that it is difficult for students to understand the connections among the disparate topics that make up the introductory course. What are students to make of a discipline that studies the social development of adolescents and the spatial memory of rats? Yet there are topics or threads that cut across the various content areas in psychology and that therefore run through the introductory course. Psychologists must draw from virtually every corner of the discipline to understand such things as sleep and dreaming, stress and adjustment, human sexual behavior, and work and careers. Therefore, I have included in the Instructor's Manual portion of the Annotated Instructor's Edition a set of cross references that show where these and other similarly broad topics are discussed in the book. Following these threads across chapters can provide students with the kind of birds-eye view that helps make the information they've learned more coherent.

The marginal annotations in the Instructor's Edition have also been greatly expanded, thanks to the thoughtful work of Ann Weber, a professor at the University of North Carolina at Asheville who not only has introduced a great many students to psychology, but also has managed to do so in a way that is both fun and illuminating. She has added points of humor and trivia, lots of extra examples to illustrate key points, dozens of new discussion questions and numerous bits of background information as well as teaching tips. The marginal annotations also contain references to lectures, films, and videos and to the related transparencies available from The Prentice Hall Slide and Transparency Series II, all of which enhance the material in the textbook.

For professors: A new set of Handout and Transparency Masters that can be used to stimulate class discussion and enhance lectures. We have pulled together a set of questionnaires and graphs that you can use as handouts or overheads. Many are adaptations of actual research questionnaires (on self-efficacy, for example), others are geared to helping students assess their own attitudes, study skills, and abilities.

Additional New Content Coverage

In a dynamic field such as psychology, there are always plenty of new discoveries to consider when revising. What follows is a partial list of the areas that have been updated and revised in the Seventh Edition.

CHAPTER ONE. New material on the process of inquiry employed by psychologists showing how the answer to one question often prompts other, more pointed questions. A new section introducing the importance of considering gender, racial, and cultural differences when analyzing the results of psychological research. New research on the extent to which the study of psychology can teach students how to be skeptical of so-called commonsense. Updated information on animal rights has also been added.

CHAPTER TWO. Updated information on hemispheric brain differences and the role they may play in dyslexia. New data from the Minnesota Twins Study supporting the role of genetics in determining who we are. This coverage of the importance of genetics is balanced by a new discussion of the role of the environment in human development. There is also new material on computer simulations of neural networks.

CHAPTER THREE. New coverage of parallel processing of sensory information in the brain, new information on motion perception, and a discussion of the way in which touch can serve as a fast and accurate substitute for sight.

CHAPTER FOUR. A new discussion of consciousness as a process rather than a series of levels or states. New coverage of Kihlstrom's work on automatic processing, the fantasy-prone, and the relationship between circadian rhythms and the effects of drugs. New research on dreams as mental housekeeping and "lucid" dreamers which shows that our physiological responses during dreams are very close to those in normal, waking life. Updated information on crack and its effects on the pleasure centers in the brain.

CHAPTER FIVE. Includes expanded coverage of Rescorla's contingency theory and the connection between contemporary research in animal learning and our understanding of human behavior. Expanded coverage of animal cognition and spatial memory in rats. Updated information on taste aversion; new coverage of optimization theory and choice behavior and their effects on economic decision-making.

CHAPTER SIX. New material on working memory, and the role vocalization may play. New coverage of schema theory: how schemas form a framework upon which we base or form recollections; also how they determine what we recall. New information on the revisability of autobiographical memory and its effect on adjustment. New coverage of the neurophysiology of memory—the role of the hippocampus in stimulating the development of new neural circuits via longterm potentiation (LTP) and the role of the receptor molecule, NMDA, in this process. New research on how restructuring of police lineups can improve the reliability of eyewitness identification and new ways of helping eyewitnesses recall more of the scene of an event. A new discussion of the sorts of memories (such as for the location of a piece of information on a page) we process automatically.

CHAPTER SEVEN. This chapter has been reorganized so that the material on problem solving and decision-making now directly follows the discussion of thinking. The discussion of language and language development now appears at the end of the chapter. New coverage of concept formation in pigeons, and expanded and updated coverage of artificial intelligence.

CHAPTER EIGHT. Expanded coverage of Sternberg's triarchic theory. Updated information on the difficulty of measuring creativity and individuals' ability to adapt to the environment. A new examination of the debate regarding the relationship between birth order and IQ scores; coverage of the effect of mothers' expectations on their daughters' math scores. Includes a new discussion of mainstreaming for the mentally retarded. Expanded discussion of the value of enrichment programs for older children.

CHAPTER NINE. Includes an expanded discussion of the relative virtues of longitudinal and cross-sectional studies; updated coverage of newborns' and infants' perceptual abilities. New discussion of the relationship between development and experience and the effects of the loss of a parent due to death or divorce. New research on working mothers and the effects of day-care on infant attachment as well as recent research on the use and abuse of television as an educational tool and as a persuasive medium.

CHAPTER TEN. New section on gender differences and similarities in sexual development; contraceptive use and the risk of AIDS among adolescents and young adults.

CHAPTER ELEVEN. Added coverage of Robert Zajonc's research on facial expression and emotion; a new section on gender differences and emotion that continues the discussion begun in Chapter One.

CHAPTER TWELVE. New coverage of the "Big Five" personality traits and coverage of the most recent revision of the MMPI. New material on the frequency and usage of personality tests. Expanded coverage of the genetic basis for differences in temperament between inhibited (shy) children and uninhibited children.

CHAPTER THIRTEEN. Redefines stress in terms of demands on adjustment. Expanded discussion of sources of stress which includes discrimination and self-imposed (cognitive) stress. Updated and expanded coverage of the physiological effects of stress including effects on the immune system.

CHAPTER FOURTEEN. Now includes an extensive discussion of gender differences in the prevalence rates of various psychological disorders. Why are women more likely to be treated for depression? Why are men more likely to suffer from personality disorders?

CHAPTER FIFTEEN. New coverage of the role and effectiveness of self-help groups in treating mental disorders. Includes a new section on gender differences in treatments and the potential for treatments to be subtly biased in favor of a male-oriented definition of what is normal or appropriate behavior.

CHAPTER SIXTEEN. New coverage of the role of schemas in social perceptions. Expanded discussion of the link between similarity and interpersonal attractiveness.

Acknowledgments

The seventh edition of a textbook naturally involves the present and past contributions of numerous people. With the publication of this edition

I wish to acknowledge all those associated with the former editions. The book continues to reflect their ideas and expertise.

The Seventh Edition has also benefitted from the extensive critical reviews by interested and knowledgeable professionals. I am indebted to the following for their invaluable assistance:

Scott Allison
University of Richmond

Carol Mohr Batt
Washington State University

Sherry Broadwell
Georgia Southern College

Albert M. Bugaj
University of Wisconsin, Richland

Andrea Colangelo
The Berkeley School

Mark K. Covey
University of Idaho

Marc Des Lauriers
Kansas City Kansas Community College

Jack W. Divine
Crowder College

Paul D. Donn
Central Michigan University

Della Ferguson
Utica College

Charles L. Fry
University of Virginia

Betty Land Gaines
Midland College

Frank X. Healey
Lackawanna Jr. College

Lyllian B. Hix
Houston Community College

Victor Indrisano
Marymount University

Pamela J. Johns
California State University, Stanislaus

Irwin Kahn
Ferris State University

Laura Kast
Washington State University

Patricia A. Kondrick
Washington State University

W. H. Lee-Sammons

Washington State University

Jerry Lehman
University of South Carolina, Spartanburg

Wayne A. Lesko
Marymount University

Susan E. MacNeill
Washington State University

Mary E. Maier
St. Louis College of Pharmacy

James R. Marks
West Los Angeles College

Cam L. Melville
Washington State University

Cindy Miller-Perrin
Washington State University

Refilwe L. Moeti
Georgia State University

George R. Mount
Mountain View College

Timothy M. Osberg
Niagara University

George L. Parrott
California State University, Sacramento

Gordon H. Raynor
Hillsborough Community College, Dale Mabry Campus

Valda Robinson
Hillsborough Community College, Dale Mabry Campus

Dale Rosenberg
North Iowa Area Community College

John S. Rosenkoetter
Southwest Missouri State University

Tirzah G. Schutzengel
Bergen Community College

Adolph Streng, Jr.
Eastfield College

Ross A. Thompson
University of Nebraska, Lincoln

Rene E. Villa
Hillsborough Community
    College, Dale Mabry Campus
Howell A. Watkins
Midland College
Georgann Wemple
Odessa College

Loren C. Wingblade
Indiana University, Bloomington
Pete Wylie
Western Oklahoma State College
Kaye Young
North Iowa Area Community
    College

We were also fortunate to have the guidance of a group of specialist reviewers whose exhaustive comments will be improving not only this edition, but those to come:

Vincent Adesso
University of Wisconsin,
    Milwaukee
Janet Andrews
Vassar College
Robert Beck
Wake Forest University
Michael Best
Southern Methodist University
Rich Carlson
Pennsylvania State University,
    University Park
Robert Guttentag
University of North Carolina,
    Greensboro
Timothy Johnston
University of North Carolina,
    Greensboro

Robin Lewis
Old Dominion University
Doug Matheson
University of the Pacific
Jim Mazur
Southern Connecticut State
    University
Jill Morawski
Wesleyan University
John Pittenger
University of Arkansas
William Ray
Pennsylvania State University,
    University Park
Ann Weber
University of North Carolina,
    Asheville
Richard M. Wielkiewicz
College of St. Benedict

Various members of the Prentice Hall staff also deserve special thanks and recognition. Editorial Director Will Ethridge; Susan Willig, Editor-in-Chief of the Social Sciences and her assistant, Shirley Chlopak; Art Director Florence Silverman; Interior Designers Linda Conway and Christine Gehring-Wolf; Manufacturing Buyer Bob Anderson; Director of Photo Archives Lorinda Morris-Nantz—all have contributed immeasurably to this edition. I would also like to mention Marketing Managers Terri Peterson and Roland Hernandez, who have put vigorous effort into this edition.

The production of the Seventh Edition was supervised by Marianne Peters, to whom I am indebted for her hard work and high degree of professionalism.

Finally, I would like to thank my editor, Leslie Carr, whose expertise, good spirits, and tireless efforts in the face of a tight schedule helped immeasurably to make this edition of the book possible.

1

The Science of Psychology

■ Thinking Critically

What am I going to get from this course? What is psychology really about?

Did psychology begin with Freud?

Why is the title of this chapter the Science of Psychology? How is psychology like physics and other sciences?

Do all psychologists see patients?

Do psychologists study behavior simply by watching people?

Is it fair to use people in experiments without telling them what the experiment is about?

Why are animals used in psychological research? What can animals tell us about human behavior? Are there protections to assure that animals are not mistreated?

Answers to these and other questions about the field of psychology appear in this chapter and in the Chapter Summary.

■ Outline

Psychology The scientific study of behavior and mental processes.

Scientific method Approach to knowledge characterized by collecting data, formulating a hypothesis, and testing the hypothesis empirically.

Why are you taking a psychology course? What would you like to learn from it? What questions would you like to have answered?

When students like you were asked these questions, they mentioned things like:

- What is motivation? Why do some people have more of it than others? Why does it sometimes disappear?
- How much of a person's behavior (if any) is inherited?
- How valid are IQ tests? Do IQ tests and tests like the SAT and ACT really tell us how well we are likely to do in school?
- What is the best and most effective way to learn?
- What effects do different types of punishment have on children's behavior?
- What influence do parents have on their children's personalities?
- How does the brain function? How does it affect our behavior?
- Does ESP exist?
- Who determines what is classified as "abnormal behavior"? Is any type of behavior truly abnormal?
- How successful is psychotherapy in curing psychological problems?
- How do you explain the similarities between twins who have grown up in different environments?
- Are humans naturally aggressive?
- Does the person shape behavior or does behavior shape the person?
- Why major in psychology? Does it have practical uses? How does psychology relate to other fields?
- Of what use is psychology to the average person in today's society?

As you can see, psychology students have a surprising number and variety of interests. Surely you share some of them. Like most people, you are probably curious about such things as intelligence testing and how heredity affects behavior; about the development of personality; about "abnormal behavior" and how psychologists treat it. And like most students, you are probably wondering what exactly psychology is and whether it is a practical field of study.

It is also likely that you have begun to develop your own answers to these kinds of questions. We all like to observe ourselves and others. We exchange our various experiences, philosophies, and advice with friends. We speculate on why people sometimes act as they do and think about how they might act in other situations. And over time, we each begin to develop our own ideas about human psychology.

Psychologists share your interest in behavior and the unseen mental processes that shape behavior. But they approach these topics in a somewhat different way. **Psychology** is the science of behavior and mental processes. Thus, psychologists use techniques based on the **scientific method** when they seek answers to questions such as these. The scientific method seeks to answer a question by collecting data through careful observation, formulating a hypothesis about the significance of those data, and testing the hypothesis empirically. Later on in this chapter, we'll look at some of the techniques that psychologists use, but first it is worth noting that psychology was not always based on the scientific method. In fact, the scientific method has been applied to psychological issues only for about the last 100 years. Before that time, psychology was not a formal discipline at all but a branch of the general field of philosophy. Let's begin with an overview of the growth of the *science* of psychology.

■ The Growth of Psychology

Wundt and Titchener: Structuralism

In 1879, Wilhelm Wundt, physiologist and philosopher at the University of Leipzig in Germany, founded the first psychological laboratory. Wundt had stated his intentions plainly five years before in his *Principles of Physiological Psychology*, in which he had argued that the mind must be studied objectively and scientifically. The book had not attracted much attention, and few people took Wundt seriously. In fact, only four students attended his first lecture.

Wilhelm Wundt

Considering how radical Wundt's views actually were, it is surprising that they went unchallenged at the time. For centuries, people had regarded their own mental processes with awe. Plato, for example, had divided the world into two realms, with mind being pure and abstract and all else physical and mundane. Yet Wundt argued that thinking is a natural event like any other—like wind in a storm or the beating of a heart. Why did this radical view go unchallenged? For one thing, British philosophers like Thomas Hobbes and John Locke had already asserted that physical sensations were the basis of thought. Moreover, by 1879 the scientific method commanded great respect in the academic community. And then, perhaps most important of all, there was Charles Darwin. The traditionalists of the day had their hands full fighting the concept of evolution. Compared to the implications of evolutionary theory, Wundt's scientific psychology seemed tame.

By the mid-1880s, however, Wundt's new psychological lab had attracted many students. Wundt's main concern at this point was with techniques for uncovering the natural laws of the human mind. In order to find the basic units of thought, he began by looking at the process by which we create meaningful patterns out of sensory stimuli. When we look at a banana, for example, we immediately think, "Here is a fruit, something to peel and eat." But these are associations based on past experience. All we *see* is a long yellow object.

Wundt and his co-workers wanted to strip perception of its associations in order to find the very *atoms* of thought. In order to do this, they trained themselves in the art of objective introspection, observing and recording their perceptions and feelings. Some days, for example, were spent listening to the ticking of a metronome. Which rhythms are most pleasant? Does a fast tempo excite, a slow beat relax? They recorded their reactions in minute detail, including measures of their heartbeats and respiration rates. However crude and irrelevant all this may seem to us today, it did introduce measurement and experiment into psychology and thus marked the beginning of psychology as a science.

Perhaps the most important product of the Leipzig lab was its students; they took the new science to universities around the world. Among them was Edward Bradford Titchener. British by birth, Titchener became the leader of American psychology soon after he was appointed professor of psychology at Cornell University, a post that he held until his death in 1927.

Psychology, Titchener wrote, is the science of consciousness—physics with the observer kept in. In physics, an hour or a mile is an exact measure. To the *observer*, however, an hour may seem to pass in seconds, while a mile may seem endless. According to Titchener, psychology is the study of such experiences. Titchener broke experience down into three basic elements: physical sensations (including sights and sounds); affections or feelings (which are like sensations, but less clear); and images (such as memories and dreams). When we recognize a banana, according to Titchener's scheme, we combine a physical sensation (what we see) with feelings (liking or disliking bananas) and images (memories of other bananas). Even the most complex thoughts and feelings, Titchener argued, can be reduced to these simple elements. Psychology's role is to identify these elements and show how they are combined. Because it stresses the basic units of experience and the combinations in which they occur, this school of psychology is called **structuralism.**

Edward Bradford Titchener

Sir Francis Galton: Individual Differences

Meanwhile, in England, Francis Galton, Darwin's half-cousin, was dabbling in medicine, experimenting with electricity, charting weather, and poring over the biographies of famous people. His motto was "Whenever you can, count" (Diamond, 1977). He also found time to explore the Sudan and Southwest Africa. Born into a rich and eminent family, Galton never had to work for a living. Throughout his life, he remained an intellectual adventurer—to the great gain of psychology and several other fields. Galton was a pioneer in the development of mental tests and the study of characteristics that distinguish one person from another. Impressed by the number of exceptional people in his own family, Galton set out to study other eminent families in England, and in the process he came to propose that genius might be hereditary. Intrigued, he invented tests to measure individual capacities and worked out ways of comparing the scores. He found a wide range of abilities and complex relations between one ability and another. Later, he became interested in mental imagery and word associations. With himself as subject, he wrote down the first two things called to mind by each of 75 words. He then tried to explain his reactions in terms of his past experiences. Madness also fascinated Galton. He decided that the best way to study madness was to become mad himself. He thus began to pretend that everyone he saw on his walks through the park was out to get him—including the dogs.

Sir Francis Galton

William James: Functionalism

William James, the first American-born psychologist, was as versatile and innovative as Galton. In his youth, he studied chemistry, physiology, anatomy, biology, and medicine. Then, in 1872, he accepted an offer to teach physiology at Harvard. There James read philosophy in his spare time and began to see a link between it and physiology. The two seemed to converge in psychology.

In 1875, James began a class in psychology at Harvard (he later commented that the first lecture he ever heard on the subject was his own). He set aside part of his laboratory for psychological experiments. He also began work on a text, *The Principles of Psychology*, which was published in 1890.

In preparing his lectures and his textbook, James studied structuralist writings thoroughly and decided that something in Wundt's and Titchener's approach was wrong. He concluded that atoms of experience—pure sensations without associations—simply did not exist. Our minds are constantly weaving associations, revising experience, starting, stopping, jumping back and forth in time. Consciousness, James argued, is a continuous flow. Perceptions and associations, sensations and emotions, cannot be separated. When we look at a banana, we see a banana, not a long yellow object.

Still focusing on everyday experience, James turned to the study of habit. We do not have to think about how to get up in the morning, get dressed, open a door, or walk down the street. James suggested that when we repeat something several times, our nervous systems are changed so that each time we open a door, it is easier to open than the last time.

This was the link he needed. The biologist in him firmly believed that all activity—from the beating of the heart to the perception of objects—was functional. If we could not recognize a banana, we would have to figure out what it was each time we saw one. Thus, mental associations allow us to benefit from previous experience.

With this insight, James arrived at a **functionalist theory** of mental life and behavior. Functionalist theory is concerned not just with learning or sensation or perception, but rather with how an organism uses its learning or perceptual abilities to function in its environment. James also argued for the value of subjective (untrained) introspection and insisted that psychology should focus on everyday, true-to-life experiences.

In 1894, one of James's students, James R. Angell, became the head of the new department of psychology at the University of Chicago. John Dewey, who had studied structuralist psychology at Johns Hopkins, became professor of philosophy at Chicago that same year. Together they made Chicago the center of the functionalist school of psychology. Both Angell and Dewey pioneered the application of functional psychology to problems and principles of education.

John B. Watson: Behaviorism

John.B. Watson was the first student to receive a doctorate in psychology from the University of Chicago. His dissertation was on learning in rats. One of the department's requirements was that he speculate on the kind of consciousness that produced the behavior that he observed in his rats. Watson found this absurd. He doubted the rats had any consciousness at all. Nevertheless, he complied with the regulations, received his degree, and returned to his laboratory to think about consciousness.

Ten years and many experiments later, Watson was ready to confront both the structuralist and functionalist schools with his own ideas about consciousness and behavior. In "Psychology as the Behaviorist Views It"

Functionalist theory Theory of mental life and behavior that is concerned with how an organism uses its perceptual abilities to function in its environment.

William James

(1913), he argued that the whole idea of consciousness, of mental life, was superstition, a relic from the Middle Ages. You cannot define consciousness any more than you can define a soul, Watson argued. You cannot locate it or measure it, and therefore it cannot be the object of scientific study. For Watson, psychology was the study of observable, measurable behavior—and nothing more.

The view that Watson adopted was based largely on Ivan Pavlov's famous experiments. Some years before Watson's article appeared, this Russian physiologist had noticed that the dogs in his laboratory began to drool as soon as they heard their feeder coming—even before they could see their dinner. Pavlov had always thought that salivation was a natural response to the presence of food, so he found the dogs' anticipatory response odd. He decided to see if he could teach them to drool at the sound of a ringing bell even when no food was in the room. He explained his successful results as follows: All behavior is a response to some stimulus or agent in the environment. In ordinary life, food makes dogs salivate. All Pavlov did was to train his animals to respond to the sound of a bell as they had previously responded to the presence of food. He called this training **conditioning.**

In a famous experiment with an 11-month-old child, Watson showed that people's behavior can also be conditioned. Little Albert was a secure, happy baby who had no reason to fear soft, furry white rats. But each time Albert reached out to pet the rat that Watson offered him, Watson made a loud noise that frightened Albert. It wasn't long before Albert was afraid of white rats (Watson & Rayner, 1920). Thus, conditioning changed the child's behavior radically.

Watson was also interested in showing that fears could also be eliminated by conditioning. Mary Cover Jones (1924), one of his graduate students, successfully reconditioned a boy who showed a fear of rabbits (not caused by laboratory conditioning) to overcome this fear. Her technique, that of first presenting the rabbit at a great distance and then gradually bringing the rabbit closer while the child was eating, is similar to techniques used today.

Watson saw no reason to refer to consciousness or mental life in order to explain this change. Little Albert simply responded to the environment—in this case, the coincidence of the loud noises and white, furry objects. Watson felt that the same was true for everyone—that all behavior could be explained with the stimulus-response formula. Psychology, he felt, must be purged of "mentalism."

In the 1920s, when Watson's behaviorist theory was first published, American psychologists had all but exhausted the structuralist approach. Wundtian experiments had lost their novelty and attraction. So Watson's orthodox scientific approach (if you cannot see it and measure it, forget it) found a warm audience.

Gestalt Psychology

Meanwhile, in Germany, a group of psychologists was attacking structuralism from another angle. Max Wertheimer, Wolfgang Köhler, and Kurt Koffka were all interested in perception, but particularly in certain tricks that the mind plays on itself. Why, they asked, when we are shown a series of still pictures flashed at a constant rate, do they seem to move

John B. Watson

Mary Cover Jones

(for example, movies or "moving" neon signs)? The eye sees only a series of still pictures. What makes us perceive motion?

The structuralists, as you will recall, wanted to break perception down into its elements. A trained Wundtian introspectionist, for example, would see nothing but six dots in Figure 1-1. But Wertheimer and his colleagues argued that anyone else looking at such a figure would see a triangle and a line formed by the dots.

Phenomena like these were the force behind a new school of thought, **Gestalt psychology.** Roughly translated from the German, *gestalt* means "whole" or "form." When applied to perception, it refers to our tendency to see patterns, to distinguish an object from its background, to complete pictures from a few cues. Like James, the Gestalt psychologists thought that the attempt to break perception and thought down into their elements was misguided. When we look at a tree, we see just that, a tree, not a series of branches.

In the 1930s, Nazism was on the rise, and the Gestalt school broke up. Wertheimer, Köhler, and Koffka all eventually settled in the United States.

B. F. Skinner: Behaviorism Revisited

Behaviorism was already thriving when the Gestalt psychologists reached the United States. B. F. Skinner was one of the leaders of behaviorism. Like Watson, Skinner believed that psychology should study only observable and measurable behavior. He too was primarily interested in changing behavior through conditioning—and in discovering natural laws of behavior in the process. But his approach was subtly different from that of his predecessor.

Watson had changed little Albert's behavior by gradually changing the stimulus. For Albert to learn a fear of white rats, Watson had to repeat the same experience over and over, making a loud noise every time Albert saw a rat. Skinner added a new element: **reinforcement.** He rewarded his subjects for behaving the way that he wanted them to behave. For example, an animal (rats and pigeons were Skinner's favorite subjects) was put in a special cage and allowed to explore. Eventually, the animal reached up and pressed a lever or pecked at a disk on the wall. A food pellet dropped into the box. Gradually, the animal learned that pressing the bar or pecking at the disk always brought food. Why did the animal learn this? Because it was reinforced, or rewarded. Skinner thus made the animal an active agent in its own conditioning.

Sigmund Freud: Psychoanalytic Psychology

It is hard to believe that **psychoanalysis** was once the dark horse of psychology. Sigmund Freud, who practiced in Vienna, was largely unknown in the United States until the late 1920s. By then, Freud had forged his clinical discoveries into a comprehensive theory of mental life that differed radically from the views of American psychologists.

Freud believed that much of our behavior is governed by hidden motives and unconscious desires. He proposed a series of critical stages that we must pass through in the first years of life. We must successfully resolve the conflicts that we meet at each stage in order to avoid psy-

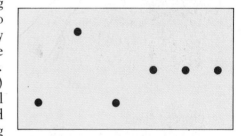

Figure 1-1

B.F. Skinner

7

Psychotherapy Use of psychological techniques to treat personality and behavior disorders.

Existential psychology School of psychology that sees the meaninglessness and alienation of modern life as leading to apathy and psychological problems.

Humanistic psychology School of psychology that emphasizes nonverbal experience and altered states of consciousness as a means of realizing one's full human potential.

Cognitive psychology School of psychology devoted to the study of mental processes generally.

chological problems later on. Unfortunately, it is possible to become "fixated" at any one of these stages and carry related feelings of anxiety or exaggerated fears with us into adulthood.

Freud not only emphasized childhood experiences, but he also maintained that many unconscious desires are sexual. A little boy at age five, Freud argued, desires his mother and wishes to destroy his father, who is his rival. Of all Freud's concepts, the influence of the sexual drive on the formation of personality has been the most controversial. Many of his colleagues rejected his viewpoint. Alfred Adler felt that it was the child's struggle to overcome a sense of inferiority that was central to forming personality. Carl Jung looked to the individual's impetus to self-realization in the context of the racial history and religious impulse of the human species.

Nonetheless, Freudian theory has had a huge impact on academic psychology (particularly on the study of personality and abnormal behavior), and it is still influential, as we shall see. Freud also founded **psychotherapy,** which uses psychological techniques to treat personality and behavior disorders.

Existential and Humanistic Psychology

Existential psychology, as the name suggests, draws on the existential philosophy made popular in the 1940s by, among others, Jean-Paul Sartre. Existential psychologists are concerned with meaninglessness and alienation in modern life, for they believe that these feelings lead to apathy, fear, and other psychological problems. Psychoanalyst Rollo May, for example, argues that modern Americans are lost souls—a people without myths and heroes. R.D. Laing, another existentialist, believes that we must reevaluate our attitude toward psychotic behavior. Such behavior, according to Laing, is not abnormal, but is rather a reasonable, normal response to an abnormal world. Existential psychology seeks to help people find an inner sense of identity so that they can achieve freedom and take responsibility for their actions.

Humanistic psychology is closely related to existential psychology. Both argue that people must learn how to realize their potential. But where existential psychology emphasizes restoring an inner sense of identity and willpower, humanistic psychology focuses on the possibilities of nonverbal experience, the unity of mind, altered states of consciousness, and letting go.

Existential and humanistic viewpoints have never predominated in American psychology, but they continue to be influential, particularly in the understanding of personality and abnormal behavior, as we shall see.

Cognitive Psychology

In the past decade or two, a new perspective has begun to emerge and shape the field of psychology. **Cognitive psychology** is the study of our mental processes in the broadest sense: thinking, feeling, learning, remembering, and so on. According to cognitive psychologists, there is more to our behavior than simple responses to stimuli. For example, once we see what happens when we respond to a stimulus, our understanding

Sigmund Freud

of that stimulus changes, and it is this cognitive understanding that guides our future behavior. Thus, cognitive psychologists are especially interested in the ways in which people perceive, interpret, store, and retrieve information.

In contrast to the behaviorists, cognitive psychologists believe that mental processes can and should be studied scientifically. Although we cannot observe cognitive processes directly, we can observe behavior and make inferences about the kinds of cognitive processes that underlie that behavior. For example, we can read a lengthy story to people and then observe the kinds of things that they remember, the ways in which their recollections change over time, and the sorts of errors that occur. On the basis of systematic research of this kind, it is possible to gain insight into the cognitive processes that underlie human memory, for example.

Although cognitive psychology is relatively young, it has already had an enormous impact on almost every area of psychology. Even the definition of psychology has changed as a result. Ten years ago, most introductory psychology texts defined psychology simply as the scientific study of behavior. Now many of those same texts point out that "behavior" includes thoughts, feelings, experiences, and so on. Other texts, including this one, now define psychology as the scientific study of behavior and mental processes. You will see the influence of cognitive psychology throughout this book.

Rollo May

■ Areas within Psychology Today

You now have some idea about the major theoretical viewpoints in psychology. Another way to view the field is to look at the kinds of interests and concerns that psychologists have. Like so many other professionals in society these days—from physicians to professional football players—psychologists have become specialists. As they study problems, they come across new questions that require examination, which raises further questions, and on and on. New areas of research continually emerge, and psychologists tend to become even more specialized. The American Psychological Association, for example, is made up of 45 divisions (see Table 1-1), each of which represents an area of special interest to contemporary psychologists.

A good way to appreciate the concerns of the various specialties of psychology is to take a single issue and see what questions each specialist might ask about it. Let's take the following question: Are there sex differences in behavior, and if so, what causes those differences?

DEVELOPMENTAL PSYCHOLOGY. The developmental psychologist studies mental and physical growth in humans from the prenatal period through childhood, adolescence, adulthood, and old age. The child psychologist is a developmental psychologist who specializes in the study of children. Developmental psychologists would be especially interested in the age at which various gender differences in behavior begin to emerge, whether the differences increase or decrease as men and women grow older, and what causes the differences.

TABLE 1-1 1989 AMERICAN PSYCHOLOGY ASSOCIATION DIVISIONS

Division*

1. General Psychology
2. Teaching of Psychology
3. Experimental Psychology
5. Evaluation, Measurement, and Statistics
6. Physiological and Comparative Psychology
7. Developmental Psychology
8. Personality and Social Psychology
9. Society for the Psychological Study of Social Issues
10. Psychology and the Arts
12. Clinical Psychology
13. Consulting Psychology
14. Society for Industrial and Organizational Psychology
15. Educational Psychology
16. School Psychology
17. Counseling Psychology
18. Psychologists in Public Service
19. Military Psychology
20. Adult Development and Aging
21. Applied Experimental and Engineering Psychologists
22. Rehabilitation Psychology
23. Consumer Psychology
24. Theoretical and Philosophical Psychology
25. Experimental Analysis of Behavior
26. History of Psychology
27. Community Psychology
28. Psychopharmacology
29. Psychotherapy
30. Psychological Hypnosis
31. State Psychological Association Affairs
32. Humanistic Psychology
33. Mental Retardation and Developmental Disabilities
34. Population and Environmental Psychology
35. Psychology of Women
36. Psychologists Interested in Religious Issues
37. Child, Youth, and Family Services
38. Health Psychology
39. Psychoanalysis
40. Clinical Neuropsychology
41. American Psychology-Law Society
42. Psychologists in Independent Practice
43. Family Psychology
44. Society for the Psychological Study of Lesbian and Gay Issues
45. Society for the Psychological Study of Ethnic Minority Issues
46. Media Psychology
47. Exercise and Sport Psychology

*There are no Divisions 4 or 11.

PHYSIOLOGICAL PSYCHOLOGY. Physiological psychologists investigate the extent to which behavior is caused by physical conditions in the body. They concentrate particularly on the brain, the nervous system, and the body's biochemistry. They would be especially interested in whether differences in behavior between men and women are due to differences in the nervous system or biochemistry.

EXPERIMENTAL PSYCHOLOGY. Experimental psychologists investigate such basic processes as learning, memory, sensation, perception, cognition, motivation, and emotion. They would be particularly interested in any differences in the way men and women store and retrieve information from memory, the way they process sensory information, and the way they go about solving complex problems.

PERSONALITY PSYCHOLOGY. Personality psychologists study the differences in traits among people, such as anxiety, sociability, self-esteem, the need for achievement, and aggressiveness. They would be interested in whether men and women differ on traits such as these, as well as on other characteristics such as intelligence and self-concept.

CLINICAL AND COUNSELING PSYCHOLOGY. About half of all psychologists specialize in clinical or counseling psychology. Clinical psychologists are interested in the diagnosis, causes, and treatment of abnormal behavior. Counseling psychologists are concerned with "normal" problems of adjustment that most of us face sooner or later, such as choosing a career or coping with marital problems. Clinical psychologists would be interested in whether men experience certain kinds of behavior disorders more or less often than women, the causes of such differences, and whether men and women differ in their responsiveness to various kinds of psychotherapy. Counseling psychologists would be more interested in gender differences in the kinds of personal day-to-day problems that men and women must face, as well as differences in the way that they cope with those problems.

SOCIAL PSYCHOLOGY. Social psychologists investigate the influence of people on one another. How are people influenced by those around them? Why do we like some people and dislike others? Do opposites really attract? Do people behave differently in groups from the way they behave when they are alone? Social psychologists would be interested in whether men and women differ in their responses to persuasive messages and in the kinds of roles that they tend to play when in groups.

INDUSTRIAL/ORGANIZATIONAL PSYCHOLOGY. Industrial and organizational psychologists address the problems of training personnel, improving working conditions, and studying the effects of automation on humans. They would be interested in whether organizations tend to operate differently under the leadership of women as opposed to men, as well as in the effect of male and female administrators on morale and productivity.

■ The Goals and Methods of Psychology

At this point, you've read about the major viewpoints in psychology and about many of the specialty areas in psychology today. By now you may be wondering whether there is any common thread to it all. What is there that draws these different viewpoints and interests together under the single heading "psychology"? One answer is that psychologists, regardless of their theoretical veiwpoints or areas of interest, share common goals and methods. Like all scientists, psychologists seek to *describe*, *explain*, *predict*, and *control* what they study.

Let's see what this means by looking at how psychologists would approach the question of whether there are sex differences in aggressiveness. Some people believe that males are naturally more aggressive than females. Others say that this may be only a stereotype, or at least that it is not always true. Psychologists would want to know first: Do men and women actually differ in aggressive behavior? A number of research studies have addressed this question, and the evidence seems

About half of all psychologists specialize in clinical or counseling psychology. Career counseling in schools and universities is one aspect of counseling psychology.

unequivocal: males do behave more aggressively than females, particularly when we consider physical aggression (Frieze et al., 1978). Having established that sex differences in aggression do exist, and having *described* those differences, psychologists then seek to *explain* the differences. Physiological psychologists might seek to explain them on the basis of anatomy or body chemistry; developmental psychologists might look to early experience and the way a child is taught to behave "like a boy" or "like a girl"; social psychologists might explain the differences as being due to societal constraints against aggressive behavior in women.

If any or all of these explanations are correct, then they should allow us both to *predict* and to *control* aggressive behavior. For example, if sex differences in aggression arise because males have a greater amount of the male hormone testosterone, then we would predict that reducing the level of testosterone would reduce aggressive behavior in men. If sex differences in aggression are due to early training, then we would predict that there would be fewer sex differences in families where parents did not stress gender differences in behavior. Finally, if sex differences in aggressive behavior are due to societal constraints against women expressing aggression, we would predict that removing or reducing those constraints would result in higher levels of aggressive behavior among women.

If any (or all) of these explanations for sex differences in aggressiveness turns out to be correct—that is, if the predictions are supported by research—we would be able to control aggressive behavior to a greater degree than was possible before. Each of these predictions could be tested through research and the results used to indicate which of the various explanations is the most successful.

Psychology is not alone in trying to describe, explain, predict, and control behavior. The behavioral sciences—anthropology, sociology, political science, and psychology—are so closely related that it is often hard to tell where one ends and the next begins. For example, all of them would regard a campus protest as a good subject for study. But how would their approaches differ?

An *anthropologist* might see the day's activities in terms of cultural patterns and rituals. He or she would note that making speeches from a soapbox is a long and honored American tradition; that linking arms to form a human barricade resembles the snake dance of Japanese protesters; that in political movements, as in primitive societies, people often call others who are not related to them "brother" and "sister."

A *sociologist* might be most interested in the interactions of the groups that form and in the bonds that are forged among people. Crowds, the sociologist would note, behave differently from individuals and from small groups. A crowd develops an organizational structure and a status system. It makes and enforces its own codes of correct and incorrect behavior.

A *political scientist* might focus on the distribution of power and authority among leaders and groups. An *economist*, being concerned mainly with the distribution of goods, would note that the students' attitude toward property differs from that of most Americans. A *historian* would compare this event to others in the past and would seek its causes.

A *psychologist* surveying the same situation would be most interested in how individuals in the crowd behave and why they behave that way.

Psychology and Common Sense

To many people, including quite a few introductory psychology students, psychology seems to be based on nothing more than common sense lightly disguised by fancy jargon. If you believe that psychological research is just a complicated process of confirming what most people already know, you may be right—sometimes.

Walter and Harriet Mischel recently investigated the possibility that even children could predict accurately the findings of some psychology experiments. The Mischels described twelve psychology experiments to fourth- and sixth-graders and asked them to predict the outcomes. On average, fourth-graders were able to guess correctly outcomes for seven of the twelve experiments. Sixth-graders did even better, correctly guessing nine out of twelve outcomes.

Does this mean that psychologists are wasting a lot of time and effort in "discovering" what even a sixth-grader could tell them? Not really. A number of studies have shown that much "commonsense" psychological knowledge is simply incorrect when put to the test. For example, Eva Vaughan (1977) gave students in an introductory psychology course a list of 23 commonly held beliefs in several areas of psychology. All 23 statements were false. However, a remarkably high percentage of the students believed many of these statements to be true. For instance, 85 percent of Vaughan's students agreed that "the basis of the baby's love for [the] mother is the fact that [the] mother fills physiological needs for food, etc." But research has shown that the infant's love for the mother is based primarily on the comfort that the infant receives from physical contact with her. Also, 80 percent of the students believed that "the best way to ensure that a desired behavior will persist after training is to reward that behavior every single time it occurs." Actually, rewarding a desired behavior only some of the time increases the likelihood that it will persist.

Studying psychology will reinforce some of your commonsense beliefs because some of what you know on the basis of your own experiences and what others have told you is quite correct. On the other hand, this course will show you that some of what you—and most people—think of as common sense is actually quite wrong. Perhaps more importantly, the study of psychology will show you how scientists tackle questions about the mind and behavior that have been puzzling us for thousands of years.

Training in psychology can also help you learn to think. In a study of graduate students in psychology, medicine, law, and chemistry, psychology students improved the most in their ability to reason during the first two years of graduate study (Nisbett, Fong, Lehman & Cheng, 1987). The reason for this? Psychology's emphasis on applying reasoning (rather than just relying on common sense) to everyday situations appears to be much more helpful in improving reasoning skills than is, for example, specialized training in chemistry.

Does their participation grow out of their political attitudes and values? Is there some underlying motive for attending the protest? Do most of the people at this particular protest also go to other protests, and if so, why?

A Process of Inquiry

In order to get answers to these and other questions about people and their thoughts, feelings, and behavior, psychologists use several kinds of research methods. These methods are designed to assure that the information psychologists gather is as accurate as possible. But even with careful planning, research data may not be complete or may be true only under certain conditions.

Thus, psychology, like all other sciences, is a process of ongoing inquiry. One research study is likely to lead to new questions and new research studies on those questions. Suppose you wanted to know whether there is any truth to the stereotype that women are more emotional than men. You might begin by asking men and women to report on how

Naturalistic observation Research method involving the systematic study of animal or human behavior in natural settings rather than in the laboratory.

emotional they are in various situations. Studies of this sort tend to find that women, on the whole, do report more emotionality than men do (Maccoby & Jacklin, 1974). But this finding leads to a new question: Are women really more emotional or is it possible that they are simply more likely than men to admit to their emotions? This new question might lead to another study that did not rely entirely on self-report to determine emotionality. Or it might lead you to study how men and women describe their emotions. Someone else might set out to study whether women report higher levels of all emotions or whether only some emotions are affected. The answers to these and other questions about emotions will be found in Chapter 11, but even those answers are likely to lead to new questions and new research as psychologists seek to refine and extend their understanding of emotions.

Throughout this text, research that supports the ideas being discussed will be identified by giving the researchers' names and the year of the study in parentheses. You will find the corresponding study listed in the references at the end of the book. By referencing work in this way, psychologists identify the evidence that supports their conclusions, and they make it easy for others to ask questions about their work and look up the studies that led to their conclusions.

The Naturalistic-Observation Method

We have all heard about the virtue of "telling it like it is." Psychologists use this method to study animal or human behavior in its natural context instead of in the laboratory under imposed conditions. Most of us use this method in everyday life without realizing it. When you watch dogs play in the park or observe how your professors conduct their classes, you are using a form of **naturalistic observation.** A psychologist with this real-life orientation might observe behavior in a school or a factory. Another might actually join a family to study the behavior of its members. Still another might observe animals in nature instead of in cages. The primary advantage of this method is that in everyday life, the observed behavior will be more natural, spontaneous, and varied than in a laboratory.

For example, W.H. Whyte (1956) wanted to see how people living in a suburban community chose their friends. He kept tabs on his subjects by reading the local newspaper. The social column told him when parties were given and who was invited. After collecting such data for some time, Whyte noticed that there were definite friendship patterns in the community. *Proximity*—people's nearness to one another—was the critical factor in determining which people became friends. Whyte concluded that all things being equal, people are more apt to make friends with those who live nearby. He might have been able to learn this by asking people, but he could not have found it out in a laboratory.

Whyte restricted his observations to one specific behavior: going to parties. It is not always possible, however, to make such restrictions. Because naturalistic observation does not interfere with people's behavior in any way, the psychologist using it has to take people's behavior as it comes. A naturalistic observer cannot suddenly yell "Freeze!" when he or she wants to study what is going on in more detail. Nor can the psychologist tell people to stop what they are doing because it is not what he or she wants to study.

There are both advantages and disadvantages to naturalistic observation. One of the central problems is *observer bias.* Any police officer will tell you how unreliable eyewitnesses can be. Even psychologists who are trained observers may subtly distort what they see in order to encourage it to conform to what they hope to see. For this reason, the behavior of subjects in observational studies is often videotaped and the tapes scored by an observer who does not know what the study is intended to discover. Also, in their detailed notes of the observation, psychologists may not record behavior that they think is not relevant. When using this method, it may be desirable to rely on a team of trained observers who pool their notes. This often results in a more complete picture than one observer could draw alone.

Another problem is that the behavior observed depends on the particular time, place, and group of people involved. Unlike laboratory experiments that can be repeated again and again, each natural situation is a one-time-only occurrence. Because of this, psychologists prefer not to make general statements based on information from naturalistic studies. They would rather test the information under controlled conditions in the laboratory before they apply it to situations other than the original.

Despite these disadvantages, naturalistic observation is a valuable tool for psychologists. After all, real-life behavior is what psychology is about. Although the complexity of behavior may present problems, naturalistic observation is a boon to psychologists. It gives them new ideas and suggestions for research. Researchers can then study these ideas more systematically and in more detail in their laboratories than could researchers in the field. It also helps researchers to keep their perspective by reminding them of the larger world outside the lab.

The Experimental Method

As we have noted, psychologists want to get at the root causes of phenomena; they want to explain thoughts, feelings, and behavior. Perhaps a psychologist has noticed that most students in her Monday morning class are unusually quiet and do not respond to her questions. She suspects this is because they stay up late on Sunday nights. Thus, the psychologist begins with a hunch, or **hypothesis:** Students who do not get enough sleep find it difficult to remember facts and ideas. But this commonsense explanation is not enough. The psychologist wants proof—facts that are unbiased. She wants to know that all other possible explanations have been ruled out. In order to test her hypothesis, she decides to conduct an experiment on the relationship between sleep and learning.

Her first step is to pick **subjects,** people whom she can observe in order to see whether her hypothesis is right. She decides to use student volunteers. In order to keep her results from being influenced by sex differences or intelligence levels, she chooses a group made up of equal numbers of men and women who scored between 520 and 550 on their College Boards.

Next, she designs a learning task. She needs something that none of her subjects will know in advance. If she chooses a chapter in a history

Hypothesis Tentative assumption that is tested empirically.

Subjects Individuals whose reactions or responses are observed in an experiment.

When people are unaware that they are being watched, they behave more naturally. A one-way mirror is thus sometimes used for *naturalistic observation.*

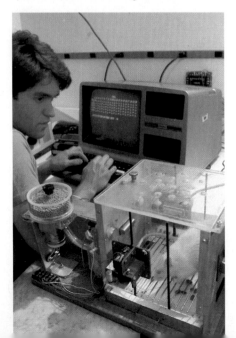

A psychology student conducting an animal learning experiment in a laboratory. The animal's responses to specific stimuli are being recorded.

book, for example, she runs the risk that some of her subjects may be history buffs. Considering various possibilities, the psychologist decides to print a page of geometric forms, each labeled with a nonsense word. Circles are "glucks," triangles "pogs," and so on. She will give the students half an hour to learn the names, then take away the study sheets and ask them to label a new page of geometric forms.

Now the psychologist is ready to consider *procedures*. Asking people if they have slept well is not a reliable measure. Some may say no to have an excuse for doing poorly on the test. Others will say yes because they do not want a psychologist to think they are unstable and cannot sleep. Then there are subjective differences: Two people who both say they slept well may not mean the same thing. So the researcher decides to intervene—that is, to control the situation a little more closely. Everyone in the experiment, she decides, will spend the night in the same dormitory. They will be kept awake until 4:00 A.M., and then they will be awakened at 7:00 A.M. sharp. She and her colleagues will patrol the halls to make sure that no one falls asleep ahead of schedule. They will check to see who is sleeping soundly between 4:00 and 7:00 A.M. By determining the amount of sleep that the subjects get, the psychologist is introducing and controlling an essential element of the experimental method: an **independent variable.** The psychologist believes that the students' ability to learn her labels for geometric forms will depend on their having had a good night's sleep. Performance on the learning task (number of correct answers) thus becomes the **dependent variable.** Changing the independent variable (the amount of sleep) should also change the dependent variable (performance on the learning task), according to the hypothesis. In particular, this group of subjects who get only three hours of sleep should do quite poorly on the test.

At this point, the experimenter begins looking for loopholes in her experimental design. How can she be sure that poor test results mean that the subjects did less well than they would have done if they had had more sleep? Their poor performance could be the result of knowing that they were participating in an experiment and therefore being closely observed. In order to be sure that her experiment measures only the effects of inadequate sleep, the experimenter divides the subjects into two groups. The two groups contain equal numbers of males and females of the same ages and with the same College Board scores. One of the groups, the **experimental group,** will be kept awake, as we have described, until 4:00 A.M. That is, they will be subjected to the experimenter's manipulation of the independent variable—amount of sleep. The other, the **control group,** will be allowed to go to sleep whenever they please. Because the only consistent difference between the two groups should be the amount of sleep they get, the experimenter can be much more confident that if the groups differ in their test performance, the difference is due to the amount of sleep they got the night before.

Finally, the psychologist questions her own objectivity. She is inclined to think that lack of sleep inhibits students' learning, but she does not want to prejudice the results of her experiment. That is, she wants to avoid **experimenter bias.** So she decides to ask a third person, someone who does not know which subject did or did not sleep all night, to score the tests.

The psychologist will interpret even the most definitive findings with some caution. Only after other researchers in other laboratories with other subjects have repeated an experiment and found the same results does the psychologist really consider the original conclusion reliable. (Psychology, like all science, is a communal enterprise.)

For some studies, a laboratory may be less suitable than a naturalistic setting. Ellsworth (1977) has noted that the laboratory is not the best setting for testing variables such as fear, conflict, grief, or love. It may be hard for subjects to express these feelings except in a limited way in the laboratory. Also, the strange and unfamiliar environment of the laboratory may affect these feelings and reactions. For example, behavior patterns between parents and children are very different in the laboratory than in the home. In the laboratory, young children are more anxious and parents behave more positively toward them than they do at home (Bronfenbrenner, 1977). Finally, since in the laboratory the subjects *know* that they are being observed by psychologists, they may try to appear healthy, normal, tolerant, and intelligent (Ellsworth, 1977). This increases the problem of testing people's true responses to situations.

The Correlational Method

An experiment is one of the most powerful ways to investigate many behaviors, but it is not always the most practical way. Suppose a psychologist wants to find out what makes a good pilot. Perhaps the Air Force has asked him to study this question because it costs thousands of dollars to train a single pilot, and each year many trainees quit. The psychologist could conduct an experiment: He might raise 10 children in playrooms filled with toy planes, cars, baseballs, and stuffed animals. This method, which studies the same group of subjects over time, is called the *longitudinal method*. It would probably tell the psychologist what he wanted to know, but both he and the Air Force would have to wait years for the result.

The **correlational method** provides a shortcut. The psychologist could begin by choosing 100 proven pilots and 100 unsuccessful ones. To gather information, he could give his pilots a variety of aptitude and personality tests. Suppose he finds that all the successful pilots score higher than the unsuccessful pilots on mechanical aptitude tests, and that all the successful pilots are cautious people who do not like to take chances. There would then seem to be some **correlation,** or degree of relation, between these traits and success as a pilot. The psychologist could therefore recommend that the Air Force use certain tests to choose the next group of trainees. Suppose he also finds that all the successful pilots play golf, come from large cities, and like pecan pie. There is no logical reason why these facts should go with piloting a plane; they just do. Puzzled, the psychologist might test another group of successful pilots for these characteristics. If he finds that these pilots, too, play golf, come from large cities, and like pecan pie, he could conclude that a correlation existed, even though he probably could not explain it.

Through correlational studies, psychologists can thus identify relations between two or more variables without needing to understand exactly why these relations exist. This method has been extremely useful

Correlational method Research technique based on the naturally occurring relationship between two or more variables.

Correlation Degree of relationship between two or more variables.

in making standardized tests. Intelligence tests, College Boards, tests for clerical and mechanical aptitude—all are based on extensive correlational studies. A person's performance on a test of clerical aptitude, for example, may be compared to success or failure in an office job.

Most psychologists use several methods to study a single problem. For example, a researcher interested in creativity might begin by giving a group of college students a creativity test that she invented in order to measure their capacity to discover or produce something new. She compares the students' scores with their scores on intelligence tests and with their grades in order to see if there is a correlation between them. Then she spends several weeks observing a college class and interviewing teachers, students, and parents in order to correlate classroom behavior and the adults' evaluations with the students' scores on the creativity test. She decides to test some of her ideas with an experiment and uses a group of the students as subjects. Her findings might cause her to revise the test, or they might give the teachers and parents new insight about a particular student.

Gender, Race, and Cultural Differences

For a long time, most psychologists were white American men and the majority of the subjects used in psychology experiments were white American male college students. The underlying assumption seemed to be that the results of these studies would apply to women, to people of other racial groups, and to people of different cultures. Psychologists have now begun to question that assumption explicitly. For example, a great deal of current research is being done in an effort to find out if some of these earlier findings hold up for women as well as for men, in different cultures, and for people of different races. Is the motivation to achieve the same for men as it is for women? Do people from India, for example, respond to stress the same way that Americans do? It's important to keep in mind that answers to these questions will in turn raise new questions. If differences are found, are they due to underlying biological differences? What role do culture and environment play?

Other research is exploring the extent to which studies by white male experimenters may have been affected by subtle, unintended biases. For example, some early research seemed to show that women were more likely than men to conform to social pressure in the laboratory (e.g., Crutchfield, 1955). However, recent research indicates that this difference disappears when the experimenter is female (Eagly & Carli, 1981). The examination of hidden biases such as this is leading some researchers to question the basic assumptions as well as the methods of research used by psychologists in their research (McHugh, Koeske, & Frieze, 1986). It is also prompting new studies designed specifically to assess racial, cultural, and gender differences in important psychological processes. For example, for many years men were the sole subjects of studies of aggression, in part because research shows that men are more aggressive than women. But the reason for this gender difference had not itself been studied until quite recently. As we saw earlier in this chapter, gender differences in aggression are now being investigated in a number of research laboratories.

Some psychologists also recommend that results for males and females should be reported separately in journal articles so that it will be easier to see similarities and differences between men and women in the processes under study (Eagly, 1987). Others are arguing for a more balanced representation between men and women as research subjects; and when selecting areas for study, psychological topics of particular interest to women (such as pregnancy and childbirth, for example) should receive more attention than they have in the past (Lott, 1986).

In various chapters of this text we discuss gender differences and similarities as they pertain to that chapter. When research findings indicate it is appropriate, you will also find discussions of cultural and racial differences and similarities on the processes under consideration.

Ethics in Research

It is likely that you will have the chance to be a subject in an experiment in your psychology department. You will probably be offered a small sum of money or class credit to participate. But it is possible that your participation may puzzle you and that you will learn the true purpose of the experiment only after it is over. Is this deception necessary for the success of psychology experiments? And what if the experiment should cause you discomfort?

Most psychologists agree that these questions raise ethical issues. And so, more than 35 years ago the American Psychological Association drew up a code for treating experimental subjects (APA, 1953). But in 1963 the issue of ethics was raised again when Stanley Milgram published the results of several experiments.

Milgram hired people to help him with a learning experiment and told them that they were to teach other people, the learners, by giving them electric shocks when they gave wrong answers. The shocks could be given in various intensities from slight to severe. The people were told to increase the intensity of the shock each time the learner made a mistake. As the shocks increased in intensity, the learners began to protest that they were being hurt. They cried out in pain and became increasingly upset as the shocking continued. The people giving the shocks often became concerned and frightened and asked if they could stop. But the experimenter politely but firmly pointed out that they were expected to continue.

This was the crux of the experiment. Milgram was investigating obedience, not learning. He wanted to find out whether anyone in the situation just described would actually go all the way and give the highest level of shock. Woud they follow their consciences or would they obey the experimenter? Incredibly, 65 percent of Milgram's subjects did go all the way, even though the learner stopped answering toward the end and many subjects worried that the shocks might have done serious damage.

So Milgram found out what he wanted to know. But to do it, he had to deceive his subjects. The stated purpose of the experiment, to test learning, was a lie. The shock machines were fake. The learners received no shocks at all. And the learners themselves were Milgram's accomplices who had been trained to act as though they were being hurt (Milgram, 1963).

Ethical Principles Governing Research Subjects

PRINCIPLE 9
RESEARCH WITH HUMAN PARTICIPANTS
The decision to undertake research rests upon a considered judgment by the indivdiual psychologist about how best to contribute to psychological science and human welfare. Having made the decision to conduct research, the psychologist considers alternative directions in which research energies and resources might be invested. On the basis of this consideration, the psychologist carries out the investigation with respect and concern for the dignity and welfare of the people who participate and with cognizance of federal and state regulations and professional standards governing the conduct of research with human participants.

a. In planning a study, the investigator has the responsibility to make a careful evaluation of its ethical acceptability. To the extent that the weighing of scientific and human values suggests a compromise of any principle, the investigator incurs a correspondingly serious obligation to seek ethical advice and to observe stringent safeguards to protect the rights of human participants.

b. Considering whether a participant in a planned study will be a "subject at risk" or a "subject at minimal risk," according to recognized standards, is of primary ethical concern to the investigator.

c. The investigator always retains the responsibility for ensuring ethical practice in research. The investigator is also responsible for the ethical treatment of research participants by collaborators, assistants, students, and employees, all of whom, however, incur similar obligations.

d. Except in minimal-risk research, the investigator establishes a clear and fair agreement with research partici-

pants, prior to their participation, that clarifies the obligations and responsibilities of each. The investigator has the obligation to honor all promises and commitments included in that agreement. The investigator informs the participants of all aspects of the research that might reasonably be expected to influence willingness to participate and explains all other aspects of the research about which the participants inquire. Failure to make full disclosure prior to obtaining informed consent requires additional safeguards to protect the welfare and dignity of the research participants. Research with children or with participants who have impairments that would limit understanding and/or communication requires special safeguarding procedures.

e. Methodological requirements of a study may make the use of concealment or deception necessary. Before conducting such a study, the investigator has a special responsibility to (i) determine whether the use of such techniques is justified by the study's prospective scientific, educational, or applied value; (ii) determine whether alternative procedures are available that do not use concealment or deception; and (iii) ensure that the participants are provided with sufficient explanation as soon as possible.

f. The investigator respects the individual's freedom to decline to participate in or to withdraw from the research at any time. The obligation to protect this freedom requires careful thought and consideration when the investigator is in a position of authority or influence over the participant. Such positions of authority include, but are not limited to, situations in which research participation is required as part of employment or in which the participant is a student, client, or employee of the investigator.

Although the design of this experiment is not typical of the vast majority of psychological experiments, it caused such a public uproar that the profession began to reevaluate its ethical health. In the wake of the controversy, a new code of ethics on psychological experimentation was approved and has been revised (APA, 1982, 1985; see Box above). Each year this code of ethics is reviewed to be sure that it is up-to-date and fully adequate to protect the subjects of research. Moreover, the federal government recently amended its Code of Federal Regulations to include an extensive set of regulations concerning the protection of human subjects. Failure to abide by these regulations can result in the termination of federal funding for the investigator and penalties for his or her institution.

But controversy about the ethics of research continues. Those favoring strict ethical controls feel that the rights of the subject are of prime

g. The investigator protects the participant from physical and mental discomfort, harm, and danger that may arise from research procedures. If risks of such consequences exist, the investigator informs the participant of that fact. Research procedures likely to cause serious or lasting harm to a participant are not used unless the failure to use these procedures might expose the participant to risk of greater harm, or unless the research has great potential benefit and fully informed and voluntary consent is obtained from each participant. The participant should be informed of procedures for contacting the investigator within a reasonable time period following participation should stress, potential harm, or related questions or concerns arise.

h. After the data are collected, the investigator provides the participant with information about the nature of the study and attempts to remove any misconceptions that may have arisen. Where scientific or humane values justify delaying or withholding this information, the investigator incurs a special responsibility to monitor the research and to ensure that there are no damaging consequences for the participant.

i. Where research procedures result in undesirable consequences for the individual participant, the investigator has the responsibility to detect and remove or correct these consequences, including long-term effects.

j. Information obtained about a research participant during the course of an investigation is confidential unless otherwise agreed upon in advance. When the possibility exists that others may obtain access to such information, this possibility, together with the plans for protecting confidentiality, is explained to the participant as part of the procedure for obtaining informed consent.

**PRINCIPLE 10
CARE AND USE OF ANIMALS**
An investigator of animal behavior strives to advance understanding of basic behavioral principles and/or to contribute to the improvement of human health and welfare. In seeking these ends, the investigator ensures the welfare of animals and treats them humanely. Laws and regulations notwithstanding, an animal's immediate protection depends on the scientist's own conscience.

a. The acquisition, care, use, and disposal of all animals are in compliance with current federal, state or provincial, and local laws and regulations.

b. A psychologist trained in research methods and experienced in the care of laboratory animals closely supervises all procedures involving animals and is responsible for ensuring appropriate consideration of their comfort, health, and humane treatment.

c. Psychologists ensure that all individuals using animals under their supervision have received explicit instruction in experimental methods and in the care, maintenance, and handling of the species being used. Responsibilities and activities of individuals participating in a research project are consistent with their respective competencies.

d. Psychologists make every effort to minimize discomfort, illness, and pain of animals. A procedure subjecting animals to pain, stress, or privation is used only when an alternative procedure is unavailable and the goal is justified by its prospective scientific, educational, or applied value. Surgical procedures are performed under appropriate anesthesia; techniques to avoid infection and minimize pain are followed during and after surgery.

e. When it is appropriate that the animal's life be terminated, it is done rapidly and painlessly.

Source: Directory of the American Psychological Association (Washington, D.C.: American Psychological Association, 1985), pp. xxx–xxxi. Copyright 1985 by A.P.A. Reprinted by permission.

importance. They believe that procedures should never be emotionally or physically distressing, and that the experimenter should first tell the potential subject what can be expected to happen (Baumrind, 1985). Some psychologists have described deliberately misleading experiments as "trickery," "fakery," and "clownery" deserving of condemnation (Rubin, 1983). They suggest, instead, the use of role-playing methods, in which subjects are asked to act "as if" they were engaged in particular behaviors for the purpose of the experiment.

Other psychologists insist that ethical rules that are too strict could damage the scientific validity of an experiment and cripple future research (Gergen, 1973). These psychologists also point out that few subjects— by their own admission—have been appreciably harmed by deceptive experiments. Even in Milgram's manipulative experiment, only 1.3 percent of the subjects reported negative feelings about their experience.

Stanley Milgram's Obedience Experiment (A) The shock generator used in the experiment. (B) With electrodes attached to his wrists, the learner provides answers by pressing switches that light up on an answer box. (C) The subject administers a shock to the learner. (D) The subject breaks off the experiment. Milgram found out what he wanted to find out, but questions about the ethics of such experimentation still remain.

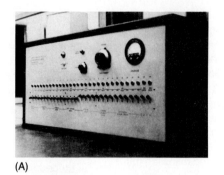

(A)

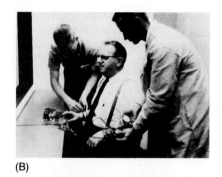

(B)

(C)

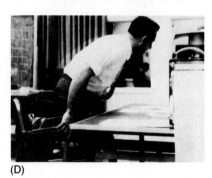

(D)

Still other psychologists suggest that the effect of experimental procedures on subjects is itself something that is deserving of research (Trice, 1986). They point out that as a science, psychology should base its ethical code on demonstrated facts, not conjecture. For example, the latest revision of the APA ethical code requires that "After the data are collected, the investigator provides the participant with information about the nature of the study and attempts to remove any misconceptions that may have arisen" (APA, 1985, p. xxxi). Presumably, this is intended to eliminate misconceptions and harmful aftereffects. But Holmes (1976b) notes that when the APA originally adopted its code, there was little or no evidence that this procedure would actually have the desired effect, although subsequent research indicates that debriefing does in fact work as intended (Marans, 1988).

Often the debate on ethical issues has focused on laboratory experiments. But questions have also been raised about the ethics of conducting naturalistic research studies. Is it ethical to study and collect data on people who are parking their cars or shopping in a store without first telling them that they are subjects of research? One study found that many people would indeed feel harassed, or that their privacy had been invaded, if they were unknowingly observed and studied (Wilson & Donnerstein, 1976). In fact, 38 percent of the people questioned stated that the public should protest against such methods of research.

In the long run, psychology can only benefit from the ethical standards controversy. Although unanimous acceptance of a formal code of ethics is a long way off, most experimenters find the APA ethical code a useful step in the right direction.

■ The Social Relevance of Psychology

Basic versus Applied Psychology

We have described the goals of psychology as description, explanation, prediction, and control. But not all research is directed equally at each of these goals. **Basic research,** or research for its own sake, is more concerned with description, explanation, and prediction. Usually, basic research is carried out to test a theory or to follow up on other research. It is only rarely a response to a pressing practical problem. Basic research may or may not eventually have practical application to social problems. **Applied psychology,** however, is the direct study of the problems of the teacher, the worker, the spouse, or perhaps of the wider social effects of racism or militarism. Applied research is often more concerned with prediction and control than with description and explanation; it is usually intended eventually to change human behavior, although it may have major theoretical importance as well.

The distinction between scholarly theory and practical use is an old one. It dates back to the different models of science proposed in the seventeenth century by René Descartes and Francis Bacon. Descartes considered all scientific endeavor intrinsically worthwhile (basic research). For Bacon, science was to be used to promote human welfare (applied research) (Fishman & Neigher, 1982).

Psychology as a discipline has dramatically increased its attention to applications in the last few years. This has come about largely in response to major federal funding cuts in areas that were seen to have little practical impact. Moreover, this trend toward increased applied research is likely to continue as psychology competes with other social sciences for limited funds to maintain research and service programs. Hatch (1982), for example, points out that psychology must pay more attention to such real-life problems as pollution, urban decay, alcoholism, smoking, and drug abuse. Not surprisingly, this proposal has caused considerable controversy within the profession of psychology as well as outside it.

Some have called for psychology to play a more active role in improving public understanding of the importance of basic science while at the same time helping people to solve difficult social problems (Bazelon, 1982). One interesting suggestion is to create partnerships between scientists and citizens on community-based research projects that can not only improve the quality of both basic and applied research but also encourage public support for research that is helping people to help themselves (Chavis, Stuckey, & Wandersman, 1983).

Fishman and Neigher (1982) also believe that the social relevance issue has become critical. The challenge, as they see it, is to improve the quality of both basic and applied research and to tie all research more directly to such social goals as public service, social policy consultation, and education and training. Unless psychology can meet these kinds of challenges, its very future as a discipline may be at stake.

Basic research Research for its own sake, usually done to test a theory or to follow up on other research rather than to solve practical problems.

Applied psychology Direct study of social problems, often with the intent to change human behavior.

■ Controversy: Guinea Pigs in Psychological Research

For the past two centuries, there has been an almost continual controversy over the use of animals in medical and psychological research. In 1876, a movement in England protesting experimental surgery on animals resulted in the British Cruelty to Animals Act, which requires that researchers acquire licenses to use living animals in their work. Today the debate about research on animals is still raging.

Several groups in this country, including Mobilization for Animals and Psychologists for the Ethical Treatment of Animals (PsyETA), are calling for more restrictive legislation regarding the use of animals in research. These groups believe that causing animal suffering is inhumane. Just as researchers would rule out harmful experimentation on human subjects, they should put an end to experimentation that causes animal suffering. Many scientists and their supporters hold an opposing view. They contend that the goals of their research—to reduce or eliminate human suffering, to enrich human life, and to deepen understanding of life forms in general—morally justify some animal suffering in order to meet those objectives (Gallistel, 1981).

The American Psychological Association has established guidelines concerning the use of animals in psychological research (see Box on pp. 20–21). Under these guidelines, the investigator is responsible for making "every effort to minimize discomfort, illness, and pain of animals"; and animals should be killed "rapidly and painlessly" when they are no longer needed.

But for many animal protection activists, the APA guidelines are not enough. Activists claim that the misuse of research animals occurs despite organizational guidelines and protective legislation. Moreover, they believe that psychological researchers unnecessarily repeat many experiments on animals and that there is little evidence that any human benefits come from this work. Also, these critics maintain that psychologists and others involved in animal research make few efforts to find alternative means of gathering data.

One target of criticism has been physiological psychologist Edward Taub, who in 1983 received a Guggenheim Fellowship to support his research on monkeys' sensory mechanisms. The award angered activists because Taub had been convicted of animal cruelty in some prior research on monkeys. PsyETA also formally protested Taub's receipt of several additional awards from the APA itself (Cunningham, 1983).

At the moment, however, there is no denying the importance of animals to basic research and, ultimately, saving lives. For example, to develop the polio vaccine, scientists relied on the use of monkeys to test it. Much of what we know about the effects of crowding stems from research with rats. The discovery and study of diseases that occur naturally in animals saves not only human lives, but those of animals as well (King, 1987). The use of animals for applied research, however, is at times questionable. Recently, as a result of protests by animal rights activists, some cosmetics companies have stopped using animals to test their products.

One important organization which opposes the protectionists' views has instituted new, more stringent policies regarding animal research. The National Institutes of Health (NIH) supports almost 40 percent of American biomedical research, much of which involves animal subjects. Henceforth, a project will not receive NIH funding unless it has first been approved by an animal research committee, including someone not affiliated with the institution doing the research; the institution's attending veterinarian; and a scientist experienced in lab animal medicine. The NIH hopes that its more restrictive policies will prevent the passage of even more limiting legislation supported by animal protectionists (Miller, 1984). Whether it also succeeds in reducing the controversy over animal research ethics remains to be seen.

Using Animals in Psychological Research

The breach between basic and applied research has raised questions about the use of animal subjects in research. Some psychologists believe that since psychology is, at least in part, the science of behavior, animal behavior is just as interesting and important as human behavior. But however interesting animal behavior may be, what possible relevance does the behavior of a 7-inch-long laboratory rat have to everyday human problems? In the short term, perhaps none. But many experiments—systematic brain surgery, for example—cannot be performed on human beings and must be done on animals if anything at all is to be learned.

Psychologists also use animal subjects because their behavior is simpler than human behavior and because their genetic histories and immediate environments can be controlled more easily. The short life spans of some animals also make it possible to study behavior over many generations, which would be highly impractical or even impossible with humans. Moreover, with animals no "social" complications exist between experimenter and subject.

The trained psychologist must reflect carefully on the limitations of making comparisons of animal and human behavior. Without analysis, animal studies may lead to grandiose and faulty conclusions about human social behavior (Mason & Lott, 1976). Certainly mental illness in a rat is different from that in a human. But if we are careful not to make any simple equation between animal behavior and human behavior, research using animals can add much to our understanding of behavior, including human behavior.

In recent times, the use of animals in psychological research has become controversial in other ways as well. Several groups have protested experimentation that causes animals to suffer. In response, the APA and other organizations have established stricter guidelines concerning the use of animals in psychological research. Despite these measures, however, the debate surrounding the ethical use of animals in research continues (see Box).

 APPLICATION

Psychology and Careers

Within the past 15 years, psychology has become one of the most popular majors in the college curriculum. In 1970–1971, 37,000 students were awarded BAs in psychology. By 1983–1984, that figure had doubled. And the trend appears to be continuing. In 1982, 2.1 percent of the college freshmen in a national survey said they were majoring in psychology; by 1985, the figure had jumped to 3.2 percent. What happens to these people? Do they all go on to careers in psychology as clinicians, researchers, and the like? What kinds of jobs do they look for and what kinds of jobs do they find once they are equipped with their hard-earned degrees?

Surveys show that between one-third and two-thirds of those who receive bachelor's degrees in psychology do not go on to graduate school in psychology. Many use their undergraduate study of psychology as a general preparation for life—an informative and worthwhile course of study that indirectly relates to and prepares them for careers in other fields. Others go directly into careers that relate to psychology.

Those with a bachelor's degree in psychology are qualified to assist psychologists in mental health centers, vocational rehabilitation, or correctional centers. They may also work as research assistants, teach psychology in high school, or take jobs as trainees in government or business.

Recently, several community colleges have started to offer associate degree programs in psychology. Graduates of these training programs are well qualified for paraprofessional jobs in state hospitals, mental health centers, and other human service settings. Job responsibilities may include the screening and evaluation of new patients, record keeping, other direct patient-contact activities, and assistance in community consultation.

Many other careers outside of psychology also draw upon one's knowledge of psychology without requiring postgraduate study. A sample: (1) Community relations officers are involved in promoting good relations with the local community. (2) Affirmative action officers specialize in recruitment and equal opportunities for minorities. (3) Recreation workers plan community recreation facilities. (4) Urban planning officers are responsible for city planning and renewal. (5) Personnel administrators deal with employee relations. (6) Health educators provide public information about health and disease. (7) Vocational rehabilitation counselors help handicapped persons find employment. (8) Directors of volunteer service recruit and train volunteers. (9) Probation officers work with parolees. (10) Day-care center supervisors supervise preschool children of working parents. (11) Research assistants perform psychological research in large hospitals, businesses, and government. (12) Laboratory assistants are involved with animal behavior research.

For those who do pursue advanced degrees, the opportunities for a career in psychology are widespread and varied. Colleges and universities currently employ nearly one-third of the people who hold advanced degrees in psychology. One-quarter of those holding advanced degrees go on to work in industry in personnel, management training, or industrial design (NSF, 1988). Holders of advanced degrees work in public schools, in prisons, in hospitals and mental health clinics, in government agencies, and the military. Nearly 20 percent of all psychologists are employed primarily in private practice; this number has been increasing in recent years. In 1976, about 30 percent of the people employed in psychology-related jobs were women; today 45 percent of those making a career in psychology are women.

Recently, the American Psychological Association (APA) developed standards later written into many state licensing laws. These standards require people in psychological settings and in private practice to be supervised by a doctoral-level psychologist. Such regulations limit the opportunities for those with master's degrees to move into higher positions. Although there are jobs available to people with master's degrees, most of them are in business, government, schools, and, to a lesser extent, hospitals and clinics.

In discussing careers in psychology, it is important to distinguish among psychiatrists, psychoanalysts, and psychologists. Although they may provide overlapping services, their main functions differ. A *psychiatrist* is a medical doctor who has completed three years of residency training in psychiatry. He or she specializes in the diagnosis and treatment of abnormal behavior. Besides giving psychotherapy, the psychiatrist also takes medical responsibility for the patient. As a physician, he or she may prescribe drugs and use other medical procedures to help a patient. A *psychoanalyst* is a psychiatrist or psychologist who has received additional specialized training in psychoanalytic theory and practice.

Most, but not all, *psychologists* hold PhD degrees in psychology—the result of four to six years of study in a graduate program in psychology. The PhD program for all psychologists includes broad exposure to the theories and findings of psychology, a special focus on a subdiscipline, such as clinical or social psychology, and extensive training in research methods. Certain subdisciplines, such as clinical and counseling psychology, require additional training in diagnosis and psychotherapy; these programs also require at least one year of training in psychotherapy in an internship program that is accredited by the APA.

Years ago, when competition for jobs was less intense than it is today, graduate students in psychology specialized in a single area, or subdiscipline, such as clinical, developmental, or educational psychology. Current employment conditions, however, require students to branch out. Psychology students on the graduate level now often specialize in two fields, such as a major in experimental psychology and a minor in industrial psychology, or school/clinical psychology, or developmental/aging, and so on. Such training provides breadth in a traditional area and depth in an applied specialty.

■ Summary

● **What am I going to get from this course? What is psychology really about?** *Psychology* is a science that studies behavior and the mental processes that shape behavior. Psychology has been a formal discipline based on the **scientific method** for about the last 100 years. The field of psychology seeks to answer a wide variety of questions about behavior—questions about intelligence, heredity, aggression, prejudice and mental disorders.

- **Did psychology begin with Freud?** Wilhelm Wundt established the first psychological laboratory at the University of Leipzig in 1879, where he intended to study the mind in an objective and scientific manner. He introduced measurement and experiment into psychology, which until then had been a branch of philosophy.

- One of Wundt's students, Edward Bradford Titchener, became professor of psychology at Cornell University and the leader of American psychology. Wundt and Titchener both believed that psychology's role is to identify the basic elements of experience and to show how they are combined. This school of psychology is known as **structuralism.**

- Sir Francis Galton pioneered the study of individual differences and the development of mental tests.

- William James, the first native American psychologist, believed that sensations cannot be separated from associations. Mental associations, he claimed, allow us to benefit from previous experience. James firmly believed that all activity is functional, and by applying biological principles to the mind, he arrived at the **functionalist theory** of mental life and behavior.

- John B. Watson confronted both the structuralist and the functionalist schools, stating that we can no more define consciousness than we can define the soul. Psychology, he maintained, should concern itself only with observable, measurable behavior. Watson's theory is part of the behaviorist school of psychology. Watson based much of his work on Pavlov's **conditioning** experiments and thought that all behavior could be explained by stimulus and response.

- While Watson was working in America, a new school of thought, **Gestalt psychology,** was being developed in Germany. Roughly translated, gestalt means "whole" or "form." Gestalt psychologists suggested that perception depends on our tendency to see patterns, to distinguish an object from its background, to complete pictures from a few cues.

- **Behaviorism** was thriving in America when B. F. Skinner replaced Watson as its leader. Skinner's beliefs were similar to Watson's, but he made the animal an active agent in the conditioning process by adding **reinforcement** to stimulate learning.

- **Psychoanalysis** was not seen as a part of psychology until the late 1920s, after Freud had worked out his theories on the effects of underlying motives and unconscious desires on behavior. His emphasis on the sexual drive in the formation of personality remains the most controversial aspect of his theories. Freud also founded **psychotherapy** with his famous "talking cure."

- **Existential psychology** is concerned with feelings of meaninglessness and alienation in modern life and how they contribute to apathy and other problems such as alcoholism and drug abuse. **Humanistic psychology** is related to existential psychology and emphasizes communication through the senses in order to achieve the realization of one's potential.

- **Cognitive psychology** is the study of our mental processes in the broadest sense. It is concerned with how people perceive, interpret, store, and retrieve information. Cognitive psychologists believe that mental processes can be studied scientifically.

- **Do all psychologists see patients?** Psychologists today practice within many specialized areas. The American Psychological Association, for example, is made up of 45 separate divisons, each of which represents an area of specialized interest. Some of the major areas within psychology are developmental psychology, physiological psychology, experimental psychology, personality psychology, clinical and counseling psychology, social psychology, and industrial/organizational psychology.

- **Why is the title of this chapter the Science of Psychology? How is psychology like physics and other sciences?** The common goal of all psychologists is to *describe, explain, predict,* and *control* human behavior. Psychologists use several different kinds of research methods to study human behavior. These scientific methods are part of an ongoing process of inquiry common to all the sciences.

- **Do psychologists study behavior simply by watching people?** The *naturalistic-observation* method is used to study animal and human behavior in natural settings, instead of in the laboratory. The *experimental method* begins with an idea or **hypothesis** about the relationship between two or more variables. To find out if they are related, the experimenter manipulates the **independent variable** to see how it affects the **dependent variable.** The experimenter uses precautionary **control groups** to help ensure that he or she is observing only the effects of one independent variable.

- The **correlational method** is a means of investigating

the relation between certain characteristics and behavior variables without needing to manipulate or change any variables.

- **Is it fair to use people in experiments without telling them what the experiment is about?** More than 35 years ago, the American Psychological Association (APA) drew up a code of ethics for psychological experimentation. Each year the code is reviewed and updated to be sure that it is fully adequate to protect the subjects of research. Although many psychologists feel this is a step in the right direction, controversy over the ethics of research continues.

- Psychology has common goals, but not all research is directed equally at each of these goals. **Basic research,** or research for its own sake, is more concerned with description, explanation, and prediction. **Applied research** directly studies real social problems and is more often concerned with prediction and control. More attention has gone to applied areas in the last few years as a direct result of cuts in the federal budget for pure research. Psychology faces the difficult challenge of maintaining high standards in pure and applied research and directing both kinds of research to the solution of important social problems.

- **Why are animals used in psychological research? What can animals tell us about human behavior? Are there protections to assure that animals are not mistreated?** Psychologists use animals in research because some types of experiments cannot be done on humans. Animals also have shorter life spans, which lets a researcher study behavior over several generations, and animals' genetic history and immediate environment can be better controlled. Psychologists are careful about generalizing from animal to human behavior. They do find, however, that animal research makes a large contribution to their knowledge of behavior. The use of animals in psychological research has become a growing ethical issue. The APA and other organizations that sponsor research have issued more stringent guidelines covering the use of animals in experimentation.

■ Review Questions

1. Psychology has been a formal discipline based on the _____ method for about the last 100 years.
2. _____ pioneered the use of tests to measure human abilities.
3. The technique of objective introspection is associated with which of the following?
   a. James and Angell   c. Freud
   b. Wundt and Titchener   d. Laing and May
4. Match the following terms with their appropriate descriptions:

   ____ structuralism
   ____ functionalism
   ____ behaviorism
   ____ psychoanalysis
   ____ existential psychology
   ____ humanistic psychology
   ____ Gestalt psychology
   ____ cognitive psychology

   A. concerned with how an organism uses its perceptual abilities to function in its environment.
   B. stresses the whole character of perception.
   C. concerned with alienation and meaninglessness in modern life and resulting psychological problems.
   D. studies only observable and measurable behavior.
   E. stresses the basic elements of experience and the combinations in which they occur.
   F. emphasizes nonverbal experience and altered states of consciousness in realizing one's potential.
   G. studies mental processes in the broadest sense.
   H. maintains that hidden motives and unconscious desires govern much of our behavior.

5. B. F. Skinner added the new element of _____ to conditioning.
6. As a result of the influence of the cognitive school, psychology is now defined as the study of _____ and _____ _____ .
7. The four goals common to all psychologists are _____ , _____ , _____ , and _____ _____ human behavior.
8. A method of research known as _____ _____ allows psychologists to see how behavior operates in real-life situations.
9. Testing done in the _____ can be repeated and information can be collected under controlled conditions.
10. The _____ variable in an experiment is manipulated to see how it affects a second variable; the _____ variable is the one observed for any possible effects.

11. The experimental method makes use of all the following EXCEPT:
    a. hypotheses   c. experimenter bias
    b. variables   d. subjects
12. The _____ method of research is used to identify naturally occurring relationships among variables without having to manipulate any variable.
13. _____ research is research done for its own sake; _____ research, by contrast, is directed at the resolution of practical problems.
14. Which of the following is a TRUE statement about ethics in research?
    a. Controversy over ethical standards has almost disappeared.
    b. The APA code of ethics in use today dates from 1953.
    c. Ethical questions only apply to laboratory experiments.
    d. Failure to follow federal regulations can result in penalties.
15. Which of the following is a TRUE statement about using animals in research?
    a. It is difficult to control an animal's immediate environment.
    b. Results can add to our understanding of human behavior.
    c. The APA has not yet issued guidelines in this area.
    d. There is little danger of making faulty comparisons between animal and human behavior.

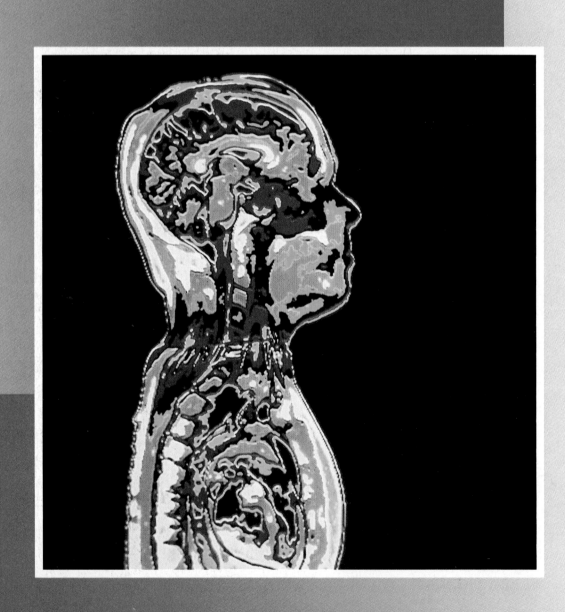

2 Physiology and Behavior

■ Thinking Critically

How are you able to distinguish hot enough from too hot when you stick your hand under the shower?

Why can coffee make us nervous?

Why do some people who have had a stroke have difficulty speaking when others do not?

What makes it possible for us to discern the sound of our name being called across a crowded, noisy room?

How do our heads know what our feet are doing?

What does it mean to calm down? How do our bodies accomplish it?

Do our genes determine who we are?

Answers to these and other questions about how our biological processes affect our psychological processes appear throughout the chapter and in the Chapter Summary.

■ Outline

Endocrine system Internal network of glands that release hormones directly into the bloodstream to regulate body functions.

Nervous system The brain, the spinal cord, and the network of nerve cells that transmit messages throughout the body.

The radio says it is 9:00 A.M., but your new watch reads 9:05, so you set it back five minutes. Later in the day, you look at your watch and see that it says 3:15 P.M., but according to the clock in the library it is only 3:00. A little annoyed, you go to a watchmaker and explain your problem. He opens the watch case and examines the maze of tiny gears and levers inside. He discovers the difficulty, replaces the mainspring, and you are back on time.

In this chapter, we are going to take our cue from the watchmaker. Psychology is the study of behavior, but often we cannot understand behavior unless we know a little about what goes on inside the human body—what makes us tick. Most of the time—when the watch is running perfectly or when the body is functioning normally—we tend to forget about the complex activities that are constantly going on. But nonetheless they continue: The cells keep functioning and reproducing themselves; the organs and glands keep regulating such diverse activities as digestion and growth; the nervous system keeps receiving, interpreting, and sending messages. And without these continuing and coordinated activities, there could be no life—certainly no psychological life—as we now know it.

The body possesses two major systems for coordinating and integrating behavior. One is the **endocrine system,** which consists of a number of glands that secrete chemical messages into the bloodstream. These chemicals perform a variety of functions, including preparation of nerves and muscles to act, control of metabolism, and regulation and development of secondary sexual traits. The second system is the **nervous system,** which relays messages in the form of nerve impulses throughout the body. The more we learn about the nervous system and the endocrine system, the more we understand how they work together to integrate the body's extraordinarily complex activities.

In order to understand how intricate these activities are, consider what happens when you burn your finger on a match. What happens next? "It's simple," you might say. "I automatically snatch my hand away from the heat." But, in fact, your body's response to a burn is not simple at all. It involves a highly complex set of activities. First, special sensory cells pick up the message that your finger is burned. They pass this information along to the spinal cord, which triggers a quick withdrawal of your hand. Meanwhile, the message is being sent to other parts of your nervous system. Your body goes on "emergency alert": You breathe faster; your heart pounds; your entire body mobilizes itself against the wound. At the same time, the endocrine system gets involved: Chemicals are released into the bloodstream and carried throughout the body to supplement and reinforce the effects of nervous system activity. Meanwhile, your brain continues to interpret the messages being sent to it: You experience pain; perhaps you turn your hand over to examine the burn; you might walk over to the sink and run cold water over your hand. In other words, even a simple event such as burning your finger results in an extremely complex, coordinated sequence of activities that involves the body's nervous system working hand-in-hand with its endocrine system.

In our effort to understand how biology affects psychological processes, we will first look at the nervous system. Then we will take a look at the endocrine system. Finally, we will consider the extent to which genes influence our behavior.

The Nervous System

The nervous system has a number of parts that all work together. These parts are various and complex, and in some cases their functions are still a mystery. Before considering the larger parts of the nervous system, we will examine its smallest unit, the individual nerve cell or neuron. This important cell underlies the activity of the entire nervous system.

The Neuron

There are more than 100 billion nerve cells, or **neurons,** in the brain of an average human being. That is more than 20 times the number of people living on the earth! And there are billions more neurons in other parts of the nervous system. Like all other cells, each neuron has a **cell body,** which contains a nucleus where metabolism and respiration take place. The nucleus contains the genetic material that directs all its functions, including the manufacture and release of the chemical messengers that enable the neuron to communicate with other cells and, ultimately, the brain. The cell body is enclosed by a cell membrane. Neurons have tiny fibers extending from the cell body that enable the neuron to receive messages from surrounding cells and pass them on to other cells. No other cells in the body are equipped to do this (see Figure 2-1).

The short fibers branching out from the cell body are called **dendrites.** The dendrites pick up messages coming in from surrounding areas and carry them to the cell body. Also extending from the cell body of the neuron is a single long fiber called an **axon.** The axon is very thin and is usually much longer than the dendrites. For example, in adults the axons that run from the brain to the base of the spinal cord, or from the spinal cord to the tip of the thumb, may be as long as 3 feet; but most axons are only 1 or 2 inches long. A group of axons bundled together like parallel wires in an electric cable is called a **nerve.** The axon carries outgoing messages from the cell and either relays them to neighboring neurons or directs a muscle or gland to take action. Although there is just one axon in a neuron, near its end the axon splits into many terminal branches. Since there may be hundreds of dendrites on a single neuron, and since the axon itself may branch out in numerous directions, one neuron can be in touch with hundreds of others at both its input end (dendrites) and its output end (axon).

Look at the neuron in Figure 2-1. Its axon is surrounded by a fatty covering called a **myelin sheath.** The sheath is pinched at intervals, which makes the axon resemble a string of microscopic sausages. Not all axons are covered by myelin sheaths, but myelinated axons are found throughout the body. As we will soon see, the sheaths help neurons act with greater efficiency as well as provide insulation to the neuron.

Although all neurons relay messages, the kind of information which they collect and the places to which they carry it help to distinguish among different types of neurons. For example, neurons that collect

Neuron Individual cell that is the smallest unit of the nervous system.

Cell body Part of the neuron that contains the nucleus and is the site where metabolism and respiration take place.

Dendrites Short fibers that branch out from the cell body and pick up incoming messages.

Axon Single long fiber extending from the cell body that carries outgoing messages.

Nerve Group of axons bundled together.

Myelin sheath Fatty covering found on some axons.

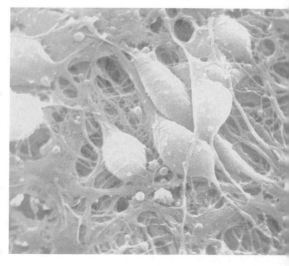

A photomicrograph of neurons, showing the cell body, dendrites, and axon.

Sensory or **afferent neurons** Neurons that carry messages from sense organs to the spinal cord or brain.

Motor or **efferent neurons** Neurons that carry messages from the spinal cord or brain to the muscles and glands.

Interneurons or **association neurons** Neurons that carry messages from one neuron to another and do most of the work of the nervous system.

Ions Electrically charged particles found both inside and outside of the neuron.

Polarization Condition of a neuron at rest when most positive ions are on the outside and most negative ions are on the inside of the cell membrane.

messages from sense organs and carry those messages to the spinal cord or to the brain are called **sensory** (or **afferent**) **neurons.** Neurons that carry messages from the spinal cord or the brain to the muscles and glands are called **motor** (or **efferent**) **neurons.** And neurons that carry messages from one neuron to another are called **interneurons** (or **association neurons**). Interneurons account for more than 99 percent of all the neurons in the central nervous system, and they perform most of the work of the nervous system.

The Neural Impulse

We have referred several times to the fact that neurons carry messages. How do these messages get started? When a neuron is resting, its cell membrane forms a partial barrier between semiliquid solutions that are inside and outside the neuron. Both solutions contain electrically charged particles, or **ions.** The charged particles outside the neuron are mostly positive ions, such as sodium, while those inside the neuron are mostly negatively charged ions. Since there are more negative ions inside the neuron than outside, the electrical charge inside the neuron is said to be negative relative to the outside, and the neuron is said to be in a state of **polarization.**

Figure 2-1
A typical myelinated neuron.

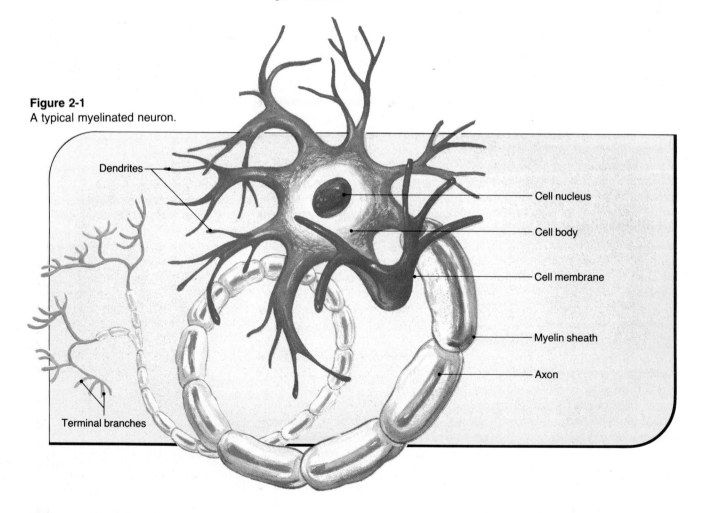

Dendrites

Cell nucleus

Cell body

Cell membrane

Myelin sheath

Axon

Terminal branches

In its resting state, a polarized neuron is like a firecracker or a loaded gun: It is ready to fire when it is properly triggered. The cell membrane lets many substances pass freely in and out. However, it tends to keep sodium ions outside of the neuron. In this way, the cell membrane keeps the neuron in a polarized state. But when a point on the cell membrane is adequately stimulated by an incoming message, the cell membrane suddenly opens at that point, allowing the sodium ions to rush in. When enough sodium has entered the neuron to make the inside positively charged relative to the outside, the cell membrane closes and no more sodium ions can enter.

The breakdown of the cell membrane does not occur at just one point. In fact, as soon as the cell membrane allows sodium to enter the cell at one point, the next point on the membrane also opens. More sodium ions flow into the neuron at the second spot and depolarize this part of the neuron. The process is repeated along the length of the neuron, creating a **neural impulse,** or **action potential,** that travels down the axon, much like a fuse burning from one end to the other (see Figure 2-2). When this happens, we say that the neuron has fired.

The neuron does not fire in response to every impulse it receives. If the incoming message is not strong enough, it may simply cause a shift in the electrical charge in a tiny area of the neuron. This **graded potential** then simply fades away, leaving the neuron in its normal polarized state. In other words, the incoming message must be above a certain *threshold* to cause a neuron to fire, just as you must pull the trigger on a gun hard enough to make it fire.

For a period of about .001 second after firing (the **absolute refractory period**), the neuron will not fire again no matter how strong the incoming

Neural impulse or **action potential** The firing of a nerve cell caused by depolarization of the neuron.

Graded potential A shift in the electrical charge in a tiny area of the neuron caused by an incoming message too weak to stimulate the neuron to fire.

Absolute refractory period A period after firing when the neuron will not fire again no matter how strong the incoming messages may be.

Figure 2-2
When a point on the *neural membrane* is adequately stimulated by an incoming message, the membrane opens at that point and positively charged sodium ions flow in, depolarizing the neuron. This process is repeated along the length of the membrane, creating the neural impulse that travels down the axon, causing the neuron to fire.

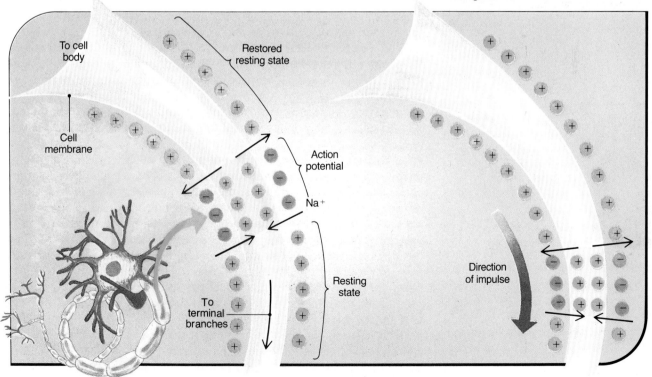

Relative refractory period A period when the neuron is returning to its normal polarized state and may refire if the incoming message is much stronger than usual.

Nodes Pinched intervals on the myelin sheaths of some axons that help speed the passage of neural impulses.

Figure 2-3

The incoming message must be above a certain threshold to cause a neuron to fire. After it fires, the cell body begins to pump potassium *ions* out of the neuron until a state of ionic equilibrium is restored. This process happens very quickly, and within a few thousandths of a second the neuron is ready to fire again. The small "bump" at the lower left represents an incoming message that was too weak to cause the neuron to fire.
Adapted from Carlson, 1981

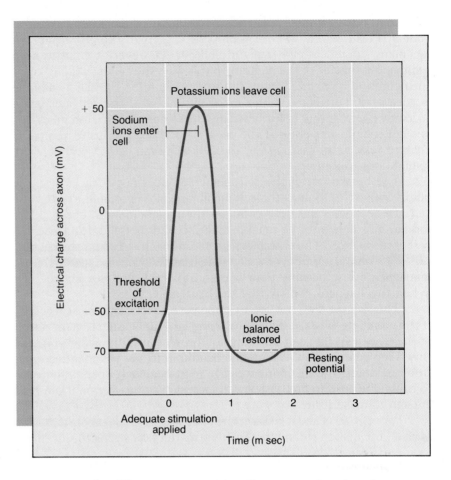

messages may be. This is not surprising if we remember that the neuron has stopped letting sodium in and is depolarized. But then, in what is called the **relative refractory period,** the cell starts to pump positive ions out again until the inside of the neuron returns to a negative charge relative to the outside. During this phase, which lasts for only a few thousandths of a second, the neuron will fire, but only if the incoming message is considerably stronger than normal. Finally, equilibrium is restored and the neuron is returned to its resting state, ready to fire again (see Figure 2-3).

This whole process occurs very quickly, but there is a wide range in the speed with which individual neurons conduct impulses. In some of the largest myelinated axons, the fastest impulses may travel at speeds of nearly 400 feet per second. Axons with myelin sheaths can conduct impulses very rapidly because the impulses leapfrog along the string of pinched intervals, or **nodes,** that lie along the sheaths. Neurons without myelin sheaths tend to be slower. Their impulses are conducted in a steady flow, like a fuse. Impulses in the slowest of these unmyelinated neurons poke along at little more than 3 feet per second.

At any instant, a neuron is either firing (on) or resting (off), just as a gun is either being fired or not. This simple on-off switching code is all the neuron can use to pass along the messages it receives. But how can such a simple on-off code communicate very complex information? Think once more about the gun. Pulling even harder on the gun's trigger will not cause the bullet to travel any faster or any farther. Either it fires because you pulled hard enough, or it does not fire because you did not pull hard enough. But if you pull the trigger again and again, and if other people around you are firing their guns at the same time, there will be a volley of shots. This will convey information very different from a single shot to someone who hears it.

The same is true of neurons. Strong incoming signals do not cause a stronger neural impulse: Each neuron fires just as strongly as before. But the neuron is likely to fire more often when stimulated by a strong signal, and neighboring neurons are also more likely to fire. The result is rapid and widespread neural firing that communicates the message, "There's a very strong stimulus out here."

The Synapse

We have been discussing the operation of a single neuron. But the billions of neurons in the nervous system work together to coordinate the body's activities. How do they interact? How does a message get from one neuron to another?

Imagine a single neuron that receives its messages from just one other neuron and transmits messages to just one neuron. The dendrites or cell body of the neuron pick up a signal; then, as we have seen, if the signal is strong enough the neuron fires, and an impulse starts down the axon and out to the end of the terminal branches. At the end of each branch, there is a tiny knob called an **axon terminal** or **synaptic knob.** In most cases, there is a tiny gap between this knob and the next neuron. This tiny gap is called a **synaptic space** (or **synaptic cleft**). The entire area composed of the axon terminal of one neuron, the synaptic space, and the dendrite or cell body of the next neuron is called the **synapse** (see Figure 2-4).

Axon terminal or **synaptic knob** Knob that forms the end of an axon terminal branch.

Synaptic space or **synaptic cleft** Tiny gap between the axon terminal of one neuron and the dendrites or cell body of the next neuron.

Synapse Area composed of the axon terminal of one neuron, the synaptic space, and the dendrite or cell body of the next neuron.

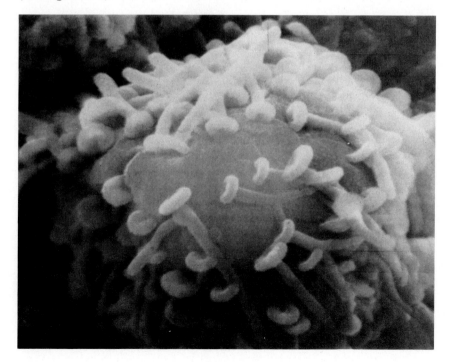

A photograph taken with a scanning electron micrograph, showing the synaptic knobs at the ends of axons. Inside the knobs are the vesicles that contain neurotransmitters.

Synaptic vesicles Tiny sacs in a synaptic knob that release chemicals into the synapse.

Neurotransmitters Chemicals released by the synaptic vesicles that travel across the synaptic space and affect the next neuron.

Receptor site A site on the other side of the synaptic space that matches a neurotransmitter, which locks into it.

Acetylcholine (ACh) A neurotransmitter that plays an excitatory role where neurons meet skeletal muscles.

Dopamine A prevalent inhibitory neurotransmitter.

Serotonin Neurotransmitter that inhibits virtually all behavior, including emotions.

Norepinephrine An adrenal hormone that causes blood pressure to rise; also, an excitatory neurotransmitter that carries nerve impulses across the synaptic gaps.

If the neural impulse is to travel on the next neuron, it must somehow travel across the synaptic space. It is tempting to imagine that the neural impulse simply leaps across the gap like an electric spark, but in reality the transfer is made by chemicals. What happens is this: Most axon terminals contain a number of tiny oval sacs called **synaptic vesicles** (see Figure 2-4). When the neural impulse reaches the end of the axon, it causes these vesicles to release varying amounts of chemicals called **neurotransmitters.** These chemical substances travel across the synaptic space and affect the next neuron.

There are more than a dozen known neurotransmitters, and their functions are still being investigated. For each such substance there are matching **receptor** (or hookup) **sites** on the other side of the synaptic space. The neurotransmitter fits into the proper receptor site just as a key fits into a lock. Some neurotransmitters "excite" the next neuron, making it, in turn, more likely to fire. **Acetylcholine** (ACh) acts as an excitatory transmitter where neurons meet skeletal muscles. ACh appears to play a critical role in such psychological processes as arousal, attention, memory, and motivation (Panksepp, 1986). Alzheimer's disease, which involves loss of memory and severe language problems, is thought to be due to a reduction in ACh and the loss of cells that respond to ACh in central portions of the brain.

Other transmitter substances "inhibit" the next neuron, making it less likely to fire. **Dopamine** is one prevalent inhibitory transmitter that seems to play an important role in schizophrenia and Parkinson's disease. **Serotonin** inhibits virtually all behavior, including emotions; it is also important in the onset of sleep. **Norepinephrine** similarly plays a role in wakefulness and arousal as well as in learning and memory.

Some of these transmitter substances have widespread effects on the nervous system. They seem to regulate or adjust the sensitivity of large

Figure 2-4
A highly simplified drawing of the synapse, showing the synaptic vesicles and the tiny synaptic space that separates most neurons from one another.

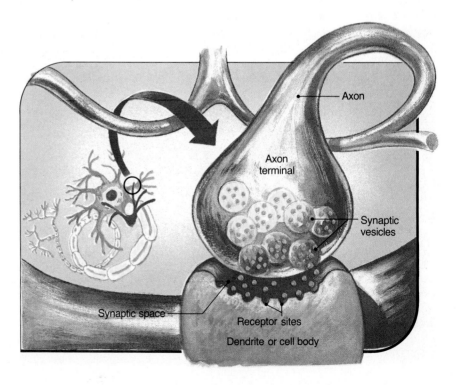

numbers of synapses, in effect "turning up" or "turning down" the activity level of whole portions of the nervous system. This process is especially clear in the case of substances that are involved in the body's own relief of pain. Both **enkephalins** and **endorphins** appear to reduce pain by inhibiting, or "turning down," the neurons that transmit pain messages in the brain. Endorphins are chains of amino acids that act like neurotransmitters. One endorphin was found to be 48 times more potent than morphine when injected into the brain, and 3 times more potent when injected into the bloodstream (Snyder, 1977) (see the Box on p.

Enkephalins and **endorphins** Chemical substances involved with the reduction of pain.

■ Neural Networks: Teaching Computers to Learn

If our brains worked the way a standard computer does, we'd be in trouble. As we grew up and were introduced to more and more people, it would take us longer and longer to remember our parents' names because, like a computer, we'd have to sort through all the names in our memories and try them one by one. Fortunately, the brain uses networks of neurons to process simultaneously all kinds of details about our parents—their faces, their voices, how we feel about them, so their names come to mind seemingly automatically. This simultaneous processing in the brain has inspired computer scientists to reconsider the step-by-step way that most computers process information. In an effort to duplicate neurons' remarkable ability to handle new information and make new connections, scientists have begun to develop *neural networks*, an exciting new development in the field of artificial intelligence that teaches computers to learn much the way the brain does.

Neural network software allows a person to create a small network of simulated neurons capable of being interconnected in various ways. As a result, the computer operator can create different types of neurons and then connect them and observe the results. Of course, artificial neural networks are not comparable to the human brain. In the first place, the brain has 100 billion neurons, while even the most complex computerized neural networks have only a few thousand (most have only a few hundred neurons). Second, nobody has yet succeeded in modeling the complex activities that occur at the synapses between individual neurons or even within a single neuron.

Despite their relative simplicity, neural networks have done some astonishing things. Simple neural networks of fewer than 20 neurons have been taught to identify defective products (bottles, cans, bars of soap) as they come off the assembly line. One network, NETalk, developed at Johns Hopkins University by Terrence Sejnowski and Charles Rosenberg of Princeton, actually enables a computer to learn to talk. At first the computer sounds are completely unintelligible, but as training proceeds, the computer sounds begin to resemble human speech. This training process is mainly trial-and-error, involving reinforcement of the computer's correct guesses. This is not entirely unlike the process children go through when learning to talk. After just 16 hours of training, NETalk learned to pronounce a 100-word passage with only 2 percent errors; and it could also pronounce similar passages it had not seen before fairly well.

What makes networks so effective at learning is that they can register similarities. Networks have been taught to recognize handwriting and human faces. Using data from underwater sensors, neural nets have learned to distinguish between different types of ships based on their distinctive sounds. They can even identify the particular make of a helicopter hovering over the surface of the ocean. At the California Institute of Technology, Carver Mead has developed a human retina and is at work on an artificial ear. By putting these neural nets on microchips, it is hoped that they will be able to help people who are blind or deaf due to eye or ear injury.

Finally, neural network software is repaying its debt of gratitude to the brain. Researchers are taking the models generated by neural networks and then going back to the brain to see if these models accurately predict brain function. Interestingly, neural network projects are showing that real neurons are far more complex and sophisticated than people have believed up until now. In fact, the individual neuron (which was once seen as simply passing information from one place to another like an electrical cord) is now being compared to a hand-held calculator as far as the complexity of the operations it can carry out all by itself (Johnson & Brown, 1988). So, far from suggesting that neurons are simple structures that will be easy to mimic, the research is making us aware of how intricate, remarkable, and sophisticated real neurons are. In fact, we've only hinted at their complexity in this text, since this is an introductory discussion.

Endorphins

Endorphins are a group of neurotransmitters involved in the natural relief of pain. In fact, they are often called the body's own narcotic. The word *endorphin* is a contraction of "endogenous morphine," meaning morphine produced within the body itself.

The discovery of endorphins took place very rapidly and in a different manner from that of other known neurotransmitters. In most cases, a transmitter substance has been identified first and its receptor sites found later. With the endorphins, it was the other way around. In the early 1970s, scientists found receptor sites in certain parts of the brain and spinal cord that bind external narcotics like morphine. Further work showed that these receptor sites are especially numerous in areas of the brain known to control the experience of pain. Investigators reasoned that such receptor sites would not exist unless the body produced narcotics that could stimulate them. The intensive search for such substances ended in 1975, when endorphins were finally isolated in brain tissue.

The exact role of endorphins in reducing pain is not yet clear. Some evidence suggests that they contribute to joggers' heightened ability to withstand pain after running: After running a mile, one group of joggers could withstand the pain of a 3-pound weight on their index finger about 70 percent longer than they could before running. Endorphins have been found to affect moods, possibly contributing to the "runner's high" that many people feel at the end of a good run. At the moment, there is no evidence to support the idea that endorphins are directly responsible for this sense of well-being experienced by many runners. However, experimental research with animals indicates that various kinds of stimulation, such as electrical shocks, raises the amount of endorphins in the brain. The same research suggests that endorphins may play a part in other processes besides pain inhibition. For instance, they may hinder certain aspects of memory in animals, as well as contribute to pleasurable sensations (Panksepp, 1986). And there seem to be endorphin-related effects on body temperature, breathing, and the circulatory system (Bolles & Faneslow, 1982).

The discovery of these natural painkilling substances raised the hope that if scientists could produce them artificially in the laboratory, they would not be as addictive as the opiates. Unfortunately, the synthetic endorphins did not live up to ex-

Running may decrease sensitivity to pain by increasing the amount of *endorphins* in the central nervous system.

pectations. Repeated administration of these substances has resulted in tolerance and dependence symptoms similar to those of drug addiction (Olson et al., 1979).

The question remains as to just why the synthetic endorphins are addictive while the natural ones are not. One explanation is that the synthetic substances are not exactly the same chemically as the real thing. The altered structure, which is necessary in order to permit the drug to penetrate the barrier between the bloodstream and the brain, may make the synthetic endorphins addictive. Then, too, synthetic endorphins are designed to retain their anesthetic effect over a longer period of time than the natural substance, which breaks down rapidly. The chemical changes necessary to achieve this may have made the synthetic substance addictive. Researchers are still looking for a nonaddictive "natural" painkiller, but so far they have been unsuccessful.

40). Enkephalins also occur naturally in the brain but seem to have smaller and shorter term pain-relieving effects (Bolles & Fanselow, 1982).

Once a chemical transmitter has been released into the synaptic space and has performed its job, what happens to it? If it remains loose, or if it continues to occupy receptor sites, it will continue to affect the next neuron indefinitely, long after the initial message or signal is over.

Some neurotransmitters (such as ACh) are simply destroyed by other chemicals in the synapse. Others (such as dopamine) are recycled—they are taken back into the vesicles to be used again. In either case, the synapse is cleared up and returned to its normal state.

Synapses and Drugs

Most drugs that affect psychological functions alter the way in which synapses work. Some drugs impede the release of transmitter chemicals from neurons into the synaptic space. For example, the toxin produced by the microorganism that causes botulism prevents the release of the transmitter ACh. The result is paralysis and sometimes rapid death. Other drugs, such as reserpine, cause transmitter chemicals to leak out of the synaptic vesicles and be rapidly broken down by enzymes. The result is a shortage of transmitters and decreased activity at the synapse. Reserpine is often prescribed to reduce blood pressure, because it decreases the activity of neurons that excite the circulatory system. Lysergic acid diethylamide (LSD) reduces the activity of serotonin, an inhibitory transmitter, and it may also affect dopamine, although as yet it is not known exactly how. You may be wondering how suppression of activity could produce the spectacular sensations of an LSD "trip." The drug provokes the effects by suppressing activity in neurons that normally inhibit other neurons in the brain. In response, impulses in the brain increase in frequency, generating hallucinations.

In contrast to drugs that reduce the amount of neurotransmitters, some, such as the venom of the black widow spider and amphetamines, speed up the release of transmitter chemicals into the synaptic space. The spider's poison causes ACh to be poured into the synapses of the nervous system. As a result, neurons fire repeatedly, causing spasms and tremors.

We have seen that some drugs produce their effect by increasing or decreasing the amount of neurotransmitters in the synapse. Other drugs work directly on the receptor sites at the other side of the synaptic gap. Morphine and other opiates are able to lock into the receptors for endorphins, the body's natural painkillers, because they have similar chemical structures. Atropine, a poison derived from belladonna and other plants, also blocks receptor sites, preventing transmitter substances from having their effect. When morphine or atropine occupy the receptor sites, chemical transmitters cannot attach themselves to the neuron, and this tends to shut down the nervous system. Curare, the poison with which some South American Indians tip their arrows, works in the same way.

Still other drugs interfere with the destruction of neurotransmitters after they have done their job. Once transmitter chemicals have bonded to receptor sites and have stimulated or inhibited the neuron, they are normally either deactivated by enzymes or reabsorbed by the vesicles from which they came. A number of stimulant drugs interfere with this process. Caffeine, for example, inhibits the action of the enzymes that break down a neurotransmitter, thus prolonging its effect. As a result, the neurons keep firing, causing a state of high arousal in the nervous system and sometimes a case of "coffee nerves." Cocaine affects the synapses in much the same way, except that it prevents transmitter chemicals from being reabsorbed. Again, the effect is continued stimulation of the receptor sites and a generalized arousal of the nervous system.

Amphetamines work in several ways: They not only increase the release of the chemical transmitters norepinephrine and dopamine, but they also inhibit reabsorption of these substances into the original axon after they have locked into receptor sites on the next neuron. As a result, the next neuron continues to fire while the overall supply of norepinephrine drops. The nervous system responds with a state of alertness or arousal—a "high."

One fascinating recent finding is that neurotransmitters in some cases may be the cause of certain kinds of mental illness. Schizophrenia, for example, seems to be associated with an overabundance of dopamine. Some drugs that have been developed to treat schizophrenia (chlorpromazine is an example) seem to reduce the symptoms of this disorder by blocking dopamine receptors. We will explore these interesting discoveries more fully in the chapters on abnormal behavior and therapy.

Divisions of the Nervous System

If the brain alone has more than 100 billion neurons, and if each neuron can be "in touch" with tens of thousands of other neurons, then our bodies must contain hundreds of trillions of synapses through which each neuron is indirectly linked to every other neuron in the nervous system. Although it is impossible to comprehend such an immense system of interconnected neurons, there really is some structure, some organization, to it all.

The nervous system is usually divided into two major parts: the **central nervous system** and the **peripheral nervous system.** The central nervous system consists of the brain and spinal cord. The peripheral nervous system connects the brain and spinal cord to everything else in the body: sense organs, muscles, glands, and so on (see Figure 2-5). Obviously, without the peripheral nervous system, the central nervous system could not do its job. What would it be like if the brain and the spinal cord were isolated from the rest of the body? In order to answer this question, we must first understand what the central nervous system normally does.

The Central Nervous System

The brain is surely the most fascinating part of the whole nervous system. Containing more than 90 percent of the body's neurons, the brain is the seat of awareness and reason, the place where learning, memory, and emotions are centered. It is the part of us that decides what to do and whether that decision was right or wrong. And it imagines how things might have turned out if we had acted differently.

THE BRAIN. As soon as the brain begins to take shape in the human embryo, we can detect three distinct parts: the hindbrain, midbrain, and forebrain. These three parts are still present in the fully developed adult brain, although they are not so easily distinguished from one another (see Figure 2-6). We will use these three basic divisions to describe the parts of the brain, what they do, and how they interact to influence our behavior.

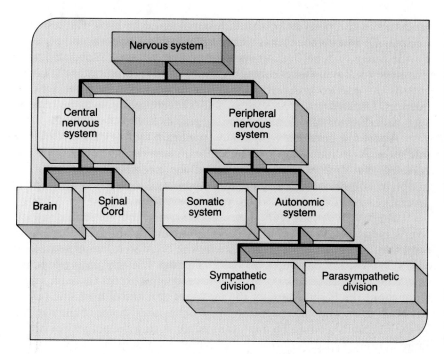

Figure 2-5
A schematic diagram of the divisions of the nervous system and their various subparts.

Since the **hindbrain** is found in even the most primitive vertebrates, it is believed to have been the earliest part of the brain to evolve. The part of the hindbrain nearest to the spinal cord is the **medulla**, a narrow structure about 1.5 inches long. The medulla controls such things as breathing, heart rate, and blood pressure. The medulla is also the point at which many of the nerves from the body cross over on their way to the higher brain centers; the nerves from the left part of the body cross to the right side of the brain and vice versa.

Above the medulla lies the **pons**, which connects the top of the brain to the section of the hindbrain called the **cerebellum**. Chemicals

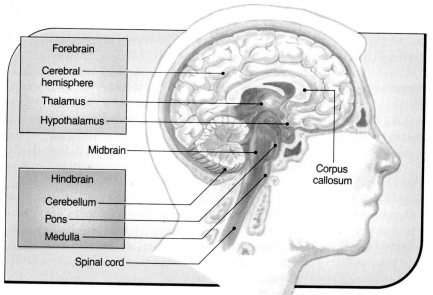

Figure 2-6
A cross-section of the brain, showing the *hindbrain*, *midbrain*, and *forebrain*.

Brain stem The top end of the spinal column that widens out to form the lower part of the brain.

Midbrain Region between the hindbrain and the forebrain; it is important for hearing and sight and is one of several places in the brain where pain is registered.

Forebrain Top part of the brain, including the thalamus, hypothalamus, and cerebral cortex.

Thalamus Area of the forebrain that relays and translates incoming messages from the sense receptors, except those for smell.

Hypothalamus Forebrain region that governs motivation and emotional responses.

Cerebral cortex The two hemispheres of the forebrain that regulate most complex behavior.

Convolutions Folds in the cerebral cortex that allow its mass to fit inside the skull.

Sensory projection areas Areas of the cerebral cortex where messages from the sense receptors are registered.

Motor projection areas Areas of the cerebral cortex where response messages from the brain to the muscles and glands begin.

Association areas Areas in the cerebral cortex where incoming messages from the separate senses are combined into meaningful impressions and outgoing messages from the motor areas are integrated.

produced in the pons help maintain our sleep-wake cycle (discussed in Chapter 4). The cerebellum is composed of two hemispheres and performs a wide range of functions. It handles certain reflexes, especially those that have to do with balance and breathing, and it coordinates the body's actions in order to ensure that movements go together in efficient sequences. Damage to the cerebellum causes severe problems in movement, such as jerky motions, loss of balance, and lack of coordination.

Above the pons and cerebellum, the **brain stem** widens to form the **midbrain.** As its name implies, the midbrain is in the middle of the brain, between the hindbrain at the base and the forebrain at the top. The midbrain is especially important to hearing and sight. It is also one of several places in the brain where pain is registered.

Supported by the brain stem, budding out above it and drooping over somewhat to fit into the skull, is the **forebrain.** In the center of the forebrain, and more or less directly over the brain stem, are the two egg-shaped structures that make up the **thalamus.** The thalamus relays and translates incoming messages from sense receptors (except those for smell) throughout the body. Many of the messages that travel from one part of the brain to another also pass through the thalamus. Some of the neurons in the thalamus seem to be important in regulating the activity of higher brain centers. Others control the activities of those parts of the nervous system outside the brain and spinal cord.

Below the thalamus is a smaller structure called the **hypothalamus.** This part of the forebrain exerts an enormous influence on many kinds of motivation. Centers in the hypothalamus govern eating, drinking, sexual behavior, sleeping, and temperature control. The hypothalamus is also directly involved in emotional behavior. Centers in the hypothalamus are responsible for such emotions as rage, terror, and pleasure. Also, in times of stress the hypothalamus appears to play a central role, coordinating and integrating the activity of the nervous system.

Above the brain stem, thalamus, and hypothalamus are the two cerebral hemispheres commonly called the **cerebral cortex.** These are what most people think of first when they talk about "the brain," and as the photo on page 48 shows, they take up most of the room inside the skull. They balloon out over the brain stem, fold down over it, and actually hide most of it from view. The cerebral cortex is the most recently evolved part of the nervous system and is more highly developed in humans than in any other animal. It accounts for about 80 percent of the human brain's weight and contains 70 percent of the neurons in the central nervous system. If it were spread out, it would cover 2 to 3 square feet, so in order to fit inside the skull, the cerebral cortex has developed an intricate pattern of folds—hills and valleys called **convolutions.** These convolutions form a pattern in every brain that is as unique as a fingerprint.

Messages from the sense receptors are registered in those areas of the cerebral cortex called **sensory projection areas.** Response messages from the brain start their return trip in the **motor projection areas,** and from there they go to the various muscles and glands in the body. There are also large areas throughout the cerebral cortex that are neither completely sensory nor completely motor. These are called **association areas,** and they make up most of the cerebral cortex. It is in the association areas that messages coming in from separate senses are combined into meaningful impressions, and where motor messages going out are integrated so the body can make coordinated movements. The association areas are involved in all of the activities that we commonly attribute to the brain: learning, thinking, remembering, talking.

The largest of the association areas is located in the **frontal lobes** of the brain, just behind the forehead (see Figure 2-7). Accounting for about half the volume of the cerebral cortex, the frontal lobes appear to

Frontal lobes Largest of the association areas; the site of such uniquely human activities as self-awareness, initiative, and planning.

■ Brain Waves

As large numbers of neurons fire in the brain, they generate sequences of rhythmic variations in electrical activity known as *brain waves*. The shape and pattern of these waves vary depending on what you happen to be doing at the time. Using electrodes placed directly on the scalp, psychologists can record brain-wave activity on an *electroencephalograph*, or *EEG*. By means of this device, investigators have uncovered a number of different types of brain waves. *Alpha waves* are commonly associated with a state of relaxation. Alphas change to higher frequency *beta waves* when a person is awake and still, but with eyes open. High-frequency *gamma waves* are characteristic of being awake and in a highly excited state. At the other extreme are the low-frequency *delta waves* that occur during deepest sleep. Also, the site of origin in the brain varies with the type of wave. Alpha waves, for instance, are usually recorded in the occipital and parietal lobes. Delta waves are much more variable in location.

Other patterns of waves arise when the brain is exposed to stimuli such as sound or light or when it enters certain psychological states. Researchers have discovered an EEG pattern that appears in the interval between some type of warning signal and a response, such as pressing a button. This seems to suggest that subtle psychological processes, such as a state of expectancy, can affect brain waves (Rosenzweig & Leiman, 1982). Because of this, brain waves can be "read" as indicators of a person's psychophysiological state, however, they do not provide information about a person's actual thoughts (Donchin, 1987).

Recently, medical researchers have discovered that epilepsy is associated with highly unusual patterns of electrical activity in the brain. When undergoing a seizure, the brain is swept by sudden and dramatic changes that have been compared to electrical storms. During these disruptions, the height of the EEG can reach 5 to 20 times that of normal brain waves (Rosenzweig & Leiman, 1982). In grand mal seizures, the EEG pattern in large areas of the brain reflects bursts of unusually rapid firing by individual neurons. The effect of these abnormalities on the behavior of the victim is striking. The person loses consciousness and the body stiffens for one or two minutes before entering a phase marked by a sequence of sudden jerks and relaxation.

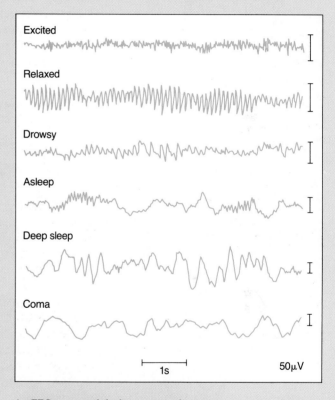

An EEG can record the brain waves of a person in a variety of states. Adapted from Penfield & Jasper, 1954. Copyright 1954 by Little, Brown. Adapted with permission.

Psychologists do not yet understand what causes these uncontrolled bursts of firing. It is known that head injuries, exposure to chemicals, and problems with metabolism can bring about seizures, but just why this happens remains a mystery. Nonetheless, researchers have developed a number of drugs that inhibit transmission of the nerve impulses that mark epilepsy, and as a result the number and severity of attacks can be reduced. In extreme cases, it is also possible to reduce epileptic seizures through brain surgery. Later in this chapter, we will discuss some fascinating discoveries that have been made as a result of this kind of "split-brain" surgery.

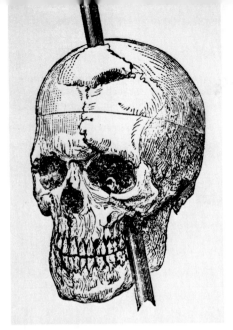

The skull of Phineas Gage, showing where the tamping iron passed through it.

be the site of mental processes that are unique to humans—self-awareness, initiative, and the ability to plan. However, the exact functions of these lobes are still obscure. In part, this is because much of our knowledge about brain function comes from research on animals, whose frontal lobes are relatively undeveloped. Therefore, in studying the frontal lobes, we have had to rely on the relatively rare cases of people with some kind of frontal lobe damage. One such famous case became public in 1848. It involved a bizarre accident that happened to a man named Phineas Gage.

Gage, who was foreman of a railroad construction gang, made a careless mistake while using some blasting powder and a tamping iron. As a result, the tamping iron tore through his cheek and severely damaged both frontal lobes. Gage remained conscious, walked part of the way to a doctor, and, to the amazement of those who saw the accident, suffered few major aftereffects. There was no physical impairment, and his memory and skills seemed to be as good as ever. He did, however, undergo major personality changes. Once a steady worker, he lost interest in work and

Figure 2-7
An interior view of the human brain The corpus callosum, which connects the two visibly distinct hemispheres of the brain, is located just above the thalamus.
From Nauta, W. J. H., & Feirtag, M. *The organization of the brain.* Copyright © 1979 by Scientific American, Inc. All rights reserved. Illustration by Carol Donner.

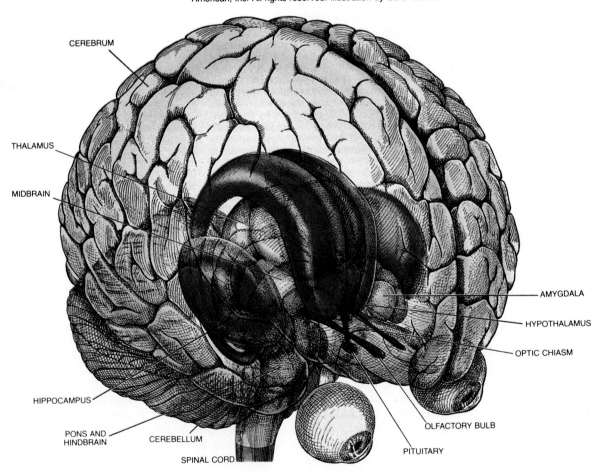

CEREBRUM

THALAMUS

MIDBRAIN

AMYGDALA

HYPOTHALAMUS

OPTIC CHIASM

HIPPOCAMPUS

PONS AND HINDBRAIN

CEREBELLUM

OLFACTORY BULB

PITUITARY

SPINAL CORD

drifted from job to job. Other personality changes were so great that, in the view of his friends, Gage was no longer the same man.

Since Gage's time, careful observation of brain-damaged people has refined these early impressions of the functions of the frontal lobes. This part of the brain seems to permit goal-directed behavior. Patients with damage to the frontal lobes have trouble completing tasks that involve following complex directions or performing tasks in which the directions change during the course of the job. The frontal lobes also appear necessary to a normal emotional life. People whose frontal lobes have been severed often seem apathetic and capable of only shallow emotions, although this apathy may be interrupted by periods of boastfulness and silliness. The frontal lobes also seem to play a role in the ability to keep track of previous and future movements of the body. Much more research needs to be done before psychologists can understand how this part of the cortex contributes to such a wide and subtle range of mental activities.

Besides their other functions, the frontal lobes receive and coordinate messages from the three other lobes of the cortex. Each of these other lobes is responsible for a different sense. The **occipital lobe,** located at the very back of the brain, receives and interprets visual information from both eyes. Next to the occipital lobe is the **temporal lobe,** which controls hearing and does some additional processing of visual information. The temporal lobe may also be the area of the brain where memories are permanently stored. The **parietal lobe** sits on top of the temporal and occipital lobes (see Figure 2-7). This lobe receives sensations of touch and bodily position and informs the brain of events worthy of special attention. Injury to any of these lobes will directly affect the sense area involved. We will look more closely at the connections between the senses and the brain areas where sensations are registered in the next chapter.

HEMISPHERIC SPECIALIZATION. We have been talking about the cerebral cortex as if it were all one piece. But if you look closely at the photos of the cortex, you will notice in the top and bottom views what appears to be a split down the middle of the cortex, running from front to back. In this case, appearance is reality: The cerebral cortex is made up of two separate hemispheres. In a sense, there is a "right half-brain" and a "left half-brain," and the only place they are directly connected is through a thick, ribbonlike band across the bottom called the **corpus callosum** (see Figure 2-6). In general, the left half of the brain receives messages from and sends messages to the right side of the body. The right half of the brain does this for the left side of the body.

Under normal conditions, the two hemispheres are in close communication through the corpus callosum and work together as a coordinated unit. Nonetheless, some evidence began to collect early in this century that the cerebral hemispheres are not really equivalent. For example, damage to the left hemisphere often seems to result in severe language problems, while similar damage to the right hemisphere seldom has that effect. Then, in the early 1960s, Sperry and his colleagues at the California Institute of Technology started treating epileptics by cutting the corpus callosum. The intent was to stop the spread of seizures from one hemisphere to the other, but the operations also cut the only direct communication link between the two hemispheres and thus made it

Occipital lobe Part of the cerebral cortex that receives and interprets visual information.

Temporal lobe Part of the cerebral cortex that controls hearing and some processing of visual information.

Parietal lobe Part of the cerebral cortex that responds to sensations of touch and bodily position and informs the brain of events worthy of special attention.

Corpus callosum Band that connects the two hemispheres of the brain and coordinates their activities.

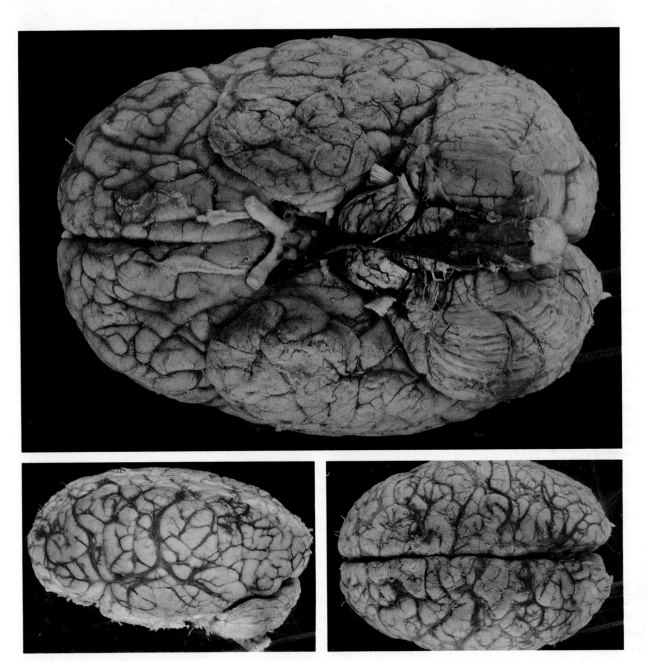

Three views of the brain Visible in the top and bottom right photos is the split down the middle of the brain. The photo at bottom left is of the blood vessels found in the brain.

possible to watch each hemisphere work on its own (Sperry, 1964, 1968, 1970). The results were startling.

When such "split-brain patients" were asked to stare at a spot on a projection screen while pictures of various objects were projected to the *right* of that spot, they were able to identify the objects verbally, and they were able to pick them out of a group of hidden objects using their right hands to feel each object in turn. When pictures of objects were shown on the *left* side of the projection screen, the reverse was found: Subjects could pick out the objects by feeling them with their left hands, yet they were unable to say what the objects were! In fact, most often when objects were projected on the left side of the screen, split-brain patients reported that they had seen "nothing" on the screen, even though they could accurately identify the objects when given a chance to touch and feel them with their left hands.

The explanation for these startling results is to be found in the way each hemisphere of the brain operates. In split-brain patients, the left hemisphere receives information only from the right side of the body and the right half of the visual field. Thus, it can match an object shown in the right visual field with information received by touch from the right hand. However, it is unaware of (and thus unable to identify) objects shown in the left visual field or touched by the left hand. Conversely, in split-brain patients the right hemisphere of the brain receives information only from the left side of the visual field and the left side of the body. Thus, it can match an object shown in the left visual field with information received by touch from the left hand. But it is unaware of any objects shown in the right visual field or touched with the right hand.

This description of the two hemispheres explains all of Sperry's findings except one: When an object is shown in the left visual field, why can't split-brain patients identify the object verbally? The answer seems to be that, for the great majority of people, language ability is concentrated almost entirely in the left hemisphere of the brain. In most split-brain patients, the right hemisphere of the brain cannot verbally identify the object that it is "seeing" in the left visual field, even though the object can be picked out by touch using the left hand. When the person is asked, "What do you see?", the left hemisphere (which monitors the right visual field) correctly reports, "Nothing."

In other words, the two hemispheres not only receive from and send information to different sides of the body, but also seem to perform somewhat different mental functions. In most people, the left hemisphere is dominant in verbal tasks, such as identifying spoken and printed words (see Figures 2-8, 2-9, and 2-10). But recent evidence shows that, in at least a few people, the right brain is not completely without verbal skills.

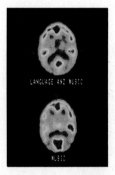

For the great majority of people, language ability appears to be concentrated almost entirely in the left hemisphere of the brain.

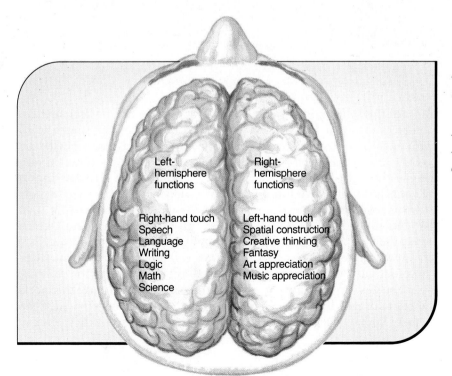

Left-hemisphere functions

Right-hemisphere functions

Right-hand touch
Speech
Language
Writing
Logic
Math
Science

Left-hand touch
Spatial construction
Creative thinking
Fantasy
Art appreciation
Music appreciation

Figure 2-8
The two hemispheres of the cerebral cortex The left hemisphere controls movements of the right hand, and the right hemisphere controls the left hand. The left hemisphere is dominant in verbal tasks, while the right hemisphere is dominant in spatial construction.

■ New Tools for Looking at the Brain

The pace of scientific discovery has long been connected to the invention of instruments that improve our powers of observation. In recent years, a number of devices designed to map various structures and operations of the brain promise to revolutionize our understanding of how the human brain works.

About 20 years ago, the invention of *computerized axial tomography (CAT) scanning* allowed scientists to photograph the brain from points around the circumference of the skull. Even more successful at producing pictures of the inner regions of the brain—its ridges, folds, and fissures—is an imaging technique called *nuclear magnetic resonance (NMR)*. Both these techniques permit unparalleled mapping of the brain's structures.

Neither CAT scanning nor NMR, however, can provide a moving picture of the brain in action. Three techniques allow

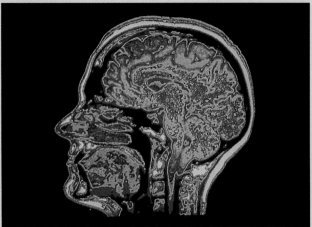

NMR image of the human head.

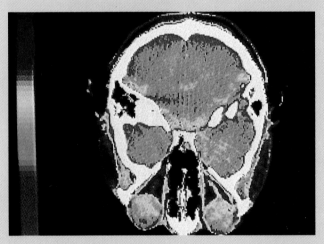

CAT scan of a normal human brain.

researchers to do just that: to observe the brain as it actually reacts to sensory stimuli such as pain, tones, and words. One technique is a kind of electroencephalography, or EEG (you read about this in the Box on p. 45), which measures the electrical activity the brain produces as it responds to stimuli. Quite recently, biophysicists have developed a technique called *EEG imaging*, by which they can measure the actual functioning of the brain "on a millisecond by millisecond basis" (Fischman, 1985, p. 18). Using 32 electrodes placed strategically on the scalp, this technique feeds information about electrical activity in the brain into a computer, which translates the information into colored moving images on a television monitor. EEG imaging was originally developed for research into convulsive seizures, but it is also promising as a technique for predicting learning disabilities in children and for mapping the brain activity of patients suffering from schizophrenia and Alzheimer's disease.

Most of the split-brain patients studied so far have had no real language ability in the right hemisphere, but some could recognize simple words with their right hemisphere, and at least a few displayed quite sophisticated verbal skills there (Gazzaniga, 1983; Zaidel, 1983). In contrast, for most people the right hemisphere appears to be responsible for some aspects of concept formation, as in being able to understand how the parts of a story fit together and what a story is all about. For example, split-brain patients studied by Gardner (1981) listened to stories and were asked to retell them. These patients could verbally describe the main details of the stories quite well. But they tended to confuse the order of sentences, leave out parts of the story, and misinterpret the point of the story.

Studies of split-brain patients like these have helped make the special functions of each hemisphere more apparent. Whereas the left hemisphere is more verbal, the right is more visually perceptive and able to pick up

The second technique is *positron emission tomography* (*PET*) *scanning*. As neurons in a given part of the brain fire, that part of the brain replenishes its energy supply by absorbing sugar from the blood. PET maps the location in the brain of radioactive sugar molecules that are released into the bloodstream. By means of this procedure, called *radioactive PET*, biophysicists can label drugs that bind to the receptors in certain neurotransmitters and trace the paths of chemicals as they travel along specific pathways in the brain, making it possible to trace specific areas of brain activity. Some of the findings have been surprising—it turns out that the brains of people with higher IQ scores are actually *less* active than those with lower IQ scores, perhaps because they process information more efficiently (Haier, 1988). Progress has been made in locating the damaged brain region in which reduced levels of the neurotransmitter dopamine contribute to Parkinson's disease, and the technique should help researchers understand more about the effects of psychoactive drugs such as tranquilizers.

A third technique is called *magnetoencephalography* (*MEG*). A regular EEG scan picks up electrical signals transmitted along nerve cells; but because these signals are distorted when they pass through the skull, it is difficult to identify their points of origin. At the same time, however, those electric currents create magnetic fields that are unaffected by bone; the MEG measures the strength of the magnetic field and identifies its source. Using this procedure, biophysicists may now be able to locate the part of the brain that does most of the work in such cognitive processes as memory and language processing. MEG is thus promising as a means of understanding such disorders as amnesia and dyslexia, and researchers also hope to be able to locate the active sites of drugs used in the treatment of such severe disorders as schizophrenia; this knowledge would be particularly valuable in understanding the drugs' serious side effects.

These advances in technology will permit neuroscientists to match anatomical structures (from CAT and NMR) with sites of energy use (PET and MEG) and areas of electrical activity in the brain (EEGs). When all these techniques are combined, scientists may finally be able to study the impact of drugs on the brain, track the formation of memories, and map the location of other mental activities in unprecedented detail.

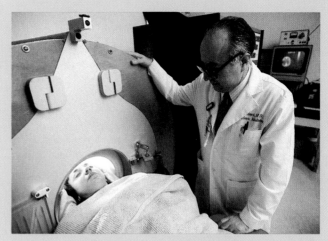

A PET scan is performed.

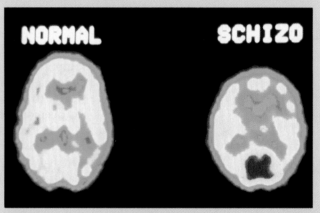

PET scan of a normal brain and the brain of a schizophrenic.

subtle emotional cues (Tucker, 1981). It now appears that in addition to being verbally dominant, the left side of the brain also functions as an interpreter (see Figure 2-11), helping us with sequencing and logic and helping us make sense of information coming in from the right hemisphere (Gazzaniga, 1985). While the left hemisphere excels at this kind of logical sequencing task, the right is better able to take in many things at once, making it more intuitive and nonverbal.

Other studies of hemispheric specialization have looked at dyslexics, people who have difficulty reading and writing. While dyslexics appear to have trouble identifying or naming words, they have no problem telling words apart. It is now believed that unlike most of us, the right side of the dyslexic's brain is the dominant one. Albert Einstein and the sculptor Auguste Rodin were both probably dyslexic. Both excelled at tasks requiring spatial and conceptual abilities. Autopsies of dyslexics have shown

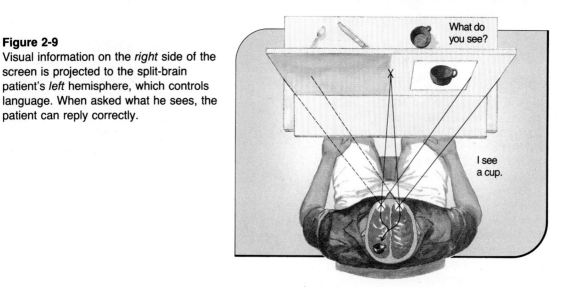

Figure 2-9
Visual information on the *right* side of the screen is projected to the split-brain patient's *left* hemisphere, which controls language. When asked what he sees, the patient can reply correctly.

that certain areas of the right hemisphere that are normally smaller than those of the left are of equal size in dyslexics. It is now hypothesized that hormones or the immune system may play a role in causing the right hemisphere in dyslexics to develop at the expense of the left. While pinpointing and then finally reversing the conditions that lead to this language disability is probably years away, techniques for teaching dyslexics to read have begun to use the strengths of the right hemisphere to overcome the weaknesses of the left.

Although the differences between the two hemispheres are intriguing, we must remember that under normal conditions, the right and left halves of the brain are in close communication through the corpus callosum and thus work together in a coordinated, integrated way. Nevertheless, in recent years a good deal of popular literature has seized on the highly publicized split-brain research and drawn all kinds of unwarranted conclusions about human behavior. In particular, some authors have inaugurated what is sometimes called a "right-brain movement" to promote the uses and virtues of supposedly right-brain skills like creativity and conceptualizing. For instance, it has been suggested that organizations increase creativity by teaming verbally oriented left-brain workers with conceptually oriented right-brain workers or by training left-brain ex-

Figure 2-10
When the image of the spoon is projected only on the *left* side of the screen, only the *right* hemisphere of the split-brain patient sees it. Since the image has not been received by the patient's language center, he cannot name the object. He can, however, pick it out by touch—if he uses his *left* hand.
Adapted from Carol Wald © *Discover* magazine, 1987

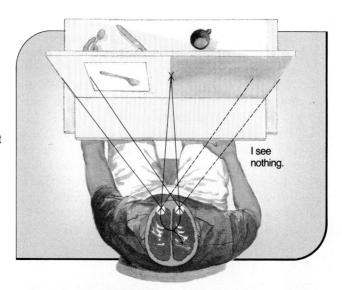

ecutives to use more effectively their right-brain skills. According to psychologist Sally Springer, the promotion of right-brain skills may be of some use in organizational management, but "to say that it works because of differential use of the two hemispheres goes well beyond what we can prove today" (McKean, 1985, p. 38). One of Sperry's colleagues, Michael Gazzaniga, adds that the right-brain movement has simply pointed out that there are normal differences among people: "You don't have to invoke one cent's worth of experimental psychological data or neuroscience to make the observation that there are some people in this world who are terribly intuitive and creative, and some who aren't" (McKean, 1985, p. 34).

THE RETICULAR FORMATION. We separated the brain into forebrain, midbrain, and hindbrain in order to simplify our discussion. But the brain itself often ignores such distinctions and sets up systems that jump across these boundaries, drawing together different parts of the brain in order to perform certain functions. One such system is the **reticular formation.**

The reticular formation (RF) is made up of a netlike bundle of neurons running through the hindbrain, midbrain, and part of the forebrain. Its main job seems to be to send "Alert!" signals to the higher parts of the brain when an incoming message is important. The RF apparently also decides which of several incoming messages is most urgent. Some messages seem to be toned down by the RF; others never reach the higher centers of the brain at all. Because of the RF, we can concentrate our attention on one message and ignore distracting messages from other sense receptors. We can read an interesting book, for example, while the television is blaring, telephones are ringing, and people are talking in other parts of the room. The RF can also be shut down. An anesthetic, for example, works largely by shutting down this system. Permanent damage to the RF can cause a coma.

THE LIMBIC SYSTEM. Another example of the interconnected nature of parts of the central nervous system is the **limbic system,** a ring

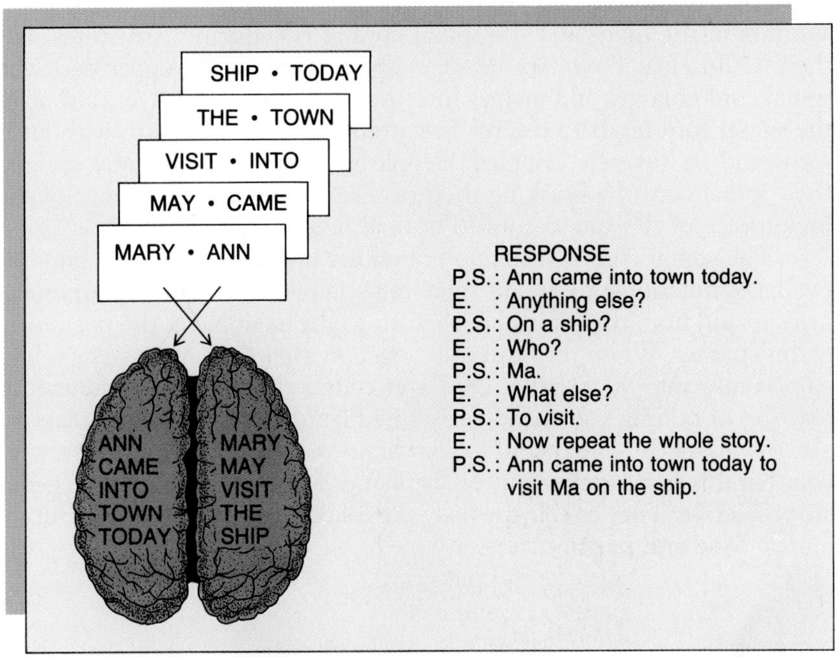

Reticular formation (RF) Network of neurons in the hindbrain, midbrain, and part of the forebrain whose primary function is to filter incoming messages and alert the higher parts of the brain to those that are important.

Limbic system Ring of structures around the thalamus that plays a role in learning and emotional behavior.

SHIP · TODAY
THE · TOWN
VISIT · INTO
MAY · CAME
MARY · ANN

ANN CAME INTO TOWN TODAY

MARY MAY VISIT THE SHIP

RESPONSE
P.S.: Ann came into town today.
E. : Anything else?
P.S.: On a ship?
E. : Who?
P.S.: Ma.
E. : What else?
P.S.: To visit.
E. : Now repeat the whole story.
P.S.: Ann came into town today to visit Ma on the ship.

Figure 2-11
When split-brain patients who have developed some language ability are presented with two different stories, one to each side of the brain, the patients' first response, when asked what the story is about, is to relate the story that was presented to the left, verbally dominant, hemisphere. But when asked if that is all there is to the story, they begin to add the details of the story presented to the right hemisphere. Because these details make no sense in relation to the first, the patients reinterpret the first story in light of the second.

Hippocampus Part of the limbic system that is vital to memory formation.

Spinal cord Complex cable of nerves that runs down the spine, connecting the brain to most of the rest of the body.

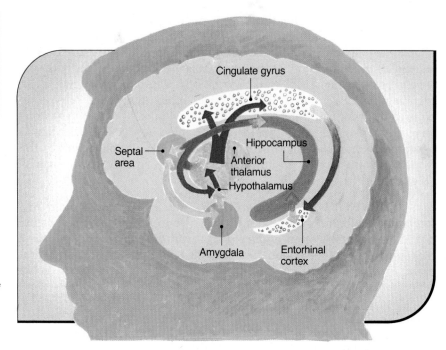

Figure 2-12
A stylized picture of the limbic system, showing how different areas of the limbic system interact during emotional stress.

From C. Levinthal, 1983. (Modified from R. A. McCleary & R. Y. Moore, *Subcortical Mechanisms of Behavior.* N.Y.: Basic Books, 1965. From F. Leukel, *Introduction to Physiological Psychology,* 3rd ed. St. Louis: Mosby, 1976, p. 299.)

of structures around the thalamus in the center of each cerebral hemisphere (see Figure 2-12). The limbic system includes the hypothalamus, part of the thalamus, and several other forebrain structures. It also contains nerve fibers that connect it to the cerebral cortex and to the brain stem.

Although much of how the limbic system functions remains a mystery, it is believed to affect or control learning and emotional behavior. For example, one of its parts, the **hippocampus,** plays an important part in memory. Patients with damage to the hippocampus cannot form new memories. They can remember things that happened years ago but will forget completely the recent death of a near relative.

THE SPINAL CORD. The complex cable of nerves that connects the brain to most of the rest of the body is known as the **spinal cord.** We talk of the brain and the spinal cord as two distinct structures, but there is no clear boundary between them since, at its upper end, the spinal cord enlarges and merges into the hindbrain. Moreover, although the spinal cord tends to receive less attention than the brain, without it we would be severely crippled. People who have accidentally severed their spinal cords by breaking their necks provide tragic evidence of the importance of the spinal cord to normal functioning.

The spinal cord is made up of bundles of long nerve fibers and has two basic functions: to permit some reflex movements and to carry messages to and from the brain. Let's return to the example at the beginning of this chapter. When you burn your finger on a match, a message signaling pain comes into your spinal cord and causes the almost instantaneous reaction of pulling your hand away (see Figure 2-13). The pain message also travels up the spinal cord to your brain, but before it even gets there, your hand is being pulled out of the flame. Most of these spinal reflexes are protective: They enable the body to avoid serious damage and maintain muscle tone and position.

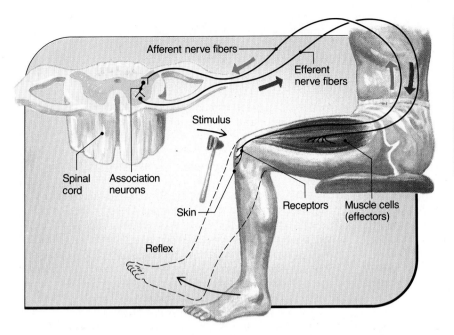

Afferent nerve fibers

Efferent nerve fibers

Stimulus

Spinal cord

Association neurons

Skin

Receptors

Muscle cells (effectors)

Reflex

Figure 2-13
Simple reflexes are controlled by the *spinal cord*. The message travels from the sense receptors near the skin through the afferent nerve fibers to the spinal cord. In the spinal cord, the messages are relayed through association neurons to the efferent nerve fibers, which carry them to the muscle cells that cause the reflex movement.

The Peripheral Nervous System

We saw earlier that the nervous system is made up of two major parts: the central nervous system (the brain and spinal cord) and the peripheral nervous system. The peripheral nervous system carries messages to and from the central nervous system. Without the peripheral nervous system, no information could get to your spinal cord and your brain, and your brain could not give directions to the muscles and glands in your body. Even the simple reflex of pulling your hand away from a flaming match would not work: The peripheral nervous system carries the pain message to your spinal cord and the instructions from the spinal cord to your hand. The peripheral nervous system is made up of two major parts: the somatic and the autonomic nervous systems.

THE SOMATIC NERVOUS SYSTEM. The **somatic nervous system** is composed of all the afferent, or sensory, neurons that carry information to the central nervous system and all the efferent, or motor, neurons that carry messages from the central nervous system to the skeletal muscles of the body. All the things that we can sense—sights, sounds, smells, temperature, pressure, and so on—have their origins in the somatic part of the peripheral nervous system. In later chapters, we will see how the somatic nervous system affects our experience of the world both inside and outside our bodies.

THE AUTONOMIC NERVOUS SYSTEM. The **autonomic nervous system** is composed of all the neurons that carry messages between the central nervous system and all the internal organs of the body (the glands and the smooth muscles such as the heart and digestive system). The autonomic nervous system obviously is necessary to such body functions as breathing and assuring a proper flow of blood. But it is also important in the experience of various emotions—a fact that makes it of special interest to psychologists.

What We Know—and Need to Know—About the Damaged Brain

Consider the case of Dr. P.:

Dr. P. was an accomplished musician and teacher at a local music academy, where his tendency to make bizarre visual mistakes was first observed. Dr. P. began to have trouble recognizing faces that should have been familiar to him. Dr. P. also began to see faces where there were no faces and to pat fire hydrants on the head and address them as if they were children. Dr. P. mistook his wife for a hat and his own foot for his shoe. He could readily identify such abstract objects as a cube, and he could identify a picture of Albert Einstein from the mustache and famous shock of white hair, but he could not readily recognize the faces in pictures of his own family members. Dr. P. was not aware of any problems in his visual behavior.

Because Dr. P. had a wonderfully developed musical cortex, neurologist Oliver Sacks concluded that his temporal lobes were intact and that his perplexing, even tragic, problem lay in his parietal and occipital lobes, particularly in his right visual cortex (Sacks, 1987).

Sacks notes that the right hemisphere of the brain and the disorders to which it is subject have traditionally been neglected by neuropsychologists, largely because it is easier to identify lesions and their effects on the brain's left side, which is more clearly demarcated than the right side. In fact, says Sacks, "we will find a thousand descriptions of left-hemisphere syndromes in the neurological and neuropsychological literature for every description of a right-hemisphere syndrome" (Sacks, 1987, p. 5).

Nevertheless, syndromes resulting from damage to the right side of the brain run from the darkly comic to the painfully tragic (Sacks also treated a patient whose vision and visual memory had been completely erased by stroke-caused damage—and who did not know that it had happened to him!). Because these cases involve remarkably selective disturbances, they provide additional impetus for researchers who focus on the relationship between specific areas and functions of the brain and mental activity. The importance of this direction in research might be illustrated by the case of a patient named M. D., who suffered global aphasia—a complete disruption of language production and comprehension—as a result of a stroke. Within 18 months, M. D. had almost completely recovered his language capabilities—except for a peculiar inability to name fruits and vegetables. M. D.'s problem suggested that the disturbance in the semantic system of his brain was extremely selective, and it would appear that the brain's "dictionary" is much more highly categorized than had previously been demonstrated (Hart, Berndt, & Caramazza, 1985).

Research on laboratory animals has suggested that aggression is linked to specific areas of the brain, and some psychologists feel that lesions in certain areas of the brain can produce aggressive behavior regardless of any environmental factors bearing on the sufferer's behavior. These findings may have implications for the understanding and treatment of violent aggression in humans, which seems in some cases to be linked to brain damage. According to a team of researchers at the Harvard University Medical School, this may be particularly true in the case of apparently senseless acts of violence committed by people who do not consider themselves sick.

Recent neuropsychological studies also suggest that our traditional concept of the relationship between the brain and the mind may be erroneous. The traditional concept is that a person makes a decision that induces the brain to trigger an act. But neurophysiologist Benjamin Libet believes that considerable brain activity *precedes* voluntary acts—precedes the instant of the decision (Libet, 1985). Libet measured the brain activity of subjects who spontaneously moved their fingers. Timing the decision to act by having the subjects note the position of a revolving spot at the moment when they made the decision, Libet detected brain activity that began, on the average, about one-third of a second before the decision. However, Libet adds that this does not mean that the will is necessarily the slave of localized brain activity; he notes that the mind has about two-tenths of a second between its awareness of intent and the projected action and can "veto" the intent.

Neurophysiologists now have access to technology with which to monitor brain activity and identify areas that seem to be linked to certain mental acts (see Box on pp. 50–51). One team of researchers has even identified certain networks of cells responsive to different musical notes. However, it should be pointed out that they have discovered not specific cells responsive to specific notes, but *networks* of responsive cells: Networks of cells located throughout the brain are believed to be involved in mental acts.

In order to understand the autonomic nervous system, we must make one more distinction. The autonomic nervous system consists of two branches: the *sympathetic* and *parasympathetic divisions* (see Figure 2-14). These two divisions act in almost total opposition to each other, but both are directly involved in controlling and integrating the actions of the glands and the smooth muscles within the body.

The nerve fibers of the **sympathetic division** are busiest when you are frightened or angry. They carry messages that tell the body to prepare for an emergency and to get ready to act quickly or strenuously. In response to messages from the sympathetic division, your heart pounds, you breathe faster, your pupils enlarge, and digestion stops. As we will see shortly, the sympathetic nervous system also tells the endocrine system to start

Figure 2-14
The sympathetic and parasympathetic divisions of the autonomic nervous system The sympathetic division generally acts to arouse the body, while the parasympathetic follows with messages to relax.

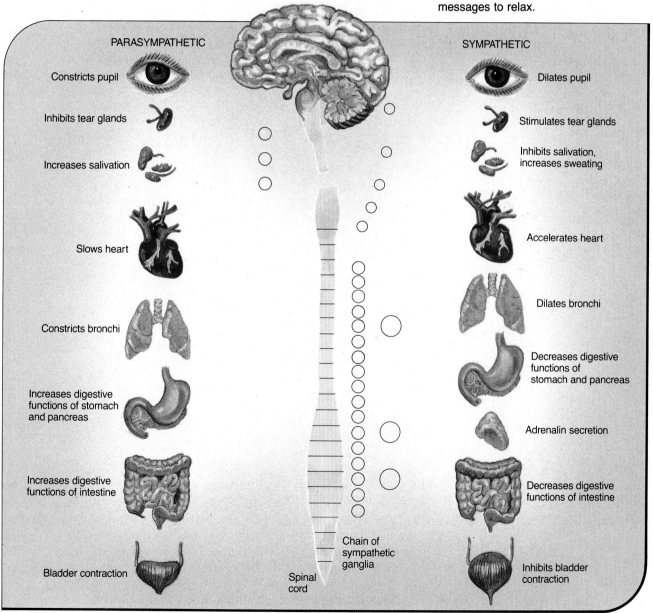

PARASYMPATHETIC

Constricts pupil

Inhibits tear glands

Increases salivation

Slows heart

Constricts bronchi

Increases digestive functions of stomach and pancreas

Increases digestive functions of intestine

Bladder contraction

Spinal cord

Chain of sympathetic ganglia

SYMPATHETIC

Dilates pupil

Stimulates tear glands

Inhibits salivation, increases sweating

Accelerates heart

Dilates bronchi

Decreases digestive functions of stomach and pancreas

Adrenalin secretion

Decreases digestive functions of intestine

Inhibits bladder contraction

Parasympathetic division The branch of the autonomic nervous system that calms the body after stress.

Hormones Chemical substances released by the endocrine glands that help regulate bodily activities.

Endocrine glands Glands of the endocrine system that release hormones into the bloodstream.

pumping chemicals into the bloodstream in order to further strengthen these reactions. Sympathetic nerve fibers connect to every internal organ in the body—a fact that explains why the body's reaction to sudden stress is so widespread. However, the sympathetic division can also act selectively on a single organ.

Parasympathetic nerve fibers connect to the same organs as the sympathetic nerve fibers, but they cause just the opposite effects. The **parasympathetic division** says, in effect, "Okay, the heat's off, back to normal." The heart then goes back to beating at its normal rate, the stomach muscles relax, digestion starts again, breathing slows down, and the pupils of the eyes get smaller. Thus, the parasympathetic division compensates for the sympathetic division and lets the body rest after stress.

Usually, these two systems work together: After the sympathetic division has aroused the body, the parasympathetic division follows with messages to relax. In most people, however, one division or the other tends to dominate. In ulcer patients, for example, the parasympathetic division tends to dominate: They salivate heavily, their hearts beat rather slowly, and their digestive systems are often overactive. People whose sympathetic division dominates show the opposite symptoms: Their mouths are dry, their palms moist, and their hearts beat quickly even when they are resting.

The autonomic nervous system was traditionally regarded as the "automatic" part of the body's response mechanism. You could not, it was believed, tell your own autonomic nervous system when to speed up or slow down your heart's beating or when to stop or start your digestive processes. These things were thought to run as automatically as a thermostat controlling the temperature of a room. The latest evidence, however, suggests that we have more control over the autonomic nervous system than we think. Many studies seem to show that people (and animals) can indeed manipulate this so-called automatic part of the nervous system. For example, it is possible to learn to control such things as high blood pressure, migraine headaches, and even ulcers. Some people have even learned to control their own heart rate and brain waves. These are all cases in which the autonomic nervous system is brought under a person's deliberate control. We will look more closely at these possibilities when we discuss biofeedback in Chapter 5.

■ The Endocrine System

The nervous system is not the only mechanism that regulates the functioning of our bodies. Let's return one more time to our earlier example. When you burn your finger on a match, you quickly withdraw it from the heat. But your response to the burn does not end with the nervous system. Chemical substances called **hormones** are also released into your bloodstream by internal organs called **endocrine glands.** These hormones are carried throughout your body, where they have widespread effects on a variety of organs. Under less dramatic circumstances, hormones, acting either singly or together, are responsible for such things as differences in

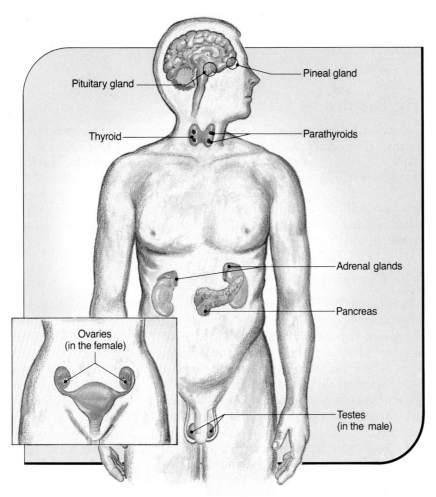

Thyroid Gland Endocrine gland located below the voice box that produces the hormone thyroxin.

Thyroxin Hormone that regulates the rate of metabolism.

Figure 2-15
The glands of the endocrine system.

vitality among people; for the readiness of nerves and muscles to react; for the rates of metabolism, growth, and sexual development; for the body's preparations for pregnancy and childbirth; and for emotional balance in general.

The locations of the endocrine glands are shown in Figure 2-15. Our discussion will focus on those glands whose functions are best understood and those whose effects are most closely related to the way we behave.

The Thyroid Gland

The **thyroid gland** is located just below the larynx, or voice box. It produces one primary hormone, **thyroxin,** which regulates the body's rate of metabolism. That is, it determines how fast or how slowly the foods we eat are transformed into the energy that we need to function normally. Differences in the metabolic rate determine how alert and energetic people are and how fat or thin they tend to be.

If your thyroid gland produces too much thyroxin, your appetite will be huge: You will eat everything in sight, although you may stay very much underweight. Your reactions may also be speeded up and extremely intense, especially your reactions to stress. Too little thyroxin

Parathyroids Four tiny glands embedded in the thyroid that secrete parathormone.

Parathormone Hormone that controls the levels of calcium and phosphate in the blood and tissue fluids.

Pancreas Organ lying between the stomach and small intestine that secretes insulin and glucagon.

Insulin and glucagon Hormones that work in opposite ways to regulate the level of sugar in the blood.

Pituitary gland Gland located on the underside of the brain that produces the largest number of the body's hormones; composed of the posterior and anterior pituitary.

Posterior pituitary Separately functioning part of the pituitary that is controlled by the nervous system.

Anterior pituitary Part of the pituitary known as the "master gland" because it produces numerous hormones that trigger the action of other glands; one of these hormones regulates body growth.

leads to the other extreme: You will want to sleep and sleep and will still feel constantly tired. Without enough thyroxin, your body is unable to maintain normal temperature, muscle tone is reduced, and metabolism is sluggish.

The Parathyroid Glands

Embedded in the thyroid gland are the **parathyroids**—four tiny pea-shaped organs. They secrete **parathormone,** which controls and balances the levels of calcium and phosphate in the blood and tissue fluids. The level of calcium in the blood has a direct effect on the excitability of the nervous system. A person with too little parathormone will be hypersensitive and may suffer from twitches or muscle spasms. Too much parathormone, on the other hand, can lead to lethargy and poor physical coordination.

The Pancreas

The **pancreas** lies in a curve between the stomach and the small intestine. The pancreas controls the level of sugar in the blood by secreting two regulating hormones: **insulin** and **glucagon.** The two hormones work against each other in order to keep the blood-sugar level properly balanced.

When the pancreas secretes too little insulin so that there is too much sugar in the blood, the kidneys attempt to get rid of the excess sugar by excreting a great deal more water than usual. The tissues become dehydrated, and poisonous wastes accumulate in the blood. The person has *diabetes mellitus* and needs insulin and a special diet to keep the blood-sugar level normal. Oversecretion of insulin, on the other hand, leads to too little sugar in the blood and the chronic fatigue of *hypoglycemia.*

The Pituitary Glands

The endocrine gland that produces the largest number of different hormones, and thus has the widest range of effects on the body's functions, is the **pituitary gland.** This gland is located on the underside of the brain and is connected to the hypothalamus. The pituitary gland has two parts that function quite separately.

The **posterior pituitary** (toward the back of the gland) is controlled by the nervous system. It secretes two hormones that signal the uterus to contract during childbirth, alert the mammary glands to start producing milk, cause the blood pressure to rise, and regulate the amount of water in the body's cells.

The **anterior pituitary** (toward the front of the pituitary gland) is controlled by chemical messages from the bloodstream and is often called the "master gland." It produces numerous hormones that trigger the action of other endocrine glands. Among the functions of the anterior pituitary is the production of the body's growth hormone, through which it controls the amount and timing of body growth. Dwarfism and giantism are the result of too little and too much growth hormone, respectively.

The functioning of the anterior pituitary provides a good example of the interaction between the endocrine system and the nervous system. The operation of the anterior pituitary is partly controlled by hormones that are released by the hypothalamus—part of the nervous system (Schally, Kastin, & Arimura, 1977). Hormones released from the anterior pituitary cause the gonads to produce still other hormones, which in turn affect the hypothalamus to produce changes in behavior or feeling. Thus, the hypothalamus affects the anterior pituitary, which indirectly affects the hypothalamus. This circular route of influence gives some idea of the two-way interaction that often takes place between the nervous system and the endocrine system.

The Gonads

The **gonads**—the *testes* in males and the *ovaries* in females—work with the adrenal glands to stimulate the reproductive organs to become mature. They also account for the appearance of what are called secondary sex characteristics—breasts, beards, pubic hair, change of voice, and distribution of body fat appropriate to males or females. As we will see in Chapter 11, hormones from the gonads play an important role in controlling the sex drive, particularly among animals.

The Adrenal Glands

The two **adrenal glands** are located just above the kidneys. Each adrenal gland has two parts: an outer covering, called the **adrenal cortex,** and an inner core, called the **adrenal medulla.** Both the adrenal cortex and the adrenal medulla are important in the body's reaction to stress. Imagine that you are walking down the street when you see a professor to whom you owe an overdue paper. As you approach each other, you realize that there is no graceful escape. You begin to experience stress. The hypothalamus secretes a hormone that causes the anterior pituitary gland to release two more hormones. One is **beta endorphin,** one of the body's natural painkillers (see the Box on p. 40). The other is **ACTH,** a messenger hormone that goes to the adrenal cortex. Alerted by ACTH from the pituitary, the adrenal cortex in turn secretes hormones that increase the level of blood sugar, help to break down proteins, and help the body respond to injury. Meanwhile, the adrenal medulla is stimulated by the autonomic nervous system so that it also pours several hormones into the bloodstream: **Epinephrine** activates the sympathetic nervous system, which makes the heart beat faster; digestion stops; the pupils of the eyes enlarge; more sugar flows into the bloodstream; the blood is prepared to clot fast if necessary. Another hormone, norepinephrine (which also acts as a neurotransmitter), not only raises the blood pressure by causing the blood vessels to become constricted, but is also carried by the bloodstream to the anterior pituitary, where it triggers the release of still more ACTH, thus prolonging the response to stress. The result is that your body is well prepared to deal with threat.

The complicated details of all these hormonal processes are much less important for our purposes than an understanding that the endocrine system plays a major role in helping to coordinate and integrate complex psychological reactions. In fact, as we have said before, the nervous system and the endocrine system work hand in hand. We will see other examples of this in Chapter 11, where we talk about motivation.

We have seen in our overview of the nervous system and endocrine

Gonads The reproductive glands—testes in males and ovaries in females.

Adrenal glands Two endocrine glands located just above the kidneys.

Adrenal cortex Outer covering of the two adrenal glands that releases hormones important for dealing with stress.

Adrenal medulla Inner core of the adrenal glands that also releases hormones to deal with stress.

Beta endorphin One of the endorphins, a natural painkiller released by the body.

ACTH Hormone released by the anterior pituitary that stimulates hormone production of the adrenal cortex.

Epinephrine Adrenal hormone that is released mainly in response to fear and causes the heart to beat faster.

Weightlifters and other athletes have used growth hormones and similar compounds called steroids to improve performance, but the potential side effects—including hypertension, blocked arteries, and a predisposition to tendon rupture—make it a questionable practice. The use of steroids changed Ben Johnson's physique dramatically, as shown in these "before and after" photos.

system a very close connection between biology and psychology. There are still other connections: Even the genes that we inherit from our parents can affect important psychological processes, as we will now discover.

■ Behavior Genetics

Charles Darwin was one of the first to recognize the impact of heredity on such psychological characteristics as intelligence, personality, and mental illness. For example, in a discussion of gestures, he described the following case:

> A gentleman of considerable position was found by his wife to have the curious trick, when he lay fast asleep on his back in bed, of raising his right arm slowly in front of his face, up to his forehead, and then dropping it with a jerk so that the wrist fell heavily on the bridge of his nose. The trick did not occur every night, but occasionally (Darwin, 1872, p. 34).

To protect the gentleman's nose, it was necessary to remove the buttons from the cuff of his nightgown. Years after the man's death, his son married a woman who observed precisely the same behavior in him. And their daughter exhibited the same gesture as well.

Darwin heard about this case from his half cousin, Francis Galton, who was the first person to try to demonstrate systematically how behavior characteristics can be transmitted genetically. Galton was especially interested in the transmission of mental traits. In order to show that high mental ability is inherited, he identified about 1,000 men of eminence in Great Britain—judges, political leaders, scholars, scientists, artists, and so on—and found that they belonged to only 300 families. Because only 1 in 4,000 people in the population was "eminent," Galton concluded that eminence must be an inherited trait.

Galton's findings were challenged by others who claimed that environmental factors such as educational and social advantages could have accounted for the concentration of eminence in just a few hundred families. In the early twentieth century, Galton's assumptions about the inherited nature of behavioral traits came under more fundamental attack from the behaviorists. The founder of behaviorism, J. B. Watson, argued that

> we have no real evidence of the inheritance of traits. I would feel perfectly confident in the ultimately favorable outcome of careful upbringing of a *healthy, well-formed* baby born of a long line of crooks, murderers and thieves, and prostitutes. Who has any evidence to the contrary? (Watson, 1930, p. 103).

The question of how much influence heredity has on various behaviors is at the heart of modern **behavior genetics** and, as we will see, psychologists still disagree on the answer to the question.

In order to begin to appreciate the "nature-nurture controversy," we need to become familiar with some of the basic mechanisms of inheritance.

Genetics

Genetics is the study of how plants, animals, and people pass traits from one generation to the next. In this context, a trait is the characteristic that is being expressed: curly hair, a crooked little finger, the inability of the blood to clot, or an allergy to poison ivy.

Gregor Mendel, a Moravian abbot, gave modern genetics its beginning in 1867 when he reported the results of his research on many years of systematically breeding peas. Mendel believed that every trait was controlled by elements that were transmitted from one generation to the next. He called these elements **genes.**

Much more is known today about genes and how they work. We know, for example, that within a cell nucleus genes are lined up on tiny threadlike bodies called **chromosomes,** which are visible under a microscope. The chromosomes are arranged in pairs, and each species has a constant number of pairs. Mice have 20 pairs; monkeys have 27; peas have 7. Human beings have 23 pairs of chromosomes in every normal cell.

The main ingredient of chromosomes and genes is **deoxyribonucleic acid (DNA),** a complex molecule that looks like two chains twisted around each other. The order of this twisting DNA forms a code that carries all our genetic information. The individual genes, which are the smallest message units of the DNA, carry instructions for a particular process or trait. It is now understood that the nucleus of every cell contains DNA with enough genetic coding to direct the development of one single cell into a fully grown adult with billions of cells!

Chromosomes, as we said, are arranged in pairs, and each pair carries a complete set of genes. Because each pair provides the coding for the same kinds of traits, a gene for a given trait may therefore exist in two alternate forms. We can think of a gene for eye color, for example, as having one form, *B*, which will result in brown eyes, and another form, *b*, which will result in blue eyes. If a boy receives *b* genes from both parents, his eyes will be blue. But if he inherits a *b* gene from one parent and a *B* gene from the other, his eyes will be brown (see Figure 2-16).

Behavior genetics Study of the relationship between heredity and behavior.

Genetics Study of how traits are passed from one generation to the next.

Genes Elements found on the chromosomes that control the transmission of traits.

Chromosomes Pairs of threadlike bodies within the cell nucleus that contain the genes.

Deoxyribonucleic acid (DNA) Complex molecule that is the main ingredient of chromosomes and genes and forms the code for all genetic information.

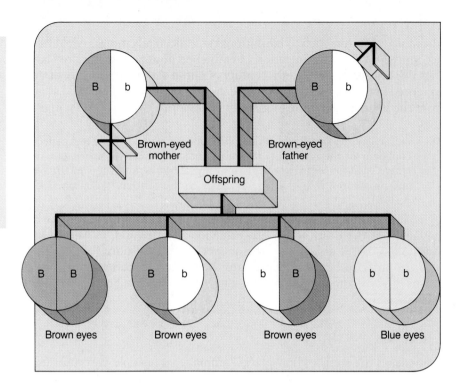

Dominant gene Member of a gene pair that controls the appearance of a certain trait.

Recessive gene Member of a gene pair that can control the appearance of a certain trait only if it is paired with another recessive gene.

Polygenic inheritance Process in which several genes interact to produce a certain trait; responsible for our most important traits.

Figure 2-16
Transmission of eye color by dominant (B) and recessive (b) genes
This figure represents the four possible mixtures of eye-color genes in these parents' offspring. Because three out of the four combinations result in brown-eyed children, the chance that any child will have brown eyes is 75 percent.

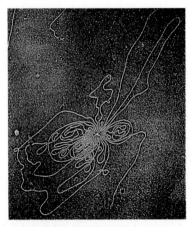

A photomicrograph of DNA molecules, showing the twisting strands. They have been magnified 6233 times.

The *B* form is thus said to be the **dominant gene,** while the *b* form is **recessive.** Although the boy with one *B* gene and one *b* gene has brown eyes, the recessive *b* gene is still present and can be passed on to offspring if it is paired with a recessive *b* gene from the other parent.

We have been talking about characteristics such as eye color that are controlled by single genes. In fact, however, most of our important characteristics, such as intelligence, height, and weight, cannot be traced back to a single gene. Rather, a number of genes make a small contribution to the trait in question in a process known as **polygenic inheritance.** Like the instruments in a symphony orchestra, each contributing separate notes to the sound that reaches the audience, the genes in a polygenic system contribute separately to the total effect.

It is also known that the effects of heredity need not be immediately or fully apparent. In some cases, expression of a trait is delayed until later in life. For example, many men inherit "male pattern baldness" that does not become apparent until middle age. In other cases, genes predispose a person to develop a particular trait, but environmental factors can alter or suppress expression of the trait. Having the proper genes provides a person with the potential for a trait, but that trait may not appear unless the environment cooperates. A person with an inherited tendency to gain weight may or may not be obese depending on diet, exercise program, and overall health. With these general principles in mind, let's look at how psychologists study the relation between genetics and behavior and see what they have learned so far.

Genetics and Behavior

To this point, we have examined the role of genetics in determining various physical characteristics, such as eye color, height, and weight. But there is increasing evidence that heredity also plays an important

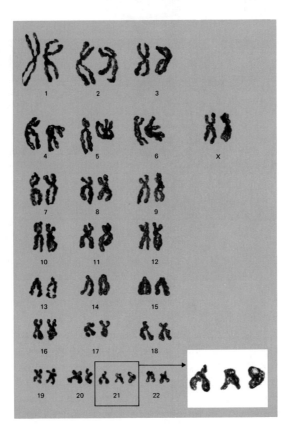

The 23 pairs of human chromosomes found in every normal cell. Twenty-two of the 23 pairs of chromosomes look exactly alike. The members of the 23rd pair, the sex chromosomes, may or may not look alike. Females have equivalent X chromosomes, while males have only one X and one Y chromosome, named for their distinctive appearance. The presence of an additional number-21 chromosome will result in Down's Syndrome, as in the inset at right.

role in a wide range of behavior, including hypertension, epilepsy, some forms of mental retardation, emotionality and responsiveness to stress, alcohol dependence, nervousness, intelligence, aggressiveness, and some forms of mental illness (Wimer & Wimer, 1985). Of course, genes do not directly cause behavior. Rather, they affect both the development and operation of the nervous system and the endocrine system, which in turn influence the likelihood that a certain behavior will occur under the proper circumstances.

In the remainder of this chapter, we will look at some of the methods used by behavior geneticists as well as some of their more interesting discoveries. We will start with methods appropriate for animal studies and then examine the techniques used to study behavior genetics in humans.

ANIMAL BEHAVIOR GENETICS. Psychologists have devised several methods to approach the problem of determining the heritability of behavioral traits (Henderson, 1982; Parke & Asher, 1983; Plomin, DeFries, & McClearn, 1980). **Strain studies** involve intensive inbreeding of close relatives, such as siblings, over many generations in order to create strains of animals that are genetically very similar to one another and different from other strains. Obviously, strain studies cannot be carried out on humans. But mice are often used because they breed so quickly and yet have relatively complex behavior patterns. When animals from different strains are raised together in the same environment, differences between them largely reflect genetic differences in the strains. Using this method, it has been shown that in mice the sense of smell, susceptibility

Drawing by Chas. Addams; © 1984 *The New Yorker Magazine*, Inc.

Artificial selection has been used to create breeds of dogs and many other animals that have desirable traits. Differences in trainability, for example, make some breeds of dogs better candidates at dog shows.

to seizures, and performance on a number of learning tasks are all affected by heredity.

Selection studies can also be used with animals to estimate heritability. If a trait is closely regulated by genes, then when animals having the trait are bred with one another, more of their offspring should have the trait than one would normally find in the general population. By measuring changes in the proportion of successive generations that have the trait, an estimate of its heritability can be made.

Artificial selection has been used for thousands of years to create breeds of dogs and many other animals that have desirable traits. Terriers, for example, were originally bred to crawl into burrows and chase out small animals living there. In France, dogs have been bred for specialized aspects of farm work, while in the United Kingdom dogs have been bred for centuries to point to hidden prey or retrieve downed birds. The fact that dog breeds differ greatly in many respects, including the development of social relationships, excitability, and trainability, suggests that these psychological characteristics are at least to some extent genetically controlled (Plomin, DeFries, & McClearn, 1980).

HUMAN BEHAVIOR GENETICS. Of course, for the purpose of studying the genetic basis of human behavior, both strain and selection studies are out of the question. A number of techniques have been developed, however, to study heritability in humans by analyzing the behavioral similarities of members of the same family. **Family studies** are based on the assumption that if genes influence a trait, close relatives should be more similar on the trait than distant relatives because close relatives share more genes. So far, family studies have uncovered strong evidence that heredity plays a role in some forms of mental illness. Siblings of schizophrenics, for example, are about eight times more likely to be schizophrenic than someone chosen randomly from the general population. And children of schizophrenic parents are about 10 times more likely to be schizophrenic than other children. Such findings, however, do not completely rule out the role of environment. Growing up in a household in which both parents are schizophrenic might cause a child to become schizophrenic, even if that child does not have the genetic potential for that disorder (Plomin, DeFries, & McClearn, 1980).

In an effort to separate more clearly the influence of heredity from that of environment on human behavior, psychologists often use **twin studies.** There are two kinds of twins. **Identical twins** develop from a single fertilized ovum and are therefore identical in genetic makeup. Any differences between them should therefore be due to environmental differences. **Fraternal twins,** however, develop from two separate fertilized egg cells and have no more in common genetically than other brothers and sisters. The differences between fraternal twins are thus due to both heredity and environment. Now, if identical twins are no more alike on some characteristics than fraternal twins, then heredity cannot be very important in that trait (assuming the various pairs of twins have similar environments).

Twin studies have provided evidence for the heritability of a number of behaviors. For example, if one identical twin is schizophrenic, about half the time the other twin will become schizophrenic. For fraternal twins, the chances are only about one in six that this second twin will become schizophrenic (Gottesman & Shields, 1982). The much greater similarity between identical twins suggests strongly that heredity plays an important role in schizophrenia.

Mental abilities also seem to be affected by heredity. Evidence from numerous studies shows that genetics plays an extremely important role in general intelligence (Loehlin & Nichols, 1976; Wilson, 1983). In Chapter 8 we will examine this relationship much more closely. Genetic differences also play a major role in specific cognitive abilities, such as verbal and spatial skills and memory. Evidence has also been found in twin studies for genetic influences on temperament and personality, such mannerisms as the strength of handshake, smoking and drinking habits, and even tastes in food (Farber, 1981).

Twins who have been reared apart provide the most compelling evidence for the degree to which genetics influence who we are. Jim Springer and Jim Lewis are identical twins separated just four weeks after birth and reunited 39 years later as part of an ongoing study of twins at the University of Minnesota. When they were reunited, they discovered that both had been married twice. Their first wives' names were Linda and their second wives' names were Betty. They had named their first sons James Allan and James Alan, respectively. Both drove the same type of blue Chevrolet, enjoyed woodworking, and had built the same kind of bench around a tree in their backyards. They had each vacationed at the same small beach in Florida and had named their dogs Toy.

Recently, researchers have become interested in **adoption studies** as well. Adoption studies focus on children who were adopted at birth

Twin studies Studies of identical and fraternal twins to determine the separate influences of heredity and environment on human behavior.

Identical twins Twins developed from a single fertilized ovum, and therefore identical in genetic makeup.

Fraternal twins Twins developed from two separate fertilized ova, and therefore different in genetic makeup.

Adoption studies Research carried out on children adopted at birth by parents not related to them with the object of determining environmental effects on human behavior.

Identical twins develop from a single ovum and consequently have the same genetic material. Fraternal twins develop from two different fertilized ova and so are as different in genetic makeup as any two children of the same parents.

Amniocentesis Technique that involves collecting cells cast off by the fetus into the fluid of the womb and testing them for genetic abnormalities.

and brought up by parents not genetically related to them. Thus, unusual similarities between adopted children and their adoptive parents are likely to be due to their shared environments, not heredity.

Adoption studies provide additional strong evidence for the heritability of intelligence and some forms of mental illness (Horn, 1983; Scarr & Weinberg, 1983). For example, one study located 47 people who had schizophrenic mothers but who had been adopted at birth and reared by normal parents. Of these 47, 5 became schizophrenic. In another group of people who had been adopted at birth but did not have a schizophrenic parent, there was no schizophrenia (Heston, 1966). Studies of biological and adoptive families have also suggested that chronic alcoholism and suicide—two phenomena that would at first appear to be tightly tied to environmental influences—have a strong genetic basis. This might help to explain why everyone who drinks does not become an alcoholic, and why only a few people turn to suicide when they despair (Kety, 1979).

Social Implications of Behavior Genetics

Science is not simply a process that takes place in a laboratory; it can have widespread effects on society at large. To the extent that we can trace such human traits as intelligence, temperament, and mental illness to their origins in chromosomes and genes, we increase the extent to which we can control human lives. And because this control permits choices that were previously not available, we face new ethical dilemmas.

Advances in genetics, for example, have improved the ability to predict birth defects in babies not yet conceived. Genetic counselors using family histories can spell out the likelihood that the children of a given marriage will inherit genetic problems. Before deciding to have a child, a high-risk couple must weigh some very serious ethical questions.

Once conception has occurred, a technique called **amniocentesis** permits detection of many genetic problems before the baby is born. Amniocentesis involves collecting some of the cells that the fetus has cast off into the fluid surrounding it in the womb and testing them for chromosomal or genetic abnormalities. In about 2 percent of the cases, genetic problems are found. Does the child nonetheless have a right to life? Do the parents have a right to abort the fetus? Should society protect all life, no matter how imperfect it is in the eyes of some? If not, which defects are so unacceptable that abortion is justified? Most of these questions have a long history, but recent progress in behavior genetics and in medicine has given them a special urgency.

The study of behavior genetics makes many people uneasy. It may lead people to conclude that who we are is written in some kind of permanent ink before we are born. Some people also fear that research in behavior genetics could be used to undercut movements toward social equality. For example, in 1969 the psychologist Arthur Jensen argued that Blacks' poor performance on intelligence tests was due to genetic influences that compensatory education programs, such as Head Start, could do nothing to improve. We will examine the debate sparked by Jensen's article in more detail in Chapter 8, but it is important to note here that far from finding human behavior to be genetically predetermined, the work of behavioral geneticists like Robert Plomin (1989) has served to illuminate just how important a role our *environment* plays in determining which genetic predispositions come to be expressed and which do not.

 ## APPLICATION

Brain Transplants

In this age of technology, most people are no longer taken aback by the idea of tissue or even organ transplants. Grafts of skin and bone removed from elsewhere in the patient's body are fairly routine. Transplants of kidneys, livers, and hearts have received a great deal of attention from the popular as well as the medical press. But to the general public, transplanting brains or even parts of the brain still belongs to the realm of horror or comedy films—or science fiction. Such things can happen to Frankenstein's monster or to characters in the films of Steve Martin and Woody Allen, but not to people in real life. Although there is no likelihood that it will ever be possible to transplant entire brains, recent advances in brain research have made transplants of live brain tissue a reality. The ability to graft tissue onto the brain is especially promising as a treatment for diseases involving the degeneration of nerve cells, such as Parkinson's disease, Huntington's chorea, and even Alzheimer's disease.

So far, most of the research on brain-tissue transplants has used rats. In the late 1970s, after experiments showed that heart tissue could be grafted to nerve fibers behind a rat's eye, researchers began to try to graft brain tissue to neurons in the brain. In particular, psychiatrist Richard J. Wyatt and neuroscientist William J. Freed, of the National Institutes of Mental Health, have explored the possibility of curing Parkinson's disease by means of brain transplants (Young, 1983). Victims of this disease lose a tiny number of cells—2,000 to 3,000—in a particular location on each side of the brain. The loss of these cells results in a deficit of the chemical transmitter dopamine, which in turn causes those stricken to lose normal control over their muscles.

Wyatt and Freed sought to learn whether dopamine-producing neurons could be transplanted into rat brains. In order to answer this question, the two investigators damaged one side of rats' brains to imitate the damage associated with Parkinson's disease. When these rats were later given a stimulant, they just walked around and around in circles. Next, Freed took dopamine-producing cells from rat embryos and injected them into the damaged area of the brain through a small hole in the skull. Several months later, many of the rats no longer engaged in the circling behavior. The implanted neurons were flourishing and apparently could fire normally. Still, the symptoms of the disease did not completely disappear in all the rats.

Later research with rats showed that cells from embryos are not the only choice for transplants. The adrenal glands of adult animals also produce dopamine, and experiments with implanting tissue from an adrenal gland in the parts of the brain affected by Parkinson's disease also succeeded in rats. The circling behavior ceased as the adrenal cells took hold and produced new supplies of dopamine (Freed et al., 1981). However, similar experiments in Stockholm, Sweden, and Mexico, on several human Parkinson's patients have produced only temporary improvement in some and no improvement, and occasionally death, in others.

Rejection of implanted brain tissues by the body's defenses is not as great a threat as with other kinds of transplants. The brain normally prevents foreign molecules from passing through the walls of blood vessels. This same barrier also keeps out elements of the body's immune system that are responsible for tissue rejection. However, this blood-brain barrier is not uniformly effective throughout the brain, which means there is some danger that implanted tissues will be rejected.

Unfortunately, a number of more serious problems remain to be solved. Experiments with rhesus monkeys have dramatized one of the major difficulties. Some time after they had injected tissue into monkeys' brains, Wyatt and his colleagues could not find the grafted tissue in many of the animals. This may have been partly because of the size of the monkey brains, or it may have been that the tissue had washed away from the implantation site rather than clinging there and growing. Still another problem is how to spread the implanted tissue throughout the target area beyond the point where it is inserted. This is essential to treating widespread degeneration, as in Alzheimer's disease and Huntington's chorea. Techniques for grafting tissues obviously must be perfected before they can be applied to humans.

If these and other obstacles can be overcome, the payoff could be quite high. Degenerative brain diseases may become curable. Patients who have suffered spinal cord damage may also be helped by tissue transplants. Research on brain-tissue transplants may also lead to new knowledge about the ability of the nervous system to heal itself after injury. The use of grafts will test the limits of this ability and extend it. The same work may also provide information about the biological basis for learning and memory.

■ Summary

- The body has two major systems that coordinate behavior. The **nervous system** conducts messages throughout the body in the form of neural impulses; the **endocrine system** sends chemical messages through the bloodstream. These two systems function together in coordinating our activities.

- The nervous system is made up of **neurons** that are specialized to send and receive information. Neurons have tiny fibers, called **dendrites**, and a single long fiber, called an **axon**, extending out from the **cell body**. The axon carries outgoing messages from the cell and either relays them to neighboring neurons or directs a muscle or gland to take action. A group of axons bundled together is called a **nerve**.

- **How are you able to distinguish hot enough from too hot when you stick your hand under the shower?** When a neuron is resting, its cell membrane keeps it in a state of **polarization**, with positive **ions** on the outside and negative ions on the inside. When sodium ions flow into the neuron and depolarize it, the process will cause the neuron to fire. The incoming message must be above a certain threshold to cause a **neural impulse** or **action potential**; otherwise the **graded potential** will fade away. During the **absolute refractory period** after firing, the neuron will not refire no matter how strong the incoming messages may be. The number of neurons firing at any given moment and the number of times they fire affect the complexity and the intensity of the message.

- The axon of every neuron ends in an **axon terminal** or **synaptic knob**. A tiny gap, called a **synaptic space** or **synaptic cleft**, separates each knob from the next neuron. A **synapse** consists of the axon terminal, synaptic cleft, and dendrite of the next neuron. When a neural impulse reaches the end of an axon, it causes tiny sacs, called **synaptic vesicles**, to release small amounts of chemicals. These chemicals, called **neurotransmitters**, travel across the synapse, where they affect the next neuron.

- There are more than a dozen known neurotransmitters with various functions. Neurotransmitters work by fitting into matching **receptor sites** on the other side of the synaptic space, just as a key fits into a lock. Some transmitters "excite" the next neuron and make it more likely to fire. Other transmitters inhibit or "turn down" the next neuron from firing and seem to regulate or adjust the sensitivity of large numbers of synapses. **Endorphins** and **enkephalins** inhibit the transmission of pain messages in the brain. After release, neurotransmitters are destroyed chemically within the synapse or cycled back into the vesicles, and the synapse returns to its normal state.

- **Why can coffee make us nervous?** Drugs that affect psychological processes interfere with chemical activity at the synapse. Some drugs cause an increase or decrease in the amounts of neurotransmitters in the synapse. Others block receptor sites for neurotransmitters across the synapse. Still others, like caffeine, work by preventing the destruction or, like cocaine, the reabsorption of neurotransmitters once they have done their job.

- The brain, the most significant element of the central nervous system, has three distinct parts: the hindbrain, midbrain, and forebrain. The **hindbrain** consists of the **medulla**, which controls breathing and many other reflexes and is the place where many nerves from other parts of the body cross on the way to the higher brain centers; the **pons** helps regulate the sleep-wake cycle and connects the forebrain to the **cerebellum**, which handles certain reflexes and coordinates the body's movements.

- Above the pons and cerebellum, the **brain stem** widens to form the **midbrain**. The midbrain is especially important to hearing and sight.

- The **forebrain** is composed of the **thalamus**, which relays messages from the sense receptors and messages from one part of the brain to another; the **hypothalamus**, which influences many kinds of motivation and emotional behavior; and the two cerebral hemispheres known as the **cerebral cortex**.

- Messages from the sense receptors are registered in those areas of the cerebral cortex called **sensory projection areas**; response messages begin in the **motor projection areas** and travel from there to the various muscles and glands; messages from the separate senses are combined into meaningful patterns in the **association areas**. The association areas are involved in all higher mental processes like thinking, learning, remembering, and talking.

- The largest of the association areas are in the **frontal lobes**. The frontal lobes are the site of uniquely human mental activities, and they contribute to a balanced emotional life. Damage to the frontal lobes can result in major personality changes. The other lobes of the cortex are each responsible for a different sense. The **occipital lobe** controls vision; the **temporal lobe** controls hearing; and the **parietal lobe** receives sensations of touch and body position.

- **Why do some people who have had a stroke have difficulty speaking when others do not?** The cerebral cortex is separated into two distinct hemispheres. In general, the left hemisphere controls the right side of the body, while the right hemisphere controls the left. The two hemispheres control different skills as well. The left hemisphere is dominant in verbal abilities; the right hemisphere is superior in spatial abilities and geometric reasoning. Therefore a stroke that damages the left hemisphere of the brain is more likely to lead to speech difficulties than a stroke on the right hemisphere.

- In the 1960s, the **corpus callosum** of several patients was cut in order to stop the spread of epileptic seizures, and it was possible to observe each hemisphere working independently of the other. For example, when such "split-brain patients" were shown objects in the left visual field, they could not identify those objects verbally. The reason for this fact seems to be that, for most people, language ability is concentrated almost entirely in the left hemisphere of the brain. In most split-brain patients, the right hemisphere of the brain cannot verbally identify the object that it is "seeing" in the left visual field, even though the object can be picked out by touch using the left hand. When the subject is asked, "What do you see?", the left hemisphere, monitoring the right visual field, reports, "Nothing." The two hemispheres not only receive from and send information to different sides of the body, but also seem to perform different mental functions. In most people, the left hemisphere is dominant in verbal tasks, while the right hemisphere appears to be responsible for some aspects of concept formation and analysis of spatial information. It is important to remember, however, that although the differences between the two hemispheres are intriguing, under normal conditions the right and left halves of the brain are in close communication through the corpus callosum and work together in a coordinated, integrated way.

- **What makes it possible for us to discern the sound of our name being called across a crowded, noisy room?** The primary function of the **reticular formation** is to filter incoming messages and alert higher parts of the brain when a message is important. The **limbic system** is thought to play a major role in learning and emotional behavior. The **spinal cord** is a complex cable of nerves that connects the brain to most of the rest of the body, sends messages to and from the brain, and controls certain reflex motions.

- **How do our heads know what our feet are doing?** The **peripheral nervous system** carries messages to and from the central nervous system, and without it, the central nervous system could not work. The peripheral nervous system consists of the **somatic nervous system**, which carries messages to the central nervous system from the senses, and from the central nervous system to the skeletal muscles; and the **autonomic nervous system**, which carries messages between the central nervous system and the body's internal organs.

- **What does it mean to calm down? How do our bodies accomplish it?** The two divisions of the autonomic nervous system work in opposite ways. The **sympathetic division** readies the body for action and triggers the release of activating chemicals into the bloodstream. The *parasympathetic division* acts to calm the body after stress. The autonomic nervous system is what controls "automatic" responses like breathing, heart rate, and digestion. It is possible to control such responses voluntarily through techniques like biofeedback.

- The *endocrine system* is made up of *glands* that secrete chemical substances called *hormones* into the bloodstream. Hormones affect such processes as metabolism, growth, and sex development and are involved in regulating emotional life. The endocrine gland that produces the largest number of hormones and has the widest range of effects is the *pituitary gland*, which is located in the brain. Hormones from the *posterior pituitary* direct preparation for childbirth; the *anterior pituitary* produces growth hormones and other hormones that trigger action of other endocrine glands. The anterior pituitary is known as the "master gland."

- The *gonads* work with the *adrenal glands* to stimulate sex development. The two adrenal glands are important in the body's response to stress. Both the *adrenal cortex* and *adrenal medulla* release hormones that prepare the body to deal with threats.

- **Do our genes determine who we are?** *Genetics* is the study of how traits are passed on from one generation to the next. *Genes* are lined up on *chromosomes* arranged in pairs within the nucleus of every cell. The chemical base of genes is the molecule *deoxyribonucleic acid*, or **DNA**. The order of the DNA molecule forms the code for all genetic information. Individual genes carry information for particular processes or characteristics.

- Psychological processes are also influenced by genes. *Behavior genetics* explores the influence of heredity on behavior. Some issues examined by behavior geneticists are the inheritance of sex characteristics, mental abilities, and forms of mental illness.

- A number of methods are used to study heritability of behavioral traits in animals. *Strain studies* employ inbreeding to create genetically similar strains of animals. *Selection studies* look at successive generations of offspring to estimate heritability. *Family studies* are based on the assumption that if genes influence a trait, close relatives should be similar on the trait.

- Psychologists use family studies as well as *twin studies* and *adoption studies* to separate out the influences of heredity and environment on various traits. Twin studies compare differences in sets of both *fraternal* and *identical twins*. Adoption studies look at children adopted at birth by parents who are not genetically related to them. Twin studies and adoption studies, along with family studies, show evidence of the role of heredity in intelligence, some forms of mental illness, and certain aspects of personality and temperament, but the role of the environment is of equal importance in determining how and what genetic traits and abilities are expressed.

■ Review Questions

1. Match the following terms with the correct definition.
   ____ neuron
   ____ nerve
   ____ axon
   ____ dendrite

   A. group of axons bundled together
   B. receives incoming messages from surrounding neurons
   C. carries outgoing messages away from the nerve cell
   D. single nerve cell

2. When a neuron is in a polarized state, there are mostly _____ ions on the outside of the cell membrane and mostly _____ ions on the inside.

3. During the _____ period, the neuron will fire only if the incoming message is considerably stronger than usual:
   A. absolute refractory
   B. relative refractory

4. A very strong incoming signal will cause a neuron to fire more strongly than before and in turn cause neighboring neurons to fire more strongly.   T/F

5. When a neural impulse reaches the end of the axon, it is transferred to the next neuron chemically through the release of _____ .

6. The _____ nervous system connects the central nervous system to all parts of the body beyond the brain and spinal cord.

7. Which of the following is NOT part of the brain's structure?
   a. hypothalamus   c. limbic system
   b. corpus callosum   d. parathyroid

8. The two cerebral hemispheres are known as the _____ _____ .

9. Match the following terms and their definitions:
   ____ sensory projection areas

   A. areas in the brain where response messages origi-

_____ association areas
_____ motor projection areas

nate and then travel to muscles and glands

B. areas in the brain where messages from the sense receptors are registered

C. areas in the brain where incoming messages from the separate senses are combined into meaningful impressions and outgoing messages from the motor areas are integrated

10. The _____ alerts higher parts of the brain to important incoming messages:
    A. limbic system
    B. reticular formation

11. The left hemisphere of the brain receives messages from the left side of the body, while the right hemisphere does this for the right side of the body.   T/F

12. Although the left and right hemispheres of the brain are specialized, they are normally in close communication through the:
    a. midbrain   c. corpus callosum
    b. temporal lobe   d. cerebellum

13. Match the following terms and their definitions:
    _____ pancreas   A. known as the "master gland" be-

_____ gonads
_____ thyroid
_____ anterior pituitary

cause it triggers the action of other endocrine glands

B. releases a hormone that regulates the body's metabolism

C. regulates the level of blood sugar

D. helps to stimulate sex development

14. Communication in the endocrine system is dependent on _____, chemicals secreted directly into the bloodstream.

15. The parts of the endocrine system that play a major role in preparing the body to deal with threats are
    a. the thyroid and parathyroid.
    b. the thyroid and the pituitary gland.
    c. the adrenal cortex and the adrenal medulla.
    d. the posterior pituitary and the anterior pituitary.

16. Match the following terms with the correct definition:
    _____ strain studies
    _____ family studies
    _____ selection studies

    A. looks at successive generations of offspring to estimate heritability.

    B. employs inbreeding to create genetically similar strains of animals.

    C. based on the assumption that if genes influence a trait, close relatives should be similar on the trait.

3 Sensation and Perception

Thinking Critically

How does information get from our eyes to our brain?

Why can't we see stars in the daytime?

How are you able to see that the blue in your sweater doesn't quite match the blue in your slacks?

Why can't you taste food if you have a stuffy nose?

How do pain relievers work?

You see a small car. How do you know it is actually a big car far away rather than a tiny car close up?

You're stopped at a traffic light. If the car next to you begins to back up, why may you suddenly step on the brake, thinking instead that you are rolling forward?

Is there such a thing as ESP?

Does subliminal perception really work?

Answers to these and other questions about sensation and perception appear throughout this chapter and in the Chapter Summary.

Outline

Sensation Experience of sensory stimulation.

Perception Process of creating meaningful patterns from raw sensory information.

Suppose you wanted to judge how far off a thunderstorm was. How would you get the necessary information? If you lived on a prairie, you could rely on your visual sense to provide relevant information, but at night you would have to rely more on your hearing sense. Some people claim that they can "smell" a storm coming or that they experience a tingling sensation in their skin. But sensation alone is not enough to represent the external world accurately. Sounds, colors, tastes, and smells are just sounds, colors, tastes, and smells until we interpret them in some meaningful way. Our *perceptual processes* enable us to understand and make sense of the sensations that we are continually experiencing; otherwise, even the most mundane tasks would become impossible. Take driving a car. As you negotiate traffic on a city street, accurate visual information about your surroundings becomes especially important. From a complicated array of colors, shapes, and patterns, you must be able to distinguish a road sign that tells you how to get to your destination from one that tells you when to stop. You depend on visual cues to judge the distance of other cars, bicycles, and pedestrians. If you see a motorist trying to enter the flow of traffic from a driveway just ahead of you, you must be able to determine whether a collision is possible. And as you drive, if you hear a siren, you must be able to determine quickly where it is coming from and how close it is so that you can yield the right of way. In all of these cases, you have to make sense out of raw sensory information and act accordingly.

In this chapter, we will see how our perceptual processes give meaning to the raw data our senses provide us from the outside world. For example, light waves bouncing off objects onto our retinas create visual images that need to be interpreted so that we can read a road sign or judge the distance of a pedestrian. First, we will discuss **sensation**—that is, the stimulation of the senses—and refer to several of the body's senses: sight, smell, hearing, balance, taste, touch, and pain. Then we will examine how we organize these sensations in order to create the **perception** of meaningful patterns. We will look at how we perceive patterns, distance, and movement, and how we are able to identify an object despite changing or even contradictory information. And finally, we will look at how characteristics of the observer influence perception.

■ The Nature of Sensory Processes

The General Character of Sensation

Described in general terms, the sequence of events that produces a sensation seems quite simple. First, some form of energy, either from an external source or from within the body, stimulates a receptor cell in one of the sense organs, such as the eye or the ear. A receptor cell is specialized to respond to one particular form of energy—light waves, for instance, or air pressure. The energy must be sufficiently intense or the receptor cell will not react to it. But given sufficient energy, the receptor responds by sending out a coded electrochemical signal. The signal varies with the characteristics of the stimulus. For instance, a very bright light might be coded by the rapid firing of a set of nerve cells, while a dim light would set off much slower firing. As the neural signal passes along the sensory nerves to the central nervous system, it is coded still further, so that by the time it reaches the brain, the message is quite precise and detailed. Thus, the coded signal that the brain receives from a flashing red light is very different from the stimulus signaling a soft yellow haze. And both of these signals differ from the code for a loud, piercing noise.

From these various signals, the brain creates sensory experiences. In a way, every sensory experience is an illusion created by the brain. The brain sits isolated within the skull, listening to the "clicking" of coded neural signals coming in over millions of nerve fibers. The clicks on an optical nerve are not any more "visual" than the clicks on an auditory nerve. But the brain interprets the clicks on the optic nerve as visual nerve energy, and thus they give rise to visual experience instead of to sounds, tastes, or smells. Even if the clicks are caused by something other than light, the brain still responds with a visual experience. Gentle pressure on an eye, for instance, results in signals from the optic nerve that the brain interprets as visual patterns. In the same way, both a symphonic recording and a stream of water trickling into the ear stimulate the auditory nerve, and both will cause us to hear something.

Sensory Thresholds

We have seen that the energy reaching a receptor must be sufficiently intense for it to have a noticeable effect. The minimum intensity of physical energy required to produce any sensation at all in a person is called the **absolute threshold.** Any stimulation below the absolute threshold will not be experienced.

How much sensory stimulation is needed to produce a sensation? How intense does a sound have to be, for example, for a person to hear it? How bright does a "blip" on a radar screen have to be for the operator to see it? In order to answer these kinds of questions, psychologists present a stimulus at different intensities and ask people whether they sense anything. You might expect that there would come a point where people would suddenly say, "Now I see the flash" or "Now I hear a sound." But actually, there is a range of intensities over which a person sometimes, but not always, can sense a stimulus. For a variety of reasons, psychologists have agreed to set the absolute threshold at the point where a person can detect the stimulus 50 percent of the time that it is presented (see Figure 3-1).

Although there are differences between people and even differences from day to day for the same person, the absolute threshold for each of our senses is remarkably low. According to McBurney and Collings (1984), the approximate thresholds are as follows:

- *Taste*: 1 gram (.0356 ounce) of table salt in 500 liters (529 quarts) of water.
- *Smell*: One drop of perfume diffused throughout a three-room apartment.
- *Touch*: The wing of a bee falling on your cheek from a height of 1 centimeter (.39 inch).

Absolute threshold The least amount of energy that can be detected as a stimulation 50 percent of the time.

Figure 3-1
Determining a sensory threshold The red line represents an ideal case—at all intensities below the threshold, the subject reports no sensation or no change in intensity; at all intensities above the threshold, the subject does report a sensation or a change in intensity. In actual practice, the ideal of the red line is never realized. The blue line shows the actual responses of a typical subject. The threshold is taken at the point where the subject reports a sensation or a change in intensity 50 percent of the time.

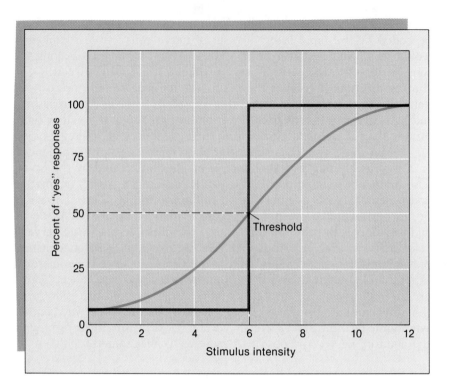

- *Hearing*: The tick of a watch from 6 meters (20 feet) in very quiet conditions.
- *Vision*: A candle flame seen from 50 kilometers (30 miles) on a clear, dark night.

Imagine now that you can hear a particular sound. How much stronger does the sound have to be before you notice that it has become louder? The smallest change in stimulation that you can detect 50 percent of the time is called the **difference threshold.** This is also called the **just noticeable difference,** or **jnd.** Like the absolute threshold, the difference threshold will vary from person to person and from time to time in the same person. But difference thresholds also vary with the absolute level of stimulation. Generally, the stronger the stimulation, the bigger the difference must be in order for you to sense it. Turning on a light at sunset is more noticeable than turning on the same light at noon on a sunny day. Adding 1 pound to a 5-pound load will certainly be noticed; adding that same pound to a 100-pound load probably will not make a noticeable difference. And finally, some of our senses are more sensitive than others to changes in stimulation: We are very good at detecting changes in the pitch of a note or the brightness of a light but much less sensitive to changes in the loudness of a sound or in pressure on the surface of our skin.

So far, we have been talking about some general characteristics of sensation, but each of the body's sensory systems works a little differently. Each one contains receptor cells that specialize in converting a particular kind of energy into neural signals. The threshold at which this conversion occurs varies with the system. So do the mechanisms by which sensory input is processed and coded and sent to the brain for still more processing.

In the following pages, we'll discuss the unique features of each of the sensory systems.

■ Vision

Animals vary in their relative dependence on the different senses. Dogs rely heavily on the sense of smell, bats on hearing, some fish on taste. But for humans, vision is probably the most important sense, and therefore it has received the most attention from psychologists. To begin to understand vision, we need to look first at the parts of the visual system, beginning with the structure of the eye.

The Visual System

The structure of the human eye, including the cellular path to the brain, is shown in Figure 3-2. Light enters the eye through the **cornea,** the transparent protective coating over the front part of the eye. Then it passes through the **pupil,** the opening in the center of the **iris,** the colored part of the eye. In very bright light, the muscles in the iris contract to make the pupil smaller and protect the eye from damage. This also helps

Cornea The transparent protective coating over the front part of the eye.

Pupil Small opening in the iris through which light enters the eye.

Iris Colored part of the eye.

Figure 3-2
A cross-section of the human eye and the layers of the retina Light must pass through the *ganglion cells* and the *bipolar neurons* in order to reach the *rods* and *cones*. The sensory messages then travel back out again from the receptor cells, through the bipolar neurons, to the ganglion cells. The axons of the ganglion cells gather together to form the *optic nerve*, which carries the messages from both eyes to the brain.
Adapted from Hubel, 1963

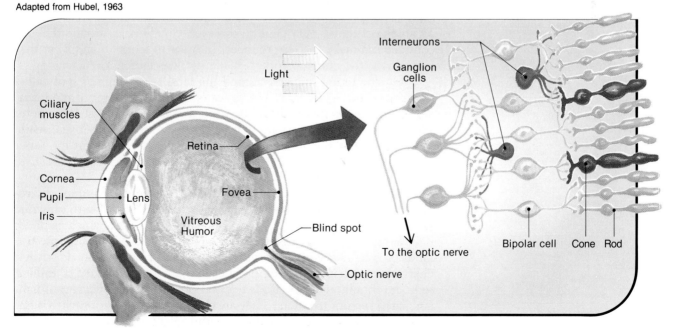

Lens Transparent part of the eye that focuses light onto the retina.

Retina Lining of the eye containing receptor cells that are sensitive to light.

Fovea Area of the retina that is the center of the visual field.

Receptor cell Specialized cell that responds to particular type of energy.

Rods Receptor cells in the retina responsible for night vision and perception of brightness.

Cones Receptor cells in the retina responsible for color vision.

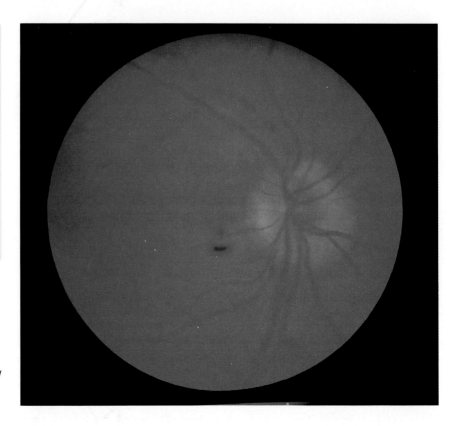

Figure 3-3
A view of the retina through an ophthalmoscope, an instrument used to inspect blood vessels in the eye. The central dark area is the *fovea*. The yellow circle marks the *blind spot*, where the optic nerve leaves the eye.

us to see better in bright light. In dim light, the muscles extend in order to open the pupil wider and let in as much light as possible.

Inside the pupil, the light passes through the **lens,** which focuses it onto the **retina,** the inner lining of the back of the eyeball that is sensitive to light. The lens changes shape in order to focus on objects that are closer or farther away. Normally, the lens is focused on a middle distance, at a point neither very near nor very far away. In order to focus on an object that is very close to the eyes, tiny muscles around the lens contract and make the lens rounder. In order to focus on an object that is far away, the muscles work to make the lens flatter.

On the retina, directly behind the lens, is a depressed spot called the **fovea** (see Figure 3-3). The fovea occupies the center of the visual field. The images that pass through the lens are in sharpest focus here. Thus, the words that you are now reading are hitting the fovea, while the rest of what you see—a desk, walls, or whatever—is hitting other areas of the retina.

THE RECEPTOR CELLS. The retina of each eye contains the **receptor cells** responsible for vision. These cells are sensitive to only one small part of the spectrum of electromagnetic energy, which includes light along with other energies (see Figures 3-4 and 3-5). There are two kinds of receptor cells in the retina—**rods** and **cones**—named for their characteristic shapes. The retina of each eye contains about 120 million rods and 8 million cones. Rods respond only to varying degrees of light and dark, and not to colors. They are chiefly responsible for night vision. Cones, on the other hand, respond both to light and dark and to colors.

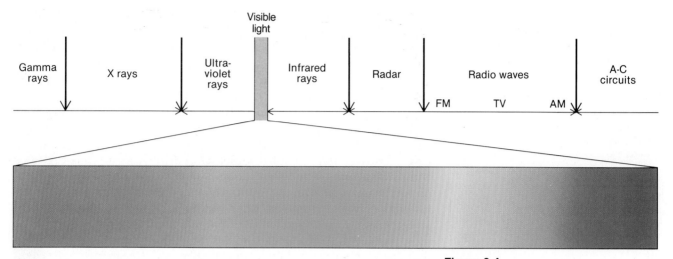

Figure 3-4
The electromagnetic spectrum. The eye is sensitive to only a very small segment of the spectrum, known as visible light.

They operate chiefly in daylight. Cones are less sensitive to light than are rods (MacLeod, 1978). In this regard, cones, like color film, work best in relatively bright light. The more sensitive rods, like black-and-white film, respond to much lower levels of illumination.

Rods and cones differ in other ways as well. Cones are found mainly, but not exclusively, in the fovea, which contains no rods. Nearly 100,000 cones are packed into the fovea, which, as you recall, is situated where images are projected onto the retina in sharpest focus. Rods predominate just outside the fovea. As we move outward from the fovea toward the edges of the retina, both rods and cones get sparser. At the extreme edges of the retina, there are no cones and only a few rods.

Rods and cones also differ in the ways that they connect to the

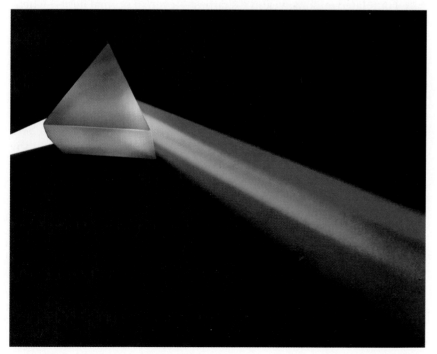

Figure 3-5
Sunlight contains the wavelengths for all the colors of the spectrum. When sunlight is passed through a prism, the wavelengths are bent at different angles and the light is separated into a color spectrum. A natural spectrum, a rainbow, occurs when sunlight is bent by the atmosphere.

nerve cells leading to the brain. Both rods and cones connect to what are called **bipolar neurons,** which are neurons with only one axon and one dendrite (see Figure 3-2). In the fovea, cones generally connect with only one bipolar neuron—a sort of "private line" arrangement. Rods are usually on a "party line"—several of them may share a single bipolar neuron.

Knowing these facts about rods and cones can help you to understand some of the more common experiences in seeing. For example, you may have noticed that at night you can see a dimly lit object better if you look slightly to one side of it rather than directly at it. This has to do with the location of the rods and cones. When you look directly at an object, its image falls on the fovea, which consists only of relatively light-insensitive cones. However, when you look slightly to one side of the object, its image falls next to the fovea and onto the highly light-sensitive rods. Moreover, such a weak stimulus will cause only a weak response in the cones, and this probably will not be sufficient to fire its bipolar neurons. But because many rods converge on a single bipolar neuron, that neuron is much more likely to fire and thereby start a sensory message to the brain.

At other times, vision is improved when more cones are stimulated. Have you ever tried to examine something but could not make out the details? You probably found that by increasing the amount of light on the object—perhaps by moving it into direct sunlight or under a lamp—you could see it better. This phenomenon results from the fact that the better the illumination, the greater the number of cones stimulated; the greater the number of cones stimulated, the more likely they are to stimulate the bipolar cells, starting a message on the way to the brain. Our ability to see increases almost without limit as light intensity increases. So for "close" activities like reading, sewing, and writing, the more light the better.

For related reasons, vision is sharpest—even in normal light—whenever you look directly at an object and its image falls on the fovea. Here in the fovea, the one-to-one connection between cones and bipolar neurons allows for maximum **visual acuity**—the ability to distinguish fine details. You can easily demonstrate acuity to yourself by doing the following: Hold the book about 18 inches from your eyes and look at the "X" in the center of the line below. Notice how your vision drops off for words and letters toward the left or right end of the line:

This is a test to show how visual**X**acuity varies across the retina.

Your fovea picks up the "X" and about four letters to either side. This is the area of greatest visual acuity. The letters at the left and right ends of the line fall well outside the fovea, where there are many more rods than cones. Rods, as you remember, tend to "pool" their signals on the way to the bipolar neurons; and while this increases sensitivity, it cuts down on the fine details in the signal that goes to the brain. Outside the fovea, acuity drops by as much as 50 percent!

ADAPTATION. The sensitivity of rods and cones changes according to how much light is available. This process is known as **adaptation.** When you go from bright sunlight into a dimly lit theater, your cones are initially fairly insensitive to light: You can see little or nothing as you look for a seat. But during the first 5 or 10 minutes in the dark, the cones become more and more sensitive to whatever light is available. After about 10 minutes, you will be able to see things directly in front of you about as well as you are going to: The cones do not get any more sensitive after this point. But the rods, which have also been adapting, continue to become more sensitive to the light for another 20 minutes or so. They reach maximum sensitivity about 30 minutes after you have entered a darkened room. The process by which rods and cones become more sensitive to light in response to lowered levels of illumination is called **dark adaptation.** But even with dark adaptation, there is not enough energy in very dim light to stimulate the cones to respond to colors. So even when your eyes are adapted to the dark, you see only a black-and-white-and-gray world of different brightnesses.

Problems with dark adaptation account in part for the much greater incidence of highway accidents at night (Leibowitz & Owens, 1977). When people drive at night, not all their visual abilities degrade equally. People are able to focus on the location of an object, such as a pedestrian, quite well: They can see that the pedestrian is in the middle of the road. However, they are not able to determine the distance of the pedestrian because of the deterioration of their sensitivity to contrast and so over-estimate their ability to stop in time. Because most drivers are generally unaware of the selective deterioration of their vision, they may drive with an exaggerated confidence in their visual abilities at night.

In the reverse process, **light adaptation,** the rods and cones become less sensitive to light. By the time you leave a movie theater, your rods and cones have become very sensitive, and the bright outdoor light sometimes hurts as a result. In the bright light, all the neurons fire at once, overwhelming you. You squint and shield your eyes and each iris contracts, all of which reduces the amount of light entering your pupils and striking each retina. As light adaptation begins, the rods and cones become less sensitive to stimulation by light, and within about a minute, both rods and cones are fully adapted to the light. At this point, squinting and shielding your eyes are no longer necessary.

You can observe the effects of dark and light adaptation by staring continuously at the dot in the center of the upper square in Figure 3-6 for about 20 seconds. Then shift your gaze to the dot in the lower square. A gray-and-white pattern should appear in the lower square (if you blink your eyes, the illusion will be even stronger). When you look at the lower square, the striped areas that were black in the upper square will now seem to be light, and the areas that were white in the upper square will now appear gray. The **afterimage** appeared because the part of the retina that was exposed to the dark stripes of the upper square became more sensitive (it dark-adapted), while the area exposed to the white part of the upper square became less sensitive (it light-adapted). When you shifted your eyes to the lower square, the less sensitive parts of the retina produced the sensation of gray rather than white. This afterimage fades within a minute as the retina adapts again, this time to the solid white square.

You can see from these examples that visual adaptation is a partial, back-and-forth kind of process. The eyes adjust—from no stimulation to stimulation, from less stimulation to more, and vice versa—but they never adapt completely. If stimulation somehow remained constant and the eyes adapted completely, gradually, all the receptors would become wholly

Figure 3-6
First stare continuously at the center of the upper square for about 20 seconds. Then shift your gaze to the dot in the lower square. Within a moment, a gray-and-white *afterimage* should appear inside the lower square.

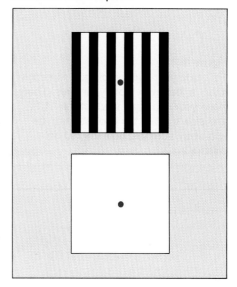

Ganglion cells Neurons that connect the bipolar neurons in the eyes to the brain.

Optic nerve The bundle of axons of ganglion cells that carries neural messages from each eye to the brain.

Blind spot Place on the retina where the axons of all the ganglion cells leave the eye and where there are no receptors.

insensitive and we would not be able to see anything at all. If you want to see a normal occurrence of full adaptation, go into a dark room with a penlight and shine the light into one of your eyes from above and to the side of your head. You will see something that looks like the branches of a tree. These are the blood vessels that run across your retina in front of the rods and cones. Normally, these vessels are invisible because their shadows are held perfectly still on the retina where they fall on the same rods and cones. But when you shine the light from a very unusual direction, as suggested here, the shadows stimulate different rods and cones, and you are thus allowed to see them.

Obviously, it is important that our eyes not adapt this way when we are trying to see objects in the real world. And they don't usually, because light stimulation is rarely focused on the same rods and cones long enough for them to become wholly insensitive. One reason for this is that small, involuntary eye movements cause an image on the retina to drift slightly and then snap it back in place again with a tiny flick. At the same time, the eyes continually show a slight, extremely rapid tremor—a tremor so minute that it goes completely unnoticed. All of these movements together keep an image moving slightly on the retina, so the receptors never have time to adapt completely.

FROM EYE TO BRAIN. Up to now, we have been focusing on the eye itself and the beginnings of visual processing in the retina. But messages from the eye must eventually reach the brain in order for a visual experience to occur. As you can imagine from Figure 3-2, the series of connections between eye and brain is quite intricate. To begin with, rods and cones are connected with bipolar neurons in many different numbers and combinations. In addition, sets of neurons called *interneurons* link receptor cells to one another and bipolar cells to one another. Eventually these bipolar neurons connect with the **ganglion cells,** leading out of the eye. The axons of the ganglion cells join to form the **optic nerve,** which carries messages from each eye to the brain. The optic nerve itself consists of only about 1 million axons. This means that in each eye, the signals from many millions of rods and cones have been combined and reduced to fit just 1 million wires that lead to the brain!

The place on the retina where the axons of all the ganglion cells join to leave the eye is called the **blind spot**—it contains no receptors. Even when light from a small object is focused directly on it, the object will not be seen (see Figure 3-7).

After they leave the eyes, the fibers that make up the optic nerves separate, and some of them cross to the other side of the head. The nerve fibers from the right side of each eye travel to the right hemisphere of the brain; those from the left side of each eye travel to the left hemisphere.

Figure 3-7
To locate your *blind spot*, hold the book about a foot away from your eyes. Then close your right eye, stare at the "X," and slowly move the book toward you and away from you until the red dot disappears.

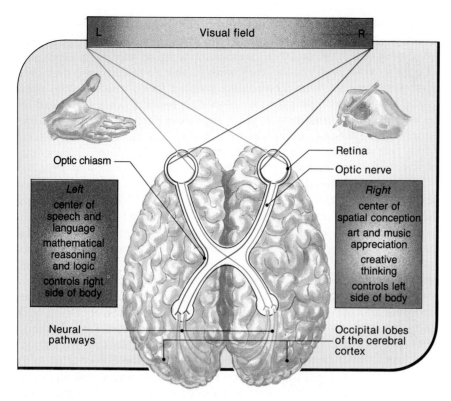

Visual field

L   R

Optic chiasm

Retina

Optic nerve

Left
center of speech and language

mathematical reasoning and logic

controls right side of body

Right
center of spatial conception

art and music appreciation

creative thinking

controls left side of body

Neural pathways

Occipital lobes of the cerebral cortex

Figure 3-8
The neural connections of the visual system Messages from the left visual field of each eye travel to the right occipital lobe; those from the right visual field of each eye go to the left occipital lobe. The crossover point is the *optic chiasm*. If a split-brain subject is shown an object in the right visual field only, it can be named because the sensory input has reached the left hemisphere of the brain, where language functions are controlled. If the object is presented to the left visual field and the sensory input reaches only the right hemisphere, which controls the memory of shapes, the subject can identify a similar object by touch alone but cannot name what he or she has seen.

The place where some of these fibers cross over is called the **optic chiasm** (see Figure 3-8). This crossing enables the fibers of the optic nerves to carry their messages to several different parts of the brain. Some messages reach the part of the brain that controls the reflex movements that adjust the size of the pupil. Others reach the part of the brain that directs the eye muscles to change the shape of the lens. But the main destinations for the messages from the retina are the visual projection areas of the cerebral cortex, where the pattern of stimulated and unstimulated receptor cells is registered and interpreted.

The fact that visual messages take different yet parallel routes once they enter the brain is supported by studies of stroke victims who, like the man described in the Highlight in Chapter 2, lose their ability to recognize faces yet still have normal visual perception in other areas. All but the most severely brain-damaged were able to tell whether faces in

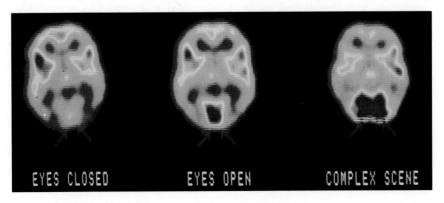

EYES CLOSED   EYES OPEN   COMPLEX SCENE

Nerve fibers from each eye cross to opposite sides of the brain, enabling the optic nerves to carry visual information to different parts of the brain. As these PET scans show, the more complex the scene, the more areas of the brain are engaged in visual processing.

Hue The aspect of color that corresponds to names such as red, green, blue.

photographs were happy or sad, surprised, disgusted, fearful, or angry (Damasio, Tranel, & Damasio, 1988). They could also tell if the faces were male or female, and they could estimate age as accurately as anyone. It appears that even though they were unable to retrieve the memories that would enable them to recognize familiar faces, in other ways these patients' visual perceptions were completely normal. They could still see as well as any normal person and they could perceive age in the lines around the eyes or emotions in the furrows in a brow, making it seem likely that the sensory messages entering the brain are routed along several pathways for simultaneous processing in a number of different areas.

Figure 3-8 also shows how visual information is routed. Visual information about any object in the left visual field will go to the right hemisphere (the pathway traced by the blue line), and information about any object in the right visual field will go to the left hemisphere (the pathway traced by the red line). What would happen if your corpus callosum were severed and these two pathways could not cross through the optic chiasm? In the early 1960s, neurosurgeons succeeded in lessening the severity of epileptic brain activity by cutting the patient's corpus callosum and preventing the abnormal activity from reverberating back and forth between the hemispheres of the cerebral cortex. Shortly thereafter, psychologists began conducting experiments to discover what could be learned about hemispheric specialization from the behavior of split-brain patients. For example, they showed a split-brain patient an object in the left visual field only; thus, all the visual information went to the right hemisphere of the patient's brain. Recall from Chapter 2 that the right hemisphere controls the memory of shapes and the motor abilities of the left half of the body: Thus, split-brain patients were able to point to the objects with their left hands. But also recall that the left hemisphere of the brain is primarily responsible for *language* functions: The same patients were thus unable to *name* the objects presented to their left visual fields because the visual information had passed only to the right side of the brain. Such phenomena remind us that the cerebral cortex is remarkably specialized in its functions, but as we saw in Chapter 2, it is important to remember that the two hemispheres of the brain are designed to work in concert.

Color Vision

Unlike many other animal species such as dogs and cats (see the Box on page 90), humans can see an extensive range of colors. In the following pages, we will first discuss some characteristics of color vision and then consider how the eyes convert light energy into sensations of color.

COLOR PROPERTIES. Look at the color solid in Figure 3-9. What do you see? Most people say they see a number of different colors: some greens, some yellows, some reds, and so forth. Psychologists call these different colors **hues;** and to a great extent, what hues you see depends on the wavelength of the light reaching your eyes (see Figure 3-4).

Now look again at Figure 3-9. You will notice that although each color patch on the green triangle is the same overall hue, the color is deepest at the left edge and tends to get paler, or more washed out, toward the right. This paleness occurs when light of other wavelengths dilutes the purity of a hue. Psychologists refer to the purity of a hue as its **saturation.** A pure color is one that is high in saturation. An impure or washed-out color is low in saturation.

Look back at the color solid in Figure 3-9 and squint your eyes so that you can barely see the colors, or turn off some of the lights in the room to make it almost dark. The colors appear darker; in fact, the purples may begin to look black. You have just reduced the **brightness** of the colors. Brightness depends mainly on the strength of the light entering your eye. The brighter the color, the whiter it seems. In the green wedge from the color solid, the colors near the top are very bright and may appear almost white; those near the bottom appear almost black.

Hue, saturation, and brightness are three separate aspects of our experience of color. While people can distinguish only about 150 hues (Coren, Porac, & Ward, 1984), different levels of saturation and brightness combine to give us more than 300,000 different colors (Hochberg, 1978; Kaufman, 1979). Some of this variety is captured in a slice from the color solid in Figure 3-9. The slice is all one hue (green), but the patches vary in saturation (from left to right) and in brightness (from top to bottom).

COLOR MIXING. For centuries, scientists have known that it is possible to produce all 150 hues simply by mixing together a few lights of different colors (see Figure 3-10). In the seventeenth century, the English physicist Isaac Newton found that combining lights of two different colors produced a new color that could be found at a place on the spectrum between the two original lights. For example, red and green lights combine to give yellow. This process of mixing lights of different wavelengths is called **additive color mixing.**

Newton also discovered that some lights combine to produce a neutral gray rather than a new hue. Such colors are termed **complementary colors.** In the color circle in Figure 3-11, colors on opposite sides of the circle are complementary. Red and blue-green are examples of complementary colors, as are blue and yellow. Other colors, such as red and

Saturation The purity of a hue.

Brightness The nearness of a color to white as opposed to black.

Additive color mixing The process of mixing lights of different wavelengths to create new hues.

Complementary colors Two hues, far apart on the spectrum, that when added together in equal intensities produce a neutral gray rather than a third hue.

Figure 3-9
The color solid The dimension of *hue* is represented around the circumference. *Saturation* ranges along the radius from the inside to the outside of the solid. *Brightness* varies along the vertical axis. The drawing (bottom left) illustrates this schematically.

Nonspectral color A hue, such as purple, that is not found in the spectrum.

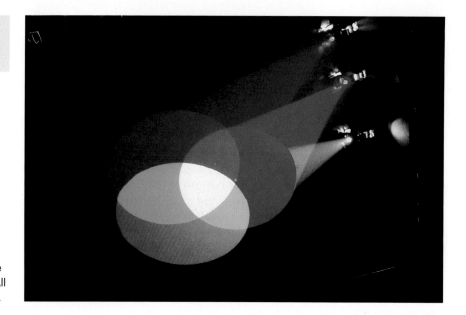

Figure 3-10
Mixing light waves is an *additive process*. When red and green lights are combined, the resulting hue is yellow. All three lights together result in white light.

blue, combine to form a hue (purple) that is not found in the spectrum—a **nonspectral color.** If you compare the color circle in Figure 3-11 with the spectrum in Figure 3-4, you will notice some colors in the circle that do not appear on the spectrum. If all the colors of the spectrum are combined, the result is white light.

Newton's work was refined in the nineteenth century, when the

Figure 3-11
The color circle The circle includes the colors found on the spectrum as well as some nonspectral colors. Colors on opposite sides of the circle are complementary; when mixed together, they produce a neutral gray.

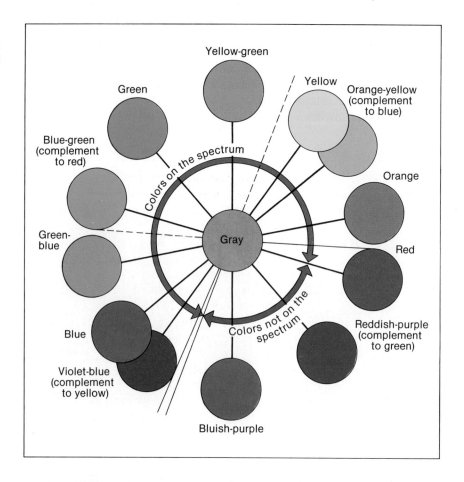

English physicist Thomas Young proposed that if red, green, and blue lights were mixed in the right intensities, they could produce any hue that the human eye can detect. James Maxwell, a Scottish physicist, confirmed that red, green, and blue are indeed **primary colors:** If mixed together in equal amounts, they produce gray; but if mixed in unequal amounts, they can be made to produce any visible hue. Maxwell discovered that many other sets of primary colors exist as well.

Most people have more experience with mixing pigments such as paints than with mixing lights. The process of mixing pigments, called **subtractive color mixing,** produces results very different from those obtained by combining lights. This is because each pigment absorbs a different part of the spectrum; thus some wavelengths are subtracted while others are reflected (see Figure 3-12). Blue paint, for instance, reflects blue light as well as some green light (which is close to blue on the spectrum), but it absorbs all other light waves. Yellow paint reflects yellow light as well as some nearby green light. When blue and yellow paints are mixed, the combined pigment reflects only green light and absorbs everything else. Thus, blue and yellow pigments absorb everything except green light, which they both reflect.

THEORIES OF COLOR VISION. We have seen so far that cones in the retina are responsible for our color vision. Somehow, the cones in the eye send a unique message to the brain in response to each of the colors that we can distinguish. But the question of how this takes place is still much debated. Consider the fact that in the fovea there are only 100,000 cones, yet we can distinguish 300,000 different kinds of colors. Obviously, there are not enough cones in the fovea to have one for every color! Somehow, relatively few kinds of cones must combine to provide both the full range of color and the clear, sharp images that we perceive when we look directly at colored objects.

A German scientist named Hermann von Helmholtz remembered that Thomas Young was able to produce all hues by mixing just three kinds of light: red, green, and blue. Helmholtz suggested that the eye contains some cones that are most sensitive to red, others that are most sensitive to green, and others that respond most strongly to blue-violet. By mixing the signals from the three receptors, then, you should be able to create any color. Yellow light, for example, would produce the sensation of yellow by stimulating the red and green receptors fairly strongly and the blue-violet receptors only weakly. Helmholtz's explanation of color vision is known as the **trichromatic theory.**

In 1878, another German scientist, Ewald Hering, proposed an alternative to this theory. He took into account the fact that we never see yellowish-blue light or reddish-green light. A mixture of red and green produces a reddish or greenish hue if the intensities of the two lights are unequal, or a neutral gray light if the two intensities are equal. However, it is possible to see yellowish reds and greenish blues. In order to explain these and other observations, Hering proposed the existence of three pairs of color receptors: a yellow-blue pair, a red-green pair, and a black-white pair. The members of each pair work in opposition to each other. The yellow-blue pair cannot relay messages about yellow and blue light at the same time, nor can the red-green pair send both red and green messages at the same time. The red-green and blue-yellow pairs determine

Primary colors A set of three colors, such as red, green, and blue, that when mixed in unequal amounts can produce any visible hue.

Subtractive color mixing The process of mixing pigments, each of which absorbs some wavelengths of light and reflects others.

Trichromatic theory Theory of color vision that holds that all color perception derives from three different color receptors in the retina (usually red, green, and blue receptors).

Figure 3-12
The process of mixing paint pigments rather than lights is a *subtractive process*, because pigments absorb some wavelengths and reflect others. A mixture of the three primary pigments absorbs all wavelengths, producing black.

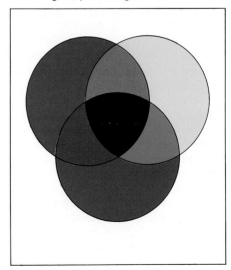

Opponent-process theory Theory of color vision that holds that three sets of color receptors (yellow-blue, red-green, black-white) respond in an either/or fashion to determine the color you experience.

Color blindness Partial or total inability to perceive colors.

Trichromats people who have normal color vision.

Monochromats Persons who are totally color blind.

Dichromats People who are blind to either red-green or yellow-blue.

the hue that you see, while the black-white pair determines brightness. Hering's theory is now known as the **opponent-process theory.**

Each of these two theories accounts for certain visual phenomena especially well. Trichromatic theory explains most efficiently the fact that three primary colors can be combined to produce any other hue. It also provides a convincing explanation for various kinds of **color blindness**— the partial or total inability to perceive hues. About 10 percent of men and 1 percent of women are color blind. People with normal color vision are **trichromats:** They can match any given hue by combining three primary colors. At the other extreme are **monochromats**—the rare people who see no color at all but respond only to shades of light and dark. More common than monochromats are **dichromats**—people who are blind to either red-green or blue-yellow. Red-green color blindness, for example, can result from a deficiency in either the red or the green receptors. In both cases, the person confuses red and green, since both red and green appear to be a desaturated yellow (see Figure 3-13).

Opponent-process theory explains other phenomena better than trichromatic theory. For example, if you look at the flag in Figure 3-14 for about 30 seconds and then look at a sheet of white paper, you will

■ Species Differences in Color Vision

When you and your cat look at the same things—the cat food that you are opening, the rug that he is sharpening his claws on, the dangerous dog next door—the two of you do not see the same things. Your cat's ability to see colors is much less developed than your own. Cats can see some colors, but only when the colored surfaces are large. Thus your cat may be able to see the color of your carpet, but you probably appreciate the multicolored label on his Nine Lives can more than he does.

In fact, compared to most other mammals, humans have unusually good color vision. The ability to see colors is nonexistent in rodents: Rats are completely color blind. Color vision among the carnivores—dogs and cats, for example—is limited, while some primitive primates, including tree shrews, can see colors moderately well. Monkeys and apes, the members of the primate order most closely related to humans, can see colors very well. It is possible that this ability evolved partly because it gave the tree-dwelling ancestors common to monkeys, apes, and humans advantages in foraging for brightly colored fruits. Color vision is not limited to a few mammals, however. Some reptiles, fish, insects, and shellfish can also distinguish colors (Rosenzweig & Leiman, 1982).

But even among animals that can see colors, there are differences in what colors they can see. For example, bees

can see ultraviolet light, but not red. Pigeons cannot see indigo and violet, monkeys cannot see some blue, indigo, and violet, and human infants are insensitive to violet. And even if an animal is sensitive to light of a certain wavelength, we do not know how that light is experienced. Deer, to their benefit, are able to distinguish the fluorescent orange that hunters are required to wear. It is not clear that they perceive the color as "orange" in the way that humans do. Rather, they probably see it as a brightness that somehow just doesn't belong to the environment. In other words, "Run!"

Animals differ not only in terms of the parts of the spectrum that they can see, but also in the ways that they divide up the spectrum into color categories. Researchers have discovered that bees lump together wavelengths that we distinguish as yellow and green. Bees that have been fed sugar water from a dish with a yellow bottom tend to return to dishes with green as well as yellow bottoms. Apparently, bees perceive the two hues as the same. Monkeys, on the other hand, perceive as quite separate colors what we see as simply shades of the same color. Such differences among animal species suggest that the receptor cells in their eyes, and the neurons to which the cells are connected, process light in somewhat different ways, although we are just beginning to discover what those differences are (Bornstein & Marks, 1982).

Figure 3-13
People who are color blind have a partial or total inability to perceive *hue*. To show what this means in everyday life, we have printed a photo of hot-air balloons both in normal color (left) and as someone with red-green color blindness would see it (right).

see an afterimage. Where the picture is green, you will see a red afterimage; where the picture is yellow-orange, you will see a bright blue afterimage; where the picture is black, you will see a bright white afterimage. The afterimage is always in the complementary color. Hering's explanation for afterimages is that the receptor pairs have adapted to the stimulation. While you were looking at the green bars in the flag, the red-green receptors were sending "green" messages; but they were also adapting to the stimulation by becoming less sensitive to green light. When you later looked at the white page (made up of light from all parts of the spectrum), the red-green receptors responded much more to wavelengths in the red portion of the spectrum, and so you saw a red bar. Can you predict in advance what kind of afterimage you will experience after you stare at the dot in the center of Figure 3-15 for about 30 seconds?

The two theories of color vision—trichromatic and opponent-process—have coexisted for over a century. Neither theory has succeeded in ousting the other. In a sense, then, current theory hypothesizes a model that combines features of both previous theories, both of which seem to be valid, although for two different stages in the visual process. We now know for certain that there are three kinds of receptors for color, just as trichromatic theory holds. But while these receptors have peaks of sen-

Figure 3-15
An afterimage always appears in complementary colors. After staring at the center of the top square for about 30 seconds and then shifting your gaze to the center dot of the bottom square, you will see *complementary afterimages*. The small yellow squares will appear as blue, and the blue squares will appear as yellow.

Figure 3-14
Stare at the white spot in the center of the flag for about 30 seconds. Then look at a blank piece of white paper and you will see an *afterimage*.

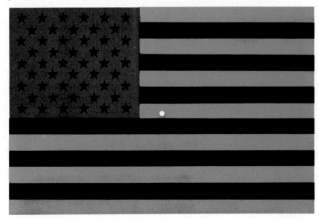

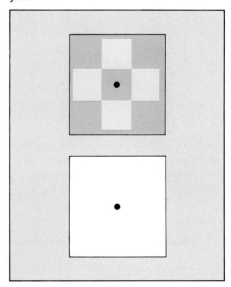

Frequency The number of cycles per second in a wave; in sound, the primary determinant of pitch.

Hertz (Hz) Cycles per second; unit of measurement for the frequency of waves.

Pitch Auditory experience corresponding primarily to frequency of sound vibrations, resulting in a higher or lower tone.

Amplitude The magnitude of a wave; in sound, the primary determinant of loudness.

sitivity at violet, green, and yellow-green, all are responsive to a broad range of colors. Moreover, contrary to the Helmholtz theory, there is no "red" receptor in the retina. We also have evidence that neurons higher up in the visual pathway code colors in an opponent-process way. DeValois and DeValois (1975) discovered that some neurons respond only to brightness and not to color: As the intensity of light increases, so does the rate at which these neurons fire. A second set of neurons increases its rate of firing when red light strikes the cones and decreases it when green light strikes them. A third set of cells fires in response to blue light and reduces its rate of firing when yellow light strikes the cones. All three sets are paired with cells that react in exactly the opposite way. Thus, Hering was not completely wrong in proposing an opponent-process mechanism.

It now seems that there are, as Helmholtz believed, three kinds of receptors for color. The messages that they transmit, however, are translated by other neurons in the visual system into opponent-process form. These complex patterns of "on" and "off" firing of neurons are what communicate the message "color" to the brain. In the brain itself are cells that respond only to color (Mollon, 1982). They too appear to work according to the opponent-process principle. In fact, certain kinds of afterimages appear when brain cells become adapted to certain colors. When heavy users of green computer monitors look away from their screens, they often notice that white objects have pink edges. This harmless phenomenon, which can last for several hours, is caused by adaptation of color cells in the brain itself. Seeing red should serve as a warning, however, of potential eyestrain, which can be serious. When doing close work on computers, take frequent breaks to give your eyes a rest.

■ Hearing

There is an ancient question that asks, "If a tree falls in the forest and there is no one there, is there a sound?" A psychologist would answer, "There are sound waves, but there is no sound or noise." Sounds and noise are psychological experiences created by the brain in response to stimulation. What kinds of stimuli cause us to hear sounds?

Sound

The physical stimuli for the sense of hearing are *sound waves*—changes in pressure caused when molecules of air or fluid collide with one another and then move apart again, transmitting energy at every bump. The simplest sound wave—what we hear as a pure tone—can be pictured as a sine wave (see Figure 3-16). The tuning fork vibrates, causing the molecules of air first to compress and then to expand. The **frequency** of the waves is measured in cycles per second, expressed in a unit called **hertz (Hz).** Frequency primarily determines the **pitch** of the sound—how high or how low it is. The human ear responds to frequencies from about 20 Hz to 20,000 Hz. A bass viola can reach down to about 50 Hz, a piano to as high as 5,000 Hz.

The height of the wave represents its **amplitude,** which, together

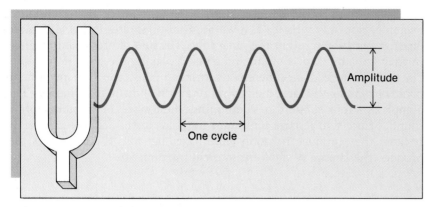

Amplitude

One cycle

Decibel Unit of measurement for the loudness of sounds.

Overtones Tones that result from sound waves that are multiples of the basic tone; primary determinant of timbre.

Figure 3-16
As it vibrates, the tuning fork alternately compresses and expands the molecules of air, creating a *sound wave*.

with pitch, determines the *loudness* of a sound. Loudness is measured in **decibels** (see Figure 3-17). As we grow older, we lose some of our ability to hear low-intensity sounds. We can hear high-intensity sounds, however, as well as ever. This is why elderly people may ask you to speak louder and then, when you oblige by speaking *much* louder, respond, "There's no need to shout!"

The sounds that we hear seldom result from pure tones. Unlike a tuning fork, which can produce a tone that is almost pure, musical instruments produce **overtones**—accompanying sound waves that are dif-

Figure 3-17
A decibel scale for several common sounds Prolonged exposure to sounds above 85 decibels can cause permanent damage to the ears.
After Dunkle, 1982

Decibels	
130	**Pain threshold**
	Sonic boom
	Air raid siren
120	Jackhammer (3 feet away)
	Jet plane (500 feet above)
	Live rock music
100	Power mower
	Subway train (20 feet away)
	Heavy truck (25 feet away)
80	**Potential ear damage**
	City traffic
	Vacuum cleaner
60	Normal conversation
	Window air conditioner
40	Average office interior
20	Whisper (5 feet away)
0	

Timbre Quality or texture of a sound caused by overtones.

Hammer, anvil, stirrup The three small bones in the middle ear that relay vibrations of the eardrum to the inner ear.

ferent multiples of the frequency of the basic tone. A violin string, for example, not only vibrates as a whole, it also vibrates in halves, thirds, quarters, and so on, all at the same time. Because of physical differences in their construction, a violin and a piano playing the same note will be "in tune" but produce different overtones. Thus, the two instruments could be playing the same melody yet retain their distinctive sounds. This complex pattern of overtones determines the **timbre,** or "texture," of the sound. Music synthesizers can mimic different instruments electronically because they produce not only pure tones but also the overtones that produce the timbre of different musical instruments.

The Ear

Hearing begins when sound waves bump up against the eardrum (see Figure 3-18) and cause it to vibrate. The quivering of the eardrum causes three tiny bones in the middle ear—called the **hammer,** the **anvil,** and the **stirrup**—to hit each other in sequence and to carry the vibrations

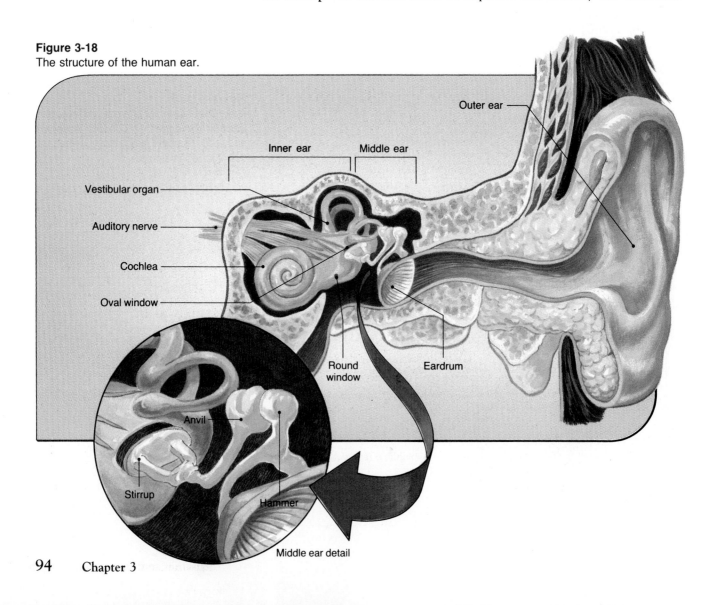

Figure 3-18
The structure of the human ear.

to the inner ear. The last of these three bones, the stirrup, is attached to a membrane called the **oval window.** Just below the oval window is another membrane, called the **round window,** which equalizes the pressure in the inner ear when the stirrup hits against the oval window.

The air waves are magnified during their trip through the middle ear. Thus, when the oval window starts to vibrate at the touch of the stirrup, it has a powerful effect on the inner ear. There, the vibrations are transmitted to the fluid inside a snail-shaped structure called the **cochlea.** The cochlea is divided lengthwise by the **basilar membrane** (see Figure 3-19). The basilar membrane is stiffer near the oval and round windows and gets gradually more flexible toward its other end. When the fluid in the cochlea begins to move, the basilar membrane is pushed up and down, rippling in response to the movement of the cochlear fluid.

Lying on top of the basilar membrane, and moving with it, is the **organ of Corti.** It is here that the messages from the sound waves finally reach the receptor cells for the sense of hearing. Embedded in the organ of Corti are thousands of tiny hair cells—the receptors. As you can see in Figure 3-20, each hair cell is topped by a bundle of fibers. These fibers are pushed and pulled by the vibrations of the basilar membrane. If the fibers bend by so much as 100-trillionths of a meter, the receptor cell

Oval window Membrane across the opening between the middle ear and inner ear that conducts vibrations to the cochlea.

Round window Membrane between the middle ear and inner ear that equalizes pressure in the inner ear.

Cochlea Part of the inner ear containing fluid that vibrates, which in turn causes the basilar membrane to vibrate.

Basilar membrane Vibrating membrane in the cochlea of the inner ear that contains sense receptors for sound.

Organ of Corti Structure on the surface of the basilar membrane that contains the receptor cells for hearing.

Figure 3-19
The cochlea When the eardrum transforms sound waves into mechanical vibrations, they are transmitted to the *oval window* of the cochlea. Pressure waves are then sent through the cochlear fluid in the directions indicated by the arrows.
Adapted from Coren, Porac, & Ward, 1984. Copyright © 1984 by Harcourt Brace Jovanovich, Inc.

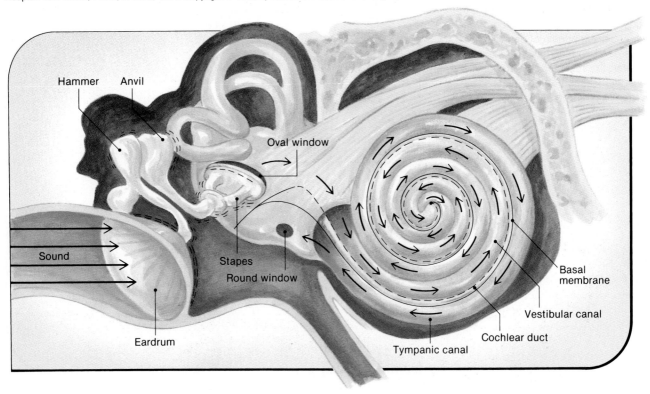

Auditory nerve The bundle of neurons that carries signals from the ear to the brain.

sends a signal to be transmitted through the **auditory nerve** to the brain. The brain pools the information from thousands of these cells to create sounds. Recently, it has been discovered that each hair cell not only sends messages *to* the brain but also receives messages *from* the brain. The brain apparently can send signals to the hair cells that reduce their sensitivity to sound in general or to sound waves of particular frequencies. It appears that the brain can in effect "shut down" the ears somewhat, but for what purpose remains one of the mysteries of research on hearing (Hudspeth, 1983).

NEURAL CONNECTIONS. The sense of hearing is truly bilateral. Each ear sends messages to both cerebral hemispheres. The switching station where the nerve fibers from the ears cross over is in the medulla, part of the hindbrain. From the medulla, other nerve fibers carry the messages from the ears to the higher parts of the brain. Some messages go to the brain centers that coordinate the movements of the eyes, head, and ears. Others travel through the reticular formation (which we examined in Chapter 2), which probably tacks on a few special "wake-up" or "ho-hum" postscripts to the sound messages. The primary destinations, of course, are the auditory projection areas in the temporal lobes of the two cerebral hemispheres. Along the way, the auditory messages pass through at least four levels of neurons—a much less direct route than in the visual system. At each stage, auditory information becomes more precisely coded.

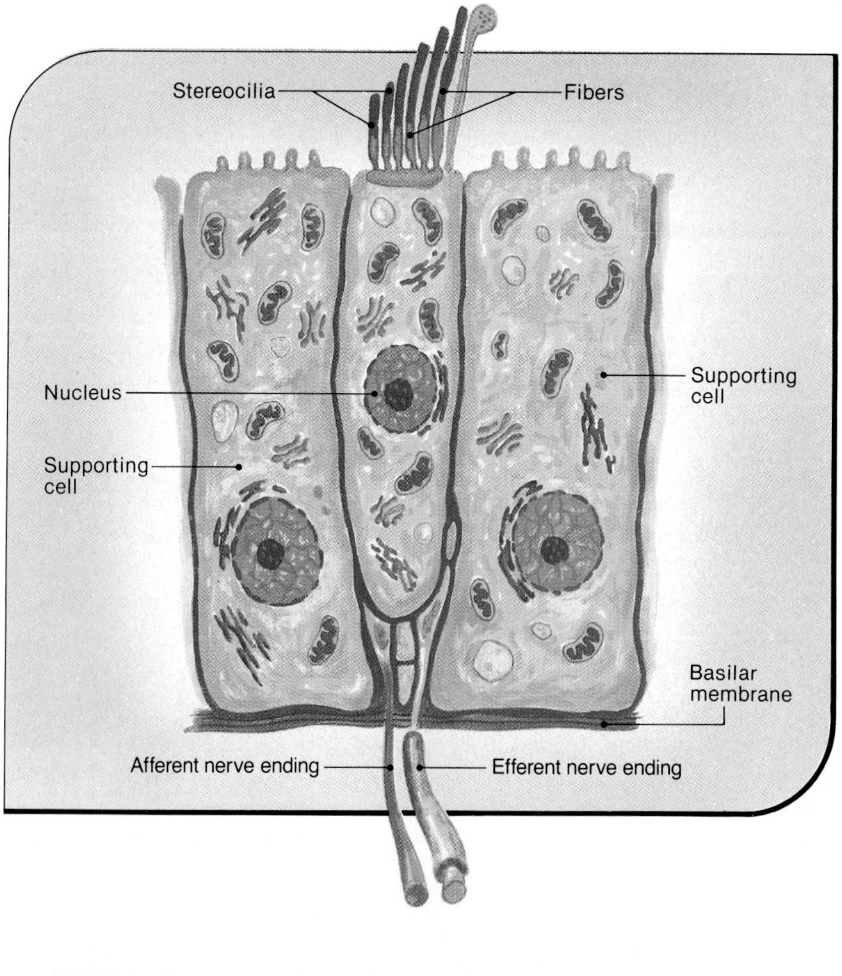

Figure 3-20
A detailed drawing of a hair cell, the receptor for hearing. At the top of each hair cell are a bundle of fibers. If the fibers bend so much as 100-trillionths of a meter, the receptor cells transmit a sensory message to the brain.
Adapted from Hudspeth, 1983. All rights reserved.

Hearing Disorders

Because the ear is so complicated, the number of possible problems that can affect our hearing is large. Deafness is one of the most common problems. Some instances of deafness result from defects in the outer or middle ear—for instance, the eardrum may be damaged or the small bones of the middle ear may not work properly. Other cases of deafness occur because the basilar membrane in the cochlea or the auditory nerve itself has been damaged. Disease, infections, and even long-term exposure to loud noise can harm the ear and cause partial or complete deafness.

Hearing aids can relieve many hearing problems, but not all. Some aids work by merely amplifying the incoming sound. However, this process will not work for people who have auditory nerve damage. Until recently, severe damage to the hairlike receptor cells in the cochlea also could not be overcome. During the last decade, however, a new surgical technique, the *cochlear implant*, has offered some hope to people who suffer from deafness due to cochlear damage. The implant operation consists of inserting a platinum electrode into the cochlea of one ear. The electrode bypasses the damaged hair cells and conveys electrical signals directly to the auditory nerve. A microphone that can be attached to the ear converts sound waves into electrical pulses that are sent to a small sound processor worn on clothing near the chest. The processor sorts out the frequencies of sounds most relevant to human needs—the sound of speech, for instance—and sends the corresponding electrical signals through a series of devices to the implanted electrode. The electrical signals reaching the auditory nerve vary with the frequency and amplitude of the sound waves that reach the microphone.

The early implants, having just one electrode, were able to present only a single noise that varied in loudness. As a result, most of the 600 profoundly deaf people who received this implant could not understand speech. But the implant did provide sound cues that improved lip reading and allowed them to hear their own voices so that they learned to adjust their own speech volume to an appropriate level. Recipients could also learn to distinguish such warning signals as horns and bells. These implants may also have given young children a vital link to spoken language at the stage in development during which exposure to words is crucial to learning how to speak normally. Many profoundly deaf children never develop normal speech. Those who received the early implants, however, learned to use words and proper pitch and loudness better than they would have without them.

Recently, experiments have been conducted with devices having multiple electrodes (Loeb, 1985). A sophisticated electronic processor filters the sound into separate frequencies for each of 22 electrodes, and each implanted electrode stimulates a different set of auditory receptors—thus reproducing electronically the kind of patterned stimulation that occurs in normal ears. Results vary greatly, but in some previously totally deaf patients these new implants have produced as much as 70 percent correct word recognition.

Far from not hearing enough sound, some people hear too much of the wrong kind and suffer greatly because of it. Almost everybody has at some time heard a steady, high-pitched hum that seems to persist even in the quietest room. The apparent sound seems to come from inside the head. In about 1 percent of the population, this tone, called a *tinnitus*, becomes unbearably loud—like the screeching of subway brakes—and does not go away (Dunkle, 1982). In a few cases, tinnitus is caused by blood flowing through vessels near the inner ear. Generally, though, tinnitus originates somewhere in the brain.

Unfortunately, medical research has not yet found a cure for this problem, although many people who suffer from severe tinnitus gain some relief from masking. A device mounted in the ear much like a hearing aid produces a sound that mutes the annoying hum. Oddly enough, in about a third of the cases, just about any weak sound has the desired effect (McFadden & Wightman, 1983). The tinnitus often remains masked for seconds or even minutes after the masking tone has been withdrawn. Researchers are at a loss to explain how masking devices work, but it is clear that they do not simply drown out the tinnitus. Another line of attack has been drugs, but those that have been tested have produced side effects worse than the problem that they were designed to cure. Researchers are working on this problem, however, and safer drugs may someday bring relief to even the most unbearable cases of tinnitus.

Theories of Hearing

The thousands of tiny hair cells in the organ of Corti send messages about the infinite variations in the frequency, amplitude, and overtones of sound waves. But so far, we have said nothing about how the different sound-wave patterns are coded into neural messages. One aspect of sound, loudness, seems to depend on how many neurons are activated—the more cells that fire, the louder the sound seems to be. The coding of messages about pitch is more complicated. There are two basic views of pitch discrimination: place theory and frequency theory. **Place theory** states that the brain determines pitch by noting the place on the basilar membrane at which the message is strongest. Helmholtz, who helped develop the trichromatic theory of color vision, proposed that for any given sound wave, there is a point on the basilar membrane at which vibrations are most intense. As the frequency of the wave changes, the point of maximum vibration also changes. According to Helmholtz, high-frequency sounds cause the greatest vibration at the stiff base of the basilar membrane. Low-frequency sounds do the same at the more flexible opposite end of the membrane (Zwislocki, 1981). The brain detects the location of most intense nerve cell activity and uses this to determine the pitch of a sound.

The **frequency theory** of pitch discrimination states that the frequency of vibrations of the basilar membrane as a *whole*, not just *parts* of it, is translated into an equivalent frequency of nerve impulses. Thus, if a hair bundle is pulled or pushed rapidly, its hair cell sends a high-frequency message to the brain. Neurons cannot fire as rapidly as the frequency of the highest-pitched sound that can be heard, however, and this problem has led theorists to suggest a **volley principle.** The nerve cells, they maintain, fire in sequence: One neuron fires, then a second one, then a third. By then, the first neuron has had time to recover and can fire again. If necessary, the three neurons together can send a rapid series of impulses to the brain.

Because neither place theory nor frequency theory alone fully explains pitch discrimination, some combination of the two is needed. The volley principle, for example, explains quite well the ear's responses to frequencies up to about 4,000 Hz. Above that, however, place theory provides a better explanation of what is happening.

■ The Other Senses

Psychologists and other scientists have focused most of their attention on the senses of vision and hearing because humans rely primarily on these two senses to obtain information about their environment. However, we also use other senses, such as smell, balance, motion, taste, pressure, temperature, and pain. Let's look at each of these senses one at a time.

Smell

Unlike many lower animals that use their noses to detect mates, predators, and prey, humans do not depend on their sense of smell for survival. Nevertheless, the sense of smell in humans is incredibly sensitive. Only a few molecules of a substance reaching the smell receptors are necessary to cause humans to perceive an odor. Certain substances that give off a large number of molecules that dissolve easily in the moist, fatty tissues of the nose can be detected in especially small amounts. Decayed cabbage, lemons, and rotten eggs are examples. According to one estimate, the sense of smell is about 10,000 times as sensitive as that of taste (Moncrieff, 1951), although sensitivity to odors appears to decrease with age (Engen, 1973).

Our sense of smell is activated by a complex protein produced in a nasal gland. As we breathe, a fine mist of this protein, called odorant binding protein (OBP), is sprayed through a duct in the tip of the nose. The protein binds with airborne molecules which then activate the receptors for this sense, located high in each nasal cavity in a patch of tissue called the **olfactory epithelium** (see Figure 3-21). The olfactory epithelium is only about one-half the size of a postage stamp, but it is packed with millions of receptor cells. Apparently, these nerve cells die and are replaced by new ones every few weeks (Graziadei, Levine, & Graziadei, 1979). These are the only nerves known to be replaced in the human body.

The axons from nerve cells in the nose carry the messages directly to the two **olfactory bulbs** in the brain. Since these fibers do not pass through the thalamus, as other sensory fibers do, the sense of smell's route to the cerebral cortex is the most direct. The olfactory bulbs can communicate "across the hall" to each other and "upstairs" to the olfactory projection areas in the cerebral cortex.

Relatively little is known about the sense of smell because of technical difficulties in studying it. For example, the olfactory epithelium is difficult to reach with measuring instruments like electrodes. Furthermore, smell is dependent on microscopic, airborne molecules whose flow through the air and through the nasal passages is quite difficult to control experimentally.

Nevertheless, psychologists have been able to uncover several interesting phenomena regarding smell. First, although the sense of smell in many other species is considerably more acute than ours, humans display

Olfactory epithelium Nasal membranes containing receptor cells sensitive to odors.

Olfactory bulb Either of the two smell centers in the brain.

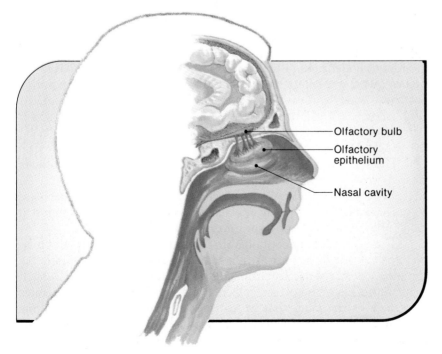

Olfactory bulb

Olfactory epithelium

Nasal cavity

Figure 3-21
The location of the olfactory epithelium.

Taste buds Structures on the tongue that contain the receptor cells for taste.

Papillae Small bumps on the tongue that contain taste buds.

some remarkable olfactory abilities. We can, for example, smell mercaptan, a foul-smelling substance added to natural gas, in concentrations as small as 1 part per 50 billion parts of air. It is also interesting to note that humans can be sensitive to the presence of odors without necessarily being able to name them. Engen (1982) found that although people could tell which one of four test tubes contained an extremely dilute odor that was different from the others, they were not successful in picking out particular odors such as menthol when asked to identify them by name. We have all had the experience of smelling something "funny" without being able to name the smell.

Odor sensitivity also appears to be related to variables like sex and age. William Doty and his research team (1984) found that subjects could determine the sex of people on the basis of breath odor. In addition, females were generally better at this task than males, reflecting a general tendency for females to have a better odor sense than males. Moreover, elderly people are less sensitive to odor than are young adults. Doty also uncovered ethnic differences in odor sensitivity. In a study of Korean-Americans, native Japanese, blacks, and whites, he discovered that the Japanese were least able to identify odors. Doty speculated that this might be due to their lack of prior exposure to the particular odors selected as stimuli for the study—a possibility that suggests that culture and learning influence smell sensitivity. Finally, our sensitivity to odor undergoes a process of adaptation similar to the adaptation of our eyes to darkness. Those of us who have lived with an odor for a while may no longer be aware of it even though visitors often find it quite objectionable.

Although we take our sense of smell for granted, its loss can be quite devastating. Complete loss of smell (known as *anosmia*) causes people to lose interest in food and even diminishes the desire for sexual activity. In a sense, we are so adapted to our sense of smell that its importance becomes apparent only when it is taken away from us.

Taste

In order to understand taste, we must first distinguish it from *flavor*. The flavor of food is a complex combination of taste and smell. If you hold your nose when you eat, most of the food's flavor will be eliminated, although you will still be able to experience sensations of *bitterness*, *saltiness*, *sourness*, or *sweetness*. In other words, you will get the taste, but not the flavor.

The receptor cells for the sense of taste lie inside the **taste buds,** most of which are found on the tip, sides, and back of the tongue. An adult has about 10,000 taste buds. The number of taste buds decreases with age, a fact which partly explains why older people lose interest in food—they simply cannot taste it as well as they used to.

The taste buds are contained in the tongue's **papillae,** small bumps that you can see if you look at your tongue in the mirror. Each taste bud contains a cluster of taste receptors, or hair cells (see Figure 3-22). About every seven days, these hair cells die and are replaced. The chemical substances in the foods that we eat are dissolved in saliva and carried down into the crevices between the papillae of the tongue, where they come into contact with the hairs of the taste receptors. The chemical

Sourness is one of the four primary taste qualities.

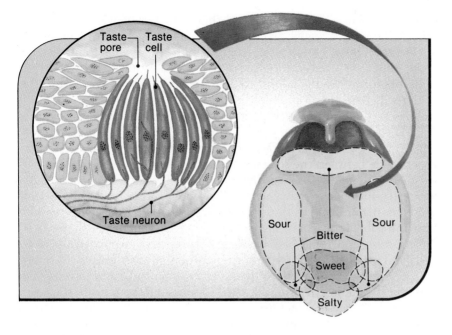

Vestibular senses Senses of equilibrium and body movement and position.

Figure 3-22
(Above) **A diagram of a single taste bud** (Below) **A schematic drawing of the tongue,** showing the locations most sensitive to the four primary taste qualities.

interaction between food substances and the taste cells causes adjacent neurons to fire, sending a nerve impulse to the brain. This happens very fast: People can accurately identify a taste within one-tenth of a second after something salty or sweet has touched the tongue (Cain, 1981). The same nerves that carry messages about taste also conduct information about chewing, swallowing, and the temperature and texture of food.

We experience only four primary taste qualities: sweet, sour, salt, and bitter. All other tastes result from combinations of these four. The tip of the tongue is most sensitive to sweetness and saltiness, the back to bitterness, and the sides to sourness (see Figure 3-22). But each area can distinguish all of the four qualities to some degree. The middle of the tongue does not respond to taste at all.

Taste, like the other senses, also displays the phenomenon of *sensory adaptation.* You may have noticed that when you first start eating salted peanuts, the saltiness is quite strong but after a while becomes less noticeable. Furthermore, exposure to one quality of taste can modify other taste sensations (Bartoshuk, 1974). This is called *cross-adaptation.* For example, many people find that after eating fresh artichokes, other foods, including just plain water, tend to have a sweet taste. Conversely, after you brush your teeth in the morning, you may notice that your orange juice has lost its sweetness. This phenomenon results partly from the fact that toothpast contains an ingredient that reduces our sensitivity to sweetness and increases our sensitivity to the sourness of the juice's citric acid.

The Vestibular Senses

The **vestibular senses** monitor equilibrium and the awareness of body position and movement. Birds and fish rely on them to tell them which way is up and in which direction they are headed when they cannot see well. Like hearing, the vestibular senses arise in the inner ear, and the

Semicircular canals Structures in the inner ear particularly sensitive to body rotation.

Vestibular sacs Sacs in the inner ear that are responsible for sensing gravitation, and forward, backward, and vertical movement.

Utricle Organ in the inner ear that provides information about horizontal movement of the body.

Saccule Organ in the inner ear that provides information about vertical movement of the body and gravitation.

While the *vestibular senses* usually monitor our sense of equilibrium and bodily position, they can produce motion sickness when confused by things like rocking boats and twisting amusement-park rides.

sense organs are hair cells that send their signals out over the auditory nerve. There are actually two kinds of vestibular sensation. The first is the sensation of *body rotation*, and it arises in the three **semicircular canals** of the inner ear. Like the cochlea, each canal is filled with fluid that shifts when the head is moved in any direction. The movement of the fluid bends hair bundles, which in turn stimulate hair cells, sending a message to the brain about the speed and direction of body rotation.

The second vestibular sense is that of *gravitation and movement* forward and backward, up and down. This sense arises from the two **vestibular sacs** that lie between the semicircular canals and the cochlea. Both sacs are filled with a jellylike fluid that contains millions of tiny crystals. The **utricle** is positioned so that when the body moves horizontally, the crystals bend hair bundles and thus start a sensory message. The **saccule** does the same thing for vertical movement. But even when your head is motionless, the crystals bend some hair bundles because they are pulled down by gravity. This gives you a sense of the position of your head at all times.

The nerve impulses from the several vestibular organs travel to the brain on the auditory nerve, but their ultimate destinations in the brain are not fully known. Some messages from the vestibular system go to the cerebellum, which controls many of the reflexes involved in coordinated movement. Others go to the areas that send messages to the internal body organs, and some go to the cerebral cortex for analysis and response.

Sensations of Motion

Motion sickness arises in the vestibular organs. Certain kinds of motion (riding in ships, cars, airplanes, even on camels and elephants) trigger strong reactions in some people. The effect is made worse if the person's head moves relative to his or her body. One theory is that motion sickness results from discrepancies between visual information and vestibular sensations: Trying to read a book while your body is being bumped up and down in a bus is one example of conflict between visual and vestibular information.

Occasionally, the vestibular sense can be completely overwhelmed by information from the visual sense. This is what happens when we watch an automobile chase scene that was filmed from inside a moving car. We feel a sensation of movement because our eyes are telling our brain that we are moving, even though the organs in our inner ear insist that we are sitting still. In fact, the sense of motion can be so strong that some people get motion sickness while sitting absolutely still as they watch a movie filmed from an airplane or a boat! This visual trick has an advantage. People who have had one or even both vestibular organs removed can function normally as long as they have visual cues on which to rely.

The Skin Senses

Our skin is actually our largest sense organ. An average person 6 feet tall has about 21 square feet of skin. Aside from protecting us from the environment, holding in body fluids, and regulating our internal temperature, the skin is also a sense organ with numerous nerve receptors distributed in varying concentrations throughout its surface (see Figure 3-23). While at least 13 different receptor types have been identified (Brown & Deffenbacher, 1979), they generally fall into a smaller number of subtypes.

The nerve fibers from all of these receptors travel to the brain through the spinal cord. Before they reach the top of the spinal cord and enter the brain, all the nerve fibers have crossed over: Messages from the left side of the body reach the projection areas in the right cerebral hemisphere; messages from the right side of the body go to the left hemisphere.

The various skin receptors give rise to what are called the *cutaneous sensations* of pressure, temperature, and pain. But the relationship between the receptors and our sensory experiences are not simple. At one time, investigators believed that the different skin sensations were each related to a specific type of receptor. But studies have failed to reveal a simple connection between the various types of receptors and the separate sensations. The **Meissner corpuscles,** abundant and close to the surface in hairless areas such as fingers, seem to be sensitive to touch, but so too are receptors around the roots of hair cells. **Pacinian corpuscles,** which lie below the surface receptors, are sensitive to pressures between internal organs and muscles. **Ruffini endings** and **Krause bulbs** are responsible, respectively, for warmth and cold. Researchers once believed that **free nerve endings** were responsible only for pain until it was pointed out that the cornea of the eye, which consists of virtually nothing but free nerve endings, is also very sensitive to pressure and temperature. Therefore, it

Meissner corpuscle Skin receptor believed to be sensitive to pressure.

Pacinian corpuscle Skin receptor believed to be sensitive to pressures between internal organs.

Ruffini ending Skin receptor believed to be responsive to warmth.

Krause bulb Skin receptor believed to be responsive to coldness.

Free nerve endings Finely branched nerve endings in the skin that serve as receptors for pain, pressure, and temperature.

Paradoxical heat Simultaneous stimulation of "warm" and "cold" receptors that is experienced as "hot."

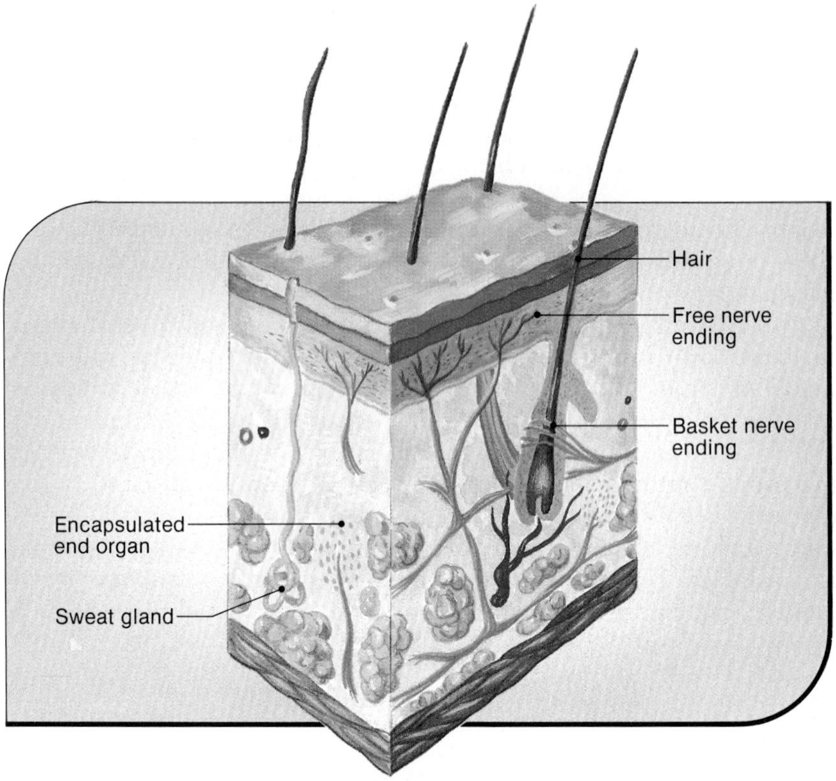

Hair
Free nerve ending
Basket nerve ending
Encapsulated end organ
Sweat gland

Figure 3-23
A cross-section of the human skin, showing several of the sensory receptors that have been identified.

now appears that there is no simple, one-to-one relationship between skin receptors and the various types of sensation.

A more complex view of skin sensation holds that, in addition to relationships between particular receptors and particular sensations, our brains may use complex information about the *patterns* of activity on many different receptors in order to detect and discriminate skin sensations. Before skin sensations reach the brain, they have undergone sufficient modification so that they bear little resemblance to the patterns of activity that started at the peripheral receptors. It may be that the pattern of different receptors firing at different rates is as important as the stimulation of particular receptors for sensitivity to various skin senses. For example, there are cold fibers that speed their firing rate as the skin cools down and slow down their firing when the skin heats up. Conversely, there are warm fibers that speed up their firing rate when the skin gets warm and slow down when the skin cools. The brain may use the combined information as the basis for determining skin temperature. If both sets of fibers are activated at once, the brain may read their combined pattern of firings as "hot." Thus, you might sometimes think that you are touching something hot when you are really touching something warm and something cool at the same time. This phenomenon is known as **paradoxical heat** (see Figure 3-24).

The way in which information is mapped onto the brain is also responsible for many aspects of skin sensation. You can actually feel the way in which your brain organizes information by testing for yourself the results of Aristotle's illusion in Figure 3-25. Touch the eraser end of a pencil with both fingers, as shown in the first picture. Because the two points on your fingers are sufficiently close together, the sensation of touch is received by a similar location on your cerebral cortex, and you have the sensation of *one* touch. Now cross your fingers and touch the pencil as shown in the second picture. The sensation of *two* touches results from the fact that these two points on your fingertips are far enough apart that the touch information is received in two quite separate locations on your cortex (Coren, Porac, & Ward, 1984).

The skin senses, like our other senses, are remarkably sensitive. For example, skin displacement of as little as .00004 inches can result in a sensation of pressure. Moreover, various parts of the body differ greatly in their sensitivity to pressure: Your face and fingertips are extremely sensitive while your legs, feet, and back are much less so (Weinstein, 1968). One way of demonstrating these differences in sensitivity is to apply a measuring device with two points to different locations on the body. How far apart must the points be before they feel like two points instead of one? On your back, they would have to be about 34 times farther apart than on your fingertips. It is no wonder that when we examine things with our hands, we tend to do so with our fingertips. Touch is a fast and accurate substitute for sight when it comes to identifying familiar objects (Klatsky, Lederman, & Metzger, 1985). As reported in the Application at the end of this chapter, this finding has practical applications both for people who are visually impaired and for the development of robotics. It is this remarkable sensitivity in our fingertips that makes possible Braille touch-reading, which requires identifying patterns of tiny raised dots distributed over a very small area.

The skin is also quite sensitive to changes in temperature, especially when large areas are stimulated at once. Apparently, many receptors together provide more precise information about temperature than do individual receptors.

The skin senses also undergo various kinds of sensory adaptation. When we first sit in a hot bath, it may be too hot to tolerate, but in a few minutes, we adapt to the heat—just as our eyes adapt to darkness—and may even add more hot water. Similarly, when we put on a slightly tight article of clothing, we may feel uncomfortable at first but not even

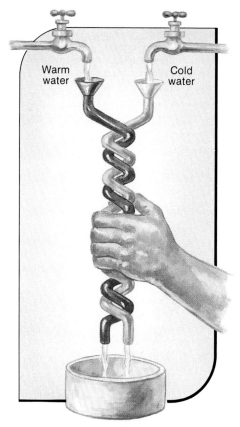

Figure 3-24
Touching a warm pipe and a cold pipe at the same time causes two sets of skin receptors to signal at once to the brain. The brain reads their combined pattern of firings as "hot," a phenomenon known as *paradoxical heat*.

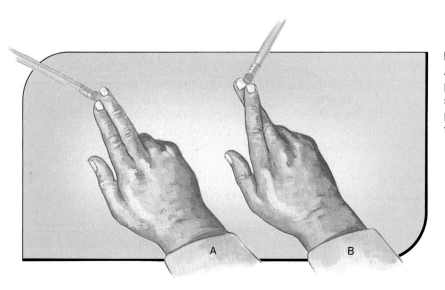

Figure 3-25
Aristotle's illusion if you touch the pencil as shown in A, you will have the sensation of one touch. If you touch the pencil as shown in B, the sensation of two touches will result.

notice later. How soon this adaptation occurs, or whether it will óccur at all, appears to be dependent on how large an area of the skin is being stimulated and the intensity of the pressure (Geldard, 1972): The larger the area and the more intense the pressure, the longer it takes for us to adapt.

Pain

Pain differs from the other senses in the extent to which people react to it. We have all experienced pain, and each of us has a pretty good idea of what it is, but people have widely different physiological reactions to pain. In fact, some people appear to be congenitally insensitive to pain (Manfredi et al., 1981). For example, there is the case of a young Canadian girl who felt nothing when she inadvertently bit off part of her tongue and received third-degree burns from kneeling on a hot radiator (Baxter & Olszewski, 1960; McMurray, 1950). Moreover, differences in pain sensations may also be attributable to psychological differences that affect perceptions of pain. If you burn your hand, you might calmly run cold water over the burn; someone else might scream out loud. Even our beliefs about pain can affect our perceptions of it. For example, one study (DiMatteo & Friedman, 1989) found that patients who believed that a given medical procedure was not painful actually did experience less pain. Another researcher (Zborowski, 1969) observed that members of different ethnic groups responded differently to surgical pain in rather predictable ways. It should not be surprising, then, that in cases of serious injury, the perception of pain does not appear to be related to the amount of tissue damage sustained (Schiffman, 1982). Because of factors such as these, it is difficult to measure typical pain thresholds or the means by which different individuals adapt to pain.

How do psychologists explain our differing sensitivities to pain? A commonly accepted explanation is the **gate control theory** of pain (Melzack, 1980). According to this theory, a "neurological gate" in the spinal cord controls the transmission of pain impulses to the brain. If the gate is open, we experience more pain than we do when it is closed. The determination of whether the gate is closed or open depends on a complex competition between different types of nerve fibers. On the one hand, there are large fibers in the sensory nerves that, when stimulated, tend to "close the gate" and thus prevent pain impulses from reaching the brain. But there are also small fibers that interact with neurons in the spinal cord to let the pain through, or to "open the gate." And certain areas of the brain stem can also close the gate from above, so to speak, by sending down signals to fibers in the spinal cord in order to close the gate. Finally, by not attending to pain, we may also experience greatly diminished feelings of pain. For example, in the locker room, athletes sometimes first become aware of injuries that went unnoticed in the heat of competition. You can see that the gate control process is quite complex, but it is already being used to develop new techniques for the control of pain. For example, some dentists are experimenting with devices that electrically stimulate the firing of large nerve fibers, block the action of small fibers, and so close the gate on pain. Patients are provided with a control so that they can adjust the amount of stimulation to their own needs.

Biochemistry may also account for some of the wide individual differences in pain sensation. In Chapter 2, we noted that morphine is a narcotic drug that blocks the transmission of pain signals across the synapses between neurons. And we also noted that researchers have discovered natural chemicals in the body called *endorphins* that have an action similar to morphine; these chemicals appear in great concentration when the body is responding to pain. A number of studies with animals have demonstrated that stress will trigger the production of pain-reducing endorphins (Lewis, Cannon, & Liebeskind, 1980; Watkins & Mayer, 1982). Rats that were given repeated electrical shocks manufactured greater quantities of endorphins and subsequently appeared to be less sensitive to pain than rats that had not experienced the preparatory shocks.

In these and other similar studies, past experience with stress apparently changed the concentration of endorphins in the nervous system and, as a result, sensitivity to pain. It is tempting to consider the possibility that other individual differences in sensitivity to pain might also be due to the concentration of endorphins. For example, we have already noted how the mental expectation of minimal pain will diminish a painful experience. If you give pain sufferers a chemically neutral pill (placebo) but tell them that it is an effective pain reducer, they will often experience less pain after taking it. Similar results occur with hypnosis and acupuncture. It may be that the common element in all these methods is their potential to stimulate the manufacture of endorphins.

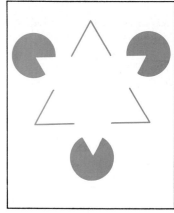

Figure 3-26
When sensory information is incomplete, we tend to create a complete perception by supplying the missing details. In this figure, we fill in the lines that let us perceive a white triangle in the center of the pattern.

Perception

As we noted in the introduction to this chapter, our senses provide us with raw data about the external world. However, without interpretation, this raw information remains what William James (1890) called "a booming, buzzing confusion." The eye records patterns of light and dark, but it does not "see" a pedestrian crossing the street. The eardrum vibrates in a particular fashion, but it does not "hear" a symphony. Experiencing *meaningful* patterns in the jumble of sensory information is what we mean by *perception*.

Ultimately, it is the brain that interprets the complex flow of information from the various senses. Using sensory information as raw material, the brain creates perceptual experiences that go beyond what is sensed. For example, looking at Figure 3-26, we tend to perceive a white triangle in the center of the pattern, although the sensory input consists only of three circles from which "pie slices" have been cut and three 60-degree angles. Or take Figure 3-27. At first glance, most people see only an assortment of black blotches. If you are told that the blotches represent a person riding a horse, suddenly your perceptual experience changes. What was meaningless sensory information now takes shape as a horse and rider.

Sometimes, as in certain optical illusions, you perceive things that could not possibly exist. The trident shown in Figure 3-28 is an example of such an "impossible" figure; on closer inspection, you discover that the object that you "recognized" is not really there. In all these cases, the brain actively creates and organizes perceptual experiences out of raw

Figure 3-27
Knowing beforehand that the black blotches in this figure represent a person riding a horse changes our perception of it.

Figure 3-28
An optical illusion In the case of the trident, we go beyond what is sensed (blue lines on flat white paper) to perceive a three-dimensional object that isn't really there.

sensory data. In the next section of this chapter, we will explore the various ways in which perceptual processes organize sensory experience.

Perceptual Organization

Early in this century, a group of German psychologists called Gestalt psychologists set out to discover the principles through which we interpret sensory information. The word *gestalt* has no exact English equivalent, but essentially it means "whole," "form," or "pattern." The Gestalt psychologists believed not only that the brain creates a coherent perceptual experience that is more than simply the sum of the available sensory information, but also that it does so in regular and predictable ways.

One important part of the perceptual process involves our being able to distinguish **figures** from the **ground** against which they appear. A colorfully upholstered chair stands out from the bare walls of a room. A marble statue is perceived as a whole figure standing out from the red brick wall behind it. The trident in Figure 3-28 stands out from the white page. In all these cases, we perceive some objects as "figures" and other sensory information as just "background."

The figure-ground distinction pertains to all our senses, not just vision. We can distinguish a violin solo against the ground of a symphony orchestra, a single voice amid cocktail party chatter, and the smell of roses in a florist's shop. In all these instances, we perceive a figure apart from the ground around it.

Sometimes, however, there are not enough cues in a pattern to permit us to easily distinguish a figure from its ground. The horse and rider in Figure 3-27 illustrate this problem, as does Figure 3-29, which shows a spotted dog investigating shadowy surroundings. It is hard to distinguish the dog because it has few visible contours of its own, and it seems as a result to have no more form than the background. This is the principle behind camouflage—to make a figure blend into its background.

Sometimes a figure with clear contours can be perceived in two very different ways because it is unclear which part of the stimulus is the figure

It is difficult for predators to see the figure of the walking stick against the background of its natural environment.

and which ground. Examples of such reversible figures are shown in Figures 3-30 and 3-31. At first glance, you perceive certain figures against a certain background, but as you look at the illustrations, you will discover that the figures eventually become ground. The result is that you have two very different perceptions of the same illustration.

Figure 3-31
Figure-ground relationship—a reversible figure Sometimes, a figure with clear contours can be perceived in two very different ways because it is unclear which part of the stimulus is *figure* and which part *ground*. At first glance, you may perceive certain figures against a certain background, but a second glance may result in just the opposite experience.

Figure 3-30
The *reversible figure* and ground in this Escher woodcut cause us to see first black devils and then white angels in each of the rings.

Figure 3-32 demonstrates some other important principles of perceptual organization. In every case, our perceptual experience is more than just a simple copy of the sensory information available to us. In other words, we use sensory information to create perceptions that are more than just sums of various parts. We tend to fill in the missing information, to group various objects together, to see whole objects and hear meaningful sounds rather than just meaningless bits and pieces of raw sensory data.

Perceptual Constancies

Surprisingly, we often continue to have the same perceptual experience even as the sensory data change. **Perceptual constancy** refers to this tendency to perceive objects as relatively stable and unchanging despite changing sensory information. Without this ability, we would find the world very confusing. Once we have formed a stable perception of an object, we can recognize it from almost any position, at almost any

Figure 3-32
Gestalt principles of perceptual organization.

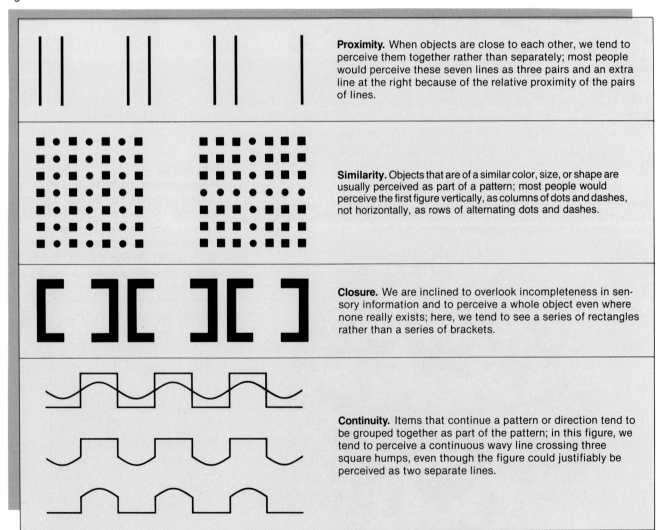

Proximity. When objects are close to each other, we tend to perceive them together rather than separately; most people would perceive these seven lines as three pairs and an extra line at the right because of the relative proximity of the pairs of lines.

Similarity. Objects that are of a similar color, size, or shape are usually perceived as part of a pattern; most people would perceive the first figure vertically, as columns of dots and dashes, not horizontally, as rows of alternating dots and dashes.

Closure. We are inclined to overlook incompleteness in sensory information and to perceive a whole object even where none really exists; here, we tend to see a series of rectangles rather than a series of brackets.

Continuity. Items that continue a pattern or direction tend to be grouped together as part of the pattern; in this figure, we tend to perceive a continuous wavy line crossing three square humps, even though the figure could justifiably be perceived as two separate lines.

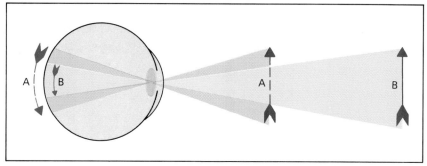

Figure 3-33
The relationship between distance and the size of the retinal image Object A and object B are the same size, but A, being much closer to the eye, casts a much larger image on the retina.

distance, under almost any illumination. A white house is perceived as a white house by day or by night and from any angle. We see it as the same house. The sensory information may change as illumination and perspective change, but the object is perceived as constant.

Objects also tend to be perceived as being their true size regardless of the size of the image that they cast on the retina. As Figure 3-33 shows, the farther away an object is from the lens of the eye, the smaller the retinal image it casts. For example, a 6-foot-tall man standing 20 feet away casts a retinal image that is only 50 percent of the size of the retinal image he casts at a distance of 10 feet. Yet he is not perceived as having shrunk to 3 feet.

Memory and experience play important parts in perceptual constancy. For example, look at Figure 3-34, which is a slightly altered photograph of British Prime Minister Margaret Thatcher. Before reading further, turn the book upside down and look at the picture again. An essentially normal face has taken on a gruesome aspect. Your experience in recognizing people and interpreting their facial expressions has accustomed you to emphasize certain perceptual cues (particularly eyes and mouths). When you look at the upside down picture, the eyes and mouth are normal, and so you perceive the entire face as being normal. In other words, you use your experience in perceiving normal human faces to perceive this (very unusual) face, and as a result, you do not perceive it as grossly distorted until you look at it rightside up.

Size constancy also depends partly on experience—information about the relative sizes of objects is stored in memory—and partly on distance cues. When there are no distance cues, size constancy has to rely solely on what we have learned from our previous experience with an object. Naturally, more errors occur when there are no distance cues, but fewer than one would expect in view of the radical changes in the size of the retinal image. We might guess that a woman some distance away is 5 feet 4 inches tall instead of 5 feet 8 inches, but hardly anyone would perceive her as being 3 feet tall, no matter how far away she is. We know from experience that adults are seldom that short.

Familiar objects also tend to be seen as having a constant shape, even though the retinal images that they cast change as they are viewed from different angles. A dinner plate is perceived as a circle even when

Figure 3-34
Look at the picture and then turn the book upside down so that the picture is rightside up. Experience leads you to use certain perceptual cues to recognize facial expressions, and the upside-down picture looks normal. Those same cues cause the rightside-up picture to look grossly distorted.

Shape constancy Tendency to see an object as the same shape no matter what angle it is viewed from.

Brightness constancy Perception of brightness as the same, even though the amount of light reaching the retina changes.

Color constancy Inclination to perceive familiar objects as retaining their color despite changes in sensory information.

Figure 3-35
Examples of shape constancy Even though the image of the door on the retina changes greatly as the door opens, we still perceive the door as being rectangular.
Boring et al., 1976

it is tilted and the retinal image is oval. A rectangular door will project a rectangular image on the retina only when it is viewed directly from the front. From any other angle, it casts a trapezoidal image on the retina, but it is not perceived as having suddenly become a trapezoidal door. These are examples of **shape constancy** (see Figure 3-35).

Two other important constancies are **brightness constancy** and **color constancy.** The former principle means that although the amount of light available to our eyes varies greatly, the perceived brightness of familiar objects hardly varies at all. We perceive a sheet of white paper as white whether we see it in candlelight or under a bright bulb. Likewise, we perceive a piece of coal as black whether we see it in a dark cellar or in noonday sunlight. This may seem obvious, but bear in mind that coal in sunlight reflects more light than white paper in candlelight, yet we always perceive white paper as being brighter. The explanation for brightness constancy is that a white object—or a black or gray one—will reflect the same percentage of the light falling on it whether that light is from a candle, a fluorescent lamp, or the sun. What is important is not the absolute amount of light that the object reflects, but how the relative reflection compares to the surrounding objects.

Similarly, we tend to perceive familiar objects as keeping their colors, regardless of information that reaches the eye. If you own a red automobile, you will see it as red whether it is on a brightly lit street or in a dark garage, where the small amount of light may send your eye a message that the color is closer to brown or black than red. But color constancy does not always operate. When objects are unfamiliar or there are no customary color cues, color constancy may be distorted—as when we buy a pair of pants in a brightly lit store, only to discover that in ordinary daylight they are not the shade we thought they were.

Throughout our discussion of these various principles, a common theme has been that our perceptual experiences often go far beyond the sensory information with which we are provided. In fact, our perceptual experiences rarely if ever correspond exactly to the information that we receive through our senses. We have already seen how neural structures

Drawing by Stuart Leeds. © 1988 The New Yorker Magazine, Inc.

"Do you enjoy being a Margarita?"

Cortical Coding and Perception

Important studies conducted decades after the original work of the Gestalt psychologists have begun to indicate how neurons in the brain organize perceptual experiences. Hubel and Wiesel (1959, 1979), who received the Nobel prize for their work, inserted an electrode into the visual cortex of an anesthetized cat. They were then able to record the activity of individual neurons when certain stimuli—such as a vertical or horizontal line—were projected onto a screen in front of the cat's eye. They found that certain cells, called *simple cells*, would respond to a line presented only in a certain orientation. For example, some cells fired only when the line was tilted 45 degrees from the vertical. When the line was displayed vertically, for example, simple cells specialized for that orientation started to respond. Cells that respond to orientation are just one type among a variety of cells called *feature detectors* that are highly specialized to respond to particular elements in the visual field. For example, other feature detectors are sensitive to movement; frogs have "bug detector" cells that are particularly suited for picking out small dark moving objects.

In addition to simple feature detectors, there are also *complex cells* that appear to coordinate information from different simple cells—for example, some complex cells respond only to a 45-degree line moving from left to right. Furthermore, there are also *hypercomplex* cells that apparently coordinate information at a still higher level of complexity, such as two different lines forming an angle.

As yet, there is still no direct confirmation of the existence of cells specialized to respond to such aspects of Gestalt organization as closure and proximity. But some psychologists believe that just as the frog has its "bug detector" cells, humans and other higher animals must have neural structures that have evolved to be sensitive to the complex patterns whose perception is crucial to their survival. We may be prewired to perceive many of the complex shapes and movements that appear in our natural environment. For example, as we will see in Chapter 9, newborns, given the choice, will spend significantly more time gazing at sketches of human faces than at other types of patterns or figures. On the other hand, it is inconceivable that we are prewired for all the unique and different objects that we encounter in the world around us, and this fact suggests that there is also an important learned component to how we organize perception.

organize sensory information. Now, we will discuss how certain "personal" variables also organize sensation.

Observer Characteristics

Clearly, our perceptual experiences depend greatly on past experience and learning. Several other factors can also affect perception, such as our particular motivations and values, expectations, cognitive style, and factors related to growing up in a particular culture. In this section, we will see how these types of variables influence the perceptual organization of sensory information.

MOTIVATION. Our desires and needs may strongly influence our perceptions. People in need are more likely to perceive something that they think will satisfy that need. For example, several interesting experiments have tested the influence of hunger on perception. Sanford (1937) found that if people were deprived of food for some time and were then shown vague or ambiguous pictures, they were apt to perceive the pictures as being related to food. Similarly, McClelland and Atkinson (1948) showed blurred pictures to people who had not eaten for varying lengths of time. Some had eaten 1 hour before; others had gone as long as 16 hours without food. Those who had not eaten for 16 hours perceived the blurred images as pictures of food more often than those who had eaten just 1 hour before.

Another experiment showed how strongly perceptions can be affected by a person's values. Nursery-school children were shown a poker chip. Each child was asked to compare the size of the chip to the size of an adjustable circle of light until the child perceived the chip and the circle of light as being the same size. The children were then shown a machine with a crank. When a child turned the crank, he or she received a poker chip that could be exchanged for candy. Thus, the children were taught to value the poker chips more highly than they had before. After the children had been rewarded with the candy for cranking out the poker chips, they were again asked to compare the size of the chips to a circle of light. This time, the chips seemed larger to the children (Lambert, Solomon, & Watson, 1949).

EXPECTATIONS. Preconceptions about what we are supposed to perceive can also influence perception. For example, in a well-known children's game, a piece of cardboard with a red stop sign is flashed in front of you. What did the sign say? Nearly everyone will say that the sign read "STOP." In fact, however, the sign is misprinted "STOPP." Because we are accustomed to seeing stop signs reading "STOP," we tend to perceive the familiar symbol rather than the misprint. Lachman (1984) demonstrated this phenomenon by asking subjects to copy a group of stimuli similar to this one:

PARIS
IN THE
THE SPRING

When the expressions were flashed briefly on a screen, the vast majority of subjects tended to omit the "extra" words and to report seeing more familiar (and more normal) expressions, such as PARIS IN THE SPRING. This phenomenon of *perceptual familiarization* or *perceptual generalization* reflects a strong tendency to see what we expect to see even when the result does not accurately reflect external reality.

COGNITIVE STYLE. As we mature, we develop a *cognitive style*—our own general method of dealing with the environment—and this also affects how we see the world. Some psychologists distinguish between two general approaches that people use in perceiving the world (Witkin et al., 1962). The first is the *field-dependent* approach. A person taking this approach perceives the environment as a whole and does not clearly differentiate the shape, color, size, or other qualities of individual items. If field-dependent people are asked to draw a human figure, they usually do not draw it so that it stands out clearly against the background. People who are *field independent*, on the other hand, tend to perceive the elements of the environment as separate and distinct from one another and to draw each element as standing out from the background.

Another way of defining cognitive styles is to distinguish between "levelers" and "sharpeners"—those who level out the distinctions between objects and those who magnify them. In order to investigate the differences between these two styles, Klein (1951) showed people sets of squares of varying sizes and asked them to estimate the size of each of the squares. One group, the "levelers," failed to perceive any differences in their sizes.

The "sharpeners," however, were aware of the differences in the size of the squares and made their size estimates accordingly.

CULTURAL BACKGROUND. Cultural background can also influence people's perceptions. As we will see in Chapter 7, the language that people speak can affect the way in which they perceive their surroundings. And cultural differences in people's experiences can also influence how people use perceptual cues. The Mbuti pygmies of Zaire, for example, seldom leave the forest and rarely encounter objects that are more than a few feet away. On one occasion, anthropologist Colin Turnbull (1961) took a pygmy guide named Kenge on a trip out onto the plains. When Kenge looked across the plain and saw a herd of buffalo, he asked what kind of insects they were. He refused to believe that the tiny black spots he saw were buffalo. As he and Turnbull drove toward the herd, Kenge believed that magic was making the animals grow larger.

■ Subliminal Perception

In 1957, an advertising executive created a controversy when he announced a new technique that supposedly could prompt consumers to buy products without being aware they had even received a message to do so. He claimed that by projecting such signs as "Buy Popcorn" on a movie screen at intervals too rapid to be perceived consciously, advertisers had been able to increase snack bar sales. This technique, called *subliminal perception* (literally, "below threshold perception") soon raised the specter of mind control—a concern intensified by popular books suggesting that George Orwell's Big Brother might soon be doing more than just watching over people's consumer behavior. More recently, the sale of audiotapes with subliminal self-help messages has become a big business, comprising anywhere from a quarter to a third of spoken-word audio cassette sales. Rather than controlling behavior, the tapes are designed to improve it. These tapes claim to carry *affirmations*, messages which are not perceptible to the ear but nonetheless affect behavior. A weight-loss tape might contain the message, "Eat less," while a tape geared toward improving self-esteem might carry the message, "I am capable." Some hour-long audiotapes hold as many as 110,000 affirmations in addition to their audible content, though the effectiveness of so many messages in such a short amount of time is disputed. Most psychologists are extremely skeptical about the effectiveness of such subliminal messages, yet the appeal of being able to improve oneself without any effort is compelling to many people who pay for and use these tapes.

Are innocent people being controlled by cleverly hidden messages? Can people actually be influenced by messages below the threshold of conscious perception? In order to establish such a claim, it would first be necessary to establish that subliminal messages are even being sent. Vokey and Read (1985) concluded that in most cases the very presence of such purported subliminal messages was mostly in the mind of the beholder. Subjects, especially when asked to look for them, found all kinds of subliminal messages in such innocuous material as the Twenty-third Psalm played backwards. Vokey and Read concluded that the very presence of subliminal messages in advertising may be in doubt.

But what if an attempt actually is made to influence us subliminally? A group of students at the University of Michigan were shown a series of geometric figures so rapidly—one every 0.001 seconds—that the subjects reported seeing only a pulse of light (Kunst-Wilson & Zajonc, 1980). Later, however, these students expressed a preference for the figures that they had been presented subliminally over ones that they were seeing for the first time. It would seem that this study supports the argument that we can perceive stimuli that we cannot describe and that our attitudes can be influenced by these perceptions. Nevertheless, the claims for mass mind control are not supported by research data. Thresholds vary from person to person—wine tasters are more skilled than most people at detecting subtle tastes and flavors—and individuals have shifting thresholds depending on such factors as fatigue or motivation. Therefore, stimuli that are subliminal for one person may be perceived clearly by someone else; if this second person responds to the message, it is certainly not a case of subliminal persuasion!

Because he had no experience of distant objects, he could not perceive the buffalo as having constant size.

Let us now look at two basic perceptual phenomena—distance and depth, and movement—to see how we use both stimulus information and past experience to create perceptual experiences.

Perception of Distance and Depth

We constantly have to judge the distance between ourselves and other objects. When we walk through a classroom, our perception of distance helps us to avoid bumping into desks or tripping over a wastebasket. If we reach out to pick up a pencil, we automatically judge how far to extend our arms. We also constantly judge the depth of objects—how much total space they occupy. We use many cues to determine the distance and the depth of objects. Some of these cues depend on visual messages that one eye alone can transmit; these are called **monocular cues.** Others require the use of both eyes, and these are called **binocular cues.** Having two eyes allows us to make more accurate judgments about distance and depth, particularly when objects are relatively near. But monocular cues by themselves are often sufficient to allow us to judge distance and depth quite accurately, as we will see in the next section.

MONOCULAR CUES. **Superposition,** when one object partly blocks a second object, is an important relative distance cue. The first object is perceived as being closer, the second as more distant (see Figure 3-36).

As all students of art know, there are several ways in which perspective can help in estimating distance and depth. Two parallel lines that extend into the distance seem to come together at some point on the horizon. This cue to distance and depth is known as **linear perspective.**

Figure 3-36
Because the king of clubs appears to have been superimposed on the blank card, we perceive it as being closer to us than the king of spades. When the cards are spaced out, however, we can see that the king of spades is actually no farther away than the king of clubs. It appears to be farther away because the other two cards seem to be superimposed on it.

Aerial perspective Monocular cue to distance and depth based on the fact that more distance objects are likely to appear hazy and blurred.

Elevation Monocular cue to distance and depth based on the fact that the higher on the horizontal plane an object is, the farther away it appears.

Figure 3-37
Because of the higher elevation and the suggestion of depth provided by the road, the tree on the right is perceived as being more distant and about the same size as the tree at lower left. Actually, it is appreciably smaller, as you can verify if you measure the heights of the two trees.

In **aerial perspective,** distant objects have a hazy appearance and a somewhat blurred outline. On a clear day, mountains often seem to be much closer than on a hazy day, when their outlines become blurred. The **elevation** of an object is another perspective cue to depth. An object that is on a higher horizontal plane seems to be farther away than one on a lower plane (see Figure 3-37).

This artist's mural painted on the side of a building creates a visual illusion and relies on *monocular cues* of depth perception.

Still another helpful monocular cue to distance and depth is **texture gradient.** An object that is close seems to have a rough or detailed texture. As distance increases, the texture becomes finer, until finally the original texture cannot be distinguished clearly, if at all. A man standing on a pebbly beach, for example, can distinguish among the gray stones and gravel beside his feet. As he looks down the beach, however, the stones will seem to become smaller and finer until eventually he will be unable to note individual stones.

Shadowing provides another important cue to distance and to the depth and solidity of an object. Normally, shadows appear on the parts of objects that are farther away. The shadowing on the outer edges of a spherical object, such as a ball or a globe, gives it a three-dimensional quality (see Figure 3-38). Without this shadowing, the object might be perceived as a flat disk. In addition to serving as cues of three-dimensionality, shadows also serve as cues as to the direction of depth—whether an object rises above or rests below the surface. We tend to assume that light comes from overhead, so when we look at Figure 3-38(c) we see a bump because the top edge is lighter the way a bump lit from above would be, while (d) appears as a dent because of the shadowing along its top edge. Looking at the image upside down reverses the effect. The shadow that an object casts behind itself also gives a cue to its depth. The presence of shadows either before or behind objects indicates how far away they are.

People traveling on buses or trains often notice that the trees or telephone poles close to the road or the railroad tracks seem to flash past the windows, while buildings and other objects farther away seem to move

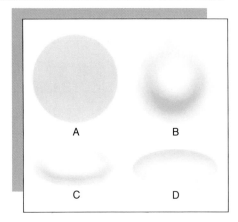

Figure 3-38
Shadowing on the outer edges of a spherical object, such as a ball or globe, gives it a three-dimensional quality (a). Without shadowing, (b), it might be perceived as a flat disk. Shadowing can also affect our perception of the direction of depth. Because we tend to assume overhead lighting, figure (c) appears to be a bump because its top edge is lit, while (d) appears to be a dent. If you turn the book upside down, the direction of depth will be reversed.

Texture gradient is a powerful monocular cue to distance and depth. As distance increases, texture becomes finer, until finally the original texture cannot be distinguished clearly.

slowly. The objects close to you are perceived as moving very quickly; those that are farther away seem to move more slowly. These differences in the speeds of *movement* of images across the retina as you move give an important cue to distance and depth. You can observe the same effect if you stand still and move your head from side to side. Also, if you move your head from side to side and focus your gaze on something in the middle distance, objects close to you seem to move in the direction opposite the direction in which your head is moving, while objects far away seem to move in the same direction as your head. This distance cue is known as **motion parallax.**

BINOCULAR CUES. All the cues discussed so far depend on the action of only one eye. Many animals, such as horses, deer, and fish, rely entirely on monocular cues. Although they have two eyes, the two visual fields do not overlap because their eyes are set on the sides of the head. Humans, apes, and many predatory animals—such as lions, tigers, and wolves—have a distinct physical advantage over these animals. Because both eyes are set in the front of the head, the visual fields overlap. The **stereoscopic vision** obtained from combining the two retinal images makes the perception of depth and distance more accurate.

Because our eyes are set approximately $2\frac{1}{2}$ in apart, each one has a slightly different view of things. The difference between the two images

Motion parallax Monocular distance cue in which objects closer than the point of visual focus seem to move in the direction opposite to the viewer's moving head, and objects beyond the focus point seem to move in the same direction as the viewer's head.

Stereoscopic vision Combination of two retinal images to give a three-dimensional perceptual experience.

Because the lion's visual fields overlap, as do ours, it has more accurate perception of depth and distance. A horse, whose visual fields do not overlap, must rely entirely on *monocular cues*.

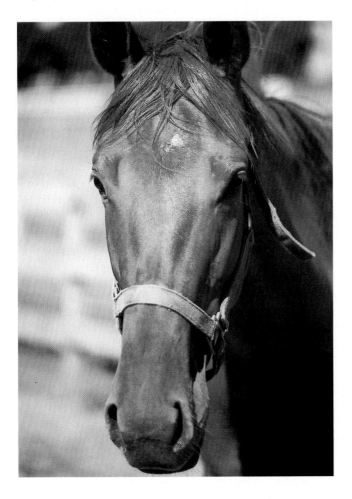

Retinal disparity Binocular distance cue based on the difference between the images cast on the two retinas when both eyes are focused on the same object.

Convergence Binocular distance cue based on sensations from the muscles that turn the eyes toward or away from each other.

Binocular depth inversion Tendency to create three-dimensional perceptual experiences that agree with past experience, despite sensory information to the contrary.

Sound localization Ability to determine where a sound originates.

Monaural cue Cue to sound location that requires just one ear alone.

Binaural cue Cue to sound location that involves both ears working together.

Figure 3-39
Cues used in sound localization Sound waves coming from source (b) will reach both ears simultaneously. A sound wave from source (a) reaches the left ear first, where it is also louder. The head casts a "shadow" over the other ear, thus reducing the intensity of the delayed sound in that ear.
Boring et al., 1976

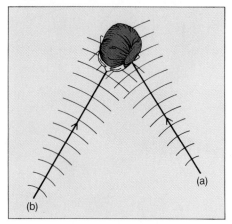

that the eyes receive is known as **retinal disparity.** The left eye receives more information about the left side of an object, and the right eye receives more information about the right side. You can easily prove that each of your eyes receives a different image. Close one eye and line up a finger with some vertical line, like the edge of a door. Then open that eye and close the other one. Your finger will appear to have moved a great distance. When you look at the finger with both eyes, however, the two different images become one.

Another binocular cue to distance comes from the muscles that control the **convergence** of the eyes. When we look at objects that are fairly close to us, our eyes tend to converge—to turn slightly inward toward each other. The sensations from the muscles that control this movement of the eyes provide another cue to distance. If the object is very close, such as at the end of the nose, the eyes cannot converge and two separate images are perceived. If the object is more than 60 or 70 feet away, the sight lines of the eyes are more or less parallel and there is no convergence.

BINOCULAR DEPTH INVERSION. Under certain special conditions, the brain appears to ignore depth and distance cues and to construct incorrect three-dimensional perceptions that more closely match our past experience. This tendency—called **binocular depth inversion**—is especially likely if the available sensory information comes from an improbable object that strongly resembles a familiar object. The best example of such an object is an inside-out human face, say the inside of a Halloween mask. If you stare at the inside of a mask that is lit from behind, you are likely to perceive a normal, rightside-out face, despite all the visual cues to the contrary. This is a particularly powerful demonstration of our tendency to create perceptual experiences that agree with past experience, despite sensory information to the contrary. A lifetime of perceiving normal faces prompts us to reinterpret the sensory data from the inverted mask in order to create a more plausible object.

LOCATION OF SOUNDS. So far, we have looked only at the perception of visual depth and distance. But sounds also occur in three-dimensional space, and to a large extent we are able to locate the source of sounds. **Sound localization** requires us to determine both distance and direction. The ability to determine the distance of a sound depends in part on **monaural** (single-ear) **cues** (see Figure 3-39). Loud sounds are perceived to be closer than faint sounds. If a sound is familiar—your best friend's voice, for instance—you can judge its distance fairly well, even with one ear covered, by judging its loudness. Changes in loudness are perceived as changes in distance, so if your friend's voice becomes louder each time he or she calls out your name, you conclude that your friend is approaching.

Our ability to locate sounds is much greater when we can use information from both ears (**binaural cues**). Thus, when your friend is off to one side of you, the sound waves of his or her voice reach one ear slightly ahead of the other. If your friend moves to a new location and calls out to you again, the shift in location will produce a slightly different time delay between the sound waves reaching your two ears. Although

During a stereo recording session, microphones are generally placed at many different locations. On playback, the twin speakers or headphones project sounds picked up by the microphones at slightly different instants, mimicking what would occur if you were hearing a live performance.

the time difference between sound waves reaching the ears is very slight—in the range of a thousandth of a second—the brain is able to process these differences for accurate judgments of location. A second important binaural cue results from the fact that sound signals arriving from a source off to one side of you are slightly louder in the nearer ear than in the ear farther from the source. The slight difference occurs because your head in effect casts a "shadow" over the ear opposite the sound source, thus reducing the intensity of sound in that ear. This relative loudness difference between signals heard separately by the two ears is enough for the brain to locate the sound source and to judge its distance. Stereo recordings sometimes use these cues to provide the illusion of depth and distance. When sound engineers record your favorite band, they may place microphones at many different locations. On playback, the two speakers or headphones project sounds at slightly different instants in order to mimic the sound patterns that would occur if you were actually listening to the group perform in front of you. In fact, we now know that some neurons in the brain are particularly sensitive to the different cues that the brain is receiving from the two ears. Some are specialized to respond to differences in the time when sounds reach the two ears, and others are more sensitive to differences in loudness.

For the most part, we are better able to locate sounds that are on the same level or plane as we are. It is more difficult to locate sounds above or below. But other species, such as birds of prey, are better able to locate sounds below them. Researchers determined that owls, for example, have a great concentration of neurons that are especially sensitive to sounds below their customary perch high in a tree.

Most of us rely so heavily on visual cues that we seldom pay much attention to the rich set of auditory information available in the world around us. Experiments with blind people, who often compensate for their lack of vision by improving their ability to perceive sounds, have shown just how much information about the environment our ears can provide. The blind can discover the presence of obstacles in their paths by listening to the echoes from a cane, their own footsteps, and their own voices. In one notable case, a blind boy was so adept at avoiding obstacles by sound that he could ride a bicycle in public places. Many blind people can judge the size and distance of one object in relation to another using nothing more than sound cues. They can also discriminate contrasting surfaces, such as glass and fabric, by listening to the difference in the echo produced when sound strikes them.

Perception of Movement

The perception of movement is a complicated process involving both visual messages from the retina and messages from the muscles around the eyes as they follow the object. At times, our perceptual processes play tricks on us and we think we perceive movement when the objects that we are looking at are, in fact, stationary. We must distinguish, therefore, between real and apparent movement.

Real movement refers to the physical displacement of an object from one position to another. The perception of real movement depends only in part on the movement of images across the retina of the eye. If you stand still and move your head to look around you, the images of all the objects in the room will pass across your retina. Yet you will probably perceive all these objects as stationary. Even if you hold your head still and move only your eyes, the images will continue to pass across your retina. But the messages from the eye muscles seem to counteract those from the retina, so the objects in the room will be perceived as motionless.

The perception of real movement seems to be determined less by images moving across the retina than by how the position of objects changes in relation to a background that is perceived as stationary. When we perceive a car moving along a street, for example, we see the street, the buildings, and the sidewalk as a stationary background and the car as a moving object. Remarkably, the brain can distinguish these retinal images of an object moving against an immobile background from all the other moving images on the retina. The perception of real movement is also remarkably accurate. Imagine you are watching a videotape of someone lifting a box of unknown weight. You would be able to predict the weight of the box fairly accurately, and you probably would also be able to tell if the person lifting the box is simply pretending it is heavier than it is (Runeson & Frykholm, 1983).

It is possible, under certain conditions, to see movement in objects that are actually standing still. One form of *apparent movement* is the **autokinetic illusion**—the perceived motion created by a single stationary object. If you stand in a room that is absolutely dark except for one tiny spot of light and stare at the light for a few seconds, you will begin to see the light drift. In the darkened room, your eyes have no visible framework; there are no cues telling you that the light is really stationary. The slight movements of the eye muscles, which go unnoticed most of the time, make the light appear to move.

Another form of illusory movement is **stroboscopic motion**—the

It is possible to perceive apparent movement in a stationary object, as in a portion of the painting *Current* by Bridget Riley.

Riley, Bridget. *Current.* 1964. Synthetic polymer paint, 58⅜″ x 58⅞″. Collection, The Museum of Modern Art, New York. Philip C. Johnson Fund.

apparent motion created by a rapid series of images of stationary objects (see Figure 3-40). A motion picture, for example, is not in motion at all. The film consists of a series of still pictures showing people or objects in slightly different positions. When the separate images are projected sequentially onto a screen, the people or objects seem to be moving because of the rapid change from one still picture to the next.

Stroboscopic motion also causes a perceptual illusion known as the **phi phenomenon.** When a light is flashed on at a certain point in a darkened room, then flashed off, and a second light is flashed on a split second later at a point a short distance away, most people will perceive a single spot of light moving from one point to another. Of course, the distance between the two points, the intensity of the two lights, and the time interval between them must be carefully controlled in order for the illusion to succeed. The same perceptual process causes us to see motion in neon signs or theater marquees, where words appear to move from one side to the other as different combinations of stationary lights are flashed on and off.

Visual Illusions

Visual illusions graphically demonstrate the ways in which we use a variety of sensory cues to *create* perceptual experiences that may (or may not) correspond to what is out there in the real world. By understanding how we are fooled into "seeing" something that isn't there, psychologists can outline how perceptual processes work in the everyday world and under normal circumstances.

Psychologists generally distinguish between *physical* and *perceptual* illusions. An example of a **physical illusion** is the bent appearance of a stick when placed in water—an illusion that can be explained by the fact that the water acts like a prism bending the light waves before they reach our eyes. This type of illusion does not startle us because it is a common and easily understood part of our experience.

On the other hand, some illusions depend primarily on our own perceptual processes, of which we are not ordinarily aware, and these illusions can be quite surprising and startling. **Perceptual illusions** occur because the stimulus contains misleading cues that cause us to create perceptions that are inaccurate or even impossible.

In Figure 3-41, for example, the strange triangle contains a false and misleading depth cue that leads us to perceive a three-dimensional figure that clearly cannot exist. Another figure that fools us by presenting false depth cues is Figure 3-42(e), in which the top line is perceived as shorter than the bottom. Our experience tells us that objects appear smaller when they are far away. In Figure 3-42(f), the railroad tracks suggest that we are looking at a three-dimensional scene and that the top bar is farther away. In the real world, this would mean that the top bar is larger than it appears to be. Therefore, we "correct" for the distance and actually perceive the top bar to be larger. We do this despite cues to the contrary: We know that the image is actually two-dimensional, but we still respond to it as if it were three-dimensional.

There are also "real world" illusions that illustrate how perceptual processes work, such as the illusion of *induced movement* when you are

Phi phenomenon Apparent movement caused by flashing lights in sequence, as on theater marquees.

Physical illusion Illusion due to distortion of information reaching receptor cells.

Perceptual illusion Illusion which is due to misleading cues in stimuli and which causes us to create perceptions that are inaccurate or impossible.

Figure 3-40
If after just the right delay (50 to 100 msec), Form 1 is replaced by Form 2 in A, B, or C, *stroboscopic motion* will be perceived as indicated by the dotted line. In A, this will be a horizontal motion of the bulb from left to right. In B, it will be a tipping of the bar from vertical to horizontal. In C, the top angular bar will appear to flip over. In all these cases, you perceive the most "reasonable" pattern of movement.

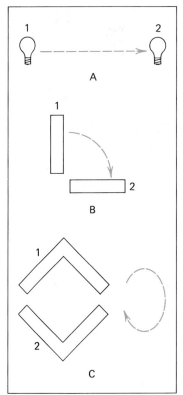

■ Extrasensory Perception

Some people claim to have an extra power of perception, one beyond those known to the normal senses. This unusual power, known as extrasensory perception, or ESP, has been defined as "a response to an unknown event not presented to any known sense" (McConnell, 1969). Examples of ESP cover a variety of phenomena, including *clairvoyance*—awareness of an unknown object or event; *telepathy*—knowledge of someone else's thoughts or feelings; and *precognition*—foreknowledge of future events. The operation of ESP and other psychic phenomena is the focus of a field of study called *parapsychology*.

Experimentation with ESP is often done with special cards called Zener cards. A deck of Zener cards contains 25 cards showing five different symbols. In order to test a subject for clairvoyance, the target cards are first arranged randomly; the order is unknown to both the subject and the experimenter. The subject is then asked to "call" the cards in order. If the number of correct guesses, called "hits," is consistently higher than would be expected by chance, ESP is presumed to be operating. In tests for telepathy, the experimenter goes through the cards and concentrates on each symbol in turn. Without being able to see the cards, the subject is asked to write down what he or she "reads" about the card in the experimenter's mind. Precognition tests call for the subject to recite the order of cards in advance. The experimenter then selects cards at random, using a computer or a pair of dice, and checks to see if the subject has called them in correct order.

C.E.M. Hansel (1966), a severe critic of ESP studies, has expressed the doubts of most psychologists about the whole subject of ESP. The most serious objections concern the unscientific manner in which some experiments are conducted and reported. Most ESP experiments, Hansel feels, are poorly designed—among other problems, there are relatively few safeguards against dishonesty. Another drawback is that the reporting of results is often inadequate or biased in favor of supporting evidence. Hansel is particularly dis-

mayed that researchers often do not seek to confirm results by conducting follow-up experiments, either with the same subjects or with different ones. To make matters worse, subjects themselves are not able to explain how they perform acts of ESP. As a result, most scientists feel that positive results with ESP are due to sloppy experiments, misinterpretation of data, and even out and out trickery (Cornell, 1984).

In view of so much professional skepticism, what accounts for the rather widespread willingness to believe in ESP? Some psychologists relate it to the difficulty that people have in sorting out random from nonrandom events. According to psychologist Lee Ross, we do not have enough information about probability in the world at large to distinguish properly natural coincidence from causal events. For example, there are hundreds of millions of people in the United States. Each of them dreams every night, and many of them have dreams seemingly predicting the future. Mathematical odds dictate that at least a few of those millions of dreams will eventually coincide remarkably well with some future events, but the coincidence is random and not the result of some causal connection between event and dream. But for those people whose dreams turn out to be "true," the experience is likely to be compelling. It is unlikely that such people will be persuaded to change their minds on the basis of some statistical data collected in a laboratory (Cornell, 1984).

Nevertheless, the possibility of ESP remains an open question for many psychologists. One survey (Wagner & Monnet, 1979) indicated that 34 percent of psychologists accepted ESP as either an established fact or a likely possibility. Even many of those who remain skeptical point not to the impossibility of ESP, but rather to the fact that experimentation has not established it as a fact or as a likely possibility. However, skeptical sentiment runs high. Whatever the possibility of ESP, the controversy over it is a striking example of how strongly held positions among psychologists can influence debate as much as objective evidence can.

sitting in a stationary car or train when a car or train next to you begins to move forward. You seem to be moving backwards. Because you have no reference point by which to tell if you are standing still, you are confused as to which car or train is actually moving. However, if you look down at the ground, you can establish an unambiguous frame of reference and make the situation clear to yourself.

Artists rely on many of these perceptual phenomena both to represent reality accurately and to deliberately distort it. For example, it is almost always necessary to distort objects deliberately as they are drawn on a two-dimensional surface in order for them to be perceived correctly

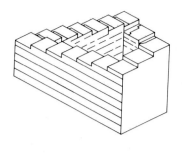
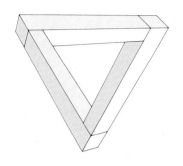

Figure 3-41
In these visual illusions, there are misleading *depth cues*. For example, the strange triangle is constructed so that a fake depth cue signals a three-dimensional object that cannot exist.
Adapted from Gregory, 1978

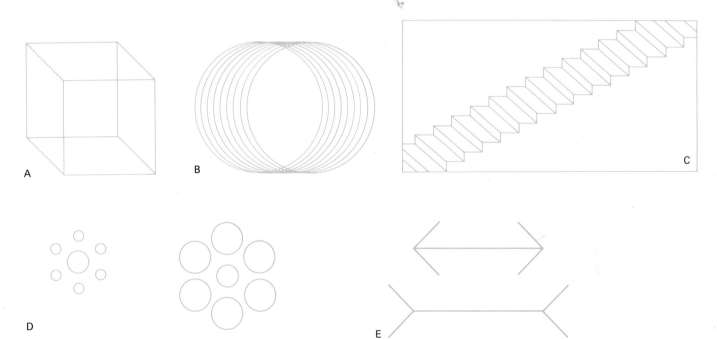

A

B

C

D

E

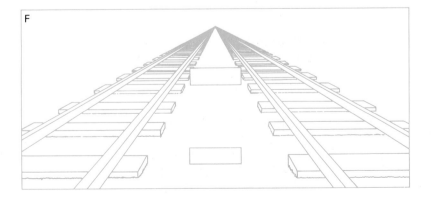

F

Figure 3-42
A, B, and C are examples of *reversible figures*. D, E, and F show that through the effects of misleading *depth cues* we misjudge the size of objects. The middle circles in D are exactly the same size. The lines in E are both the same length, and the rectangular bars in F have the same dimensions.

by viewers. Railroad tracks, for instance, are always drawn closer together in the distance—see Figure 3-42(f). In Figure 3-43, you can readily see how an artist can use distance cues not only to give realistic depth to a picture, but to create perceptual experiences that don't correspond to anything in the real world. 3-D movies also work on the principle that the brain can be deceived into seeing three dimensions if slightly different images are presented to the two sides of the brain. Thus, our understanding of perceptual illusion enables us to manipulate images for deliberate effect—and to delight in the results.

Figure 3-43
The artist has manipulated distance cues in order to create the *perceptual illusion* of water traveling uphill.

Perception and the Blind

A woman who had been blind from birth finally had an operation that would enable her to see. One of her first sights after the operation was her own reflection in a mirror. Her response: "I thought I was better looking."

This story illustrates what many people have always suspected: Blind people have visual images even though they may never have actually seen anything. Of great interest to psychologists and researchers in the field of perception and sensation is a twofold question: How do blind people visualize the world and where do they get their information?

In the 1930s, Marius von Senden, a German scientist, studied the perceptions of people who had been born blind and were later cured. One patient thought that people and trees looked alike because they both have central trunks that you can put your arms around, no sharp edges, and limbs that emerge from the trunk. She was quite surprised to discover, upon being cured, that people and trees look so different. Much later, Hollins (1985) reported that the ability of blind people to produce imagery on the basis of how something "feels" is related to whether the person was born blind or later became blind. Blind adults had significantly better abilities at visualizing correctly objects that were sensed by touch than people who never had vision.

John Kennedy, a psychologist at the University of Toronto, has studied how blind people perceive by asking them to draw various objects. Since the blind perceive objects only through touch, Kennedy wished to see if they could convey their sense of objects through line drawings. He was surprised to note that the blind people in his study quickly realized that some aspects of reality must be sacrificed in a drawing—that you cannot draw all sides of an object, for example. The blind artists devised various ways to represent objects, such as a cup or a table, that were readily understood by people who could see. Kennedy was especially fascinated to find that his blind subjects understood the idea of occlusion—that objects in front will partly or totally obscure objects behind them.

Other studies designed by Kennedy have revealed that blind people have an intuitive grasp of several other principles of graphic imagery. The blind seem to understand linear perspective, which—as we saw earlier—is the tendency of parallel lines to converge at a point in the distance. Some blind subjects were also able to represent the near edge of a surface with a thick line and the far edge with a thin line. When blind subjects touched tactile drawings, they understood that lines can represent changes in depth. Thus, they could distinguish between foreground and background, just as sighted people can. Finally, in a fascinating series of experiments, Kennedy asked people who had been blind from birth to portray the idea of movement. They accomplished the task in a number of ways. Some showed figures in postures of movement, such as a man with knees bent. Others represented movement abstractly instead of literally. One subject, for example, indicated that a figure of a man was running by drawing a line trailing behind one foot. Another drew a wheel with curved spokes (Kennedy, 1983). It seems clear that though the usual cues discussed in this chapter do help us perceive motion and depth, they are not the only sources of information regarding these perceptions.

Apparently, when blind people are cured, their initial sense impressions are very much like a newborn baby's—they see patches of brightness and darkness but can barely perceive the details of objects. One blind man, who was cured at age 53, could not discern what a lathe was—although he had worked with one every day for years while blind—until he could touch and handle it. In the blind, touch appears to fill much of the void left by the lack of sight. It also seems that active blind people when they are cured learn to see more quickly than passive blind people.

■ Summary

- The study of *sensation* is the study of how the various receptor cells in the sense organs translate forms of physical energy into neural messages; how those messages reach the central nervous system; and the different experiences that result. The related process of *perception* is the interpretation of sensory data by the brain.

- **How does information get from our eyes to our brain?** In all sensory processes, some form of energy stimulates a receptor cell in one of the sense organs. The receptor cell then changes the energy that it receives into a neural signal. As the neural signal travels along the sensory nerves to the central nervous system, it is coded further. By the time it reaches the brain, its message is quite precise. The brain creates the "illusion" of sensory experience by interpreting the "clicks" on various nerve fibers, such as the optic and auditory nerves.

- **Why can't we see stars in the daytime?** The minimum intensity of physical energy that is required to produce sensation half the time it is present is called the **absolute threshold.** The absolute threshold for each of our senses is remarkably low. The smallest detectable change in stimulation is called the **difference threshold** or the **just noticeable difference (jnd).** Generally, the stronger the overall stimulation, the bigger the change needed for you to be able to sense it.

- The physical stimulus for the sense of vision is only a small segment of the spectrum of electromagnetic energy. There are two kinds of receptors in the retina—**rods** and **cones.** Cones operate mainly in daylight and respond to colors; rods are chiefly responsible for night vision when there is not enough light to stimulate the cones. The *fovea* contains thousands of cones but no rods.

- Several rods generally connect with a single bipolar neuron, while most cones are connected to their own bipolar neuron. The one-to-one connection in the fovea between cones and bipolar neurons allows for maximum **visual acuity,** the ability to distinguish fine details. Thus, vision is sharpest when the image falls directly on the fovea; outside the fovea, acuity drops dramatically.

- The sensitivity of rods and cones changes according to how much light is available, a process known as *adaptation.* When you go from bright sunlight into a dimly lit theater, your cones are initially fairly insensitive to light, and you can see little as you look for a seat. After 10 minutes **dark adaptation** occurs as the rods and cones become more sensitive to light and you begin to see better. When you leave the theater, the opposite process, **light adaptation,** a decreased sensitivity to light, occurs.

- Neural messages originate in the retina, but they must get to the brain for a visual sensation to occur. Within the retina, rods and cones connect to **bipolar** **neurons,** which in turn connect to the **ganglion cells.** The axons of the ganglion cells converge to form the **optic nerve,** which carries messages from the eye to the brain. The optic nerve fibers from the right side of each eye travel to the right hemisphere of the brain; those from the left side travel to the left hemisphere. The fibers cross one another at the **optic chiasm.** Some messages travel to parts of the brain that control retinal movements. Others are headed for the visual projection areas in the brain.

- **Hue, saturation,** and **brightness** are three separate aspects of our experience of color. *Hue* refers to what most of us call color (e.g., red, green, blue). *Saturation* refers to the purity of the hue; and *brightness* refers to the intensity of the hue (from bright to dark).

- **How are you able to see that the blue in your sweater doesn't quite match the blue in your slacks?** There are two main theories of color vision. According to the **trichromatic theory,** the eye contains three different kinds of color receptors that respond to red, green, and blue light, respectively. By mixing these three basic colors, the eye can detect any color in the spectrum, even subtle differences among colors that are nearly the same. The **opponent-process theory** accepts the notion of three different kinds of receptors, but claims that each receptor responds to either member of three basic color pairs: red-green, yellow-blue, and black-white (dark and light).

- Modern research has established support for the operation of both theories. We now know that there are three types of color receptors in the retina. In addition, bipolar neurons or ganglion cells process coded signals from the receptors according to an opponent-process principle. When these signals reach the brain, color receptors in the visual cortex process them further, in an opponent-process manner.

- The physical stimuli for the sense of hearing are sound waves that produce vibration of the eardrum. Vibration of the eardrum causes three bones in the middle ear—the **hammer, anvil, and stirrup**—to vibrate in sequence. These vibrations are magnified in their passage through the middle ear deep into the inner ear. There, the vibrations cause fluid inside the **cochlea** to vibrate, pushing the **basilar membrane** and **organ of Corti** up and down. Inside the organ of Corti are tiny hair cells that are the receptors for hearing. Stimulation of these receptors produces auditory signals that are transmitted through the **auditory nerve** to the brain.

- The *place theory of hearing* states that the brain determines pitch by noting the place on the basilar membrane where the message is strongest. **Frequency theory** states that the frequency of vibrations of the basilar membrane as a whole is translated into an equivalent frequency of nerve impulses. Neurons, however, cannot fire as rapidly as the frequency of the highest pitched sound. This suggests a **volley principle,** whereby nerve cells fire in sequence to send a rapid series of impulses to the brain.

- The sense of smell is activated by substances carried by airborne molecules into the nasal cavities. There they activate the receptors for smell, which are located in a patch of tissue called the **olfactory epithelium.** The messages are then carried directly to the two **olfactory bulbs** in the brain. Humans are more adept at detecting the presence of odors than identifying their source.

- **Why can't you taste food if you have a stuffy nose?** The receptor cells for the sense of taste lie in the **taste buds** on the tongue. Each taste bud contains a cluster of taste receptors, or hair cells, that cause their adjacent neurons to fire when they become activated by the chemical substances in food. We experience only four primary taste qualities—sweet, sour, salty, and bitter—and these combine to form all other tastes. *Flavor* is a complex combination of taste and smell.

- The **vestibular senses** tell us what position our body is in, whether it is moving, and which way is up. The receptors for this sense are located in the vestibular organs in the inner ear. Motion sickness originates in the vestibular organs and may result from discrepancies between vestibular sensations and visual information.

- Skin receptors give rise to what are called the *cutaneous sensations* of pressure, temperature, and pain. However, studies have failed to reveal a simple connection between the various types of receptors and the separate sensations. The **Meissner corpuscles** seem to be sensitive to touch, but so too are receptors around the roots of hair cells. **Pacinian corpuscles** are sensitive to pressures between internal organs and muscles. **Ruffini endings** are responsible for warmth, and **Krause bulbs** are responsible for cold. Once believed responsible only for pain, **free nerve endings** constitute virtually the whole of the cornea and are also quite sensitive to pressure and temperature.

- **How do pain relievers work?** A commonly accepted explanation of our sensitivity to pain is the **gate control theory,** according to which a "neurological gate" in the spinal cord controls the transmission of pain impulses to the brain. If the gate is open, we experience more pain than we do when it is closed. Whether the gate is open or closed depends on a complex competition between different types of nerve fibers, and certain areas of the brain stem can also close the gate by sending signals down to fibers in the spinal cord. Pain relievers like morphine block the transmission of pain signals across the synapse.

- Perception is creating meaningful sensory experiences out of raw sensory information. Perceptual experiences go beyond what is sensed and may even lead us to perceive objects that couldn't possibly exist.

- Gestalt psychologists were the first to describe some of the ways in which perceptions are created. A **figure** is distinguished from the **ground** against which it appears. In a *reversible figure*, parts of the stimulus shift from being figure to being ground. The principle of *closure* refers to the tendency to overlook incompleteness in sensations and to perceive a whole object where none really exists. The concept of *continuity* states that objects that continue a pattern or a direction tend to be perceived as a group. Likewise, the principle of *proximity* supposes that objects seen or heard close together tend to be perceived as a group. The principle of *similarity* states that objects that look alike are perceived as part of a pattern. According to the principle of *common fate*, objects that are in motion together are perceived as distinct from the objects around them.

- **You see a small car. How do you know it is actually a big car far away rather than a tiny car close up?** *Perceptual constancy* refers to the tendency to perceive objects as relatively stable and unchanging, despite changing sensory information. Experience seems to compensate for the changing sensory information, leading to **size constancy, shape constancy**, and **color constancy.**

- Our desires and needs may strongly influence our perceptions. We tend to perceive things as we wish them to be. How an object is interpreted also depends on a person's values, expectations, cognitive style, and cultural background.

- We can perceive distance or depth through **monocular cues**—from one eye—or **binocular cues**—which depend on the interaction of both eyes. Binocular cues increase the accuracy of depth and distance perception. Each eye has a slightly different view of things. The difference between the images that the two eyes receive is called **retinal disparity.** Other binocular cues include **stereoscopic vision** and **convergence.**

- **Sound localization** is the ability to determine where a sound originates. **Monaural cues** such as loudness convey information about distance, while **binaural cues,** such as discrepancies in arrival time of sound waves and their volume, help to locate the source of a sound. Blind people are particularly adept at using sound cues to determine information about their environment.

- **You're stopped at a traffic light. If the car next to you begins to back up, why may you suddenly step on the brake, thinking instead that you are rolling forward?** Perception of *movement* is a complicated process involving both the visual messages from the retina and messages from the muscles around the eye as they shift to follow a moving object.

- The perception of *real movement*—the physical displacement of an object from one position to another—seems to be determined chiefly by changes in the position of objects in relation to a background that is perceived as stationary.

- *Apparent movement* involves the perception of movement in objects that are actually standing still. The **autokinetic illusion** refers to the apparent motion of a stationary object such as a point of light in a dark room. **Stroboscopic motion** is the apparent motion created by a rapid series of images of stationary objects, such as in motion pictures. It is responsible for the perceptual illusion known as the **phi phenomenon.**

- **Is there such a thing as ESP? Does subliminal perception really work?** Among psychologists, ESP, or extrasensory perception and *subliminal perception* remain controversial. Neither have been proven to exist though there is also no conclusive evidence proving that they do not exist. Those who believe in ESP may be confusing coincidence with causality. When it comes to subliminal perception, it is difficult to determine whether a stimulus has been perceived subliminally because sensory thresholds can vary from person to person and among situations.

■ Review Questions

1. The _____ threshold is the smallest change in simulation that can be detected 50 percent of the time.
   A. absolute
   B. difference

2. Match the following terms with their definitions:
   ____ cornea   A. colored part of the eye
   ____ pupil   B. center of the visual field
   ____ iris   C. receptor cell responsible for color vision
   ____ lens
   ____ fovea   D. protective layer over front part of the eye
   ____ retina
   ____ rod   E. contains the receptor cells that respond to light
   ____ cone
      F. focuses light onto the retina
      G. receptor cell responsible for night vision
      H. opening in the iris through which light enters

3. The process whereby the rods and cones adjust to become more sensitive to lowered levels of illumination is known as _____.
   A. dark adaptation
   B. light adaptation

4. The place on the retina where the axons of all the ganglion cells come together to leave the eye is called the:
   A. fovea   C. optic chiasm
   B. blind spot   D. visual cortex

5. _____ , _____ , and _____ are three separate aspects of our experience of color.

6. The process of mixing pigments is known as _____ color mixing.
   A. additive
   B. subtractive

7. As a sound wave moves from the outer ear to the inner ear, number the following in the order that it would reach them:
   ____ oval window
   ____ anvil
   ____ cochlea
   ____ auditory nerve
   ____ round window

8. Match the following theories with their definitions:
   ____ frequency theory   A. groups of cells fire in sequence, not each individually
   ____ volley principle
   ____ place theory
      B. rate at which hair cells in the cochlea fire determines pitch
      C. different parts of basilar membrane respond to different frequencies

9. The organs that monitor equilibrium and awareness of body movement are called the _____ organs.

10. The receptor cells for taste lie in the _____ _____ on the tongue and give rise to to the four

basic taste sensations _____ , _____ , _____ , and _____ .

11. The process by which we create meaningful experiences out of the jumble of sensory information is called _____ .

12. In the case of reversible figures, we have difficulty distinguishing the _____ from the _____ behind it.

13. Match the following principles of perception with their definitions:

_____ similarity
_____ continuity
_____ common fate
_____ proximity
_____ closure

A. tendency to perceive a whole object even where none exists
B. objects in motion together appear to stand out from their surroundings
C. elements that continue a pattern are likely to be seen as part of the pattern
D. objects that are like one another tend to be grouped together
E. elements found close together tend to be perceived as a unit

14. Next to each depth cue, put B if it is a binocular cue and M if it is a monocular cue:

_____ retinal disparity
_____ texture gradient
_____ shadowing
_____ convergence
_____ motion parallax
_____ accommodation
_____ stereoscopic vision
_____ linear perspective
_____ superposition

15. The perception of loud sounds as being closer than faint sounds is a common _____ cue to sound localization:
A. monaural
B. binaural

16. Autokinetic illusion, stroboscopic motion, and phi phenomenon are three examples of _____ movement.

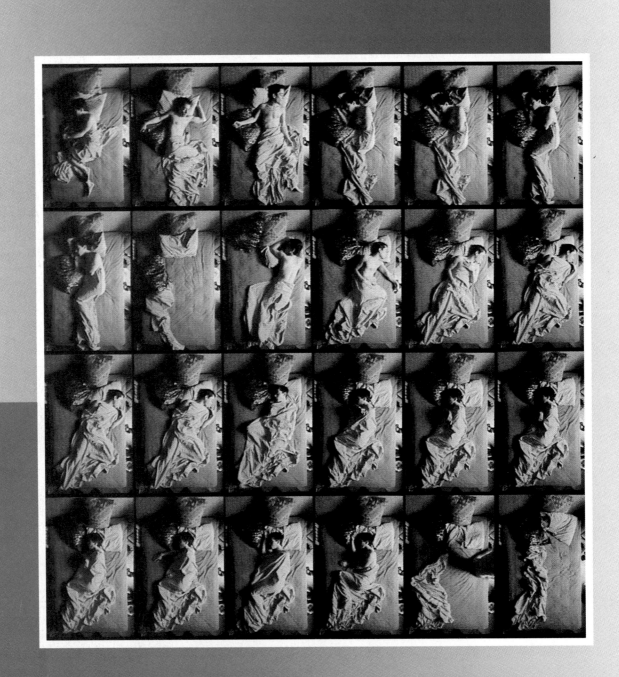

4 States of Consciousness

■ Thinking Critically

What is consciousness? What purpose does it serve?

Is daydreaming undesirable? Why do we do it?

How many hours of sleep do we need? Can going without sleep hurt you?

Do dreams really reveal our unconscious desires?

Is hypnosis safe? Does it really work?

Does getting drunk on the weekends mean a person is an alcoholic?

What does it mean to be addicted to drugs or alcohol?

What is crack? Why is it such a problem?

Answers to these and other questions about the nature and processes of consciousness appear throughout the chapter and in the Chapter Summary.

■ Outline

Consciousness Our awareness of such cognitive processes as sleeping, dreaming, concentrating, and making decisions, among many others.

Waking consciousness State of consciousness that includes the thoughts and feelings that occur when we are awake and reasonably alert.

Altered state of consciousness (ASC) State of awareness that differs noticeably from states that we experience when awake and alert.

Consider the following scenario. You wake up and begin the day by deciding what to eat for breakfast and what to wear; after breakfast, you sit down to memorize some history facts for an upcoming exam, but after a while you find yourself daydreaming about last night's date or next summer's vacation. A deliberate focusing of attention may then be required before you can return to concentrating on your history test. During lunch, you drink a cup of coffee or tea to keep yourself alert. After lunch, you may spend some time reflecting on such grand questions as the meaning of life; or perhaps you meditate for a short while in order to get rid of some of the anxiety that you feel about the upcoming test. If it's Friday, perhaps you go out for dinner and have a glass of wine or beer with your meal. Finally, the day ends as you fall asleep and, shortly thereafter, experience the first of several dreams that you will have before morning.

This description of an imaginary day in your life demonstrates clearly the great variety of cognitive processes that occur in human beings: making decisions, remembering, daydreaming, concentrating, reflecting, sleeping, and dreaming are only a sample of the kinds of mental processes that we experience. Our awareness of these various mental processes is called **consciousness.**

Generally psychologists divide the study of consciousness into two broad areas. **Waking consciousness**—or conscious awareness—includes all the thoughts and feelings that occur when we are awake and reasonably alert. But there are also times when we experience **altered states of consciousness (ASC)**—times when our mental state differs noticeably from our experience when we are awake and alert. Some altered states (such as daydreaming, sleep, and dreaming) are quite normal and seem to occur spontaneously. Other ASCs (such as hypnosis, meditation, and intoxication) involve deliberate attempts to alter our normal consciousness.

Recently, a new view of consciousness has been emerging. This view sees consciousness as an information-processing function, similar to the workings of a computer (Rumelhart & McClelland, 1986). Instead of looking at states of consciousness, the information processing approach, as it is sometimes called, is concerned with *processes of consciousness.* From this perspective, the conscious processes are those aspects of our mental life to which we devote conscious attention, such as studying a textbook. Unconscious processes are those that are automatic; they happen without our having to be aware of them (Kihlstrom, 1987). For example, you are reading the words on this page, recognizing them without having to be *consciously* aware of each letter, or even each word. Hopefully, you *are* paying attention to the ideas these letters and words help express.

From an evolutionary perspective, consciousness has important survival value. Throughout history, humans have compensated for their relative shortcomings in strength and speed by developing mental skills that enabled them to think, to reason, to remember, to plan, and to predict. Moreover, human beings appear to be unique in their development of self-consciousness: we are apparently the only organism to have developed an awareness of our own existence.

Both consciousness and self-awareness were important factors in the early development of psychology. You will recall from Chapter 1 that scientific psychology began with the structuralists and their efforts to discover the basic elements of human experience. At about the same time, William James drew attention to the constant flow of our thoughts as they start and stop and jump from one thing to another. For James, consciousness resembled a kaleidoscopic flow or "stream" of external and internal information. James's concept of the "stream of consciousness" also had parallels in the art and literature of the time. For example, his novelist brother Henry James and, more notably, James Joyce wrote fiction that tried to capture the flow of subjective experiences in our conscious life.

In this century, the study of consciousness has passed in and out of favor among psychologists. Despite psychology's roots in the study of consciousness, many researchers in the early part of this century concluded that a truly scientific study of mental life could never succeed and so turned their attention elsewhere. Behaviorism, first under James Watson and later under B. F. Skinner, became influential because it dealt only with observable and verifiable behavior. Watson (1919) promised his followers "no discussion of consciousness and no reference to such terms as sensation, perception, attention and the like. . . . I frankly don't know what these mean, nor do I believe anyone else can use them consistently." Psychology, in the words of one observer, suffered a "loss of consciousness."

However, in the 1950s and 1960s, psychology's interest in consciousness reawakened. Aside from the commonsense observation that such processes do indeed form a part of our psychological functioning, advances in technology have made it possible to study indirectly various aspects of consciousness in ways that are far more scientific than the early method of introspection. For example, we saw in Chapter 2 that the techniques of electroencephalography (EEG), PET and CAT scans, and magnetoencephalography (MEG) have made it possible to study with some precision the nature of brain activity during various states of consciousness. By linking data from those techniques to subjective reports of conscious processes, it may be possible to make tremendous strides in our understanding of consciousness.

Social events have also influenced psychology's renewed interest in consciousness. In the 1960s, many young people began experimenting with psychedelic, mind-altering drugs. Others became interested in Eastern religions—or mystical aspects of Western religion—as alternative means of insight into a reality not available to our normal, workaday experience.

These recent technological and cultural developments have renewed psychologists' interest in the study of consciousness (Hilgard, 1980). As you will see, throughout this book we will repeatedly have occasion to look closely at various aspects of normal waking consciousness. Such processes as sensation and perception, learning, memory, cognition, and intelligence are now so important in psychology that whole chapters are devoted to them. But you will find that the remaining chapters also have a great deal to say about waking consciousness. Therefore, in the remainder of this chapter our emphasis will be on altered states of consciousness. We will look first at nonconscious mental processes and then examine normal variations in consciousness such as daydreaming, sleep, and dreaming. Then we will turn our attention to various techniques that are used deliberately to alter normal states of consciousness.

■ Variations In Consciousness

In our ordinary waking life, we are continually exposed to a variety of external and internal stimuli. Externally, there are sounds, sights, smells, and so on. Internally, there are thoughts, memories, and feelings associated with our bodies. However, we are not normally aware of all these competing stimuli at the same time. In order to survive and make sense of our environment, we must continuously select only the most important information to attend to and filter out everything else. The way in which we do this is discussed at some length in Chapter 6. For our present purposes, it is simply important to note that the hallmark of normal waking consciousness is the highly selective nature of attention.

Nevertheless, we are subject to numerous processes, undergo numerous experiences, and perform numerous tasks without being consciously aware of them. For example, we are not usually aware of such vital bodily processes as control of blood pressure or respiration. And most of us are able to walk down the street or ride a bicycle without consciously thinking about every movement. In fact, there are times when things go better if we are not consciously aware of them. You probably have no trouble at all signing your name; you probably do it many times a day "without giving it a thought." In fact, if you think carefully about each movement of your pen or pencil, you will find that

© 1987 S. Gross

"YOU'RE NOT ON THE LIST. YOU MUST BE HAVING AN OUT OF BODY EXPERIENCE."

signing your name so that it looks normal becomes exceedingly difficult. Similarly, if you are driving your car along the familiar route that you always take to work or school, the process can be so automatic that you remain largely unaware of your actions.

Many psychologists believe that there are also important mental processes, such as recognizing a word or a friend's face, that go on outside of normal waking consciousness. As we saw in Chapter 1, Sigmund Freud believed that many of the most important influences on our behavior—such as erotic feelings toward our parents—are kept out of consciousness even though they continue to play an important role in shaping our behavior. According to Freud, the conscious part of our minds is only the tip of an iceberg: The real driving forces behind human actions are sexual and aggressive instincts that remain mostly hidden. Freud, however, believed that these hidden thoughts and feelings can be revealed, and made conscious, through such alterations to consciousness as hypnosis and dreaming. We will have occasion to explore the notion of nonconscious mental processes as we consider various altered states of consciousness in this chapter and especially when we consider behavior disorders in Chapter 14.

Daydreaming

In James Thurber's book *The Secret Life of Walter Mitty*, the protagonist mentally departs from his humdrum daily existence for a series of fantastic and heroic ventures. In the comic strip "Peanuts," Snoopy is well known for his imaginary adventures as the archrival of the Red Baron. A college student sitting in psychology class may actually be lost in thoughts of summer sun and fun on the beach. Although it requires deliberate effort to enter an ASC via hypnosis, drugs, or meditation, **daydreaming** is an ASC that occurs seemingly without effort.

Typically, daydreaming occurs when you would rather be somewhere else or be doing something else—escaping from the demands of the real

Daydreaming Alteration in consciousness that occurs seemingly without effort and, typically, when we would prefer to escape momentarily the demands of the real world.

Daydreaming is an altered state of consciousness that occurs seemingly without effort—typically when you would rather be somewhere else.

world for a moment. You may reminisce pleasantly about last year's vacation or leave the daily college grind behind and fantasize about your future as a business tycoon. And sometimes, as in the case of Walter Mitty or Snoopy, you may project yourself into fantastic, unlikely adventures. Daydreams provide the opportunity to write, act in, and stage-manage a private drama for which you are the only audience.

Although daydreaming may seem to be a random and effortless process, psychologists have discovered that people's daydreams tend to fall into a few distinct patterns and that different people tend to prefer different kinds of daydreams (Singer, 1975). People who score high on measures of anxiety tend to have fleeting, loosely connected daydreams related to worrying. They take little pleasure in their daydreaming. In contrast, people who are strongly achievement oriented tend to have daydreams that concern achievement, guilt, fear of failure, and hostility. These daydreams often reflect the self-doubt and competitive envy that accompanies great ambition. Still other people derive considerable enjoyment from their daydreams and use them to solve problems, think ahead, or distract themselves. These "happy daydreamers" tend to have pleasant fantasies uncomplicated by guilt or worry. And finally, some daydreamers display unusual curiosity about their environment and place great emphasis on objective thinking. These people tend to have daydreams whose contents are closely related to the objective world and are marked by controlled lines of thought. About 4 percent of people are considered *fantasy-prone*, that is, they spend more than half their time not just daydreaming, but lost in elaborate reveries. Studies of the fantasy-prone show that they are generally highly creative, able to become completely absorbed in their fantasies (Lynn & Rhue, 1988). One fantasy-prone woman actually found herself shivering uncontrollably while watching the movie, *Dr. Zhivago* (which takes place in Siberia). For many of these people, it appears that fantasy serves as an escape from difficult circumstances. A majority of those studied by Lynn and Rhue said they felt lonely and isolated as children. In some cases they were abused or suffered severe emotional problems.

Intelligence, as well as personality, also affects our daydreaming. One group of researchers discovered that intellectually gifted adolescents—those who have experienced considerable academic success—tend to have daydreams with less guilt and fear of failure than their less gifted peers.

If daydreaming is nearly universal, does it serve any useful function? Can Walter Mitty justify his fantasies on a practical basis? Some psychologists argue that daydreams have little or no positive or practical value. These psychologists hold that daydreams are essentially a retreat from the real world that occurs when inner needs cannot be expressed in actual behavior. We daydream, they claim, when the world outside does not meet our needs or when we want to do something but cannot; they suspect that the daydream may actually substitute for more direct and effective behavior.

By contrast, other psychologists have stressed the positive value of daydreaming and fantasy. Freudian theorists have traditionally held that daydreams allow us to express and deal with various desires, generally about sex or hostility, that would otherwise make us feel guilty or anxious (Giambra, 1974). And Pulaski (1974) suggests that daydreaming can build cognitive and creative skills and help people survive difficult situations. For example, it is difficult to imagine an artist or a writer succeeding without an active fantasy life. Pulaski notes that daydreaming has also helped prisoners of war survive torture and deprivation. Her view suggests that daydreaming and fantasy can provide welcome relief from everyday—and often unpleasant—reality and can reduce internal tension and external aggression.

Singer goes one step further in proposing that daydreams are not just a substitute for reality or a form of tension-relief, but an important part of our ability to process information (see Chapter 6). Singer suggests that during the daytime, as we process the vast, potentially overwhelming array of information received through our senses, we single out some of the material for later review and further processing during quieter moments when we have less to do. When the opportunity arises—perhaps during a dull moment—we rework some of this information and transform it into new and more useful forms. Daydreams and dreams provide a window through which we can watch this process of dealing with "unfinished business." In the long run, then, although daydreaming temporarily distracts us from the real world, Singer believes that it also allows us to take care of important unfinished business so that we are in fact better able to cope with our environment when the pace of real-world activity quickens again.

Sleep and Dreaming

We spend about one-third of our lives in an ASC—namely, sleep. Throughout history, people have paid varying degrees of respect to sleep and to its product, dreams. Some societies have held that great universal truths are revealed in dreams, while others view sleep as an essential, but basically nonproductive, activity. Only recently have sleep researchers begun to analyze the fascinating complexity of sleep, its function, and its influence on human activity.

SLEEP. Nobody who has tried to stay awake for any length of time can doubt that sleep is necessary. There are some individuals who claim that they do not sleep, but when they are observed under laboratory conditions some actually sleep soundly without being aware of it, while others engage in short periods of "microsleep," dozing for a second or two at a time. It appears that merely resting doesn't satisfy us as does actual sleep. And when an organism is deprived of sleep, it craves it just as strongly as it would food or water after deprivation.

Although the need for sleep certainly exists, nobody is yet certain why we need to sleep. Many scientists believe that sleep serves to restore the effectiveness of the body and the brain. This view implies that during our waking life, the body is depleted of certain chemicals that are restored during sleep. But little evidence exists to support this idea. Protein synthesis in the brain speeds up during sleep, but whether protein depletion is a cause of sleep remains unclear. A chemical called the s-factor (Maugh, 1981) from the brains of animals and from human urine that induces deep sleep when injected into the brain has been isolated. But again, there is no evidence yet that a buildup of s-factor is the normal cause of

Biological Clocks: From Jet Lag to Cancer Treatment

In a world organized by mechanical clocks, time schedules, and calendars, it is easy to forget that your body has its own natural rhythms. It's often not until something happens to trip them up, like a cross-country flight or a cup of coffee that keeps you up too late at night, that you are likely to notice how these inner timepieces help keep us going. Scientists are discovering that our natural biological rhythms can be harnessed to help fight disease. They are also learning that ignoring them can be extremely dangerous, both for ourselves and others (see Highlight Box on The Effects of Sleep Deprivation on Human Performance).

Each of us has our own set of biological rhythms. Some are at their best in the morning, others don't come alive until late at night. Many of these rhythms follow a roughly daily or circadian cycle (from Latin *circa diem*, which means "about a day"). Others, such as women's menstrual cycles, do not. The rhythms and chemistry of all these different cycles are in tune with one another, and a shift in one can bring about a shift in another.

The sleep–wake cycle is only one of a number of circadian rhythms; body temperature, blood pressure, and the levels of many endocrine secretions change in daily cycles as well. How much are these circadian gears in our biological clocks affected by the daily cycle of the sun? One study chose a particularly dramatic way of exploring this question. In 1988, Veronique Le Guen, a 32-year-old Frenchwoman, spent 111 days in a cave in Southern France. She lived without a watch or radio. Nothing but her own natural rhythms guided her day. At one point she slept for 31 hours. At another, she took a nap that lasted for 18 hours, even though she thought she had only dozed for a few minutes. In another, similar study, after two months of living under constant illumination, volunteers slept only every 36 to 50 hours, although they still spent a third of their total time sleeping. Clearly, the sun has some effect when it comes to the timing of our normal sleep–wake cycle. It also seems to affect the delicate balance of our moods. The "Christmas blues" may not be so much related to feelings of being left out of good times during the holidays as to the fact that late December is marked by the shortest days of the year with the least daylight. Some sufferers of depression and elderly people who don't get outside very often are given "light treatments" that provide artificial light that closely replicates the spectrum of sunlight, in an effort to prevent their natural rhythms from running down.

Jet lag is one of the most dramatic disruptions of our biological clocks. When you fly across a continent or ocean you are rapidly traversing several time zones. You might leave New York at 7 P.M. and arrive in London at 9 A.M. (London time)—just time to start the day. But your biological clock tells you that it's only 3 A.M.—past your bed time. Travelers going such distances at such rates will experience a disjunction between biological and environmental cues, causing drowsiness, irritability, and digestive disorders, among other symptoms. Our biochemistry will be telling us to sleep while our perceptual information tells us it's daytime.

In order to deal with this effect, researchers suggest that travelers adjust to their new schedule prior to the trip and immerse themselves in the schedule of the new time zone as soon as possible. One study (Klein & Wegmann, 1974) found that travelers who stayed indoors upon reaching their destinations adjusted more slowly than those who forced themselves to adjust activity and sleep in accord with the new time zone.

While we only tend to notice our biological rhythms when they break down, most of the time they function in perfect, health-promoting harmony. In a promising line of research, scientists are finding that by working with the body's own natural rhythms, they may be able to combat disease more effectively. Anticoagulant medication has been found to be more effective when administered at night when the blood is already somewhat thinner. (Many coronaries occur in the morning, apparently because the blood is more prone to clotting at that time.) Laboratory studies have shown that animals' ability to tolerate cancer drugs is high at certain times of the day and low at others. Since some of those in cancer treatment die not from cancer, but from the powerful drugs they must take to try to combat the cancer, timing cancer treatments so that they occur during times of greater tolerance of the drugs may save lives and actually improve the effectiveness of treatment. Researchers are even looking into the possibility that the cycles of cancer cells themselves can be shifted so they are least able to resist the drugs when the body is most tolerant making the drugs safer and even more effective at the same time.

These findings may have serious implications for drug testing and the procedures used to determine whether a substance or particular dosage is safe for human use. Animals tested at the peak of their biological cycles have proven to be able to withstand doses of poisons that would kill them at other times. This means that "safe dosages" may not be safe for a person taking them at a low point in their body's cycle. The Food and Drug Administration is presently looking into requiring drug research to be sensitive to the biological clocks of laboratory animals (many of which arrive in labs suffering from jet lag as a result of being shipped in for testing from breeders) in hopes of gaining a more accurate assessment of the maximum doses of potentially lethal substances.

sleep or that sleep somehow reduces the level of s-factor in the body. Another hypothesis concerning the function of sleep comes from evolutionary theory. Sleep may be an adaptive mechanism that evolved to encourage organisms to remain inactive and to conserve energy during times of the day when their food supplies were low or their predators were especially numerous. Despite these suggestive hypotheses, scientists have so far been unable to piece together a completely satisfactory explanation of the role of sleep.

Although the function of sleep continues to be uncertain, scientists have recently learned a great deal about sleep and the dreams that accompany it. Researchers do not usually enter people's homes in order to study the ways in which they sleep. Instead, they find volunteers who are willing to spend one or more nights in what is called a "sleep lab." With electrodes that are painlessly attached to their skulls, the volunteers sleep comfortably while brain waves, eye movements, muscle tension, and other physiological data are monitored. Information from such studies shows clearly that although there are significant individual differences in sleep behavior, everyone goes through several stages while sleeping (Anch, 1988).

"Going to sleep" means losing awareness and failing to respond to a stimulus that would produce a response in the waking state. Brain waves during this "twilight" state (as measured by an EEG) are characterized by irregular, low-voltage *alpha waves* (see Figure 4-1). This pattern of brain waves is typical of relaxed wakefulness, such as lying on a beach or in a hammock or perhaps resting after a big meal. People who are in this twilight state with their eyes closed often report seeing flashing lights and colors, geometric patterns, and visions of landscapes. Sometimes, there is also a floating or falling sensation, followed by a quick jolt back to consciousness.

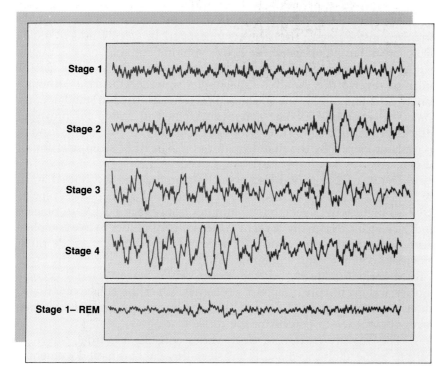

Figure 4-1
The brain wave patterns typical of the five stages of sleep—the four NREM stages and the first REM stage. The brain waves in REM sleep closely resemble Stage 1 of NREM sleep, but the person in REM is very deeply asleep.
From Luce and Segal, 1966

During sleep research, electrodes monitor subjects' brain waves, eye movements, muscle tension, and other physiological data.

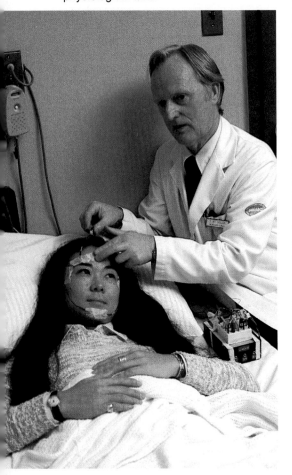

Following this initial twilight phase, the sleeper enters Stage 1 of sleep. Stage 1 brain waves are of very low amplitude and are "tight," much as they are when a person is alert or excited. But in contrast to normal waking consciousness, Stage 1 of the sleep cycle is marked by a slowing of the pulse, muscle relaxation, and side-to-side rolling movements of the eyes. This rolling eye movement is the most reliable measure of the initial sleep process (Dement, 1974). Stage 1 usually lasts only a few moments, and if the easily aroused sleeper is awakened, he or she may be unaware of having been asleep at all.

Stages 2 and 3 represent progressively deeper sleep. Brain waves increase in amplitude and they tend to become slower. Figure 4-1 clearly shows this transition to long, slow, brain waves. At this stage, the sleeper is hard to awaken and does not respond to such stimuli as noises or lights. Heart rate, blood pressure, and temperature continue to drop.

Stage 4 sleep is marked by very slow *delta* waves. Heart rate, breathing rate, blood pressure, and body temperature are as low as they will get during the night. In young adults, delta sleep occurs in 15- to 20-minute segments—interspersed with lighter sleep—mostly during the first half of the night. Delta sleep lessens with age but continues to be the first sleep to be made up after sleep has been lost.

About an hour after first falling asleep, the sleeper begins to ascend from Stage 4 sleep to Stage 3, Stage 2, and back to Stage 1-REM—a process that takes about 40 minutes. The brain waves return to the low-amplitude, saw-toothed shape of Stage 1 and waking alertness. Heart rate and blood pressure also increase, yet the muscles of the body become more relaxed than at any other point in the sleep cycle, and the person is very difficult to awaken. The eyes move rapidly under closed eyelids. **Rapid eye movement** (or **REM**) distinguishes this sleep stage from all others (called **non-REM** or **NREM**) that precede and follow it.

REM sleep is usually called **paradoxical sleep,** because while the brain activity, heart rate, blood pressure, and so on closely resemble waking consciousness, the sleeper appears to be deeply asleep and is incapable of moving because the body's voluntary muscles are essentially paralyzed. When researchers made lesions on the brain stems of cats in order to reverse this paralysis, the results were spectacular. Although otherwise sound asleep, the cats raised their heads, tried to stand up, and sometimes succeeded. Some cats even seemed to search for prey and attack it (Morrison, 1983). Obviously, the ability to inhibit this kind of movement caused by the muscle paralysis makes REM sleep safer for all of us.

The first REM period lasts about 10 minutes and is followed again by Stages 2, 3, and 4 of NREM sleep. This sequence of sleep stages repeats itself all night long, averaging 90 minutes from Stage 1-REM to Stage 4 and back again. Normally, a night's sleep consists of four to five complete sleep cycles of this sort. But the pattern of sleep changes as the night progresses. Stages 3 and 4 dominate at first; but as time passes, the Stage 1-REM periods gradually become longer, while Stages 3 and 4 become shorter and eventually disappear altogether. Over the course of a night, about 45 to 50 percent of the time is spent in Stage 2, while REM sleep takes up another 25 percent of the total.

This nightly pattern of sleep varies considerably from person to person. Some adults need hardly any sleep. Researchers have documented the cases of a Stanford University professor who slept for only three to four hours a night over the course of 50 years, and a woman who lived a healthy life on only one hour of sleep per night (Rosenzweig & Leiman, 1982). Sleep patterns also change with age. Infants tend to sleep much longer than adults—13 to 16 hours during the first year—and much more of their sleep is REM sleep. Infants also enter REM sleep immediately after falling asleep, unlike adults, and change sleep stages often. The elderly, on the other hand, tend to sleep less than younger adults, wake up more often during the night, and spend much less time in the deep sleep of Stages 3 and 4.

DREAMS. On the average, people dream about two hours every night, even though most dreams are quickly forgotten. **Dreams** are vivid visual and auditory experiences that occur primarily during REM periods; subjects awakened during REM sleep report vivid dreams about 80 to 85 percent of the time (Berger, 1969). Less vivid experiences that resemble "thinking" tend to occur during NREM sleep. REM dreams can be so realistic at times that it is hard to distinguish them from reality. In some primitive cultures, in fact, dreams are thought to be real experiences of a world that is not available to us in our waking lives. Similarly, most young children have great difficulty distinguishing between dreams and waking experiences. One possible reason that REM dreams appear to be so vivid and real has to do with the state of brain arousal during REM sleep. Recall that REM, or paradoxical, sleep is characterized by brain activity that closely resembles normal waking consciousness. But during REM sleep, the brain is relatively insensitive to outside sensory input. Thus, during REM sleep, you have a brain that to all appearances is alert and excited and whose only input is internal images from memory (Koulack & Goodenough, 1976).

Psychologists have long been fascinated by dream activity and the contents of dreams. Sigmund Freud (1900), whose theories will be discussed more comprehensively in Chapter 12, called dreams the "royal road to the unconscious." He believed that dreams represent wishes that have not been fulfilled in reality. In this regard, he suggested that dreams provide valuable insight into the motives that guide people's behavior—motives of which people may remain consciously unaware. In sleep, according to Freud, people can express primitive desires that are relatively free of conscious controls or moral considerations. For example, a person who is otherwise unaware of hostile feelings toward a loved one may have dreams about murder. However, even in a dream these feelings may become transformed into a highly symbolic form whereby, for example, a desire to terminate someone is transformed into the dream image of seeing them off at a train "terminal." According to Freud, this process of censorship and symbolic transformation accounts for the fact that dreams often take on a highly illogical character. Untangling these disguised meanings becomes one of the main tasks of psychoanalysts in their work with clients.

Recently, a neurophysiological interpretation has been offered for the illogical and disjointed nature of many dreams. J. Allan Hobson and Robert McCarley (1977) propose that dreams are generated by random outbursts of nerve cell activity. The brain, responding to these internal stimuli, many of which affect brain cells used in vision and hearing,

Dreams Vivid images or experiences that occur primarily during REM periods of sleep.

Though there is some evidence that dreams are generated by random outbursts of nerve cell activity, others argue that often dreams just *seem* illogical and disjointed because we don't remember them very well.

Chagall, Marc *Over Vitebsk*. 1915–20 (after painting of 1914). Oil on canvas, 26⅜ x 36½". Collection, The Museum of Modern Art, New York. Acquired through the Lillie P. Bliss Bequest.

attempts to synthesize them or make sense of them by drawing on memory and other stored information to create the images and scenes we experience as dreams. The brain is sufficiently aroused to provide a narrative of events, but cannot do this in more than a primitive, concrete fashion.

Still other researchers suggest that dreams are actually the brain's effort to free itself of repetitious thoughts or associations so that it is more open to new information (Crick & Mitchison, 1983). The fact that dreams may be generated by the brain as a form of mental housekeeping or as a result of being fooled by spontaneous nerve impulses does not necessarily make them any less meaningful clues to a person's individual psychological concerns (Hobson, 1988.)

Whatever the ultimate explanation, dream content is related to a number of different factors. For example, when you are closest to waking, your dreams are apt to be about recent events. Since the last dream that you have before waking is also the one that you are most likely to remember, it follows that most of the dreams that you remember are likely to be about recent events. In the middle of the night, however, more of your dreams are likely to involve childhood or past events. Furthermore, dream content can be modified by presleep events. In one study (Hauri, 1970), subjects who had engaged in six hours of strenuous exercise before sleep tended to have dreams with relatively little physical activity. Hauri concluded that, to some extent, dream content may complement and compensate for waking experiences. Consistent with this suggestion is the fact that subjects who had experienced a day of social isolation had dreams with a great amount of social interaction (Wood, 1962), and subjects who had been water-deprived dreamed of drinking (Bokert,

1970). These compensatory effects may be only temporary, however. In some cases at least, long-term deprivation leads to a reduction in related dream content. For example, recently paralyzed individuals reported more physical activity in their dreams than did long-term paralyzed individuals (Newton, 1970), which suggests that compensatory dreams die, so to speak, when they cannot be supported by an underlying reality.

Dreams also vary according to sex and age. One repeated finding is that female dreams tend to be about indoor settings (Brenneis, 1970; Cohen, 1973) and that male dreams are more aggressive. Before menstruation, women often dream about waiting. And before childbirth, they are likely to dream more about babies or their mothers than about their husbands. On the other hand, both sexes dream equally about being pursued or victimized.

Young children's dreams closely resemble their waking life, but children also often dream about scary animals. Since, as we have noted, children have greater difficulty in distinguishing dreams from reality, the intrusion of such elements makes their dreams all the more nightmarish.

Some people are actually conscious of dreaming and can be trained to signal the start of a dream by making regular eye movements even while they remain asleep. Research on the physiological measures of experiences during dreaming shows that dreaming about singing or sexual activity, for example, is even more like actually being engaged in that activity than *imagining* being engaged in that activity (LaBerge, 1986).

Most dreams last about as long as the events would in real life; they do not flash on your mental screen just before waking, as was once believed. Generally, they consist of a sequential story or a series of stories. Stimuli, both external and internal, may modify an ongoing dream, but they do not initiate dreams. One interesting experiment used three different external stimuli on subjects who were dreaming; a five-second tone just below the waking threshold, a flashing lamp, and a light spray of cold water. The water was incorporated into 42 percent of the dreams, the light into 23 percent, and the tone into 9 percent (Dement & Wolpert, 1958). Another experiment by Dement and Wolpert (1958) showed that when a tape recording of the subject's voice was played back to the subject while dreaming, the principal actor in the dream became more active and self-assertive. Thus, while these external stimuli are perceived during dreaming, their origin is often not perceived as being external. Their presence in the dream is usually personal and subjective rather than literal. Interestingly, significant external stimuli—such as the sleeper's name being spoken—are most likely to spur awakening.

Are all the dreams dreamt in a single night related to one another? Unfortunately, experimenters run into a methodological problem when they try to anwer this question. Each time the subject is awakened to be asked about a dream, the natural course of the dream is interrupted and usually lost forever. If one particular problem or event weighs heavily on the dreamer's mind, however, it will often show up in dreams throughout the night (Dement, 1974).

What if you set up a tape recorder to play back information while you sleep? Will you painlessly absorb this material? Unfortunately, no learning of complex material during sleep has ever been demonstrated. Even experiments designed to teach sleepers simple pairs of words have failed. Very rudimentary forms of learning may be possible, however. The first time that a stimulus such as a loud noise is presented to a sleeper, it produces signs of arousal. Repetition of the stimulus causes less and less arousal, suggesting that the sleeper has learned that the stimulus is not a cause for alarm.

Attempts to influence dream content through presleep suggestions have also had mixed results. Success seems to depend on such subtleties as the phrasing of the suggestion, the tone in which it is given, the relationship between the suggester and the subject, and the setting (Walker & Johnson, 1974). If these variables could be refined and controlled, the presleep suggestion technique could be important for both sleep researchers and psychotherapists.

NEED FOR DREAMS. You will recall that psychologists are uncertain about why we need to sleep; the explanation for why we dream is even less clear. Freud suggested that dreams provide a psychic safety valve, giving harmless expression to otherwise disturbing thoughts that are often transformed into highly symbolized forms. If this theory is correct, then depriving people of the opportunity to dream should have significant effects. Dement (1965) studied the effects of dream deprivation by awakening subjects just as they entered REM sleep. He found that subjects who were deprived of REM sleep became anxious, testy, and hungry, had difficulty concentrating, and even hallucinated in their waking hours. But we now know that some dreams occur in NREM sleep, so eliminating REM sleep is not the same as eliminating all dreams. Moreover, in later experiments on the loss of REM sleep, Dement found no evidence of harmful changes in people who were kept from REM sleep for 16 days, nor in cats deprived for 70 days (Dement, 1974). "A decade of research," he wrote, "has failed to prove that substantial ill effects result even from prolonged selective REM deprivation" (Dement, 1974).

This does not mean that stopping people from entering REM sleep has no effect at all. When people have been deprived of REM sleep and are then allowed to sleep undisturbed, the amount of REM sleep nearly doubles. This phenomenon is called *REM rebound*. Interestingly, schizophrenics show little or no REM rebound. Persons who show signs of dreaming during the day also show less REM rebound (Cohen, 1976). These facts suggest that we can make up for the loss of REM sleep either in NREM sleep or in dreamlike fantasies during waking life (Dement et al., 1970). In passing, it is worth noting that the REM rebound phenomenon may be one reason why it is difficult for some people to break the habit of using sleeping pills or a "nightcap" to help them sleep. Alcohol and most sleep medications are central nervous system depressants that reduce the amount of REM sleep and dreaming. The rebound effect that occurs when these drugs are discontinued is too disturbing for many people. The sharp increase in bizarre dreams drives them back to using the drugs again in an attempt to avoid dreaming. And studies of alcoholics indicate that REM deprivation caused by a disturbance in sleeping patterns may even produce a kind of REM rebound during waking life. This is delirium tremens—the "DTs"—which are vivid hallucinations experienced during alcohol withdrawal (Greenberg & Pearlman, 1967).

At the neurophysiological level, Oswald (1973, 1974) suggests that REM sleep may be related to brain "restoration" and growth. There is some evidence that there is a greater rate of protein synthesis during REM

The Effects of Sleep Deprivation on Human Performance

Have you ever wondered what effect lack of sleep has on you? At some point in your college career you will probably pull an all-nighter, staying up twenty-four hours straight, cramming for the next day's must-pass exam. Is that extra studying worth the effort? Or are you likely to lose as much as you gain by being exhausted on the day of the test?

The effect of sleep deprivation on your test-taking ability depends on the type of exam questions. If they're multiple choice or true/false questions, a night without sleep won't affect your ability to deal with them. The reason is that in answering such questions you rely on familiar, established problem-solving techniques, an ability unaffected by the loss of one night's sleep. If, however, your exam included essay questions, you'd be in trouble. To answer this type of question you need to think flexibly, and this ability is diminished after only a single sleepless night.

These findings seem to support the view that a basic function of sleep is to repair the cerebral cortex from the wear and tear of conscious activity. The loss of creative ability is a signal that lack of sleep causes something to go wrong in the cerebral function, thereby disturbing something fundamental in the decision-making process.

Besides the practical help they may offer you in studying, these findings also have important implications for those whose job requires that they stay awake through the night. For example, sleep deprivation may hinder the ability of people in high-risk positions such as pilots, hospital residents, and nuclear power station operators to cope effectively with an on-job emergency, requiring creative thinking.

In fact, sometimes lack of sleep or shifts in personnel's work cycles—and therefore in their sleep cycles—may be a factor, if not the cause of an accident. For example, the three control room operators at the Three Mile Island power station the morning of the nuclear accident were working a slow shift rotation—days for a week, evenings for a week, then late nights for a week. According to biologists, the slow rotation shift may result in the worst possible human performance because it disrupts the body's biological clock—especially the sleep cycle.

Indeed during the first 100 minutes of the Three Mile Island accident, the operators made an unusual number of errors. Fourteen seconds after the trouble began, one of them failed to notice two warning lights. A few seconds afterwards, they didn't realize that a valve that should have closed was open. In the words of the president's investigating commission, the operators "ignored or failed to recognize the significance of several things that should have warned them they had an open valve and a loss-of-coolant accident. . . ." The commission concluded that human failure had converted a minor incident at Three Mile Island into a major accident.

More research may be needed on how people deprived of sleep are affected by normal bodily rhythms and incentives such as higher pay for successful performance. The new awareness of the relationship of sleep deprivation to accidents has, nevertheless, led policy makers to intervene to change working patterns of high-risk personnel. For example, regulations restricting hospital residents' hours have already been established in some parts of the country. Thus, New York State now requires that they work no longer than an average of 80 hours a week per month. As a spokesperson for the State's Health Department explains, "We think most patients would rather have a well-rested doctor than a zombie working on one-hour's sleep."

Sources: *The Mind* for Horne's study. The article reports that the study appears in the current issue of *Sleep*; The *New York Times*, 1/5/89, p. 19 for Deaconson study.

---

sleep compared to NREM sleep, a fact which may be the neurophysiological indication of the integration of new and old information into creatively restructured patterns. Rossi (1973) even argues that this biochemical activity "serves as the organic basis for new developments in the personality." But these ideas are just possibilities at this stage—nobody really knows what functions dreams serve.

SLEEP DISORDERS. Up to now, we have emphasized typical or average patterns of sleep. But anyone who has spent a sleepless night tossing and turning has firsthand knowledge that eight hours of sleep each night is not always possible. The scientific study of sleep has also opened the way to an understanding of sleep disorders such as **insomnia,** which

Insomnia Sleep disorder characterized by difficulty in falling asleep or remaining asleep throughout the night.

by one estimate afflicts as many as 30 million people in the United States. One recent survey of adults revealed that 6 percent of males and 14 percent of females reported problems either in falling asleep or remaining asleep throughout the night (Kripke & Gillin, 1985). Insomnia usually grows out of stressful events and is temporary. But for some victims, insomnia is a persistent life disruption. In such cases, the simple remedy of sleeping pills is often counterproductive, since sleeping pills lose their effectiveness over time and, as we have noted, can cause such unpleasant effects as REM rebound.

In some cases, insomnia may be the result of enduring psychological problems, such as depression (Kales et al., 1976), and its cure depends on treatment of the underlying disorder. In other cases, the insomniacs appear to be physiologically different from normal sleepers, having a biological system that is always overaroused. A biological predisposition to insomnia and the associated distress about sleeplessness can combine to form a cycle in which the biological and emotional factors reinforce one another. Worrying about not sleeping will create an attitude of desperation whereby bedtime rituals, such as brushing the teeth and getting dressed for bed, "become harbingers of frustration, rather than stimuli for relaxation" (Hauri, 1982). Furthermore, bad sleep habits—such as varying bedtimes—and distracting sleep settings may aggravate or cause insomnia on their own. Even the shortage of copper or iron or excessive amounts of aluminum trace elements in the diet have been associated with the occurrence of sleep disorders (Penland, in press).

It is often the case that a simple change in routine (such as changing the temperature of the bedroom or avoiding certain foods before bedtime) will result in a marked improvement in quality of sleep. Similarly, in-

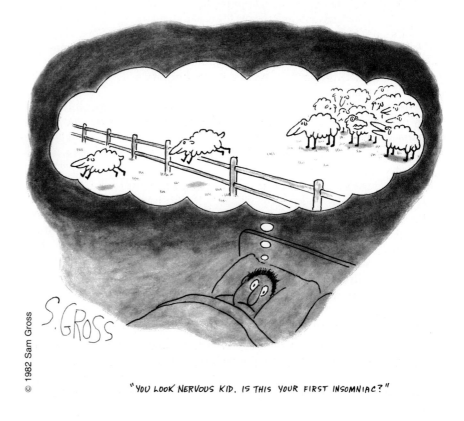

© 1982 Sam Gross

"YOU LOOK NERVOUS KID. IS THIS YOUR FIRST INSOMNIAC?"

somnia sufferers are often helped by maintaining regular bedtime hours and not sleeping late on weekends. In general, sleep researchers advise regularity in sleep habits, avoiding drugs (including alcohol and caffeine), avoiding anxious thoughts while in bed, and not fighting insomnia when it occurs. The old saying "If I can't sleep, I mop the kitchen floor" makes sense to sleep researchers, who counsel their clients to get out of bed and engage in unrelated activities until they feel sleepy again. Along with this strategy, insomniacs are often advised to set aside regular times during the day—well before bedtime—to deliberately mull over their worries. This technique may be supplemented by training in how to relax using such techniques as biofeedback, hypnosis, or meditation. Finally, tryptophan, a protein that promotes sleep, may be used. This protein is found in a glass of warm milk, confirming another folk remedy for sleeplessness. In general, the key seems to be to avoid using the bed as a battlefield against insomnia.

Insomniacs may envy those who have no problem sleeping. But too much sleep can also be a sleep disorder. A major cause of this problem is **apnea,** a condition associated with breathing difficulties during the night. In severe cases, the victim actually stops breathing after falling asleep. When the level of carbon dioxide in the blood rises to a certain point, apnea sufferers are spurred to a state of arousal just short of waking consciousness. Because this can happen hundreds of times in a night, apnea patients typically feel exhausted and fall asleep repeatedly the next day. This sleep disorder is particularly prevalent among the elderly, who are also the major consumers of sleeping medications. As with insomnia, apnea may only be aggravated by medications; and since sleeping pills may further suppress breathing, they may pose a serious medical risk for some people with apnea. The preferred treatment for this problem is somewhat similar to that for insomnia, involving regular bedtimes and wake-up times. Along with this, weight loss and changes in sleeping position can also be helpful. For severe sufferers, a device that keeps the breathing passages unobstructed may be used, as well as medications that stimulate breathing.

Another cause of too much sleep is **narcolepsy,** a hereditary condition that causes victims to nod off without warning in the middle of a conversation or other alert activity. A study of 190 patients who claimed they couldn't stay awake during the day revealed that 65 percent had narcolepsy (Dement, 1974). Narcoleptics will often experience a sudden loss of muscle tone upon expression of any sort of emotion. A joke, anger, sexual stimulation—all bring on a feeling of weakness. Another symptom of the disorder is immediate entry into REM sleep, which produces frightening hallucinations that are in fact dreams that the narcoleptic experiences while still partly awake. Narcolepsy is thought to arise from a defect in the central nervous system, and this disorder can be treated—as can some forms of apnea—with prescription drugs.

Sensory Deprivation

Daydreams and dreams are the most common alterations of normal consciousness, and they both occur naturally under normal conditions. And both daydreaming and sleep are likely to occur when sensory stimulation is reduced (e.g., when the eyes are closed, the environment is quiet).

Apnea Sleep disorder characterized by breathing difficulty during the night and feelings of exhaustion during the day.

Narcolepsy Hereditary sleep disorder characterized by sudden nodding off during the day and sudden loss of muscle tone following moments of emotional excitement.

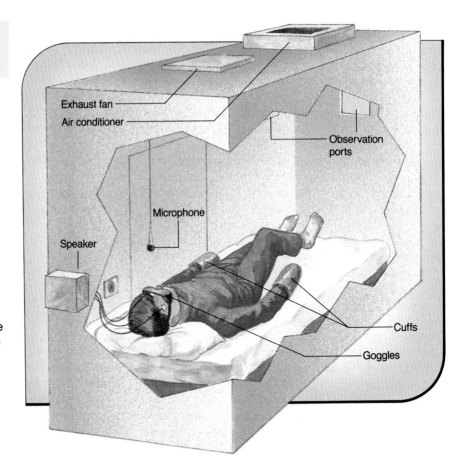

Figure 4-2
A schematic drawing of a sensory deprivation chamber The subject lies on a cot. Cardboard cuffs are placed over the subject's hands and forearms and translucent goggles over the eyes. The only sound is the monotonous noise of the exhaust fan. A microphone allows experimenters to monitor any speech, and the wires attached to the subject's head record brain waves.

After W. Heron, 1961. Reprinted by permission.

This raises an intriguing question: What would happen if we were to be deprived of all sensory stimulation? Would it just leave us feeling deeply restful? Or would it have more profound effects on our consiousness?

In the 1950s and 1960s, experimenters explored the effects of such **sensory deprivation**—the radical reduction of sensory stimuli. The results were somewhat surprising. The primary study was done at McGill University in Montreal in the late 1950s. Student volunteers were put in special sensory deprivation chambers (see Figure 4-2). They were then masked and bandaged, severely restricting their visual, auditory, and tactile stimulation. They were released from these constraints only for three meals a day and for trips to the bathroom. The results were dramatic. The subjects were increasingly unable to do the mental tasks that they had set for themselves. Some had planned to mentally review their studies. Others had intended to think about papers they had to write. The subjects grew increasingly irritable and eventually began to hallucinate. When released from their cubicles, they performed poorly on a number of tests in comparison with a control group given the same tests (Heron, 1957). Other research has modified both the techniques for studying deprivation and the initial findings of the McGill study. Investigators learned to vary the mode of sensory deprivation in three ways. First, the patterns that normally characterize stimulation could be eliminated with translucent goggles or white noise. Second, the variability on sensory input could be reduced by immobilizing part or all of the subject's body in a frame. Third, the absolute level of sensation could be reduced by placing volunteers in dark, quiet chambers or by immersing them in water (Suedfeld & Borrie, 1978).

No matter how deprivation was induced, its effects were similar. Subjects hallucinated, although not as often as first reported; they experienced altered perceptions, both similar to and different from those discovered among the McGill subjects; and they dreamed, daydreamed, and fantasized. Subjects reported flashes of light, geometrical forms, noises, and various complex images of objects or living beings. Some volunteers also described nonexistent odors, such as tobacco smoke, and the feeling that the room or they themselves were moving. Subjects emerging from solitary confinement to face a battery of perceptual tests had impaired color perception and reaction time. However, visual acuity and perception of brightness remained relatively unimpaired, and some faculties, such as pain and taste sensitivity, were actually heightened by systematic deprivation. Some of these effects, which were most powerful after about two days of deprivation, lasted for up to a day after the end of the experiment (Suedfeld & Borrie, 1978). And within a few hours of entering the chamber, most subjects began to pass through alternating states of drowsiness, sleep, and wakefulness. Because the distinctions among wakefulness, drowsiness, and sleep became blurred in the chamber, it was difficult for most subjects to distinguish between waking hallucinations and dreams (Suedfeld, 1975).

Meditation

Of course it is not necessary to be isolated in a sensory deprivation chamber in order to experience an alternation in consciousness. For centuries, people have used various forms of **meditation** to achieve the same end (Benson, 1975). Each form of meditation focuses the meditator's attention in a slightly different way. Zen meditation concentrates on respiration. Sufism, on the other hand, relies on frenzied dancing and the use of prayer (Schwartz, 1974). Transcendental Meditation (TM) uses a mantra, which is a sound especially selected for a student by a teacher of TM. According to proponents of TM, concentrating on the mantra keeps all other images and problems at bay and lets the meditator relax more deeply (Deikman, 1973; Schwartz, 1974).

Despite its diverse forms, meditation reduces the activity of the sympathetic nervous system. In Chapter 2, we noted that this portion of the nervous system helps prepare the body for strenuous activity during an emergency. Meditation produces a lower rate of metabolism (see Figure 4-3) as well as a reduction in heart and respiratory rates. Alpha brain waves (which accompany relaxed wakefulness) noticeably increase during meditation, and there is a decrease in blood lactate, a chemical that appears to be linked to stress.

Meditation has been used to treat certain medical problems, including drug abuse. Some studies have found that a high percentage of mediators who used drugs stop using them. For example, Benson and Wallace (1972) found that among people who meditated using TM, marijuana use fell from 78 percent to 22 percent after 21 months. Among those who used LSD, 97 percent had ceased taking the drug after an average of 22 months of meditation. The subjects of this study were

Meditation Any of various methods of concentration, reflection, or focusing of thoughts that reduce the activity of the sympathetic nervous system.

Meditation lowers metabolic, heart, and respiratory rates. The same changes, however, can also be achieved by deep relaxation.

Hypnosis Trancelike state in which the subject responds readily to suggestions.

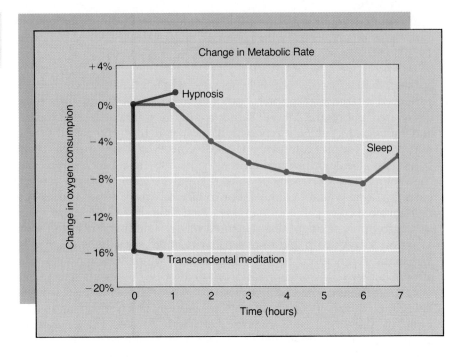

Change in Metabolic Rate

Figure 4-3
A graph depicting the lowered rate of metabolism during meditation, as measured by reduced absorption of oxygen in the bloodstream.

Wallace et al., 1972. Copyright © 1972 by Scientific American, Inc. All rights reserved.

already committed to TM when they were surveyed. Among other populations, the effects are not always so dramatic (Benson et al., 1979). Meditation has also been shown to reduce high blood pressure (Benson, Alexander, & Feldman, 1975; Stone & DeLeo, 1976).

Meditation has other effects as well. People often report experiencing themselves and their surroundings. They may also experience increased sensory awareness, euphoria, strong emotions, and a sense of timelessness and expanded awareness (Deikman, 1973). Peace of mind, a sense of well-being, and total relaxation have also been reported (Dean, 1970).

Nevertheless, there remains some controversy about whether meditation significantly alters normal states of consciousness. For example, the same physical changes can be obtained simply from deep relaxation (Holmes, 1984). Others reply that this fact does not rule out the possibility that meditation produces some unique beneficial effects.

Hypnosis

Hypnosis, while sharing some attributes with other ASCs, has a distinct history dating back to mid-eighteenth-century Europe, where Anton Mesmer, a Viennese physician, fascinated audiences by putting patients into trances and curing a variety of illnesses. Although the term *mesmerism* was first used to describe the phenomenon, *hypnosis* has since become the preferred term (Hypnos was the Greek god of sleep). Mesmer's abilities were initially discredited by a French commission chaired by Benjamin Franklin; but later in the nineteenth century, certain respectable physicians revived interest in hypnosis when they discovered that it could be used to treat certain forms of mental illness. Even today, however, there remains considerable disagreement about how to define hypnosis and even about whether it is indeed a valid ASC.

Although several techniques are in use today, most methods of hypnotic induction share common features. The hypnotist begins by focusing a willing subject's attention. The subject will be asked to concentrate on the hypnotist's voice, and this instruction may be supplemented by asking the subject also to concentrate on a particular object or to visualize a particular scene, such as a relaxing day at the beach. The focus may be sharpened by a kind of guided imagery; for example, a subject who imagines being at the beach might be asked to think about how he or she is progressively becoming more and more relaxed lying in the sand. As the subject enters the trance, its effects may be heightened and tested by some preliminary suggestions. For example, the subject may be told that at the count of ten it will be impossible to open his or her eyes. Sometimes, these suggestions are put in a "paradoxical" form. Subjects will be told, for example, that the harder they try to open their eyes, the more tightly they will remain closed. More suggestions of relaxation will follow until eventually the person appears to be in a state of complete relaxation.

Using hypnosis, it is usually relatively easy to convince suggestible subjects that they cannot open their eyes or that their arms are too heavy to lift. It is more difficult to produce anesthesia, whereby the subject is insensitive to such pain as a pinprick. And it is still more difficult to obtain recollections of lost memories or to create hallucinations (Hilgard, 1965).

Moreover, people vary greatly in their susceptibility to hypnosis. The ability to be carried away by a book or a movie is an excellent predictor of susceptibility to hypnosis. The depth to which a subject can enter a hypnotic trance can be measured more precisely using Hilgard's Stanford Susceptibility Scale. About 10 percent of the people tested show almost no response to hypnosis at all. At the other extreme, about 25 percent are able to undergo deep hypnosis, including such effects as anesthesia. But only about 5 to 10 percent are able to achieve the most dramatic effects, such as experiencing hallucinations (Hilgard, 1965). These individual differences in susceptibility appear to be partly learned and partly inherited. Growing up with parents who have good imaginations and who encourage imaginative play seems to contribute to hypnotic susceptibility (Kihlstrom, 1985). But so too does growing up with severely punishing parents, perhaps because such an experience predisposes one to be highly obedient in response to the hypnotist's suggestions. On the genetic side, there is evidence that identical twins are more similar to each other in their suggestibility than are fraternal twins (Morgan, 1973). And age is also a source of variability in susceptibility. There is considerable evidence that children are, on the whole, more susceptible to hypnotic induction than adults (Banyai & Hilgard, 1976).

Given the great differences between people in hypnotic susceptibility, it stands to reason that clinical and therapeutic uses of hypnosis will not be universally effective. But hypnosis is being used in a variety of medical and counseling situations. The anesthetic effects of hypnosis, in addition to being a measure of the depth of induction, have been found to be more effective than morphine in alleviating certain types of pain. Dentists have been relying for years on this effect in their use of hypnosis as an anesthetic. More recently, its usefulness has been demonstrated in the treatment of children with leukemia who have to undergo repeated bone marrow biopsies. This procedure is extremely painful, but children

Using hypnosis, it is usually relatively easy to convince suggestible subjects that they cannot open their eyes or that their arms are too heavy to lift. This woman has been told to hold her hand over the flame of a cigarette lighter.

who are able to imagine themselves living temporarily in a world outside their bodies can learn to tolerate the procedure quite well (Hilgard, Hilgard, & Kaufmann, 1983). A somewhat different use of hypnosis is the control of bleeding among hemophiliacs undergoing dental treatment. In one study, a group of hemophiliacs under hypnosis imagined that their mouths were filled with ice; these patients, who would normally have required several pints of blood and a week in the hospital, needed no blood and were not hospitalized (Lucas, 1975).

Still other uses of hypnosis include aid in quitting smoking, in dieting, and in improving athletic performance. In such cases hypnotists may rely on *posthypnotic suggestions*. While hypnotized, the subject may be told, for example, that after awakening from the trance the very sight of a cigarette will induce a feeling of nausea. This suggestion will be reinforced with follow-up visits to the hypnotist. The effectiveness of hypnosis on habit change, however, has been disputed. It has been pointed out that if a person really wants to change a behavior, he or she is likely to do so without hypnosis. Hypnosis may provide additional encouragement, but so might joining a mutual support group such as Weight Watchers. In other words, it is not clear that posthypnotic suggestions are any more effective than other kinds of supportive help provided with no hypnosis whatsoever.

One of the striking aspects of hypnosis is its ability to retrieve lost memories. Police departments sometimes employ hypnosis to enable witnesses to retrieve memories of crime scenes that they cannot otherwise recall. Related to this is the phenomenon of age regression. Subjects undergoing age regression will not only *remember* events long past, but will feel as if they are reliving the events. Sometimes, they may perform such feats as speaking in forgotten childhood languages. Fromm (1970) reports the case of a Japanese-American who had forgotten his childhood language but began speaking it fluently under hypnosis. Despite these impressive memory feats, there remains some doubt regarding the accuracy of memories retrieved under hypnosis. While a hypnotized subject may recount in detail and with great conviction the circumstances surrounding a childhood birthday party, this does not mean that the account is accurate. In some cases, it has been possible to demonstrate that these "memories" are actually fantasies similar to vivid nighttime dreams that seem at the time to be absolutely real.

We have seen that there is some controversy about the effects of hypnosis and about whether it is necessary to use hypnosis at all in order to achieve some of the results that have been reported. There is also controversy about whether the hypnotic trance *is* in fact an altered state of consciousness. Hypnosis appears to have no clearly measureable effect on blood pressure, heartbeat, brain waves, or other vital signs that would allow us to distinguish a hypnotic trance from a normal resting state (Hilgard, 1974). Although some psychologists have suggested that the increase in suggestibility that occurs under hypnosis is sufficient to class it as an ASC, nonhypnotized subjects under orders from an authoritative experimenter are capable of doing virtually everything hypnotized subjects can do. Yet a recent study (Zamansky & Bartis, 1985) indicates that people who are hypnotized have a distinctly different experience while they are performing feats than do people who are not hypnotized. So the jury is still out on whether there needs to be a separate, definable state of consciousness known as the "hypnotic trance" or whether suggestibility alone explains the many observed "hypnotic" behaviors.

■ Drug-Altered Consciousness

So far, our discussion has been concerned with ASCs produced without drugs. Meditation, hypnosis, daydreams, sleep, and dreaming can all occur without chemical intervention. In this final section of the chapter, we will look at ASCs that are induced with the help of drugs.

Since ancient times, drugs have been used to alter consciousness for social, religious, and personal reasons. Wine is mentioned often in the Bible and plays a sacramental role in several major religions. Marijuana is mentioned in the herbal recipe book of a Chinese emperor in 2737 B.C.; and the Jivaro Indians of Ecuador, who consider the world of the senses an illusion, use drugs to contact the "real world" of supernatural forces. In our own culture, the use of some substances to alter mood or behavior is, under certain circumstances, regarded as normal behavior. This includes moderate intake of alcohol and of the caffeine in coffee, tea, or cola. It also includes the use of tobacco and, in various subcultures, such illegal substances as marijuana, cocaine, and amphetamines.

There has even been some speculation that altering consciousness with drugs is one way to counteract the limiting effects of "straight," logical, and uninsightful thinking (Weil, 1972). For example, there are claims that drugs improve creativity. Coleridge reported that his poem "Kubla Khan" was the result of an opium dream. Ken Kesey's novel *One Flew Over the Cuckoo's Nest* was written while the author used drugs. Nevertheless, there remain questions about whether drug-altered consciousness can produce creative output that is not already present in the creator.

Apart from the possibly beneficial use of some kinds of drugs to alter consciousness, the problems associated with drug abuse have also been recognized since ancient times. The Greeks advocated moderation in all things, including the use of wine. And the Bible preaches against the sin of alcohol abuse. Yet, as we will shortly see, a very large percentage of Americans today abuse drugs.

We have seen that there are contradictory claims about the benefits of drug use. How do we know whether in fact a given drug has positive or negative effects? Until fairly recently, answers to such questions relied in large part on anecdotal reports of drug experiences. Today, however, drug effects are most often studied in carefully controlled scientific experiments. In most cases, experimenters compare behavior prior to the administration of the drug to the behavior that follows its administration. But special precautions must be taken to ensure that any observed changes in behavior are actually due to the drug. For example, simply *expecting* that a drug will produce a particular effect is often enough to produce the effect. If the active ingredient is removed from marijuana or the caffeine removed from coffee unbeknownst to users, the effect of the drug is usually unchanged: Subjects act just as if they have been administered marijuana or caffeine! Similarly, if an experimenter expects that alcohol will slow down behavior, he or she may be more likely to look for and observe that phenomenon.

In order to eliminate such sources of error, most drug researchers use a **double-blind procedure.** Some subjects receive the active drug while others receive a neutral, inactive substance called a **placebo;** neither the researcher nor the subjects know which subjects got the active drug and which got the placebo. Then, after data are collected, the researcher can compare the behavior of subjects who actually received the drug with the behavior of subjects who unknowingly received a placebo. If the groups differ in their behavior, the cause is likely to be the active ingredient in the drug.

Studying drug-altered consciousness is further complicated by the fact that most drugs not only affect different people in different ways, but also produce different effects in the same person from one occasion to another or from one setting to another. For example, some people are powerfully affected by even small amounts of alcohol, while others are not. And drinking alcohol in a convivial family setting produces somewhat different effects than alcohol imbibed under the watchful eye of a scientist! Researchers must carefully control all these variables in order to be sure that the observed drug effects reflect only those of the chemical that is under scrutiny.

In the discussion of the effects of particular drugs, it is convenient to group them under the categories of *depressants*, *stimulants*, and *hallucinogens*. This grouping helps us to organize our knowledge of drugs even though these are not rigid categories.

Depressants

Generally, **depressants** are chemicals that slow down behavior and thinking by either speeding up or slowing down nerve impulses. In general, alcohol, barbiturates, and the opiates have depressant effects.

ALCOHOL. Our society recognizes many appropriate occasions for the use of alcohol: to celebrate important events, to reduce tensions, to break down social isolation and inhibitions, and to promote group harmony. Earlier in this chapter, we also noted the long-standing use of alcohol in religious sacraments. Perhaps because of its social acceptability and legality, **alcohol** is the most widely used drug in our society. Users of alcohol outnumber users of all other drugs combined, and about 500 million gallons of alcoholic beverages are consumed annually in the United States. But according to a government survey, 39 percent of American

Alcohol Depressant that is the intoxicating ingredient in whiskey, beer, wine, and other fermented or distilled liquors.

■ Drug Use and Abuse

The line between "drug use" and "drug abuse" is not a sharp one. According to the American Psychiatric Association, *substance abuse* is defined by three conditions: (1) a pattern of pathological use such as intoxication throughout the day, an inability to cut down or stop, a need for its daily use in order to function adequately, and the continuing use of the substance even if it makes a physical disorder worse; (2) disturbance in social relationships or deterioration of occupational functioning; and (3) signs of disturbance lasting for at least one month. The person who regularly goes on drinking binges, for example, that are severe enough to cause him or her ill health and problems within the family or on the job is involved in alcohol abuse.

For many drugs, including alcohol, continued abuse over a period of time can lead to *substance dependence* (sometimes called *addiction*). Interestingly, as we will see, many potent drugs do not produce dependence, even after prolonged and heavy use. In any event, substance dependence is much more serious than substance abuse and is marked by evidence of either *tolerance*—increasing amounts of the drug needed to achieve the same effect—or *withdrawal* symptoms—physical and psychological problems that appear if a person reduces or stops using the substance (APA, 1980). Both these conditions are present in the following case:

A 42-year-old executive in a public relations firm was referred for psychiatric treatment by his surgeon, who discovered him sneaking large quantities of a codeine-containing cough medicine into the hospital. . . . An operation on his back five years previously had led his doctor to prescribe codeine to help relieve the incisional pain at that time. Over the intervening five years, however, he had continued to use codeine-containing tablets and had increased his intake to 60–90 5-mg tablets daily. He stated that he often "just took them by the handful—not to feel good, you understand, just to get by." He had tried several times to stop using codeine, but had failed. During this period he lost two jobs because of lax work habits and was

divorced by his wife of 11 years (Spitzer et al., 1981, p. 255).

Considering the difficulties that substance abuse and dependence cause for the abuser, we may wonder why some people come to abuse drugs at all. The various schools of thought within psychology each provide somewhat different answers to this question. The *psychoanalytic* thinkers, for example, consider abuse to be an expression of an unconscious emotional problem. In particular, they believe that people who abuse drugs have an exaggerated need to feel dependent and to be taken care of. *Behaviorist* thinkers are more likely to point to the role of learning. Many addicts, for example, learn drug use as part of a deviant subculture. And some abusers accidentally learn that some drug relieves their anxiety or distress and then find themselves turning to it more and more often to solve their problems. *Physiological* psychologists see abusers as to some extent victims of their body chemistry: Some people, they believe, metabolize drugs differently and become addicted much more quickly—and powerfully—than others. Whatever the initial cause, however, frequent, heavy abuse can turn into actual dependence, at which point the person is physically "hooked" on continued use of the drug, as in the aforementioned case of the codeine addict. The body needs the substance just to function "normally."

Finally, *social* factors play a role in both substance abuse and dependence. In our society, alcohol and many drugs are widely available—perhaps more so now than at any time in our history. Moreover, we have come to expect that drugs solve problems, having learned this lesson from the prescriptions so readily dispensed by physicians and from a constant barrage of advertising for "medicine" to cure every conceivable ailment, to help us sleep or take off weight, to make us feel young and vigorous, and so on. Under the circumstances, it is hardly surprising that some people turn to drugs to make them feel better. For most of us, use does not become abuse. But in those people who are psychologically troubled or physiologically vulnerable—or both—abuse or dependence are both very real possibilities.

Perhaps because of its social acceptability and legality, alcohol is the most widely used drug in our society. One out of every ten Americans uses alcohol compulsively, and half the adult population abuses alcohol.

adults and 34 percent of American youths do not consider alcohol to be a drug; and only 7 percent of the public think alcoholism is a serious drug problem, compared to 53 percent who hold this attitude toward all other drugs. Nonetheless, 1 out of every 10 Americans uses alcohol compulsively, and half of the adult population abuses alcohol (National Commission on Marijuana and Drug Abuse, 1973a). Furthermore, there has been a sharp upsurge recently in the use of alcohol by adolescents.

The biochemical effects of alcohol are not completely understood. There is some evidence that it has an effect on the nervous system that is similar to general anesthetics (McKim, 1986). The effects of alcohol are not limited to a specific neural location, and it has many effects on a variety of tissues. There are also suggestions that when metabolized by the body, alcohol produces byproducts that are similar to the opiates that we will be discussing shortly (Wadja, 1979). This may partly explain its mood-elevating effects—for example, why it can make us feel happy. Prolonged or excessive use of alcohol can damage the brain, liver, and other organs, affect the development of fetuses, and even permanently damage the personality of the user.

But although alcohol is a depressant, subjectively it is experienced as a stimulant. This is because it depresses or inhibits centers in the brain that are used for critical judgment and for the inhibition of impulsive behavior. As a result, a person's diminished self-control under the influence of alcohol can produce behavior that results in social embarrassment, injury, or even death. In our sober moments, we may be afraid to tell off the boss because the negative consequences of getting fired outweigh the positive feelings that would ensue from telling the boss exactly what we think. Under the influence of alcohol, however, we are likely to be less concerned with the negative consequences of our behavior and thus more likely to speak our mind. In this sense, alcohol may be thought of as a "truth serum," reflecting the wisdom of the ancient Roman saying *in vino veritas* ("in wine there is truth").

A study by Murial Vogel-Sprott (1967) neatly illustrates this phenomenon. She had subjects participate in an experiment in which certain behaviors resulted in both painful shocks and money. Some subjects were given alcohol before the experiment began; others received only a placebo. The subjects who received a placebo sharply reduced the behaviors that were accompanied by shock—the money just wasn't worth the pain. But subjects under the influence of alcohol showed no such inhibition. They weathered the shocks in order to get the money. It was as though the negative consequences of their behavior (the shocks) were no longer important. This may explain, at least in part, why some people drink alcohol before potentially stressful or unpleasant events and also why alcohol is involved in half of all murders, assaults, and rapes. Under the influence of alcohol, the negative or unpleasant consequences of behavior simply lose their importance.

Alcohol also has numerous effects on perceptual and motor processes. Alcohol diminishes visual acuity, depth perception, and the perception of the differences between bright lights and colors, although it appears to improve the ability to perceive dim lights. Some aspects of hearing, such as the perception of loudness, are not affected, but the ability to discriminate between different rhythms and pitches is impaired by a single dose of the drug. Smell and taste perception are uniformly diminished,

and the perception of time also becomes distorted. Most people report that time seems to pass more quickly when they are "under the influence" (NCMDA, 1973b).

Motor responses and reaction time also deteriorate rapidly under the effect of alcohol. Reaction time is slowed by about 10 percent with a dose of 80 mg to 100 mg. In tasks requiring attention to several simultaneous stimuli, both speed and accuracy of responses are greatly reduced. And doses as low as 10 mg significantly interfere with people's ability to follow a moving target with a marker (McKin, 1986). From these data it can be concluded that only 50 mg of alcohol is sufficient to impair seriously one's ability to perform the many complicated tasks in driving a car.

Alcohol also has significant effects on memory. Heavy drinkers may experience blackouts that render them unable to remember any of the events that occurred when they were drinking.

Although many of these effects can be traced to the way in which alcohol affects the central nervous system, alcohol can also have an effect due to the person's *expectations* about what it is supposed to do. For example, experimental evidence indicates that men become more aggressive when they *believe* they are drinking alcohol even if they are not

■ Who Drinks?

All of us have equal access to alcohol—a highly addictive drug—yet not all of us become alcoholics. What accounts for this difference?

From a global point of view, there are several cross-cultural consistencies. Men drink more than women and do so in peer groups away from women and family. Alcohol is generally more acceptable among soldiers and others who work to master the environment than among those charged with preserving tradition, like priests, mothers, and judges (Robinson, 1977).

There are, however, many differences in drinking among both individuals and cultures. In some cases, people will go on binges and then generally refrain from alcohol between drinking bouts. In some cultures, such as among the French, people will consume large amounts of alcohol over the course of the day without exhibiting the symptoms of excessive alcohol consumption.

Although men do drink more than women, when effects of body weight are removed, it appears that women who are social drinkers achieve the same level of alcohol in the blood (Vogel-Sprott, 1984). Advancing age also seems to reduce the amount of alcohol that a person will drink (Vogel-Sprott, 1984).

Among alcoholics, there is a fairly regular pattern of consumption. When a group of alcoholics was given free access to alcoholic beverages, they tended to consume great amounts for several days and followed this with several days of reduced consumption that were accompanied by the appearance of withdrawal symptoms (Griffiths, Bigelow, & Henningfield, 1980).

Despite these regularities, it remains difficult to define *alcoholism* precisely. According to McKim (1986), some researchers define alcoholism as a condition that interferes with normal functioning, while others think of it as a metabolic or psychiatric disorder that is a definable disease. However, these criteria have fuzzy boundaries, and McKim proposes that the best definition of *alcoholic* may simply be "a person who consumes sufficient alcohol to attract the attention of the police or the medical authorities."

There does appear to be some evidence of a genetic link to alcohol abuse. For example, identical twins are far more likely to have similar drinking patterns than fraternal twins. It has also been discovered that an adopted child of a biological parent who is an alcoholic is more likely to become one also, particularly if one of the adoptive parents has a drinking problem (Shields, 1977). Ricardo Cruz-Coke (1971) identified a recessive gene which is related to both alcohol predisposition and color blindness. Color blindness is indeed more common among alcoholics.

From an environmental perspective, urban dwellers are more likely to drink than those who live in the country. And people in such professions as bartenders, waitresses, and stevedores are more likely to be alcoholics than farmworkers or carpenters. Unstable home conditions, such as broken homes or families with a dominant mother or antagonistic father, are also more likely to produce alcoholics (McCord, 1972).

Although anybody is capable of becoming an alcoholic under the right circumstances, there are some features that appear to characterize the personality of an alcoholic. According to one investigation, alcoholics suffer from feelings of inferiority that they overcome with attempts at dominance and control. Drinking makes them feel that they can behave more effectively. On the other hand, there are many alcoholics who do not exhibit this personality type, and there are many people with "alcoholic personalities" who do not become excessive drinkers.

Furthermore, there is controversy over whether an alcoholic can control his or her drinking or whether total abstinence is the only way to cure alcoholism. Alcoholics Anonymous is the primary advocate of total abstinence and reacts with alarm and political pressure to any suggestion that an alcoholic can become a social drinker. This point of view holds that any use of alcohol by an abstaining alcoholic will lead to a total loss of self-control. Nevertheless, several studies have discovered that some long-term alcoholics have reverted to moderate use (Davis, 1962). The Rand Report on Alcoholism (Armor, Polach, & Stambul, 1978) concluded that controlled drinking may be an attainable treatment goal.

actually doing so. They also become more sexually aroused and less anxious in social situations when they mistakenly believe they are drinking alcohol (Marlatt & Rohsenow, 1981). Thus, in part at least, the effects of alcohol (and other drugs as well) depend on the expectations of the user.

Alcohol abuse and dependence, as the most serious substance abuse problem in our society, has been an area of particular challenge for researchers. Although we have no definitive answer to the question of

Barbiturates Potentially deadly depressants, first used for their sedative and anticonvulsant effects, now used only to treat such conditions as epilepsy and arthritis.

Even though alcohol is a depressant, it is often experienced as a stimulant. Many people *expect* drinking alcohol to help them be less anxious in social situations, and their behavior may be affected by the expectation.

what causes alcoholism, we do have some suggestive evidence. First, we know that people turn to alcohol in order to relieve stress from life problems. As a depressant, alcohol does exert a calming effect on the nervous system. The problem, of course, is that too-frequent use of this calming agent can produce more life stress (family crises, loss of job). Some researchers have tried to identify an "alcoholic personality," in the belief that alcoholics are often emotionally immature and needy, have low self-esteem, and do not tolerate frustration well (Coleman et al., 1984). On the other hand, since many people who have these characteristics do not become alcoholics, this personality profile cannot be the whole answer.

Going beyond the individual, some researchers have suggested that *culture* can be an important influence. Sometimes, spouses and parents are powerful models in introducing people to a pattern of heavy drinking. And in some ethnic cultures, alcohol is more acceptable than in others. Orthodox Jews, who frown on the use of alcohol, and Muslims, who prohibit it, have low rates of alcoholism.

Another line of research has sought to find *biological* factors in alcoholism. Some investigators have suggested that alcoholics may be born with a genetic vulnerability to alcoholism. Since some groups of people are known to metabolize alcohol differently from others (Asians and American Indians, for example, react more strongly to alcohol than do Europeans), it is possible that there are inborn individual differences in alcohol tolerance as well (Coleman et al., 1984).

BARBITURATES. **Barbiturates**—popularly known as "downers"—include such medications as Amytal, Nembutal, and Seconal. This class of depressants was discovered about a century ago and was first used by physicians for its sedative and anticonvulsant effects. The use of barbiturates declined in the 1950s, when researchers became acutely aware of their potentially deadly effects, particularly when combined with alcohol. This decline in popularity was also hastened by the introduction of a new class of sedatives, the "minor tranquilizers," which include the very popular drug Valium (see the Box in Chapter 15). Nonetheless, barbiturates are often used today to treat such diverse conditions as insomnia, anxiety, epilepsy, arthritis, and bedwetting (Reinisch & Sanders, 1982).

The effects of barbiturates are very similar to those of alcohol: Taken on an empty stomach, 150 mg will cause light-headedness, silliness, and poor motor coordination (McKim, 1986). Larger doses, 400 mg to 700 mg, can yield effects such as slurred speech, loss of inhibition, and increases in aggressive behavior (Aston, 1972). As is the case with alcohol, the effect of the drug varies from one setting to another. A dose that causes aggressive behavior at a party may cause only drowsiness when taken in the privacy of one's home.

Another noteworthy effect of barbiturates involves their effects on memory. While barbiturates can cause amnesia, as does alcohol in the form of blackouts, in smaller doses they also can enhance memory; the "truth serums" of spy thrillers are actually barbiturates.

THE OPIATES. Heroin is the best known of the **opiates,** but it is a relative newcomer on the scene. A Sumerian tablet from 4000 B.C. refers to a "joy plant" that is thought to have been the poppy plant from which the drug opium is derived. Ancient Greek and Roman physicians prescribed opium for a number of conditions. Among royalty, it was a popular poison for killing rivals. The use of opium spread from the Middle East into China, where for centuries its uses were primarily medicinal. However, in 1644, when tobacco smoking was banned by the Chinese emperor, smokers replaced tobacco with opium in their pipes, and the use of the drug to produce an ASC was firmly established.

In the United States, during most of the nineteenth century and for the early part of this century, opium was a widely used ingredient in a variety of over-the-counter (patent) medicines. Chiefly in the form of *laudanum*—opium dissolved in alcohol—the drug was used to treat a variety of ailments and was marketed under such innocuous names as "Mrs. Winslow's Soothing Syrup" and "Street's Infant Quietness." During

The opium poppy The flower and distinctive fruit (left); the fruit of a smaller variety (right).

the same period, the drug morphine (named after Morpheus, the Greek god of sleep) was chemically isolated from opium and it too was relatively easy to obtain (although a prescription was required). During the latter portion of the nineteenth century, people began to recognize the fact that opiates are highly addictive. Somewhat ironically, heroin—a further refinement of opium discovered in 1898—was originally proposed as a cure for morphine addiction. Although the nonmedicinal distribution of opiates was banned early in this century, the problem of opiate **dependence** remains with us today.

Generally, the opiates produce subjective feelings of euphoria, well-being, and relaxation. However, controlled studies show that the pleasant effects are not long-lived and are quickly replaced by undesirable changes in mood and behavior. A study by Meyer and Mirin (1979), for example, demonstrated that addicts who are given relatively free access to heroin do experience euphoria and reduced tension for the first few days of use. However, **tolerance** to heroin soon sets in. Users find that more of the drug is necessary to produce the positive effects and reduce the unpleasant sensations associated with **withdrawal.** In Meyer and Mirin's study, users also reported that the pleasant feelings lasted for only a short time after several days of use and that more frequent injections became necessary to sustain the "high." The researchers also observed increases in aggressive behavior and social isolation, along with decreases in general physical activity and social interaction.

The unpleasant withdrawal symptoms that follow discontinuance of heroin add to its addictive potential. The first symptom of withdrawal is restlessness, accompanied by fits of yawning, chills, and hot flashes. The skin often breaks out into goose bumps resembling the texture of a plucked turkey (thus the term "cold turkey"). This is often followed by periods of prolonged sleep lasting up to 12 hours. When awake, the addict experiences severe cramps, vomiting, and diarrhea, along with convulsive shaking and kicking. All this is accompanied by profuse sweating. In about a week's time, the withdrawal symptoms diminish and disappear.

For the most part, the social problems associated with heroin arise from the fact that addicts must take increasingly larger doses in order to get the positive mood-alteration effects. Lesser doses simply provide some relief from the terrible pains of withdrawal. In advanced stages of addiction, heroin becomes less a means to alter consciousness than a painkiller. Since heroin is illegal and expensive, addicts must spend a great deal of time—often in criminal activities—obtaining it.

Stimulants

The drugs classified as **stimulants**—amphetamines and cocaine—have legitimate medicinal uses, but they also produce feelings of optimism and boundless energy. Therefore, their use can be highly reinforcing, and the potential for abuse is high.

AMPHETAMINES. Although there are reports of amphetamine-like substances that date back more than 5,000 years, it was not until the early part of this century that researchers began to discover the medicinal value of amphetamines. **Amphetamines** are chemically similar to epinephrine, a neurotransmitter that stimulates the sympathetic nerv-

Dependence Strong physical need for a substance, such as some drug.

Tolerance Phenomenon whereby higher doses of a drug are required to produce its original effects or to prevent withdrawal symptoms.

Withdrawal Unpleasant physical or psychological effects that follow the discontinuance of a dependence-producing substance.

Stimulants Drugs, including amphetamines and cocaine, that stimulate the sympathetic nervous system and produce feelings of optimism and boundless energy.

Amphetamines Stimulant drugs that initially produce "rushes" of euphoria often followed by sudden "crashes" and, sometimes, severe depression.

Cocaine Drug that, while producing a sense of euphoria by stimulating the sympathetic nervous system, also produces anxiety, depression, and addictive cravings.

Up until the early part of this century, opiates—including heroin—were used as the active ingredients in a variety of patent medicines.

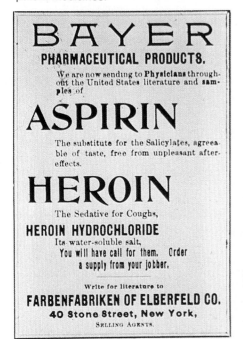

BAYER

PHARMACEUTICAL PRODUCTS.

We are now sending to **Physicians** throughout the United States literature and samples of

ASPIRIN

The substitute for the Salicylates, agreeable of taste, free from unpleasant after-effects.

HEROIN

The Sedative for Coughs,

HEROIN HYDROCHLORIDE

Its water-soluble salt,
You will have call for them. Order
a supply from your jobber.

Write for literature to

FARBENFABRIKEN OF ELBERFELD CO.
40 Stone Street, New York,
SELLING AGENTS.

ous system (see Chapter 2). Because of this chemical similarity, amphetamines have been used for the treatment of asthma because they open respiratory passages and ease breathing. They have also been used as mild stimulants and for the treatment of narcolepsy. Until quite recently, it was very easy to receive prescriptions for these medications, and their popularity was further enhanced by their wide use by the military during World War II. Truck drivers and students also came to rely on amphetamines to stay awake and alert. And since amphetamines tend to suppress the appetite, they were widely used for a time as "diet pills." In fact, amphetamines became so popular that by the 1970s, an estimated 10 percent of the U.S. population over the age of 14 had used them (Greaves, 1980). This represented 10 billion pills per year, or 50 pills a year for every man, woman, and child in the United States.

Unfortunately, it is now known that amphetamines have a tremendous potential for abuse because of their effects on consciousness and behavior. One of the side effects of amphetamines is their ability to make people feel happy. Higher doses increase this effect, and when injected, users report "rushes" of euphoria. The downside of these effects, however, is serious. After the effects of the drug wear off, users experience a "crash" accompanied by severe depression (Gunne & Anggard, 1972). In order to avoid the crash, users tend to take more amphetamines (or other drugs). High doses of amphetamines also produce a condition known as *amphetamine psychosis*, even in people who are otherwise normal and who have had no previous psychiatric history. This condition, similar to paranoid schizophrenia, is characterized by delusions, hallucinations, and paranoia.

Habitual amphetamine use can also stimulate aggressive, violent behavior. To a great extent, the popular image of a "dope fiend" is an appropriate description of the amphetamine addict. These changes in behavior are not caused directly by the drug itself; rather, they grow out of the profound personality changes—particularly paranoia—that come from excessive use (Rylander, 1969). Because of the addictive potential of amphetamines, their medicinal use is now restricted to the treatment of narcolepsy and hyperactivity in children.

COCAINE. **Cocaine** is also a stimulant and, like the amphetamines, it can cause euphoric moods. Cocaine is extracted from the leaves of the coca bush, which is native to the Andes Mountains in South America. The original method for ingesting this drug, which is still practiced today in South America, involves chewing the leaves of the coca bush. The Spanish Conquistadors, who used coca as a means of payment for laborers on plantations and in gold and silver mines, found that they could extract more labor from their workers because of the stimulant effects of the drug. At the same time, they could cut down on food rations, because the drug suppressed the appetite (McKim, 1986).

Among Europeans, the drug remained generally unknown until the middle 1800s, when it became popular to blend coca into wine and other drinks. The Coca-Cola Company used chemically active coca leaves as a substitute for the alcohol in its original formula. To this day, Coca-Cola—and other colas—are blended with coca leaves that have had the active ingredient removed. Among the more famous users of cocaine was Sigmund Freud, who had very positive personal experiences with the drug

■ Coffee and Cigarettes

In 1604, King James I of England described the smoking of tobacco as "a custome lothsome to the eye, hateful to the Nose, harmefull to the braine, dangerous to the Lungs, and in the blacke stinking fume thereof, neerest resembling the horrible Stygian smoke of the pit that is bottomlesse." About 60 years later, a petition circulated around London lamenting, "What a curse it is that ordinary working men should sit the whole day in coffee houses simply to chatter about politics, while their unhappy children are wailing at home for lack of bread!" Sound familiar?

Coffee and cigarettes—two things that go together well—are powerful mind-altering drugs. And quite aside from their harmful physical effects, they share many characteristics of the "more serious" drugs that we are discussing in the text. Caffeine, occurring naturally in coffee, tea, and cocoa, belongs to a class of drugs known as *xanthine stimulants*. Its effects are not completely understood, but caffeine generally appears to act as a stimulant suppressing inhibitory neurotransmitters and releasing stimulatory neurotransmitters—thus promoting neuron firing. *Nicotine*, occurring naturally only in tobacco, has similarly stimulant effects, although at higher doses it begins to act as depressant. It also acts directly on the reticular system (see Chapter 2), promoting general arousal.

Coffee is best known for its ability to maintain wakefulness and alertness. Actually, many of the supposed effects of caffeine are illusory. One study asked subjects to perform a series of motor and perceptual tasks after being administered a dose of caffeine. All the subjects thought that they were doing better when they were on caffeine, but their actual performance was not improved over their performance without caffeine. On the other hand, another study concluded that although caffeine does not aid intellectual performance, it reduces the effects of boredom and fatigue on motor and perceptual tasks. It doesn't help you to perform better than you normally do, but it helps to keep you from perfoming at your worst. With regard to sleep, caffeine, the primary ingredient in over-the-counter stimulants, reduces the total number of sleep minutes and increases the time it takes to fall asleep. Interestingly, it is the only stimulant that does not appear to alter sleep stages or cause REM rebound, making it much safer than amphetamines.

Nicotine is not nearly as safe. The general effect of increased heart rate and constricted blood cells causes smokers to lose skin color, have cold hands, and to wrinkle and age faster (Daniell, 1971). The effects of nicotine on mood are somewhat paradoxical. Biochemically, it appears to be a stimulant, but most smokers report that a cigarette will relax them. Long-reformed smokers will experience tobacco craving in times of stress. Some of the relaxing effects of smoking may come from the ritual itself: holding the cigarette, lighting it, inhaling. Most importantly, however, the relief from withdrawal symptoms may be the primary relaxant. The smoker breathes a sigh of relief from the agony of not having a cigarette.

This phenomenon points to the most striking aspect of tobacco consumption—how difficult it is to quit. Many exheroine addicts report that tobacco should be as easy to quit. The withdrawal symptoms include nervousness, insomnia and drowsiness, headaches, irritability, and an intense craving for nicotine (McKim, 1986). This craving may last as long as nine years for some exsmokers (Fletcher & Doll, 1969). Research on treatment outcomes indicates that as few as 15 percent of smokers are able to quit permanently. One mechanism responsible for this is the nicotine-bolus. When ingested through smoking, the nicotine tends to concentrate together and arrive at the brain all at once following each puff (Russell, 1976). This "rush," very much like what happens when heroin is injected, keeps the brain craving for more.

Caffeine is generally more benign, but large doses—5 to 10 cups a day—may cause a disorder called *caffeinism*, which is characterized by delirium and excitement. It appears that caffeine suppresses the transmission of naturally occurring chemicals that have calming effects (in this respect, it is similiar to Valium—see Box in Chapter 15.) For this reason, caffeine will interfere with prescribed medications like tranquilizers and sedatives. Coffee also appears to exaggerate the symptoms of a variety of psychiatric patients. DeFreitas and Schwartz (1979) switched patients on a psychiatric ward to decaffeinated coffee—unbeknownst to both the patients and the staff. It was found that there was a decrease in symptoms like anxiety and an increase in socially appropriate behavior. These effects were reversed when regular coffee was served again.

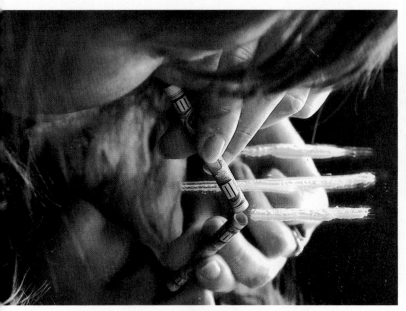

A cocaine user about to inhale the white powdery substance.

In many parts of the country the use of crack, a crystalline form of cocaine, has become epidemic. Because they interfere with pleasure centers in the brain, crack and cocaine produce a feeling of euphoria that is quickly followed by a crashing, pleasureless low that fosters even greater craving and dependency.

and urged its use on his friends and relatives. He also promoted its use as a cure for alcoholism and morphine addiction. Although he eventually became disillusioned with the drug, one of his colleagues developed what is still the only legitimate medical use for cocaine—as a local anesthetic. Novocaine is a familiar form of cocaine.

The use of cocaine as a recreational drug gradually declined in the first half of the twentieth century, in part because it became associated in the popular imagination with narcotics and opiates, even though it is chemically quite distinct from them. Today, cocaine is the most popular illegal drug in use. In its crystalline form, known as "crack," cocaine can be smoked easily in a pipe or cigarette. The media speak quite freely of what has become known as the "crack epidemic," and estimates now range as high as 20 million cocaine users in the United States. What makes crack such a serious problem is that many users report becoming dependent on the drug almost immediately and that, because of the way the drug acts on the brain, the craving for it is difficult to break.

The effects of cocaine are very similar to those of the amphetamines, although shorter in duration, and the effects of crack even faster and more intense. Along with the feelings of euphoria, energy, and perceived clarity of thought, physiological effects include stimulation of the sympathetic nervous system, an increase in the heart rate, a rise in blood pressure, and a constriction of blood vessels. Large doses also raise the body temperature and dilate pupils. After relatively large doses wear off, however, some users experience a "crash" characterized by anxiety, depression, and a strong craving for more cocaine. Siegel (1982) surveyed habitual users and discovered that one-third to one-half also experienced such mood and behavioral symptoms as paranoia, visual hallucinations, cravings, and attention and concentration problems. When smoked as crack, molecules of cocaine reach the brain in less than 10 seconds, producing a high that lasts from 5 to 20 minutes and is followed by a swift and equally intense depression. Crack and cocaine stimulate a pleasure center in the base of the brain, an area that, as we will see in Chapter 11, is responsible for our emotions. As the levels of cocaine in the brain drop, users begin to feel depressed and anxious. With crack, this pleasureless state begins to set in within 30 minutes. Because it interferes with the chemistry of this pleasure center and subsequently the brain's ability to reestablish emotional balance, the craving for the drug is doubly painful and difficult to overcome. The compulsion to take cocaine can become so great that it can impoverish even wealthy users. During periods of active use, or "runs," the cost can be as high as $1000 a day.

Hallucinogens and Marijuana

The hallucinogens include LSD ("acid"), mescaline, peyote, psilocybin, and phencyclidine (PCP, or "angel dust"). Marijuana is sometimes included in this group, although its effects are normally less powerful. The term *hallucinogen* comes from the fact that, even in very small doses, these drugs will often produce visual effects that are something like hallucinations. Although many other drugs will, in large enough doses, also produce hallucinatory experiences, hallucinogens will do so in less than toxic doses.

HALLUCINOGENS. Many of the **hallucinogens** occur in natural forms such as mushrooms or other fungi. In this form, they share with other consciousness-altering drugs an ancient history. Mescaline, for example, occurs naturally in the peyote cactus, and there is evidence that it has been used for at least 8,000 years by Native Americans. In fact, the Native American Church still uses peyote in its religious sacraments.

In contrast, the story of **LSD,** the drug that triggered the current interest in the hallucinogens, begins in this century. In 1943, an American pharmacologist synthesized lysergic acid diethylamide (LSD), and after ingesting it, he reported experiencing "an uninterrupted stream of fantastic pictures and extraordinary shapes with an intense, kaleidoscopic play of colors." These effects led others to experiment with LSD as a means of altering normal consciousness. In the 1960s, the development of LSD as a street drug was prompted in large part by Timothy Leary, a Harvard psychologist who, after trying the chemically related drug psilocybin, underwent a kind of religious experience and, along with his colleague Richard Alpert, proclaimed a new religion. His message—"Turn On, Tune In, and Drop Out"—became the byword of the hippie movement in the 1960s. LSD continues to be widely sampled, but regular use has waned since its peak in the 1960s and early 1970s.

Studying the consciousness-altering effects of the hallucinogens is particularly difficult. As is true for other drugs, setting, mood, and expectations have a profound effect on the reactions to these drugs. But unlike cocaine and the opiates, which produce "rushes," the effects of most hallucinogens are more subtle, and their onset is often delayed for an hour or more. After taking LSD, subjects sometimes find researchers' questions hilarious or irrelevant, while at other times they either refuse to answer them or are unable to do so (NCMDA, 1973a). And of course there is the added difficulty of trying to measure subtle changes in perceptual experiences. Siegel (1977) solved some of these problems by training his subjects to use a code to classify their subjective impressions

Hallucinogens Any of a number of drugs, such as LSD and mescaline, that distort visual and auditory perception.

LSD (lysergic acid diethylamide) Hallucinogen or "psychedelic" drug that produces hallucinations and delusions similar to those occurring in a psychotic state.

of a series of color slides when not under the influence of LSD. After they were well trained in the use of the code, they were administered LSD or a placebo and their responses were again recorded and classified. During the testing, neither the subjects nor the experimenters know whether the drug or placebo had been administered. With the placebo, subjects reported mostly black and violet forms. But under LSD, they reported stronger colors such as orange, red, and yellow. LSD also produced perceptions of "violent" movement. Furthermore, the subjects taking LSD had the subjective experience of actually entering into and becoming part of the scene at which they were looking. At higher doses, the figures lost their geometric qualities and began to take on the shape of meaningful objects that would change rapidly like motion pictures.

In addition to its visual effects, LSD also changes auditory perception in a variety of ways. Some people report hearing imaginary conversations, fully orchestrated original symphonies, or foreign languages previously unknown to them. Auditory acuity may be increased, making the person keenly aware of low sounds like breathing, heartbeats, or the light rustle of leaves in the wind.

In addition to these perceptual experiences, many people, like Leary and Alpert, attach great significance to their experiences with LSD. The writers Humphrey Osmond and Aldous Huxley coined the term "psychedelic" to describe this aspect of the LSD experience; *psychedelic* means "mind manifesting" or "mind expanding" (Osmond, 1957). One account of such an experience comes from R. Gordon Wasson, who described the experience as permitting him "to see more clearly than our perishing mortal eyes can see, to see vistas beyond the horizons of this life, to travel backwards and forwards in time, to enter other planes of existence, even . . . to know God" (Wasson, 1972). In addition to these effects, some users report powerful insights into their own lives, somewhat akin to the experiences of those undergoing psychotherapy (McKim, 1986). In describing such an experience, Osmond reported:

> "I cried . . . for all the people around me that I botched in the giving or to whom I cannot give because I am depleted. . . . I expressed great hostility toward both my parents and . . . analyzed my feelings as they derived from my relationship with each of them" (Aaronson & Osmond, 1970).

The negative effects of LSD and the other hallucinogens are somewhat different from those of the drugs that we have discussed so far. For example, there appear to be no withdrawal effects from the use of hallucinogens. On the other hand, tolerance can build up quite rapidly: if LSD is taken repeatedly, after a few days no amount of the drug will produce its effects until administration is halted for about a week (McKim, 1986). This rapid development of tolerance is a built-in deterrent to continuous use—a fact that helps to explain why in most cultures LSD is taken episodically rather than habitually. After a time, users seem to get tired of the experience and decrease or discontinue its use, at least for a period of time.

Other negative effects of some hallucinogens include "bad trips," which are unpleasant experiences caused by a change in dosage or a change in setting or mood. During a bad trip, the drug user may not realize that the experiences are being caused by the drug, and panic may set in. The treatment for this involves "talking down" the user by reminding him or her that it is the drug that is causing the "bad trip" and by providing an atmosphere of support and relaxation. More serious are the stories of users who kill themselves by thinking they can fly out of a window or who commit murders while they are under the influence of the drug. In rare cases, some users have developed enduring mental illnesses from repeated use of hallucinogens—apparently because the drug triggers a powerful emotional response that in turn sets off a preexisting tendency toward psychotic behavior.

Marijuana Plant containing a mild hallucinogen and producing a "high" often characterized by feelings of euphoria, a sense of well-being, and swings in mood from gaiety to relaxation.

MARIJUANA. **Marijuana,** *Cannabis,* was cultivated as long as 5,000 years ago in China. There are reports of its use in the Bible, and the ancient Greeks were also aware of its existence. It has also been used in India for centuries because of its intoxicating effects, although it is only in this century that a similar use of marijuana has been made in the United States. During the 1920s, the use of marijuana spread and created great alarm, as reflected in the film *Reefer Madness,* which proclaimed that the drug could seduce innocent youth into violence and madness. By the end of the 1930s, the drug had all but dropped out of sight. Nevertheless, the use of marijuana underwent a revival in the 1960s, and there are currently an estimated 50 million Americans who have tried marijuana at least once.

Although the active ingredient in marijuana, tetrahydrocannabinol (THC), shares some chemical properties with hallucinogens like LSD, it is far less potent and affects consciousness far less profoundly. In fact, first-time users often report that they feel none of the effects. It often takes several trips to notice the subtle effects. And the effects of marijuana are particularly sensitive to the user's mood and the setting in which the drug is taken. The marijuana "high" is often marked by euphoric feelings and a sense of well-being accompanied by swings from gaiety to relaxation. On the other hand, there may also be feelings of anxiety and paranoia. Which of these effects occurs depends in large part on the mood of others in the setting and on whether they are also using marijuana.

Many users also report an increased sensitivity to sights and sounds, although objective measures usually fail to confirm these changes (Jones, 1978). On the other hand, the time-distorting effect of marijuana has been confirmed under experimental conditions. In addition, marijuana can produce alterations in attention and memory. The "high" is characterized by an inability to maintain attention on many types of tasks, and this fact contributes to concern about a person's ability to drive a car after using marijuana (DeLong & Levy, 1974). The effects on short-term memory are marked by an inability to retain information for later use. Weil and Zinberg (1969) reported that it is not unusual for a person to begin a sentence and then forget what he or she was talking about before the sentence is completed. There have also been reports that marijuana stimulates creativity, but research data have not confirmed this impression (Grinspoon, 1977).

With regard to tolerance, there is actually evidence of *reverse* tolerance in humans. Some users report that they need less of the drug to get high as they become more experienced. This phenomenon, however, may be related to the fact that experienced users become more adept at inhaling the drug and learn to perceive its effects more quickly. In mod-

Marijuana (*Cannabis*) It is by the pointed, serrated leaves that marijuana can be recognized.

erate regular usage, the drug retains its subjective potency from day to day. There are also some reports of withdrawal effects, such as restlessness, irritability, and insomnia (Jones & Benowitz, 1976), but these effects appear to be associated with the continuous use of extremely high doses.

The negative physical effects of marijuana seem to be chiefly those that ensue from the smoking of any substance: potential respiratory and cardiovascular damage. However, there are also some reports of "apathy, loss of effectiveness, and diminished capacity to carry out complex, long-term plans, endure frustration, concentrate for long periods, follow routines, or successfully master new material" (McGlothlin & West, 1968). It is difficult to determine whether these reports describe changes produced by marijuana in normal people, or whether people who are predisposed toward apathy are just more likely to select and use marijuana for a long

Table 4–1

Adapted from Sarason and Sarason, 1987

TABLE 4.1 DRUGS: CHARACTERISTICS AND EFFECTS

	Typical Effects	Effects of Overdose	Tolerance/Dependence
Depressants			
Alcohol	Tension reduction "high", followed by depressed physical and psychological functioning	Disorientation, loss of consciousness, death at extremely high blood-alcohol levels	Tolerance; physical and psychological dependence; withdrawal symptoms
Barbiturates Tranquilizers	Depressed reflexes and impaired motor functioning, tension reduction	Shallow respiration, clammy skin, dilated pupils, weak and rapid pulse, coma, possible death	Tolerance; high psychological and physical dependence on barbiturates, low to moderate physical dependence on such tranquilizers as Valium, although high psychological dependence; withdrawal symptoms
Opiates			
Opium Morphine Heroin	Euphoria, drowsiness, "rush" of pleasure, little impairment of psychological functions	Slow, shallow breathing, clammy skin, nausea, vomiting, pinpoint pupils, convulsions, coma, possible death	High tolerance; physical and psychological dependence; severe withdrawal symptoms
Stimulants			
Amphetamines Cocaine/Crack Caffeine Nicotine	Increased alertness, excitation, euphoria, increased pulse rate and blood pressure, sleeplessness	For amphetamine and cocaine: agitation, and with chronic high doses, hallucinations, paranoid delusions, convulsions, death For caffeine and nicotine: restlessness, insomnia, rambling thoughts, heart arrythmia, possible circulatory failure. For nicotine: increased blood pressure.	For amphetamine and cocaine: tolerance; psychological but probably not physical dependence For caffeine and nicotine: tolerance; physical and psychological dependence; withdrawal symptoms
Hallucinogens			
LSD PCP (dissociative anesthetic)	Illusions, hallucinations, distortions in time perception, loss of contact with reality	Psychotic reactions, particularly with PCP; possible death with PCP	No physical dependence for LSD, degree unknown for PCP; psychological dependence for PCP, degree unknown for LSD
Marijuana			
	Euphoria, relaxed inhibitions, increased appetite, possible disorientation	Fatigue, disoriented behavior, possible psychosis	Psychologial dependence

period of time. One study of 2,000 college users (Brill & Christie, 1974) found no difference in grade point average between users and nonusers, although the users were slightly more uncertain about their career goals. The observed differences were rather small, and the study did not determine whether marijuana use caused these differences or whether some other factor might have been at play. A laboratory study in which subjects could earn money for work showed no difference in effort between casual users and heavy users of marijuana (Mendleson et al., 1976).

Although marijuana by itself is neither totally harmless nor a "killer weed," many people have protested against its use because users may go on to sample more powerful and hazardous drugs. Studies do reveal, for example, that almost all heroin users used marijuana before their heroin addiction developed. But it does not follow that use of marijuana *led* to heroin addiction in these people. Moreover, very few marijuana users go on to use heroin. On the other hand, there may well be some indirect relationship between marijuana use and the subsequent development of a heroin habit in some people. It may be, for example, that people who are predisposed toward addictive drug behavior by using marijuana place themselves in settings that provide them with the opportunity to sample other drugs. It also may be that the personality characteristics of curiosity and risk taking that prompt a person to try marijuana, coupled with an inclination to try drugs as a way of altering consciousness, will increase the likelihood that they will use other drugs as well (McKim, 1986).

Marijuana smoking has the same negative physical effects attributable to smoking any substance—potential respiratory and cardiovascular damage.

 APPLICATION

Medical versus Legal Aspects of Drug Policy

The recent concern over the spread of the disease AIDS brings to light important conflicts regarding public policy and drug abuse. It is well documented that one of the prime routes for the transmission of the AIDS virus is the practice of sharing contaminated needles among intravenous drug users. This fact has prompted the recommendation by some authorities that drug addicts be provided with sterile needles in order to help prevent the spread of the disease. In this country, such proposals, although advanced seriously, have made little headway. Opponents object to the public condoning of any aspect of drug abuse, even though significant benefits may accrue to both non-drug users and society in general from the recommended policy. The concerns expressed by those opposed to "free needles" are reflected in some quarters by the banning in some states of any paraphernalia designed for illict drug use. In Massachusetts, for example, it is illegal to sell a pipe that is primarily designed for smoking hashish or marijuana.

At one extreme, the "wrongness" of drug abuse outweighs any considerations of a more tolerant public policy. Drug use is seen as a crime that should be punished. The preponderance of law enforcement efforts has traditionally been directed at the curtailment of supply by the apprehension of suppliers. Some law enforcement officials argue, however, that arresting even major suppliers will not check the supply of drugs as long as a huge public demand remains. This position has prompted the development of policy in urban centers like New York and Miami that involves the organization of drug "sweeps" concentrating on the apprehension of drug buyers and users. The idea is that demand for drugs may lessen if users develop a realistic fear of arrest and punishment.

Somewhat opposed to this is the notion, at least a century old, that drug abuse is a disease and should be treated as such. It makes no more sense, according to this point of view, to deprive a heroin addict of his drug than it would to deprive a diabetic of insulin. By maintaining heroin's status as an illegal drug, addicts are only encouraged to commit crimes in order to secure their supply. In Great Britain, addicts have long been able to receive heroin as a prescription drug. In addition to its value in crime prevention, the partisans of this policy argue that addicts, freed from having to devote their lives to the continual task of obtaining heroin, are able to concentrate on becoming productive members of socity. In the United States, the use of a substitute opiate, methadone, has the same aim of addiction control as would legal access to heroin.

These policies although they do have some social benefits, do not constitute a cure for addiction any more than insulin cures the underlying condition that causes diabetes. Midway between a purely punitive, legalistic approach and providing free access to drugs is the belief that although drug abuse is a disease, it is a treatable one. Programs like Synanon and Alcoholics Anonymous do not believe that substance abuse can be *cured*, but they argue that removing the abuser from negative influences and providing group support with peers can promote abstinence. Other treatment approaches include traditional psychotherapy and the use of antagonist drugs that block the effects of the abused drug. A British writer (Bewley, 1974) has commented that treating abuse as a medical problem removes the seductive aura of drug use: "Sickness is generally less attractive than sin."

Nevertheless, overall only about 10 percent of participants in drug treatment programs achieve control over their drug use. Furthermore, this is probably an overestimation of the numbers of users who become abstainers. Moreover, the already low cure rates do not reflect the drug abusers who are not motivated to seek treatment.

Given these sobering numbers, the debate over public policy continues. The legalistic group argues that even if drug abuse is a disease, treatment is ineffective and law enforcement remains the only viable option. However, those who still believe drug abuse to be a medical problem argue that the high failure rate of treatment is only one more reason to provide freer access to some drugs; they also argue that law enforcement is as ineffective at curbing society's appetite for drugs as is medical treatment. They propose that legalizing or decriminalizing certain drugs brings their use out into the open and prevents crime and self-destructive behavior. Law enforcement people reply that any free access to drugs runs the risk of their abuse by nonusers.

We have seen, of course, that drug abuse and its negative social and personal consequences are not confined to illegal drugs. To a great extent, historical and political circumstances determine, more than medical or social considerations, which drugs will be banned and which will be legal. Alcohol, whose negative consequences are possibly as great as those from the opiates and arguably greater than marijuana, was prohibited for more than a decade earlier this century. Prohibition did little to check usage but did much for the fortunes of organized crime. Some have noted that the legality of alcohol is related to the fact that users tend to include large numbers of white males—that is, the people who enact and enforce laws. Heroin, on the other hand, is a drug of the disenfranchised "under-class" and marijuana is a drug of the young—of those people who do not play an active role in the political process.

The conflicts over drug use and policy conspire to create contradictory patterns of policy and enforcement. These inconsistencies make it harder for the nonuser who is at risk to detect a clear societal attitude toward drug use. It is something of a platitude, but ironically true, that a child of social drinkers or perscription drug users will find it difficult to understand that he or she should avoid drugs whose only apparent negative quality is their illegality. In fact, illegality may only tempt certain people into drug usage.

■ Summary

- **What is consciousness? What purpose does it serve?** Psychologists divide the study of *consciousness* into two broad areas. *Waking consciousness* includes all the thoughts and feelings that occur when we are awake and alert. *Altered states of consciousness* are those when our mental state differs noticeably from our experience when we are awake, including such states as daydreaming, sleep and dreaming, hypnosis, meditation, and intoxication.

- Our waking consciousness is highly selective, and

we normally attend to only the most important information in our environment, filtering out almost everything else; in other words, the hallmark of normal waking consciousness is the highly selective nature of consciousness. However, many psychologists believe that there are important mental processes that go on in addition to waking consciousness that are highly influential on our behavior.

- **Is daydreaming undesirable? Why do we do it? *Daydreaming*** allows you to escape from the demands of the real world and be somewhere else for the moment. Daydreams vary with personality and may be a way of processing "unfinished business" that is made possible by a reduction of external stimuli. There appear to be three main patterns of daydreams. The first type reflects anxiety in the dreamer; the second reflects self-doubt and fear of failure; the third type reflects happier fantasies uncomplicated by guilt or anxiety.

- **How many hours of sleep do we need? Can going without sleep hurt you?** The function of *sleep* remains unclear, but it appears to be a necessity even though many psychological functions can be maintained during periods of sleep deprivation. Many scientists believe that sleep serves to restore the effectiveness of the brain and the body, but little evidence supports this idea directly. From the evolutionary perspective, sleep is an adaptive mechanism that encourages organisms to remain inactive when food supplies are low or predators numerous.

- There are four stages of sleep. Stage 1 lasts only a few minutes and is a borderline between true sleep and waking. Sleep becomes progressively deeper in Stages 2 and 3. Stage 4, delta sleep, is the deepest stage. After Stage 4, **REM** (rapid eye movement) sleep begins. The other stages of sleep are referred to as **NREM** (nonrapid eye movement) sleep. The sequence of sleep repeats itself four or five times per night, with Stage 2 taking up about half of total sleep time and REM about a quarter. The nightly pattern of sleep varies widely from person to person, with infants sleeping longer than adults and older adults sleeping less than younger adults. It does appear that a lack of sleep hinders creativity and problem solving.

- **Do dreams really reveal our unconscious desires? *Dreams*** occur in both REM and NREM sleep, but are more frequent and detailed in REM sleep. Dreams reshape and recreate material into new and often illogical forms and can be a source of creative ideas.

A dream may reflect the dreamer's unconscious wishes, needs, and conflicts, but whatever the ultimate explanation, dream content is related to a number of different factors. While you are closest to waking, your dreams are likely to be about recent events—and are the dreams that you are most likely to remember. During the middle of the night, however, your dreams are apt to involve childhood or past events. Dream content can be modified by pre-sleep events and may, to some extent, complement and compensate for waking experiences. Most dreams last about as long as the same events would last in real life, generally consisting of a sequential story or series of stories. Both internal and external stimuli can modify ongoing dreams but cannot initiate them.

- Sleep disorders include *insomnia*, which is normally related to stress and is temporary. Some people suffer from chronic insomnia that may have a basis in an overaroused biological system. Insomniacs may also develop cycles during which their anxiety about falling asleep further contributes to the problem. This disorder can be treated most effectively by methods that allay anxiety about sleeplessness and induce the ability to relax and avoid distractions. *Apnea* is a sleep disorder marked by breathing difficulties during sleep; hundreds of times a night, sufferers are spurred to a state of arousal just short of waking consciousness and, not surprisingly, are usually exhausted the next day. *Narcolepsy* is a sleep disorder characterized by sudden sleeping spells in the middle of daytime activity. It is believed to arise from a defect in the central nervous system that can be treated with medication.

- *Sensory deprivation* results from the radical reduction of sensory stimuli. It produces an altered state of consciousness that can lead to hallucinations, altered perceptions, dreams, daydreams, and fantasies. Research indicates that hearing, touch, sensitivity to pain, and taste become more acute after sensory deprivation, while other sensory capacities are either unaffected or reduced.

- *Meditation* can take many different forms. Successful meditation produces deep relaxation and may be useful in reducing drug use and other problems.

- **Is hypnosis safe? Does it really work?** Psychologists disagree about whether the trance induced by *hypnosis* is a true altered state. Some suggest that the variability of suggestibility can account for all the phenomena attributed to the hypnotic trance.

Nonetheless, hypnosis and suggestibility have been shown to alter some people's perception and behavior. Even though the therapeutic uses of hypnosis are not universal, hypnosis has been useful in a variety of medical situations, particularly as a powerful anesthetic. Another striking aspect of hypnosis is its ability to retrieve lost memories.

- The use of drugs to alter consciousness has a long history. The effect that any drug has on consciousness depends on set—the person's state of mind at the time the drug is taken—and setting—the physical, social, and emotional atmosphere in which the drug is taken.

- Scientific studies of drug effects often employ the *double-blind procedure*. In this type of study, neither the experimenters nor the subjects know whether they are receiving an active drug or an inactive *placebo*. After the data are collected, the researcher can compare the behavior of subjects who received the drug with that of those who received the placebo. Differences in behavior can then generally be attributed to the active ingredient in the drug.

- *Depressants* are chemicals that slow down behavior and thinking by either speeding up or slowing down nerve impulses. They include alcohol, barbiturates, and opiates.

- **Does getting drunk on the weekends mean a person is an alcoholic?** *Substance abuse* is characterized by (a) an inability to cut down or stop using the substance; (b) disturbed social relationships and/or functioning on the job; and (c) signs of disturbance, such as binge drinking, lasting at least one month.

- **What does it mean to be addicted to drugs or alcohol?** *Dependency*, or addiction, is even more serious. It is marked by an increased *tolerance* or need for more and more of the substance to achieve the effect and symptoms of physical or psychological *withdrawal* if the person tries to cut back or stop using the substance.

- *Alcohol* is a depressant which can lessen a person's normal inhibitions but which has a temporary stimulating effect. Alcohol impairs some kinds of perception. The behavior of people who have been drinking is influenced by ideas about how drinkers should act as well as by the alcohol itself. Since alcohol is the most commonly abused substance in our society, researchers are quite interested in the causes of alcoholism. Although it has been difficult to identify an "alcoholic personality," there is evidence that both cultural and biological factors are influential. While occasional nights of heavy drinking probably do not signal alcoholism, a consistent pattern of drinking binges that interfere with a person's personal relationships or job or school performance is frequently an indication of alcoholism and may lead to more continuous heavy drinking over time.

- *Barbiturates* are depressants that have the same potential as alcohol for creating physical and psychological dependence. They were first used primarily for their sedative and auticonvulsive effects, but their popularity declined when researchers became aware of their serious—and potentially deadly—side effects.

- *Opiates*, a class of depressants that includes heroin, induce subjective feelings of euphoria, well-being, and relaxation, but these effects are shortlived and give way to undesirable changes in mood and behavior. In addition, opiates are highly physically addictive. Users become tolerant to the drug and need larger doses to achieve the same effects after using it for a long period of time. Physiological withdrawal is characterized by painful physical and psychological symptoms.

- *Stimulants* produce feelings of optimism and boundless energy. They are highly reinforcing and have a strong potential for abuse. *Amphetamines* were originally developed for their stimulant properties and were also used as appetite suppressants. Although they can induce an initial "rush" of euphoria, a "crash"—sometimes accompanied by severe depression—may follow when their effects wear off.

- **What is crack? Why is it such a problem?** Another stimulant, *cocaine*, is becoming a predominant drug problem in our society, particularly when smoked as crack. As a stimulant of the sympathetic nervous system, cocaine increases the heartbeat, raises blood pressure, and constricts the blood vessels. It also produces a sense of euphoria. Users can develop strong dependency and tolerance. Compulsive use can cause loss of sleep, paranoia, and hallucinations. Because of all these factors and the expense of maintaining a crack or cocaine dependence, this drug has been the source of a tremendous rise in violent crime.

- The *hallucinogens* include *LSD,* mescaline, peyote, and psilocybin. They have a low dependence rate and rarely cause psychosis. Hallucinogens have profound effects on visual and auditory perception. Although there appear to be no withdrawal effects, tolerance can be built up quite rapidly.

- The most common hallucinogen, **marijuana**, does not appear to cause mental and physical deterioration if it is used moderately. Long-term use, however, may cause physical harm. Its effects include euphoria, a heightened sense of humor, impairment of short-term memory, heightened sensory sensitivity, increased visual imagery, and distortion of the sense of time. Moreover, there are the negative physical effects associated with the smoking of any substance: potential respiratory and cardiovascular damage.

■ Review Questions

1. We experience _____ consciousness when our mental state differs noticeably from that which we experience when we are awake and alert.
2. The hallmark of normal waking consciousness is highly selective _____ .
3. According to Freud, the real driving forces behind human actions are _____ instincts that are hidden but made conscious through such states as dreaming and hypnosis.
4. Psychologists have a clear understanding of the biological and psychological necessity for sleep. T/F
5. REM sleep is usually called _____ sleep because while such things as heart rate closely resemble waking consciousness, the sleeper's voluntary muscles appear to be paralyzed.
6. The increase in dreaming that occurs after the cessation of dream deprivation is known as ___ _____ .
7. Match the sleep disorder with the symptoms:
   ___ insomnia   A. excessive, unpredictable sleeping sessions
   ___ apnea   B. breathing difficulties and day-after exhaustion
   ___ narcolepsy   C. acute or chronic inability to sleep
8. Sensory deprivation results in a state in which most subjects cannot distinguish between dreams and waking _____ .
9. Despite its diverse forms, meditation reduces the activity of the _____ system.

10. Many psychologists feel that the effects of hypnosis can be accounted for by the variable of _____ .
11. Although alcohol is a _____ , it is experienced subjectively as a _____ .
12. _____ are commonly known as "downers."
13. The crystalline form of cocaine is known as:
    a. LSD   c. crack
    b. angel dust   d. opium
14. Match the following types of drugs with their descriptions:
    ___ alcohol   A. produces feelings of optimism and boundless energy
    ___ amphetamines   B. addictive drugs that dull the senses
    ___ barbiturates   C. effects vary with quantity consumed and manner and setting in which it is taken
    ___ opiates
    ___ cocaine   D. responsible for the most serious drug problem in the U.S. today
    ___ hallucinogens   E. causes profound effects on visual and auditory perception
                         F. depressants that affect memory and perception of time

(handwritten answers, left column)

1 - altered state.
~~2. experience of consciousness~~
~~2.~~
2 - attention
3 - sexual & aggressive
4 - F
5 - paradoxical
6 - REM Rebound
7 - C B A

(handwritten answers, right column)

8 - hallucinations
9 - sympathetic (nervous
10 - suggestibility
11 - depressant, stimulant
12 - Barbiturates
13 - C
14 -

(handwritten letters beside question 14 matches)
D alcohol
A amphetamines
F barbiturates
B opiates
C cocaine
E hallucinogens

5 Learning

■ Thinking Critically

You and your boyfriend or girlfriend have a favorite song. After you break up, you can't bear to listen to it. Why?

Can looking at a photograph taken from a very tall building help a person who is afraid of heights to overcome his or her fear?

Is promising yourself you can go to a movie after you've finished reading and reviewing this chapter likely to help you study in the future?

How can you train a tiger to jump through a flaming hoop?

How do we know to carry an umbrella when it looks like rain?

Why do some people eat when they are especially happy or sad?

Why do people gamble even though they lose more money than they win?

Why are migrant workers usually paid by the basket, bin, or bushel instead of by the week or hour?

Why do the children of violent people frequently become violent?

Answers to these and other questions about how we learn appear in this chapter and in the Chapter Summary.

■ Outline

As unlikely as it seems, the following situations have something in common:

• Upon completion of a training course at the National Zoo, the star students demonstrate their special behaviors: Junior, a young orangutan, cleans up his cage for the chance to blow on a whistle; a pair of 18-inch-long lizards jump 2 feet in the air to snatch insects from the tip of a forceps; a chinchilla weighs itself by hopping into a basket on top of a scale; and Peela the tiger retrieves a floating keg from the moat in his exhibition area.

• In the chronic schizophrenia ward of a mental hospital, patients who once had to be fed, cleaned, and clothed by caretakers now do their own laundry, eat meals together in a dining room, and wash and comb their own hair. The ward operates as a token economy: For performing tasks, patients earn tokens that will buy things like candy, soap, magazines, and trinkets.

• Joey, a city kid, goes away to summer camp for the first time. Being from the city, he hasn't done much in the way of boating, hiking, camping, and so on. But by the end of eight weeks at Camp Winnepesaka, Joey can row a canoe and sail a sunfish, pitch camp, and blaze a trail; he can even distinguish poison ivy from poison sumac and pick out constellations in the nighttime sky.

Although all these situations take place outside a school classroom, **learning** is nonetheless going on. Most people think of learning as "studying." But psychologists define it more broadly as the process by which experience or practice results in a relatively permanent change in behavior. This certainly covers classroom learning and studying, but it covers many other types of learning, too: learning to turn off lights when we leave a room; learning which way to put the key into a car ignition; learning how to avoid falling down on skis; learning how to dance.

Some kinds of learning are quite simple. Young children and even animals have little difficulty in learning to avoid a hot flame. On the other hand, learning some things, such as how to play the violin or how to calculate the volume of an irregular solid object, is difficult for many people and impossible for others.

Some of the simplest, most basic learning is called conditioning. **Conditioning** is a general term—used for animals as well as for human beings—that refers to the acquiring of fairly specific patterns of behaviors in the presence of well-defined stimuli. There are two main types of conditioning: classical and operant.

Our discussion begins with the first of these processes: classical conditioning. This simple kind of learning provides a convenient starting point for examining what the learning process is and how it can be observed.

▪ Classical Conditioning

Pavlov's Conditioning Experiments

Classical conditioning was discovered almost by accident by Ivan Pavlov (1849–1936), a Russian physiologist who was studying the digestive processes. Since animals salivate when food is placed in their mouths, Pavlov

Learning is the process by which experience or practice results in a relatively permanent change in behavior.

inserted tubes into the salivary glands of dogs in order to measure how much saliva they produced when they were given food. He noticed, however, that the dogs salivated before the food was in their mouths: The mere sight of food made them drool. In fact, they even drooled at the sound of the experimenter's footsteps. This aroused Pavlov's curiosity. What was making the dogs salivate even before they had the food in their mouths? How had they learned to salivate in response to the sound of the experimenter's approach?

In order to answer these questions, Pavlov set out to teach the dogs to salivate when food was not present. He devised an experiment in which he sounded a bell just before the food was brought into the room. A ringing bell does not usually make a dog's mouth water, but after hearing the bell many times just before getting fed, Pavlov's dogs began to salivate as soon as the bell rang. It was as if they had learned that the bell signaled the appearance of food, and their mouths watered on cue even if no food followed. The dogs had been conditioned to salivate in response to a new stimulus, the bell, which would not normally have caused that response (Pavlov, 1927) (see Figure 5-1).

Generally speaking, **classical conditioning** involves learning to transfer a natural response from one stimulus to another, previously neutral stimulus. Pavlov's experiment illustrates the four basic elements of classical conditioning. The first is an **unconditioned stimulus (US),** like food, which invariably causes a certain reaction—salivation, in this case. That reaction—the **unconditioned response (UR)**—is the second element and always results from the unconditioned stimulus: Whenever the dog is given food (US), its mouth waters (UR). The third element is the neutral stimulus—in this case, the ringing of the bell—which is called the **conditioned stimulus (CS).** At first, the conditioned stimulus does not bring

Classical conditioning Type of learning in which an organism learns to transfer a response from one stimulus to another, previously neutral stimulus.

Unconditioned stimulus (US) Stimulus that invariably causes an organism to respond in a specific way.

Unconditioned response (UR) Response that takes place in an organism whenever an unconditioned stimulus occurs.

Conditioned stimulus (CS) Originally neutral stimulus that is paired with an unconditioned stimulus and eventually produces the desired response in an organism when presented alone.

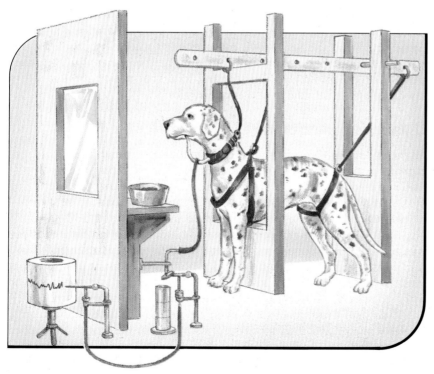

Figure 5-1
Pavlov's apparatus for classically conditioning a dog to salivate. The experimenter sits behind a one-way mirror and controls the presentation of the conditioned stimulus (bell) and the unconditioned stimulus (food). A tube runs from the dog's salivary glands to a vial, where the drops of saliva are collected as a way of measuring the strength of the dog's response.

Conditioned response (CR) Response an organism learns to produce when a conditioned stimulus is presented.

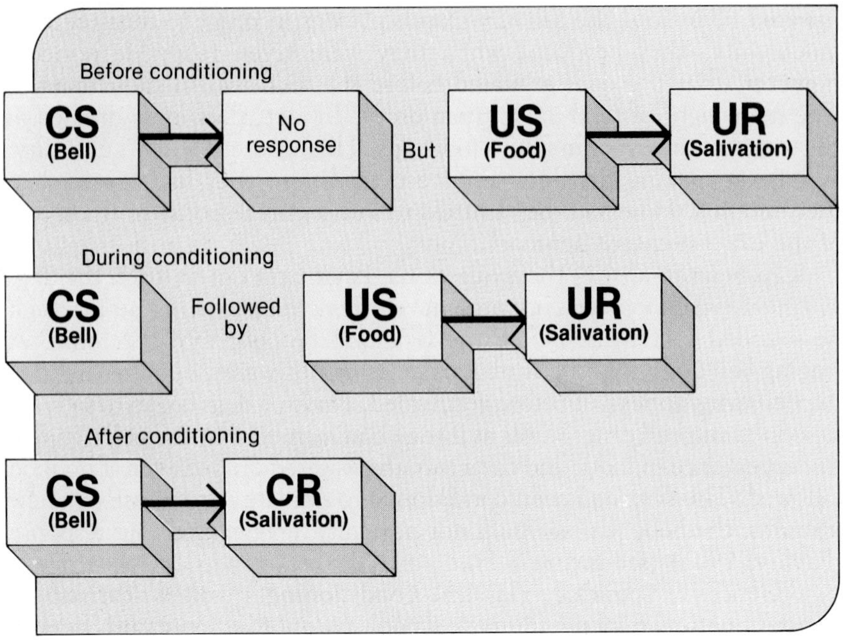

Figure 5-2
A paradigm of the classical conditioning process.

about the desired response. Dogs do not normally salivate at the sound of a bell—unless they have been conditioned to react in this way. Such a reaction is the fourth element in the classical conditioning process: the **conditioned response (CR).** The conditioned response is the behavior that the animal has learned to produce in response to the conditioned stimulus. Usually, the unconditioned response and the conditioned response—salivation, in our example—are basically the same (see Figure 5-2).

Without planning to do so, you may have conditioned your own pet in a way very similar to Pavlov's experiments. Many cats and dogs come running at the sound of a can opener or a certain cupboard door, rubbing around their owners' legs, looking in the dishes in which they are fed, or otherwise preparing for the food that they have learned to associate with particular sounds or activities.

Classical Conditioning in Human Beings

So far, we have been focusing on classical conditioning in animals, but humans respond to these same principles. For example, the sight of a menu, the sound of silverware being placed on the dinner table, the ring of the oven timer signaling that a favorite casserole is ready to be served—all of these can cause a hungry person to salivate.

You may also be subject to classical conditioning any time that you watch a television commercial or read a magazine advertisement. Consumer researchers have demonstrated that pairing pleasant or unpleasant music with pictures of a product can lead us to prefer that product even when competing products are otherwise basically the same (Gorn, 1982).

Classical conditioning can even be used to teach newborn infants. Babies who are only 5 to 10 days old can learn to blink their eyes when they hear a tone (Lipsitt, 1971). Babies blink naturally when a puff of air is blown in their eyes. The puff of air is an unconditioned stimulus.

Blinking—the babies' natural reaction—is an unconditioned response. If a tone—a conditioned stimulus—is sounded just before the puff of air is blown into their eyes, the babies soon begin to blink their eyes whenever they hear the tone. By blinking as soon as they hear the tone, the babies are producing a conditioned response.

Classical conditioning can also result in some strange kinds of learning. For example, one group of experimenters conditioned a group of asthma sufferers to react to substances that had not previously affected them. They first exposed the asthmatics to something to which they were allergic, like dust or pollen—an unconditioned stimulus. Of course, the dust or pollen caused an attack of asthma (an unconditioned response). Then the experimenters presented a neutral substance (a conditioned stimulus). Initially, the asthmatics had no reaction to this neutral substance. But when the neutral substance was repeatedly followed by dust or pollen, the asthma sufferers began to wheeze and sniffle as soon as the neutral substance was presented. These attacks were conditioned responses: The subjects had to *learn* to react in this way. In one study, even a picture of the conditioned stimulus could trigger an attack of asthma (Dekker, Pelser, & Groen, 1957). This study and others like it help to explain why asthma attacks are sometimes brought on by such seemingly neutral events as hearing the national anthem, seeing a waterfall, or listening to a political speech!

One of the best-known examples of classical conditioning in humans is the case of John Watson's experiment with an 11-month-old boy (Watson & Rayner, 1920). The experimenters started by showing Albert a white rat. At first, the child displayed no fear. He crawled toward the rat and wanted to play with it. But every time he approached the rat, the experimenters made a loud noise by striking a steel bar. Since nearly all children are afraid of loud noises, Albert's natural reaction was fear. After just a few times, Albert began to cry and crawl away whenever he saw the rat. This is a simple case of classical conditioning. An unconditioned stimulus—the loud noise—caused the unconditioned response of fear. Next, Albert learned to associate the loud noise with the rat, so that the rat (conditioned stimulus) then caused him to be afraid (conditioned response).

Several years later, psychologist Mary Cover Jones demonstrated a method by which children's fears can be unlearned using classical conditioning (Jones, 1924). Her subject was a three-year-old boy who, like Albert, had a fear of white rats. Jones paired the sight of a rat with a pleasant experience—eating candy. While Peter sat alone in a room, a caged white rat was brought in and placed far enough away so that he would not be frightened. At this point, Peter was given plenty of candy to eat. On each successive day of the experiment, the cage was moved closer and was followed by candy, until eventually Peter was not afraid of the rat. In this case, eating candy (US) elicited a pleasant response (UR). By pairing the candy with the sight of the rat (CS), Jones was able to teach Peter to respond with pleasure (CR) when the rat was present.

Many years later, psychiatrist Joseph Wolpe adapted Jones's method to the treatment of certain kinds of anxiety (Wolpe, 1973, 1982). Wolpe reasoned that since irrational fears and anxieties are learned or conditioned, it should also be possible to unlearn them through conditioning.

Desensitization therapy Conditioning technique designed to gradually reduce anxiety about a particular object or situation.

He noted that it is not possible to be both fearful and relaxed at the same time; therefore, if people could be taught to relax in fearful or anxious situations, their anxiety should disappear. His **desensitization therapy** begins by teaching the person a system of deep-muscle relaxation techniques. Then the therapist helps the person construct a list of situations that create various degrees of fear or anxiety. These situations are then rated on a scale from zero (the person would feel absolutely calm and relaxed) to 100 (the person would be terrified). For example, a person who is afraid of heights might rate "standing on top of the Empire State Building" near the top of the scale, while "standing on the first rung of a ladder" might be rated near the bottom. Then the person enters a state of deep relaxation during which he or she imagines the least distressing situation on the list. When the person succeeds in remaining relaxed

Who's Afraid of the Big Bad Wolf?

One very interesting phenomenon in human learning is the formation of *phobias*. Phobias are irrational fears of particular things, activities, or situations. People have had their lives disrupted by fears of high places (acrophobia), closed places (claustrophobia), cats, spiders, snakes, and busy public places (agoraphobia), among others. Many of us are fearful of a visit to the dentist or of making a speech, but in some people these situations can provoke a major panic attack in which the sufferer is unable to catch his or her breath, sweats profusely or shakes from an uncontrollable chill, and even has convulsions and passes out.

Sigmund Freud explained phobias in terms of unresolved inner conflicts in which the phobic object (the thing that is feared) represents some other problem or situation that troubles the patient. They may also be learned through observational learning (Cook, Mineka, Wolkenstein, & Laitsch, 1985). A different explanation has been suggested by Wolpe and Rachman (1960), who see phobias simply as a case of classical conditioning: An object comes to be feared after being linked with a frightening stimulus. Although phobias can be classically conditioned in this way, in other respects they do not follow most rules of classical conditioning.

In the first place, phobias are not affected by standard extinction procedures. For example, a woman has developed a fear of dogs because of one frightening experience in the past. According to traditional learning theory, each time she sees a dog and nothing frightening happens, her fear of dogs should decrease. But this does not happen. Her fear may become stronger each time she sees a dog or even thinks about dogs.

Furthermore, phobias, like food aversions, can sometimes be learned in one trial, which is not the case with typical

Many people are nervous about flying but for some the fear is so great that it prevents them from traveling by air. This person is part of a class designed to help her overcome her fear of flying.

laboratory fear conditioning. Moreover, the range of stimulus objects that result in phobic fear is limited. Classical conditioning theory would lead us to expect that any object could become a source of a phobia if it were paired with a stimulus that arouses fear and anxiety. But this is not true for most phobias. "Only rarely, if ever, do we have pajama phobias, grass phobias, electric-outlet phobias, hammer phobias, even though these things are likely to be associated with trauma in our world" (Seligman, 1972, p. 455).

Seligman suggests that all these nonconformities can be explained by the concept of *preparedness*. All the common objects of phobia—heights, snakes, cats, the dark, and so on—represent "events related to the survival of the human species through the long course of evolution" (p. 455). Thus, humans may be prepared to develop phobias about these things.

while imagining that situation, he or she progresses to the next one, and so on until the person experiences no anxiety even when imagining the most frightening situation on the list. We will discuss desensitization therapy in greater detail in Chapter 15, but for the moment, it is sufficient for you to realize that it is just one way in which classical conditioning can be used to change human behavior.

Necessary Factors in Classical Conditioning

We have seen that classical conditioning can occur quite easily, but it is not automatic. Learning does not occur unless certain requirements are met. The more carefully all these factors are controlled, the more likely it is that learning will take place. For example, the conditioned stimulus must be sufficiently strong and distinctive for the subject to perceive it easily. Another factor that significantly affects the success of the learning process is the order in which the conditioned stimulus and the unconditioned stimulus are presented. The most effective method is the one used in all of the experiments that we have described: presenting the conditioned stimulus just before the unconditioned stimulus. Remember that Pavlov rang his bell just before he gave the dogs their food. Presenting the conditioned stimulus and the unconditioned stimulus together is usually less effective. If the bell had rung at the same time that the dogs had gotten their food, they probably would not have salivated later at the bell alone. *Backward conditioning*—presenting the unconditioned stimulus before the conditioned stimulus—seldom results in effective learning. It would have been very difficult for Pavlov's dogs to learn to salivate when they heard a bell if they had already received their food before the bell rang.

The amount of time between the occurrence of the conditioned stimulus and the unconditioned stimulus is also critical to the success of learning. If this time-lapse—called the **interstimulus interval**—is either too short or too long, it will impair learning. The most effective interstimulus interval is usually somewhere between a fraction of a second and a few seconds, depending on which animal is being conditioned and what it is supposed to learn. Pavlov found that if the interval between the sounding of the bell and the presentation of the food was too long, the dogs would not learn. Moreover, one trial is usually not enough for any significant learning to occur. Most classical conditioning requires repeated trials to build up the learned association between the conditioned stimulus, like Pavlov's bell, and the unconditioned stimulus, like food. Pavlov had to pair the bell with the food several times before the bell alone would cause a dog's mouth to water.

Conditioning is usually cumulative. Each trial builds on the learner's previous experience. This does not mean that learning will increase indefinitely or by an equal amount on each successive trial. At first the strength of the conditioned response—one way of measuring the effectiveness of classical conditioning—increases greatly each time the conditioned stimulus and the unconditioned stimulus are paired. Learning eventually reaches a point of diminishing returns: The amount of each increase gradually becomes smaller until finally no further learning occurs and the response continues at the same strength on subsequent trials.

Where learning does take more than one trial, the *spacing* of trials

Interstimulus interval Time lapse between the presentation of the conditioned stimulus and the unconditioned stimulus.

is as important as their number. If the trials follow each other rapidly, or if they are very far apart, the subject may need many trials to achieve the expected response strength. If the trials are spaced evenly, neither too far apart nor too close together, learning will take fewer total pairings of the CS and US. Care must also be taken that the learner is rarely exposed during learning to the CS or US alone. The irregular pairing of the CS and US is called **intermittent pairing,** and it reduces both the rate of learning and the final level of learning achieved.

Classical conditioning generally requires a short interval between presentation of the conditioned stimulus and the unconditioned stimulus and more than one occasion on which the two are paired. An interesting exception to these principles is **conditioned food aversion.** It rarely takes an animal two occasions of being poisoned to learn not to eat a particular food. This phenomenon was discovered by accident by John Garcia in the midst of experiments on the effects of exposure to radiation (Garcia et al., 1956). Garcia was exposing rats in a special chamber to high doses of radiation that made them sick. He noticed that the rats were drinking less and less water when in the radiation chamber, although they drank normally in their "home" cages. Garcia realized that the water bottles in the radiation chamber were plastic, perhaps giving the water a different taste from the water offered in glass bottles in the home cages. Garcia theorized that the taste of the water from the plastic bottles had served as a conditioned stimulus that the rats associated with becoming ill, so that they learned to avoid the plastic-tasting water.

This hypothesis has since been tested in a number of animals by Garcia as well as a number of other researchers, and a great deal has been learned about this phenomenon (Braveman & Bronstein, 1985). We now know, for example, not only that conditioned food aversion can take place after only one bad experience, but also that the interval between eating the food (the CS) and falling ill (the US) can be quite long—up to 12 hours among rats. In one experiment, after rats experienced a single pairing of salty water (CS) with illness (US) induced by drugs, they avoided salty water for more than a month (Garcia, Hankins, & Rusiniak, 1974). Another unusual feature of food aversion is that an animal that has been poisoned learns to avoid only the food it ate but not any of the other stimuli that were present while it was eating, such as the room in which it ate the food or the container in which the food was kept (Dickinson & Mackintosh, 1978). In fact, if the animal eats both familiar and novel foods before it becomes ill, it subsequently avoids only the novel foods!

The research on food aversion suggests that some behaviors can be learned by classical conditioning much faster than others. Taste-illness combinations may produce rapid learning because they increase an organism's chances of survival. Garcia believes that evolution plays a part in the rat's ability to learn quickly what foods to avoid. Over thousands of generations, rats have evolved a nervous system that helps them remember taste-illness combinations (Garcia & Koelling, 1966). Clearly, this is an advantage to a scavenger like the rat, which comes into contact with potentially toxic foods quite often.

One interesting application of this research is the use of conditioned food aversion to stop coyotes from preying on ranch sheep in the western United States. Sheep carcasses were laced with a drug that induces nausea and vomiting and left at the edges of ranch areas. Coyotes that ate the poisoned meat and became ill appeared to avoid attacking sheep (Gustavson & Gustavson, 1985). However, not all the studies of this method have had the same results, and it remains quite controversial.

Of course, the learning of food aversions is not limited to lower animals—people have been found to develop aversions based on a variety of cues, including taste, appearance, and smell. For example, if we become ill several hours after trying a new dressing on our regular salad, we are apt to develop a strong aversion to that dressing, no matter how much we enjoyed it. One study found that over half the college students surveyed had at least one taste aversion (Logue, Ophir, & Strauss, 1981). The conditioned food aversion response is so ingrained that even when food is not the cause of illness we are still likely to form an aversion. One psychologist described a dinner party at which he and several other guests all picked up an intestinal virus that left many of them with an aversion to tarragon chicken (the main dish) or any food with tarragon spicing (Mazur, 1986). Even though they knew that the tarragon chicken was not the source of their illness they were unable to overcome the powerful conditioned response.

Extinction and Spontaneous Recovery

Let's go back to Pavlov's dogs. What happens when the dog has learned to salivate upon hearing a bell, but after hearing the bell repeatedly fails to get food? The dog's response to the bell—the amount of salivation—will gradually decrease until eventually the dog will no longer salivate when it hears the bell. This process is known as **extinction.** If the conditioned stimulus (the bell) appears alone so often that the learner no longer associates it with the unconditioned stimulus (the food) and stops making the conditioned response (salivation), extinction has taken place.

Once a response has been extinguished, is the learning gone forever? Pavlov trained his dogs to salivate when they heard a bell, then caused the learning to extinguish. A few days later, the same dogs were again taken to the laboratory. As soon as they heard the bell, their mouths began to water. The response that had been learned and then extinguished reappeared on its own, with no retraining. This phenomenon is known as **spontaneous recovery.** The dogs' response was only about half as strong as it had been before extinction, but spontaneous recovery does indicate that learning is not permanently lost (see Figure 5-3).

Extinction Decrease in the strength or frequency of a learned response due to withholding of reinforcement (operant conditioning) or to failure to continue pairing the US and CS (classical conditioning).

Spontaneous recovery The reappearance of an extinguished response after the passage of time, without further training.

Figure 5-3
From point *A* to point *B*, the conditioned stimulus and the unconditioned stimulus were paired and learning continued to increase. From *B* to *C*, however, the conditioned stimulus was presented alone. By point *C*, the response had been extinguished. After a rest period from *C* to *D*, spontaneous recovery occurred—the learned response reappeared at about half the strength that it had at point *B*. When the conditioned stimulus was again presented alone, the response extinguished rapidly (point *E*).

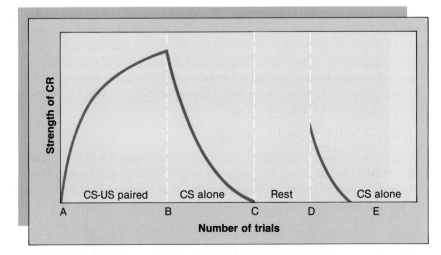

185

Stimulus generalization Transfer of a learned response to different but similar stimuli.

Stimulus discrimination Learning to respond to only one stimulus and inhibit the response to all other stimuli.

In order to understand spontaneous recovery, we have to take a closer look at what happens during extinction. Let us begin with a dog that has learned a particular response, like salivating when it hears a bell. If the bell is rung over and over again but is not followed by the appearance of food, the conditioned response becomes extinguished—the animal's mouth no longer waters when it hears the bell. We are not, however, simply teaching this learned behavior and then erasing it. Extinction is the result of new learning that works in the opposite direction from the original learning. When the animal will no longer produce the conditioned response, extinction is complete.

Generalization and Discrimination

Certain situations or objects may resemble one another enough so that the learner will react to one as he or she has learned to react to the other. Pavlov noticed that after his dogs had been conditioned to salivate when they heard a bell, their mouths would often water when they heard a buzzer or the ticking of a metronome. Their conditioned response had been generalized to other noises that sounded like the bell. Reacting to a stimulus that is similar to the one to which you have learned to react is called **stimulus generalization.**

Recall the case of Little Albert and his conditioned fear of white rats. When the experimenters later showed Albert a white rabbit, he cried and tried to crawl away. He had generalized his fear from the white rat to the similar stimulus of the white rabbit. In fact, his fear generalized to a number of white furry objects—cotton balls, a fur coat, and even a white Santa Claus mask.

Wolpe's desensitization therapy, mentioned earlier, provides another example of stimulus generalization. In the example that we used, while the person most fears great heights (such as standing at the top of a tall building), the fear response has generalized to a wide variety of more or less similar situations: flying in an airplane, standing on a ladder, perhaps even watching a circus high-wire performer. Even pictures taken from the tops of tall buildings may trigger fear, despite the fact that the person is sitting safely at home while looking at them.

It is also possible to train animals and people not to generalize, but rather to give a learned response only to a single specific object or event. This process is called **stimulus discrimination,** and in effect it is the reverse of generalization. When there are several objects, only one of which is followed by the unconditioned stimulus, the subject will learn over time to respond only to that stimulus and to inhibit the response in the presence of all other stimuli.

Learning to discriminate is very important in everyday life. As we noted earlier, most children fear loud noises. Since thunder cannot harm a child, however, it would be helpful if children learned not to be afraid every time they heard it. Not all mushrooms are good to eat, and not all strangers are unfriendly. Thus, discrimination is one of the most important parts of learning.

Higher-Order Conditioning

Once a subject has learned to give a conditioned response in the presence of a conditioned stimulus, it is possible to build on that learning in order to get new kinds of learning. For example, after Pavlov's dogs had learned to salivate when they heard a bell, Pavlov was able to use the bell (without food) to teach the dogs to salivate at the sight of a black square. Instead of showing them the square and following it with food, he showed them the square and followed it with the bell. The dogs eventually learned to salivate when they saw the square. The bell was used as an unconditioned stimulus and the black square was used as a conditioned stimulus. This procedure is known as **higher-order conditioning,** not because it is more complex or because it involves any new principles, but simply because it is learning based on previous learning.

A study by Marlin (1983) shows clearly how it is possible to use conditioning as a building block for further learning. Marlin taught a group of rats to fear being put in a particular cage by pairing a mild electric shock to their feet (the US) with placement in the experimental cage (CS). The conditioned response (CR) was fear. Once the fear response was well established, the electric shocks were stopped and a new stimulus (a tone) was introduced. After a few trials, the rats indicated that they had learned to fear the tone, even though it had never been paired with shock. Apparently, the learned fear of the experimental cage was the foundation of the new learning: fear of the tone.

Higher-order conditioning is difficult to achieve because it races against extinction. The dogs that learn to respond to a square are no longer getting any food. In fact, the square is a signal that the bell will *not* be followed by food, and so the dogs will soon stop salivating when they hear the bell. To avoid this problem, food must be given to the dogs once in a while at the sound of the bell, so that their mouths will continue to water when they hear the bell. Similarly, the rats in Marlin's study will soon learn that the tone is a signal that the shock will *not* be turned on, and their fear will decrease over time unless shock is occasionally reinstated.

Classical conditioning is now well accepted as at least one of the ways in which animals and people learn. Much of the current research into classical conditioning is aimed at tracing the physical changes that take place in the learner's nervous system during conditioning. Some of this research focuses on rats and lower animals, such as insects and mollusks, because of their simpler nervous systems. Some very sophisticated forms of learning—including higher-order conditioning, extinction and spontaneous recovery, and stimulus specificity and generalization—have been demonstrated in these simple animals and their neurobiological effects traced (Hawkins & Kandel, 1984). Other work with mammals such as rabbits has also focused on the changes in levels of certain neurotransmitters that appear to occur when learning is taking place (Thompson, 1986). However, classical conditioning is not the only way in which learning can occur, as we will see in the rest of this chapter.

Higher-order conditioning Conditioning based on previous learning; the conditioned stimulus is used as an unconditioned stimulus in further training.

■ Operant Conditioning

Classical conditioning is concerned with behavior that invariably follows a particular event: the salivation that automatically occurs when food is placed in the mouth; the blink of the eye that always results when a puff of air strikes the eye. In classical conditioning, we usually learn to transfer

Operant behavior Behavior designed to operate on the environment in a way that will gain something desired or avoid something unpleasant.

Operant or **instrumental conditioning** Type of learning in which the likelihood of a behavior is increased or decreased by the use of reinforcement or punishment.

Reinforce To present a stimulus that increases the probability that the preceding response will recur in the future.

this reaction to another stimulus that would not normally produce it: salivating at the sound of a bell, blinking to a tone. In a sense, classical conditioning is passive. The behavior is initially *elicited* by the unconditioned stimulus.

Most behavior, however, initially seems to be *emitted* rather than elicited; that is, most behavior is usually voluntary rather than inevitably triggered by outside events. Dogs do not usually wait passively to have food placed in their mouths—they beg at the dinner table. You wave your hand in a particular way to signal a taxi or bus to stop for you. Children pick up their toys either to avoid punishment or to gain some particular reward from their parents. These and similar actions can be classified as **operant behavior.** They are learned behaviors that are designed to *operate* on the environment in a way that will gain something desired or will avoid something unpleasant. This kind of learning is called **operant** (or **instrumental) conditioning.** Anyone who has ever trained a dog to do tricks such as sitting up, fetching, or rolling over knows that the best method of training is to reward the dog with a bit of food each time it gives the desired response. This is operant conditioning. You use the food to **reinforce** the correct behavior. Incorrect behavior may be either ignored (no reward) or punished (by a swat with a rolled-up newspaper, for example). This is the essence of operant conditioning: Correct responses are reinforced; incorrect responses are either ignored or punished.

Response Acquisition

We have said that classical conditioning deals with behavior that is initially a natural, automatic response. This implies that it is relatively easy to produce the desired responses. All Pavlov had to do when he wanted his dogs to salivate was to put food in their mouths. But operant behavior does not automatically follow from a stimulus. Thus, the first problem in operant conditioning is to make the desired response occur so that it can then be reinforced and learned.

One of the most common ways of getting the desired behavior is simply to wait for the subject to hit upon the correct response. The first time babies say "Mama" is by accident. But if their mothers smile and hug them, they will learn to repeat the sound. However, this can be a slow and tedious process: If you were an animal tamer for a circus, imagine how long you would have to wait for a tiger to decide to jump through a flaming hoop so that you could reward that behavior!

In the laboratory, there are several ways to speed up the process and make it more likely that the desired response will occur. One possibility is to increase motivation: A hungry laboratory rat is more active and thus more likely to give the response you are looking for than a well-fed rat. But imagine that you want the rat to learn to press a bar or lever in order to get food. A rat has a set of natural responses to hunger, but pressing a bar is not one of them. So until it learns to press the bar, you will have to see that the rat goes hungry.

One way to speed up the process of learning is to eliminate a large number of potential responses, thereby improving the chances that the correct response will occur. This can be done by restricting the environment and then allowing the subject to respond freely within these bounds.

Learning and the Birds and the Bees

Birds, bees, and other animals can learn about their environment in remarkable detail, but their genes seem to define rigidly when and how this learning takes place (Gould & Gould, 1981). In order to survive, honey bees must be able to record and recall the location of nectar-bearing blossoms and the location of the home hive. Thus, a bee must learn the sensory details of the two locations and landmarks in between. Many people have difficulty with such tasks, yet bees perform them easily and consistently. But bees, unlike many other organisms (including people), are greatly constrained in terms of when this learning can occur. For example, they can learn the location of their hive only when they first leave it in the morning. If the hive is moved at all after the first flight out, the returning bees become confused. Similarly, bees can learn the odor of a flower only when they are perched directly on it. Their remarkable learning abilities are inflexibly programmed by their genetic makeup to act only under certain very specific conditions.

Because genetic programming varies from species to species, animal species differ in terms of what and when they can learn. This is especially apparent in *imprinting*—extremely rapid learning that occurs only when a certain kind of stimulus is presented at a certain time (see Chapter 9). Newborn animals quickly learn to recognize their mother when they hear her make a call that triggers in them the response of following her. As they follow her around, they memorize certain traits of the mother that distinguish her from all other possible mothers. Despite variation, imprinting serves the same function for all species: Being able to recognize their mother greatly improves the chances for survival of the young.

These are all examples of *preparedness*: Each species is prepared or preprogrammed for certain types of learning that are important to its survival. We noted earlier that preparedness may play a role in the development of phobias and in conditioned taste aversions. One especially clear demonstration of preparedness is a study of food aversions in rats and quails (Wilcoxon, Dragoin, & Karl, 1971). The subjects were fed water that was flavored with salt, colored blue, and contained a chemical that would make the animals ill. Later, they were offered a choice between water just colored blue and water just flavored with salt. The rats chose the blue water and avoided the salty water; the quails did the reverse. The explanation seems to be that the rats had associated the *flavor* cue with their illness, while the birds had associated a *visual* cue. Actually, each species was doing its best to avoid the water that had made it ill. Knowing how rats and quail find their food in nature makes good sense of these findings. Rats are scavengers who may nibble at almost anything. If it tastes like something that made them sick before, they will not eat any more of it. Quail, on the other hand, find their food by sight and recognize visually the foods that have or have not been good for them before. Many insect species use this dependence of birds on visual cues to disguise themselves, either to blend into their backgrounds or to look like another species that is poisonous.

Preparedness shows up in other ways as well. For example, researchers have found that there is a definite limit to the new tricks that an old dog can learn (Rescorla & Holland, 1982). Keller and Marian Breland (1972), husband-and-wife psychologists, trained animals to perform in shows. They tried to condition a bantam chicken to stand still on a platform for 12 to 15 seconds as part of a complex stunt, but the chicken insisted on scratching until the Brelands gave up and billed it as a "dancing chicken." A raccoon was trained to insert a coin into a container for food but reverted to its natural "washing" response. It was content to rub the coins together and handle them and refused to give them up to the food dispenser.

In all these cases, we see remarkable differences between species in what behaviors they can learn and the circumstances under which learning will be effective. These species differences put significant constraints on both classical and operant conditioning.

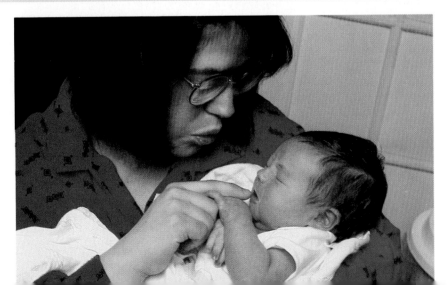

While early research supported the popular belief that immediately comforting a crying child served as a positive reinforcer of crying, more recent studies indicate that ignoring a child's crying may contribute to more crying.

One pioneer of operant conditioning used both of these techniques. Around the turn of the century, while Pavlov was busy with his dogs, Edward Lee Thorndike, an American psychologist and educator, was conducting experiments to determine how cats learn. His basic apparatus, which he called a "puzzle box," was a simple wooden cage, just big enough for a cat to move around in, but not big enough for the cat to feel comfortable (see Figure 5-4). The cats were kept hungry before each trial, and after a cat was in the box, a bit of food was placed just outside the cage, where the cat could see it and smell it. To get to the food, the cat had to open the latch on the cage door. Sometimes, this was a simple matter of stepping on a pedal on the floor or pushing on a rod in the middle of the cage; in other experiments, escape could be achieved only through a series of two or three actions. Cats don't generally like being confined in boxes, especially when they are hungry and food is available just outside. Like most cats in similar situations, Thorndike's cats tried to scratch or push their way out. The boxes were essentially bare, except for the latch mechanisms, so that the cats had few options for action other than working on the latches, and they generally discovered fairly quickly the action that led to reward (Thorndike, 1898).

Another laboratory device for speeding up operant conditioning is even better known and more widely used today: the **Skinner box,** named after B.F. Skinner, an American psychologist who developed many modern techniques and theories of operant conditioning. A Skinner box for rats is small, with solid walls, and bare except for a bar with a cup underneath it. In this simple environment, it doesn't take long for an active, hungry rat to happen to step on the bar, thereby releasing food pellets into the cup and thus reinforcing bar-pressing behavior (see Figure 5-5). The Skinner box for pigeons is also bare, and when the pigeon, exercising its natural food-finding behavior, pecks at a disk on the wall of the box, food is released into a cup.

The first time, that an operant response occurs and is reinforced is important, but it rarely produces strong learning. Thorndike carefully timed how long it took each cat to open the door to get food. On the

Figure 5-4

A cat in a Thorndike "puzzle box" The cat can escape and be rewarded with food by tripping the bolt on the door. As the graph shows, Thorndike's cats learned to make the necessary response more rapidly after an increasing number of trials.

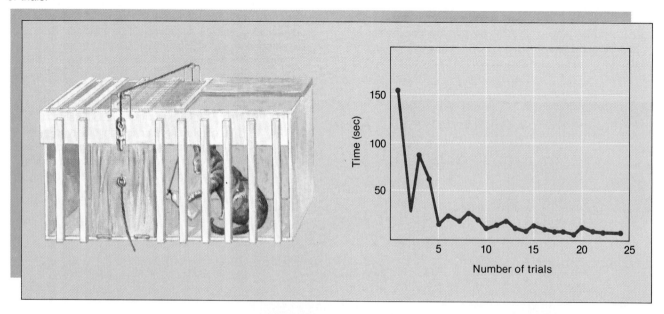

first trial, it took a while for the cat to open the door. After eating its meager reward, the cat was put back in the box and the timer started again. On the second trial, the cat would still thrash around a good bit before it managed to escape, but not as long as it had the first time. On each successive trial, the cat took less and less time, until finally it could escape from the box in almost no time at all (see Figure 5-5). Thus, operant conditioning is a gradual process: The strength of a desired response increases a bit every time that it is reinforced, and it takes a little less time to occur in the future.

Unfortunately, it is rarely possible to arrange the environment outside the laboratory so conveniently. And in some cases, as with the tiger and the flaming hoop, you would probably wait forever for the desired behavior to occur. In these situations, a very effective procedure for acquiring a new response is the reinforcement of *partial responses*—the small bits of behavior that make up the whole. Little by little, the complete response is shaped by successive approximations. This approach, called **shaping,** was used to teach a severely disturbed little boy named Dickey to wear his eyeglasses. Dickey, age six, had just had cataracts removed from his eyes, and his physicians feared that without the glasses his vision would deteriorate permanently. At the mere mention of eyeglasses, however, Dickey threw terrible temper tantrums. Researchers at the University of Washington tried a shaping procedure to ease him into the idea of wearing his glasses. Dickey was deprived of his breakfast so that food could be used as a reward for behavior in the right direction. Then an empty glasses frame was left in Dickey's room, and he received a bit of food each time he picked it up. Later in the procedure, he had to put the glasses on in order to receive a reward, and finally he had to keep the glasses on in order to be reinforced. Within 18 days, Dickey had learned through these gradual steps to wear his glasses for 12 hours a day (Wolf, Mees, & Risley, 1964).

Shaping is probably most familiar in the context of animal training. For instance, in order to teach a circus tiger to jump through a flaming hoop, the tiger might first be reinforced for jumping up on a certain

Shaping Reinforcing successive approximations to a desired behavior.

Figure 5-5
A rat in a Skinner box By pressing the bar, the rat releases food pellets into the box, reinforcing the bar-pressing behavior.

The first problem in operant conditioning is to make the desired response occur so that it can be reinforced and learned. The animal trainer uses *shaping,* reinforcing smaller bits of behavior, to teach animals complicated tricks.

pedestal, then for leaping from that pedestal to another. Next, the tiger might have to jump through a hoop between the pedestals in order to gain its reward. Finally, the hoop would be set afire and the tiger would have to leap through the burning hoop to be rewarded. Shaping has also been used in managing uncooperative zoo animals. At the National Zoological Park in Washington, D.C., a polar bear suffered from a broken tooth, and keepers needed a safe way of getting close enough to treat the problem. The bear was rewarded with food first for sticking its nose through a slot in the cage door, then for allowing a keeper to lift its lip and touch its teeth. Shortly thereafter, a veterinarian was able to treat the damaged tooth while the bear waited placidly for its familiar reward (Pryor, 1981).

Types of Reinforcement

We have seen that in operant conditioning, once the desired response occurs, we increase the likelihood that it will occur again by providing reinforcement. Thorndike's understanding of the importance of reinforcement is reflected in his **law of effect:** In a given stimulus situation, a response that consistently brings about a satisfying effect (reinforcement) will be "stamped in," and responses that bring about an annoying effect will be "stamped out." When presented with the stimuli of confinement and hunger, each cat tried out a variety of responses. When a response worked—when it allowed the cat to escape the puzzle box and eat—the connection or association between that response and the stimuli was strengthened, and the cat was more likely to try that response again in the presence of those stimuli. When a response didn't work (was not reinforced), the connection between that response and the stimuli was weakened, and the cat was less likely to try that response again.

Whenever something we do is followed closely by a reinforcer, we will tend to repeat the action—even if the reinforcement is not produced directly by what we have done. In one of Skinner's experiments (1948), a pigeon was placed in a cage that contained only a food hopper. There was nothing the bird could do directly to get food, but at random intervals Skinner dropped a few grains of food into the hopper. He found that the pigeon began to repeat whatever it had been doing just before it was given food: standing on one foot, hopping around, or strutting around with its neck stretched out. None of these actions had had anything to do with getting the food. It was pure coincidence that the food appeared when the bird was standing on one foot, for example. But that action would usually be repeated. Skinner called the bird's behavior "superstitious." It is possible that some human superstitions are learned in the

Shaping can also be used for some types of human learning. A gymnast's movements are developed and perfected through a series of successive approximations.

same way. If we happen to be wearing a particular piece of jewelry or carrying a rabbit's foot when we are reinforced, we may come to believe that our behavior caused the reinforcement. This phenomenon was illustrated in a laboratory study conducted by Catania and Cutts (1963) in which college students were asked to push one of two buttons when they saw a light. Reinforcement was given only when they pushed the right-hand button, but not every time they pushed this button. Virtually no subjects learned to push only the right-hand button. Instead, most of the students developed elaborate sequences of left/right button pushing that they later said were the "key" to getting reinforced!

POSITIVE AND NEGATIVE REINFORCEMENT. Psychologists distinguish between several kinds of reinforcers. One important distinction is between **positive** and **negative reinforcers.** Describing a reinforcer as "positive" simply means that it *adds* something rewarding to a situation, such as food or pleasant music. Negative reinforcement is effective because it *subtracts* something *un*pleasant from the situation; the reinforcement consists of *removing* the stimulus. You might find it helpful to use the plus symbol (+) to refer to a positive (+) reinforcer that adds (+) something rewarding to the environment and the minus sign (−) to refer to a negative (−) reinforcer that subtracts (−) something negative or unpleasant from the environment. Animals will learn to press bars and open doors not only to get food and water (positive reinforcement) but also to get away from electric shocks or loud noises (negative reinforcement).

Note that both positive and negative reinforcement result in the learning of new behaviors and the strengthening of existing behaviors. A child might practice the piano in order to receive praise (positive reinforcement) or to escape doing tedious homework for a while (negative reinforcement). A dog that learns to open the back door with its paws may be doing so either for the positive reinforcement of getting outside to play or for the negative reinforcement of getting away from the bothersome family cat. If a child is scolded for eating spaghetti with his fingers and the scolding stops when he picks up a fork and uses it, he is more likely to use a fork in the future. This is an example of a negative reinforcer, because reducing or terminating unpleasant events (such as punishment) increases the likelihood that behavior going on at the time will recur. And if at the same time you add positive reinforcement ("Good boy! That's the way grown-ups eat their spaghetti!"), the new behavior is even more likely to happen again in the future.

PRIMARY AND SECONDARY REINFORCEMENT. Another important distinction is between primary reinforcers and secondary reinforcers. A **primary reinforcer** is one that is rewarding in and of itself, without any association with other reinforcers. Food, water, and sex are primary reinforcers. A **secondary reinforcer** is one whose value must be learned through association with other reinforcers. It is referred to as secondary not because it is less important, but because it is learned. A rat learns to get food by pressing a bar; then a buzzer is sounded every time the rat presses the bar and gets food. Even if the rat stops getting the food, it will continue to press the bar just to hear the buzzer. Although the buzzer by itself has no value to the rat, it has become a secondary reinforcer.

Negative reinforcer Any event whose reduction or termination increases the likelihood that ongoing behavior will recur.

Positive reinforcer Any event whose presence increases the likelihood that ongoing behavior will recur.

Primary reinforcer Reinforcer that is rewarding in itself, such as food, water, and sex.

Secondary reinforcer Reinforcer whose value is learned through association with primary reinforcers.

Skinner found that the bird would repeat whatever action it had been doing just before food was dropped into the box—a form of *superstitious behavior.*

Money is a secondary reinforcer. Although money is just paper or metal, through its association with food, clothing, and other primary reinforcers, it becomes a powerful reward. Children come to value money only after they learn that it will buy such things as candy (a primary reinforcer). Then the money becomes a secondary reinforcer. Chimpanzees have learned to work for poker chips, which they insert into a vending machine to get a primary reinforcer, raisins. The poker chips have become secondary reinforcers for the chimps. Tokens have been used successfully as reinforcers for school children, prisoners, and chronic schizophrenics. For example, students can be rewarded for remaining quiet during study periods, or for paying attention, by being given a token, such as a poker chip, that can be collected and later exchanged for books or privileges (Packard, 1970). These *token economies* have proved especially effective in encouraging mental patients to improve their personal hygiene and to engage in more social interactions (Schaefer & Martin, 1966). We will discuss this approach to therapy in greater detail in Chapter 15.

DELAYED REINFORCEMENT. Finally, it is important to recognize that quite often there is an unavoidable delay between the time that the desired behavior occurs and the time that reinforcement is given. The length of this delay is important to the success of learning: The longer the interval, the less effective the reinforcement. In one study (Azzi et al., 1964), the experimenters varied the time interval between the moment when rats pressed a lever and the delivery of reinforcement. A delay of only a few seconds sharply reduced the rate at which the rats pressed the bar. Delayed reinforcement can affect choices we make, particularly those involving self-control (Mazur, 1986). A dieter may choose to eat a piece of cake because that primary reinforcer is much more immediate than the reinforcement of weight loss.

The reduced effectiveness of delayed reinforcement appears to be due to distracting events that interfere with the learning process (Wickelgren, 1977). By minimizing the distractions to which the learner is subjected between the behavior and the reinforcement, it is possible to delay reinforcement without decreasing learning too much. The same effect may be achieved with humans by repeatedly reminding the learner that the reinforcement is coming or by explaining why the person is being reinforced when it finally does arrive. This forms a connection between the learner's response and the delayed reinforcement that follows.

Some behaviors are so intrinsically reinforcing that there is no delay at all in reinforcement. For example, the stalking and sexual behaviors of animals are considered intrinsically reinforcing—that is, reinforcing all by themselves. As the behavior occurs, the animal is immediately rewarded by the behavior itself. As you might expect, such behaviors are very hard to eliminate.

Schedules of Reinforcement

Seldom, either in life or in the laboratory, are we rewarded every time we do something. And this is just as well, for *partial reinforcement*, in which rewards are given for some correct responses but not for every one, results in a behavior that will persist longer than one learned by continuous reinforcement. The program for choosing which responses to reinforce is called the **schedule of reinforcement.** Schedules can be either fixed

Would You Rather Have $100 Now or $120 Later? Choosing Between Reinforcers

In a Skinner box, an animal often has little choice about what operant behavior it can perform and what reinforcer it will receive. There may be only one response bar in the chamber, and pressing the bar may always produce the same type of reinforcer, a food pellet. In everyday life, however, people must often choose among different behaviors, and each behavior can lead to a different type of reinforcer. If on a Saturday night you stand in line to buy a ticket for a hockey game, this behavior will be followed by one type of reinforcer. If instead you drive to a party at a friend's house, this will be followed by other types of reinforcers. Sometimes our choices involve larger reinforcers. If you have worked long and hard to save enough money to buy a car, the possible reinforcers (different makes and models) are numerous indeed.

Both psychologists and economists have tried to understand how people behave when faced with choices like these. One theory that is popular among economists is *optimization theory*. Stated simply, this theory maintains that individuals will choose whatever behavior they think will optimize their satisfaction or happiness. This strategy certainly sounds sensible, and in many cases people do indeed make the optimal choice. Thus your selection of a car or of an activity for Saturday night will probably be based on your guess as to which choice will bring you the most satisfaction.

Nevertheless, some psychologists who study choice have come to the conclusion that optimization theory is not an accurate theory of human choice behavior (Herrnstein & Mazur, 1987). The problem is that people frequently make non-optimal choices when they ought to know better. One common situation in which people often fail to make the optimal choice is when they must choose between reinforcers that will be delivered at different times in the future. Suppose you have won a raffle, and as your prize you can choose either (1) $100 right now, or (2) $120 to be delivered in one week. Herrnstein and Mazur (1987) found that when given a hypothetical choice like this, many people choose the immediate $100. This choice is not necessarily non-optimal: Perhaps for these people, waiting an additional week is not worth the extra $20. But suppose the prize in a different raffle is either (1) $100 to be delivered in one year, or (2) $120 to be delivered in one year and one week. In this case, almost everyone chooses to wait the additional week for the extra $20, even those who would not wait the extra week in the first example. Yet if it is worth an additional week's wait to get the extra $20 in the second example, why is it not worth the wait in the first example? This inconsistency in choice behavior is difficult for optimization theory to explain.

Research with both people and animals has suggested that this type of non-optimal behavior is caused by a tendency to be overly influenced by immediate reinforcers (Ainslie,

Money is a secondary reinforcer; we learn to value it because of what it will buy.

1975). Consider a student who has an early morning class in a course where it is important to attend each lecture. The night before a class, the student decides that a good grade in the course (a delayed reinforcer) is much more important than an hour of extra sleep, and he sets his alarm accordingly. When the alarm rings on the following morning, however, the student changes his mind, now choosing the extra sleep over a good grade. The immediate reinforcer, extra sleep, now has greater control over his behavior than the delayed reinforcer, a good grade. The power of immediate reinforcers can be seen in many other situations, as when a person on a diet is confronted with a piece of chocolate cake, or when someone trying to save money sees an attractive item in a store window.

Psychologists have developed a variety of techniques that dieters, impulsive spenders, and those who tend to oversleep can use when trying to avoid the power of immediate reinforcers (Watson & Tharp, 1985). For example, a student with an early morning class can ask a classmate to stop by on the way to class, thereby making it awkward and embarrassing to stay in bed. An impulsive spender may be advised to carry no credit cards and very little cash, thereby making it more difficult to go on a spending spree. According to Herrnstein and Mazur (1987), the need for such techniques is in itself evidence that optimization theory is not an accurate theory of human behavior. If people naturally tended to make the optimal choice, they would have no need for techniques designed to help them avoid the temptation of an immediate reinforcer.

or varied and can be based either on the number of responses or on the elapsed time between responses. The most common reinforcement schedules are the fixed-interval and the variable-interval schedules, which are based on time, and the fixed-ratio and the variable-ratio schedules, which are based on the number of correct responses.

On a **fixed-interval schedule,** subjects are reinforced for the first correct response after a certain time has passed after the previous correct response: They learn to wait for a set period before responding. Subjects begin making responses shortly before the set amount of time has gone by, in anticipation of the reinforcement that is to come. For example, although a cake recipe may say, "Bake for 45 minutes," you will probably start checking to see if the cake is done shortly before the time is up. With fixed-interval schedules, performance tends to fall off immediately after the reinforcement, and tends to pick up again as the time for the next reinforcement draws near. On a fixed-interval schedule, a rat may have to wait at least five minutes after pressing a bar before the bar-press will again produce food. Usually, the rat will stop pressing the bar right after it gets its food, but will begin pressing it more frequently as the five-minute time limit approaches.

A **variable-interval schedule** reinforces correct responses after varying lengths of time. One reinforcement might be given after six minutes, the next after four minutes, the next after five minutes, the next after three minutes. Subjects learn to give a slow, steady pattern of responses, being careful not to be so slow as to miss all the rewards. When exams are given at fixed intervals—like midterms and finals—students tend to increase their studying just before an exam; studying then decreases sharply right after the exam until shortly before the next one. On the other hand, if several exams are given during a semester at unpredictable intervals, students have to keep studying at a steady rate all the time, because on any given day there might be an exam (see Figure 5-6).

Figure 5-6
Response patterns to schedules of reinforcement On a *fixed-interval* schedule, the number of responses increases and the slope becomes steeper as the time for reinforcement approaches. On a *variable-interval* schedule, the response rate is relatively constant. The *fixed-ratio* schedule is characterized by a high rate of response and a moderate pause after each reinforcement. On a *variable-ratio* schedule, there is a high rate of response with a slight pause after each reinforcement.

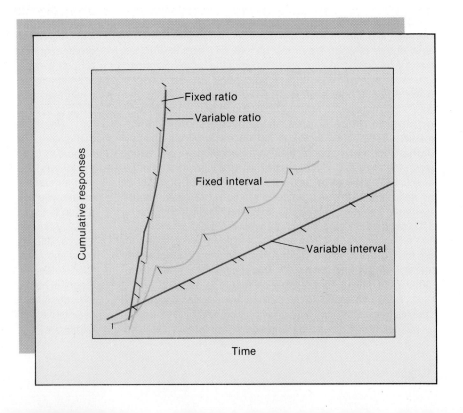

A fixed-ratio schedule—such as being paid on a piecework basis—usually results in a high response rate. There is incentive to make many responses in a short time in order to get more rewards.

On a **fixed-ratio schedule,** a certain number of responses must occur before reinforcement is presented. This results in a high response rate because it is advantageous to make many responses in a short time in order to get more rewards. Being paid on a piecework basis is an example of a fixed-ratio schedule. A migrant worker might get $3 for every 10 baskets of cherries he picks. The more he picks, the more money he makes. A fixed-ratio schedule results in a pause after reinforcement is received, then a rapid and steady response rate until the next reinforcement.

On a **variable-ratio schedule,** the number of responses necessary to gain reinforcement is not constant. The slot machine is a good example of a variable-ratio schedule. It may pay off, but you have no idea when. Since there is always a chance of hitting the jackpot, the temptation to keep playing is great. Subjects on a variable-ratio schedule tend not to pause after reinforcement and have a high rate of response over a long period of time. Since they never know when reinforcement may come, they keep on trying.

Aversive Control

Up to this point, we have concentrated on the effect of reinforcers on behavior. A reinforcer can be anything that increases the likelihood that a response will be repeated when it is presented after the response. Praise, food, money, a smile—all are positive reinforcers for most of us. If they follow some behavior, we are more likely to behave that way in the future.

But behavior can also be controlled by **punishment.** For most of us, receiving a fine for speeding or littering reduces the likelihood that we will speed or litter in the future. Being rudely turned down when we ask someone for a favor makes it less likely that we will ask that person for a favor again. In all these cases, the unpleasant aftereffect makes it less likely that we will repeat our behavior.

It seems obvious, therefore, that punishment works. But we can

Because the reinforcement is unpredictable, a *variable-ratio schedule* tends to yield a very high rate of response. This is the attraction of slot machines and lotteries. Since there is always a chance of hitting the jackpot, the temptation to keep playing is great.

think of situations where it does not work. Children often continue to misbehave even after they have been punished repeatedly. Some drivers continue to drive recklessly despite repeated fines. The family dog continues to sleep on the couch at night despite being punished for this every morning. So it is important to ask: Under what conditions does punishment work?

The effectiveness of punishment depends entirely on how and when it is used. Punishment should be *swift*. Children who misbehave should be punished right away so that they know that what they have done is wrong. If punishment comes too late, it may not be clear to children why they are being punished. Punishment should also be *sufficient* without being cruel. If a parent merely warns a child not to bully other children, the effect may be less than if the warning is accompanied by the threat of being "grounded" for a day. Moreover, the common practice of making the punishment for each successive misdeed more severe than the last is not so effective as maintaining a constant level of punishment. Effective punishment is also consistent, or *certain*. The parent should try to punish the child each and every time he or she misbehaves. Otherwise, the misbehavior may persist.

One of the problems with using punishment is that it can often disrupt the learning process. When children are learning to read and the teacher scolds them every time they mispronounce a word, they may only become frightened. As they become more frightened and confused, they mispronounce more words and get scolded more often. In time, they may become so scared that they will not want to read at all. Moreover, punishment can provoke aggressive behavior. Laboratory studies show that monkeys that are punished tend to attack other monkeys, pigeons other pigeons, and so on (Schwartz, 1984). Similarly, punishment often makes people angry, and angry people are likely to be more aggressive and hostile.

Despite obvious negative side effects, punishment used properly works quickly, and in some cases speed is especially important. A child who likes to play in the street or who likes to poke things into electric outlets must be stopped quickly, and in these cases punishment has a role to play. Similarly, some severely disturbed children repeatedly injure themselves by banging their head against the wall or by hitting themselves in the face with their fists. Punishment can stop this self-destructive behavior so that other forms of therapy can proceed.

By itself, punishment simply inhibits or suppresses behavior. It doesn't teach an alternative behavior to replace what is being punished. Scolding a child for misbehaving does not in itself teach the child how he or she should have behaved. But when punishment is *stopped*, any behavior going on at the time is reinforced and is more likely to occur in that situation in the future. Thus, if punishment must be used to suppress undesirable behavior, it should be terminated when more desirable behavior occurs (in order to negatively reinforce that behavior). Positive reinforcement (praise, rewards) should also be used to strengthen the desired behavior. This approach is more productive than punishment alone, since it teaches an alternative behavior to replace what is being punished. The positive reinforcement also makes the learning situation less threatening in general.

As a method for controlling behavior, punishment is an unpleasant alternative. It is often carried out ineffectively, and it can have negative side effects. Most of us would prefer to avoid using punishment at all, perhaps relying only on the *threat* of punishment if behavior is getting out of control. In this case, a change to more desirable behavior can prevent the punishment from ever occurring. Psychologists call this **avoidance training.**

Avoidance training with animals usually includes some sort of warning device, like a light or a buzzer. For example, an animal might be placed in a box with a wire floor that can deliver a mild shock. The experimenter first sounds a buzzer, then a few seconds later turns on the shock. If the animal presses a bar after hearing the buzzer, no shock will be delivered. Pressing the bar after the shock has already started will have no effect. The animal must learn to press the bar after hearing the buzzer, but before the shock starts, in order to prevent the shock from occurring. At first this usually happens accidentally. But once the animal learns that pressing the bar prevents the shock, it will run to the bar whenever it hears the buzzer and will avoid the shock altogether.

Avoidance training is usually helpful to us, as when we learn to carry an umbrella when it looks like rain or not to drink from bottles labeled "Poison." But sometimes avoidance learning persists after it is no

Avoidance training Learning a desirable behavior in order to prevent an unpleasant condition such as punishment from occurring.

Table 5-1
From Landy, 1987, p. 212. Adapted by permission.

TABLE 5-1 EXAMPLES OF REINFORCEMENT IN EVERYDAY LIFE	
Continuous reinforcement (reinforcement every time the response is made)	■ Using a token to ride the subway. ■ Putting a dime in the parking meter. ■ Putting coins in a vending machine to get candy or soda.
Fixed-ratio schedule (reinforcement after a fixed number of responses)	■ Being paid on a piecework basis—in the garment industry workers may be paid so much per 100 dresses sewn. ■ Taking a multi-item test. This is an example of negative reinforcement—as soon as you finish those items on the test, you can leave!
Variable-ratio schedule (reinforcement after a varying number of responses)	■ Playing a slot machine—the machine is programmed to pay off after a certain number of responses have been made, but that number keeps changing. This type of schedule creates a steady rate of responding, because players know if they play long enough, they will win. ■ Hunting—you probably won't hit something every time you fire, but it's not the amount of time that passes, but the number of times you shoot that will determine how much game you are able to catch. And the number of times you shoot will no doubt vary—you won't hit something every time. ■ Sales commissions—you have to talk to many customers before you make a sale, and you never know whether the next one will buy. Again, the number of sales calls you make, not how much time passes, will determine when you are reinforced by a sale. And the number of sales calls will vary.
Fixed-interval schedule (reinforcement of first response after a fixed amount of time has passed)	■ You have an exam coming up, and as time goes by and you haven't studied, you have to make up for it all by a certain time, and that means cramming. ■ Picking up a salary check, which occurs every week or every two weeks.
Variable-interval schedule (reinforcement of first response after varying amounts of time)	■ Surprise quizzes in a course cause a steady rate of studying because you never know when they'll occur, and so you have to be prepared all the time. ■ Dialing a friend on the phone and getting a busy signal. This means that you have to keep dialing every few minutes because you don't know when your friend will hang up. Reinforcement doesn't depend on how many times you dial; it depends on dialing *after* the other person has hung up. ■ Watching a football game, waiting for a touchdown. It could happen anytime—if you leave the room to fix a sandwich, you may miss it, so you have to keep watching continuously.

Response generalization Giving a response that is somewhat different from the response originally learned to that stimulus.

Though punishment can disrupt the learning process and result in aggressive behavior, there are situations where, used properly, it is valuable in stopping dangerous behaviors quickly.

longer effective. A child who learns not to go into deep water may avoid deep water even after he or she has learned how to swim. In other cases, avoidance behavior may persist even after the fear has been removed. It seems that the fear that was essential for learning the avoidance response is not necessary in the long run for sustaining the learned response.

Generalization and Discrimination

As we saw in our discussion of classical conditioning, a response can generalize from one stimulus to a similar one. Conversely, the same stimulus will sometimes bring about different, but similar, responses. An example of stimulus generalization in operant conditioning is a baby who is hugged and kissed for saying "Mama" when he or she sees the mother, and then begins to call everyone "Mama"—including the mailman. Although the person whom the baby sees—the stimulus—changes, the baby responds with the same word. In the same way, the skills that you learn when playing tennis may be generalized to badminton, Ping-Pong, and squash.

Response generalization occurs when the same stimulus leads to different, but similar, responses. The baby who calls everyone "Mama" may also call the mother "Dada" or "gaga"—other sounds that have been learned—until he or she learns that only "Mama" is correct. In response generalization, the response changes but the stimulus remains constant.

The ability to tell the difference, or discriminate, between similar stimuli—or even to determine whether the right stimulus is present—is as essential in operant conditioning as it is in classical conditioning. Knowing what to do has little value if the learner does not know when to do it.

Discrimination in operant conditioning is taught by reinforcing a

If the expected reinforcement for an action does not occur—the woman shown here expects to receive food for the money that she put in the machine—the behavior of the subject often becomes more intense (here the women kicks the machine) before it disappears altogether (extinction).

response only in the presence of certain stimuli. In this way, pigeons have been trained to peck at a red disk but not at a green one. First the pigeon is taught to peck at a disk. Then it is presented with two disks, one red and one green. The bird gets food when it pecks at the red one but not when it pecks at the green. Eventually, it learns to discriminate between the two and will only peck at the red disk. Babies who call everyone "Mama" learn to discriminate between their own mothers and other people and to use "Mama" only for their own mothers. Of course, this could be done by punishing the children for calling other people "Mama." But more commonly, we teach children to discriminate by reinforcing them for using "Mama" correctly and not reinforcing them when they use the term for other people.

Extinction and Spontaneous Recovery

Extinction was discussed earlier in connection with classical conditioning. In operant conditioning, extinction is the result of withholding reinforcement. Withholding reinforcement does not usually produce an immediate decrease in the frequency of the response. When reinforcement is first discontinued, there is often a brief increase in responding before it declines. The behavior itself also changes at the start of extinction. It becomes more variable and often more forceful. For instance, if you try to open a door by turning the knob and pushing the door but find that it will not open, you may continue to try. You may turn the knob more violently and you may even kick or pound on the door. But if the door still will not budge, your attempts will decrease, and you will finally stop trying to get the door open altogether.

Several factors affect how easy or how hard it is to extinguish learned actions. The stronger the original learning, the harder it is to stop the action from being performed. The greater the variety of settings in which learning takes place, the harder it is to extinguish it. Rats trained to run in a single straight alley for food will stop running sooner than rats trained in several different alleys that vary in width, brightness, floor texture, and other features. Complex behavior is also much more difficult to extinguish than simple behavior. Since complex behavior consists of many actions, each single action contributing to the total behavior must be extinguished.

The schedule of reinforcement used during conditioning also has a major effect on the extinction process. Partial reinforcement creates stronger learning than continuous reinforcement. This is because the subject does not expect reinforcement for each response and has learned to continue responding in anticipation of eventual reinforcement. During extinction, it will take the subject longer to learn that no reinforcement will be presented and longer to stop responding.

Avoidance behavior, or any behavior learned on the basis of punishment rather than reinforcement, is especially hard to extinguish. Once the subject has learned how to avoid the punishment, whether by not responding to a stimulus or by giving an alternate response, there is no easy way to let the subject know that the punishment has been removed. The subject has learned that punishment follows a particular response, and if that response is never given, the subject will never know that the punishment does not follow. If you have been repeatedly attacked by a

"THIS IS A STICKUP!"

"THIS IS A STICKUP!"

"THIS IS A STICKUP!"

Merely paying attention to someone's behavior can be reinforcing, particularly if the person is "starved for attention." Withdrawal of the reinforcing attention results in the elimination of the behavior.

Drawing by Opie © 1961. The New Yorker Magazine, Inc.

particularly nasty dog when you jogged down one street, you may change your route and jog down a different street. However, because you have no way of knowing whether the dog's owner has moved away and made it safe for you to jog on your original route, you probably will continue to jog on the new, alternate route.

One way to speed up the extinction of any kind of learning is to put the learner in a situation that is different from the one in which the response was learned. The response is weaker in the new situation, and it will disappear more quickly. When the learner is returned to the learning surroundings after extinction, the response may show spontaneous recovery, just as in classical conditioning; but it is likely to be weaker than it was initially, and it should be relatively easy to extinguish once and for all.

■ A Review of Classical Conditioning and Operant Conditioning

In our examinations of classical and operant conditioning, we have noted a number of similarities and some differences between the two. Both focus on the building of associations between stimuli and responses. Both are subject to extinction and spontaneous recovery and generalization and discrimination. In these respects, operant conditioning and classical conditioning appear to be quite similar learning processes.

The main difference between them is that in classical conditioning, the learner is passive and the desired behavior is involuntary; in operant conditioning, the learner is active and the desired behavior is likely to be voluntary. However, some psychologists have begun to wonder whether the two kinds of learning are really very different—whether in fact they are simply two different ways of bringing about the same kind of learning. For example, classical conditioning can be used to shape voluntary movements (Brown & Jenkins, 1968). Moreover, operant conditioning of involuntary processes has occurred in autonomic conditioning studies in which both humans and animals have been taught to control certain biological functions, such as blood pressure, heart rate, and skin temperature. (In the Application at the end of this chapter, we'll discuss how autonomic conditioning, incorporated into a technique called biofeedback, has become an important tool for treating a variety of health problems.) Finally, in operant conditioning, once the operant response becomes linked to a stimulus, the operant response looks and acts very much like an unconditioned response. If a rat is trained to open a door when a light goes on, the light elicits the door-opening behavior just like an unconditioned stimulus in classical conditioning.

These facts, together with the fact that there are few differences between classical and operant conditioning in such things as extinction and generalization, suggest that classical and operant conditioning may in fact simply be two different procedures for achieving the same end (Hearst, 1975). If so, psychologists have been overstressing the differences and paying too little attention to the similarities between the two. Learning occurs in both cases, and the nature of learning itself remains open to new theories. In the next section, we discuss several of these new theories.

■ Cognitive Learning

Cognitive learning Learning that depends on mental processes that are not able to be observed directly.

Latent learning Learning that is not immediately reflected in behavior change.

Classical and operant conditioning concern the learning of observable, external, objectively measurable responses. But it would appear that, at least in the case of humans, there's often more to learning than meets the eye. We learn to find our way around a building or neighborhood, we learn what to expect from a given situation, we learn abstract concepts, and we can even learn about situations that we have never experienced firsthand. While stimulus-response associations may be part of this learning, it seems that **cognitive** (or internal) **learning** is also important. As we will see in this portion of the chapter, much of the recent research in the area of learning has been concerned with identifying what cognitive learning is and how it works—what goes on *inside* us when we learn.

Cognitive Maps and Latent Learning

Work on cognitive learning actually began shortly after the pioneering work in both classical and operant conditioning. One of the pioneers in the study of cognitive learning was Edward Chace Tolman. In his presidential address to the American Psychological Association, Tolman (1938) acknowledged that the psychology of learning "has been and still is primarily a matter of agreeing or disagreeing with Thorndike, or trying in minor ways to improve upon him." For his part, Tolman disagreed with Thorndike on two important points. First, Tolman felt that Thorndike's Law of Effect neglected the inner drives or motives that made learners pursue the "satisfying state," and he felt that the concept of response needed to include a range of behaviors—a *performance*, in Tolman's word—that would allow learners to reach their goal. Second, Tolman felt that learning occurs even before the subject reaches the goal and occurs whether or not the learner is reinforced. In Tolman's view, the cats in Thorndike's cages, for example, were constantly storing up knowledge about what worked and what didn't as they explored the cage and tried out various behaviors. This idea of **latent learning** is the concept for which Tolman is best known.

Tolman demonstrated latent learning in a famous experiment conducted with C. H. Honzik in 1930. Hungry rats were placed in a maze and required to find their way from a start box to an end box. One group of rats consistently found food pellets in the end box; a second group of rats found nothing in the end box when they finally reached it. Operant conditioning theory predicts that the food reinforcement would make the first group of rats learn the maze faster than the second group. For 10 days, the rats ran the maze and the experimenters charted both the time that it took each rat to run the maze and the number of wrong turns that each rat took. And indeed, after 10 days the first group of rats—those that were reinforced with food when they reached the end of the box—did run the maze faster and with fewer errors than did the rats who were

Drawing by Chas. Adams: © 1981 The New Yorker Magazine, Inc.

not reinforced. On the basis of external, observable behavior, it would appear that one group of rats had learned how to run the maze while the other group had not. But then Tolman did an interesting thing: He took some of the rats in the second, unreinforced group and started to give them food when they reached the goal box. Almost immediately, these rats were running the maze as quickly and with as few errors as the rats that had been trained with food reinforcement for 10 days (see Figure 5-7).

Tolman explained his dramatic findings by suggesting that the unrewarded rats had learned a great deal about the maze as they wandered around inside it. In fact, they may actually have learned *more* about the maze than had the rats that rushed directly to the end box in order to get their food reinforcement. He contended that the unrewarded rats' learning was *latent*—stored internally in some way but not yet reflected in their behavior. When the rats were given a good reason to run quickly to the end of the box (in this case, a food reward), they showed that they were quite capable of finding their way—they put their latent learning to use.

Since Tolman's time, there has been a great deal of work on just what the nature of this latent learning might be. In learning how to get around a maze, a building, or a neighborhood with many available routes, the mechanism for storing latent learning has been taken to be a sort of mental image, or **cognitive map,** of the whole area. When the proper time comes, the learner can call up the stored image or map and put it to use.

In response to Tolman's theory of latent learning, Thorndike proposed an experiment to test whether a rat could in fact learn and store away an image of the most direct route through a maze without the rat ever running the route itself. He suggested that the experimenter put a

Figure 5-7
Maze used to study latent learning in rats The results of the classic Tolman-Honzik study are revealed in the graph. Group A never received a food reward; Group B was rewarded each day. Group C was not rewarded until the eleventh day, but note the significant change in their behavior on Day 12.
From Tolman and Honzik, 1930

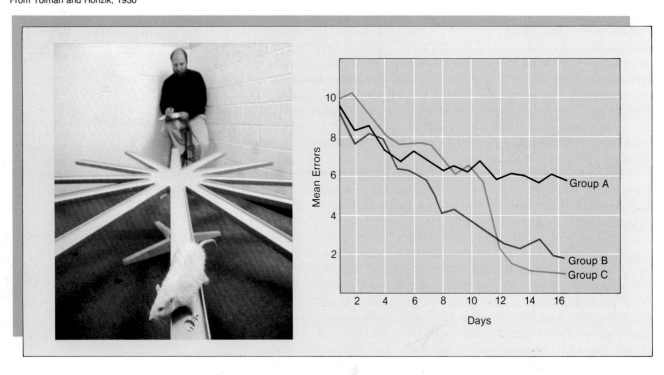

rat in a small container, perhaps made of wire, and carry it in this container several times through a maze, rewarding the rat at the end of each trial as if it had run the maze itself. He predicted that such a rat would show little or no evidence of learning compared to rats that had learned the same maze by their own trial and error.

Thorndike never carried out this test himself, nor did Tolman. In 1956, however, three experimenters at the University of Kansas followed Thorndike's design quite closely (McNamara, Long, & Wike, 1956). They used a simple maze, but instead of taking the passive rats through the "correct" path, they carried each passenger over the same path that a free-running partner rat had taken on the same trial. They discovered that the passenger rats indeed learned the maze just as well as their active counterparts. In a second version of the experiment, McNamara and his co-workers eliminated as far as possible the cues from outside the maze that might tell the rats where they were. They covered windows and masked the lights in the room so that the rats would have only the directional cues of running the maze to orient them. Under these conditions, the passenger rats seemed not to have learned to run the maze at all, performing only as well as they might do by chance.

The first experiment seems to verify that latent learning of cognitive maps can occur just as Tolman suggested. The second experiment suggests that the rats used information from their surroundings as an important part of their cognitive maps. More recent research confirms this picture of cognitive learning in animals. It appears that animals have a great deal more flexibility when it comes to solving problems and making choices than can be explained by simple conditioning (Domjan, 1987). In a series of experiments with rats in a radial maze, rats consistently recalled which arms they had previously traveled down and which they hadn't, even when scent cues were removed and all arms contained a bait reward. It seems that these rats had developed a cognitive map or spatial memory of their experiences in the maze (Olton & Samuelson, 1976). The important point for our purposes is that, even in rats, learning seems to involve more than just a change in observable behavior; rather, it appears to involve changes in unobservable mental processes that may (or may not) be reflected at some future time in the subject's behavior.

Insight

Another phenomenon that highlights the importance of cognitive processing in learning is **insight,** the sudden "coming together" of the elements of a situation so that the most efficient path is clear or a problem is solved. In this case, learning does not progress slowly and gradually on a smooth curve, but suddenly shoots up from unsuccessful trial and error to instant success.

During World War I, the German Gestalt psychologist Wolfgang Köhler conducted a series of experiments on the nature of insightful learning. Köhler's most famous experiments (1927) focused on the ways in which chimpanzees solved problems, such as reaching a banana placed on the ground just outside their cage. The chimps almost always tried first to reach the food with their hands and often very noisily and actively showed their frustration at their lack of success. After a while, however, the chimps would start looking at what was lying about the cage, including

Insight Learning that occurs rapidly as a result of understanding all the ingredients of a problem.

a stick left there by the experimenters. Sometimes quite suddenly, a chimp would grap the stick, poke it through the bars of the cage, and drag the banana within reach. If the stick was too short but a longer stick was within reach, the chimps quickly learned to retrieve the longer stick and, if necessary, to connect the two sticks together in order to reach the banana. In another famous problem, Köhler hung the banana from the roof of the cage, just out of the chimps' reach. Instead of sticks, the chimps were provided with boxes, which they quickly learned to move to the spot under the banana so that they could stack them up high enough to reach the food.

Köhler also worked with chickens, which did not demonstrate as great a capacity for insightful learning as the apes. This was not surprising to Köhler, who expected only higher animals such as apes and humans to be capable of the complex cognitive processes that produce insight. In 1984, however, four Harvard University psychologists (Epstein et al., 1984) presented the banana-and-box problem to a small group of pigeons. Since moving boxes around is not as natural a behavior for pigeons as it is for chimps, the researchers first conditioned the pigeons, through standard shaping procedures, to push a box toward a particular target—a green spot on the wall of the training cage. On separate occasions, the pigeons were also taught to climb onto a box that was stuck to the floor and to peck at a small picture of a banana. The question then was: Could the pigeons put the two new behaviors together to solve the problem of the banana and the box? When the pigeons were presented with the hanging banana and a box, Epstein and his co-workers reported that each pigeon showed confusion and, just like Köhler's chimps, looked for a while from the banana to the box. Then, fairly suddenly, each pigeon began to push the box toward the banana, stopping now and then to sight the banana and to check the direction in which to push the box. With the box underneath, each of the pigeons then climbed on top and pecked at the picture of the banana in order to receive its reward.

Epstein and his co-workers felt that the main reason that pigeons couldn't solve the problem without preliminary training is that pigeons (unlike chimps) don't already know how boxes can be pushed around and used in various ways, nor do they normally value bananas. When pigeons are given the right tools and are taught how to use them, they show that they can solve quite complex cognitive problems. In other words, in this view, Köhler's chimps learned quickly how to reach the banana because they already knew how to use sticks and boxes to get objects, and they valued bananas.

The way in which previous learning can be used to speed up new learning is demonstrated clearly in a series of studies by Harry Harlow with rhesus monkeys (Harlow, 1949). Harlow presented each monkey with two boxes—say, a round green box on the left side of a tray and a square red box on the right side. A morsel of food was put under one of the boxes. The monkey was permitted to lift just one box; if it chose the correct box, it got the food. On the next trial, the food was put under the same box (which might have been moved to a new position) and the monkey again got to choose just one box. Each monkey had six trials to figure out which box covered the food no matter where that box was located. Then the monkeys were given a new set of choices—say, between

Köhler's insightful chimps One of Köhler's chimps has arranged a stack of boxes in order to reach some bananas hanging from the roof of the cage.

a blue triangular box and an orange pentagonal one—and another six trials, and so on with other shapes and colors of boxes.

How long do you think it took the monkeys to figure out that in any set of six trials, food was always under the same box? Initially the monkeys seemed to choose boxes randomly, by trial and error; sometimes they would find food, but just as often they would not. However, after a while, their behavior changed: They would turn over one or two boxes and then choose the correct box consistently until the experimenter supplied new boxes. They seemed to have learned the underlying principle—that the food would always be under the same box—and they used that learning to solve almost instantly each new set of choices presented by the experimenter.

Harlow concluded that the monkeys had "learned how to learn" or that they had established **learning sets:** Within the limited range of choices, they had discovered how to tell which box would give them what they wanted. By extension, Köhler's chimps could be said to have established learning sets for various ways of obtaining food that was just out of reach. When presented with the familiar problem of reaching the banana, the chimps simply called up the appropriate learning sets and solved the problem. In contrast, Epstein's pigeons first had to be taught the appropriate learning sets, and then they too were able to solve the problems. In both cases, the animals seemed to have learned more than just specific behaviors—they apparently learned how to learn.

Learning set Ability to become increasingly more effective in solving problems as more problems are solved.

▪ Contingency Theory

We have seen clearly that learning is a very complex process that involves mental processes even in fairly simple animals, such as rats and pigeons. In the late 1960s, some researchers began to wonder whether even simple classical conditioning is more complex than it at first appears. Did Pavlov's dogs salivate when they heard a bell only because the bell and food had been paired on a few previous occasions, or did the bell perhaps *tell the dogs something* about the coming of food?

Robert Rescorla (1976) tested some of these ideas by trying out various different ways of pairing a tone (the CS) with electric shocks (the US) administered to dogs. One group of dogs heard the tone followed consistently by a shock, just as in classical conditioning studies. These dogs learned to fear the sound of the tone, much as Pavlov would have predicted. Another group received an equal number of tones and shocks, but the tone was never followed immediately by a shock; the two were always unpaired. According to classical conditioning theory, this second group should have demonstrated no learning of any association between the tone and shock. Rescorla found, however, that the dogs learned that the tone was insurance against a shock—that they were never shocked when the tone was present but might be shocked when they didn't hear the tone. When the tone was on, the dogs were calm, but when there was no tone, they became alert and fearful. For a third group of dogs, the tones and shocks were presented at random, entirely independently

Blocking Prior conditioning prevents conditioning to a second stimulus even when the two stimuli are presented simultaneously.

Contingency theory Proposes that for learning to take place, the stimulus must provide the learner with information about the likelihood of other events occurring.

Learned helplessness Apathy and passivity learned in a situation where one's behavior has no effect on reward and punishment.

of one another; occasionally, a tone and shock were paired by chance. According to Pavlov's theory, even this occasional pairing should have produced some learning, but the dogs in this group did not in fact learn to fear the tone. Apparently, Rescorla concluded, the tone told the dogs in the third group nothing about the likelihood of being shocked, and in the absence of this information, no learning took place.

Further support for this view of classical conditioning comes from some research by Leon Kamin (1969). Kamin first paired noise (CS) with a brief shock (US) to the feet of some rats. The rats quickly learned to react with fear to the onset of the noise. After this association had become well established, Kamin added a second CS (a light) along with the noise and the shock. Since the light and the noise were both being paired with shock, you might expect that after a while, the rats would learn to fear both the light and the noise. But this was not the case: The rats showed no sign of fear when only the light was presented. It was as if they did not realize that the light was also a signal that a shock was forthcoming. Kamin concluded that the original learning had a **blocking** effect on new learning. Once the rats learned that noise signaled the onset of shock, adding yet another cue (a light) provided no new information about the likelihood of shock, and so no new learning took place. In other words, according to Kamin, classical conditioning occurs only when a CS tells the learner something new or additional about the likelihood that the US will be forthcoming.

On the basis of these and many other studies, we now know that Pavlovian conditioning does not happen automatically when a conditioned and unconditioned stimulus are paired. The environment in which the pairing occurs, the nature of the two stimuli being associated, and previous experiences with either or both of the stimuli all are crucial factors in determining whether or not conditioning, or learning, occurs (Domjan, 1987).

It appears that the close appearance in time of two events (US and CS) not only does not explain why classical conditioning occurs; it isn't even necessary to classical conditioning (Rescorla, 1988). Instead, the important thing is that the conditioned stimulus must tell you something about whether the unconditioned stimulus is going to occur. The buzzer or tone must signify *contingency*—that if one thing occurs, something else is likely to occur. This and related proposals have since been grouped under the heading **contingency theory.** Conditioning is now seen as the learning of relations among events or stimuli rather than the simple, causal combination of the reward strengthening the response, as it was originally thought to be.

The studies by Rescorla and Kamin concerned classical conditioning, but similar cognitive processes also seem to be involved in operant conditioning (Rescorla & Holland, 1982). One especially interesting line of research concerns the phenomenon of **learned helplessness.** Learned helplessness was first produced in a study of avoidance training by Overmier and Seligman (1967). Two groups of dogs were given shocks to their feet. One group was able to escape the shock by leaping over a barrier into another section of the box; the other group was restrained in harnesses that made it impossible to escape the shock. After several trials, both groups were put in a situation where they could escape and were again shocked. The group that had originally been harnessed did not try to escape when they had the chance; they just whined and lay down in the experimental chamber, apparently resigned to a fate that they had come to believe they could not control.

Seligman and his colleague Stephen F. Maier have since conducted numerous experiments in learned helplessness and have produced similar results in both animals and humans (Maier & Seligman, 1976). On the basis of this research, it appears that once learned helplessness is established, the subject is less motivated to try different responses that might bring relief from the unpleasant situation; moreover, even if a response does bring relief, the learner seems to have difficulty recognizing that the response had anything to do with the relief. For example, college students who are faced with a series of unsolvable problems eventually give up and make only halfhearted attempts to solve new problems, even when the new problems are solvable. Moreover, success in solving new problems has little effect on their behavior—they continue to make only halfhearted attempts as if they had never had any success at all.

Even young infants are able to distinguish between situations in which they can control delivery of a reward and those in which they cannot. This was the conclusion of experimenters who worked with infants lying in a crib, their heads resting on a pillow. For one group, beneath the pillow was a switch; whenever the infant shifted its head, a mobile on the opposite side of the crib would move for a few seconds. For the other group, the mobile was moved by the experimenters independently of what the infants did. The babies in the first group quickly learned to move the mobile and repeatedly shifted their heads, taking obvious pleasure in the result. The babies in the second group also smiled and cooed when the mobile moved, but only for a time. Apparently, because they realized they could not control the mobile, the rate at which they turned their heads stayed even and they soon lost interest in the mobile. The reinforcing power of the mobile seems to have depended on the infants' awareness that they controlled its movement (Watson, 1971).

All of these studies suggest that classical and operant conditioning are more complex than they at first appear. Contingency theorists believe that animals and humans continually collect, code, and distill information about their environments. Classical and operant conditioning procedures are simply two ways of providing that information to the subjects. In this sense, the distinction between classical and operant conditioning is not very great. Moreover, this line of reasoning suggests that there may be other, more effective procedures by which to provide this information and thus to cause learning, at least for some organisms. In the next section of the chapter, we will explore this possibility further.

Social Learning Theory

In the past two decades, another group of psychologists has challenged the idea that most or all human learning involves classical or operant conditioning. The foremost representative of this group is Albert Bandura, and the point of view which he represents is called **social learning theory** (Bandura, 1977). Social learning theorists are impressed by the extent

Social learning theory View of learning that emphasizes the ability to learn by observing a model or receiving instructions, without firsthand experience by the learner.

Observational or vicarious learning
Learning by observing other people's behavior.

to which we learn not just from firsthand experience—the kind of learning explained by classical and operant conditioning—but also from watching what happens to other people or by being told about something. In fact, we can learn new behaviors without ever actually carrying them out or being reinforced for them. The first time you drive a car, you are likely to drive carefully because you have been told to do so, you have been warned about driving carelessly, you have watched people drive carefully, and you've seen what happens if people drive carelessly. In other words, you have learned a great deal about driving without ever actually sitting behind the wheel of a car.

This kind of **observational** (or **vicarious**) **learning** is quite common. By watching models, we can learn such things as how to start a lawn mower and how to saw wood. We also learn how to show love or respect or concern, as well as hostility and aggression. When the Federal Communications Commission (FCC) banned cigarette commercials on TV, they showed their belief that modeling a response—lighting up a cigarette—would encourage people to imitate it. They removed the model to discourage the habit.

But obviously we do not imitate everything that other people do. Social learning theory accounts for this in several ways (Bandura, 1977). First, you must not only see but also *pay attention* to what the model does; this is more likely if the model (such as a famous or attractive person or an expert) commands attention. Second, you must *remember* what the model did. Third, you have to *convert* what you learned into action: It is possible to learn a great deal from watching a model but have no particular reason to convert what you have learned into behavior. This distinction between *learning* on the one hand and *performance* on the other is very important to social learning theorists: They stress that learning can occur without any change in outward behavior.

In a classic experiment, Bandura (1965) demonstrated that people can learn a behavior without being reinforced for doing so, and that learning a behavior and performing it are not the same thing. Bandura randomly divided a group of 66 nursery-school children (33 boys and 33 girls) into three groups of 22 subjects. Next, each child was led individually into a darkened room, where he or she watched a film. In the film, an adult model walked up to an adult-size plastic doll and ordered it to clear the way. When the doll failed to obey, the model exhibited a series of aggressive acts. He set the doll on its side, punched it in the nose and exclaimed, "Pow, right in the nose, boom, boom." He also hit it with a rubber mallet, kicked the doll around the room, and threw rubber balls at it.

In *observational* or *vicarious learning*, we learn by watching a model perform a particular action and then trying to imitate it correctly.

The film ended differently for children in each of the three groups. Children in the *model-rewarded condition* watched the model being rewarded by a second adult, who brought a large supply of candies and soft drinks and praised him. Children in the *model-punished condition* observed the second adult shaking his finger, scolding, and spanking the model for his behavior. Children in the *no-consequences condition* saw the same film, but without an ending showing either of these consequences to the model. Immediately after seeing the film, the children were escorted individually into a room in which a doll, rubber balls, a mallet, and many other toys were available for play. While a child played alone for 10 minutes, observers coded his or her behavior from behind a one-way

Modifying Your Own Behavior

Can people modify their own behavior? The answer is yes. The first thing to do is to decide what behavior you want to acquire—the "target" behavior. What if you want to get rid of some behavior? Behavior modification specialists emphasize a positive approach called "ignoring." Much better results are achieved when the emphasis is on the new behavior to be acquired rather than on the behavior to be eliminated. For example, instead of setting a target of being less shy, you might define the target behavior as becoming more outgoing or more sociable. Other possible target behaviors are behaving more assertively, studying more, and getting along better with your roommate. In each case, you have focused on the behavior that you want to acquire rather than on the behavior that you want to reduce or eliminate.

The next step is to define the target behavior precisely: What exactly do you mean by "assertive" or by "sociable"? One way to do this is to imagine situations in which the target behavior could be performed. Then describe in writing these situations and the way in which you now respond to them. For example, in the case of shyness, you might write: "When I am sitting in the lecture hall, waiting for class to begin, I don't talk to the people around me." Next, write down how you would rather act in that situation: "Ask the people sitting next to me how they like the class or the professor; or ask if they have seen any particularly good films recently."

The next step is to monitor your present behavior by keeping a daily log of activities related to the target behavior in order to establish your present rate of behavior. At the same time, try to figure out if your present, undesirable behavior is being reinforced in some way. For example, if you find yourself unable to study, record what you do instead and try to determine how that undesirable behavior is being reinforced.

The next step—the basic principle of self-modification—is to provide yourself with a positive reinforcer that is contingent on specific improvements in the target behavior. You may be able to use the same reinforcer that now maintains your undesirable behavior, or you may want to pick a new reinforcer. Watson and Tharp (1981) use the example of a student who wanted to improve his relationship with his parents. He first counted the times he said something pleasant to them and then rewarded himself for improvement by making his favorite pastime, playing pool, contingent on the predetermined increases in the number of pleasant remarks he made. You can also use tokens: Give yourself one token for every 30 minutes of studying and cash in those tokens for reinforcement. For an hour of TV, you might charge yourself three tokens, while the privilege of going to a movie might cost six.

Remember that behavior need not be learned all in one piece. You can use shaping or successive approximations to change your behavior bit by bit over a period of time.

If you would like to attempt a program of self-modification, a book by David Watson and Roland Tharp entitled *Self-Directed Behavior* (1985) is extremely useful, as it provides step-by-step instructions and exercises.

---

mirror. Every time the child spontaneously repeated any of the aggressive acts seen in the film, he or she was coded as *performing* the behavior. After 10 minutes, an experimenter entered the room and offered the child treats in return for imitating or repeating things the model had done or said to the doll. Bandura used the number of successfully imitated behaviors as a measure of how much the child had *learned* by watching the model (see Figure 5-8).

Analysis of the data revealed that (1) children who had observed the model being rewarded were especially likely to *perform* the models' behavior spontaneously; but (2) children in the three groups had *learned* equal amounts about assaulting the doll. That is, when they were offered rewards for showing what they had learned, the children in all three groups could imitate the model's behavior equally well, and quite accurately at that (see Figure 5-9).

Notice that the children in this study learned aggressive behavior without being reinforced for it. In fact, the children learned even when the model was neither reinforced nor punished for behaving aggressively. While reinforcement of a model is not necessary for vicarious learning to occur, seeing a model reinforced or punished nonetheless provides us

Figure 5-8
Bandura's experiment in learned aggressive behavior After watching an adult behave aggressively with an inflated doll, the children in Bandura's study imitated many of the aggressive acts of the adult model.

with useful information. It tells us what the correct or incorrect behavior is and what is likely to happen to us if we imitate the model. In short, we learn what behaviors are valued and are therefore able to anticipate the consequences of acting in various ways. Human beings have not only sight but also insight, hindsight, and foresight. We use all of these to interpret our own experience and that of others (Bandura, 1962).

Finally, Bandura stresses that humans beings are capable of setting performance standards for themselves and then rewarding (or punishing) themselves for achieving or failing to achieve those standards. In other words, people can be their own source of reinforcement or punishment and can thus regulate their own behavior. Because of its emphasis on expectations, insight, information, self-satisfaction, and self-criticism, social learning theory has great potential for widening our understanding not only of how people learn skills and abilities, but also of how attitudes, values, and ideas pass from person to person. Social learning theory can also teach us how *not* to pass something on. For example, suppose you want to teach a child not to hit other children. A traditional learning theorist would advise you to slap the child as punishment to change the behavior, while reinforcing more desirable behavior. But a social learning theorist would tell you that slapping the child only demonstrates a better way of hitting. You and the child would both be better off if you demonstrated a less aggressive model of dealing with other people (Bandura, 1973, 1977). Such advice, combined with traditional discrimination training and reinforcement, can indeed help people to change their behavior. Because social learning theory borrows the best principles from

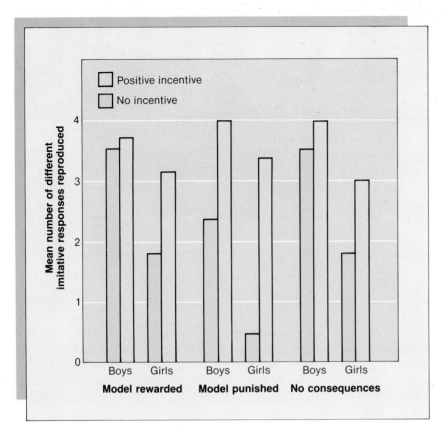

Figure 5-9
As the graph shows, even though all of the children in Bandura's study of imitative aggression learned the models' behavior, they *performed* differently depending on whether the model was rewarded or punished.

Bandura, 1965, p. 592. Copyright © 1965 by the American Psychological Association. Reprinted by permission.

operant conditioning and combines them with the "human element" ignored by traditional learning theories, it has attracted a great deal of interest and has become a major trend in research into learning.

 APPLICATION

Shaping Better Health through Biofeedback

For 20 of her 29 years, a woman had suffered from tension headaches. The dull aching would begin in the morning and last all day. Members of the clinic where she sought help traced her problem, as in many cases of tension headache, to excessive contraction of the frontalis muscle, the main muscle in the forehead. They therefore set about teaching their patient to relax this muscle by providing her with *biofeedback*. Electrodes attached to her forehead measured the degree of contraction in the frontalis muscle. The machine registered the contraction with an audible tone—the less the contraction, the lower the pitch of the tone. If the patient relaxed the muscle even slightly, the tone dropped noticeably. The patient worked to relax the muscle more and more, using the dropping pitch of the tone as her guide. Over the course of several dozen 30-minute training sessions spread over nine weeks, the woman became more and more able to control the level of frontalis contraction. At a follow-up three months after therapy had begun, the woman reported virtually no further tension headaches (Budzynski, Stoyva, & Adler, 1970).

Biofeedback training, which has been used for a number of disorders, is an operant conditioning procedure in which instruments are used to inform the learner about some biological response over which he or she wishes to gain control. Some sort of instrument is used to collect information about a biological response—for example, muscle contractions, blood pressure, or heart rate—of which people normally have little or no awareness. Information about the response is provided to the subject in the form of a light, a tone, or some other signal that can be varied according to the measured level of the response. The feedback information—the tone or light—serves as a secondary reinforcer, and the response is learned bit by bit, as in shaping techniques of learning.

The effectiveness of biofeedback depends on some of the same factors that determine success in operant conditioning. Feedback should be rapid, consistent, and precise. When feedback is *rapid*, reinforcement is most effective. Each time the tone drops, for example, it immediately reinforces the muscle relaxation response. *Consistent* feedback is also crucial. Suppose that early in the training, the tone dropped several times, but the muscle had actually contracted rather than relaxed. Learning how to relax the muscle would have been much harder, if not entirely impossible. Finally, especially at the start of training, feedback must be *precise*, indicating even the slightest changes in response. This permits the shaping of the desired behavior by successive approximations.

In recent years, biofeedback has become a well-established treatment for a number of medical problems, including not only tension headaches but also migraine headaches, asthma, and peptic ulcers. Migraine headaches, which plague about 10 percent of the population to varying degrees, can be eased or stopped by a biofeedback approach that differs in some details from that used to treat tension headaches. Migraines typically affect a localized area of the head, cause intense pain, and are sometimes associated with nausea, vomiting, and sensitivity to light. Just before the headaches start, blood vessels carrying blood to the brain constrict, reducing the blood supply to nerve cells in the brain. Shortly afterward, these vessels expand rapidly, causing nerve cells surrounding the vessels to fire off messages of intense pain. Research has discovered that with migraine sufferers, changes in the blood supply to the hands, and hence changes in the

Although paralyzed from the neck down, this woman has learned through biofeedback to control her blood pressure, to sit upright—and to lead a more normal life. The monkey has been trained through shaping to assist her in a variety of tasks.

skin temperature of the hands, are associated with changes in the supply of blood to the brain. The mechanism behind this effect is not fully understood, but biofeedback therapists can teach victims to change the skin temperature of their hands and thereby counteract the changes in brain blood supply that cause migraines. Generally, a temperature sensor placed on a finger causes changes in a tone, which can be used effectively as feedback to increase or decrease skin temperature and blood supply to the brain. The training period is longer and more difficult than for tension headaches. Nevertheless, significant reductions in the frequency of migraines have been reported consistently (Olton & Noonberg, 1980).

Biofeedback has effectively relieved medical problems other than headaches, including asthma. During an asthma attack, the victim suffers from shortness of breath and difficulty in breathing. These symptoms are due in part to the contraction of muscles around the air passages in the lungs, partly blocking the movement of air through the lungs. In order to keep the passages partly open, the lungs must remain partly inflated, limiting the efficiency with which air is exchanged. Biofeedback has been employed successfully to train people to change the volume of air they exhale. In one approach, a device measures resistance to breathing in the lungs and converts this into an audible tone, which can in turn be used to learn to reduce resistance in the air passages.

Finally, peptic ulcers—small areas of the lining of the stomach or small intestine that have been destroyed by digestive acids—have also been treated by means of biofeedback. The behavior to be shaped in this case is a reduction in the amount of acid that is secreted by the stomach. Acid levels in the stomach are measured either by extracting liquid through a tube inserted into the nose and swallowed, or by swallowing a meter that transmits readings to a receiver outside the body. When acid measurements are converted into a biofeedback signal, some subjects can successfully train themselves to reduce the amount of acid secreted. Although the amount of reduction has been great enough to be valuable, so far it has not been so great that biofeedback can be clearly recommended over other modes of treatment.

Biofeedback has some drawbacks. Patients must invest considerable time and effort in shaping their behavior. They must also have the discipline to practice their new technique, a quality that many patients do not display. Nevertheless, biofeedback does place the control of treatment in the patient's own hands, a major advantage over other kinds of treatment, and has achieved impressive success in treating certain kinds of problems (Olton & Noonberg, 1980).

Biofeedback has been hailed as a panacea and damned as quackery, and the debate still rages (Roberts, 1985). The main points of contention are the scientific rigor of the studies that have evaluated biofeedback and the professionalization of the technicians who operate the various biofeedback instruments. Advocates of the procedure have responded by arguing that when biofeedback is viewed properly, as an aid to learning self-regulation of biological processes rather than as a therapy, and evaluated on those terms, it can stand up to any level of scientific rigor (Norris, 1986).

■ Summary

- **Learning** is the process by which relatively permanent changes in behavior are brought about through experience or practice. Some of the simplest kinds of learning are called *conditioning*—the acquisition of specific patterns of behavior in the presence of particular stimuli.

- **You and your boyfriend or girlfriend have a favorite song. After you break up, you can't bear to listen to it. Why?** In *classical conditioning*, the subject learns an association between a response that is invariably elicited by one stimulus and another stimulus that does not normally produce such a response. This process was first demonstrated by Ivan Pavlov, who conditioned dogs to salivate upon hearing a bell.

- Four elements define any classical conditioning situation: The stimulus that invariably elicits the response is the *unconditioned stimulus* (US). The reaction to the unconditioned stimulus is the *unconditioned response* (UR). The neutral stimulus to which the subject learns to respond is the *conditioned stimulus* (CS). The response associated with the conditioned stimulus is the *conditioned response* (CR).

- If a CS is repeatedly presented without the US, learning will fall off fairly rapidly and may disappear altogether, a situation called *extinction*. After extinction has occurred, if the CS is not presented for a period of time, most subjects show *spontaneous recovery*: The CR will return, although it will usually be weaker and more easily extinguished.

- **Can looking at a photograph taken from a very tall building help a person who is afraid of heights to overcome his or her fear?** Once a response has been conditioned to one CS, it may also be elicited by other, similar stimuli. This is *stimulus generalization*; its opposite is *stimulus discrimination*. A subject can be taught to discriminate among stimuli, responding only to one CS and inhibiting the conditioned response to others. *Desensitization* therapy is one form of stimulus generalization.

- After a response to a conditioned stimulus has been learned, the conditioned stimulus itself can be used as an unconditioned stimulus in further training, or *higher-order conditioning*.

- **Is promising yourself you can go to a movie after you've finished reading and reviewing this chapter likely to help you study in the future?** In *operant conditioning*, *reinforcement* is used to increase the likelihood that a target response such as effective studying will recur. Since **operant behaviors** are emitted rather than elicited by unconditioned stimuli, motivation may be manipulated and special efforts must be made to increase the likelihood of obtaining the target behavior in the first place. E. L. Thorndike confined hungry cats to *puzzle boxes* until they performed the behaviors required to escape; in **Skinner boxes**, hungry animals have few options other than the simple behavior, such as pressing a lever, that triggers the release of a food reinforcement.

- **How can you train a tiger to jump through a flaming hoop?** *Shaping* is a particular instance of operant conditioning in which the learner is reinforced first for partial approximations of the desired behavior and is then gradually required to approximate the target behavior more and more closely in order to get reinforcement.

- **How do we know to carry an umbrella when it looks like rain?** Reinforcement may be *positive*—adding something pleasant to the environment—or *negative*—subtracting an aversive stimulus from the environment. The opposite of reinforcement is *punishment*, which may also be positive (adding an *aversive* stimulus) or negative (subtracting or removing a *rewarding* stimulus).

- In *escape training*, a subject learns to remove an aversive or punishing stimulus, thus earning a negative reinforcer. In **avoidance training**, a subject learns to respond to a signal stimulus that precedes the onset of punishment, thus earning the negative reinforcer of not being punished.

- **Why do some people eat when they are especially happy or sad?** A *primary reinforcer* is rewarding to the subject in and of itself; food, sex, and other immediately pleasurable stimuli are examples. A *secondary reinforcer* is one whose value has to be learned through association with other reinforcers; money is a common example of a secondary reinforcer.

- The highest response rates in operant conditioning are obtained when reinforcement is not given on every response. *Schedules of reinforcement* can be based either on the number of responses (*fixed* or *variable-ratio*) or on elapsed time since the last reinforced response (*fixed-* or *variable-interval*). Learners respond differently to each schedule of reinforcement.

- **Why do people gamble even though they lose more money that they win?** The strongest and steadiest response rate is obtained through a variable-ratio schedule on which, like a slot machine, the number of responses necessary to gain reinforcement is not constant; subjects tend to respond at a high rate over a long period of time. On a fixed-interval schedule, subjects are reinforced for the first correct response after a predetermined time following the previous correct response. On a variable-interval schedule, correct responses are reinforced after varying lengths of time.

- **Why are migrant workers usually paid by the basket, bin, or bushel instead of by the week or hour?** On a fixed-ratio schedule, a certain number of responses are necessary before reinforcement is provided. This tends to encourage a high rate of response over a long period of time.

- Stimulus generalization and discrimination occur in operant conditioning as well as in classical conditioning. In addition, operant conditioning may produce *response generalization*, in which the stimulus remains the same but the response changes. *Discrimination* depends on several factors, including the strength of the original learning and the number of settings in which learning took place.

- *Cognitive learning* theorists look beyond directly observable, external learning processes. They seek to explain how animals, and especially humans, learn things that they have never experienced directly, how complex responses can be remembered for long periods without practice or reinforcement, and why some learning appears to be sudden or insightful rather than slowly incremental.

- Edward Chace Tolman demonstrated that learning could take place even before the learner was reinforced for demonstrating what had been learned. Unreinforced learning may be **latent**, or stored internally. When reinforcement is introduced, the learning is demonstrated just as if it had been built up gradually through trial and error. Particularly when the learning concerns spatial relationships, the storage of latent learning may be thought of as a **cognitive map**.

- Often, learning, especially in higher animals and humans, seem to "come together" all at once to produce the solution to a stimulus problem. This *insight* may be based on prior acquisition of **learning sets**, or packages of information about how to learn or to solve particular problems.

- *Contingency theory* proposes that a simple pairing in time of an unconditioned stimulus and a conditioned stimulus, or of response and reinforcement, is not enough to explain learning. In this view, for learning to take place, a stimulus must provide the learner with specific new information that something else will or will not happen. An unconditioned stimulus must "surprise" the learner, causing the subject to "look back" over other recent stimuli for something new that can be associated with the new or changed unconditioned stimulus. A conditioned stimulus that cannot be associated with a surprising unconditioned stimulus will be **blocked**, and no learning will be seen.

- **Why do the children of violent people frequently become violent?** *Social learning theory* emphasizes *vicarious* or *observational learning*—the ability to learn complex stimulus-response-reinforcement interactions by watching another individual model them.

- Conditioning and cognitive theories of learning can be seen as complementary and interactive, rather than competitive. Most learning in the real world is probably a mixture of the methods examined and defined by learning theorists, and the various approaches have been mixed in several useful therapies and learning strategies.

■ Review Questions

1. The simplest type of learning is called _____ . It refers to the establishment of fairly predictable behavior in the presence of well-defined stimuli.
2. For the most effective learning in classical conditioning, should the conditioned stimulus (CS) be presented before or after the unconditioned stimulus (US)?
3. To extinguish classical conditioning, you must break the association between which pair?
   a. CS and CR
   b. US and UR
   c. US and CR
4. After extinction and a period of rest, a CS may again elicit a CR; this phenomenon is known as _____ _____ .
5. The process by which a learned response to a specific stimulus comes to be associated with different but similar stimuli is known as _____ .
6. A type of learning that essentially involves reinforcing the desired response is known as _____ _____ .
7. In the technique called _____ , a new response is acquired by successively reinforcing partial responses.
8. Which kind of reinforcement is administered when an aversive stimulus is turned off?
   a. positive reinforcement
   b. negative reinforcement
   c. positive punishment
   d. negative punishment
9. Classify the following as (1) primary or (2) secondary reinforcers:
   ___ food   ___ money
   ___ diploma   ___ sex
10. Identify the following schedules of reinforcement as (FI) fixed interval, (VI) variable interval, (FR) fixed ratio, or (VR) variable ratio:
    ___ The subject is reinforced on the first response after two minutes have passed.
    ___ The subject is reinforced on every sixth response.
    ___ The subject is reinforced after four correct responses, then after six more correct responses, then after five more correct responses.
    ___ The subject is reinforced on the first correct response after three minutes have passed since the last reinforcement, then the first correct response after six minutes since reinforcement, then the first correct response after five minutes since reinforcement.
11. Unreinforced, or latent, learning may be stored internally. Particularly when this learning concerns spatial relationships, it is called a _____ _____ .
12. An ape examines a problem and the tools available for solving it. Suddenly, he leaps up and quickly executes a successful solution. This is an example of
    a. insight.
    b. operant conditioning.
    c. trial and error learning.
13. Which of the following factors have been identified by contingency theorists as necessary for learning?
    a. a surprising UCS
    b. strong reinforcement
    c. blocking
14. According to social learning theorists, what is the source of reinforcement?
    a. internal standards of behavior
    b. external rewards
    c. both a and b

6 Memory

■ Thinking Critically

How do we know the difference between "*You* did it!" and You *did* it!"

Why is it easier to recall an unfamiliar name or phone number once you've seen it written down?

Why does standing in the phone booth repeating the number the operator just gave you help you to remember it long enough to place your call?

You wake up at 4 A.M. vividly recalling the dream you were having and then go back to sleep. When you get up at 7 A.M. you recall waking up but remember nothing of the dream itself. Why?

Is it a mistake to remember things as better than they were?

Why does studying help you remember things better?

Why can a certain odor or song bring back memories of a time or place you haven't thought of in years?

The answers to these and other questions about how memories are formed, stored, retrieved, and forgotten appear throughout this chapter and in the Chapter Summary.

■ Outline

- The famous conductor Toscanini was known to have memorized every single note of every instrument in about 250 symphonies and all the music and lyrics of about 100 operas. Once, when he could not locate a score of Joachim Raff's Quartet No. 5, he sat down and reproduced it purely from memory—despite not having seen or played the score for decades. Nonetheless, when a copy of the quartet was finally found, it was discovered that with the exception of one single note, Toscanini had reproduced it perfectly (Neisser, 1982).
- A waiter named John Conrad never writes down a single item of a customer's order. He routinely handles parties of 6 and 8 in a busy Colorado restaurant, remembering everything from soup to salad dressing. Once he handled a party of 19, distributing 19 complete dinners among his customers without a single error (Singular, 1982).
- Before being stricken with a viral illness, a 29-year-old woman (known as MZ) could remember "the exact day of the week of future or past events of almost anything that touched my life . . . all personal telephone numbers . . . colors of interiors and what people wore . . . pieces of music . . . recalling a picture, as a painting in a museum, was like standing in the museum looking at it again" (Klatzky, 1980).

These accounts of people with extraordinary memories raise numerous questions about the nature of memory. Why are some people so much better at remembering things than others? Are they simply born with good memories or do they learn to remember unusually well? Could I learn to remember as much as these people do? And why is it that remembering can sometimes be so simple (as when a baseball fan remembers every batting average on his favorite team) and yet so difficult at others (as when groping for answers on an exam)? Why do we find it so difficult to remember something that happened only a few months ago, yet find ourselves able to recall every vivid detail of some other event that happened 10, 20, or even 30 years ago? Just how does memory work and what makes it fail? We will be exploring all these and other questions about memory in this chapter.

Since we can only remember those things that we perceive in the first place, we will start by looking at what happens to the vast amounts of information that continually bombard our senses. We begin by selecting some of this information to think about and potentially remember.

■ The Sensory Registers

If you look slowly around the room, you will see that each glance—which may last for only a fraction of a second—takes in an enormous amount of visual information, including colors, shapes, textures, relative brightness, shadows, and so on. At the same time, you are taking in sounds, smells, and other kinds of sensory data. All this raw information flows from your senses into what are known as the **sensory registers.** These are like waiting rooms. Information enters, stays for a very short time, and then is either processed further or lost. Although there are registers for each of our several senses, the visual and auditory registers have been studied most extensively, and it is to them that we now turn.

Visual and Auditory Registers

In order to understand how much visual information we take in, and how quickly it is lost, take an instant camera into a darkened room and take a photograph using a flashbulb. During the split second that the room is lit up by the flash, your visual register will take in a surprising amount of information about the room and its contents. Try to hold on to that visual image, or *icon,* as long as you can. You will find that it fades rapidly and, in a few seconds, is gone. Then compare your remembered image of the room with what you actually saw at the time, as captured in the photograph. You will notice that there was far more information taken in by the visual register than you were able to retain for even a few seconds.

A clever set of experiments by George Sperling (1960) clearly demonstrates the speed with which information disappears from the visual register. Sperling flashed groups of letters, such as those in Figure 6-1, on a screen for just a fraction of a second. When the letters were gone, he then sounded a tone in order to tell his subjects which row of letters they should try to recall: A high-pitched tone meant that they should try to remember the top row of letters; a low-pitched tone meant that they should recall the bottom row; and a medium-pitched tone signaled them to recall the middle row. Using this *partial-report technique,* Sperling found that if he sounded the tone immediately after the letters were flashed, his subjects could usually recall 3 or 4 of the letters in any of the three rows: That is, they seemed to have at least 9 of the original 12 letters in their visual registers. But if he waited for even one second before sounding the tone, his subjects were able to recall only 1 or 2 letters from any single row; in just one second, they apparently had lost all but 4 or 5 of the original set of 12 letters.

In fact, there is some evidence that under normal circumstances, visual information may disappear from the visual register even more rapidly than Sperling thought. In real life outside the laboratory, new visual

Even though our *sensory registers* may take in an enormous amount of visual and other sensory information, we are able to enlist our attention—the process of sensing selectively and giving meaning to incoming sensory information—to help us function and make sense of such situations.

Attention Selection of some incoming information for further processing.

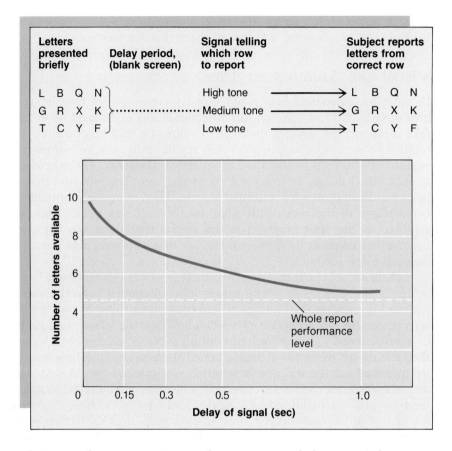

Figure 6-1
Sperling's partial-report technique is illustrated at the top; the results are given in the graph. The longer the signal was delayed, the more the number of recalled letters decreased.

information keeps coming into the register, and this new information replaces or "erases" the old information almost immediately. This is just as well, because otherwise the visual information would simply pile up in the sensory register and get hopelessly scrambled. Under normal viewing conditions, visual information is erased from the sensory register in about a quarter of a second and is replaced by new information long before it has a chance to fade out by itself.

Auditory information fades more slowly than visual information. The auditory equivalent of the icon is the *echo*. The echo tends to last for several seconds, which, given the nature of speech, is fortunate. Otherwise, "*You* did it!" would be indistinguishable from "You *did* it!" because we would be unable to remember the emphasis on the first words by the time the last words were registered.

Initial Processing

If information disappears from the sensory registers so rapidly, how do we remember anything for more than a second or two? The answer is that we select some of the incoming information and hold it for further processing and, perhaps, for remembering permanently (see Figure 6-2). No matter how hard we try, we simply cannot be aware of all the details that bombard our senses. We constantly select which information is chosen for further processing. This is what we call **attention:** the process of selective looking, listening, smelling, tasting, and feeling. In the process of attending, we also give *meaning* to the information that is coming in.

Information in the sensory registers is just meaningless raw data. Look at the page in front of you. You will see a series of black lines on a white page. Until you recognize these lines as letters and words, they are just meaningless marks. In order for you to make sense of this jumble of data, the information in the sensory registers must be processed for meaning.

Suppose you are sitting at a desk reading this book. Your roommate is listening to a talk show on the radio. There are traffic sounds outside. The water you are heating to make tea starts to boil. Even if you turn off the kettle and ask your roommate to take the radio into the other room, there will still be at least a vague hum from the radio, the traffic noises will continue, and you will taste the tea as you read. In situations like this, how do we select which information to pay attention to?

Broadbent (1958) suggested that there is a filtering process at the entrance to the nervous system. All incoming stimuli are accepted into the sensory registers, where they are sorted out by physical properties such as color, size, loudness, location, shape, and so on. Only those stimuli that meet certain requirements are allowed through the filter. According to Broadbent, only those stimuli that get through the filter are compared with what we already know, so that we can recognize them and figure out what they mean. If you are sitting at a restaurant table listening to a friend talk, you filter out all other conversations taking place around you. Although you may be able to describe certain physical characteristics of those other conversations, such as whether they were spoken by men or women or spoken loudly or softly, according to Broadbent you would normally be unable to describe what was being said. Because the conversations were filtered out, processing did not reach the point at which you could understand the meaning of what you heard.

According to Broadbent's theory, information will draw our attention if it is made to stand out because of its physical properties—intensity,

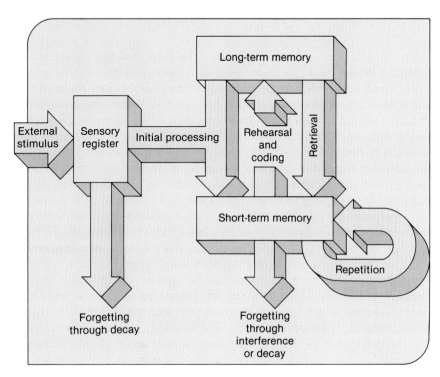

Figure 6-2
The sequence of information processing in memory Raw information flows from the senses into the *sensory registers*, where it is either further processed or lost. Information chosen for further processing enters *short-term memory*, from which it is either forgotten or transferred into *long-term memory*.

The First Scientific Research on Memory

In the middle of the nineteenth century, the psychology of learning and memory was still pretty much in the realm of philosophy. Hermann Ebbinghaus, a German psychologist, designed the first real memory experiment with well-defined independent and dependent variables and controls for other factors. The only real problem with Ebbinghaus's experimental design, as compared with modern research, was that he used a single subject—himself. Nevertheless, Ebbinghaus was the first person to attempt an essentially scientific study of the phenomenon of memory.

Ebbinghaus tested the number of times that he had to read through a list of single syllables before he could repeat the list from memory. After once achieving "mastery" over a list, he allowed some time to pass, during which he worked with other lists of syllables in order to prevent himself from rehearsing the list that he was testing. Then, he went back to the original test list and again measured how many times he needed to read it through before he could recite it from memory. Even when he could remember none of the list after having first returned to it, Ebbinghaus found that he could relearn any such list more quickly than he had learned it the first time. The difference in times required for learning, or "savings," was Ebbinghaus's dependent variable.

To be sure that he was looking only at memories formed as he learned each list and not at associations formed earlier in his life, Ebbinghaus chose to use random lists of consonant-vowel-consonant syllables. He constructed the lists by combining all the possible beginning and ending consonant

Hermann Ebbinghaus and his learning curve Ebbinghaus found that the amount of previously learned material that could be retrieved decreased systematically over time, but not necessarily at a steady rate.

sounds and middle vowel or diphthong sounds to make almost 2,300 syllables. Most of the syllables were meaningless, although many certainly formed words familiar to Ebbinghaus from the several languages that he spoke. He then arranged the syllables in meaningless lists, with no inherent associations between words (Gundlach, 1986).

The *"cocktail-party" phenomenon* states that we can shift our *attention* if we sense something particularly meaningful. Thus, if someone around us in a restaurant were to speak our name, we would very likely shift our attention to their conversation.

color, sudden starts or stops. Yet most of us have had the experience of reading a book only to have our attention swing to a particularly meaningful word farther down the page—perhaps our own last name or the name of our hometown. Or, to return to the restaurant example, if someone around us were to speak our name, in all likelihood our attention would shift to their conversation. This is called the *cocktail party phenomenon* (Cherry, 1966). There is no physical reason why that one word should have stood out. In fact, according to Broadbent's theory, since we were not attending to it and it was presumably filtered out, we should not even have heard the word, much less understood what it meant!

Treisman (1960, 1964), among others, modified the filter theory to account for these exceptions. She suggested that the filter is not a simple on or off switch, but a variable control like the volume control on a radio that can "turn down" unwanted signals without rejecting them entirely. According to this view, many signals are passed on from the sensory registers at the same time. All this information gets at least some processing, during which time it begins to become meaningful—we begin to understand what we are seeing and hearing, tasting and touching. Although we may be paying attention to only some of this incoming information, we monitor the other signals at a low level. In this way,

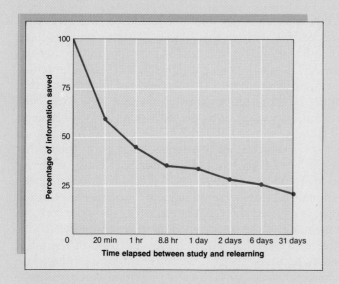

As you might expect, Ebbinghaus found that the longer he waited between trials to recite a list, the more he forgot. What was slightly more surprising was his discovery that this loss did not progress at a steady rate. The difference from one interval to another was greatest at the shortest intervals— say between one hour and two—and leveled out at intervals of days or weeks, as shown in the learning curve. In Ebbinghaus's terms, the difference between the memory savings at 20 minutes and the savings at one hour might be 20 percentage points, while the difference between one day and two might be less than 10 percentage points. Ebbinghaus found that he forgot more in the first 20 minutes after he first learned a list than in the next week.

Ebbinghaus manipulated the variables of his experimental design in many ways over several years. He compared the results when the relearned list was systematically scrambled despite containing the same syllables as the original list. He tried learning the list backward the second time. In both cases, while it took longer to relearn an altered list than to relearn the same list, it still took fewer trials than it had taken in order to learn the list in the first place. Ebbinghaus also varied the length of the list and demonstrated that it not only took longer to learn a longer list, but apparently took longer to learn each item whenever the total list was lengthened; it took more than twice as long to learn a list of 24 items than it did to learn a list of 12 items. In order to demonstrate the importance of using meaningless lists of syllables for his experiments, Ebbinghaus memorized an 80-syllable passage from a poem and a list of 80 of his random syllables. It took him many fewer repetitions to learn the poem in the first place, and his savings on relearning was much greater, presumably because the poem provided ready-made associations with which Ebbinghaus could process the material into long-term memory.

Finally, Ebbinghaus documented that there is value in *overlearning* material. In some trials, after he could repeat a list perfectly, Ebbinghaus continued to read it over for a set number of repetitions. When he tested the repetitions needed to relearn those lists after varying intervals, he found greater savings of learning time than when he stopped the original learning as soon as he achieved mastery. This is at least one point with direct application to the task of studying for exams: Even after you're sure you know the material, read it over a few more times, and you're likely to remember it even better.

although we are not normally aware of extraneous stimuli, we can shift our attention if we sense something particularly meaningful. This automatic processing works even when we are asleep: A classic example is the mother who wakes immediately to the sound of her baby crying yet sleeps through other, louder noises. The mother is paying attention without being aware of it. Similarly, most of us would wake up immediately to the words "The house is on fire," while we would probably sleep through less important phrases like "The car is for sale." When taking a practice test, you may recall where on a page a particular definition or explanation occurs without being able to recall just what that definition or explanation is. You processed its location automatically (Johnston & Dark, 1986).

Let's look more closely at the evidence for this alternative view of attention. How do we know that apparently "unattended" messages are not completely filtered out (and thus forgotten) at the level of the sensory registers? Norman (1969) gave subjects separate messages in each ear at the same time and asked them to *shadow*, or verbally repeat, one of these messages and to ignore the other. Nonetheless, he found that people could remember parts of the irrelevant message if they were interrupted during the experiment or asked to recall the message immediately afterward. Moray (1959) also found that if it had been preceded by the subject's name, part of an unattended message could be remembered immediately after the message ended. But without this "signal," Moray's subjects could remember little or nothing of the unattended message. In another experiment, MacKay (1973) asked subjects to shadow ambiguous sentences delivered to one ear while ignoring in the other ear information that clarified the meaning of those sentences. For example, the word *bank* can refer to a financial institution or to the sides of a river. All subjects shadowed an ambiguous sentence delivered to one ear which contained the word *bank*. For some subjects, an unattended message in their other ear suggested that the word *bank* referred to a financial bank, while for other subjects the unattended message suggested that *bank* referred to a riverbank. Even though subjects were subsequently unable to recall the unattended message, it affected their interpretation of the word *bank*. In other words, the meaning of the unattended message was understood.

To summarize, we know that we attend to very little of the information in our sensory registers. In part, we select information based on certain physical characteristics—such as color, a certain voice quality—and process those signals further in an effort to recognize and understand them. But other ignored signals get at least some initial processing, so that we can shift our attention to focus on something particularly meaningful. But what happens to the information that we do attend to? It enters our short-term memory.

■ Short-Term Memory

Short-term memory (STM) is what we are thinking about at any given moment. It is sometimes referred to as *consciousness*. When you listen to a conversation or a piece of music, when you watch a ballet or a tennis tournament, when you become aware of a leg cramp or a headache—in all these cases you are using STM to both hold on to and think about new information coming in from the sensory registers. STM therefore has two main tasks: to store new information briefly and to work on that (and other) information. Thus, STM is sometimes called *working memory*.

Capacity of STM

The arcade fanatic absorbed in a game is oblivious to the outside world. Chess masters at tournaments demand complete silence while they ponder their next move. And you shut yourself in a quiet room to study for final exams. All these examples illustrate the fact that there is a definite limit on how much information STM can handle at any given moment. In fact, psychologists have determined that STM can hold only 5 to 10 bits of information at the same time (Miller, 1956; Sperling, 1960). You can demonstrate this for yourself. Read the first row of letters in the following list just once. Then close your eyes and try to remember the letters in the correct sequence before going on to the next row:

1. C X W
2. M N K T Y

Chess players demand complete silence as they ponder their next move. This is due to the fact that there is a definite limit on how much information STM can handle at any given moment.

3. R P J H B Z S

4. G B M P V Q F J D

5. E G Q W J P B R H K A

Like most people, you probably found row 1 and 2 fairly easy, row 3 a bit harder, row 4 very hard, and row 5 impossible to remember after just one reading. This gives you an idea of the relatively limited capacity of STM.

Now try reading through the following set of 12 letters just once and see if you can repeat them: TJYFAVMCFKIB. How many letters were you able to recall? In all likelihood, not all 12. But what if you had been asked to remember the following 12 letters instead: TV FBI JFK YMCA. Could you do it? Almost certainly the answer is yes. These are the same 12 letters as before, but here grouped into four separate "words." This way of grouping and organizing information so that it fits into meaningful units is called **chunking.** The 12 letters have been chunked into four meaningful items that can be readily handled by STM. Here's another example of chunking. Try to remember this list of numbers:

1 0 6 6 1 9 4 5 1 8 1 2

Remembering 12 separate digits is usually very difficult, but try chunking the list into three groups of four:

1066   1945   1812

Particularly if you are interested in military history, these three chunks will be much easier to remember than 12 unrelated digits.

By chunking words into sentences or sentence fragments, we can process an even greater amount of information in STM (Aaronson & Scarborough, 1976, 1977; Tulving & Patkau, 1962). For example, suppose you want to remember the following list of words: *tree, song, hat, sparrow,*

Memory   **227**

box, *lilac, cat.* One strategy would be to cluster as many of them as possible into phrases or sentences: "The sparrow in the tree sings a song"; "a lilac hat in the box"; "the cat in the hat." But isn't there a limit to all this? Would five sentences be as easy to remember for a short time as five single words? Simon (1974) found that as the size of any individual chunk increases, the number of chunks that can be held in STM declines. Thus, STM can easily handle five unrelated letters or words simultaneously, but five unrelated sentences are much harder to remember.

A dramatic example of the power of chunking was reported by Chase and Ericsson (1981). The subject in this case, known as SF, was a young man who had spent more than 250 hours in the laboratory over two years, purposefully using chunking to increase his short-term memory for strings of digits. At the time of the report, SF could accurately recall strings of more than 80 digits. He accomplished this feat by associating groups of digits with his already vast knowledge of common and record times for running races of particular lengths. The digit string 3492 might be broken out, for instance, as a chunk associated with a near-record time for the mile, 3 minutes, 49.2 seconds. SF, by the way, was no better than average at remembering strings that he could not relate to running, such as strings of letters.

Keep in mind that STM usually has more than one task to perform at once. During the brief time you spent memorizing the rows of letters on pages 226–27, you probably gave them your full attention. But normally, you have to attend to new incoming information while you work on whatever is already present in short-term memory. Competition between these two tasks for the limited workspace in STM means that neither task will be done as well as it could be. In one experiment, subjects were given six random numbers to remember and repeat while performing a simple reasoning task. As a result, they performed their reasoning task more slowly than subjects who had simply been asked to repeat the numbers 1 through 6 throughout the task (Baddeley & Hitch, 1974). Similarly, if you had been asked to count backward from 100 while trying to learn the rows of letters in our earlier example, you would have been much less successful in remembering them. Try it and see.

Coding in STM

There has been a good deal of controversy over how we *code* information for storage in STM. Much of the early research on STM looked at how we remember strings of letters or numbers, like our earlier lists. And the evidence seemed to indicate that these kinds of information were stored *phonologically* in STM, or in a manner based on speech (Baddeley, 1986). In other words, we code verbal information according to the way it sounds even if we see the word, letter, or number on a page rather than hear it spoken. How do we know that information is stored phonologically? Because numerous experiments have shown that when people try to retrieve material from STM, they are likely to mix up items that sound alike and that are spoken alike even if they are visually dissimilar (Sperling, 1960). Thus, the letters B and V are often confused, while V and Y seldom are. The sequence PTGZDBVC is generally harder to remember than FJYQKRMH. Moreover, words that sound alike and are pronounced alike are often confused in STM. For example, a list of words such as *mad, man, mat, cap* is much harder for most people to recall accurately than is a list such as *pit, day, cow, bar* (Baddeley, 1986).

It used to be assumed that this difficulty was because the words sounded alike or were acoustically similar. It now appears that it is the fact that they are spoken similarly rather than their acoustic similarity that is the key to the difficulty in recalling these words. When saying "mat" or "mad" the movements of your mouth and vocal chords are very nearly the same, making it difficult for the STM to distinguish among them. In a series of studies designed to test this idea, subjects who were presented with items visually and prevented from articulating them did a significantly poorer job of recalling them, indicating that our short term memories are stimulated by vocalization and subvocalization rather than hearing. It appears that there is some truth to the old saying, "Say a word three times and it's yours."

Vocalization or articulation also seems to play a part in reading. This is particularly true for poor or beginning readers; but even experienced readers tend to *subvocalize*—that is, to pronounce words to themselves silently or audibly. This slows our reading down, of course, to the rate of speaking. In fact, the technique of speed-reading is based in part on learning to process printed words visually only. Yet Levy (1978) and others have found that subvocalizing printed words helps us to understand more complex material better. You can test this for yourself very simply. Try to suppress subvocalizing by counting from 1 to 10 quickly and steadily while reading something simple like a shopping ad; then try it again while reading something more complex, like an editorial. When you are prevented from subvocalizing, you will probably have much greater difficulty understanding and remembering the editorial than the shopping ad.

But not all material in short-term memory is stored phonologically. At least some material is stored in visual form, while other information is retained in terms of its meaning. For example, we don't have to convert things like maps, diagrams, and paintings into sound before we can code them into STM and think about them. And, of course, deaf people rely primarily on shapes rather than on sounds to retain information in STM (Conrad, 1972; Frumkin & Ainsfield, 1977).

In fact, it appears that the capacity of STM is actually greater with visual coding than it is with phonological coding (Reed, 1982). A good illustration of the superiority of visual coding in STM is the experiment done by Nielsen and Smith (1973). They asked subjects to pay close attention either to a verbal description of a face or to an actual picture of a face for four seconds. The subjects were then asked to match features of a test face with the features they had just seen or heard described. It took much longer to recognize the face from the verbal description ("large ears," "small eyes," etc.), a fact which suggests that visual images tend to be more efficiently coded and decoded than verbal ones.

Retention and Retrieval in STM

Without looking back, try to recall the five rows of letters you learned on pages 226–27. In all likelihood, if you haven't gone back to study those lists again, you will not be able to recall them. The reason is that material in short-term memory disappears in 15 to 20 seconds unless it is rehearsed or practiced (Bourne et al., 1986).

Why do we forget material stored in short-term memory? According to the **decay theory,** the passing of time in itself will cause the strength of memory to decrease, thereby making it harder to remember. Most of the evidence supporting the decay theory comes from experiments known as *distractor studies.* For example, Peterson and Peterson (1959) gave subjects a sequence of letters to learn, like *PSQ.* Then subjects heard a three-digit number, like 167. They were then asked to count backward from 167 by threes: 167, 164, 161, and so on, for up to 18 seconds. At the end of that period, they were asked to recall the three letters. The results of this test astonished the experimenters. The subjects showed a rapid decline in their ability to remember the letters (see Figure 6-3). Since counting backward was assumed to be a task that would not interfere with remembering, the fact that subjects forgot the letters seemed to prove that the letters had simply faded from short-term memory in a very short time. Later experiments by Reitman (1974) and Shiffrin and Cook (1978) led to the same conclusion. Decay, then, seems to be at least partly responsible for forgetting in short-term memory.

But Shiffrin and Cook also found that interference can lead to forgetting from STM. **Interference theory,** unlike decay theory, holds that information gets mixed up with, or pushed aside by, other information and thus becomes harder to remember. Some of this forgetting may be due simply to the limited capacity of STM, with new information pushing out old. This process is most pronounced, however, when the new information is in some way similar to the old. If you are counting items, keeping a running total in your head, or repeating a phone number over and over in order to remember it, you may not lose your line of thought if someone talks to you about the beautiful poem that he or she has just read. If, however, someone begins counting another set of items or calls

Figure 6-3
The graph shows the results of Peterson and Peterson's distractor study. The experiment measured the length of time that short-term memory lasts without rehearsal. Subjects showed a rapid decline in their ability to remember a sequence of letters.

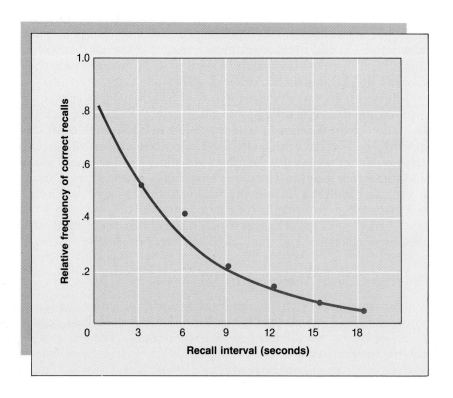

your attention to some other group of numbers, you will quickly become confused about which set of digits was yours.

Once information is lost from STM, it is gone forever. If you can't recall now those lists of letters from earlier in the chapter, you probably never will! Usually it is just as well that this sort of forgetting takes place. Not only does this process provide space in STM for new information, but it keeps us from being overwhelmed with a jumble of irrelevant, trivial, or unrelated data. In this sense, forgetting from STM is usually not a "problem." But there are two exceptions to this general principle: Sometimes we need to hold on to some information for a bit longer than 15 or 20 seconds, while at other times we need to remember a new piece of information permanently. How can we avoid forgetting these kinds of information?

Rote Rehearsal

If you want to hold on to information for just a minute or two, the most effective device is **rote rehearsal.** You talk to yourself, repeating information over and over, silently or out loud. Through constant rote rehearsal, information can be held indefinitely in short-term memory (Klatzky, 1980). Although this is hardly the most efficient way to remember something permanently, it can be quite effective for a short while. In fact, if you repeat something to yourself long enough, even if you cannot recall it later, you may recognize the information when you

Rote rehearsal Retaining information in STM simply by repeating it over and over.

■ Drugs and Memory

Memory can be both enhanced and impaired by the use of drugs. To date, most of the research in this area has focused on the short- and long-term effects of alcohol. Overall, the results show that alcohol interferes with the ability to encode new information but has relatively little effect on the retrieval of data already stored in long-term memory (Birnbaum et al., 1978). Heavy use of alcohol, however, may result in significant memory loss. In some cases, *everything* that was said or done while intoxicated is completely blocked out of memory. The person may fail to remember even highly significant events—such as having injured somebody! In extreme cases, chronic alcoholism may result in *Korsakoff's psychosis*, a disorder characterized by gross memory defects and disorientation. Sufferers of Korsakoff's psychosis may lose track of their own names, where they came from, or where they are.

The effects of marijuana on memory are far less clear. In one study, subjects who had smoked marijuana experienced unusual difficulty in transferring information from short- to long-term memory. They could recall items for a brief period, but as time progressed, they forgot more and more of the information (Klatzky, 1980). Like alcohol, marijuana appears to interfere with the ability to encode and store data in long-term memory.

There are drugs that actually enhance memory. Perhaps the most promising of these is DDAVP, a synthetic drug related to the hormone *vasopressin*, which is secreted by the pituitary gland. Vasopressin appears to increase a person's motivation and enjoyment of learning, and these are important factors in improving one's memory. Taken in the form of a nasal spray, DDAVP has significantly increased subjects' ability to recall information on cue.

Another hormone, *epinephrine*, may also aid memory. Gold and Delaney (1981) discovered that the memory-enhancing effects of epinephrine were greatest when it was administered right after a learning session. Delays in administering the epinephrine markedly reduced its effectiveness. These results suggest that naturally occurring memory problems may be due in part to inadequate levels of vasopressin or epinephrine (McGaugh, 1983).

Rote rehearsal, simply repeating material over and over, is a very common memory strategy. Repetition without any intent to learn, however, does not seem to enhance memory.

hear or use it again. If you look up a telephone number and then 20 minutes later you are asked, "What was the telephone number?" you are not likely to recall it. But if someone asks instead, "Were you dialing 555–1356?", you might recognize the number if you had repeated it often enough (Glenberg, Smith, & Green, 1977).

Rote rehearsal, simply repeating material over and over, is a very common memory strategy. Millions of students have learned their ABCs and multiplication tables by doggedly repeating letters and numbers. But mere repetition without any intent to learn does not seem to enhance memory. A child may see the same mailboxes day after day for years on the way to school and still be unable to recall the names on the mailboxes along the way. The mail carrier, however, probably could. Or think of the number of times in your life that you have handled (and presumably recognized) pennies. Stop here and try to draw from memory the front side of a U.S. penny. When you have finished your drawing, turn to Figure 6-4 on p. 234 and pick the illustration which you believe matches a real penny. For most people, this task is surprisingly difficult: Despite seeing and handling tens of thousands of pennies, most people cannot accurately draw one or even recognize one when it is shown in a drawing (the correct penny, incidentally, is C in Figure 6-4) (Nickerson & Adams, 1979). A well-known example of this same phenomenon is the case of Edmund Clarke Sanford, a noted psychologist of the early twentieth century. Professor Sanford described his inability to recall a group of prayers that he had read aloud "at least 5,000 times in the last 25 years, usually at 24-hour intervals." He was so used to reading these prayers that he could do so with very little attention. Still, when he actually tested his memory of them, he found that he could only repeat an average of three to six words before having to refer to the text for help.

Laboratory experiments have also shown that repeating an item more often does not always improve later recall. Craik and Watkins (1973) asked subjects to keep track of the last word beginning with a given letter in a 21-word list. For example, if the given letter was G, a typical list might include: *daughter, oil, rifle, garden, grain, table, football, anchor, giraffe,* and so on. Subjects would hold *garden* in short-term memory by repeating it silently until *grain* was heard, *grain* until *giraffe* was heard, and so on. As you can see from the list, *garden* was held in STM for just an instant since *grain* followed it immediately. But *grain* was held in STM for quite a while until *giraffe* finally replaced it. Nonetheless, subjects were equally likely to recall that *garden* and *grain* were on the list, despite the difference in rehearsal times for the two words. In other words, it is not the *amount* of rehearsal that increases memory, but rather the *type* of rehearsal. Rote memorizing for a long time is unlikely to be effective.

Elaborative Rehearsal

If simple rote repetition is not sufficient, what do we have to do to assure that information in STM will be remembered for a long time? Most researchers believe that **elaborative rehearsal** is necessary (Postman, 1975). Elaborative rehearsal involves relating new information to something that we already know. Suppose that you had to remember that the French word *poire* means *pear*. You are already familiar with *pear*, both as a word and as a fruit. *Poire*, however, means nothing to you. In order

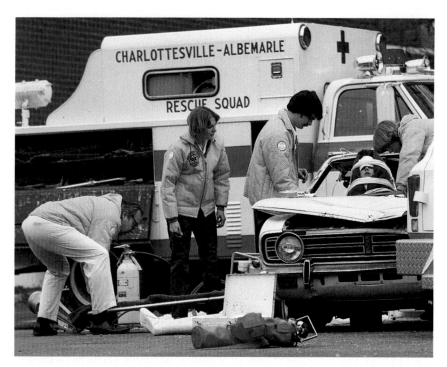

Elaborative rehearsal The linking of new information in short-term memory to familiar material stored in long-term memory.

Retrograde amnesia Inability to recall events immediately preceding an accident or injury, but without loss of earlier memory.

A person who suffers a concussion may not be able to recall what directly preceded the injury. This happens because the injury interferes with *elaborative rehearsal*.

to remember what it means, you have to link it up with *pear*. To do this, you might make up a sentence: *Pear* and *poire* both begin with *p*. Or you might associate *poire* with the familiar taste and image of a pear.

You can see that elaborative rehearsal involves a deeper and more meaningful processing of new data than does simple rote repetition. Unless material gets rehearsed in this way, it will quickly be forgotten. For example, consider for a moment what happens when elaborative rehearsal is either interrupted or prevented. Frequently, a person who has suffered a concussion cannot recall what directly preceded the injury even though he or she can remember what happened some time before the injury. A severe electric shock can have the same effect. This condition is known as **retrograde amnesia.** The events right before the accident were at the short-term memory level and had not been rehearsed enough to be remembered for more than a short time. Thus, they were completely forgotten.

Dreams also occur in STM, and unless they are rehearsed or repeated, they will quickly be forgotten. Cohen (1974) asked one group of subjects to call the weather report on the telephone immediately after they woke up and to write down the day's expected temperature. This effectively prevented them from rehearsing their dreams. A second group of students was instructed to lie still for 90 seconds upon waking—the approximate time the first group took to call the weather report—and then to write down their dreams. This group could think about and rehearse their dreams while waiting. Only 33 percent of the first group could recall their dreams, while 63 percent of the second group remembered theirs.

Barring disruptions such as these, elaborative rehearsal seems to be necessary if you want to remember something more or less permanently. But before we go further in understanding the nature of this process, we need to understand more about long-term memory.

Figure 6-4
Which of these accurately illustrates a real U.S. penny?

Long-term memory (LTM) Portion of memory that is more or less permanent and that corresponds to everything we "know."

Procedural memory Portion of long-term memory that contains learned associations between stimuli and responses.

Semantic memory Portion of long-term memory that stores general facts and information.

Episodic memory Portion of long-term memory that stores more specific information that has personal meaning.

■ Long-Term Memory

Everything that we "know" is stored in **long-term memory (LTM):** the words to a song, the results of the last election, the meaning of "justice," how to ride a bicycle. One portion of LTM contains the kinds of basic, learned associations between stimuli and responses that we discussed in Chapter 5. Links between conditioned stimuli and conditioned responses, between cues and operant behaviors—all these are stored in the portion of LTM that Tulving (1985) calls **procedural memory.** These associations provide blueprints for actions. They are learned by direct experience and are expressed in overt behavior. They make it possible for us to drive a car, to ski down a hill, to use a knife and fork, to operate vending machines—all of these are complex stimulus-response patterns that we have learned through experience, and they are all part of long-term memory.

Other portions of LTM consist of general knowledge: We know that 2 and 2 make 4 and that George Washington was the first president of the United States. We also understand the meanings of the various words in this sentence, as well as abbreviations like TV, FBI, JFK, and YMCA. Psychologists call this portion of LTM **semantic memory.** Semantic memory is much like a dictionary or encyclopedia, filled with general facts and information. When you see the words *George Washington*, you can call up a great variety of additional information from LTM: 1776, the first president, Father of Our Country, Mt. Vernon, crossing the Delaware, wooden teeth, a holiday in February. You may have learned these things by reading, by being told about them, or by observing places and enactments; and you can use the information in an infinite variety of ways.

Still other information in LTM is more personal and specific: what you ate for dinner last night, the date you were born, and what you are supposed to be doing tomorrow at 4 P.M. This personal kind of knowledge is called **episodic memory** (Tulving, 1972, 1985). Episodic memory is made up of specific events that have personal meaning for us. If semantic memory is like an encyclopedia or dictionary, episodic memory is more like a diary, although it may also include events in which you did not participate but which are important to you. Episodic memory lets you "go back in time" to a childhood birthday party, to the day you were in an auto accident, to the story of how your parents met, to the great time you had with your best friend last Washington's Birthday.

It should be clear by now that unlike STM, LTM contains a stag-

Pathology of Memory

Forgetting is a normal, even healthy part of remembering. As we have seen, both decay and interference commonly lead to forgetting in short-term memory. Any information that has been poorly encoded may be very difficult to retrieve from long-term memory. These are fairly normal occurrences of forgetting. But sometimes forgetting can become uncontrollable and persistent. When it actually interferes with our normal memory processes, we consider it to be a pathology of memory. Most often, pathological memory conditions result from traumatic events like accidents or disease.

Head injuries like concussions are a common cause of retrograde amnesia, ordinarily a temporary condition in which events just prior to an accident cannot be recalled. Also, damage to the hippocampus region of the brain may cause *hippocampal amnesia*. This too entails a breakdown in the transference of data from short- to long-term memory and usually results in more extended memory loss. More devastating still is the memory damage caused by a brain disorder known as *Milner's syndrome*. In 1959, Brenda Milner studied one young man who had lost part of his temporal lobes and hippocampus in a brain operation. His IQ did not decline after the operation. He could remember events that preceded the operation as well as anyone else, but nothing that had happened *since* the operation stuck in his mind. His family moved to a new house shortly after his stay in the hospital, and although he remembered his old address perfectly well, the new one eluded him. He might use the lawn mower on a Tuesday, but on Wednesday his mother would have to tell him all over again where to find it. He read the same magazines over and over—and each time the material was new to him (Milner, 1959).

A person with this syndrome can remember events from the distant past before brain damage occurred. He or she can also retain new information for a short time if it is repeated. But the person cannot transfer new material from short-term memory to long-term memory, even though long-term memory is still "working" well enough to retrieve "old" memories from the distant past (Klatzky, 1980).

Forgetfulness also plays a prominent role in various degenerative diseases. *Alzheimer's disease*, for example, is an untreatable neurological disorder that involves severe memory loss.

The causes of memory pathology are invariably traced to brain damage. But what causes brain damage? Nutritional imbalances may be an important factor in some cases. Accidents, including those caused inadvertently during surgical operations, are another. Other research shows that supposedly beneficial drugs like antibiotics can cause varying degrees of forgetfulness, apparently by inhibiting essential protein synthesis (Rosenzweig & Leiman, 1982).

gering amount of information. Yet we nonetheless reach down and retrieve almost instantly such things as the number of days in a year, the name of the current president, and the temperature at which water freezes. How can we retrieve isolated facts like these so quickly from the vast storehouse of LTM? The answer is *organization*. The information in LTM is highly organized and cross-referenced like a cataloging system in a library or the index at the back of this book. The more carefully we

Information in LTM is highly organized and cross-referenced like a cataloging system in a library.

organize and cross-reference information when it goes into LTM, the more likely it is that we will be able to retrieve it later. Let's look more closely at the ways in which information is placed in LTM and then see how the nature of these processes affects the storage and retrieval of long-term memories.

Coding in LTM

Can you picture the shape of Florida? Do you know what a trumpet sounds like? Can you recall the smell of a rose or the taste of coffee? When you answer the telephone, can you sometimes identify the caller immediately, just from the sound of the voice? The fact that you can do most or all these things suggests that at least some long-term memories are coded in terms of nonverbal images: smells, tastes, and so on.

But most of the information in LTM seems to be coded in terms of meaning. If material is especially familiar (the national anthem, perhaps, or the opening of Lincoln's Gettysburg Address) you may have stored it verbatim in LTM, and with a little luck you can retrieve it word-for-word when you need it. More often, however, we do not use verbatim storage in LTM. If someone tells you a long, rambling story, complete with flashbacks, you may listen to every word but you certainly will not try to remember the story verbatim. Instead, you will extract the main points of the story and try to remember those. Even simple sentences are usually coded in terms of their meaning. For example, the sentences "Tom called John" and "John was called by Tom" differ in what psychologists call their **surface structure**—the particular arrangement of words in each sentence. But they both mean the same thing—their **deep structure** is identical—and under normal conditions they are both stored in LTM in the same way. Thus, when people are asked to remember that "Tom called John," they often find it impossible to remember later whether they were told "Tom called John" or "John was called by Tom." They usually remember the meaning of the message (the deep structure) but not the exact words (the surface structure) (Bourne et al., 1986).

You will remember that information in STM gets transferred to LTM if it is rehearsed. *Elaborative rehearsal* involves extracting the meaning of the information and then linking the new information to as much of the material already in LTM as possible. The more links or associations you can make, the more likely you are to remember the new information later, just as it is easier to find a certain book in a library if it is catalogued under many headings rather than just one or two. This is one reason why we tend to remember semantic material better than episodic. Episodic material is quickly dated; we code fewer cross-references for it. For instance, you may remember that you ate a hamburger last night, but normally there is no good reason to relate that piece of information to anything else in LTM, and so it is not something you are likely to remember for very long. But if you have been a vegetarian for years and find the very thought of eating beef disgusting, then eating that hamburger was a very meaningful event, and it is probably linked to all kinds of other facts in your LTM. As a result, you are unlikely to forget it for quite some time.

We have been talking as if there were only one kind of elaborative rehearsal, but in fact there are many different ways of rehearsing material. Think for a moment about the way in which you might study for an examination in this course. If you expect a multiple-choice test, the way in which you study is likely to be quite different than if you expect a fill-in-the-blank or short-answer test. And if you expect to be asked to write answers to essay questions, your approach to studying would almost certainly be very different.

In other words, there are various ways of rehearsing material for storage in LTM, and our choice of method depends at least in part on the way in which we expect to retrieve the information at a later time. We believe that the way in which we encode material will have an effect on the ease with which we can retrieve it later, and research data confirms this belief (Flexser & Tulving, 1978; Leonard & Whitten, 1983). We will discuss this principle in greater detail when we examine ways in which memory can be improved.

Storage and Retrieval in LTM

We saw earlier that information in short-term memory disappears in less than 20 seconds unless it is repeated. But at least some information placed in long-term memory apparently does not disappear over time. In fact, under the proper circumstances, we can often dredge up an astonishing amount of information from LTM. In one study, for example, elderly adults who had graduated from high school more than 40 years earlier were still able to recognize the names of 75 percent of their classmates (Bahrick, Bahrick, & Wittlinger, 1974).

Some researchers have suggested that the effort put into encoding a memory may affect how long it lasts. Walker and his colleagues (1983) asked their subjects to read a series of paragraphs and then to recall the last sentence of each. These sentences contained more or less ambiguous references to other material in the paragraph, and that "more or less" was the independent variable. The researchers' hypothesis was confirmed: The subjects who read the most ambiguous sentences and therefore had to work harder to encode them remembered the sentences better than the subjects who read clearer sentences. These findings have not been verified, however, by some other studies of the effect of making an effort (Garret & Langer, 1983; Zacks et al., 1983); and the subject of the effect of cognitive effort remains open to inquiry.

But not everything stored in LTM can be remembered when we need it. Can memories be lost from long-term memory in the same way that they are lost from short-term memory? We concluded that loss from STM could be explained by some combination of decay and interference. Decay does not seem very likely to explain loss from LTM; recall your last conversation with one of your grandparents about his or her childhood or youth.

That leaves us with interference as an explanation. Experiments have in fact shown that competing information can interfere with long-term memory. Interference can come from two directions. First, new material may interfere with material already in long-term memory—**ret-**

Information placed in long-term memory apparently does not disappear over time. With the aid of retrieval cues, older adults have stored up a great deal of information in LTM, and those attending class reunions have often been able to recognize the names of a high percentage of their classmates.

Figure 6-5
Diagram of experiments measuring retroactive and proactive interference
In the case of *retroactive interference*, the experimental group usually does not perform as well on tests of recall as the control group, which does not suffer from retroactive interference from the list of words in Step 2. In the case of *proactive interference*, the experimental group suffers the effects of proactive interference from the list in Step 1 and, when asked to recall the list from Step 2, performs less well than the control group.

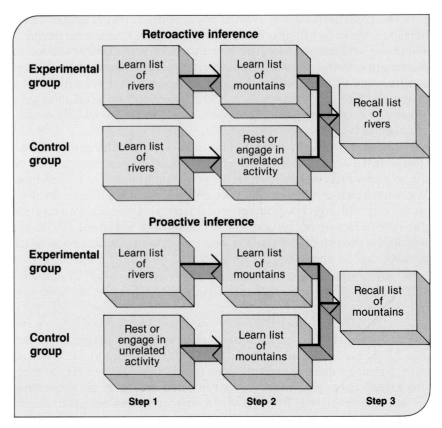

roactive interference (Figure 6-5). If you learn a new way of doing something, you may find it difficult to recall how you had done it for years. Second, the interference may also go the other way, with the old information blocking a similar new memory—**proactive interference** (see Figure 6-5).

Let's look at interference from another angle. Exactly how does it work? It could be a storage loss or a failure to retrieve a memory that is actually there—a retrieval loss. Retroactive interference seems to be due to storage loss; new information simply pushes the old out. It appears that proactive interference is due primarily to retrieval problems. The old and new memories are both there, but they may be retrieved by the same cues, and seniority seems to take precedence.

RECONSTRUCTIVE MEMORY. Some very interesting research on long-term memory was done by a British psychologist named Frederick C. Bartlett (1932). Bartlett had his subjects read a story or examine a drawing, then recount the story or describe the drawing at various intervals. In some experiments, he had one subject tell the story to another, who told it to another, and so on. Bartlett studied the ways in which the stories and drawings were transformed in successive accounts. For example, one of the stories he used is known as "The War of the Ghosts," a complex American Indian tale rich in the stuff of legend and symbolism. Bartlett's subjects, most of whom were students at Cambridge University, tended to drop out or alter many of the details of the story, especially details unfamiliar to their own culture. The name of the town from which the characters in the story came, Egulac, was almost never mentioned. The characters were often described as "natives" rather than Indians, and their canoe became merely a boat. While the story mentioned that the characters were hunting seals, many of the subjects described them as fishing, a more familiar activity. Yet the subjects seemed quite unaware that they had altered the story; they had recounted the tale just as they remembered it.

Bartlett's research shows that material in LTM interact in interesting ways. Memories change but may not really be lost. They may be transformed into something at least partly different. This phenomenon of *reconstructive memory* is very well recognized in the accounts of witnesses to, or victims of, crimes and accidents (see the Application on pages 250–51). People also rewrite their memories of past events to fit their current view or their desired view of themselves. Nor is this always a bad thing. A study of children whose home life had been so troubled that they had spent time in a child guidance clinic found that rewriting one's early history could make a difficult, disadvantaged life less of a liability. Of those original subjects interviewed 30 years later, those who incorrectly recalled their childhoods as fairly normal had been able to develop a basically stable, conventional life of their own (Robins, et al., 1985).

Reconstructive memory can be used for social or personal self-defense. Each time you tell someone the story of an accident, you may unconsciously make subtle changes in the details of the story—you like to think of yourself as more reasonable than that, and maybe the other guy wasn't quite that big—and these changes are encoded as part of the memory. When an experience doesn't fit with our view of the world or ourselves, we tend, unconsciously, to adjust it or to blot it out of memory altogether. This is the general phenomenon Freud described as *repression*.

At its most extreme, repression can cause hysterical amnesia. Screenwriters have gotten a lot of footage over the years of amnesia victims, and we are all familiar with some form of the story: A man wakes up in a strange city, unable to remember his name or where he came from or how he got there, but perfectly capable of reciting the alphabet or frying an egg. The memory of any personal information is gone. It makes a good melodramatic story—and it does happen. In hysterical amnesia, there is no apparent organic reason for the failure of memory. Usually, something in the person's life has been so frightening or so unacceptable that he or she has totally repressed all personal memories rather than remember that one incident.

The conditions of hysterical amnesia have been approximated experimentally. In one study, college students were taught a list of word pairs. After learning the list of pairs, they were read a second list of words, some of which were consistently accompanied by a mild but unpleasant electrical shock. This second list was composed of words that appeared to be related to the word pairs in the first list. If the students had learned the pair *thief* and *steal*, for example, the corresponding word on the second list was *take*. When they were tested for their retention of the first list, the apparent association of the "shocked" word with the word pair led to a significant drop in their ability to remember the original pair, even though the paired words had had no shock directly attached to them (Glucksberg & King, 1967).

USING SCHEMAS. The idea that past reactions and experiences can affect memory led Bartlett to develop his *schema theory*, a theory of the way in which people use past reactions and past experiences to organize and interpret their perceptions of an episode in the present. Modern schema theory has refined Bartlett's ideas somewhat, but the concept of schema remains at the center of the way psychologists view memory. A **schema** is like a script that past experience has begun writing for you with details to be filled in by your present experience. It is an unconscious mental representation stored in memory of an event, object, situation, person, process, or relationship that is stored in memory and used to compare current perceptions. For example, you may have schemas for going to the mall, eating in a restaurant, what Italians are like, driving a car, or attending a class lecture. A class lecture schema might include a large room, seating arranged in rows, a space in the front of the room where the professor or lecturer will stand, a podium or lectern, a blackboard, a screen, and other physical characteristics common to your experience of attending lectures. You enter, sit down, open your notebook; the professor or lecturer enters and addresses the class from the front of the room.

Schemas appear to serve memory in several ways (Brewer & Nakamura, 1984). They serve as a framework into which incoming information is fitted. For example, if you enter a restaurant and identify it as a fast-food restaurant, you know you should go to the counter. Schemas may also influence the amount of attention you pay to a given event. If you attend a lecture on acid rain, it is likely you will pay more attention than if you happen to overhear a conversation on the same topic in the cafeteria. Schemas may also help determine what you recall. In this way, schemas are means by which you engage in forming stereotypes. Schemas can help you fill in missing information or make inferences. If Bob is in a really bad mood one day and you find out later that he had a flat tire, your schema or mental representation of what it is like to fix a tire would help you to understand why Bob was so nasty at dinner.

In the preceding examples, schemas served to improve your comprehension of present circumstances. They also appear to help people *retrieve* information from memory. In one study, college undergraduates read a story about two boys playing hooky from school. The story related what the boys did at one of their homes while skipping school. Many details about the home were given in the course of the story. Later, the students were asked to recall as many details of the home as possible—either from the point of view of someone looking to buy a new home or from that of a burglar. Next, some were asked to do the same thing all over again, but this time from the other perspective. When students changed perspective, previously "forgotten" information was recalled, even though in both cases they were asked to recall as many details of the original story as they could. Students whose second perspective was that of the burglar suddenly recalled more of the possessions in the home, such as jewelry and crystal, than they had been able to recall when they described the details of the house from the perspective of the potential home buyer. Those who recalled the story as home buyers recalled things such as the leaky roof in the original story that they had not recalled earlier when taking the perspective of a burglar (Anderson & Pichert, 1978). Schemas seem to help people streamline their retrieval processes, so they recall what they need to know and filter out memories that are not pertinent to the present situation.

Other factors also affect retrieval from long-term memory. The more cues we have, and the more extensively the information was linked to other material when it was first entered in LTM, the more likely it is that our search will end in success. For example, if someone asks you to recite a poem you once learned, you may be able to do it without help: You have perfect *recall* of the poem. But suppose you get stuck halfway through and cannot remember the next line or phrase. When someone tells you what it is, you probably *recognize* it as soon as you hear it. If you are asked, "Who was the twenty-second president of the United States?", you might have difficulty recalling his name, since the only useful retrieval cue is *twenty-second*. If you were told, "His name is the same as that of a large city in Ohio," the additional cues might help you recall his name. But if you were asked, "Was it John Sherman, Thomas Bayard, or Grover Cleveland?", you would probably recognize the correct answer as Grover Cleveland immediately. His name is a powerful retrieval cue.

We can use not only randomly related material but hierarchically related information in order to retrieve material from long-term memory (see Figure 6-6). We don't have to stop and ponder whether both trout and tuna have fins, because we have placed both species in the category of fish, and all the information that we have stored for fish applies equally to both trout and tuna. Bower and his associates (1979) tested the memories of several groups of people for a set of 112 words. Some groups were given the words in sets arranged hierarchically into four categories of 28 words each. Other groups studied jumbled groupings. When the subjects' recall was tested, those who had learned hierarchical groups remembered more than three times as many words as those who had learned unorganized groups.

We have talked about retrieval mostly in terms of a conscious search

Figure 6-6
Diagram depicting hierarchically related material When information is learned in hierarchical groups, it is more completely retrieved from LTM.

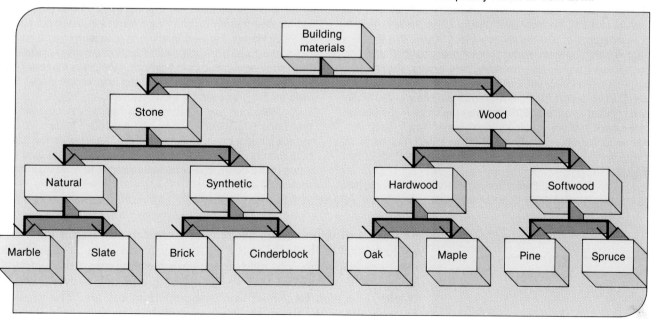

■ Flashbulb Memories

"I was standing by the stove getting dinner; my husband came in and told me." "I was fixing the fence, can go within a rod of the place where I stood. Mr. W. came along and told me. It was 9 or 10 o'clock in the morning." "It was in the forenoon; we were at work on the road by K's mills: A man driving past told us." These were three responses to the question, "Do you recall where you were when you heard that Abraham Lincoln was shot?" Other accounts were even more detailed. In fact, of 179 people interviewed, 127 recalled precisely the time and place at which they first heard of the assassination. That is a very high percentage, considering that the question was asked by a researcher 33 years after the event (Colegrove, 1982).

Being able to remember vividly a certain event and the incidents surrounding it for a long time has come to be known as *flashbulb memory*. Events that are shocking or otherwise highly significant are often remembered in this way. The death of a close relative, a time when we were seriously hurt, a graduation or wedding day may all elicit flashbulb memories.

There are several theories about how people form such memories. According to the "now print" theory, a mechanism starts up in the brain when something especially significant, shocking, or noteworthy is at hand. The entire event is captured and then "printed," much like a photograph. The "print" is then stored, like a photograph in an album, for long periods, perhaps for a lifetime. It is periodically reinforced, since such an important event is bound to be remembered and discussed many times throughout the years.

But this theory raises other questions. Why are very insigificant features remembered along with the main event— "standing by the kitchen stove," "mending the fence"? The answer given by the "now print" theory is that the entire event is registered, not just the main subject. Again, this is like a photograph. You may decide to photograph your mother sitting on the couch on her silver wedding anniversary. Your mother is the main subject, yet that same picture may capture the way the living room furniture was arranged, the way the family dog climbed into the picture, the way the crack in the plaster of the back wall seemed to be much larger than it really was. We were not taking a picture of those things, but because they were in the background, they too were registered (Brown & Kulik, 1977).

The "now print" theory implies, among other things, that

Even years from now, many people will have a *flashbulb memory* of where they were and what they were doing at 11:38 A.M. EST on January 28, 1986—if they are reminded that this is the moment when the space shuttle *Challenger* exploded.

flashbulb memories are accurate, that they are created at the time of an event, and that they are remembered better because of their highly emotional content. All these implications have been questioned. First of all, flashbulb memories are certainly not always accurate. Although this is difficult to test, let us consider just one case in point. Psychologist Ulric Neisser recalled the day that he heard about the Japanese attack on Pearl Harbor. He was listening to a baseball game on the radio, and it was interrupted with the shocking announcement. The problem with this vivid flashbulb memory is that baseball is not played in December when the attack took place! The vivid memory was simply incorrect (Neisser, 1982).

Moreover, even if an event is registered accurately, it may undergo periodic revision. We are bound to discuss and rethink a major event many times over. As a result, the flashbulb memory may become more (or less) accurate over the years until it bears little or no resemblance to what we initially remembered.

for a piece of information. But retrieval cues can also trigger memories without your deliberately trying to remember anything. If a professor mentions Napoleon, you may remember something about the Battle of Waterloo. But *Napoleon* may also conjure up a French pastry, a trip to Naples, or a man you know who is shorter than you are. The smell of an apple pie in the oven, the taste of apple pie, or the words *apple pie* printed in a book can all lead you to remember a particular experience of apple pie.

Thus, long-term memory offers a vast storage space for information that we can retrieve in a variety of ways. Its capacity is virtually limitless, and material stored in LTM never seems to decay, although it may be transformed. By comparison, short-term memory has a very limited capacity, and information may be lost from STM by decay as well as interference and simply running out of storage space. In order to maintain information in STM, we must refresh it constantly through rehearsal, or we may transfer it to long-term memory through processing. The sensory registers have an even smaller capacity for less permanent memories and no ability to process memories. Together, these three stages of memory characterize the information-processing view of memory (see Table 6-1).

Our discussion thus far has focused on the ordinary workings of memory. In the next section, we take a brief look at some examples of extraordinary memory and then turn our attention to ways in which memory can be improved. As you will see, exceptional memory essentially relies on developing the skills used in ordinary memory.

■ Special Topics in Memory

Extraordinary Memory

Some people seem to have truly extraordinary memories. For example, from time to time the newspaper will carry a report of a person with a "photographic memory." Such people can apparently create unusually sharp and detailed visual images of something that has been seen—a picture, a scene, a page of text. **Eidetic imagery,** as this phenomenon is called by psychologists, enables a person to see the features of an image in minute detail, sometimes even to read a page of a book that is no longer present. Eidetic imagery is much more common in children, but some adults also seem to have it.

Eidetic imagery Ability to reproduce unusually sharp and detailed images of something that has been seen.

TABLE 6-1 MEMORY AS AN INFORMATION-PROCESSING SYSTEM					
SYSTEM	*Means by which information is encoded*	*Storage organization*	*Storage duration*	*Means by which information is retrieved*	*Factors in forgetting*
SENSORY	Visual and auditory registers	None	From less than 1 second to only a few seconds	Reconsideration of registered information	Decay
SHORT-TERM	Visual and, especially, phonological representation	None	Usually 15 to 20 seconds	Rote or elaborative rehearsal	Interference or decay
LONG-TERM	Comprehension of meaning, elaborative rehearsal	Logical frameworks, such as hierarchies or categories	Perhaps for an entire lifetime	Retrieval cues linked to organized information	Retrieval failure, interference, or decay

Haber (1969) screened 500 elementary school children before finding 20 with eidetic imagery. The children were told to scan a picture for 30 seconds, moving their eyes to see all its various parts. The picture was then removed, and the children were told to look at a blank easel and report what they saw. They needed at least 3 to 5 seconds of scanning in order to produce an image, even when the picture was familiar. Once the image had been described, it faded away. Imagery usually could not be prolonged or recalled, but the children could "erase" the images by blinking or looking away from the easel.

The quality of eidetic imagery seems to vary from person to person. One girl in Haber's study could move and reverse images and recall them several weeks later. Three children could produce eidetic images of three-dimensional objects, and some could superimpose an eidetic image of one picture onto another and form a new picture. However, the children with eidetic imagery performed no better than their noneidetic classmates on other tests of memory.

No less dramatic are the more frequent cases of people who dazzle their friends and acquaintances with what seem to be impossible feats of memory. Such people are called **mnemonists.** One of the most famous mnemonists is the Russian newspaper reporter named Shereshevskii ("S"), who was studied for over 20 years by a distinguished psychologist, Alexander Luria. In *The Mind of a Mnemonist* (1968), Luria described how "S" could recall masses of senseless trivia as well as detailed mathematical formulas and complex arrays of numbers. He could easily repeat lists of up to 70 words or numbers after having heard or seen them only once.

These and other people with exceptional memories were not born with a special gift for remembering things. Rather, they have carefully developed memory techniques using the same principles that we have been discussing in this chapter. For example, Luria (1968) discovered that as "S" studied long lists of words, he would form a graphic image for every item. As these images became more numerous and complex, he would find a way of "distributing" them in a "mental row or sequence" so that one followed from another. "S" became so adept at this that he could repeat lengthy lists backward or forward, and even years later he could recall them perfectly. His technique essentially involved coding verbal material visually in a way that allowed him to see various complexities and relationships. When read a long and random list of words, for example, "S" might visualize a well-known length of a certain street, specifically associating each word with some object along the way. When asked to recite the list of words, he would take an imaginary walk down that street, recounting each object and the word with which it was associated. By organizing his data in a way that was meaningful to him, he could more easily link it to existing material in his long-term memory. In turn, this connection provided him with many more retrieval cues than he would have had for isolated, meaningless facts.

Developing an exceptional memory takes time and effort. Virtually all the mnemonists discussed thus far had strong reasons for developing their memories as they did. "S" used it to advantage as a newspaper reporter. The waiter we spoke about in our introduction used it to establish a clientele who gave him significantly larger tips for his memory feats (Singular, 1982). As we will see in the next chapter, chess masters also sometimes display astonishing recall of meaningful chess board configurations (Chase & Simon, 1973; de Groot, 1965). For example, some master chess players are able to recall the position of every single piece on the board after only a five-second exposure to a particular pattern. Yet when these same masters are shown a totally random and meaningless array of chess pieces, their recall is no better than yours or mine (Ericsson & Chase, 1982).

Mnemonics Techniques that make material easier to remember.

One memory researcher concluded:

> One of the most interesting things we've found is that just trying to remember things does not insure that your memory will improve. It's the active decision to get better and the number of hours you push yourself to improve that makes the difference. Motivation is much more important than innate ability (Singular, 1982, p. 59).

But even if you are motivated, what should you do to improve your memory? That is the subject of the next section.

Improving Your Memory

The key to improving memory lies in organizing and coding material more effectively when it is first entered into LTM. There are certain techniques called **mnemonics** that can be used to assist in this task. Such devices are based on the coding and retrieval principles that we have discussed in this chapter. When we use mnemonic devices, we deliberately impose some sort of order on the material that we want to learn.

Some of the simplest mnemonic devices are the rhymes and jingles that we often use to remember dates and other facts. "Thirty days hath September, April, June, and November" helps us recall how many days there are in a month. "I before E, except after C, or when sounded like A, as in 'neighbor' and 'weigh' " helps us spell certain words. Other simple mnemonic devices involve making words or sentences out of the material to be recalled. The colors of the visible spectrum—red, orange, yellow, green, blue, indigo, violet—can be remembered by using their first letters to form the name *ROY G. BIV*. In remembering musical notes, the spaces in the treble clef form the word *FACE*, while the lines in the clef may be remembered by "Every Good Boy Does Fine."

Greek and Roman orators used a topical system of mnemonics to memorize long speeches. They would visit a large house or temple and walk through the rooms in a definite order, noting where specific objects were placed within each room. When the plan of the building and its contents were memorized, the orator would go through the rooms in his mind, placing images of material to be remembered at different places in the rooms. In order to retrieve the material during the speech, he would imagine himself going through the building and, by association, would recall each point of his speech as he came to each object and each room.

Imagery is also a great aid to understanding and recalling verbal material. In experiments, subjects who are taught to memorize word lists by forming mental pictures related to the meaning of each word show better recall than subjects who use other learning strategies. If you were

Figure 6-7
Which of these two images is more memorable? The word pair *man—horse* could be recalled more readily if you imagined the two interacting. Although it was long assumed that using "bizarre" imagery—a man throwing a horse—was a more effective technique for recalling word pairs or lists, some recent research indicates that using plausible images—a horse throwing a man—is more effective.

asked to recall the word pair *man—horse*, your best bet would be to imagine a horse and man somehow interacting. You could visualize the horse trying to throw the man, for instance (see Figure 6-7). This strategy can also be applied to long pieces of writing. As you read, try to picture the people, events, and ideas described by the author. Sometimes, a single image can bring meaning to an entire paragraph. The more you visualize, and the more dynamic your images, the better you will recall what you have read.

Most memory improvement books are filled with mnemonic devices such as these, and they do in fact work if you are willing to spend the time to learn how to use them. For example, a study by Bower (1973) showed that mnemonic techniques were far more effective than simple rehearsal for remembering long lists of items. College students were asked to study five successive "shopping lists" of 20 unrelated words each. They were given five seconds to study each word and time to study each list as a whole. At the end of the session, they were asked to recall all 100 items. Subjects using mnemonic devices remembered an average of 72 items, but the control group—generally relying on simple rehearsal— remembered only 28. The subjects trained in mnemonic techniques were also much more successful at recalling the position of each item and the list on which it appeared.

How can you use the principles in this chapter to help you remember the material that you have been reading? You could simply reread the chapter until you have drummed it into your head. A more efficient approach, however, is active rehearsal, or recitation. After reading the chapter, close the book and try to remember what you have read. The more time that you spend recalling or attempting to recall the material, the better you will learn it within a given time. But there is an even more efficient strategy that begins *before* you have read the chapter.

IMPROVING YOUR MEMORY FOR TEXTBOOK MATERIAL. As we have said, the key to storing new material in long-term memory is making associations between the new material and information that is already stored. Several researchers have examined just how to apply this principle to learning material from textbooks. One of the most important elements of success seems to be starting with a framework or outline of the material so that you have associations, and especially hierarchical associations, ready when you get to the meat of the material. You can get such a framework from summaries and outlines provided in many books, especially textbooks, or from scanning the headlines on sections of a chapter or even the first sentences of paragraphs. In fact, one study (Reder & Anderson, 1980) found that, of two groups of students who spent the same total amount of time studying, those who studied only a summary of the material remembered more than those who read the whole text, whether the questions were taken directly from the text or required the students to combine material and draw inferences. The differences in performance persisted even when the main points of the material were underlined for the students reading the whole text. This certainly is not to suggest that you limit your study to scanning summaries—the details given in any text may be interesting and important, such as suggestions for improving your memory for textbook material. Reder and Anderson's findings demonstrate, however, that summaries can be useful tools, especially in studying for tests.

As you study, you should also try to relate the material that you want to learn to material that you already know and to confirm the relationship in your own words. This *elaboration* requires that you reprocess the material for storage (recall the difference between rote and elaborative rehearsal). You can also work with a friend, taking turns challenging each other with questions that combine material from different sections or paragraphs. Again, integrating and elaborating the material forces you to process it and to form new associations among the pieces of information that you are storing. This procedure provides more retrieval cues to help you get to the material when you need it.

THE SQ3R METHOD. Probably the most effective system for studying written material is known only by the letters of its five stages: SQRRR (or SQ3R, for short). SQRRR involves five steps.

Survey (1). Before you even start to read, look quickly at the chapter outline, the headings of the various sections in the chapter, and the chapter summary. This will give you an overview of what you will read and make it easier to organize and interrelate the material in the chapter.

Question (2). Also before you start to read, translate each heading in the chapter into questions about the text to follow. This helps you compare the new material with what you already know. It gets you actively involved in thinking about the topic. It also helps to bring the main points into sharp relief. Before you had read this chapter, for example, you might have translated the heading "Short-Term Memory" on page 226 into questions such as "Why is it called 'short-term'?" "Is there another type of memory that lasts longer?" "What good is a short-term memory?" "Why do memories fade?" It is usually helpful to write these questions out.

Read (3). Now read the first section in the chapter. Look for the answers to the questions that you have posed. If you find major points not directly related to your questions, try either to revise or refine your old questions to include the new material or make up new questions especially for this material.

Recite (4). When you have finished reading the section, close the book and recite from memory the answers to your questions and any other major points that you can remember. It may help to jot down your answers in outline form or even to recite them aloud to somebody. Then open the book and check to be sure that you have covered all the major points in the section. Repeat steps 2, 3, and 4 for each section of the chapter.

Review (5). After you have completed the chapter, review your notes and then recite your questions and answers from memory. Relate the material to other ideas, to your life, or to things with which you are familiar. Try to think of particularly good examples or illustrations. Get involved. The *SQ3R* method forces you to react—to have a kind of dialogue with the text. This interaction makes the material more interesting and meaningful and improves your chances of recalling it. It also organizes the material and relates it to what you already know. As we have seen, this process is important for transferring the material to long-term memory. Although this seems time-consuming, you will probably

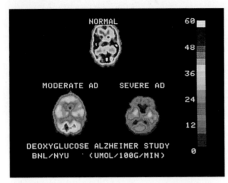

When compared to that of a normal brain, this CAT scan of the brain of a person with Alzheimer's disease provides a graphic illustration of the idea that memory is not centered in only one part of the brain.

spend less time overall because studying for exams later should go much more quickly.

Biological Bases of Memory

What physiological processes take place inside of us when we are remembering something? Where is memory stored and retrieved? These are the questions that we address now.

For the past 100 years, psychologists have attempted to determine if memory is localized in a certain part of the brain. In Chapter 2 we learned that some functions, such as vision and speech, are localized in this way. Early in the nineteenth century, it was believed that this was also true of memory.

We now know that no single part of the brain is solely responsible for memory. Lashley (1950) performed a pivotal experiment in which he removed various parts of rats' brains. Although their memories were found to be weakened by losing any part of the brain, the memories were still present. The amount of memory remaining seemed to depend primarily on the amount of brain tissue that Lashley removed, not on the particular portion of the brain that was removed. From this discovery Lashley concluded that a single memory can be stored in numerous parts of the brain, so that removal of any one part can diminish but not erase the whole memory.

Some of the learning by classical conditioning (see Chapter 5) may be stored in the cerebellum (McCormick et al., 1982). Rabbits blink when a puff of air is blown on their eyes, and a conditioned stimulus such as a tone can be paired with the unconditioned stimulus of a puff of air, so that the rabbits blink (conditioned response) when they hear the tone. After some rabbits had learned this conditioned response for just one eye, the researchers removed a tiny part of the rabbits' cerebellums on the same side as the eye that had been trained. After the operation, the rabbits did not respond to the conditioned stimulus with the eye that had been trained before, although the unconditioned response—blinking at a puff of air—was intact and the rabbits were still perfectly able to learn the conditioned response for the other eye.

It has been much more difficult to study memory for higher kinds of learning, primarily because these kinds of learning are mostly seen in humans and ethics prohibits tampering with the brains of living humans. However, the limited studies that have been possible—studying learning sets (see Chapter 5) in monkeys—have found a connection between higher learning and the cerebral cortex, where one would expect such learning to be stored. Thus, evidence seems to indicate that some memories may be stored in specific regions of the brain, while other memories are stored throughout many regions (Carlson, 1985). Studies have also examined many hormones, neurotransmitters, and other chemicals that are active in the brain and that may contribute to the way memories are transmitted, processed, and stored.

One possible explanation for the widespread storage of most memories is that several different senses seem to be involved in any one memory.

A single experience might be stored in the brain's visual areas, auditory areas, and areas for smell and touch—all at the same time. Another explanation is that the processing centers that retrieve stored material are widely distributed. Damaging the brain may interfere with only some retrieval mechanisms.

Recent evidence also suggests that specific parts of the brain are necessary for the *formation* of memory. At the base of the cortex is a section of the brain called the *limbic system* (see Chapter 2). It appears that in humans, the hippocampus—which is part of the limbic system— is instrumental in transferring factual information from short-term to long-term memory (see Figure 6-8). People with hippocampal damage can remember events that have just occurred (STM) but often have to write everything down to remember it for any length of time (LTM). For example, electroconvulsive shock therapy (see Chapter 15) disrupts the hippocampus, and patients who undergo this therapy for severe depression tend not to remember things that happened in the two or three hours just before the treatment—memories that might still be undergoing processing by the hippocampus when it was disrupted.

Recall the discussion of cognitive maps in Chapter 5. Normal rats had no trouble learning the maze and avoiding runs where they had already eaten food; but when their hippocampi were removed, the rats become very inefficient, spending a good deal of time revisiting spokes of the maze that were empty (Olton, Becker, & Handelmann, 1980). O'Keffe and Nadel (1978) traced the electric firing of neurons along rat's hippocampi and found that a different neuron fired as the rat reached each spot along a run.

A famous case of hippocampal damage is that of the patient known as HM (Milner, 1959). HM had his hippocampus removed from both sides of his brain in an attempt to relieve him of an incapacitating form of epilepsy. While his seizures were indeed eased, HM lost his capacity to process short-term memories into long-term storage (see the Box on amnesia for more on HM). Interestingly, the one kind of memory that HM can still acquire and store as effectively as ever is the memory of how to do things—procedural memory. Once he is taught to solve a particular puzzle, for example, he can solve it again, although he swears he has never seen the puzzle before.

It is now believed that the hippocampus helps the brain form memories by stimulating it to form new synapses; to make new connections among the neurons in the brain. Neurons in the adult brain do not reproduce. They do form new synapses, however, which is one reason we are able to continue to learn new ideas, improve our throwing arm, and form new memories long after our brains have fully developed. How are these new connections engraved in the brain's circuitry? Scientists have found that when a portion of the hippocampus is stimulated by an electric current, a small response can be measured farther down a neural pathway. If this area of the hippocampus is stimulated again, these circuits react much more vigorously, seemingly sensitized by the earlier stimulation. It appears that stimulation through the hippocampus causes new synapses to form and strengthens the synapses that already exist. This process is called *long-term potentiation*, or *LTP*, and it appears it be the primary means by which learning, and consequently memory, takes place.

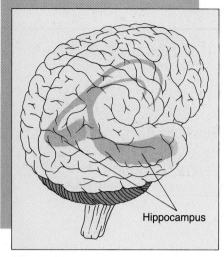

Figure 6-8
The hippocampus, part of the limbic system, is instrumental in transferring factual information (such as names, faces, or telephone numbers) from short-term to long-term memory.

No wonder Lashley was unable to find a single part of the brain responsible for memory. Different kinds of learning are stored in different parts of the brain, different systems of memory are stored in different parts of the brain, and different kinds of memories are processed in different parts of the brain.

⬤ APPLICATION

Eyewitness Testimony

Jurors in court cases are generally willing to believe eyewitnesses. Faced with conflicting or ambiguous testimony, it is tempting to put faith in someone who actually "saw" an event with his or her own eyes. However, this faith in eyewitnesses may be unjustified (McCloskey & Egeth, 1983). While there is no denying that eyewitness accounts are a unique and essential form of courtroom testimony, studies show clearly that people who say "I know what I saw" often mean "I know what I *think* I saw." And they can be wrong (Loftus, 1983).

Consider this scenario. Two women enter a bus station and leave their belongings unattended on a bench while they check the bus schedule. A man enters, reaches into their baggage, stuffs something under his coat, and leaves. One of the women returns to her baggage and, after checking its contents, exclaims, "My tape recorder has been stolen!" Eyewitnesses sitting nearby confirm her story when contacted by insurance investigators; many eyewitnesses are able to provide a detailed description of the missing tape recorder, including its color, size, and shape. In fact, there never was a tape recorder! The man and women were assisting psychologist Elizabeth Loftus in a study of the fallibility of eyewitness testimony (Loftus, 1983).

Increasingly, the courts have begun to recognize the eyewitness problem. For example, judges instruct juries to be skeptical of eyewitness testimony and to evaluate it critically. How serious are these reservations about traditional courtroom procedures? Take the case of Father Bernard Pagano, a Roman Catholic priest who found himself accused of a series of armed robberies in Wilmington, Delaware. After one witness contacted police to say that Father Pagano looked a great deal like the man in a sketch being circulated by the local media, no less than seven eyewitnesses positively identified the priest as the perpetrator. In the middle of the trial, however, another man—a man whose resemblance to Father Pagano was not close—confessed to the crimes (see the accompanying photographs). How did the court manage to become embroiled in such a potential miscarriage of justice? Well, it seems that the notion of a larcenous priest became plausible because the media had highlighted the fact that the culprit was unusually "gentlemanly"—polite, articulate, well-dressed, and so on. Furthermore, in presenting pictures of suspects to eyewitnesses, the police had apparently mentioned that the culprit could be a priest. Naturally, Father Pagano was the only suspect in clerical garb, and it would seem that the witnesses' memories adjusted to accommodate the fact that they were presented with the picture of a priest. Needless to say, Father Pagano was more fortunate than some accused criminals.

The structure of police lineups is part of the problem. In one study, hundreds of college students saw videotapes of staged robberies. Some of the students saw videotapes of traditional police lineups of suspects appearing simultaneously. Thirty-nine percent of the students identified an innocent person as the robber under these conditions. Other students saw videotapes of suspects who appeared one at a time. The error rate under these conditions fell to 19 percent (Cutler & Penrod, 1988). Clearly, eyewitness testimony is fallible, but there are some ways that its reliability can be improved.

In recent years, some courts have also begun admitting "expert testimony" from psychologists about eyewitness testimony in an effort to inform jurors of the potential pitfalls. What do psychologists tell jurors about eyewitness testimony? First of all, they make them more aware of factors that may interfere with a witness's memory. For example, information is subject to change or distortion even after it has been encoded in long-term memory. There is a marked tendency, especially with highly meaningful information, to shift it around until it is more to our liking or matches up more favorably with other recollections. Juries are also warned that cross-racial identification by eyewitnesses is extremely questionable. People have more trouble recognizing faces belonging to people of other races than they do remembering someone of their own race. And whites tend to be less accurate than other racial groups in identifying minority members.

Other errors in testimony may result from the way in which eyewitnesses are questioned by police, lawyers, and investigators. In one classic experiment, a group of students was shown a film of a car accident. They were then questioned about the film. Some were asked, "How fast was the car going when it passed the barn while traveling along the country road?" A week later, all the students were asked whether there had been a barn in the film. Nearly 20 percent of the students "remembered" the barn. In fact, there was no barn in the film (Bazelon, 1980; Loftus, 1980; Loftus, Miller, & Burns, 1978). Obviously, then, the strategies according to which questions are posed to witnesses can make differences in subsequent eyewitness accounts.

It might seem that a simple "Just give me the facts" is all that is necessary, but research has proven that helping eyewitnesses mentally travel back to the scene of the crime, having them recall the weather, the time of day, and the sounds and smells of the scene can make a big difference in how much they remember.

Father Bernard Pagano (left) was identified as an armed robber by seven eyewitnesses and nearly convicted for crimes actually committed by the man pictured on the right.

Then, once their description of the scene is completed, questions about details of the incident they've described should be asked in a reverse order—from the end of the story back to the beginning. This often yields more information than asking them to go back through the story from beginning to end. By looking at their memories in reverse order, eyewitnesses take a new look at the scene, again making it more likely that they'll recall new material.

On the other hand, expert psychological testimony has also become the target of considerable controversy. Lower courts have often denied the need for expert testimony, maintaining that it is within the scope of juries to decide on the merit of eyewitness testimony. Higher courts, however, have sometimes ruled differently, citing the usefulness of expert testimony. Psychologists, too, have expressed their own reservations. Some question whether expert testimony is either useful or necessary. Others maintain that research in this area is not sufficiently developed. Still others are wary of intruding into judicial proceedings where they may do harm (Loftus, 1984).

■ Summary

- Memory has three main structural components, each of which plays a particular role in the way memory works. The **sensory registers** have very limited capacity, and sensory memories fade very rapidly. Short-term memory has a larger but still limited capacity. Long-term memory, on the other hand, has a virtually limitless capacity.

- **How do we know the difference between "*You* did it!" and "You *did* it!"** The *sensory registers* receive sensory information from the external world. They may be thought of as the "waiting rooms" of memory.

They have a huge capacity, but retention time is extremely brief; if old information is not replaced by new information, it fades from the sensory registers in only a few seconds. Using the *partial report technique*, George Sperling discovered that the sensory registers hold much more information than we can retrieve from them. Auditory information fades much more slowly than does visual information, so words "echo" for several seconds after we've heard them.

- We are continually bombarded by sensory information; some of this information is selected for further processing. According to Broadbent, we pay *attention* to information that in some way stands out because of its physical properties. Other material is filtered out immediately and receives no further processing.

- An alternative view of attention holds that unattended signals get at least *some* initial processing for meaning. This allows us to shift attention to something particularly meaningful even if it doesn't otherwise stand out from the background.

- The information that we select for further processing enters our *short-term memory* (STM). The main tasks of short-term memory are to store new information briefly and actively process it and other information. STM is sometimes referred to as "consciousness" or "working memory."

- It is generally thought that the capacity of STM is limited to between 5 and 10 items at a time. We can process greater amounts of information by *chunking* material into meaningful units. However, as individual chunks increase in size, the number of them that can be held in short-term memory declines.

- **Why is it easier to recall an unfamiliar name or phone number once you've seen it written down?** There has been considerable debate over how we code information for temporary storage in short-term memory. It is now known that some verbal information is coded *phonologically*, while other information is coded in visual form. The capacity of short-term memory is greater with visual coding than with phonological coding.

- Material in short-term memory will disappear rapidly unless it is rehearsed or practiced. There are two basic explanations for why this happens. The *decay theory* states that time causes the strength of the memory to fade. The *interference theory* claims that other information simply gets in the way of remembering. It now appears that decay and interference both cause short-term memory loss.

- **Why does standing in the phone booth repeating the number the operator just gave you help you to remember it long enough to place your call?** Some information can be held indefinitely in STM by *rote rehearsal*—repeating the item over and over again, either out loud or silently. The amount of repetition an item gets does not always improve later recall, particularly if there is little or no intent to remember the material permanently.

- **You wake up at 4 A.M. vividly recalling the dream you were having and then go back to sleep. When you get up at 7 A.M. you recall waking up but remember nothing of the dream itself. Why?** To retain material more or less permanently, *elaborative rehearsal* is necessary. When elaborative rehearsal is either interrupted or prevented, information in STM is lost. For example, a blow to the head can cause **retrograde amnesia**—the inability to recall what was stored in short-term memory immediately preceding the injury. Dreams, which also occur in STM, will be quickly forgotten upon waking unless they are rehearsed.

- *Long-term memory* (LTM) is the storehouse for all we know. It has a seemingly unlimited capacity. It is also a highly organized and relatively permanent storage. There are three systems of long-term memory: **Procedural memory** contains learned associations that provide blueprints for action. **Semantic memory** stores general facts and information. **Episodic memory** stores the "stories" of specific events that have personal meaning.

- Although some information in LTM is coded visually, most of the information in LTM seems to be coded according to its meaning. People usually remember the meaning of a verbal message (its **deep structure**) but not the exact arrangement of words (the **surface structure**).

- Material does not seem to be lost from long-term memory by decay, but interference can block retrieval of long-term memories. **Proactive interference** occurs when old material in LTM gets in the way of new material and causes retrieval problems. **Retroactive interference** occurs when new material pushes out similar old material—a storage loss.

- **Is it a mistake to remember things as better than they were?** We tend to transform or "reconstruct" difficult memories to fit categories with which we are familiar or comfortable. As a form of psychological self-defense, reconstructive memory was identified by Freud as repression. In its extreme form, repression can cause hysterical amnesia.

- **Why does studying help you remember things better?** The more links that can be made between new and old information in LTM, the easier it is to retrieve new information later on. Organizing and cross-referencing information when it enters LTM makes it more likely that we will be able to retrieve it later. As a general rule, it is easier to remember semantic material than episodic material because more "cross-references" exist for it. Hierarchies are an especially effective way to organize material in LTM. One broad category of information may provide retrieval cues for many subgroups of information.

- One form of exceptional memory is *eidetic imagery*—the ability to reproduce images photographically. This ability is inborn, but other exceptional memory skills are ones that are carefully developed and practiced. Most memory experts, or *mnemonists*, are individuals who are strongly motivated to improve their memories.

- The key to improving memory lies in organizing and coding material more effectively when it is first entered into long-term memory. *Mnemonics* are techniques that help us remember material by imposing a meaningful order on it. Forming images or mental pictures is another aid in recalling verbal material.

- **Why can a certain odor or song bring back memories of a time or place you haven't thought of in years?** Some memories are stored in specific regions of the brain, and others are stored throughout the brain. One explanation for the widespread storage of memories is the involvement of different senses in any one memory. When certain senses are stimulated, we are often able to retrieve memories that haven't been accessible for quite a while. Another explanation is that the processing centers are widely distributed. Finally, there is some evidence that a part of the brain called the limbic system is specifically involved in the formation of memories.

■ Review Questions

1. Raw information from the senses flows into the ____ ____ before being either lost or processed further.
2. The selection process that allows us to retain information after it has arrived from the senses is termed ____.
3. We sometimes find ourselves shifting our attention to something that we had supposedly tuned out. This is called the ____ ____ phenomenon.
4. ____ ____ memory is what we are thinking about at any given moment. Its function is to briefly store new information and to work on that and other information.
5. According to ____ theory, the passing of time in itself will cause the strength of memory to decrease. By contrast, ____ theory holds that information gets mixed up with, or pushed aside by, other information and thus becomes harder to remember.
6. To assure that information in short-term memory will be remembered for a long time, the best strategy to use is ____ rehearsal, which involves relating new information to something that we already know.
7. ____ rehearsal, or simply repeating information over and over, is an effective way of retaining information for just a minute or two.
8. Two parts of long-term memory are ____ memory, which is filled with general facts and information, and ____ memory, made up of events that have personal meaning for us.
9. Usually the inability to recall items from long-term memory can be traced to inadequate ____ ____.
10. When the operator gives you the telephone number you requested, you have trouble remembering it because it resembles your friend's number. This is an example of ____ interference.
11. The psychological term for the detailed visual images that serve as the basis for photographic memory is ____ imagery.
12. Mnemonists are able to accomplish their feats of memory by
    a. repeating facts until recall is automatic.
    b. making use of unrefined natural ability.
    c. using carefully developed memory techniques.
    d. using the SQ3R method.
13. Arrange the following steps of the SQ3R method in the proper sequence: question, read, review, survey, recite.
14. Some memories are stored in specific regions of the brain, while others are stored throughout many regions.   T / F

7 Cognition and Language

Thinking Critically

What do you think of when you think of home?

How do we know that a lion is not a bird, but a penguin is?

You are driving to your friends' house in Spokane. Why might you be inclined to use a formula like $t = d/r$ (time = distance divided by rate of travel) when figuring out how long it will take to get there?

Why is it often helpful to draw a map when giving directions?

You must decide between an inexpensive, noisy apartment with neighbors who are a nuisance, and a quieter, more expensive apartment with nice neighbors. How might you go about making a decision?

Do these two sentences mean the same thing?

The ocean is unusually calm tonight.

Tonight the ocean is particularly calm.

Can animals be taught to use language?

Answers to these and other questions about how we think, solve problems, make decisions, and develop and use language appear in this chapter and in the Chapter Summary.

Outline

Cognition The processes of thinking.

Image A mental recollection of a sensory experience.

If someone were to ask you, "What is **cognition,** or thinking?" you might respond with something as broad as "Thinking is what goes on inside your head." And indeed this is not a bad answer. Cognitive processes play a role in many psychological functions. A clue to the vast range of things involved in thinking can be seen in the different ways we use the word. "I've given it some thought" implies reflection or meditation. "I think this town is like the one I grew up in" indicates conceptualization. "What does she think of all this?" is a way of asking for an evaluation. "Aha! I think I have the answer!" reflects problem-solving and insight. "I think I'll buy the red one" indicates a decision. These are all examples of thinking. Thinking includes the processing and retrieval of information from memory. But in addition, it requires manipulation of information in various ways.

In previous chapters, we have seen that thinking is relevant to such diverse processes as attention, sensation and perception, learning, memory, and forgetting. Later in this book, we will see how cognition bears a crucial relation to intelligence, coping and adjustment, abnormal behavior, and interpersonal relations. In this chapter, we will first look at the building blocks of thought—the kinds of things we think *about*—and then study the ways in which we use these building blocks in problem-solving and decision-making. Then we will examine language and the role it plays in thinking.

Building Blocks of Thought

Images and concepts are the two most important building blocks of thought. When you say that you are thinking about your father, you may have an image of him—probably his face, but perhaps also how he sounds when he is talking or the scent of his favorite after-shave lotion. But you can also think about your father by using various concepts or categories that help you to recall him—concepts like *man, father, taxpayer, butterfly collector, gentle, strong.* In the first part of this chapter, we will consider the role that images play in thinking. Then we will explore concepts and their relationship to thought.

Images

Stop reading and think for a moment about Abraham Lincoln. Then think about being outside in a summer thunderstorm. Your thoughts of Lincoln probably included such words as *President, slavery, Civil War,* and *assassinated.* But you probably also had some mental images concerning Lincoln: his bearded face, perhaps, or his lanky body, or a log cabin. When you thought about the thunderstorm, you probably formed mental images of wind, rain, and lightning. An **image** is a mental representation of a sensory experience; it can be used to think about things. We can visualize the Statue of Liberty or astronauts hopping around on the surface of the moon; we can smell Thanksgiving dinner; we can hear Martin

Luther King, Jr., saying, "I have a dream!" In short, we can think by using sensory images.

Moreover, researchers have found that we not only visualize things in order to think about them, we *manipulate* mental images. Shepard and Metzler (1971), for example, presented subjects with pairs of geometrical patterns (see Figure 7-1). In some cases, the two pictures were of the same pattern rotated to provide different views; see Figures 7-1(A) and 7-1(B). In other cases, the two pictures were of different patterns; see Figure 7-1(C). Subjects were asked to determine whether each pair of patterns was the same or different. The researchers discovered that subjects invariably rotated the image of one pattern in their minds until they could see both patterns from the same perspective. Then subjects tried to see if the mental image of one pattern matched the other pattern. The more a pattern had to be rotated, the more time it took to match it to the other. In other words, a pattern that had to be mentally rotated 180 degrees would take longer to compare than one that had to be rotated 90 degrees. Subsequent tests have supported these findings. It seems that we can and do manipulate mental images in order to help us think about things.

Images allow us to think about things in nonverbal ways. Albert Einstein relied heavily on his powers of visualization in order to understand phenomena that would later be described by complex mathematical formulas. Einstein believed that his extraordinary genius resulted in part from his skill in visualizing the possibilities of abstract conceptions (Shepard, 1978). Although few of us manage to match Einstein's brilliance,

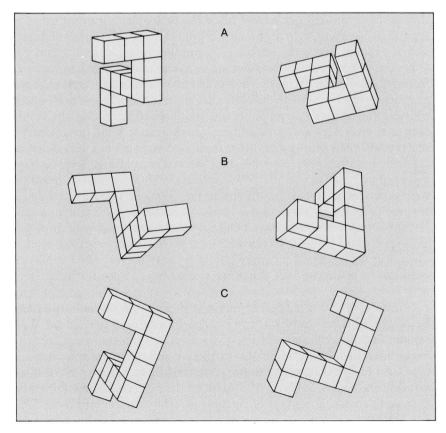

Figure 7-1
Examples of the pairs of geometrical patterns used in Shepard and Metzler's (1971) experiment The researchers found that subjects first rotated an *image* of one pattern in their minds until they could see both patterns from the same perspective. They then matched the mental images of the pairs of patterns to decide if they were the same (A and B) or different (C).

we nonetheless use imagery as an effective aid in thinking about and solving problems. All of us have watched a teacher clarify a difficult idea by drawing a quick, simple sketch on a blackboard. Many times, when words make a tangled knot of an issue, a graphic image drawn on paper straightens out the confusion. Images also allow us to use concrete forms to represent complex and abstract ideas. For example, you have no doubt seen a pie chart of a budget in which each item is represented by a wedge, the size of which varies according to its percentage of the budget. You can mentally compare the sizes of each wedge and imagine how the pie would look if a particular item received a larger or smaller wedge. Thus, images are an important part of thinking and cognition. Now let's examine concepts, another important building block of thought.

Concepts

Concepts are mental categories for classifying specific people, things, or events based on their common features. *Dogs*, *books*, and *cars* are all concepts that let us categorize objects in the world around us. *Fast*, *strong*, and *interesting* are also concepts that we can use in categorizing objects. When you think about an object—say a Ferrari—you usually think of the concepts that apply to it: for example, *fast*, *sleek*, *expensive car*. Thus, concepts help us think more efficiently about things; without the ability to form concepts, we would need a different name for every individual object.

Concepts also give meaning to new experiences. We do not stop and form a new concept for every new experience. We draw on concepts that we have already formed and place the new object or event into the appropriate categories. In the process, we may modify some of our concepts to better match the world around us. Consider, for example, the concept of *professor*. You probably had some concept of *professor* before you ever attended any college classes. In all likelihood your concept changed somewhat after you actually met some professors and took your first college courses. Perhaps your concept became more accurate: You might realize now that professors are not all absentminded, that some professors are not even 30 years old—in fact, that most professors are not very different from all the other people whom you have come to know. Your concept will become fuller as you add new information about professors based on your experiences at college. In the future, because you have formed a concept of *professor*, you will not have to respond to each new professor as a totally new experience; you will know what to expect and how you are expected to behave. Conceptualizing *professor* (or anything else) is a way of grouping or categorizing experiences so that every new experience need not be a surprise. We know, to some extent, what to think about it.

Interestingly, some recent research suggests that humans may not be unique in their ability to form concepts. For example, Edward Wasserman and his colleagues at the University of Iowa trained pigeons to peck different buttons when shown pictures of cats or people, flowers, cars, and chairs (Bhatt, Wasserman, Reynolds, & Knauss, 1988; Wasserman, Kiedinger, & Bhatt, 1988). Once the pigeons mastered the task, they were shown a new set of pictures of cats, flowers, and so on. Remarkably, the pigeons were able to correctly categorize the new pictures

"If only he could think in abstract terms. . . ."

about 70 percent of the time. It seems that they had learned the essential features that distinguish, say, cats from other objects, and were able to apply that learning to pictures they had never seen before.

PROTOTYPES. It is tempting to think of concepts as simple and clear-cut. But psychologists have discovered that most of the concepts that people use in thinking are neither clear nor unambiguous (Rosch, 1973, 1978). Rather, they are "fuzzy": They overlap one another and are often poorly defined. For example, most people can tell a mouse from a rat. But most of us would be hard pressed to come up with an accurate list of the critical differences between mice and rats.

If we cannot explain the difference between *mouse* and *rat*, how can we use these concepts in our thinking? The answer seems to be that we construct a model (or **prototype**) of a representative mouse and another prototype of a representative rat, and then use those prototypes in our thinking. Our concept of *bird*, for example, does not consist of a list of key attributes like *feathered*, *winged*, *two feet*, and *lives in trees*. Instead, most of us have a model bird, or prototype, in mind—such as a robin or a sparrow—that captures for us the essence of *bird*. When we encounter new objects, we compare them to this prototype in order to determine if they are in fact birds. And when we think about birds, we usually think about our prototypical bird.

Most people would agree that a robin somehow expresses "birdness" more than a penguin does. It more nearly fits our prototypical image of a bird. But prototypes are seldom perfect models. Robins, for example, do not contain every single feature that can be possessed by birds. For example, they do not have the talons of an eagle. Because natural categories are fuzzy, prototypes are only the best and most suitable models of a concept, not perfect and exclusive representations of it. As Lindsay and Norman (1977) point out, "The typical dog barks, has four legs, and eats meat. We expect all actual dogs to be the same. Despite this, we would not be too surprised to come across a dog that did not bark, had

Most of us rely on a model bird or *prototype* to think about the concept of bird. When confronted with a bird that does not readily fit that prototype, we rely on degree of *category of membership* to decide that a penguin is a "bird."

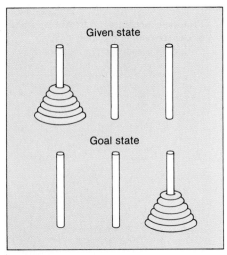

Figure 7-2
The given state (top) and goal state (bottom) for the disk-transfer problem
The goal is to transfer all six disks to one of the other two spikes without ever permitting a larger disk to rest on top of a smaller disk.

only three legs, or refused to eat meat" (p. 386). We would still be able to recognize such an animal as a dog.

How, then, do we know which objects belong to a concept? For instance, how do we know that a lion is not a bird but that a penguin is a bird? The answer is that we decide what is most probable or most sensible, given the facts at hand. This is what Rosch calls relying on the *degree of category membership*. For example, a lion and a bird both have two eyes. But the lion does not have wings, it does not have feathers, and it has four feet and a mouth full of teeth—all of which indicate that it is quite unlike our prototype for a bird. Thus, we are able to eliminate lions from the general category of *birds*. On the other hand, penguins share many features that belong to our prototype for a bird. As a result, we recognize these Arctic creatures as members of the bird family even though they lack feathers and don't fly.

So far we have seen how images and concepts form the building blocks of thought. In the next section we will turn our attention to the ways in which we use images and concepts to solve problems and make decisions.

■ Problem-Solving

Consider the following problems:

1. Six disks are placed on a stake, with the smallest disk on the bottom of the pile and the largest on top. Transfer these disks to another stake so that the largest disk is on the bottom and the smallest is on top.

2. You have three jugs; one is filled with 12 cups of water, the other two are empty but have a capacity of 3 cups of water each. Divide the water among the jugs so that the largest jug has 6 cups of water left in it.

Most people find these two problems very easy to solve. But now consider more elaborate versions of the same two problems:

3. There are three identical spikes and six disks, each with a different diameter but each having a hole in the center large enough for a spike to go through. At the beginning of the problem, the six disks are placed on one spike, one on top of another, with the largest disk on the bottom, then the next largest, and so on, in order of decreasing size up to the smallest disk, which is on top (see Figure 7-2). You are permitted to move only one disk at a time from one spike to another spike, with the restriction that a larger disk must never be moved on top of a smaller disk. The goal is to transfer all six disks to one of the other two spikes (without ever permitting a larger disk to rest on top of a smaller disk) (Wickelgren, 1974, p. 102).

4. You have three jugs, which we will call A, B, and C. Jug A can hold exactly eight cups of water. B can hold exactly five cups, and C can hold exactly three cups (see Figure 7-3). A is filled to capacity with eight cups of water. B and C are empty. We want to find a

way of dividing the contents of A equally between A and B so that both have four cups. You are allowed to pour water from jug to jug (Mayer, 1983, p. 173).

Most people find the last two problems much more difficult to solve than the first two. Why should this be the case? In part, it is because the solutions to Problems 3 and 4 simply take longer to work out than the solutions to the first two problems. But there is more to it than that. The first two problems are considered trivial because what you are asked to do is obvious; the strategy for solving them is simple and easily identified, and it is easy to verify that each step is moving you closer to a solution. The last two problems, however, require some interpretation, the strategy for solving them is not at all obvious, and it is much harder to know whether any given step has actually helped move you closer to a solution.

Let's examine each of these aspects of the problem-solving process. After we have looked at the principles of solving a problem and the steps and strategies involved in the process, we will turn to common obstacles that people face when they tackle a problem. To conclude, this section will present several techniques for sharpening your skills at problem-solving.

The Interpretation of Problems

The first step in solving a problem is called **problem representation,** which means interpreting or defining the problem. It is tempting to leap ahead and try to solve a problem just as it is presented, but this impulse often leads to poor problem solutions. For example, if your business is losing money, you might sit down to figure out how to cut costs. But by defining the solution narrowly as cost-cutting, you have ruled out the possibility that the best way to stop losing money might be to increase income rather than to cut costs. A better representation of this problem would be to discover ways to cut costs or increase income or both.

Now consider these problems:

1. Nine dots are arranged in a square pattern—three rows of three (see Figure 7-4). Without lifting your pencil from the paper, connect all the dots by drawing only four continuous straight lines.

Figure 7-4
The nine-dot problem Without lifting your pencil from the page, connect all nine dots by drawing four straight lines. One solution is given in Figure 7-6.

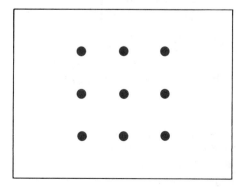

Problem representation Defining or interpreting a problem.

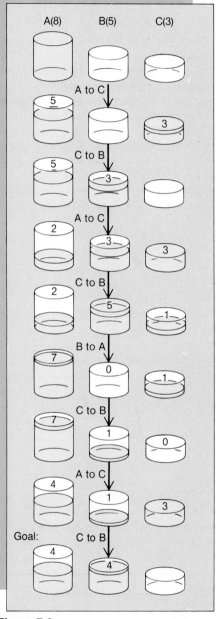

Figure 7-3
A version of a water jug problem The given state is eight cups of water in jug A and none in jugs B and C. The goal is to have four cups of water in jug A and four in jug B.

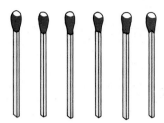

Figure 7-5
The six-match problem Arrange the six matches so that they form four equilateral triangles. The solution is given in Figure 7-7.

2. Arrange six kitchen matches into four triangles (see Figure 7-5). Each side of every triangle must be only one match length.

In working the nine-dot problem, many people assume that the lines must be drawn within the square formed by the dots (see Figure 7-6 for a solution). If they persist too rigidly with this assumption, they may develop "conceptual blocks." Similarly, on the kitchen match problem it is easy to assume that the triangles must all be in only two dimensions— that is, lying flat—or that one match cannot serve as the side of two triangles (see Figure 7-7 for a solution). In each case, easy assumptions have served as conceptual blocks against success in problem-solving. These two problems also illustrate another key factor in successful problem-solving: the way in which a problem is presented or interpreted. A narrow definition of a problem obscures the key to its solution.

Let us turn to a more difficult example. Carroll, Thomas, and Malhotra (1980) asked two groups of subjects to work on two different problems. One group was given a problem that dealt with *time*: organizing seven stages of a manufacturing process, taking into account specific guidelines or constraints. The other group received a problem that dealt with *space*: organizing the location of seven business offices on a corridor, again taking into account specific constraints. Although the two problems appeared to be quite different, they were actually the same: They had the same number of variables and constraints, and they had the same solution. Nonetheless, the subjects who worked on the spatial problem were far more successful than those who worked on the time problem. Why should this be so? The answer seems to be that both groups simply accepted the initial representation of the problem. The subjects who received the space problem automatically represented or interpreted the problem in visual terms. They all drew diagrams that showed how the offices could be arranged. This approach made this particular problem easy to solve. Most of the subjects working on the time problem, however, did not interpret it visually. They used no maps or other visual images. After many attempts, they became tangled in a complex maze of language and logic. When the researchers repeated the experiment but instructed all subjects to use a graphic approach to solving the problem, the two problems turned out to be equally easy to solve.

Another aspect of problem interpretation is deciding what class or category of problem the problem belongs to. Properly categorizing a problem can provide clues about how to solve it. In fact, once a simple problem has been properly categorized, its solution may be as easy as painting by numbers. For example, many people find the following problem difficult to solve:

> A farmer is counting the hens and rabbits in his barnyard. He counts a total of 50 heads and 140 feet. How many hens and how many rabbits does the farmer have? (Reed, 1988, p. 277)

This problem becomes much easier to solve when you realize it belongs to the same category as the following, more familiar problem:

> Bill has a collection of 20 coins that consists entirely of dimes and quarters. If the collection is worth $4.10, how many of each kind of coin are in the collection? (Reed, 1988, p. 277)

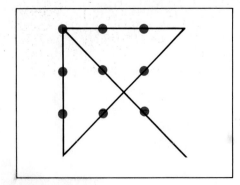

Figure 7-6

Quite often, people who seem to have a knack for solving problems are actually just very skilled at interpreting and representing them in effective ways. Star chess players, for example, can readily categorize a new game situation by comparing it to various standard situations stored in their long-term memories. This strategy helps them to interpret the current pattern of chess pieces with greater speed and precision than the novice chess player. A seasoned football coach may quickly recognize that a certain situation on the gridiron calls for a particular kind of defense. He has interpreted the game in terms of familiar categories. To a great extent, gaining expertise in any field, from football to physics, consists in increasing your ability to represent and categorize problems in such a way that they may be solved more quickly and effectively (Mayer, 1983).

Producing and Evaluating Solutions

Once you have properly interpreted a problem, the next step is to select a solution strategy that best suits the problem. When casting about for the right strategy, you must choose from a rich assortment of possibilities. In the following pages, we will examine some of the strategies that are often available.

TRIAL AND ERROR. One possibility is simple **trial and error,** but this strategy usually wastes many hours since it may take a very long time for the solution to appear. Moreover, many problems can never be solved strictly through this scattershot approach. How many guesses would it take, for example, to come up with the name of the seventh caliph of the Islamic Abbasid dynasty? Or, how soon could you guess the square root of the product of two sides of a given triangle? You could well go on guessing for the rest of your life.

To solve most problems, it is necessary to choose some strategy other than trial and error. The particular strategy you use should be based on an accurate categorization and representation of the problem. But it should also take into account the limits of short-term memory. We have to be able to retrieve information and work on it without overcrowding the limited work space of short-term memory. With this in mind, let's look at some of the alternative problem-solving strategies that are available.

INFORMATION RETRIEVAL. In some cases, the solution to a problem may be as simple as retrieving information from long-term memory. **Information retrieval** is an important option when a solution must be found quickly. For example, a pilot is expected to memorize the slowest speed at which she can fly a particular airplane before it stalls and heads for the ground. When she needs this information, she has no time to sit back and calculate the correct answer. Because time is of the essence, she simply refers to her long-term memory for an immediate answer.

ALGORITHMS. More complex problems require more complex methods. In some cases, you may be able to use an **algorithm.** Algorithms are problem-solving methods that guarantee a solution if they are appropriate for the problem and are properly carried out. For example, an algorithm for solving an anagram (a group of letters that can be rearranged to form a word) entails trying every possible combination of letters until

Trial and error A problem-solving strategy based on successive elimination of incorrect solutions until the correct one is found.

Information retrieval A problem-solving strategy that requires only the recovery of information from long-term memory.

Algorithm A step-by-step method of problem-solving that guarantees a correct solution.

Like a great football coach or chess player, an experienced conductor's expertise helps him or her represent and categorize the problems presented by a piece of music more easily and effectively.

Figure 7-7

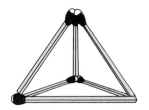

we come up with the hidden word. Suppose we are given the letters *acb*. We try *abc*, *bac*, *bca*, *cba*, and finally come up with *cab*, whereby the problem is solved. To calculate the product of 323 and 546, we multiply them according to the rules of multiplication (the algorithm). If we do it accurately, we are guaranteed to get the right answer. To convert temperatures from Fahrenheit to Celsius, we use the formula $C = \frac{5}{9}(F - 32)$. This formula, like all formulas, is an algorithm.

HEURISTICS. Many of the problems that we encounter in everyday life, however, cannot be solved by using algorithms. In these cases, we often turn to heuristics. **Heuristics** are rules of thumb that help us to simplify problems. They do not guarantee a solution, but they may bring it within reach. Some heuristic methods work better in some situations than in others. Some heuristics have special purposes only, such as those applied to chess or word puzzles. But other general heuristics can be applied to a wide range of human problems. Part of problem-solving is to decide which heuristic is most appropriate for a given problem (Bourne et al., 1986).

A very simple heuristic method is **hill-climbing.** In this process we try to move continually closer to our final goal without ever digressing or going backward. At each step, we evaluate how far "up the hill" we have come, how far we still have to go, and precisely what the next step should be. On a multiple-choice test, for example, one useful strategy in answering each question is to eliminate the alternatives that are obviously incorrect. Even if this does not leave you with the one correct answer, you are closer to a solution. In trying to balance a budget, each reduction in expenses brings you closer to the goal and leaves you with a smaller deficit with which to deal.

There are other problems, however, for which the hill-climbing heuristic is not optimal. Problems 3 and 4 on pp. 260–61 are of this sort. In each case, there comes a point where you *must* digress, or actually move backward, in order to make ultimate progress toward your goal.

Let us consider some other examples for which the hill-climbing strategy is inappropriate. You have probably played checkers at one time or another. At a decisive moment you may have had to "give up" a piece in order to maneuver toward a more strategic position on the board. Although losing that one piece seemed to push you further from victory, the move in fact nudged you closer to your goal. In baseball, a pitcher can prevent a good hitter from batting in runs at a critical time by giving him or her an "intentional walk." This tactic puts an extra player on base and seems to work against the goal of keeping runners off the bases. But the shrewd pitcher knows that by conceding a walk to a strong batter, he or she will get to pitch to the next batter, a weaker hitter who is less likely to score runs.

Another problem-solving heuristic is to create **subgoals.** By setting subgoals, we can often break a problem into smaller, more manageable pieces, each of which is easier to solve than the problem as a whole. Consider the problem of the Hobbits and the Orcs. You are at a river with three Hobbits and three Orcs. Your clearly specified main goal is to get them across the river. One constraint is that if Orcs outnumber Hobbits—on either side of the river—they will assault them. The boat that you have to use will carry only two creatures at a time. How do you

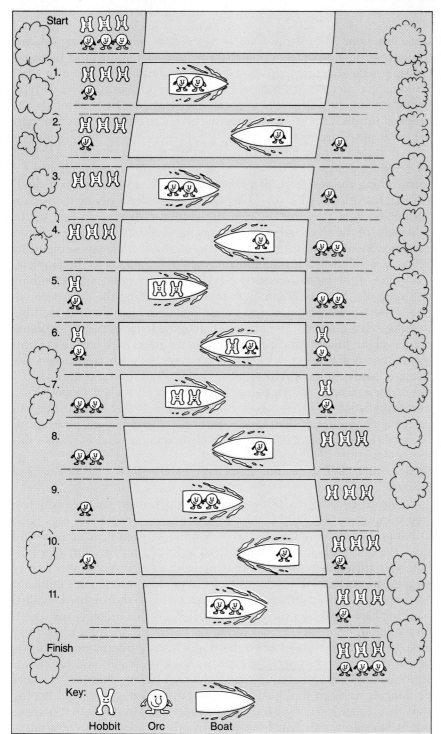

Figure 7-8
The Hobbits and Orcs problem The problem of getting all the creatures across the river without Orcs ever outnumbering Hobbits can be solved by establishing *subgoals*.

get them all across the river without creating a situation whereby Hobbits are outnumbered by Orcs?

The solution to this problem may be found by thinking of it in terms of a series of subgoals. As suggested by Figure 7-8, let us consider what has to be done to get just one or two creatures across the river at a time—leaving aside, temporarily, the main goal of getting everyone across. We could first send two of the Orcs across. Then, while working on this subgoal, we might perceive that there is no constraint against having a creature make a return trip. So, if we have one of the first two Orcs return alone after the first trip, we could then send over a Hobbit without creating a situation where Orcs outnumber Hobbits. By working on the problem in this fashion—concentrating on subgoals—we can eventually get everyone across safely.

A student whose goal is to write a history paper might set subgoals by breaking down the work into a series of separate tasks: choosing a topic, doing the research, preparing an outline, writing the first draft, editing, rewriting, and so on. Subgoals make problem-solving more manageable because they free us from the burden of having to "get to the other side of the river" all at once. This tactic allows us to set our sights on closer, more manageable goals. Of course, the overall purpose of setting subgoals is still to reach the ultimate goal—the solution to the problem.

One of the most frequently used heuristics combines hill-climbing and subgoals. **Means-end analysis** involves analyzing the difference between the current situation and the desired end, then doing something to reduce that distance. We progress through a series of points involving choices about how to proceed further, and we assess each choice in terms of whether it will bring us closer to our goal. At each point, we make the most likely choice and continue to the next point. Wickelgren (1979) notes, for example, that a person driving toward a clear landmark—a mountain range—with no specific directions to guide him or her will probably choose roads that appear, from his or her present position, to be headed in that direction. If the road then curves and leads in a different direction than was expected, the person might decide. "I'll go another mile and if I'm not any closer by then, I'll turn around and go back."

Means-end analysis moves very carefully through subgoals from one step to another. Like hill-climbing, it is always forward-looking. Such attention to what lies ahead is often helpful, because if we stray too far from the end goal, it may vanish from sight altogether. But, like hill-climbing, this strategy may prompt us to overlook digressions or temporary steps backward that are absolutely necessary for the solution of a problem.

An alternative heuristic method that is not so shortsighted is called **working backward** (Bourne et al., 1986). With this strategy, the search for a solution begins at the goal and works backward toward the "givens." This method is often used when the goal has more information than the givens and when the operations can work both forward and backward. If, for example, we wanted to spend exactly $100 on clothing, it would be difficult to reach that goal by simply buying some items and hoping that they totaled exactly $100. A better strategy would be to purchase one item, subtract its cost from $100 in order to determine how much money is left, then purchase another item, subtract its cost, and so on until we have spent $100.

Up to this point, we have seen how various strategies can be used to solve problems. Yet in real life, problem-solving often bogs down and we find ourselves either unable to arrive at a solution or faced with a solution that is not effective. In the next section, we will examine various obstacles to problem-solving.

Obstacles to Solving Problems

Problem-solving is affected by many factors other than those we have already discussed. One such factor is level of motivation, or emotional arousal. In Chapter 11, we will see that the "peak," or optimum state of performance, in problem-solving is achieved at intermediate levels of excitement or arousal. Moreover, the more complex the problem-solving task, the lower the level of emotion that can be tolerated without interfering with performance. Generally, we must whip up a certain surge of excitement in order to motivate ourselves adequately to solve a problem, but too much arousal can hamper our ability to find a solution.

■ Teaching Problem-Solving

Does education contribute to the development of good reasoning skills? A recent study suggests that the answer to this question is no. In this study, a group of 320 men and women were asked to prepare speeches on a number of social issues, such as television violence and the military draft. The subjects varied from high school dropouts to graduate students. Their speeches were taped and rated for quality of reasoning. The researchers found that education level made very little difference in the quality of the reasoning used in support of an argumentative position and concluded that most educational practice does little to prepare students for reasoning out open-ended issues. But even if education presently does not promote greater reasoning skills, might it be possible to devise programs that have such an effect?

A number of psychologists and educators believe that it is possible to improve reasoning skills by teaching students scientific aspects of thinking and problem-solving. For example, students have been taught a variety of problem-solving strategies in the belief that this will improve problem-solving in a wide range of situations. In one such study, the researchers discovered that fifth- and sixth-graders who were doing poorly in math did not realize that they should use different strategies for familiar as opposed to unfamiliar problems (Hasselbring, Goin, & Bransford, 1985). The researchers discovered that for the most part, the children made few attempts on their own to distinguish between the problems they knew (and could solve from memory) and the problems which they did not know and which required a different problem-solving strategy. With specific instruction, however, they learned that some problem-solving situations require a change in strategies, and they were then better able to draw upon a wide range of relevant strategies to improve their performance. Similar approaches have been used in situations as different as military training (Halff, Hollan, & Hutchins, 1986) and expository writing (Hayes & Flower, 1986).

But it has also become clear that training in several problem-solving strategies is not the only thing that is necessary for effectively solving new problems. Acquisition of knowledge is also important. In a study of chess experts, de Groot (1965) discovered that the important difference between chess masters and novices was not that the masters could *conceive* a greater number of moves; rather, it was the fact that the chess masters' years of experience enabled them to recognize more quickly and accurately the significance of various board positions. They were able to recognize a situation as resembling one with which they were already familiar, and this recognition had a significant effect on their next moves.

As a result of research such as this, psychologists have come to recognize that improving problem-solving will require both the acquisition of relevant knowledge and an awareness of how to organize that knowledge efficiently so that it is available for problem solving (Bransford et al., 1982). Because a given learner may be stronger in one of these areas and weaker in the other, it is important that the instructor assess each learner's strengths and weaknesses before beginning instruction. Some children, for example, may have memorized the multiplication table but be unaware of the law of communicativity ($5 \times 6 = 6 \times 5$). For them, the emphasis should be on learning rules and strategies. Others may understand the rules but be deficient in organizing and remembering multiplication facts; for these students, the somewhat unhappy task of rote memorization may have to be emphasized.

Another factor that can either help or hinder problem-solving is **set,** which refers to our tendency to perceive and to approach problems in certain ways. This can be helpful if we have learned certain operations and perceptions in the past that we can apply to the present. For example, people tend to do better when they solve problems for the second or third time because they have learned more effective strategies for choosing moves and because they understand the problem better (Reed, Ernst, & Banerji, 1974). Much of our education involves learning sets and ways to solve problems (i.e., heuristics and algorithms), although it may seem that we are learning only specific information. We are taught to integrate new information into forms that we already know or to use methods that have proved effective in the past. In fact, the strategies that we use in problem-solving are themselves a set. We have learned that approaching a problem in a certain logical order is the best way to solve it.

But sets do not always help solve problems. If a problem requires you to apply your previous experience in a new and different way, a strong set could become a serious obstacle. People who are most successful in solving problems often are those who have many different sets at their disposal and can judge when to change sets or when to give up a set entirely. Great ideas and inventions come out of such a balance. Copernicus was familiar with the sets of his time, but he had the flexibility to see that they might not be relevant to his work. Only by putting aside these sets could he discover that the earth revolves around the sun. The point is to use a set when it is appropriate, but not to let the set use you—not to be so controlled by learned ways of approaching a problem that you are closed to new approaches to solving it.

One set that can seriously hinder problem-solving is **functional fixedness.** Consider Figure 7-9. Do you see a way to mount the candle on the wall? The more you use an object in one way, the harder it is to see new uses for it. When you get used to seeing or using something in only one way, you have assigned it a fixed function. To some extent, of course, part of the learning process is to assign correct functions to objects. We teach a child that the "right" function of a spoon is stirring, not pounding. Much of how we form concepts involves learning the "right" functions of objects. But it is important to remain open enough to see that an object can be used for an entirely different function if need be. In Figure 7-9, for example, many people have trouble realizing that the box of tacks can be used as a candleholder (see Figure 7-10, p. 270).

Birch and Rabinowitz (1951) studied functional fixedness with the two-string problem (see Figure 7-11, p. 271). In this problem, the subject is asked to hold two dangling strings simultaneously. The strings are positioned in such a way that the subject cannot stretch out to reach them at the same time. Lying on a table in the room are also an electrical switch and a relay that can be used as a pendulum to set one of the strings swinging so that both strings can be reached together. When subjects were specifically reminded of the normal functions of these additional items, they were unlikely to employ them as a pendulum. But when not told their normal functions, subjects were more likely to use them to solve the problem (see Figure 7-12, p. 272).

We have been talking about functional fixedness in terms of objects, but the idea can also be applied to problems with people. For example, the problem of the elderly has been given much attention recently. Older

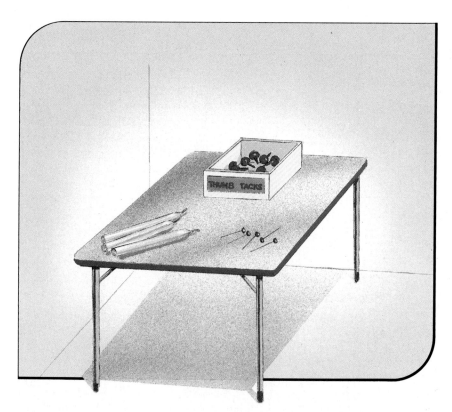

Tactic of elimination A problem-solving strategy in which possible solutions are evaluated according to appropriate criteria and discarded as they fail to contribute to a solution.

Figure 7-9
In order to test the effects of *functional fixedness*, subjects might be given the items shown on the table and asked to mount a candle on the wall. A solution is given in Figure 7-10.

people who are put into institutions often feel useless and depressed. Unwanted children who live in institutions also do not always receive the time and care they need. Instead of seeing the elderly as people to be looked after, someone grasped the idea that they might serve as foster grandparents to the children in institutions. This was a case of suspending the fixed function of both groups. The "grandparents" gave the children love and attention, and the children gave the older people the feeling of being useful. Two human problems were solved with one wise, new, and compassionate solution.

Despite the many pitfalls that we may encounter when trying to solve problems, there are many techniques for sharpening our performance on such tasks. Let us take a look at some of the ways to become better and more efficient problem-solvers.

Becoming Better at Problem-Solving

As you will recall, the first step in reaching a solution to a problem is often to try out various ways of interpreting or representing the problem. You can then experiment with a number of solution strategies, shifting your perspective of the problem from one angle to another. Let's look more closely at how some of these strategies work.

TACTIC OF ELIMINATION. If in a given problem you are more sure of what you do *not* want than of what you do want, the **tactic of elimination** can be very helpful. The best approach is to create first a list of all the possible solutions that you can think of. Then you evaluate

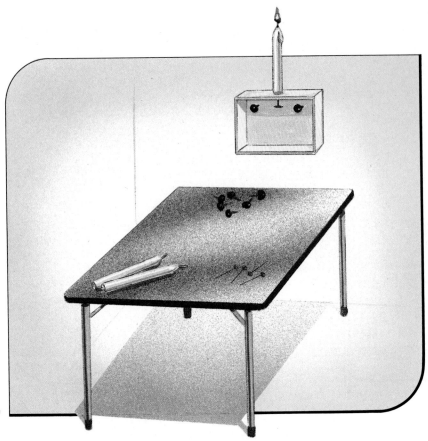

Figure 7-10

and discard choices by applying the appropriate criteria. When working with this strategy, however, remember that you have assumed that a good solution to the problem exists in your list of possible choices. This assumption may prove false, however, and as a result you could very well eliminate all the possible solutions!

VISUALIZING. Other useful tactics are **visualizing,** diagramming, and charting various courses of action (Adams, 1980). For example, in the Hobbit and Orc problem, it might help to draw a picture of the river and show the Hobbits and Orcs at each stage of the problem as they are ferried back and forth. By drawing a diagram of a problem, or even constructing a simple model of it, we often find it easier to grasp the principle of the problem and to avoid irrelevant or distracting details. Some chess masters, for example, can visualize chess games in their heads; as a result, they are able to play blindfolded as many as 50 simultaneous games! Similarly, members of the Canadian National Women's Basketball Team could learn more effectively the patterns of new plays than a group of psychology graduate students. The basketball players were able to visualize the new plays based on their wide basketball experience. The psychology students had to learn the plays piece by piece.

CREATIVE PROBLEM-SOLVING. Many problems, of course, do not lend themselves to straightforward strategies, but rely more on the use of flexible and original thinking. For example, how many unusual uses can you think of for an ordinary object like a brick? It's easy to think of a few good uses for a brick but quite another task to come up with 50 or 60 distinct uses. Psychologists sometimes refer to this type of thinking as **divergent thinking,** in contrast to **convergent thinking** (Guilford, 1967). A problem requiring convergent thinking has only one or a very few solutions—for example, a math problem. Problems that have no single correct solution and that require a flexible, inventive approach call for divergent thinking. A multiple-choice test is a convergent-thinking problem; an essay test calls for divergent thinking.

People differ greatly in their convergent- and divergent-thinking abilities. As we will see in Chapter 8, people who score high on standard tests of intelligence (convergent thinking) tend to be above-average in creativity as well (divergent thinking). But some people with high IQ scores have great difficulty with divergent-thinking problems—and vice versa (Kershner & Ledger, 1985).

Because creative problem-solving requires thinking up new and original ideas, it appears that the process is not always aided by planning and the deliberate use of problem-solving strategies. Solutions to many problems rely on insight, often a seemingly arbitrary flash "out of the blue" that solves a problem. Many of us have had this experience of suddenly seeing our way to a solution that previously had seemed all but impossible. Henri Poincaré, the French mathematician, has written about his own experiences with this phenomenon:

> One evening, contrary to my custom, I drank black coffee and could not sleep. Ideas rose in crowds; I felt them collide until pairs interlocked, so to speak, making a stable combination. By the next morning I had established the existence of a new class of Fuchian functions (Poincaré, 1924).

Many people have provided strikingly similar accounts of their own processes of creative thinking. Whatever careful attention they may have

Divergent thinking Thinking that meets the criteria of originality, inventiveness, and flexibility.

Convergent thinking Thinking that is directed toward one correct solution to a problem.

Figure 7-11
Birch and Rabinowitz's two-string problem In another test of *functional fixedness*, subjects were asked to solve the problem of how to grasp both strings at the same time. The solution is given in Figure 7-12.

Brainstorming A problem-solving strategy in which an individual or a group collects numerous ideas and evaluates them only after all ideas have been collected.

Figure 7-12

paid to heuristics, strategies, and the like, the solution does not appear to emerge logically from the preparation. Poincaré may have been trying to solve his problem by normal means, but his sudden insight does not appear related to a deliberate problem-solving strategy. Note that he does not say he brought the ideas together, but that he "felt them collide." Something other than logic seems to have been involved.

This phenomenon suggests that if you cannot arrive at a solution to a problem after careful preparation and step-by-step efforts at problem-solving, you might be advised to stop thinking about the problem for a while in order to return to it later and approach it from a new angle (Murray & Denny, 1969). It is easy to get so enmeshed in the details of a problem that you lose sight of what might be obvious. Taking a rest from a problem may allow you to discover a fresh approach.

Another creative strategy is to *redefine* the problem. For example, recall the business that was losing money, the only solution to which seemed to be cost-cutting. However, the range of solutions was expanded to include increasing income, and the business was presented with a new array of possibilities.

Thus, it is important to develop a questioning attitude toward problems. It is easy to look at problems just as they are presented to us—to assume, for example, that we cannot move out of the square in the nine-dot problem. A more questioning attitude—"What is the *real* problem here? Can the problem be interpreted in other ways?"—can open up new avenues to creative solutions. At the same time, it is often crucial to maintain an uncritical attitude toward potential solutions. The method of **brainstorming**—which can proceed in groups or individually—encourages people to produce ideas without evaluating them prematurely. Only after lots of ideas have been collected are they subjected to review and criticism (Haefele, 1962).

Finally, there is evidence that people will become more creative when exposed to creative peers and teachers who can be role models (Amabile, 1983). Although some creative people work well in isolation, many find it stimulating to work in teams with other creative people and employ such group problem-solving strategies as brainstorming.

THE DEVELOPMENT OF EXPERTISE. The ability to think creatively is important, but there are many situations in which creativity is relatively useless in the absence of relevant knowledge. Visualization, for example, is a good skill to have when working in particle physics, but it is doubtful whether a visually talented person like an artist could think creatively about the structure of matter without the training and knowledge of a physicist.

Many occupations require training that involves the learning of specific bodies of knowledge and skills particularly related to a given area. An experimental physicist needs to learn both theory and how to operate various types of apparatus. Experience also allows an auto mechanic to know that a particular color of exhaust smoke indicates that an engine may be burning oil. An expert mechanic develops a multitude of such rules, as well as a mental map of the internal combustion engine. This type of knowledge allows an expert to work efficiently on problems without the elaborate preparation that a new problem would require of a beginner (Gentner & Stevens, 1983).

Many of the problems that you must solve each day require you to make decisions. What to wear, what to say to your boss, what to eat—these are just a few examples. Usually, you must pick one of several choices. For instance, do you wear the red striped shirt, the yellow one, or the blue plaid one? Do you ask your boss about your next assignment, your vacation plans, or your next raise? When you are pushing your cart along the aisles of the supermarket, which bread do you buy? Do you choose the dark or light rye, the brand for which you have saved a coupon, or the loaf that is most nutritious? In the next portion of the chapter, we will examine in greater detail the processes involved in this particular kind of problem-solving.

Even everyday decisions, such as what brand to buy at the supermarket, call for rating and choosing among alternatives.

■ Decision-Making

Decision-making differs from other kinds of problem-solving in that we already know all the possible solutions (choices). The task is to select the best alternative by using a predetermined set of criteria. Sometimes we have to juggle a fairly large and complex set of criteria. As this set grows, so do the difficulties in reaching a good decision. For example, suppose that we are looking for an apartment. The amount of rent is important, but so are the neighbors, location, level of noise, and cleanliness. If we find a noisy apartment with undesirable neighbors but a bargain-basement rent, should we take it? Is it a better choice than the apartment in a more desirable location with less noise, but with a somewhat higher rent? How can we weigh the various characteristics in order to ensure that we make the best possible decision from among the various choices?

If you were to proceed logically, you would use some kind of **compensatory model** to arrive at a decision. In this case, you would rate all of the choices on each of several criteria in order to see how the attractive features of each choice might compensate for the unattractive ones. For example, if you are buying a house, one criterion might be that you prefer a brick house. You might, however, buy a wooden house if it is located in a good school district, has a pleasing floor plan, and is reasonably priced. In this case, the attractive features compensate for the fact that the house is not brick.

One of the most useful compensatory models is shown in Table 7-1. The various criteria are listed, with each assigned a weight according to its importance. Here the decision involves the purchase of a new car, and only three criteria are considered: price (which is not weighted heavily), gas mileage, and repair record (which are given fairly heavy weights). Each car is then rated from 1 (poor) to 5 (excellent) on each of the criteria. You can see that Car 1 has an excellent price (5) but relatively poor gas mileage (2) and service record (1); Car 2 has a less desirable price but a fairly good mileage and repair record. Each rating is then multiplied by the weight for that criterion (e.g., for Car 1, the price rating of 5 is multiplied by the weight of 4) and the result is put in parentheses next to the rating. Then the numbers in parentheses are added to give a total for each car. Clearly Car 2 is the better choice: It has a less desirable price, but that fact is offset by the fact that its mileage and service record are better and these are more important than price to this particular buyer.

Using a table like this one allows you to evaluate a large number of choices on a large number of criteria. It can be extremely helpful in making choices such as which college to attend, which job offer to accept, which career to pursue, and where to take a vacation. If you have properly weighted the various criteria and correctly rated each alternative in terms of each criterion, then you can be sure that the alternative with the highest total score is in fact the most rational choice given the information available to you.

Most people, however, do not follow such a precise system of making decisions. Rather, they use various **noncompensatory models.** Especially popular is the *elimination-by-aspects* tactic (Reed, 1988). In this case, we toss out specific choices if they do not meet one or two of our requirements, regardless of how good they are on other criteria. For example, we might eliminate Car 2, regardless of all its advantages, because "it costs more." As you might guess, noncompensatory models tend to be shortsighted. They do not help us weigh the values of particular features, nor do they

When it comes to major decisions, such as which car to buy, *compensatory models* are the best choice in decision-making.

TABLE 7-1 COMPENSATORY DECISION TABLE FOR PURCHASE OF A NEW CAR				
	Price (weight = 4)	Gas mileage (weight = 8)	Service record (weight = 10)	Weighted total
Car 1	5(20)	2(16)	1(10)	(46)
Car 2	1(4)	4(32)	4(40)	(76)
Ratings: 5 = Excellent 1 = Poor				

invite us to compare all the alternatives. As a result, such a model can lead to a decision that is merely adequate, but not the best.

Sometimes, we mix both compensatory and noncompensatory strategies to settle on a decision. When there are many alternatives and many criteria, we may use a noncompensatory approach to eliminate any choices that are especially weak on one or more criteria, even though they may be strong on other criteria. When the field has been narrowed to a few alternatives, all of which are at least average on the various criteria, then we might adopt some form of compensatory decision model.

We also decide among different decision models according to how much is at stake. We are more likely to use a compensatory model when the stakes are high: buying a home or choosing a college. When the stakes are low, the noncompensatory model usually helps us to decide quickly such casual matters as which shoes to wear or who we think might win an Academy Award.

But even in important matters it is not always easy to make rational decisions. Sometimes, for example, information about an alternative is uncertain. In the case of the two cars, we may not know the repair record of either car, perhaps because both are new models. In this case, we have to make some estimates based on information about past repair records, which then help us to predict the repair records of these new models. In the absence of any reliable information at all, we may have to guess about some of the facts that we need to make a decision, and research indicates that in many cases our guesses may not be correct.

Tversky and Kahneman (1973) conducted one experiment in which students at a particular university were asked to choose whether a student who was described as "neat and tidy," "dull and mechanical," and a "poor writer" was a computer science major or a humanities major. More than 95 percent chose computer science as the major. Even after they were told that more than 80 percent of the students at their school were majors in humanities, the estimates remained virtually unchanged. This exemplifies how people use the heuristic of **representativeness:** A decision is made on the basis of certain information that matches a stereotyped model. For example, many people discriminate vocationally against the elderly without considering a particular person's ability to do the job. They have a stereotype of the elderly being incapable of certain tasks and judge a *given* individual as being representative of the *general* model.

Another common heuristic is **availability.** In the absence of full and accurate information, we often make decisions based on whatever information is most easily retrieved from memory, even though this information may not be accurate. In one experiment, subjects were asked whether the letter *r* appears more frequently as the first or third letter in English words. Most people said first, but the correct answer is third. Their estimates were incorrect because they relied on the most readily available information in their memories, and it is easier to recall words that begin with *r* than words that have *r* as their third letter.

As we all know, however, people do manage to make serviceable decisions in the real world. In part, this is because it is often possible to revise decisions if it appears that an initial choice is not optimal. Moreover, real-world decisions often don't have to be ideal or optimal, as long as the results are acceptable. An investment that returns a 20 percent profit in one year is still a fine investment, despite the fact that another in-

Representativeness A heuristic by which a new situation is judged on the basis of its resemblance to a stereotypical model.

Availability A heuristic by which a judgment or decision is based on information that is most easily retrieved from memory.

Medical Decision-Making

You have a sore throat and a high fever accompanied by severe back pains. You are examined by a doctor, who asks a few questions, listens to your heart and lungs, looks down your throat, and then takes your blood pressure. Finally, you are given a drug prescription and told that you should be feeling better by the day after tomorrow. How did your doctor arrive at that decision so quickly?

Medical decisions are not nearly as clear-cut and objective as they might seem. Elstein, Shulman, and Sprakfa (1978) found that most physicians tend to form a few initial general hypotheses almost immediately. These guide the search for additional information, the choice of diagnostic tests, and perhaps the choice of some initial medication. These hypotheses are then modified or changed as new data are found. If evidence refutes this initial diagnosis, new hypotheses will be generated partly on the basis of the results of the tests and partly on the basis of the doctor's knowledge and past experience. These hypotheses, too, will be tested until it appears that the problem has been correctly diagnosed, though a well-trained physician will remain alert for evidence that a diagnosis is still not quite correct.

If all possible diagnoses are considered, each one tested thoroughly, and the results evaluated according to a compensatory model, then medical decision-making can be very effective. But because subjective judgment plays such a large role in the medical decision process, it can also go awry relatively easily, especially when an inexperienced physician is making the decision. With this in mind, Elstein and his colleagues (1978) recommend following three stages in medical decision-making: (1) produce a list of alternative hypotheses, (2) collect data selectively, and (3) assemble all the data and plot a course of action. In Stage 1, physicians should start with the most common diagnoses that fit the case. However, they should also keep in mind other, less common diagnoses that, if overlooked, could seriously endanger the patient. In the second stage, physicians should order labo-

Accurate diagnosis is crucial to medical decision making. Doctors sometimes use computer programs which generate an exhaustive list of potential diagnoses based on a given set of symptoms to bring to mind less common diagnoses they might otherwise overlook.

ratory tests that will either confirm or rule out the most common diagnoses as well as those for which the patient would be at serious risk if he or she were not treated. At this stage, the physician must balance the harm that these tests might cause the patient—as well as the costs of the tests—with the likely benefits. When interpreting the data in Stage 3, it is important to remember that a patient with several complaints may well suffer from more than one ailment. Moreover, in sifting through all the data in an effort to confirm or rule out hypotheses, it is critical to remember that the patient may have an uncommon illness, and as a result *none* of the preliminary diagnoses may be correct. Finally, when charting a course of treatment, the physician must weigh the probability that the diagnosis is accurate against the benefits and risks that can follow from the chosen regimen of treatment.

vestment might have returned 25 percent or 30 percent. Einhorn (1980) discusses a similar case regarding strategies for accepting people into a professional school. The admissions officers may adopt a strategy that leads to an 80 percent success rate among those applicants accepted. They would conclude that they had a good admissions model, even if the reality is—unknown to the admissions officers—that 90 percent of the rejected applicants also would have been successful students.

On the other hand, there are situations in which "close is not good enough." Spettle and Liebert (1986) studied the potential for error in decision-making among operators at nuclear power plants. They found that in addition to the kinds of heuristic errors that we have been discussing, the stress of an emergency situation causes decision-making to deteriorate further. Great stress may even erode performance to the point of panic. On the other hand, they suggest that people can be trained to meet novel situations in which quick and accurate decisions are crucial. With training that simulates actual emergency conditions, people can be better prepared to use efficient and effective decision-making strategies. The Outward Bound program was originally developed because British sailors whose boats were torpedoed panicked and died when calm decision-making would have ensured their survival. This program puts people in a variety of stressful wilderness situations in the belief that people will learn effective personal strategies that can be transferred to a wide variety of everyday situations.

So far in this chapter, we have examined images and concepts and the ways in which these two building blocks of thought can be used in problem-solving and decision-making. In the next section, we will examine how humans develop their ability to use language and the relationship between language and thought at various ages. We will also look at the question of whether nonhumans are capable of using language, as well as the implications of this possibility for understanding the nature of thought in lower animals.

Phonemes The basic sounds that make up any language.

Morphemes The smallest meaningful unit of speech such as simple words, prefixes, and suffixes.

■ Language

The Nature of Language

Language is based on universal sound units called **phonemes.** The sounds of *t*, *th*, and *k*, for instance, are phonemes. There are about 45 phonemes in English, and as many as 85 in some languages (Bourne et al., 1986). By themselves, phonemes are meaningless and therefore seldom play an important role in helping us to think. The sound *b*, for example, has no inherent meaning. But phonemes can be grouped together to form words, prefixes (*un-*, *pre-*), and suffixes (*-ed*, *-ing*). These are called **morphemes,** which are the smallest *meaningful* units in a language. Morphemes play an extremely important role in human cognition. By themselves, they can represent important ideas such as *red* or *calm* or *hot*. The suffix *-ed* captures the idea of *in the past* (as in *mowed* or *liked* or *cared*). The prefix *pre-* reflects the idea of *before* or *prior to* (as in *preview* or *prewar*).

But morphemes can also be combined to make up complex words that represent quite complex ideas, such as *pre-exist-ing*, *un-excell-ed*, *psycho-logy*. In turn, words can be combined to form *phrases*, and *sentences*, which can represent even more complex thoughts. When thinking about something—say the ocean or a sunset—our ideas about it rarely reflect the single thoughts expressed by morphemes like *red* or *calm*. Instead, our ideas usually are made up of phrases and sentences, such as "The ocean is unusually calm tonight."

In Chapter 6, as you may recall, we saw that sentences have both a surface structure (the particular words and phrases) and a deep structure (the underlying meaning). The same deep structure can be conveyed by various different surface structures, as in the following example:

- The ocean is unusually calm tonight.
- Tonight the ocean is particularly calm.
- Compared to most nights, tonight the ocean is calm.

When you wish to communicate an idea, you start with a thought, then choose words and phrases that will express the idea, and finally produce the speech sounds that make up those words and phrases. You can see in Figure 7-13 that the movement is indeed from top to bottom. When you want to understand a sentence, your task is reversed. You must start with speech sounds and work your way up to the meaning of those sounds.

Just as rules exist for combining phonemes and morphemes, so do they exist for structuring sentences and their meanings. These rules are what linguists call a **grammar** (Chomsky, 1957). They are what enable speakers and listeners to perform what Chomsky calls the *transformations* that allow a person to go up and down, as it were, from surface to deep structure. Two major components of a grammar are semantics and syntax. **Semantics** describes how we assign meaning to the morphemes that we use. Some rules describe how a word may refer to an object—for example, that a large striped cat is a *tiger*. Other semantic rules explain how different combinations of morphemes affect meaning, such as adding the suffix *-ed* to a verb like *play* to put the action in the past or adding the prefix *un-* to *necessary* to reverse its meaning. **Syntax** is the system of rules that governs how we combine words to form grammatical sentences. After all, a random jumble of individually meaningful words doesn't communicate very much! In the English language, for example, there is a rule that adjectives come before nouns. The reverse is true in some European languages.

Figure 7-13
The direction of movement in speech production and comprehension
Producing a sentence involves movement from thoughts and ideas to basic sounds; understanding a sentence requires movement from basic sounds back to the underlying thoughts and ideas.

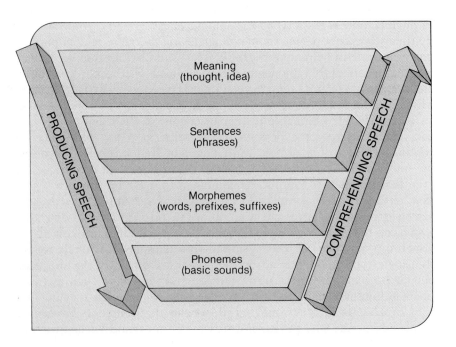

Language Development

A BRIEF CHRONOLOGY. The development of language begins with the sounds that infants produce. These sounds are quite complex, and their appearance follows a recognizable pattern. At about two months of age, an infant begins to coo—a nondescript word for nondescript sounds. In another month or two, the infant enters the "babbling" stage and starts to repeat sounds. At the beginning of babbling the infant will tend to produce a single expression like *da*. A few months later, the infant may string together the same sound, as in *dadadada*. Finally, the infant will form combinations of different sounds, as in *dabamaga* (Ferguson & Macken, 1983).

At the same time, the pattern of an infant's babbling gradually takes on other important features of adult language. At about age four to six months, the infant's speech begins to show signs of *intonation*, the rising and lowering of pitch that allows adults to distinguish, for example, between questions ("You're tired?") and statements ("You're tired."). At about the time children reach their first birthday, they show signs of using intonation to indicate commands and questions (Greenfield & Smith, 1976). A child might look at his or her bottle, for example, and utter a sound with a rising pitch, or inflection. Toward the end of the first year, children also show signs of understanding what is said to them and they begin not only to imitate what others say but also to use sounds to get attention. Overall, during the first year of life, vocalization becomes less solitary and more socially directed.

The culmination of all this preparation is the utterance of the first word at about 12 months, usually *dada*. During the next 6 to 8 months, children build a vocabulary of one-word sentences: [Pick me] "Up!"; [I want to go] "Out!"; [Tickle me] "Again!" These action words tend first to describe the child's own behavior before they are used to describe the action of others (Huttenlocher, Smiley, & Charney, 1983). Children may also use compound words such as *awgone* [all gone]. To these they add words that they use to address people—*Bye-bye* being a favorite—and a few exclamations, such as *Ouch!*

In the second year of life, as children begin to distinguish between themselves and others, possessive words become a big part of the vocabulary: [The shoes are] "daddy's." But the overwhelming passion of two-year-olds is naming. With little or no prompting, they will name virtually everything that they see in their environment. As we will see in Chapter 9, children at this age think very concretely. They are fascinated by objects and the way that objects appear. If a child doesn't know the name of an object, he or she will simply invent one or use another word that is almost right. Stone and Church (1984) described a child who called all red cars *engines*—apparently derived from red fire engines—long before he used the word *red* or had grasped the more abstract concept of colors or the differences between cars and fire engines. A somewhat older child might refer to skywriting as "a scar on the sky." This label is not a careless error, but rather reflects the child's efforts to link together two familiar experiences (a scar that slowly disappears and the sky) in order to describe a new experience or concept for which the child has not yet learned the proper word (Mendelsohn et al., 1984).

During the third year of life, a child begins to form two- and three-word sentences. Typical beginners' sentences are *Baby crying, My ball, Dog barking*. Mother-child conversations have been recorded at this age in order to see just what children pick up and what they omit. Children at this age most noticeably omit auxiliary verbs—[Can] "I have that?" "I [am] eating it up"—and prepositions and articles— "It [is] time [for] Sarah [to] take [a] nap." Apparently, children seize on the most important words, possibly those that their parents stress (Bloom, 1970).

At three to four years of age, children begin to fill in their sentences: *Billy school* becomes *Billy goes to school*. They start to use the past tense as well as the present. They ask more questions and learn to use "Why?" effectively—and sometimes monotonously. By the age of five or six, most children have a vocabulary of over 2,500 words and can make sentences of six to eight words.

THEORIES OF LANGUAGE DEVELOPMENT. This chronology shows that most children enjoy making sounds and learning words and that they pick up the complex rules for putting words together into sentences quite easily. But what prompts children to learn to talk in the first place? And how do they learn to speak so well so quickly?

There are two very different theories about how language develops. B.F. Skinner (1957) believes that parents and other people around the infant listen to the cooing and babbling and *reinforce*, or reward, the child for making those sounds that most resemble adult speech. If a child says something that sounds like *mama*, the father or mother reinforces the behavior with a hug. As the child gets older, he or she is reinforced only for sounding more and more like an adult and for using words correctly. Children who call an aunt "mama" are less likely to be hugged; that is, they are reinforced only when they call the right person "mama." Similarly, children slowly learn by trial and error what words belong where in a sentence, how to use prefixes and suffixes, and so on. All these little bits of language learning are put together into what G.J. Whitehurst has called "a patchwork of thousands of separately acquired frames, patterns, responses, rules, and small tricks. The elegance of the final product belies the chaos of its construction" (1982, p. 368).

But most psychologists and linguists now believe that simple reinforcement alone cannot explain the impressive speed, accuracy, and originality with which children learn to use language. Noam Chomsky (1965), the most influential advocate of this point of view, rejects the notion that children must be *taught* language. Instead, he argues that children are born with an *internal* device for processing the adult speech that they hear around them. This mechanism enables them to understand the basic rules of grammar, to make sense of what they hear, and to form their own sentences. It conforms to a transformational grammar and is universally "wired-in" to all humans. This internal language acquisition device is like a street map (Whitehurst, 1982). Children don't approach language like strangers without maps encountering a new city, blundering this way and that, taking wrong turns, getting lost, and finally learning what leads where. Instead, they are born with an internal "map" of language, an overview of the neighborhood and its divisions (for example, the division between "doers" and "what they do," or what we know as nouns and verbs).

Most psychologists today agree that children are born with a biological capacity for language, but this potential must be stimulated by their environment—the speech that they hear from the day they are born. Both French and English children, for example, go through similar stages of development in their native languages, but obviously children in France grow up speaking French and not English.

We also know that without a social environment—people with whom to talk—children are slow to pick up words and rules that enable them to communicate and learn. Babies raised in institutions, who have no smiling adults to reward their efforts, babble like other children but take much longer to begin talking than children raised in families (Brown, 1958). Deaf children, who cannot hear themselves make noise, also babble at the same age as other children but they require special training if they are to learn to talk (Gibson, Shurcliff, & Yonas, 1970). Clearly feedback, in the form of listening to oneself and to others, influences language development.

However, some aspects of children's speech are highly resistant to adult influence. McNeill (1972) recorded a mother-child interchange in which a child refused to alter "nobody don't like me" to "nobody likes me" as corrected by his mother. Finally, the child uttered "Oh! Nobody don't likes me." Until children are ready—in this case, to use the verb conjugation rule correctly—no amount of correction or reinforcement will change the rule that they are using at the current state of their language development. In another case, a child was talking about a "fis" (Moskowitz, 1978). The adult repeated "fis" and the child became annoyed. "Fis!" the child said, expressing frustration. Eventually, the adult tried "fish," and the child, satisfied at last, said, "Yes, fis."

These errors, and others like them, indicate that during the first years of life, children have a grammar of their own that guides their use of language (see Figure 7-14). A two- or three-year-old might proudly announce, "I saw some sheeps" or "I digged a hole." Obviously, the words *sheeps* and *digged* were not learned by imitating adults. Rather, the child applied some logical rules for making plurals and past tenses, unaware that some words are irregular. In other words, children seem to know what they *want* to say before they can say it correctly by adult standards.

We have seen that all children share an innate ability to learn language in a structured, rule-guided fashion. In the next section, we will explore the question of whether this ability to use language is unique to humans.

Figure 7-14
A standard test of children's syntax
Nonsense words are used in order to ensure that memorized knowledge does not interfere with the child's performance. The ability to generalize the correct plural indicates that the child has arrived at a more complex language stage.

Primate Language

Language has long been regarded as a uniquely human capability that sets us apart from all other animals. But what if language can be linked to cognitive processes found in other species? For example, certain animals are capable of representational thought: They can relate a symbol of an object to the object itself. And we know that other species communicate in various ways. Do these abilities—symbolic representation and communication—indicate that nonhumans can represent their world through language?

Von Frisch (1974) demonstrated that honeybees go through an intricate dance in order to inform their hive mates of the location and distance of a pollen source. However, these communications are somewhat inflexible, unlike human language, and may be inaccurate if the bee has to fly upwind back to the hive. Human language is marked by its ability to adapt to novel situations. The rigid communication system of the bee cannot accommodate subtle changes in the environment (McNeill, 1972).

Other species, however, have been viewed by psychologists as better candidates for language. The great apes (chimpanzees, gorillas, orangutans, and gibbons) and humans are classified as primates and are, loosely speaking, cousins to one another. A number of intriguing experiments have been conducted in an effort to determine whether apes can be taught to use language.

In 1933, W.A. and L.N. Kellogg raised a chimpanzee named Gua with their own son Donald. At first, Gua developed some skills more rapidly than the human child. Gua more quickly developed motor skills, such as the ability to move around and grasp objects. The chimpanzee also showed good problem-solving abilities, learned socialized actions like kissing for forgiveness, and demonstrated the ability to respond to verbal commands. But unlike Donald, the chimpanzee demonstrated no ability to approximate human vocalizations. Hayes and Hayes (1951) also raised a chimpanzee in their home, combining a homelike atmosphere with operant conditioning (see Chapter 5). Even with strong reinforcement, their chimpanzee, Viki, could approximate the human vocalizations of only four words: *mama*, *papa*, *cup*, and *up*.

In commenting on this work, Kellogg (1968) noted that physical limitations on the chimpanzee's vocal apparatus may have played a major role in the relative failure of the early chimpanzee language experiments. Is it possible that chimpanzees can acquire the ability to communicate with language by means other than sounds? Allen and Beatrice Gardner (1969, 1975, 1977) attempted to teach American Sign Language (Ameslan) to a chimpanzee named Washoe. Washoe was raised in an environment where she never heard oral speech but was communicated with only by signing. The Gardners' method relied on the chimpanzee's well-known ability to imitate gestures, and appropriate responses were reinforced by operant conditioning.

At age two, Washoe had learned 38 signs, 85 at age four, and 160 by age five. Washoe also learned to make combinations of one-word signs into two-word telegraphic sentences, such as *more milk*. She was reported to have invented these new combinations on her own, without having been specifically taught them. Another feature of Washoe's development that paralleled development in children was her ability to generalize signs so that they applied to a variety of objects. For example, she was able to sign *dog* not only for an actual dog, but for the picture of a dog as well. And she was able to adapt her use of signs to novel situations. For example, after seeing a swan, she signed *water-bird*, even though the sign had never been modeled to her. This behavior has been duplicated with other chimpanzees. Fouts (1973) observed a chimpanzee named Lucy create the sign *drink fruit* for a watermelon.

Premack (1971, 1976) used a slightly different method to study language acquisition in chimpanzees. With the aid of reinforcements, he taught a chimpanzee named Sarah to communicate by arranging plastic chips on a magnetic board. Each chip stood for a different word, and the

Instead of teaching them American Sign Language, some researchers have used a geometric keyboard connected to a computer in an effort to see if chimpanzees can learn to represent their world through language.

order in which they could be arranged on the board could also convey meaning. Sarah, like Washoe and Lucy, learned a large number of signs. She too could arrange the chips to form telegraphic sentences like *Place orange dish*. Sarah even learned how to construct sentences that involve conditional relationships (*If Sarah take apple, then Mary give Sarah chocolate. If Sarah take banana, then Mary no give Sarah chocolate*).

Another group of researchers (Rumbaugh, 1977; Rumbaugh et al., 1974; Rumbaugh & Savage-Rumbaugh, 1978) worked with a chimpanzee named Lana, who learned to type messages on a geometric keyboard connected to a computer. Reportedly, Lana was able to comprehend complex human sentences. For example, she was able to respond correctly to such questions as "What is the name of the object that is green?" Moreover, Lana also demonstrated the ability to create original messages, such as *apple which is orange* for an orange. These researchers (Greenfield & Savage-Rumbaugh, 1984) have also reported that apes, like human children, will use their newly developed language to comment on their environment.

Finally, Patterson (1978, 1980, 1981) extended these studies beyond chimps by training a gorilla named Koko to use sign language. Koko too could arrange signs in new combinations, such as *white tiger* for zebra. Patterson observed that Koko would sign to her dolls when she was alone, and she seemed to express a sense of self-awareness when she referred to herself as a *fine animal gorilla*. She was observed signing back and forth with another gorilla and has been known to express emotions like happiness and to swear, joke, and lie.

Do these fascinating studies establish that other species share with humans the ability to acquire and use language? There is a great deal of controversy about the answer to this question, and the findings, while intriguing, remain inconclusive. For example, Straub and colleagues (1979) pointed out that pigeons, by the use of operant conditioning, can be taught to peck a sequence of keys in order to get grain. No one would claim that this is evidence that pigeons are capable of developing language. And Limber (1977) noted that apes require a tremendous amount of intensive reinforcement to develop their still very limited linguistic skills.

Human children learn language effortlessly and swiftly, without the necessity of deliberate, intensive adult instruction. Even deaf, retarded, and deprived children outpace apes in their acquisition of language.

Terrace (1979) carefully studied videotapes of an ape named Nim Chimpsky who had been taught sign language and concluded that Nim was essentially just imitating his trainer's signs. No spontaneous combination of words into novel phrases occurred, nor did Nim's phrases eventually increase in length or complexity. Terrace also claims that other researchers have produced no unedited videotapes "that show that an ape's utterances are spontaneous and . . . not whole or partial imitations of the teacher's most recently signed utterance" (Terrace, 1985). He concludes that apes fail to develop language that is truly flexible, rule-driven, and capable of expressing abstract concepts. The "linguistic" apes, according to Terrace, have not developed a syntactical use of language—the ability that allows humans to understand and produce complex sentences that have never been heard or uttered before.

Given this controversy, it is still not possible to arrive at a consensus about the linguistic behavior of apes. Experimentation continues, and Terrace (1985) notes that the ability to use a sign in order to refer to an object is an impressive achievement in itself—even if it is not quite language. Moreover, Premack (1983) points out that language training has the side effect of improving apes' abilities to perform various other reasoning tasks. Recent work with pygmy chimps has shown that some chimps can begin to pick up language spontaneously (Savage-Rumbaugh et al., 1986). Whatever the eventual outcome of this debate, humans have already benefited from the research on apes. For instance, a computer-based language originally designed to instruct chimpanzees has been successfully applied to the teaching of severely retarded humans. By means of this technique, they are able to communicate their needs and wants to others, and in many cases their behavior no longer reflects the frustration that can result from an isolating communication disorder.

We have seen in our discussion so far that language is closely tied to the expression and understanding of thoughts. You might also have noticed that many words in our language—such as *friend*, *family*, *airplane*, *love*—correspond to concepts which, as we have seen, are among the building blocks of thought. By putting words together into sentences, we are able to link concepts to other concepts and form complex thoughts and ideas. Since our language determines not only the words we use but also the ways in which we combine those words into sentences, is it possible that language determines how we think and what we can think about? In the next, and final, section of this chapter, we will examine the relationship between language and thinking.

Language and Thought

Some theorists believe that language does indeed determine the way we think and the things we can think about. Recall that in Chapter 6 we noted that language affects long-term memory. To illustrate this effect, Brown and Lenneberg (1954) asked subjects to look at color patches and assign each one a name. Colors that were quickly and easily named (like *blue*) were more readily coded and retrieved than those that took longer to name and were given less common labels (like *sky blue* or *pale blue*).

This indicates that the ease with which we remember an experience is closely related to the ease and speed with which we name and encode that experience. As Lindsay and Norman (1977) point out, "memory for single perceptual experiences is directly related to the ease with which language can communicate that experience" (p. 483).

If language affects our ability to store and retrieve information, it should also affect our ability to think about things. Benjamin Whorf (1956) is the strongest spokesman for this position. According to Whorf's **linguistic relativity hypothesis,** the language that one speaks determines the pattern of one's thinking and one's view of the world. For Whorf, if a language lacks a particular expression, the thought to which the expression corresponds will probably not occur to the people who speak that language. Whorf notes that the Hopi Indians have only two nouns for everything that flies. One noun refers to birds. The other is used for everything else, whether airplanes, kites, or dragonflies. Thus, according to Whorf, the Hopi would interpret all flying things in terms of either of these two nouns—something in the air would be either a bird or a nonbird.

Think for a moment about how linguistic relativity might apply to what you are learning in this course. Phrases like *linguistic relativity hypothesis* or *surface and deep structure* capture very complex ideas. To the extent that you understand those terms, you probably do find it easier to think about the relationship between language and thought, or between words and sentences and their underlying meaning. The technical vocabulary of any field of study permits people to think and communicate more easily, more precisely, and in more complex ways about the content of that field. But this example also illustrates some of the criticisms of Whorf's hypothesis. The idea of deep structure occurred before someone

Linguistic relativity hypothesis Whorf's idea that patterns of thinking are determined by the specific language one speaks.

■ Slips of the Tongue

We are all familiar with embarrassing slips of the tongue— for example, when the doctor asks someone named Phil, "How would you like to be *killed*?" instead of "*billed*." Sigmund Freud proposed that such linguistic mistakes are the conscious manifestation of unconscious thoughts and feelings. According to Freud, the doctor in the example may have been harboring unconscious feelings of hostility toward the patient.

Other psychologists reject the notion that unconscious emotional conflict causes slips. Rather, these researchers note that the words in our mental dictionary can be compared to central crossing points in a spider's web. When we try to say a particular word, other nearby words are also activated primarily on the basis of meaning, sound, and grammar. Thus, the doctor might have said *kill* instead of *bill* possibly because of the similarities in sound.

Nevertheless, there is some evidence that emotional factors may also contribute to verbal slips. Motley (1985) conducted an experiment in which male subjects were asked to complete sentences like, "Tension mounted at the end, when the symphony reached its————." When the subjects were administered the test by a man, they tended to complete the sentence with words such as *finale* or *conclusion*. However, when the test was administered by an attractive female, they were more likely to use the word *climax*. Motley concluded that emotional factors may interact with cognitive ones to determine our choice or words—and of slips of tongue—in a variety of communication situations. The doctor who says that he wants to "kill Phil" may have misspoken himself both because of the similarity of the words and because of unconscious hostility toward his patient.

■ Schizophrenic Language

As we will see in Chapter 14, schizophrenia involves a major disorder of both thought and language. Schizophrenic thought appears to be highly illogical, and it often goes off on unpredictable and disconnected tangents (Rutter, 1985). Bleuler (1950) provides this example of one subject's thought patterns: "I always liked geography. My last teacher in that subject was Professor August A. He was a man with black eyes and other sorts too. I have heard it said that snakes have green eyes." Each sentence seems to lead to the next, but there is no overall structure to the line of thinking; one idea leads to another by means of loose associations, and the verbal expression reflects this disorder. An even more extreme example of schizophrenic thought disorder is called *word salad*—strings of apparently unconnected words with the occasional addition of gibberish, somewhat like infant babbling.

Shakow (1963) proposed that schizophrenics have a basic inability to maintain attention. According to this view, schizophrenic speech simply reflects a mind that wanders uncontrollably from one topic to another. But others emphasize the fact that there is a structure underlying schizophrenic speech. Gibberish, for example, is not a loosely arranged sequence of words such as might be caused by a wandering mind. Rather, the words are connected to one another, though the connections are not always immediately obvious. On closer examination, it often appears that the schizophrenic's disconnected language is actually similar in many ways to normal slips of the tongue. If this viewpoint is correct, then the task of understanding schizophrenic language becomes one of explaining why schizophrenia causes such an extraordinary emphasis on sequences of word associations and why the person suffering from schizophrenia is unable (or unwilling) to censor these associations. For example, for most of us thinking of a person with black eyes would not be linked immediately to the fact that snakes have green eyes, and even if it were we would probably not mention it in a conversation about school and teachers.

According to the *linguistic relativity hypothesis*, once expressions such as *powder snow* make their appearance in the language, they shape the way skiers subsequently think about snow.

thought up that particular phrase. Similarly, you were able to identify and think about basic speech sounds before you learned that they are called *phonemes*. And you certainly recognize the difference between what someone says and what that person means without having to know that these are called surface structure and deep structure, respectively.

In the same vein, some critics of the linguistic relativity hypothesis point out that it is more likely that the need to think about things differently changes a language than vice versa. For example, if the Hopi Indians had been subjected to air raids, they would probably have created a word to distinguish a butterfly from a bomber! Closer to home, most English-speaking people know only one word for snow. But skiers, realizing that different textures of snow can affect their downhill run, have coined such specific words for snow as "powder," "corn," and "ice." But Whorf may still be correct in pointing out that once such phrases as "powder snow" and "corn snow" make their appearance, they shape the way skiers subsequently think about snow. Language can help us organize our thoughts into concepts that serve as a kind of shorthand for a whole array of meanings. When a skier hears that conditions indicate powder snow, the verbalized information has clear and automatic implications—almost requiring no thought—for the type of wax and technique that he or she might use. In short, experience may shape language, which in turn may shape subsequent experience.

While language efficiently organizes human thought, it may capture only *some* of the experiences of the people who speak it. Nonskiers may call all types of snow simply "snow," but they can think about the differences among icy snow, slush, wet snow, and snow flurries. The Dani of New Guinea have no words for colors—everything is either dark/cool or light/warm; nonetheless, they remember basic colors like red, green, and yellow better than other colors. Furthermore, when taught the names of these basic colors, they learn them faster than they learn the names of other colors. And the Dani judge the similarity of colors much as English-speaking people do (Heider & Oliver, 1972; Heider, 1972; Rosch, 1973). In other words, the Dani think about colors much as we do, even though their language has no words for specific colors. Moreover, Berlin and Kay (1969) have discovered that the complexity of a society is a good predictor for the number of color terms that its language will contain. As a primitive society becomes more complex, its people have no trouble adding the necessary words to accommodate their expanded concepts. Thus, people from different cultures with very different languages think about some things, such as color, in very similar ways. Even though language and thought are intertwined, people can think about things for which they have no words in their language.

We have seen that the linguistic relativity hypothesis somewhat overstates the relationship between language and thought. Nonetheless, we have also seen that language is closely related to the expression and understanding of thoughts: Language reflects and organizes a person's thoughts, it changes as a person's way of thinking changes, and, to a limited extent, it shapes what people can think about and remember most effectively. By all accounts, then, language plays an important role in thinking.

Artificial intelligence Use of computers to simulate human cognitive processes.

 APPLICATION

Artificial Intelligence

We are all familiar with the science fiction computer and its ability to think and even feel like a human being. In some respects, this fantasy is actually becoming reality. For the last several decades, computers have been used for many tasks that require fairly mechanical kinds of "thinking"—doing mathematical calculations, storing and retrieving data, and performing well-structured tasks. It is relatively easy, for example, to program computers to use problem-solving algorithms, which (as we have seen) consist of formulas or a discrete list of steps to go from a beginning state to a conclusion. Sophisticated algorithms are already being used in computers that do complex tasks like word processing, calculation, and graphic illustration. In most such cases, computers actually perform these tasks faster and with greater accuracy than humans.

But are computers capable of duplicating more complex cognitive processes as well? That is the ques-

tion being asked by researchers in the field of **artificial intelligence** (AI). The results so far have been mildly encouraging: Computers have been programmed to simulate a variety of complex cognitive processes. For example, despite the complexity and indeterminacy of heuristic thinking, computers have been programmed to use heuristics in problem-solving. Chess, for example, is a game in which there are trillions of possible moves. Human chess masters rely on heuristics to identify the most promising moves and to select the optimal move. Chess-playing computers have been programmed to use similar heuristics, with the result that these computers can defeat all but the most expert human players (Best, 1989).

Another area in which artificial intelligence has had some success is *expert systems*. Expert systems are computer programs that attempt to simulate human experts. For example, MYCIN is an expert system that diagnoses bacterial infections and recommends treatments (Shortliffe, 1976). The computer first gathers information about the patient's symptoms and past history as well as the results of pertinent lab tests. Using this information and its knowledge of diseases, the computer then attempts to make a diagnosis and recommend medication. Another expert system, PROSPECTOR, uses its knowledge and heuristics as well as geological information about an environment to identify underground ore deposits. Both MYCIN and PROSPECTOR have turned out to be quite good at their tasks (Frenzel, 1987).

Computers have also been taught to understand some aspects of natural language, an accomplishment that has traditionally been seen as uniquely human. If you have ever tried to program a computer, you know that it is usually necessary for you to learn the computer's language, since computers do not understand plain English. But efforts are afoot to change all that. For example, Terry Winograd (1972) developed a robot named SHRDLU that could communicate with its operator and carry out instructions in a small area filled with blocks of various shapes, sizes, and colors. The following is an excerpt from one conversation between Winograd and SHRDLU (the computer comments are italicized):

Winograd: Pick up a big red block.
SHRDLU: *OK.*
W: Grasp the pyramid.
S: *I don't understand which pyramid you mean.*
W: Find a block which is taller than the one you are holding and put it in the box.
S: *By "it" I assume you mean the block which is taller than the one I am holding. OK.*
W: What does the box contain?

S: *The blue pyramid and the blue block.*
W: What is the pyramid supported by?
S: *The box.*
W: How many blocks are in the box?
S: *Four of them.*
W: Is at least one of them narrower than the one which I told you to pick up?
S: *Yes, the red cube.*
W: Is it supported?
S: *Yes, by the table.*
W: Can the table pick up blocks?
S: *No.*

(Boden, 1987, pp. 115–17)

In all the aforementioned cases, human programmers provided the computers with the necessary knowledge and the rules to use in order to go about their tasks. But in recent years, researchers in AI have begun exploring ways in which computers can learn from experience what they need to know in order to perform a task. This aspect of artificial intelligence was discussed in Chapter 2 in the Box on neural networks.

It is too early to conclude whether computers will ever approach the full range of thinking of which humans are capable. Griffin (1984) points out that "Human minds do more than process information; they think and feel. We experience beliefs, desires, fears, expectations, and many other subjective mental states." More recently, a similar critique has been made by Dreyfus and Dreyfus (1986). But others, like Simon (1981), argue that if all these supposedly more human attributes eventually can be understood by psychologists, there is no reason why they also could not be replicated by machines.

■ Summary

- **Cognition** involves diverse thinking processes that play a role in many psychological functions. Cognition refers to reflection, conceptualization, problem-solving, and decision-making, as well as to various ways of manipulating information, including the processing and retrieval of information from memory.

- **Images** and **concepts** are the two most important building blocks of thought.

- **What do you think of when you think of home?** When we are thinking about things, we rely on sensory images, which we also manipulate to aid our thinking about things from various perspectives. Images allow us to think in nonverbal ways, to clarify difficult concepts, and to make complex abstractions concrete.

- **How do we know that a lion is not a bird, but a penguin is?** In practice, concepts tend to be "fuzzy" and ambiguous rather than clear-cut and precise. In everyday thinking, we rely on models or **prototypes** of concepts. We decide which objects belong to a particular concept according to what seems most probable and sensible given the facts at hand.

- **Problem representation,** or interpretation, is the first step in figuring out a solution to a problem. People show a strong tendency to accept the initial representation of a problem even though it may not be the most appropriate. Those who are skilled at problem-solving are adept at representing problems in various ways.

- Different types of problems require different solutions. In some cases, solving a problem is simply a matter of retrieving information from long-term memory and applying it to the situation at hand.

- **You are driving to your friends' house in Spokane. Why might you be inclined to use a formula like $t = d/r$ (time = distance divided by rate of travel) when figuring out how long it will take to get there?** *Algorithms* are problem-solving methods that guarantee the correct solution if they are appropriate for the problem and are properly carried out.

- *Heuristics* are rules of thumb that help in simplifying problems and bringing solutions within reach. Part of problem-solving is deciding which heuristic best fits the problem at hand. Hill-climbing, subgoals, means-end analysis, and working backward are four heuristic methods. *Hill-climbing* involves the effort to move continually closer to a final goal without digressing or backing up. In setting *subgoals,* we break a problem into smaller and more manageable goals, each of which is easier to solve than the problem as a whole. *Means-end analysis* is a combination of setting subgoals and hill-climbing. Each subgoal (each end) is evaluated in terms of whether it will bring us closer to our final goal (the end). *Working backward* is a problem-solving strategy whereby we begin at the goal and work backward toward the "givens"—the information at hand.

- A number of conditions can affect problem-solving. The peak state of performance in problem-solving is achieved at intermediate levels of arousal. A state of high emotional arousal can interfere with problem-solving.

- *Set* refers to our tendency to perceive and approach problems in certain ways. Set can be helpful by allowing us to benefit from past experiences in learning certain operations and ways of perceiving. But if we rely too heavily on set and fail to look for new methods to solve problems, we may overlook more creative strategies. *Functional fixedness* occurs when we get used to perceiving something in a certain way and cannot perceive it in any other way.

- **Why is it often helpful to draw a map when giving directions?** Becoming better at problem-solving requires trying out various ways of representing problems and experimenting with different solution strategies. The **tactic of elimination** requires listing possible solutions and then evaluating choices according to appropriate criteria. **Visualizing** involves the diagramming or charting of a simple model that allows us to focus on important details and to ignore distracting details.

- Creative problem-solving requires the solution of problems that do not lend themselves to straightforward strategies. This type of problem-solving relies on **divergent thinking** that is flexible and inventive. It is often marked by *insight*—a "flash out of the blue" that solves a problem—and can often be enhanced by maintaining a willingness to redefine a problem in imaginative ways and by maintaining a questioning attitude. **Brainstorming** can also facilitate creative problem-solving.

- *Expertise* can rely on creativity, but it also depends on knowledge about a particular subject area. The knowledge that comes from experience enables the expert to define a problem quickly and to eliminate counterproductive strategies.

- Decision-making differs from other kinds of problem-solving in that we know the available options but need to select the best one. In making this selection, we often evaluate our options by using a predetermined set of criteria. The more complex our criteria, the greater the difficulty we encounter in reaching a solution.

- **You must decide between an inexpensive, noisy apartment with neighbors who are a nuisance, and a quieter, more expensive apartment with nice neighbors. How might you go about making a decision?** *Compensatory models* allow us to rate and compare different choices on each of several criteria. Such rational models of decision-making allow us to evaluate a large number of criteria. They are the models of choice in making important decisions.

- In everyday decision-making we tend to use less logical and formal methods. **Noncompensatory models,** such as the elimination-by-aspects method, do not involve weighing the various criteria and making comparisons among alternatives. Because they are shortsighted and are often unduly influenced by the **representativeness** and **availability** heuristics, noncompensatory models result in adequate but not always the best decisions.

- *Phonemes* are the basic, universal sounds of all languages. Phonemes are meaningless in themselves but are combined to form **morphemes,** the smallest meaningful units in language. We express our ideas in phrases and sentences (combinations of morphemes) rather than in single concepts.

- **Do these two sentences mean the same thing?**
  The ocean is unusually calm tonight.
  Tonight the ocean is particularly calm.
  We move from deep structure to surface structure to communicate ideas. We use the reverse process, movement from surface structure to deep structure, in order to comprehend ideas. The same deep structure can be communicated by various different surface structures, as in the two previous sentences.

- In order for speakers and listeners to communicate effectively, language must follow rules. These rules constitute *grammar.* Speakers and listeners use grammar to perform *transformations* that allow them to move up and down from surface structure to deep structure. The two major components of grammar are *semantics* (how meaning is assigned to *morphemes*) and *syntax* (how words are combined to make sentences).

- The development of language begins with the sounds that infants produce—sounds that are actually quite complex and whose development follows a regular pattern. After producing single expressions like *da*, the infant will begin stringing the same sounds together, as in dadadada. Gradually, infant babbling takes on features of adult speech, including *intonation*. At about 12 months of age, the infant will utter a first word and will soon build a vocabulary of one-word sentences. In the second year of life, the child develops a passion for naming things and thinks in very concrete terms. Two- and-three-word sentences begin occurring during the third year of life, and at age three to four, children begin to fill in sentences with properly used syntactical items such as past-tense verbs.

- There are two very different theories about how language develops. B.F. Skinner believes that children develop language skills through trial and error and reinforcement. The more current belief is that children have an innate capacity for learning language which is stimulated by hearing speech and by having people around with whom to communicate.

- **Can animals be taught to use language?** The ability to develop language is universal among humans, but some researchers maintain that primates are also capable of rule-guided communication if they are taught to use various forms of sign language or other symbols instead of spoken words. Although some researchers have produced some intriguing results, critics have pointed out that children learn language without the intensive instruction given the apes and argue that the apes simply imitate their trainers' signs without developing the ability to use specific rules or to express abstract concepts.

- Language itself significantly affects our ability to think about things. The **linguistic relativity hypothesis** maintains that thinking is patterned by language and that the language one speaks determines one's view of the world. Although this theory has been strongly criticized, evidence suggests that the way we think affects the words we use, and that once words make their appearance in a language, they shape the way we think about things. However, people from different language backgrounds appear to think about some things—like color—in very similar ways. Thus, people are able to think about things for which no equivalent words exist in their language; that is, to some extent, thinking occurs independently of language.

■ Review Questions

1. The term that psychologists use to refer to the processes of thinking is _____.
2. _____ and _____ are the two most important building blocks of thought.
3. Categories for classifying specific people, things, or events are
   a. concepts.   c. phonemes.
   b. images.   d. morphemes.

4. Images help us think about things because images are more concrete than words.   T / F
5. People decide which objects belong to a concept by comparing the facts to a model or prototype.   T / F
6. Match each problem-solving strategy with its definition:
   ____ algorithm   a. rules of thumb that help in
   ____ heuristics   simplifying and solving

_____ hill-climbing
_____ means-end analysis
_____ working backward

a. problems, although they do not guarantee a correct solution
b. strategy in which each step moves you progressively closer to a solution
c. step-by-step method that guarantees a solution
d. a strategy in which one moves from the goal to the starting point
e. strategy that aims to reduce the discrepancy between the current situation and the desired goal at a number of intermediate points

7. All of the following are potential obstacles to problem-solving except
   a. sets.
   b. excitement.
   c. functional fixedness.
   d. hill-climbing.

8. Bill is trying to decide between taking a ski vacation in Vermont and a beach vacation in the Caribbean. To make the choice, he sets up some criteria for a good vacation and then rates the two alternatives on each in order to see how they stack up against each other. Bill is using a _____ model of decision-making.

9. Our tendency to perceive and to approach problems in certain ways is termed a _____ .

10. The tendency to perceive only a limited number of uses for an object, a tendency which interferes with the process of problem-solving, is known as _____ .

11. In making decisions, most people use a compensatory model.   T / F

12. Decision-making models that do not try to systematically weigh comparisons among alternatives are _____ models.

13. People are most likely to use a compensatory model when
    a. the stakes are low.
    b. the stakes are high.
    c. others are observing them.
    d. the problem is simple.

14. In language, universal sounds, called _____ , are combined to form the smallest meaningful units, which are called _____ . These meaningful units can then be combined to create words, which in turn can be used to build phrases and whole _____ .

15. We use _____ to link concepts with other concepts and thus form more complex thoughts.

16. According to Whorf's _____ _____ hypothesis, the language that one speaks determines the pattern of one's thinking and one's view of the world.

17. According to Chomsky, language users employ rules or _____ to allow them to go from the surface to the deep structure of language.

8

Intelligence

■ Thinking Critically

Is there more than one kind of intelligence?

What is IQ?

How well do tests like the SAT and GRE predict grades in college?

Do intelligence tests discriminate against people from other cultures?

What do IQ scores tell us?

Can the environment in which we grow up make us more intelligent, or is our intelligence genetically predetermined?

Is mental retardation the result of brain damage?

Are creative people more intelligent?

The answers to these and other questions about the nature and measurement of intelligence appear in this chapter and in the Chapter Summary.

■ Outline

1. Describe the difference between *laziness* and *idleness*.
2. Which direction would you have to face so your right hand would be toward the north?
3. What does *obliterate* mean?
4. In what way are an *hour* and a *week* alike?
5. Select the item that completes the following series of four figures:

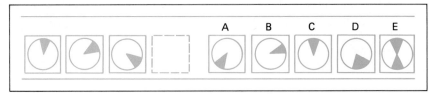

6. Choose the lettered block that best completes the pattern in Figure 1.

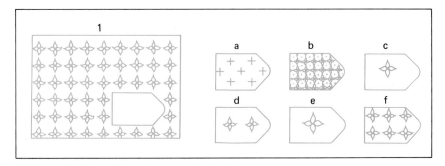

7. The opposite of hate is:
   (a) enemy   (b) fear   (c) love   (d) friend   (e) joy
8. If three pencils cost 25 cents, how many pencils can be bought for 75 cents?
9. A bird does not always have:
   (a) wings   (b) eyes   (c) feet   (d) a nest   (e) a bill
10. Choose the word that is most nearly *opposite* in meaning to the word in capital letters:
    SCHISM: (a) majority   (b) union   (c) uniformity
    (d) conference   (e) construction
11. Choose the set of words that, when inserted in the sentence, best fits in with the meaning of the sentence as a whole:
    From the first, the islanders, despite an outward _____, did what they could to _____ the ruthless occupying power.
    (a) harmony . . . assist
    (b) enmity . . . embarrass
    (c) rebellion . . . foil
    (d) resistance . . . destroy
    (e) acquiescence . . . thwart
12. Select the lettered pair that best expresses a relationship similar to that expressed in the original pair:
    CRUTCH: LOCOMOTION:: (a) paddle: canoe
    (b) hero: worship   (c) horse: carriage   (d) spectacles: vision
    (e) statement: contention

13. The first three figures are alike in some way. Find the figure at the right that goes with the first three.

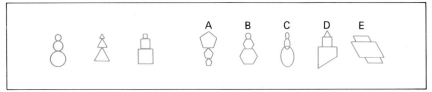

14. Decide how the first two figures are related to each other. Then find the one figure at the right that goes with the third figure in the same way that the second figure goes with the first.

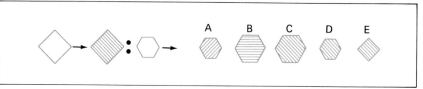

15. For each figure, decide whether or not it can be completely covered by using all the given blue pieces without overlapping any.

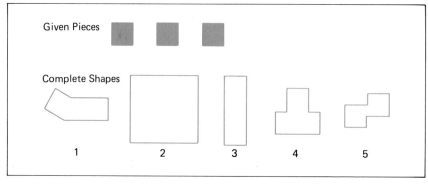

These questions have been taken from various **intelligence tests** designed to measure general mental abilities. Obviously, we cannot see the complex mental processes that are involved in **intelligence.** We have to approach the subject indirectly—by watching what people do when situations require the use of intelligence. But what do these tests actually tell us? Do they sample all the kinds of ability that we consider "intelligence"? What is intelligence anyway? And is it related to creativity? If you do well on tests such as these, will you be more successful in school, in a job, or in your personal life than someone who does less well? We will address these and related questions in this chapter. We'll begin by looking at what is meant by intelligence.

■ Intelligence

What does "intelligence" mean to you? Take a few minutes to write down on a sheet of paper some behaviors that you believe to be characteristic of intelligent people. In particular, what behaviors distinguish them from unintelligent people?

Sternberg and his associates (Sternberg et al., 1981; Sternberg, 1982) conducted a study to find out how various people define intelligence. They studied both laypersons with no expertise in psychology and psychologists who specialize in studying intelligence. In each group, the researchers asked a large number of people to list characteristics of intelligence and then to rate various kinds of people on the basis of those characteristics. The results showed that most laypersons think of intelligence as practical problem-solving ability, verbal ability, and social competence. Practical problem-solving ability includes using logic, connecting ideas, and viewing a problem in its entirety. Verbal ability includes using and understanding both written and spoken language in well-developed ways. Social competence concerns interacting well with others—being open-minded about different kinds of people and showing interest in a variety of topics. Experts described intelligence as being made up of verbal intelligence, problem-solving ability, and practical intelligence. This corresponds fairly closely to the layperson's view (see Table 8-1). The main difference in thinking between the two groups is one of emphasis. Whereas laypersons stress social competence, experts do not consider this an essential component of intelligence. Experts, on the other hand, consider motivation an important factor, while this characteristic does not appear on the laypersons' list.

Though many experts, such as those in Sternberg's study, agree on some of the major characteristics of intelligence, a more recent study by Snyderman and Rothman (1987) indicates that there is not yet a consensus among experts as to what kinds of behaviors qualify as "intelligent." Over three-quarters of those psychologists and educators surveyed also felt dissatisfied with our ability to measure adequately creativity and individuals' ability to adapt to their environment—qualities that a majority felt to be important aspects of intelligence. As we will see throughout this chapter, part of what makes intelligence difficult to define is that reliable measurements of it are difficult to develop and therefore to test.

Before we go on, you might find it interesting to compare your own description of intelligence with those of Sternberg's laypersons and experts. Which one seems to match your own definition most closely? Now that you can compare all three definitions, which one do you think is the best? Why do you think so?

Psychologists have thought about the nature of intelligence for many years, and in the process they have developed several formal theories of intelligence. We will turn our attention first to those formal theories and then to the ways in which psychologists go about measuring intelligence.

■ Formal Theories of Intelligence

Basically, there are two kinds of theories of intelligence—"lumpers" and "splitters" (Mayr, 1982). Lumpers see intelligence as a general capacity for acquiring knowledge, while splitters see it as many different types of abilities. Charles Spearman, a British psychologist, began working on a theory of intelligence around 1900. It struck him that people who are bright in one area often seem to be bright in other areas. So Spearman

TABLE 8-1 SOME CHARACTERISTICS OF INTELLIGENCE AS SEEN BY LAYPERSONS AND EXPERTS

Laypersons	Experts
I. Practical problem-solving ability Reasons logically. Makes connections among ideas. Can see all sides of a problem. Keeps an open mind. Responds thoughtfully to the ideas of others. Good at sizing up situations. Interprets information accurately. Makes good decisions. Goes to original source for basic information. Good source of ideas. Perceives implied assumptions. Deals with problems in a resourceful way.	**I. Practical intelligence** Sizes up situations well. Determines how best to achieve goals. Shows awareness of world around him or her. Shows interest in the world at large.
II. Verbal ability Speaks articulately. Converses well. Is knowledgeable about a particular field. Studies hard. Reads widely. Writes without difficulty. Has a good vocabulary. Tries new things.	**II. Verbal intelligence** Has a good vocabulary. Reads with high comprehension. Is intellectually curious. Sees all sides of a problem. Learns rapidly. Shows alertness. Thinks deeply. Shows creativity. Converses easily on a wide range of subjects. Reads widely. Sees connections among ideas.
III. Social competence Accepts others as they are. Admits mistakes. Shows interest in the world at large. Arrives on time for appointments. Has social conscience. Thinks before speaking and acting. Shows curiosity. Avoids snap judgments. Makes fair judgments. Assesses the relevance of information to the problem at hand. Is sensitive to others. Is frank and honest with self and others. Shows interest in the immediate environment.	**III. Problem-solving ability** Makes good decisions. Displays common sense. Shows objectivity. Is good at solving problems. Plans ahead. Has good intuition. Gets to the heart of problems. Appreciates truth. Considers the results of actions. Approaches problems thoughtfully.

Source: Sternberg, 1982.

Operations According to Guilford, the act of thinking.

Contents According to Guilford, the terms we use in thinking, such as words or symbols.

Products According to Guilford, the ideas that result from thinking.

argued that intelligence is more than an accumulation of specific skills. Instead, he maintained, intelligence is quite general, a kind of well, or spring, of mental energy that flows into every action. The intelligent person understands things quickly, makes good decisions, carries on interesting conversations, and so on. He or she behaves intelligently in various situations. All of us are quicker in some areas than in others. We may find math easy, for example, but will spend hours writing an essay. But Spearman saw these differences as simply ways in which the same underlying general intelligence is revealed in different activities. To return to the image of a well or spring, general intelligence is the fountain from which specific abilities flow like streams of water in different directions.

L. L. Thurstone, an American psychologist, partly agreed with Spearman, but he thought the differences between various abilities needed more attention. From the results of various intelligence tests, Thurstone made a list of seven primary mental abilities (Thurstone, 1938):

S—Spatial ability*   M—Memory
P—Perceptual speed   W—Word fluency
N—Numerical ability   R—Reasoning
V—Verbal meaning

Unlike Spearman, Thurstone believed that these abilities are relatively independent of one another. A person with high spatial ability might be low on word fluency, for example. But together, Thurstone felt, these primary mental abilities are what we mean when we speak of general intelligence. According to Thurstone, one or more of these abilities can be found in any intellectual activity. To read a book, you need verbal meaning, word fluency, and reasoning. To study that same book for an exam, you also need memory. Thurstone thus presented a somewhat more complex model of intelligence than Spearman's.

According to Thurstone, one or more primary mental abilities is involved in any intellectual activity. To read a book, for example, you need verbal meaning, word fluency, and reasoning.

J. P. Guilford found both Spearman's and Thurstone's models of intelligence incomplete. Guilford distinguished three basic kinds of mental ability: **operations,** the act of thinking; **contents,** the terms in which we think—such as words or symbols; and **products,** the ideas we come up with (Guilford, 1961). Each of these categories can be broken down further. The result is the three-dimensional model shown in Figure 8-1.

According to Guilford, all mental activity involves an operation on some kind of *content* that results in some *product.* For example, you are reading a newspaper column about the candidates in a mayoral election. Reading involves three operations: cognition, memory (you recall the candidates' speeches and ads), and evaluation (you ask yourself if the columnist and the candidates are making sense). In performing these operations, you use two kinds of contents: semantic (the words) and behavioral (the activities or behavior described). The products of your reading are inferences (this person would make a good mayor, that person would not) and classes (two candidates are liberal, the third is conservative). You may also discover some relationships: Perhaps the candidate born in the central city understands its problems better than the two who were raised in the suburbs.

Formal theories about intelligence can become incredibly complex.

* Spatial ability is the ability to perceive distance, recognize shapes, and so on.

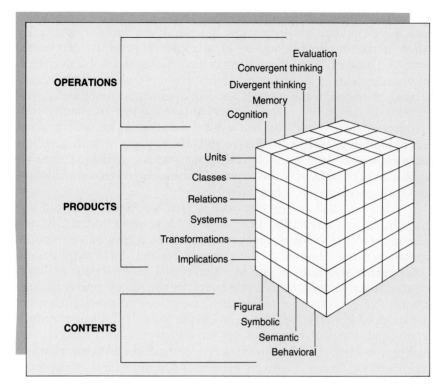

Triarchic theory of intelligence
Sternberg's theory that intelligence involves mental skills (componential aspect), insight and creative adaptability (experiential aspect), and environmental responsiveness (contextual aspect).

Figure 8-1
Guilford's three-dimensional model of intelligence The model consists of 120 small cubes, or factors. Each factor can be classified according to operation, product, and content.

For example, most people find the 120 cubes in Guilford's model overwhelming! Some recent research has been directed at developing simpler theories of intelligence. Psychologist R. B. Cattell believes that there are just two clusters of mental abilities, with only minor differences between the specific abilities within each cluster (Cattell, 1971). The first cluster is what Cattell calls *crystallized intelligence*, or abilities such as reasoning and verbal and numerical skills. These are the kinds of abilities stressed in school, and as a result, Cattell believes, the scores on tests of crystallized intelligence are greatly affected by experience and formal education. The second cluster of abilities makes up what Cattell calls *fluid intelligence*, or skills such as spatial and visual imagery, the ability to notice visual details, and rote memory. Scores on tests of fluid intelligence are much less affected by experience and education.

Robert Sternberg (1985, 1986) proposed a **triarchic theory of intelligence** that takes a very different approach to understanding intelligence. Sternberg never did very well on standard tests of intelligence. In fact, he says, "I really stunk on IQ tests. I was just terrible" (Trotter, 1986, p. 56). Understandably, Sternberg became quite curious not only about the cognitive processes that are necessary to answer questions on standard IQ tests, but also about the relationship between these processes and intelligent behavior in real life. After studying these questions in some depth, Sternberg concluded that human intelligence encompasses a much broader variety of skills than imagined by previous theorists and that skills necessary for effective performance in the real world are just as important as the more limited skills assessed by traditional intelligence tests.

In fact, Sternberg's theory is itself very much grounded in his own real-world experience. As a professor at Yale, he found himself working with three graduate students whom he calls Alice, Barbara, and Celia. Alice fit the standard definition of intelligence perfectly. She scored extremely well on tests of intelligence and had nearly a 4.0 average as an undergraduate. Her analytical abilities were excellent. Barbara's undergraduate record was not great, and her Graduate Record Exam (GRE) scores were quite low by Yale's standards, yet she had excellent recommendations from those who had worked with her as an undergraduate and found her to be highly creative and able to come up with good new ideas and to do good research. The third graduate student, Celia, was somewhat in the middle of the other two. She had good recommendations and fairly good scores on her GRE.

Alice excelled in her first year of graduate work. Celia did well enough, but not terrifically. Because of her low scores on the GRE and despite Sternberg's own recommendation to the admissions committee, Barbara was not admitted to the program. Instead, Sternberg hired her as a research associate because he believed her creativity and ability to do good research could be valuable assets. By the second year of graduate school, Alice was having trouble developing her own research ideas and had dropped from the top of the class to the lower half. Celia continued to do good, but not great, work yet turned out to have the easiest time finding a good job. Barbara proved to be very much the associate Sternberg had hoped for. In fact, Sternberg believes that some of his most important work has been done in collaboration with her.

Each of these three students seemed to have a different kind of intelligence, causing them to excel in different ways. Alice, Barbara, and Celia each represent one of the three aspects of Sternberg's triarchic theory. Alice represents the *componential* aspects of intelligence. These are the mental processes or skills that are emphasized by most of the previous theories of intelligence, such as the ability to learn how to do things or acquire new knowledge and carry out tasks effectively.

Barbara exhibited the greatest strength in what Sternberg calls the *experiential* aspects of intelligence—being able to adjust to new tasks, to use new concepts, to respond effectively in new situations, to gain insight, and to adapt creatively. This aspect of intelligence involves being able to process at least some kinds of information efficiently and effectively with minimal effort, and perhaps without conscious thought.

Celia had the easiest time finding a job because she was strong in the *contextual* aspects of intelligence. This aspect involves the ability to select environments in which one can function effectively, to adapt to the environment, and to reshape it if necessary. Intelligent people, according to Sternberg, are very good at capitalizing on their strengths and compensating for their weaknesses. They make the most of their talents by seeking situations that match their skills, by shaping those situations so that they can make maximal use of their skills, and by knowing when to seek out new situations that better fit their talents.

You can see that for Sternberg, intelligence is tightly tied to a broad variety of skills that are important to functioning effectively in the real world. In this sense, Sternberg's theory of intelligence is quite close to the informal view that most laypersons hold of intelligence (see Table 8-1).

Despite the differences between them, formal theories of intelligence are important because they provide a standard view of intelligence that can be used as the basis for the measurement of intelligence. Formal theories supply the means to develop intelligence tests to measure the abilities of large numbers of people and to compare them to one another. From formal definitions of the components of intelligence, psychologists can create corresponding questions and problems to tap those components. But because intelligence tests are not based on everyday views of intelligence, they will not precisely match people's ideas about what they should include, as we shall see in the following pages.

Intelligence Tests

The Stanford-Binet Intelligence Scale

The first "intelligence test" was designed for the French public school system by Alfred Binet, director of the psychological laboratory at the Sorbonne, and his colleague, Theodore Simon. Binet and Simon developed a number of questions and tested them on schoolchildren in Paris to find out which children were retarded or had trouble learning.

The first **Binet-Simon Scale** was issued in 1905. It consisted of 30 tests arranged in order of increasing difficulty. With each child, the examiner started at the top of the list and worked down until the child could no longer answer questions. By 1908, enough children had been tested to predict what the normal average child could do at each age level. From these average scores Binet developed the concept of *mental age*. A child who scores as well as an average 4-year-old has a mental age of 4; a child who scores as well as an average 12-year-old has a mental age of 12.

In the next 10 years, a number of Binet adaptations were issued, the best known of which was prepared at Stanford University by L. M. Terman and issued in 1916. Terman introduced the now-famous term **IQ (intelligence quotient)** to establish a numerical value of intelligence and set the score of 100 for a person of average intelligence. An approximate distribution of IQs in the population is shown in Figure 8-2.

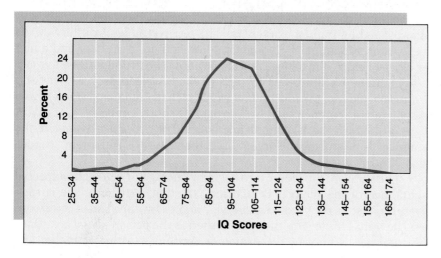

Figure 8-2
The approximate distribution of IQs in the population.

Designated area	Subtest	Age span
Verbal Reasoning	Vocabulary	2 to 23
	Comprehension	2 to 23
	Absurdities	2 to 14
	Verbal Relations	12 to 23
Abstract/Visual Reasoning	Pattern Analysis	2 to 23
	Copying	2 to 13
	Matrices	7 to 23
	Paper Folding and Cutting	12 to 23
Quantitative Reasoning	Quantitative	2 to 23
	Number Series	7 to 23
	Equation Bulding	12 to 23
Short-Term Memory	Bead Memory	2 to 23
	Memory for Sentences	2 to 23
	Memory for Digits	7 to 23
	Memory for Objects	7 to 23

TABLE 8-2 AREAS, SUBTESTS, AND AGE SPANS FOR STANFORD-BINET: FOURTH EDITION

Alfred Binet

For two reasons, the **Stanford-Binet Intelligence Scale** has been revised three times since 1916. First, any test must be updated as the meanings and usage of words change. Second, Terman and his colleagues found that some questions were easier for people from one part of the country than for those from another, that some were harder for boys than for girls (and vice versa), and that some failed to discriminate among age levels since nearly everyone tested could answer them. Such questions were replaced. Questions 1 and 2 at the start of this chapter were drawn from the revised Stanford-Binet. In 1972, the norms for scoring the test were restandardized and included the scores of non-whites for the first time. The test items themselves were not changed (Sattler, 1982).

As shown in Table 8-2, the 15 different subtests of the Stanford-Binet are designed to measure skills in four areas closely related to the characteristics of intelligence described by most theorists: verbal reasoning, abstract/visual reasoning, quantitative reasoning, and short-term memory. The subtests are designed to provide information about a person's memory and reasoning abilities and to serve as the basis for developing, at the most interpretive level, a measurement of a general intelligence factor (Sattler, 1982). The Stanford-Binet test is not simply passed out to a roomful of students. Instead, each test is given individually and administered by trained examiners. The test resembles an interview. It takes about 30 minutes for young children and up to an hour and a half for older ones. For instance, 3-year-olds are asked to identify a toy cup as something "we drink out of" and to name objects such as *chair* and *key*; 6-year-olds are asked to define words such as *orange* and *envelope* and to complete a sentence such as "An inch is short; a mile is _____ ." A 12-year-old might be asked to define *skill* and *juggler* and to complete the sentence: "The streams are dry _____ there has been little rain" (Cronbach, 1970).

The standard procedure is to begin by testing just below the expected mental age of the subject. If a person fails that test, he or she is then given the test at the next lowest level, and so on, until the subject can pass the test. This level is then established as the person's *basal age*. Once the basal age is known, the examiner continues testing at higher and higher levels until the person fails *all* the tests. Then the tests stop. After scoring the tests, the examiner determines the subject's mental age by adding to the basal age credits for each test passed above that age level.

The Wechsler Intelligence Scales

The individual test most often given to adults is the **Wechsler Adult Intelligence Scale—Revised (WAIS-R).** The original WAIS was developed by David Wechsler, a psychologist at Bellevue Hospital in New York City. Wechsler objected to using the Stanford-Binet for adults on three grounds: First, the problems had been designed for children and seemed juvenile to adults. Second, the mental-age norms of the Stanford-Binet did not apply to adults. Finally, while the Stanford-Binet emphasizes verbal skills, Wechsler felt that adult intelligence consists more in the ability to handle the environment than in the skill to solve verbal and abstract problems.

The WAIS-R is divided into two parts: One part stresses verbal skills, the other performance skills. The verbal scale includes tests of information ("Who wrote *Paradise Lost?*"); tests of simple arithmetic ("Sam had three pieces of candy, and Joe gave him four more. How many pieces of candy did Sam have then?"); and tests of comprehension ("What should you do if you see someone forget a book on a bus?"). All of these tests require a verbal or written response. The performance scale also measures routine tasks. People are asked to "find the missing part"— buttonholes in a coat, for example; to copy patterns; and to arrange three to five pictures so that they tell a story. Questions 3 and 4 at the start of this chapter are taken from the WAIS.

Although the questions and instructions might be more sophisticated on the WAIS-R than on the Stanford-Binet, the problems are not especially adult ones. Wechsler's chief innovation was in scoring. First, the person is given separate verbal and performance scores as well as an overall IQ score. Second, on some items the person can earn one or two extra points, depending on the complexity of the answer given. This

Wechsler Adult Intelligence Scale— Revised (WAIS-R) Individual intelligence test developed especially for adults; measures both verbal and performance abilities.

The *Wechsler Intelligence Scales* are designed for both adults (WAIS-R) and children (WISC-R).

innovation credits the reflective qualities that we expect to find in adults. Third, on some questions, both speed and accuracy affect the score.

Wechsler has also developed a similar intelligence test for use with school-age children. Like the WAIS-R, the **Wechsler Intelligence Scale for Children—Revised (WISC-R)** yields separate verbal and performance scores as well as an overall IQ score.

Group Tests

The Stanford-Binet, the WAIS-R, and the WISC-R are individual tests. The examiner takes the person to an isolated room, spreads the materials on a table, and spends from 30 to 90 minutes giving the test. The examiner may then spend another hour or so scoring the test according to detailed instructions in the manual. Obviously, this is a time-consuming, costly operation. Moreover, the examiner's behavior may greatly influence the score.

For these reasons, test makers have devised **group tests,** written intelligence tests that a single examiner can give to large groups. Instead of a person sitting across the table asking you questions, you receive a test booklet that contains questions for you to answer within a certain amount of time. Questions 6 through 12 at the start of this chapter are all from group tests.

When most people talk about intelligence tests, they are usually referring to group tests, because this is usually the means by which they were themselves tested in school. Schools are among the biggest users of group tests. From fourth grade through high school, tests such as the *School and College Ability Tests* (SCAT) and the *California Test of Mental Maturity* (CTMM) are used to measure students' specific abilities. The *Scholastic Aptitude Tests* (SAT)—questions 10 through 12 at the start of this chapter—and the *American College Testing Program* (ACTP) are designed to measure a student's ability to do college-level work. The *Graduate Record Examination* (GRE) performs the same function on the graduate level. Group tests are also widely used in different industries, the civil service, and the military.

Group tests have some distinct advantages. They eliminate bias on the part of the examiner. Answer sheets can be scored quickly and objectively. And since more people can be tested in this way, more useful norms can be established. But there are also some distinct disadvantages to group tests. The examiner is less likely to notice if a person is tired, ill, or confused by the directions. People who are not used to being tested tend to do less well on group tests than on individual tests. Emotionally disturbed children also seem to do better on individual tests (Anastasi, 1982).

Performance and Culture-fair Tests

Deaf children take longer to learn words than children who can hear. Immigrants who may have been lawyers or teachers in their own countries may need time to learn English. Infants and preschool children are too young to understand directions or answer questions. How can we test these people? One way is to use problems that minimize or eliminate the use of words—that is, **performance tests** or nonverbal tests of various sorts.

Schools are among the biggest users of group tests of intelligence

One of the earliest performance tests, the *Seguin Form Board*, was devised in 1866 to test the mentally retarded. The form board is essentially a puzzle. The examiner removes specifically designed cutouts, stacks them in a predetermined order, and asks the person to replace them as quickly as possible. Another performance test, the *Porteus Maze*, consists of a series of increasingly difficult printed mazes. The examiner asks the person to trace his or her way through the maze without lifting the pencil from the paper. This test gives the examiner the equivalent of a mental age based on the most difficult maze that a person negotiates.

One of the most effective tests used for very young children is the *Bayley Scales of Infant Development*. The Bayley Scales are used to evaluate the developmental abilities of children from two months to two and a half years of age. One scale tests perception, memory, and the beginning of verbal communication; another measures sitting, standing, walking, and manual dexterity. The Bayley Scales can detect early signs of sensory and neurological defects, emotional problems, and troubles in a child's home environment (Graham & Lilly, 1984).

Culture-fair tests are designed to measure the intelligence of people who are outside of the culture in which the test was devised. Like performance tests, culture-fair tests minimize or eliminate the use of language. Culture-fair tests also try to minimize skills and values—such as the need for speed—that vary from culture to culture. A good example of this is the *Goodenough-Harris Drawing Test*. The subject is asked to draw the best picture of a person that he or she can. The drawing is scored for proportions, correct and complete representation of the parts of the body, detail in clothing, and so on. It is not scored for artistic talent.

Cattell's *Culture-fair Intelligence Test* combines some questions that demand verbal comprehension and specific cultural knowledge with other questions that are culture-fair. By comparing scores on the two kinds of questions, cultural factors can be isolated from general intelligence. An example of a culture-fair item from the Cattell test is question 5 at the start of this chapter.

Another culture-fair test is the *Progressive Matrices* (question 6 at the start of this chapter). This test consists of 60 designs, each with a missing part. The person is given six to eight possible choices to replace the part. The test involves various logical relationships, requires discrimination, and can be given to one person or to a group.

▬ What Makes a Good Test?

All the tests that we have looked at so far claim to measure a broad range of mental abilities, or "intelligence." How can we tell if they really do measure intelligence? And how can we decide whether one test is better than another? Psychologists address these questions by referring to a test's reliability and validity.

Reliability

By **reliability** psychologists refer to the dependability and consistency of the scores yielded by a given test. If your alarm clock is set for 8:15 A.M. and goes off at that time every morning, it is reliable. But if it is set for

Culture-fair tests Intelligence tests designed to eliminate cultural bias by minimizing skills and values that vary from one culture to another.

Reliability Ability of a test to produce consistent and stable scores.

Split-half reliability A method of determining test reliability by dividing the test into two parts and checking the agreement of scores on both parts.

Correlation coefficients Statistical measures of the degree of association between two variables.

8:15 and rings at 8:00 one morning and 8:40 the next, you cannot depend on it; it is unreliable. Similarly, a test is reliable when it yields consistent results. On the other hand, if you score 90 on a verbal aptitude test one week and 60 on the same or an equivalent test a week or two later, something is wrong.

How do we know if a test is reliable? The simplest way to find out is to give the test to a group and then, after a short time, give the same people the same test again. If they score the same each time, the test is reliable. For example, look at Table 8-3, which shows the IQ scores of eight people tested one year apart on the same test. This is a very reliable test. Although the scores did change slightly, none changed by more than six points.

But there is a serious problem with this way of determining reliability. Because the exact same test was used on both occasions, people might simply have remembered the answers from the first testing and repeated them the second time around. In order to avoid this, *alternate forms* of the test are often used. In this method, two equivalent tests are designed to measure the same ability. If a person gets the same score on both forms, the tests are reliable. One way to create alternate forms is to split a single test into two parts—for example, to assign odd-numbered items to one part and even-numbered items to the other. If scores on the two halves agree, the test is said to have **split-half reliability.** Most intelligence tests do in fact have alternate equivalent forms—for example, there are many versions of each college admission test.

These methods of testing reliability can be very effective. But is there some way of being more precise than simply calling a test "very reliable" or "fairly reliable"? Psychologists express reliability in terms of **correlation coefficients,** which measure the relationship between two sets of scores.[*] If test scores on one occasion are absolutely consistent with those on another occasion, the correlation coefficient would be 1.0. If there is no relationship between the scores, the correlation coefficient would be zero. In Table 8-3, where there is a very close, but not perfect, relationship between the two sets of scores, the coefficient is .96.

How reliable are intelligence tests? In general, the reliability coefficients are around .90—that is, people's IQ scores on most intelligence tests are about as stable as the scores in Table 8-3. Performance and culture-fair tests are somewhat less reliable. However, scores on even the best tests vary somewhat from one day to another. Therefore, many testing services now report a person's score along with a range of scores that allows for variations due to chance. The person might be told that his or her score was 105 with a range of 95–115. This implies that the true score almost certainly lies somewhere between 95 and 115 but is most likely within a few points of 105. But even with the *best* intelligence tests, differences of a few points in IQ scores have little meaning and should not be the basis for major decisions, such as putting a child in an accelerated or remedial program.

We have seen that many intelligence tests are reliable. But do these tests really measure "intelligence"? We know that the scores on intelligence tests are fairly consistent from day to day, but how do we know

Table 8-3 IQ Scores on the Same Test Given One Year Apart		
Person	First Testing	Second Testing
A	130	127
B	123	127
C	121	119
D	116	122
E	109	108
F	107	112
G	95	93
H	89	94

[*] For more information on correlation coefficients, consult the appendix on measurement and statistical methods at the end of this book.

that the consistency is due to "intelligence" and not to something else? When psychologists ask these questions, they are concerned with test validity.

Validity

Validity is a test's ability to measure what it has been designed to measure. How can you determine if a given test actually measures what it claims to measure?

CONTENT VALIDITY.   One measure of validity is known as **content validity**—whether or not the test contains an adequate sample of the skills or knowledge that it is supposed to measure.

Do IQ tests adequately cover the kinds of mental abilities that they set out to include? The answer is somewhat mixed. Alfred Binet specifically designed his test to measure qualities like judgment, comprehension, and reasoning, and so the test was more heavily verbal than perceptual or sensory. Binet himself felt that his intelligence test measured not some single entity called "intelligence," but rather sampled various different mental operations, all of which are part of intelligence. As we saw earlier, Binet's original test has been revised and updated several times. At the earliest age levels, the test now requires eye-hand coordination, discrimination, and the ability to follow directions. Children build with blocks, string beads, match lengths, and so on. Older children are tested on skills that they learn in school, like reading and math. The tests still rely heavily on verbal content: vocabulary, sentence completion, and interpreting proverbs, for instance. And even the tests that are not strictly verbal still require understanding of fairly complex verbal instructions.

Most people would agree that the content of the Stanford-Binet is at least part of what we commonly consider "intelligence," so we can conclude that the Stanford-Binet does have at least some content validity. But the heavy emphasis on verbal skills suggests that the test may not adequately sample all aspects of intelligence equally well.

As we saw earlier, it was partly the Stanford-Binet's emphasis on verbal skills that prompted Wechsler to devise the WAIS and the WISC. Wechsler believes that taken together, his subtests adequately measure what we call "intelligence," which he defines as "the aggregate or global capacity of the individual to act purposefully, to think rationally, and to deal effectively with his environment." In fact, the WAIS-R and WISC-R do appear to cover many of the primary abilities that Thurstone included under "intelligence" and that Cattell grouped under the headings of "fluid" and "crystallized" intelligence. So the WAIS-R and WISC-R also appear to have some content validity as intelligence tests.

Most group intelligence tests, such as those from which questions 6 through 12 at the beginning of this chapter were taken, also seem to measure at least some of the mental abilities that make up intelligence. In general, then, the content of most intelligence tests does cover many of the abilities considered to be components of intelligence. These include concentration, planning, memory, understanding language, and writing (Carroll & Horn, 1981). As we saw earlier, most people would agree that these abilities are part of intelligence. Yet intelligence tests do not cover every type of mental ability. Some tests cover skills that other tests

Validity Ability of a test to measure what it has been designed to measure.

Content validity Refers to a test's having an adequate sample of the skills or knowledge it is supposed to measure.

Criterion-related validity Validity of a test as measured by a comparison of the test score and independent measures of that which the test is designed to measure.

leave out, and each intelligence test emphasizes the abilities that it measures in a slightly different way.

CRITERION-RELATED VALIDITY. Is test content the only way to determine if an intelligence test is valid? Fortunately, it is not. For example, if both the Stanford-Binet and the WISC-R measure intelligence in children, high scores on one should go with high scores on the other. And if school grades reflect intelligence, then students with good grades should be high scorers on the Stanford-Binet and other intelligence tests. In each case, we can compare scores on the test with some other "direct and independent measure of that which the test is designed to predict" (Anastasi, 1982, p. 137) in order to determine **criterion-related validity.**

In fact, various intelligence tests do relate well with each other despite the differences in their content. People who score high on one test tend to score high on the others. Again, we can use the correlation coefficient to describe the strength of the relationship. The Stanford-Binet and Wechsler Scales correlate around .80. The SAT and Wechsler Scales correlate about .60 to .80. The Progressive Matrices and the Porteus Maze Test correlate .40 to .80 with other intelligence tests. The Goodenough-Harris Drawing Test correlates about .50 or better with other tests. Thus, despite their differences in surface content, most intelligence tests do seem to be measuring similar things.

Do IQ tests predict academic achievement? Even the strongest critics agree that this is one thing that IQ tests do well. The Stanford-Binet was designed specifically to predict school performance, and it typically performs this function quite well. Correlations between grades and IQ of .50 to .75 are quite common. Like the Stanford-Binet, the Wechsler Scales also correlate highly with school grades, especially the verbal IQ score. The SAT and ACT college admission tests correlate around .40 with college grades, and the GRE is a good predictor of performance in graduate school. Evidence on the various performance and culture-fair tests is scanty but suggests that these tests do not predict school grades as well as other intelligence tests do (Blum, 1979).

We have seen that intelligence tests are quite reliable: Scores on these tests are consistent from day to day. These tests also seem to include many of the qualities that psychologists define as components of intelligence. And intelligence test scores seem to agree with one another and with other indicators of intelligence, such as school grades. Nonetheless, in the past decade or so, intelligence tests have been the subject of severe criticism.

Criticisms of IQ Tests

TEST CONTENT AND SCORES. One major criticism of IQ tests is directed at their content. Many critics believe that intelligence tests are concerned with only a very narrow set of skills: passive verbal understanding; the ability to follow instructions; common sense; and, at best, scholastic aptitude (Ginsberg, 1972; Sattler, 1975). For example, one critic observes, "Intelligence tests measure how quickly people can solve relatively unimportant problems making as few errors as possible, rather than measuring how people grapple with relatively important problems, making as many productive errors as necessary with no time factor" (Blum, 1979, p. 83).

These critics suggest that if there is one thing that all intelligence tests measure, it is the ability to take tests. This would explain why people who do well on one IQ test also tend to do well on others. And it would also explain why intelligence tests correlate so closely with school performance, since academic grades also depend heavily on test scores. But whether this ability applies to other, real-life situations that require successful intellectual activity is questionable (Blum, 1979). Thus it should not be surprising that there is a growing trend to "abandon the term IQ and replace it with a more accurate descriptor, such as school ability or academic aptitude" (Reschly, 1981, p. 1097).

Still other critics suggest that the content and administration of IQ tests discriminate against minorities. In part, this may be because minority children tend to see such tests as "just a game" and so make less of an effort to do well (Palmer, 1979). But it is also suggested that the unique language skills of black and minority children are not measured by most IQ tests (Blum, 1979). Moreover, examiners often complain that they "cannot understand" how poor black children talk, and this complication obviously does not encourage good test performance (Sattler, 1975). In addition, certain questions may have very different meanings for a white middle-class child and for a black ghetto child. The Stanford-Binet, for instance, asks, "What's the thing for you to do if another boy hits you without meaning to do it?" The "correct" answer is, "Walk away." But for a ghetto child, whose survival may depend on being tough, the logical answer might be, "Hit him back." This answer, however, receives zero credit on the Stanford-Binet. One of the ways cross-cultural tests have traditionally attempted to overcome cultural differences has been to eliminate the major basis for those differences. This might mean creating a test where language or reading are not necessary or allowing plenty of time so that people from cultures that do not value quick responses, as ours does, will not be penalized for responding slowly (Anastasi, 1988).

Even culture-fair tests may accentuate the very cultural differences that they were designed to minimize (Linn, 1982). Nonverbal tests can be more culturally loaded than verbal ones. For example, when given a picture of a head with the mouth missing, one group of Oriental children responded by saying that the body was missing, thus receiving no credit. To them, the absence of a body under the head was more remarkable than the absence of the mouth (Ortar, 1963). And nonverbal tests often require abstract thinking styles that are typical of Western middle-class cultures (Cohen, 1969). Cattell's Culture-fair Test, for example, may be easier for those cultural groups accustomed to working with pencil and paper or those motivated to do well on tests.

There are many other reasons why minority children might perform more poorly on IQ tests than middle-class whites (Sattler, 1975). Studies suggest that minority children are more wary of adults, more eager for adult approval, less motivated to get "the right answer" just for the sake of being right, and less driven to achieve. Such emotional and motivational factors could be reflected in test performance.

Although these concerns are real, the best evidence available indicates that "the major, widely used and widely studied tests" are not biased against minorities (Bersoff, 1981; Cole, 1981; Reschly, 1981).

The content of IQ tests, including culture-fair tests, has been criticized for discriminating against minorities. The best evidence to date, however, indicates that the major and widely used IQ tests are not biased against minorities.

While some test items do appear to be biased, these items are so few that they have little or no effect on the IQ scores of various groups. Nonetheless, as Cole (1981) points out, this does not mean "that the use made of the tests is necessarily socially good nor that improvements in the tests cannot be made" (p. 1075).

USE OF IQ SCORES. If IQ tests were just used for some obscure research purposes, perhaps the criticisms would carry less weight. But because IQ tests have been used for so many significant purposes, their evaluation is very important.

Alfred Binet developed the first IQ test to help the French public school system identify students who needed to be put in special classes. In fact, Binet believed that courses of "mental orthopedics" could be used to help those with low IQ scores. But the practice of using IQ tests to put a person into a "track" or "slot," as in school classes, can backfire. To the extent that a child gets a low score on an IQ test because of test bias, language handicap, or disinterest, the administrative decision to label children "slow" or "retarded" and put them into special classes apart from "normal" students can have a disastrous effect—one that may get worse, not better, with time. Moreover, as we shall see later in this chapter, mental retardation involves a great deal more than simply low IQ scores.

Although IQ tests are useful for predicting academic performance and for reflecting past learning, there is much that they do not measure—motivation, emotion, and attitudes, for example. Yet in many situations these other characteristics may have more to do with one's success and effectiveness than IQ does. Let's look briefly at the relationship between IQ scores and success.

IQ AND SUCCESS. Despite their limitations, IQ tests do predict school performance. What does this fact mean and how important is it?

IQ scores should correlate well with academic performance because both involve some intellectual activity and both stress verbal ability. Moreover, both academic achievement and high IQ scores require similar kinds of motivation, attention, and continuity of effort. And since academic success depends largely on test-taking ability, the correlation is not surprising. But critics suggest that there may be another, less attractive, reason for the relationship between school performance and IQ test scores. If teachers expect a student to do well in school—on the basis of his or her IQ scores—they may encourage that student. By the same token, a student with a low IQ score may not be expected to perform as well and may be neglected as a result.

Whatever the reason, IQ scores do predict success in school with some accuracy. Moreover, people with high IQ scores tend to become engaged in high-status occupations: Physicians and lawyers tend to have high IQs while truck drivers and janitors tend not to. But critics point out that this can be explained in various ways. For one thing, because people with higher IQs tend to do better in school, they stay in school longer and earn advanced degrees, which, in turn, open the door to high-status jobs. Moreover, children from wealthy families are more likely to have the motivation and the money needed for graduate school and occupational training. They also tend to have helpful family connections.

Perhaps most importantly, they grow up in environments that encourage academic success and reward good performance on tests (Blum, 1979).

In fact, studies have shown that IQ scores and grades in college have very little to do with later occupational success (McClelland, 1973). We now know that when education and social class are held constant, in a wide range of jobs people with high IQs do not perform better than people with lower IQs. As early as 1921, Edward L. Thorndike observed that the Stanford-Binet test was useful in predicting a child's academic achievement but less helpful in determining "how well he will respond to thinking about a machine that he tends, crops that he grows, merchandise that he buys and sells and other concrete realities that he encounters in the laboratory, field, shop, and office. It may prophesy still less accurately how well he will succeed in thinking about people and their passions and in responding to these" (Sattler, 1975, p. 21).

In this section, we have reviewed several criticisms that have been leveled at IQ tests and their use. But criticism does not always mean that the critics want IQ tests to be eliminated altogether. Instead, many of these critics simply want to make IQ tests more useful. For example, J. R. Mercer has developed a "System of Multicultural Pluralistic Assessment" (SOMPA), which can be used to test children between the ages of 5 and 11. SOMPA takes into account both the dominant school culture and the family background, and IQ scores (based on the Wechsler Scales) are then adjusted accordingly (Rice, 1979). And Sternberg is presently at work developing a new intelligence test that will tap the very broad set of skills that he believes to constitute intelligence.

In any event, it is important to remember that an IQ score is *not* the same as intelligence. Tests measure a person's ability level at a certain point in time and in relation to the norms for his or her age group. IQ scores do not tell us why someone performs poorly or well. Moreover, "intelligence" is not a single entity; rather, it is a combination of abilities required for adaptation to, and effective behavior in, the real world (Anastasi, 1982; Frederickson, 1986; Sternberg, 1985, 1986). Obviously, these abilities will vary to some extent from culture to culture and from one age to another. Those abilities considered most important in one culture will tend to increase in that culture; abilities that are deemphasized will tend to decrease (Levinson, 1959). And finally, an IQ score is really a very simplistic way of summing up an extremely complex set of abilities. Maloney and Ward (1976) point out that we do not describe a person's personality with a two- or three-digit number. Why, then, he asks, should we try to sum up something as complex as intelligence by labeling someone "90" or "110"?

■ Determinants of Intelligence

Heredity

About 50 years ago, R. C. Tryon began wondering if the ability to run mazes could be bred into rats. Horse breeders and cattle farmers have long known that selective breeding—for example, crossing a fast horse with a strong one—can change the physical characteristics of animals.

Could the same technique alter mental abilities? Tryon isolated eligible pairs of "maze-bright" rats in one pen and "maze-dull" rats in another. The animals were left free to breed. Within a few generations, the difference between the two groups was astounding: The maze-dull rats made many more mistakes learning a maze than their bright counterparts (Tryon, 1940; see Figure 8-3).

It is difficult to explain how maze ability was transmitted. Perhaps the brighter rats inherited better eyesight, larger brains, quicker reflexes, greater motivation, or a combination of these advantages. Still, Tryon did demonstrate that a specific ability can be passed down from one generation of rats to another.

Obviously, it is impossible to perform laboratory experiments in the selective breeding of humans. Nature, however, gives us nearly perfect experimental subjects for measuring heredity in humans: identical twins. Unlike siblings and fraternal twins, whose genes come from the same parents but have combined differently, identical twins have exactly the same genetic inheritance. If, as Tryon's experiment suggests, intelligence is inherited, identical twins should have identical IQs. Any difference between them would have to be attributed to environment or experience.

Studies of twins begin by comparing the IQ scores of identical twins who have been raised together. The correlation, shown in Figure 8-4, is very high. But these twins grew up in the same environment: They shared parents, home, schoolteachers, vacations, and probably friends and clothes, too. These common experiences may explain their similarity. In order to check this possibility, researchers look for identical twins who were separated early in life—generally before they were six months old—and raised in different families. The correlation between IQs of separated twins is nearly as high as that between twins raised together, but there is some evidence of environmental influence.

At this point, the case for heredity seems to be won: Identical twins have about equal IQ scores even when they have not been raised together. For several reasons, however, twin studies are not "final proof." First, it is so difficult to find identical twins who were separated at birth that very few such pairs have been studied. Second, adoption agencies tend to match natural and foster parents. If the twins were born to educated middle-class parents, it is highly likely that the adopted twin was placed with educated middle-class foster parents. Finally, even if the twins grew up in radically different environments, they lived for nine months in the same mother: Their prenatal experiences were identical. Therefore, at least some of their similarity may actually be due to similarity of environment. It is here that the case for environmental influence begins.

Figure 8-3
Errors made by Tryon's maze-bright and maze-dull rats in learning a maze
The colored line shows what percentage of the parent group made equal numbers of errors. The black lines show the errors of the eighth generation of rats. Notice that almost all the maze-dull rats made more errors than the maze-bright rats.

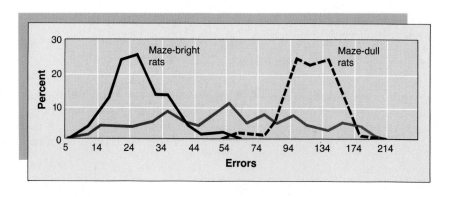

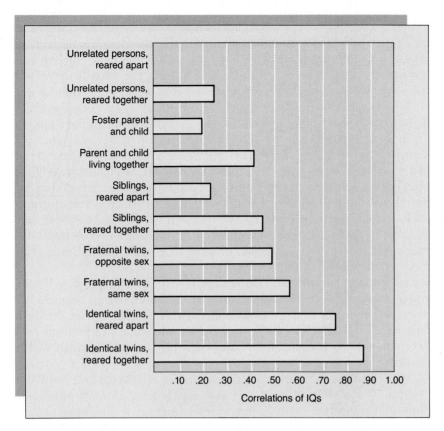

Figure 8-4
Correlations of IQ scores and familial relationships.
Adapted from L. Erlenmeyer-Kimling and L. F. Jarvik, "Genetics and Intelligence: A Review," *Science*, 1963, *142*, 1477–79. Copyright 1963 by the American Association for the Advancement of Science.

Environment

Proponents of the environmental factor do not deny that some part of intelligence is inherited, but they feel this is only the start. Each of us inherits a certain body build from our parents, but our actual weight depends on what we eat and how much we exercise. Similarly, even

Separated at birth, the Mallipert twins meet accidentally.
Drawing by Chas. Addams; © 1981 The New Yorker Magazine, Inc.

Though studies of the IQ scores of identical twins seem to indicate that there is a strong genetic component to intelligence, it is still not possible to rule out prenatal and environmental influences.

though we inherit certain mental capacities, the development of our intellectual abilities depends on what we see around us as infants, how our parents respond to our first attempts to talk, the schools we attend, the books we read, the TV programs we watch—and even what we eat.

In fact, since a number of studies show that prenatal nutrition affects IQ scores, the environmental case begins even before birth. For example, psychologists studied a group of pregnant women who were economically deprived and therefore rarely enjoyed "three square meals a day." Half of the women were given a dietary supplement, and half were given placebos—in order to guard against the possibility that merely taking pills would make the women feel better and that this factor, not nutrition itself, would affect their babies. When given intelligence tests between the ages of three and four, the children of the mothers who had taken the supplement scored significantly higher than the other children (Harrell, Woodyard, & Gates, 1955).

Extreme malnutrition during infancy can lower IQ scores. For example, severely undernourished children in South Africa averaged 20 points lower in IQ than similar children with adequate diets (Stock & Smythe, 1963). If children do not get an adequate diet early in their development, both their mental and their physiological growth will be stunted.

None of this is surprising: Common sense tells us that we need food to grow. But is that all we need? Apparently not. Many psychologists think that surroundings are as important to mental development as diet. The first hint of this fact came from studies of the effect of light deprivation on sight. Chimpanzees, kittens, rabbits, and other animals raised in total darkness for 16 to 18 months and then moved to a normal environment could never see as well as animals exposed to daylight since birth. There was nothing wrong with these animals' eyes at birth. It seems that the cells and nerves that we use to see do not develop without stimulation (Wiesel & Hubel, 1963). It is probable that the same is true for other parts of the nervous system, including the brain.

Even more revealing was a further study of Tryon's maze-bright and maze-dull rats conducted in the 1950s. Psychologists raised one group of mixed bright and dull rats in absolutely plain surroundings and another group in a stimulating environment that contained toys, an activity wheel, and a ladder. When the rats were grown, they were tested on the mazes. There was no difference between genetically bright and dull rats that had been raised in a restricted environment: The inherited abilities of the bright rats had failed to develop, and they acted just like dull rats. Among the rats raised in the unusually stimulating environment, there was also little difference in performance. They all acted like bright rats. Apparently, the genetically maze-dull rats were able to make up through experience what they lacked in heredity. The researchers performed autopsies on both groups and found that the rats brought up in a stimulating environment had heavier brains than the others regardless of whether or not they had inherited maze-brightness (Cooper & Zubek, 1958).

Quite by chance, one researcher found evidence that IQ scores among children also depend on stimulation. In the 1930s, psychologist H. M. Skeels was investigating orphanages for the state of Iowa. Then as now, the wards were terribly overcrowded: Often three or four attendants were responsible for washing, dressing, feeding, and cleaning up

IQ Scores, Family Size, and Birth Order

Zajonc and Markus (1975) present some striking findings about the relationship between IQ scores, family size, and birth order. After reviewing research conducted by Belmont and Marolla (1973), who collected IQ and birth-order statistics on 386,114 young men in the Netherlands, Zajonc and Markus concluded:

> Intelligence declines with family size; the fewer children in your family, the smarter you are likely to be. Intelligence also declines with birth order; the fewer older brothers or sisters you have, the brighter you are likely to be.

Zajonc and Markus constructed a model of the intellectual environment of a family in order to account for these findings. Their model suggests that when a newborn baby enters a family, the average intellectual environment of the family is lowered. Each parent is arbitrarily given an "intellect score" of 100. But the zero score assigned to the newborn baby lowers the average intellectual environment in the family to a level of 67. If a second child is born two years later, the family's average score will drop to nearly 50. One simple way to explain this principle is to imagine the intellectual capacity of the parents being spread among a number of young children. The more children there are, the smaller the amount that will be passed to each child.

In order to maximize the intellectual environment of your children, the authors suggest that you have no more than two children and that you have them at least three years apart. One of the benefits enjoyed by firstborn children is the opportunity to teach things to their younger siblings. Contrary to popular belief, only children are not at an intellectual advantage. This is probably because they lack this teaching opportunity.

The Zajonc and Markus model has received a good deal of support. For example, the model predicted a decline in SAT scores until 1980 and a rise thereafter until the year 2000—a pattern reflecting increases and decreases in family size. So far, the figures match the predictions almost perfectly (Zajonc, 1986). However, a number of critics have raised questions about Zajonc's conclusions (Flynn, 1988; Lang &

One of the benefits firstborn children have is the chance to teach their younger siblings.

Reifman, 1988; Rodgers, 1988; Roznowski, 1988). One of these questions has to do with Zajonc's use of aggregate or group statistics to explain *individual* performance. Others question his assertion that birth order *causes* differences in intelligence, when all that one can safely say is that the two are correlated—that when birth order rises, SAT scores tend to fall. Finally, some believe that race, socioeconomic status, and the war in Vietnam (which encouraged many young men during those years to seek a college education to avoid the draft), could have affected the results but were not taken into account. In fact, family size appears to be much less important in determining mental abilities than social class and ethnic background. Although there is not enough research on the question, the origins of these influences may be related to such factors as education and environment. Children with well-educated parents who provide a rich intellectual climate are likely to have a better chance to develop their intellectual skills than children whose parents cannot provide them with these benefits (Page & Grandon, 1979). Given these legitimate and important questions, the relationship between birth order and IQ remains an open question, and research is continuing.

after as many as 35 children. There was rarely time to play with the children, to talk to them, or to read them stories. Many of the children were classified as subnormal, and it was fairly common for the state to transfer them to institutions for the mentally retarded when the orphanages ran out of space. Skeels became interested in two such children who, after 18 months in an orphanage, were sent to a ward for severely retarded adult women. When Skeels first tested these girls, they did seem retarded, but after a year on the adult ward, their IQs were normal (Skeels, 1938). Skeels regarded this fact as quite remarkable—after all, the women

Figure 8-5
Changes in IQ of the institutionalized children studied by Skeels.
Adapted from H. M. Skeels, "The Study of the Effects of Differential Stimulation on Mentally Retarded Children: A Follow-up Report," *American Journal of Mental Deficiencies*, 1942, *46*, 340–50.

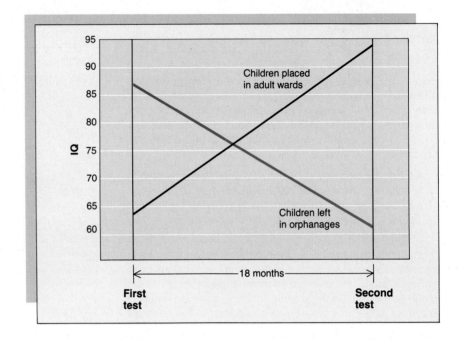

with whom the girls had lived were themselves severely retarded. Skeels decided to repeat the experiment and placed 13 slow children as houseguests in adult wards (Skeels, 1942) (see Figure 8-5). Within 18 months, the mean IQ of these children had risen from 64 to 92 (within the normal range)—all because they had had someone to play with them, to read to them, to cheer when they took their first steps, and to encourage them to talk. During the same period, the mean IQ of a group of children who had been left in orphanages dropped from 86 to 61. Such dramatic changes could not occur if intelligence were stable and hereditary. Thirty years later, Skeels found that all 13 of the children raised on adult wards were self-supporting, their occupations ranging from waitress to real estate salesperson. Half of the contrasting group were unemployed, four were still in institutions, and all those who had jobs were dishwashers (Skeels, 1966).

Taking their cue from Skeels, some researchers suggest that child-rearing patterns contribute to class differences in IQ. They point out that lower-class mothers, especially mothers with large families, often do not play with their children as much as middle-class mothers do. Nor do they reward them consistently for achievements, such as learning to crawl or to tell time. Middle-class parents also encourage their children to talk, asking them to describe what they are building with blocks, to identify shapes, colors, and sizes. Those who claim that intelligence depends on stimulation explain the lower IQs of some poor children in terms of thwarted curiosity, an underdeveloped attention span, and a general mistrust of adults.

This is the essence of the case for environment as a factor in the development of successful intellectual ability: True, some general abilities are inherited, but without stimulation a child's intelligence will not develop. The effects of early deprivation—whether the extreme loneliness of the institutionalized child or the relative isolation of some lower-class children—may not be reversible in later life. When it comes to considering

Environmentalists claim that intellectual development depends on environmental stimulation and encouragement. Naturally environments vary, and because mental stimulation has a wide variety of practical purposes, it takes different forms in different cultures.

these sorts of group differences, the question as to whether intelligence is mainly genetically or environmentally determined is not so much the issue as, "Can intelligence be changed?" (Angoff, 1988). Given what we know about the effects of providing a more stimulating environment, for example, the answer appears to be that it can.

The Jensen Controversy

The recent furor over IQ testing was triggered in large part by a 1969 article by psychologist Arthur Jensen that criticized such compensatory education programs as Operation Head Start. The purpose of Operation Head Start was to act as a kind of foster-middle-class environment for disadvantaged children. Its purpose was not only to teach children basic concepts, but also to encourage them to put their perceptions into words. The program sought to teach children to trust adults, to feel comfortable in a schoolroom, and to exercise their curiosity—in other words, to get children ready for school. We will examine Head Start and other compensatory programs more closely in the Application at the end of this chapter, but for the moment we will focus on Jensen's argument that race differences in IQ scores are largely inherited.

Jensen's views on racial differences in IQ are highly controversial. As both sides point out, however, comparisons of average scores of any group tell us very little about what we can expect of any one member of the group.

In the first part of his article, Jensen examines the evidence that intelligence is inherited and concludes that heredity accounts for at least 80 percent of the variation in IQ scores. He then turns to the question of the effect of race differences on intelligence: Black Americans average 15 points lower than whites on most IQ tests. Jensen claims that socioeconomic class does not explain these differences. For one thing, blacks in the upper and middle classes, as well as those in lower classes, have lower IQ scores than their white counterparts. For another, American Indians, who are worse off than blacks in every way, score higher on IQ tests than blacks. Jensen concludes that discrimination and prejudice cannot explain the gap. According to Jensen, one must conclude that the gene pool of blacks differs from that of the general population. Although Jensen concluded that heredity is strongly implicated in IQ differences between groups, he did caution against drawing conclusions about any one person's IQ on the basis of such group generalizations.

Jensen's work generated a furious controversy among educators and social scientists over the validity of IQ testing, the heritability of intelligence, and the relationship between race and intelligence. Between 1969 and 1973 alone, 117 articles were published in response to Jensen's original piece in the *Harvard Educational Review* (1969). Critics have pointed to the potential effects of generations of systematic discrimination: They claim that the effects of discrimination are evident in the fact that IQ scores for blacks from the northern part of the United States are significantly higher than those for Southern blacks, suggesting that a higher level of discrimination in the South depresses IQ scores. They also argue that teachers tend to expect less from black students and will communicate this, however subtly. The effects of low expectations and low self-esteem mount over the years. Finally, whereas Jensen appears to assume that blacks and whites from the same class live in the same environments, few researchers would agree. For example, while the average white construction worker owns his own home, his black co-worker, with the same salary and references, has a much more difficult time finding a home and getting a mortgage.

It is difficult to sort out the conflicting data and claims involved in the argument over Jensen's work. This is especially true since most of the participants, including Jensen and many of his critics, agree that *both* hereditary and environmental factors affect IQ. Dobzhansky (1973) insists that we simply do not have conclusive evidence to prove that there is, or is not, a genetic basis for racial differences in IQ scores. Moreover, as Jensen himself points out, we should remember that comparisons of average scores of any group tell us very little about what we can expect of any one member of the group.

Gender Differences in Cognitive Abilities

Another area of recent concern is the relationship between gender and cognitive abilities. Do males show greater abilities than females in some areas? Do females have more abilities in some areas than males? These questions have become increasingly important since women have entered the work force in larger numbers. Employment statistics show that many occupations are dominated by one sex or the other. Engineering, for example, is almost exclusively a male field (U.S. Bureau of the Census, 1984). Is it possible that these occupational differences reflect real gender differences in cognitive abilities?

In 1974, psychologists Eleanor Maccoby and Carol Jacklin published a review of psychological research on sex differences in a number of areas. In most of the studies that they examined, they found no differences at all between the two sexes. But a few differences did appear in the area of cognitive abilities. Maccoby and Jacklin found that girls tend to have greater verbal ability than boys and that boys tend to have greater visual-spatial and mathematical abilities.

More recently, Alan Feingold (1988) studied the results of aptitude tests given between 1947 and 1980. Though he found some gender differences in verbal and spatial ability, he also found that these differences had *declined* considerably over the years he surveyed. The gap between boys' and girls' scores on tests of spatial relations had declined by half. Only in the area of advanced high-school mathematics did boys' superior performance remain constant.

Psychologist Janet Shibley Hyde (1981) believes that as a result of the Maccoby and Jacklin study, many people have exaggerated the importance of these male-female differences. She points out that although the differences identified by Maccoby and Jacklin were consistent, they were also very small. In fact, the differences appear only in studies with very large numbers of subjects. In small groups, these differences are often too slight to detect. These concerns are echoed by Caplan, MacPherson, and Tobin (1985), who conclude that "it is by no means clear as yet" that sex differences in spatial abilities exist (p. 797). In fact, widespread beliefs of males' superiority in math may become a self-fulfilling prophecy. One study by Eccles and Jacobs (1986) found that the girls whose mothers believed that math is more difficult for girls than for boys were actually likely to take fewer math courses.

It seems clear that gender differences in cognitive abilities should not be used for vocational counseling of individuals. Considering how small the differences are and the fact that they are declining, it would be a mistake to conclude that females as a group should not enter careers that rely on visual-spatial skills or math abilities or to expect that individual women cannot demonstrate outstanding skills in these areas. It now appears that math anxiety, parents' beliefs about the difficulty of mathematics, and students' perceptions about the value of math, are major contributors to the differences in mathematical achievement between males and females. The role of biological sex differences appears far less important (Jacklin, 1989). By the same token, it would be a mistake to assume that these small differences in cognitive abilities should keep men out of professions that rely on strong verbal skills. It is also important to remember that, because sex differences do not appear at all on many tests, it is difficult to determine how important they are when they do appear. Finally, as we discussed earlier, since overall IQ scores are not good predictors of career success, very small sex differences on specific abilities are even less likely to be reliable predictors of future job performance.

Mental retardation Condition of significantly subaverage intelligence combined with deficiencies in adaptive behavior.

The very slight gender differences in cognitive abilities make it clear that they should not be used in vocational counseling.

Extremes of Intelligence

The average IQ score on intelligence tests is 100. Nearly 70 percent of all people have IQs between 85 and 115, and all but 5 percent of the population falls between 70 and 130. In this section, we will focus on those people who score at the two extremes of intelligence—the mentally retarded and the gifted.

Mental Retardation

Mental retardation is a broad heading that covers a large number of very different kinds of mental deficits with a wide variety of causes, treatments, and outcomes. The American Association on Mental Deficiency

(AAMD) defines mental retardation as "significantly subaverage general intellectual functioning existing concurrently with deficits in adaptive behavior and manifested during the developmental period" (Grossman, 1983, p. 8). There are several important points to this definition. First, mentally retarded people are well below normal in intelligence. *Mild retardation* corresponds to Stanford-Binet IQ scores ranging from a high of 68 down to a low of 52. *Moderate retardation* includes people with IQ scores ranging from 51 to 36. Those with IQ scores between 35 and 20 are considered *severely retarded*, and the *profoundly retarded* are those whose scores are below 19 (see Table 8-4).

But a low IQ score is not in itself sufficient for identifying someone as mentally retarded. The person must also be lacking in the kinds of daily living skills everyone needs to function independently (Wielkiewicz & Calvert, 1989). Therefore, evaluations of the mentally retarded usually include tests of motor development and social adaptation as well as of intelligence. One widely used group of motor development tests is the *Oseretsky Tests of Motor Proficiency*. These tests measure control of facial muscles, hand and finger coordination, and posture. Two measures of social adaptation are the *Adaptive Behavior Scale* (ABS) and the *Vineland Social Maturity Scale*. Both are based on observations of the individual's behavior in everyday situations. In the ABS, the person is scored in such areas of adaptation as language development, understanding and use of number and time concepts, domestic activity, responsibility, and social action. Another section focuses on the individual's maladaptive behaviors, such as withdrawal, hyperactivity, and violent behavior.

What causes mental retardation and what can be done to overcome it? In most cases, the cause of retardation is simply not known (Hallahan, Kauffman, & Lloyd, 1985). This is especially true in cases of mild retardation, which account for nearly 90 percent of all retardation. Only 25 percent of those who have been identified as mentally deficient show evidence of biological complications. The rest are considered to be *psychosocially retarded*, a term that suggests the wide variety of environmental, social, nutritional, and other risk factors that can combine to produce

Table 8-4
Based on DSM-III-R, 1985 and Grossman, 1983

TABLE 8-4 LEVELS OF MENTAL RETARDATION

Type of retardation	IQ Range*	Level of functioning
Borderline retardation Mild retardation	70-85 50-55- +70	The individual may be able to function adequately in society. The individual is "educable": He or she can learn academic skills comparable to those of a sixth-grader and can be minimally self-supporting, although requiring special help at times of unusual stress.
Moderate retardation	35-40- 50-55	The individual is " trainable": He or she can learn on a second-grade level, and perform skilled work in sheltered workshop if provided with supervision and guidance.
Severe retardation	20-25- 35-40	The individual does not learn to talk or to practice basic hygiene until school years, and while he or she cannot learn vocational skills, simple tasks can be carried out with supervision.
Profound retardation	Below 20- 25	The individual requires constant care and supervision.

mental retardation of varying degrees of severity (Scott & Carran, 1987). The more severe forms of retardation often appear to involve genetic or biological disorders. One such cause is a genetically based disease known as phenylketonuria, or PKU. When a person suffers from PKU, the liver fails to produce a certain enzyme necessary for early brain development. PKU occurs in about one person out of 25,000 (Minton & Schneider, 1980). Another cause of severe mental retardation is chromosomal abnormality, as in Down's syndrome. Severe mental retardation can also be caused by brain damage in infancy or early childhood and by severe environmental deprivation.

As you might guess, little can be done to reverse the biological conditions that underlie many cases of severe mental retardation once they have developed. But steps can be taken to reduce the effects of retardation, whether mild or severe, through education and training. For those with severe brain damage combined with other physical limitations, learning abilities may be only slight. For others with no physical impairment but with a history of social and educational deprivation, education and social contact may have a dramatic impact. The majority of handicapped students are educated within local school systems (Schroeder, Schroeder & Landesman, 1987), a process called *mainstreaming*, which helps ensure that these students are more likely to socialize with nonhandicapped peers. In a similar way, there has been a movement in recent years to take mentally retarded people out of large, impersonal institutions and to place them in smaller community homes that offer them a greater opportunity for normal life experiences and therefore growth (Landesman & Butterfield, 1987).

In order to fully assess individuals and to place them in appropriate treatment and educational programs, mental health professionals need information on emotional adjustment, physical health, and social adjustment. The passage of the Education for All Handicapped Children Act in 1977 instituted four required procedures. First, handicapped children must be tested to identify their disabilities. Second, a team of specialists must determine each child's educational needs. Third, an educational program that meets those needs must be provided. Finally, children are to be periodically retested to determine if the program is adequate.

In the assessment phase, special attention must be paid to possible biases in measuring instruments. In a landmark case in California, a judge ruled that the state's education department may not place black children in self-contained classes for the "educable mentally retarded" (EMR) on the basis of standardized intelligence tests. The judge's ruling was based on the assertion that standardized intelligence tests can be used to limit some minority students' educational achievement by labeling and classifying them as EMR and then restricting their school experience to special classes outside of the mainstream (Bersoff, 1981; Reschly, 1981).

Giftedness

At the other extreme of the intelligence scale are "the gifted"—those with exceptional mental abilities as measured by scores on standard intelligence tests. As with mental retardation, the causes of **giftedness** are largely unknown.

Giftedness Refers to superior IQ combined with demonstrated or potential ability in such areas as academic aptitude, or creativity, or leadership.

Although little can be done to reverse the biological conditions underlying many cases of mental retardation, its effects can be reduced through education and training that help to modify behavior, as in the Special Oympics, where participation, rather than simply winning, is rewarded.

Recently, there has been a national movement to recognize gifted children and to establish special educational programs for them (Horowitz & O'Brien, 1985, 1986). Even so, questions remain as to what mental abilities are involved in giftedness and as to how these abilities can best be measured. And there is the related question of whether giftedness is a matter of potential alone or a combination of both potential and demonstrated achievement (Fliegler & Bish, 1959).

The first and now classic study of giftedness was begun by Lewis Terman and his colleagues in the early 1920s. Terman's (1925) was the first major research study in which giftedness was defined in terms of academic talent and measured by an IQ score in the top 2 percent. More recently, there has been an effort to broaden the definition of giftedness beyond that of simply high IQ. Renzulli (1978), for instance, proposes thinking of giftedness as the interaction of above-average general ability, exceptional creativity, and high levels of commitment. Sternberg and Davidson (1985) define giftedness as especially effective use of what we earlier called "componential" aspects of intelligence: planning, resource allocation, acquiring new knowledge, and carrying out tasks effectively. In 1971, a significantly broadened definition of giftedness was drafted by Congress. Gifted children were to include those with demonstrated achievement and/or potential ability in any of the following areas, singly or in combination: (1) general intellectual ability, (2) specific academic aptitude, (3) creative or productive thinking, and (4) leadership ability.

Various criteria have been used to identify gifted students, including scores on intelligence tests, teacher recommendations, and scores on achievement tests. Most school systems also use diagnostic testing, interviews, and evaluation of student academic and creative work. These selection methods seem to work well for identifying students with a broad range of talent, but they do not do the best job of distinguishing specific abilities, such as a talent for mathematics or music. This fact has led to the development of specialized programs, such as the Study of Mathematically Precocious Youth (SMPY), to identify children who are gifted in one or more specific areas without necessarily exhibiting general intellectual superiority overall (Fox, 1981). As yet, however, there has been little systematic study of programs for the gifted, making it difficult to document their effectiveness (Reis, 1989).

The gifted movement is not without critics, who have pointed out that some fundamental assumptions about gifted children may not be true. One such notion is that gifted people are a distinct group, demonstrably superior to other people in all areas of intelligence and creativity. People gifted in one area, however, may not be gifted in others. For example, Gardner (1983) found that gifted children performed no better than other bright children on tests of moral and social reasoning.

A second assumption is that gifted children will contribute greatly to society when they become adults. As we have seen, there is no evidence that high IQ scores by themselves predict such things as professional success or leadership. Even in Terman's group, where there was a remarkably high level of professional achievement overall, not everyone was successful in his or her chosen field. While some minimal level of intelligence may be required for success, more recent studies show that other factors—determination, self-reflection, daringness, and encouragement, among others—are needed as well (Gardner, 1983). These data

There are many different ways in which children can be "gifted," and some educational programs are designed for children with any of a variety of special abilities, not just those who do well on intelligence tests.

indicate that it makes little sense to identify giftedness in terms of IQ alone. However, to the extent that educational programs select gifted students using a broad range of criteria, including such things as outstanding achievement, leadership, creativity, and initiative, it is possible that the students selected for these programs are indeed tomorrow's leaders.

Critics of the gifted movement have also expressed concern that present measures may fail to identify gifted students in minority populations (Baldwin, 1985). Some of the alternatives devised thus far are an abbreviated Stanford-Binet for the disadvantaged (Bruch, 1971) and the Mercer and Lewis (1978) System of Multicultural Pluralistic Assessment. In both cases, intelligence test scores are adjusted to take into account a child's sociocultural group. In addition, the multiple screening methods used by many schools tend to increase the participation of minority students in special programs. However, it is still too soon to predict the effectiveness of these alternatives.

Yet another reservation about programs for gifted children is how students themselves feel about being labeled exceptional. Some children, it would seem, would rather not be thought of as "brains." And gifted children may chafe under the pressure to perform. Finally, there is a growing controversy over creativity and its relationship to giftedness. Guilford (1967), among others, has pointed out that some types of thinking involved in creative problem-solving are not adequately assessed by achievement and aptitude tests. And Getzels and Jackson (1962) have found that some children who score only moderately high on intelligence, but high on creative measures, are capable of high levels of achievement. We will look more closely at the relationship between creativity and intelligence in the next section.

■ Creativity

In ancient Greece, the mathematician Archimedes noticed that the water overflowed when he got into his bath. From this observation he formulated his theory of displacement: A body or an object immersed in water will

Creativity The ability to produce novel and unique ideas or objects.

displace an amount of water equal to its own volume. Centuries later, the Impressionist painters noticed that as the sun moves across the sky, the light on a haystack changes. They realized that they could paint this light just as easily as they could paint the haystack. Few previous artists had regarded light itself as a subject for painting. Creativity is not, of course, limited to inventors and artists. Shoppers who compare prices in a quest for bargains are acting intelligently—they are examining the available information and making rational decisions. But the shopper who first thought of organizing a co-op, with one family going to the wholesale market every week to buy food for the whole group, was exercising **creativity**—the ability to produce novel and unique ideas or objects ranging from philosophy to paintings, from music to mousetraps.

Some researchers believe that creative ability is simply one aspect of intelligence. For example, in the Sternberg (1981) study discussed earlier in the chapter, it was found that experts on intelligence included creativity as part of verbal intelligence (although laypersons did not include creativity in their view of intelligence). Guilford also included creativity as part of what he called intelligence. His complex model of intelligence (Figure 8-1) includes five kinds of operations, one of which is "divergent thinking." Divergent thinkers expand on the facts, letting their minds go wherever each piece of evidence leads. Instead of looking

Creativity Tests

Although many psychologists consider creativity an aspect of intelligence, there is less certainty about the best way to go about testing creativity. How can we measure creative responses with questions that can only be answered true or false, a or b? One solution has been the development of more open-ended tests. Instead of asking for one predetermined answer to a problem, the examiner asks the test taker to think of as many answers as possible. Scores on the tests are based on the number and originality of the subject's answers.

In one such test, the *Torrance Test of Creative Thinking*, the examiner shows the subject a picture and then asks the subject to explain what is happening in the picture, how it came about, and what its consequences are likely to be. The *Christensen-Guilford Test* asks the subject to list as many words containing a given letter as possible; to name things belonging to a class—such as liquids that will burn; and to write four-word sentences beginning with the letters *RDLS*—Rainy days look sad, Red dogs like soup, Renaissance dramas lack symmetry, and so on.

One of the most widely used creativity tests, Mednick's (1962) *Remote Associates Test* (RAT), asks the subject to produce a single verbal response that relates to a set of three apparently unrelated words. For example, the three stimulus words might be *poke*, *go*, and *molasses*. A desirable response—although not the only possible one—relates them through the word *slow*: *slow*-poke, go *slow*, *slow* as molasses. Arriving at such responses is not easy, especially since the stimulus words have no apparent connection to one another.

The newer *Wallach and Kogan Creative Battery* focuses on having the subject form associative elements into new combinations that meet specific requirements. Children are asked to "name all the round things you can think of" and to find similarities between objects—for example, a potato and a carrot. While it is possible for people who do not have high IQs to receive high scores on the Wallach and Kogan test, the Torrance test seems to require a reasonably high IQ for adequate performance. But the validity of neither of these tests is conclusive (Crockenberg, 1980; Anastasi, 1982).

How creative are people who do well on creativity tests? The correlation between test scores and the products that we associate with creativity—paintings, poems, operas, inventions, cures for cancer—is relatively low. Some psychologists explain these disappointing results by pointing out that creativity appears to depend on more than intellectual abilities alone. For example, Tryk (1968) sees *motivation* as a critical factor in creative output. Great artists, scientists, and writers have more than simple "talent" or "genius." They have intense dedication, ambition, and perseverance.

Creativity is not, of course, limited to inventors and artists; in fact, some researchers believe that creative ability is simply one aspect of intelligence.

for the "right" answer, divergent thinkers develop numerous possibilities and try to produce different solutions that can then be evaluated or combined. And Sternberg includes creativity and insight as important elements in the experiential component of human intelligence.

Although some psychologists believe that creativity is one aspect of intelligence, most IQ tests do not include measures of creativity, and many researchers in the area would argue that "intelligence" and "creativity" are not the same thing. What is the relationship between intelligence and creativity? Are people who score high on IQ tests likely to be more creative than those who score low?

In one study, Getzels and Jackson (1962) gave creativity and IQ tests to a group of bright fifth- through twelfth-graders in a private school. Scores on the creativity tests correlated .27 on average with the tests of intelligence. That is, there was slight tendency for those children who scored high on the creativity tests also to score high on the IQ tests, but the relationship between the two scores was not very strong. Wallach and Wing (1969) studied the divergent-thinking ability of a sample of college freshmen and compared this to the students' scores on Scholastic Aptitude Tests as a measure of intelligence. Again, there seemed to be little direct relationship between scholastic aptitude and divergent-thinking ability.

One criticism of these studies, however, is that they used only bright students. For example, the average IQ of the students tested by Getzels and Jackson was 132! Perhaps there is little relationship between creativity and IQ once IQ reaches a certain level. In fact, there is considerable evidence that this may be the case. The threshold theory of the relation between intelligence and creativity states that in order for a person to be considered creative, he or she must first be at least slightly more intelligent than average. But above that point, there seems to be little relation between the two variables. One study found that intelligence and creativity correlated .88 for people with IQs below 90, .69 for those with IQs ranging from 90 to 110, − .30 for those with IQs between 110 and 130, and −.09 for those with IQs above 130. That is, below an IQ of 110, higher IQ scores were accompanied by higher creativity, but above this point there was little or no relationship between IQ and creativity. Other studies have borne out these findings (Barron, 1963; Yamamoto & Chimbidis, 1966). This evidence supports the view that while creativity is based on a certain amount of intelligence, once intelligence passes a threshold level, creativity and intelligence are related only moderately, if at all.

Since all these studies rely heavily on tests of creativity, any conclusions drawn from them must be qualified by what many experimenters regard as the dubious relationship between creativity test scores and real-life creativity. But other studies at least partially avoid this problem by studying adults who have demonstrated outstanding creativity in their lives. These studies (e.g., Barron, 1963; Cattell, 1971; Helson, 1971; Bachtold & Werner, 1973) show that creative people tend to be highly intelligent—that is, highly creative artists, writers, scientists, and mathematicians tend, as a group, to score high on intelligence tests. But for individuals in this special group, there is little relationship between IQ scores and levels of creative achievement. These data further support the threshold theory of creativity and intelligence.

Interestingly, creative people are often *perceived* as more intelligent than less creative people who have equivalent IQ scores. In one study of architects, for example, psychology staff members perceived creative architects as more intelligent than less creative architects even though their IQ scores were, in fact, equivalent (MacKinnon, 1962). This finding brings us back to everyday ideas of intelligence that we discussed early in the chapter. Perhaps some characteristic that creative people share—possibly "effectiveness" or some quality of social competence—conveys the impression of intelligence even though it is not tapped by IQ tests (Barron & Harrington, 1981).

APPLICATION

Intervention Programs—Do They Improve IQ?

We have seen that, to some extent, IQ scores are affected by experience. Nutrition, environmental stimulation, and child-rearing patterns can all influence scores on IQ tests. A number of researchers have become interested in whether it is possible to increase IQ scores deliberately.

One way to go about this process is to provide *coaching*. Coaching includes specific instruction and practice in taking intelligence tests in order to promote higher scores. Sometimes, this means just practicing

the kinds of questions and problems that may appear on the test. Coaching may also include some tutoring in an educational area in which the student is deficient. While intensive short-term coaching with practice questions may increase an IQ score, the increase is seldom great. Also, while this kind of coaching may achieve the desired results in the form of higher test scores, it does not seem to produce any improvement in underlying mental abilities, since school and college grades do not also improve (Linn, 1982).

Apart from coaching, efforts have been made to intervene in more substantial ways in order to increase mental abilities. These intervention programs attempt to increase not only IQ scores but also "intelligence" itself, and thereby to improve academic performance as well as test scores. In 1961, Heber launched the Milwaukee Project. Its purpose was to see if intervening in a child's family life could alter the effects of cultural and socioeconomic deprivation on IQ. Heber and his associates worked with 40 poor, mostly black families in the Milwaukee area among whom the average IQ of the mothers was under 75 on the Wechsler Scales. The pregnant women were split into two groups. One group was given job training and sent to school. As they found jobs, they were also instructed in child care, home economics, and personal relationships. The control group received no special education or job training. When all 40 women had had their babies, the research team began to concentrate on the children. The children of the mothers who were being given special training were taken to an infant education center at the age of three months. For the next six years, these children spent the better part of each day at the center. They were given nourishing meals and an educational program that included a wide range of educational toys. They were cared for by paraprofessionals who behaved like nonworking mothers in affluent families.

All of the children were periodically given IQ tests. Those in the experimental group ended with an average IQ score of 126—which was 51 points higher than their mothers' scores. The average score of the children in the control group, whose lives had not been changed as much, was 94—still much higher than their mothers' average scores, perhaps because they had become accustomed to taking tests, an experience their mothers had never had.

Sandra Scarr and Richard Weinberg went a step further than Heber and his associates. They studied black children who had been adopted by well-educated white families with moderate incomes. They found that children who had been adopted early in life and who had warm, intellectually enriched family environments got higher IQ scores than the national average score for blacks, and also did better in school (Scarr-Salapatek & Weinberg, 1976).

The largest program designed to improve educationally disadvantaged children's chances of school achievement is Head Start, a program that began almost 20 years ago. Head Start focuses on preschoolers between the ages of three and five who are from low-income families. The purpose of the program is to provide the children with some educational and social skills before they get to school, as well as to provide information about nutrition and health to the children and their families. The Head Start program has stressed parental involvement in all its aspects, from daily activities to administration of the program itself. The acceptance of cultural differences between children, as opposed to an emphasis on the poverty of their families and what they lack in comparison with middle-class children, has distinguished Head Start from other intervention programs (Zigler & Berman, 1983).

Several studies have evaluated the long-term effects of Head Start. Brown and Grotberg (1981), after reviewing many of these studies, concluded that the program has indeed brought about lasting improvements in children's cognitive abilities. There is also some evidence that the involvement of parents in the Head Start program has been crucial to its success (Ryan, 1974).

Head Start, designed to improve educationally disadvantaged children's chances of school achievement by providing them with preschool intellectual stimulation, is the largest *intervention program* in the U.S.

Another study evaluated the effects of the Perry Preschool Program in Ypsilanti, Michigan. The children in this study were 123 black preschoolers from poor families, 58 of whom attended the program while 65 did not. The children who participated in the program scored higher on tests of academic skills, were more likely to finish high school and plan to go to college, and had a higher employment rate and lower arrest rate than those who did not participate in the program (Schweinhart & Weikart, 1980).

These studies provide clear evidence that cognitive abilities can be enhanced through extensive training in educational skills. Most of these programs focus on preschoolers. Some researchers believe that the effectiveness of programs introduced later in life is limited, although older children, adolescents, and adults may benefit from such training (Anastasi, 1988). Others feel that the successes of preschool programs like Head Start have not been adequately applied to the creation of programs for older children. The gains made by children in Head Start tend to decline after a few years (Haskins, 1989). This may be due in part to the lack of long-term programs affecting the influences of family, school, and community throughout childhood (Woodhead, 1988).

Hobbs and Robinson (1982) propose that intervention programs have overemphasized the early childhood period. These researchers believe that academic skills can be taught at any age through adolescence and that the development of intelligence occurs over a lifetime rather than stopping at some point during childhood. Problem-solving skills and abstract thinking abilities, according to these authors, also appear to be modifiable in adolescence and early adulthood. Hobbs and Robinson recommend further research on junior and senior high-school students and an increase in programs designed to develop cognitive abilities in adolescents who show learning deficits.

■ Summary

- **Is there more than one kind of intelligence?** Laypersons define *intelligence* as a combination of practical problem-solving ability, verbal ability, and social competence. Experts view intelligence similarly, as a combination of verbal ability, problem-solving ability, and practical intelligence. *Intelligence tests* are intended to measure a person's mental abilities.

- Spearman viewed intelligence as a single kind of mental energy that flows into every action. Thurstone identified seven somewhat independent mental abilities that combine to form general intelligence. Guilford constructed a three-dimensional model of intelligence composed of *operations* performed on *contents* with a resulting *product.* Cattell views intelligence as two clusters of abilities: "crystallized intelligence" (reasoning and verbal and numerical skills) and "fluid intelligence" (visual-spatial skills and rote memory). Sternberg proposed a *triarchic theory of intelligence: componential* aspects of intelligence include mental processes such as acquiring new knowledge; *experiential* aspects include such abilities as adapting to new situations and understanding new concepts; *contextual* aspects include such abilities as adapting to or reshaping the environment in order to make maximal use of one's skills.

- **What is IQ?** The first test of intelligence was the *Binet-Simon Scale,* designed by French psychologists for use in the French public school system. This was later adapted by Terman into the *Stanford-Binet Scale.* Terman also introduced the term **IQ (intelligence quotient)** to mean a numerical value of intelligence and based it on a score of 100 for average intelligence. The Stanford-Binet Scale emphasizes verbal skills and is administered individually by a trained examiner. The test score is used to calculate the mental age at which the subject performs. The *Weschler Adult Intelligence Scale—Revised* was designed especially for adults. It includes a verbal scale and a performance scale, and yields separate scores on the two scales, as well as an overall IQ. Like the Stanford-Binet, it is administered individually.

- **How well do tests like the SAT and GRE predict grades in college?** *Group tests* are written tests of intelligence designed to be administered by a single examiner to many people at one time. Two advantages of group tests are efficiency in testing and the elimination of bias on the part of the examiner. One of the disadvantages is that there is less chance of the examiner detecting problems a subject might be experiencing at the time of the test that could interfere with the score. Examples of group tests are the School and College Ability Tests (SCAT), the Scholastic Aptitude Tests (SAT), and the Graduate Record Examination (GRE). The SAT and GRE are both fairly good predictors of performance in college.

- **Do intelligence tests discriminate against people from other cultures?** *Performance tests* are non-verbal intelligence tests for people who are unable to take standard intelligence tests, such as non-English-speaking people, the handicapped, and preschool children. These tests generally substitute puzzles or mazes for written questions. The Bayley Scales of Infant Development, for example, are used to measure the developmental abilities of very young children. *Culture-fair tests* are an attempt to measure the intelligence of people who are outside the culture in which the test was devised. These intelligence tests try to minimize the use of skills and values that vary from one culture to another and that can affect test scores.

- In a test, *reliability* means that scores are consistent and stable. Reliability can be measured by retesting people at different times and comparing the results, by using alternate forms of the same test, or by dividing the test into two parts and checking for *split-half reliability.* Reliability is expressed in terms of *correlation coefficients.* If test scores correlate perfectly, the correlation coefficient is 1.0; if there is no correlation between the scores, the coefficient is zero. The most widely used individual tests—the Stanford-Binet and the WAIS-R—are very reliable.

- *Validity* is a test's ability to measure what it has been designed to measure. **Content validity** is a measure of whether the test contains an adequate sample of the skills or knowledge it is supposed to measure. Most intelligence tests are thought to have content validity in that they cover many of the abilities considered to be components of intelligence. **Criterion-related validity** is measured by a comparison of the test score and independent measures of that which the test is designed to measure. The independent measure against which the test is evaluated is called the criterion. With the exception of various performance and culture-fair tests, most IQ tests are good predictors of academic performance. In addition, most IQ tests relate well with one another, despite differences in content.

- **What do IQ scores tell us?** Many critics have found fault with the content of intelligence tests, claiming that they are actually concerned with only a narrow set of skills, particularly academic abilities and the ability to take tests. Others believe that for many reasons IQ tests discriminate against minorities, though recent evidence suggests that most major, widely used intelligence tests are not biased. In any case, standardized intelligence tests should not be used to place children in an educational "slot" that may do them more harm than good by restricting their possibilities for educational achievement.

- IQ scores predict success in school fairly reliably, but they are of little value in predicting career success. However, even though there is no evidence that people with high IQ scores do better in their careers than those with lower scores, they are more likely to hold high-status jobs. A probable reason for the low correlation between IQ scores and career success is that success in a chosen field also depends on a variety of factors—such as motivation, emotional stability, and adaptability—that IQ tests do not measure.

- **Can the environment in which we grow up make us more intelligent, or is our intelligence genetically predetermined?** Heredity and environment are both determinants of intelligence. In support of heredity, psychologists point to significantly higher correlations between IQ scores of identical twins than between those of fraternal twins or other members of the same family. Environmentalists agree that some part of intelligence is inherited, but state that how intelligence develops depends on environmental factors as we grow up. Several studies have demonstrated that stimulating a child's family life to alter the effects of deprivation can dramatically improve IQ scores. Without such early stimulation, it appears that the effects of childhood deprivation may not be reversible in later life.

- The Jensen controversy refers to the claim made by psychologist Arthur Jensen that race differences, as revealed in IQ scores, are largely inherited. Jensen's work stirred furious argument over the validity of IQ testing, the heritability of intelligence, and the relationship between intelligence and race. Research on the question continues, but most critics strongly insist that we have no conclusive evidence to prove that there is, or is not, a genetic basis for racial differences in IQ scores.

- Some studies on cognitive abilities have found that girls tend to have greater verbal ability than boys and that boys tend to have greater visual-spatial and mathematical abilities. Critics argue, however, that these findings should not be used for vocational counseling of individuals. Recent studies emphasize that sex differences in many abilities are extremely small and appear only in studies with very large numbers of subjects; in small groups, differences in ability are often too difficult to detect. Given that IQ scores are not good predictors of career success, very small sex differences on specific abilities are even less likely to be reliable predictors of job performance.

- **Is mental retardation the result of brain damage?** *Mental retardation* refers to significantly subaverage intellectual functioning combined with deficiencies in adaptive behavior. Mild retardation corresponds to IQ scores between 68 and 52, moderate retardation to scores between 51 and 36, and severe retardation to scores between 35 and 20. The profoundly retarded are those whose scores are below 19. The causes of mental retardation include genetic disease, chromosomal abnormality, brain damage, and severe environmental deprivation. Ninety percent of all retardation consists of cases that are considered mild; and in most of these cases, the causes of retardation remain unknown. However, biological or genetic disorders are usually the cause of severe retardation. Educational and social contact may have a dramatic effect on some forms of mental retardation, and federal law requires that handicapped children be properly evaluated and placed in educational programs appropriate to their needs.

- **Giftedness** refers to a combination of superior IQ and demonstrated or potential achievement in such areas as academic performance, creativity, or leadership. The gifted movement seeks to identify gifted students and to place them in special educational programs. This movement has been criticized on a number of counts, including its ability to predict future leadership and professional success. While critics have objected to identifying giftedness in terms of IQ alone, the selection methods now used by most school systems include a broad range of criteria.

- **Are creative people more intelligent?** *Creativity* is the ability to produce novel and unique ideas or objects. Most IQ tests do not include measures of creativity, despite the fact that many psychologists consider it an important component of intelligence. The threshold theory of the relation between intelligence and creativity states that a certain level of intelligence is a necessary precondition for creativity. Beyond this threshold level, however, creativity and intelligence appear to be only mildly related, if at all. Creative people are nonetheless very often perceived as being more intelligent than less creative people who have equivalent IQ scores.

▮ Review Questions

1. Match each of the following with his concept of intelligence:

   ____ Cattell
   ____ Spearman
   ____ Sternberg
   ____ Thurstone
   ____ Guilford

   a. proposed a triarchic theory of intelligence
   b. identified seven somewhat independent mental abilities
   c. argued that intelligence is general
   d. proposed two clusters of mental abilities
   e. proposed that operations performed on contents result in a product.

2. According to Sternberg, the three complex aspects of intelligence are the _____ aspects, which include the acquisition of new knowledge; the _____ aspects, which include the ability to understand new concepts; and the _____ aspects, which include the ability to adapt to or reshape the environment.

3. In 1916, the Stanford psychologist L. M. Terman introduced the term _____ and set the score of _____ for a person of average intelligence. His test was based on the first intelligence test, the _____ _____ _____, designed by Alfred Binet.

4. The IQ test that L. M. Terman constructed is called the Stanford-Binet Intelligence Scale. T/F

5. The individual IQ test most often given to adults is the _____ _____ _____ _____.

6. Written tests of intelligence designed to be administered by a single examiner to many people at one time are termed _____ _____. Which of the following is NOT such a test?
   a. GRE
   b. SAT
   c. Wechsler Adult Intelligence Scale
   d. SCAT

7. _____ tests eliminate or minimize the use of words. They are designed for people who cannot speak English and for preschoolers and handicapped people. Like these tests, _____ _____ tests also minimize the use of language, but they also include questions that minimize the use of skills and values that vary across cultures.

8. Which of the following makes a good test?

a. high reliability   c. correlation coefficients
b. high validity   d. a and b

9. If you take a test several times and score about the same each time you take it, your results suggest that the test is _____ .

10. Which of the following is a measure of reliability?
   a. correlation coefficient   c. criterion validity
   b. median   d. average

11. _____ is a test's ability to measure what it has been designed to measure.

12. IQ scores predict success in _____ pretty well, but not _____ success.

13. Arthur Jensen argued that
   a. the races do not differ in terms of average IQ.
   b. racial differences in IQ are largely due to environmental factors.
   c. racial differences in IQ are largely due to genetic factors.
   d. racial differences in IQ are due equally to environmental and genetic factors.

14. Significant sex differences in mental ability have not been established.   T/F

15. The ability to produce novel and unique ideas or objects, ranging from philosophy to paintings, from music to mousetraps, is termed
   a. creativity.   c. fluid intelligence.
   b. IQ.   d. wit.

9 Infancy and Childhood

■ Thinking Critically

Can stress affect a child's prenatal development?

Are babies born with distinct personalities?

Why do babies like stripes?

At roughly what age do babies first recognize themselves?

Does all development proceed in a carefully ordered sequence of stages?

Are babies who explore a little, and then come back to their mothers, likely to be too dependent?

Do firstborn children develop differently from those born later?

Are the differences between the sexes the result of development?

How does our understanding of what a friend is change as we grow older?

The answers to these and other questions about the ways in which we develop throughout infancy and childhood appear throughout this chapter and in the Chapter Summary.

■ Outline

Developmental psychology Study of the psychological and physical changes that take place throughout life.

An old king, realizing that his end was near, summoned his three sons to his bedside. "My sons," said the dying monarch, "I must decide which among you is to inherit my kingdom. I will ask each of you one question, and this is it: If you could spend your childhood over again, how would you spend it?"

The first son sprang forward. "I would spend it with reckless abandon!" he said. "Childhood is the only time we are not held accountable for the consequences of our actions."

The second son regarded his brother reproachfully. "I would not spend it at all," he said. "I would save it carefully until I grew old enough to appreciate it fully."

"And you, my son?" said the aged ruler to his third son. "If you could spend your childhood over again, how would you spend it?"

"I would neither spend it foolishly nor hoard it selfishly," said the third son. "I would invest in the pursuit of love, knowledge, and experience so that my later years might reap the dividends."

"Truly, such a wise answer should not go unrewarded," said the king. "The kingdom shall be yours."

If each of us were asked to answer the old king's question, our responses would be varied and would reflect our individual experiences from our earliest moments of life to the present day. We may remember our childhoods with fondness or with regret—or we may hardly remember them at all. Yet none of us can deny the importance and the apparent miracle of childhood. When it ends, a helpless infant should have acquired most of the capabilities of an adult.

▐ Methods and Issues in Developmental Psychology

Developmental psychology is the study of the psychological and physical changes that take place throughout a person's life. Some developmental psychologists are mainly interested in charting the course of significant psychological changes as people grow older. For example, when do children first learn to speak and how does their speech change as they develop and mature? Do creativity and intelligence increase, decline, or remain unchanged as we get older? How early can we identify gifted children and what becomes of such children later in life?

Other developmental psychologists are more concerned with the reasons *why* developmental changes occur. What causes changes in the way we speak as we grow older? What causes increases or declines in creativity or intelligence as we age? What causes some children to be "gifted," and why do some gifted children make outstanding contributions as adults while others never distinguish themselves?

The methods psychologists use to study these questions are the same as those discussed in Chapter 1: *the naturalistic-observational method*; *the correlational method*; and *the experimental method*. Because they are interested in studying these changes over time, however, developmental psychologists rely on two particular types of studies. In **longitudinal studies,** researchers follow a fixed group of people over a period of time. The same subjects are observed, interviewed, or tested at several ages. In **cross-sectional studies** researchers look at samples of people of different ages at one point in time so that comparisons can be made among different age groups.

Longitudinal study Study of a fixed group of people at selected intervals over an extended period of time.

Cross-sectional study Study of the different comparisons between people of different ages at just one point in time.

Both longitudinal and cross-sectional studies can be undertaken using experimental, correlational, or naturalistic-observational methods. Suppose, for example, that a psychologist wants to know how children's environments affect IQ scores. He or she might decide to study this question longitudinally using a naturalistic-observational method. After selecting a group of newborns to study, the psychologist and a group of research assistants might spend one day per week for 10 years in the homes of these children observing the environment of the household and parent-child interactions and relating those data to the child's IQ scores. Another psychologist might be interested in studying this problem cross-sectionally using the correlational method. In this case, the psychologist might choose a group of children aged 6, 9, 12, and 15 and then interview their parents, correlating this information with the children's IQ scores at each age.

The question of the effect of the environment on IQ scores could also be approached experimentally using a longitudinal approach. A psychologist might start with a group of two-year-olds from disadvantaged backgrounds and divide them in three groups. The first group would be exposed to an enriched environment for a year starting at age two. The second group would be exposed to an enriched environment for a year starting at age four, and the third group would be exposed to the enriched environment for a year at age six. This would enable the psychologist to study the effects of an enriched environment at different ages.

Each of these approaches to studying development over time has its own strengths and weaknesses. Often, psychologists will use data gathered from all of them. These *converging data* are then combined to provide a fuller picture than any one method could afford. In this chapter and the next, we will see examples of all these research methods as they are used to help us understand psychological development.

Besides using various methods to study human development, psychologists often approach their studies from varying points of view. Some psychologists, as we saw in Chapter 2, emphasize the importance of heredity while others stress experience or environmental influences. Some see change as abrupt and discontinuous while others view development as a gradual, continuous process. In this chapter and in the next, we will see how these differing viewpoints come into play as we discuss the various aspects of human development from infancy through adulthood.

■ Prenatal Development

Scientists once thought that the development of the child before birth was simply a process of physical growth. Only at birth, they believed, did experience and learning begin to influence psychological develop-

Prenatal development Physical and psychological changes in an organism before birth.

Placenta Organ that connects the developing fetus to the mother's body, providing nourishment to it and filtering out some harmful substances.

Fetus An unborn infant at least eight weeks old.

ment. Today, we know that the unborn baby is profoundly affected by its environment. Some psychologists believe that this period of prenatal development may be the single most important developmental period of our lives. Although most experts don't go as far as this, they do agree that there is much more going on during the prenatal period than mere physical growth.

The Prenatal Environment

During the earliest period of **prenatal** (before birth) **development,** survival is the most important issue. Immediately after conception, the fertilized egg divides many times, beginning the process that will change it from a one-celled organism into a highly complex human being. The cell ball implants itself in the uterus, and around it grows a **placenta,** which carries food to it and waste produces from it as the organism grows. In time, the major organ systems and physical features develop. If all goes well, by the end of this stage of development the organism is recognizably human and is now called a **fetus.** The fetal period begins in the eighth week after conception and lasts until birth. (It is usually early in this period that a woman discovers that she is pregnant.) The important role of this period is the preparation of the fetus for independent life.

From the second week after conception until birth, the baby is linked to its mother, and thus to the outside world, through the placenta. Many changes in the mother's body chemistry, whether as a result of nutrition, drugs, disease, or prolonged stress or excitement, affect the fetus directly through the placenta. However, the placenta is not merely a passive tube connecting mother and fetus; it is an active organ with some ability to select and provide substances that the developing fetus needs. Unfortunately, although it can filter out some harmful substances, it cannot protect the fetus from the toxic effects of alcohol, narcotics, medications, and a variety of other chemicals.

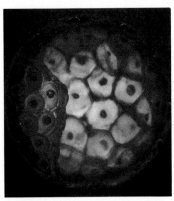

A fertilized human egg, shortly after conception when it has divided many times.

Good nutrition is at least as important for the fetus as it is for us. Yet many mothers, especially in developing countries, subsist on diets that are not substantial enough to nourish them or their babies properly. Even in the United States, expectant mothers' diets are often inadequate. Malnutrition in the prenatal period can result in seriously deprived babies and often permanent damage. These babies may have smaller brains and bodies and be weak, listless, and disease-prone (Stechler & Halton, 1982). During childhood, they often show impaired intellectual functioning that is usually difficult or impossible to improve.

This two-month-old human fetus can be affected by changes in its mother's body.

Besides malnutrition, drugs constitute a particular threat to the unborn child. If the mother is a heavy drinker, her baby may be born mentally retarded, be unusually small and slow to develop, and suffer from other serious abnormalities (Clarren & Smith, 1978). If the mother is a heavy user of drugs, her baby may be born with an addiction and may experience withdrawal symptoms immediately after birth. If she smokes, the baby may be premature, underdeveloped, or deformed (Evans, Newcombe, & Campbell, 1979).

Certain diseases can also injure the fetus, particularly early in pregnancy. German measles (rubella) is especially dangerous and can lead to eye damage, heart malformations, deafness, and mental retardation. Other diseases, such as syphilis and diabetes, can also produce serious defects in the fetus.

Moreover, prolonged stress or excitement on the part of the mother can directly affect the health of the fetus. There is some evidence that when pregnant women experience emotional stress, their fetuses move more frequently and forcefully than usual (Sontag, 1964). In one study, it was found that women who were under severe stress (most often from extremely unhappy marriages) gave birth more often to children who were sickly and slow to develop and whose behavior was abnormal. Critics of these and similar studies have pointed out, however, that the connection between maternal stress and developmental problems in children is by no means clear. For example, since many of the mothers under stress in these studies were also poor, it may have been that growing up in a deprived household was more responsible for the children's problems than was prenatal stress (Sameroff & Chandler, 1975).

As we saw in Chapter 2, it is possible to detect many fetal disorders before the baby is born, using the technique of *amniocentesis*. Moreover, it should be kept in mind that despite the hazards to the fetus that we have mentioned, most babies develop normally. If a pregnant woman is careful to eat well, maintain her health, and avoid exposure to harmful substances and communicable diseases, she should not worry about whether stress at home or on the job will harm her child. Young children are resilient and with proper care can often recover completely from minor problems related to prenatal development. As human beings, we have a long period of childhood, and most of our development, as we will see, occurs after we are born.

Neonate A newborn baby.

Rooting reflex A reflex in newborn babies that causes them to turn their heads and search for a nipple when they are picked up.

Sucking reflex A reflex in newborns that causes them to suck on anything that touches their faces.

■ The Newborn Baby

Recent research has challenged the traditional idea that newborn babies— or **neonates,** as they are often called—are passive creatures that merely eat, and sleep, and remain oblivious to the world around them. We now know that newborn babies see, hear, and understand far more than they've been given credit for. Most of their senses operate fairly well at birth or shortly thereafter. Neonates absorb and process information from the outside world almost as soon as they enter it. They learn quickly who takes care of them and begin to form close attachments to those people.

It's easy to see why neonates were once thought to be passive and relatively unresponsive to the outside world. For one thing, they sleep most of the time—up to 16 or 20 hours a day. For another, they are helpless. Left lying in their cribs, they can neither lift their heads nor turn over by themselves. They are totally dependent on the care of the adults around them. They are, however, equipped with a number of reflexes. When someone picks up a newborn, the baby begins searching for a nipple with its head and mouth, grasping the adult with surprising strength. The **rooting reflex,** as this is called, directs babies toward the food that they need. Another reflex crucial for the neonate's survival is the **sucking reflex.** Shortly after birth, newborns will suck on anything that touches their faces: a bottle, a pacifier, a finger. Within a few days,

Although it was once assumed that pregnant women should avoid undue exertion, it is generally recognized today that proper exercise contributes to the good health that helps lessen stress during pregnancy.

Grasping reflex A reflex in newborns that causes them to clasp their fingers around anything that is put in their hands.

if all goes well, they suck rhythmically and efficiently while being fed. Another reflex is **grasping,** which will lead the newborn to cling vigorously to an adult's hands or fingers or to any object placed in their hands. All these reflexes help to ensure that babies can cling to their mothers and receive the nourishment vital to life.

But newborns are capable of much more than reflex behavior. They seem prepared by nature to make contact with adults and to communicate with them. Neonates will turn their heads toward a voice (interestingly, they prefer the higher-pitched voices of women). They will wave their arms and legs in time with the rhythms of human speech. They will follow a human face (or a picture of one) with their eyes—but they will not follow a scrambled drawing of a face. Within a few weeks, newborns can recognize their parents and distinguish their voices from those of other adults.

Most parents will testify that their babies seem to have distinctive personalities—recognizable almost from birth. Psychologists have found that there is some basis for this notion. Differences in temperament can

■ Temperament

It is tempting to talk about children as if they were all the same, but from birth onward, infants display individual differences. One baby curls quietly in an adult's arms; another squirms and kicks. One sleeps through a rock concert while another wails when a dog barks two houses away. One baby feels almost limp when picked up; another is always tense and rigid. What do these differences mean? Some researchers have suggested that these individual characteristics express the child's inborn temperament. One study concluded that there are three general kinds of babies: "easy," "difficult," and "slow-to-warm-up" (Thomas, Chess, & Birch, 1970). "Easy" babies are those who are relaxed and adaptable from birth. In later life, such children find school quite agreeable and learn rather easily how to make friends and how to play by the rules. "Difficult" babies, on the other hand, are moody and intense. They react violently to new people and new situations, sometimes withdrawing from them, sometimes protesting until the well-meaning adult gives up. "Slow-to-warm-up" babies are relatively inactive, withdrawn, and slow to react. Unlike tantrum-prone "difficult" babies, these children seem reluctant to express themselves. In later life, they often have difficulty in competitive and social situations. Another developmental psychologist has proposed a similar set of distinctions: quiet babies, active babies, and average babies (Brazelton, 1969, 1973). In both sets of distinctions, it is suggested that children retain the same general temperament from birth to adolescence.

Other psychologists are cautious about categorizing babies as "quiet" or "active," "easy" or "difficult." These psychologists point out that the same baby may go through all these states in a single day. While one style or another will usually dominate, it should not be thought of as unchanging. Moreover, about one-third of the children in the Thomas study did not fit any of the three categories.

Still other psychologists flatly reject the idea that temperament is inborn or predetermined. True, some children who were grumpy at birth are nasty at the age of 8 and impossible at 12, but this is not necessarily because they were "born that way." Rather, these psychologists suggest that infants behave the way they do because they are part of a social system in which various people—the infant, the mother, the father, siblings, and so on—influence one another's behavior and temperament (Bronfenbrenner, 1977). Suppose, for example, that an infant has digestive troubles and cries constantly. An inexperienced mother or father might consider such a child difficult and hard to please. Yet another set of parents might react quite calmly to the same situation. Studies indicate that the "goodness of fit" between the temperaments of children and their parents affects development (Thomas & Chess, 1977). Since the two sets of parents would treat a child who cries a lot differently, the two children would probably grow up having different temperaments. It's important to keep in mind the extremely important role that parents and others play in the development of the child.

sometimes be observed in the earliest days of life. Some babies cry much more than others, and some are much more active than others. Some are cuddly, and some seem to dislike being picked up and held. Neonates have even been found capable of expressing several basic emotions: for example, their faces show different expressions for surprise, distress, and disgust (Trotter, 1983). And they have their likes and dislikes: In one experiment, babies only a few hours old showed pleasure at the taste of sweetened water and smell of vanilla, but grimaced at the taste of lemon juice and the smell of rotten eggs (Steiner, 1979).

It is obvious from this new evidence that neonates are aware of the world around them—and research continues to document the sophistication of their perception (Hay, 1986). Because infants cannot communicate directly, it is difficult to devise experiments that measure their cognitive and perceptual abilities. Studies of infant perception by Andrew Meltzoff and Keith Moore (1985) and others seem to indicate that infants arrive in the world with far greater perceptual and cognitive abilities than had been previously thought. Though still controversial, these studies show that almost from birth, infants display a skill at imitating certain facial expressions. This imitative skill peaks at about two months and then begins to decline over the first six months (Bjorklund, 1989). Neonates only hours old are surprisingly adept at imitating adults opening their mouths and, to a lesser degree, sticking out their tongues, indicating that they are not only able to see these expressions, but also to perceive and control their own facial muscles well enough to reproduce them. This coordination of vision, and the proprioceptive, or felt, senses seems to set the stage for later cognitive development (Bjorklund, 1989). Yet only a few decades ago, neonates were thought to have such poor vision and coordination that this would have been impossible.

Newborn babies, then, are advanced in some ways, but they have a long way to go. The simple act of picking up a toy, for example, requires that the baby judge how far away the toy is, crawl or walk up to it, and coordinate an arm and hand to pick it up. It takes most babies almost a year to be able to cross a room and grab something that they want. Much of the rest of this chapter concerns how babies develop these and other abilities.

Physical and Motor Development

Certainly one of the most visible changes during infancy and childhood is physical growth. The child increases in size, of course, but there are also marked changes in body proportion (see Figure 9-1). The body becomes longer and the head proportionally smaller, so that the child's overall shape becomes more like that of an adult. Height and weight increase steadily from early childhood, with an additional spurt taking place during adolescence.

The physical development of a child follows a regular course known as **maturation**—a more or less automatic unfolding of development that begins with conception. It is as if the body had certain goals—say, a height of 6 feet. Physical maturation follows a somewhat different sequence

Maturation Automatic unfolding of development in an organism over time.

Newborns are equipped with a number of reflexes. The *grasping reflex* causes infants to grasp adult hands and fingers and helps insure that they can cling to their mothers and receive nourishment.

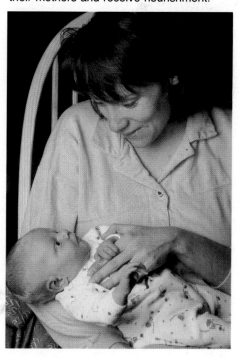

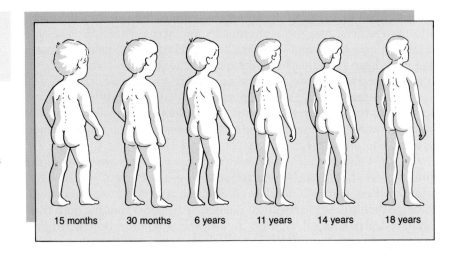

Figure 9-1
Body proportions at various ages As the child grows, the head becomes relatively smaller and the legs longer in proportion to the rest of the body.
Adapted from Bayley, 1956. Reprinted with the permission of the Society for Research in Child Development, Inc.

15 months 30 months 6 years 11 years 14 years 18 years

in boys and girls. Girls develop more quickly in the prenatal period than boys do, but boys grow faster in their first few months of life. Girls then surpass boys in growth until they are about four. After the age of four, both sexes grow at approximately the same rate until puberty. There are, however, sex differences in children's body compositions. Proportionately, girls have more fat than boys and less muscle tissue. Girls' skeletal systems are more mature than those of boys of the same age throughout childhood. The greatest sex differences, of course, become evident at puberty, which girls experience as much as two years earlier than boys do. With the advent of puberty, both sexes go through a period of rapid growth, followed by the development of the secondary sexual characteristics.

Physical maturation follows such a predictable timetable that psychologists have been able to establish **developmental norms,** or standards, that indicate the age by which an average child should reach various developmental milestones. By about 10 months, for example, infants can stand up; by about 13 months, they can begin to walk by themselves. Some infants, however, develop much faster than these norms, and others do so more slowly. There is a *range* of normal development: Some babies may be several months ahead of or behind schedule and yet be perfectly normal. Norms, then, are general guidelines—they can't predict the day or the week at which a child should develop a particular skill. They do, however, alert parents and doctors to extremes. For example, brain damage may not be discovered until a parent notices than an infant has not tried to lift his or her head by the age of 4 months. At the opposite extreme, the infant who walks at 11 months, starts talking at 14 months, and is throwing a ball at three years may be ready to start school a year early. The child who develops more slowly than the norm will not always lag behind. Albert Einstein, the story goes, did not begin to talk until he was three years old—about 18 months late, according to most norms. Given these individual differences, parents should not be alarmed if their babies seem a little "behind schedule" in developing a particular skill. Virtually all babies eventually catch up. What should be cause for concern is a lengthy developmental lag.

Less visible than growth during the infant's first years is the development of the central nervous system (see Figure 9-2). An infant's brain grows rapidly, reaching three-quarters of its adult size by the time the child is two. Besides simply becoming larger, the infant's brain becomes more complex. Interconnections among nerve cells and among regions of the brain are formed. It is this brain development that makes it possible for babies to get their bodies under control, first raising their heads and then sitting up, crawling, and walking.

The physical maturation of infants also makes new behavior possible. Within a year after birth, most babies are sitting up, crawling around, and beginning to walk with a little help. As soon as they can walk unaided, they try to jump and climb. At each stage, their view of the world changes markedly. By the age of 7 months, they are curious about everything that they see; by 10 months, they can act on their curiosity, crawl through open doors, and push books off tables. Along the way, they work out a number of techniques, like crawling, that they will later abandon.

In describing infants' motor development, psychologists focus on walking and grasping. Although both appear as reflexes in newborns, neither is of much use to them at that point. Held up, with their bodies dangling, newborns pump their legs up and down like runners. This reflex seems to disappear after seven to nine weeks. When they begin to practice walking again at 6 to 11 months, the picture is quite different, for by then infants can pull themselves up. Gradually, their attempts become more deliberate, and with only a little support they begin to walk forward. They soon learn heel-to-toe coordination, and after practice (and many falls) they straighten up and walk.

What happens if parents do not encourage their babies to walk even when they are ready? Hopi Indian babies who have been strapped to stiff, confining cradleboards during the first year learn to walk just as easily as Hopi babies who have been allowed to scramble around as they liked

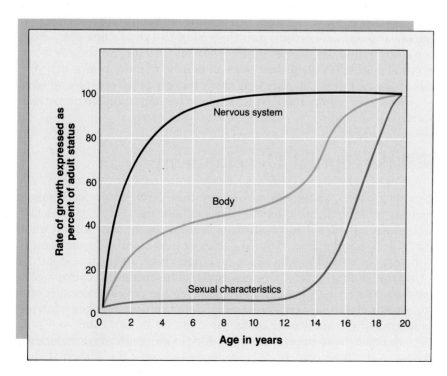

Figure 9-2
Patterns of growth of various parts of the body The nervous system develops relatively early; sexual characteristics do not appear until puberty (see Chapter 10).

Adapted from Jackson, 1928. Used by permission.

(Dennis & Dennis, 1940). There seem to be *critical periods* when a child is most able to start certain activities. Children who are bedridden from the age of 13 to 18 months (the average "walking readiness" period) find learning to walk after this period much more difficult.

Does encouragement or training help a child to walk sooner? One experiment indicated that early encouragement does, indeed, produce results. A group of one-week-old babies was trained by their mothers in walking and "foot-placing" exercises each day for a seven-week period, while a second group of babies was not. The babies who had been helped through the motions of walking were significantly more active and walked sooner than the others.

Walking, of course, is not the only motor skill young children master: They quickly learn to run, skip, climb, and balance themselves as their muscles and bones mature and their coordination develops. At three and four, they begin to attempt to use their hands for increasingly complex tasks—first learning how to put on mittens and shoes, then grappling with buttons, zippers, and shoelaces. Grasping a crayon firmly in the fist gives way to holding it in a more controllable way with the fingers. All these skills develop rapidly, some after considerable adult coaching and others almost spontaneously as children imitate the motions of their older siblings and parents.

We have described physical and motor development as gradual, steady processes: that is, as children get older and bigger, most seem to become more proficient at any kind of task. But T. G. R. Bower (1976) points out that this isn't always the case. Sometimes, infants acquire a particular ability, lose it for a while, and then regain the skill later during the course of their development. For example, newborn infants show a striking aptitude for imitation—a talent that requires a high degree of coordination between the baby's senses and muscles. Newborns can mimic adults who stick out their tongues, open their mouths, or widen their eyes. Yet as the infant develops, this remarkable ability seems to disappear quickly and does not return until the end of the child's first year. Also, as we saw earlier, infants show the reflex of "walking" in their first two months. The reflex then disappears until real walking begins near the end of the first year. So although much human development is gradual and steady, it is important to remember that development sometimes occurs in "fits and starts" that are much less orderly.

■ Perceptual Development

Newborn babies, as we saw earlier, are now given credit for being far more aware of their environment than was once thought. Babies, in fact, were once considered to be virtually blind at birth, but we now know that this is not the case. Normal babies can both see and hear at birth, although not as well as adults can, and their vision and hearing continue to improve during infancy. One question that has intrigued developmental psychologists is: To what extent does perception develop naturally with the growth of a child? Is it a process of maturation and therefore relatively independent of experience? Many psychologists do not think so.

Animals have been studied in order to determine how experience relates to the development of perception. In one of the earliest studies,

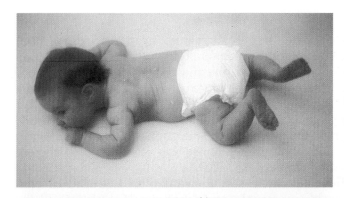

The normal sequence of motor development Newborns are only capable of simple reflex movements. At about 1 month, they begin to lift their shoulders. They start to crawl at about 4 to 6 months. By 9 months, they can sit up by themselves. They can stand upright at about 10 months, and they begin to walk at about 13 months.

Riesen (1947) sought to discover whether chimpanzees that had been raised in darkness for 16 months could perform visually oriented tasks when exposed to light. He found that the chimpanzees' visual responsiveness had been severely inhibited. Objects with which they were familiar through touch—their feeding bottle, for example—were not visually recognized for a long time. "Visual learning," Riesen explained, "so characteristic of the normal adult primate, is thus not an innate capacity independent of visual experience, but requires a long apprenticeship in the use of the eyes" (p. 108).

Studies with young kittens have shown that the *kind* of visual stimulation that infants receive may also affect their visual functioning. Blakemore and Cooper (1970) placed one group of two-week-old kittens in cages covered with black-and-white vertical stripes. They placed another group in similar cages covered with horizontal stripes. After five months, both groups of kittens showed permanent visual defects, including clumsy movements and the inability to perceive objects properly. Moreover, kittens raised in a horizontally striped cage ignored vertically oriented objects, and those raised in a vertically striped cage ignored horizontally oriented objects. The researchers concluded that the brain's visual cortex may adjust permanently to the kind of visual stimulation that it receives during maturation.

Another experiment with kittens seems to support this idea. In this case, kittens that had had one eye covered between their fourth and twelfth weeks of life never developed normal binocular vision—that is, sight involving the coordination of a different image from each eye. If the eye was covered only before the fourth week or only after the twelfth week, this effect did not occur. This suggests that there is a critical period for the development of binocular vision in cats—and perhaps in human infants as well (Pines, 1982).

Other factors besides the quantity and quality of visual stimulation may also affect visual functioning. Studies have shown that feedback from movements that are self-produced may also influence the development of perception. Held and Hein (1963) placed two young kittens in a special apparatus that allowed one kitten to move relatively freely as it pulled the other kitten, whose movements were restrained. Although both kittens received the same visual stimulation, the passive, restrained kitten failed in a number of visual tests. It had not received the sensory-motor feedback needed to develop normal visual functioning.

Do the effects of visual deprivation from an early age also apply to humans? Research on this question has, of course, been limited. Evidence suggests that people who are born blind and whose sight is restored through surgery often have permanent visual defects that may stem from a lack of early visual stimulation (Riesen, 1950). Less severe eye disorders may also interfere with visual development and result in permanent deficits. Thus there is good evidence to suggest that stimulation, experience, and learning all contribute to perceptual development. The ability to perceive is inborn, but without experience it will not develop properly.

Acuity and Pattern Perception

How well can infants see? How "sharp" are their eyes? As we've suggested, neonates cannot see as well as adults can. For one thing, they lack visual acuity, or the ability to distinguish fine details (Acredolo & Hake, 1982). If you hold this book about 18 inches from your eyes, you should have little or no difficulty identifying separate letters on the page, or even seeing parts of each letter. But an infant would not see separate letters. Rather, words would appear simply as gray blurs with white spaces between blurs and lines.

We know, then, that infants can perceive lines and dots as long as they are not too small or too thin. But can they perceive patterns? Can they tell the difference between, say, a human face and a balloon? Some of the first experiments that sought to answer this question were conducted by Robert Fantz. His method was simple: He showed infants a variety of pictures and patterned cards in order to see which ones they liked best. Preference was measured by how long the infant looked at a card. In one experiment, Fantz showed 1- to 15-week-old babies two cards with black-and-white facial patterns and one card that was a plain oval. All the infants spent more time looking at the patterned cards (Fantz, 1961) (see Figure 9-3). Similar techniques show that infants prefer faces to other stimuli and bright colors to pastels. Still other studies have demonstrated that infants can abstract various kinds of information from a series of pictures. For example, they can recognize a woman's face as being different from a series of men's faces. Not only can infants perceive such differences in the stimuli presented to them, but they also have been found to prefer more and more complex stimuli as they grow older (Acredolo & Hake, 1982).

We know from these studies that infants perceive patterns and can recognize the human face at an early age. But what about depth and distance perception? Before babies learn to crawl and learn from experience that it takes effort to go from the crib to the door, do they realize

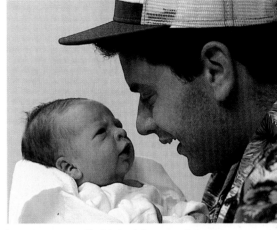

It now appears that infants' perceptions are far more advanced than was believed originally. For example, they can recognize a woman's face as being different from a man's.

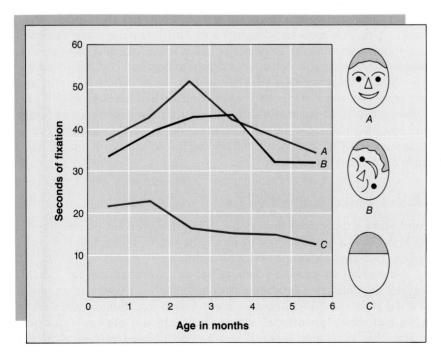

Figure 9-3
Fantz's experiment on pattern perception Infants were shown the three shapes at the side of the graph. At almost every age, the babies spent more time looking at the patterned faces and less time looking at the plain oval.
From Fantz, 1965

that the door is far away? Before they have dropped a rattle from their crib a hundred times, do they perceive depth?

Distance and Depth Perception

Psychologists created an ingenious device—the *visual cliff*—for some classic experiments on depth perception. The device consists of a table divided into three parts. The center is a solid board. On one side, the table surface is dropped 1 inch or so; on the other side (the visual cliff) the drop is about 40 inches. The side with the visual cliff is covered with glass an inch below the center board so that infants who cross over will not fall. The three parts are covered with a checkerboard pattern in order to make it easier to distinguish where one part ends and the next begins. An infant is placed on the center board, and his or her mother stands on one side or the other, encouraging the infant to crawl toward her.

All of the 6- to 14-month-old infants tested by Walk and Gibson (1961) refused to crawl over the deep side to their mothers. Some peered down over the cliff, others cried, and still others patted the glass with their hands. When their mothers stood on the shallow side, however, the babies crawled to them. Obviously, then, 6-month-olds perceive depth. What about younger babies? Because infants younger than 6 months cannot crawl, they were placed on one side or the other of the center board and their pulse rates measured (Campos, Langer, & Krowitz, 1970). When they were placed on the deep side of the board, the infants' hearts slowed down—a reaction typical of infants and adults who stop to orient themselves in new situations. Although they did not know how to react, babies younger than 6 months did seem to know that something was different on the deep side.

More recently, scientists have developed another technique to measure babies' depth perception. This method, known as the *loom-zoom procedure*, presents the infant with a shape that seems to approach on an apparent collision course (loom) and then zoom back to its original position. Although some experiments with this technique have suggested that infants can perceive an object's motion toward them (Bower, 1977), it is not clear that this constitutes depth perception.

Since babies younger than six months have imperfect vision and immature nervous systems, it is likely that if they have any depth perception, it is limited. It also seems likely that the experience of seeing and touching objects at various distances—for example, reaching out to a piece of furniture for support and finding it too far away to grasp—helps to develop depth perception.

Object Perception

Adults take it for granted that people and objects are solid. At the movies, we know that if we reach out to touch the actors, all we will feel is the screen. But does an infant understand this?

It seems that even as young as one or two months of age, infants can tell the difference between a flat photograph or drawing of an object and the three-dimensional object itself. Given the choice, babies prefer to look at three-dimensional objects (Fantz, 1961). Studies with three-month-olds have found that infants are more likely to reach out to three-

When placed on the *visual cliff*, babies 6 months of age and older will not cross the deep side, even to get to their mothers. However, when their mothers stand on the shallow side, the babies crawl to them. This is evidence that 6-month-olds perceive depth.

dimensional objects than to pictures—a fact which suggests that they somehow sense the graspable nature of the object (Bower, 1972; DiFranco, Muir, & Dodwell, 1978). Going a step further, other investigators have found that five-month-old infants can identify a person in a photograph. After looking at a person for a while, the babies were shown two photos—one of the person they'd been looking at and one of a strange face. The babies preferred to look at the photograph of the strange face—as if they'd become bored with the face that they'd already seen in the flesh (Dirks & Gibson, 1977).

Another aspect of three-dimensional objects that adults take for granted is **object permanence.** We assume that a box locked in the closet will be there when we come back. But does an infant realize that a ball that rolls under a chair does not change into something else or even disappear forever?

Experiments conducted by Bower (1971) suggest that infants develop a sense of object permanence when they are about 18 weeks old. Bower used a toy train that went behind a screen. When 16-week-old and 22-week-old infants watched the toy train disappear behind the left side of a screen, they looked to the right, expecting it to reappear. If the researcher took the train off the table and lifted the screen, all the babies seemed surprised not to see the train. This seems to indicate that both the 16-week-old and the 22-week-old infants had a sense of object permanence. But the second part of the experiment showed that this was not really the case. After the train went behind the screen, the researchers exchanged it for a ball. When the screen was lifted, the 22-week-old babies seemed puzzled and looked back to the left side for the original object, but the 16-week-old infants did not seem to notice the switch. Thus, the 16-week-old babies seemed to have a sense of "something permanence," while the 22-week-old babies had a sense of object permanence based on a specific object.

Bower also tested the concept of *person permanence.* Using mirrors, he showed infants multiple images of their mothers. Bower found that infants less than 20 weeks old were generally pleased with the multiple images. However, older infants were disturbed; they seemed aware that there should be only one mother (Bower, 1971).

Other Senses

Babies don't experience the world only through their eyes. Normal newborns, as we have seen, can hear fairly well. This fact is familiar to all new mothers and fathers who have seen their babies wake up when a door slams or wail when a fire truck screeches down the street. Beyond simply taking in sounds, infants can also. tell sounds apart. They react differently to speech sounds, for example, than to nonspeech sounds. And infants only a few months old can distinguish between different consonant sounds; they can recognize the difference between "pa" and "ba," for example (Eimas & Tartter, 1979). Infants thus seem especially well prepared to hear speech even at a remarkably early age, even before birth.

In one recent study, babies whose mothers read a particular passage aloud each day during the last six weeks of their pregnancy showed a marked preference for that same passage after birth (DeCasper & Spence,

Object permanence Realization that objects hidden from view nonetheless still exist.

1986). It also appears that infants are better at distinguishing sounds in all languages than are adults. For example, in one study, Japanese infants had no trouble telling the difference between "ra" and "la," but by the time they were one year old, they had lost this auditory ability (Werker, 1989).

Infants also make contact with the world by touching, tasting, and smelling it. They squirm or cry if clothing binds them or a pin pokes them. But they also eagerly reach out to touch things, exploring the folds of their clothes and blankets and grasping whatever toys or objects are held out to them. As for taste and smell, we noted earlier that even newborns have been found to have their preferences. They like sweet flavors, and this choice persists through infancy and childhood. They also seem to prefer many of the smells that adults find pleasant, although some things that smell good to most adults (shrimp, for example) provoke expressions of disgust in babies.

It should be kept in mind that the senses do not work in isolation. When you shake a jingling toy in front of an infant, the baby will probably grab the toy and chew on it. This simple action involves five different senses: hearing the toy jingle, seeing it held within reach, touching it, and finally tasting and smelling it. Babies are born with some "communication" between their senses: Shortly after birth, they will turn their eyes toward a soft tone played at one side of the head. Somewhat older infants will search for the source of a sound by moving their eyes and turning their heads. Even as early as three or four months, babies appear to know that certain sights and sounds go together (mother's face and her voice, for example). Vision and touch likewise seem to be coordinated in infants only a few months old. In one experiment (Bahrick & Watson, 1985) infants were placed in an infant seat that prevented them from seeing their legs and seated in front of two video screens. On one screen the baby's own legs were displayed "live." On the other, the legs of a different infant were shown. Babies watched the screen with the different legs twice as much as their own, presumably because the discrepancy between their own movement and what they saw on the screen caught their attention.

Even though infants can sense many things, their perceptions of the world grow sharper and increasingly meaningful as they grow older. Two factors are important in this development. The first is nervous system maturation, which progresses rapidly in infancy. The second is experience in the world—taking in sights, sounds, textures, smells, and tastes through the senses. As children become able to experience the world more actively, their perceptions sharpen, and the people and things immediately at hand come more clearly into focus.

■ Memory Development

We've just seen that infants are capable of perceiving a great deal. But do they remember what they see or hear? In an attempt to answer this question, one investigator repeatedly showed infants a pattern displayed on a screen until they became familiar with it. Then a new pattern was displayed alongside the old one. The babies preferred the novel pattern, apparently recognizing the other as one they knew well already (Fantz, 1965).

What does this tell us? For one thing, it tells us that babies, too, can become bored. But more importantly, the experience implies that the babies could *remember* the old pattern. Otherwise, they would not prefer the new one. In another study, 18-, 24-, and 30-week-old babies were shown different photographs—one of a familiar female face looking in various directions and another of a female face that they had never seen before. The younger babies reacted only to the changes in direction. They did not indicate that they understood either that it was the same face seen from different angles or that there were two different faces in the photographs. But the 30-week-old babies appeared to recognize both the changes in direction and the change in an unfamiliar face (Cohen, 1979). In another experiment, five-month-old infants who were given only two minutes to become familiar with a face still remembered things about that face 2 weeks later (Fagan, 1973). Yet another study has shown that infants as young as 2 to 4 weeks can remember for several days a word that has been repeated to them over and over (Ungerer, Brody, & Zelazo, 1978).

So very young infants apparently can remember. But their memories are primitive compared with those of older children (Kail, 1984). Memory improves dramatically as children develop, and psychologists have long sought to identify what causes this expansion of memory. Age alone cannot account for it, nor can some kind of age-related increase in brain capacity. But the acquisition of language profoundly affects our ability to "record" and store what we experience. Related to children's acquisition of language is their ever-increasing store of knowledge about the world. A child is more likely to remember, for example, that the striped animal encountered at the zoo is a zebra if she already knows that it's something like that familiar creature called a horse, which is an animal and not a plant or an inanimate object. As their knowledge grows, children are better able to sort out the new bits of information that they encounter and relate that information to what they already know. During middle childhood, when children begin formal schooling, they also develop specific strategies for remembering. Some of these are taught directly by the school ("*i* before *e* except after *c*"), and others are learned less formally as part of the whole school experience. (Chapter 6 discusses in detail the effects of language, previous experience, and learning strategies on our ability to remember.) In addition, as children grow older, they learn for the first time that remembering things is important, a fact which further contributes to memory development.

▪ Cognitive Development

In this section, we look at changes in the way children think about the world. Perhaps the most influential view of children's cognitive development is that of Swiss psychologist Jean Piaget. We will look at his theory in some detail and then consider some recent criticisms of that theory.

TABLE 9-1 PIAGET'S STAGES OF MENTAL DEVELOPMENT		
Stage	**Age**	**Illustrative behavior**
Sensory-motor	birth to 2 years	Infants know the world only by looking, grasping, mouthing, and other actions.
Preoperational	2 to 7 years	Young children form concepts and have symbols such as language to help them communicate. These images are limited to their personal (egocentric), immediate experience. Preoperational children have very limited, sometimes "magical" notions of cause and effect and have difficulty classifying objects or events.
Concrete operations	7 to 11 years	Children begin to think logically, classify on several dimensions, and understand mathematical concepts, provided they can apply these operations to concrete objects or events.
Formal operations	11 to 15 years	Individuals can explore logical solutions to both concrete and abstract concepts: They can systematically think about all possibilities, project into the future or recall the past, and reason by analogy and metaphor.

Adapted from Craig, 1986, p. 40. Reprinted by permission.

Piaget's Approach

Jean Piaget (1896–1980) entered the field of cognitive development through a back door: He was trained as a biologist, a perspective that is evident in his work. For example, Piaget saw all behavior in terms of a person's adapatation to the environment. Unlike animals, people have few reflexes, so they must learn how to deal with their environment. Piaget first became interested in human adaptation while watching his own children at play. Observing them with the trained eyes of a scientist, he began to see their games as confrontations with their surroundings. In other words, through play they were learning to adapt.

As Piaget's children grew, he noticed that their approach to environmental problems changed dramatically at different ages. Was it simply that their coordination improved or did the older children think differently from their younger brothers and sisters? Piaget became an avid child watcher: He played with children, asked about their activities, and devised games that would indicate how they were thinking.* Gradually, he discerned a pattern—a series of stages through which, in his view, all children pass (see Table 9-1).

Jean Piaget

SENSORY-MOTOR STAGE (*birth–2 years*). As Piaget saw it, the baby's first step is to apply the skills that he or she has at birth—sucking and grasping—to a broad range of activities. Small babies delight in putting things into their mouths: their own hands, their toys, and so on. Gradually, they divide the world into what they can suck and what they cannot. Similarly, young babies will grasp a rattle instinctively. Then, at some point, they realize that the noise being produced comes from the rattle. They begin to shake everything they get hold of, trying to reproduce the sound, and eventually start to distinguish between things that make

---

* Piaget's approach is unusual. In developing theories, most researchers test as many children as they can in order to arrive at solid generalizations. Piaget chose instead to study a small number of children intensively as they went about their daily lives. This is a form of naturalistic observation, which is discussed in Chapter 1.

noise and things that do not. In this way, infants start to organize their experiences, fitting them into categories. **Schemes,** as these simple frameworks are called, constitute the first step toward intentional behavior and adaptive problem solving. Unusual things that do not fit into existing schemes, such as a strange adult or a moving mechanical dog, are apt to disturb children at this stage (Kagan, 1976).

Schemes Piaget's term for the frameworks one uses to organize experience, which change as one develops.

By the end of the sensory-motor stage, as we saw earlier, children have developed a sense of object permanence. When a ball rolls under a chair, the child realizes that the ball still exists. Also, by the end of this stage, children have a sense of self-recognition—the ability to name themselves correctly in a mirror (Berntenthal & Fischer, 1978). Object permanence is crucial to cognitive development, for it enables the child to begin to see how things happen.

PREOPERATIONAL THOUGHT (2–7 years). Children are action-oriented when they enter the preoperational stage. Their thought is tightly bound to physical and perceptual experiences. But as their ability to remember and anticipate grows, children begin to use symbols to represent the external world. The most obvious example of representation is language, and it is in this stage that children begin to use words to stand for objects.

But preoperational thinking differs in many ways from the thinking of older children and adults. Small children, for example, are extremely egocentric: They have great difficulty distinguishing between the way things *appear* to be and the way they really *are* (Flavell, 1986). They also assume that objects have feelings, just as they do; they consider their own psychological processes—for example, dreams—to be real, concrete events. According to Piaget, children in the preoperational stage cannot put themselves in someone else's place. For example, a four-year-old boy was asked if he had a brother, and he replied, "Yes." The child was then asked the brother's name: "Jim." "Does Jim have a brother?" "No." The child could not think of himself as somebody else's brother, nor could he work backward to reason that if Jim was his brother, he must be Jim's brother (Phillips, 1969).

Although they may be self-centered most of the time, under certain conditions even four-year-olds seem to take into account the perspectives of other people (M. L. Hoffman, 1977). In one study, four-year-olds chose birthday presents that were appropriate for their mothers. If the children had been entirely self-centered, they probably would have picked toys that they liked as gifts for their mothers (Marvin, 1975). In other studies, four-year-olds were found to use simple forms of speech when talking to two-year-olds (Gelman, 1979), and they gave very detailed directions to people who they thought could not see (Maratsos, 1973)—both of which suggest that preoperational children do not always think in egocentric ways.

Piaget also suggested that children in the preoperational stage tend to focus on the one aspect of a display or event that attracts their attention and to ignore all the others. In a famous experiment, he asked preoperational children to fill two identical short, wide containers with beads (Figure 9-4). When they had finished, he poured the beads from one container into a tall, narrow container and asked the children whether it had more beads in it than the other. The children always said that

Figure 9-4
In this famous Piagetian experiment, once the beads from one of the short, wide containers have been poured into the tall, narrow one, the child at the preoperational stage will usually say that the tall container has more beads in it. Children at this stage apparently can concentrate on only one aspect of a thing at a time: height, width, number or color.

the tall one had more, even though Piaget had not added or taken away any beads. In a more recent experiment, Gelman (1979) found that very young children (age two and a half to four years) could identify changes that occurred as a result of adding or subtracting objects even if they did not see the changes occur. If the color or shape of the objects was also changed, however, the children became confused and could not tell if the numbers of objects had changed. These results indicate that very young children can concentrate on only one aspect of a thing at a time: height, width, number, or color. The dominant feature of what a child sees becomes the center of his or her attention.

The children were also confused in these experiments because young children cannot mentally retrace their steps in order to reach a conclusion: "If we poured the beads back into the original container, it would look the same as before. The number of beads must therefore be the same."

CONCRETE OPERATIONS (7–11 years). During this stage, children become more flexible in their thinking. They learn to retrace their thoughts, correct themselves, and start over if necessary. They learn to consider more than one dimension of a problem at a time and to look at a single object or problem in different ways.

Another bead game illustrates all these abilities and shows how children between the ages of 7 and 11 have grown intellectually. Piaget gave children of different ages a box of 20 wooden beads, two of them white and the rest brown. He asked them whether the wooden beads or the brown beads would make the longest necklace. Children under 7 decided that there were more brown beads, ignoring the fact that *all* the beads were wooden. Children 7 and older laughed at the question: They knew that all the beads were wooden (Piaget & Szeminska, 1952).

By about age 10, children also become better able to infer what another person knows or may be thinking (Schantz, 1975). At about the same time, they become aware that the other person may be equally capable of inferring their thoughts.

Although quite logical in their approach to problems, children in the concrete operations stage can think only in terms of concrete things that they can handle or imagine handling. In contrast, adults can think in abstract terms, can formulate hypotheses and accept or reject them without first testing them. This ability develops in the next stage.

FORMAL OPERATIONS (11–15 years). In order to test the development of abstract thinking, Piaget gave children in the concrete and the formal operations stages a variety of objects and asked them to separate the objects into two piles: things that would float and things that would not (Inhelder & Piaget, 1958). The objects included cubes of different weights, matches, sheets of paper, a lid, pebbles, and so on. Piaget then let the children test their selections in a pail of water, asking them to explain why some things floated while others sank.

The younger children were not very good at classifying the objects. When questioned, they gave *individual* reasons for each object's performance: The nail sank because it was too heavy, the lid floated because it had edges, and so on. The older children seemed to know what would float. When asked to explain their choices, they began to make comparisons and cross-comparisons, gradually concluding that neither weight nor size alone determined if an object would float: It was the relation between these two dimensions that was important. Thus they approximated Archimedes' law: Objects float if their density is less than that of water.

Younger children solve complex problems by testing their ideas in the real world; their explanations are concrete and specific. Adolescents can think in abstract terms and can test their ideas internally, with logic. As a result, they can go beyond the here-and-now to understand things in terms of cause and effect, to consider the possibilities as well as the realities, and to develop *concepts*, or categories of objects that share some characteristic. We will explore in greater detail the kinds of cognitive changes that occur during adolescence and adulthood in Chapter 10.

Criticisms of Stage Theory

Piaget's work has led to a good deal of research. Developmental psychologists have focused on two of his assumptions: that there are distinct stages in cognitive development and that a person must go through each stage in order to reach the next.

T. G. R. Bower (1976) has argued that development does not always progress in this schematic and sequential way. He found that during their first 11 or 12 years, children appear to master and then to lose the concept of conservation of weight; for example, they do not realize that a pound of feathers weighs the same as a pound of lead, even though the feathers make a bigger pile. Children finally reach a stable understanding of this concept when they are about 13 years old. There also appear to be "fits and starts" in children's memory development that do not follow Piaget's outline (Liben, 1974; Samuels, 1974).

J. L. Horn (1976) feels that much of the evidence that seems to support the idea of developmental stages has been misinterpreted. For example, simple observation tells us that an average child can do things at the age of four that he or she could not do at the age of two. But that does not necessarily mean that something happens to a child of two that prepares him or her to have the skills of a four-year-old. Horn suggests that a child can reach a later developmental stage (and perform the tasks associated with it) without having gone through the earlier stages, just as some children can walk without ever having crawled. Research by Scott Paris and Jill Weissberg (1986) supports the idea that development may be more a result of greater experience than specific stages of ability. They observed a group of children ages three through six as they tried to recall a shopping list containing six items. All the children who were familiar with the technique of rehearsal (see Chapter 6), no matter what their age, were able to recall more items on the list. The older children were more likely to use the strategy of rehearsal and so performed better, but the younger children performed just as well when they had rehearsed the list, indicating that it was the technique of rehearsal, not a specific stage of cognitive development, that improved performance.

Perhaps it would be better to see Piaget's model as an incomplete rather than a comprehensive picture of cognitive development. The interests and abilities of a particular child and the demands of the environment may influence development of cognitive abilities in ways not accounted for by Piaget (Kagan, 1976). Thus, cognitive development

Imprinting Rapid formation by a young animal of a strong bond to the first moving object with which it comes into contact, generally its mother.

Attachment Social bond that develops between an infant and its primary caregiver.

might be better viewed as an ongoing process rather than as a series of separate stages with "breaks" between them.

■ Social Development

One of the important aspects of human development is the process by which a child learns to relate to other people. Early in life, a child's primary relationship is to his or her parents or other caregivers. By early childhood, various other relationships begin to form—with siblings, playmates, and others outside the family circle. The social world expands still further as children begin school and encounter an increasing number and variety of social relationships—with teachers, classmates, friends, teammates, neighbors, and so forth. As we will see, social development is the result of both constant and changing influences over time. How does social development occur?

Social Development during Infancy

In nature, young animals of many species follow their mothers around. Why? Because they have **imprinted** on their mothers: In a short time the young animals have formed a strong bond to the first moving object with which they have come into contact. In nature, this object is usually the mother. But in laboratory experiments, certain species of animals, such as ducks and geese, have been hatched away from their mothers and have imprinted on decoys, toy balls, and even human beings (Hoffman & DePaulo, 1977; Lorenz, 1935) (see Figure 9-5).

Imprinting of this particular type clearly does not occur with human babies. A newborn child separated from its mother will not attach itself to a manikin or a toy. But infants will form a close **attachment,** or social bond, to the person who cares for them, and in most cases in our society this person is the mother. For a long time, it was thought that feeding of the infant is the primary souce of attachment. After all, feeding is the infant's first and most important experience of the world. To the extent that the mother satisfies her baby's need for food, the infant should begin to see her in a positive way, and this relationship might cause the baby's first social attachment to form. Certainly the experience of feeding contributes to the development of attachment, but researchers no longer think that food and oral gratification are so overwhelmingly important. Parents and caregivers also provide warmth and "contact comfort": They talk to, hold, and smile at the baby. All these actions help to develop attachment, although psychologists disagree about which is most important.

The infant's attachment to his or her mother grows slowly over the first months of life. By six months, infants normally show a clear preference for their mothers, reacting with smiles and coos at her appearance and whimpers or cries when she goes away. At around seven months, infants begin to appear even more deeply attached. They will reach out their arms to be picked up and will crawl into their mother's lap and cling to her. They begin to be wary of strangers, sometimes reacting with tears and wails at even the friendliest approach by someone whom they don't

Figure 9-5
Imprinting Newly hatched goslings follow biologist Konrad Lorenz, on whom they have imprinted—they have established a very strong bond with the first moving object with which they have come into contact.

know. Infants of this age may also react negatively if they are separated from their mothers, even for a few minutes. Parents are sometimes puzzled by these new reactions in their previously friendly, well-adjusted infants, but they are perfectly normal developments. Psychologists think that anxiety over strangers and separation from mother indicate that the infant is becoming more aware of the world: He or she knows that mother is a comforting presence and that there are people and things "out there" that may pose a threat.

Eventually, infants do learn that the world beyond mother's lap is not necessarily frightening. They crawl away cautiously, then more boldly, to investigate things and people around them. This exploration is necessary for children to develop **autonomy,** or a sense of independence and trust in their own abilities and powers. At first glance, autonomy and attachment may seem to be polar opposites, but they are in fact simply different sides of the same coin. Recent research indicates that the stronger the attachment between mother—or principal caregiver—and child, the more autonomous the child is likely to be. This may seem paradoxical,

Autonomy A sense of independence and trust in one's own abilities and powers.

Surviving Childhood Trauma

In 1959, psychologist Harry Harlow published the results of an experiment with rhesus monkeys—a bit of research that has since become very famous (Harlow, 1959). Harlow separated baby monkeys from their mothers and raised them in cages by themselves. Even though they were adequately fed, some of the monkeys died, and those that survived were decidedly abnormal—they were irritable, antisocial, and withdrawn. This experiment provided dramatic evidence that mothering and social relationships are important to normal development. It also supported an idea widely held at least since the time of Sigmund Freud: that trauma in childhood, such as separation from the mother, can produce abnormalities in the adult personality.

Although there is a large body of additional research in abnormal psychology that supports this notion, some experimental and child psychologists have begun to suggest that the relationship between youthful trauma and adult maladjustment is not quite so clear-cut. Children may be far more resilient than was once thought. For example, Jerome Kagan, a developmental psychologist at Harvard University, has said, "You can predict very little from experiences at ages 0 to 3, even when they include a number of traumatic events" (*Newsweek*, January 18, 1982). Although Harlow's monkeys were not accepted by their peers because they were too immature, some of these motherless monkeys were then raised with younger monkeys and began to develop normally.

Kagan's view is also supported by a later study con-

ducted by Harlow and Stephen Suomi. Suomi and Harlow (1977) found that much of the trauma of maternal separation in rhesus monkeys could apparently be erased if one-year-old monkeys raised in isolation were put into a cage with normal two- and three-month-old monkeys. The normal monkeys, outgoing and sociable, apparently rehabilitated the maladjusted monkeys. It seems that under some circumstances early traumas can be overcome if social support and affection are forthcoming. This discovery has implications for the treatment of children who have the misfortune to suffer child abuse, the death of a parent or sibling, or some other painful event. If family members, teachers, friends, or some other people are available to comfort the child, he or she may recover from the trauma with no ill effects.

More recently, research on young children who have suffered the loss of a parent to death or divorce has shown that the quality of the child's relationship with the remaining parent greatly affects the degree to which a child is traumatized by the loss. Children with a parent who is able to offer emotional support do not show evidence of the cycle of vulnerability to stress, elevated hormone levels, and depression that characterizes the development traumatized children (Breier, 1988). In fact, it appears that poor parenting, particularly those cases where the child feels burdened by the remaining parent's own need for emotional support, can have a far more negative impact on a child's development than the loss of a parent early in life.

Socialization Process by which children learn the behavior and attitudes appropriate to their family and culture.

As soon as they can crawl, all infants begin to leave their mothers in order to investigate things and people around them. This exploration is necessary for children to develop *autonomy*.

but it makes more sense if we remind ourselves that a strong mother-child attachment provides a sense of *security*.

Studies of children with varying degrees of attachment to their mothers have shown that, in new situations, children who feel that they have a secure "home base"—a secure relationship with their mothers—are more likely to venture out from that base to explore these new situations. These children apparently know that when they finish exploring, they can return to the haven of maternal protection (Ainsworth et al., 1979). Studies of children from the ages of one through six years have also shown that babies who are securely attached to their mothers at the age of one are later more at ease with other children, more interested in exploring new play situations, and more enthusiastic and persistent when presented with new tasks (Main, 1973; Matas, Arend, & Sroufe, 1978; Waters, Wippman, & Sroufe, 1979). Therefore, mother-child attachments, far from being a sign of excessive dependency, actually seem to strengthen the child's growing desire for autonomy.

At about two years of age, children begin to test their strength by refusing everything: "No, I won't get dressed." "I won't go to sleep." The child's first efforts to be independent, however, may not be entirely welcome to the parents. The parents' attachment to the child, the mischief that children get into as they begin to explore, and the extra demands on the parents' time and energy may explain this reaction, although research on these questions is far from conclusive (Haith & Campos, 1977). The usual outcome of these first moves toward independence is that the parents begin to discipline the child. Children are expected to eat at a particular time, not to pull the cat's tail or kick their siblings, and to respect other people's rights. The constant push-and-pull between such restraints and the need for independence often causes difficulties for both parents and children. But it is an essential step in developing a balance between dependence and autonomy.

Social Development during Childhood

As children grow up, they are **socialized**—that is, they learn the behaviors and attitudes appropriate to their family and culture. Their social world expands: They play with their siblings; they make friends; they go off to nursery school, kindergarten, and finally school itself. But it is important to remember that throughout this period of encounters with new people and influences, children's parents continue to have a major influence on their social development. Here, too, the security of a child's attachment to his or her mother seems particularly important because it provides a base from which the child explores the world (Hartup, 1989).

When children are still tiny, most parents are concerned mainly with seeing to their physical and emotional needs. Yet even at this early stage in parents' interaction with their children and children's interaction with their parents, some rudimentary two-way teaching is going on. For example, a mother will vary the way she talks or plays with an infant in order to maintain the child's interest and match what appear to be the child's competencies at that point (Hodapp & Mueller, 1982). When children reach the toddler stage, the parents' role shifts very strongly to one of teaching (although the physical and emotional needs of the child still demand attention, of course). From using the toilet, to tying shoe-

Day-care: Rearing Children Away from Home

More mothers than ever before are working at full-time jobs—in many cases because their income is needed to help support their families, but in some cases because they are pursuing rewarding careers. When mothers of young children work outside the home—and about half now do—some provision for the children is obviously needed. Some mothers hire full-time baby sitters, if they can afford to, or leave their children in the care of relatives during the day. But as more and more young children are cared for in commercial day-care centers, psychologists and parents have begun to ask, is it a good idea to leave young children with substitute caregivers in day-care centers?

There is not yet a clear answer to this question, and as frequently happens in research on important social issues, one set of findings raises a new set of questions. For example, some psychologists have found that infants left in day-care are less securely attached to their mothers and are more likely to assert themselves than are children cared for at home (Belsky & Rovine, 1988). However, other psychologists interpret this same evidence as indicating that babies in day-care are simply more independent than their peers cared for at home (Clarke–Stewart, 1989). More recent research indicates that if an infant is insecurely attached to his or her mother to begin with, day-care may hinder rather than help the situation. For securely attached children, day-care does not appear to be an unsettling experience (Clarke–Stewart, 1989).

One thing that is clear is that day-care in a variety of forms is here to stay. Some psychologists are exploring what elements go into making day-care a positive experience in the development of children. One of the factors that appears to be most important is the particular facility and the services that it offers. If the center is well run (clean, attractive, with well-scheduled activities) and adequately staffed (no more than three or four children per adult attendant), the likelihood is that children will do as well in day-care as they would at home with mother (Craig, 1989). The important thing to consider is that the caregiver be consistently there (frequent staff turnover is undesirable) and be a loving, supportive person—a "second mother," in short (Browning, 1982). Some experts recommend enrolling children either before or after the stranger/anxiety period (approximately 7 to 15 months) so

Although little is known about the long-term effects of day-care, available evidence suggests that the *setting* in which the care takes place is not as important as the *quality* of the care.

that they don't have to adjust to life at a center at just the time when they are most distressed at separation from mother and interaction with strangers (Hall, 1982).

It now appears that in some respects good day-care may be even better for the child than staying at home. Children reared in day-care centers are sometimes more sociable with other children and more at ease with strangers than children brought up in the more isolated environment of home. A long-term study found that older children from disadvantaged backgrounds may actually benefit intellectually from day-care if it offers a structured educational program (Scarr, 1984). Another found that easy babies actually gained more in IQ when raised in a day-care center than if they were at home (Ramey, MacPhee, & Yeates, 1982). And Hoffman (1983, 1989), who has reviewed all the studies done in the last 50 years on maternal employment, has found no consistent effects on children of mothers working outside the home and leaving their children in the care of others.

If should be noted that we know rather little about the long-term effects, if any, of day-care. Studies have yet to be done comparing the adolescent and adult adjustment of day-care versus home-care children. Evidence now available, however, suggests that it is not so much the setting (whether home or center) that is important, but rather the quality of care that the child receives. Most psychologists seem to agree that *good* day-care has no ill effects on children (Rutter, 1982).

---

laces, to holding a crayon, children need the help of patient teaching—and their first teachers are usually their parents. At the same time, the parents' role becomes less one of actively doing for the child and more a combination of overseeing what the child does and verbal (rather than physical) intervention (Hartup, 1989).

Parents instruct their children in how to do things, but they teach them in other, less direct ways as well. They serve as models of behavior, and they make their expectations known through punishing and rewarding children's behavior. There is a large body of evidence showing that styles of parenting—the ways in which parents act toward their children and the demands they make of them—can have a lasting effect on children's behavior. Baumrind (1972), who has done extensive research on parenting, has found that authoritarian parents, who control their children's behavior rigidly and require total obedience, are likely to produce children who are withdrawn and distrustful. On the other hand, the children of parents who exert little control tend to be more dependent and to have less self-control than children whose parents provide structure and guidance. Other researchers have also found that restrictiveness often leads to dependence and submissiveness in children and that extremes of either restrictiveness or permissiveness can lead to social problems later on (Craig, 1989). The best parenting approach, according to Baumrind, seems to be firmness without being controlling combined with a great deal of warmth and encouragement. Parents who use this approach seem most likely to have children who are self-reliant and socially responsible, but this does not mean that this approach is correct for every parent or every child at every stage of growing up. There are simply no guarantees that any single method or combination of methods will produce a socially competent child. The best evidence thus far indicates that certain approaches are more likely to succeed than others and that the appropriate parenting style for a given child is likely to change somewhat as the child grows, especially as new influences from the world outside the family begin to intrude (Hall, 1982).

Along with parents, brothers and sisters also play an important socializing role in a child's life. Siblings are more than occasional playmates—they constitute a younger child's first peer group. Like parents, they act as powerful models. Indirectly or directly, older siblings teach motor skills and language to their younger brothers and sisters. They show them how to play with toys or put on clothes or answer the telephone. And if siblings are close in age (and especially if they are of the same sex), they also provide the child's first experience with competition as they struggle to establish their own identities and outdo the other.

Besides siblings' direct influence on one another, a child's early social development is influenced by *birth order*. The evidence available thus far indicates that certain personality traits are connected with birth order. Firstborn children are generally more achievement-oriented than later siblings and seem to have a greater need for adult approval. Second and third children are usually more socially adept than firstborns and better able to get along well outside the family. A probable reason for this fact is that later siblings do not get exclusive attention from parents and depend to a greater extent on social contact with older brothers and sisters. Although the connection between birth order and personality tendencies is fairly well established, psychologists agree that the effects are modified by other factors in need of more study, such as the number and sex of siblings in a family and the proximity of siblings in age.

Not all children have siblings, of course, but virtually all do have some contact with playmates and friends before going to school. Like siblings, these playmates help to teach and socialize the young child. Preschoolers quickly learn some of the rules of social life, such as sharing

Research on parenting has found that authoritarian parents who control their children's behavior rigidly and require total obedience are likely to produce children who are withdrawn and distrustful.

and cooperation, although adult prodding is often called for. They also learn new social behaviors, such as how to act at birthday parties. Children of this age learn in part by imitating and instructing one another—a process that can result in the acquisition of new skills, whether valuable (such as riding a tricycle) or not so valuable (such as flushing the family's washcloths down the toilet). But they also learn through reward and punishment. Children tend to do the things that are rewarded or reinforced by other children and to avoid the things that are punished (Hall, 1982).

Eventually, of course, all children leave the protection of home and family for the new world of school. Here they are separated from parents or caregivers, perhaps for the first time, and enter a world filled with unfamiliar adults and peers. The impact of school is felt immediately. No matter what kind of school a child attends, there are new codes of behavior that are different from those of home. In even the most favorable school environments, individual attention is limited, and children must learn quickly to ask questions, explore things independently, and to do certain things (for example, to tie a shoelace or to put on a coat) for themselves. While the school environment encourages independence and self-sufficiency, at the same time it demands cooperation with others and participation in structured group activities. Children are expected to be self-controlled and to follow orderly procedures, such as raising their hands before speaking, lining up for recess, and asking permission to leave the room. And in all their various school activities, children must learn to control aggression, to be considerate of others, and to follow basic rules of social behavior.

Not surprisingly, this restructuring of their social world can be a dramatic adjustment for many children. But the adjustment to school is likely to be easier if a child has had a supportive family and has already begun to develop social skills within family relationships. Teachers also make a difference in the social development that takes place in the classroom. Like parents, teachers are models, and their role definitions of themselves have an influence on children's behavior (Strommen, Mc-Kinney, & Fitzgerald, 1983). Another important consideration is the role of teachers in helping children adjust to school. As they oversee classroom activities, teachers are often instrumental in reinforcing peer activities and encouraging more isolated children to take part in the group.

The school environment also calls on children to develop the social skills needed to cope with a variety of peers. As we have seen, peers begin to have an influence on a child's social development as early as late infancy, but their influence is strongest at the time when children begin school. We have also looked at some of the ways in which peers influence one another by serving as models and punishing or rewarding each other's behavior. But as peers begin to take on more definite roles in the school setting (the smartest, the most athletic, the most popular, the toughest) and thus to exert greater control over one another, there is far more pressure than before to cooperate with one's peers and feel accepted by them. Studies of schoolchildren show that the way in which children relate to their peers is an important determinant of popularity. Asher and Renshaw (1981), for example, have pointed out that popular children have the ability to initiate friendships and to communicate effectively and positively with other children.

During the school years the influence of peers is especially strong. In particular, successful peer relations in class, outside school and in organized activities such as team sports are a factor in popularity.

The importance of being accepted by one's school peers shows up strongly when psychologists study unpopularity and its effects. Studies show that aggressive children who have difficulty making friends and being accepted by their peers are more likely to drop out, engage in criminal behavior, and show evidence of psychopathology later in life (Parker & Asher, 1987). While it is not clear that poor relations with peers *causes* these problems, they do serve as predictors for children who are likely to be at risk.

Along with the social environment that school provides, school is also a major influence on a child's sense of competence and achievement. Once at school, children may find it necessary to revise their own expectations of themselves, depending on how well they do at school, and their estimates of their efforts when compared to their classmates' (Entwisle & Hayduk, 1978). Studies show that children who are successful at school and who view themselves as successful are likely to develop a positive outlook. Children who face more disappointments and frustration may begin to lower their expectations and even give up (Seligman, 1975). In many respects, then, school is the first encounter between a child and the social system outside the family; and success at school—or the lack thereof—in the early years can exert a lifelong influence.

Sex Typing and Sex Roles

Parents treat their sons and daughters differently, starting with the blue or pink blanket in which they wrap the new baby. Until recently, this differential treatment was thought perfectly natural and appropriate since it was believed to reflect inherent differences between boys and girls. But in the last decade, psychologists have begun to examine closely the extent to which differences between boys and girls are the *result* of different treatment and the extent to which they may be due to a few inherent differences between the sexes (Deaux, 1985).

For example, from very early childhood, boys tend to be more aggressive than girls (Wolman, 1978). Males are also more competitive (Spence & Helmreich, 1983). Are these differences the result of biology or culture? Boys might be more aggressive because they have higher levels of the hormone testosterone, which is thought to be related to aggressive behavior. But aggression and competitiveness are also areas where parents often have very different expectations for boys and girls (Sears, Macoby, & Levin, 1957). As a result, any inborn sex differences in aggressiveness might be increased by learning and parents' teaching.

In fact, most of the differences assumed to distinguish women from men now appear to be primarily, if not entirely, the result of culture rather than biology. Newborn baby girls behave like baby boys, and two-year-old girls and boys are about equal in cognitive development and social skills. A two-year-old boy is just as likely to be fearful, dependent, and interested in caring for others as girls have been thought to be (Williams, 1977). As children get older, however, their behavior conforms more and more to our culture's version of how men and women should act.

How are children socialized into these stereotyped sex roles? First, they learn about sex-appropriate behavior from their parents, and parents' attitudes have a great influence on their children's feelings about being a boy or a girl. In one study in which parents were asked to describe their newborn children, the parents were much more likely to describe their newborn daughters as delicate, beautiful, and weak; newborn sons, on the other hand, were characterized as strong, well-coordinated, and robust (Rubin, Provenzano, & Luria, 1974). As all the babies were the same height and weight, these descriptions appeared to reflect the parents' expectations rather than actual physical characteristics.

In one study, adults saw a videotape of a nine-month-old infant reacting to a jack-in-the-box. Those who had been told the baby's name was "David" tended to interpret "his" reactions as being angry. Those who had been told that the same child's name was "Dana" attributed the emotional reaction on the tape to "her" fear (Condry & Condry, 1976).

It is also possible that infants *themselves* notice differences between their father's and mother's roles. If mothers assume caregiving tasks, while fathers interact with their children through vigorous play, children may develop quite different ideas about what it means to be male and female (Lamb, 1979).

As more women work outside the home, however, fathers will become more active in child rearing (L. W. Hoffman, 1977). This trend pleases many observers who believe that as both mother and father share in child care and work outside the home, children will have a family model that avoids rigid sex roles. The working mother provides a self-sufficient model for her children, especially if the father takes on some of the household chores. Children who observe their parents sharing domestic duties learn that there is not "men's work" and "women's work"—there is just work.

But these changes in role modeling may have some unexpected effects. In several studies, fathers have been found to be more likely than mothers to treat sons and daughters differently. Fathers are much more likely to prefer male children to female children (Coombs, Coombs, & McClelland, 1975) and to describe infants in sex-typed language (Fagot, 1974; Rubin, Provenzano, & Luria, 1974). Fathers are more concerned with their sons' than with their daughters' cognitive development; they encourage their daughters more than their sons to develop social skills (Block, Block, & Harrington, 1974). Fathers also tend to encourage their daughters to "daydream" or to wonder about life. They are more willing to comfort them, and they generally have warmer relations with their daughters than with their sons (Block, 1976, 1979).

These studies suggest that as fathers become more directly involved in child care, there could be *more* sex-role differentiation and a resulting decrease in the options made available to young children. Perhaps, however, as men become more aware of the rewards of nurturance and more flexible in their own parental roles, they will encourage their children to be equally "liberated" from traditional sexual stereotypes.

Of course, socialization only begins in the home. Schools and the mass media express cultural values and are apt to be slow in reflecting changes in attitudes. For example, textbooks still frequently portray women and girls in subordinate roles. The mass media—particularly television—also reinforce sexual stereotypes. The harried housewife in commercials, the macho cops and private eyes, and the bikini-clad females who sell cars—all these stereotypical figures teach children certain values about being men and women. Even *Sesame Street* has come under fire for

Children are socialized into *stereotyped sex roles* by their parents, and parents' attitudes greatly influence how a child feels about being a boy or a girl.

Social cognition A mental understanding of the social world and one's place in it.

Many more fathers are becoming increasingly active in parenting. While some observers feel that certain paternal behavior may result in *more* sex-role differentiation among children, others believe that as more men experience the rewards of nurturance, many children will enjoy a family model that avoids rigid sex roles.

rigid sexual stereotyping and negative female role models (Bergman, 1974).

Thus, most children are subtly bombarded with pressures to conform to sexual stereotypes. Many girls still assume that they can be happy only as wives and mothers, that they should be beautiful, and that they must find a man to whom to attach themselves. Boys learn that they are expected to be domineering and that it is normal to be aggressive. Parents who do not accept such stereotypes can provide their children with more alternatives, but they also have to be aware that much socialization takes place outside the home.

Social Cognition

As children's social horizons begin to extend beyond their own families, they become more aware of a complex social world. They become capable of understanding other people, social relationships, and, finally, social institutions. This mental understanding of the social world and their place in it is called **social cognition.** Cognitive psychologists believe that there are predictable changes in children's social cognition. They believe, too, that the ability to understand the social world depends, in part, on what stages children have reached in other areas of their development.

As we have seen in our discussion of cognitive development, there are limits to the way children can think about the world. An infant's view of the world is egocentric; although the child soon forms an important attachment to his or her mother (or other caregiver), the relationship does not include the ability to understand the mother or her needs. An infant can't think, "She's had a long day already, so I'd better not cry tonight and disturb her sleep." Further along in the socialization process, infants and young children are more aware of the existence of a surrounding social order, but they are still incapable of understanding that other people have thoughts and feelings of their own. And they remain egocentric in the belief that others see the world and respond to it exactly as they do (Hall, 1982). Only as children lose their egocentrism do they start to see themselves and others as distinct individuals and realize that there are many different perspectives in the world besides their own.

Overcoming egocentrism is a lengthy process, and it is only in middle childhood (around the time they begin school) that children begin to gain some real understanding of others. In coming to recognize that other people have their own thoughts and feelings, children develop a first and essential component of social knowledge: They can begin to infer what other people's thoughts and feelings are—"Mother is angry with me"; "Dad looks happy today." It will take years before a child is fully capable of understanding someone else's perspective, but children can begin to act on this new knowledge in their own social relationships and friendships.

Children in middle childhood also begin to see themselves in a way that indicates greater awareness of their own personal characteristics: "I'm shy"; "I don't like hard work"; "I want to be a doctor when I grow up." Moreover, in middle childhood, children begin to compare these attributes with other children's and in this way begin to evaluate their own relative strengths and weaknesses (Ruble, Parsons, & Ross, 1976).

It is also in middle childhood that children develop the ability to think about social relationships. Selman (1981) has discovered, for example, that children under the age of seven consider "friends" to be people who live nearby, who have nice toys, and who play with them. "Friend" means "playmate." Around age seven, children begin to define friends as "people who do things for me"; therefore friends are important because they meet the child's needs. Later, at about age nine, children begin to understand that "friendship" is a two-way street and that while friends do things for us, we are also expected to do things for them. But throughout these years, friendships come and go at a dizzying speed. Friendship lasts only as long as needs are being satisfied. It is not until late childhood or early adolescence that friendship is viewed as a stable and continuing social relationship that requires trust, confidence, and mutual support regardless of day-to-day problems or dissatisfactions.

 ## APPLICATION

Television and Children

It may seem unlikely that watching cartoon characters flatten each other or TV cops and robbers shoot it out could cause children to behave aggressively themselves. But a large body of research on the relationship between television viewing and aggression shows that this is indeed what happens.

Over the last two decades, psychologists, educators, and parents have expressed a great deal of concern about the influence of television on children's behavior. Singer and Singer (1983) find that preschoolers spend about four hours a day watching television and note that viewing time increases as children get older. They also note that, overall, children spend more time watching television than they do attending school. In fact, even though estimates of the time children spend in front of the television set vary greatly (from 11 to 28 hours per week), all indicate that American children spend more time watching TV than any other single activity besides sleep (Huston, Watkins, & Kunkel, 1989).

One of the reasons why television's influence on children is studied so carefully is not only that children watch a lot of television, but also that they are vulnerable to its messages, particularly those in commercials (Huston, Watkins, & Kunkel, 1989). Children under the age of eight do not distinguish the persuasive messages of commercials from those of the program. Even older children are likely to be easily mislead by the subtly deceptive promises of advertisers (Kunkel, 1988).

In 1982, the National Institute of Mental Health published a comprehensive review of research on the psychological effects of television on young viewers. The many conclusions of the study have ignited a new controversy over their issue—a controversy focused primarily on the findings that watching violent television programs can promote or increase aggressiveness in children.

L. D. Eron (1982) has conducted a number of long-term studies to determine when television violence begins to affect children and what it is about TV violence that impresses youngsters. He determined that the degree to which children are affected by watching violence depends on how closely they identify with the programs' characters and how realistic they believe the programs to be. Eron also asked children to rate one another on aggressiveness and then tied these results to television viewing. Children who identified strongly with TV characters on programs that contained a lot of violence were rated highly aggressive by their peers; children who believed these programs to be very realistic were also rated highly aggressive.

The television networks often argue that although their programs may include a good deal of violence, they also conclude with good winning out over evil. Thus, claim the networks, these programs teach children a positive lesson. Much to the contrary, the NIMH report argues that young children have not yet reached a stage of cognitive development at which they can understand the relationship between violent actions observed during a show and their final consequences (punishment) at the end of the show (Rubinstein, 1983).

The NIMH report also shows that children who watch a lot of TV tend to develop a distorted view of the world. Heavy viewers see the world as a place in which many more unpleasant and scary events take place than actually occur.

While research confirms the negative impact of television on children, it also supports the idea that television can have positive influences. Children's receptivity to television also makes television a valuable educational tool. Infants as young as 10 months old are able to learn physical tasks from watching television (Meltzoff, 1988). Television also can serve as a talking picture book for infants, helping them learn to identify and name objects (Lemish & Rice, 1986). While most children's programs tend to be fast-paced and lively, programs that are deliberately slow and repetitive can also hold children's attention. A program such as *Mr. Roger's Neighborhood* can stretch children's imaginations, acquaint them with letters and numbers, and teach them valuable social lessons. Singer and Singer

While some reports argue that children who watch TV heavily may develop a distorted view of the world, other studies suggest that properly designed programs can teach children certain cognitive skills.

(1983) have also found that for some children, a combination of certain parental attitudes with television watching can aid academic performance in the early school years. Among families of low socioeconomic status in which the mother describes herself as curious and imaginative, these researchers found that heavier viewing can lead to better reading comprehension. For these children, television perhaps provides the opportunity to learn and practice certain skills that they might otherwise find difficult to acquire.

■ Summary

- *Developmental psychology* is the study of psychological and physical changes over time, from the fetal stage through adulthood. Developmental psychologists employ various methods to gather data and study changes in human development. Using a **longitudinal study,** a researcher studies a fixed group of people over a period of time. **Cross-sectional studies** enable a researcher to compare a sample of people of different ages at one point in time.

- To uncover the reasons why developmental changes occur, developmental psychologists can use the naturalistic-observational method, the correlation method, or the experimental method. Actually they often use converging data from all three of these methods, since this gives them a more complete idea of the reasons behind developmental changes.

- **Can stress affect a child's *prenatal development*?** Psychologists now know that the **prenatal** (before birth) environment profoundly affects the unborn fetus. The *placenta* links the *fetus* to its mother and filters food in and waste products out. The placenta cannot filter out all harmful substances, however, so the pregnant woman should maintain a healthy diet and avoid drugs (including alcohol), communicable diseases, and stressful environments.

- **Are babies born with distinct personalities?** Newborns, or *neonates,* begin to absorb and process information from the outside world almost as soon as they are born; most of their senses operate at birth or shortly thereafter. Neonates are equipped with reflexes that prepare them to make contact and communicate with the adults around them. Three important reflexes that are present at birth are **rooting, sucking,** and **grasping.** In addition, neonates will respond to human voices and faces by turning their heads or their eyes toward them. Newborns seem to be born with "personalities" and react differently to certain tastes and smells.

- *Maturation* is an automatic unfolding of development that begins with conception. Boys and girls mature at different rates and have different body compositions. The greatest sex differences become evident at puberty, when both boys and girls go through a period of rapid growth followed by the development of the secondary sexual characteristics. *Developmental norms* are standards of growth that indicate the ages by which an average child should reach various developmental milestones. Normal development can occur within a range of ages, so these norms are only general guidelines.

- The development of the central nervous system makes it possible for babies to get their bodies under control. The brain grows rapidly and becomes more complex, making new behavior possible. Motor abilities such as walking and grasping are present at birth, but develop in sequence. Walking progresses from lifting up the head, sitting up, crawling around, and walking with help to walking unsupported. There seem to be critical periods when a child is most able to start certain activities. Much of human development is gradual and steady, but sometimes development occurs in spurts that are less orderly.

- Normal babies can both see and hear at birth, although not as well as adults can, and vision and hearing continue to improve during infancy. Visual perception seems not to be an innate capacity independent of visual experience. There is good evidence to suggest that stimulation, experience, and learning all contribute to a child's perceptual development. The ability to perceive is inborn, but without experience it will not develop properly.

- **Why do babies like stripes?** Neonates lack **visual acuity**—the ability to distinguish fine details. Infants can perceive lines and dots as long as they are not too small or too thin. They can also recognize patterns and have been found to prefer increasingly complex stimuli as they grow older.

- Developmental psychologists use a device called a *visual cliff* to test infants' distance and depth perception. When allowed to crawl freely around the cliff, babies will not cross what appears to them to be a deep hole; they will, however, cross over a hole that appears to be shallow and therefore not dan-

gerous. Because babies under six months have imperfect vision and immature nervous systems, it is likely that their depth perception is limited. The experience of seeing and touching objects at various distances probably helps develop depth perception.

- Infants as young as one or two months old can tell the difference between a picture of an object and the actual object. They are also more likely to reach out toward an actual object than toward a picture of it, indicating that they sense the graspable nature of objects. **Object permanence** is the knowledge that an object continues to exist even if it is not in sight. Infants develop a sense of object permanence at about 18 to 20 weeks of age.

- Infants experience and make contact with the world through all their senses. Even very young infants can hear fairly well and can distinguish between speech and other types of sounds. Infants will often reach out to touch, smell, and taste objects around them; and they even demonstrate preferences in tastes and smells. Infants' perceptions of the world grow sharper and more meaningful as they grow older. This is both because the nervous system is maturing and because they are gaining in firsthand experience of the world.

- *Cognitive development* refers to changes in the way children think about the world as they grow older. Jean Piaget saw all behavior in terms of a person's adaptation to the environment. He noticed that as children grow older their strategies for adapting and coping with their surroundings become more sophisticated. From his observations Piaget developed his theory of cognitive development, consisting of a series of stages through which all children must pass.

- **At roughly what age do babies first recognize themselves?** The first in Piaget's theory of cognitive development is the *sensory-motor stage* (birth–2 years). Babies in this stage apply the reflexes of sucking and grasping to a broad range of activities. Infants will begin to organize their experiences into categories and devise **schemes** with which to deal with their world. At the end of the sensory-motor stage children develop object permanence and a sense of self-recognition.

- *Preoperational thought* (2–7 years) is the next stage in Piaget's theory. During this time the child learns to use symbols to represent the external world. The child is egocentric most of the time and can center on only one aspect of an event at a time. In this stage a child cannot mentally reverse a situation.

- During the *concrete operations stage* (7–11 years), the child learns to retrace his or her thoughts, to consider more than one dimension of a problem at a time, and to look at a single object or problem in several ways. By about age 10, children usually become more able to infer what another person knows or may be thinking and also become aware that another person may be able to infer what they are thinking.

- The *formal operation stage* (11–15 years) marks the development of abstract thinking and the ability to formulate concepts.

- **Does all development proceed in a carefully ordered sequence of stages?** Piaget assumed that there are distinct stages of cognitive development and that an individual must go through each stage in order to reach the next. Other developmental psychologists question these assumptions and suggest that cognitive development may proceed by "fits and starts," that there may be no sharp "breaks" between stages, and that it may not be necessary to go through earlier stages to reach a later stage.

- In nature, young animals of many species **imprint** on the first moving object they come in contact with after birth, usually the mother, and will follow her around. Imprinting creates a strong bond between the young animal and its mother.

- Human babies form a close **attachment** to their mothers during the first few months of life. This attachment is the beginning of the child's social development. The mother satisfies the infant's need for food and gives warmth, contact, and auditory and visual stimulation. At around seven months, children begin to show anxiety around strangers and react negatively to being separated from their mothers.

- **Are babies who explore a little, and then come back to their mothers, likely to be too dependent?** As soon as most babies can crawl, they begin to explore and to separate themselves from their mothers. They begin to develop a sense of **autonomy.** A strong mother-child relationship actually fosters autonomy because it provides the child with a secure base from which to explore new situations.

- Throughout childhood, children continue to develop socially both within and outside the family. Parents significantly influence their children's social development through direct teaching as well as by serving as models of behavior. Research shows that styles of parenting can have a lasting effect on children's behavior. Certain parenting approaches seem more likely to succeed than others in producing a socially competent child, and in any event it is necessary that parenting styles change somewhat as children grow older.

- **Do firstborn children develop differently from those born later?** Siblings also play an important *socializing* role in a child's life. Older siblings help teach younger ones language and behaviors. Sibling relationships expose children to competition, as siblings seek to establish their own identities. Among siblings, firstborns tend to be more achievement-oriented and to seek adult approval; later siblings are often more competent socially. Besides siblings, other peers help to teach and socialize the preschool child.

- School is a child's first encounter with the social system outside the family and it calls for learning new social behaviors and skills. School encourages independence but at the same time it demands co-operation, interaction with peers, and conformity to the rules of social behavior. The socializing influence of peers is strongest during the school years. Successful relationships with peers become an important determinant of popularity and are a means of developing competence in social roles. Successes and failures at school may have a lasting effect on a child's sense of competence and achievement.

- **Are the differences between the sexes the result of development?** Psychologists have begun to examine the extent to which differences between the sexes are the result rather than the cause of differences in treatment. Most research on the subject does not support the notion of profound sexual differences. Males, however, do tend to be more aggressive than females. This difference may be hormonal at first, but socialization and parents' expectations probably account for the discrepancy later. Many societies presume the existence of significant sex differences, and assign distinctive (and often opposite roles) to each sex. As more women work outside the home and more men become involved in childcare, sex roles in the United States have begun to loosen. However, many parents continue to treat their sons and daughters differently. Schools and the media, too, continue to reinforce sexual stereotypes.

- **How does our understanding of what a friend is change as we grow older?** Children gradually develop **social cognition,** a mental understanding of the social world and their place in it. Infants and very young children are egocentric. As they lose their egocentrism, children in middle childhood develop a greater understanding of others and can make assumptions about others' thoughts and feelings. They are also more self-aware and begin to assess their own strengths and weaknesses relative to others. Around this time children start to think about social relationships. Before age seven they consider friends simply as playmates. After age seven friends are important because they meet certain needs. Around age nine there begins an understanding of the reciprocal nature of friendship. The fuller understanding of friendship as a stable social relationship does not come until late childhood or adolescence.

Review Questions

1. In a _____ study the researcher compares people of different ages at one point in time.
2. The very earliest, or _____ period of development, is now thought to involve psychological as well as physical changes in an organism.
3. Neonates are only capable of simple reflexes and thus remain relatively unresponsive to the outside world. T/F
4. Physical development follows a regular, more or less automatic, course, which psychologists refer to as _____.
5. Match the following terms with their correct definitions:

   ____ rooting reflex
   ____ grasping reflex
   ____ sucking reflex

   a. causes newborns to clasp anything that is put in their hands
   b. causes newborns to suck on anything that touches their faces
   c. causes newborns to search for a nipple when they are picked up

6. Psychologists have agreed on some general guidelines and timetables in predicting the course of development. These guidelines are called _____ _____.
7. Match the following terms with the appropriate definition:

   ____ perceptual ability
   ____ depth perception
   ____ visual acuity
   ____ object permanence

   a. ability to distinguish fine details
   b. is innate, but requires experience for proper development
   c. awareness that objects hidden from view still exist
   d. awareness of how close or far away an object is relative to oneself.

8. Through a special device called the _____ _____, psychologists are able to measure the extent of depth perception in infants.
9. The fact that an infant prefers a new pattern to an old one shows that it has the ability to remember. The acquisition of _____ will further enhance this ability.
10. Match Piaget's stages of cognitive development with their appropriate descriptions:

    ____ sensory-motor
    ____ preoperational
    ____ formal operations
    ____ concrete operations

    a. marked by egocentrism and a narrow focus of attention
    b. increased logical aptitude and intellectual flexibility, but no ability to think abstract thinking
    c. marked by the development of abstract thinking
    d. a sense of self-recognition and object permanence develops by the end of this stage.

11. According to Piaget, the _____ one first uses to organize experience change as one grows older.
12. The bonding between an infant and its primary caregiver is called _____.
13. Children's development of _____ cognition gives them a fuller picture of the social world and their place within it.

10 Adolescence and Adulthood

■ Thinking Critically

Does culture affect the experience of adolescence?

What is it that makes adolescence a psychologically difficult period for some?

How do people go about developing a sense of their own identity?

Why are adolescents often passionate social and political activists?

What kinds of adolescents are most at risk for suicide?

Do we know why we age?

How does one choose a career?

Is work less satisfying for women than for men?

Do we become better at different kinds of thought processes as we grow older?

Does sexual activity generally end at a certain age?

Do older adults fear death?

The answers to these and other questions about the developmental changes that occur during adolescence and adulthood appear in this chapter and in the Chapter Summary.

■ Outline

illiam James, the nineteenth-century American psychologist and philosopher, believed that our character was "set like plaster" by the age of 30. Since James's day, psychologists have suggested even earlier ages as the point at which development is more or less finished. In fact, until recently many psychologists believed that most important developmental changes occurred before the beginning of adolescence.

However, recent research suggests that significant developmental changes occur throughout the life span. We now know that adolescence and adulthood are important developmental periods for human beings—not just years during which people simply play out their lives according to the patterns established in early childhood.

In this chapter, we will explore the ways in which adolescents and adults grow and change—physically, intellectually, and socially. We will learn that adolescence, adulthood, and old age bring significant changes in the way that people think. We will examine the ways in which people react to physical change and to their sexuality. We will also examine changes over the life span in social relationships and in personality. We begin our discussion at the end of childhood and the start of adolescence.

■ Adolescence

In the late nineteenth century, adolescence was generally seen as a stage of life characterized by periods of instability and strong emotion and accompanied by awakening intellectual capabilities. For example, G. Stanley Hall portrayed adolescence as a period of inevitable "storm and stress," suffering, passion, and rebellion against adult authority (Hall, 1904). Sigmund Freud and his followers shared this **classical view of adolescence** as a period of considerable conflict, anxiety, and tension. In fact, Hall and Freud believed that if an adolescent did *not* experience turmoil and confusion it was a sign of future developmental problems.

Anthropologist Margaret Mead (1928, 1930) questioned the classical view of adolescence and suggested instead that the apparent chaos of adolescence may be unique to highly industrialized nations. On the remote islands of Samoa, for example, she found that adolescence was not a time of crisis or stress, but was rather a time for the orderly development of a set of slowly maturing interests and activities. More recent research suggests that the classical view is also not an accurate description of adolescence in the United States. Studies of midwestern boys and a national sample of 3,000 adolescents (Douvan & Adelson, 1966) have all reported that for the great majority of adolescents, life is not filled with turmoil and chaos. If turbulence exists for some adolescents, so too does stability for others. While some adolescents seem to progress with almost routine steadiness of purpose, others experience cycles of ups and downs, while still others undergo prolonged inner turmoil, as manifested in serious behavior problems. For the most part, it now appears that adolescents whose development has proceeded smoothly up to this point in their lives typically experience little storm and stress, while those whose prior development has been stressful are likely to experience a stressful adolescence as well (Bronfenbrenner, 1986; Offer & Offer, 1975).

Reactions to Physical Changes

THE GROWTH SPURT. Adolescence is ushered in by a series of dramatic physical changes. The most obvious change is the so-called **growth spurt**—a rapid increase in both height and weight that begins at about age 8 or 9 in girls and age 10 or 11 in boys. In the next seven years, most adolescents will attain 98 percent of their adult height.

In both sexes the growth spurt results in a lengthening of the body trunk, with the legs reaching their peak growth before the trunk. This pattern of growth gives rise to the "leggy" look of young adolescents. Other physical features also change during this period. Boys begin to develop heavier bodies, more substantial musculature in relation to body size, larger hearts, higher systolic blood pressure, and greater oxygen-carrying capacity in the blood (Petersen & Taylor, 1980). In contrast, girls begin to accumulate proportionally larger amounts of fat in their arms, chests, hips and legs, and they begin to look more like adult women (see Figure 10-1).

Adolescents are acutely aware of these rapid changes in their bodies.

Growth spurt Rapid increase in height and weight that begins at about age 8 or 9 in girls and 10 or 11 in boys.

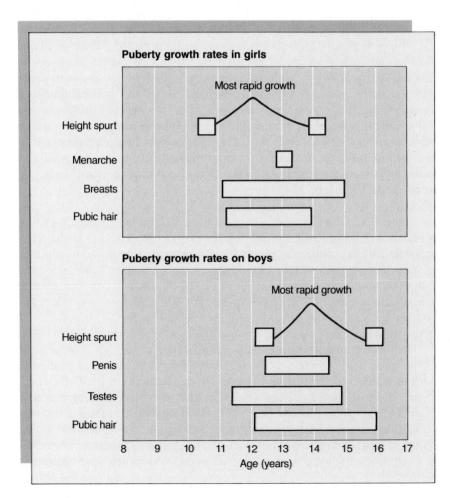

Figure 10-1
Chart showing growth rate and sexual development for boys and girls during puberty The bars indicate average ages at onset and completion.

Adapted from Tanner, 1973. Copyright © 1973 by Scientific American, Inc. All rights reserved.

Girls generally enter the *growth spurt* at about age 8 or 9, boys generally at about age 10 or 11. However, there are sometimes significant differences in the ages at which the growth spurt occurs, and these differences can have psychological consequences.

They are particularly concerned about whether they are the "right" shape or size, whether they measure up to the "ideal" adolescent portrayed on television and in magazines. Predictably, few adolescents approximate the ideal, and so it is not surprising that when young adolescents are asked what they most dislike about themselves, physical appearance is mentioned more often than anything else (Conger & Petersen, 1984). In fact, approximately one-third of boys and one-half of girls in early adolescence report distress about some aspect of their physical appearance. Especially among adolescent girls, satisfaction with one's appearance is tied to satisfaction with one's self (Lerner & Karabenick, 1974). Adolescents who are least satisfied with their physical appearance also have the lowest self-esteem, maintain the least stable self-image, and are the most self-conscious about how they look (Adams & Gullota, 1983). Thus, physical appearance is not at all a minor matter for adolescents.

Individuals differ greatly in the age at which the growth spurt occurs, and this fact also has psychological consequences. Among boys, maturing early seems to have distinct advantages (Dreyer, 1982; Seigel, 1982). Boys who mature earlier do better in sports and social activities and thereby gain greater respect among other boys. In contrast, boys who mature later are more likely to feel inadequate, anxious, and self-conscious (Jones, 1958; Jones & Bayley, 1950; Mussen & Jones, 1957, 1958). These personality characteristics tend to persist into early adulthood, although they become less marked and often disappear as time goes by (Jones, 1965; Peskin, 1967, 1973).

For girls, early maturation appears to be a mixed blessing. A girl who matures earlier may be admired by other girls but is likely to be taunted or treated as a sex object by boys (Clausen, 1975). Her larger size and more adult physique may also make her feel conspicuous and awkward, especially compared with boys of her own age. For these reasons, the late-maturing girl often finds adolescence a little easier than her early-maturing peer (Siegel, 1982). But as with boys, the consequences of early- and late-maturation decrease over time. Most early-maturing girls who found adolescence stressful are well-adjusted and at ease with themselves in adulthood (Peskin, 1973).

SEXUAL DEVELOPMENT. Maturation of the reproduction system is another striking feature of adolescence, and it too occurs at different times for different individuals—as is obvious to anyone observing youngsters in a seventh- or eighth-grade gym class. The first visible signs of **puberty** (which refers to the onset of sexual maturation) appear about a year after the start of the growth spurt. The full growth of secondary sex characteristics (genital development, pubic and body hair, breast development, and so on) takes approximately four years for both sexes.

In boys, the first indication of approaching puberty is enlargement of the testes and scrotum. This is followed by growth of pubic and body hair and, later on, by a deepening of the voice as the larynx and vocal chords increase in size. By age 15, about half of teenage boys are capable of producing sperm (Chumlea, 1982). Budding of the breasts is the first indication of approaching puberty in girls. At about the same time, pubic hair develops, and rapid growth starts in the uterus and vagina. The onset of menstruation (or **menarche**) occurs about two years after the beginning of breast and genital development. When a girl's period becomes regular a year or so later, she is capable of conceiving a child.

Sexual maturation, like other aspects of physical change, has significant psychological consequences for adolescents. Among boys, the increasing frequency of erections and concomitant ejaculations are often a source of pride and a sign that the transition to manhood has begun. However, some boys become concerned about their occasional inability to control their erections, and their resulting embarrassment may give way to some shyness and self-consciousness, at least in the short term. And some boys worry that the ejaculation of seminal fluid is abnormal, a sign of some serious physical problem.

Many adolescent girls also welcome the onset of menstruation as a sign that they are finally becoming "women" and are crossing the threshold into adulthood. But evidence indicates that most girls are much less positive about menarche (Grief & Ulman, 1982). For many girls, menstruation (sometimes called "the curse") is at best something to be tolerated and at worst a source of considerable psychological and physical discomfort. A negative reaction to menarche is even more likely if it arrives unusually early or unusually late, if the girl has received little or no preparation, if family members and friends stress the negative aspects of menstruation, if it is in fact accompanied by physical discomfort, or if the girl is not psychologically "ready" to move on to adulthood.

Sexual maturation has other psychological consequences as well. In particular, patterns of sexual behavior change tremendously with the arrival of sexual maturity, as we will see in the next portion of this chapter.

Traditional standard Expectation that adolescents will postpone the expression of sexual needs until they are responsible married adults.

Adolescents are acutely aware of the physical changes that are taking place. Many become anxious about measuring up to an ideal physical attractiveness.

Social, Interpersonal, and Personality Development

SEXUAL BEHAVIOR. The adolescent's capacity to reproduce is considered the single most important developmental event of adolescence. It sets the stage for all other intellectual and social changes that occur during this period of life (Dreyer, 1982). But the subject of adolescent sexuality is confusing in our society. According to the **traditional standard,** adolescents are expected to postpone the expression of sexual needs until they are responsible married adults. This standard made sense 100 years ago, when the average age of menarche was between 15 and 17 years of age. But over the past century, sexual maturation (and the resulting increase of interest in the opposite sex) has been occurring at an earlier and earlier age. Largely because of improved food programs and better health care, the age of menarche has declined an average of four months for each decade over the past century, although it is not expected to decline further in developed countries. In less developed parts of the world, menarche still occurs very late—between 15.5 and 18.4 years in New Guinea, for example (Chumlea, 1982). Whether boys now mature earlier is difficult to determine; nevertheless, the advent of voice change is reported to have decreased from 18 years to 13 or 14 years of age (Chumlea, 1982).

With an earlier onset of sexual maturity and an earlier interest in the opposite sex, patterns of sexual behavior have also clearly changed

Double standard Expectation that females, but not males, will postpone the expression of sexual needs until they are married.

over the last century. Both the traditional standard and the **double standard,** which demands virginity for females but not for males, are being challenged. For example, national surveys indicate that girls are only slightly slower to become sexually active. By age 18, 60 percent of white boys have had intercourse; and 60 percent of white girls had had intercourse by age 19, just one year later. For blacks, there is a two-year difference between boys and girls: Sixty percent of black males have had intercourse by the time they are 16; 60 percent of black girls have been sexually active by age 18 (Hofferth & Hayes, 1987). These percentages are especially striking when compared with figures drawn from samples of teenage girls before 1950. These indicate that only about 7 percent of teenage girls reported that they had had intercourse by age 16 (Kinsey et al., 1948).

Earlier sexual maturation, coupled with the heavy emphasis on sexuality in today's society, combine to increase the importance of sexuality in the lives of most contemporary adolescents. For many adolescents today, sex is a means of communication, a new experience, an index of maturity, a source of peer approval and status, a challenge to restrictive parents or society, and an escape from loneliness or other pressures of life. Yet these same adolescents are no more mature psychologically than were their grandparents at the same age. One consequence of this growing discrepancy between sexual maturity and psychological immaturity is a tremendous increase in unwanted pregnancies, as we will see in the next section.

SEXUALLY TRANSMITTED DISEASES AND UNWANTED PREGNANCIES. Over 20 percent of all adolescent girls conceive a child by age 18, despite the widespread availability of sex education programs. In large part, the explanation for this shocking statistic is to be found in the fact that most young adolescents are still at the level of thinking which Piaget described as concrete operational thought (see Chapter 9). Planning for sex, acknowledging that sexual intercourse will eventually occur, and recognizing that pregnancy is a possible result are simply not characteristic of adolescent thinking. One girl's remarks illustrate this fact well: "And like you really don't connect it, you know, until once you've been pregnant. Because when it's never happened you say, 'Why should it happen?' or 'It's never happened yet!' You just don't worry about it. You don't believe it can happen to you" (Sorensen, 1973). In one study, 82 percent of female adolescents who never used birth control reported that they didn't *think* about becoming pregnant (Sorensen, 1973). And over 70 percent of all adolescents disapprove of planning for sex (Sorensen, 1973). Among those adolescents who do use birth control methods, 45 percent admit to carelessness in their use.

American adults as well as adolescents tend to see the use of contraceptives as difficult and problematic (Brooks-Gunn & Furstenberg, 1989). As a result, married couples in their 30s are more likely to choose sterilization over other forms of contraception (Jones et al., 1988). The awkwardness and inconsistency that characterizes the attitudes of so many toward the use of contraceptives places sexually active adolescents and adults at risk, not just for pregnancy, but also for sexually transmitted diseases. Teens are at especially high risk for these diseases (Cates & Rauh, 1985). In particular, the number of cases of acquired immune

Among adolescents who do use birth control methods, 45 percent admit to being careless in their use. About 10 percent of all adolescent girls will conceive a child this year, and the risk for girls under the age of 15 is much higher than for those over the age of 15.

deficiency syndrome (AIDS) among adolescents has been doubling in recent years, and it may be that only the long incubation period for this disease has kept the actual numbers of adolescents with the disease relatively low. In fact, one-fifth of all AIDS cases have occurred in 20- to 29-year-olds, which suggests that many contracted the AIDS virus as teenagers (Curran et al., 1988).

For those teenagers who become parents, the consequences of parenthood, unfortunately, are often catastrophic—particularly for those who are without parental support or who live in impoverished communities (Crockenberg, 1985; Furstenberg, 1983; Furstenberg, Brooks-Gunn, & Chase-Lansdale, 1989). This is especially true of teen mothers for whom motherhood usually has serious and negative effects on education, economic prospects, and marital stability (Hofferth & Hayes, 1987).

The emergence of sexual feelings in adolescence is closely followed by and intertwined with the need for intimacy. Most teenagers are eager to develop a relationship with an opposite-sex partner in order to help solidify sexual identity and to bolster fragile self-esteem, as we will see in the next section of this chapter.

IDENTITY. After puberty, the next major life event experienced by adolescents is separation from parents. In order to make this transition from dependence on parents to dependence on one's self, the adolescent must develop a stable sense of self, or **identity** (Erikson, 1968). Adolescents begin to question whether their past and present experiences will prepare them for the future. They begin to discover that some of the roles they play feel false, feel "not me." And some roles that were easy to identify during childhood—family, ethnic, and group membership, for instance—are no longer so clear-cut. The overwhelming question for adolescents becomes, "Who am I?"

Marcia (1980) has identified four possible outcomes of an adolescent's attempts to achieve a stable sense of identity (see Table 10-1). **Identity achievers** have succeeded in making personal choices about the goals that they should pursue. They are comfortable with their various

Identity Erikson's term for the stable sense of self necessary to make the transition from dependence on others to dependence on oneself.

Identity achievers According to Marcia, adolescents who achieve identity by making personal decisions about goals.

"What? Not <u>another</u> identity crisis."

Table 10-1
Adapted from Marcia, 1980. © 1980 by John Wiley & Sons, Inc.

TABLE 10-1 MAJOR CHARACTERISTICS OF MARCIA'S FOUR STATUSES	Identity achievement	Foreclosure	Moratorium	Indentity diffusion
Experience a crisis period	Yes	No	Yes	Yes
Committed to an occupation	Yes	Yes	No	No
Have adopted values, ideologies	Yes	Yes	No	No
Females	High fear of success; positive psychological benefits	Low fear of success; positive psychological benefits	High fear of success; uncertainty, instability, low self-esteem	Low fear of success; uncertainty, instability, low self-esteem
Males	Low fear of success; high self-esteem	High fear of success; low self-esteem	Low fear of success; high self-esteem	High fear of success; low self-esteem
Feelings about parents	Balanced feelings	Strong positive ties	Bonds of love, hate	Feelings of rejection, detachment from parents

Foreclosure According to Marcia, accepting an identity provided by others rather than one chosen by oneself.

Moratorium According to Marcia, period during which an adolescent delays developing an identity while exploring alternatives and choices.

Identity diffusion According to Marcia, failure to develop a clear sense of one's own identity.

Peer group Age-mates who provide a supportive network for the adolescent.

roles and are confident that their values and actions meet with the approval of others. In contrast, other adolescents adopt **foreclosure:** They prematurely settle on an identity that is provided for them by others and become what those others want them to be. Still other adolescents declare a **moratorium** and set aside the problem of developing an identity while they continue to explore various alternatives and choices. In a sense, they put everything on "hold." Finally, some adolescents experience **identity diffusion:** They are dissatisfied with their present place in society, but they are also unable to develop a new identity that "feels right." They can't "find themselves" and may resort to escapist activities in order to counter the anxiety that they feel (Adams & Gullota, 1983).

What determines whether an adolescent will (or will not) achieve a sense of self or identity? In part, the answer is to be found in the family itself. Numerous studies reveal that high self-esteem and a clear sense of self are both associated with positive perceptions of and rewarding relationships with parents (Conger, 1977; Siegel, 1982; Walker & Green, 1986). Most adolescents share their parents' fundamental values, although there may be disagreements about less important matters, such as tastes in dress and music (Hill, 1980). Thus, the family itself plays a tremendously important role in the extent to which adolescents can achieve a sense of independence and of personal identity.

SOCIAL RELATIONSHIPS. Part of identity formation also involves a measure of separation from one's family. For most adolescents, the **peer group** of age-mates provides a supportive network that makes it possible to become autonomous and to experiment with different cultural values while at the same time meeting their needs for emotional closeness. The *friendship group* also helps each adolescent to create his or her own social

■ Selected Facts about Teenage Pregnancy

- The earlier a girl goes steady, the more likely she is to become pregnant (Rodgers, 1983)
- Many teenage girls engage in sexual intercourse only a few times before becoming pregnant (Ktsanes, 1980; Zelnick & Kanter, 1978).
- The younger the teenager at first intercourse, the greater the risk of pregnancy (Zabin, Kanter, & Zelnick, 1979).
- Many inner-city youth, among whom the risk of pregnancy is greatest, live in families where misinformation or no information exists about reproduction and contraception (Hardy, 1985).
- Sixty-two percent of teenagers who never use a contraceptive method become pregnant (Zabin, Kanter, & Zelnick, 1979).

- Repeated pregnancy is common among teenagers (Hardy, 1985).
- The child born to a teenage mother is at greater biological and social risk than a child born to an older mother (Hardy, 1985).
- The rate of teenage pregnancy in the United States is much higher than in any other developed country; Sweden, for example, has a higher frequency of adolescent sexual intercourse but a frequency of pregnancy less than half that of the United States (Hardy, 1985).
- Almost 50 percent of all federal funds allocated for Aid to Families with Dependent Children goes to families with teenage mothers (Moore, 1978).

style (P.R. Newman, 1982). Adolescents often feel a desperate need for their friends to approve their choices, their views, and their preferred patterns of behavior. They continually question whether their behavior is appropriate and find it difficult to tolerate criticism. The result is often a rigid conformity to peer and friendship group values.

We have seen that peers and friends are important to normal adolescent development. But exactly *how* important depends in large part on the adolescent's relationship with his or her family (Walker & Green, 1986). Adolescents with strong family ties tend to associate with similarly raised friends and use those friends not only to develop and refine their skills, but also to provide advice on interpersonal matters. These adolescents continue to rely on their parents for help on moral issues and questions about the future (Wilks, 1986). Adolescents without such strong family ties often depend more heavily on peers both to increase their self-esteem and to allow them to act out commonly held antisocial wishes. In addition, adolescents whose parents provide structure and allow them to participate in decision-making report less dependence on peers than do other adolescents (Steinberg & Silverberg, 1986).

Although we have seen that friends are important to all adolescents, the nature of friendship changes significantly during the adolescent years. Friendship groups in early adolescence tend to be small, unisex groups (called *cliques*) of three to nine members. Cliques provide the adolescent with intimacy and closeness. Over time, unisex cliques break down and are replaced by mixed-sex groups, which in turn slowly dissolve as "the couple" becomes the dominant form of intimate relationships (Dunphy, 1963). At first, adolescents tend to have short-term heterosexual relationships within the group. These relationships fulfill mutual needs but carry no connotations of "going steady," engagement, or marriage (Sorensen, 1973). Such relationships do not demand love and can dissolve overnight. But between the ages of 16 and 19, most adolescents settle into more stable dating patterns; no longer crowd-oriented and better able to accept their sex roles, they begin to gain competence and confidence with more intimate long-term relationships. At this point, the well-adjusted adolescent has begun to develop a stable sense of identity and has experienced some mature and intimate relationships—both of which provide a platform for the transition to young adulthood.

Cognitive Development

During adolescence, a dramatic change also occurs in cognitive processes. Piaget described this progression as a change from concrete operations to **formal operations**—a change from a concrete to an abstract way of thinking about the world. Younger children can think logically, but only in terms of concrete things. Adolescents can manipulate and understand abstract concepts (Piaget, 1969). With this ability, adolescents can formulate general rules about the world and then test them against available facts. Thought is no longer dependent on direct experience. Adolescents can speculate about alternative possibilities, can reason in hypothetical terms, and can understand analogies and metaphors.

Not all adolescents reach the stage of formal operations, and those who do may not reveal formal operational thinking in all of the everyday problem-solving situations that they face (Gardner, 1982). For example,

Formal operations Fourth and final stage in Piaget's theory of cognitive development, characterized by the transition from concrete to abstract thinking.

■ Caution: Youth Working

A 15-year old girl leaves school at 4:00 P.M. and walks a few short blocks to a neighborhood restaurant, where she dons an apron and goes to work as a kitchen helper for four hours. In exchange for her work she receives the minimum wage, a free dinner—and the benefits of working: discipline, a sense of responsibility, and job skills. Her work experience is likely to make her more mature, more self-reliant, and more successful as a student.

According to psychologist Ellen Greenberger, however, this story reflects a popular misconception: that after-school work experience is necessarily a good thing for teenagers (Greenberger, 1983). Americans, with their high regard for work, tend to assume that it is valuable for everyone—even 14- and 15-year-olds. When the U.S. Department of Labor in 1982 proposed to increase the number of hours that young teenagers might legally work (from 18 to 24 hours per week during the school year), Greenberger testified against the proposal before a House of Representatives subcommittee.

According to Greenberger, who has done research on youth employment for several years, working while in school *does* have some of the benefits that its proponents claim. Teenagers who work are likely to gain a better understanding of money and increased feelings of responsibility and self-reliance. But they are also likely to spend less time on their schoolwork and less time with their families—circumstances that Greenberger considers to be among the major disadvantages of working. Greenberger and her associates found a significant relationship between the number of hours that teenagers worked and their grade-point averages: generally, the more work, the lower the GPA. Moreover, working during the teenage years is associated with increased use of cigarettes, alcohol, and marijuana.

Teens who work are likely to spend less time on their schoolwork and less time with their families.

In other industrialized countries, it is the exception rather than the rule for teenagers (even 16- and 17-year olds) to work while attending school. For example, in 1979 over 60 percent of American 16- and 17-year-olds were working, while less than 2 percent of Japanese young people worked. And as Greenberger (1983) points out, employment of 14- and 15-year-old students is now higher than it has been since 1940 (the first year the U.S. Census compiled a separate record of working students). This movement of youth into the workplace, she suggests, may be one reason for our nation's declining educational performance. At a time when we are concerned with encouraging high school students to spend more time on their studies, it would seem poor public policy to urge them to spend additional hours on the job.

many young adolescents cannot yet understand the ambiguity of moral judgments or appreciate irony; they cannot sufficiently distance themselves from their thoughts in order to achieve true objectivity. Similarly, as we saw earlier in this chapter, some adolescents fail to use formal operational thinking to plan for the prevention of pregnancy.

Nonetheless, the growing ability to think more abstractly accounts in part for some profound changes in the ways adolescents relate to other people and to the world around them. Adolescents are able to think not only about the way things are, but also about how they might be different (and perhaps better). Adolescents also tend to become immersed in introspection and self-analysis (Elkind, 1968). As they reflect in more complex ways on their feelings, attitudes, and actions, they may feel that they are "onstage"—that their peers are always judging their appearance and behavior. They continually play to an imaginary audience by dressing in a particular way, cultivating a distinctive image, and so on. Newly introspective adolescents may also believe that their feelings are unique in content and intensity. This sense of self-importance is what Elkind (1969) has called a "personal fable." The adolescent feels that no one else can reach the same heights of ecstasy or descend to the same depths of misery. This self-preoccupation has led many an adolescent to pour out anguished feelings in poetry or love letters. Toward the end of adolescence, a more mature perspective is gained. As older teenagers reach out to others and form more mature relationships, they begin to judge themselves more realistically.

Peer groups help adolescents develop identities apart from family influences; *cliques* are small friendship groups which provide intimacy but which also tend to be exclusive.

Adolescent Reactions to Situational Stress

Our discussion so far has focused on the mastery of normal life events during adolescence. In this section, we explore the adolescent's reaction to more unique crises and to unusual kinds of stress. Before we proceed, it is worth noting that because adolescents are in a state of transition and because they have not yet achieved a stable identity or developed a stable life-style, they are particularly vulnerable to stress. This vulnerability is increased still further by the fact that adolescents are for the most part unable to think through the long-term consequences of their actions. Therefore, crises which are normally stressful for anybody are especially so for adolescents. Adolescents especially need support, discipline, and structure from an involved, caring family in order to cope effectively with the stressors to which they are exposed.

When adolescents become more confident about intimate long-term relationships—usually between the ages of 16 and 19—they begin to develop stable dating patterns.

COPING WITH DIVORCE. Adolescents are idealists who tend to have unrealistic expectations for themselves and others. Therefore, parental divorce can have a profound effect on adolescents, who may conclude that "you can't count on anyone anymore." They are likely to feel that they are being abandoned or being required to grow up too quickly. And when the discipline, order, and control provided by the parents temporarily disappears, adolescents have to cope suddenly with much greater independence, and the result is not always favorable.

Under these circumstances, it is not unusual for adolescents to become disillusioned about relationships and commitments and to doubt their own ability as sexual partners and their ability to succeed in marriage. Even well-adjusted adolescents may come to believe that somehow they were personally responsible for the parental split. And they may fear that talking about their pain, loneliness, sense of betrayal, and feelings of responsibility will reveal them to the world as failures. In order to defend themselves against their vulnerability, they may express great anger and rage (Van Ornum & Mordock, 1983).

Many of the disruptive effects of divorce, however, can be minimized if the parents are not engaged in great conflict, if the adolescent has regular contact with the noncustodial parent, if effective discipline and support are available from the custodial parent, if open discussion of divorce-related issues is encouraged and facilitated, and if the financial security of the child's household is assured.

Adolescents who do not have to cope with divorce nonetheless are likely to encounter other crises, such as broken romances, school failure, frequent moves, or injury. The majority of adolescents will weather these

■ Moral Reasoning and the Growth of Conscience

One of the most important changes that occurs during adolescence is the development of moral reasoning. Prior to the onset of adolescence, children adopt what Lawrence Kohlberg (1979, 1981) called a "preconventional" perspective on morality. At the *preconventional level*, very young children interpret behavior in light of its concrete consequences— whether they are rewarded or punished for it. Somewhat older children at this level define "right" behavior as that which satisfies needs, particularly their own.

With the arrival of adolescence and the gradual shift to formal-operational thought, the stage is set for the progression to Kohlberg's second level of moral reasoning—the *conventional level*. At this level, the adolescent at first defines right behavior as that which pleases or helps others and is approved by them. Around mid-adolescence, there is a further shift toward considering various abstract social virtues such as "doing one's duty," being a "good citizen," respecting authority, and maintaining the social order. Both forms of conventional moral reasoning require an ability to think about such abstract values as "duty" and "social order," to consider the intentions that lie behind behavior, and to put oneself "in the other person's shoes." In turn, these require formal-operational thinking. But, as we will see shortly, being able to think in formal-operational ways does not in itself guarantee that moral thought will progress to the conventional level.

The third level of moral reasoning—the *postconventional level*—also requires advanced formal-operational thought. This level is marked by an emphasis on abstract principles quite apart from the concern with existing social rules and the power of those who enforce them. Justice, liberty, and equality become the guideposts for deciding what is moral and correct, whether or not this corresponds to the rules and laws of a particular society at a particular time. For the first time, the person may become aware of discrepancies between what appears to be "moral" and what is "legal," and this awareness may lead to conflicts over following one's conscience as opposed to obeying the law.

A couple of points are worth making about Kohlberg's view of the development of moral reasoning in adolescence. First, research indicates that most people—both adolescents and adults—never progress beyond conventional moral reasoning (Conger & Petersen, 1984; Lerner & Shea, 1982). In fact, in one study a number of college students and young adults were found to be reasoning predominantly at the pre-conventional level (Haan, Smith, & Block, 1968). Second, although the development of formal-operational thought is necessary before a person can reach higher levels of moral reasoning, it is no *guarantee* of advanced morality (Kohlberg, 1976; Walker & Richards, 1979; Carroll & Rest, 1982). In other words, attaining the formal-operational level of thinking may make you capable of conventional and postconventional moral reasoning, but this does not mean that you will necessarily reason about morality in those ways. Nor does your ability to engage in higher levels of moral reasoning necessarily mean that you will behave more morally, although there is some evidence that this tends to be the case (Blasi, 1980; Lerner & Shea, 1982; Bornstein & Lamb, 1988).

Kohlberg's concept of moral stages is not without its critics. For example, some social scientists argue that Kohlberg's theory fails to take cultural differences into account: Concepts of what is and is not moral vary from one culture to another (Baumrind, 1978). These critics maintain that moral development results from a culture's efforts to make its social life possible, not from universal principles that apply to all people everywhere.

In addition, there are criticisms leveled at Kohlberg's methodology. The most substantial support for Kohlberg's theories has come from a longitudinal study conducted over 20 years by Colby, Kohlberg, and others and completed in 1983. At three- and four-year intervals, the researchers interviewed 58 boys and evaluated their judgments about several hypothetical moral problems. Psychologist Carol Gilligan (1982) points out that this is an inadequate means of testing theories that are supposed to apply to all people regardless of gender. She suggests that more in-depth studies of women's values and moral judgments—including concerns for charity and kindness—would produce a very different picture of the way moral reasoning develops in adults of both sexes.

Finally, other critics, observing that the Colby-Kohlberg longitudinal study began in the 1950s, point out that subjects of that study have lived through the civil rights movement, Vietnam, Watergate, and the women's movement. Their judgments about such matters as social justice and human frailty are not likely to be the same as the judgments of a generation that grew up with the Great Depression, World War II, and the Cold War. And they are not likely to be the same as the generation that grows up in the next 20 or 30 years.

crises and move forward in development. But for some, the outcome may be alienation, disillusionment, cynicism, and hopelessness. This result is especially likely when the crises are continual, when the adolescent experiences prolonged lack of family support, and when the adolescent lives in a socially disorganized and deteriorated ethnic ghetto or a rural slum. Adolescents in such settings have little chance of developing self-esteem, constructive relationships with others, and a confident sense of their own identity. Delinquency and suicide are both symptoms of such alienation.

DELINQUENCY. Minor delinquent acts are said to characterize the behavior of all adolescents. Petty thievery, for example, is widespread in early adolescence. In their rejection of parental values and in their experimentation with varying roles, most young people will engage in deviant acts at some time. But chronic delinquency is another matter entirely. Estimates of the incidence of delinquency vary from as low as 2 percent for boys and half a percent for girls up to 16 percent (Lefrancois, 1986). The discrepancy in these estimates is due largely to reporting problems and to variations in the legal adjustment of cases (plea-bargaining from "delinquent" to "person in need of supervision"). No single factor is responsible for a youth becoming delinquent; stress, skill deficiencies, and situational constraints all combine to produce problem behavior. Families of delinquents typically experience a multitude of problems. These difficulties, in combination with poverty, school problems, and deviant peers, result in an adolescent being at high risk for delinquency. The adolescent who is most likely to engage in delinquent behavior is one who does not value academic achievement, who is overly concerned with independence from adult figures, who sees society as problematic, who is not religious, and who experiences little or no guilt related to transgressions. In addition, parents who expect unquestioning obedience from their children and who continually assert their power over them are more likely to have delinquent offspring.

SUICIDE. The rate of suicide among adolescents and young adults in America has doubled since 1970 (see Table 10-2). For adolescents, it is now the second leading cause of death after accidents. Studies from the National Center for Health Statistics indicate that approximately 5,000 young people between the ages of 10 and 19 kill themselves each year.

Perhaps as many as one-third of all adolescents will experience a single-parent family situation. The effects of divorce can be minimized if there is regular contact with the noncustodial parent and discipline and openness available from the custodial parent.

TABLE 10-2 U.S. SUICIDE RATE PER 100,000 POPULATION IN WHITE MALE, ACCORDING TO AGE		
	1970	1980
5–14 years	.5	.7
15–24	13.9	21.4
25–34	19.9	25.6
35–44	23.3	23.5
45–54	29.5	24.2
55–64	35.0	25.8
64 and over	41.1	37.5
U.S. Bureau of the Census		

Table 10-2
White males are more vulnerable to suicide than black males and females of both races. Note the dramatic increase in occurrence during adolescent years. Suicide is the second leading cause of death among adolescents (accidents are the leading cause).
U.S. Bureau of the Census, 1984

And for every "successful" suicide, many, many more young people make an attempt. Over 100,000 teenagers will attempt suicide this year, and about 250,000 will contemplate it. Although the suicide rate rises with age, with the highest rates occurring in white males over 45, the recent significant increase in adolescent suicides has been cause for alarm.

We saw that, for some adolescents, life appears chaotic and confused. Moreover, lacking the stability of a background of life experiences yet able to anticipate the future, adolescents often believe that what they are feeling at a given moment will be felt forever; they are not yet convinced that "time heals all wounds." Consequently, some adolescents turn to a permanent solution to temporary problems.

The majority of suicidal adolescents have experienced an erosion of meaningful family and social ties and a pervasive sense of isolation and helplessness. Both those who consider suicide as well as those who actually attempt it have often experienced extreme parental anger, parental depression, and poor parent-child relationships.

But adolescent suicide can also occur in families that appear to be loving and caring—a fact which suggests that pressures other than overt family discord contribute to suicide attempts (Husain & Vandiver, 1984). A closer look suggests that, in some cases at least, parents who outwardly express such values as individuality, self-understanding, and need for egalitarianism actually are trying to avoid assuming parental responsibility. By setting up the family as a "pseudodemocracy," they leave their adolescent children without the kinds of support needed to deal with the complexities of their environment. Having too much responsibility and too many privileges, these adolescents may not know how to cope effectively with pressure. Having no one to talk to and obtain help from, the teen may decide on a course of action based on hopelessness and despair (Conger, 1985).

The Transition to Adulthood

The transition from childhood to adolescence is fairly well defined by the physical changes of puberty. Yet there is no clear-cut line to cross at the end of adolescence: No rites of passage exist in our society to mark the official beginning of adulthood. As we have no other obvious point at which we can declare that adolescents have assumed an adult identity, the end of formal education and/or the assumption of a job adequate for self-support is often considered the beginning of the adult years (Siegel, 1982).

■ Early and Middle Adulthood

As we have seen, the study of adolescence tends to focus on reactions to dramatic physical changes, identity formation, and autonomy and independence. During adulthood, the focus shifts somewhat to the framework that helps an individual navigate his or her life course and to a closer consideration of the way in which each person engages with society

(Levinson, 1986). Like adolescents, adults must respond to some physical changes. But adults must also set and achieve realistic goals, exercise considerable responsibility, think critically, form a personal philosophy of life, make maximal use of skills, and contribute to society. As we will see, adults typically perform these tasks within the context of work and marriage.

In their efforts to understand adult development, psychologists use three approaches to research, two of which (cross-sectional and longitudinal studies) were discussed in Chapter 9. The third method is the biographical approach. Of these various approaches, cross-sectional studies are the most popular, because data on a large number of people can be collected in a relatively short time. In contrast, a longitudinal study of the same people could take 50 years or more to complete! Cross-sectional studies, however, cannot distinguish age differences from cohort differences. The term **cohort** refers to the total population of individuals born during the same period of historical time. "Cohort differences," therefore, are differences between individuals who were born and grew up at different times. If in 1989 we conduct a cross-sectional study that compares 18-year-olds with 37-year-olds, we don't know whether the differences we find are due to the 20-year age difference or to the fact that the 37-year-olds grew up in the 1950s and 1960s while the 18-year-olds grew up in the 1970s and 1980s. Consider another example. A woman who is 60 years old in 1989 lived the first 20 years of her life during the Great Depression and World War II. By contrast, her son, who is only 35 years old in 1989, grew up in the relatively prosperous and less turbulent 1950s and 1960s. Any observable differences between mother and son may reflect differences in age, cohort differences, or both.

Longitudinal studies solve some of these problems, since the same people are observed over many years. But as we noted, a longitudinal study of adulthood would take decades to complete. Thus, some researchers have turned to a third way of studying adulthood: the **biographical approach.** With this approach, researchers try to reconstruct a person's past by interviewing the person and by consulting various other sources, much as a biographer does in writing a book-length account of someone's life. This method provides insight into the ways that a particular group of individuals develop over a span of many years, and yet the research can be completed in a fairly short period of time. The major disadvantage, of course, is that people's recollections of the past are not always accurate, and so biographical data are likely to be less precise and reliable than either longitudinal or cross-sectional data collected from the same people. Since each of these methods has different strengths and weaknesses, they are all used to study development during adulthood, and you will see examples of all of them in this chapter.

Levinson (1986) describes adult development as a stepwise progression through three eras, each of which is initiated by a major period of transition. The eras are early adulthood (17 to 45), middle adulthood (40 to 65), and late adulthood (60 and older). Levinson's view of the tasks that adults must master within each era appear in Table 10-3. The next section of this chapter is devoted to a discussion of the developmental tasks in early and middle adulthood. Then, in the closing pages of the chapter, we will examine development in late adulthood.

Cohort Total population of individuals born during the same period of historical time.

Biographical approach Method of research that tries to reconstruct an individual's past.

TABLE 10-3
LEVINSON'S MODEL OF THE DEVELOPMENTAL SEQUENCES IN A MAN'S LIFE

Stage	Task
Entering the adult world (22–28)	Resolution of the conflict between exploring available options & establishing a stable life structure — "I will keep my options open."
Age–30 ... transition (28—33)	Tentative commitments and life goals re-examined & questioned — "Did I make the right choices?"
Settling down & becoming one's own man (33–40)	Achieving stability, security & comfort — actively carving out niche in society — "I want to make my place in this world."
Mid-life transition (40–45)	Assessment of accomplishments & evolvement of another life structure — "What is it I really want ?"
Mid-life (45–50)	Accepting one's fate — "What I have achieved is OK."
Age–50 ... transition and mid-life culmination (50–60)	Finding security and self acceptance — "What I have become is OK."
Late adult transition (60 +)	Achieving a satisfactory life outlook — "My life has been OK and will continue to be OK."

Reaction to Physical Changes

Between the ages of 19 and 30, most people reach the peak of their physical condition. In the 20s, physical strength reaches its maximum, the cardiovascular system is strongest, vision is as sharp as it is ever likely to be, and psychomotor skills (running, gymnastics, skiing) are at their peak (Marshall, 1973).

But beginning in the early 30s and continuing into the 40s, adults undergo a gradual and inevitable decline in life processes (Hendricks & Hendricks, 1977). Typically, most of us are at first unaware of the decline, in part because the changes are small and in part because we develop strategies for minimizing their impact: We rest a bit more after participating in vigorous exercise, we hold our reading material a little closer to the light, and we work harder to keep ourselves in shape. But eventually, evidence of the decline is undeniable. Weight and blood pressure start to increase; speed, strength, and agility decrease; vision and hearing become less sharp; we react more slowly to stimuli. Wrinkles appear, gray hairs emerge, aches and pains are more common, and sleep comes less readily (LaRue & Jarvik, 1982; B.M. Newman, 1982).

There are several theories about why we age. The most obvious is that our bodies simply wear out (Timiras, 1972). Yet since many bodily systems are able to replace or repair their worn components (wounds heal, for example, and skin cells are constantly being generated), this version cannot be the whole story. A related theory is that as they undergo repeated divisions, more and more cells in our bodies contain genetic errors and do not function properly. Yet another theory holds that our body chemistry loses its delicate balance over the years (Timiras, 1978). For example, our excretory system, after years of filtering pollutants from our bloodstream, becomes less efficient, and the resulting change in our blood chemistry can produce a variety of other malfunctions. Finally,

Most people attain peak physical strength during their 20s but undergo an inevitable physical decline beginning in their 30s and continuing into their 40s.

according to another theory, our bodies tend with age to reject some of their own tissues (Beaubier, 1980).

Whatever the reason, the processes of aging go forward in everyone, although they do so at different rates in different people. Much depends, for example, on whether a person has a nutritious diet and gets regular exercise and whether skills are practiced. And these behaviors in turn depend a great deal on the ideas and thoughts that the individual has about the fact of aging. For example, we now know that lack of exercise is a primary reason for the physical decline that is often seen in the 40s and 50s; but we also know that if people believe that rapid aging is inevitable, they are likely to do very little to slow it down (B.M. Newman, 1982). Similarly, the widespread belief that memory fails as we age is not altogether true. Many memory tasks are performed equally well by old and young adults (Ronch, 1982).

THE CHANGE OF LIFE. One major physical change in middle age is the **climacteric,** or the decline in function of the reproductive organs. In women, the amount of estrogen, the principal female hormone produced by the body, drops sharply. Breasts, genital tissues, and the uterus begin to shrink slowly, and menstrual periods become less frequent before ceasing altogether. The cessation of menstruation is called **menopause.** These hormonal changes often cause a characteristic pattern of physical symptoms such as hot flashes, shortness of breath, and sometimes pain in the breasts or lower abdomen (B.M. Newman, 1982).

We saw earlier that onset of menstruation signals adolescent girls that they have crossed the threshold to womanhood. Does the arrival of menopause also result in changed self-perceptions? Menopause certainly signals to a woman that her reproductive years are over. Current evidence suggests that women who strongly identify with the role of mother and who are anxious about growing old and losing their physical attractiveness do indeed sometimes experience considerable psychological distress at menopause. The result may be depression, irritability, or anxiety. But most women find that menopause is not the difficult period that they had been led to expect, either physically or psychologically. For some, menopause signifies the beginning of a period during which energies can be directed toward new activities and new sources of personal fulfillment (B.M. Newman, 1982).

In middle-aged men, a gradual decline in the male hormone testosterone results in reduced production of sperm and seminal fluid. Erection occurs more slowly, ejaculation occurs with less force, and orgasm is shorter. Although these biological changes are less drastic and final than those that occur in women (for example, men can father children at virtually any age), they, too, signal the waning of the active reproductive years. Since the changes in men are less clearly observable, and since society puts less emphasis on men's attractiveness and reproductive role, the male climacteric usually produces few major psychological problems.

Social, Interpersonal, and Personality Development

Most young adults enter the world of work, marry, and have children all in the short span of less than 10 years. In this section of the chapter, we will examine how these major life events affect adult development and how they change during the course of adulthood.

CAREER CHOICE. The choice of job and career were not always important issues in early adulthood. Years ago, men followed in their fathers' footsteps or took whatever apprenticeships were available in their communities. Women stayed home and raised families. Today, the choices are far more numerous for both men and women. The number of women in the work force has increased dramatically in the last 50 years; today, 9 out of 10 women enter the labor force at least once during their lifetimes. Over 50 percent of married women work during their child-rearing years, and a third of those working have children under the age of six (Havinghurst, 1982). Consequently, the need to make decisions about jobs and careers has become an important part of young adulthood for both men and women.

How does one choose a career? Prior to 1950, it was assumed that at a given point in time, an individual simply assessed his or her personal abilities, surveyed the employment opportunities available, and selected the job that offered the greatest chances for satisfaction and success. However, during the 1950s, alternative theories began to appear that were more concerned with *why* and *how* people choose one career over another. Two common threads running through all these theories are the premise that personality is at least as important as ability in selecting a career and that career choice goes on over a considerable period of time rather than in just a few years at the end of adolescence and the beginning of young adulthood. Ginsberg (1972), for example, proposed that vocational choice occurs in three stages. During the **fantasy period** (before adolescence), children try out various occupational roles as they play. During adolescence they enter the **tentative choice period,** during which

Today, 9 out of 10 women will enter the labor force at least once in their lives, and while women still do not enjoy the same professional opportunities as men, many previously male-dominated professions are being opened to them.

they begin to match their interests, abilities, and values with various career opportunities. In late adolescence and young adulthood, they enter the **realistic choice period.** The realistic period involves active exploration of various kinds of work, a further narrowing of alternatives, and finally a more or less permanent commitment to one or another career.

During the process of occupational choice, personality, interests, values, and abilities all play a role. But other factors also enter into the deliberations. For example, sons show a strong tendency to choose an occupation similar to their fathers' (Mortimer, Lorence, & Kumka, 1986). When the father's job is viewed as prestigious and the son is close to his father, this tendency is even greater. For girls, career choice is often influenced by their mothers' career choices. Daughters of employed mothers more often aspire to a career outside the home and more often choose a traditionally masculine occupation. In addition, fathers having high occupational status more often promote such achievement in their daughters; this is especially true for oldest daughters and in families with no sons (Bronfenbrenner, 1986; Vondracek & Lerner, 1982).

While initial career choices are made during late adolescence and early adulthood, for many people the process of occupational choice goes on throughout life as interests change, new abilities are discovered, and new job opportunities become available. For example, there are more adult college students today than there are college students in the 18–22 age bracket (Datan, Rodeheaver, & Hughes, 1987). Many of these adult learners have reached middle age and have developed concerns for people beyond their immediate families, for future generations, and for the nature of the world in which those generations will live. Many middle-aged persons also devote a great deal of time and energy to activities such as professional associations, civic organizations, unions, and youth leadership, and these activities in turn may awaken interests in new and different careers.

Still other people may have achieved many of their goals or see no chance to achieve them, and they may experience boredom, fatigue, and a feeling of being trapped by unchangeable routines. Some observers speak of this period as a "mid-life crisis"—a time when success in one area of life leaves the individual feeling unfulfilled and ready for a decisive shift in career or life-style. Data suggest, however, that most individuals go through much less dramatic conceptualizations of self, time, and purpose and make renewed commitments to marriage, work, and family (B.M. Newman, 1982). Levinson calls this process the **mid-life transition,** a period when the adult assesses his or her accomplishments, determines whether they have been satisfying, formulates new goals, and evolves yet another life structure to guide behavior into the future (see Table 10-4).

THE EFFECTS OF WORK. Once a career has been chosen, what effect does working have on adults? Studies of job satisfaction indicate that the vast majority of workers, in virtually all occupations, are moderately or highly satisfied with their jobs and would continue to work even if they didn't have to do so because work gives meaning to their lives. This meaning varies, of course, as jobs vary. For some adults, jobs are a way of passing time or of obtaining economic independence. For others, the job is a source of self-respect or respect from others and provides a life purpose. And people in all occupational groups say that they value

Realistic choice period Ginsberg's third stage of vocational choice, during which young adults actively explore various kinds of work and make a commitment to a career.

Mid-life transition According to Levinson, process whereby adults assess the past and formulate new goals for the future.

Women report fewer opportunities to leave unsatisfactory jobs or to receive promotions—two ways by which men reduce work-related stress.

TABLE 10-4 HYPOTHESIZED RELATIONSHIP BETWEEN SELECTED CHARACTERISTICS AND OUTCOMES OF YOUNG MARRIAGES — FORECAST OF MARITAL COMPETENCE AND SATISFACTION

Characteristic	Poorest	Intermediate	Best
Ages at marriage	Both seventeen or younger	Female seventeen, male twenty or older	Female at least eighteen, male twenty or older
Educational attainment	Both school dropouts	Female dropout, male high school graduate	Both high school graduates; male, at least, with some post-high school education
Pregnancy	Premarital pregnancy	No premarital pregnancy; pregnancy immediately following marriage	Pregnancy delayed until at least one year following marriage
Acquaintance before marriage	Less than six months; no engagement period, formal or informal	One year, at least, with at least six months understanding or engagement to marry	Several years, with at least six months understanding or engagement to marry
Previous dating patterns	Limited number of dating partners; went steady immediately, or short period between first date and first date with fiancé	Some dating experience before dating fiancé	Numerous dates, played the field; some previous experience with going steady
Personality dynamics	Generally poor interpersonal skills; lacking maturity; limited interests; poor personal and social adjustment	Mixed	Generally competent in interpersonal relations; flexible, mature; maintaining healthy and pleasurable relations with others
Motivation for marrying	Drifted into marriage; because of pregnancy; seemed like the thing to do; just wanted to; other impulsive reasons with no strong emphasis on marital and parental roles	Mixed; marriage preferred to career, though had previous post-high school educational aspirations and, for females, perhaps tentative plans to work, etc.	No post-high school educational aspirations; and, for females, marriage, family, and homemaking preferred over working, living independently; positive emphasis upon role as wife and mother
Status of families	Both lower class	Mixed; lower and middle or upper class	Both middle or upper class
Parental attitudes before marriage	Strongly opposed	Mildly opposed or resigned acceptance	Supportive, once the decision was clear
Wedding	Elopement and civil ceremony		Conventional, hometown, church-sanctioned
Economic basis	Virtually completely dependent on relatives	Low dependence on relatives; mostly independent income, even if near hardship level	At least assured income above self-perceived hardship level
Residence	Always lived with in-laws or other relatives	Doubled up with relatives some of the time, independent other times	Always maintained own independent place of residence
Postmarriage parental views	Rejecting or punitive, assistance provided as a method of controlling the marriage	Cool	Psychologically supportive, sincerely want to help, assistance provided with no strings attached

Table 10-4

Burchinal, 1965. Copyright 1965 by The National Council on Family Relations.

the peer group relationships that they experience as a result of work. Moreover, increases in job status during adulthood contribute to feelings of self-esteem. For these and other reasons, it comes as no surprise that men and single women who are employed are healthier than those who are unemployed.

However, the picture is not universally bright, especially for women. Many jobs available to women are less satisfying than home management.

Women also may experience sex discrimination on the job and feel undervalued. Women report fewer opportunities to leave unsatisfactory jobs or to receive promotions—two ways by which men reduce work-related stress (Aranya, Kushnir, & Valency, 1986). Even in professionally challenging jobs, career advancement for women involves considerable risk-taking, assertiveness, initiative in creating opportunities, and persistence (Sodano & Baleris, 1983). Yet, despite these problems, most women report increases in self-esteem when they are employed, especially when they experience emotional support from their husbands and children (Baruch & Barnett, 1986; Rudd & McKenry, 1986).

MARRIAGE. We saw earlier that more than 90 percent of Americans will marry at some point in their lifetimes (Doherty & Jacobson, 1982). In our society, the usual prelude to marriage is the selection of a mate. Most Americans view love as the overriding factor in this selection; yet research indicates that most people are likely to marry someone of similar race, religion, education, and background. There are probably many reasons for this phenomenon, including the fact that people from the same social background tend to come into contact more frequently and to discover shared interests and compatibilities.

There is considerable evidence that marriage is an important determinant of overall life satisfaction: Married people report the highest levels of happiness, followed by the widowed, the separated-divorced, and the never-married or single (Campbell, 1976). Marital satisfaction, however, varies during the marriage and affects men and women in different ways: Husbands report most dissatisfaction during the years before retirement; wives report most dissatisfaction during the parental years (Rollins & Feldman, 1970).

A host of factors contributes to marital satisfaction, most notably the ability to resolve rather than avoid conflicts (suggesting that arguments are not necessarily harmful), empathic skill, communication skill, egalitarian attitudes, mutual problem-solving, openness, competence, strong affectional bonds, quality and quantity of shared time, and financial security (Argyle & Furnham, 1983; Lewis & Spanier, 1979; Rettig & Bubolz, 1983). Marital timing is also important to marital success and satisfaction. Both teenage and late marriages are less stable. Young people are likely to be immature and to lack preparation, and older people have fewer opportunities to find mates with similar life-styles (Bitter, 1986).

Nevertheless, many marriages endure in the face of declines in satisfaction, commitment, expression of love, romantic feelings, and friendship (Belsky, Lang, & Roving, 1985; Swensen & Trahaug, 1985). Many couples remain married because the commitment is to the institution of marriage and not to the particular individual. Others simply prefer to avoid major life changes. Still others prefer "the security of misery to the misery of insecurity."

SEXUAL BEHAVIOR. Sexual behavior also changes during the adult years when, for most people, sexual behavior becomes intertwined with a special relationship with a permanent partner. More than 90 percent of Americans eventually marry, and more than half of all married adults report having no sexual activity outside of marriage (Thompson, 1984). Surveys reveal that one-third of married couples rate their sex

Marriage is an important factor in overall life satisfaction, but teenage marriages are not typically stable. Generally speaking, the younger a couple marries, the more likely they are to divorce.

lives as very good, another third as good, and the remaining third poor to very poor (Broderick, 1982). The majority of adult women (about 60 percent) report that they have orgasms during intercourse most, if not all, of the time, although most studies find that, on average, the husband's interest in sexual intimacy is greater than the wife's at every age surveyed (Broderick, 1982).

However, frequency of sexual intercourse and other physical expressions of affection between married couples tend to decline over the years (Masters & Johnson, 1970), even though most couples remain interested in sex and continue to have sexual intercourse several times a month, on average (Broderick, 1982). Although aging may produce bodily changes that require some adjustment in technique or timing, a healthy person is able to continue sexual activity into advanced age. And contrary to popular belief, the physiological changes of menopause have no effect on a woman's level of sexual interest (Comfort, 1976). To the extent that some older couples do become sexually inactive, the reason is most often their belief that sexuality after a certain age is no longer expected or "nice" or the absence of a partner because of ill health or death.

PARENTHOOD. The arrival of children signals a major turning point in most adults' lives. Raising a family can be a source of immense satisfaction. As children grow, their parents can experience a sense of achievement and pride. And for most adults, loving (and being loved by) one's children is an unparalleled source of fulfillment. Caring for, nurturing, and guiding one's children is a unique experience that can give added meaning and sense of purpose to one's life.

However, with the birth of the first child, many adjustments have to be made in a marriage. "Husband" and "wife" become "father" and "mother"; "couple" becomes "family." Friendship and romance give way to a working relationship that requires the willingness to regulate cycles of work, procreation, and recreation. Young children demand considerable time, attention, and energy, and these demands may leave husband and wife with little time to be alone with each other. Inexperienced parents may be terrified of responsibility, plagued by inadequacy, and stricken by guilt over mixed emotions about the baby. The husband may feel "left out" (Lamb, 1976) while the wife may resent her husband's freedom from child care.

On top of these stresses, conflicts may arise between the parents' pursuit of careers and their responsibilities at home. This can be a real crisis, for the woman especially. If she has been involved in a career, she may suddenly have conflicting values: She may feel frustrated if she abandons her career and anxious or guilty if she continues to work. For women, this conflict between employment and domestic work is added on top of normal worries about being an adequate wife and mother (Warr & Perry, 1982). Thus, it should come as no surprise that women feel the need for cooperation more strongly during this period of life than do men (Belsky, Lang, & Roving, 1985). And while fathers today do tend to spend more time with their children, nevertheless mothers continue to bear the greatest responsibility for housework and child rearing. Consequently, mothers report more marital dissatisfaction during the child-rearing years than at any other time.

When the "couple" becomes a "family," major adjustments must be made, but while parenthood can be a major source of stress and conflict, it is a source of immense satisfaction for most adults.

Once children leave the home, many parents find renewed marital satisfaction. In fact, married couples with "empty nests" are often among the happiest (Campbell, 1975; Miller, 1976; Rollins & Feldman, 1970). For the first time in years, they can be alone together and enjoy one another's company. In a study of older couples, more than 50 percent said that their marriage had improved with time; and most of those polled felt that the later years of their marriage were the best (Stinnett, Carter, & Montgomery, 1972).

DO PERSONALITY CHARACTERISTICS CHANGE IN ADULTHOOD? We have seen that various major life events in adulthood require considerable change and adaptation. Do they also lead to significant changes in personality? Actually, relatively few studies have systematically examined the effects of specific life events on adult personality development. Data suggest that with increasing age, both sexes display less self-centeredness and better coping skills (Neugarten, 1977). Those whose occupations require self-direction also reveal changes in intellectual flexibility (Kahn & Shooler, 1983). One longitudinal study found that 45-year-olds are more sympathetic, giving, productive, and dependable than they were at age 20 (Block, 1971). And another study reported that the middle years of life bring about increasing commitment and responsibility for others, development of new and more mature ways of adapting, and greater interpersonal comfort (Vaillant, 1977). Orderly changes in adaptive strategies and moral growth in adult life also occur (Gould, 1972, 1978; Hauser, 1976; Kohlberg, 1976; Levinson, 1978, 1986, 1987). Yet still other research employing personality tests suggests either that personality does not change greatly during the adult years (McCrae & Costa, 1984) or that changes occur in only some personality characteristics (Hann, Millsap, & Hartke, 1986).

Cognitive Development

In Chapter 9, we noted that Piaget's model of cognitive development stops with the acquisition of formal operations in adolescence. Piaget (1967) hinted that there might be further changes in styles of thinking during adulthood, but only recently have a number of investigators begun to explore the ways in which an adult's thinking may differ from that of an adolescent.

Earlier in this chapter, we saw that the development of the ability to think in abstractions allows adolescents to operate in a world of possibility, thus contributing to their increased flexibility. The tasks of adulthood, however, involve making commitments. Careers must be started, bonds of intimacy formed, and children raised. From a multitude of possible alternatives, adults must restrict their courses of action. The ability to make choices and commitments is one mark of cognitive maturity.

In many other respects as well, adult thinking differs appreciably from that of adolescents. The acquisition of knowledge is often less important in adulthood than knowing how to apply knowledge to the solution of social problems. Many adults are also better at identifying new problems rather than simply solving problems posed by others. In professions such as architecture, writing, and the sciences, the height of creative invention and the ability to forge powerful intellectual syntheses often are not realized until mid-life (Perlmutter & Hall, 1985). Some investigators feel that becoming aware of the genuine complexity of our social system is another hallmark of adult thinking. Moreover, mature adults see many problems as open-ended and ambiguous with no single "correct" solution, and they realize that the best approach to such problems is likely to be an effort to reduce ambiguity (Labouvie-Vief, 1986).

It has been suggested that these changes in adult thinking occur as a result of experience with the kinds of complex problems that arise in adult life. Thinking within social contexts requires movement away from the literal, formal, and somewhat rigid thinking of young adulthood (Labouvie-Vief, 1986). Executive thinking, for example, involves goal-setting, self-regulation, and self-actualization; it also involves give-and-take, participation with others in planning, and anticipating what others will think. Of necessity, adults come to recognize the limitations of pure reasoning for solving problems that need to be viewed from many different perspectives, and so formal reasoning gives way to complex social reasoning (Zabrucky, Moore, & Schultz, 1987).

Adult Reactions to Situational Stress

Earlier in the chapter, we looked briefly at several important sources of stress during adulthood. In this section, we will look more closely at the ways in which adults react to one particular source of situational stress: divorce.

Half of those married today will eventually divorce, yet mutually shared decisions to divorce are uncommon. More often, one partner takes the initiative in ending the relationship after a long period of slowly growing dissatisfaction and emptiness. Once the decision is made, however, the result is almost always a dramatic increase in turmoil, indecision, and apprehension.

For most people, being told they are no longer loved or wanted is an extraordinarily stressful experience. Feelings of humiliation and utter powerlessness can be overwhelming. The common response to this shattered self-esteem is anger and depression. Moreover, despite numerous arguments and threats of divorce, many spouses are completely unprepared for their partner's decision; surprise and shock are common. The shock of rejection, feelings of helplessness, and a sense of dependence on another person for survival—all of these join to cause severe disequilibrium and disorganization as well as uncontrolled and unpredictable behavior (Kelly, 1982).

For a time at least, the stress of the separation may be more traumatic than the stress of the unsatisfactory marriage. The bitter conflict of the divorce, the many changes, the new learning required by a shift to single status, the struggle for a new identity, and the temporary economic hardship all contribute to a high level of stress. However, in spite of the trauma, most men and women develop and change in gratifying ways in the aftermath of divorce. Divorced adults often report that the divorce was a positive step that eventually resulted in greater personal contentment and healthier psychological functioning, although a substantial minority seem permanently affected by the divorce (Kelly, 1982).

A full early life predicts a full late life, and hence the later years result in accentuation of early and middle-life characteristics rather than an alteration of them.

Later Adulthood

The almost 26 million Americans over 65 constitute the group typically identified as "the aged." This group currently represents over 11 percent of the population, but estimates are that about one out of every five Americans—an estimated 50 million people—will be over 65 by the year 2030 (see Table 10-5). The increase is due mainly to new medical discoveries and improved health care. In 1900, the average life expectancy was 47 years, and only 4 percent of the population was 65 and older. By 1979, the average life expectancy had increased to 73 years. More and more people have and will continue to have an opportunity to live longer lives (see Table 10-6).

Because of the increased number of older adults in our society, increased attention has been drawn to their needs. The political strength of older persons is growing: Almost 90 percent of older adults are registered to vote, and two-thirds vote regularly (a greater percentage than in any other age group), and older people are organizing themselves for political action and influence (Butler & Lewis, 1982). As a result of advocacy efforts, the first White House Conference on Aging was held in 1981, followed by the United Nations World Assembly on Aging on 1982. Predating these major events and contributing to their occurrence was the addition of the National Institute on Aging to the existing 10 National Institutes of Health, as well as the founding of the American Association for Geriatric Psychiatry in 1978. Many colleges and universities have also introduced courses pertaining to later adulthood into their curricula, and some 300 institutions of higher education now offer at least one course in gerontology.

As a result of these developments, knowledge about the aging process and the challenges of late adulthood has increased rapidly. And all the research points in one direction: Late adulthood is welcomed by those who learn to manage and use it to the fullest. Andrés Segovia gave acclaimed concerts on the classical guitar until his death in 1987 at the age of 93; Bob Hope continues to entertain and golf his way around the world in his 80s; the late Claude Pepper served in Congress for 41 years until his death at the age of 88; Agatha Christie wrote mysteries after age 85; statesman Konrad Adenauer and cellist Pablo Casals are other well-known examples of those remaining active and making major contributions after age 85.

These famous people simply illustrate the more general point that most older people remain active and productive when they are free from disease and serious economic hardship. Many carry on those activities that they enjoyed in their younger years, suggesting that a full early life predicts a full late life (McGuire & Dottario, 1987). The later years result in accentuation of early and middle-life characteristics rather than alteration of them. Nonetheless, just as change and development characterize the early years of life, the later years also require that the individual grow, develop, and change. Physical abilities are somewhat diminished, but the capacity to control the environment still exists. Loved ones have been lost, but the need to love still exists. Dependence on others has increased, but independence is still valued. The task, then, is to clarify,

TABLE 10-5
THE AGING OF THE POPULATION: PERCENTAGE OF THE POPULATION 65 YEARS AND OVER.

Year	Total
1950	8.1%
1960	9.2
1970	9.8
1980	11.3
Projected	
1990	12.3
2000	12.2
2010	12.7
2020	15.6
2030	18.3

Table 10-5
Historical figures from the *Statistical Abstract of the United States*, 1981; projected figures from Allan & Brotman, 1981

Table 10-6
Statistical Abstract of the United States, 1981; National Center for Health Statistics, 1984

TABLE 10-6
THE INCREASE IN THE AVERAGE LIFE EXPECTANCY IN THE UNITED STATES.

Year	Life expectancy Male	Female
1920	53.6	54.6
1930	58.1	61.6
1940	60.8	65.2
1950	65.6	71.1
1960	66.6	73.1
1970	67.1	74.8
1979	69.9	77.8
1982	70.9	78.2

deepen, and accept one's own life and to use one's experiences to manage personal change (Schell & Hall, 1979).

Reactions to Physical Changes

During later adulthood, the hair grays or turns white and becomes sparse. The skin becomes increasingly wrinkled. Chests are no longer as full or as broad. Bones become spongy and fragile and more easily broken. Muscles can atrophy and joints can stiffen. The heart does not react as quickly during exercise or exposure to stress, and once stimulated it takes longer to return to normal rates of beating. Circulation slows, blood pressure rises, and because the lungs hold less oxygen, the older adult has less energy for activity and fewer reserves to deal with stress. Vision, hearing, touch, taste, and smell are all less sensitive than they once were (LaRue & Jarvik, 1982).

These physical changes are inevitable during later adulthood, but none of them is crippling or incapacitating. While they call for some adjustment and change in life-style, it is quite possible to lead an active and full life despite the changes. This fact brings us to a very important point: The most important fact is not *what* biological changes occur in later life, but rather how the individual *responds* to those changes. We all know people who "look older than their years" and others who are "young at heart." And there's a good deal of truth in the saying "You're

■ The Myths of Aging

People over 65 constitute the fastest-growing segment of the U.S. population. If you are like most people, you probably assume that the majority of older adults are lonely, poor, and troubled by ill health. This view is not only inaccurate, but also causes many problems for older people. As Eisdorfer (1983) notes: "Our beliefs, based in fiction and nonfiction alike, have relegated the aged to a nonproductive, impaired, incapable, and useless status with the loss of virtually everything that contributes to the personal capacity, performance, roles, and status of individuals in the world" (p. 198). For example, doctors and other health professionals sometimes assume that it is "natural" for elderly patients to be ill. Symptoms that would indicate treatable disease in younger people are taken simply as signs that "Martha just isn't what she used to be." Numerous psychological problems, such as depression, can be wrongly blamed on a fictitious process of mental decline that is expected to begin in old age.

In this chapter, we have seen that one myth about aging is the belief that senility is widespread and inevitable. Other false notions about old people are that they are helpless and dependent on their families for care and financial support.

This is true of a small minority of the aged—mostly the very old. The majority of people over 65 live independently and maintain an acceptable style of life—they are not living in heatless tenements worrying about how to make it to the store to buy their next loaf of bread.

In 1975, the National Council on the Aging reported the results of a survey of the elderly. More than half the people questioned reported that they were just as happy as they were when younger. Three-quarters thought that they were involved in activities that were as interesting as ever (Birren, 1983).

All this is not to deny that for a significant minority of older adults, advancing age *does* present problems. For the poor, and especially for minorities, late adulthood may be bleak. A lifetime of poor health care may culminate in serious illness, and lack of money may have made putting aside any assets for old age impossible. (And most jobs held by poor working people do not provide pensions or other retirement benefits.) These people face the same conditions in late adulthood that they did earlier in life: poor housing, lack of opportunity, lack of resources. With advancing age, these problems are even more burdensome.

only as old as you feel." These observations underscore the fact that chronological age is not a very good indicator of aging.

Research supports these impressions, and psychologists are now beginning to use functional, adaptational, or psychological age as a better predictor of a person's response to life's demands. For example, as we noted earlier, proper exercise—even into the 80s and beyond—significantly slows down the deterioration of bodily functions. Proper exercise also seems to improve mental functioning. Even rapid walking for a 30-minute period three to four times a week can provide considerable rejuvenation. With proper exercise, men and women of 60 and 70 can become as fit and energetic as those 20 to 30 years younger (deVries, 1986).

Although exercise can forestall some of the physical changes that occur in later life, it is also important for older adults to learn effective ways to conserve strength and use resources more effectively. Body monitoring, or the need to look after those bodily processes that formerly took care of themselves, demands more time. For example, significant hearing loss occurs in about 30 percent of older people. Because they are unable to hear conversations, some older adults may withdraw from situations where communication takes place in order to avoid embarrassment from frequent misunderstandings. They may even become depressed, as if it were somehow their own fault for not hearing well (Hull, 1982). In contrast, other people will closely monitor their ability to hear, seek devices that will at least partially offset the hearing loss, pay closer attention to lip movements, and encourage others to sit closer to them and to speak a bit louder so that they can understand what is being said. Visual problems restrict mobility and leisure time activity and increase feelings of vulnerability to danger and crime. But here, too, there are great individual differences in ability to adapt. Some people will become frustrated at the loss of some visual ability and resign themselves to a less-fulfilling life. Others will avail themselves of all available technology, make some appropriate adjustments in their lives, and go on living a full and satisfying life.

You may be wondering if this isn't perhaps a too optimistic picture of adaptation during later adulthood. "What happens when people become senile?" you might ask. First of all, **senility** is by no means a natural or inevitable result of aging. Very few people actually become senile. Second, senility is brought on by disease, not the simple passage of time (Reisberg, 1983). Two-thirds of all cases of senility, for example, are caused by Alzheimer's disease, an organic brain disorder. Senility is thus no more "natural" than a brain tumor or any other disease affecting the nervous system. Third, many behaviors that we may be quick to label as signs of senility are actually the results of older people's exclusion from an active role in society as well as a consequence of taking large numbers of drugs and experiencing higher levels of depression. If they seem unable to comprehend current events, for example, it is usually because they have given up reading the newspaper—since they have no one to discuss the news with or feel that their opinions don't matter to anyone anymore.

The point to be remembered is that there is naturally some physical decline in later adulthood, and even in the best of worlds, there will continue to be some decline. But what is often attributed to "aging" is in many cases really a result of disease or of being rendered "useless" by

Senility Mental and physical deterioration brought on by disease that occurs in some older adults.

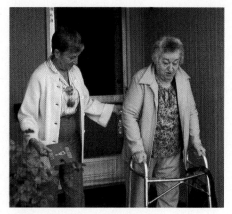

Older adults often experience reduced mobility and must depend on others for assistance in getting around. Adjustments in attitude and life-style may be required, but physical decline need not necessarily be incapacitating.

Proper exercise can keep men and women over 60 as fit and energetic as those twenty to thirty years younger.

a society that emphasizes youth and vigor. To the extent that diseases such as Alzheimer's can be brought under control, to the extent that adults are careful to exercise and eat proper foods, and to the extent that attitudes toward the aged become more positive, the research evidence suggests that for the vast majority of people, the physical decline in later adulthood can be both slow and gentle, requiring only modest adjustments and changes in life-style

Social, Interpersonal, and Personality Development

SEXUAL BEHAVIOR. Another misconception about the aged is that they are not sexual. In large part, this misconception reflects our attitudes about the elderly. To the extent that we see the aged as physically less attractive, we may find it difficult to believe that they (or, worse yet, our parents) are sexually active (Ronch, 1982). And it is true that older people respond more slowly and are less active sexually, but the vast majority of older adults are orgasmic and can enjoy sex. Seventy percent of 70-year-old males are sexually active if they are married (Clanan, 1966), and some men and women become even more sexually active as they age (Pfeiffer, 1977).

Nonetheless, several factors work against sexual satisfaction in old age. First, some older adults accept the myth that they should be disinterested in sex, and as a result they attempt to deny their sexual urges in order to avoid disapproval. Second, older women, most of whom are widows, have no available partners and so tend to lose some interest in sex. Poor health is another factor that may curb sexual activity. And finally, there are cohort differences to consider: Today's older adults grew up in the early part of this century, when attitudes toward sexual behavior were quite different from what they are today. Thus, their sexual attitudes and behaviors are likely to reflect that generational difference at least as much as they reflect the normal process of growing older.

SOCIAL RELATIONSHIPS. The phenomenon of aging takes place in a social context. While social and personal constraints during the later years may limit or alter social behavior, the later years present many new opportunities and gratifying social experiences for the elderly (Kahana, 1982). Social behavior in the later years, just as in youth, is influenced by two important factors: the personal characteristics of the individual and the social network and supports available.

Four-fifths of those over 65 have living children; among this group, 94 percent are grandparents. Grandparenting can often be more rewarding than parenting. Relieved from the major responsibility of child care and its accompanying doubts and anxieties, grandparents may actually enjoy their grandchildren more than they did their own children. Grandparents provide a useful function in society, giving love and guidance to children without asking much in return. Wisdom is imparted to youth—a process which benefits both the giver and the receiver. Many human beings feel a need to leave something behind when they die. Many also feel the need to share the knowledge that they have gained over their years and to counsel or guide younger persons—a process often referred to as "eldering." Grandparenting provides one way to meet these needs and to remain connected with younger generations.

In addition, friendships are especially important in late adulthood (Baldassare, Rosenfield, & Rook, 1984; Larson, Mannell, & Zuzank, 1986). While relationships with family members often come to emphasize dependency and caretaking functions, friends provide enjoyment and companionship characterized by openness and reciprocity. Having a confidante is especially important. Those whose self worth is bolstered by others take better care of themselves and have better health (Cutrona, Russell, & Rose, 1986). Consequently, they can face the normal challenges of late adulthood with less disruption.

RETIREMENT. Ultimately, of course, everyone must face the prospect of retirement. But people's reactions to retirement differ greatly, in part because the role of the retiree is, at best, ambiguous. Are retirees supposed to sit on the porch and watch life go by, or should they join civic groups, play golf, and be foster grandparents? Since there are few clear expectations about what retirees should do, there is a great deal of latitude for individuals to structure retirement as they please.

Money certainly has an effect on people's attitudes toward retirement and on their behavior during retirement. If retirement means a major loss of financial freedom, a person will be less eager to retire and will be more constrained in what he or she can do during the retirement years.

But more than money is involved. People's attitudes toward retirement are tied to their attitudes toward work. People who are fulfilled by their jobs are often less interested in retiring than those whose jobs are unrewarding (Atchley, 1976). Blue-collar workers, for example, often look forward to retirement; professionals more often do not. Other factors, such as education and age, are also important. Highly educated men are less interested in retiring than uneducated ones, although well-educated women tend to leave the work force earlier than their less-educated counterparts.

Table 10-7
U.S. Bureau of the Census, 1980

TABLE 10-7 DEMOGRAPHIC CHARACTERISTICS OF PEOPLE OVER 65 YEARS OLD	Male	Female
Population (in millions)	9.8	14.0
Marital status (in % of people over 65)		
Single	5.1	5.9
Married	77.6	39.7
Widowed	13.6	51.0
Divorced	3.7	3.4
Employment status (in % of people over 65)		
Employed	18.6	7.9
Unemployed	.5	.3
Not in labor force	80.9	91.8
Living arrangements (in % of people over 65)		
Living in household alone	14.7	40.9
Living in household with spouse	75.5	38.0
Living in household with someone else	9.7	20.8
Not in household	.1	.3

The death of one's spouse may be the most severe challenge to be faced during adulthood. Because they are not accustomed to taking care of themselves, men tend to suffer more from spousal loss, but there are many more widows

WIDOWHOOD. The death of one's spouse may be the most severe challenge to be faced during adulthood. Both men and women respond to such loss with initial disbelief. Numbness follows. Only later is the full effect of the loss felt, and its impact can be severe. For example, a long-term study of several thousand widowers 55 years of age and older revealed that nearly 5 percent of them died in the first six months following their spouse's death, a figure that is well above the expected death rate for married men of the same age. Thereafter, the mortality rate fell gradually to a more normal level (Butler & Lewis, 1982).

Adjusting to the loss of a spouse can take a very long time, although the amount of time required can be somewhat reduced if the individual has at least one close friend who can provide nurturance and support during the adjustment period (Lowenthal & Haven, 1968). Support from a loving family and time to prepare for the death in advance are also important factors in easing the transition.

Because they are not used to taking care of themselves, men are said to suffer more from spousal loss. But because there are many more widows than widowers, men are also much more likely to remarry. More than half the women over 65 are widowed, and half of them will live another 15 years without remarrying. Thus, for somewhat different reasons, the burden of widowhood falls heavily on both men and women (Feinson, 1986).

Cognitive Development

For a number of years, comparisons of the intellectual performance of younger and older adults suggested that cognitive functioning declined in later adulthood (Datan, Rodeheaver, & Hughes, 1987). However, more recent research indicates that those whose behavior and attitudes remain flexible, who are involved in a broad spectrum of intellectually stimulating activities, and who practice their problem-solving skills can maintain a high level of functioning in old age (Denney, 1982; Schaie, 1984). Memory, comprehension, and even some fine motor skills can remain well-developed. Although performance on artificial laboratory problem-solving tasks does tend to decline during adulthood, the ability to solve practical, real-life problems actually increases. In addition, specialized training can greatly reduce the decline in cognitive performance in later adulthood (Willis, 1985; Willis & Schaie, 1986).

The elderly also are more skilled at solving problems that require an appreciation of the social context in which the problem occurs. For example, one study of 150 members of the 1971–74 Vermont legislature reported that younger legislators produced twice as many bills as older ones, but the likelihood of an older legislator's bill being passed was twice that of a younger legislator's bill. On closer examination, the researcher discovered that the younger politicians worked on a trial-and-error basis, proposing many bills in hopes that at least a few would survive. In contrast, the older politicians displayed greater caution and deliberation and tended to produce bills that reflected a more mature grasp of the problems being addressed (Fengler, 1976).

In later adulthood there is also often an increase in introspection and consequent reorganization of value systems. These changes can lead to renewed interest in philosophical and religious pursuits. In Japan, many old men turn to writing poetry (Butler & Lewis, 1983). Perhaps these changes also account in part for the extraordinary creative achievements late in life by Leonardo da Vinci, Titian, Rembrandt, Rodin, Grandma Moses, Cervantes, Voltaire, Goethe, Tolstoi, and Picasso—all of whom continued to be extraordinarily productive in later life.

Reactions to Situational Stress

As we have seen, later adulthood is inevitably a stressful period of life (Ronch, 1982). Parents, siblings, and spouses die, friends die or move away, retirement occurs, income is reduced, and the body begins slowly to decline. In the face of these changes, older adults must accomplish "unique developmental work" (Butler & Lewis, 1982).

How one handles the stresses of old age depends on an intricate balance of physical, social, and emotional factors. An older person who is lonely may eat poorly and become malnourished—a condition that, in turn, can cloud mental functioning. Depression, particularly following the loss of a spouse, may lead to a decline in health or to increased consumption of alcohol, both of which make further coping more difficult. In contrast, individuals who have a continuing sense of usefulness, who are self-starters, and who can initiate and structure new contacts, who maintain old or initiate new activities, and who feel control over their lives have the lowest rates of disease and the highest survival rates (Butler & Lewis, 1982; Caspi & Elder, 1986; Liberman & Tobin, 1983; Rodon, 1980).

These and other findings suggest that one's life history determines to a great extent whether the stresses of old age are approached with a sense of fulfillment and gratitude or with feelings of bitterness and missed opportunity. The mental health that the individual brings to later adulthood most often determines how effectively these pressures will be handled (Cutrona, Russell, & Rose, 1986).

Coping with the Prospect of Death

Fear of death is seldom a central concern for people in later adulthood. In fact, research data suggest that it is a greater problem in young adulthood or in middle age, when the first awareness of mortality coincides with a greater interest in living (Kimmel, 1974). For example, a study undertaken to compare attitudes toward death and dying among young adults and people over age 65 found that 19 percent of the young adults were afraid of death, compared with only 1.7 percent of the older adults (Rogers, 1980). The elderly person, while aware of the imminence of death, is more often concerned with taking stock of past accomplishments. Butler (1963) asserts that such a life review is virtually universal among those in later adulthood. This is not to suggest that the elderly brood about the past. Rather, life review occurs alongside concerns with the present.

The elderly do have two major fears associated with dying. They fear the pain, indignity, loneliness, and depersonalization that they may experience during dying, as well as the possibility of dying alone. They

Elisabeth Kübler-Ross and the American Way of Dying

Psychiatrist Elisabeth Kübler-Ross (1969) interviewed more than 200 dying people of all ages to try to understand the different aspects of the dying process. From these interviews, she isolated five sequential stages through which people pass as they react to their own impending deaths:

Denial: The individual denies the prognosis, refuses to believe that it is his or her death that is approaching, insists that an error has been made, and seeks more acceptable diagnoses.

Anger: Accepting the accuracy of the diagnosis and the reality of the situation, the individual expresses resentment toward and envy of those whose plans and dreams may yet be fulfilled; the patience and understanding of other people is particularly important at this stage.

Bargaining: The individual desperately tries to buy time, negotiating with doctors, family members, clergy, and God in what seems to be a healthy attempt to cope with the reality and realization of death.

Depression: As the efforts to bargain fail and time begins running out, the individual succumbs to depression, contemplating and lamenting failures and losses than can no longer be redressed.

Acceptance: Typically tired, weak, and unemotional, the individual enters a state of "quiet expectation," submitting to his or her fate.

According to Kübler-Ross (1969), the central problem that Americans have in coping with death is that we fear and deny it. Because we do not believe that we could possibly die of natural causes, we associate death with "a bad act, a frightening happening" (p. 2). She observes that while some other cultures are *death affirming*, American culture is *death denying*. "We are reluctant to reveal our age; we spend fortunes to hide our wrinkles; we prefer to send our old people to nursing homes" (Kübler-Ross, 1975, p. 28). We also shelter children from death and dying. By trying to "protect" children from unpleasant realities, we may actually make them inordinately fearful of death.

Kübler-Ross believes that we depersonalize dying people at a time when they badly need comfort and compassion. In part, this may be because relating to dying people can be very painful for family and friends—and for nurses, doctors, and mental health professionals as well (Pattison, 1977). Often, dying people are separated from everyone and everything that is familiar and meaningful to them and are "segregated" with other sick and dying people in a hospital or nursing home. It is even more difficult to cope with fears about dying when a person feels alone and perhaps discarded (Kübler-Ross, 1975).

Kübler-Ross's work has increased our understanding of the emotional needs of the dying person (Kastenbaum & Costa, 1977). In the last decade, medical and other professional schools have begun to expound the principle that death is a natural event and that families should be helped to accept it.

There is, however, some doubt, about the accuracy of Kübler-Ross's five-stage model of dying. Shibles (1974) suggests that the stages are too narrow and fixed. Kastenbaum (1977) has argued that there is no evidence that every person moves through all five stages. Pattison (1977) believes that a dying person, like someone who is not dying, has a continual ebb and flow of emotions.

Even more seriously, some health-care professionals apply the Kübler-Ross model in a rigid and destructive manner. Clinical personnel may patronize the dying person. Or *they* may become angry if a person does not move neatly into the "next" stage. In extreme cases, professionals actually demand that individuals "die in the right way" (Pattison, 1977, p. 304). Pattison points out that Kübler-Ross cited many examples of people who did not precisely follow the five-stage model. He adds, "From my own personal contacts with Dr. Kübler-Ross, I believe she would be dismayed at the manner in which her stages of dying have been misused to force artificial patterns of dying upon the dying person" (p. 304).

also worry about burdening their survivors with the expenses of dying and burial. Moreover, as a result of our own fears about dying and the pain of relating to those who are dying, we depersonalize dying people at just the time when they most need comfort and compassion (Kübler-Ross, 1975). For more promising developments in the care of the dying, see the Application at the end of this chapter.

APPLICATION

Hospice Care for the Dying

In the Middle Ages, a "hospice" was a way station and a refuge where pilgrims and travelers could find food, rest, and comfort on their journey. Today's *hospice* is a center for the dying that seeks to minister to their medical, psychological, and social needs.

"I am less afraid of death than I am of dying" is a remark often heard by doctors and counselors from dying patients. And, in truth, the pain and loneliness of the dying are often fearsome—and to a certain extent inescapable. Yet the American way of dying may have made things worse. In the past, most people who had terminal diseases suffered and died at home and were consoled somewhat by familiar faces and surroundings. Today, the terminally ill are more apt to spend their last days, or even months, in a hospital or a nursing home. Seventy percent of all Americans now live part of their last year in one of these facilities.

There is now a new health-care facility for the terminally ill: the hospice. With in-patient facilities and home-care services, the hospice helps a dying patient and his or her family live with as little pain and as much comfort as possible until the patient's death. The key features that distinguish a hospice from a hospital or nursing home are the treatment of people who cannot be cured and the attention given to their families. Hospitals seek to help the patient recover from disease. Nursing and convalescent homes exist to provide long-term care for the elderly or the handicapped. Neither is equipped to deal with those patients suffering from an incurable disease and who may expect to live for less than a year. Moreover, hospitals and nursing homes have only minimal resources for helping these patients' families deal with the emotional trauma of watching a loved one die. By contrast, hospices exist solely to deal with the dying and their survivors, not with the ill or the elderly.

The first goal of hospice care is to control pain, not to try to cure its causes. For example, Hospice, Inc., in New Haven, Connecticut, uses a mixture of morphine and water to relieve pain while allowing the patient to be active and alert. But the hospice also recognizes that pain control succeeds best when it is related to the patient's mental and emotional well-being. Hospice treatment, therefore, includes a con-stant program of comfort, counseling, and care designed to help patients cope with the situation. Allaying patient fears is a major part of this program. At Hospice, Inc., Dr. Sylvia Lack, the head physician, tries to prepare dying patients for the inevitable. She explains that 50 percent of terminal patients do not experience pain; that pain, if it comes, does not have to be endured; and that pain control should start when pain is mild—patients should not feel guilty about asking for relief even in the earliest stages (Dubois, 1981).

Hospice patients spend their last days either in the facility itself or, in most cases, at home with their families. An important goal of the hospice is to allow the patient to be comfortable and to live (as much as possible) in a familiar way. Patients wear their own clothes, not hospital gowns, and they are encouraged to bring in favorite possessions for their rooms. Family visits are welcome at any time, and when family members come, they find the person they know and love—not a supine body attached to tubes, dials, and machines.

Hospices also recognize the need to comfort the family and friends of the dying patient throughout the whole period of grief, which means after death as well as before it. Dr. Elisabeth Kübler-Ross found that it was often harder for the family to accept death than it was for the dying patient. In the Hospice program, outside professionals can advise the bereaved on insurance policies, bills, lawyers, and funeral preparations. A grieving person can turn to the hospice staff for help at any time.

Besides the psychological and spiritual uplift provided by hospices, there are also noteworthy dollar savings. Professional planners of the hospice movement report that "61 percent of one hospice's patients die at home (compared with the 2 percent of all American deaths which occur at home)" (Dubois, 1981). According to the American Hospital Association, in 1978 the average cost of a day's hospital care was $151.79. Hospice, Inc., placed the cost of its Home Care Service at approximately $750 per patient over a three-month period.

All of the benefits of hospices, however, depend

on how well they can overcome the negative American attitudes toward death and dying and toward institutions associated with them. People who lived near Hospice, Inc., for example, feared that a "death house" was coming to their neighborhood. In order to dispel this image, the hospice was designed to appear as pleasant as possible.

It is in accepting death as part of the life process that the hospice movement renders perhaps its greatest service to the dying and their families. Hospices can encourage people to share their needs and fears and thus help them overcome their dread of what they may not want to accept—but cannot avoid.

■ Summary

- It was once thought that an individual's development ended with childhood. More recent evidence shows that development continues through adolescence, adulthood, and later adulthood. Human beings appear to undergo physical, personal, social, and cognitive changes throughout life. In addition, our strategies for reacting to stress develop over the life span.

- **Does culture affect the experience of adolescence?** According to the *classical view of adolescence,* adolescence is a period of "storm and stress" accompanied by conflict, anxiety, and tension. More recently, it has been argued that this experience may not be universal, since in some nonindustrial societies adolescence can be a time of orderly development and slowly maturing interests and activities. It now appears that adolescents whose development has proceeded smoothly experience little storm and stress, while those whose prior development has been stressful are also likely to experience a stressful adolescence.

- Adolescence begins when a child's body shows signs of becoming an adult's body. In both sexes, it begins with the physical changes of *puberty,* preceded by rapid *growth spurt*. On the average, girls grow faster in the beginning and show signs of sexual maturity at an earlier age than boys. **Menarche** usually occurs somewhere between the ages of 10 and 17. Boys usually catch up and surpass girls in height; by about the age of 16 or 17 boys usually have an advantage in strength and motor development due to greater muscle growth in adolescence.

- **What is it that makes adolescence a psychologically difficult period for some?** The physical changes that occur during puberty have a psychological impact on adolescents. Adolescents are acutely aware of these changes and are concerned about whether their physical appearance matches their image of the "ideal" adolescent. Some boys and girls mature faster physically during puberty than others. Maturing early or late contributes to psychological difficulties during adolescence. Eventually, however, everyone goes through puberty, and differences between early and late maturers become less marked as time goes on. Changes in puberty also reflect the maturation of the reproductive system and have significant psychological consequences. Both males and females have feelings of pride about their ability to function as sexual beings—as men and women—but also experience negative feelings and embarrassment about sexual functioning, such as menstruation for girls and ejaculations for boys.

- According to the *traditional standard,* adolescents are expected to postpone the expression of sexual needs until they are married adults. But with an earlier onset of sexual maturity and an earlier interest in the opposite sex, patterns of sexual behavior have begun to change. Most studies confirm the impression that sexuality is an important aspect of contemporary adolescent experience: It can be a means of communication, a new experience, a source of peer approval, and an escape from loneliness or other pressure. Yet adolescents are no more psychologically mature than were their grandparents at the same age, and among the consequences of this growing discrepancy between sexual maturity and psychological immaturity is a tremendous increase in teenage pregnancies.

- **How do people go about developing a sense of their own identity?** Along with the emergence of sexual feelings in adolescence is the need for intimacy. Most teenagers are eager to develop a relationship with an opposite-sex partner in order to help solidify sexual identity and bolster fragile self-esteem. Erikson notes that adolescents have to develop an *identity* in order to make this transition. Marcia has identified several outcomes of an adolescent's attempts to achieve a stable sense of identity. Some adolescents are ***identity achievers*** who have succeeded in making personal choices about their goals, while others ***foreclose*** on a particular identity, prematurely setting on goals that have been chosen for them. Others put a ***moratorium*** on identity choice and continue to explore alternatives. Still others experience ***identity diffusion,*** feeling that they are unable to find an identity that "feels right."

- Another part of identity development comes from ***peer groups.*** Within these groups, adolescents find acceptance but also experience desperate needs for peer approval. In addition, the group adolescent culture functions to instill many conformist attitudes and behaviors among its members. Studies indicate that adolescents with strong family ties tend to rely less on peers and more on family members for advice and guidance; those without strong family ties tend to rely more heavily on peers to provide self-esteem.

- **Why are adolescents often passionate social and political activists?** Cognitive development occurs as the adolescent begins to think more like an adult and less like a child. According to Piaget, adolescence marks the change from the concrete operations stage to the ***formal operations*** stage. Adolescents begin to think about the world in abstract ways. At this stage, adolescents often become preoccupied with problems in society and may speculate on how things could be different. They tend to become immersed in introspection and may feel as though they are always being watched and judged. To the adolescent, his or her feelings are unique in content and intensity. Toward the end of adolescence, teenagers begin to form more mature relationships and judge themselves more realistically.

- Sources of situational stress among adolescents include parental divorce, delinquency, and suicide. As idealists, adolescents can have profound reactions to divorce. They may feel abandoned and develop difficulties of their own regarding relationships with the opposite sex. They may also have feelings of responsibility for parental difficulties. Many of these problems can be minimized if effective communication can be maintained within the family. Good family relationships help adolescents weather the "normal" crises of development, but intact families that are unsupportive may leave adolescents feeling alienated and helpless when confronted by crisis.

- To some extent, minor delinquency characterizes the behavior of all adolescents. But chronic delinquency affects a minority of adolescents who come from multiple-problem families. Other contributors are poverty, school problems, and deviant peers. No single factor, however, can predict whether a child will become delinquent. The result seems to be dependent on a multitude of factors working together.

- **What kinds of adolescents are most at risk for suicide?** The suicide rate among adolescents has doubled since 1970. Adolescent suicide can occur in both problem families and families that are loving and caring. This suggests that pressures other than family discord can contribute to suicide attempts. To some extent, families that stress individuality and independence in their children may find that their adolescent children have difficulty in finding someone with whom to communicate their hopelessness and despair.

- In our society, there is no set time when one "officially" ends adolescence and enters adulthood. But commonly, it is the time when formal schooling ends and a person begins employment with the intention of self-support. For practical reasons, cross-sectional, rather than longitudinal, studies are more commonly used in doing research on adults though cross-sectional studies cannot separate age differences from ***cohort*** differences. Adulthood is not homogeneous, and people continue to confront developmental challenges during the adult years.

- **Do we know why we age?** Most people reach the peak of their physical condition during their 20s. Beginning in the late 20s and continuing thereafter, everyone undergoes a gradual and inevitable decline in life processes. Several theories attempt to explain why we age. One is that our bodies simply wear out. A second theory states that with repeated divisions, more and more cells in our bodies contain genetic errors and do not function properly. A third theory is that our body chemistry loses its delicate balance over the years. A fourth contends that our bodies tend to reject some of their own tissues as we age. People age at different rates, and the effects of aging depend on how well a person takes care of his or her body. Heredity is also a factor, since some people are predisposed genetically to show signs of age earlier than others.

- One of the major changes in middle age is the ***climacteric,*** or the decline in the function of the reproductive organs. Among women, the amount of estrogen drops sharply, and eventually ***menopause,*** the cessation of menstruation, occurs. Women who are strongly identified with the role of mother and are anxious about getting old may experience significant psychological stress at menopause. But for many other women, menopause signifies the beginning of a period during which energies can be directed toward new activities and new sources of fulfillment. Among men, there is also a reduced ability in sexual function. But the changes are less drastic, and since society puts less emphasis on men's reproductive role, the male climacteric produces few major psychological problems.

- **How does one choose a career?** Career choice is another important issue in early adulthood. Although the importance of career choice was once primarily a male concern, today career choices are important for both men and women. Current theories hold that personality is an important contributor to career choice, in addition to ability and opportunity. Another factor influencing career choice is one's parent's career. Career choices may also shift during adulthood as interests change and new opportunities become available.

- Some adults who may have achieved many of their goals or see no chance to achieve them may feel trapped by routine and experience a "mid-life crisis." However, data suggest that this is not a common phenomenon; most individuals go through less dramatic reactions (the so-called *mid-life transition*) and make renewed commitments to marriage, work, and family.

- **Is work less satisfying for women than for men?** Studies of job satisfaction indicate that the vast majority of workers are at least somewhat satisfied with their jobs and would continue to work even if they didn't have to. The meaning of work varies from person to person. To some, it is a source of self-respect and life purpose. For others, work is a means of passing time. To still others, it is primarily a source of financial independence. Among women, available work is often less satisfying than home management. Yet, most women report increases in self-esteem when employed, especially if they experience support from their families.

- Marriage remains an important determinant of overall life satisfaction. Married people report the highest levels of happiness. Timing is important in promoting successful marriages. Young people are relatively unprepared for the tasks of marriage, and older people have more difficulty finding mates with compatible life-styles. Although love is popularly considered to be the overriding factor in mate selection, most people are likely to marry someone

because his or her background is similar. The ability to resolve conflict productively appears to be a key to successful marriage, although many couples remain married despite feeling overall discontent.

- During adult years, sexual behavior tends to be focused within a special relationship with a permanent partner. In contemporary society, a majority of women have great sexual interest, but males' interest in sexual intimacy appears to be greater among every age group. Married couples typically sustain interest in sexual activity even though a decline in frequency is common. Contrary to popular belief, menopause has no effect on women's level of arousal.

- The experience of raising a family presents many new challenges, responsibilities, and role changes for men and women. With young children, it is necessary to regulate cycles of work, procreation, and recreation. Conflicts also arise between career and home responsibilities. This conflict may be especially acute for working women, who also have to live up to expectations associated with motherhood. As middle age approaches and children leave home, couples who can be alone together and enjoy each other's company may find renewed satisfaction in their marriage.

- **Do we become better at different kinds of thought processes as we grow older?** There is disagreement on what sort of cognitive changes occur through adulthood, but recent studies indicate important ways in which an adult's thinking differs from an adolescent's. For one thing, the acquisition of knowledge is often less important than the skill in applying knowledge to social problems. In addition, adult thinking at about mid-life is generally necessary for the forging of powerful intellectual synthesis. Understanding the complexity of the social system also seems to be a hallmark of adult thinking.

- Older adults are becoming an increasingly more important sector of society. Gerontology is becoming an increasing concern of behavioral scientists. Growth and development, despite diminishing physical abilities, continues in important ways.

- During later adulthood certain physical changes characteristic of aging occur, but none are necessarily crippling or incapacitating. The crucial task for older adults is not that physical changes occur, but how they are psychologically and behaviorally responded to. An optimistic outlook will enable a person to continue an active and fulfilling life. Other behaviors such as exercise can preserve more youthful functioning. Nevertheless, adapting effectively to diminished physical capabilities remains one of the tasks of later adulthood.

- *Senility* is not a normal consequence of old age. Two-thirds of senility is caused by Alzheimer's disease, an organic brain disorder. Senility is not a characteristic developmental progression.

- **Does sexual activity generally end at a certain age?** The notion that older adults are not sexual is a misconception. However, there are some social factors that contribute to a belief among some older adults that they should be uninterested in sex. For one thing, there are cohort differences to consider: Today's older adults grew up in the early part of the century, when attitudes toward sexual behavior were quite different than they are today. Poor health is another factor that may diminish sexual behavior.

- The loss of a spouse by death is the most severe crisis of adulthood. Many survivors experience illness or may even die themselves soon after. Because they are not used to taking care of themselves, men are more liable to suffer from spousal loss. They are also more likely to remarry than widows.

- Recent research indicates that adults who remain intellectually active can maintain a high level of cognitive functioning well into advanced age. The ability to solve practical, real-life problems actually increases. Later adulthood is also marked by greater introspection and reorganization of value systems.

- **Do older adults fear death?** In later adulthood, reactions to situational stress are highly dependent on one's life history and can determine whether the stresses of old age can be approached with a sense of fulfillment and gratitude or bitterness and feelings of missed opportunities. Fear of death is seldom a central concern of later adulthood, but concern about the process of dying may be of greater concern than death itself. Older adults do express concern about the loneliness and depersonalization imposed on them by the American way of dying. The practice of institutionalizing the terminally ill and segregating them from what is familiar to them exacerbates the problem.

■ Review Questions

1. Adolescence begins with _____, the point at which sexual reproduction becomes possible.
2. An important physical change for adolescent girls is _____, the onset of menstruation.
3. Match Marcia's four possibilities of adolescent identity achievement with their proper definitions:

____ moratorium
____ identity achievement
____ identity diffusion
____ foreclosure

    a. setting aside the problem of achieving an identity while exploring alternatives
    b. experiencing dissatisfaction with current status but unable to develop a comfortable new identity
    c. settling prematurely on an identity provided by others
    d. succeeding in making personal decisions about goals to be pursued

4. About _____ percent of all adolescent girls in this country will conceive a child this year:
    a. 3   b. 6
    c. 8   d. 10

5. Adolescents often depend on _____ _____ to approve their choices, views, and patterns of behavior.
6. Piaget described _____ _____ as a change from concrete to abstract ways of thinking about the world.
7. Approximately _____ young people between the ages of 10 and 19 kill themselves each year.
    a. 1,500   b. 3,000
    c. 5,000   d. 6,000
8. The _____ is the decline in function of the reproductive organs.
9. According to Levinson, the process of _____ _____ is the period during which the adult assesses his or her accomplishments and perhaps formulates new goals.
10. Sociological theories of choice of mate would predict that girls will select mates like their fathers.   T/F
11. More than adolescents, adults tend to think in terms of _____ contexts.
12. _____ _____ significantly slows down the deterioration of bodily functions.
13. Two thirds of all cases of senility are caused by _____ _____.
14. One effect of physiological chances in late adulthood is loss of interest in sexual activity.   T/F

11 Motivation and Emotion

■ Thinking Critically

Why do we have emotions? What purpose does motivation serve? Is motivation inborn?

What makes us hungry?

What causes sexual desire?

Is being highly competitive necessary for achievement?

How do emotions affect performance? Is a musician or football player likely to perform better when feeling emotional?

Someone stands you up for a date you'd been looking forward to. Why are some people likely to feel angry about this, while others will feel hurt and sad?

The answers to these and other questions about motivation and emotion are found throughout the chapter and in the Chapter Summary.

■ Outline

Motive A specific need, desire, or want such as hunger, thirst, or achievement, that energizes and directs goal-oriented behavior.

Emotion A feeling such as fear, joy, or surprise, that energizes and directs behavior.

In order to see the manipulation of motivation and emotion at a sophisticated level, we turn to a detective story. At the beginning, all we know is that a murder has been committed: After eating dinner with her family, sweet little old Miss Jones collapses and dies of strychnine poisoning. "Now, why would anyone do a thing like that?" everybody asks. The police ask the same question, in different terms: "Who had a *motive* for killing Miss Jones?" In a good mystery, the answer is: "Practically everybody."

The younger sister—now 75 years old—still bristles when she thinks of the tragic day 50 years ago when Miss Jones stole her sweetheart. The next-door neighbor, a frequent dinner guest, has been heard to say that if Miss Jones's poodle tramples his peonies one more time, he intends to. . . . The nephew, a major heir, is deeply in debt. The parlor maid has a guilty secret that Miss Jones knows. All four people were in the house on the night that Miss Jones was poisoned. All four had easy access to strychnine, which was used to kill rats in Miss Jones's basement. All four had strong emotional reactions to Miss Jones—envy, anger, shame, guilt. And any one of them could have been motivated to kill her.

Motivation and emotion also play a role in some of the less spectacular events in the story. Motivated by hunger, the family gets together to eat a meal. The poodle, motivated by curiosity or the call of nature, is attracted to the neighbor's peonies. The next-door neighbor visits because he is lonely and wants company. The parlor maid's guilt stems from activity to satisfy sexual needs. The tragedy of Miss Jones's death brings the family closer together out of a need for affiliation. But the fear that results from the murder causes the self-preservation drive to take over, and each person involved becomes suspicious of the others.

In this story, motivation and emotion are so closely related that it is difficult to draw distinctions between them. A **motive** is an inner directing force—a need or want—that arouses the organism and directs behavior toward a goal. All motives are triggered by some kind of stimulus: a bodily need, such as hunger or thirst; a cue in the environment, such as the peonies in the garden; or a feeling, such as loneliness, guilt, or anger. When one or more stimuli create a motive, the result is goal-directed behavior (see Figure 11-1). **Emotion** refers to the experience of such feelings as fear, joy, surprise, or anger. Like motives, emotions also activate and affect behavior, although it is more difficult to predict the kind of behavior that will result. If a man is hungry, we can be reasonably sure that he will seek food. If, however, this same man experiences a feeling of joy or surprise, we cannot know with certainty how that feeling will affect his behavior.

Figure 11-1
A *motive* is triggered by some kind of *stimulus*—a bodily need or a cue in the environment. A motive, in turn, activates and directs *behavior*.

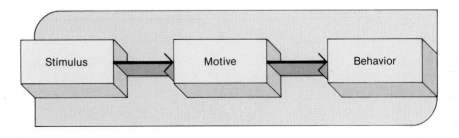

Stimulus → Motive → Behavior

The important thing to remember about both motives and emotions is that they move us to some kind of *action*—whether it be as drastic as murder or as mundane as drumming our fingers on a table because we are nervous. Motivation takes place whether we are aware of it or not. We do not have to know that we are feeling hungry in order to go to the refrigerator, or to be aware of a need for achievement in order to study for an exam. We do not have to think that we are feeling fearful in order to step back from a precipice or think that we are angry in order to raise our voice at someone. Also, the same motivation or emotion may produce different behaviors in different people. Ambition might motivate one person to go to law school and another to join a crime ring. Feeling sad might lead one person to cry and another to talk to a friend. On the other hand, the same behavior might result from different motives or emotions: You might buy liver because you like it, because it is inexpensive, or because you know that your body needs the iron contained in it. You may go to a movie because you are happy, bored, or lonely. The workings of motives and emotions can be very complex.

In this chapter, we will first look closely at the various kinds of motives that seem to play an important role in human behavior. Then we will turn our attention to emotions and the various ways in which they can be expressed.

■ Perspectives on Motivation

Around the turn of the century, psychologists were inclined to explain motivated behavior by attributing it to **instincts**—innate tendencies to behave in certain ways in the presence of the proper stimulus. In 1890, William James suggested that human behavior could be accounted for by such diverse instincts as hunting, rivalry, fear, curiosity, shyness, love, shame, and resentment. Thirty years later, thousands of human instincts had been identified, and psychologists were beginning to look elsewhere for better explanations of behavior. After all, not all human behavior is inborn, and attributing every conceivable behavior to a corresponding instinct is really no explanation at all.

An alternative view of motivation holds that bodily needs (such as the need for food or the need for water) create a state of tension or arousal called a drive (such as hunger or thirst). According to **drive reduction theory,** motivated behavior is an attempt to reduce this unpleasant state of tension in the body and to return the body to a state of **homeostasis,** or balance. When we are hungry, we seek out food in order to reduce the hunger drive. When we are tired, we go to sleep. When we are thirsty, we find something to drink. In each of these cases, behavior is directed toward reducing a state of bodily tension or arousal.

But drive reduction doesn't explain all motivated behavior. For example, when we are bored, we may actually seek out activities that *increase* tension and arousal. People go to horror movies, go jogging, learn skydiving, and take on all kinds of new challenges. It is difficult to see how these kinds of motivated behavior reduce states of arousal. Rather, it seems that organisms seek to maintain an optimum state of

Instinct Inborn, goal-directed behavior tendency that fulfills specific biological needs and contributes to an organism's survival.

Drive reduction theory The theory that motivated behavior moves the organism toward a reduction of arousal.

Homeostasis State of balance and stability in which the organism functions effectively.

Incentive An external stimulus that prompts goal-directed behavior.

Primary drive A physiologically based unlearned motive (e.g., hunger).

arousal: If arousal is too high, efforts will be made to reduce it; if arousal is too low, efforts will be made to increase it.

In addition, some behavior doesn't seem to be triggered by internal states at all. After a satisfying meal, for example, the smell of a bakery may cause us to eat more food; a sample copy of a new magazine, a demonstration of a new product, or a store window display may lead us to buy something we would not have otherwise bought. In other words, objects in the environment (called **incentives**) can also motivate behavior (Bolles, 1972; Rescorla & Solomon, 1967).

In the next section of this chapter, we will begin by exploring hunger and thirst, two motives that are especially influenced by internal biological states. Then we will examine sexual behavior, which is responsive to both internal states and external incentives. We will then look at several behaviors, such as curiosity and manipulation, that are particularly responsive to external environmental cues. Finally, we will explore several learned motives that play a major role in human social relationships.

■ Primary Drives

As we have seen, all motives are aroused by some kind of stimulus—a bodily need such as hunger or thirst or a cue in the environment such as a picture of a juicy hamburger and a cool milkshake. When a motive is aroused, the result is goal-directed behavior—perhaps a trip to the nearest fast-food restaurant. Thus, one or more stimuli create a motive, which in turn activates and directs behavior. But motives differ in the kinds of stimuli that arouse them as well as in the effects that they have on behavior.

Some motives are unlearned and are common to every animal, including humans. These motives are called **primary drives.** Primary drives, such as hunger, thirst, and sex, are strongly influenced by stimuli from within the body. These stimuli are part of the biological arousal associated with the survival of the organism or, in the case of sex, the survival of the species.

Hunger

When you are hungry, you eat. If you cannot do so, your need for food will increase the longer you are deprived of it. But your appetite, your feeling of hunger, will not necessarily increase. Suppose you decide to skip lunch in order to play tennis. Your need for food will remain nonetheless, and it will increase throughout the day. But your hunger will come and go. You will probably be hungry around lunchtime; then your hunger will probably decrease during the tennis game. But it is likely that by dinnertime no concern will seem as pressing as getting something into your stomach. The psychological state of hunger, then, is not the same as the biological need for food, although it is often set in motion by biological processes.

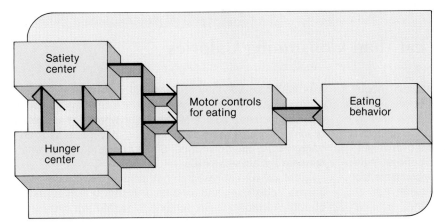

Glucose A simple sugar that is the main source of body energy.

Figure 11-2
A diagram of the dual mechanisms in the brain that control hunger and eating The *hunger center* signals when you are hungry and stimulates eating. The *satiety center* reduces the feeling of hunger and the desire to eat.

We now know that two centers in the brain are especially important in controlling hunger. One, the *hunger center*, stimulates eating; while the other, the *satiety center* (*satiety* means being full to satisfaction), reduces the feeling of hunger. Both centers are located in the hypothalamus.

Since the 1950s, scientists have explored the ways in which these two centers function. If the neurons in either center are stimulated, the neurons in the other center will fire less often. Thus, if your hunger center "tells" you that you are hungry, you will get few signals from the satiety center to contradict this message (see Figure 11-2). It has also been discovered that these two centers alone do not regulate hunger. Neurons that pass through the hunger and satiety centers on their way to other parts of the brain also have some influence. So does another part of the brain near the hypothalamus, called the amygdala, but its exact role has not been precisely defined.

How do these areas of the brain "know" when to signal hunger? It appears that the brain monitors the level of a simple sugar called **glucose** in the blood. When the level of glucose falls, neurons in the hunger center are stimulated, while those in the satiety center are inhibited. An increase in the level of fats in the blood as the body draws down reserve energy supplies appears to have the same effect.

The brain also monitors the amount and kind of food that you have eaten. Receptors in the stomach apparently can sense not only how much food it holds but also how many calories the food contains. A stomach full of salad is far less satisfying than a stomach full of filet mignon with all the trimmings. Signals from these receptors are sent to the brain, where they stimulate the satiety center, with the result that you feel less hungry. In addition, there is some evidence that when food enters the small intestine, a hormone is released into the bloodstream and carried to the brain, where it also stimulates the satiety center (Smith & Gibbs, 1976).

These hunger mechanisms regulate our day-to-day intake of food. But there appears to be yet another hunger regulator, one that operates on a long-term basis to regulate the body's weight. With the exception of humans and some domesticated animals, very few animals ever become grossly overweight. The body seems to have a way of monitoring its own

The precise role played by the brain in hunger is not known, but after lesions were made in the hypothalamus of this rat, it ate so much that it increased its body weight to over three times its normal weight.

There's More to Being Fat than Consuming Calories

Fitness is America's obsession: People now worry about cellulite the way they used to worry about crabgrass. Thin is in, and the generous proportions so admired in the past by artists like Rubens and Renoir are decidedly not chic today.

But unfashionable or not, many people *are* overweight, and some are heavy enough to be considered obese. Why do people become fat? It is not simply that they consume too many calories. Two people who maintain the same level of activity can consume the same number of calories, but one might gain weight and the other might not (Rodin, 1981b). The causes of obesity are many and complex, and they underscore the fact that eating is more than a simple response to a chemical imbalance in the blood.

Biological factors, which may be hereditary, can contribute to being overweight. Some people are born with an oversupply of fat cells—a condition that increases the body's ability to store excess calories. There also may be a link between a biochemical defect and overeating. McLaughlin, Peikin, and Boile (1984) discovered that obesity may be caused by a hormone-related inability to sense fullness. Although they found the hormone that signals satiety, cholecystokinin (CCK), to be present in adequate amounts in obese rats, these rats did not have enough receptors on which the hormone could bind. Thus, the obese rats never experienced satiety, and they continued eating.

Eating experiences during childhood also influence body weight. People who were overfed as babies may retain fat cells that stay with them in later life. In addition, poor eating habits learned during childhood may persist into adulthood. Yesterday's child who constantly had a hand in the cookie jar may turn into today's obese adult—still with a hand in the cookie jar.

Emotional factors also play an important part in how much we eat. Some people eat when they are lonely, bored, or anxious. Infants who are fed whenever they cry may come to associate food with a feeling of comfort, and as adults they may eat whenever they are upset. If feeding was the only source of attention during childhood, socially isolated adults may use food as a source of stimulation when they are bored or lonely. In anxious individuals, food may serve as a distraction from other problems. Some people eat more when they are not active sexually.

Much current research has emphasized the role that internal bodily cues and external environmental cues play in obesity. According to Schachter (1971a, 1971b), overweight people are less sensitive than people of normal weight to internal signals of hunger, such as hunger pangs and low blood sugar. Schachter believes that obese people are more sensitive to environmental cues and that their eating is controlled by these cues. The sight of a big bowl of ice cream on the table before us comes with the incentive to eat it, the means to do so, and the prospect of enjoying it. We are all receptive to such stimuli, but Schachter believes that fat people are more vulnerable to such cues.

However, Schachter's hypothesis has come under criticism. Judith Rodin (1981a, 1985) has concluded from her research that not all overweight people are externally overresponsive, nor are all normal-weight people internally responsive. In fact, the link between eating and obesity is not terribly strong: Some people who are very thin may eat what seems like a large amount of food, and some people who eat very little are nonetheless overweight. The key to obesity, then, is to be found not only in a person's eating behavior but also in the number of calories that their bodies need in order to maintain their daily energy levels. This difference in the amount of food needed can be explained in part by individual differences in metabolism or amount of physical activity. With all other factors being the same, a construction worker is likely to need more calories per day than an office worker. In fact, some researchers believe that level of activity is a greater factor in determining obesity than how much one eats.

fat stores and regulating the intake of food in order to provide just enough energy to maintain normal activities without storing up excessive fat deposits.

As we mentioned earlier, hunger does not always stem from a biological need for food. External cues, like the smell of a cake baking in the oven or the sight of golden brown french-fried potatoes, can trigger the desire to eat at almost any hour of the day. Sometimes, just looking at the clock and realizing that it is dinnertime can make us hungry. One intriguing line of research suggests that such external cues may actually set off internal, biological processes that mimic real internal needs. For example, Rodin (1985) found that the mere sight, smell, or thought of food causes an increase in insulin production, which in turn lowers glucose levels in the body just as if the body has a physical need for food. This means that the aroma wafting out of a nearby restaurant may not only be an incentive to eat: It might arouse the primary drive of hunger.

The hunger drive can be affected by emotions. Suppose you are very hungry and in the midst of preparing a meal when you have a very disturbing argument with your boyfriend or girlfriend. If you become very upset by the argument, you may not want to eat for hours. Or what if just as you are sitting down to dinner you receive a phone call notifying you that one of your favorite relatives has died? You probably would not want to eat right away. On the other hand, some people become hungry when they are anxious or nervous. In these cases, motivation is affected by emotions. Feelings of being hurt, happy, sad, angry, nervous, or anxious affect the extent to which you experience hunger.

Social influences also affect your motivation to eat. The typical business lunch is a good example. If you are busy trying to impress a prospective client, you may not feel very hungry even though it is an hour past your usual lunchtime. Conversely, social situations can prompt you to eat when you are not hungry. Suppose one morning after having slept late and eaten a large breakfast, you are invited to your grandparents' house for dinner. When you arrive, you discover, much to your dismay, that a wonderful home-cooked meal will be served in a few minutes. Although you are not very hungry, you may decide to eat again out of courtesy so as not to hurt your grandparents' feelings.

The ways in which a person responds when he or she is hungry vary with each individual's experience and are for the most part governed by learning and social conditioning. Most Americans eat three meals a day at regular intervals. A typical family, for example, may eat at 7 A.M., noon, and 6 P.M. But in Europe, people often have dinner much later in the evening. In Italy, for example, people rarely eat dinner before 9

Hunger does not always result from a biological need for food. It can also be triggered by external cues—perhaps even the sight of delectable foods laid out on a buffet table.

All types of social occasions have grown up around the offering and acceptance of food—from the informal American picnic to the ritualized Japanese tea ceremony.

Eating Disorders

"When people told me I looked like someone from Auschwitz [a Nazi concentration camp], I thought that was the highest compliment anyone could give me." This is the confession of a young woman who suffered from *anorexia nervosa* when she was a teenager. She was 18 years old, 5 feet 3 inches tall, and weighed 68 pounds. This young woman was lucky: She managed to overcome anorexia and has since maintained normal body weight. Others are not so fortunate. In 1983, singer Karen Carpenter died of cardiac arrest following a battle with anorexia. At one point, perhaps as many as 6 percent of anorexics died as a result of the disorder (Agras & Kraemer, 1983).

What is anorexia nervosa? The American Psychiatric Association's *Diagnostic and Statistical Manual of Mental Disorders* (*DSM-III-R*) describes it as follows:

A. Intense fear of becoming obese, which does not diminish as weight loss progresses.
B. Disturbance of body image (for example, claiming to "feel fat" even when emaciated).
C. Weight loss of at least 25 percent of original body weight or, if under 18 years of age, weight loss from original body weight plus projected weight gain expected from growth charts may be combined to make the 25 percent.
D. Refusal to maintain body weight over a minimal normal weight for age and height.
E. No known physical illness that would account for the weight loss (APA, 1987, pp. 66–67).

Who suffers from anorexia nervosa? About 90 percent of all anorexics are upper-middle- and upper-class young women who display an inordinate interest in virtually every aspect of food except the proper use of it (Romeo, 1984; Gilbert & DeBlassie, 1984). Generally, the anorexic enjoys a normal childhood and adolescence and does not appear to experience developmental difficulty. Anorexics are usually successful students and cooperative, well-behaved children.

In short, they are not likely candidates for physical and psychological disorder.

So what does lead to anorexia? It's not an easy question to answer, but several explanations have been proposed. Cultural factors are probably involved: The media promote the notion that in order to be attractive, a woman must possess the physique of a pencil-thin fashion model. American women do tend to overestimate their body size (Bruch, 1980; Fallon & Rozin, 1985). Thompson and his colleagues (1986) found in one study that over 95 percent of their female subjects thought that they were about one-fourth larger than they actually were in the waist, thighs, and hips.

Physiological disturbance could be involved in anorexia, and some research emphasizes the role of "situational pressures" (Polivy & Herman, 1985). Investigations into the family backgrounds of anorexics suggest that they have often been encouraged to develop a dependence on parents that may, in extreme cases, result in such developmental difficulties as fear of sexual maturity. Because anorexia interferes with sexual development (menstruation may cease), it may reduce anxiety over sexuality. Many anorexics are young women susceptible to pressures to conform to sexual stereotypes that include physical attractiveness, and many feel that they are subject to forces beyond their control. From this perspective, anorexics are individuals who diet "not because their physiology requests it; they diet for personal reasons usually at variance with physiological well-being" (Polivy & Herman, 1985, p. 198).

Anorexia is frequently compounded by the disorder known as *bulimia*. The *DSM-III-R* lists the following diagnostic criteria for bulimia:

A. Recurrent episodes of binge eating (rapid consumption of a large amount of food in a discrete period of time, usually less than two hours).
B. At least three of the following:
   1. consumption of high-caloric, easily ingested food during a binge

P.M. What we choose to eat is also influenced by our culture. Most Americans love milk, but the Chinese have a strong aversion to it (Balagura, 1973). While a cola drink may provide both the sweetness of orange juice and the stimulation of coffee, most people would not choose to drink it in the morning with their breakfast. So although hunger is basically a biological drive, it is not merely an internal state that we satisfy when our body tells us to. Both the motivation to eat and overeating behavior are influenced by psychological, cultural, and environmental considerations in addition to biological factors.

resembles other drives in these respects, it differs from them in one important way: Hunger and thirst are vital to the survival of the individual, but sex is vital only to the survival of the species.

BIOLOGICAL FACTORS IN AROUSAL. The sex drive is powerfully affected by hormones, the chemical messengers secreted into the bloodstream by the various endocrine glands (see Chapter 2). The circulatory system carries hormones to the sites in the body where they act. For both men and women, **testosterone** is the major biological influence on the sex drive (Masters, Johnson, & Kolodny, 1982). A decline in the level of testosterone in either men or women can lead to a drop in sexual desire. Men may have difficulty in getting and sustaining an erection (Kolodny, Masters, & Johnson, 1979). A high level of testosterone, on the other hand, spurs intense interest in sex. It is important to keep in mind, however, that the testosterone level does not completely determine sexual desire. Despite low testosterone levels, some people maintain an active interest in sex. As we'll see, in human sexuality psychological influences are at least as important as biological factors.

The possibility also exists that the sex drive in human beings, as in other animals, may be affected by subtle smells. Many animals have been found to secrete substances called **pheromones** that, when smelled by the opposite sex, affect sexual readiness. Some evidence indirectly suggests that humans may secrete such pheromones through the sweat glands of their armpits as well as from the genitals (LeMagnen, 1952; Michael, Bonsall, & Warner, 1974). Research with rhesus monkeys has shown that females secrete fatty acids called *copulins* that have an aphrodisiac effect on males. It now appears that human females also secrete copulins (Morris & Udry, 1978). At the present time, however, researchers are not in agreement about the role, if any, that such secretions play in human sexual arousal.

The nervous system also exerts controls over the sex drive. Once sexual arousal begins, stimulation of the genitals and other parts of the body becomes important. In the male, signals are sent to an "erection center" located at the bottom of the spinal cord. This center in turn sends neural messages to muscles that control an erection. A similar reflex center higher in the spine stimulates ejaculation, except that this process is subject to some voluntary control. Little is known so far about how similar mechanisms may affect the sexual drive in women (Hyde, 1982).

Not surprisingly, the brain exerts a powerful influence on the sex drive. Just how the brain affects sex remains unclear, although some evidence suggests that the limbic system, located deep in the brain, influences sexual excitement (see Chapter 2). When experimenters implanted electrodes in the limbic system of male monkeys, they located three areas that, when stimulated, caused erections (Hyde, 1982). Two human subjects who had electrodes placed in their limbic systems for therapeutic reasons reported intense sexual pleasure when the electrodes were electrically stimulated (Heath, 1972).

PSYCHOLOGICAL INFLUENCES ON SEXUAL MOTIVATION. In both human beings and other animals, the sex drive is affected by hormones and by the nervous system. But human sexual motivation, especially in the early stages of excitement and arousal, is much more

Testosterone Hormone that is the primary determinant of the sex drive in both men and women.

Pheromones Substances secreted by some animals that, when scented, enhance the sexual readiness of the opposite sex.

Sexually explicit material may be a source of arousal for some people but not for others. The rate of arousal is much faster for most men than for women.

dependent on experience and learning. In fact, the number of stimuli that can activate and shape the sex drive in humans is almost infinite.

What kind of stimulus can have this effect? It need not be anything as immediate as a sexual partner. People respond sexually to fantasies, pictures, words, and to things that they see, touch, or hear. Magazines stress the aphrodisiac effects of soft lights and music. One person may be unmoved by an explicit pornographic movie but aroused by a romantic love story, while another may respond in just the opposite way. Popular music captures some of the many things that can be sexually attractive. The Beatles sang about "something in the way she moves." Fred Astaire told Audrey Hepburn, "I love your funny face." And Cole Porter admired "the way you sing off-key." Human sexual response is also affected by social experience, sexual experience, nutrition, emotions—particularly feelings about one's sex partner—and age. In fact, just thinking about or having fantasies about sex can arouse the sex drive in humans.

Although there is a great variety of stimuli that can trigger the human sex drive, men and women tend to be sexually aroused in different ways. Men are more aroused by visual cues, whereas women respond more to touch (Schulz, 1984). A man may be aroused to erection simply by watching his partner undress, while a woman may need to have her body caressed in order to achieve the same state of arousal. And although descriptions or scenes of sexual activity are arousing to both men and women, the rate of arousal in women is slow compared to the instantaneous response of most males (Heiman, 1977; Byrne, 1977; Christensen, 1986). The focus of interest also differs for males and females: Men tend to favor close-ups of sexual acts, while women respond more to the style, setting, and mood of the material (Masters, Johnson, & Kolodny, 1982).

Aside from differences between men and women, there are individual differences in how we become sexually aroused—differences based on learning from past experience and influenced by culture, age, and economics. Despite the possibility that bodily secretions may have aphrodisiac properties, most Americans tend to find odors from the genitals, underarms, mouth, and feet unpleasant or even disgusting. Since this is not true of young American children and adults of many other cultures, we can assume that this is due to social conditioning.

What we find attractive is also heavily influenced by culture. In some cultures, most men prefer women with very large breasts, while in other cultures the preference is for small, delicate breasts. In some groups in Africa, elongated ear lobes are considered very attractive. In our own culture, what we find attractive often depends on the styles of the time. Long hair on men, for example, which may have been considered attractive in the early 1970s, is not as attractive today. Culture and experience can also influence the extent to which we learn to find articles of clothing sexually arousing. What's important to keep in mind is that although sex is a primary biological drive, the environmental cues that lead to arousal are determined largely by learning.

Finally, just as sexual drive in humans can have both biological and psychological sources, so too can the lack of sexual drive be traced to both biological and psychological factors. Sexual dysfunctions will be discussed in Chapter 14.

Social conditioning and culture—including standards of physical attractiveness—are among the stimuli that affect the *sex drive* in humans. While the American male might well be attracted to the fashion model on the left, the Taureg nomad of Niger would no doubt prefer the woman in festive makeup on the right.

In our discussion so far, we have moved from motives that are heavily dependent on biological needs (hunger and thirst) to a motive that (in humans at least) is considerably more sensitive to external cues (sex). In the next section, we will continue this progression and examine some motives that are even more responsive to environmental cues.

Stimulus Motives

Like primary drives, **stimulus motives** seem to be largely unlearned, but in all species these motives are more dependent than primary drives on external stimuli—things in the world around us. Moreover, unlike the primary drives, their main function extends beyond the bare survival of the organism or species to a much less specific end—dealing with information about the environment in general. Motives such as *activity, curiosity, exploration, manipulation,* and *contact* push us to investigate, and often to change, the environment.

Activity

People need to be active. Most people get bored when they are confined to a small space with nothing to do. They wander around, drum their fingers on the table, or study the cracks in the wall. Of course, age, sex, health, genetic makeup, and temperament affect the need for *activity* to various degrees. One person may be comfortable sitting in the same position for hours, while another may begin to fidget in five minutes.

Although all animals need activity, scientists are not sure if it is a motive in itself or a combination of other motives. Most of the experiments to determine if there is a separate "activity motive" have been done with rats. A rat put into a cage so small that it cannot move around will be more active than normal when it is released (Hill, 1956). But before we conclude that activity is an unlearned motive, we should consider other experiments. Food deprivation increases activity, but running is affected more than other types of restless behavior (pawing, climbing, moving around aimlessly). Experiments with female rats (Wang, 1923) show that peak activity coincides with peak sexual receptivity. So it is still unclear whether the need for activity is a separate motive by itself or simply the result of other motives.

Exploration and Curiosity

Where does that road go? What is that dark little shop? How does a television set work? What is that tool used for? Answering these questions has no obvious benefit for you. You do not expect the road to take you anywhere you need to go or the shop to contain anything you really want. You are not about to start a TV-repair service or use an unknown tool. You just want to know. *Exploration* and *curiosity* appear to be motives activated by the new and unknown and directed toward no more specific a goal than "finding out." Even animals will learn a behavior just to be allowed to explore the environment. The family dog will run around a new house, sniffing and checking things out, before it settles down to eat its dinner.

Animals also seem to prefer complexity, presumably because more complex forms take longer to know and are therefore more interesting (Dember, Earl, & Paradise, 1957). Placed in a maze that is painted black, a rat will explore it and learn its way around. The next time, given a choice between a black maze and a white one, it will choose the white one (Dember, 1965). Apparently, the unfamiliarity of the unknown maze has more appeal. The rat seems to be curious to see what the new one is like (see Figure 11-3).

There are, of course, reservations. At times, we have all found the unknown more distressing than stimulating or found something—an argument, a symphony, or a chess game—too complex for us. A young child accustomed only to her parents may withdraw from a new face and scream with terror if that face has a beard. Unusual clothing or a radical piece of art or music may be rejected, scorned, or even attacked. But here again, learning is important. Familiarity may change the face, the

Figure 11-3
On the first trial, a rat explores either one of the grey arms of the maze at random. On the second trial, however, given a choice between a grey arm and an arm of a different light intensity, a rat will consistently choose the unfamiliar one.

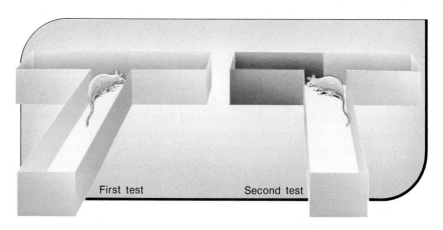

First test   Second test

Is Work a Stimulus Motive?

What would you do if you won $10 million in a lottery? Your first reaction might be, "I'd spend the rest of my life on the beach (or skiing or traveling)." But in all likelihood you, like most other people who receive financial windfalls, would seek some kind of work eventually. A variety of motives keeps people working, even when they don't need a paycheck to survive. If you've ever worked as a volunteer, you know that helping someone can be more satisfying than receiving pay. Work also provides a sense of identity. Actress Carol Channing expressed it this way: "I'm not going to sit and stagnate. If I'm not working, I'm not living." However, enjoyment of work is not limited to members of the glamour professions. One man aged 81 said, "I've been in the fabric business since I was a kid, and I still get a kick out of it." People also work because they feel an urge to keep solving problems, making discoveries, or perfecting their crafts. Linus Pauling, a Nobel laureate in his late eighties, said, "I keep working because there is always the chance that I will think of something new."

Studies suggest that rats, pigeons, and children sometimes work to gain rewards even if they can get the same rewards without working (D'Amato, 1974):

> Rats will run down an alley tripping over hundreds of food pellets to obtain a single, identical pellet in the goal box, . . . and pigeons will peck a key, even on intermittent schedules of reinforcement, to get exactly the same food that is freely available in a nearby cup. Given the option of receiving marbles merely by waiting an equivalent amount of time for their delivery, children tend to prefer to press a lever . . . to get the same marbles. (p. 95)

Why would animals or humans work for food or other rewards when they can get the same payoff without working? Isn't there an inherent tendency to "freeload"? Apparently just the opposite is true: There seems to be an inherent need to work. Both animals and people prefer to earn their rewards. In fact, external rewards or incentives may even undermine the *intrinsic* motivation to perform a task. In one experiment, monkeys manipulated puzzles without any reward until the puzzles were baited with a raisin. Once they realized that they could get a raisin by manipulating a puzzle, the monkeys lost interest in the unbaited puzzle (deCharms, 1968).

Why would people and animals prefer to work for their rewards? Working for rewards may help us to control our environment. Such control is necessary for survival and is basic in both animals and human beings. In a number of experiments, animals that could not control their rewards and punishments became passive and apathetic; they simply "gave up." This *learned helplessness* has received considerable attention as an explanation for some cases of severe depression (Seligman, 1975; see Chapter 14).

---

clothing, or the symphony from the unacceptable to the novel and interesting. A child who at age 2 is only up to "Three Blind Mice" welcomes the complexity of a popular song at age 12 and perhaps of a Mozart string quartet at age 22. As we learn—and as we continually explore our environment—we raise our threshold for the new and complex, and our explorations and our curiosity become much more ambitious.

Manipulation

Why do you suppose that museums have "Do Not Touch" signs everywhere? It is because the staff knows from experience that the urge to touch is irresistible. Unlike curiosity and exploration, *manipulation* is directed toward a specific object that must be touched, handled, played with, and felt before we are satisfied. Manipulation is a motive that seems to be limited to primates, which have agile fingers and toes.

The desire to manipulate seems to be related to two things: a need to know about something at a tactile level and sometimes a need to be soothed. The Greek "worry beads"—a set of beads on a short string that are moved back and forth during a conversation—are examples of this second type of manipulation. Under stress, people "fiddle" with a ciga-

Curiosity is a stimulus motive that pushes us to investigate unfamiliar stimuli, and as we learn to explore our environment, our curiosity becomes more ambitious.

An infant monkey with Harlow's "surrogate mothers"—one made of wire, the other covered with terrycloth. The monkey clings to the terrycloth "mother," even though the wire "mother" provides both food and warmth.

rette, a paper napkin, a fountain pen. Children are always manipulating the objects around them. Eyeglasses, earrings, flowers, dogs' tails—everything must be touched and played with. The brighter the object, the more mixed its colors, the more irregular its shape, the more appealing it is as a potential object for manipulation.

Contact

People also want to touch other people. The need for *contact* is broader and more universal than the need for manipulation. Furthermore, it is not limited to touching with the fingers—it can involve the whole body. Manipulation is active, but contact can be passive.

In a famous series of experiments (Harlow, 1958; Harlow & Zimmerman, 1959), newborn baby monkeys were separated from their mothers and given two "surrogate mothers." Both were the same shape, but one was made of wire and offered no soft surfaces. The other was cuddly—layered with foam rubber and covered with terry cloth. A nursing bottle was put in the wire "mother," and both "mothers" were warmed by means of an electric light placed inside them. Thus the wire "mother" fulfilled two physiological needs for the infant monkeys: the need for food and the need for warmth. But it was to the terry-cloth "mother," which did not provide food, that the babies went. When they were frightened, they would run and cling to it as they would to a real mother. Since both mothers were warm, it seems that the need for affection, cuddling, and closeness goes deeper than a need for mere warmth.

■ Learned Motives

We are not born with all our motives intact. We have already seen that even motives that appear to be unlearned—such as hunger, thirst, and sex—are actually learned in part. As we develop, our behavior becomes governed by new motives that are almost entirely learned. Although these new motives are learned rather than innate, they can exert just as much control over our behavior as unlearned drives and motives do.

One very important learned motive is aggression. Another major class of learned motives, **social motives,** centers around our relationships with other people. We will first look at aggression and then consider some of the most important of these social motives.

Aggression

Aggression in human beings includes all behavior that is intended to inflict physical or psychological harm on others. Intent is an important element of aggression (Beck, 1983). If you accidentally hit a pedestrian with your car, you have inflicted harm, but without intent to do so. If, however, you spot the man who mugged you last week and try to hit him with your car as he crosses the street, you are doing something intentionally harmful. This is an act of aggression.

Judging from the statistics (which often underreport certain types of crimes), aggression is disturbingly common in this country. There were approximately 19,300 murders committed in the United States in 1983; there were 78,900 reported rapes, 639,500 aggravated assaults, and 500,200 robberies (FBI, 1984). Violence in the family is also common. In a study of some 2,000 married couples in this country, investigators found that more than 25 percent of those questioned had engaged in some form of physical violence in their married lives (Straus, 1977). Some fairly recent data indicate that perhaps as many as 6 million wives are physically abused each year; between 2,000 and 4,000 wives are beaten to death each year (*Time*, September 5, 1983). Frequently, aggression is directed at children: By 1982, the number of cases of child abuse reported each year had approached 1 million (*Time*, September 5, 1983).

Why is aggression so widespread? One view is that aggression is part of an unlearned instinct, a vestige of our past that is triggered by pain or frustration (Lorenz, 1968). There is some evidence that, in fact, pain and frustration can motivate aggressive behavior. In one experiment, a pair of rats received electric shocks through a grid in the floor of their cage; finding escape impossible, they turned to fighting with each other. The fighting increased in proportion to shock frequency and intensity (Ulrich & Azrin, 1962). In humans as well, the role of frustration in aggression has also been demonstrated repeatedly. For example, in one experiment, Kulik and Brown (1979) divided subjects into two groups and told each group that they could earn money by soliciting charitable donations over the telephone. One group was told that previous callers had been quite successful in eliciting pledges; the other group was told that its predecessors had been quite unsuccessful. Each group was given a list of prospective donors, all of whom were accomplices with instructions to refuse to pledge any money. The subjects who had been led to expect a high rate of success tended to express considerable anger, exchanging harsh words with their respondents and even slamming down the receiver.

People who behave aggressively are intending to inflict physical or psychological harm on others. In the U.S., *aggression* is disturbingly common within the family as well as among strangers.

While studies such as this one indicate a link between frustration and aggression, this is not always the case. In response to frustration, some people seek help and support, others withdraw from the source of frustration, and some even escape into drugs or alcohol. In other words, it appears that frustration generates aggression only in those people who have learned to be aggressive as a means of coping with unpleasant situations (Bandura, 1973). Moreover, aggression may be learned as a response to a number of different stimuli. According to Berkowitz (1983), research indicates that almost any unpleasant event can lead to aggression. Foul odors, high room temperature, frightening information, and irritating cigarette smoke have all been found to increase hostility in human subjects. Thus, frustration is only one of many types of unpleasant experiences that can provoke aggression.

Freud also viewed aggression as an innate drive, similar to the hunger and thirst drives, that continues to build up until it is released. Freud believed that one important function of society is to direct the expression of the aggressive drive into constructive and socially acceptable channels, such as sports, debating, and various forms of competition. If Freud's view is correct, then watching a violent activity should reduce the aggressive drive. But while there is some evidence that angry people who are encouraged to express their aggression do in fact become less angry and aggressive, in nonangry people the opposite seems to be true. When encouraged to express aggression, nonangry people are either unaffected or actually become more aggressive (Doob & Wood, 1972).

Faced with evidence that aggression in humans is not an innate response to pain or frustration, along with evidence that there is no aggressive drive that periodically builds up until it is released, most psychologists today take a somewhat different view of human aggression: that it is largely a learned response. One important way of learning aggression is to observe aggressive models, especially models who get what they want (and avoid punishment) when they behave aggressively. For example, in contact sports acts of aggression are seldom condemned, and are in fact often praised (Bredemeier & Shields, 1985). In professional hockey, fistfights between players often elicit as much enthusiasm from the crowd as goal scoring.

Even violence on television can contribute to learning. One study of television viewing habits and aggressiveness in children asked 8-year-

Aggression and Rape

Murder, violence, and child and spouse abuse are easily recognized as acts of aggression. But rape is also primarily an act of aggression rather than sexual passion. Most rapes are premeditated: They are not the result of a rapist's spontaneous submission to his sexual urges (Harrington & Sutton-Simon, 1977). Many rapists also ignore or reject willing sexual partners and feel satisfied only with sex that they force on an unwilling victim (Gager & Schurr, 1976). In fact, about half of all rapists are married.

Groth and his colleagues (Groth, Burgess, & Holmstrom, 1977) studied 225 accounts of rape and found that in almost two-thirds of the cases, the predominant motive was power—a desire to intimidate and conquer the victim, often as a way of shoring up a sense of personal weakness. In the remaining cases, the predominant theme was anger. A small percentage of these rapists were sadists—individuals who get sexual pleasure from the suffering of their victims. Unlike power-oriented rapists, angry rapists are much more dangerous and likely to brutalize their victims. Their sexual satisfaction in the act is minimal and may not even occur. In fact, many anger-dominated rapists are disgusted by the idea of normal sex.

Laboratory research confirms the link between rape and aggression. In one study (Malamuth, 1981), subjects rated the likelihood that they would commit rape if they could not be caught. Then, the same subjects were mildly rejected and insulted by a woman. Men who had said that they were more likely to commit rape reported feeling more anger toward the woman and a stronger desire to hurt her. They also behaved more aggressively toward her when given the opportunity.

Does violent pornography encourage the expression of such aggressive behavior? In 1986, the United States Attorney General's Commission on Pornography declared that exposure to materials in which sex occurs in a context of violence does indeed increase the likelihood of aggression. For example, after being exposed to sexually violent stories, especially when the experimenter appears to approve of violence against women, men in one study did indeed act more aggressively toward women in a laboratory setting (Malamuth & Donnerstein, 1984). So far, however, laboratory research indicates that exposure to violent erotic material increases arousal and aggression only in assaultive men and in those men who report that they might rape if they felt that they would not be punished (Malamuth & Check, 1980). Certainly, violent erotica is degrading to members of both sexes, and there is some evidence that people who are aroused by depictions of coercive sex have a callous attitude toward rape and rape victims (Allgeier & Allgeier, 1984). But there is as yet no answer to the practical question of whether the prohibition or, alternatively, the broader availability of pornographic material would have an impact on either social values or the frequency of sexual violence.

old children to rate their favorite television programs. Ten years later, the researchers rated the aggressiveness of these same subjects. They found that children who rated violent TV shows as their favorites were significantly more aggressive when they were observed 10 years later (Lefkowitz et al., 1972).[*]

Achievement motive The need to excel, to overcome obstacles; a social motive.

But what if the aggressive model is itself not particularly effective or is even punished? The concept behind the ancient custom of public executions and punishments, like flogging and stocks, is that punishing a person for aggressive acts will deter others from committing those acts. In one study, one group of children was shown a film in which an aggressive character was punished. Another group was shown a film in which the character was rewarded for the same behavior. A third group watched a film with no violence in it at all. Then all the children were given the chance to act aggressively under circumstances like those depicted in the violent films. Those children who had seen the aggressive model being punished were less aggressive than those who had seen the aggressive model rewarded, but both groups of children were *more* aggressive than those who had seen *no* aggressive model at all. Simply seeing an aggressive model seems to increase aggression among children, whether the model is punished or rewarded.

Aggression can also be "unlearned." For example, aggression can be ignored and nonaggressive behavior rewarded. Davitz (1952) used this approach with two playgroups of children. One was rewarded for constructive behavior, while the other was rewarded for aggressive behavior. Next, the children in both groups were deliberately frustrated, a situation that would ordinarily lead to aggression. The children who had been rewarded for constructive behavior were far less aggressive than the children in the other group.

These data support the idea that aggression is a learned motive. A number of important social motives also seem to be learned, and we turn to them now.

Achievement

Climbing Mount Everest "because it is there," sending rockets into space, making the dean's list, rising to the top of a giant corporation—all these actions probably have mixed underlying motives. But in all of them there is a desire to excel, "to overcome obstacles, to exercise power, to strive to do something difficult as well and as quickly as possible" (Murray, 1938, pp. 80–81). It is this interest in achievement for its own sake that leads psychologists to suggest a separate **achievement motive.**

As with all learned motives, need for achievement varies widely from person to person. McClelland (1958) developed several ways to measure need for achievement experimentally. One method uses responses from the Thematic Apperception Test (see Chapter 12). For example, one picture in the test shows an adolescent boy sitting at a classroom desk. A book lies open in front of him, but the boy's gaze is directed toward the viewer. Subjects are asked to make up stories about the picture. Subjects' stories are presumed to reflect their own motiva-

---

[*] We will examine more closely the link between television violence and aggression in Chapter 9.

tions; therefore, those stories in which the major character accomplishes something difficult or unique, sets relatively high standards of excellence, or takes significant pride in success score high on need for achievement. One person who scored high on the need for achievement responded: "The boy in the picture is trying to reconcile the philosophies of Descartes and Thomas Aquinas—at the tender age of 18. He has read several books on philosophy and feels the weight of the world on his shoulders." Another response was in sharp contrast: "Ed is thinking of leaving home for a while in the hope that this might shock his parents into getting along." This second response was from someone who scored low in need for achievement (Atkinson & Birch, 1970; Atkinson & Raynor, 1975).

Helmreich and Spence (1978) used a self-report questionnaire called the Work and Family Orientation (WOFO) scale to study achievement motivation. They discovered that there are three separate but interrelated aspects of achievement-oriented behavior: *work orientation*, the desire to work hard and do a good job; *mastery*, the preference for difficult or challenging feats with an emphasis on improving one's past performance; and *competitiveness*, the enjoyment of trying one's skills against those of other people.

How do individual differences in the three aspects of achievement motivation relate to people's attainment of goals? Surprisingly, Helmreich and Spence discovered that having a high degree of competitiveness may actually interfere with achievement. In one study, students' grade point averages (GPAs) were compared to their WOFO scores. As you might expect, students who scored low in work, mastery, and competitiveness had lower GPAs. But students who were high in work, mastery, and competitiveness did not have the highest GPAs. The students with the highest grades were those who had high work and mastery scores but who were low in competitiveness. The counterproductive effect of competitiveness on achievement has also been observed in other groups of subjects, such as business people, elementary school students, and scientists. No definitive explanation has been found for this phenomenon, although researchers speculate that highly competitive people may alienate people who would otherwise help them, or that preoccupation with winning may distract such people from the actions necessary and appropriate for this attainment of goals. Or perhaps, as we will see later in this chapter, the overwhelming need to succeed makes for a level of arousal that is too high for optimum performance on complex tasks.

There are three separate but interrelated aspects of achievement-oriented behavior: *work orientation*, the desire to work hard and do a good job; *mastery*, the preference for challenging feats; and *competitiveness*, the enjoyment of seeing how one's skills stack up against those of others.

■ Avoidance of Success

Is there a motive to *avoid* success? According to Horner (1969), both men and women develop the need to achieve, but women also develop a fear of success (FOS). Horner asked undergraduate men at the University of Michigan to finish a story that began: "After first-term finals, John finds himself at the top of his medical school class." Undergraduate women got the same story, but with "Anne" substituted for "John." Only about 10 percent of the men revealed doubt or fear about success. But the women worried about social rejection, picturing Anne as "acne-faced," lonely and dateless, and "unsexed."

Horner attributed FOS to the way many women are raised in our society. If a girl grows up hearing women who achieve outside the home called "sexless," "unfeminine," or "hard," achievement—or the prospect of it—may make her feel guilty and anxious. Horner believes that unless these feelings can be resolved, such women will not make full use of their opportunities.

Other researchers who have followed up Horner's research have obtained mixed results. Some have been able to reproduce Horner's data, although they usually find less pronounced differences between the sexes' level of FOS. Others have found high levels of FOS in samples of men and yet others have reported no sex differences at all in FOS (Frieze et al., 1979; Zuckerman & Wheeler, 1975). In order to explore the reasons behind these different findings, Monahan and his colleagues (1974) expanded Horner's original study design. Using a sample population of 11- to 16-year-olds, Monahan had half of the males respond to the John story and the other half to the Anne story. The females were also divided half and half between the John and Anne stories. A comparison of the results among the four experimental groups provided interesting insights into the phenomenon of FOS. The majority of subjects of both sexes imagined much happier outcomes for John, while both boys and girls overwhelmingly predicted dire consequences for Anne. Indeed, the boys showed an even higher percentage of negative responses for Anne than the girls did. All in all, 21 percent of the boys and 30 percent of the girls gave negative responses to the John story, while 68 percent of the boys and 51 percent of the girls responded negatively to the Anne story. Monahan concluded that Horner's findings reflect fear of punishment for sex-role-inappropriate behavior, rather than fear of success itself. Judging from the hostile responses given to the Anne story by several boys, women's fear of punishment for crossing sex-stereotype boundaries is not unrealistic. Backing up these conclusions, a study by Feather (1975) examined responses to a story in which a woman succeeds in a "sex-appropriate" field such as nursing. Responses showed little evidence of FOS. Besides sex-role appropriateness, the importance that a person places on doing well at a particular pursuit also figures into FOS. Subjects may have felt that it

Cultural stereotypes about appropriate sex roles for women may account for a learned motive to avoid success. But this may be changing as women observe more role models who demonstrate the value of achievement. Pictured here is astronaut Sally Ride.

was important for John to succeed in his medical career but that it was less so for Anne (Eccles, 1983).

Even though there is little or no evidence of gender differences in FOS, some people do seem to have a genuine fear of success: Their anxiety about doing well actually inhibits their achievement-oriented behavior. For example, we've all known bright individuals who do little with their talents and other people who seem to have a knack for "snatching defeat from the jaws of victory." In some such cases, of course, the reason may simply be little or no achievement motivation. But in other cases, the cause is more indirect. In success-fearing people, a good performance that is acknowledged as such is immediately followed by a decline in the performance of similar tasks (Canavan-Gumpert, Garner, & Gumpert, 1978). Why do some people apparently fear success? Tresemer (1977) suggests three possible reasons. Some people simply desire to avoid the continued high levels of effort required of a successful person. Think of a college athlete who begins the season brilliantly. This athlete may subsequently be criticized harshly if his or her performance falls off, while a mediocre teammate will not ordinarily be subjected to the same close scrutiny. Another source of FOS may be a desire to behave in ways that are consistent with one's self-image. If you think of yourself as a "C" student and receive an "A" for a difficult assignment, you may feel that a high grade is out of character for you. It can be uncomfortable to have to reassess and redefine yourself, even in a more positive light. Finally, some people are concerned about the social ostracism that may come with success. Those who outperform the rest of us may be envied, rejected, or pressured to conform. There can be real costs and punishments for performing too well.

From tests and personal histories, psychologists have discovered some general traits of people who are high in need for achievement. These people do best in competitive situations and are fast learners. They are driven less by the desire for fame or fortune than by the need to live up to a high, self-imposed standard of performance. They are self-confident, take on responsibility willingly, and are relatively resistant to outside social pressures. They are energetic and allow few things to obstruct their goals. But they are also apt to be tense and to have psychophysiological disorders—that is, real physical disorders such as ulcers and headaches that seem to have psychological causes.

Power

Another important learned motive is the **power motive,** or need for power. The power motive may be defined as the need to win recognition or to influence or control other people or groups. Like the achievement motive, the power motive can be scored from stories written in response to pictures in the Thematic Apperception Test. Images that concern vigorous actions, behavior that greatly affects others, and interest in reputation or position lead to high scores on the power motive (Winter, 1973).

College students who score high on need for power tend to occupy "power positions," such as offices in student organizations, residence counseling positions, and membership on important committees. They tend to participate in sports involving direct contact between competitors. They also tend to be interested in such careers as teaching, psychology, and business (Beck, 1983).

David Winter (1973) studied the power motives of 12 American presidents from Theodore Roosevelt to Richard Nixon. He scored the concerns, aspirations, fears, and plans for action of each president as revealed in his inaugural speech. The highest scorers in terms of power drives were Theodore Roosevelt, Franklin Roosevelt, Harry Truman, Woodrow Wilson, John Kennedy, and Lyndon Johnson. Except for Theodore Roosevelt, all were Democrats, and all six men were action-oriented presidents. All also scored high in the need for achievement. By contrast, Republican presidents—such as Taft, Hoover, and Eisenhower—were more restrained and scored much lower in power motivation and in the need for achievement. Richard Nixon scored quite high in the need for achievement but relatively low in power motivation. According to Winter, the effect of this kind of mixed achievement/power score is a tendency to vacillate in the exercise of power. Winter (1976) also studied Jimmy Carter when he was still a presidential candidate, finding his power motive to be about average and his need to achieve somewhat above average—about the same as Theodore Roosevelt's. Winter suggests a number of interesting relationships between the power motive and specific presidential policy decisions and actions:

1. Those presidents in power when the country entered wars tended to score high on power motive.
2. Power motive scores of presidents seem to be related to the gain or loss of territory through wars, expansion, treaties, and independence struggles.

John F. Kennedy is among the six recent American presidents scoring highest on the *power motive*. Kennedy also scored high on the need for achievement.

3. Presidents with high power motive scores tended to have the highest turnover in cabinet members during their administration.

Affiliation

Sometimes you want to get away from it all—to spend an evening or a weekend alone, reading, thinking, or just being by yourself. But generally, people have a need for affiliation, a need to be with other people. If people are isolated from social contact for a long time, they may become anxious. Why do people seek one another out? How are groups formed, and why does a handful of isolated people become a group?

For one thing, the **affiliation motive** is aroused when people feel threatened. Esprit de corps—the feeling of being part of a sympathetic group—is important among troops going into a battle. A football coach's pregame pep talk is important to the team. Both are designed to make people feel that they are working for a common cause or against a common foe.

Often, affiliation behavior results from another motive entirely. For example, you may give a party to celebrate getting a job because you want to be praised for your achievement. It has also been suggested that fear and anxiety are closely linked to the affiliation motive. When rats, monkeys, or humans are put in anxiety-producing situations, the presence of a member of the same species who is not anxious will reduce the fear of the anxious one. If you are nervous on a plane during a bumpy flight, you may strike up a conversation with the calm-looking woman sitting next to you because the erratic flight of the plane does not seem to be worrying her.

One study of the affiliation motive involved two groups of college students who agreed to participate in psychology experiments. Upon arriving at the lab, one group was brought into a room filled with ominous-looking equipment. An unsmiling, white-coated scientist warned the students that the experiments would entail "quite painful" electric shocks. The other group was welcomed by a friendly, casually dressed researcher who also told them to expect shocks but who emphasized that the shock would be "more like a tickle than anything unpleasant" (Schachter, 1959). Both groups were told that the experiment would begin in 10 minutes. They could either wait alone or with other subjects, as they preferred. More of the subjects who expected painful shocks indicated that they wanted to be with other people compared to the subjects who expected a mild shock. And both groups preferred to wait with subjects like themselves: The high-fear group wanted to wait with other people who were also expecting painful shocks, and the low-fear group preferred to wait with other low-fear subjects. On the basis of these and other similar findings, Schachter concluded that one of the reasons that people affiliate is the need to interpret unfamiliar situations. Just how scared should they be? Should they refuse to participate? In order to answer such questions as these, it is not sufficient to say that "misery loves company"; rather, "misery loves *miserable* company"!

A more recent theory of affiliation proposes that people seek company or solitude depending on how much benefit they can expect from being with other people (Rofe, 1984). In ambiguous situations like the one created by Schachter, people are indeed likely to seek out others

Affiliation motive The need to be with others.

Affiliation behavior is a result of internal and external factors. The *affiliation motive* is related to most people's need to be part of a sympathetic group.

Unconscious Motives

A new car is advertised, and a man decides that he would like to own one. Why? He may tell you that his old car is running down and that this one looks "pretty good" to him. But there may be other reasons why he wants this new car—reasons of which is he unaware.

Theories of *unconscious motivation* vary. Freud's is probably the most extreme. Freud believed that every act—however trivial—derives from a host of unconscious motives. A Freudian might see the man's choice of car as the desire to conquer a sexual object—a desire encouraged by advertisements touting it as "sleek," "purring," and "packed with power." Freudian theory also proposes aggression as a possible reason—the man may feel a need to zoom down Main Street with as much horsepower as possible under his control.

Some psychologists maintain not only that behavior is influenced by unconscious motives, but also that some kinds of behavior occur *only* when we are unaware of our motives (Brody, 1980). This is in line with the Freudian theory of the unconscious.

But we do not need to explain all acts in Freudian terms in order to realize that they can spring from unconscious motives. The man who buys a certain car may be expressing a desire for social approval—"Be the first one on your block to own one!"—or he may be rewarding himself for hard work.

He could be trying to bolster a sagging self-image or he could be consoling himself for the loss of a promotion or a girlfriend.

Unconscious motives are not a particular *class* of motives, as physiological, learned, and stimulus motives are. As we pointed out in the discussion of physiological drives, we do not have to be aware of hunger and thirst in order to act to satisfy them. An unconscious motive is one that we are acting to satisfy without quite knowing why.

It is difficult to learn about unconscious motives because we have to rely on what people *say* about their motives. For example, when people report their motives, they are recalling something that has already occurred, and their memories may be inaccurate. People may also experience things on different levels of consciousness, and these experiences may be too subtle for them to put into words.

Subjects under hypnosis, for example, are functioning on two levels of consciousness; on one level, they are conscious of what they are experiencing, but the other level remains hidden. Hypnosis can allow them to give expression to experiences on the hidden level. In one experiment, for example, people were hypnotized and told that they would experience no pain. Subsequently, they said they had felt no pain, but other behaviors indicated that they were indeed suffering (Hilgard, 1977).

like themselves to help them assess the situation. But in less ambiguous settings, people may actually prefer to be alone or to be with people who are not facing the same problems. For example, Rofe, Hoffman, and Lewin (1985) found that patients with major illnesses preferred being with healthy people rather than being with other seriously ill patients or being alone. They also preferred not to talk about their illnesses.

In any case, it is clear that affiliation behavior (like most behavior) results from a subtle interplay of factors both inside and outside of the person. Whether you strike up a conversation with the person sitting next to you on a bumpy flight depends on how friendly you are normally, how scared you feel, how calm or nervous your neighbor appears to be, and how turbulent the flight is, among other things.

A Hierarchy of Motives

You have probably noted that our discussion has gradually moved from primitive motives, shared by all creatures, to motives that are more sophisticated, complex, and human. Maslow (1954) arranged all motives in such a hierarchy, from lower to higher. The lower motives are relatively simple: They spring from bodily states that *must* be satisfied. As the motives become higher, they arise from other things: the desire to live as comfortably as possible in our environment, to deal as well as we can with other human beings, and to make the best impression on others that we can. Maslow's hierarchy of motives is shown in Figure 11-4.

According to Maslow's theory, higher motives appear only after the more basic ones have been satisfied. This is true on both an evolutionary and an individual scale. If you are starving, you will probably not care what people think of your table manners.

Maslow believed that the most highly "evolved" motive in the hierarchy is self-actualization. This may be described as a desire to make the best one can out of oneself. It does not concern the respect of other human beings and their judgments of us, but rather what we ourselves want to be. People differ in how important self-actualization is in their behavior, but to some extent, all of us are motivated to live according to what is necessary for our personal growth. The people who are the most self-actualizing, Maslow said, think of themselves as whole beings, not as parcels of hunger, fear, ambition, and dependency.

Maslow's conclusions were based primarily on his observations of people whom he believed to be "self-actualized." They included historical figures, famous living individuals, and even friends whom he admired greatly. Not surprisingly, his approach has been criticized as being unscientific (Wahba & Bridwell, 1976). Moreover, we can all think of people who were able to achieve greatness without having all their more basic needs satisfied. Nonetheless, in the real world, Maslow's theories provide a useful way of thinking about what factors motivate normal, healthy people. Maslow's insights into the features of people who are living up to their potential also fill a gap left by many earlier psychological theorists who concentrated their efforts on understanding disturbed patients.

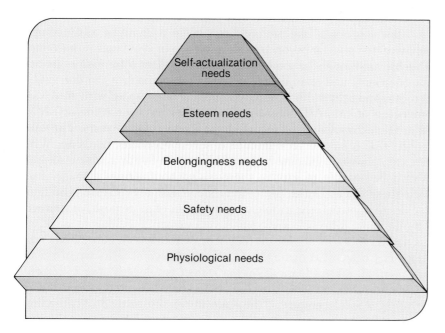

Figure 11-4
A pyramid representing Maslow's hierarchy of emotions From bottom to top, the stages correspond to how fundamental the motive is for survival and how early it appeared in both the evolution of the species and the development of the individual. According to Maslow, the more basic motives must be satisfied before higher motives can appear.
After Maslow, 1954

■ Emotions

In the first part of this chapter, we saw that motives can both arouse and direct our behavior. Emotions do the same. "She shouted for joy," we say, or "I was so angry I could have strangled him." The fact that emotions arouse and shape behavior provides a rich source of profits for advertising agencies. By manipulating our emotions, advertisers can get us to buy everything from cars to mouthwash.

To some extent, we can classify emotions according to whether they cause us to turn *to* or *away* from objects (Arnold, 1960). On this basis, there appear to be three fundamental categories of emotion. Imagine that you overhear this conversation among three people whose television set has just gone out during a midsummer thunderstorm:

A. Just when the movie was getting good! I've wanted to see it for years, and now *this* happens. (*Fiddles with set, to no avail, and switches it off disgustedly.*) Things like this always happen at the worst time. It makes me furious!

B. I *hate* thunderstorms, I always have. Don't you think we ought to turn off all the lights so we won't attract the lightning? My grandmother used to hide in a closet till it stopped, and I don't blame her. She used to say it was God's vengeance for our sins.

C. (*Going to window.*) Look at it, it's fantastic—the way the blue flashes light up everything! It makes the whole world different. I've always loved thunderstorms—they're so wild and happy. They make me feel liberated and crazy!

"A" is frustrated and angry. This category of emotions moves us to *approach* something, but in an aggressive or hostile way. "B" is fearful and anxious. These emotions make us want to *avoid* something. "C" is happy and experiencing a sense of release and joy. These emotions make us want to *approach* something in a positive way.

But emotions, like motives, can begin a chain of fairly complex behavior that goes far beyond simple approach or avoidance. For example, if we are anxious about something, we may collect information about it, ask questions, and then decide whether to approach it, to flee from it, or to stay and fight it. Imagine a hypothetical family faced with an anxiety-provoking situation: The husband and father has been termporarily laid off at the factory where he's worked as a foreman for 25 years. The family realizes that it faces several months of severe economic hardship. Where can supplementary income be found? How can family goals be adjusted? Will it be possible to survive the crisis without serious damage? Faced with these uncertainties and the anxiety that they create, the family decides to approach the problem with a series of more positive strategies. The husband, who is knowledgeable about cars and likes to work with his hands, goes to work for his neighbor, who owns an automobile repair shop. His wife, who managed an office for several years when she was first married, takes advantage of her former employer's offer to return to a part-time position with the company. Their daughter accepts a scholarship at a local campus of the state university instead of attending a more expensive private school. In short, the family's emotional anxiety has focused the performance of its members and triggered a complex sequence of goal-directed behavior in much the same way that motives do.

Of course, sometimes our emotions have less beneficial effects. Most of us have been in situations in which we desperately wanted to think rationally but could not because our emotions had disrupted our concentration. Under what circumstances does emotion hinder what we do, and when does it help? There seems to be no single, simple answer. It is largely a question of degree—of both the strength of the emotion and the difficulty of the task. The **Yerkes-Dodson law** puts it this way: The more complex the task, the lower the level of arousal that can be tolerated without interfering with performance. You may feel very angry while boiling an egg, and it may not make much difference, but the same degree of emotional arousal may interfere with your ability to drive safely. Moreover, although a certain minimum level of arousal is necessary for good performance, a very high level may affect your performance for the worse (see Figure 11-5).

Yerkes-Dodson law States that there is an optimal level of arousal for the best performance on any task; the more complex the task, the lower the level of arousal that can be tolerated before performance deteriorates.

Basic Emotional Experiences

As we saw earlier, emotions can be broadly grouped according to the ways in which they affect our behavior—whether they motivate us to approach or to avoid something. But within these broad groups, how many different emotions are there?

One of the most influential attempts to identify and classify emotions was made by Robert Plutchik (1980). He proposed that animals and human beings experience eight basic categories of emotions that motivate

Figure 11-5
Graphs illustrating the Yerkes-Dodson law A certain amount of arousal is needed to perform, but a very high level of arousal interferes with performance. The level of arousal that can be tolerated is higher for a simple task than for a complex one.
After Hebb, 1955

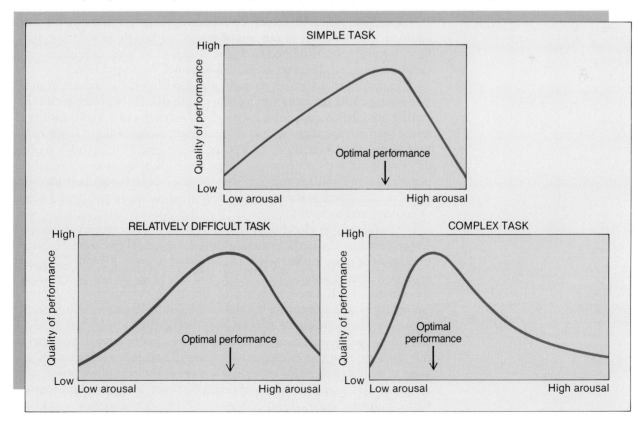

Figure 11-6

Plutchik's eight basic categories of emotions Emotions that lie next to one another on his emotion "circle" are more similar than those that lie opposite one another or are further apart. When adjacent emotions are combined, they yield new but related emotions. For example, sadness mixed with surprise leads to disappointment.

Plutchik, 1980

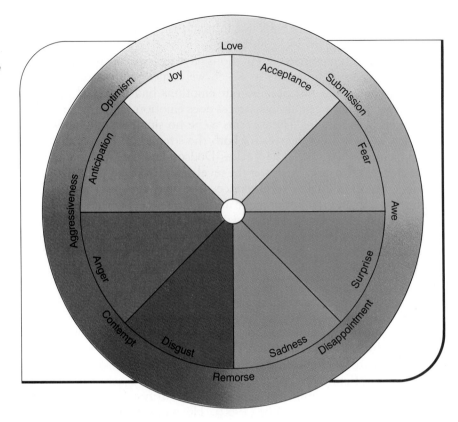

various kinds of adaptive behavior. Fear, surprise, sadness, disgust, anger, anticipation, joy, and acceptance—each of these emotions helps us to adjust to the demands of our environment, although in different ways. Fear, for example, is related to flight, which helps protect animals from their enemies, while anger is related to attack or destruction.

Emotions that lie next to each other on Plutchik's emotion "circle" (see Figure 11-6) are more similar than those that lie opposite each other or that are farther away from each other. Amazement is more similar to terror than to rage; ecstasy and adoration are more similar to each other than either is to loathing. Moreover, according to Plutchik's model, different emotions can combine to produce an even wider range of experience. Anticipation and joy, for example, combine to become optimism; joy and acceptance make us feel love; disappointment is a blend of surprise and sadness.

Within any of Plutchik's eight categories, emotions vary in *intensity* (represented by the vertical dimensions of the model in Figure 11-7). At the top—the most intense—end of the model lie rage, vigilance, ecstasy, adoration, terror, amazement, grief, and loathing. As we move toward the bottom, each emotion becomes less intense, and the distinctions among the emotions become less sharp. Anger, for example, is less intense than rage, and annoyance is even less intense than anger. But all three emotions—annoyance, anger, and rage—are closely related. In general, the more intense the emotion, the more it motivates behavior. If you want to mail an important letter and you get to the post office one minute after it closes, your basic emotion might be anger, and you might respond with a muttered curse. If you only wanted to buy some stamps, you would probably feel annoyed and might just walk away. But if you wanted to mail an income tax form that had to be postmarked by midnight that night, you might feel rage and end up banging on the post office door or perhaps even kicking it.

Thus, although Plutchik claims that there are only eight categories or families of emotions, within each category the emotions vary in intensity, and this fact greatly expands the range of emotions that we experience. From a very simple model such as this, it is possible to account for a large number of different emotions and a wide variety of associated behaviors.

Theories of Emotion

Why do we feel on top of the world one minute and down in the dumps the next? What causes emotional experiences?

In the 1880s, William James formulated the first modern theory of emotion, and at almost the same time a Danish psychologist, Carl Lange, reached the same conclusions. According to the **James-Lange theory,** stimuli cause physiological changes in our bodies, and emotions are the result of those physical changes. If you come face-to-face with a grizzly bear, the perception of the stimulus (the bear) causes your muscles, skin, and viscera (internal organs) to undergo changes: faster heart rate, enlarged pupils, deeper or shallower breathing, flushed face, increased perspiration, butterflies in the stomach, and a gooseflesh sensation as the body's hairs stand on end. The emotion of fear is simply your awareness of these changes. All of this, of course, happens almost instantaneously and in a reflexive, automatic way.

We now know that facial expressions can affect our emotions. In

James-Lange theory of emotion States that physical reactions precede experienced emotions.

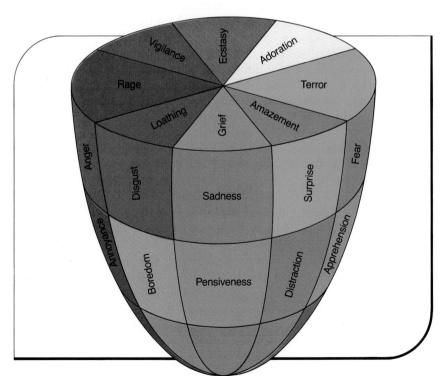

Figure 11-7
Plutchik's three-dimensional model of the eight basic emotions Within any of the categories, emotions vary in intensity. Intensity is represented on the vertical dimension of the model, ranging from maximum intensity at the top to a state of deep sleep at the bottom. The model tapers inward at the bottom to indicate that emotions are less clearly distinguishable from one another at low intensities.
Plutchik, 1980

Cannon-Bard theory of emotion States that the experience of emotion occurs simultaneously with biological changes.

Cognitive theory of emotion States that emotional experience depends on one's perception or judgment of the situation one is in.

one study, subjects reported that facial expressions such as those associated with words containing the sounds *ah* or *ee* (as in *about* or *cheese*) gave them a pleasant feeling. Facial expressions such as those produced when pronouncing words containing the sound *ooh* (as in *loose*) made them feel more negative. One explanation is that facial expressions that open the sinus cavity cause a warmer flow of blood to the brain and create a more pleasant emotional experience than do those that constrict the sinus cavity and produce a cooler flow (Zajonc, Murphy, & Inglehart, 1989). This process may not apply to all emotions, however.

If peripheral body changes alone *cause* specific emotions, then we should be able to pinpoint different body changes for each emotion. Perhaps butterflies in the stomach make us afraid and blushing causes shame or guilt. There is some evidence that the physiological changes associated with fear and anxiety are somewhat different from those associated with anger and aggressiveness (Funkenstein, King, & Drolette, 1953; McGeer & McGeer, 1980). But beyond this, psychologists have not found distinct bodily states that could cause all of our various emotions. All strong emotions, for example, are accompanied by a rapid pulse rate. But a rapid pulse rate does not tell you *which* strong emotion you are feeling. Most of the physiological "signs" of emotion say only that some kind of emotion is present and tell how intense it is. They cannot tell us whether we are experiencing terror or joy.

How, then, can we explain the differences among emotions? Nearly 70 years ago, an alternative theory of emotions, the **Cannon-Bard theory,** proposed that emotions and bodily responses occur simultaneously, not one after the other. Thus, when you see the bear, you run and are afraid—with neither reaction preceding the other. This model makes an important point: What you see (or hear or otherwise perceive) plays an important role in determining the emotional experience that you have. Recently, cognitive psychologists have developed and extended this idea by suggesting that our perception or judgment of situations (cognition) is absolutely essential to our emotional experience (Lazarus, 1982). All emotional states consist of a diffuse and general arousal of the nervous system. According to the **cognitive theory of emotion,** the situation that we are in when we are aroused—the environment—gives us clues as to what we should call this general state of arousal. Thus, our cognitions tell us how to label our diffuse feelings in a way suitable to our current thoughts and ideas about our surroundings (see Figure 11-8).

A fascinating test of the cognitive theory of emotion was undertaken by Spiesman (1965). People were shown a gory film that aroused strong emotional responses, as measured by autonomic responses like heart rate and electrical conductivity of the skin, and as reported in interviews. Spiesman decided to explore how different kinds of sound tracks would affect the level of emotional response in this stress-inducing film, as measured by skin conductivity. He compared the arousal effects of the original silent film with three different sound tracks. The first he called the *trauma* track; this track simply narrated what was happening in the film. The second track was *intellectual*; its description was detached and clinical, allowing the viewer to maintain emotional distance from the events on the screen. The third sound track was the *denial* track; it tended to gloss over, deny, or speak in glowing terms about what was depicted.

The subjects were selected from two groups: university students and

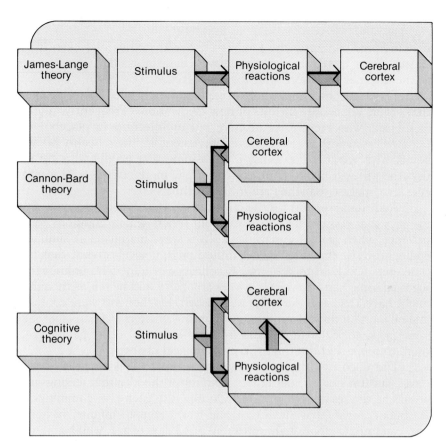

Figure 11-8
A summary of the three major theories of emotion According to the *James-Lange theory*, the body first responds physiologically to a stimulus, and then the cerebral cortex determines which emotion is being experienced. In the *Cannon-Bard theory*, impulses are sent simultaneously to the cerebral cortex and peripheral nervous system; thus the response to the stimulus and the emotion are experienced at the same time, but independently. *Cognitive theorists* propose that the cerebral cortex and peripheral nervous system work jointly to determine which emotions we feel.

business executives. Each person saw the film alone, seated in a comfortable chair, with the device to measure skin conductivity attached throughout the showing. The results clearly showed that the different verbal settings provided by each sound track affected the subjects' emotional responses. Those who heard the trauma track were much more emotional than those who had seen the film with no accompanying narration. Those who heard the intellectual and denial tracks were much less emotional. These results show quite clearly that our emotional responses are directly and sharply affected by how we interpret a situation.

However, some more recent attempts to repeat these experiments have failed to yield the same results (Hogan & Schroeder, 1981). In an effort to explain these different findings, Pennebaker and Skelton (1981) suggested that a two-part process is involved in interpreting emotional states. People, they suggest, respond to emotional arousal with a quick appraisal of their feelings, and then they search for environmental cues to back up their assessment; in the process, more attention is paid to internal cues that agree with external cues. Support for this viewpoint comes from an experiment in which subjects were asked to report their reactions to harmless white noise. One group was told that their skin temperatures would increase during exposure to the noise. A second group was told that skin temperature would decrease during noise exposure. A third group was given no expectations. Actual skin temperatures in all three groups fluctuated both up and down during the course of the experiment, with more frequent fluctuations occurring in the two groups that expected some kind of change. But subjects *reported* experiencing predominantly the kind of change that they had been led to expect. Thus, it appears that subjects were biased toward paying attention to the internal sensations that they expected.

This same process may help to explain the so-called "placebo effect" that occurs commonly in tests of new medications. Frequently, a group of subjects who receive an inactive pill or injection (a placebo) will nonetheless report measureable improvement in their health or well-being. This effect makes sense if we assume that people who are told that the pill will make them feel better pay more attention to internal cues that suggest that they are in fact getting better.

Additional support for the cognitive theory of emotion comes from the fact that people have to learn from others which emotions to experience when smoking marijuana. In a way, marijuana is similar to epinephrine. It produces vague, diffuse physiological arousal that first-time users find hard to describe. A colleague of mine who unknowingly ingested some marijuana in brownies at a party said he felt as though he might have "had a stroke"—he was flushed, his thoughts were confused, and he found it difficult to think. Beginning smokers learn to label these same physiological symptoms as a "high"—that is, other people teach them to name and interpret the physiological changes.

The cognitive theory of emotion seems to make a great deal of sense, but it is not without critics, who reject the idea that feelings must always be the result of cognitions. Quoting the poet e. e. cummings, R. B. Zajonc argues that "feelings come first." Human infants, he points out, can imitate emotional expressions at 12 days of age, well before they acquire language. Animals rely on their sense of danger to survive: A rabbit doesn't evaluate the possibilities that might account for a rustle in the bushes before it runs away (Zajonc, 1980).

Zajonc suggests instead that the affective (or emotional) system responds instantaneously to the situations in which we find ourselves. But the affective reaction is likely to be fairly diffuse and difficult to explain. Therefore, we invent explanations for our feelings: Cognition comes *after* emotion. Think for a moment about the way in which you form opinions of people whom you meet. According to Zajonc, you have an immediate emotional reaction of some sort (perhaps attraction or repulsion) toward your new acquaintance, and you begin sizing up how the person feels about you. Then you invent ways to make the emotional reaction seem rational (Zajonc, 1984).

C. E. Izard (1971) is another researcher whose theory challenges head-on some of the assumptions of the cognitive theory of emotions. Cognitive theorists tend to believe that infants do not experience distinct emotions because they have not yet learned to interpret the physiological arousal that accompanies all emotion. Izard, however, thinks that babies are born with 10 basic, distinct emotions that are quite similar to Plutchik's 8 fundamental emotions. The ability to experience these basic emotions is innate and has evolved over thousands of generations, because emotion helps both infants and adults to survive. Disgust, for instance, promotes removal of possibly dangerous things from the mouth.

Also contrary to cognitive theory, Izard claims that emotions can be experienced without the intervention of cognition. In his view, a situation such as separation or pain provokes a unique pattern of facial movements and body postures. These responsive patterns are unlearned and are the result of activity in the nervous system that may be completely independent of conscious thought (Trotter, 1983). When information about our facial expressions and posture reaches the brain, we automatically experience the corresponding emotion. We experience surprise, for instance, once a complex pattern of muscular—and especially facial—activities has "told" the brain that we are feeling surprise rather than anger or shame. According to Izard, then, the James-Lange theory was essentially right in suggesting that emotional experience arises from bodily reactions. But Izard's theory stresses the face and body posture as crucial to the experience of emotion, while the James-Lange theory emphasizes visceral reactions.

If Izard is right, then an important element in determining our emotional experience is our own expressive behavior, which is the next—and final—topic in this chapter.

■ The Expression of Emotion

Sometimes you are vaguely aware that a person makes you feel uncomfortable. When pressed to be more precise, you might say, "You never know what he is thinking." But you do not mean that you never know his opinion of a film or what he thought about the last election. It would probably be more accurate to say that you do not know what he is *feeling*. Almost all of us conceal our emotions to some extent in order to protect our self-image or to conform to social conventions. But usually there are some clues to help us determine another person's emotions.

Verbal Communication

It would be simplest, of course, if we could just ask people what they are feeling. Sometimes we do, with varying results. If your roommate finishes washing the dishes and says acidly, "I hope you are enjoying your novel," her words are quite clear, but you know very well that she is not saying what she means. If she were to say, "I am furious that you did not offer to help," she would be giving you an accurate report of her emotions at that moment.

For many reasons, we may not be able or willing to report our emotions accurately. In some situations, people simply do not know what their emotions are. A father who abuses his child may sincerely profess affection for the child, yet act in ways that reflect another set of emotions hidden from his own awareness. Even when we are aware of our emotions, we sometimes dimish the degree of emotion that we are feeling, as when we say that we are "a little worried" about an upcoming exam, when in fact we are terrified. Or we may deny the emotion entirely, especially if it is negative. This may be done out of politeness or out of self-protection, as when we claim to like someone either because we do not want to hurt that person or because we feel that he or she has some kind of power over us.

Whatever the reason, often what people *say* does not reflect accurately what they are *feeling*. Thus, it is sometimes necessary to resort to other cues to emotion if we are to understand them fully.

Nonverbal Communication

"Actions speak louder than words," the saying goes, and people are often more eloquent with their bodies than they realize or intend. We transmit a good deal of information to others through our facial expressions, body postures, vocal intonations, and physical distance; in fact, our bodies often send emotional messages that contradict our words.

Here's an extended example of this process at work. At a county fair, a political rally, or a football game, a pickpocket goes to work. Standing behind someone, the nimble-fingered thief prepares to relieve him of his wallet. Slowly, the thief's hand moves toward the victim's back pocket and is almost touching the wallet, when suddenly it pulls back empty. The pickpocket moves casually through the crowd, whistling. What went wrong? What gave the thief a clue that his intended victim might have been about to reach for his wallet? It could have been any one of many signs to a pickpocket skillful enough to stay out of jail. The hairs on the back of the victim's neck might have bristled slightly; there might have been a slight stiffening of the back, a twitch in a neck muscle, a subtle change in skin color, a trickle of sweat. The victim might not yet have been aware that his pocket was about to be picked, but these physiological signals showed an awareness that something was afoot.

As we noted earlier, these physiological changes are not normally under our control. They tend to function independently of our will and often, indeed, against it.

Facial expressions are the most obvious emotional indicators. We saw earlier that facial expressions can cause some emotional experiences. Facial expressions are also good indicators of the emotions that a person is experiencing, from whatever source. We can tell a good deal about a person's emotional state by observing whether that person looks as if he or she is laughing, crying, smiling, or frowning. Many facial expressions are innate, not learned. Children who are born deaf and blind use the same facial gestures to express the same emotions that other children do. Charles Darwin originated the idea that most animals share a common pattern of muscular facial movements. For example, dogs, tigers, and humans all bare their teeth in rage. Darwin also suggested that expressive behaviors serve a basic biological, as well as a social, function. His idea that emotions have an evolutionary history and can be traced across cultures as part of our biological heritage laid the basis for many modern investigations of emotional expression (Izard, 1982) (see Figure 11-9).

It turns out, however, that some emotions are easier to express facially than others. Thompson and Meltzer (1964) asked their subjects to fake certain emotions. They found that most people had no trouble expressing love, fear, determination, and happiness. Suffering, disgust, and contempt were more difficult to express convincingly. These feelings were also more difficult for other people to "read." And widely different emotions are easier to tell apart than are related emotions such as fear and surprise (Tomkins & McCarter, 1964).

Body language is another means by which messages can be communicated nonverbally. When we are relaxed, we tend to stretch back into a chair; when we are tense, we tend to sit more stiffly with our feet together. Slumping and straightness of the back supply clues about which emotion someone is feeling. Birdwhistell (1952) has made the study of

Sadness
Brows' inner corners raised, drawn out and down.

Interest
Brows raised or knit, mouth softly rounded, lips pursed.

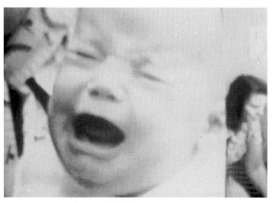

Distress
Eyes tightly closed, mouth, as in anger, squared and angular.

Fear
Brows level, drawn in and up, eyelids lifted, mouth retracted.

Anger
Brows drawn together and downward, eyes fixed, mouth squarish.

Joy
Mouth forms smile, cheeks lifted, twinkle in eyes

Figure 11-9
Infant facial archetypes Working from Charles Darwin's theory that certain emotional and facial expressions have an evolutionary history and are universal, psychologist Carroll Izard believes that he has isolated 10 distinct emotions that can be interpreted in the facial expressions of infants. Six characteristic expressions are illustrated here.

Different emotions can be communicated nonverbally. After giving a speech and then forgetting to introduce her husband, Nancy Reagan is obviously embarrassed; the former President is obviously amused.

The meaning of body language, distance, and gesture varies from culture to culture. Most Americans would interpret Soviet premier Mikhail Gorbachev's gesture as a gesture of triumph. For Russians, however, it is a symbolic gesture of friendship.

body language into a science called *kinesics*. He believes that every movement of the body has a meaning, that no movement is accidental, and that all of our significant gestures and movements are learned. In a study similar to that of Thompson and Meltzer, Beier (1974) videotaped subjects acting out six emotions: anger, fear, seductiveness, indifference, happiness, and sadness. He found that most subjects could portray successfully two out of the six emotions, but that the rest of their portrayals did not reflect their intentions. One girl appeared angry no matter what emotion she tried to project; another was invariably seductive.

Body language may sometimes contradict verbal messages in the communication of what we are feeling (Birdwhistell, 1974). In a family, for example, one might first notice that the mother verbally defers to her husband and children by asking for and taking their advice. But a closer inspection may reveal her to be the true leader when she leans forward and all the other family members unconsciously imitate her (Fast, 1970).

Just as people send out complex and contradictory emotional messages by nonverbal cues, they also show considerable variety in their ability to read such messages. Rosenthal and his colleagues (1974, 1979) developed a test of sensitivity to nonverbal cues—the Profile of Nonverbal Sensitivity (PONS)—that assesses people's ability to judge the meaning of vocal intonations and face and body movements. In the test, the subjects watch a film that shows an actress or actor portraying various emotional states. Sometimes, the portrayal is accompanied by spoken phrases, but certain tones and rhythms that identify them as distinct words have been removed. The viewer then picks one of two possible interpretations of the scene.

The study showed that women were consistently better than men at understanding nonverbal cues, although men in the "nurturant" professions—psychiatrists, psychologists, mental hospital aides, and teachers—along with artists, actors, and designers, scored as high as women. The study also showed that sensitivity to nonverbal cues increases with age, probably because we accumulate more experience in judging vocal tones and observing body movements as we grow older.

Closely related to the ability to read other people's emotions is *empathy*—the arousal of emotion in an observer that is a vicarious response to the other person's situation (Parke & Asher, 1983). Empathy depends not only on your ability to identify someone else's emotions, but also on the capacity to put yourself in his or her place and to have an appropriate emotional response. Just as sensitivity to nonverbal cues increases with age, so does empathy: The cognitive and perceptual abilities required for empathy develop only as a child matures.

In addition to body language, another kind of body communication is *distance*. The normal distance between people differs from culture to culture. Two Swedes conversing would ordinarily stand much farther apart than would two Arabs or Greeks. Within every culture, there seems to be a distance that is generally thought appropriate for normal conversation. If someone is standing closer than usual to you, it may indicate aggressiveness or sexuality; if farther away than usual, it may indicate withdrawal or repugnance.

Explicit *acts*, of course, can also be nonverbal clues. When we receive a 2:00 A.M. telephone call, we expect that what the caller has to say is urgent. A slammed door tells us that the person who left the room is angry. If friends drop in for a visit and you invite them into the living room, you are probably less at ease with them than you are with people whom you ask to sit down at the kitchen table. *Gestures*, such as a slap on the back or an embrace, can also indicate feelings. Whether a person shakes your hand briefly or for a long time, firmly or limply, can tell you something about what he or she feels toward you.

A word of caution is needed here. Although overt behavior can be a clue to emotion, it is not always infallible as a clue to a person's feelings. Laughing and crying sound alike, for example, and we bare our teeth in smiles as well as in snarls. Crying can "mean" sorrow, joy, anger, nostalgia, or that you are slicing an onion. Moreover, as with verbal reports, it is always possible that someone is putting out false clues. And we all have done something thoughtlessly—turned our backs, frowned because we were thinking about something else, laughed at the wrong time— that has given offense because these acts were taken to express an emotion that we were not, in fact, feeling at that time.

■ Gender Differences and Emotion

Experience tells us that males and females differ considerably in how they express emotion and the emotions they choose to express. As noted in Chapter 1, for example, men are often perceived as being less emotional than women. But does it follow that men *feel* less emotion, or is it that men are less likely to express the emotions that they feel? And are there some emotions that men are *more* likely to express than women?

Recent research sheds some light on these questions. In one study, when men and women were shown people in distress, the men showed little emotion whereas the women expressed feelings of concern and distress for the other person (Eisenberg & Lennon, 1983). However, physiological measures of emotional arousal (such as heart rate and blood pressure) showed that the men in the study were actually just as affected emotionally as were the women, but the men inhibited the expression of their emotions whereas the women were more open about their feelings. O'Leary and Smith (1988) have pointed out that emotions such as sympathy, sadness, empathy, and distress are often considered to be "unmanly," and boys are trained from an early age to inhibit the expression of those emotions in public settings.

In other circumstances, men and women react with very different emotions to the same situation. For example, Brody (1985) described one study in which subjects reacted to hypothetical situations in which they were betrayed or criticized by another person. Males usually said that they would feel angry, while females were likely to report that they would feel hurt, sad, or disappointed in the same situation.

It appears that when men are angered, they tend to interpret the cause of their anger as something or someone in the environment around them, and they are likely to turn their anger outward toward other people and toward the situation in which they find themselves. Women, on the other hand, are more likely to see themselves as the source of the problem and to turn their anger inward against themselves. Given these differences, it is perhaps not surprising that men are four times more likely than women to be violent, while women are much more likely than men to be depressed.

APPLICATION

Truth Is More than Skin-Deep—The Lie Detector

As credibility and trust have declined in American society, the popularity of lie detectors has increased. Once limited to law enforcement applications, lie detectors (also called polygraphs) came to be routinely used by corporations, banks, and even fast-food chains to question job applicants about their honesty in past jobs. In 1983, President Reagan ordered polygraph tests of certain federal employees in an effort to plug leaks to the press of classified or embarrassing information.

But by December of 1988, the Employee Protection Act prohibited the use of polygraphs for random examinations or as part of a preemployment screening process. The growing use of the polygraph brought to the fore a controversial question: What does a lie detector measure? Is it only the act of telling a lie that produces the telltale patterns of inked lines on graph paper? Or can other factors, such as emotional reactions to the content of the questions or the testing situation itself, cause truthful people to appear to be liars?

Lie detectors do not register lies; they rely on the fact that emotions and inner conflict are typically accompanied by physiological changes. When a person lies, there are changes in blood pressure, in breathing, and in the resistance of the skin to electrical current, known as *galvanic skin response*. There is no single pattern of responses unique to lying, however; the pattern varies from person to person.

In a typical lie detector examination, failing the test can have serious consequences. Subjects are thus generally quite nervous as a blood pressure cuff is strapped to one arm, sensors designed to measure breathing are attached to the chest and stomach, and electrodes are placed on the fingertips to measure galvanic skin response. Because the blood pressure cuff soon becomes uncomfortable, the examination must be short—three to four minutes long.

The form and mix of questions is a key to the examination. A typical set of questions includes just a few that are critical: "Did you take money from the cash register on the evening of July 21?" The rest are control questions, designed to be answered dishonestly even if the subject is telling the truth about the relevant questions. For example, to a control question such as "Have you ever taken anything in your life?" even most truthful people will choose to lie, given the circumstances, since just about everyone has stolen something sometime. Polygraph examiners assume that an otherwise truthful person will react more strongly to the control questions, while an untruthful subject will react more strongly to the relevant ones (Mayer, 1982).

Lie detectors are far from error-free. Figures vary widely, but according to one estimate, examinations in the field correctly identify about 75 percent of those lying. Unfortunately, about 49 percent of those telling the truth are also identified as lying (Horvath, 1977). One major source of error is the fact that galvanic skin response changes in reaction to all kinds of emotions, not just those connected with deception (Lykken, 1975). When someone is asked if he or she committed a murder, the lie detector is likely to jump. Of course, this may reflect guilt, but it may also reflect anxiety, fear, or loathing—all possible reactions to being questioned about a murder. If a suspect were questioned about marital problems, relationships with parents, or even attitudes toward work, the polygraph might make a similar jump in emotional response regardless of whether the person told the truth when answering (Stern et al., 1981).

It is also easy to fool the polygraph machine,

given the proper knowledge. Some tactics do not work, however. Conscious efforts not to sweat or not to alter one's respiratory patterns will not succeed. Nor will efforts to increase one's response to control items, such as by clenching one's teeth (Waid & Orne, 1982). But taking tranquilizers does seem to reduce the physiological response to lying. So does not paying attention to the questions. In one experiment, subjects counted backward by sevens during their examination to distract themselves from the questions, and they were able to escape detection more often as a result (Waid, Orne, & Orne, 1981).

Personal and social factors can also affect the physiological signs monitored by the machine. The galvanic skin response of some people changes spontaneously at a high rate, thus increasing the chances that their truthful answers will appear to be lies. Finally, the degree to which examiner and subject are matched in terms of sex, age, race, or ethnicity may also have an effect. In one study, the lie detector was least successful when examiner and subjects shared the same ethnicity, possibly because the subjects felt most at ease in this situation (Waid & Orne, 1981).

It is possible to increase the accuracy of polygraphs by testing only for "guilty knowledge"—that is, knowledge about details of the crime that only the

Lie detectors make use of the fact that inner emotions are typically accompanied by measurable physiological changes.

guilty person could know. For example, if a list of banks is read, a guilty suspect should react more strongly to the name of the bank that he or she actually robbed. However, in many of the 500,000 to 1 million testings that take place each year in the United States, the most sophisticated methods are not used in formulating the questions or interpreting the results, partly because the vast majority of the 4,000 to 8,000 examiners have had little or no training in physiology or psychology (Lykken, 1975).

■ Summary

- **Why do we have emotions? What purpose does motivation serve?** Motives and emotions both energize and direct our behavior. The two are closely related and can activate us even without our awareness. **Motives** are triggered by bodily needs, cues in the environment, and such feelings as loneliness or guilt. When such stimuli combine to create a motive, goal-directed behavior results. Like motives, **emotions**, which usually refer to such complex feelings as anger, fear, or love, activate behavior; but it is more difficult to predict the behavior and goals affected by emotion than those stimulated by motives.

- **Is motivation inborn?** One of the earliest explanations of motivated behavior focused on **instincts**—innate tendencies to behave in certain ways. But since not all human behavior is inborn, psychologists began to look for other explanations of motivation. According to **drive reduction theory**, bodily needs create a state of tension or arousal called a *drive;* motivated behavior is seen as an attempt to reduce this tension and return the body to a state of **homeostasis** or balance. However, other theories remind us that even such common activities as learning new skills tend to increase arousal and suggest that motivated behavior reflects our efforts to maintain an optimal state of arousal. Moreover, some behavior is triggered by objects in our environment (**incentives**) rather than by internal states.

- **Primary drives** are unlearned motives that are common to every animal. They include hunger, thirst, and sex. The primary drives are triggered by physiological stimuli and by both internal and external cues. All of them are subject to learning and experience.

- **What makes us hungry?** Hunger is influenced by two centers in the brain. The *hunger center* stimulates the desire to eat, while the *satiety center* signals when to stop. The hunger center is stimulated in response to a drop in the level of *glucose* in the blood or an increase in the level of fats in the blood. Receptors in the stomach send signals to the brain, where they stimulate the satiety center. Another hunger regulator operates on a long-term basis to regulate the body's weight. The hunger drive can be affected by emotions, and social influences may also affect the motivation to eat: The ways in which people respond when they are hungry vary with their experiences and are largely governed by learning and social conditioning.

- The thirst drive is related to balances of fluids within the body. One thirst regulator monitors the level of fluid inside the body's cells, and a second thirst regulator signals when there is a drop in the level of fluid outside the cells. We drink until we have consumed enough fluid to restore water to our tissues, but it is not fully understood how we know when to stop drinking. Like hunger, thirst is influenced by learned and cultural factors, and even such environmental cues as a TV commercial can influence not only our motivation to drink but our choice of what to drink.

- **What causes sexual desire?** Sexual desire is affected by hormones, mainly **testosterone;** it is also affected by sensory stimulation and by stimulation of a portion of the brain called the limbic system. In humans as in other animals, it may also be affected by the smell of **pheromones.** *Sexual dysfunction,* the loss or impairment of ordinary sexual function in men and women, is sometimes caused by organic factors but is more often due to psychological factors.

- A second set of motives that is largely innate depends more on external stimuli than on internal physiological states. These **stimulus motives,** such as curiosity, activity, exploration, manipulation, and contact, push us to investigate, and often to alter, our environment.

- Some motives are learned as we develop. Aggression is one of these *learned motives.* **Aggression** includes all behavior that is intended to inflict physical or psychological harm on others and implies intent to do harm. Some theories hold that aggression is an innate drive, but most psychologists today believe that aggression is largely a learned response. They argue that aggression can be learned by watching models whose aggressive behavior either gets them what they want or avoids punishment. They add that even watching aggressive behavior on television can contribute to the learning of such behavior.

- **Is being highly competitive necessary for achieve-**

ment? Various **social motives** are also learned, including achievement, power, and affiliation. The **achievement motive** is a desire to excel, to overcome obstacles, to achieve for its own sake. There appear to be three interrelated aspects of achievement-oriented behavior: *work orientation*—the desire to work hard and do a good job; *mastery*—the preference for challenging activities; and *competitiveness*—the enjoyment of matching one's skills against those of others. Surprisingly, a high degree of competitiveness may interfere with achievement, because preoccupation with the end of "winning" may distract people from the means of achieving their goals. The **power motive** is the need to control or influence other people or groups. Finally, the **affiliation motive,** the need to be with others, is usually aroused when people feel threatened. One recent theory of affiliation suggests that people seek company or solitude depending on how much benefit they can expect from being with other people.

- Abraham Maslow proposed that all motives can be arranged in a hierarchy, from lower to higher. Higher motives will appear only after the more basic ones have been satisfied. The most evolved motive in Maslow's hierarchy is *self-actualization.*

- **How do emotions affect performance? Is a musician or football player likely to perform better when feeling emotional?** Emotions, like motives, arouse and direct our behavior. We can classify emotions in terms of whether they cause us to avoid something (fear), approach something aggressively (anger), or approach something with acceptance (joy, love). Emotions can either help or hinder performance. The **Yerkes-Dodson law** states that the more complex the task, the lower the level of emotional arousal that can be tolerated before performance declines.

- Robert Plutchik proposed a more detailed classification of eight basic emotions, each of which helps the individual adapt to the environment in some way. Each emotion also varies in intensity. Different basic emotions can combine like primary colors to produce more complex emotions.

- There are three basic theories about emotion. The **James-Lange theory** maintains that emotion is the result of visceral or peripheral reactions. The perception of a stimulus causes the body to undergo certain physiological changes that are the cause of emotion.

- The **Cannon-Bard theory,** unlike the James-Lange theory, holds that emotions and bodily responses occur simultaneously, not one after the other. Thus, one's perception of a situation strongly influences one's emotional experience. This theory is a forerunner of cognitive theories of emotion.

- **Someone stands you up for a date you'd been looking forward to. Why are some people likely to feel angry about this, while others will feel hurt and sad?** *Cognitive theories of emotion* state that emotion results from the interaction of cognitive and physiological processes. Our cognitions—our perceptions and expectations—tell us how to label our physiological states in ways that reflect our surroundings and experiences. Cognitive theories of emotion hold that our cognitions tell us what emotions we are experiencing, that our emotional responses are affected by our perceptions and expectations can even influence the way we respond to internal sensations.

- Izard has challenged the cognitive theory of emotions by proposing that humans are born with the ability to experience a number of distinct emotions. In his view, situations evoke a unique pattern of facial expressions and body postures, which the brain translates into an appropriate emotional experience.

- Nonverbal communication—facial expressions, position, posture, distance between people, explicit acts, and gestures—can be a useful clue to emotion. Often, nonverbal communication contradicts a person's verbal message. Many *facial expressions* do not appear to be learned but are universal in humans. The rest of the body also sends messages through its position and posture, an idiom called *body language*. Women, on the average, tend to understand nonverbal clues better than men.

Review Questions

1. Both _____ and _____ direct our behavior and can activate behavior even without our awareness.
2. Motivation begins with which of the following?
   a. emotion   c. stimulus
   b. drive   d. arousal
3. According to drive reduction theory, the state of balance toward which motivated behavior is directed is called _____.
4. Primary motives are not at all affected by learning or experience.   T / F
5. In the brain, signals from the _____ center stimulate eating, while those from the _____ center reduce the desire to eat.
6. Thirst regulators monitor the level of _____ inside and outside the body's cells.
   a. water   c. sodium
   b. nutrients d. fluids
7. The hormone _____ stimulates sexual arousal in both men and women.
8. A class of wants or needs that are set in action by external stimuli and push us to investigate our environment are called _____ motives.
9. Next to each of the motives listed, mark U if it is an unlearned motive and L if it is a learned motive.
   ____ sex   ____ aggression
   ____ curiosity   ____ manipulation
   ____ affiliation   ____ achievement
   ____ activity   ____ contact
   ____ power
10. You might accidentally hit a dog that is crossing the street, but deliberately running over your neighbor's dog would be considered an act of _____.
11. A person who is willing to contend with the high risks of a career in sales is probably motivated by a high _____ motive.
12. The _____ motive is sometimes aroused when a person needs to be consoled or supported by a group of peers.
13. According to Maslow's hierarchy, the higher motives can only appear after the basic ones have been satisfied.   T / F
14. According to the _____ _____ law, there is a relationship between the complexity of a task and the level of emotional arousal that can be tolerated while performing the task.
15. According to Robert Plutchik, emotions vary in _____, a fact that accounts in part for the great range of emotions we experience.
16. Match the following theories of emotion with their definitions:
   ____ Cannon-Bard
   ____ cognitive theory
   ____ James-Lange

   a. says that physical reactions come before experienced emotions
   b. says that emotions and bodily responses occur simultaneously
   c. says that emotional experience depends on perception of a given situation
17. Izard's theory of emotion stresses the importance of:
   a. cognition.
   b. expressive behavior.
18. Two important nonverbal clues to emotion are _____ _____ and _____ _____.

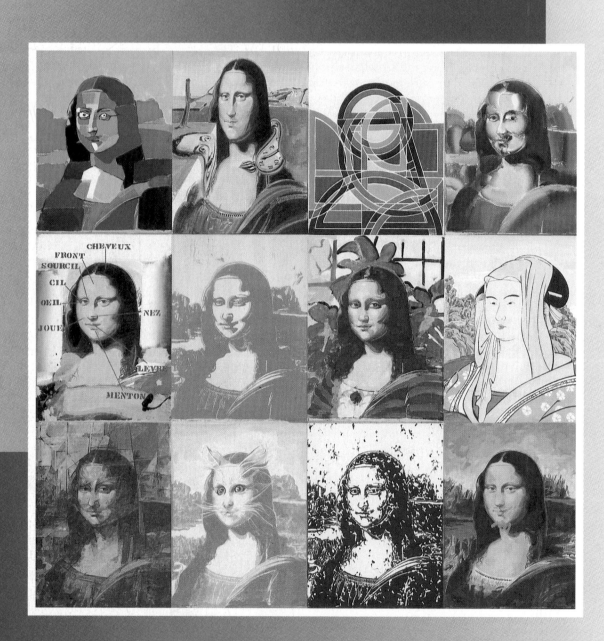

12 Personality

■ Thinking Critically

Are people usually aware of the reasons why they behave as they do?

Why do so many ancient myths and legends contain characters who are easily recognizable today?

What is it that makes people strive for accomplishment and perfection?

What role do the relationships within your family play in forming your personality?

Does personality develop through a predictable series of stages?

If you say someone is stingy or easygoing, to what are you referring?

Are they likely to be consistently stingy or easygoing in every situation?

Do people's expectations guide their personalities?

Are personalities learned from experiences?

How can a person's response to an inkblot provide information about his or her personality?

The study of personality has given rise to a number of theories that provide tentative answers to these and other questions discussed in this chapter and in the Chapter Summary.

■ Outline

Woodcut of Freud by Jean Cocteau
Transforming the lower body into a human profile is Cocteau's way of symbolizing the effect of the id on "higher" principles of human behavior.

Sigmund Freud

People often talk about personality as if it were a commodity, like a bright tie that adds life to an old suit. Moreover, we sometimes talk as if personality consisted only of appealing, admirable traits: affection, charm, honesty. But as we shall see in this chapter, to a psychologist personality is much more complex than the ordinary use of the word implies, and it includes negative as well as positive personal qualities.

It is easy to talk about aspects or traits of personality without defining the term itself. And we often do: "I don't trust that man. He isn't honest," we might say. Or, "I love Anne. She's good-hearted." But a broad definition of personality is difficult, partly because personality is not one characteristic or ability, but a whole range of them. Even psychologists have a hard time agreeing on a single definition of personality. One current definition, and the one we will use, is that **personality** is the "pattern of characteristic thoughts, feelings, and behaviors that persists over time and situations and that distinguishes one person from another" (Phares, 1984, p. 673). That's quite a mouthful, but notice two important parts of this definition. First, personality refers to those aspects that distinguish a person from everybody else. Personality is a person's psychological signature: the behaviors, attitudes, motives, tendencies, outlooks, and emotions with which he or she responds to the world. In this sense, personality is both characteristic of and unique to a particular person.

A second aspect of our definition is that personality persists over time and across situations. Whether we are reflecting on our own behavior or interpreting the actions of someone else, we expect to find consistency. If a person is friendly one day, we would be surprised if he or she were unfriendly the next. If a relative who is usually quiet and mannerly suddenly turns loud and disrespectful, we are concerned and seek explanations. We know that life is not as predictable as a television serial, but we do expect a degree of consistency, a pattern of behavior that reflects each person's unique personality. And when we are faced with inconsistency, we suspect that something is wrong. Thus, the concept of personality lends a degree of predictability and stability to an individual.

Thoughtful people have always tried to comprehend the variety of human personality. But it was only a century ago that scientists began to make systematic scientific observations of personality and to draw conclusions from them. Some theorists emphasize early childhood experiences; some stress heredity. Others attribute the key role to the environment. Some researchers even question just how consistent people are from situation to situation and from time to time and play down the importance of the whole concept of a unique and consistent personality. In this chapter, we will look at some of the major personality theories in contemporary psychology and at ways to assess personality.

■ Psychodynamic Theories
Sigmund Freud

To this day, Sigmund Freud is the best-known and most influential personality theorist. Freud specified an entirely new perspective for the study of human behavior. Up to his time, psychology had focused on consciousness—that is, on those thoughts and feelings of which we are aware. Freud, however, stressed the **unconscious**—all the ideas, thoughts, and feelings of which we are not normally aware. Although many of his views were modified by later research (actually, Freud himself revised and expanded his theories throughout his life), his ideas still form the basis of **psychoanalysis,** and they influence our language, literature, customs, and child-rearing practices.

BASIC CONCEPTS. According to Freud, the basis of human behavior is to be found in various unconscious instincts, or drives. He distinguished two classes of instincts: life instincts and death instincts. Relatively little is known about the **death instincts,** which show up as self-destructive, suicidal tendencies when directed toward the self and as aggression or war when directed toward others. Under **life instincts** Freud included all those instincts involved in the survival of the individual and of the species: hunger, thirst, self-preservation, and especially sex. It is important to note that Freud used the term *sexual instincts* to refer not just to erotic sexuality but to the desire for virtually any form of pleasure. In this broad sense, Freud regarded the sexual instinct as the most critical factor in the development of personality.

The life and death instincts are part of what Freud called the id (see Figure 12-1). The **id** is a "seething cauldron" of unconscious urges and desires that are continually seeking expression. The id operates according to the **pleasure principle:** It tries to obtain immediate gratification and thus to pursue pleasure and avoid pain. Just as soon as an instinct arises, the id seeks to gratify it. But since the id is not in contact with the real world, it has just two ways of obtaining gratification. One is by reflex actions, such as coughing, which relieve unpleasant sensations at once. Another is by what Freud termed *wish fulfillment,* or **primary-process thinking:** A person forms a mental image of an object or situation that partially satisfies the instinct and relieves the uncomfortable feeling. Primary-process thought is most clearly evident in dreams and daydreams, but it can occur in other ways. If you are angered by someone and spend the next half hour imagining all the brilliant things that you might have said or done to get even, then you are engaging in a form of primary-process thinking.

Mental images of this kind can provide fleeting relief, but they are not very effective in fully satisfying most needs. Just thinking about being with someone you love can be gratifying, but it is a poor substitute for actually being with that person. Therefore, the id by itself is not very effective in gratifying instincts. It must ultimately have contact with reality if it is to relieve its discomfort. The id's link to reality is the ego.

Freud thought that the **ego** controls all thinking and reasoning activities. Through the senses, the ego learns about the external world. The ego also controls the satisfaction of the id's drives in the external world. We noted earlier that in seeking to replace discomfort with comfort, the id acts according to the pleasure principle. In contrast, the ego operates by the **reality principle.** By means of intelligent reasoning, the ego tries to delay satisfying the id's desires until it can do so safely and successfully (see Figure 12-2). For example, if you are thirsty, your ego will attempt to determine how best to obtain something to quench your thirst effec-

Unconscious In Freud's theory, all the ideas, thoughts, and feelings of which we are not and cannot normally become aware.

Psychoanalysis Both Freud's personality theory and his form of therapy.

Death instincts In Freud's theory of personality, the group of instincts that lead toward aggression, destruction, and death.

Life instincts In Freud's theory of personality, all those instincts involved in the survival of the individual and the species, including hunger, self-preservation, and sex.

Id In Freud's theory of personality, the collection of unconscious urges and desires that continually seek expression.

Pleasure principle According to Freud, the way in which the id seeks immediate gratification of an instinct.

Primary-process thinking In Freud's theory, the process by which the id achieves immediate partial satisfaction of an instinct through mental images such as dreams and daydreams.

Ego According to Freud, the part of the personality that mediates between environmental demands (reality), conscience (superego), and instinctual needs (id); now often used as a synonym for "self."

Reality principle According to Freud, satisfaction of instincts safely and effectively in the real world, characteristic of the ego.

Secondary-process thinking In Freud's theory, the process by which the ego uses intelligent reasoning to find safe and effective ways to gratify id instincts in the real world.

Superego According to Freud, the social and parental standards the individual has internalized; the conscience and the ego ideal.

Ego ideal That part of the superego that consists of standards of what one would like to be.

Libido According to Freud, the energy generated by the sexual instinct.

Fixation According to Freud, a partial or complete halt at some point in a person's psychosexual development.

Oral stage First stage in Freud's theory of personality development, in which the infant's erotic feelings center on the mouth, lips, and tongue.

Figure 12-1

Diagram of the structural relationship formed by the id, ego, and superego

The *ego* is partly unconscious, partly conscious, and derives knowledge of the external world through the senses. The *superego* is also partly conscious and partly unconscious. But the *id* is entirely unconscious. The open space beneath the id indicates the limitlessness of the unconscious id.

Adapted from *New Introductory Lectures on Psychoanalysis* by Sigmund Freud. New York: Carlton House, 1933.

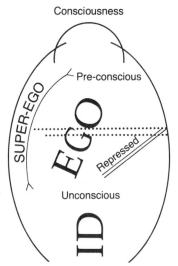

Consciousness

Pre-conscious

SUPER-EGO

EGO

Repressed

Unconscious

ID

tively and safely. Freud called this type of realistic thinking **secondary-process thinking.**

A personality that consisted only of ego and id would be completely selfish. It would behave effectively but unsocially. Fully adult behavior is governed not only by reality but also by morality—that is, by one's conscience or the moral standards that people develop through interaction with their parents and society. Freud called this moral guardian the **superego.**

The superego is not present in a child at birth. As young children, we are amoral and do whatever is pleasurable. As we mature, we assimilate, or adopt as our own, the judgments of our parents about what is "good" and "bad." In time, the external restraint applied by our parents is replaced by our own internal self-restraint. The superego, eventually acting as conscience, takes over the task of observing and guiding the ego, just as the parents observe and guide the child.

According to Freud, the superego also compares the ego's actions with an **ego ideal** of perfection and then rewards or punishes the ego accordingly. Unfortunately, the superego may be too harsh in its judgments. Dominated by such a punishing superego, an artist, for example, may realize the impossibility of equaling Rembrandt or Michelangelo and give up painting.

Ideally, the id, ego, and superego work in harmony. The ego satisfies the demands of the id in a reasonable, moral manner approved by the superego. We are then free to love and hate and to express our emotions sensibly and without guilt. When our id is dominant, our instincts are unbridled and we are apt to be a danger to ourselves and to society. When our superego dominates, our behavior is checked too tightly and we cannot enjoy a normal life.

PSYCHOSEXUAL STAGES. Freud's theory of personality development gives center stage to the way in which the sexual instinct is satisfied during the course of life. Recall that Freud thought of the sexual instinct not just as a desire for sexual activity but, in broader terms, as a craving for sensual pleasure of all kinds. Freud called the energy from the sexual instinct **libido.** As an infant matures, his or her libido becomes focused on different sensitive parts of the body. During the first one and a half years of life, the dominant source of sensual pleasure for the child is the mouth. At about 18 months, sensuality shifts to the anus, and at about age three it shifts again, this time to the genitals. The child's experience at each stage stamps his or her personality with tendencies that endure into adulthood. If the child is deprived of pleasure (or allowed too much gratification) from the part of the body that dominates a certain stage, some sexual energy may remain permanently tied to that part of the body. This is called **fixation,** and as we will see, it can lead to immature forms of sexuality and to certain characteristic personality traits. Let's look more closely at the psychosexual stages that Freud identified and their relationship to personality development.

During the **oral stage** (birth to 18 months), the infant derives most of its sensual pleasure from its mouth, lips, and tongue. Moreover, the child depends completely on other people to satisfy its needs. In the early portion of the oral stage, the child relieves sexual tension by sucking and swallowing and feels frustrated when it cannot do so. By about 8 months of age, when baby teeth have developed, children can also obtain oral pleasure by chewing and biting.

According to Freud, a child's experience during the oral stage can have a profound effect on later personality. Infants who are given too much oral gratification may become both overly optimistic and extremely dependent on other people to meet their needs. However, infants who receive too little oral gratification may become pessimistic and respond with hostility when frustrated in later life. Lack of confidence, gullibility, sarcasm, and argumentativeness are also personality traits that Freud attributed to fixation at the oral stage.

With the onset of the **anal stage** (roughly 18 months to $3\frac{1}{2}$ years), the primary source of sexual pleasure shifts from the mouth to the anus, although oral stimulation continues to provide some pleasure. Just about the time children begin to derive pleasure from holding in and excreting feces, toilet training takes place, and they must learn to regulate the new pleasure. Here again, if the parents are too strict or too lenient, the child may become fixated at the anal stage. For example, if parents are too rigid about toilet training, some children will throw temper tantrums and in later life will be messy and destructive. Other children will respond by retaining feces even to the point of constipation; later in life, these children are likely to be obstinate, stingy, overly precise, and excessively orderly.

During the **phallic stage** (after age three or so), children discover their genitals and the pleasure of masturbation. It is at this time that the child develops a marked attachment for the parent of the opposite sex and becomes jealous of the parent of the same sex. Freud called this the **Oedipus complex.** In Greek mythology, Oedipus killed his father and married his mother; he is thus a model for boys, who, Freud believed,

Anal stage Second stage in Freud's theory of personality development, when a child's erotic feelings center on the anus and on elimination.

Phallic stage Third stage in Freud's theory of personality development, when erotic feelings center on the genitals.

Oedipus complex According to Freud, a child's sexual attachment to the parent of the opposite sex and jealousy toward the parent of the same sex.

Figure 12-2
Diagram showing how Freud conceived the working of the pleasure and reality principles Note that according to the reality principle, the *ego* uses rational thought in order to postpone the gratification of the *id* until its desires can be satisfied safely.

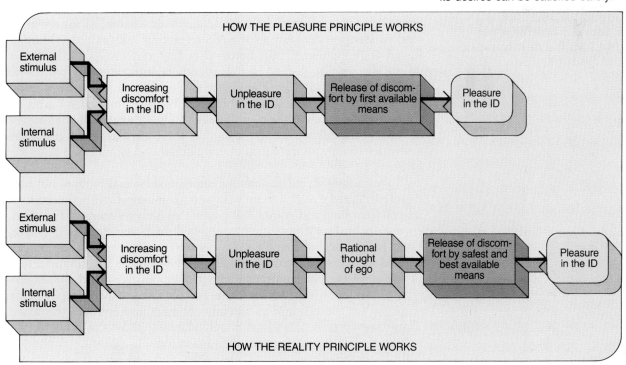

Latency period In Freud's theory of personality, a period after the phallic stage in which the child appears to have no interest in the opposite sex.

Genital stage In Freud's theory of personality development, the final stage of normal adult sexual development.

Freud believed that during the *oral stage*, when infants are dependent on others to satisfy their needs, they derive sensual pleasure from the mouth, lips, and tongue. Lack of confidence is thus among the traits that he attributed to *fixation* at this stage.

sexually desire their mothers and would like to kill their fathers for blocking their goals. Because the boy is powerless to carry out his desire to remove his father, he has no choice but to repress these unacceptable impulses. Moreover, he is afraid that his father knows what he is thinking and is going to punish him. The result is that the boy is attracted to, but repelled by, his mother, and afraid of, but violently jealous of, his father. Freud believed that girls go through a corresponding conflict involving love for their fathers and jealousy toward their mothers.

Most children eventually resolve the Oedipus complex by identifying with the parent of the same sex. But once again, excessive frustration or gratification at this stage can result in fixation. According to Freud, one possible result of fixation at the phallic stage is vanity and egotism. Men often express these characteristics by taking great pride in their sexual prowess and treating women with contempt. Women are more likely to become flirtatious and promiscuous. Freud also suggested that phallic fixation can lead to low self-esteem, a feeling of worthlessness, shyness, and an avoidance of heterosexual relationships.

At the end of the phallic period, Freud believed, children lose interest in sexual behavior and enter a **latency period.** Beginning around the age of 5 or 6 and lasting until age 12 or 13, boys play with boys, girls play with girls, and neither sex takes much interest in the other.

At puberty, we enter the last psychosexual stage, which Freud called the **genital stage.** At this time, our sexual impulses reawaken. Now, however, they are directed toward members of the opposite sex. In lovemaking, the adolescent and the adult are able to satisfy unfulfilled desires from infancy and childhood. Ideally, immediate gratification of these desires is replaced by mature sexuality, in which postponed gratification, a sense of responsibility, and caring for others all play a part.

Unfortunately, many of Freud's concepts are difficult to translate into experimental terms, but his theory has received some limited confirmation from research. For example, people who eat and drink too much tend to mention oral images when interpreting inkblot tests (Masling, Rabie, & Blondheim, 1967; Bertrand & Masling, 1969). Orally fixated people also seem to depend heavily on others, as Freud predicted (Fisher & Greenberg, 1985). Some evidence suggests that a few traits of anally fixated people also appear together. For instance, individuals who are stingy are also likely to be neat (Fisher & Greenberg, 1985). However, no strong research evidence shows that these various personality characteristics stem from the kinds of early-childhood experiences described by Freud.

Freud's beliefs, particularly his emphasis on sexuality, were not completely accepted even by those who were members of the psychoanalytic school. Carl Jung and Alfred Adler were two early followers of Freud who eventually broke with him and formulated their own theories of personality. Jung accepted Freud's stress on unconscious motivation but expanded the scope of the unconscious well beyond the selfish satisfactions of the id. Adler believed that humans have positive—and conscious—goals that guide their behavior. Other psychodynamic theorists put greater emphasis on the ego and its attempts to gain mastery over the world. These neo-Freudians, such as Karen Horney, also focus more on the influence of social interaction on personality.

Carl Jung

Carl Jung's beliefs differed from Freud's in many ways. Jung contended that libido, or psychic energy, represents *all* the life forces, not just the sexual ones. Both Freud and Jung emphasized the role of the unconscious in determining human behavior. But where Freud saw the id as a "cauldron of seething excitations" that the ego had to control, Jung saw the unconscious as the ego's source of strength and vitality. Jung believed that there were two distinct levels of the unconscious: a personal unconscious and a collective unconscious. The **personal unconscious** contains our repressed thoughts, forgotten experiences, and undeveloped ideas. These ideas may rise again to consciousness if some incident or sensation triggers their recall.

The **collective unconscious,** which is perhaps Jung's most original concept, consists of the memories and behavior patterns inherited from past generations. Jung believed that just as the human body is the product of a million years of evolution, so too over the centuries the human mind has developed "thought forms," or collective memories, of experiences that people have had in common since prehistoric times. He called these thought forms **archetypes.** Archetypes give rise to certain typical mental images or mythical representations (see Figure 12-3). Since all people have mothers, the archetype of "mother" is universally associated with the image of one's own mother, with Mother Earth, and with a protective presence. The archetype of the "hero" can be represented equally by a primitive tribal chieftain, by Joshua at the battle of Jericho, or by Nelson Mandela, depending on the particular moment in history.

Among the many archetypes, Jung felt that some play special roles in shaping personality. The **persona** is an archetype whose meaning is derived from the Latin word for mask. The persona is the part of our personality by which we are known to other people—a shell that grows around our inner self. Some people become so identified with their public selves that they lose touch with their inner feelings. Such over-emphasis on one aspect of the personality is, for Jung, an important source of personality maladjustment.

Two other important archetypes are anima and animus. The **anima** is the female side of the male personality, the expression of female traits that guides male interactions with the opposite sex. The **animus** plays a corresponding male role in female personality. Thus, Jung considered aggressive behavior in females or nurturant behavior in males to be manifestations of, respectively, the animus or the anima in action.

Jung also suggested that people can be divided into two general attitude types: introverts and extroverts. **Extroverts** are concerned with the external world. They are "joiners," and are interested in other people and in events going on around them. **Introverts** are more concerned with their own private worlds. They tend to be unsociable and lack confidence in their dealings with people. Everyone, Jung felt, possesses some aspects of both attitude types, but one is usually dominant, while the other is largely submerged.

Jung further divided people into rational and irrational categories. **Rational people** regulate their actions by the psychological functions of thinking and feeling. In making decisions, they may be guided principally

Personal unconscious According to Jung, one of the two levels of the unconscious; the personal unconscious contains the individual's repressed thoughts, forgotten experiences, and undeveloped ideas.

Collective unconscious In Jung's theory of personality, the part of the unconscious that is inherited and common to all members of a species.

Archetypes In Jung's theory of personality, thought forms common to all human beings, carried in the collective unconscious.

Persona According to Jung, our public self, the mask we put on to represent ourselves to others.

Anima In Jung's theory, the feminine side of masculine personality.

Animus The masculine side of feminine personality.

Extrovert According to Jung, a person who usually focuses on social life and the external world instead of his or her internal experience.

Introvert In Jung's theory, a person who usually focuses on his or her own inner thoughts and feelings.

Rational people According to Jung, those people who regulate their actions by the psychological functions of thinking and feeling.

Carl Jung

by thought, or they may give more weight to emotional factors and value judgments. In contrast, **irrational people** base their decisions on perception, either through the senses (sensation) or through unconscious processes (intuition). Most people exhibit all four psychological functions: thinking, feeling, sensing, and intuiting. Jung felt, however, that one or more of them is usually dominant. Thus, a thinking person is rational and logical and decides on the basis of facts. The feeling person is sensitive to his or her surroundings, acts tactfully, and has a balanced sense of values. The sensing type relies primarily on surface perceptions and rarely uses imagination or deeper understanding. And the intuitive type sees beyond obvious facts to predict future possibilities.

While Freud emphasized the sexual instincts, Jung stressed rational and spiritual qualities. While Freud considered development to be set in childhood, Jung thought that full psychic development occurred only during middle age. And while Jung had a sense of historical continuity, believing that the roots of the human personality extend back through our ancestral past, he also contended that a person moves constantly toward self-realization—toward blending all parts of the personality into a harmonious whole. Because Jung broke with Freud and because of the mystic tendencies and symbolism and mysticism that characterize his theory, Jung's ideas have been somewhat neglected by psychologists. Recently, perhaps because of the popular interest in mysticism, Jung has been "rediscovered," and there is renewed interest in his theories.

Figure 12-3
The artistic expression of archetypes from the collective unconscious
Each of these artworks depicts the same mythological female figure—a goddess of love and fertility. Bottom left is a fertility goddess from Catal Huyuk in West Asia and dates from about 6000 B.C. The top left is an early figure of Venus from 150 B.C., and the bottom right, also of Venus, is from the 15th century. Despite their obvious differences, there are also striking similarities. The differences are obvious, but so are the similarities. According to Jung, mythological figures represent *archetypes*, or thought forms stored in a *collective unconscious*. He believed that because archetypes are stored as images passed on from generation to generation, they inspire the artistic imagination from generation to generation.

Alfred Adler

Alfred Adler developed a theory of personality that sharply differed from Freud's. According to Freud, personality develops out of the conflict between the self-denying demands of society and the self-gratifying impulses of the individual. Adler, in contrast, believed that individuals to a great extent possess innate *positive* motives and strive toward personal and social perfection. Adler, a frail child who almost died of pneumonia at the age of five, originally proposed that the main shaper of personality was the individual's attempt to overcome physical weaknesses. He labeled this effort **compensation.** Examples include the blind person who, like Stevie Wonder, develops particularly acute auditory abilities or the disabled child who, like Wilma Rudolph, becomes an Olympic medalist.

Adler later modified his views and suggested that people try to overcome *feelings* of inferiority that may or may not have a basis in reality. Developing children, for example, often feel inferior to the seemingly all-powerful parents on whom they are dependent. These feelings of inferiority may be further intensified by comparisons to siblings, teachers, or seemingly more competent peers—even if such feelings do not have much basis in reality. Adler, who placed great importance on birth order, maintained that it is not important that a second child is in fact inferior in athletic ability compared to his or her older brother or sister; but it is important if he or she *believes* that to be the case. The attempt to overcome such feelings of inferiority was for Adler a primary governor of human behavior and a crucial determinant of adult personality.

Adler did not consider the common human feeling of inferiority to be a necessarily negative characteristic. Rather, he felt that such feelings stimulate positive development and personal growth. Nevertheless, some individuals become so fixated on their feelings of inferiority that they become paralyzed by them and develop what Adler termed an **inferiority complex.**

Later in his life, Adler shifted the emphasis of his theory from overcoming inferiority feelings to a more positive emphasis on strivings for superiority and perfection according to which the individual strives for personal perfection and for the perfection of the society to which he or she belongs. In this regard, Adler developed the concept of **fictional finalism,** which means that people set up important goals for themselves that guide their behavior. It is not crucial whether personal goals are actually attainable, but it is important that the person *act* as if these goals were attainable. Although all people share the common goal of individual and social perfection, each individual's movement toward a fictional finalism leads to the development of a particular set of meanings and beliefs that become his or her **style of life.** He believed that an individual's style of life develops at an early age—by age four or five.

Adler's emphasis on positive, socially constructive goals and on strivings for perfection are in marked contrast to Freud's vision of the selfish person locked into eternal conflict with society. In a sense, Adler reintroduced the idea—which Freud had deleted—that a person's voluntary effort toward personally positive and socially beneficial goals is an important part of human personality and its development.

Adler also believed that individuals are not passively controlled by their environment but can operate creatively on it. Here Adler clearly

Compensation According to Adler, the person's effort to effect or overcome imagined or real personal weaknesses.

Inferiority complex In Adler's theory, the condition by which an individual is emotionally paralyzed by feelings of inferiority.

Fictional finalism According to Adler, motivating goals that people establish to guide their behavior even though such goals might not be actually attainable.

Style of life According to Adler, each individual's development of a particular set of meanings and beliefs.

"All right, deep down its a cry for psychiatric help—but at one level it's a stick-up."
PUNCH/Rothco

Alfred Adler

Anxiety A feeling like fear without an identifiable source.

Neurotic trends In Horney's view, irrational strategies for coping with emotional problems and minimizing anxiety.

Compliant type In Horney's theory, a person whose relations to others are marked by deference and submission.

Aggressive type According to Horney, the individual who customarily relates to others aggressively.

Detached type According to Horney, a person who relates to others in a basically detached manner.

set himself apart from Freud by making the individual the master of his or her own fate. Many psychologists believe that this emphasis on voluntary striving toward positive and social goals marks Adler as the father of what has become known today as humanistic psychology.

Karen Horney

Karen Horney is another personality theorist greatly indebted to Freud but in disagreement with some of his ideas, particularly his analysis of women and his stress on sexual instincts. From her experience as a practicing therapist in both Germany and the United States, Horney concluded that environmental and social factors are the most important influences in shaping personality and that the most vital of these factors are the human relationships with which the child grows up.

Horney believed that overemphasizing sexual drives produced a distorted picture of human relationships. Although sexuality is important to the development of personality, nonsexual factors, such as a need for a sense of basic security, also play a vital role. For example, all people share the need to feel loved and nurtured by their parents, quite aside from whatever sexual feelings they might have about them. Conversely, a parent's protective feelings toward his or her children are shaped not only by biological forces but also by society's injunction that the nurturance of children is an important human value.

For Horney, **anxiety**—an individual's reaction to real or imagined dangers or threats—is a stronger motivating force than the sexual drive. Whereas Freud held that anxiety usually arises from sexual conflicts, Horney stressed that feelings of anxiety also originate in a variety of nonsexual contexts. In childhood, anxiety arises because children depend on adults for their very survival. They feel anxious because they are insecure about receiving continued nurturance and protection. Because they come to feel that their parents are not completely dependable as providers of these needs, they develop inner protections, or defenses, that provide both satisfaction and security; and they experience more anxiety when those defenses are threatened.

Horney (1937) believed that there are several general strategies, or **neurotic trends,** that help individuals cope with emotional problems and ensure safety, albeit at the expense of personal independence: moving toward people (submission), moving against people (aggression), and moving away from people (detachment). Each person's characteristic reliance on one or another of these strategies is reflected in their patterns of behavior or *personality type*. For Horney, a **compliant type** is an individual who has an overriding need to give in or submit to others and feels safe only when receiving their protection and guidance. This is neurotic, according to Horney, because the resulting friendliness is superficial and masks feelings of aggression and anxiety. In contrast, the **aggressive type** masks his or her submissive feelings and relates to others in a hostile and domineering manner. He or she, however, is also hiding basic feelings of insecurity and anxiety. Finally, the **detached type** copes with basic anxiety by withdrawing from other people. This person seems to be saying, "If I withdraw, nothing can hurt me."

Well-adjusted people also experience threats to their basic security and experience basic anxiety. But because the environment better enables

Karen Horney

them to satisfy their basic emotional needs, they are able to develop without becoming trapped in neurotic life-styles.

Horney's emphasis on cultural as opposed to biological forces had a profound effect on her views of human development. For example, she believed that adults can continue to develop and change throughout the life cycle. Because biology is not destiny, the adult may come to understand the source of his or her basic anxiety and try to do away with neurotic anxiety. And Horney also opened the way to a more constructive understanding of male and female personality. By emphasizing that culture and not anatomy determines many of the personality traits that differentiate women from men, and by pointing out that cultural forces can be changed, she challenged the prevailing notion that there are inevitable differences between the personality characteristics of men and women. To the extent that men are more aggressive and less nurturant than women, for example, Horney suggests that the explanation is to be found in society and in culture, not in biology.

Erik Erikson

Erik Erikson, who studied with Freud in Vienna, is another theorist who takes a socially oriented view of personality development. In addition, the workings of the ego play a prominent role in his theory. He also extends his interest to development throughout the life cycle.

Erikson agrees with much of Freud's thinking on sexual development and the influence of libidinal needs on personality. But also important for Erikson is the *quality* of parent-child relationships. Children can be disciplined in a way that leaves them with a feeling of being loved or of being hated. The difference is largely due to the atmosphere of the home. The important point is that children should feel that their own needs and desires are compatible with those of society. Only if children feel competent and valuable, in their own eyes and in society's, will they develop a secure sense of identity. This is an example of how Erikson shifts the focus of personality theory to ego development.

Erik Erikson

In expanding his interest to the continued development of the personality throughout life, Erikson (1963) outlined "eight ages of man," and suggested that success in each age depends on a person's adjustments in previous stages (see Figure 12-4):

1. *Trust versus mistrust.* During the first year of life, babies are torn between trusting and not trusting their parents. If needs are generally met, the infant comes to trust the environment and himself or herself. The result is faith in the predictability of the environment and optimism about the future. The frustrated infant becomes suspicious, fearful, and overly concerned with security.

2. *Autonomy versus shame and doubt.* During their first three years, children's growing physical development allows them increasing autonomy and greater contact with their surroundings. They learn to walk, hold onto things, and control their excretory functions. If the child repeatedly fails in trying to master these skills, self-doubt may grow. One response to self-doubt is the practice of abiding compulsively by fixed routines. At the other extreme is the hostile rejection of all controls, both internal and external. If parents and

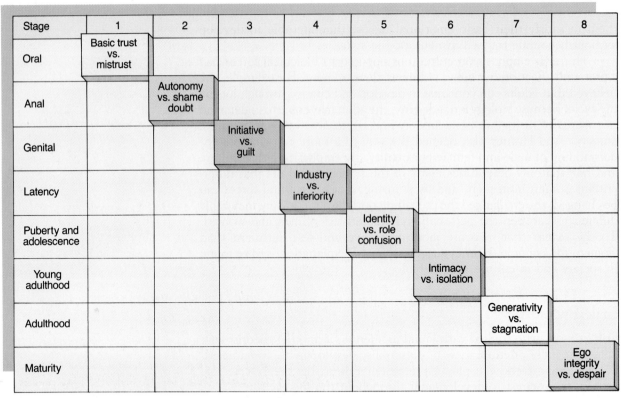

Stage	1	2	3	4	5	6	7	8
Oral	Basic trust vs. mistrust							
Anal		Autonomy vs. shame doubt						
Genital			Initiative vs. guilt					
Latency				Industry vs. inferiority				
Puberty and adolescence					Identity vs. role confusion			
Young adulthood						Intimacy vs. isolation		
Adulthood							Generativity vs. stagnation	
Maturity								Ego integrity vs. despair

Figure 12-4
Erikson's eight stages of personality development Each stage involves its own developmental crisis, whose resolution is important to adjustment in successive stages.

Adapted from *Childhood and Society* by Erik H. Erikson, by permission of W. W. Norton & Company, Inc. and The Hogarth Press. Copyright 1950, © 1963 by W. W. Norton & Company, Inc. Renewed 1978 by Erik H. Erikson. Used by permission.

other adults belittle a child's efforts, the child may also begin to feel shame and acquire a lasting sense of inferiority.

3. *Initiative versus guilt.* Between the ages of three and six, children become increasingly active, undertaking new projects, manipulating things in the environment, making plans, and conquering new challenges. Parental support and encouragement for these initiatives can lead to a sense of joy in exercising initiative and taking on new challenges. However, if the child is unable to acquire a sense of initiative, strong feelings of guilt, unworthiness, and resentment may persist.

4. *Industry versus inferiority.* During the next six or seven years, children encounter a new set of expectations at home and at school. They must learn the skills needed to become fully functioning adults, including personal care, productive work, and independent social living. If children are stifled in their efforts to become a part of the adult world, they may conclude that they are inadequate, mediocre, or inferior and lose faith in their power to become industrious.

5. *Identity versus role confusion.* At puberty, childhood ends and the responsibilities of adulthood loom large. The critical problem of this stage is to find one's identity. In Erikson's view, identity is achieved by integrating a number of roles—student, sister or brother, friend, and so on—into a coherent pattern that provides a sense of inner continuity, or identity. Failure to forge an identity leads to role confusion and despair.

6. *Intimacy versus isolation.* During young adulthood, men and women must resolve a new critical issue: the question of becoming intimate

with a member of the opposite sex. Marriage is usually the form that this attempt ultimately takes. To love someone else, Erikson argues, we must have resolved our earlier crises successfully and feel secure in our identities. To form an intimate relationship, lovers must be trusting, autonomous, and capable of initiative and must exhibit other hallmarks of maturity. Failure at intimacy brings painful loneliness and a sense of being incomplete.

7. *Generativity versus stagnation.* During middle adulthood, roughly between ages 25 and 60, the challenge is to remain productive and creative in all aspects of one's life. People who have successfully negotiated the six earlier stages are likely to find meaning and joy in all the activities of life—career, family, community participation. For others, life becomes a drab routine, and they feel dulled and resentful.

8. *Integrity versus despair.* With the onset of old age, everyone must try to come to terms with the approach of death. For some, this is a period of despair at the loss of former roles, such as employee, parent, Little League coach, and so forth. Yet, according to Erikson, this stage also represents an opportunity to attain full selfhood. By this Erikson means an acceptance of one's life, a sense that it is complete and satisfactory. People who have gained full maturity by resolving earlier stages possess the integrity to face death with a minimum of fear.

Relatively little of Erikson's theory has been verified by research. Nevertheless, some aspects of it have been studied. The concept of identity resolution has probably attracted the most attention. Waterman, Beubel, and Waterman (1970) asked whether people who were successful in handling the crises of the first four stages were more likely to achieve a stable source of identity in the fifth stage. Their data suggest that this is indeed the case. While resolution of earlier crises may not be essential for ego identity, it does seem to be important. Other research has examined the link between the formation of identity in Stage 5 and the achievement of intimacy in Stage 6. Is it necessary to achieve identity in order to achieve intimacy? The answer, again, seems to be yes. Orlofsky, Marcia, and Lesser (1973) found that college men who were the least isolated socially were also those with the clearest sense of self. In a follow-up study of the same group of college men, Marcia (1976) observed that identity was still related to intimacy: Achieving a sense of personal identity apparently does enable an individual to have successful personal relationships. Yet another study found that the relationships between identity and intimacy are quite similar for both sexes. Both men and women believe that a positive sense of identity is the basis for achieving satisfactory relationships (Orlofsky, 1978).

■ Humanistic Personality Theories

In the first portion of this chapter, we saw that Freud believed that personality grows out of the resolution of unconscious conflicts and developmental crises. Many of his followers—including some who modified his theory and others who broke away from him—also embraced this basic point of view. But in the theory of Alfred Adler, we glimpsed a very different view of human nature. You will recall that Adler wrote about forces that contribute to positive growth and a motive for personal perfection. For these reasons, Adler is sometimes considered the first humanistic personality theorist. **Humanistic personality theory** emphasizes the fact that humans are positively motivated and progress toward higher levels of functioning—that there is more to human existence than dealing with hidden conflicts and life crises.

William James

William James is another early psychologist whose ideas anticipated the humanistic view of personality. In his book *The Principles of Psychology* (1890), James devoted a great deal of attention to the psychological concept of the **self**. For James, the self is the sum total of everything that a person calls his or hers: possessions, family, job, friends, enemies. Anything that can fill in the blank in the sentence "This is my ————" constitutes a part of the self. James divided the self into four parts: the material self, the social self, the spiritual self, and the pure ego. The material self refers to material possessions. The social self (perhaps like Jung's persona) is descriptive of how we are viewed by other people. The spiritual self refers to psychological faculties, like reasoning, or emotional dispositions, like aggressiveness or passivity. Finally, pure ego is simply the individual's internal stream of consciousness.

James's concept of self and Adler's concept of striving for perfection laid the groundwork for later humanistic personality theorists such as Carl Rogers, to whom we now turn.

Carl Rogers

Carl Rogers

As we saw in Chapter 1, humanistic psychologists believe that life is a continuing process of striving to achieve our potential, of opening ourselves to the world around us and experiencing joy in living. Carl Rogers, who died early in 1987, is perhaps the most famous of several humanistic theorists who believe that men and women develop their personalities in the service of positive goals. According to Rogers, every organism is born with certain innate capacities, capabilities, or potentialities—"sort of genetic blueprint, to which substance is added as life progresses" (Maddi, 1989, p. 102). The goal of life, according to Rogers, is to fulfill this genetic blueprint, to become whatever each of us is inherently capable of becoming. Rogers called this biological push toward fulfillment the **actualizing tendency.** It is worth noting that Rogers believed that the actualizing tendency characterizes all organisms—plants, animals, and humans. But in the course of life, human beings also form images of themselves, or self-concepts. Just as we try to fulfill our inborn biological potential, so too do we attempt to fulfill our self-concept, our conscious sense of who we are and what we want to do. Rogers called this striving the **self-actualizing tendency.** If you think of yourself as "intelligent," for example, you will strive to live up to that particular image of yourself.

If another of your self-concepts is "athletic," you will attempt to fulfill that image as well.

When an individual's self-concept is closely matched with his or her inborn capacities, then that person is likely to become what Rogers called a **fully functioning person.** Such people are self-directed: They decide for themselves what it is they wish to do and to become, even though their choices may not always be sound ones. They are not unduly swayed by what other people think they ought to be or what others expect them to become. Fully functioning people are also open to experience—to their own feelings as well as the world and other people around them—and thus find themselves "increasingly willing to be, with greater accuracy and depth, that self which [they] most truly [are]" (Rogers 1961, pp. 175–76).

According to Rogers, people are likely to become more fully functioning if they are brought up with **unconditional positive regard.** This means that they feel themselves valued by others regardless of their own feelings, attitudes, and behaviors. The warmth, respect, acceptance, and love that they receive from others is unconditional.

But often parents and others offer what Rogers called **conditional positive regard.** This means that only certain aspects of an individual are valued and accepted. The acceptance, warmth, and love that a person receives from others depends on his or her behaving in certain ways and fulfilling certain conditions. The condition can be expressed very explicitly, such as "Daddy won't love you if . . ." or "Mommy doesn't love girls who. . . ." But it can also be expressed subtly, such as "That's a nice idea, but wouldn't you rather do. . . ?" The message here is twofold: The other person finds your feelings or behavior questionable and proposes alternatives that he or she believes are better for you. Not surprisingly, one response to conditional positive regard is a tendency to change one's self-concept to include those things that one "ought to be," to become more like the person one is expected to be. In the process, one's self-concept becomes less and less like one's inborn capacity, and life begins to deviate from the genetic blueprint.

When people lose sight of their inborn potential, they become constricted, rigid, and defensive. They feel threatened and anxious and experience considerable discomfort and uneasiness. Because their lives are directed toward what other people want and value, they are unlikely to find much real satisfaction in what they do. Some of these people realize that they don't really know who they are or what they want.

Fully functioning person According to Rogers, individuals whose self-concepts closely resemble their inborn capacities or potentials.

Unconditional positive regard The acceptance and love for another person regardless of that person's behavior.

Conditional positive regard The acceptance and love for another person that depends on that person's behavior.

■ Constitutional and Trait Theories

The preceding personality theories, although different in emphasis, are quite similar in several respects. They all emphasize the importance of early childhood experiences, and they each put forward a set of principles that attempt to account for all the varieties of human personality.

Other personality theorists take a different point of view. Instead of concentrating on how personality develops, they concentrate on the ways in which already developed adult personalities differ from each other.

William Sheldon

One of the earliest theories of personality is **constitutional theory,** which asserts that body type and personality are related. The most fully researched and documented version of this theory, that of William Sheldon, divides the human physique into three types: *endomorphs* (round, soft bodies with large abdomens), *mesomorphs* (sturdy, upright bodies with strong bones and muscles), and *ectomorphs* (thin, small-boned, fragile bodies). Most people have some characteristics of all three of these **somatotypes,** with one type dominant.

Sheldon also divided temperament, or personality, into three types: *viscerotonia*, characterized by sociability, fondness for food and people, and love of comfort; *somatotonia*, characterized by love of physical adventure, risk, and vigorous activity; and *cerebrotonia*, characterized by restraint, self-consciousness, and love of privacy. Sheldon asserted that chubby endomorphs were likely to be high in viscerotonia, athletic mesomorphs high in somatotonia, and thin ectomorphs high in cerebrotonia. Sheldon also believed that personality type is caused by body type. Although most researchers today seriously question the effect of physique on personality, Sheldon's work has been influential in identifying several quite different types of human temperament (Sheldon, Stevens, & Tucker, 1970).

Trait Theories

Trait theorists reject Sheldon's idea that only a few clear-cut personality types exist. They suggest instead that people differ on a number of dimensions or traits, such as dependency, anxiety, aggressiveness, and sociability. Each person possesses each of these **personality traits** to a greater or lesser degree.

Of course, traits cannot be directly observed. We cannot see sociability in the way that we can see long hair, blue eyes, or a taste for loud colors. But we can *infer* a trait from how a person behaves. If a person consistently throws parties, goes to great lengths to make friends, and is regularly seen in groups, we might conclude that he or she has the trait of sociability.

Traits can be classified in terms of whether they are cardinal, central, or secondary. *Cardinal traits*—relatively rare—are so general that they influence every act a person performs. An example might be a person who is so selfish that virtually every gesture reveals this attribute. More typical are *central traits*, which are often, but not always, detectable in behavior. For example, a person may be generally aggressive but not display this central trait in every situation. Finally, *secondary traits* are attributes that do not form a vital part of the personality but come into play only in particular situations. An otherwise assertive person may be submissive, for example, when confronted by his or her boss. People possessing particular traits tend to be relatively consistent in their behavior over time and across situations. Thus, a person who possesses the trait of aggressiveness will be aggressive in a variety of situations and remain aggressive from year to year.

Our language has many words that describe personal behavior traits. Gordon Allport, along with his colleague H. S. Odbert (1936), looked through the dictionary and found 17,953 words that in some way refer to personality traits. For Allport, traits literally exist in the nervous system and are structures that guide consistent behavior across a wide variety of situations. Allport also believed that while traits describe behaviors that are common to many people, each individual personality contains a unique constellation of traits. He opposed the idea of dividing people into various types and argued that each individual can be understood only in terms of his or her uniqueness and individuality.

Only about 4,500 of the words on Allport and Odbert's list concern the kinds of stable or enduring characteristics that we would identify as personality traits, but that is still a massive list with which to work. When synonyms and near-synonyms are removed, the number of possible personality traits drops to around 200. Psychologist Raymond Cattell (1965), using a statistical technique called **factor analysis,** has demonstrated that when people are rated on those 200 characteristics, various traits tend to cluster in groups. Thus, if a person is described as persevering or determined, he or she is also likely to be thought of as responsible, ordered, attentive, and stable. Moreover, it is unlikely that he or she would be described as frivolous, neglectful, and changeable. On the basis of extensive research, Cattell concluded that just 16 traits account for the complexity of human personality, though more recently he has suggested that it might be necessary to add 7 more traits to the original list (Cattell & Kline, 1977). Each individual consists of a relatively unique constellation of those basic traits.

Factor analysis A statistical technique used by Cattell to identify a set of basic personality traits.

Gordon Allport

Raymond Cattell

Extroverts tend to be sociable, like parties, have many friends, and act impulsively.

"Big Five" Dimensions of Personality

SURGENCY or EXTRAVERSION

Talkative, bold, active, boisterous, forceful, assertive, spontaneous, active, demonstrative, energetic, enthusiastic, adventurous, outgoing, outspoken, loud, noisy, ambitious, dominant, sociable.

AGREEABLENESS or PLEASANTNESS

Warm, kind, cooperative, unselfish, flexible, fair, polite, trustful, forgiving, helpful, pleasant, affectionate, gentle, good-hearted, sympathetic, trusting, generous, flexible, considerate, agreeable.

CONSCIENTIOUSNESS or DEPENDABILITY

Organized, dependable, conscientious, responsible, hardworking, efficient, planful, capable, deliberate, painstaking, precise, practical, thorough, thrifty, cautious, serious, economical, reliable.

EMOTIONAL STABILITY

Unemotional, unenvious, relaxed, objective, calm, at ease, even-tempered, good-natured, stable, contented, secure, imperturbable, undemanding, steady, placid, peaceful.

CULTURE or INTELLIGENT or SOPHISTICATION

Intelligent, perceptive, curious, imaginative, analytical, reflective, artistic, insightful, inventive, wise, witty, refined, creative, sophisticated, knowledgeable, intellectual, resourceful, versatile, original, deep, cultured.

Figure 12-5

However, other trait theorists believe that Cattell used too many traits to classify personality. For example, Tupes and Christal (1961) demonstrated that personality traits can be boiled down to just five basic dimensions: extraversion, agreeableness, conscientiousness, emotional stability, and culture. This finding has been confirmed repeatedly in subsequent research (see Figure 12-5) (Norman, 1963; Borgatta, 1964; Goldberg, 1981, 1982; Botwin & Buss, in press). While there is some disagreement about whether the fifth dimension should be "culture" or "openness to experience" (McCrae & Costa, 1985, 1987, 1989) or "intellect" (Digman & Takemoto–Chock, 1981), there is a growing consensus that the "big five" personality dimensions may indeed capture the most salient dimensions of human personality (John, 1988).

■ Personality Theories and the Question of Consistency

All the personality theories that we have been discussing assume that behavior is generally consistent across both situations and time. According to this view, an aggressive person is likely to be aggressive in a wide variety of situations and to remain more or less the same from day to day and year to year. Such consistently aggressive behavior is also evidence for the underlying personality trait, or disposition, of aggression.

Some theorists, however, question whether humans are in fact con-

Androgyny

The concept of *androgyny*, meaning the fusion of male and female sides in one nature, is popular today largely because the women's movement has focused attention on what it means to be feminine—and thus also masculine—in our society.

Psychologists, too, have become interested in sex typing and androgyny. In order to measure how masculine, feminine, or androgynous a person is, Sandra Lipsitz Bem (1974, 1975) designed the Bem Sex Role Inventory (BSRI), which is made up of a list of 60 personality characteristics. It includes 20 traits that our society considers "masculine" (ambition, self-reliance, assertiveness); 20 traits that are considered "feminine" (affection, gentleness, understanding); and 20 traits that are neutral (honesty, friendliness, amiability). Bem arrived at this list after studying how a group of undergraduates rated the desirability of various traits for each sex. On the test, people describe themselves on each of these traits by using a scale of 1 (never or almost never true) to 7 (always or almost always true). The difference between the total points assigned to masculine and feminine adjectives tells how sex-typed a person is. If someone has approximately equal masculine and feminine scores, that person is considered androgynous.

Bem and her colleagues tested more than 1,500 undergraduates and found that half of them stuck with the "appropriate" sex role, 15 percent identified with the opposite sex, and about 30 percent were androgynous. Bem then went on to test whether androgynous people are actually more adaptable. She tested students for independence—a typically "masculine" trait—and conformity—a typically "feminine" trait. Students came to a lab for what they thought was an experiment on humor. Each person sat in a booth equipped with earphones and a microphone and watched cartoons that had already been rated according to how funny they were. As each cartoon appeared on the screen, subjects heard the experimenter ask each student in turn to rate the film. Actually, what the students were hearing was a preprogrammed tape on which people claimed that funny cartoons were not funny, and vice versa. "Feminine" women found it much harder to be assertive and to resist conforming to these opinions than "masculine" men or androgynous students.

Other researchers have found connections between androgyny and personal adjustment. Androgynous people tend to feel happier and to tolerate stress better than do subjects who conform to traditional sex roles (Shaw, 1982). Androgynous people also tend to be seen by others as well adjusted (Major, Carnevale, & Deaux, 1981). Finally, Heilbrun (1981) found that among women, androgyny is associated with higher self-esteem.

Despite the groundswell of enthusiasm for androgyny, the concept has encountered some pointed criticism. First, not all research shows that androgynous people are better adjusted. In one study in which subjects were given the BSRI and a battery of other tests, the better-adjusted individuals of both sexes had high masculinity scores (Jones, Chernovertz, & Hansson, 1978). Moreover, critics have argued that the ideal of androgyny ignores a fundamental principle of social organization. We are born with a sex, and this biological status inevitably affects the way others behave toward us and the way we see ourselves and the world. According to these critics, to believe that a lifetime of socialization can be shed and androgyny adopted at will is naive (Locksley & Colten, 1979).

sistent in their behavior. For example, the marine sergeant who is aggressive toward his recruits may be quite submissive when the captain comes to conduct an inspection. A given situation, moreover, may elicit similar behavior from a wide variety of people no matter what personality traits they possess. For example, most people wait their turn at a checkout counter no matter how aggressive they may otherwise be. Some theorists have suggested that the idea of consistent personality traits is something of an illusion. They suggest that we rely on the concept of personality because of a human need to believe in consistency, even though the empirical evidence for consistency may be meager, and even though situational variables often explain more about behavior than do personality traits (Kelley, 1955; Mischel, 1969). Some of these theorists take an even more radical approach and argue that external, situational variables account for *all* behavior. In the following section, we will examine this challenge to traditional views of personality.

Situationism The theory that views behavior solely as a response to external stimuli.

Situationism and Interactionism

Walter Mischel is one of the primary proponents of the **situationist** perspective. He reviewed many studies of personality and found that the consistency of behavior across situations was actually quite low—that, in fact, people act in quite different ways across a range of situations (Mischel, 1968). Mischel concluded that any approach to personality that relied solely on internal dispositions or traits would be, at best, inadequate (Mischel, 1977).

How, then, do we account for the *apparent* consistency in people's behavior? In part, Mischel proposed that behavior sometimes appears to be consistent because we see a person only in a limited variety of situations that tend to elicit the same behavior. The apparent consistency in an individual's behavior is really a result of the narrow range of situations in which we see that person. But in addition, Mischel found that observers often read consistency into the behavior of others even when there is none. We all tend to overestimate the consistency of a person's actions and to ignore behaviors that do not square with our preexisting image of that person. Hayden and Mischel (1976) performed an experiment in which subjects read vignettes about people and then formed impressions of their personality traits. When the subjects were given further information about those persons, they discounted information that was inconsistent with their initial impressions. For example, subjects would ignore evidence of assertiveness in people whom they had previously rated to be shy but were very perceptive in recognizing further evidence of shyness. Mischel concluded that people have a strong need to believe in the consistency of others' behavior, regardless of the evidence.

Recently, Mischel has moderated his position somewhat. He now concedes that at least *some* behaviors are relatively consistent over time and across situations. For example, intelligence, as measured by intelligence tests, appears to be highly consistent in a variety of situations (Mischel, 1968). Similarly, academic achievement is quite consistent from course to course and grade level to grade level (Rushton & Endler, 1977). Even such characteristics as expectancies and value systems are apparently relatively consistent over time and across situations (Mischel 1979). In addition, Block (1971) showed that students rated as dependable by high school peers tended to be rated again as dependable by independent observers 10 years later.

Moreover, research shows that some people are more consistent than others. Bem and Allen (1974) evaluated a group of subjects on the traits of friendliness and conscientiousness. Ratings were obtained from the subjects themselves, from their parents, and from peers. In addition, the subjects were rated on friendliness according to their actual behavior in a small group and on conscientiousness by a neatness score based on their personal appearance. Finally, the subjects were asked to rate themselves on the consistency of their own behavior.

Bem and Allen discovered that for the trait of friendliness those subjects who rated themselves as consistent were indeed scored consistent: They were rated as friendly by the behavioral scales, by outside raters, and according to self-rating. With regard to conscientiousness, however, results were more mixed: Subjects who had rated themselves as conscientious were not necessarily rated so by the other measures. But

Walter Mischel

the study did show that at least some people—those who saw themselves as consistent—will indeed display some consistency across a variety of situations.

It seems that a fully satisfactory theory of personality will have to account for both consistencies and inconsistencies in behavior. One approach to this involves considering the *interaction* between personal and situational factors (Bowers, 1973). A person may not be consistently aggressive in all situations, but there are likely to be situations in which he or she will almost always be aggressive and situations in which he or she will be reliably submissive. Bandura (1977) expanded this view by suggesting that there is always an interaction between three factors: the person, the situation, and the feedback obtained from a person's actual behavior in the situation. A person evaluates a situation according to certain internal **expectancies** such as personal preferences. This evaluation produces some type of behavior. Environmental feedback that follows the actual behavior also refines a person's behavioral expectancies for the future. In this way, expectancies shape behavior in a given situation, and the results of the behavior in turn shape expectancies.

In a similar way, Julian Rotter (1954) proposed that **locus of control** is a prevalent expectancy, or cognitive strategy, by which people evaluate situations. Some people have an *internal* locus of control. They believe that they can control their own fate. By hard work, skill, and training, they believe it is possible to find reinforcements and avoid punishments. People with an *external* locus of control believe that they do not have control over their fate. They believe that chance, luck, and the behavior of others determine their destiny and that they are helpless to do anything about it. These expectancies shape their behavior in different situations and are themselves shaped by the person's experiences over time.

Expectancies In Mischel's view, what a person anticipates in a situation or as a result of behaving in certain ways.

Locus of control According to Rotter, an expectancy about whether reinforcements are under internal or external control.

Albert Bandura

■ The Genetic Basis for Personality

Does heredity have a hand in the development of personality? A growing body of research suggests that indeed it does (Goldsmith, 1983; Kagan, 1989). Comparative studies of identical and fraternal twins have shown that identical twins, who share exactly the same genetic material, are much more similar to one another than are fraternal twins on such personality characteristics as emotionality, activity, sociability, and impulsiveness. Thus, if one twin cries easily (a sign of emotionality), his identical twin brother is five times more likely than a fraternal twin to cry easily, too. Similarly, if one twin cannot sit still long (a sign of activity), an identical twin brother is three times more likely than a fraternal twin brother to act in the same way (Buss, Plomin, & Willerman, 1973).

Moreover, whether a person is more introverted or extroverted also seems to be powerfully influenced by genetics (Henderson, 1982). For example, Jerome Kagan (1989) found that most children who are extremely shy, timid, and inhibited at 21 months of age are still unusually inhibited six years later; he concludes that inhibited and uninhibited children differ genetically. However, no firm evidence exists that specific traits, such as assertiveness, reliability, or optimism, are inherited. A person who inherits a tendency to be extroverted may be inclined to be impulsive, active, sociable, and talkative, but experience plays an important role in the development of these specific personality characteristics. Similarly, a person who inherits a tendency to be emotionally reactive may or may not be anxious or moody or restless or aggressive, depending on his or her experiences.

■ Locus of Control: Who Runs Your Life?

Suppose you have made plans to watch a late-night movie on TV. You walk around the corner to the convenience store to buy some beer and pretzels—only to find that the storekeeper has just locked up for the night. Would you be more likely to say to yourself, "Just my rotten luck!" or "It's my own fault: I should have left the house a few minutes earlier"?

People differ in the extent to which they believe what happens to them is due to external forces ("Just my luck!") or internal ones ("It's my own fault"). Recently, psychologists have studied this personality disposition that they call *locus of control*. Externally oriented people feel that their behavior is generally rewarded or punished by forces beyond their control, such as fate, other people who are powerful, and luck. At the opposite extreme are the individuals who believe that they are the source of their own reinforcements and rewards.

Many "externals," for example, believe that success depends on "being in the right place at the right time." They also tend to have faith in chance or fate. They are the buyers of lottery tickets, the readers of horoscopes, the owners of lucky charms. In the extreme, they see promotions as going to whomever the boss happens to like, marriage as depending on who chances to fall in love with whom, and life itself as a case of "whatever will be, will be."

Those with an "internal" orientation tend to see themselves as masters of their own fate. Rather than lottery tickets, they buy self-improvement books. They believe that promotion depends on hard work, on what you know rather than whom you know.

Rotter (1966) developed a test of internal versus external control that has been widely used by experimenters. The test consists of 17 questions that require the subject to choose between two alternatives. For example:

a. In the long run, people get the respect they deserve in this world.
b. Unfortunately, an individual's worth often passes unrecognized no matter how hard he tries.

Internals would be likely to choose (a), while externals would be likely to choose (b).

People who answer many of these questions in the external direction are morely likely to conform to the views and wishes of others. Because they feel that they cannot control what happens to them, they tend to be more willing to rely on others for direction. By contrast, people who answer mostly in the internal direction are much more independent and resist attempts by others to influence them (Phares, 1984). For example, one study (Ritchie & Phares, 1969) found that externals tended to adopt the opinions of people whom they regarded as authorities. Internals, on the other hand, paid more attention to the content of the opinion than they did to the reputation of its source.

Internals differ from externals in a number of other ways

People with an external *locus of control* tend to have faith in chance or fate.

as well. They tend to be more intelligent, possibly because brighter people can in fact control what happens to them more certainly than can those who are less talented (Mischel, 1981). Internals are also more success-oriented and tend to take more reasonable risks (Strickland, 1979). If internals tend to be more intelligent and success-oriented than externals, do they also fare better in school and in college? Prociuk and Breen (1975, 1977) found that internals outperformed externals in academic subjects. Phares (1978) observed that internal elementary-school students received higher grades than their external classmates, but he found no comparable differences among college students.

Locus of control may also be related to the ways in which people respond to the threat of disaster. Sims and Baumann (1972) arrived at this conclusion after investigating a curious fact. They noticed that over the course of a number of years, fewer people in Illinois were killed by tornadoes than in Alabama, although both states had about equal numbers of such storms. Sims and Baumann hypothesized that a larger proportion of the people living in Alabama reacted to tornado watches with resignation rather than preparation. Research bore out their hunch: A significantly higher proportion of Alabamians endorsed external locus-of-control statements (Lazarus & Monat, 1979).

It is one thing to react passively to the threat of tornadoes, which are to a certain extent out of our control. But what about health care, which *is* under our control? The evidence is that here, too, externals tend to be more passive: They take fewer precautions to protect their health, participate less in physical activities, and seek less information about health maintenance (Strickland, 1979). All in all, people with an internal locus of control work harder for good health. This suggests that if physicians could determine which of their patients are external and which internal, they could better tailor the treatment to the individual. For example, since externals prefer structure imposed by others and tend not to take the initiative, they might require more active supervision by the doctor (Phares, 1984).

Both Bandura and Rotter have tried to combine personal variables (such as expectancies) with situational variables in an effort to understand the complexities of human behavior. However, another group of theorists puts an even greater emphasis on the environment as a source of behavior, as we will see in the next section.

B. F. Skinner and Behaviorism

If trait theorists believe that you do what you are, B. F. Skinner and other behaviorists believe that you are what you do. Such theorists deny that internal personality variables (such as traits or expectancies) are at all necessary for explaining behavior (Skinner, 1953). Behavior, they suggest, is explained by learning, which is in turn controlled by reinforcement, as we saw in Chapter 5. Only observable and measurable behavior can form the basis for predicting, explaining, and controlling behavior. Therefore, Skinner concentrates on finding the observable links between behavior and the conditions that cause or control it. For example, Skinner does not believe that drives like hunger and thirst are necessary to explain behavior. He argues that thirst simply describes a relationship between a stimulus condition and the drinking behavior to which it leads. In other words, a hot day and a dry throat are stimuli that result in a behavioral response: drinking water. It adds nothing to the explanation to speculate about an internal feeling of being thirsty. In the same way, our behavior toward another person is determined by aspects of that person and by the situation in which we find ourselves.

Skinner points out that although the specific situation determines the response, not all people react the same way to a given situation. Hall and Lindzey (1978) illustrate this concept with the example of two people seeking a raise from the same employer. One person may approach the situation aggressively, the other passively. It all depends on what has worked for each of them in the past. If a behavior has been followed by a reward in the past, it is more likely to occur again in that same situation in the future. If a behavior has not been rewarded in the past, it is less likely to recur in the future.

Skinner agrees with the traditional personality theorists that early development is especially important for explaining patterns of adult behavior. However, he relies solely on specifying the **reinforcement contingencies** that a person experiences in his or her development. Thus, a child who is rewarded when he or she shows curiosity will show a greater tendency to exhibit curiosity behavior in a variety of situations, not only during childhood but also in adulthood. Such learned behavior patterns become the basis for the kinds of consistencies that we call "personality." Similarly, a child who tries to avoid being questioned in school may learn to say "I don't know" whenever he is called on by a teacher. He learns that this strategy is successful for avoiding more questioning. The success of this strategy may result in a shy, evasive, and escape-oriented adult (Lundin, 1974).

Although early experiences may influence patterns of adult responses, according to Skinner, behavior can still be modified by new reinforcements. The shy adult may learn to become assertive if rewarded for that type of behavior. And in fact, reinforcement has been shown to be an effective modifier of highly ingrained adult behavior. For example,

B. F. Skinner

Token economies A means of behavioral change whereby members of an institution receive tokens, which may be exchanged for tangible reinforcements, for adaptive behaviors.

Performance standards In Bandura's theory, standards that people develop to rate the adequacy of their own behavior in a variety of situations.

Self-efficacy According to Bandura, the expectancy that one's efforts will be successful.

as we saw in Chapter 5, some mental hospitals use token economies in order to change the behavior of patients (Kazdin, 1976). Patients are given the opportunity to earn tokens for behaving in responsible and socially appropriate ways. They can then spend the tokens on special foods or extra privileges. The use of this type of reinforcement can greatly modify even long-term and highly stable behavior patterns. Even patients who have been socially unresponsive for years will begin to interact with their environment in order to obtain tokens.

Social Learning Theory

As we saw in Chapter 5, social learning theory shares the Skinnerian outlook that behavior is controlled by reinforcement. But according to social learning theory, reinforcement alone does not account for the learning of all the behaviors that constitute personality. Albert Bandura (1977) suggested that people observe which behaviors are rewarded and which are punished and that these observations eventually lead them to develop unique **performance standards** by which they guide their behavior. For example, the hard-driving business executive's child, in addition to learning the assertive behavior modeled by the parent, also learns that the display of such behavior will meet with parental approval—that is, reinforcement. Under these circumstances, it is likely that the child will include assertiveness in his or her own performance standards and use those standards to guide future behavior accordingly.

Bandura suggests that people continuously evaluate their current behavior against an individually developed standard of excellence and are variously successful in meeting the performance standards that they have internalized. A math professor's son may not have a good quantitative aptitude, while his daughter may be particularly talented in that area. Both children might develop a performance standard that calls for achievement in mathematics, but the son will feel incapable of meeting the standard while the daughter will experience great success. The daughter, according to Bandura, will also develop a high sense of **self-efficacy.** She will develop the attitude that she is capable of meeting her personal performance standards. Her brother, however, may come to develop a low sense of self-efficacy and thus feel generally incapable of meeting his goals.

Some personality theorists feel that children may learn to behave aggressively if they find aggression to be a successful response to such stimuli as a sibling's teasing.

But Bandura also emphasizes the fact that people are capable of self-regulation. The frustrated brother may modify his behavior and seek reinforcement for other learned behaviors. In other words, his performance standard may be modified by his experiences with the environment. He may pursue other academic interests at which he can excel and which are not necessarily unrelated to his original performance standard.

Bandura calls such interactions between personalities and their environment **reciprocal determinism.** Personality variables, situational variables, and actual behaviors are constantly interacting with one another. A person may be prone to display aggressive behavior. But whether the person will actually behave aggressively is determined by his or her perception of a given situation, which likely involves other people as well. People who are considering behaving aggressively will likely ask themselves if they are prepared to cope with aggressive behavior in return. Furthermore, the consequences that follow their behavior will affect their behavior in new situations. They learn where and when it will be rewarding to be aggressive. According to Bandura, human personality develops out of this continuous interaction of personal standards (learned by observation and reinforcement), situations, and behavioral consequences.

In a similar vein, Walter Mischel (1981) has proposed a set of **person variables** that grow out of personal experiences and that play a role in shaping future behavior. For example, people develop expectancies as to whether or not they will be successful in attaining goals that are important to them. To a great extent, these expectancies reflect differences in competency. In our example of the professor's son, because of his relative incompetency in math he might well develop a low expectancy of success in this area and redirect his attention to areas in which he may have a greater expectancy of success or which he may value more highly. His sister, on the other hand, who is quite competent in math will probably expect to be successful in it. Nevertheless, she might not personally value math achievement and therefore also might direct her attention to other areas. What is crucial in all this is that both Bandura and Mischel believe that people internally organize their expectancies and values in order to control their own behavior. These personal standards form a relatively unique constellation for each person, one that grows out of his or her unique life history. Social learning theorists have thus developed personality theories based on the cognitive processing of life experiences.

We have seen that there is great diversity in the way psychologists view personality. As yet, there is no consensus on which of these views is most accurate, as each of them seems to add to our understanding of human personality. There is also disagreement among psychologists on the best way in which to measure or assess personality, as we will see in the next portion of this chapter.

Reciprocal determinism In Bandura's model, proposal that the person influences the environment and is in turn influenced by the environment.

Person variables According to Mischel, cognitive processes that influence behavior in different situations.

■ Personality Assessment

In some ways, testing personality is a great deal like testing intelligence (see Chapter 8). In both cases, we are trying to measure something that we cannot touch or see. And in both cases, a "good test" has to be both reliable and valid. It must give dependable and consistent results, and it has to measure what it claims to measure. But special difficulties occur in the measurement of personality that are not found in the measurement of intelligence and academic ability. As we mentioned earlier, personality reflects *characteristic* behavior—how a person usually reacts to his or her environment. In assessing personality, then, we are not interested in someone's *best* behavior. We want to find out what that person's *typical* behavior is—how that person usually behaves in ordinary situations. This process is complicated further by the fact that such things as fatigue, desire to impress the examiner, and fear of being tested can profoundly affect a person's behavior in a personality assessment situation.

In the intricate task of measuring personality, psychologists use four basic tools: the personal interview, the direct observation of behavior, objective tests, and projective tests.

The Personal Interview

Essentially, an *interview* is a conversation with a purpose: to get information from the person being interviewed. Interviews are often used in a clinical setting in order to find out, for example, why someone is seeking treatment and to help diagnose the problem. They can also be used to check on a client's progress in therapy. Such interviews are likely to be *unstructured*. That is, the interviewer is free to ask the client questions about material that comes up and to ask follow-up questions whenever appropriate. Ideally, the interviewer should try to direct the conversation over a wide range of subjects, and encourage the person to discuss freely his or her experiences, feelings, and attitudes. The interviewer also pays attention to the other person's behavior, such as his or her way of speaking, poise, or tenseness about certain topics. Quite often, interviews of this kind are used in combination with more objective tests of personality.

When conducting systematic research on personality, investigators more often rely on the *structured interview*. Here, the order and content of the questions are fixed ahead of time, and the interviewer tries not to deviate from the format. This kind of interview is less personal, but it assumes that the interviewer will obtain comparable information from everyone interviewed. It is also more likely to be effective in drawing

The *personal interview* is a basic tool of personality assessment. The structured interview follows a fixed order and content of questioning.

out information about sensitive topics that might not be fully discussed in an unstructured interview.

For both kinds of interviewing, the skill and the behavior of the interviewer are important. He or she should establish a sympathetic relationship with the person being interviewed but not become too emotionally involved. The most effective interviewers are warm, interested in what the respondent has to say, calm, relaxed, and confident (Saccuzzo, 1975; Feshbach & Weiner, 1982). But because the behavior of the interviewer can make such a difference in the outcome of an interview, the results of interviews are often unreliable. Structured interviews tend to be better in this respect, because the behavior of the interviewer is less likely to affect what the respondent says.

Observation

Another way to find out how a person usually behaves is to *observe* his or her actions in everyday situations over a long period of time. Behaviorists and social learning theorists prefer this method. Observing behavior in different situations gives a much better view of the effect that situation and environment have on behavior and of the range of behaviors that a person might exhibit. Since most people are self-conscious when they suspect that they are being watched, observation is most valuable with young children or with people who have problems with language. But observation can be used successfully with people of almost any age and in many settings—a company cafeteria, an assembly line, or wherever people work or socialize together.

Direct observation lets the observer see the person's behavior firsthand. The observer does not have to rely on self-report. And if several careful observers give unbiased and factual accounts of a person's behavior over a period of time, the composite picture of that person's behavior can be quite accurate. However, there are drawbacks to direct observation. An observer may misinterpret the true meaning of some act. For example, the observer may think that a child is being hostile when the child is merely protecting himself against the class bully. In addition, observation is an expensive, time-consuming method of research and must therefore be used selectively. Finally, as we have said, the mere presence of an observer can affect the behavior of the subject and interfere with the results.

In recent years, the techniques of observation have been refined somewhat. For one thing, most observations are now quantified. If, for example, aggression is being studied, the investigator typically determines in advance exactly what behaviors will be considered aggressive and then counts the frequency with which the subject displays those behaviors. Moreover, it is now typical for experimenters to videotape behavior. This allows an entire research team to view a person's behavior repeatedly and at various speeds. Quite recently, with the introduction of small, inexpensive radio "beepers," a number of researchers have begun to use people's observations of themselves as a source of data. At various times during the day, the psychologist activates the beeper; the subject then stops what he or she is doing and either makes an entry in a notebook or fills out a brief questionnaire describing his or her behavior or thoughts or feelings at the moment the beeper went off.

Videotaped *observations* permit an entire research team to view the same behavior repeatedly and at different speeds.

Objective Tests

Objective tests Personality tests that are administered and scored in a standard way, such as the Minnesota Multiphasic Personality Inventory.

Sixteen Personality Factor Questionnaire Objective test designed by Cattell to provide scores on his 16 basic personality traits.

Minnesota Multiphasic Personality Inventory (MMPI) The most widely used objective personality test, originally intended for psychiatric diagnosis.

In an attempt to devise measuring instruments that do not depend on the skills of an interviewer or the interpretive abilities of an observer, psychologists have created **objective tests,** or personality inventories. Generally, these are written tests that are given and scored according to a standard procedure. The tests are usually constructed so that the person merely chooses between a "yes" or "no" response or selects one answer among many choices.

Because of their interest in accurately measuring personality traits, trait theorists in particular have favored objective tests. Cattell, for example, developed a 374-question personality test called the **Sixteen Personality Factor Questionnaire.** Not surprisingly, the 16PF (as it is usually called) provides scores on each of the 16 traits identified by Cattell. The questions on the 16PF include the following:

> I prefer to marry someone who:
> (a) commands general admiration
> (b) in between
> (c) has artistic literary gifts
> My friends consider me a highly practical realistic person
> (a) yes
> (b) in between
> (c) no
> I think I am better described as
> (a) polite and quiet
> (b) in between
> (c) lively and active

Research on the 16PF has gone on for more than 30 years, and one reviewer concluded: "No other personality measuring instrument has a more substantial scientific foundation. Nor has any instrument undergone a more thorough examination by critics. . . . When evaluated by reasonable standards, the 16PF compares favorably with any other inventory that purports to measure variations in normal personality functioning" (Bolton, 1978, p. 1080). Other recent reviews are more critical, although they agree that the 16PF can be useful for some research purposes if used with care (Anastasi, 1982; Graham & Lilly, 1984).

The most widely used objective personality test is the **Minnesota Multiphasic Personality Inventory (MMPI)** (Lubin, Larsen, Matarazzo, & Seever, 1985). Published in 1942 by Hathaway and McKinley, the MMPI was originally developed to help diagnose psychiatric disorders (see Figure 12-6). A number of psychiatric groups, such as schizophrenics and manic-depressives, were given this test, and it was observed that they provided distinctive patterns of response to the 550 items (to which a person answers "true," "false," or "cannot say"). Some typical items are: "Once in a while I put off until tomorrow what I ought to do today." "At times I feel like swearing." "There are persons who are trying to steal my thoughts and ideas." Some of the items repeat very similar thoughts in different words: "I tire easily." "I feel weak all over much of the time." This redundancy contributes to ease of scoring and provides a check on the possibility of false or inconsistent answers.

The MMPI also has several scales that check the validity of the

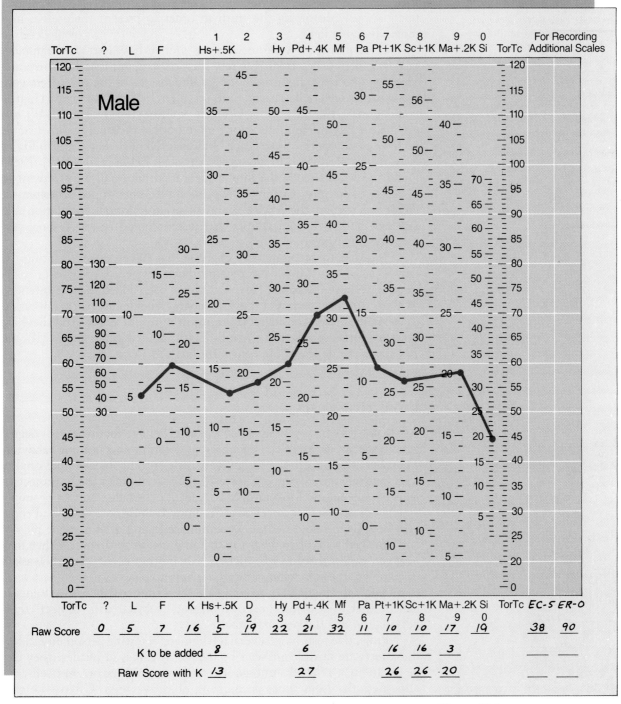

Figure 12-6
An MMPI profile.
University of Minnesota Press

responses. For example, if a person has answered too many items "cannot say," the test is considered invalid. The L, or lie, scale is scored on 15 items scattered throughout the test. Sample items rated on this scale include "I do not always tell the truth" and "I gossip a little at times." Most of us would have to admit that despite our best intentions, our answers to these two questions would have to be "true." People who mark these and many other similar terms "false" are probably consciously or unconsciously distorting the truth in order to present themselves in a more favorable light.

By analyzing subjects' answers, researchers have extracted a number of personality scales from this test such as masculinity-femininity, depression, and hypochondriasis. These dimensions of the MMPI are generally highly regarded as useful tools for differentiating among psychiatric populations (Anastasi, 1982; Graham & Lilly, 1984). The MMPI can also be used to differentiate among more normal personality dimensions, such as extroversion-introversion and assertiveness, but the validity of most such scales is still in question. Although Lubin et al. (1984, 1985) found the MMPI to be the most widely used personality instrument in a variety of settings, Costa and McCrae (1980) performed an extensive factor analysis on the MMPI scores of a large normal population and failed to find significant factors that discriminated among normal personality dimensions.

In order to accommodate changes that have occurred during the last 50 years, the MMPI has recently been revised. Outdated or sexist items have been reworded. New items have been added that are intended to assess disorders such as Type A behavior, suicide, and eating disorders that have received considerable attention in recent years. And there are now two forms of the test: the full-length, adult form of the MMPI has 704 items, while the adolescent form has 654 items.

Projective Tests

As we saw earlier, psychodynamic theorists believe that to a great degree people are not aware of the unconscious determinants of their behavior. Therefore, these psychologists put very little faith in objective personality tests that rely on self-reports. Instead, they often prefer to use **projective tests** of personality. Most projective tests of personality consist of simple ambiguous stimuli that can elicit an unlimited number of responses. People may be shown some essentially meaningless material or a vague picture and be asked to explain what the material means to them. Or they may be given two or three words, such as "My brother is. . . ," and be asked to complete the statement. They are given no clues as to the "best way" to interpret the material or to complete the sentence. Many psychologists believe that in devising their own answers, subjects will "project" their personality into the test materials.

Projective tests have several advantages in testing personality. Since these tests are flexible and can be treated as games or puzzles, they can be given in a relaxed atmosphere, without the tension and self-consciousness that sometimes accompany objective tests. Often, the true purpose of the test can be hidden, so that responses are less likely to be faked. Some psychologists believe that the projective test can uncover unconscious thoughts and fantasies, such as latent sexual or family problems. In any event, the accuracy and usefulness of projective tests depends greatly on the skill of the examiner.

The **Rorschach test** is probably the best known of the projective personality tests. It is named for Hermann Rorschach, a Swiss psychiatrist

"Rorschach! What's to become of you?"
© 1976 by Sidney Harris, *Saturday Review*

who in 1921 published the results of his research on interpreting inkblots as a key to personality. Much work on the inkblot technique had already been done when Rorschach began to practice, but he was the first to use the technique to evaluate a person's total personality. After 10 years of testing thousand of blots, he finally chose 10 that seemed to arouse the most emotional responses in people (see Figure 12-7).

Each inkblot design is printed on a separate card and is unique in its form, color, shading, and white space. Five of the blots are black and gray; two have red splotches; three blots have patches of several colors. The cards are given to the subject one at a time and in a specific order. The subject is asked to specify what he or she sees in each blot. The test instructions are kept to a minimum so that the subject's responses will be completely his or her own. Although no specific permission is given, the subject may turn the card and look at the blot from any angle and may make as many interpretations of each blot as he or she wants. After interpreting all the blots, the subject goes over the cards again with the examiner and explains which part of each blot determined each response.

Many psychologists interpret the Rorschach responses intuitively. That is, they draw inferences from the responses just as they would from anything else that a person says or does. But it also possible to score Rorschach responses systematically and in great detail, although the procedure is extremely complex and requires extensive training (Exner & Weiner, 1982). In formal scoring, attention is paid to such things as the part of each inkblot that the person used and how those portions were used to create the response. For example, was the person greatly influenced by the shape of the blot or by its color or shading? Did the person see movement in the inkblot (e.g., "This is a man running up a hill")? What kind of content did the person create (e.g., animals, people)?

Somewhat more demanding is the **Thematic Apperception Test (TAT),** developed at Harvard by H.A. Murray and his associates. It consists of 20 cards picturing one or more human figures in various poses (see Figure 12-8). Some of the pictures suggest a basic story; others give few plot hints. A person is shown the cards one by one. He or she has to make up a complete story for each picture, including what led up to the scene depicted, what the characters are doing at that moment, what their thoughts and feelings are, and what the outcome will be.

Although various scoring systems have been devised for the TAT, the examiner usually interprets the stories in the light of his or her personal knowledge of the subject. An important part of the evaluation is to determine if the subject seems to identify with the hero or heroine of the story or with one of the minor characters. Then the examiner must determine what the attitudes and feelings of the character reveal about the storyteller. The examiner also assesses each story for content, language, originality, organization, and consistency. Certain themes, such as the need for affection, repeated failure, or parental domination, may recur in several plots.

Both the Rorschach and the TAT are controversial personality tests. Frequently, they are not administered in a standard fashion, despite the fact that the way in which the test is administered significantly affects the results (Anastasi, 1982). To make matters worse, the tests are seldom scored objectively, and often the final interpretation of the results differs

Thematic Apperception Test (TAT) A projective test composed of ambiguous pictures about which a person writes stories.

Figure 12-7
Inkblots like those used on the *Rorschach projective test*.

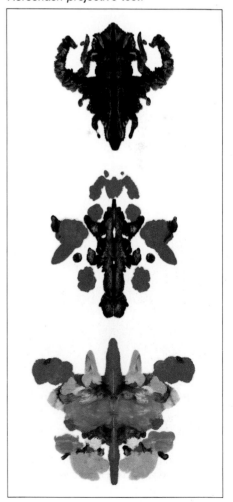

Figure 12-8
Sample item from the *Thematic Apperception Test* (TAT).

greatly from one examiner to another. It is not difficult to understand, therefore, why they are not well regarded tests (Peterson, 1978; Swartz, 1978; Anastasi, 1982; Graham & Lilly, 1984). However, they do seem to have value as a form of supplementary interview which, when interpreted by a skilled examiner, can provide insight into a person's attitudes and feelings.

● APPLICATION

A Case Study in Behavior and Personality

Jaylene Smith is 30 years old, single, and shows plenty of promise as a physician. Yet she is troubled by some aspects of her social life and has entered therapy. Here is a profile of Jay (adapted from Lazarus & Monat, 1979, pp. 23–25, 216–18).

Acquaintances describe Jay in glowing terms— for example, as highly motivated, intelligent, attrac-

tive, and charming. But Jay, unbeknownst to others, is terribly insecure and anxious. When asked once by a psychologist to pick out some self-descriptive adjectives, Jay selected introverted, shy, inadequate, and unhappy—not an enviable self-image!

Jay was the firstborn in a family of two boys and one girl. Her father is a quiet and gentle person who married when he was 35 years old. Although an excellent diagnostician, he decided to pursue medical research rather than enter private practice. Since his work often allowed him to study at home, he had extensive contact with his children, especially when they were young. Although he loved all his children, he favored Jay. His ambitions and goals for Jay were extremely high, and as she matured, he responded to her every need and demand almost immediately and with full conviction. He wanted to instill in her a strong desire for achievement so that someday she would strive to become successful and independent. He wanted very much to be proud of his little "bundle of joy," as he affectionately referred to Jay. Their relationship remains as close today as it was during Jay's childhood.

Jay's mother, who was 30 years old when she married, worked long hours away from home as a store manager and consequently saw her children primarily at nights and on an occasionally free weekend. Tired when she was with her family, she had little energy for "nonessential" interactions and devoted what efforts she could to feeding the children (especially the younger ones) and to making certain the house was in order. Mrs. Smith has always been career-oriented but has frequently experienced considerable conflict and frustration over her roles as full-time mother, housekeeper, and financial provider. Much of this conflict, unfortunately, was communicated subtly to the children, especially when they were quite young. Mrs. Smith was amicable toward all her children but tended to argue and fight more with Jay than with the others—at least until Jay was about 6 or 7 years of age (when the bickering subsided). Today, their relationship is cordial but lacks the closeness apparent between Jay and Dr. Smith. Interactions between Dr. and Mrs. Smith also were occasionally marred by stormy outbursts over seemingly trivial matters. These episodes were always followed by periods of mutual silence lasting for days at a time.

Jay's first brother, born when she was two years old, was for some time a threat and a source of irritation to Jay, although she does not remember too clearly the details of their early relationship. Her parents recall that Jay would sometimes have temper tantrums when the new infant demanded and received a lot of attention (especially from Mrs. Smith) while she herself now received relatively little. The temper tantrums intensified when Jay's second brother was born just one year after the first. As time went on, the brothers seemed to form an alliance to undermine Jay's supreme position with their father. In the process, Jay became closer to her father, while greater than average jealousy and rivalry characterized Jay's relationships with her younger brothers from early childhood to the present. Throughout elementary and high school, Jay was popular and did well academically. When asked once by a favorite teacher about future goals, Jay replied definitively, "I plan on going into medicine because I enjoy helping people, particularly when they are sick and must be taken care of." Yet despite Jay's lofty goals and ambitions, off and on between the ages of 8 and 17, there were strong feelings of loneliness, depression, insecurity, and confusion—feelings perhaps common to everyone during this age period, but stronger than in most youngsters and all too real and distressing.

Jay's college days, when she was away from home for the first time, proved exciting and challenging—a period of great personal growth and pain. New friends and responsibilities gave Jay increased self-confidence and zeal for pursuing a medical career. However, several unsuccessful romantic involvements proved disheartening and led Jay to increase her study efforts. Interpersonal relationships would always be troublesome for Jay. This aspect of life—the failure to achieve a stable and long-lasting relationship with that "special someone"—bitterly gnawed at Jay. "After all," she would muse, "aren't people supposed to fall in love and marry? What is wrong, why can't I ever maintain a serious relationship for any length of time?"

Two representative incidents regarding Jay and various boyfriends are worth noting. Although her disposition in most other circumstances is even-tempered, perhaps even inhibited, she often has an explosive fit of anger that terminates an important relationship. Her relationships with other women, although more stable than those with men, are usually casual, uncommitted, and of short duration.

When Jay was 13, she became good friends with a male classmate named Mark. They had many hours of conversation, although Jay never was able "to be herself" and really express her feelings. The relationship continued to blossom until one fatal day when a minor disagreement suddenly erupted into a major altercation. Jay ran away and tearfully professed that she did not want to see Mark again. Despite Mark's persistent efforts to talk with her and despite sharing some classes in school, Jay refused to have anything further to do with him.

Much later, while finishing her undergraduate education, Jay met Ted, a graduate student some 15 years older than herself. At 21, Jay felt that she was falling in love again, but this time it was the "real" thing. Unfortunately, their relationship had lasted for only about two months when disaster struck. Although Jay and Ted were close and trusted one another, an innocent conversation between Ted and a female classmate triggered Jay's rage. When Jay caught sight of the two, she turned quickly and hurried away. Ted finally caught up with her, but she screamed angrily in his face that she never wanted to see him again. And she never did.

Thanks to her excellent work during college, Jay was admitted to medical school. After the initial excitement, however, the hard realities took hold—more years of difficult work, intense competition, and, naturally, possible failure. The severe pressures and work load forced Jay to ignore potential romantic involvements although she had many casual friends whom she could always contact for brief diversions. While she tried not to dwell on personal feelings and conflicts during this period of her life, they crept through periodically: "I don't deserve to be a doctor"; "I won't pass my exams"; "Who am I and what do I want from life?"; "Why can't I meet that special person?" At graduation, Dr. and Mrs. Smith were as proud as they could possibly be. Their daughter was now, officially, Dr. Jaylene Elizabeth Smith, and she had graduated at the top of her class!

How can we describe and understand Jaylene Smith's personality? How did she become what she is? Was she affected by being the oldest child in her family and by having only brothers with whom to grow up? In what ways is she like her father and in what ways like her mother? Why does Jay feel insecure and uncertain despite her obvious success? Why do her friends see her as charming and attractive while she describes herself as introverted and inadequate? And what can we learn about Jay from the personality theories reviewed in this chapter?

Had Freud been Jay's therapist, he probably would have concluded that Jay has not yet effectively resolved the Oedipal complex. According to Freud, personality characteristics such as insecurity, introversion, feelings of inadequacy and worthlessness often arise from fixation at the phallic stage of development. Working from this start, Freud would have predicted that Jay's relationship with her father was either very distant and unsatisfying or unusually close and gratifying. We know, of course, that it was the the latter.

In all likelihood, Freud would also have predicted that at around age five or six, Jay would undoubtedly have become aware that she could not actually marry her father and do away with her mother, as Freud would say she wished to do. It is interesting that the arguments and fights between Jay and her mother subsided when Jay was "about 6 or 7 years of age." Moreover, we know that shortly thereafter, Jay began to experience "strong feelings of loneliness, depression, insecurity, and confusion." Clearly, something important happened in Jay's life when she was six or seven, although we can only speculate about what it was.

Finally, the continued coolness in Jay's relationship with her mother and the unusual closeness with her father would probably have confirmed Freud's suspicion that Jay has still not satisfactorily resolved the Oedipal complex. Thus, Freud would have predicted that Jay would have problems making the progression to mature sexual relationships with other men. Jay, of course, is very much aware that she has problems relating to men, at least when these relationships get "serious," although she has not attributed her problems to conflicts over sexuality.

And what does Erikson's theory tell us about Jaylene Smith's personality? Recall that for Erikson, one's success in dealing with later developmental crises depends on how effectively one has resolved earlier crises. The fact that Jay is having great difficulty in dealing with intimacy (Stage 6) suggests that she is still struggling with problems from earlier developmental stages. Erikson would look for the source of these problems in the quality of Jay's relationships with others. We know that her mother "subtly" communicated her own frustration and dissatisfaction to her children and spent little time on "nonessential" interactions with them. These feelings and behavior patterns would be unlikely to result in the kind of basic trust and sense of security that Erikson believes are essential to the first stage of development. In turn, Jay's failure to establish basic trust would be expected to make future development more difficult. In addition, her relationship with her mother and brothers continued to be less than fully satisfactory. It is not surprising, then, that Jay had some difficulty working through subsequent developmental crises. Although her father certainly provided a close and caring relationship, Jay was surely aware that in part his affection depended on her fulfilling the dreams, ambitions, and goals that he had for her.

Humanistic personality theory would focus on the discrepancy between Jay's self-concept and her inborn capacities. For example, Rogers would point out that Jay is intelligent and achievement-oriented but nevertheless feels that she doesn't "deserve to be a doctor," worries about whether she will ever be "truly happy," and remembers that when she was 13, she "never was able 'to be herself' and really express her feelings," even with a good friend. Her unhappiness, fearfulness, loneliness, insecurity, and other dissatisfactions similarly reflect the fact that Jay has not been able to become what she "most truly is." Rogers would also certainly expect to find that in Jay's life, acceptance and love were conditional on her living up to other people's ideas of what she should become. We know that throughout most of her life, Jay's father appears to have been her primary source of positive regard. We don't know with certainty that Dr. Smith made his love for Jay conditional on her living up to his goals for her, but it seems probable that he unintentionally did so.

The psychologist working from the trait perspective would infer the existence of certain traits from Jay's behavior. When we observe that Jay chose at an early age to pursue medicine, did well academically year after year, elected the necessary courses to qualify for medical school, persisted through four difficult years of medical study, and graduated first in her class, it seems reasonable to infer a trait of "determination" or "persistence" in order to account for her behavior. Similarly, you might reasonably conclude from the previous description of Jay that she also has traits of sincerity, motivation, and intelligence, as well as insecurity, introversion, shyness, and anxiety. These relatively few traits account for a great deal of Jay's behavior, and they also provide a relatively brief summary of "what Jay is like."

Yet other psychologists would suggest that Jaylene may have *learned* to be shy and introverted because she was rewarded for spending time by herself studying. It is possible that her father rewarded her for devoting herself to her studies. Certainly, she earned the respect of her teachers, and long hours of studying helped her avoid the somewhat uncomfortable feelings that she experienced when she was around other people. Reinforcement may have shaped other parts of Jay's personality as well. It seems likely that her father and her teachers helped form her trait of self-discipline and her need to achieve in school through a series of reinforcements. Even her aggression toward men may have been learned as a successful response to her brothers' teasing. If her hostility put an end to their taunts and was also rewarded by her father's affection, she may have learned to react with aggression to threats not only from her brothers but also from men in general.

In Jaylene's case, it is also likely that at least some aspects of her personality were learned by observing her parents and brothers. Her aggressive behavior with boyfriends, for example, may have grown out of watching her parents fight. As a young child, she may have observed that some people effectively deal with conflict by means of outbursts. Moreover, Jay surely noticed that her father, a "successful medical researcher," enjoyed and prospered in both his career and his family life, while her mother's two jobs as housewife and store manager left her somewhat frustrated and overtired. This contrast may have contributed in part to Jay's own interest in medicine and to her mixed feelings about the desirability of having a close relationship that might result in marriage.

Finally, it is possible that Jaylene Smith inherited tendencies toward introversion and emotional instability. But her experience in dealing with other people, including her brothers and her parents, probably had a great deal to do with making her less stable in her relationships with men than with women, more insecure and anxious than restless or excitable, and more self-sufficient and suspicious than reserved and aloof.

In the final analysis, it seems reasonable to say that, as a reflection of her personality, Jay's behavior is the product of a complex interaction of inherited predispositions, life experiences that include important family influences, learned behaviors, and the continual needs to resolve tension between life expectancies and real-life contingencies.

■ Summary

- Psychologists do not agree on a single definition of personality. One current definition is that **personality** refers to the pattern of characteristic thoughts, feelings, and behaviors that persists over time and situations and distinguishes one person from another. A wide variety of theories have been developed to explain not only the common types of personality, but also how people come to have the unique psychological signatures that are called our personalities. The first part of this chapter discussed the different theories put forth to explain personality. The second part of the chapter examined how personality is tested and assessed.

- **Are people usually aware of the reasons why they behave as they do?** Sigmund Freud proposed the first major *psychoanalytic theory* of personality. He stressed the *unconscious* (the thoughts and feelings of which we are not normally aware) and believed that personality is composed of three interrelated parts—the id, the ego, and the superego—that form an integrated whole. The *id* is a repository of unconscious urges seeking expression. The energy from the *life* and *death instincts* of the id is set in motion by a state of deprivation, which causes discomfort or tension. The id relieves this discomfort by reflex actions or by wish fulfillment, which Freud called *primary-process thinking.* The id acts according to the *pleasure principle.* The *ego* operates on the *reality principle.* It controls thinking and reasoning and directs the personality. The ego derives its energy from the id. It also controls the id and directs its energy into effective, realistic channels, a process known as *secondary-process thinking.* The *superego,* the moral guardian of behavior, compares the ego's actions with an *ego ideal* and then rewards or punishes the ego.

- As part of his theory of personality development, Freud identified five psychosexual stages through which children must pass: the *oral, anal, phallic, latency,* and *genital* stages. Strong attachment to the parent of the opposite sex and jealousy of the parent of the same sex—which develops during the phallic stage—is called the *Oedipus complex.*

- **Why do so many ancient myths and legends contain characters who are easily recognizable today?** Carl Jung believed that there are two distinct aspects of the unconscious that influence behavior and contribute to the development of personality. The *personal unconscious* contains our repressed thoughts, forgotten experiences, and undeveloped ideas; the *collective unconscious* consists of the memories and behavior patterns inherited from past generations. Among the images of the collective unconscious are *archetypes* that give rise to mythical representations. The *anima* is the archetypal female side of the male personality—the expression of female traits that guides male interactions with the opposite sex; the *animus* is the corresponding archetype in the female personality. Jung also conceived of two general attitude types. *Extroverts* are concerned with the external world—with other people and with events going on around them; *introverts* are more concerned with their own private worlds.

- **What is it that makes people strive for accomplishment and perfection?** Alfred Adler believed that we are not at the mercy of instinctual urges. Each of us is free to choose our own destiny and to develop in any way that will help us reach our goals. Adler believed that a person's motivation is a striving toward superiority, based in part on their feelings of inferiority in relation to their parents. Eventually, Adler shifted his emphasis from overcoming inferiority feelings to a more positive emphasis on strivings for superiority and perfection. With the concept of *fictional finalism,* he stressed that people set up important goals to guide their behavior.

- **What role do the relationships within your family play in forming your personality?** Karen Horney was influenced by Freud but believed that environmental and social factors are the most important influences shaping personality. The most important of these factors are family interpersonal relationships. She felt that *anxiety* arising from conflicts in these relationships is a stronger factor in personality than sexual drives alone. According to Horney, some people develop strategies or *neurotic trends* that help them cope with characteristic emotional problems. By emphasizing that culture and not anatomy determines many of the personality traits that differentiate women from men, Horney also challenged the prevailing notion that there are inevitable differences between the personality characteristics of men and women.

- **Does personality develop through a predictable series of stages?** In contrast to Freud, Erik Erikson feels that personality continues to develop during the life span. He describes eight stages of personality development, each of which involves the resolution of a crisis: *trust versus mistrust; autonomy versus shame and doubt; initiative versus guilt; industry versus inferiority; identity versus role confusion; intimacy versus isolation; generativity versus stagnation;* and *integrity versus despair.* According to Erikson, success in each stage depends on a person's adjustment in the previous stages. Erikson strongly believes in the necessity of achieving a positive personal identity (Stage 5) if one is to be able to form successful personal relationships.

- *Humanistic personality theories* look on life as a process of striving to realize our potential and thus view personality as one aspect of our efforts to develop and fulfill ourselves. According to Carl Rogers, all organisms are born with biological capacities and have the *actualizing tendency* to fulfill their inborn potential. In addition, human beings form self-concepts; the *self-actualizing tendency* drives them to live up to their images of themselves. Individuals whose self-concepts form a close match with their inborn capacities are more likely to realize their potential and become *fully functioning persons.* Fully functioning persons have been brought up with **unconditional positive regard** from others and are directed toward their own goals and ambitions. People who have been brought up with **conditional positive regard** deviate from their inborn potential and attempt to fulfill the goals that others have set for them. People who are not fully functioning are likely to feel threatened and anxious in general and dissatisfied with what they do.

- One of the earliest theories of personality is the **constitutional theory,** which suggests that there is a relationship between physique and behavior. William Sheldon identified three basic dimensions of a person's **somatotype:** *endomorphy, mesomorphy,* and *ectomorphy.* He found that somatotype ratings were often related to temperament.

- **If you say someone is stingy or easygoing, to what are you referring?** *Trait theorists* also maintain that a unique pattern of traits possessed by each person determines that person's behavior, but they disagree with Sheldon that constitutional factors alone determine these traits. They define **personality traits** as relatively permanent and consistent dispositions to behave in characteristic ways. They disagree on how many personality traits there might be and how they arise. Gordon Allport argued that there are potentially thousands of terms that can be used to describe human personality traits. Raymond Cattell, using a statistical approach called **factor-analysis,** identified 16 basic traits. More recently, it has begun to appear that personality traits can be boiled down to just five major dimensions: *extraversion, agreeableness, conscientiousness, emotional stability,* and *culture.*

- **Are they likely to be consistently stingy or easygoing in every situation?** There has been much controversy over trait theory. The central dispute is whether there are in fact appreciable consistencies in behavior and, if so, whether they are due to consistencies in a person, to consistencies in the environment, or to the person and the environment interacting. Proponents of the **situationist** perspective, notably Walter Mischel, argue that behavior sometimes appears to be consistent because we observe a person only in a limited variety of situations that tend to elicit the same behavior. The apparent consistency in an individual's behavior is really a result of the narrow range of situations in which we

observe that individual. Moreover, we tend to overestimate the consistency of a person's actions and to ignore behaviors that do not square with our preexisting concept of that person.

- **Do people's expectations guide their personalities?** In moderating the situationist position, other researchers note that some behaviors are consistent across situations, while others are more situationally dependent. A compromise outlook is called *interactionism,* which holds that knowledge both of a person and of the environment is necessary to predict and explain a person's behavior. Some interactionists argue that people develop **expectancies**—such as the expectation of success or failure—that guide their perceptions of social situations and their actions within them. One prevalent expectancy is **locus of control.** People who believe that they can control their own fate and that hard work, skill, and training make it possible to find reinforcements and avoid punishments have an *internal* locus of control; those who tend to believe that chance, luck, and the behavior of others determine their destiny have an *external* locus of control. These expectancies shape behavior in different situations and are themselves shaped by a person's experiences over time.

- **Are personalities learned from experiences?** *Behaviorism,* exemplified by the views of B. F. Skinner, claims that behavior is determined solely by learned experience guided by reinforcement. Skinner concentrates on finding the observable links between behavior and the conditions that cause or control it; these links are called **reinforcement contingencies.** Skinner does feel that there are consistencies in personal behavior because a person will respond to a new situation in ways that have been previously reinforcing.

- *Social learning theory* shares the outlook that behavior is controlled by reinforcement. But theorists such as Albert Bandura emphasize that factors such as observations contribute to the learning of new behaviors whose actual performance is then dependent on reinforcement histories. These theorists also agree that particular life circumstances develop a set of **person variables** (expectancies or characteristic strategies) that can help predict how a person will confront new situations. Behavior is viewed as a process of **reciprocal determinism,** which involves an interaction between person variables, situational variables, and continued feedback from actual behavior in new situations.

- Psychologists use four basic tools to assess personality: personal interviews, direct observation of behavior, objective tests, and projective tests.
- During an *interview* the interviewer seeks to evaluate another person by listening to what the person says and by observing his or her behavior. In an unstructured interview, the conversation may range over a number of subjects, and the person is encouraged to freely discuss experiences, feelings, and attitudes. In a structured interview, the content of questions is fixed beforehand and the interviewer tries not to deviate from the format. Because the behavior of the interviewer can make a difference in the outcome of an interview, structured interviews are considered more reliable in doing systematic personality testing.
- *Observation* is done to find our how a person behaves in everyday situations over a period of time and to determine the influence that situations and environments have on the range of behaviors a person might show. An advantage of direct observation is that the observer does not have to rely on a subject's own description of his or her behavior. Some disadvantages are the possibility of misinterpreting a behavior and the fact that the mere presence of an observer can affect the behavior of a subject.

- *Objective tests* of personality are given and scored according to standardized procedures. Such tests, like the **Sixteen Personality Factor Questionnaire** and the **Minnesota Multiphasic Personality Inventory (MMPI),** are usually constructed as questionnaires requiring yes-or-no responses or the selection of one answer among multiple choices. Because all objective tests rely on self-report, their effectiveness depends on the honesty with which the questions are answered. The advantages of objective tests are that they are inexpensive to use, easy to score, and do not depend on the interpretive skills of an observer or interviewer.
- **How can a person's response to an inkblot provide information about his or her personality? Projective tests** of personality use ambiguous stimuli that can elicit an unlimited number of responses. It is believed that a person will project his or her personality into the test material. Two well-known projective tests are the **Rorschach test,** consisting of 10 inkblot designs that subjects are asked to interpret, and the **Thematic Apperception Test (TAT),** consisting of 20 pictures about which subjects are asked to make up stories.

■ Review Questions

1. Personality is the pattern of thoughts, feelings, and behaviors that persists over _____ and _____ and that distinguishes one person from another.

2. Match the following of Freud's terms with their appropriate definitions:
   ____ unconscious
   ____ id
   ____ superego
   ____ ego
   ____ ego ideal
   ____ libido

   a. energy that comes from the sexual instinct
   b. mediator between reality, the superego, and the id
   c. unconscious urges seeking expression
   d. that part of the superego concerned with standards
   e. ideas and feelings of which we are not normally aware
   f. moral guardian of the ego

3. According to Freud, the _____ operates according to the reality principle, while the _____ acts according to the pleasure principle.

4. According to Freud, _____-process thinking is the means by which the id partially relieves the discomfort of instinctual drives through formal mental images:
   a. primary
   b. secondary

5. Match the following of Jung's terms with their appropriate definitions:
   ____ persona
   ____ animus
   ____ collective unconscious
   ____ archetype

   a. typical mental image or mythical representation
   b. memories and behavior patterns inherited from past generations
   c. aspect of the personality by which one is known to other people
   d. expression of male traits that guides female interactions with the opposite sex

6. Match the following of Adler's terms with their appropriate definitions:
_____ style of life
_____ inferiority complex
_____ compensation
_____ fictional finalism

a. fixation on or belief in a negative characteristic
b. individual's effort to overcome weaknesses
c. individual's particular set of meanings and beliefs
d. individual's tendency to set up goals to guide their behavior

7. Horney believed that _____ is a stronger source of emotional disturbance than sexual urges.

8. Match Erikson's "eight stages of man" with their appropriate descriptions:
_____ industry versus inferiority
_____ trust versus mistrust
_____ generativity versus stagnation
_____ intimacy versus isolation
_____ identity versus role confusion
_____ autonomy versus shame and doubt
_____ initiative versus guilt
_____ integrity versus despair

a. the infant appreciates the predictability of the environment and learns optimism about the future
b. the child's independence and contact with the environment increase
c. children become increasingly active, undertake new projects, and manipulate things in the environment
d. children encounter new expectations and begin learning adult skills
e. childhood ends and the responsibilities of adulthood loom large
f. the question of becoming intimate with the opposite sex arises
g. the adult faces the challenge of remaining productive and creative
h. individuals access life roles and face death

9. Rogers believed that a person strives to live up to and fulfill a self-image; he called this a person's _____ _____ tendency.

10. _____ argue that behavior is not highly consistent over time:
a. Trait theorists
b. Situationists

11. Social-learning theorists believe that people develop _____ (such as locus of control) that largely explain their behavior in different situations.

12. According to behaviorists, _____ accounts for the behavior to which personality is commonly attributed.

13. _____ tests require people to fill out questionnaires, which are then scored according to a standardized procedure.

14. In _____ tests of personality, people are shown ambiguous stimuli and asked to describe them or make up a story about them.

13 Stress and Adjustment

■ Thinking Critically

Why is it that even a pleasant event, like falling in love, can be stressful?

You've been planning to attend a concert for three weeks. On the day of the concert, your car won't start. How are you likely to feel and why?

Your best friend never seems to become nervous or flustered, while another friend always seems to be having a crisis about something. Are some people more resistant to stress?

Why do people often become silly when they are in a situation that makes them nervous?

What is one reason why a good run or game of basketball can make you feel better after a difficult day?

Do the unsettling symptoms of stress, such as increased heart rate and sweaty palms, serve any purpose? Can they cause physical harm?

What does it mean to be well-adjusted?

The answers to these and other questions about what causes stress and how we can cope with it appear throughout this chapter and in the Chapter Summary.

■ Outline

Let's begin the study of stress and adjustment with a few true stories.

• In 1979, Iranian militants stormed the United States embassy in Teheran and took 52 Americans hostage. For 444 days, the hostages lived in fear of their lives and endured the humiliations of captivity. To feel less like a prisoner and more like a person in charge of his life, one hostage saved food from meals and then played gracious host by offering it to other hostages who visited him in his cell. A diary kept by one American records other strategies: "Al's working on his painting. . . . Dick's walking his daily three miles back and forth across the room, and Jerry's lying on his mattress reading."

• When Eric de Wilde, an orphan, found a bag of jewels worth $350,000 on a Florida railroad track, it seemed like a fairy tale come true. But salespeople and reporters hounded him, and schoolmates and others kept calling him up with demands and threats. "Life is very difficult for the young man—a lot of things have happened to him in a hurry," said the lawyer whom de Wilde was forced to retain. But when the boy arrived in New York to sell his jewels at a public auction, he conducted himself with such dignified restraint that he managed to maintain his privacy and self-possession.

• When Janet Lodge had her first baby, she was filled with special joy, because at age 34 she had feared she would never become pregnant. But she found taking care of the baby, along with her other responsibilities, exhausting. Her husband Michael resented her constant fatigue and the fact that he didn't seem to come first in her life anymore. In an effort to solve these problems, Janet and Michael used some of their savings to pay for household help. Michael also took a more active role in looking after the baby, playing with her, and watching her development. This relieved some of Janet's burden and left her with more time and energy for her other responsibilities and for her life with Michael.

These three brief stories seem very different, but they have much in common. All the people involved were faced with significant new demands from their environments, they had to find ways of coping with new events, and they all seemed to adjust about as well as could be expected under the circumstances. Like these people, each of us must adjust to a life that is less perfect than we would like, a life in which even pleasures seem to come with built-in complications. We need to adapt not just to crises or to unexpected strokes of good fortune, but also to the constant minor demands of everyday life.

Every **adjustment** is an attempt—successful or not—to balance our desires against the demands of the environment, to weigh our needs against realistic possibilities, and to cope as well as we can within the limits of the situation. The student who fails to get the lead in the school play may quit the production in a huff, accept a smaller role, serve as theater critic for the school paper, or perhaps join the debating team. Each response is an adjustment to failure, although some responses may be less constructive in the long run than others.

This chapter will discuss the kinds of problems that people face in the course of living and the various ways in which they try to cope with these problems. Along the way, we will see that most people's problems are numerous and complex and that coping with stress is rarely easy. Finally, we will examine what psychologists mean when they refer to someone as "well-adjusted."

Sources of Stress

Stress refers to any adjustive demand that creates a state of tension or threat and that requires change or adaptation. Many situations require that we change our behavior in some way: A traffic light turns red and we stop our car; we change channels on the television set in order to see a new program; we go inside when it starts to rain. Under normal circumstances, these situations are not stressful because they are not usually accompanied by tension or threat. Now imagine that when the light turned red you were rushing to make an important appointment; or that someone watching TV with you has indicated that they definitely do not want to switch the channel; or that you are about to host a large outdoor party when it starts to rain. Under these conditions, the same events can become quite stressful.

Before we look at some of the major sources of stress, it is worth making several points about stress in general. Some things, of course, are inherently stressful, such as wars and natural disasters. Here the danger is very real: Lives are threatened, and often there is little or nothing people can do to save themselves. But even in naturally stressful situations, the time of greatest stress is not necessarily the time when danger is at its height, as Seymour Epstein (1962) demonstrated when he studied the effects of anticipated stress on a group of 28 parachutists. Each man was asked to describe his feelings before, during, and after his jump. All reported an increase of fear and of desire to escape as the time for the jump approached. Once the men were in line and realized that they could not turn back, however, they began to calm down. By the time they reached the most dangerous part of the jump—when they were in free-fall and waiting for their chutes to open—their fears had subsided. The time of greatest stress thus proved to be the period when the parachutists were *anticipating* danger.

But stress is not limited to life-and-death situations, nor, as two of our introductory anecdotes show, to unpleasant ones. The good things that happen to us, as well as the bad ones, cause stress because they carry with them adjustive demands that "require change or adaptation if an individual is to meet his or her needs" (Morris, 1990). A wedding is exciting, but it is also a stressful event—most weddings are very complicated affairs, and in addition they mark a profound change in one's relationships with one's parents, friends, old boy- or girlfriends, and of course one's new spouse. A promotion at work is satisfying—but it brings with it the need to relate to new people in new ways, to learn to do new things, and perhaps to dress differently and keep different working hours.

"As we feared, Harkness was stunned by the news."
Copyright © 1977, Henry R. Martin

Change

Notice that all the stressful events that we have considered so far involve change. But most people have a strong preference for a sense of order, continuity, and predictability in their lives. Therefore, any event, whether good or bad, that causes change and discontinuity in people's lives will be experienced as stressful. Put the opposite way, the stressfulness of various situations can be determined by the amount of change that they require. In 1967, Holmes and Rahe devised the Social Readjustment Rating Scale (SRRS) to measure how much stress a person has undergone in any given period. The two researchers began by compiling a list of several dozen events deemed stressful because they create change, for better or worse, in the pattern of a person's life and therefore require adjustment. Each event was assigned a point value—depending on the amount of change that it required (see Table 13-1). The most stressful event on the list is the death of a spouse. It has a rating of 100. At the bottom of the scale, a minor brush with the law is rated 11.

Note that the stressfulness of these events has little to do with whether they are desirable or undesirable. "Change in responsibilities at work" carries 29 "stress units," whether it is due to a promotion to more interesting work or to being assigned a much bigger volume of boring work. "Change in living conditions" carries 25 "stress units," whether it means moving into a wonderful new house or leaving an attractive large apartment that costs too much for a small dreary one with a more affordable rent.

Using the SRRS scale, you simply add up the stress ratings of all the events that people have lived through in a given period of time in order to determine the amount of stress that they have experienced. In general, a total score of 150 or less is considered normal; 150–199 corresponds to mild stress; 200–299 suggests a moderate crisis; and 300 or higher indicates a major life crisis. For example, marital reconciliation (45), together with pregnancy (40), a new mortgage (31), a change in living conditions (25), and a change in social activities (18), totals 159 points, or mild stress.

Even desirable major life events—getting married, having a baby, moving into a new house—can cause stress and, in turn, psychological and medical problems.

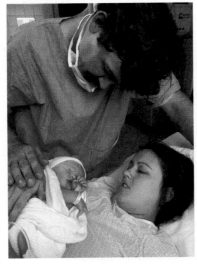

TABLE 13-1 SOCIAL READJUSTMENT RATING SCALE	
LIFE EVENT	**LIFE-CHANGE UNITS**
Death of one's spouse	100
Divorce	73
Marital separation	65
Jail term	63
Death of a close family member	63
Personal injury or illness	53
Marriage	50
Being fired at work	47
Marital reconciliation	45
Retirement	45
Change in the health of a family member	44
Pregnancy	40
Sex difficulties	39
Gain of a new family member	39
Business readjustment	39
Change in one's financial state	38
Death of a close friend	37
Change to a different line of work	36
Change in number of arguments with one's spouse	35
Mortgage over $10,000	31
Foreclosure of a mortgage or loan	30
Change in responsibilities at work	29
Son or daughter leaving home	29
Trouble with in-laws	29
Outstanding personal achievement	28
Wife beginning or stopping work	26
Beginning or ending school	26
Change in living conditions	25
Revision of personal habits	24
Trouble with one's boss	23
Change in work hours or conditions	20
Change in residence	20
Change in schools	20
Change in recreation	19
Change in church activities	19
Change in social activities	18
Mortgage or loan of less than $10,000	17
Change in sleeping habits	16
Change in number of family get-togethers	15
Change in eating habits	15
Vacation	13
Christmas	12
Minor violations of the law	11

Table 13-1

The SRRS assigns "life-change units" to several dozen stressful events. Holmes and Rahe linked the number of units to risk for medical problems. Note that the mortgage sum of $10,000 reflects economic realities of over 20 years ago.

Reprinted with permission from Holmes and Rahe, "The social readjustment rating scale," in *Journal of Psychosomatic Research*, 11, 1967. © 1967, Pergamon Press.

Hassles

Holmes and Rahe emphasize stress that arises from fairly dramatic, one-time life events. But other psychologists (Lazarus & De Longis, 1983; Lazarus et al., 1985) point out that much stress arises from nonevents; that is, from "chronic or repeated conditions of living—boredom, continuing tension in a family relationship, lack of occupational progress, isolation and loneliness, absence of meaning and commitment" (Lazarus, 1981, p. 60).

The heart of Lazarus's thinking is the concept of "hassles," which he defines as petty annoyances, irritations, and frustrations. Such seemingly minor matters as being stuck in traffic, misplacing the car keys or

Exam Anxiety and Grandma's Health

Every student knows that examination time can be a source of great stress. In the following article, Professor John J. Chiodo of Clarion University describes some truly extraordinary effects of exam-related stress and suggests a variety of ways in which faculty members can help to alleviate the problem.

I entered the ranks of academe as well prepared as the next fellow, but I was still unaware of the threat that midterm exams posed to the health and welfare of students and their relatives. It didn't take long, however, for me to realize that a real problem existed. The onset of midterms seemed to provoke not only a marked increase in the family problems, illnesses, and accidents experienced by my students, but also above-normal death rates among their grandmothers.

In my first semester of teaching, during the week before the midterm exam, I got numerous phone calls and visits from the roommates of many of my students, reporting a series of problems. Mononucleosis seemed to have struck a sizable portion of my class, along with the more common colds and flu.

A call from one young woman awakened me with the news that her roommate's grandmother had died, so she (my student) would be unable to take the exam. I expressed my condolences, and assured the caller that her roommate would not be penalized for such an unexpected tragedy.

Over the next few days I received many more calls—informing me of sickness, family problems, and even the death of a beloved cat. But the thought of three grandmothers passing away, all within the short exam period, caused me a good deal of remorse. But the term soon ended and, with the Christmas break and preparations for the new semester, I forgot all about the midterm problem.

Eight weeks into the second semester, however, I was once again faced with a succession of visits or phone calls from roommates about sick students, family problems, and, yes, the deaths of more grandmothers. I was shaken. I could understand that dorm meals and late nights, along with "exam anxiety," might well make some students sick, but what could account for the grandmothers? Once again, though, other things occupied my mind, and before long I had stopped thinking about it.

I moved that summer to a large Midwestern university, where I had to reconstruct my teaching plans to fit the quarter system. I taught three classes. By the end of the first midterm exams two of my student's grandmothers had died; by the time the year was over, a total of five had gone to their reward.

I began to realize the situation was serious. In the two years I had been teaching, 12 grandmothers had passed away; on that basis, if I taught for 30 years 180 grandmothers would no longer be with us. I hated to think what the universitywide number would be.

I tried to figure out the connection. Was it because grandmothers are hypersensitive to a grandchild's problems? When they see their grandchildren suffering from exam anxiety do they become anxious too? Does the increased stress then cause stroke or heart failure? It seemed possible; so it followed that if grandmothers' anxiety levels could be lowered, a good number of their lives might be prolonged. I didn't have much direct contact with grandmothers, but I reasoned that by moderating the anxiety of my students, I could help reduce stress on their grandmothers.

With that in mind, I began my next year of teaching. On the first day of class, while passing out the syllabus, I told my students how concerned I was about the high incidence of grandmother mortality. I also told them what I thought we could do about it.

To make a long story short, the results of my plan to reduce student anxiety were spectacular. At the end of the quarter there had not been one test-related death of a grandmother. In addition, the amount of sickness and family strife had decreased dramatically. The next two quarters proved to be even better. Since then, I have refined my anxiety-reduction system and, in the interest of grandmotherly longevity, would like to share it with my colleagues. Here are the basic rules:

- *Review the scope of the exam.*
- *Use practice tests.*
- *Be clear about time limits.*
- *Announce what materials will be needed and what aids will be permitted.*
- *Review the grading procedure.*
- *Review the policies on makeup tests and retakes.*
- *Provide study help.*
- *Make provision for last-minute questions.*
- *Allow for breaks during long exams.*
- *Coach students on test-taking techniques.*

I have been following these rules for 13 years now, and during that time have heard of only an occasional midterm-related death of a grandmother. Such results lead me to believe that if all faculty members did likewise, the health and welfare of students—and their grandmothers—would surely benefit.

getting into a trivial argument may be as stressful, he holds, as major life events like those on the Holmes-Rahe scale. This does not mean that Lazarus discounts big events. Rather, he believes that big events matter so much not because they create stress directly, but because they trigger little hassles that give rise to stress. Thus, a major event creates a ripple effect. "In sum," Lazarus says, "it is not the large dramatic events that make the difference, but what happens day in and day out, whether provoked by major events or not" (1981, p. 62).

We have been speaking of external events and situations, both major and minor, as sources of stress. The reason that these events are stressful is that they give rise to feelings of pressure, frustration, conflict, and anxiety. Each of these emotional experiences contributes to our overall feeling of stress. Let's take a look at each of them before we consider the differences in the ways people perceive and adjust to stress.

Pressure

Pressure is another common source of stress. Pressure occurs when we feel forced to speed up, intensify, or shift the direction of our behavior or to meet a higher standard of performance (Morris, 1990). In part, pressure can arise from within us, from very personal goals and ideals. Because of our concern about our intelligence, appearance, popularity, or talents, we may push ourselves to reach even higher standards of excellence. This kind of pressure can be constructive. It may lead, for example, to a serious effort to learn to play a musical instrument, which can ultimately bring us great pleasure. On the other hand, internal pressure can be destructive if our aims are impossible to achieve.

A sense of pressure may also derive from outside influences. Among the most significant and consistent of these are seemingly relentless demands that we compete, that we adapt to the rapid rate of change in our society, and that we live up to what our family and close friends expect of us. The forces that push us to compete affect nearly all relationships in America life. We compete for grades, for popularity, for sexual and marital partners, and for jobs. We are taught to see failure as shameful. Hence the pressure to win can be intense.

Frustration

Frustration also contributes to stress. Frustration occurs when a person is prevented from reaching a goal because something or someone is in the way (see Figure 13-1). A teenager madly in love with a popular singer may learn that she is happily married; a high-school student who does poorly on his College Boards may not get into his father's alma mater. These people must either give up their goals as unattainable or find some way to overcome the obstacles blocking them.

The teenager with a crush will probably recover quickly, but the student faces a more complex problem. Most likely his first reaction will be to get angry—at himself for not having studied harder, at his father for pushing him to apply to that college, at the admissions board for not taking into account the bad cold he had the day he took the College Boards. He may not be able to express his anger directly; he may not even realize or admit how disappointed he is. Nevertheless, he must either

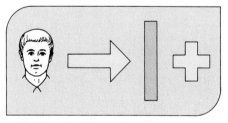

Figure 13-1
A diagram of frustration The person is prevented by a barrier (the vertical line) from reaching a goal (+).

Conflict Simultaneous existence of incompatible demands, opportunities, needs, or goals.

Approach/approach conflict Result of simultaneous attraction to two appealing possibilities.

find a new way to reach his goal or change it and be satisfied with another school.

Morris (1990) identifies five basic sources of frustration above and beyond daily hassles. *Delays* are hard for us to accept because our culture stresses the value of time. Anyone who has been caught in a traffic jam is familiar with the frustration of delay. Also, because advertising makes consumer goods so attractive, we may become frustrated if something that we would like to own is out of our immediate economic reach. *Lack of resources* is especially frustrating to low-income Americans, who cannot afford the new cars or vacations that TV programs and magazine articles would have us believe everyone must have. *Losses*, such as the end of a love affair or a cherished friendship, are frustrating because they often make us feel helpless, unimportant, and worthless. *Failure* is a frequent source of frustration in our competitive society. The aspect of failure that is hardest to cope with is guilt. We imagine that if we had done certain things differently, we might have succeeded, and so we feel responsible for our own or someone else's pain and disappointment. *Discrimination* can also be a source of frustration. Being denied opportunities or recognition simply because of one's sex, age, religion, or skin color, regardless of one's personal qualifications or accomplishments, is immensely frustrating.

Conflict

Of all life's troubles, **conflict** is probably the most common. A student finds that both of the required courses that he or she wanted to take this year meet at the same time. In an election, the views of one candidate on foreign policy reflect our own, but we prefer the domestic programs proposed by an opponent. A boy does not want to go to his aunt's for dinner, but neither does he want to listen to his parents complain if he stays at home.

Conflict arises when we face two or more incompatible demands, opportunities, needs, or goals. There is never any way to resolve conflict completely. We must either give up some of our goals, modify some of them, delay our pursuit of some goals, or learn to accept the fact that not all of our goals can be fully attained. Whatever we do, we are bound to experience some frustration; knowing this adds to the stressfulness of conflicts.

In the 1930s, Kurt Lewin described conflict in terms of two opposite tendencies: *approach* and *avoidance*. When something attracts us, we want to approach it; when something frightens us, we try to avoid it. Lewin (1935) showed how different combinations of these tendencies characterize three basic types of conflict.

The first, diagrammed in Figure 13-2, he called **approach/approach conflict**. A person is simultaneously attracted (the arrows) to two appealing goals (the plus signs). For example, a woman may want to pursue a career and also to raise a family. As a rational person, she considers the alternatives. She could accept a job now and delay having children, or she could have children now and look for work later on. Alternatively, she could modify both goals by hiring a housekeeper. Or she and her husband could share child-care duties. Here the solutions are numerous, but this is not always the case. Suppose the same woman wanted a career that

Figure 13-2
A diagram of approach/approach conflict The person is attracted to two incompatible goals at the same time.

required frequent and often prolonged travel—say, in international sales. She might conclude that a career would necessitate neglecting her family. If she is right, it might in fact be impossible for her to attain both goals simultaneously.

The reverse of this dilemma is **avoidance/avoidance conflict,** when a person is confronted with two undesired or threatening possibilities (Figure 13-3). When faced with an avoidance/avoidance conflict, people usually try to escape. If escape is impossible, they cope in one of a number of ways, depending on how threatening each alternative is. Students who must choose between failing an exam or studying something that they find terribly boring will probably decide to study, at least for a time. Otherwise, they may have to repeat the course—an even less pleasant alternative. Making that kind of choice is not very stressful. Consider, in contrast, the situation of a police officer assigned to a high-crime area. There is risk involved in answering every radio call; but since a police officer risks job, self-esteem, and the lives of fellow officers by failing to respond, he or she will almost surely respond—and the cost in stress will be high.

People caught in avoidance/avoidance conflicts often vacillate between one threat and another, like the baseball player caught between first and second base. He starts to run toward second, then realizes that he will be tagged and turns around, only to realize that he will be tagged on first if he tries to go back there. In no-exit situations like this, many people simply wait for events to resolve their conflict for them.

Approach/avoidance conflict (see Figure 13-4), in which a person is both attracted to and repelled by the same goal, are also difficult to resolve. A football player recovering from an operation may want to return to his team, but he knows that he may limp for the rest of his life if he is injured again. A woman knows that she will disappoint her present employer if she moves to a new and better job, but she realizes that she will feel resentful toward him or her if she stays in her present job. People whose parents taught them that sex is dirty and sinful may find themselves in adulthood simultaneously attracted to and repelled by members of the opposite sex.

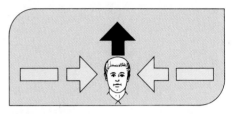

Figure 13-3
A diagram of avoidance/avoidance conflict Repelled by two undesirable alternatives at the same time, the person is inclined to try to escape (the black arrow), but often other factors prevent such an escape.

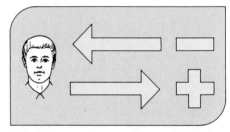

Figure 13-4
A diagram of approach/avoidance conflict The person is both repelled by and attracted to the same goal.

Beginning parachutists often report an *avoidance/avoidance conflict*—they're fearful of the jump but too proud to abandon their commitment. Once they are in line and it becomes apparent that they cannot turn back, they become calmer, and during the jump itself, their fears subside further. Anticipating the jump seems to be more stressful than making it.

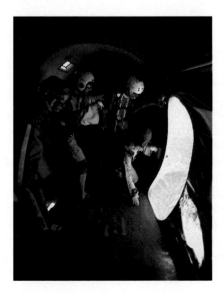

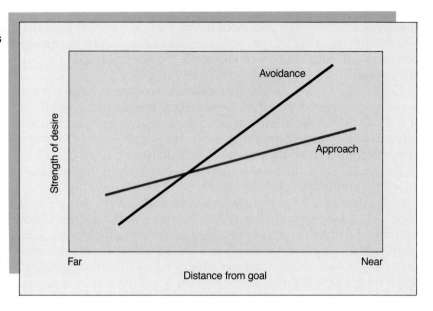

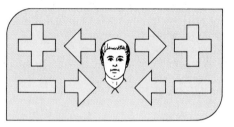

Figure 13-6
A diagram of double approach/ avoidance conflict We are caught between two goals, each of which has good and bad features.

The desire to approach a goal grows stronger as we get nearer to it, but so does the desire to avoid it. The avoidance tendency usually increases in strength faster than the approach tendency. In an approach/avoidance conflict, therefore, we approach the goal until we reach the point at which the tendency to approach equals the tendency to avoid the goal (see Figure 13-5). Afraid to go any closer, we stop, fall back, and approach again, vacillating until we have to make a decision or until the situation changes.

Approach/avoidance conflicts are often combined in complex patterns. A mother who loves classical music may dream that her son will be a great pianist. His father might want him to be an athlete. If the child practices the piano, he pleases his mother but upsets his father; if he stays after school for football practice, he disappoints his mother but pleases his father. *Double approach/avoidance conflict*, as Lewin called this, is diagrammed in Figure 13-6.

Self-imposed Stress

So far we have considered sources of stress that, for the most part, lie outside the individual. However, sometimes people create problems for themselves quite apart from stressful events in their environment. Albert Ellis (Ellis & Harper, 1975) has proposed that many people carry around a set of irrational, unreasonable, self-defeating beliefs that add unnecessarily to the normal stresses of living. For example, according to Ellis, some people believe "It is essential to be loved or approved by almost everyone for everything I do"; for people who share this belief, any sign of disapproval will be a source of considerable stress. Other people believe "I must be competent, adequate, and successful at everything I do"; for such people, the slightest sign of failure or inadequacy is taken as evidence that they are worthless human beings. Still other people believe "It is disastrous if everything doesn't go the way I would like"; if things don't go perfectly, these people feel upset, miserable, and unhappy. As we will see in the next chapter, Aaron Beck (1967, 1976) believes that many cases of depression arise from self-defeating thoughts such as these.

Stress and Individual Differences

Some people cope with major life stresses without experiencing great difficulty, while others have difficulty with even minor problems. What accounts for the difference? The answer seems to be individual differences in perceiving and reacting to potentially stressful events.

An obstacle that looks like a molehill to one person looks like a mountain to another. An experienced construction worker thinks nothing of eating his or her lunch on a girder hundreds of feet above the ground, but just watching him or her may be enough to make a passerby anxious. One patient facing a serious operation may feel less anxious than someone else going to a doctor for a routine physical exam. The person who gets fired from a job and the soldier who gets caught behind enemy lines may feel equally threatened. In short, how much stress we experience depends partly on the way we interpret the situation.

Several factors determine whether or not we find a particular situation stressful (Kessler, Price, & Wortman, 1985). Someone who is self-confident, who feels adequate to cope with life events, is less likely to find a given situation stressful than someone who lacks such self-assurance. For example, students who know that they can study when they have to and have done well in the past are likely to be calmer the night before an exam than those who have done poorly on previous exams. People who have handled job changes well in the past are likely to find the next change less stressful than those who have had great difficulty adjusting to previous job changes.

Kobasa (1979) studied closely a group of people who either tolerated stress exceptionally well or actually thrived on it. What these stress-resistant people had in common was a trait that Kobasa called *hardiness*: They felt very much in control of their lives, were deeply committed to their work and their own values, and experienced difficult demands from the environment as challenging rather than frightening. Kobasa's study suggests that people's response to stress depends partly on whether they believe they have some control over events or whether they feel helpless. Research cited by Seligman (1975) shows that people in seemingly hopeless situations not only become apathetic but, when the situation changes, fail to recognize that it is now possible to cope more effectively. They remain passive even when there are opportunities for improving the situation.

So much for individual differences in the susceptibility to stress. What about behavior under stress once it does occur? Here, too, there are differences among people. In natural disasters, for example, some people immediately mobilize their forces to save themselves. Others fall apart. Still others are shaken but regain their composure—and ability to respond—almost immediately. And then there are those who refuse to admit that there is any danger. In the next section, we will consider in detail what people choose to do—or not do—when they are under stress.

An obstacle that looks like a molehill to one person may strike another as a mountain. The mere sight of these construction workers may be enough to make a passerby nervous.

■ How People Cope with Stress

Whatever its source, stress calls for adjustment. Psychologists distinguish between two general types of adjustment: direct coping and defensive coping. *Direct coping* refers to any action that we take to change an uncomfortable situation. When our needs or desires are frustrated, we attempt to remove the obstacles between ourselves and our goal or we give up. Similarly, when we are threatened, we try to eliminate the source of the threat, either by attacking it or by escaping from it.

Defensive coping refers to the different ways people convince themselves that they are not really threatened or that they do not really want something they cannot get. A form of self-deception, defensive coping is characteristic of internal, often unconscious conflicts. We are emotionally unable to bring a problem to the surface and deal with it directly because it is too threatening. In self-defense, we avoid the conflict.

Direct Coping

When we are threatened, frustrated, or in conflict, we have three basic choices for coping directly: confrontation, compromise, or withdrawal. We can meet a situation head-on and intensify our efforts to get what we want (confrontation). We can give up some of what we want and perhaps persuade others to give up part of what they want (compromise). Or we can admit defeat and stop fighting (withdrawal).

Take the case of a woman who has worked hard at her job for years but is not promoted. She learns that the reason is her stated unwillingness to move temporarily from the company's main office to a branch office in another part of the country in order to get more experience. Her unwillingness to move is an obstacle between her and her goal of advancing in her career. She has several choices. Let's look at each in turn.

CONFRONTATION. **Confrontation** means facing a stressful situation forthrightly, acknowledging to oneself that there is a problem for which a solution must be found, attacking the problem head-on, and pushing resolutely toward one's goal. The hallmark of the "confrontational style" (Golden, 1982) is making intense efforts to cope with stress and to accomplish one's aims. This may involve learning skills, enlisting other people's help, or just trying harder. Or it may require trying to change either oneself or the situation. The woman whom we have been describing might decide that if she wants very much to move up in the company, she will have to agree to relocate. But she might, instead, try to change the situation itself in one of several ways. She could challenge the assumption that the branch office would give her the kind of experience that her supervisor thinks she needs. She could try to persuade the boss that although she has never worked in a branch office, she nevertheless has enough experience to handle a better job in the main office. Or she could remind the supervisor of the company's need to promote more women to top-level positions.

Confrontation may also include expressions of anger. Anger can be effective, especially if we have really been unfairly treated and if we express our anger with restraint instead of exploding in rage. A national magazine once reported an amusing, and effective, example of controlled anger in response to an annoying little hassle. As a motorist came to an intersection, he had to stop for a frail old lady crossing the street. The driver of the car behind honked his horn impatiently, whereupon the first driver shut off his ignition, removed his key, walked back to the other car, and handed the key to the second driver. "Here," he said, "*You* run over her. I can't do it. She reminds me of my grandmother."

COMPROMISE. **Compromise** is one of the most common, and effective, ways of coping directly with conflict or frustration. We often recognize that we cannot have everything we want and that we cannot expect others to do just what we would like them to do. In such cases, we may decide to settle for less than we originally wanted. A young person who has loved animals all his life and has long cherished the desire to become a veterinarian may discover in college that he has less aptitude for biology than he had hoped and that he finds dissecting specimens in the lab so distasteful that he could never bring himself to operate on animals. By way of compromise, he may decide to become an animal technician, a person who works as an assistant to a veterinarian.

WITHDRAWAL. In some circumstances, the most effective way of coping with stress is to withdraw from the situation. A person at an amusement park who is overcome by anxiety just looking at a roller coaster can move on to a less threatening ride or even leave the park entirely. The woman whose promotion depends on temporarily relocating might simply quit her job and join another company. Or she might withdraw figuratively from the stressful situation by deciding that promotion no longer matters to her and that she has already advanced in her career as far as she wants to go.

We often equate **withdrawal** with simply refusing to face problems. But when we realize that our adversary is more powerful than we are, or that there is no way we can effectively change ourselves, alter the situation, or reach a compromise, and that any form of aggression would be self-destructive, withdrawal is a positive and realistic adjustment. In seemingly hopeless situations, such as submarine and mining disasters, few people panic (Mintz, 1951). Believing that there is nothing they can do to save themselves, they give up. If the situation is in fact hopeless, resignation may be the most effective way of coping.

Perhaps the greatest danger is that withdrawal will turn into avoidance of all similar situations. We may refuse to go to any amusement park or carnival again. The woman who did not want to move to a branch office may quit her job without even looking for a new one. In such cases, coping by withdrawal becomes maladaptive avoidance, and we begin to suspect that the adjustment is not really effective. Moreover, people who have given up are in a poor position to take advantage of a more effective solution if one comes along. For example, one group of fifth-grade students was given unsolvable problems by one teacher and solvable problems by another. When the "unsolvable" teacher later presented the students with problems that *could* be solved, the students were unable to solve them, even though they had solved nearly identical problems given by the other teacher (Dweck & Repucci, 1973).

Compromise Deciding on a more realistic solution or goal when an ideal solution or goal is not practical.

Withdrawal Avoiding a situation when other forms of coping are not practical.

"This toy is designed to hasten the child's adjustment to the world around him. No matter how carefully he puts it together, it won't work."
Drawing by Joe Mirachi; © 1964 The New Yorker Magazine, Inc.

Though there are times when withdrawal can be the most effective way of coping with a difficult or frightening situation, if it becomes an habitual avoidance, it can leave the individual unable to take advantage of more effective solutions when they come up.

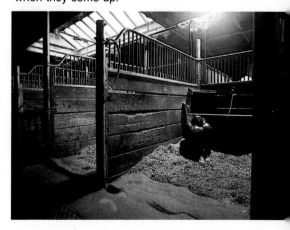

Withdrawal, in whatever form, is a mixed blessing. Although it can be an effective method of coping, it has built-in dangers. The same tends to be true of defensive coping, to which we now turn.

Defensive Coping

Thus far, we have been speaking of coping with stress that arises from recognizable sources. But there are times when we either cannot identify or cannot deal directly with the source of our stress. For example, you return to a parking lot to discover that someone has damaged your new car and then left the scene. Or your vacation trip must be delayed because the airport is buried under 3 feet of new snow. In other cases, a problem is so emotionally threatening that it cannot be faced directly. Perhaps you find out that someone to whom you are close is terminally ill. Or you learn that after four years of hard study you have failed to be admitted to medical school and may have to abandon your lifelong ambition of becoming a physician.

In all these cases, you are under stress and there is little or nothing you can do to cope with the stress directly. In such situations, people

■ Social Class and Stress

Abnormal behavior—as seen in crime, delinquency, family violence, and neurosis—is often linked to low socioeconomic status. Why should there be such a connection?

Several studies point to a one-word answer: stress. People who belong to the lower socioeconomic class are both more exposed to stress and more vulnerable to it. Pearlin and Schooler (1978) put it this way: "The less educated and the poorer are more exposed to hardships and, at the same time, are less likely to have the means to fend off the stresses resulting from the hardships. Not only are life problems distributed unequally among social groups and collectivities, but it is apparent that the ability to deal with the problems is similarly unequal" (p. 17).

Kessler (1979) reached similar conclusions. He analyzed interviews done in 1967 and 1969 with 720 people and collected information about specific events that had occurred in the lives of those people in the same two years. In addition, he reviewed data on his subjects' physical and financial status and on how much emotional distress they felt roughly 10 years after the events. When he compared members of the upper and lower classes, he found that the latter had had to face more stressful experiences than the former (e.g., poor housing, dangerously crime-ridden neighborhoods, and long-term joblessness). His data also suggested that those in the lower classes had not coped with their difficulties as well as those in the upper class. And he found that stressful events of the same severity had had more impact on the emotional lives of lower-class subjects.

Several studies indicate that not only do people from lower socioeconomic classes have more difficult experiences to cope with than do members of other classes, but they are also more likely to suffer as a result. There are several possible reasons for this. Liem and Liem (1978) concluded that lower-class members have fewer people and fewer community resources to which to turn for help in getting through hard times. Wills and Langer (1980) propose that low income and lack of education are associated with ineffective coping styles. Perhaps lower-class members tend to believe in an external locus of control (see Chapter 12)—that is, that external factors are responsible for what happens to them and that they themselves have little personal control over their lives. Furthermore, there is evidence that lower-class members often doubt their ability to master difficult situations and have poor self-esteem.

None of this proves that social class itself is the direct cause of all the difficulties that its members experience. It may be that lower-class membership offers few opportunities to learn effective methods of coping with stress. Alternatively, it may be that poor coping skills (which can be seen in any class) cause people to drift downward into the lower classes.

are likely to turn to **defense mechanisms** as a way of coping. Defense mechanisms are ways of deceiving oneself about the causes of a stressful situation so that pressure, frustration, conflict, and anxiety are reduced. The self-deceptive nature of such adjustments led Freud to conclude that they are entirely unconscious. Freud was particularly interested in distortions of memory and in irrational feelings and behavior, all of which he considered symptoms of a struggle against unconscious impulses. Therefore, he believed that defensive ways of coping always spring from unconscious conflicts and that we have little or no control over them. Not all psychologists accept this interpretation. Often we *realize* that we are pushing something out of our memory or otherwise deceiving ourselves. All of us have blown up at one person when we knew we were really angry with someone else.

Whether or not defense mechanisms operate unconsciously, they do provide a means of coping with stress that might otherwise be unbearable. Let's look more closely at some of the major defense mechanisms.

DENIAL. One common defense mechanism is **denial,** or the refusal to acknowledge a painful or threatening reality. As we saw in Chapter 10, the first reaction of most people when they learn that they are dying is denial. Lazarus (1969) cites the example of a woman who was near death from severe burns. At first, she was depressed and frightened, but after a few days she began to feel sure that she would soon be able to return home and care for her children, although all medical indications were to the contrary. By denying the extent of her injuries, this woman was able to stay calm and cheerful. She was not merely putting on an act for her relatives and friends: She *believed* she would recover. In a similar situation, C.T. Wolff and his colleagues (1964) interviewed the parents of children who were dying of leukemia. Some parents denied their children's condition; others accepted it. Physical examinations revealed that those who were denying the illness did not have the physiological symptoms of stress, such as excessive stomach acid, found in those who accepted their children's illness.

Many psychologists would suggest that in these situations denial is a positive solution. But in other situations it clearly is not. Students who deny their need to study and instead spend more nights at the movies may well fail their exams. Heroin addicts who insist that they are merely experimenting with drugs are also deluding themselves.

REPRESSION. Perhaps the most common mechanism for blocking out painful feelings and memories is **repression.** Repression, a form of forgetting, means excluding painful thoughts from consciousness. The most extreme form of this defense is *amnesia*—the total inability to recall the past. Soldiers who break down in the field often block out the memory of experiences that led to their collapse (Grinker & Spiegel, 1945). But forgetting that you are supposed to go for a job interview Thursday morning or forgetting the embarrassing things you said at a party last night may also be instances of repression.

Many psychologists believe that repression is a sign of struggle against impulses that conflict with conscious values. For example, most of us are taught that violence and aggression are wrong. But it is only human to feel anger at least sometimes. This conflict between our feelings and our

Defense mechanisms Self-deceptive techniques for reducing stress, including denial, repression, projection, identification, intellectualization, reaction formation, displacement, and sublimation.

Denial Refusing to acknowledge a painful or threatening reality.

Repression Excluding uncomfortable thoughts from consciousness.

Projection Attributing one's own repressed motives, feelings, or wishes to others.

Identification Taking on the characteristics of someone else to avoid feeling incompetent.

values can create stress, and one way of coping defensively with that stress is to repress our feelings—to block out completely any awareness of our underlying anger and hostility.

Denial and repression are the most basic defense mechanisms. In denial, we block out situations with which we can't cope. In repression, we block out unacceptable impulses or thoughts. These mechanisms form the bases for other defensive ways of coping.

PROJECTION. If a problem cannot be denied or repressed completely, it may be possible to distort its nature so that it can be more easily handled. One example of this is **projection,** the attribution of one's own repressed motives, ideas, or feelings to others. We ascribe feelings that we do not want to someone else, thus locating the source of our conflict outside ourselves. A corporation executive who feels guilty about the way he rose to power may project his own ruthless ambition onto his colleagues. He is simply doing his job, he believes, while his associates are all overly ambitious and preoccupied with power. A high-school student talks his girlfriend into sneaking away with him for the weekend. It is a bad experience for both of them. Days later he insists that it was she who pushed him into it. He is not lying—he really believes that she did. Perhaps he feels guilty for insisting that they sneak away together, angry with her for not talking him out of it, and disturbed by what he felt during the experience. To pull himself together, he locates the responsibility outside himself. In both cases, the stressful problem has been repressed and then translated into a form that is less stressful and easier to handle.

Dana Bramal (1962) demonstrated projection with an experiment in which heterosexual male subjects were assigned a partner, and some were led to believe that they had measurable homosexual tendencies. Others were not so deceived. Bramel then studied the ways in which the deceived subjects tried to cope with the presumably disturbing "evidence" that they had homosexual tendencies. Many subjects used projection: In interviews after the experiment, many more experimental than control subjects attributed homosexual tendencies to their *partners*. In other words, they dealt with the stress by locating the problem outside themselves.

IDENTIFICATION. The reverse of projection is **identification.** Through projection, we *rid* ourselves of undesirable characteristics that we have repressed by attributing them to someone else. Through identification, we *take on* the characteristics of someone else in order to share in that person's triumphs and to avoid feeling incompetent. The admired person's actions become a substitute for our own. Identification is sometimes considered a form of defensive coping because it enables people to resolve conflicts vicariously. A parent with unfulfilled career ambitions may share emotionally in a child's professional success. When the child is promoted, the parent may feel as if he or she has triumphed.

Identification is often used as a form of self-defense in situations where a person feels utterly helpless. Psychoanalyst Bruno Bettelheim, once a prisoner in a Nazi concentration camp, described how some prisoners gradually came to identify with the Nazi guards. Over the years, they began to copy the speech and mannerisms of the guards, and sometimes even their values. Bettelheim explains that the prisoners were completely dependent on the guards, who could treat them however they liked. The relationship between prisoner and guard was similar to that between child and parent. Bettelheim suggests that the guards may have consciously been trying to make the prisoners feel like children. For example, prisoners had to ask permission to go to the bathroom. Sometimes permission was denied, forcing grown men to suffer the indignity of wetting their pants. Reduced to a childlike, helpless condition, prisoners reverted to a pattern developed in childhood: They identified with the aggressor (Bettelheim, 1943, 1960). Like children in conflict with a powerful and threatening adult, they admired their enemy and became like him as a way of defensively coping with unbearable and inescapable stress.

REGRESSION. People under severe stress, like the concentration camp victims described by Bettelheim, may revert to other kinds of childlike behavior as well. This is called **regression.** In Chapter 12, for example, we noted that people who become fixated at one of the early Freudian stages (oral, anal, or phallic) are especially likely to display the immature childlike traits associated with those stages whenever they come under stress.

Why do people regress? Some psychologists say that it is because an adult cannot stand feeling helpless. Children, on the other hand, are made to feel helpless and dependent every day. Becoming more childlike can make total dependency or helplessness more bearable.

But regression is not always the result of imposed dependency. Adults who cry when their arguments fail may expect those around them to react sympathetically, as their parents did when they were children. Other adults may use temper tantrums in a similar way. In both examples, people are drawing on childish behaviors to solve current problems, in the hope that someone will respond to them the way adults did when they were children. Inappropriate as it may seem, such immature and manipulative behavior often works—at least for a while.

INTELLECTUALIZATION. This defense mechanism is a subtle form of denial. We realize that we are threatened but detach ourselves from our problems by analyzing and intellectualizing them, almost as if they concerned other people and did not bother us emotionally. Parents who sit down to discuss their child's difficulties in a new school and hours later find themselves engaged in a sophisticated discussion of educational philosophy may be intellectualizing. They appear to be dealing with their problems but may in fact have cut themselves off from their emotions.

Like denial, **intellectualization** can be a useful defense under some circumstances. Doctors and nurses see pain and suffering every day of their working lives. They must keep some degree of detachment if they are to remain objective. Bettelheim reports that he felt completely detached on his journey to a concentration camp. He simply did not feel that the experience was happening to him (Bettelheim, 1943).

REACTION FORMATION. The term **reaction formation** refers to a behavioral form of denial in which people express with exaggerated intensity ideas and emotions that are the opposite of their own. *Exag-*

Regression Reverting to childlike behavior and defenses.

Intellectualization Thinking abstractly about stressful problems as a way of detaching oneself from them.

Reaction formation Expression of exaggerated ideas and emotions that are the opposite of one's repressed beliefs or feelings.

Displacement Shifting repressed motives and emotions from an original object to a substitute object.

geration is the clue to this behavior. The man who praises a rival extravagantly may be covering up jealousy about his opponent's success. The woman who is overly cordial and claims, "I've never had an angry moment in my life" may be coping defensively with repressed hostile feelings that she finds intolerable. Reaction formation may also be a way of convincing oneself that one's motives are pure. The man who feels ambivalent about being a father may devote a disproportionate amount of time to his children in an attempt to prove to *himself* that he is a good father.

DISPLACEMENT. **Displacement** is the redirection of repressed motives and emotions from their original objects to substitute objects. Displacement permits repressed motives and feelings to find a new outlet.

■ The Ethics of Stress Research

A group of students who has assembled for a seminar suddenly notice that smoke is seeping under the door of the room where they are meeting. When they try to flee, they discover that the door is locked. This is not the prelude to a campus tragedy, but rather a psychology experiment (with a simulated fire to make it seem like real life) designed to investigate the effects of prior organization on group behavior under stress.

In the scientific community, such experiments are highly controversial, and some psychologists believe that they should be banned. No one doubts that such research has yielded important insights into stress. But many people fear that the new knowledge has been gained at a price that's too high. As they see it, some research on stress is unethical because it can harm participants emotionally. The unwitting subjects in the simulated fire might have been badly frightened and, under stress, might have behaved in ways that would later give them cause for self-reproach. (There might have been physical harm inflicted as well had they panicked in their efforts to escape.) In other experiments, critics argue, researchers have led subjects to believe that they have failed important tests, that they have latent homosexual tendencies, or that they have caused pain or injury to others. Subjects have sometimes been deceived about the true nature of a study, coerced into participating, or even allowed to remain unaware that they were taking part in research (Cook, 1976).

At one extreme are the scientists who rank the obligation to protect subjects above all other considerations. They argue that researchers must never mislead subjects, must rule out research situations that subjects might find physically or emotionally stressful, and must brief potential participants thoroughly before seeking their consent to serve as subjects.

At the other extreme are those scientists who say that these restrictions cannot really minimize distress or prevent outright harm, but can only hamper research. When the obligation of scientists to protect human dignity is mentioned, this group cites the right of scientists to investigate and of society to profit from fruitful studies.

Many people on both sides of the controversy do not take such extreme positions. They hold, instead, that resourceful researchers can find ways to safeguard subjects without abandoning important research topics. In designing stress research, for example, psychologists can take advantage of situations in which stress occurs naturally. One way of doing this is to interview people in a dentist's waiting room, hospital patients about to undergo surgery, or students preparing for examinations.

As we saw in Chapter 1, the American Psychological Association has adopted a set of "Ethical Principles in the Conduct of Research with Human Participants" (APA, 1985). Three of these ethical principles are especially important to stress research. First, investigators must tell potential subjects in advance about any aspect of a study that could make the subjects reluctant to take part in the study if they knew about it. Second, they must inform research subjects about possible risks and protect the subjects from "physical and mental discomfort, harm, and danger." Finally, if any harmful consequences occur inadvertently, the investigators must assume responsibility "to detect and remove or correct" those consequences.

The man who has always wanted to be a father and learns that he cannot have children may feel inadequate. As a result, he may become extremely attached to a pet or to a sibling's child. The woman who must smile and agree with her boss all day may come home and yell at her husband or children. The new object may not be a fully satisfactory substitute, but it probably provides at least some relief and perhaps allows the person to cope more effectively than would otherwise be possible.

SUBLIMATION. **Sublimation** involves transforming repressed motives or feelings into more socially acceptable forms. Aggressiveness might be transformed into competitiveness in business or sports. A strong and persistent desire for attention might be shaped into an interest in acting or politics. Curiosity about the human body might be transformed into an interest in painting or photographing nudes.

From the Freudian perspective, sublimation is not only necessary but desirable. If people can transform their sexual and aggressive drives into more socially acceptable forms, they are clearly better off. The instinctual drives are at least partially gratified with relatively little anxiety and guilt. Moreover, society benefits from the energy and effort channeled into the arts, literature, science, and other socially useful activities.

We have seen that there are many different ways of coping defensively, with stress. Is defensive coping a sign that a person is immature, unstable, on the edge of a "breakdown"? The answer is no. The effects of prolonged stress can be so severe, as we will see in the next section, that in some cases defensive coping not only becomes essential to survival but even contributes to our overall ability to adapt and adjust. But even in less extreme situations people can profitably use defense mechanisms to cope with problems and stress. As Coleman et al. (1987) point out, defenses are "essential for softening failure, alleviating tension and anxiety, repairing emotional hurt, and maintaining our feelings of adequacy and worth" (p. 190). But when a defense mechanism interferes with a person's ability to function or creates more problems than it solves, it is considered maladaptive.

Sublimation Redirecting repressed motives and feelings into more socially acceptable channels.

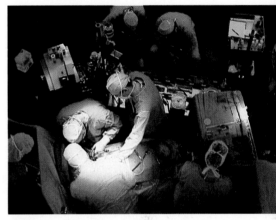

While it would seem natural that surgeons would experience a great deal of stress, they call on their training and skills to control their situation, make its outcome more predictable, and lessen its stressfulness.

■❙ What Stress Does to People

In 1976, Canadian physiologist Hans Selye proposed that we react to physical and psychological stress in three stages that he called the General Adaptation Syndrome (or GAS for short). These three stages are alarm reaction, resistance, and a final stage of exhaustion. The sequence may be repeated several times in a single day as new demands arise.

Stage 1, the *alarm reaction*, is the first response to stress. It begins when the body recognizes that it must fight off some physical or psychological danger. Emotions run high. We become more sensitive and alert. Respiration and heartbeat quicken, muscles tense, and other physiological changes occur. These changes help us to mobilize our coping resources in order to regain self-control. At this stage, we might use either direct or defensive coping strategies. If neither of these approaches reduces the stress, we eventually enter Selye's second stage of adaptation.

Coping with a highly stressful situation can cause such physiological reactions as quickened respiration and heartbeat, muscle tension, and even changes in hormonal levels.

During Stage 2, that of *resistance*, physical symptoms and other signs of strain appear as we struggle against increasing psychological disorganization. We intensify our use of both direct and defensive coping techniques. If our efforts succeed in reducing the stress, we return to a more normal state. But if the stress is extreme or prolonged, we may turn in desperation to inappropriate coping techniques and cling rigidly to them despite evidence that they are not helping very much. If that happens, physical and emotional resources are further depleted and signs of wear and tear become even more apparent.

In the third stage, *exhaustion*, the person uses increasingly ineffective defense mechanisms in a desperate attempt to bring the stress under control. Some people lose touch with reality and show signs of emotional disorder or mental illness. Other people may show signs of "burnout," such as inability to concentrate, irritability, procrastination, and a cynical belief that nothing is worthwhile (Freudenberger & Richelson, 1980; Maslach, 1982; Freudenberger, 1983). At times, physical symptoms such as skin or stomach problems occur, and some victims of burnout turn to alcohol or drugs in an effort to cope with stress. If stress continues, irreparable physical or psychological damage may occur—even death.

One of the most startling implications of Selye's theroy is the possibility that prolonged psychological stress may cause disease, or at least make certain diseases worse. This idea is controversial, but recent studies strongly support the belief that psychological factors lie at the root of some of our worst afflictions, including heart disease.

How can psychological stress lead to physical illness? When people experience stress, their hearts, lungs, and nervous systems, among other bodily functions, are forced to work harder, and it is not surprising that when such conditions are prolonged, a person is more likely to experience some kind of physical debility. The human body simply is not designed to be exposed for long periods of time to the powerful biological changes that accompany alarm and mobilization.

For example, stress is known to be an important factor in the development of coronary heart disease (CHD), which is the leading cause of death and disability in this country. Although heredity is also an important factor, even among genetically identical twins the incidence of CHD is linked closely to attitude toward work, problems in the home, and amount of leisure time (Kringlen, 1981). Another study found that Japanese-Americans were more likely to experience CHD than Japanese living in Japan; and Japanese-Americans who had embraced American cultural values had a higher rate of CHD than those who followed traditional Japanese cultural values (Marmot & Syme, 1976).

We also know that occupation and accompanying stress are also factors in CHD: For instance, London bus drivers are far more likely to have CHD than are the conductors who sell the bus tickets but do not have to contend with the strain of driving in heavy traffic (Fox & Adelstein, 1978). And among those who have suffered heart attacks for whatever reason, life stress and social isolation have been shown to be significant predictors of survival or mortality (Ruberman et al., 1984).

Animal studies also demonstrate a connection between stress and cancer. In one study, a group of mice known to be vulnerable to cancer was kept for 400 days in standard housing in which they heard noise made by people and other animals. By the end of this period, 92 percent

© 1987 S. Gross

■ Cancer and Stress

To many psychotherapists, *illusion* is a bad word. In their view, staying in touch with reality is the hallmark of mental health, and people who cherish too many illusions, especially about important things, are not truly well-adjusted.

Shelley E. Taylor (1983) takes a strikingly different view: "Far from impeding adjustment," she says, "illusion may be essential for adequate coping" (p. 1171).

Taylor reached this conclusion after a two-year study of women with breast cancer. The women who coped best with the stress of disfiguring surgery, painful follow-up treatment, and fear of death proved to be those who constructed comforting illusions about themselves and their illness. Taylor defined illusions as beliefs that were based on an overly optimistic view of the facts or that had no factual basis at all.

The helpful illusions grew out of the women's attempts to do three things: to understand the causes of their cancer and its significance in their lives; to gain a sense of mastery over the disease in particular and their lives in general; and to restore their self-esteem in the face of a devastating experience.

Here are some of Taylor's findings on each of these points:

1. Although the causes of cancer are not fully understood, 95 percent of the women nevertheless believed that they knew why their cancer had occurred. Some blamed the stress of an unhappy marriage. Others mentioned birth control pills, heredity, or diet. The women's erroneous belief that they had pinpointed the reason for their illness seemed to make them feel better psychologically. It may have helped them to feel that they were not at the mercy of a capricious fate. Whatever the reason, even highly improbable explanations—like having been hit in the breast with a Frisbee—seemed useful.

   Moreover, many women took comfort from the belief that having cancer had in some ways made their lives better. "I have much more enjoyment of each day," said one. "You find out that things like relationships are really the most important things you have—the people you know and your family—everything else is just way down the line," said another (Taylor, 1983, p. 1163).

2. Having cancer is a very sobering experience that can make people feel powerless. To counter that feeling, two-thirds of the women expressed the conviction that if they thought the right thoughts and did the right things, they could prevent the recurrence of cancer. As one woman put it, "I think that if you feel you are in control of it, you can control it up to a point. I absolutely refuse to have any more cancer" (Taylor, 1983, p. 1163).

3. Numerous studies show that undergoing a major stressful experience often lowers self-esteem, even if the victim is blameless. That may explain why the women tried to feel better about themselves by drawing comparisons with others whom they chose to regard as less fortunate. "I think I did extremely well under the circumstances," said one woman, remarking that there are "some women who aren't strong enough, who fall apart and become psychologically disturbed" (Taylor, 1983, p. 1165).

It is clear that illusions promoted the adjustment of the women in Taylor's study. But relying on illusions would seem to be a very risky way of adjusting: If the illusion is shattered, then it seems that the person's sense of well-being should collapse as well. For example, imagine that a woman suffers a recurrence of cancer despite following a rigorous diet or practicing positive thinking in the firm belief that it would keep her well. What happens to this woman's ability to cope?

Oddly enough, the women in Taylor's study did not seem to be overly troubled when their theories turned out to be wrong, their self-protective measures useless. Of course, they were disheartened by their failing health. But their adjustment seemed none the worse because they had embraced an illusion and seen it fall to pieces. What they usually did then was simply take a new approach to coping, try to control another aspect of their lives, or seek to bolster their self-esteem in a new way.

The struggle to remain continuously in close touch with unrelieved reality is sometimes too much to bear. At such times, Taylor suggests, the well-adjusted people may be those who allow themselves to nurture their illusions and who "are ultimately restored by those illusions (p. 1168).

---

of the mice had developed cancer. In contrast, when a comparable group of mice was kept in quiet, low-stress conditions, only 7 percent developed cancer. In other experiments, cancer was diagnosed earlier and death occurred sooner in mice that got frequent shocks with no escape possible than in mice that were allowed to cope with the stress of shocks by escaping (Anderson, 1982).

Other research has demonstrated a connection between stress and such diseases as tuberculosis, arthritis, diabetes, leukemia, herpes, colds, stomach disorders, back pain, and mononucleosis (Levy, 1982; Fox, 1983; Jemott & Locke, 1984; Sarason et al., 1985). How can stress lead to such a wide variety of diseases? It appears that stress does not directly *cause* specific diseases; rather, stress apparently weakens the body's immune system. As a result, the person under stress is more vulnerable to all kinds of diseases, ailments, and illnesses. In recent years, for example, scientists have demonstrated significant reductions in the body's immune system in response to a wide variety of stressful situations: significant life change, intense pressure, being deprived of sleep, and experiencing profound grief or depression (Krantz, Greenberg, & Baum, 1985; Maier, 1987; Glaser & Kiecolt-Glaser, 1988; Kiecolt-Glaser & Glaser, 1988). Finally, laboratory experiments have demonstrated that immune system activity in rats can be increased or decreased through conditioning, a kind of learning process that we studied in Chapter 5. And, when mice are subjected to loud noises, their immune systems do not work as well as usual. The effect is similar when animals undergo the stress of capture (Anderson, 1982).

Thus, a great deal of evidence supports the theory of an important relationship between psychological stress and physical illness. The connection between stress and illness is especially marked when a person can do nothing directly to control the source of stress, as in the loss of a job or the death of a relative (Glass, 1977). Furthermore, the relationship between psychological factors and physical health is a two-way street. When you get sick, you are more likely to experience feelings of anxiety or helplessness. Obviously, someone with a serious illness will experience feelings of depression and frustration, but even catching a cold is likely to affect a person psychologically.

Sources of Extreme Stress

Outside the laboratory, stress comes from a variety of sources, ranging from unemployment to wartime combat, from violent natural disaster to rape. In this section, we will look briefly at some of these major stressors, the effects they have on people, and how people try to cope with them.

1. *Unemployment.* Joblessness is a major source of stress. One researcher found that when the jobless rate rises, so do first admissions to psychiatric hospitals, infant mortality, deaths from heart disease, alcohol-related diseases, and suicide (Brenner, 1973, 1979). In a study of aircraft workers who lost their jobs, Rayman and Bluestone (1982) found that many of the workers reported suffering from high blood pressure, alcoholism, heavy smoking, and anxiety. Other studies have found signs of family strain. "Things just fell apart," one worker said after he and his wife both had lost their jobs.

People seem to react to the stress of unemployment in several stages (Powell & Driscoll, 1973). First comes a period of relaxation and relief, in which they take a vacation of sorts, confident that they will find another job. Stage 2, marked by continued optimism, is a time of concentrated

Type A and Type B personalities
Concerned with the quality of his work and the urgency of completing it on time, the Type A executive may be raising both his blood pressure and his chances of coronary heart disease. The Type B businessman, on the other hand, is more concerned with both the quality of his work and the quality of his life.

S.GROSS

job hunting. In Stage 3, a period of vacillation and doubt, people become moody, their relationships with family and friends deteriorate, and they scarcely bother to look for work. By Stage 4, a period of malaise and cynicism, people have simply given up.

It is important to note that these effects are not universal, although they may be quite frequent. Moreover, there are some indications that joblessness may not so much create new psychological difficulties as bring previously hidden ones to the surface. Finally, two studies have shown that death rates go up and psychiatric symptoms get worse not just during periods of unemployment but also during short, rapid upturns in the economy (Eyer, 1977; Brenner, 1979). This finding lends support to the idea that we discussed earlier—that change (whether good or bad) causes stress. Unemployment is simply one source of major life change.

2. *Divorce and separation.* As Coleman et al. (1988) observe, "the deterioration or ending of an intimate relationship is one of the more potent of stressors and one of the more frequent reasons why people seek psychotherapy" (p. 155). The partners may feel that they have failed at one of life's most important endeavors. Strong emotional ties frequently continue to bind the pair. If only one spouse wants to end the marriage, that one may feel sadness and guilt at hurting a once-loved partner; the rejected spouse may suffer from anger, feelings of humiliation, and self-recriminations over his or her role in the failure. Even if the decision to separate was shared, ambivalent feelings of love and hate can make life confusing. Under these circumstances, it is common to find a great deal of defensive coping; denial and projection in particular are often used to cushion the impact of divorce or separation.

3. *Bereavement.* "But O the heavy change, now thou art gone,/Now thou art gone, and never must return." So John Milton wrote of the death of the young Lycidas, and few people who have lost someone to death would take issue with the poet's sentiments.

Most people come through the experience of bereavement without suffering permanent harm, but usually not without going through a long process that Freud called the "work of mourning." Janis and his colleagues (1969) have described normal grief as beginning with numbness and

Joblessness is a major form of stress. People who are unemployed often smoke heavily and frequently suffer from high blood pressure, alcoholism, and anxiety.

progressing through months of distress in which anger, despair, intense grief and yearning, depression, and apathy may all appear.

In his classic study of widows in London, Parkes (1976) offers poignant glimpses of typical grief. "It's like a dream," one widow said. "I feel I'm going to wake up and it'll be all right. He'll be back again." Several widows recognized in themselves an irrational need to try to find their dead husbands. "Everywhere I go I am searching for him," one widow said. "In crowds, in church, in the supermarket. I keep scanning faces. People must think I'm odd." In the same vein, another widow said, "I go to the grave . . . but he's not there." Most of the women spoke of being angry. At the height of their grief, they sometimes blamed doctors for not doing more, God for taking the husband away, or even the husband himself, as if he had deserted them on purpose. "Why did he do this to me?" one woman said.

All these reactions are attempts to cope defensively with an inescapable and extremely painful reality. In most cases, they allow the survivor to gather strength for more direct coping efforts later on—such as selling belongings and moving out of the home that he or she shared with the dead person.

4. *Combat.* There have always been people who find it impossible to hold up under the extreme stress of battle. Disabling reaction to combat stress was called "shell shock" in World War I, "operational fatigue" or "war neurosis" in World War II, and "combat exhaustion" in the Korean and Vietnam wars. In each war, the symptoms were the same. The first sign of disintegrating self-control might be crying over small frustrations or bursting into rage in response to a harmless remark. The initial reaction later gives way to inability to sleep, cringing at sudden noises, psychological confusion, crying without being able to stop, or sitting silently and staring into space. In World War II, about 5 percent of combat soldiers were discharged for psychiatric reasons, and some of these veterans are still hospitalized as a result of the stress that they experienced.

The very nature of military combat—including physical exhaustion, separation from family, and aggressiveness heightened by training—makes it an extraordinary stressor. Feelings of guilt and helplessness may also intensify the stressfulness of the situation.

Posttraumatic Stress Disorders

If all human behavior followed simple, strict rules of logic, then the symptoms of stress would disappear when the stressful events that caused them came to an end. But psychologists recognize that some stress disorders—those known as *posttraumatic stress disorders*—can arise *after* a person has suffered a severe trauma or crisis.

The kinds of events that can lead to posttraumatic stress disorders are usually outside the realm of ordinary grief and loss. They are experiences that even the best-adjusted among us would find terrifying and anxiety-provoking: rape, for example, or military combat, or a devastating flood.

In some cases, posttraumatic disorders set in either right after a traumatic event or within a short time. But in other cases, months may go by, during which the victim appears to have recovered from the experience; then, without warning, psychological symptoms suddenly develop. In some instances, the symptoms disappear quickly, although they may recur repeatedly; in others, they continue for weeks or months.

Symptoms are often striking. For example, after a flood in which 125 people perished, one man whose wife and children were among the dead could not sleep unless he left a light burning in his room. Darkness reminded him of the awful moment when the power had failed just before the flood waters engulfed his house and killed his wife and children. Dramatic nightmares in which the victim seems to reexperience the terrifying event exactly as it happened are common. So are daytime flashbacks, in which there is also a feeling of reliving the trauma. Generally, the victims of posttraumatic disorders cannot function well in their day-to-day existence, and they may withdraw from social life and from job and family responsibilities.

Combat veterans appear to be especially vulnerable to such problems. The Center for Policy Research in New York found that more than a third of the men who took part in heavy combat in Vietnam showed signs of serious posttraumatic distress. Certainly, many Vietnam veterans have had unusual difficulty in readjusting to civilian life. Indeed, their symptoms tend to be so serious that the posttraumatic stress disorder in Vietnam returnees has been given its own name: the Vietnam syndrome.

Recovery from posttraumatic stress disorder depends a great deal on how much emotional support victims get from family, friends, and community.

Some of its manifestations are the same as in any posttraumatic disorder, but many Vietnam veterans have experienced additional problems, among them paranoia, inability to love or trust others, alienation from their own emotions, feelings of guilt about their combat experiences, and, most notably, feelings of uncontrollable anger that sometimes erupt in violence. Rates of drug and alcohol abuse have been higher than average in Vietnam returnees, and some of the veterans have been arrested for crimes that they attribute to their emotional difficulties.

Many Vietnam veterans have sought psychiatric treatment. Psychiatrists and psychologists who work with them cite two factors that perhaps contribute to the severity of the symptoms. For one thing, civilian casualties in the Vietnam War were higher than in most wars, a fact that may give rise to feelings of guilt. Another presumably important factor is the unpopularity of the war. Instead of being welcomed home as heroes, returning Vietnam soldiers were often cold-shouldered, as if they had been responsible for the war and its excesses. These critical attitudes are significant, for recovery from any posttraumatic disorder depends a great deal on how much emotional support victims get from family, friends, and community.

Even soldiers who cope relatively effectively with stress during combat often cannot do so after they leave the battlefield. This is one form of *posttraumatic stress disorder*, a topic that is examined more closely in the box above.

5. *Natural and man-made catastrophes.* Natural and man-made catastrophes include floods, earthquakes, violent storms, fires, and plane crashes. Psychological reactions to all such stressors have much in com-

Psychological reactions to natural and man-made disasters have much in common. Victims progress from the initial shock stage to a suggestible stage to a final recovery stage.

United Feature Syndicate, Inc.

mon. At first, in the *shock* stage, "the victim is stunned, dazed, and apathetic," and sometimes even "stuporous, disoriented, and amnesic for the traumatic event." Then, in the *suggestible* stage, victims are passive and quite ready to do what rescuers tell them to do. In the third phase, the *recovery* stage, emotional balance is regained, but anxiety often persists and victims may need to describe their experiences over and over again. (Morris, 1990). And some investigators report that in later stages survivors may feel irrationally guilty because they lived while others died. Said a stewardess who survived a plane crash, "It's not fair. Everyone else is hurt. Why aren't I?" (*Time*, Jan. 15, 1973, p. 53).

■ The Well-adjusted Person

Psychologists hold different opinions about what constitutes good adjustment. Some base their evaluation on a person's ability to live according to social norms. Everyone has hostile and selfish wishes; everyone dreams impossible dreams. People who learn to control forbidden impulses and to limit their goals to those that society allows are, by this definition, well-adjusted. A woman who grows up in a small town, attends her state university, teaches for a year or two, then settles down to a peaceful family life might be considered well-adjusted to the extent that she is living by the predominant values of her community

Other psychologists disagree strongly with this conformist viewpoint. Barron (1963) argues that "refusal to adjust . . . is very often the mark of a healthy character." Society is not always right. To accept its standards blindly—to say, for example, "My country, right or wrong"—is to renounce the right to make independent judgments. Barron suggests that well-adjusted people *enjoy* the difficulties and ambiguities of life; they do not sidestep them by means of unthinking conformity. They accept challenges and are willing to experience pain and confusion. Confident of their ability to deal with problems in a realistic and mature way, they

The Self-actualizing Person

One view of the well-adjusted person has been detailed by Abraham Maslow. People who are well-adjusted attempt to "actualize" themselves: That is, they live in a way that they believe is best for their own growth and fulfillment regardless of what others may think. After studying a number of famous people and a group of college students, Maslow (1954) compiled a list of 15 traits that he believed were characteristic of self-actualizing people:

1. *More efficient perception of reality.* They judge people and events realistically and are better able than others to accept uncertainty and ambiguity.
2. *Acceptance of self and others.* They take others for what they are and are not guilty or defensive about themselves.
3. *Spontaneity.* This quality is shown more in thinking than in action. As a matter of fact, self-actualizing people are frequently quite conventional in behavior.
4. *Problem centering.* They are more concerned with problems than with themselves and are likely to have what they consider important goals.
5. *Detachment.* They need privacy and do not mind being alone.
6. *Autonomy.* They are able to be independent of their environment.
7. *Continued freshness of appreciation*, even of often-repeated experiences
8. *Mystical experiences, or the oceanic feeling.* This feeling, which Maslow includes under the heading of "peak experiences," frequently involves wonder, awe, a feeling of oneness with the universe, and a loss of self.
9. *Gemeinschaftsgefühl, or social interest.* This is a feeling of unity with humanity in general.
10. *Interpersonal relationships.* Deep close relationships with a few chosen individuals characterize self-actualizing people.
11. *Democratic character structure.* Self-actualizing people are relatively indifferent to such matters as sex, birth, race, color, and religion in judging other people.
12. *Discrimination between means and ends.* They enjoy activities for their own sake, but also appreciate the difference between means and goals.
13. *Sense of humor.* Their sense of humor is philosophical rather than hostile.
14. *Creativeness.* Their creativity in any field consists mostly in the ability to generate new ideas.
15. *Resistance to enculturation.* While not rebellious, they are generally independent of any given culture.

Maslow did not consider self-actualizing people perfect—disregard of others is one of their possible faults. Moreover, having the characteristics on this list does not mean that you are self-actualizing, only that self-actualization is important to you and that you are the type of person who tries to achieve it.

can admit primitive or childish impulses into consciousness. Temporary regression does not frighten them. Barron sees flexibility, spontaneity, and creativity as signs of healthy adjustment.

Still other psychologists suggest that well-adjusted people have learned to balance conformity and nonconformity, self-control and spontaneity. They can let themselves go at times but can control themselves in situations where acting on their impulses would be damaging. They can change themselves when society so demands, but they try to change society when this seems the better course. Such flexibility is often considered a sign that these people can judge *realistically* both the world around them and their own needs and capabilities. They both know their strengths and admit their weaknesses. As a result, they have chosen an approach to life that is in harmony with their inner selves. They do not feel that they must act against their values in order to be successful. Their self-trust enables them to face conflicts and threats without excessive anxiety and, perhaps more important, lets them risk their feelings and self-esteem in intimate relationships.

Another means of evaluating adjustment is to use specific criteria, such as the following (Morris, 1990):

1. *Does the action meet the adjustive demand, or does it simply postpone resolving the problem?* Various forms of escapism—drugs, alcohol, and even endless fantasizing through books, movies, and television—may divert us from our pain. But they do not eliminate the causes of our difficulties. Thus, completely relying on escapism can never make for truly effective adjustment to a stressful situation.

2. *Does the action meet the individual's needs?* Often we act to reduce external pressures without considering our personal needs. People may abandon their own career goals because of the goals of a spouse. In the short run, external pressure may be reduced, but they may be frustrated and disappointed for the rest of their lives. A solution that creates such inner conflict is often not an effective adjustment.

3. *Is the action compatible with the well-being of others?* Some people satisfy their needs in ways that hurt others. A young executive who uses people and manipulates co-workers may "get ahead" through such actions. But even if he does succeed in becoming vice president of his company, he may find himself without friends. He may fear that others will treat him as he treated them. Ultimately, this situation can become seriously stressful and frustrating. Good adjustment must take into consideration both individual needs and the well-being of others.

We have seen that there are many different standards for deciding if a person is well-adjusted. It is apparent that a person considered well-adjusted by one standard may not be considered well-adjusted by other criteria. The same holds true when we try to decide what behaviors are "abnormal"—the topic of the next chapter.

 APPLICATION

The Stockholm Syndrome

One of the clearest illustrations of adaptation to extraordinary stress is the reaction of hostages to their captors. The stress of being taken hostage is sudden, unexpected, and intense. Hostages, captors, and outside authorities often have little control over events as they unfold. What kinds of adjustment mechanisms do people use in such situations?

One particularly striking pattern of coping has come to be known as the Stockholm Syndrome. The most remarkable feature of this pattern is that hostages side with their captors—and the captors come to sympathize with their captives. The term *Stockholm Syndrome* derives from a 1973 bank robbery in Stockholm, Sweden, in which robbers held four hostages captive for six days. By the end of the ordeal, the hostages had become more loyal to the bank robbers than to the police. They ultimately refused to testify against their former captors. One woman hostage became so emotionally attached to one of the robbers that she broke her engagement to another man after the incident.

Psychologists define three stages of the syndrome:

1. The hostages begin to feel warm toward their captors.
2. The hostages develop negative feelings toward the authorities who are trying to rescue them.
3. The captors develop positive feelings toward their victims. Both groups are isolated and terrorized and therefore come to believe. "We are in this together."

Why would a hostage come to like or even love a captor? Dr. Frank Ochberg, director of the Michigan Department of Mental Health, explains. "When someone captures you and places you in an infantile position, he sets the stage for love as a response to infantile terror—he could kill you but he does not and you are grateful" (*Time*, Dec. 24, 1979).

Dr. Robert Jay Lifton of Yale University writes of the "psychology of the pawn" (1961). Manipulated through constant fear of injury or death to act as instructed, pawns adapt to events beyond their control. They adopt certain behaviors for coping, such as submissiveness. Like other human beings, pawns are deeply sensitive to their limitations and unfulfilled potential. They are vulnerable to any feelings of guilt that the captors may try to induce.

Lorraine Berzins, an officer with the Canadian Penitentiary Service, offers other insights into why a hostage develops a positive feeling toward a captor. In 1970, she was taken hostage at knifepoint by an inmate. She had been professionally trained to deal with violent behavior, and eventually she got her captor to trust her. She observes:

> There may be a clash between our different perceptions of a person's "good" qualities alongside his criminal behavior. . . . If a person is not trained or experienced enough to be able to accommodate the seeming contradiction of the two, he may need to deny one in order to preserve the other. The hostage, to preserve the trust that his survival depends on, may need to see his captor as "all good" to resolve the dissonance and maintain harmony between them (Schreiber, 1978).

Why do the hostages develop negative feelings toward the authorities who are trying to rescue them?

> For the authorities the desired outcome is the capture of the kidnappers and the recovery of persons and property. Having been on the outside and indulged in some of those same calculations himself as he followed other kidnap episodes in the news, the hostage is deeply distrustful of the negotiators. Suppose they overreact. . . . "I had

Patty Hearst as "Tania" the urban terrorist Forcibly removed from her customary world and completely isolated by her captors, she seemed to have joined them as a member of a small faction alienated from the outside world—even to the point of wielding an automatic rifle while they robbed a bank.

this very strong feeling that my life wasn't as important to the negotiators as it was to me," says Berzins (Schreiber, 1978).

Berzins also states, "If your way of coping with anxiety is to project blame onto other people, you're obviously not going to project it onto the hostage-taker because it's too dangerous. . . . The easiest target is the outside authorities."

The prisoner sometimes feels that he or she and the hostage-taker constitute a small group facing a hostile world. Isolated from outside information, kidnapped heiress Patty Hearst was told that her parents and society no longer cared about her. This lie was seemingly confirmed by the police raid on the Los Angeles hideout of her six captors in which they burned to death (Conway & Seigelman, 1980).

A hostage may be unclear as to exactly what principles of the outside authorities he or she is defending. Lifton says that one of the ex-hostages in Iran viewed resistance to his captors partly as a matter of suffering for the sake of the Shah, whom he did not wholeheartedly support. The Iranians led him to focus on a questionable cause and to overlook the fact that he was being held illegally (*U.S. News & World Report*, Dec. 31, 1979).

Why would captors develop positive attitudes toward their victims? Confronted by authorities who want to demonstrate that hostage taking cannot succeed, captors know that they may very well die. Concern about the pain and discomfort of their victims helps keep their minds off the stress that they themselves are feeling. Also, despite their proclamations of willingness to die for their cause, they often compromise their ideals. In order to survive, they often refrain from harming their hostages.

The Stockholm Syndrome does not always occur. According to Lifton, if hostages have a "relatively strong belief system" or a "varied knowledge and a fluid kind of identity," they can withstand shocking challenges to their viewpoints (*U.S. News & World Report*, Dec. 31, 1979). Moreover, captors may overmanipulate their victims, causing captives who were initially fearful to become angered by their humiliating treatment. These manipulations may be heavy-handed, easily perceived, and countered by hostages who reflect on them and discuss them with one another.

Resentment at overmanipulation led the American hostages in Iran to develop strategies that main-tained their pride. Resourceful secret communication systems and humorous cartoons mocking the Iranians enabled the Americans to enjoy outwitting their captors. Other strategies used by these hostages to preserve their individuality included demanding better food, maintaining a neat appearance, observing a busy daily schedule, and attempting to escape.

The effects of captivity on a hostage continue after liberation. They can include:

1. Feelings of guilt about hostages who have died or about people who are still hostages.
2. Lack of any feelings, which gives way periodically to an intense need to talk.
3. Suspicions that they are being deceived, especially by established authorities.
4. Hostility, in particular toward employers who expect ex-hostages to return to normalcy quickly.
5. Loss of confidence in the world, requiring continual reasssurances from family and friends that the ex-hostage's life will not be violently interrupted again.
6. Need to find meaning in the ordeal, which leads some hostages to feel a sense of rebirth or a resolve to "turn over a new leaf."

If you have understood this chapter, you will recognize that all these aftereffects are normal responses to extreme stress and that all of them are attempts to cope effectively with overwhelming pressure. Thus they illustrate, in exaggerated form, the same coping processes that we all use in extraordinary situations.

■ Summary

- *Adjustment* refers to any attempt to adapt to your physical and social environment and to achieve harmony between your desires and the demands and constraints imposed on you by the environment.

- **Why is it that even a pleasant event, like falling in love, can be stressful?** *Stress* refers to any adjustive demand that includes a state of tension or threat and that requires change or adaptation. Pleasant and unpleasant situations can be stressful if they cause change and discontinuity in one's life. The Social Readjustment Rating Scale is used to measure how much stress a person has undergone within any given period.

- While significant life changes are obviously stressful, it is possible that little daily frustrations—"hassles"—cause at least as much stress. Both major and

minor events are stressful in that they give rise to feelings of pressure, frustration, conflict, and anxiety. Minor frustrations may be triggered by major life events such as death or divorce.

- *Pressure* occurs when we feel forced to speed up, intensify, or redirect our behavior, or to meet a higher standard of performance. We may pressure ourselves to live up to some internal standard of excellence. External sources of pressure include competition, change, and the expectations of family and friends.

- **You've been planning to attend a concert for three weeks. On the day of the concert, your car won't start. How are you likely to feel and why?** *Frustration* occurs when people are prevented from achieving a goal. They must either give up the goal, find some new way to achieve it, or adjust to living with their disappointment. The five leading sources of frustration are delays, lack of resources, losses, failure, and discrimination.

- **Conflict** is probably the most common problem to which people must adjust. Conflict occurs when a person is faced with two or more incompatible demands, opportunities, needs, or goals.
- One way of describing conflict is in terms of two opposite tendencies: approach and avoidance. We want to approach things that attract us and avoid things that repel us. These contradictory feelings produce three basic types of conflict.
- In an *approach/approach conflict* we are attracted to two goals at the same time and must either make a choice between them or modify one or both of them in some way.
- In an *avoidance/avoidance conflict* we face two undesired or threatening, yet unavoidable, alternatives and must either choose the one that causes the least discomfort or, in certain extreme instances, sit the situation out and wait for the inevitable.
- In an *approach/avoidance conflict* we are both attracted to and repelled by the same goal. Both the desire to approach and the desire to avoid a goal grow stronger as we near it, with the avoidance tendency growing at a faster rate. In double approach/avoidance conflict there are good and bad features associated with both goals.
- **Your best friend never seems to become nervous or flustered, while another friend always seems to be having a crisis about something. Are some people more resistant to stress?** In addition to environmental sources of stress, people often impose unnecessary stress on themselves as a result of unreasonable, self-defeating beliefs and expectations. People also differ in perception of stress. Stress-resistant people are inclined to feel committed, challenged, and in control of events in their lives.
- There are two general types of coping with stress; direct coping and defensive coping. Direct coping refers to any action people take to change an uncomfortable situation: either by *confronting* problems directly, *compromising,* or withdrawing from the situation entirely. *Withdrawal* can sometimes be the most realistic form of adjustment; the danger of withdrawal, however, is that it may turn into avoidance of all similar situations.
- Defensive coping is a means of coping with situations that people feel unable to resolve. Defensive coping involves the use of *defense mechanisms.* In using defense mechanisms, people deceive themselves about reality in order to reduce stress. The most common defense mechanisms are denial, repression, projection, identification, regression, intellectualization, reaction formation, displacement, and sublimation.
- **Denial** is the refusal to acknowledge that a painful or threatening situation exists. **Repression,** a form of forgetting, is probably the most common means of blocking out awareness of underlying anger and hostility. **Projection** involves attributing one's own motives, feelings, or wishes to others. The reverse is *identification*—taking on the characteristics of someone else in order to share that person's successes and avoid feelings of personal incompetence.
- **Why do people often become silly when they are in a situation that makes them nervous?** *Regression* refers to the reversion to childlike, even infantile behavior in situations where no form of adult behavior will work. **Intellectualization** is a subtle form of denial in which we detach ourselves emotionally from our problems by analyzing them in purely rational terms. **Reaction formation** is exhibited when we exaggeratedly express emotions of ideas that are the opposite of what we really feel or believe.
- **What is one reason why a good run or game of basketball can make you feel better after a difficult day?** *Displacement* is the redirection of repressed motives or emotions from original objects to substitute objects. **Sublimation** is the redirection of repressed motives or emotions into more socially acceptable forms such as physical activity or creative pursuits.
- Defense mechanisms can be an adaptive means of coping with stress, particularly prolonged stress. They are considered maladaptive only when they interfere with a person's ability to function or when they create more problems than they solve.
- Hans Selye believes that people react to stress in three stages that he calls the General Adaptation Syndrome: alarm, resistance, and exhaustion. In Stage 1 the body mobilizes itself against the physiological effects of stress, and people begin to employ either direct or defensive coping strategies. Psychosomatic symptoms tend to appear in the second stage, and the use of coping strategies intensifies. The third stage is characterized by the application of increasingly ineffective defense mechanisms that can result in mental and physical exhaustion. If stress continues, irreparable physical and psychological damage may follow, including death.

- **Do the unsettling symptoms of stress, such as increased heart rate and sweaty palms, serve any purpose? Can they cause physical harm?** A growing body of research points to a connection between prolonged stress and the weakening of the body's immune system. Some investigators have found a correlation between the ability to tolerate stress and such major diseases as heart disease and cancer.

- The major stressors—including unemployment, divorce and separation, bereavement, combat, and natural and manmade disasters—create major difficulties in adjustment and may produce disabling symptoms a long time after the events themselves are over.

- The psychological reaction to unemployment typically follows a pattern that ends in physical illness, strained relationships, and total apathy and resignation. Divorce and separation are stressful because they bring about the end of an intimate relationship, and also because they induce feelings of sadness, guilt, rejection, failure, and ambivalence. The adjustment to loss requires working through an extended period of mourning. Combat stress may result in immediate disabling reactions such as loss of self-control or withdrawal from reality. This form of stress may also manifest itself later on as posttraumatic stress disorder. People's psychological reactions to natural and manmade catastrophes generally progress from a shock stage, to a passive and suggestible stage, and finally to a recovery stage. Anxiety may persist through the recovery stage, with victims continuing to relive their experience and to feel guilty for having survived.

- **What does it mean to be well-adjusted?** Psychologists differ in their opinions about what makes a well-adjusted person. Some believe that good adjustment depends on people's ability to conform to social norms, to control their drives, and to strive for goals of which society approves. Others feel that people are well-adjusted when they are able to face the difficulties and ambiguities of life with flexibility, spontaneity, and creativity. Still others suggest that the well-adjusted person is able to balance conformity and nonconformity, self-control and spontaneity. Finally, some psychologists evaluate a person's adjustment according to specific criteria, such as how well the adjustment actually solves the problem and satisfies both personal needs and the needs of others.

▣ Review Questions

1. _____ refers to any attempt to deal with stress; to adapt to your physical and social environment; and to achieve harmony between your desires and the demands and constraints imposed by the environment.
2. People's reactions to situations in which they feel threatened, pressured, frustrated, anxious, or in conflict are known collectively as _____.
3. Both pleasant and unpleasant situations can be stressful.   T / F
4. _____ occurs when we feel forced to speed up, intensify, or redirect our behavior, or to meet a higher standard of performance.
5. _____ occurs when people are prevented from achieving a goal.
6. Probably the most common problem to which people must adjust is _____.
7. Match each type of conflict with its definition:
   ___ approach/approach
   ___ avoidance/avoidance
   ___ approach/avoidance
   ___ double approach/ avoidance

   a. We must choose between two undesired, yet unavoidable alternatives.
   b. We are both attracted and repelled by the same goal.
   c. We are attracted to two goals at the same time.
   d. We are forced to choose between two goals, each of which has positive and negative features.

8. _____ is a form of stress in which people experience all the symptoms of fear but cannot identify what is frightening them.
9. There are two general types of coping, _____ and _____.
10. Confronting problems, compromising, or withdrawing from the situation entirely are all forms of _____ coping.
11. _____ coping is a means of coping with situations that people feel unable to resolve.
12. Match each of the following defense mechanisms with its definition.
   ___ Denial
   ___ Repression
   ___ Projection
   ___ Identification
   ___ Regression

   a. a form of forgetting
   b. detachment from problems through rational analysis
   c. reversion to less mature, even childlike behavior

_____ Intellectualization
_____ Reaction formation
_____ Displacement
_____ Sublimation

d. expression of emotions or ideas that are the opposite of what we really feel or believe

e. redirection of motives or emotions to other objects

f. refusal to acknowledge that a painful or threatening situation exists

g. attributing one's own motives and feelings to others

h. redirection of motives or emotions into more socially acceptable forms

i. taking on the characteristics of someone else in order to share that person's successes and avoid feelings of personal incompetence

13. The General Adaptation syndrome consists of three stages of reaction to stress: _____, _____, and exhaustion.

14. Research so far has been unable to find a connection between stress and the strength of the body's immune system.   T / F

14 Abnormal Behavior

Thinking Critically

What is the difference between someone who is simply eccentric and someone who exhibits abnormal behavior?

Physicians make diagnoses by looking at a person's physical symptoms. How are mental disorders diagnosed?

Why would someone wash their hands every time they touch something or check the front door of their house again and again to make sure that it is locked?

Can a psychological problem lead to *real* physical disorders, or are such physical ailments always psychosomatic?

Most people feel depressed from time to time. Are these feelings of depression the same as those experienced by people who are treated for depression?

What is a personality disorder?

Can environmental stresses, such as poor living conditions and economic hardship, contribute to the onset of some mental disorders?

These and other questions about the nature of different mental disorders are discussed in this chapter and in the Chapter Summary.

Is this a woman who is homeless because she cannot afford a place to live, or is she someone for whom it is impossible to live normally? Mental health professionals have four major criteria they use in determining whether someone's behavior is abnormal: distorted perception; inappropriate behavior; discomfort and danger to oneself or to others.

W hen does behavior become abnormal? The answer to this question is more complicated than it may seem. There is no doubt that the man on a street corner who claims to be George Washington or the woman who insists that elevators are trying to kill her is behaving abnormally, but what about the 20 students who cram themselves into a telephone booth, or the business executive who has three martinis every day for lunch? Whether these behaviors are classified as abnormal depends on whose standards and system of values are being used: society's, the individual's, or the mental health professional's.

Table 14-1 presents three different views on mental health; each uses different standards to judge normal and abnormal behavior. Society's main concern is whether behavior conforms to the existing social order. The individual is concerned with his or her own sense of well-being. The mental health professional is concerned with characteristics of personality. Because these views are often at odds, it is difficult for psychologists to derive a single definition of normal and abnormal behavior that includes them all.

To some extent, psychologists use *intrapersonal standards* of normality—that is, they try to evaluate people in terms of their own lives. Consider the following examples:

- A bookkeeper falls behind in her work because no matter how often she erases stray pencil marks on her ledger, she cannot get the page clean enough. Her employer does not understand. Finally, one morning, she cannot get up to go to work.
- The adolescent son of a wealthy suburbanite has a substantial allowance of his own, yet one night he is arrested for trying to hold

Table 14-1
Adapted from Strupp & Hadley. Copyright 1977 by the American Psychological Association. Adapted by permission of the authors.

TABLE 14-1 VIEWPOINTS ON MENTAL HEALTH		
	STANDARDS/VALUES	MEASURES
Society	Orderly world in which people assume responsibility for their assigned social roles (e.g., bread-winner, parent), conform to prevailing mores, and meet situational requirements.	Observations of behavior, extent to which a person fulfills society's expectations and measures up to prevailing standards.
Individual	Happiness, gratification of needs.	Subjective perceptions of self-esteem, acceptance, and well-being.
Mental Health Professional	Sound personality structure characterized by growth, development, autonomy, environmental mastery, ability to cope with stress, adaptation.	Clinical judgment, aided by behavioral observations and psychological tests of such variables as self-concept, sense of identity, balance of psychic forces, unified outlook on life, resistance to stress, self-regulation, ability to cope with reality, absence of mental and behavioral symptoms, adequacy in love, work, and play, adequacy in interpersonal relationships.

Prevalence of Psychological Disorders

Psychologists have become increasingly concerned about the extent of mental health problems in this country, and recent studies have collected important data on both the prevalence and incidence of mental health problems in the United States. *Prevalence* refers to the frequency with which a given disorder occurs at a given time; *incidence* refers to the number of new cases of a disorder that arise during a given period. For example, if there were 100 cases of severe anxiety in a surveyed population of 1,000, the prevalence of anxiety would be 10 percent. If 10 more people in the population reported severe anxiety during the next year, the incidence rate would be 1 percent per year.

In recent years, *epidemiologists*—scientists who study the distribution of physical and psychological disorders—have uncovered some alarming data about the prevalence of psychological disorders in the United States. As a result of a landmark study sponsored by the National Institute of Mental Health, J.K. Myers and his associates (1984) have concluded that at any given time, over 29 million American adults—about one out of every five—suffer from some form of psychological disorder. Over 13 million Americans suffer from various anxiety disorders, and 10 million abuse drugs or alcohol. Schizophrenia, one of the most severely disabling of mental disorders, afflicts only 1 percent of the population—but the figure corresponds to 1.4 million people. Over 25,000 Americans commit suicide every year, and another 200,000 attempt it (Dohrenwend et al., 1980; Dohrenwend & Dohrenwend, 1982). For each person who is suffering from a psychological disorder, there are many more—family, friends, relatives—who are indirectly affected. It is probably safe to say that every American is in some way, directly or indirectly, affected by mental illness.

up a gas station. He insists that there is nothing wrong with his actions.

- A quiet, well-behaved child suddenly covers the living room walls with paint. When questioned, she explains that "Johnny" did it. Within a few weeks, the child is spending all her time alone in her room talking with her imaginary friend.

Each of these people is acting in an impaired, self-defeating manner. The bookkeeper has set herself an impossible task. Her need for neatness is so exaggerated that she cannot possibly succeed. The young man is surprised at the reactions of people to his robbery attempt. "Why all the fuss?" he asks. "So I got caught." His failure to accept certain basic social values is a psychological problem. All children use their imaginations: They invent people when they play and make excuses for unacceptable behavior. But the girl in the third example is unable—or unwilling—to turn her imagination off. Perhaps Johnny protects her from punishment, loss of love, loneliness. Johnny does all the things that she cannot.

The behavior of these people is considered abnormal because their perception of reality is distorted and their ability to cope with life's demands is impaired. The bookkeeper is struggling to reach an impossible goal: perfection. The young man grasps neither the effects of his action on his intended victim nor the basic immorality of his behavior. The child, on the other hand, perceives her own normal impulses as terribly wrong, but since she cannot control them, she invents a second self. In each case, the important point about abnormal behavior is that the person's *interpretation of reality* makes adjustment impossible. Within that interpretation of reality, the person is trying to cope effectively. But each person's behavior creates more problems than it solves. Distorted perception, inappropriate behavior, and discomfort are three criteria of abnormal behavior.

A fourth criterion is *danger*—to oneself or to others. The person who is likely to attempt suicide or to harm someone else in a sudden outburst is an obvious threat. So, in a more general—though usually less dangerous—way, is the person who behaves irrationally. We all depend on being able to predict how people will act. We expect drivers to stop for red lights, grocers to give us food in exchange for money, friends to respect our feelings and be sympathetic. When people violate these written and unwritten rules, they create problems for themselves and for those around them. When these violations are extreme, we understand that such people need help. But this has not always been so.

■ What Is Abnormal Behavior?

Historical Views of Abnormal Behavior

No one knows for sure what was considered abnormal behavior thousands of years ago. On the basis of studies of contemporary primitive tribes, however, we can hazard a general description: In such cultures, nearly everything was attributed to supernatural powers. Madness was a sign that spirits had possessed a person. Sometimes people who were "possessed" were seen as sacred, and their visions were considered messages from the gods. At other times, the tribal wise men diagnosed the presence of evil spirits. Presumably, this supernatural view of abnormal behavior dominated early societies.

The ancient Greeks viewed strange behavior differently. Hippocrates (c. 450–c. 377 B.C.), for example, maintained that madness was like any other sickness—a natural event arising from natural causes. Epilepsy, he reasoned, was caused by the brain melting down into the body, resulting in fits and foaming at the mouth. Melancholia, an imbalance in the body

The witchcraft trial of a young woman in colonial Massachusetts Abnormal behavior was once considered the work of demons, and the disturbed person was believed to be possessed by the devil.

fluids, was cured with abstinence and quiet. Although Hippocrates' ideas may seem fanciful to us, they had a positive influence on the treatment of disturbed people, who as a result received care and sympathy like that offered to others suffering from physical ailments.

In the Middle Ages, disturbed behavior, like almost every aspect of life, was seen in a spiritual context. The people of the time sought supernatural explanations for melancholy, incoherence, self-abusive, violent behavior, or mere eccentricity. Abnormal behavior was often considered the work of demons; the disturbed person was often believed to be a witch or possessed by the devil. Exorcisms, from mild to hair-raising, were performed, and a number of unfortunate people endured horrifying torture. Some were burned at the stake.

Not all disturbed people were persecuted or tortured. Beginning in the late Middle Ages and continuing throughout the fifteenth and sixteenth centuries, there were public and private asylums where mentally ill people could be confined (if not well cared for). Although some of these institutions were founded with good intentions, most were little more than prisons. In the worst cases, inmates might be chained down and given little food, light, or air. Although the idea of offering disturbed people some kind of "asylum" was an advance over treating them as witches, little was done to make sure that humane standards prevailed in these institutions until the late eighteenth century.

The year 1793 was a turning point in the history of the treatment of the mentally ill. In that year, Philippe Pinel became director of the Bicêtre Hospital in Paris. Under his direction, the hospital was drastically reorganized: Patients were removed from their chains and allowed to move about the hospital grounds, rooms were made more comfortable and sanitary, and dubious and violent medical treatments, such as bleeding, were abandoned. Pinel's reforms were soon followed by similar efforts in England and, somewhat later, in America. The most notable American reformer was Dorothea Dix (1802–1887), a schoolteacher from Boston who led a nationwide campaign for humane treatment of mentally ill people. The very concept of mental illness dates back to Dix; under her influence, the country's asylums were gradually turned into hospitals staffed by doctors, nurses, and attendants.

In 1735, William Hogarth's *A Rake's Progress* depicted two upper-class women enjoying a tour of St. Mary's of Bethlehem, an asylum better known as Bedlam.

At about the same time that institutional reforms were beginning, Franz Anton Mesmer was achieving considerable fame for his success in curing everything from melancholy to blindness through hypnosis. Although Mesmer was something of a showman, a number of doctors took him seriously, among them the neurologist Jean-Martin Charcot. Charcot sought connections between the workings of the brain and the miraculous effects of hypnosis. Sigmund Freud, who studied under Charcot, based much of his early psychoanalytic work on the effects of hypnosis on disturbed people. Thus, Mesmer's experiments had a lasting indirect influence on our understanding of abnormal behavior.

Although the idea that disturbed behavior might have an organic or physiological basis dates back to Hippocrates, this notion had little experimental support until 1894. In that year, Fournier published an explanation of *paresis*—an overall breakdown of the mind and the body that was common among nineteenth-century merchants and soldiers. He found that most of them had at some point contracted syphilis. Fournier concluded that syphilis caused the massive mental deterioration that characterized paresis. Thus began the search for medical cures for all forms of madness.

Current Views of Abnormal Behavior

Today, there are several different viewpoints on abnormal behavior, each of which has a substantial following. Here, in brief, are some of the explanations that psychology has offered for abnormal behavior.

THE PSYCHOANALYTIC MODEL. The **psychoanalytic model** was developed by Freud and his followers. According to this model, behavior disorders are symbolic expressions of unconscious internal conflicts. For example, a man who behaves toward women in a violent way may be unconsciously expressing rage at his mother for being unaffectionate toward him during his childhood. The psychoanalytic model argues that people must become aware that the source of their problems lies in their childhood and infancy before they can resolve those problems effectively.

THE BEHAVIORAL MODEL. According to the **behavioral model,** abnormal behavior, like all behavior, is the result of learning. Fear, anxiety, frigidity, and similar behaviors are learned according to the principles we discussed in Chapter 5. And they can be unlearned using those same principles, without the probing of an analyst or the use of drugs.

THE COGNITIVE MODEL. As we saw in the section on cognitive learning in Chapter 5, cognitive psychologists believe that internal processes (such as expectations and awareness of contingencies) play an important role in learned behavior. According to the **cognitive model,** abnormal behavior is best understood as the result of such internal processes. Unlike the psychoanalytic model, the cognitive model stresses

Philippe Pinel removing the chains from patients in the Bicêtre Hospital in Paris.

mental processes of which the individual is aware and sees the individual as an active processor of information. For example, a bright student who considers himself academically inferior to his classmates and who believes that he doesn't have the ability to perform well on a test may not study for the test with much care or confidence. Naturally, he performs poorly, and his poor performance confirms his belief that he is academically inferior. This student is caught up in a vicious circle in which self-defeating beliefs lead to failure which then further strengthens the self-defeating beliefs (Turk & Salovey, 1985). According to cognitive psychologists, then, a therapist who sets out to modify abnormal behavior must first modify the person's cognitive processes.

Biological model of abnormal behavior View that abnormal behavior has a biochemical or physiological basis.

Diathesis-stress model of abnormal behavior View that people biologically predisposed to a disorder will exhibit that disorder when particularly affected by stress.

THE BIOLOGICAL MODEL. The **biological model** holds that abnormal behavior is caused at least in part by hereditary factors as well as malfunctioning of the nervous system and the endocrine glands. As we shall see, evidence is growing to the effect that genetic factors are involved in disorders as diverse as schizophrenia, mental retardation, and criminality. We will also see that some cases of depression and schizophrenia seem to stem from disturbances in the biochemistry of the nervous system. In other cases, it appears that there is a biological *predisposition* to develop a particular disorder, although some kind of stressful circumstance is necessary before the predisposition shows up in behavior (Rosenthal, 1970). According to this **diathesis-stress model,** some people appear to be biologically vulnerable to certain kinds of stress, while other people are immune to even extreme trauma.

None of the competing points of view can claim to be the only correct theory. Each has shed light on certain types of abnormality, and each is likely to continue to do so. Given the many ways in which abnormal behavior is manifested and the difficulty of studying abnormality in humans (brains of living people can't be put under the microscope, for example), it is not surprising that no single theory has yet been proved right in every respect. We will examine each of these perspectives in greater detail throughout this chapter. Because psychologists do not agree on which model is superior to the others, our discussion emphasizes the interaction of biological and learning factors in the development of mental disorders. In effect, we will take the diathesis-stress model as a point of view from which to examine both mental disorders and the ways in which psychologists interpret them.

Classifying Abnormal Behavior

We have been talking about abnormal behavior as if it were all of a kind, but there are in fact many different kinds of psychological disorders. For nearly 40 years, the American Psychiatric Association (APA) has issued an official manual describing and classifying the various kinds of abnormal behavior. This publication, the *Diagnostic and Statistical Manual of Mental Disorders* (DSM), has gone through three editions: The first appeared in 1952, the second in 1968, and the third in 1980. The manual currently in use, which is known as *DSM-III-R,* differs from its predecessors in being far more detailed and comprehensive.

DSM-III-R was designed to provide a complete list of mental disorders, with each category painstakingly defined in terms of significant behavior patterns so that diagnoses would be both valid and reliable. For example, a person diagnosed as schizophrenic should indeed be suffering from schizophrenia and not some other disorder, and most professionals using the *DSM* criteria should arrive at the same diagnosis for that person. The manual is silent as to the *causes* of disorders (still a matter of dispute in most cases, even for familiar disorders). The designers of the manual hoped that it would stand up well to professional scrutiny and be acceptable as a working tool to psychologists and psychiatrists of many theoretical persuasions.

The *DSM*, however, has not been without its critics. Some experts object to the very notion of classifying psychological and behavioral disorders as if they were diseases and publishing the classification in a medically oriented handbook. Others charge that the manual includes too many kinds of behavior that have nothing to do with mental illness. As one group of commentators wrote:

> *DSM-III* includes many behaviors which have little or no medical relevance and belong properly in the province of the psychologist, e.g., gambling, malingering, antisocial behavior, academic and occupational problems, parent-child problems, marital problems, and the curious "substance use disorders," which apparently would bring almost any kind of behavior within the compass of psychiatry—drinking coffee, having sex, eating wiener schnitzel (Eysenck, Wakefield, & Friedman, 1983, p. 189).

These critics see the manual as an attempt by medical doctors to define all behavioral problems, whatever their nature and severity, as diseases, even though some might be more appropriately classified as "problems in living" (Smith & Kraft, 1983).

Still other critics object to specific *DSM* categories for a variety of reasons. For example, many psychologists have criticized the diagnostic category *premenstrual dysphoric syndrome* as sexist and as improperly labeling as "illness" what may actually be a normal psychological reaction to significant biological changes in the body. Similarly, many psychologists objected that there is insufficient scientific evidence to classify ego-dystonic homosexuality as a mental disorder (as it was classified in the 1980 version of *DSM-III*).

In 1986, however, when the American Psychiatric Association revised *DSM-III* and compiled the current manual, *DSM-III-R*, both premenstrual dysphoric syndrome and ego-dystonic homosexuality were included as diagnostic categories despite much criticism. Some psychologists continue to be dissatisfied with the revised diagnostic manual, and there is growing interest in the possible development of an alternative classification manual more appropriate to psychology. At present, however, *DSM-III-R* is still widely used in diagnosing abnormal behavior and will probably continue to be the standard manual for some time to come. *DSM-IV* is scheduled for publication in 1993.

In the remainder of this chapter, we will look more closely at a variety of psychological disorders. As you read through the chapter, you may occasionally feel an uncomfortable twinge of recognition. This is only natural and is nothing to worry about. Much abnormal behavior is simply normal behavior that is greatly exaggerated or displayed in inappropriate situations. Moreover, the similarities between yourself and a person with psychological problems are likely to be as instructive as the differences.

Anxiety Disorders

In some disorders, people experience "persistent feelings of threat and *anxiety* in facing the everyday problems of living" (Carson et al., 1988, p. 183), or they experience severe anxiety when they try to change various behavior patterns that they find troublesome. Although all of us are afraid from time to time, we usually know why we are fearful, our fear is caused by something appropriate and identifiable, and it passes with time. But in the case of **anxiety disorders,** the person either does not know why he or she is afraid or the anxiety is inappropriate to the circumstances. In either case, the person's fear and anxiety don't seem to make sense.

Until recently, these disorders were part of the broader category of *neurosis*, and people experiencing them were called neurotic. But psychologists and psychiatrists have found it difficult to agree on precisely what neurosis means, and the term *neurotic* has become so widely used in everyday language ("I cleaned my room three times today—I guess that's pretty neurotic!") that it has little clinical usefulness. Therefore, the most recent system for classifying abnormal behavior, the *DSM-III-R*, has essentially dropped the term *neurosis*. Although some psychologists believe that the abandonment of the idea of neurosis is premature, we will follow *DSM-III-R* and treat the various neurotic disorders separately in this chapter.

The clearest examples of anxiety disorders are **panic attacks,** which are sudden, unpredictable attacks of intense fear or terror. During a panic attack, a person may also have feelings of impending doom, chest pain, dizziness or fainting, and a fear of losing control or dying. A panic attack usually lasts only a few minutes, but such attacks recur for no apparent reason. For example:

> A 31-year-old stewardess . . . had suddenly begun to feel panicky, dizzy, had trouble breathing, started to sweat, and trembled uncontrollably. She excused herself and sat in the back of the plane and within ten minutes the symptoms had subsided. Two similar episodes had occurred in the past: the first, four years previously, when the plane had encountered mild turbulence; the second, two years earlier, during an otherwise uneventful flight, as in this episode. (Spitzer et al., 1981, p. 219)

In contrast to panic attacks, which seem to occur without any obvious cause or triggering event, **posttraumatic stress disorder,** as its name implies, is clearly related to some original stressful event. People who have lived through fires, floods, tornadoes, or the horrors of combat may experience episodes of fear and terror years afterward; sometimes these involve "reliving" the traumatic event. We discussed this disorder at some length in Chapter 13.

Another form of anxiety disorder is **obsessive-compulsive disorder.** *Obsessions* are involuntary thoughts or ideas that keep recurring despite the person's attempt to stop them. *Compulsions* are repetitive, ritualistic

Anxiety disorders Disorders in which anxiety is a characteristic feature or the avoidance of anxiety seems to motivate abnormal behavior.

Panic attack A sudden unpredictable feeling of intense fear or terror.

Posttraumatic stress disorder A condition in which episodes of anxiety, sleeplessness, and nightmares are the result of some disturbing event in the past.

Obsessive-compulsive disorder A disorder in which a person feels compelled to think disturbing thoughts and perform senseless rituals.

Panic attacks are sudden, unpredictable attacks of intense fear or terror. During a panic attack, a person may have feelings of impending doom, chest pain, dizziness or fainting, and a fear of losing control or dying.

Phobic disorder A condition characterized by intense phobias and compulsive avoidance behavior.

Phobia Excessive unreasonable fear attached to an apparently harmless stimulus.

Simple phobia Phobia directed at a specific situation (such as being in the dark) or a specific object (such as snakes).

Agoraphobia Excessive fear of being alone and, in severe cases, of leaving home and being in open spaces.

Edvard Munch's *The Scream*. Some see in this painting the fear and terror produced by a *panic attack*.

behaviors that a person feels compelled to perform. Obsessive thoughts are often of a horrible nature. One patient, for example, reported that "when she thought of her boyfriend she wished he were dead; when her mother went down the stairs, she 'wished she'd fall and break her neck'; when her sister spoke of going to the beach with her infant daughter [she] 'hoped that they would both drown' " (Carson et al., 1988, p. 189). Truly compulsive behaviors may be equally dismaying to the person who feels a need to perform them. They often take the form of washing or cleaning, as if the compulsive behavior were the person's attempt to "wash away" the contaminating thoughts. One patient reported that her efforts to keep her clothes and body clean eventually took up six hours of her day, and even then, "washing my hands wasn't enough, and I started to use rubbing alcohol" (Spitzer et al., 1981, p. 137).

At times, anyone can experience mild obsessions or compulsions. Most of us have occasionally been unable to get a particular song lyric out of our head or have felt that we *had* to walk so as to avoid stepping on cracks in the sidewalk. But in an obsessive-compulsive disorder, the obsessive thoughts and compulsive behavior are of a more serious nature. For example, a man who checks his watch every five minutes when his wife is late coming home is merely being normally anxious. But a man who feels that he must go through his house every hour checking every clock for accuracy, even though he knows there is no reason to do so, is showing signs of an obsessive-compulsive disorder.

Since people who experience obsessions and compulsions often do not seem particularly anxious, you may wonder why this disorder is considered an anxiety disorder. The answer is that if such people try to *stop* their irrational behavior, or if someone else tries to stop them, they experience severe anxiety. In other words, it seems that the obsessive-compulsive behavior acts in some way to keep their anxiety down to a tolerable level.

Finally, **phobic disorders** are also closely linked to feelings of anxiety. A **phobia** is an intense, paralyzing fear of something in the absence of any real danger—a fear of something that most other people find bearable. This fear is often recognized by the person suffering from it as unreasonable, but it persists nonetheless.

Of course, many people have irrational fears. Fears of height, water, closed rooms, and cats are all common phobias. But when people are so afraid of snakes that they cannot go to a zoo, walk through a field, or even look at pictures of snakes without trembling, they may be said to have a phobic disorder. For example, one woman was so afraid of thunderstorms that she became anxious and would stay inside whenever the sky became overcast or the weather forecast predicted rain (Spitzer et al., 1981). Such phobias are generally categorized as **simple phobias** and also include such fears as those of darkness, infections, and even running water.

Perhaps the most common phobic disorder is **agoraphobia,** "a marked fear of being alone, or being in public places from which escape might be difficult" (APA, 1980, p. 226). Sufferers avoid such things as elevators, tunnels, and crowds, especially crowded stores or busy streets. Because of the severity of its effects on the sufferer's day-to-day functioning, agoraphobia is the most common phobia encountered in the clinic; 50 percent to 80 percent of phobics seeking therapy suffer from agoraphobia

(Foa, Steketke, & Young, 1984). For reasons that are not yet fully understood, most agoraphobics are women (Brehony & Geller, 1981). One possible explanation is the fact that traditionally it was more acceptable for a woman to be housebound. It is also possible that women more readily admit to the problem.

Another important category of phobias is **social phobias,** which are fears generally connected with the presence of other people. Fear of public speaking is a social phobia. For some people, even eating in public can cause severe anxiety. Like agoraphobia, social phobias generally begin during adolescence, when an individual is experiencing growing awareness of his or her interactions with other people.

What causes anxiety disorders? Most psychoanalytic theorists believe that they are the result of unconscious conflict. Unacceptable impulses or thoughts (usually sexual or aggressive) threaten to overwhelm the ego and break through into full consciousness. The person is still unaware of the unconscious impulses or thoughts but experiences the early warning signal of anxiety nonetheless, perhaps in the form of a panic attack. One way to minimize or avoid the anxiety is to concentrate intensely on ritualistic behavior. For example, a young man who is about to finish his medical internship is repeatedly tortured by the thought that he has made a mistake in his career choice and in his decision to marry early. Hostility toward his wife begins to surface. Then he discovers that if he concentrates on a list of medical symptoms that he memorized years ago, he can escape his worries about his life. Reciting lists becomes more and more frequent. Later he realizes that his wife is hinting that they should start a family. Every time the topic comes up, he becomes tense and anxious and goes to the bathroom to wash his hands. This, too, may reduce his anxiety, and he increasingly responds with this kind of behavior as a means of escaping tension and worry. Soon these trivial rituals—reciting lists, washing his hands—hold his life together, and also eat up more and more of his time and energy. In other words, repeated thoughts and actions—obsessive-compulsive behavior—that once helped control the tension and anxiety have now become problems themselves.

According to the psychoanalytic view, phobias are a result of **displacement.** People feel threatened by unconscious impulses, and by converting their vague anxiety into a fear of something specific, like elevators or spiders, they gain the temporary illusion of controlling their fears.

Behaviorists, on the other hand, believe that people who suffer from anxiety disorders have learned to associate fear and anxiety with an apparently harmless situation. It may be that the fear has generalized from some other, similar situation that really *was* harmful. Or the person may have had a terrifying experience in the past and been unable to unlearn that terror. For example, a young boy is savagely attacked by a large dog. Because of this experience, he is now terribly afraid of all large dogs. Even other children who saw the attack or heard about it may also come to fear dogs. As we saw in Chapter 5, because phobias are often learned after only one such event and are extremely hard to change, some learning theorists see them as *prepared responses*—responses built into us biologically through evolution. Seligman (1972) suggests that this is why there is a relatively limited range of phobic objects.

Obsessive-compulsive behavior may also be learned. The learning may occur by trial and error, as when the intern in our example discovered

Social phobia Phobia centered on the fear of being with other people.

Displacement Conversion of a vague anxiety resulting from threatening unconscious impulses into a fear of something specific.

While some people suffer little or no discomfort from such things as great heights, others may experience a paralyzing fear of height in the absence of any real danger; in that case, the individual suffers from a *phobic disorder* known as *acrophobia*.

Somatoform disorders Disorders in which there is an apparent physical disorder for which there is no organic basis.

Somatization disorder Disorder characterized by recurrent vague somatic complaints without a physical cause.

Agoraphobia includes the fear of being in public places from which escape might be difficult. Sufferers avoid such things as elevators and crowded subways.

While many people suffer some discomfort when asked to speak in public, others suffer an irrational fear of doing so. Such fear is a *social phobia*.

that reciting lists reduced his anxiety. It can also be an exaggerated version of behavior that succeeded when we were children—washing our hands is a "good" action that parents praise (Dollard & Miller, 1950). If the behavior reduces anxiety, it is reinforced and is more likely to recur. Whatever the source of the behavior, if it succeeds in reducing anxiety, it will be more likely to recur when anxiety reappears.

From the cognitive perspective, the feeling that one is not in control of one's life is central to all forms of anxiety. Research indicates that if people believe they have control over stressful events, they experience less anxiety than if they believe that they have little or no control. In some instances, this is the case even when the perceived control is only imaginary.

Psychologists working from the biological perspective point out that even when there is the same opportunity to learn phobic or obsessive-compulsive behavior, some individuals develop unrealistic fears while others do not. By way of explanation, these psychologists point out that the activity of the autonomic nervous system is involved in all kinds of fear. Moreover, there is considerable evidence that autonomic responsiveness is genetically determined, at least in part. Thus, there is a distinct possibility that the predisposition to anxiety disorders may be inherited (Cattell, 1965; Eysenck, 1970; Sarason & Sarason, 1987). In fact, there is some evidence that anxiety disorders tend to run in families (Carey & Gottesman, 1981; Torgersen, 1983). However, there is no evidence that specific kinds of anxiety disorders are inherited. In addition, as we shall see in the next chapter, while such tranquilizer drugs as Valium can significantly reduce anxiety, this does not mean that the anxiety was *caused* by a biological problem of some kind.

Somatoform Disorders

Somatoform disorders involve physical symptoms of serious bodily disorders without any physical evidence of organic causes for them. Sufferers from these disorders do not consciously seek to mislead people about their physical condition: The symptoms are real and not under voluntary control (APA, 1980).

In cases of **somatization disorder,** the person feels vague, recurring, physical symptoms for which medical attention has been sought repeatedly but no organic cause found. Complaints often involve back pains, dizziness, partial paralysis, abdominal pains, and sometimes anxiety and depression. The following case is typical:

> An elderly woman complained of headaches and periods of weakness that lasted for over six months. Her condition had been evaluated by doctors numerous times; she was taking several prescription medications, and she had actually undergone thirty operations for a variety of complaints. She was thin, but examination showed her to be within normal limits in terms of physical health (except for numerous surgical scars). Her medical history spanned half a century, and there can be little doubt that she suffered from somatization disorder. (Quill, 1985)

Less often, people complain of more bizarre symptoms, such as paralysis, blindness, deafness, seizures, loss of feeling, or false pregnancy.

Sufferers from such **conversion disorders** have intact muscles and nerves, yet their symptoms are very real. (For example, a person with such a "paralyzed" limb has no feeling in it, even if stuck with a pin.) A related somatoform disorder is **hypochondriasis** (commonly known as hypochondria). In this case, the person interprets some small sign or symptom—perhaps a cough, bruise, or perspiration—as a sign of a serious disease. Although the symptom may exist, there is no evidence that it reflects a serious illness. Nevertheless, repeated assurances of this sort have little effect, and the person is likely to visit one doctor after another looking for one who will share his or her conviction.

Sometimes it is easy to determine that there is no organic cause for a conversion disorder. Some symptoms are anatomically impossible, as in *glove anesthesia*, which is a lack of feeling in the hand from the wrist down. There is no way that damage to the nerves running into the hand could cause such a localized pattern of anesthesia. Another clue that the disorder has psychological causes is that the person sometimes may be quite cheerful about it. Psychologists call this attitude *la belle indifference*, or beautiful indifference: The person seems blithely unconcerned about a serious medical condition. Psychologists also look for evidence that the "illness" resolves a difficult conflict or relieves the patient of the need to confront a difficult situation. For example, a housewife reported that she had serious attacks of dizziness, nausea, and visual disturbances that came on in the late afternoon and cleared up at about 8:00 P.M. After ruling out any physical cause for her problems, a therapist discovered that she was married to an extremely tyrannical man, who shortly after coming home from work in the evening would abuse her and her children verbally, criticizing her housekeeping, the meal she had prepared, and so on. Her attacks, while very real to her, served to remove her from this painful situation: Her psychological distress was unconsciously converted to physical symptoms (Spitzer et al., 1981).

Psychoanalysts see all somatoform disorders as a displacement—or conversion—of emotional problems to physical problems. Freud concluded that the physical symptoms were always related to traumatic experiences buried in a patient's past: A woman who, years earlier, saw her mother physically abused by her father suddenly loses her sight; a man who was punished for masturbating later loses the use of his hand. By unconsciously developing a handicap, people punish themselves for forbidden desires or behavior, prevent themselves from acting out those desires or repeating that forbidden behavior, and regress to an earlier stage when others took care of them. Moreover, constant worry over physical symptoms can serve, as in the case of an obsession, to keep an unconscious impulse from rising to awareness.

Behaviorists, on the other hand, look for ways that the symptomatic behavior could have been learned and for signs that it might still be rewarding. They would suggest that the person learned in the past that sickly behavior, aches, pains, and so on can be used to avoid unpleasant situations. (Timely headaches and stomachaches have "solved" a lot of problems over the years.) In addition, a person who is ill often gets a good deal of attention, support, and care, which can be indirectly rewarding to at least some people some of the time.

From the biological perspective, research indicates that individuals suffering from hypochondriasis seem to be unusually sensitive to their

Conversion disorder Disorder in which a dramatic specific disability has no physical cause and instead seems related to psychological problems.

Hypochondriasis A condition in which a person interprets small and insignificant symptoms as signs of serious illness in the absence of any organic symptoms of such illness.

own internal processes (Hanback & Revelle, 1978; Tyrer, Lee, & Alexander, 1980). However, no hereditary basis for somatoform disorders has yet been established.

Psychophysiological Disorders

Psychophysiological disorders are *real* physical disorders that seem to have psychological causes. Many cases of ulcers, migraine headaches, asthma, high blood pressure, and other disorders are thought to be psychological in origin. In each case, the complaints have a valid *physical* basis, but they are thought to be caused or exacerbated by stress, anxiety, and other psychological factors. Indeed, modern medicine is beginning to accept the idea that many physical ailments are to some extent psychophysiological—since stress, anxiety, and various states of emotional arousal alter body chemistry, the functioning of bodily organs, and the body's immune system.

It is important to distinguish between psychophysiological disorders and hypochondriasis. A person with a psychophysiological disorder is really sick; a hypochondriac is not. In hypochondriasis, the person believes that he or she is seriously ill despite the *absence* of any substantial symptoms and despite reassurances to the contrary from physicians. The hypochondriac might almost be said to be suffering from disease phobia—fear that he or she has a serious disease.

As we said, however, an individual suffering from a psychophysiological disorder is physically ill. In fact, since virtually every physical disease may be linked to psychological stress, *DSM-III-R* does not list all the serious diseases as such. Rather, the manual categorizes psychophysiological disorders according to the part of the body that is affected. For example, psychophysiological respiratory disorders include bronchial asthma and the hiccups; psychophysiological musculoskeletal disorders include backache and tension headache. In Chapter 13, we examined a number of psychophysiological disorders and their causes in the discussion of the effects of prolonged stress.

Dissociative Disorders

Dissociative disorders are among the most puzzling forms of mental disorders, both to the observer and to the sufferer. Dissociation means that part of an individual's personality is separated or dissociated from the rest, and for some reason the person cannot reassemble the pieces. It usually takes the form of memory loss; a complete—but usually temporary—change in identity; or even the presence of several distinct personalities in one person.

Loss of memory without an organic cause may be a reaction to intolerable experiences. People often block out an event or a period of their lives if it has been extremely stressful. During World War II, some hospitalized soldiers could not recall their names, where they lived, where they were born, or how they came to be in battle. But war and its horrors are not the only causes of **amnesia.** The man who betrays a friend to complete a business deal or the unhappily married man who reserves a single ticket to Tahiti may also forget—selectively—what he has done. He may even assume an entirely new identity, although this phenomenon is unusual.

Total amnesia, in which people forget everything, is quite rare, despite its popularity in novels and films. In one unusual case, the police picked up a 42-year-old man after he became involved in a fight with a customer at the diner where he worked. The man reported that he had no memory of his life before he drifted into town a few weeks earlier. Eventually, he was found to match the description of a missing person who had wandered from his home 200 miles away. Just before he disappeared, he had been passed over for promotion at work and had had a violent argument with his teenage son (Spitzer et al., 1981).

Even rarer and more bizarre than amnesia is the disorder known as **multiple personality,** in which a person has several distinct personalities that emerge at different times. This dramatic disorder, which has been the subject of popular fiction and films, is actually extremely rare. In the true multiple personality, the various personalities are distinct people, with their own names, identities, memories, mannerisms, speaking voices, and even IQs. Sometimes, the personalities are so separate that they don't know that they inhabit a body with other "people"; sometimes, personalities do know of the existence of others and will even make disparaging remarks about them. Consider the case of Maud and Sara K., two personalities that coexisted in one woman:

> In general demeanor, Maud was quite different from Sara. She walked with a swinging, bouncing gait contrasted to Sara's sedate one. While Sara was depressed, Maud was ebullient and happy. . . . Insofar as she could Maud dressed differently from Sara. . . . Sara used no make-up. Maud used a lot of rouge and lipstick, [and] painted her fingernails and toenails deep red. . . . Sara was a mature, intelligent individual. Her mental age was 19.2 years, IQ, 128. A psychometric done on Maud showed a mental age of 6.6, IQ, 43. (Carson et al., 1988, p. 206)

It is typical for multiple personalities to contrast sharply with each other. It is as if the two (and sometimes more) personalities represent different aspects of a single person—one the more socially acceptable, "nice" personality, the other the darker, more uninhibited or "evil" side.

A far less dramatic (and much more common) dissociative disorder is **depersonalization disorder.** Its essential feature is that the person suddenly feels changed or different in a strange way. Some people feel that they have left their bodies, others that their actions are mechanical or dreamlike. A sense of losing control of one's own behavior is common, and it is not unusual to imagine changes in one's environment. This kind of feeling is especially common during adolescence and young adulthood, when our sense of ourselves and our interactions with others changes rapidly. Only when the sense of depersonalization becomes a long-term or chronic problem, or when the alienation impairs normal social functioning, can this be classified as a dissociative disorder (APA, 1980). For example, a 20-year-old college student sought professional help after

Amnesia Loss of memory for past events.

Multiple personality disorder Condition in which more than one personality seems present in a single person.

Depersonalization disorder Condition in which a person feels unreal and unconnected to his or her body.

Jane Doe was near death when discovered by a Florida park ranger in 1980. She was also suffering from *amnesia* and could not remember her name, her past, or her ability to read or write. Despite later renewed ties to the past, Jane Doe never regained her memory.

■ Multiple Personality Disorder: Is It Real?

Multiple personality disorder is surely one of the most mysterious of all psychological abnormalities. How can a person have more than one distinct personality? How is it possible that some people have seemed to have more than *20* distinct personalities?

Most people know about multiple or split personalities from popular sources such as movies like *The Three Faces of Eve*, the story of a young woman who assumed three very different personalities. In fact, there really was an Eve White, who was the subject of a famous case study of Thigpen and Cleckley in 1954. Eve's "three faces" consisted of Eve White, a gentle, sexually reserved young woman; Eve Black, a buoyant, more sexually assertive personality; and Jane, a third personality who seemed more mature and stable, who seemed to know all about the two Eves, and who seemed to regard Eve Black more highly than Eve White.

A more recent case is that of Billy Milligan, who was arrested in 1977 for a series of rapes. Under questioning, Milligan began to introduce an impressive array of personalities, including an intellectual with a British accent who deemed it beneath his dignity to take an IQ test; a teenaged drummer who was the only smoker among the personalities; a three-year-old girl who liked to draw butterflies; and a lesbian who was considered to be the personality responsible for the rapes. In 1978, Milligan was acquitted on grounds of multiple personality disorder.

Such cases as Milligan's, in which the patient's behavior involves criminal activity, draw professional and public attention to the position of psychologists who doubt that true multiple personalities exist. According to these critics, famous cases in the literature like Eve White and Billy Milligan are fraudulent. Either these people were clever enough to fool the therapists or the therapists themselves accidentally planted the multiple personalities in their patients' heads. And once the person shows "evidence" of having an additional personality, this argument runs, the avid interest of the therapist in an exotic and rare disorder serves to reinforce the abnormal behavior and make it more likely to recur.

Billy Milligan

Some intriguing research, however, supports the existence of multiple personality disorder. A team of investigators at the National Institutes of Mental Health has discovered that each of a person's different personalities has a distinct pattern of brain waves (Putnam, 1982). When normal people were trained to create "multiple personalities" through elaborate rehearsal, their brain-wave patterns were the same no matter which "personality" was tested. But people with real multiple personalities showed markedly different patterns of brain waves as they switched from one personality to another. In fact, the brain waves were as different as if they had come from completely different people. This finding not only seems to show that multiple personality disorder is real; it seems to offer one way in which real cases of multiple personality disorder can be distinguished from fakes.

The issue of abnormal behavior and the law is discussed further in the Application section at the end of this chapter.

experiencing episodes of feeling "outside" himself for two years. At these times, he felt groggy, dizzy, and preoccupied. Since he had had several episodes while driving, he had stopped driving alone. Although he was able to keep up with his studies, his friends began to notice that he seemed "spacy" and self-preoccupied (Spitzer et al., 1981).

Psychoanalytic theorists believe that some dissociative disorders, like amnesia, are the result of a person's completely blocking out thoughts or impulses that arouse anxiety (or any associated thoughts that might possibly trigger anxiety). Multiple personality, on the other hand, involves a kind of projection in which each personality can say of the others, in effect, "It's not *me* who's thinking or saying these terrible things." Depersonalization works in much the same way, although much less dramatically.

Behaviorists would not agree that dissociative disorders arise from unconscious conflicts, but they would agree that these behaviors can, under some circumstances, be learned and maintained. They point out that amnesiacs who cannot recall personally important information are frequently individuals who are not well-prepared to deal with emotional conflict; for them, blocking out disturbing thoughts and avoiding stress are rewarding forms of behavior.

■ Affective Disorders

As their name suggests, **affective disorders** are characterized by disturbances in *affect*, or emotional state. Most people have a wide affective range—that is, they are capable of being happy or sad, animated or quiet, cheerful or discouraged, overjoyed or miserable, depending on the circumstances. In people with affective disorders, this range is greatly restricted. These people seem stuck at one end or the other of the emotional spectrum, either consistently happy or consistently sad, with little regard for the circumstances of their lives. In other cases, they alternate between extremes of happiness and sadness.

The most common affective disorder is **depression,** a state in which a person feels overwhelmed with sadness, grief, and guilt. Depressed people are unable to experience pleasure from activities that they once enjoyed and are tired and apathetic—sometimes to the point of being unable to make the simplest everyday decisions. They may feel as if they have failed utterly in life, and they tend to blame themselves for their problems. Seriously depressed people often have disturbed patterns of sleeping and eating (insomnia is common, and the individual may lose interest in food). In very serious cases, depressed people may be plagued by suicidal thoughts or may even attempt suicide.

It is important to distinguish between the clinical disorder known as depression and the "normal" kind of depression that all people experience from time to time. It is entirely normal to become depressed when a loved one has died, when you've come to the end of a romantic relationship, when you have problems on the job or at school—even when the weather's bad or you don't have a date for Saturday night. Most psychologically healthy people get "the blues" occasionally for no apparent reason. But in all these instances, the depression either is related to a "real world" problem or passes quickly. Only when depression is serious, lasting, and seemingly unrelated to any stressful life event can it be classified as an affective disorder (APA, 1980). For example:

> A 50-year-old widow was transferred to a medical center from her community mental health center, to which she had been admitted three weeks previously with severe agitation, pacing, and handwringing, depressed mood accompanied by severe self-reproach, insomnia, and a 6–8 kg [15-pound] weight loss. She believed that her neighbors were against her, had poisoned her coffee, and had bewitched her to punish her because of her wickedness. Seven years previously, after the death of her husband, she

When suffering from depression, individuals feel overwhelmed with sadness and guilt, may believe that they have failed completely, blame themselves for their problems, and are sometimes reduced to crying in solitude.

Mania Disorder in which a person is overly excited and hyperactive.

had required hospitalization for a similar depression, with extreme guilt, agitation, insomnia, accusatory hallucinations of voices calling her a worthless person, and preoccupation with thoughts of suicide. (Spitzer et al., 1981, pp. 28–29)

But affective disorders do not always involve depression. Less commonly, people experience a state of **mania,** in which they become hyperactive and excessively talkative, are easily distracted, are euphoric or "high," and seem extremely flamboyant. People in a manic state have unlimited hopes and schemes but often have little interest in carrying

■ Suicide

In the United States alone, more than 200,000 people attempt suicide each year (Rosenhan & Seligman, 1984). More women than men attempt suicide, but more men actually succeed at it, in part because men often choose more violent lethal means, such as firearms. Disturbing increases in the number of adolescents and young adults attempting suicide have become a focus of growing concern. Adolescents account for 12 percent of all suicide attempts, and suicide is the second leading cause of death among adolescents, after accidents (Weiner, 1982). However, no convincing explanation has been offered for the increase. The stresses of leaving home, meeting the demands of college or career, and surviving loneliness or broken romantic attachments are particularly great at this time. It may be that in recent years, problems from the outside world—unemployment, the emotional and financial costs of attending a prestigious college, the feeling that one's personal future may be threatened by a nuclear war—are adding to people's personal problems.

Several myths have grown up around the subject of suicide. These include the idea that the person who talks of committing suicide will never do it. In fact, most people who kill themselves have mentioned their intent beforehand. Such comments should *always* be taken seriously by the person's friends and family. A related misconception is that a person who has attempted suicide and failed is not serious about it. Often a failed suicide will try again, picking a more deadly method the second or third time. (And any suicide attempt is a sign that a person is deeply troubled and in need of help.) Another erroneous idea is that those who commit suicide are life's losers—people who have failed vocationally and socially. In fact, many people who kill themselves seem to have every reason to live—prestigious jobs, families, and so on. Physicians, for example, have a suicide rate several times that of the general population—which is probably related to the stresses of their work.

People considering suicide are overwhelmed with hope-

Disturbing increases in the number of adolescents and young adults attempting suicide have become a growing concern. Though the reasons for these increases remain unclear, what is clear is that most suicidal people do want help, however much they may despair of obtaining it.

lessness. They feel that things *cannot* get better and that there is no way out of their difficulties. This is depression in the extreme, and it is not a state of mind that someone is easily talked out of. It will do little good to tell such a person that things aren't really so bad. The person will only take this as further evidence that no one understands his or her suffering. But most suicidal people *do* want help, however much they may despair of obtaining it. If a friend or family member seems at all suicidal, make sure that person is not left alone, and seek professional help for him or her as soon as possible. Your local community mental health center is a good starting place, or you can call one of the national suicide hot lines (see telephone numbers in Chapter 15).

them out. They sometimes become aggressive and hostile toward others as their self-confidence becomes more and more unrealistic. In an extreme case, people going through manic episodes may become wild, incomprehensible, or violent until they collapse from exhaustion.

Manic episodes rarely appear by themselves; rather, they usually alternate with depression. Such an affective disorder, in which both mania and depression are present, is known as **bipolar disorder** (the person alternates between two "poles" of mania and depression). Occasionally, bipolar disorder is seen in a mild form: The person has alternating moods of unrealistically high spirits followed by moderate depression.

Perspectives on Affective Disorders

Most psychologists agree that the key to understanding affective disorders lies in understanding depression. We will conclude our discussion of affective disorders by surveying some of the more important theories about the causes of depression.

PSYCHOANALYTIC THEORY. Freud viewed depression as excessive and irrational grief. He believed that the source of the grief was to be found in the individual's relationship with the person on whom he or she was most dependent as a child. Depression is believed to originate in some disturbance of that relationship, usually the real or imagined loss of a parent. Because the "loss" provokes intense anger and anxiety, it is repressed and the person is no longer consciously aware of it. However, a subsequent event can trigger the anxiety; in a defensive effort, the person may then identify with the "lost" person, perhaps in an effort to reverse the loss. By identifying with the "lost" person, the individual may in fact be able to reduce some anxiety, but there is an unexpected cost involved in this defensive maneuver: The anger and resentment that the individual feels about having been deserted are now turned inward against the self. Thus, psychoanalytic theory also holds that depression is the result of anger turned against oneself. While this is an intriguing theory, it has been difficult to establish a direct connection between early loss and risk of depression in adult life (Crook & Eliot, 1980), and critics of the psychoanalytic model point out that there is no direct evidence to support the contention that the depressed individual interprets loss as desertion or rejection.

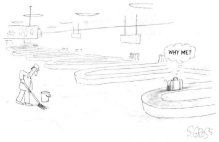

© 1987 S. Gross

BEHAVIOR THEORY. Behaviorists view depression differently. They believe that there is a direct relationship between depression and lack of reinforcement (see Chapter 5). For example, Lewinsohn and his associates believe that depression is linked to a deficiency in social skills (Lewinsohn, 1974; Lewinsohn & Hoberman, 1982). Individuals who lack sufficiently effective social skills receive relatively little positive reinforcement from other people; as a result, they may exhibit the form of passive behavior that characterizes depression. Furthermore, other people tend to avoid depressives, and their avoidance decreases even further the depressive's rate of positive reinforcement and thereby serves to intensify the depression (Lewinsohn & Arconad, 1981). In this view, depressed people become trapped in a vicious circle. Some support for this view is found in studies showing that depressives do generate anxiety and even hostility in other people (Coyne, 1976) and that this is in part because they tend to require more emotional support from other people than those who feel comfortable in giving (Coyne, 1982).

COGNITIVE THEORY. The cognitive theory of depression also rests on the principle that, at least in part, depression is learned behavior. In comparison to behaviorists, however, cognitive theorists put more emphasis on the thought processes that the person has developed as a result of his or her experience. According to Aaron Beck (1967, 1976), during childhood and adolescence, some individuals may undergo such experiences as the loss of a parent, difficulties in gaining parental or social approval, or criticism from teachers and other adults. One response to such experience is to develop a negative self-concept—a feeling of incompetence or unworthiness that has little to do with the reality of the situation but that is maintained by a distorted and illogical interpretation of the real events. When a new situation arises that resembles the situation under which the self-concept was learned, these same feelings of worthlessness and incompetence may be activated and result in depression.

Beck describes several kinds of illogical thinking that can contribute to feelings of depression:

1. *Arbitrary inference.* The individual arrives at a conclusion about himself or herself despite the scarcity or absence of evidence. For example: A man thinks of himself as professionally incompetent because his car won't start on the morning that he is to make an important presentation at work.
2. *Selective abstraction.* The individual arrives at a conclusion based on only one of numerous factors influencing a situation. For example: An athlete blames themself for his or her team's performance even though several other members of the team also performed poorly.
3. *Overgeneralization.* The individual arrives at a sweeping conclusion based on a single, sometimes trivial, event. For example: A high school student concludes that she is not worthy of admission to the college of her choice because of poor performance on a minor quiz for which she was not prepared.
4. *Magnification and minimization.* The individual tends to magnify difficulties and failures while minimizing accomplishments and successes. For example: A man who has been driving for 20 years without an accident minimizes that evidence of skillful motoring and focuses instead on the slight dent that he put in his car while trying to back out of a tight parking space.

Some research provides support for Beck's view of depression. In tests designed to allow respondents to express their immediate thoughts, researchers have found the thoughts of depressed persons to be generally more illogical than the thoughts of people who are not depressed (White, Davison, & White, 1985). Depressed people also seem to perceive and recall information in more negative terms (Roth & Rehm, 1980). However, it has also been pointed out that such negative responses may be the result of depression instead of the cause (Hammen, 1985). As we shall see in Chapter 15, therapy based on Beck's theories has proved quite successful in the treatment of depression.

According to the cognitive theory of depression, an athlete who blames themself for his or her team's failure even though other team members also performed poorly practices *selective abstraction*—arriving at a conclusion based on only one factor out of several pertinent possibilities.

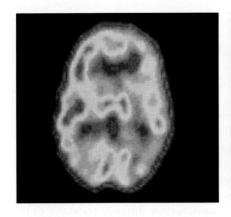 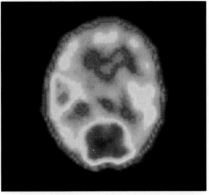

Some research has begun to link *affective disorders* with chemical imbalances in the brain. PET (positron emission tomography) scans can reveal the rates at which glucose is consumed in the brain. The normal brain in the left photo suggests moderate levels of consumption (here indicated by yellow and blue). The brain in the right photo is of someone diagnosed as bipolar and suggests higher levels of consumption (indicated by red).

BIOLOGICAL THEORIES. From the biological perspective, it is important to note that there is strong evidence that genetic factors play an important role in the development of depression (Goodwin & Guze, 1984; Kety, 1979). But just what is it that some people seem to inherit and others do not? Presumably, it is some biological defect that makes some people more likely to become depressed than others, especially when they are under stress.

But there is no clear-cut indication of just what this defect might be. In fact, there is some evidence that the biological mechanism may vary from one family to the next (Lingjaerde, 1983). However, some promising research has linked affective disorders to certain chemical imbalances within the brain—principally, to high and low levels of certain neurotransmitters, which are chemicals involved in the transmission of nerve impulses from one cell to another (see Chapter 2) (Bunney et al., 1979). For example, some researchers have had success in increasing and decreasing depressed behavior in rats by lowering and raising the level of the neurotransmitter norepinephrine (Weiss, Glazer, & Pohorecky, 1975). Other researchers suspect that the key factor is not simply the level or amount of neurotransmitters involved, but rather a dysfunction in the way that neurotransmitters transfer impulses from one neuron to another (Sulser, 1979). In any case, even though such research remains promising, the specific genetic mechanisms involved in depression are not currently known.

■ Psychosexual Disorders

Ideas about what is normal and what is abnormal in sex vary with the times—and with the individual. As Alfred Kinsey and his associates showed years ago (1948, 1953), most Americans enjoy sexual activities forbidden by laws that do not recognize current sexual mores. As a result, the definition of what constitutes abnormal sexual behavior has narrowed considerably in recent years. *DSM-III-R* recognizes two main types of psychosexual disorder: sexual dysfunction and paraphilias. In the pages that follow, we will discuss each of these in turn.

Sexual dysfunction The loss or impairment of the ordinary physical responses of sexual function.

Impotence In men, the inability to achieve or keep an erection.

Frigidity In women, the inability to become sexually aroused or reach orgasm.

Inhibited sexual desire Psychosexual dysfunction involving lack of sexual interest.

Inhibited sexual excitement Psychosexual dysfunction characterized by an inability to achieve or sustain arousal during sexual activity.

Orgasm Peaking of sexual pleasure and release of sexual tension.

Inhibited orgasm Psychosexual dysfunction characterized by an inability to achieve orgasm even when aroused and adequately stimulated.

Dysfunction

Sexual dysfunction consists of an inability to function effectively during sex. In men, this may take the form of **impotence,** the inability to achieve or keep an erection. In women, it is often **frigidity,** the inability to become sexually excited or to reach orgasm. These dysfunctions are common, especially in their milder forms. Only when such dysfunction becomes typical, when enjoyment of sexual relationships becomes impaired, should it be considered serious. Most truly impotent men and frigid women, for example, cannot have satisfying sexual relations even after repeated attempts with a partner whom they desire.

Psychosexual dysfunction may occur during any of a number of points in the sexual response cycle. Some people find it difficult or impossible to experience any desire for sexual activity. This **inhibited sexual desire** involves lack of sexual interest. It is more common among women than among men and may play a part in 40 percent of all sexual dysfunctions (Southern & Gayle, 1982). It is difficult to analyze the extent and causes of this disorder, because some people may simply have a normally low motivation for sexual activity; their reports of low interest in sex would be normal for them and would not necessarily reflect any sexual disorder. Some people report no anxiety about or aversion to sex but exhibit physiological indicators of inhibited desire (Wincze, Hoon, & Hoon, 1978). This fact has led some researchers to conclude that the disorder may sometimes be biological in nature. In cases where people report feeling neutral about sex or actually having an aversion to it, investigators suggest that the problem may originate in earlier traumatic experiences or unfulfilling relationships.

Other people are able to experience sexual desire but either cannot achieve physical arousal and its accompanying pleasure or cannot sustain arousal until the end of intercourse. This dysfunction is called **inhibited sexual excitement.** Masters and Johnson (1970) recommend that inhibited sexual excitement should be diagnosed only when the male fails to attain erection and vaginal entry on 25 percent of his attempts. Causes of this dysfunction include anxiety-provoking attitudes deriving from parental or social teaching, fear of pregnancy or inadequate performance, and inexperience on the part of one or both partners. In one study, Cooper (1969) found that situational anxiety, including such fears as fear of ridicule, inadequate genital size, and especially performance failure, was a primary factor in erectile dysfunction. That many impotent men report satisfactory arousal in response to such stimuli as sexually explicit films supports this conclusion.

Still other people are able to experience sexual desire and maintain arousal but are unable to reach **orgasm** (the peaking of sexual pleasure and the release of sexual tension). This is termed **inhibited orgasm.** However, some studies indicate that about only 30 percent of the women surveyed reported experiencing orgasm regularly during intercourse (Hoch et al., 1981). Does this fact reflect widespread sexual dysfunction among women? Pointing to the number of females who experience this pattern of response, Hoch et al. (1981) suggest that it may be normal for a majority of women. Inhibited male orgasm—the inability to ejaculate even when fully aroused—is rare but, interestingly enough, seems to be becoming more common as more men find it desirable to practice the delay of orgasm

(Rosen & Rosen, 1981). Masters and Johnson (1970) attribute the disorder primarily to such psychological factors as traumatic experiences, and it would appear to be a side effect of some medications, such as tranquilizers (Munjack & Kanno, 1979).

Problems other than the aforementioned can also occur during the sexual response cycle. Men may experience *premature ejaculation*, which Masters and Johnson (1970) define as the male's inability to inhibit orgasm long enough for a partner to climax in at least 50 percent of his encounters. Women may experience *functional vaginismus*: During sexual excitement, they have involuntary muscle spasms in the outer part of the vagina and intercourse becomes impossible. It should be pointed out that such problems are probably quite common, and *DSM-III-R* considers them dysfunctions only if they are "recurrent and persistent." In addition, what is a problem for one person or couple may not necessarily be a problem for another. In order to evaluate possible dysfunctions, psychologists thus try to find out whether a problem has always existed or occurs only periodically, whether it occurs in all sexual situations or only in some, and whether it occurs in similar or different degrees during each stage of the sexual response cycle. Only in this way can an accurate assessment be made of the level of sexual distress that is being experienced (Shover et al., 1982).

Paraphilias Unconventional objects or situations that cause sexual arousal in some people.

Fetishism The reliance on nonhuman objects as the preferred or exclusive method of achieving sexual excitement.

Voyeurism The desire to watch others having sexual relations or to spy on nude people.

Exhibitionism The compulsion to expose one's genitals in public in order to achieve sexual arousal.

Transvestism Dressing in the clothing of the opposite sex to achieve sexual gratification.

Sadomasochism Obtaining sexual gratification from aggression.

Paraphilias

A second group of psychosexual disorders involves the use of unconventional sex objects or situations known as **paraphilias.** Most people have unconventional sexual fantasies at some time, and this fantasizing is often a healthy outlet that stimulates normal sexual enjoyment. The repeated use of nonhuman objects, however—a shoe, for instance, or a belt—as the preferred or exclusive method of achieving sexual excitement is considered a psychosexual disorder. It is known as **fetishism.** Fetishes often involve articles of clothing, and the fetish is frequently associated with someone a person was close to in childhood. Fetishists are usually men, and Nagler (1957) suggests that the fetishist's behavior reflects a fear of his masculine social role. The fetishist often steals the object that arouses him, and this behavior may represent an assertion of masculinity.

Other unconventional patterns of sexual behavior are **voyeurism,** watching other people have sex or spying on people who are nude in order to achieve arousal; **exhibitionism,** the compulsion to expose one's genitals in inappropriate situations in order to achieve sexual arousal; and **transvestism,** wearing clothes of the opposite sex for sexual excitement and gratification. Transvestism seems to be exclusively male behavior, and there is really no explanation for it. There is no evidence of any hormonal or genetic abnormality (Buhrich et al., 1979). One explanation is that childhood experience with cross-dressing may have been associated with sexual play and arousal. One sample of transvestites found that 78 percent were either married or formerly married (Prince & Bentler, 1972), and marital friction is one of the main reasons that transvestites seek therapy.

Sadomasochism ties sexual pleasure to aggression. To attain sexual gratification, sadists humiliate or physically harm their sex partners. Mas-

The Seattle shoe bandit displayed characteristics of *fetishism*—accosting women on the street, he stole one shoe from each. Here, police examine the collection of shoes eventually found in his apartment.

Pedophilia Desire to have sexual relations with children as the preferred or exclusive method of achieving sexual excitement.

Personality disorders Disorders in which inflexible and maladaptive ways of thinking and behaving cause distress and conflicts.

Schizoid personality disorder Disorder in which a person is withdrawn and lacks feelings for others.

ochists cannot enjoy sex without accompanying emotional or physical pain. As with sexual dysfunction, most psychologists see the choice of unconventional sexual objects as indicating fear of heterosexual intimacy.

Certainly one of the most serious paraphilias is **pedophilia,** which is technically defined as "the act or fantasy of engaging in sexual activity with prepubertal children" (APA, 1980, pp. 271–72). Child sexual abuse is not uncommon. Statistics indicate that approximately 88 percent of the victims of child sexual abuse are girls whose mean age is about $9\frac{1}{2}$ years (Jaffe, Dynaeson, & Tenbensel, 1975; Mohr, Turner, & Jerry, 1964). Between 20 percent of the men and 25 percent of the women in one study reported having had childhood sexual contact with an adult male (Herman & Hirschman, 1981).

Pedophiles are almost invariably men under the age of 40 (Makstein, McLaughlin, & Rogers, 1979). Most of them are known to the victims as relatives, friends, or acquaintances; they are often people to whom the child's care has been entrusted (Mohr et al., 1964). Although there is no single reason that accounts for pedophilia, some of the most common reasons are that pedophiles cannot adjust to the sexual role of an adult male and have been interested exclusively in children as sex objects since adolescence, that they turn to children as sexual objects in response to stress in adult relationships in which they feel inadequate, or that they have records of unstable social adjustment and generally commit sexual offenses against children in response to a temporary aggressive mood (Cohen, Seghorn, & Calmas, 1969; Fitch, 1962; Groth & Birnbaum, 1979). Studies also indicate that the majority of pedophiles have histories of sexual frustration and failure, tend to perceive themselves as immature, and tend to be dependent and unassertive.

■ Personality Disorders

In Chapter 12, we saw that a person's personality is his or her unique and enduring pattern of thoughts, feelings, and behavior. And we also saw that people normally have the ability to adjust their behavior to fit the needs of different situations, despite certain characteristic views of the world and ways of doing things. But some people develop inflexible and maladaptive ways of thinking and behaving that are so exaggerated and rigid that they cause serious distress and social problems. People with such **personality disorders** may range from the harmless eccentric to the cold-blooded killer. Recently, it has been estimated that at least half of those who seek help for a psychological problem show some evidence of a personality disorder.

One group of personality disorders is characterized by odd or eccentric behavior. For example, people who exhibit **schizoid personality disorder** lack the ability or desire to form social relationships and have no warm or tender feelings for others. Such loners cannot express their feelings and are perceived by others as cold, distant, and unfeeling. Moreover, they often appear vague, absentminded, indecisive, or "in a fog." Because their withdrawal is so complete, schizoids seldom marry and may have trouble holding jobs that require them to work with or relate to others (APA, 1980). For example:

A 36-year-old electrical engineer was "dragged" to a marital therapist by his wife because of his unwillingness to join in family activities, failure to take an interest in his children, lack of affection, and disinterest in sex. . . . The patient's history revealed long-standing social indifference, with only an occasional and brief friendship here and there (Spitzer et al., 1981, p. 66).

People with **paranoid personality disorder** also appear to be odd. They are suspicious and mistrustful even when there is no reason to be, and are hypersensitive to any possible threat or trick. They refuse to accept blame or criticism even when it is deserved. They are guarded, secretive, devious, scheming, and argumentative, although they often see themselves as rational and objective. In one case, for example, a construction worker began to get into disputes with his co-workers because he was afraid that they might let his scaffolding slip in order to kill or injure him. Upon examination by a psychologist, he thought that his examiner was "taking their side" against him (Spitzer et al., 1981, p. 37).

A second cluster of personality disorders is characterized by dramatic, emotional, or erratic behavior. For example, people with **narcissistic personality disorder** display nearly total self-absorption, a grandiose sense of self-importance, a preoccupation with fantasies of unlimited success, a need for constant attention and admiration, and an inability to love or really care for anyone else (APA, 1980). The word *narcissism* comes from a character in Greek mythology named Narcissus, who fell in love with his own reflection in a pool and pined away because he could not reach the beautiful face that he saw before him. For example, a male graduate student sought help because he was having difficulty completing his PhD dissertation. He bragged that his dissertation would revolutionize his field and make him famous—but he had not been able to write much of it yet. He blamed his academic adviser for his lack of progress, called his fellow students "drones," and stated that everyone was jealous of his brilliance. He had frequent brief relationships with women, but few lasting friendships (Spitzer et al., 1981). Although excess self-esteem would seem to be the prominent problem here, this may not be the case. Otto Kernberg observes that the self-esteem of the narcissistic person is really very fragile: "The pathological narcissist cannot sustain his or her self-regard without having it fed constantly by the attentions of others" (Wolfe, 1978, p. 55).

Many psychologists believe that narcissism begins early in life. While all infants tend to be narcissistic, most grow out of it. But for reasons that we do not yet understand, the narcissistic person never makes the change. Some social critics assert that certain tendencies in modern American society—such as our worship of youth and beauty and our disregard for old age—have contributed to an apparent boom in narcissistic personality disorders (Lasch, 1979). Clinical data, however, do not support this speculation. While acknowledging that our society stimulates narcissism, Kernberg argues that this cannot be the root of the disorder: "The most I would be willing to say is that society can make serious

Paranoid personality disorder Disorder in which a person is inappropriately suspicious and mistrustful of others.

Narcissistic personality disorder Disorder in which a person has an exaggerated sense of self-importance and needs constant admiration.

© 1987 S. Gross

psychological abnormalities, which already exist in some percentage of the population, seem to be at least superficially appropriate" (Wolfe, 1978, p. 59).

One of the most widely studied personality disorders is **antisocial personality disorder.** People who exhibit this disorder lie, steal, cheat, and show little or no sense of responsibility, although often they are intelligent and charming on first acquaintance. The "con man" exemplifies many of the features of the antisocial personality, as does the person who compulsively cheats his or her business partners because he or she knows their weak points. The antisocial personality rarely shows the slightest trace of anxiety or guilt over his or her behavior. Indeed, these people blame society or their victims for the antisocial actions that they themselves commit.

Unfortunately, antisocial personalities are often responsible for a good deal of crime and violence, as seen in this case history of an antisocial personality:

> Although intelligent, the subject was a poor student and was frequently accused of stealing from his schoolmates. At the age of 14, he stole a car, and at the age of 20, he was imprisoned for burglary. After he was released, he spent another two years in prison for drunk driving and then eleven years for a series of armed robberies.
>
> Released from prison yet one more time in 1976, he tried to hold

Borderline Personality Disorders

Currently, it is estimated that borderline personality disorders may afflict up to 5 percent of the United States population (Grinspoon, 1985). Although characteristic behavior varies widely, some general tendencies can be identified. Borderline individuals tend to exhibit instability in their self-images, their moods, and their interpersonal relationships. They experience uncertainty about such things as loyalties and career choices. They tend to act impulsively and often in self-destructive ways. They feel uncomfortable about being alone, and they often manipulate self-destructive impulses in an effort to control or solidify personal relationships. Such self-destructive behavior includes promiscuity, drug and alcohol abuse, and threats of suicide (Gunderson, 1984). Arkema (1981) reports the following case:

> Ms. C., a 22-year-old unemployed woman, had been assaulted by her boyfriend and had cut both her forearms. . . . [The couple] had been at a nightclub the previous evening. He felt she was dancing too seductively, they argued, and he slapped her in the face. She ran from the club, later cut both arms, became fearful something terrible would happen to her boyfriend, and spent the rest of the night looking for him, damaging her car in the process. . . . In the hospital, with much support, she appeared to understand the advisability of terminating the destructive relationship. As soon as she was free on a pass, however, she would become "desperate" and seek him out again. She observed, "If I have someone else right away I can do it; I can leave him. But it's the only way." (pp. 174–75)

Borderline personality disorders are both serious and common. At present, psychologists are able to say that more women suffer from these disorders than men and that they run in families (McGlashan, 1983; Loranger, Oldham, & Tulis, 1983). These disorders are often accompanied by depressive and bipolar disorders, and this overlapping has led some psychologists to question whether borderline personality disorders actually constitute a separate and distinguishable category (Pope et al., 1983). On the other hand, family studies show that relatives of people diagnosed as borderline individuals are much more likely to be treated for borderline disorders than for certain other types. This finding supports the position that borderline disorders are in fact a true category of affective disorders.

Like Gary Gilmore, Ted Bundy was a highly intelligent serial killer who, though he may have killed as many as 50 women, apparently felt no guilt or anxiety. When a witness for the prosecution pointed at the defendant, identifying him as the man she saw leaving her sorority house with a baseball bat on the night two women were murdered, he referred to himself in the third person, telling the jury, "That's Mr. Bundy."

down several jobs but succeeded at none of them. He moved in with a woman whom he had met one day earlier, but he drank heavily (a habit that he had picked up at age 10) and struck her children until she ordered him out of the house at gunpoint. On at least two occasions, he violated his parole but was not turned in by his parole officer. In July of 1976, he robbed a service station and shot the attendant twice in the head. He was apprehended in part because he accidentally shot himself during his escape. "It seems like things have always gone bad for me," he later said. "It seems like I've always done dumb things that just caused trouble for me" (Spitzer et al., 1983, p. 68).

Under psychiatric evaluation, he was found to have a superior IQ of 129 and a remarkably good store of general knowledge. He slept and ate well and exhibited no significant changes of mood. He admitted to having "made a mess of my life" but added that "I never stew about the things I have done."

The subject was named Gary Gilmore, and on January 17, 1977, he was the first person to be executed in the United States in 11 years. While awaiting an execution that was postponed several times, he became the subject of numerous news stories detailing his fight for his announced "right to be executed." He twice attempted suicide.

Perhaps 3 percent of American men and less than 1 percent of American women suffer from antisocial personality disorder. However, it is very difficult to make sound judgments about the prevalence of this disorder, because the only reliable laboratory setting so far has been prison. One study categorized 50 percent of the populations of two prisons as antisocial personalities (Hare, 1983), but other studies show that many of the most common criteria also apply to large numbers of people raised in economically deprived environments. One researcher placed the following advertisement in an underground Boston newspaper:

> WANTED: charming, aggressive, carefree people who are impulsively irresponsible but are good at handling people and at looking after Number One. Send name, address, phone, and short biography proving how interesting you are . . . (Widom, 1978, p. 72).

Of 73 respondents, about one-third seemed to satisfy the typical criteria for antisocial personality disorder. Widom was forced to conclude that about the only difference between prison samples and the people in her own study was the fact that her subjects had somehow avoided being apprehended by the police.

Not surprisingly, these same problems complicate efforts to explain antisocial behavior. Some psychologists feel that it is the result of emotional deprivation in early childhood. Respect for others is the basis of our social code, but if you cannot see things from the other person's perspective, rules about what you can and cannot do will seem to be only an assertion of adult power to be broken as soon as possible. The child for whom no one cares, say psychologists, cares for no one. The child whose problems no one identifies with can identify with no one else's problems.

Social learning theorists base their explanations on the nature of family influences. They reason that a person who has been rejected by one or both parents is not likely to develop adequate social skills and appropriate social behavior. They also point out the high incidence of antisocial behavior in people with an antisocial parent and suggest that antisocial behavior may in part be a result of modeling that parent's behavior (Robins, 1966).

Cognitive theorists emphasize the role of arrested moral development. For example, between the ages of about 7 and 11, all children are apt to respond to unjust treatment by behaving unjustly toward someone else who is vulnerable. At about age 13, however, they are better able to reason in abstract terms, and most children begin to think more in terms of fairness than vindictiveness. This seems to be especially true if new cognitive skills and moral concepts are reinforced by parents and peers (Berkowitz & Gibbs, 1983). From this standpoint, cognitive psychologists feel that antisocial behavior is the result of development arrested during the period at which children do not estimate the effects of their behavior on other people.

An entirely different perspective seeks the roots of antisocial personality disorder in biology. For example, there is some evidence that the impulsive and aggressive tendencies characteristic of antisocial behavior correlate with abnormalities in the brain (Hill, 1952). Impulsive violence and aggression have also been linked with abnormal levels of certain neurotransmitters (Virkkunen, 1983). Other findings suggest that heredity is a factor in the development of antisocial behavior (Bonham et al., 1982; Hutchings & Mednick, 1977). Although none of this research is definitive, it does suggest that some antisocial personalities may be victims of their nervous systems as much as of their upbringings—an explanation that we have seen repeatedly throughout this chapter.

▮ Schizophrenic Disorders

It is a common misconception that schizophrenia means split personality. This is not the case at all. The disorder commonly meant by the term *split personality* is actually multiple personality disorder, which, as we have seen, is a dissociative disorder. The misunderstanding comes from the fact that the root *schizo-* comes from the Greek verb meaning to split.

But what is split in schizophrenia is not so much the personality as the mind itself.

Schizophrenic disorders are marked by disordered thought and communication, inappropriate emotions, and bizarre behavior that lasts for months. Schizophrenics are out of touch with reality. They often suffer from **hallucinations** (false sensory perceptions) which most often take the form of hearing voices—although some schizophrenics experience visual, tactile, or olfactory hallucinations. Schizophrenics usually have **delusions** (false beliefs about reality with no factual basis) that distort their relationships with their surroundings and with other people. They may think that a doctor wishes to kill them or that they are receiving radio messages from outer space. They often regard their own bodies—as well as the outside world—as hostile and alien. Because their world is utterly different from the one most people live in, they usually cannot live anything like a normal life. Often, they are unable to communicate with others, for when they speak, their words are a total confusion. (See Table 14-2 for the *DSM-III-R* criteria for schizophrenia.)

The following case illustrates some of schizophrenia's characteristic features:

> [The patient is a 35-year-old widow.] For many years she has heard voices, which insult her and cast suspicion on her chastity. . . . The voices are very distinct, and in her opinion, they must be carried by a telescope or a machine from her home. Her thoughts are dictated to her; she is obliged to think them, and hears them repeated after her. She . . . has all kinds of uncomfortable sensations in her body, to which something is "done." In particular, her "mother parts" are turned inside out, and people send a pain through her back, lay ice-water on her heart, squeeze her neck, injure her spine, and violate her. There are also hallucinations of sight—black figures and the altered appearance of people—but these are far less frequent . . . (Spitzer et al., 1981, pp. 308–9).

There are actually several kinds of schizophrenic disorders, which differ from one another in terms of characteristic symptoms.

Disorganized schizophrenia includes some of the more bizarre symptoms, such as giggling, grimacing, and frantic gesturing. People suffering from disorganized schizophrenia show a childish disregard for social conventions and may urinate or defecate at inappropriate times. They are active but aimless, and they are often given to incoherent conversations.

The primary feature of **catatonic schizophrenia** is a severe disturbance of motor activity. People in this state may remain immobile, mute, and impassive. At the opposite extreme, they become excessively excited, talking and shouting continuously. They may behave in a robot-like fashion when ordered to move, and some have even let doctors mold their arms and legs into strange and uncomfortable positions that they then can maintain for hours.

Paranoid schizophrenia is marked by extreme suspiciousness and quite complex delusions. Paranoid schizophrenics may believe themselves to be Napoleon or the Virgin Mary or may insist that Russian spies with laser guns are constantly on their trail because they have learned some great secret. These people may actually appear more "normal" than other schizophrenics if their delusions are compatible with everyday life; they are less likely to be incoherent or to look or act "crazy." However, they

Schizophrenic disorders Disorders in which there are disturbances of thoughts, communication, and emotions, including delusions and hallucinations.

Hallucinations Sensory experiences in the absence of external stimulation.

Delusions False beliefs about reality with no basis in fact.

Disorganized schizophrenia Type of schizophrenia in which bizarre and childlike behaviors are common.

Catatonic schizophrenia Type of schizophrenia in which disturbed motor behavior is prominent.

Paranoid schizophrenia Type of schizophrenia characterized by extreme suspiciousness and complex, bizarre delusions.

"Doctor, this is Mr. Gusset. Mr. Gusset thinks he's the Empire State Building."
© 1987 S. Gross

Undifferentiated schizophrenia Type of schizophrenia in which there are clear schizophrenic symptoms that don't meet the criteria for another type.

TABLE 14-2 THE DSM-III-R CRITERIA FOR SCHIZOPHRENIA

A. Active phase: At least one of these categories of behavior must occur for at least two weeks:
1. At least two of the following:
   a. Delusions
   b. Hallucinations lasting more than a brief time that may occur through the day for several days or several times a week for several weeks
   c. Incoherent thinking or a marked loosening of associations
   d. Catatonic behavior (a disturbance in motor behavior in which the person may "freeze" into an apparently uncomfortable pose or become extremely overactive)
   e. Lack of changes in affect or grossly inappropriate affect
2. Bizarre delusions such as thought broadcasting or mind control
3. Prominent auditory hallucinations, such as hearing a voice that keeps up a running commentary on one's behavior, or hearing two or more voices talking to each other

B. Level of functioning in work, social relations, and self-care is clearly below the highest level achieved in the past. If the individual is a child, the level of social functioning does not meet that expected for his or her age group.

C. If severe depression or manic behavior is present, it occurred relatively briefly.

D. There must be continuous signs of illness for six months, including at least two weeks of psychotic symptoms. This period may include phases both before and after the psychotic period and in each case must include at least two of the following behaviors:
1. Marked social isolation or withdrawal
2. Marked impairment in functioning at work or in school
3. Markedly peculiar behavior, for example, collecting garbage or talking to oneself in public
4. Impaired personal hygiene and grooming
5. Blunted, flat, or inappropriate emotional expression
6. Digressive, vague, overelaborate, or circumstantial speech, or poverty of speech or speech content
7. Odd or bizarre ideation or magical thinking, for example, being able to see the future, having a sixth sense, believing that "others can feel my feelings"
8. Unusual perceptual experiences, for example, sensing the presence of a force or person not actually present
9. Apathy or lack of initiative

E. Not due to any organic mental disorder

F. If there is a history of autistic disorder, prominent delusions or hallucinations must also be present before a schizophrenic disorder can be diagnosed.

Table 14-2

Adapted with permission from the *Diagnostic and Statistical Manual of Mental Disorders, Third Edition, Revised.* Copyright © 1987 American Psychiatric Association.

---

may become hostile or aggressive toward anyone who questions their thinking or tries to contradict their delusions (Sarason & Sarason, 1989).

Finally, **undifferentiated schizophrenia** refers to those people who have several of the characteristic symptoms of schizophrenia, such as delusions, hallucinations, or incoherence, yet do not show the typical symptoms of any other subtype.

Since schizophrenia is a very serious disorder, considerable research has been directed at trying to discover its causes. As we saw in Chapter 2, it is now clear from a wide range of studies that there is some genetic

Schizophrenics often suffer from *hallucinations*, false sensory perceptions that can be aural as well as visual. This woman hears voices accusing her of horrific crimes that she has not committed.

component to schizophrenia. People who are schizophrenic are more likely than other people to have schizophrenic children, even when those children have lived with foster parents since birth (Heston, 1966). And if an identical twin becomes schizophrenic, the chances are about 50 percent that the other twin will also become schizophrenic; but if a fraternal twin becomes schizophrenic, the chances are only about 10 percent that the other twin will also become schizophrenic (Rosenthal, 1970). But note that even with identical twins, who are genetically exactly the same, half of the twins of schizophrenics do not themselves become schizophrenic.

These studies and others indicate that some kind of biological predisposition to schizophrenia is inherited (McGuffin, Reveley, Holland, 1982; Zerbin-Rüdin, 1972). Recent research suggests that the problem may lie in excess amounts of *dopamine* in the central nervous system. Drugs that alleviate schizophrenic symptoms also decrease the amount of dopamine in the brain and block dopamine receptors. On the other hand, amphetamines increase the amount of dopamine in the brain, increase the severity of schizophrenic symptoms, and if taken in excess lead to what is called amphetamine psychosis, which is very similar to schizophrenia.

However, research indicates that many people who are genetically vulnerable to schizophrenia do not become schizophrenic. Environmental factors—in particular, disturbed family relations—are also involved in determining whether a person will become schizophrenic. McGuffin,

Reveley, and Holland (1982) reported on a set of identical triplets who all suffered from chronic psychotic disorders. But while two brothers had clear and severe schizophrenic symptoms and were unable to function between psychotic periods, the third brother was able to function at a higher level and hold down a job between periods. His IQ was higher and his relationship with his family less troubled. Environment and experience can increase or decrease the effects of any inherited tendency, and the result is often a significant difference between two individuals' levels of functioning.

Along these same lines, a number of studies have demonstrated a relationship between social class and schizophrenia (Hollingshead & Redlich, 1958). In general, the incidence of schizophrenia is decidedly higher in the lower class than in other social classes. One theory holds that the lower-class socioeconomic environment, offering little education, opportunity, or reward, is a cause of schizophrenia; another holds that the motivational and cognitive impairments suffered by schizophrenics subject them to a downward social drift into lower classes. There appears to be some truth to both theories, but no causal link has been firmly established.

Similarly, some psychologists regard family relationships as a factor in the development of schizophrenia. The evidence in support of this position is mixed. It is true that schizophrenics experience more parental conflicts than other people, and communication between their parents is inferior to that of parents of nonschizophrenics (Fontana, 1966). And one study found that communication problems between parents themselves was an effective predictor of schizophrenia in their children (Goldstein & Rodnick, 1975). And it is clear that families have a significant impact on patients' adjustment after they leave the hospital (Leff, 1976). It is much less clear exactly how all of these family factors combine with biological predispositions so that some people but not others experience schizophrenia. That is the continuing challenge of research not only into schizophrenic disorders but into all other forms of abnormal behavior.

Although quite different in emphasis, the various views of schizophrenic disorders are by no means mutually exclusive. Many theorists believe that a combination of some or all of these factors produces schizophrenia, and in practice, many psychologists use a combination of drugs and therapy to treat schizophrenia. Most psychologists consider the diathesis-stress model to be the most useful theory for further research into the causes of schizophrenia. Genetic factors predispose some people to schizophrenia, and stress activates the predisposition. Unfortunately, the exact sources of stress have not yet been pinned down.

Estimated prevalence of major maladaptive behavior patterns in the United States in 1984

1,672,000 cases of schizophrenia
946,000 cases of major affective disorder
13,090,000 cases of anxiety-based disorders
9,218,000 cases of personality disorder
31,020,000 cases of "functional" mental disorder
60,500,000 cases of uncomplicated "demoralization"

■ Gender Differences in Abnormal Behavior

Throughout this chapter, we have proceeded as though men and women are similar with respect to mental disorders. In fact, however, there are substantial differences between men and women in terms of abnormal behavior. Many studies show that women (especially women 25 to 45 years old and minority women) have a higher rate of psychological disorders than men. There are also differences in the kinds of disorders men and women experience: Women are much more likely to suffer from anxiety disorders and depression, while men are more likely to suffer from substance use disorders and from antisocial personality disorder (Russo, 1985; Basow, 1986; Cleary, 1987).

What do these differences mean? Are women perhaps genetically more vulnerable to psychological disorders than men? The evidence suggests that this is not the case. First, there are no significant sex differences in those disorders (bipolar disorder, schizophrenia) for which a genetic basis has been most clearly demonstrated (Basow, 1986). Second, during childhood, boys are much more likely than girls to experience mental disorders (Basow, 1986). Third, during adulthood, divorced women, widowed women, and women who never married all have lower rates of mental illness than comparable groups of men.

Thus, there is no evidence that women are genetically more susceptible to mental illness than men. How, then, can we account for the fact that married women have higher rates of mental illness than married men? First, it is important to realize that for both men and women, marriage reduces the likelihood of psychological disorder: Married women are much less likely to experience psychological problems than are single women, and the same is true for men (see Table 14-3). But the same data also show that marriage is less beneficial for women than it is for men (Russo, 1985; Basow, 1986; Cleary, 1987). Therefore, while men benefit psychologically from marriage, women benefit less; the result is a higher prevalence of psychological disorders and higher rates of admission to mental health facilities among married women than among married men (Carmen et al., 1981; Russo & Sobel, 1981; Cleary, 1987).

What accounts for these differences? For women, marriage, family relationships, reproduction, and childrearing are likely to be more stressful than they are for men (Russo, 1985; Basow, 1986). In addition, women are more likely than men to be the victims of incest, rape, and marital violence. In other words, while marriage and family life provide a refuge for both men and women, women tend to find the experience of marriage and family more stressful than do men. Interestingly, recent research indicates that for some married women, employment outside the home can provide the kind of refuge that family life provides for many men. In particular, employment can provide "stimulation, self-esteem, adult

Table 14-3

TABLE 14-3 RATE OF RESIDENCY IN MENTAL HOSPITALS AS A FUNCTION OF MARITAL STATUS (Persons per 100,000), 1975			
	Men	Women	Men/Women
Married	672.1	1101.6	0.61
Divorced	5318.8	4690.7	1.13
Widowed	1095.7	925.7	1.18
Never married	1937.5	1500.0	1.29
Adapted from Rosenstein and Milazzo-Sayre, 1981, Table 1.			

contacts, escape from the repetitive routines of housework and child care, and a buffer against stress from family roles" (Hoffman, 1989, p. 284), though these benefits are likely to accrue only to the extent that the woman freely chooses to work, has a satisfying job, receives support from her family and friends, and is able to set up stable childcare arrangements (Basow, 1986; Hoffman, 1989).

To compound the problem, as we saw in Chapter 13, the effects of stress are greater to the extent that a person feels alienated, powerless, and helpless. These factors are more prevalent in women than in men. They are especially prevalent among minority women, and indeed the prevalence of psychological disorders is greater among minority women than among nonminority women (Russo & Sobel, 1981). And these factors play an especially important role in anxiety disorders and depressive disorders—precisely those disorders experienced most often by women (Carmen et al., 1981).

Therefore, the best account of sex differences in psychological disorders seems to be that women are generally less disturbed than men under most conditions, but they do not benefit as much as men from marriage and family life. Confronted by the normal stresses of marriage and family living, and feeling relatively alienated and powerless, married women are more likely to experience psychological problems, especially during the childrearing years (25 to 45).

 APPLICATION

Mental Illness and the Law

When David Berkowitz, better known as "Son of Sam," was arrested in New York in August 1977, he was taken into custody by a cordon of some 30 police officers wearing bulletproof vests and carrying shotguns. Public emotions were running high. Berkowitz was suspected of murdering six young people and wounding seven others in a killing spree that had attracted headlines around the world. Berkowitz explained that he was part of an army led by someone he called General Jack Cosmo. The army was made up largely of "demon dogs" that roamed the world telling people to kill. Periodically, when Berkowitz was out driving around at night, he would hear orders to kill, and when he followed those orders, the demon dogs would "move in and feast."

Two court-appointed psychiatrists decided that Berkowitz was not fit to stand trial. But the psychiatrist appointed by the prosecutor's office later declared that Berkowitz could understand the proceedings against him and assist in his own defense, and the judge agreed with him. Within two weeks of being found competent to stand trial, Berkowitz entered a plea of guilty over the strong objections of his attorneys. Thus, the question of his insanity at the time of the murders was never considered by the courts, and he is now serving a 365-year sentence in Attica prison in New York State.

Two quite separate questions were raised in the Berkowitz case: Was he competent to stand trial? And was he insane at the time of the killings? "Competence to stand trial" means that at the time of the trial (often months or years after the crime was committed), the defendant has a reasonable understanding of the proceedings, can make decisions, and offer testimony, and understands the charges, pleas, and penalties. If an accused person is found unfit to stand trial, he or she is usually sent to a mental hospital until psychiatrists and the judge agree that the defendant is competent to return to the courtroom. In some cases, this means never. In fact, it is possible for an accused person to be sentenced (in effect) to spend the rest of his or her life in an institution without ever being found guilty of a crime!

If at some point the person is declared competent to stand trial, then the court must determine whether he or she was insane at the time of the crime. The following rule is used by most courts to determine insanity: A person is not responsible for criminal conduct if, at the time of such conduct, as a result of mental disease or defect, he or she lacks substantial capacity either to appreciate the criminality (wrongfulness) of his or her conduct or to conform to the requirements of law.

The court ruled that Berkowitz was in fact competent to stand trial, but in order to rule on his insanity, the court would have had to decide whether at the time of the killings Berkowitz understood that what he was doing was wrong and that he was "substantially in control" of his behavior. If the answer to *either* of these questions had been no, then he would have been declared legally insane at the time that he committed the crimes and been hospitalized until he no longer represented a threat to society, at which point he would have been released as a free man. In the case of John W. Hinckley, who pleaded insanity to the charge of trying to assassinate President Ronald Reagan, the jury found that the prosecution had failed to prove Hinckley *sane* when he committed the act. To some people, this is a rather roundabout way of saying that Hinckley was *insane* at the time of the assassination attempt, and the decision remains controversial.

The insanity plea is quite rare: It arises in less than 1 percent of serious criminal cases, according to most estimates (*U.S. News & World Report*, May 7, 1979, p. 42). But it is extremely controversial for many different reasons. Since criminals who are declared legally insane are not subject to punishment for their actions, the court system relies heavily on the advice and testimony of forensic psychologists and psychiatrists, who help determine the mental state of suspects both at the time of the crime and at the time of the trial. These experts also help in deciding questions about rehabilitation, parole, or fitness to stand trial at a later date (Robitscher & Williams, 1977). The influence of these experts on the outcome of court cases is increasingly controversial.

David Berkowitz, New York's "Son of Sam" killer

How large a part, if any, should these mental health experts play in deciding the fate of people who have violated the law? Some, like the well-known psychiatrist Thomas Szasz, feel that psychiatrists and psychologists should stay out of the legal arena altogether. He points to the danger of a "therapeutic state," in which dependence on psychiatric opinion might lead to a massive loss of personal liberties. Other critics are concerned that psychiatrists and psychologists are under pressure to testify as defense or prosecution attorneys want them to. At the other extreme, psychiatrist Bernard Diamond feels that psychiatry and psychology should play a larger role in the judicial process and in some cases even determine guilt. He believes that forensic psychiatry is an important way to educate the public, reform the law, and change social attitudes toward mental illness. In the middle of this dispute lies a skeptical public, which may distrust psychological jargon and feel that psychiatrists and psychologists "let off" dangerous criminals who pose a continuing threat to the community. In fact, the evidence suggests that forensic experts have compiled a poor record on being able to predict who will be dangerous in the future (Tierney, 1982). Trial lawyer F. Lee Bailey claims that jurors often say, "I know this guy is nuts, but we're not going to put him in some institution where some psychiatrist can let him out" (*Newsweek*, August 29, 1977, p. 28). And still other mental health experts, like Karl Menninger, believe that psychiatrists should stay out of the courtroom, but should be consulted after the trial on such matters as length of sentence, rehabilitation methods, and parole (Robitscher & Williams, 1977).

Other critics claim that clever defendants can fool the experts and, in some cases, be set free to commit additional crimes. Thomas Vanda, a Chicago man acquitted in 1975 after stabbing a teenage girl, later advised a fellow inmate to "act crazy" in front of psychiatrists. When Vanda offered this advice, it was in 1979—when he was back in jail, charged with stab-

bing another young woman. And once again, he was pleading insanity.

Other critics of forensic psychiatry argue from the opposite point of view—the defendant's. It is almost impossible for someone to get a fair trial, they say, once he or she has been hospitalized as "incompetent." And, according to these critics, confinement in a mental hospital is in many respects more punitive and restrictive than being sent to prison (Brooks, 1974).

■ Summary

- **What is the difference between someone who is simply eccentric and someone who exhibits abnormal behavior?** The distinctions between normal and abnormal behavior are unclear. Four criteria that are widely used to distinguish normal from abnormal behavior are: a distorted perception of reality, inappropriate behavior, discomfort, and danger to oneself or to others.

- Various approaches have been taken to explain and treat abnormal behavior over the centuries. Primitive societies probably attributed it to supernatural causes. The ancient Greeks looked for natural causes and treated disturbed people, like those with physical illnesses, with care and sympathy. In the Middle Ages, abnormal behavior was considered a sign of possession by the devil, punishable by exorcism and even physical torture. This period also saw the rise of asylums for the confinement of the mentally ill. Reform efforts began in the late eighteenth century, in both Europe and America, to turn asylums into appropriately staffed hospitals for the mentally ill. The pioneering efforts of Fournier in the late nineteenth century redirected attention to the search for medical cures for all forms of abnormal behavior.

- Today, several models of mental disorder coexist. Most important among these are the *psychoanalytic model,* which sees abnormal behavior as the result of unconscious conflict left over from childhood; the *behavioral model,* which holds that abnormal behaviors are due to faulty learning; the *cognitive model,* which understands abnormal behavior as the result of internal processes that play an important role in learned behavior; and the *biological model,* which holds that abnormal behavior is caused at least in part by hereditary factors and malfunctioning of the nervous system and the endocrine system. Fi-

nally, the *diathesis-stress model* holds that some people are biologically more vulnerable to certain kinds of stress than are other people.

- **Physicians make diagnoses by looking at a person's physical symptoms. How are mental disorders diagnosed?** Abnormal behavior is classified and diagnosed according to an official *Diagnostic and Statistical Manual of Mental Disorders* of the American Psychiatric Association. The current manual, *DSM-III-R,* was published in 1980 and revised in 1986. The manual attempts to classify abnormal behavior according to objective behavioral symptoms, while remaining silent as to the *cause* of a disorder. This classificatory scheme does have some critics, who object to classifying behavioral disorders as diseases and then publishing the classifications in a medically oriented handbook; others claim that several behaviors have no medical relevance, should be considered relatively normal reactions to particular life situations, and should be treated by psychologists rather than medical doctors.

- **Why would someone wash their hands every time they touch something or check the front door of their house again and again to make sure that it is locked?** *Anxiety disorders* are those in which *anxiety* is either a prominent feature or in which abnormal behavior seems prompted by a need to avoid anxiety. These include *panic attacks,* abrupt feelings of intense fear or terror for no apparent reason; *posttraumatic stress disorder,* in which spells of anxiety are related to a disturbing event in the past; *obsessive-compulsive disorder,* in which a person feels compelled to think disturbing thoughts and/or perform irrational actions to avoid anxiety; and *phobic disorder,* in which anxiety is provoked by a definite (and apparently harmless) stimulus.

- Psychoanalytic theorists think that anxiety disorders are largely the result of threatening unconscious conflicts. A person attempts to avoid anxiety by engaging in behavior that creates the temporary illusion of being in control. Behavior theorists, on the other hand, believe that anxiety results from the learned association of fear with earlier situations that may or may not have been harmful. Cognitive psychologists hold that the belief that one is not in control of one's life is central to all forms of anxiety and point out that if people believe that they have control over their lives, they experience less anxiety than if they believe that they have little or no control. Psychologists working from the biological perspective point out that the activity of the autonomic nervous system is involved in all kinds of fear and suggest that the predisposition to anxiety disorders may be inherited.

- *Somatoform disorders* involve physical symptoms of disease with no apparent organic cause. These include *somatization disorders,* which are characterized by recurring vague physical symptoms such as aches, pains, and dizziness; *conversion disorders* (once known as hysteria), in which a dramatic physical disability, such as blindness or paralysis, seems related to psychological needs; and *hypochondriasis,* in which a person who has no real disease symptoms nevertheless feels certain that he or she is ill.

- **Can a psychological problem lead to *real* physical disorders, or are such physical ailments always psychosomatic?** *Psychophysiological disorders* are *real* physical disorders, such as migraine headaches, ulcers, or asthma, that seem to have psychological causes. Psychological stress can lead to physical illness because it causes people's bodies to work harder in order to cope. Modern medicine has begun to accept the idea that many physical ailments are to some extent psychophysiological, because stress and anxiety can alter body chemistry and the functioning of bodily organs. Conversely, the experience of physical illness can in turn have adverse emotional effects, such as anxiety and depression.

- *Dissociative disorders* are those in which a person's personality seems fragmented. These disorders include *amnesia,* or loss of memory; *multiple personality disorder,* in which more than a single personality seems present in one person; and *depersonalization disorder,* in which a person experiences feelings of unreality and loss of control over the body.

- **Most people feel depressed from time to time. Are these feelings of depression the same as those experienced by people who are treated for depression?** *Affective disorders* are those characterized by disturbances in *affect,* or emotional state. The most common is *depression,* in which a person feels sad, apathetic, and self-reproachful. Its apparent opposite is *mania,* in which a person feels overly excited and hyperactive. Mania may actually be a defense against the depressed state. In *bipolar disorder* the person alternates between periods of mania and periods of depression. Only when depression is serious, lasting, and seemingly unrelated to any stressful life event can it be classified as an affective disorder.

- Most psychologists believe that the key to understanding affective disorders lies in understanding depression. Psychoanalysts, in the tradition of Freud, have viewed depression as excessive and irrational grief, usually over the real or imagined loss of a parent; the individual feels deserted and may eventually turn his or her anger and resentment inward. Behaviorists hold that there is a direct connection between depression and lack of reinforcement; they argue that people with ineffective social skills receive little positive reinforcement from others and may thus exhibit the form of passive behavior that characterizes depression. Cognitive psychologists also believe that, at least in part, depression is learned behavior, but they place more emphasis on the thought processes that the individual has developed as a result of his or her experience. Theorists working from the biological perspective point out evidence for the role of genetic factors in depression; they emphasize the possibility that a biological defect makes some people more likely to become depressed than others.

- *Sexual dysfunction* consists of an inability to function effectively during sex. In men this may mean *impotence,* the inability to achieve or keep an erection. In women it may mean *frigidity,* the inability to become sexually excited or reach orgasm. Other sexual disorders include *paraphilias,* which involve the use of unconventional sex objects. Among these are *fetishism,* the use of nonhuman objects *exhibitionism,* the compulsion to expose one's genitals to others inappropriately *transvestism,* the urge to wear the clothes of the opposite sex *sadomasochism,* the linking of sexual pleasure and pain; and *pedophilia,* the act or fantasy of engaging in sex with young children.

- **What is a personality disorder?** *Personality disorders* involve certain inflexible and maladaptive patterns of behavior that cause a person distress and conflict with society. Among them are *schizoid personality disorder,* in which a person is withdrawn and distant from any social relationships *paranoid personality disorder,* in which a person is unrealistically suspicious and mistrustful of others; and *narcissistic personality disorder,* in which a person is self-absorbed and unable to form normal emotional ties to others. The most serious personality disorder—at least in its effects on society—is *antisocial personality disorder,* which involves a pattern of violent, criminal, or unethical and exploitative behavior together with no affectionate feelings for other people. Some psychologists feel that antisocial behavior results from emotional deprivation in childhood. Social learning theorists point out family influences, reasoning that a person who has been rejected by one or both parents is less likely to develop appropriate social behavior. Cognitive theorists emphasize the role of moral development, observing that moral adjustment is more likely when new moral concepts are reinforced by parents and peers. Others seek its basis in physiological impairment, such as a malfunction in the brain region that inhibits behavior.

- **Can environmental stresses, such as poor living conditions and economic hardship, contribute to the onset of some mental disorders?** *Schizophrenic disorders* are the most serious mental disturbances, involving a disintegration of the personality and disturbances in thought, communication, and emotions. *Delusions* (mistaken beliefs about reality) and *hallucinations* (false sense perceptions) are characteristic features. There are several subtypes of schizophrenia. These include *disorganized schizophrenia,* in which bizarre and childlike behaviors are common *catatonic schizophrenia,* in which disturbed motor behavior is most characteristic and prominent *paranoid schizophrenia,* in which there are extreme suspiciousness and bizarre delusions, especially delusions of grandeur; and *undifferentiated schizophrenia,* in which a person shows several schizophrenic symptoms without fitting into one of the above categories. Schizophrenic disorders are serious and disabling, although they can sometimes be controlled by drugs so that the person can lead a more nearly normal life. Both biological and social factors seem to play a role in the development of schizophrenia; there seems to be a hereditary component to the disorder, but environmental stresses, such as economic hardship, also seem to play a part.

- There are significant **gender differences** in psychological disorders. Boys and single adult males are more likely than girls and single adult females to experience psychological disorders. But married females (especially those 25 to 45 years of age and minority women) are more likely than comparable married males to experience disorders. Moreover, while men are more likely than women to suffer from substance use disorders and antisocial personality disorder, women are more likely to suffer from anxiety disorders and depression. The explanation for these differences seems to be that marriage is less beneficial for women than it is for men, and that women traditionally have felt more alienated, powerless, and helpless than men.

▪ Review Questions

1. Using four major criteria, psychologists can readily distinguish abnormal from normal behavior.   T / F
2. Match the model of abnormal behavior with the appropriate explanation or approach:

____ cognitive
____ psychoanalytical
____ biological
____ behavioral

   A. Behavior disorders are symbolic expressions of unconscious internal conflicts.

   B. Abnormal behavior is caused at least in part by hereditary factors as well as malfunctioning of the nervous system and the endocrine glands.

   C. Abnormal behavior is the result of learning and can be unlearned.

   D. Abnormal behavior is best understood as the result of faulty thought processes.

3. *DSM-III-R,* the classification system for mental illness, was developed by
   a. psychologists.
   b. physicians.
   c. the federal government.
4. Panic attacks, phobias, and obsessive-compulsive disorder are three examples of _____ disorders.

5. A feeling of fear of losing control that happens without an obvious cause is characteristic of _____ :
   a. panic attacks.
   b. postraumatic stress disorder.
6. In cases of _____ , a person feels recurring, vague physical symptoms that cannot be linked to any organic cause.
   a. somatization disorder
   b. hypochondriasis
7. A psychophysiological disorder involves a real physical symptom with a psychological cause.   T / F
8. Multiple personality and depersonalization disorder are two types of _____ disorders, characterized by signs of fragmented personality.
   a. personality
   b. dissociative
9. _____ disorders are those characterized by disturbances in emotional state.
   a. affective
   b. dissociative
10. One theory about depression is that it is a form of self-punishment.   T / F
11. An affective disorder involving swings between mania and depression is known as _____ disorder.
12. Match the following terms with their correct definitions:

____ sexual dysfunction   A. inappropriate exposure of one's genitals in public
____ paraphilias
____ fetishism   B. sexual gratification derived from inanimate objects
____ pedophilia
____ exhibitionism   C. inability to function effectively during sex
____ sadomasochism
   D. disorders involving the use of unconventional sex objects or situations
   E. sexual pleasure tied to aggression
   F. desire for sexual relations with children

13. Match the following personality disorders with their correct definition:

____ schizoid personality disorder   A. characterized by extreme suspicion and mistrust of others
____ paranoid personality disorder   B. marked by a pattern of criminal or exploitative behavior
____ narcissistic personality disorder   C. characterized by withdrawal from social contact and lack of feeling for others
____ antisocial personality disorder   D. marked by extreme self-absorption and need for admiration

14. Delusions, hallucinations, and disordered thought are symptomatic of _____ disorders.

15 Therapies

■ Thinking Critically

What is free association?

Are therapists basically silent observers who listen to their patients talk?

Can people be taught new ways of behaving, much the same way they are taught anything else?

If a person's problems stem from relationships within the family, can a therapist work with the whole family to deal with those problems?

How effective is psychotherapy?

Is electroconvulsive or shock therapy still used?

Why are there so many mentally disturbed people living on city streets?

What can be done to prevent mental illness?

Are women more likely than men to be mentally disturbed?

The answers to these and other questions about therapy appear in this chapter and in the Chapter Summary.

■ Outline

To many people, the term **psychotherapy** still evokes an image of a psychologist or psychiatrist sitting silently in a chair while a client, reclining on a nearby couch, recounts traumatic events in his or her life. As the anxious client reveals dreams, fantasies, fears, and obsessions, the therapist nods, scribbles a few words in a notebook, and perhaps asks a question or two. The therapist rarely offers the client advice and never reveals details of his or her own personal life.

This cliché of psychotherapy has some truth to it—scenes like this one do occur. But there are many other forms of psychotherapy. And while some therapies have much in common, others bear little or no resemblance to one another.

Despite its prevalence in our society, relatively few people know what psychotherapy is or what to think about it. Some consider it a disgrace to be in therapy. Others see it as self-indulgent because they believe that people should work out their problems on their own. Asking for help—and paying for it—seem to them signs of a weak character. Surprisingly too, psychotherapy is as controversial among psychologists as it is among laypeople. Many experimentally oriented psychologists look on therapy as a vague and poorly defined art. They maintain that, in a practical sense, it is impossible to measure the effectiveness of one treatment as opposed to another. Many other psychologists feel differently and suggest that particular therapies may be better suited to certain kinds of people and problems.

Although there are many forms of psychotherapy to choose from, most therapists today do not adhere strictly to one technique; rather, they borrow from several to meet the needs of their clients. In this chapter, we will survey the various therapies used in private practice and in institutions and describe some recent developments. We will explore the effectiveness of different psychotherapies in treating psychological disorders. Finally, we will look at the traditional treatment of severe emotional disturbance and consider some alternatives.

■ Insight Therapies

A variety of therapies used in both private practice and institutions fall under the heading of **insight therapy.** While insight therapies differ from one another in orientation and technique, their main goal is to give people a better understanding and awareness of their feelings, motivations, and actions. In this section, we will consider the major insight therapies as well as some recent developments in the area.

Psychoanalysis

Psychoanalysis, the classic approach to psychotherapy, is based on the belief that the anxiety and problems that cause a person to seek help are symptoms of repressed problems from childhood. Usually, these problems concern aggressive or sexual drives that the child thought were dangerous or forbidden. Psychoanalysis reverses this process and brings these repressed feelings to consciousness, so that the person can deal with them more effectively.

Successful psychoanalysis depends on two conditions. First, the person must not inhibit or control thoughts and fantasies. Slips-of-the-tongue and associations between seemingly unrelated thoughts are clues to underlying problems. The procedure for bringing underlying thoughts or feelings to the surface of consciousness is called **free association** (see Figure 15-1). Second, the analyst must remain completely neutral and mostly silent. Usually, the client lies on a couch, and the analyst sits behind him or her so that the analyst cannot be easily seen. The analyst's silence becomes a blank screen on which the client projects feelings that might otherwise be suppressed.

Analysis typically proceeds in stages. After the initial awkwardness wears off, most people enjoy the chance to talk without interruption and like having someone interested in their problems. After a few sessions, they may test their analysts by talking about desires and fantasies that they have never revealed before. When they discover that their analysts are not shocked or disgusted, clients are reassured and see their analysts as warm and accepting. At this point, many people feel that they are getting better and express confidence in their analysts' ability to help them. Because people will often carry over to their analysts feelings that

Free association In psychoanalysis, the uninhibited disclosure of thoughts and fantasies as they occur to the client.

Figure 15-1
An artist's conception of free association. You can see how each figure seems to grow out of the one before it.
Picture Collection, the Branch Libraries, New York Public Library

The consulting room where Freud met his clients Note the position of Freud's chair at the head of the couch. In order to encourage *free association*, the psychoanalyst is not easily seen and functions as a blank screen onto which the client can project his or her feelings.

Positive transference Development of warm feelings toward one's therapist.

Negative transference Displacement of hostility felt for a parent or other authority figure to one's therapist.

Insight An awareness of how and why we feel and act as we do.

they have about other figures from their experience, this process is known as *transference*. When the client feels good about the analyst, the process is called **positive transference.**

This euphoria gradually wears off. As people expose their innermost feelings, they experience a terrible vulnerability. They want reassurance and affection, but their analysts remain silent. Their anxiety builds. Threatened by their analysts' silence and by their own thoughts, clients may feel cheated and accuse their analysts of being money-grabbers. Or they may feel that their analysts are really disgusted by their disclosures or are laughing about them behind their backs. This **negative transference** is a crucial step, for it reveals people's negative feelings about authority figures and their resistance to uncovering repressed emotions.

At this point in therapy, analysts begin to interpret their clients' feelings. The goal of interpretation is **insight:** People must see why they feel and act as they do and how their present state of mind relates to childhood experiences. Analysts encourage clients to confront events that they have only mentioned briefly and to recall them fully. In this way, they help their clients to relive their childhood traumas and to

■ Psychoanalytic Therapy: An Illustration

The interview that follows is one that would take place during the early stages of psychoanalysis and demonstrates free association. The analyst remains fairly quiet while the client, a 32-year-old male teacher with recurring headaches, talks about whatever occurs to him:

Client: This is like my last resort. I've been to so many doctors for this headache. But I tell you . . . I don't want . . . I know that there's something wrong with me though. I've known it since I was a kid. Like I started to tell you, when I was 17, I knew there was something wrong with me, that . . . and I told my father that I needed to see a doctor, and he laughed at me and said it was just foolishness, but he agreed to take me to his doctor, Dr._____on 125th Street, and I never went in; I chickened out.

Therapist: You chickened out, then. How'd you feel about that chickening out?

Client: I don't know. I don't feel *proud* that I wasn't able to talk over these . . . this feeling I had. . . . I wouldn't have wanted my father to know about my . . . some of my problems. 'Cause my father, he just . . . you know, I told him, my father, that there was something wrong, that I needed help, and he'd laugh at me and, you know, just to pacify me, you know, he took me to Dr._____, but I didn't know Dr._____. He was a friend of my father's,

yeah, I don't know if. . . . I don't remember thinking about it, but if I had talked to Dr._____about my problems like the problems I talk about in here, and my father found out, he might get pretty mad. Yeah.

Therapist: Well, this would be insulting to him? He'd feel it would be a bad reflection on his upbringing of you, if you went to a doctor like this? Would this humiliate him?

Client: Yeah. I've got. . . . My father and I didn't get along too well, and to tell the truth, I was ashamed of my father. He was born in Poland, and he was a self-made man. He went to the University of Warsaw and then Fordham. He was a pharmacist, but he was . . . he didn't care how he dressed. He was all sloppy and dirty, and he was short. He's about five foot one and stoop-shouldered. . . . We used to go to restaurants, my mother and him and me, and he would never leave a tip, never leave a tip, never leave a tip. I used to sneak back and I'd throw a few cents that I might have on the table, but he was so stingy, so tight. When we went on a train, when we went somewhere, I would try to pretend I wasn't with them. I'd want. . . . I'd go in another. . . . I do need some help, and I know I've got to do the talking. That's the hardest part for me, that you won't give me any guidelines, that I have to do everything myself, and you'll analyze me. . . . I didn't ever think I'd. . . . I didn't want to think I was gonna end up resolve conflicts that they could not resolve in the past. *Working through* old conflicts provides people with a second chance to review and revise the feelings and beliefs that underlie their problems.

This description applies to traditional, or orthodox, psychoanalysis. But only a handful of people who seek therapy go into traditional analysis. For one thing, as Freud himself recognized, analysis depends on people's motivation to change and on their ability to deal rationally with whatever analysis uncovers. Schizophrenics freely talk about their fantasies and unconscious wishes, but they often cannot use the analyst's interpretations effectively. Psychoanalysis is best suited to "potentially autonomous" people (Hersher, 1970)—not to severely disturbed people. Moreover, orthodox analysis may take five years or more, and most traditional analysts feel that at least three and sometimes five sessions a week are essential. Thus, few people can afford psychoanalysis, and many others need immediate help for immediate problems.

Furthermore, some psychologists believe that orthodox psychoanalysis is outdated. Freud invented this technique in the late nineteenth century. He worked primarily with upper-class women who were struggling

here. I hate to think that this is the problem, but . . . (Hersher, 1970, pp. 135–39).

Somewhat later in therapy, the analyst takes a more active role, as shown in this excerpt from a session with a different client:

Therapist (summarizing and restating): It sounds as if you would like to let loose with me, but you are afraid of what my response would be.

Client: I get so excited by what is happening here. I feel I'm being held back by needing to be nice. I'd like to blast loose sometimes, but I don't dare.

Therapist: Because you fear my reaction?

Client: The worst thing would be that you wouldn't like me. You wouldn't speak to me friendly; you wouldn't smile; you'd feel you can't treat me and discharge me from treatment. But I know this isn't so; I know it.

Therapist: Where do you think these attitudes come from?

Client: When I was 9 years old, I read a lot about great men in history. I'd quote them and be dramatic, I'd want a sword at my side; I'd dress like an Indian. Mother would scold me: Don't frown; don't talk so much. Sit on your hands, over and over again. I did all kinds of things. I was a naughty child. She told me I'd be hurt. Then, at 14, I fell off a horse and broke my back. I had to be in bed. Mother then told me on the day I went riding not to, I'd get hurt because the ground was frozen. I was a stubborn, self-willed child. Then I went against her will and suffered an accident that changed my life, a fractured back. Her attitude was, "I told you so." I was put in a cast and kept in bed for months.

Therapist: You were punished, so to speak, by this accident.

Client: But I gained attention and love from Mother for the first time. I felt so good. I'm ashamed to tell you this: Before I healed, I opened the cast and tried to walk, to make myself sick again so I could stay in bed longer.

Therapist: How does that connect up with your impulse to be sick now and stay in bed so much? *(The client has these tendencies, of which she is ashamed.)*

Client: Oh. . . . *(pause)*

Therapst: What do you think?

Client: Oh, my God, how infantile, how un-grownup *(pause)*. It must be so. I want people to love me and be sorry for me. Oh, my God. How completely childish. It is, *is* that. My mother must have ignored me when I was little, and I wanted so to be loved.

Therapist: So that it may have been threatening to go back to being self-willed and unloved after you got out of the cast *(interpretation)*.

Client: It did. My life changed. I became meek and controlled. I couldn't get angry or stubborn afterward.

Therapist: Perhaps if you go back to being stubborn with me, you would be returning to how you were before, that is, active, stubborn, but unloved.

Client (excitedly): And, therefore, losing your love. I need you, but after all, you aren't going to reject me. But the pattern is so established now that the threat of the loss of love is too overwhelming with everybody, and I've got to keep myself from acting selfish or angry (Wolberg, 1977, pp. 560–61).

with the strict moral and social codes of a Victorian society. But society has changed. Today it may be harder for people to *find* rules for behavior than to break them.

Finally, and perhaps most importantly, psychodynamic personality theory has changed since the turn of the century (see Chapter 12), and these changes are reflected in different approaches to therapy. For example, although Freud felt that to understand the present one had first to understand the past, most neo-Freudians try to get their clients to cope with current problems rather than with unresolved conflicts from the past. Also, neo-Freudians favor face-to-face discussions, and most take an active role: They interpret clients' statements freely, suggest topics for discussion, illustrate comments by role playing, and so on.

Client-centered Therapy

Carl Rogers, the founder of **client-centered** (or **person-centered**) **therapy,** took bits and pieces of the neo-Freudians' views and revised and rearranged them into a radically different approach to therapy. The goal of therapy, in Rogers's view, is to help clients become fully functioning, to open them up to all of their experiences and to all of themselves. Rogers called his approach to therapy client-centered because he did not feel that the

■ Client-centered Therapy: An Illustration

Client: I guess I do have problems at school. . . . You see, I'm chairman of the Science Department, so you can imagine what kind of a department it is.

Therapist: You sort of feel that if you're in something that it can't be too good. Is that. . . .

Client: Well, it's not that I. . . . It's just that I'm. . . . I don't think that I could run it.

Therapist: You don't have any confidence in yourself?

Client: No confidence, no confidence in myself. I never had any confidence in myself. I—like I told you—like when even when I was a kid I didn't feel I was capable and I always wanted to get back with the intellectual group.

Therapist: This has been a long-term thing, then, it's gone on a long time.

Client: Yeah, the *feeling* is—even though I know it isn't, it's the feeling that I have that—that I haven't got it, that—that—that—people will find out that I'm dumb or—or. . . .

Therapist: Masquerade. . . .

Client: Superficial, I'm just superficial. There's nothing below the surface. Just superficial generalities, that. . . .

Therapist: There's nothing really deep and meaningful to you.

Client: No—they don't know it, and. . . .

Therapist: And you're terrified they're going to find out.

Client: My wife has a friend, and—and she and the friend got together so we could go out together with her and my wife and her husband. . . . And the guy, he's an engineer and he's, you know—he's got it, you know; and I don't want to go, I don't want to go because—because if—if we get together he's liable to start to—to talk about something I don't know, and I'll—I won't know about that.

Therapist: You'll show up very poorly in this kind of situation.

Client: That I—I'll show up poorly, that I'll —that I'll just clam up, that I. . . .

Therapist: You're terribly frightened in this sort of thing.

Client: I—I'm afraid to be around people who—who I feel are my peers. Even in pool—now I—I play pool very well and— if I'm playing with some guy that I—I know I can beat, *psychologically,* I can run 50, but—but if I start playing with somebody that's my level, I'm done. I'm done. I—I— I'll miss a ball every time.

Therapist: So the . . . the fear of what's going on just immobilizes you, keeps you from doing a good job (Hersher, 1970, pp. 29–32).

Carl Rogers   Albert Ellis

Rational-emotive therapy (RET) A highly directive therapeutic approach based on the idea that an individual's problems have been caused by his or her misinterpretations of events and goals.

image of a patient seeking advice from an expert, the doctor, is appropriate. The best experts on individual people are the individuals themselves.

Rogers's ideas about therapy are quite specific. As we saw in Chapter 12, Rogers believed that defensiveness, rigidity, anxiety, and other signs of discomfort arise because people have experienced conditional positive regard. They have learned that love and acceptance are conditional on becoming what other people want them to be. Therefore, the cardinal rule in person-centered therapy is for the therapist to express *unconditional positive regard*. That is, therapists must show that they truly accept and value their clients—no matter what clients may say or do. Rogers felt that this is a crucial first step toward getting clients to accept themselves. Rather than taking an objective approach, Rogerian therapists try to understand things from the clients' point of view. They are also emphatically *nondirective*. They do not suggest reasons why clients feel as they do or how they might better handle a difficult situation. Instead, they try to reflect clients' statements, sometimes asking questions and sometimes hinting at feelings that clients have not put into words. Rogers felt that when therapists provide an atmosphere of openness and geunine respect, clients can find themselves.

Rational-Emotive Therapy

Unlike Rogerians, *rational-emotive therapists* look on themselves as experts and on their clients as people who have become trapped by irrational and self-defeating beliefs. According to Albert Ellis (1973), most people compare themselves to other people and then rate themselves. This prevents them from accepting their natural faults and usually results either in self-contempt or in a pose of defensive superiority. Regardless of what might have happened in the past, rational-emotive therapists insist that people are solely responsible in the present for how they feel about themselves and for their happiness. The goal of **rational-emotive therapy (RET)** is to show clients that their own misinterpretations of events are causing their problems and to teach clients to see themselves more rationally.

RET therapists believe that people seek help when they find themselves acting in self-defeating ways. For example, some people feel that something is wrong with them if everyone they meet does not immediately love and admire them. Others "beat their brains out" trying to solve problems beyond their control. Still others simply refuse to examine obvious evidence and persist in thinking that they are weak, sinful, or stupid. In order to correct these illogical and self-defeating beliefs, RET therapists use a variety of techniques, including persuasion, confrontation, challenge, commands, and even theoretical arguments. They do not "baby" their clients, and some people find their toughness hard to accept. They may go so far as to give "homework" assignments, encouraging clients to argue with their bosses, to ask the girl down the hall for a date,

■ Rational-Emotive Therapy: An Illustration

Client: . . . I always doubt that I have what it takes intellectually. . . .

Therapist: Well, let's suppose you haven't. Let's just suppose for the sake of discussion that you really are inferior to some degree, and you're not up to your fellows—your old peers from childhood or your present peers. Now what's so catastrophic about that, if it were true?

Client: Well, this is a fear, I'm not . . . if they found out, then . . . if I can't keep my job teaching, then I . . . I couldn't support my family.

Therapist: How long have you been teaching?

Client: Seven years.

Therapist: So, being inferior, you've done pretty well in keeping your job. You're not that concerned about your job.

Client: I know my wife says this. She says that somebody would find me out, but I . . . still feel that I . . . I'm kidding everybody, that I have to be very careful what I say and what I do, because if they should find out that I haven't got it, then I don't know what I would do. If I don't feel that I'm capable of being a teacher, then I shouldn't be a teacher.

Therapist: Who said so?

Client: I don't know.

Therapist: I know. You said so. Don't you think there are lots of teachers in the school system who are not very good teachers?

Client: Yes, I know there are a lot of them, and I don't respect them. I don't feel they should be teachers if they aren't qualified.

Therapist: So you're saying you don't respect yourself, if you act ineffectively as a teacher. Right?

Client: Yes, I wouldn't respect myself.

Therapist: Why not?

Client: Because if . . . well, it wouldn't be right to say that I'm teaching when . . . if I haven't got the qualifications, if I'm not capable to do the job.

Therapist: Let's assume you're a lousy teacher. Now why are you tying up your performance? Lousy teacher, we're assuming now. You are a lousy teacher and may always be a lousy teacher. Why are you tying that aspect of you up with your total self? I am a slob because my teaching is slobbish. Now do you see any inconsistency with that conclusion?

Client: No, but I agree that I would be . . . it would be a terrible thing if I were to teach and it wouldn't . . . and I wouldn't be capable. That it wouldn't be right. That would be like I was a fraud.

Therapist: But the terrible thing is that you would be a slob, a no-goodnik, a louse who couldn't respect you.

Client: It would be dishonest of me.

Therapist: Well, yeah. What's terrible about that?

Client: Well, it's terrible.

Therapist: But according to you, about half or more of the teachers in the school system are not-so-hot teachers. Right?

Client: Yes, and if I were the administrator, I would have to do something about that.

Therapist: Meaning fire them?

Client: Fire them.

Therapist: And then who would teach the kids?

Client: You mean, if I was the administrator I'd have to. . . .

Therapist: Tolerate.

Client: To tolerate it. . . . (Hersher, 1970, pp. 64–66).

■ Computer Therapy

Does a therapist have to be a person? The increasing popularity of microcomputers has led inevitably to the development of software packages that focus on many of the same problems and strategies encountered in person-to-person therapy. Programs now exist to help with a wide variety of psychological concerns: making friends, losing weight, staying in school, changing jobs, managing stress, stopping smoking, and becoming more assertive. The value of such programs is still under debate.

Ironically, one of the first and most widely known therapy programs, ELIZA, was written as a joke—and then taken very seriously. Developed in 1964 by Dr. Joseph Weizenbaum to illustrate the absurdity of artificial intelligence, ELIZA simulates a traditional conversation between therapist and client. The client types in any message, and ELIZA types out its response. The resulting "dialogue" has many of the properties of spoken conversation:

Program: Was there much friction between you and him [your father] when you were growing up?
Person: Yes, we fought all the time.
Program: Perhaps you were afraid of him.
Person: I certainly was. He used to really blow up.
Program: Perhaps you are still a little fearful of older men.
Person: Let's talk about something else.
Program: Okay. Go ahead. I will try to follow what you have to say about it.

When it became clear that people *liked* ELIZA and were often more honest talking to a computer than they would be talking to a human therapist, the stage was set for the development of more therapeutic software.

Psychotherapists were quick to point out, however, that emotions such as empathy, sympathy, and understanding lie outside the realm of any machine. The therapeutic significance of pauses, silences, and confrontations may also be missed by a computer. Moreover, computers cannot deal effectively with bizarre conversation, as is illustrated by the following "dialogue":

Program: Do you say that because no one else will listen to you for some special reason?
Person: Et cetera.
Program: I'm not sure I fully understand you.
Person: Abracadabra. Heresahellofafunnybobo.
Program: Earlier you said your brother beats you up all the time . . . (Spero, 1978, p. 282).

In the 1970s, a computerized Device for Automated Desensitization (DAD) was developed to treat phobias. The device instructs patients to relax while showing them a program of pictures related to the things that they are afraid of. Comparisons indicate that DAD is about as effective as a human therapist in administering this type of treatment (Arieti, 1975). In other cases, computerized devices teach children to speak. The children "play" with the computer, which is programmed to reward their success in speaking.

Advocates of electronic therapy observe that computers are uniquely suited to fostering psychological development. For one thing, programs can be self-modifying to fit the information supplied by the client. Any suggestions offered can then be specifically tailored to dealing with the problem at hand. For another, programs are interactive: Clients can make choices and then see their immediate consequences. Clients can also rate their own performances. And the computer can provide many possible outcomes for a given behavior, depending on circumstances; the computer can demonstrate to the client that more than one "suitable" pattern exists.

Some psychologists are now automating their offices and using therapeutic programs both for testing and as adjuncts to one-on-one therapy. Programs especially targeted to the needs of people who never receive professional attention could be a boon as well. However, the standards for *effective* software still remain to be worked out.

---

to pat the dog that frightens them. In short, RET therapists are very directive.

Recent Developments

Recent years have seen an explosion of insight therapies, possibly as many as several hundred, each gaining a degree of popularity and prominence for a time. Bookstores are filled with books on how to change oneself, and self-help has been one of the major fads of the 1970s and 1980s. Even among the mainstream insight therapies, there has been considerable divergence from the traditional form of "couch" psychotherapy.

One general trend is toward shorter term "dynamic therapy" for

Behavior therapies Therapeutic approaches aimed at teaching new behavior and based primarily on applying the principles of conditioning.

Behavioral contracting A form of operant conditioning therapy in which client and therapist set reinforcements for reaching behavioral goals.

most people—usually once a week for a fixed duration. Because they now operate within such a time-limited framework, insight therapies have become more problem- or symptom-oriented. Instead of slowly and patiently trying to construct a "narrative of the psyche"—the aim of traditional Freudian analysis—contemporary therapists are more likely to try to help their clients correct the immediate problems in their lives. Unlike Freudians, they see the individual as more in control and less at the mercy of early-childhood events. Although childhood is not discounted as a source of formative experiences, the focus is on the client's current life situation and relationships. In addition, therapists give clients more direct guidance and feedback, commenting on what they are told rather than just eliciting responses in a neutral manner. This movement toward briefer therapy is supported in a recent article by Howard et al. (1986). The authors reviewed more than 30 years of research on therapy with more than 2,400 patients. They found that about 50 percent of the patients showed improvement after only 8 sessions and that about 75 percent improved within 26 sessions.

Another notable trend in therapies in the past quarter century has been the proliferation of behavior therapies. Like the new insight therapies, they contrast in several respects with the traditional approach to therapy. Behavior therapists are active rather than neutral; they concentrate on overt behavior rather than on its rationale; the therapy is brief rather than open-ended; and research evaluation is considered important (Garfield, 1981). In the next section, we will examine several types of behavior therapies.

■ Behavior Therapies

Behaviorists do not consider disorders to be symptoms of hidden emotional conflicts that need to be uncovered and resolved. Nor are disorders a sign of irrational and self-defeating ways of thinking. Rather, they argue that the behavior disorder *is* the problem. They feel that if they as therapists can teach people to respond with more appropriate behavior, they have in effect "cured" them.

Behavior therapies are based on the belief that all behavior, normal and abnormal, is learned. Hypochondriacs *learn* that they get attention when they are sick; schizophrenics *learn* that they are safe when they withdraw from reality. Therapists do not need to know how or why people learned to behave as they do; their job is to teach people more satisfying ways of behaving. Behaviorists use several techniques to build new habits.

Operant Conditioning

As we saw in Chapter 5, *operant conditioning* techniques are based on the idea that a person learns to behave in different ways if new behaviors are reinforced and old ones are ignored or punished. In one form of operant conditioning called **behavioral contracting,** the therapist—or anyone trying to help someone change a behavior pattern—and client agree on behavioral goals and on the reinforcement that the client will receive when the goals are reached. These goals and reinforcements are often written down in a contract that binds both the client and the therapist as if by legal agreement. The contract specifies the behaviors to be followed, the penalties for not following them, and any privileges to be earned (Harmatz, 1978). One such contract might be: "For each day that I smoke fewer than 20 cigarettes, I will earn 30 minutes of time to go bowling. For each day that I exceed the goal, I will lose 30 minutes from the time that I have accumulated." Another form of operant conditioning is called the **token economy.** Token economies are usually employed in institutions like schools and hospitals, where controlled conditions are most feasible (Wilson & O'Leary, 1980). Subjects are rewarded with tokens or points for behavior considered desirable and adaptive; in turn, the tokens or points can be exchanged for desired items and privileges. On the ward of a mental hospital, for example, improved grooming habits might earn points that can be used to purchase special foodstuffs or weekend passes. Token economies have proved effective in modifying the behavior of patients who are considered resistant to other forms of treatment, such as chronic schizophrenics (Ayllon & Azrin, 1965; Paul, 1982; Paul & Lentz, 1977). Interestingly, the use of token economies has also led to an increase in hospital staff morale (Ullman & Krasner, 1975).

Aversive Conditioning

Aversive conditioning is aimed at eliminating undesirable behavior patterns. Therapists teach clients to associate pain and discomfort with the behavior that they want to unlearn. This form of behavior therapy has been used successfully to treat alcoholism, obesity, and smoking.

Sometimes the therapist uses real physical pain. Some clinics, for example, treat alcoholism by pairing the taste and smell of alcohol with drug-induced nausea and vomiting. It doesn't take long before patients feel sick just seeing a bottle of liquor. A follow-up study of nearly 800 patients who completed alcohol-aversion treatment at one clinic in 1978 and 1979 found that 63 percent maintained continuous abstinence for at least 12 months after treatment (Wiens & Menustik, 1983). Convicted child molesters have been cured by showing them pictures of naked children and then giving them electric shocks. The use of electric shock as an aversive stimulus has declined in recent years because its effectiveness has been questioned: Although it can create avoidance in the presence of the certainty of punishment, unwanted behaviors may well continue in real-life situations when no such threat exists. More recently, people have been taught to block behavior with unpleasant fantasies. For example, without undergoing shock treatment, child molesters can learn to associate things they fear with pictures of children and to associate things they enjoy with pictures of adults.

Desensitization

In some cases, aversive conditioning may be harmful. For example, if a little boy who is afraid of dogs is taken by the hand and urged to approach the dog that bit him, he might well be terrified the next time someone takes his hand. In such cases, **desensitization,** a method for gradually

Ads such as this use classical conditioning to link unpleasant stimuli with undesirable behavior. They can begin to make people aware of the positive associations they may have for behavior that is fundamentally undesirable.

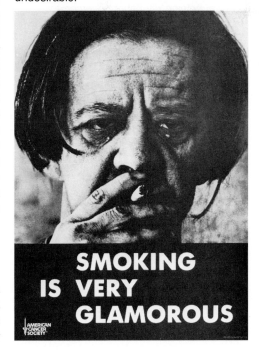

SMOKING IS VERY GLAMOROUS

AMERICAN CANCER SOCIETY

Therapies   573

Modeling Type of learning in which a person learns by observing someone else perform a desired behavior.

"Leave us alone! I am a behavior therapist! I am helping my patient overcome a fear of heights!

© 1975 by Sidney Harris/Medical Tribune

In addition to its usefulness in treating problem behavior, *modeling* has been used to help retarded individuals learn skills and self-management techniques.

reducing irrational fear, would be a more useful technique (Wolpe, 1973). For example, a politician tells the therapist in his first session that he is very anxious about speaking to crowds. The therapist looks for more details. He or she asks if the man is more threatened by an audience of 500 than by an audience of 50, more tense when addressing men than when speaking to both men and women, and so on. Perhaps this politician feels more anxious talking to adolescents than to small children. Thus, the therapist establishes a *hierarchy* from the least to the most anxiety-provoking situations.

After establishing a hierarchy, the therapist teaches the client to clear his or her mind, to release tense muscles, and to relax. In some cases, drugs or mild hypnosis help the client to relax. Once clients have mastered the technique of deep relaxation, they begin to work at the bottom of their anxiety hierarchy. Therapists ask clients to imagine the least threatening situation and to signal when they begin to feel tense. At the signal, the therapists tell the clients to forget the scene and to concentrate on relaxing. After a short time, they instruct them to return to the scene. This process is repeated until the clients feel completely relaxed about that scene. Then they advance up the hierarchy this way until they can imagine the situation of which they are most afraid without anxiety. Wolpe reports that most clients transfer what they learn in his office to real-life situations.

Modeling

The behavior therapies we have discussed so far rely on classical and operant conditioning principles to change behavior. But as we saw in Chapter 5, much human behavior can be learned by **modeling**—the process of learning by watching someone else perform various behaviors. This technique can also be used to treat problem behavior. In one experiment, Bandura, Blanchard, and Ritter (1969) tried to help people overcome snake phobias by showing them films in which models confronted snakes and gradually moved closer and closer to them. The researchers reported notable reduction in the people's fear of snakes (see Figure 15-2). Similar techniques have been successful in reducing such

Figure 15-2
Desensitization therapy at work The clients in these photographs are overcoming a simple phobia—fear of snakes. Having practiced a technique of deep relaxation, the client begins working from the bottom of his or her *anxiety hierarchy* and advances to the situation that provokes the greatest anxiety. Here, clients progress from handling rubber snakes (top left) to viewing live snakes through a window (top center) and finally to handling live snakes. This procedure can also be conducted in the therapist's office, where clients combine relaxation techniques with imagining anxiety-provoking scenes.

common fears as fear of dental work (Melamed et al., 1975). Moreover, a combination of modeling and positive reinforcement was successful in helping schizophrenic patients to learn appropriate behavior not inside the hospital but outside it as well (Bellack, Hersen, & Turner, 1976). Modeling has also been used to teach retarded individuals to learn job skills and the appropriate behavior in response to problems encountered in job situations (La Greca, Stone, & Bell, 1983).

Aaron Beck

Cognitive Behavior Therapy

Like rational-emotive therapists, *cognitive behavior therapists* believe that their clients suffer from misconceptions about themselves and their relationship to their environment. For example, Aaron Beck (1967) proposed that depression results from negative patterns of thought that some people develop about themselves. For instance, a salesman might come to believe that if he is competent, he will never lose an important account. This is an unrealistic expectation, yet when he does inevitably lose an account, he concludes that he is an incompetent person. The result is a sense of helplessness and depression in a situation where other people would feel only disappointment. As long as he continues to have unrealistic expectations, he is likely to continue to feel hopeless and depressed in the face of moral disappointment.

Cognitive behavior therapy A type of psychotherapy that emphasizes changing the client's perceptions of his or her life situation as a way of modifying behavior.

Stress-inoculation therapy Form of cognitive behavior therapy that trains clients to cope with stressful situations by understanding their misconceptions about them.

Cognitive behavior therapy focuses the client's attention on such negative and unrealistic ways of thinking and tries to break the vicious circle by prompting the client to think more logically, realistically, and positively about life situations. One technique that the therapist might use is to have a depressed person record his or her moods at regular intervals during the day. Usually, the person finds that those moods vary over the course of time. The therapist uses this insight to help the client realize that it is not necessary to be depressed all the time—that the person is capable of being happy or enthusiastic or optimistic. The therapist then tries to help the client modify his or her behavior in order to increase the likelihood of successful experiences. These successes can then be used to challenge and change the person's negative way of thinking.

A related form of cognitive behavior therapy is called **stress-inoculation therapy,** which trains the client to cope more effectively with situations that are stressful largely because of the client's misconceptions about them (Meichenbaum & Cameron, 1982). This form of therapy involves three stages. First, client and therapist explore the way the person thinks about stressful situations. It is not unusual to find that people respond to stress with a number of negative self-statements: "This is terrible. I'm going to fall apart. I just can't handle this." Of course these self-statements make a difficult situation even more stressful. The task of therapy, then, is to develop new and more adaptive self-statements in the face of stress. This is the second stage in stress-inoculation therapy: New self-statements are learned and practiced. For example, a client who feels overwhelmed by fear might rehearse such self-statements as "When fear comes, just pause"; "Label your fear from 0 to 10 and watch it change"; "It's not the worst thing than can happen" (Meichenbaum, 1974, p. 16). Finally, the client applies the rehearsed strategies in actual stress-producing situations; he or she is placed first in situations that are moderately easy to cope with and then in stressful situations that are more difficult.

How effective is cognitive behavior therapy? Rush and his associates (1977) divided a group of severely depressed men and women into two groups. One group was treated with a drug commonly used in the treatment of depression; the other underwent 20 sessions of cognitive behavior therapy. After 12 weeks, Rush and his colleagues reported that 79 percent of the group that had undergone therapy had significantly improved, compared to only 20 percent of those in the group that had been treated with medication. A number of other studies also indicate that cognitive behavior therapy can be very effective, particularly in the treatment of depression (Jarvik et al., 1982; Kovacs et al., 1981; Steuer & Hammen, 1983; Wilson, Goldin, & Charbonneau-Powis, 1983).

▮ Group Therapies

Both insight and behavioral therapies are limited to the interaction of a client with a therapist. Many psychologists think this is less than ideal. People may attach great importance to their therapists' real and imagined reactions. But since therapists are human, there is always some degree of **countertransference** (the process whereby therapists project their own emotions onto clients). Furthermore, therapy sessions are unlike everyday life: People seldom find the psychoanalyst's neutrality or the Rogerian therapist's unconditional positive regard among their friends and family. It may be hard to transfer the insight and confidence gained in therapy to other situations.

Group therapies allow both therapist and client to see how the person acts with others. They also let people shed inhibitions and express themselves in a safe setting. Finally, groups are a source of reinforcement. Traditional therapy groups are an extension of individual psychotherapy. The participants may also be seeing the therapist individually. Such groups meet once or twice weekly, for about an hour and a half.

Family Therapy

A special form of group therapy is **family therapy** (Molineux, 1985). This therapy is based on the theory that if one person in the family is having problems, it is often a signal that the entire family unit needs assistance. Family therapists feel that most psychotherapists treat people in a vacuum. There is no attempt to meet the person's parents, spouse, and children. The primary goals of family therapy are improving family communication, encouraging family members to become more empathic, getting members to share responsibilities, and reducing conflict. In order to achieve these goals, all family members must see that they will benefit from changes in their behavior. Family therapists concentrate on changing the ways in which family members satisfy their needs rather than on trying to change those needs or the individual members' personalities (Horn, 1975).

Family therapy is indicated when problems exist between husband and wife, parents and children, or other family members. It is also indicated when a client's progress in individual therapy seems to be slowed by his or her family or when a family member has trouble adjusting to a client's improvement. Goldenberg (1973) notes, however, that not all families may benefit from family therapy. Some problems are too entrenched; important family members may be absent or unwilling to cooperate; one family member may monopolize the session to the extent that the therapy becomes unworkable. In such cases, a different therapeutic approach might work better.

Another form of group therapy is **marital therapy,** which is designed to assist couples who are having difficulties with their relationship. Most marital therapists concentrate on improving the couple's patterns of communication and mutual expectations. Various techniques are practiced by marital therapists, with videotaping becoming one of the increasingly popular techniques. For example, a wife might point out that her husband interrupts her and doesn't seem to respect her opinions; the husband might respond that his wife complains about family finances and seems to undermine his self-respect as a provider. Each may see the spouse's flaws clearly enough but be blind to his or her own shortcomings. By watching videotapes of their conversations, both partners may be helped to gain some insight into the real nature of their behavior. Other therapists favor behavioral techniques. For example, a couple might be helped to develop a schedule for exchanging specific caring actions. This approach is based on the theory that scheduled exchanges of benefits can result in

Traditional *therapy groups* allow both therapist and client to see how a person acts with others.

Family therapy works toward improving communication among family members. All members need to see that they will benefit from changes in their behavior.

the learning of behavior that benefits both partners (Thibaut & Kelley, 1959). It isn't terribly romantic, but its supporters point out that any strategy that breaks the cycle of dissatisfaction and hostility is an important step in the right direction.

Whatever form of therapy a couple chooses, research indicates that marital therapy for both partners is more effective than therapy for only one of them (Gurman & Kniskern, 1978). One study found that when both partners underwent therapy together, 56 percent were still married five years later; among those couples who underwent therapy separately, only 29 percent had remained married (Cookerly, 1980).

Group Therapy and the Interpersonal Perspective

Both family and marital therapy developed out of the **interpersonal theory** of personality and personality disorders. Interpersonal theory was first systematized by the American psychiatrist Harry Stack Sullivan, who felt that anxiety can be aroused during the course of an individual's early development as a result of his or her relationships with others (Sullivan, 1953). For example, if a young child feels rejected in a relationship with someone else, notably a parent, a pattern of anxious behavior can begin. The experience contributes to the child's developing sense of self, which may thus be distorted. Because distorted perceptions shape a person's behavior toward other people, they contribute to unsatisfactory relationships and become more severe. The result can be characterized as anxiety.

Interpersonal theory thus strongly emphasizes unsatisfactory relationships as a factor in maladaptive behavior. Supporters of this position have argued that the DSM-III-R (see Chapter 14) is flawed as a diagnostic instrument because it ignores the social context in which maladaptive behavior occurs. For example, they argue that depression might be redefined as the result of a person's belief that he or she is being blamed or accused by another person who is perceived as hostile; depression results when the blame or accusation is internalized and becomes self-blame or self-accusation. Depression can be seen as hostility toward oneself (Benjamin, 1982; McLemore & Benjamin, 1979).

Sullivan emphasized that the client's relationship with the therapist is also an important interpersonal relationship and encouraged therapists to organize sessions in which the client could develop self-confidence that could be transferred to other situations. He thus saw the therapist as a participant-observer who must continually be aware of the conscious and unconscious attitudes that he or she might project into the client-therapist relationship. Therapists should be aware that a client's anxieties might prompt them to express their own. For example, a client might say something like "Sometimes I get so mad I feel like throttling someone." The therapist might respond by saying, "That's not an uncommon thought, and thinking about killing someone isn't the same thing as doing it." The therapist may in this case be reassuring himself about his own anxieties over the client's hostility—and may in fact be reinforcing the client's anxiety. A more appropriate response would be an acknowledgement that everyone has the urge to express pent-up feelings and a recommendation that the client talk about other situations in which he

Harry Stack Sullivan

or she experiences similar feelings. By resolving their own feelings about the client, therapists are better able to establish a pattern of interaction whereby the client can develop a self-image that is compatible with his or her relationships with other people in a variety of real-life situations. As we shall see, interpersonal therapy has been found to be quite effective in the treatment of depression.

Gestalt Therapy

Gestalt therapy is largely an outgrowth of the work of Frederick (Fritz) Perls at the Esalen Institute in California. Perls began his career as a psychoanalyst but later turned vehemently against Freud and psychoanalytic techniques. He felt that "Freud invented the couch because he could not look people in the eye" (1969, p. 118). Gestalt therapy emphasizes the here-and-now and encourages face-to-face confrontations.

Gestalt therapy is designed to make people self-supporting. It can

> **Gestalt therapy** Form of therapy, either individual or group, that emphasizes the wholeness of the personality and attempts to reawaken people to their emotions and sensations in the here-and-now.

■ Gestalt Therapy: An Illustration

Therapist: Try to describe just what you are aware of at each moment as fully as possible. For instance, what are you aware of now?

Client: I'm aware of wanting to tell you about my problem, and also a sense of shame—yes, I feel very ashamed right now.

Therapist: Okay. I would like you to develop a dialogue with your feeling of shame. Put your shame in the empty chair over here (*indicates chair*), and talk to it.

Client: Are you serious? I haven't even told you about my problem yet.

Therapist: That can wait—I'm perfectly serious, and I want to know what you have to say to your shame.

Client: (*awkward and hesitant at first, but then becoming looser and more involved*): Shame, I hate you. I wish you would leave me—you drive me crazy, always reminding me that I have a problem, that I'm perverse, different, shameful—even ugly. Why don't you leave me alone?

Therapist: Okay, now go to the empty chair, take the role of shame, and answer yourself back.

Client: (*moves to the empty chair*): I am your constant companion—and I don't *want* to leave you. I would feel lonely without you, and I don't hate you. I pity you, and I pity your attempts to shake me loose, because you are doomed to failure.

Therapist: Okay, now go back to your original chair and answer back.

Client: (*once again as himself*): How do you know I'm doomed

to failure? (*Spontaneously shifts chairs now, no longer needing direction from the therapist; answers himself back, once again in the role of shame.*) I know that you're doomed to failure because *I* want you to fail and because I control your life. You can't make a single move without me. For all you know, you were *born* with me. You can hardly remember a single moment when you were without me, totally unafraid that I would spring up and suddenly remind you of your loathsomeness.

Client: You're right; so far you *have* controlled my life—I feel constantly embarrassed and awkward. (*His voice grows stronger.*) But that doesn't mean that you'll continue to control my life. That's why I've come here—to find some way of destroying you. (*Shifts to the "shame" chair.*) Do you think *he* can help you? (*Bill, as shame, points to the therapist.*) What can he do? He hardly knows you as I know you. Besides, he's only going to see you once or twice each week. I am with you every single moment of every day!

Therapist: Bill, look how one hand keeps rubbing the other when you speak for shame. Could you exaggerate that motion? Who does that remind you of?

Client: (*rubbing his hands together harder and harder*): My mother would do this—yes, whenever she was nervous she would rub her hands harder and harder.

Therapist: Okay, now speak for your mother. (Shaffer, 1978, pp. 92–93) be done with individuals, but it is more frequently done in a group setting. The therapist is active and directive and usually concentrates on one person at a time. The emphasis in Gestalt therapy is on the *whole* person, and the therapist's role, as Perls describes it, is to "fill in the holes in the personality to make the person whole and complete again" (Perls, 1969, p. 2). Gestalt therapists try to make people aware of their feelings and to awaken them to sensory information that they may be ignoring. Many techniques may be used—people are told to talk about themselves in the first person ("I keep looking away" instead of "My eyes keep looking away"). In this way, therapists remind clients that they alone are responsible for everything they do. If clients want to discuss a third person, they must speak directly to that person or act out a conversation if that person is absent. Gestalt therapy, like psychoanalysis, uses people's dreams to help uncover information. Often, clients are asked to act out all parts in their dreams—both people and objects.

Large-Group Awareness Training

In the past decade, various types of large-group awareness training have developed, the best known of which is **est** (Erhard Seminar Training). By 1980, more than 250,000 people had participated in est training—as many as several hundred at a time in a single training seminar.

Est begins with a pretraining session at which trainees agree to certain conditions, such as staying seated and silent unless called on and using the bathroom, eating, and smoking only during breaks. The training itself occurs over the following two weekends; it is conducted by an authoritarian trainer who derides trainees and their accomplishments. Trainees must raise their hands if they wish to stand and speak and must remain standing until they are thanked by the trainer and applauded by the audience. If trainees express criticism or anger, they are met with studied indifference by the trainer, who reminds them that they themselves chose to take est training.

Est trainees learn that their lives can be made to work only if they experience reality directly—and that their belief systems, understanding, and reasonableness are isolating them from such an experience (Finkelstein, Wenegrat, & Yalom, 1982). Powerful feelings are released as trainees examine images from their past, including their childhoods. Trainees subsequently learn that although they may not have voluntarily caused their misfortunes, they are totally responsible for their present experience of them.

In the final sessions, trainees learn that the emotional upsets of life result from machinelike, illogical associations that link the experiences of the present with past threats or losses. In other words, they are mechanical, illogical "feeding tubes."

Est graduates seem to indicate a general satisfaction with the training. One unpublished study (Hosford et al., 1980) shows that compared with control groups awaiting est training, est graduates show changes on psychological tests that indicate improved mental health. Another unpublished study that was more effectively designed (Hoepfner, 1975) shows no effect of est training. Although severely disturbed clients are least likely to benefit from est training, research has shown that they are not likely to be permanently harmed by it either (Finkelstein et al., 1982).

est A form of large-group awareness training that emphasizes the direct experience of reality.

■ Nonprofessional "Therapists"

If you suffer from a physical ailment that doesn't clear up, the chances are that you'll soon see a doctor. If you're emotionally troubled, however, statistics show that you're much less likely to visit a mental health professional. Instead, you are more likely to talk things over with someone whom you already know, such as your supervisor, hairdresser, bartender, or lawyer. According to Cowen (1982), "For the most part, people do *not* bring their personal troubles to mental health professionals at *any* point in their unfolding, least of all in response to early, sometimes keenly important, signs of distress" (p. 385). Among the reasons for this reluctance are the high cost of such services, their geographic or practical inaccessibility, and their ideological unacceptability to some people. "Even when such barriers do not exist," Cowen says, "many troubled individuals prefer to talk with people who are known and trusted in more natural contexts—people who are willing to listen when they are ready to talk" (p. 385). And there is some evidence that at least some of these nonprofessional "therapists" are as effective as trained therapists in helping people (Strupp & Hadley, 1979).

Cowen (1982) surveyed 325 of these nonprofessional "therapists," such as bartenders and hairdressers. He found that discussions of personal problems do indeed arise with "substantial frequency" and that the sorts of problems raised—children, health, marriage, depression, anxiety, jobs, money, and sex—were not different from those raised with mental health professionals. And the amateur therapists perceived themselves as being somewhat helpful. On the whole, they rated themselves in the "moderately effective" range, with hairdressers rating themselves a bit higher and bartenders a bit lower than lawyers and supervisors. When the groups were asked about their effectiveness, Cowen says, the general response was, "We're coping and doing a decent job, but there are gaps and we could use help" (Cowen, 1982, p. 393).

Among the tactics most frequently cited by the amateurs were "offering support and sympathy," "trying to be light-hearted," and "just listening." Lawyers, however, emphasized asking questions, giving advice, and pointing out the consequences of bad ideas in addition to giving support and sympathy. Cowen notes that women were called on to deal with personal problems more often than men, that they felt more at home in this role and preformed it more patiently and sympathetically, and that they used more engaging, task-oriented strategies than their male counterparts.

Interestingly, the amateurs said that they saw helping others with their problems as a normal and sometimes very important part of their jobs. As one hairdresser put it, "to be perfectly truthful, I regard myself as a B− hairdresser. But my business is booming. Mostly that's because I listen to people, care about their personal concerns, and try to be helpful. The guy down the street is really an A+ hairdresser—one of the best in town. But he's going to go out of business because he can't stand people and is incapable of listening sympathetically to *anyone's* problems" (Cowen, 1982, p. 390).

■ Effectiveness of Psychotherapies

Although insight therapy, behavior therapy, and group therapy represent different approaches to the goal of improved mental health, they all share one characteristic: All are *psycho*therapies—that is, they deal with disorders by using psychological methods. But is psychotherapy *effective*? Is it any better than no treatment at all? And if it is, how *much* better is it?

One of the first studies to consider these questions was done by Eysenck (1952), who surveyed 19 published reports covering more than 7,000 cases. Eysenck concluded that individual psychotherapy was no more effective against neurotic disorders than no therapy at all: "Roughly two-thirds of a group of neurotic patients will recover or improve to a marked extent within about two years of the onset of their illness whether they are treated by means of psychotherapy or not" (p. 322).

Although Eysenck's conclusions caused a storm of controversy in the psychological community, his study immediately stimulated more research. A later review of the literature done by Meltzoff and Kornreich (1971) found more "good" or acceptable results than did Eysenck and therefore concluded that psychotherapy is effective and superior to no treatment. Bergin and Lambert (1978) also found evidence of treatment-related improvement. They questioned the "spontaneous recovery" of the control subjects in the studies that Eysenck surveyed, noting that even though they received no formal therapy, many of them did get help from friends, clergy, physicians, and teachers. They concluded that the improvement rate among people in psychotherapy was greater than that of untreated control subjects. Sloane and his colleagues (1975), who compared people who had received psychoanalytic psychotherapy, those who had had behavior therapy, and a control group of people who were on a waiting list for therapy, found that both therapies were superior to the control condition in reducing major symptoms.

In 1977, a dramatically new approach was taken to the effectiveness question. Smith and Glass (1977) reported an averaging of the results of a large number of studies, from which they concluded that the typical therapy client is better off than 75 percent of untreated controls. But is this result due simply to the fact that the therapy patients believed they would be helped, or is it due to the actual treatment itself? Landman and Dawes (1982) concluded that while initiating *any* treatment will create a small improvement, actually receiving therapy leads to a much greater improvement. In other words, the effects of receiving therapy appear to be due to more than just *believing* that you are going to get better.

The issue of effectiveness raises a second set of questions. Is any particular form of psychotherapy better than the others? Is group therapy or behavior therapy, for example, more effective than insight therapy? In general, the answer seems to be no: Several recent reviews have concluded that there are few if any differences in the results obtained by various forms of therapy (Garfield, 1983; Michelson, 1985; Smith, Glass, & Miller, 1980). However, other psychologists question these conclusions; they point out that there is no agreement on appropriate methods

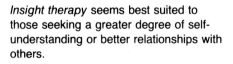

Insight therapy seems best suited to those seeking a greater degree of self-understanding or better relationships with others.

for determining the relative effectiveness of different types of therapy (Eysenck, 1985; Piroleau, Murdock, & Brody, 1983; Shapiro, 1985). It is dismaying that the debate over such an important issue has not yet been resolved, but the debate itself continues to spur careful well-managed studies conducted in the hope of making a breakthrough.

It does seem, however, that some kinds of psychotherapy may be particularly appropriate for certain people and problems. Insight therapy, for example, seems to be best suited to people seeking extensive scrutiny of themselves or profound self-understanding, relief of inner conflict and anxiety, or better relationships with others. On the other hand, behavior therapy is probably most appropriate in cases where there is a specific behavioral problem. Desensitization, for example, is most effective with conditioned avoidance responses such as phobias and anxiety disorders. Aversive techniques are successful in producing impulse control, and modeling combined with positive reinforcement has helped in learning complex or appropriate responses to unfamiliar or threatening situations. Behavioral approaches have also been successful with sexual dysfunctions such as frigidity and impotence.

The trend in psychotherapy is toward eclecticism—that is, toward a recognition of the value of a broad treatment package rather than commitment to a single form of therapy. Although an eclectic model doesn't guarantee greater effectiveness—an inconsistent hodgepodge of techniques and concepts could result instead—the majority of therapists now identify with this approach.

Biological Treatment

Sometimes therapists find that they cannot "reach" clients with any of the therapies that we have described because the clients are extremely agitated, disoriented, or totally unresponsive. In these cases, therapists may decide to use **biological treatment** to change clients' behavior so that they can benefit from therapy. Biological treatment is also used both to restrain clients who are dangerous to themselves and to others and in institutions where there are only a few therapists for many patients.

Electroconvulsive Therapy

Electroconvulsive therapy (ECT) is most often used for cases of prolonged and severe depression that do not respond to other forms of therapy. Until recently, the technique of ECT has remained largely unchanged. One electrode is placed on each side of the patient's head, and a mild current is turned on for a very short time (about one and a half seconds). The electrical current passes from one side of the patient's brain to the other, producing a brief convulsion, followed by a temporary loss of consciousness. Muscle relaxants administered in advance prevent dangerously violent contractions. When patients awaken several minutes later, they normally have amnesia for the period immediately before the procedure and remain confused for the next hour or so. With repeated treatments, people often become disoriented, but this condition usually

Biological treatment Treatment of behavior disorders with such methods as electroconvulsive therapy, insulin shock treatment, psychosurgery, and drug therapy.

Electroconvulsive therapy (ECT) A physical therapy in which a mild electrical current is passed through the brain for a short period, often producing convulsions and temporary coma; used to alleviate sudden and severe depression.

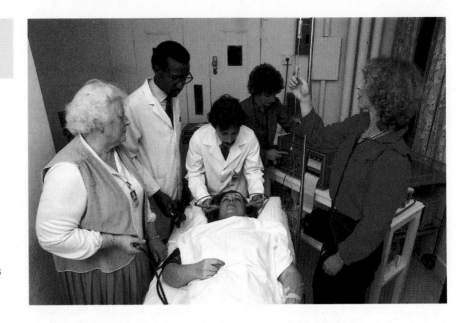

Psychosurgery Brain surgery used in the treatment of severe mental disorders.

Although no one knows precisely why *electroconvulsive therapy* works, it has been successful in treating cases of severe and prolonged depression.

clears after treatment concludes. Treatment normally consists of fewer than a dozen sessions of ECT.

An important recent development is *unilateral ECT*. In this procedure, the current is passed through only one side of the brain, usually the nondominant hemisphere (see Chapter 2). Evidence suggests strongly that this new method reduces such side effects as memory impairment and confusion without decreasing the effectiveness of the therapy (Daniel & Crovitz, 1983). In addition, some therapists have begun using less powerful electric currents, a modification that also seems to lessen the severity of side effects.

No one knows exactly why ECT works, but most researchers believe that convulsions produce both physiological and psychological changes (Sarason & Sarason, 1989). While ECT appears to be effective in alleviating certain severe depressions, it has many critics and its use is extremely controversial. For example, the procedure is clearly capable of damaging the brain. Such damage has been found in animals sacrificed immediately after ECT treatment, and it is possible that each treatment destroys a number of central nervous system neurons.

Nevertheless, defenders of ECT insist that it is highly effective and works relatively quickly, which is an important factor when dealing with suicidally depressed people. Recent studies also indicate that complications are less widespread than was once believed and that memory impairment following treatment generally disappears completely (Holden, 1985). In any case, ECT is considered a highly effective short-term therapy (Scovern & Kilmann, 1980), especially in severe cases in which other methods have failed or where medication cannot work quickly enough.

Psychosurgery

As we saw in Chapter 2, changing a person's behavior and emotional state by brain surgery is a drastic step, especially since the effects of **psychosurgery** are difficult to predict. In a prefrontal lobotomy, the frontal lobes of the brain are severed from the deeper centers beneath them, on the assumption that in extremely disturbed patients the frontal lobes intensify emotional impulses from the lower brain centers (chiefly the thalamus and hypothalamus). Unfortunately, lobotomies can work with one person and fail completely with another—possibly producing permanent undesirable side effects, such as an inability to inhibit impulses or a virtually total absence of feeling.

Prefrontal lobotomies are rarely performed today. In fact, no psychosurgical procedures are used except as desperate measures to control such conditions as intractable psychoses, severe and debilitating disorders that do not respond to any other treatment, and occasionally for pain control in a terminal illness.

Drug Therapies

Psychiatrists today generally prefer drugs to either ECT or psychosurgery. There are two major advantages to the use of drugs: They produce only temporary changes in body chemistry, and the side effects are easier to predict. Moreover, the dosage can be varied from one person to another.

ANTIPSYCHOTIC DRUGS.   Before the mid-1950s, drugs were not used widely in therapy because the only available sedatives induced sleep as well as calm. Then the major tranquilizers *reserpine* and the *phenothiazines* were introduced. In addition to alleviating anxiety and aggressive behavior, both drugs reduce psychotic symptoms, such as hallucinations and delusions. Thus they are called *antipsychotic drugs*. The first of the phenothiazines was *chlorpromazine* (Thorazine), and it became the treatment of choice for schizophrenia.

How do antipsychotics work? Research with animals indicates that, in part, phenothiazines inhibit the functioning of the hypothalamus, which controls arousal. Brain-wave studies further suggest that this prevents internal arousal signals from reaching the higher portions of the brain (Sarason & Sarason, 1989). In addition, it appears that virtually all the antipsychotics block dopamine receptors in the brain.

As the following case study shows, the antipsychotics can sometimes have dramatic effects (Grinspoon, Ewalt, & Shader, 1972):

> Ms. W. was a 19-year-old, white, married woman who was admitted to the treatment unit as a result of gradually increasing agitation and hallucinations over a three-month period. Her symptoms had markedly intensified during the four days prior to admission. . . . She had had a deprived childhood, but had managed to function reasonably well up to the point of her breakdown.
>
> At the outset of her hospitalization, Ms. W. continued to have auditory and visual hallucinations and appeared frightened, angry, and confused. . . . Her condition continued to deteriorate for more than two weeks, at which point medication was begun. . . .
>
> She responded [to thioridazine (Mellaril)] quite dramatically during the first week of treatment. Her behavior became, for the most part, quiet and appropriate, and she made some attempts at socialization. She continued to improve, but by the fourth week of treatment began to show signs of mild depression. Her medication was increased, and she resumed

Because it produces only temporary changes in body chemistry and because its side effects are predictable, *drug therapy* is generally preferred over electroconvulsive therapy and psychosurgery.

■ Valium

In addition to antipsychotic and antidepressant drugs, a third group of drugs, known as *antianxiety drugs* or *minor tranquilizers*, is often prescribed for the relief of anxiety and tension. One of the most commonly prescribed of these drugs is Valium. After its introduction in 1963, Valium rapidly became the most widely prescribed drug in the United States. In 1978, about 68 million prescriptions were written for Valium, Librium, and other related tranquilizers at a wholesale market value of $360 million (*Newsweek*, Sept. 24, 1979).

The benefits of Valium do not come without substantial costs. Side effects of drowsiness and motor impairment are sometimes responsible for car accidents. It can cause negative effects when taken with other drugs, including alcohol. Valium may also interfere with serotonin, a natural brain chemical that is an antidepressant and aids in normal sleep. Valium, with its anxiety-easing properties, may also mask clinically significant symptoms and could prevent a person from seeking needed psychotherapy (Carson et al., 1988).

But perhaps the most serious worry is that Valium users will become dependent on the drug. The drug does have addictive potential, and critics are concerned that it is too freely prescribed. Moreover, an abrupt discontinuation of the drug can cause serious withdrawal symptoms such as tremors, nervousness, weakness, weight loss, nausea, retching, abdominal pain and cramping, insomnia, muscle twitches, facial numbness, and muscle cramps (Pevnick, Jasinski, & Haertzen, 1978).

Despite the arguments against it, Valium's value should not be overlooked. Although side effects and dependency may develop—even with the prescribed dosage—Valium is relatively safe and helps people deal with profound anxiety. Caution and restraint, however, should be exercised by physicians in prescribing the drug. It should be reserved for those seriously affected by anxiety and not be regarded as a cure for all the stresses and strains of everyday life. Also, Valium is not a cure in itself. Whenever possible, it should be used in combination with psychotherapy to help people deal with the causes of their problems.

her favorable course. By the sixth week she was dealing with various reality issues in her life in a reasonably effective manner, and by the ninth week she was spending considerable time at home, returning to the hospital in a pleasant and cheerful mood. She was discharged exactly 100 days after her admission, being then completely free of symptoms.

However, antipsychotic drugs have a number of undesirable side effects (Van Putten et al., 1981). Blurred vision and constipation are among the common complaints. More serious side effects include *tardive dyskinesia*, a disturbance of motor control, particularly in the muscles of the face, which can only be partially alleviated with other drugs. And some schizophrenic patients not only fail to respond to antipsychotic drugs but are made worse by them (Buckley, 1982).

In addition, while antipsychotic drugs do allow many schizophrenic patients to leave the hospital, the drugs by themselves are of little value in treating social incapacity and other difficulties in adjusting to life outside the institution. As a result, relapse is disturbingly common. In the last decade, attention has turned to ways in which psychoactive drug therapy can be combined with some form of psychotherapy in an effort to reduce or prevent relapse.

ANTIDEPRESSANT DRUGS. A second group of drugs is used to combat depression. These drugs seem to work by increasing the amounts of serotonin and norepinephrine in the brain (Berger, 1978). Unlike the use of antipsychotic drugs to treat schizophrenia, the use of antidepressant compounds to treat depression has been dramatically successful in some cases. When taken even after acute episodes of depression, some antidepressant drugs have been shown to reduce drastically the likelihood of relapse (Prien et al., 1984).

However, individuals suffering from depressive disorders have been known to respond to a wide variety of treatments–and sometimes to no treatment at all. In a 1987 study sponsored by the National Institute of Mental Health, 239 depressive patients were divided into four groups. One group was treated with the antidepressant imipramine, a second underwent cognitive therapy, while a third underwent therapy based on interpersonal principles. A fourth group received harmless pills called placebos and minimal supportive consultations with a psychiatrist. After 16 weeks, between 50 and 60 percent of the patients in the first three groups recovered fully: The recovery figures were the same for drug therapy, cognitive therapy, and interpersonal therapy. Thus, even though prescription of antidepressant drugs has been considered a standard treatment for depression, this study indicates that such drugs are no more effective than psychotherapy in treating depression. Moreover, almost 30 percent of the people in the fourth group (who received placebo pills and minimal counseling) also recovered fully over the 16-week period with hardly any therapy at all.

This NIMH study is important for several reasons. It underscores the fact that antidepressant drugs are simply not effective in a significant proportion of cases. In fact, it is sometimes necessary to go from one drug to another until an effective one is found for a given individual. Also, while drugs alleviate some symptoms, it is often necessary to follow up pharmacological therapy with some form of psychotherapy even after "full recovery" is achieved. The NIMH study strongly suggests that even though drugs remain the quickest and least expensive form of therapy for depression, therapists should not hastily discard psychotherapy as an alternative treatment where time and resources permit its use.

Institutionalization

For the severely mentally ill, hospitalization has been the treatment of choice in the United States for the past 150 years. Of all the money spent on mental health in this country, 70 percent goes to hospital care (Kiesler, 1982a), and the direct cost of inpatient services is estimated to exceed $6 billion a year. More than 1.8 million people are admitted to mental hospitals annually.

However, mental hospitals are often large, isolated, state-run institutions in which patients face rather bleak prospects. Most such institutions are severely understaffed and cannot afford intensive therapy for all patients, so only the patients who seem to have the best chance of being cured, or at least of improving, are given therapy. Others receive only custodial care—the staff looks after them and sees that they are washed, dressed, and fed and that they take their medicine; but these patients may see a psychologist or psychiatrist for only a few minutes a week. Some hospitals have good recreational and vocational facilities; others have only a television set. Not surprisingly, patients on many wards are apathetic and seem to accept a permanent "sick role."

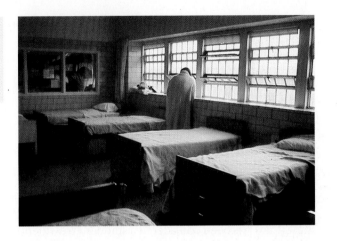

Deinstitutionalization The practice of providing patients with continued mental health care in the local community rather than keeping them in institutions.

Contrary to popular belief, mental hospitalization is increasing far faster than the population rate. More than 1.8 million people are admitted to mental hospitals annually.

Contrary to popular belief, (1) mental hospitalization is increasing far faster than the population rate; (2) mental hospitals—both state and private—account for only 25 percent of admissions for mental illness (most admissions for mental illness are to general hospitals without psychiatric units); (3) lengths of stay have decreased only at state and Veterans Administration psychiatric hospitals (where they still average six and five months, respectively); (4) several more effective alternatives to hospitalization exist; and (5) mental hospitalization accounts for 25 percent of total hospital days in the United States (Kiesler, 1982b).

Hospitalization as a treatment for mental illness is no bargain. What are the more effective—and more cost-effective—alternatives?

■ Alternatives to Institutionalization

Deinstitutionalization

The advent of antipsychotic drugs in the 1950s created a favorable climate of opinion for the policy of **deinstitutionalization**—releasing patients back into the community. The idea of deinstitutionalization was further strengthened in 1963, when Congress passed legislation that established a network of community mental health centers around the nation. The practice of placing patients in more humane facilities or returning them under medication to care within the community intensified during the 1960s and 1970s. The many community-based mental health centers that were starting up at the time made deinstitutionalization appear quite feasible. In fact, by 1975 there were 600 regional mental health centers, which accounted for 1.6 million instances of outpatient care.

However, deinstitutionalization has run into serious problems. Discharged patients are often confronted with poorly funded community mental health centers and a lack of adequate follow-up care. Moreover, they are often poorly prepared to live in the community and receive little guidance in coping with the mechanics of daily life. Patients who return home can become a burden to their families, especially if they don't get close follow-up care. Residential centers, such as halfway houses, vary

Deinstitutionalized patients often receive inadequate follow-up care, and programs for releasing patients back into the community may be a significant factor in the number of mentally disabled people who are homeless.

in quality, but many provide inadequate medical and psychological care and minimal contact with the outside world. In any case, the dearth of sheltered housing forces many former patients into nonpsychiatric facilities often located in dirty, unsafe, and isolated neighborhoods. And former patients are further burdened by a social stigma, which is perhaps the largest single obstacle to their rehabilitation (Bassuk & Gerson, 1978). Moreover, although deinstitutionalization and outpatient care are presumed to be well-established national policy objectives in mental health, Medicare, Medicaid, Blue Cross-Blue Shield, and other large insurers typically cover inpatient care completely but discourage outpatient care by requiring copayments and limiting the number of treatment visits.

The full effects of deinstitutionalization are not entirely known, because the number of follow-up studies on discharged patients has been inadequate—in part because patients are transient and difficult to follow for long periods. Some psychologists argue that deinstitutionalization should be discouraged until more research is done on the practice and its alternatives. They fear that the potential cost to society of burgeoning numbers of vagrants and mentally disabled people living in lonely hotels and dangerous streets could be vast—much greater than the cost of supporting the hospitals that would otherwise accommodate them. Others say that despite all the problems, deinstitutionalization is an essential part of mental health treatment.

The success or failure of deinstitutionalization hinges on the quality of continuing care available in the community. In order to succeed, the process requires better planning, more funding, and greater community support than it generally receives at present. Full-spectrum services are required, as are staff trained to cope with the problems of the mentally ill living in the community. In addition, short-term rehospitalization arrangements should be available for those who need them.

Alternative Forms of Treatment

Deinstitutionalization assumes that institutionalization occurred in the first place. Recently, however, forms of treatment that avoid hospitalization altogether have received increasing attention. Kiesler (1982a) examined 10 controlled studies in which seriously disturbed patients were

Primary prevention Techinques and programs for preventing or reducing the occurrence of mental illness by promoting mental health.

randomly assigned either to hospitals or to an alternative program. The alternative programs took many forms: patients living at home who were trained to cope with daily activities; a small homelike facility in which staff and residents shared responsibility for residential life; hostels offering therapy and crisis intervention; family crisis therapy; day-care treatment; visits from public health nurses combined with medication; and intensive outpatient counseling combined with medication. Whatever the specific form of alternatives, all involved daily professional contact and skillful preparation of the community to receive the patients. On the other hand, the hospitals to which some people were assigned provided very good patient care, probably substantially above average for institutions in the United States. Nevertheless, in 9 out of 10 studies, the outcome was more positive for alternative treatments than for hospitalization, even though hospitalization cost 40 percent more than the alternative programs. Moreover, patients given alternative care were less likely to undergo hospitalization later—a fact which suggests that to a degree, hospitalizing mental patients is a self-perpetuating process. Many such people "could be treated in alternative settings more effectively and less expensively," Kiesler concludes (1982a, p. 358).

Prevention

Yet another approach is to prevent the onset of mental illness in the first place. Although many preventive programs have been shown to be effective in eliminating or reducing disturbance, no more than 2 percent of the money spent on mental health goes for prevention (Albee, 1982). Practically all current efforts are targeted at treatment *after* mental illness develops. However, advocates of prevention observe that there are many more disturbed people in this country than could possibly be seen individually by mental health professionals. For example, Albee (1982) has estimated that "the mental health community actually sees fewer than one in five of the seriously disturbed people" (p. 1043). Since treatment programs cannot begin to reach all those in need, the desirability of making greater efforts at prevention becomes clear.

Suicide hot lines and other crisis intervention programs are *secondary prevention* measures designed to serve individuals and groups at high risk for mental disorder.

Prevention means reducing the incidence of emotional disturbance right from the start. In turn, this requires finding and eliminating the conditions that cause or contribute to behavior disorders and fostering well-being instead.

Currently, the concept of prevention has taken three related but distinguishable forms: *primary prevention*, which is aimed at lessening the likelihood of mental disease and at promoting general mental health; *secondary prevention*, or the effort to reduce the impact and spread of a currently existing problem and to prevent it from becoming more severe; and *tertiary prevention*, which involves strategies to reduce the long-term consequences of mental disorders to individuals who suffer from them.

Primary prevention includes family planning and genetic counseling. Prospective parents can get assistance in thinking through such questions as how many children to have and when. Tests can be conducted to diagnose genetic defects, and advances in genetic research sometimes make it possible to alleviate potential defects even before a baby is born. Primary prevention also involves programs for increasing personal and social competencies among a wide variety of groups. For example, one program might help mothers to encourage the development of problem-solving skills among their children; another program might enhance competence and adjustment among the elderly. Current campaigns to educate young people about the consequences of drugs are also examples of primary prevention measures.

Secondary prevention requires the identification of groups that are at high risk for mental disorders—for example, abused children, people who are recently divorced, and people laid off from their jobs. The main thrust of secondary prevention is *intervention*—detecting maladaptive behavior early and treating it promptly. One form of intervention is crisis intervention, which includes such programs as suicide hot lines; another is the establishment of short-term crisis facilities at which a therapist can provide face-to-face counseling and support for high-risk individuals and families.

The main objective of **tertiary prevention** is to help individuals adjust to community life after release from a mental hospital. Hospitals, for example, often grant passes to encourage patients to leave the institution for short periods of time prior to their release. Tertiary prevention

Secondary prevention Techniques and programs emphasizing early detection of maladaptive behavior and prompt treatment in high risk groups.

Tertiary prevention Techniques and programs for reducing the long-term consequences of mental illness by facilitating an individual's readjustment to family and community life.

■ Self-help Groups

This chapter emphasizes the treatment and therapy that trained professionals provide. But there are simply not enough mental health professionals to provide treatment for everyone who needs or wants it (Lieberman, 1986). For example, in Chapter 14 we saw that at any given time, nearly 30 million adult Americans suffer from some form of psychological disorder (Regier et al., 1988); counting children and adolescents, the total rises to 40–45 million. Only a fraction of those people can be served by mental health professionals.

As a result of this gap in the mental health system (as well as the high cost of many forms of professional treatment), more and more people are turning to low-cost, self-help groups to obtain support and help when they are faced with life crises (Tyler, 1980). According to recent conservative estimates, more than 6 million adult Americans presently belong to self-help groups, and that number is expected to grow to at least 10 million by the end of the century (Jacobs & Goodman, 1988).

What are self-help groups and how do they work? Most self-help groups are small, local gatherings of people who share a common problem or predicament and who provide mutual assistance for each other at a very lost cost (Katz, 1981; Jacobs & Goodman, 1988). Alcoholics Anonymous is a particularly well-known self-help group, but there are also groups for people suffering from anorexia, arthritis, cancer, divorce, drug abuse, as well as for parents whose children have died or are chronically ill or handicapped, for adolescents, for retirees, overeaters, compulsive gamblers, AIDS victims, former mental patients, people suffering from depression or anxiety—in short, there are self-help groups for virtually every conceivable life problem.

Do self-help groups work? The evidence is that, in many cases, apparently they do. Alcoholics Anonymous has developed an enviable reputation for helping people to cope with alcoholism. And both the number of self-help groups and their rapid growth in the 1980s reflect their widespread appeal. Research confirms that most group members express strong support for their groups (Riordan & Beggs, 1987). And the few studies that have directly measured the effectiveness of self-help groups have demonstrated that they can indeed be effective (Galanter, 1984; Videka-Sherman, 1982).

Though more research is needed before we will know for certain how self-help groups can be used most effectively, it seems likely that such groups will play an especially valuable role in preventing psychological disorders by reaching out to people who are nearing the limits of their ability to cope effectively with life stress. By providing social support, and by increasing their members' coping skills through information and advice, self-help groups may significantly reduce the likelihood that their members will develop more serious psychological problems that will require professional treatment.

measures also include halfway houses, where patients can find support and skills training during the period of transition, and nighttime and outpatient programs that provide supportive therapy while the patients continue to lead normal family lives and to hold down jobs. Tertiary prevention also involves efforts to educate the community that the patient must reenter.

A good example of a variety of preventive measures being implemented is the aftermath of the Hyatt Regency Hotel disaster in Kansas City in 1981, when the sudden collapse of two aerial walkways in the midst of a crowded "tea dance" killed 111 people and injured more than 200. The disaster had a major emotional impact on the rescuers and survivors, as well as on hotel and media employees, medical personnel, hotel guests, and the family and friends of the dead and injured (Gist & Stolz, 1982). An estimated 5,000 people faced psychological consequences; because virtually all the victims were local, and entire community felt the impact.

By the Monday after the Friday evening disaster, all the community mental health centers in the area had organized support group activities. Training was arranged for the professionals and natural caregivers, such as ministers, who would respond to Hyatt-related emotional problems. In addition, a major campaign was undertaken to publicize the availability of psychological services and to "legitimize the expression and acceptance of psychological reactions to the disaster" (Gist & Stolz, 1982, p. 1137). Press releases delivered a consistent message to the community, describing the reactions that were to be expected after such a disaster, emphasizing that they were normal responses that needed to be shared and accepted, and reminding people that help was available. As a result of these preventive steps, the number of serious delayed reactions was far below what would otherwise have been expected.

Preventing behavior disorders rather than treating them afterward has been the ideal of the mental health community—if not the reality—since 1970 at least, when the final report of the Joint Commission on Mental Health of Children called for prevention as a new focus in mental health work. Ironically, because preventive programs are often long-range in scope and indirect in focus, they may be the first to be eliminated in times of economic hardship, when cuts are being made on the basis of cost-effectiveness.

■ Gender Differences in Treatments

In Chapter 14, we saw that there are significant differences between men and women in the prevalence of many psychological disorders. There are also important similarities and differences in the treatment that men and women receive. First, women are more likely than men to be in psychotherapy (Williams, 1987). In part, this undoubtedly reflects the higher rate of mental illness among women. But in addition, it is likely that women are more willing than men to admit that they have psychological problems and that they need help solving those problems. Moreover, psychotherapy is more socially accepted and approved for women than for men (Williams, 1987). Whatever the reasons for the difference, it is estimated that in 1977 5.6 percent of all females visited ambulatory health care facilities for treatment of psychological problems, compared to 3.5 percent of males (Russo, 1985; Williams, 1987). A 1980 national survey arrived at a similar finding: Sixty percent of the people seeing psychologists and psychiatrists were women (Williams, 1987).

In most respects, the treatment received by women is the same as that received by men, but this fact has come to be a source of some concern in recent years. Most therapists are male, and most vocational and rehabilitation programs are male-oriented. This, in turn, opens the possibility that women in therapy may be encouraged to adopt traditional, male-oriented views of what is "normal" or "appropriate," that there may be a tendency for male therapists to encourage women to adapt, adjust, or conform to their surroundings passively, and that male therapists may not be sufficiently sensitive to the extent to which some of the stress experienced by women derives from the world in which they live (APA, 1975; Asher, 1975). In response to these concerns, there has been an increase recently in the number of "feminist therapists," who attempt to help their clients become more aware of the extent to which their problems derive from external controls and inappropriate sex roles, become more conscious of and attentive to their own needs and goals, and to develop a sense of pride in their womanhood and not passively accept or identify with the status quo (Williams, 1987).

There is one important respect in which the therapeutic treatment received by women often differs from that received by men: Women receive a disproportionate share of drugs prescribed for psychological disorders. Overall, more than 70 percent of all prescriptions written by psychiatrists are for women, although women account for only 58 percent of psychiatrists' office visits (Russo, 1985; Basow, 1986). Similarly, although women account for only two-thirds of the cases of depressive disorders, they receive 70–80 percent of all antidepression medications. Researchers have not yet identified the reasons for this sex bias in drug prescriptions, but it has become a source of considerable concern. The willingness to prescribe drugs to women may encourage women to see their problems as having physical causes and thus as being their own fault. Moreover, the readiness to prescribe drugs for women may in part account for the fact that women abuse prescription drugs more often than men do (Russo, 1985).

As researchers continue to explore these various issues, the American Psychological Association (1978) has issued the following guidelines regarding treatment of women in psychotherapy:

1. The conduct of therapy should be free of constrictions based on gender-defined roles, and the options explored between client and practitioner should be free of sex role stereotypes.
2. Psychologists should recognize the reality, variety, and implications of sex-discriminatory practices in society and should facilitate client examination of options in dealing with such practices.
3. The therapist should be knowledgeable about current empirical findings on sex roles, sexism, and individual differences resulting from the client's gender-defined identity.

4. The theoretical concepts employed by the therapist should be free of sex bias and sex role stereotypes.

5. The psychologist should demonstrate acceptance of women as equal to men by using language free of derogatory labels.

6. The psychologist should avoid establishing the source of personal problems within the client when they are more properly attributable to situational or cultural factors.

7. The psychologist and a fully informed client mutually should agree on aspects of the therapy relationship such as treatment modality, time factors, and fee arrangements.

8. While the importance of the availability of accurate information to a client's family is recognized, the privilege of communication about diagnosis, prognosis, and progress ultimately resides with the client, not with the therapist.

9. If authoritarian processes are employed as a technique, the therapy should not have the effect of maintaining or reinforcing stereotypic dependency of women.

10. The client's assertive behaviors should be respected.

11. The psychologist whose female client is subjected to violence in the form of physical abuse or rape should recognize and acknowledge that the client is the victim of a crime.

12. The psychologist should recognize and encourage exploration of a woman client's sexuality and should recognize her right to define her own sexual preferences.

13. The psychologist should not have sexual relations with a woman client nor treat her as a sex object.

 APPLICATION

How to Find Help

As we have seen in this chapter, there is no such thing as *therapy* in a definitive sense; there are only *therapies*. There are probably as many approaches to therapy as there are practicing psychologists. While we have referred to a number of therapies in this chapter, there are others—many of them developed through a synthesis of various techniques and practices. Whole books could be (and have been) written to list the many people and organizations dedicated to helping those who feel that they need some kind of counseling.

It should be clear by now that therapy and psychological counseling are not just intended to help "crazy" people. Unfortunately, the notion that seeking help for your problems is a sign of weakness or mental illness is hard to dispel. But the fact is that tens of thousands of people have been helped through psychological counseling and therapy. These people include business executives, artists, sports heroes, celebrities, and students. They are, in short, people like you and me. Therapy is a common, useful aid in coping with daily living.

College is a time of stress and anxiety for many students. The pressure of work, the competition for grades, the exposure to different people with different views, the tension of relating to your peers—these and other factors add up to considerable emotional and physical stress. These problems can be made worse because many students are away from home for the first time. Most colleges and universities have their own counseling services—many of them as sophisticated as the best clinics in the country. Most communities also have community mental health programs. As an aid to a potential search for the right counseling service, we are including a list of some of the other available resources for people seeking mental health professionals. Many of these services have national offices that, if contacted, will provide you with local branches and the appropriate people to contact in your area.

FOR HELP LOCATING AN APPROPRIATE SELF-HELP GROUP NEAR YOU:

National Self-Help Clearinghouse
Graduate School and University Center of the
City University of New York
33 West 42nd Street, Room 1227
New York, NY 10036
(212) 840-1259

ALCOHOL AND DRUG ABUSE

Alcohol and Drug Problems Association
1130 17th St. NW
Washington, DC 20036

National Clearinghouse for Alcohol Information
P.O. Box 2345
Rockville, MD 20852

National Clearinghouse for Drug Abuse Information
Room 110
1400 Rockville Pike
Rockville, MD 20852

Veterans Administration
Alcohol and Drug Dependency Services
810 Vermont Ave. NW
Washington, DC 20005

Association of Halfway Houses
Alcoholism Programs, Inc.
786 E. 7th St.
St. Paul, MN 55106

General Service Board
Alcoholics Anonymous, Inc.
P.O. Box 459, Grand Central Station
New York, NY 10017

FOR THOSE WITH A FRIEND OR RELATIVE WHO HAS AN ALCOHOL PROBLEM:

Alanon Family Group Headquarters, Inc.
P.O. Box 182, Madison Square Station
New York, NY 10010

National Association for Children of Alcoholics
31582 Coast Highway, Suite B
South Laguna, CA 92677
(714) 499-3889

SMOKING

The National Congress of Parents and Teachers
700 North Rush St.
Chicago, IL 60611

Weight and Smoking Counseling Service
400 E. 59th. St.
New York, NY 10022
(212) 755-4363

DEPRESSION AND SUICIDE

Mental Health Counseling Hotline
33 East End Ave.
New York, NY 10028
(212) 734-5876

International Association for Suicide Prevention
Suicide Prevention Center
1041 S. Menlo Ave.
Los Angeles, CA 90006
(213) 381-5111

Payne-Whitney Suicide Prevention Program
525 E. 68th St.
New York, NY 10021
1-800-822-2694

National Save-A-Life League
815 Second Ave., Suite 409
New York, NY 10017
(718) 492-4067

SEXUAL AND SEX-RELATED PROBLEMS

Community Sex Information, Inc.
P.O. Box 2858, Grand Central Station
New York, NY 10017

Sex Information and Education Council of the United States (SIECUS)
137-158 N. Franklin St.
Hempstead, NY 11550
(516) 483-3033

National Rape Task Force Coordinator
National Organization for Women Legislative Office
1107 National Press Building
Washington, DC 20004
(202) 347-2279

Association of Women in Psychiatry
Women's Studies Dept., University of Delaware
34 W. Delaware
Newark, DE 19711

Association of Gay Psychiatrists
P.O. Box 29527
Atlanta, GA 30359
(404) 231-0751

Homosexual Community Counseling Center, Inc.
30 E. 60th St.
New York, NY 10022
(212) 517-3171

STRESS

American Academy of Stress Disorders
8 S. Michigan Ave.
Chicago, IL 60603
(312) 263-7343

Neurotics Anonymous
1341 G St. NW, Room 426
Washington, DC 20005

National Commission Against Mental Illness
1101 17th St. NW
Washington DC 20036
(202) 296-4435

FOR HELP IN SELECTING A THERAPY:

Psychiatric Service Section
American Hospital Association
840 N. Lake Shore Drive
Chicago, IL 60611

Mental Health Help Line
789 West End Ave.
New York, NY 10024
(212) 222-7666

Psychotherapy Selection Service
3 E. 80th St.
New York, NY 10021
(212) 861-6387

GENERAL INFORMATION ON MENTAL HEALTH
AND COUNSELING

The National Alliance for the Mentally Ill
1901 N. Fort Meyer Drive, Suite 500
Arlington, VA 22209

Mental Health Association
1800 N. Kent St.
Arlington, VA 22209
(703) 528-6405

The American Psychiatric Association
1700 18th St. NW
Washington, DC 20009

The American Psychological Association
1200 17th St. NW
Washington, DC 20036

The National Institute of Mental Health
1400 Rockville Pike
Rockwall Bldg. Room 505
Rockville, MD 20850

Community Psychology Division
The American Psychiatric Association
c/o Barbara Dohrenwend
CUNY Graduate Center
33 W. 42nd St.
New York, NY 10036

Counseling Division
The American Psychiatric Association
c/o Norman I. Kagan
Department of Education
Michigan State University
East Lansing, MI 48823

Rehabilitation Psychiatry Division
The American Psychiatric Association
c/o Durand Jacobs
VA Hospital
10701 East Boulevard
Cleveland, OH 44106

■ Summary

- *Psychotherapy* is a general term for a variety of therapist-client relationships that seek to aid the client in resolving personal problems. Many experimentally oriented psychologists consider therapy a vaguely defined procedure, but others feel differently and point out that various types of therapy have been shown to be suited to certain people and certain problems. Most therapists employ techniques from a number of different types of therapy in their work.

- **Insight therapy** is a general term that comprises a variety of therapies used in private practice and institutions. Insight therapies try to give people a better understanding and awareness of their feelings, motivations, and actions.

- **What is free association? Psychoanalysis**, as developed by Freud, is based on the belief that the anxiety and problems that cause a person to seek help are symptoms of repressed problems from early childhood. Psychoanalysis brings these repressed problems to consciousness so that the person can deal directly with them by working through them. This entails healing with *positive* and *negative transference* toward the therapist. Successful analysis depends on the person's effort not to inhibit or control his or her thoughts and fantasies, but to express them in a process of *free association*. The goal of analysis is *insight*.

- **Are therapists basically silent observers who listen to their patients talk?** The analyst remains neutral and for the most part, silent, but many psychologists believe that therapists should take an active role in trying to get their clients to focus on coping with current problems rather than on resolving past conflicts. According to Carl Rogers's *client-centered* or *person-centered therapy,* the goal is to help people become fully functioning; to open them up to all of their experiences and to all of themselves so that they have no reason to act defensively. The client-centered therapist is nondirective and tries only to reflect the client's statements.

- **Rational-emotive therapy** (RET) assumes that people have become trapped by irrational and self-defeating beliefs. RET therapists directly show their clients how their misinterpretations of events cause their problems and teach their clients to see themselves and events more rationally.

- **Can people be taught new ways of behaving, much the same way they are taught anything else?** Behaviorists reject the idea that behavior disorders are symptoms of hidden emotional conflicts and hold instead that the behavior disorder itself is the problem. **Behavior therapies** are based on the belief that all behavior is learned. The behavior therapist seeks to teach the client more satisfying behavior by applying principles of conditioning. In *operant conditioning*, people learn to behave in different ways if new behaviors are reinforced and old behaviors ignored or punished. **Behavioral contracting** is a form of operant conditioning in which client and therapist agree to preset goals and conditions.

- **Aversive conditioning** is aimed at eliminating undesirable behavior patterns by teaching clients to associate pain and discomfort with the undesirable response. It has been used successfully to treat alcoholism, obesity, and smoking.

- Irrational fears and anxiety have been successfully treated using **desensitization.** Wolpe believes that chronically anxious people may not know why they feel tense, but that they can distinguish among different levels of anxiety. The therapist establishes a *hierarchy* from the least to the most anxiety-producing situations, and then teaches the person to relax. The therapist begins with the least threatening scene and works up to the most threatening one.

- **Cognitive behavior therapists** believe that their clients suffer from misconceptions about themselves and their relationship to their environment. Therapists using this method focus their clients' attentions on their negative and unrealistic ways of thinking and try to get clients to think more logically and realistically about life situations. A related form of therapy, **stress-inoculation therapy,** asks clients to attend to self-statements about their responses to stressful situations and tries to develop strategies for applying new attitudes to those situations.

- **Group therapies** allow both the therapist and the client to see the client interacting with others. They also give clients a chance to shed inhibitions and express themselves in a safe atmosphere, and provide them with a source of reinforcement.

- **If a person's problems stem from relationships within the family, can a therapist work with the whole family to deal with those problems?** *Family therapy* is a special form of group therapy. It is based on the idea that when one family member has problems, the whole family may need help. It aims to improve communication and empathy among family members and to enable them to share leadership and reduce conflict. One form of group therapy is **marital therapy**, which concentrates on improving couples' patterns of communication and mutual expectations.

- Both family and marital therapy developed out of the **interpersonal theory** of personality first systemized by Sullivan, who felt that such disorders as anxiety could be aroused as a result of an individual's early relationships with others. Therapies derived from Sullivan's position encourage the therapist to establish a pattern of interaction whereby the client can develop a self-image that is compatible with his or her relationships with other people in a variety of real-life situations.

- **Gestalt therapy** emphasizes the whole person and attempts to reawaken a person to his or her feelings. *Large-group awareness training,* such as **est,** has become popular in recent years. Est teaches people to experience reality directly, instead of experiencing automatic associations with the past.

- **How effective is psychotherapy?** The question of *effectiveness* of psychotherapy has become an important one. Although one early survey by Eysenck suggested that psychotherapy was no more effective than no treatment, the majority of subsequent well-controlled surveys of outcome indicate that the effectiveness of psychotherapy is moderately high. Although no particular form of psychotherapy seems inherently superior to any other, different forms are especially suited to different problems.

- **Is electroconvulsive or shock therapy still used?** Among the **biological treatments** for mental illness, the use of **electroconvulsive therapy** (ECT), which may be helpful with some severe depressions, is decreasing in frequency. **Psychosurgery** such as lobotomy, which is irreversible, is even more rare. *Drug therapy* has been a powerful tool in the treatment of mental illness. The *antipsychotic drugs* have been important in the treatment of major disorders such as schizophrenia, reducing anxiety and aggression, and decreasing hallucinations and delusions. *Antidepressant drugs*—namely, *monoamine oxidase* (MAO) *inhibitors* and the *tricyclics*—can be extremely effective in reversing depression.

- Severe mental illness is most often treated by the hospitalization of the patient. Many mental institutions are large, impersonal, state-run facilities that have been criticized as mere "warehouses" for the mentally ill, providing little real treatment and little real expectation of recovery. The rate of mental institutionalization has risen in spite of the growing popularity of the idea of deinstitutionalization.

- **Why are there so many mentally disturbed people living on city streets?** *Deinstitutionalization,* or the release of mental patients from large institutions to more humane facilities or back to the community, has not been a great success. The process requires more follow-up care, more funding, and more community support than it has received. As a result, many formerly institutionalized people now live as vagrants.

- Some forms of treatment for mentally ill people seek to avoid hospitalization altogether. Patients have been treated at home or in small-group living situations with frequent contact with mental health professionals. Several studies suggest that this type of treatment, which does not begin to remove the client from normal surroundings, is more effective than hospitalization and can be obtained at a lower cost.

- **What can be done to prevent mental illness?** Preventing mental illness is even less costly than the most efficient methods of treating it. **Primary prevention** includes family planning and genetic counseling. **Secondary prevention** attempts to identify people who are at high risk for mental illness, such as abused children, and provides services to prevent the appearance of serious disturbance. **Tertiary prevention** provides services to patients released from mental treatment facilities in order to avoid rehospitalization.

- **Are women more likely to be mentally disturbed than men?** Women are more likely than men to receive therapy for psychological disorders. This appears to be due in part to the greater prevalence of psychological disorders among women, but also to a greater willingness on the part of women to admit that they have problems and need help, as well as greater social approval for women to be in therapy. The treatment received by women is generally similar to that received by men, but concerns have been raised not only about the effectiveness of male-oriented therapies for women but also about the disproportionate use of prescription drugs with women.

▪ Review Questions

1. Which of the following is the goal of working through problems in psychoanalysis?
   - a. free association
   - b. positive transference
   - c. countertransference
   - d. insight

2. Match the terms at left with the appropriate descriptions at right:
   - ____ psychoanalysis
   - ____ client-
   - a. aimed at teaching clients to stop misinterpreting events

centered therapy

_____ cognitive behavior therapy

_____ rational-emotive therapy

and to see themselves more rationally

b. based on the idea that anxiety stems from repressed problems from childhood

c. goal is to help clients become more fully functioning

d. seeks to relieve clients of their misconceptions about themselves and their relationship to their environment

3. Rogerian therapists show that they value and accept their clients by providing _____ _____ regard.

4. In contrast with _____ therapies, which seek to increase clients' self-awareness, _____ therapies try to teach people more appropriate ways of acting.

5. A client begins therapy to get rid of an irrational fear of elevators. A technique that the therapist is likely to employ is _____
   a. desensitization.
   b. behavior contracting.

6. The behavior therapy known as _____ _____ discourages undesired behaviors by associating them with pain and discomfort.

7. Match the therapies at left with their descriptions at right:

_____ Gestalt

_____ large-group awareness training

a. emphasizes that reality should be experienced directly rather than linked with the past

_____ est

_____ interpersonal therapy

b. teaches people to experience reality directly and to avoid illogical associations with past experiences

c. emphasizes the whole person and awareness of feelings

d. assists people in developing a self-image compatible with relationships in real-life situations

8. Family therapists concentrate on changing the needs and personalities of individual family members. T / F

9. Behavior therapy has generally been found to be more effective than insight therapy for most types of problems. T / F

10. Drugs that help to control schizophrenia are called _____
    a. barbiturates   c. lithium.
    b. tricyclics.   d. antipsychotics.

11. The practice of treating severely mentally ill people in large, state-run facilities is known as _____.

12. The mentally ill who receive alternative care are less likely to undergo hospitalization later on. T / F

13. The establishment of halfway houses and similar facilities within the community is an example of the movement toward _____.

14. Crisis intervention and hot lines are two examples of _____, that is, coping with mental illness before it occurs.

16 Social Psychology

■ Thinking Critically

How do we form first impressions?

If a friend says, "Sam is a lot of fun," is it likely that you will like him when you meet him?

You run into a friend at the supermarket and greet him warmly, but he barely acknowledges you, mumbling "Hi" and walking away. What affects how you interpret his reaction?

When it comes to love, do opposites attract?

If someone who has never particularly liked the city accepts a great job in Manhattan, are their feelings about city life likely to change?

If you're in a crowded shopping mall and you see someone sitting on the floor, crying, possibly because they've fallen, why is it unlikely that you will walk over and ask if they need help?

What makes a person a leader?

How does the environment in which we live and work affect our relations with others?

The answers to these and other questions about why people behave the way they do in relationships and in groups are discussed in this chapter and in the Chapter Summary.

■ Outline

Social psychology The scientific study of the way in which the thoughts, feelings, and behaviors of one individual are influenced by the real, imagined, or implied behavior or characteristics of other people.

We all spend much of our time alone thinking about our relations with other people. We try to explain to ourselves why we like one person and dislike another. We attempt to make sense of other people's behavior given various situations and our own behavior. We examine our attitudes and think about how they compare to those of the people around us. We meet with others in groups and wonder whether the group will be effective in solving problems.

Social psychologists address the same questions, but they do so with more systematic methods than we use at home in our armchairs. **Social psychology** is the scientific study of the way in which the thoughts, feelings, and behaviors of one individual are influenced by the real, imagined, or inferred behavior or characteristics of other people.

We begin by exploring the ways in which people form impressions of and make judgments about each other as well as the factors that influence whether or not people are attracted to one another. Next we will consider the ways in which people's attitudes and behaviors are shaped and changed by others. Then our discussion will shift to relationships between people in small groups and large organizations. Finally, we will examine the ways in which the environment influences people's feelings, attitudes, and behaviors.

■ Social Perception

Before we meet someone, we want to know what kind of person he or she is so that we can adjust our expectations and behavior accordingly. Unfortunately, such information is often difficult to acquire, so we are forced to form first impressions of people using only scanty evidence.

Impression Formation

In forming our first impressions of someone, we use external cues to fit the person into categories.

How do we form our first impressions of people? What external cues do we use? And how accurate are we?

When we meet someone for the first time, we may notice a number of things about that person—clothes, gestures, manner of speaking, tone of voice, firmness of handshake, and so on. We then use these cues to fit the person into ready-made *categories*. No matter how little information we may have or how contradictory it may be, no matter how many times in the past our initial impressions of people have been wrong, we still classify and categorize people. Associated with each category is a *schema*, which, as we saw in Chapter 6, is a set of beliefs or expectations about something (in this case, people) that is based on past experience and that is presumed to apply to all the people in that category. For example, if a person is wearing a white coat and has a stethoscope around her neck, we might reasonably categorize her as a doctor and as a result conclude that she is a highly trained professional, knowledgeable about diseases and their cures, qualified to prescribe drugs, and so on. These various conclusions follow from most people's schemas of *doctor*.

Schemas serve a number of important functions. For one thing, they allow us to make inferences about other people. We assume, for example, that a friendly person is also likely to be good-natured, to accept a social invitation from us, or to do us a small favor. We may not know these things for sure, but our schema for *friendly person* allows us to infer them.

Schemas also play a crucial role in how we interpret and remember information. In fact, research shows that people have difficulty with information that does not fit an established schema. For example, in one study, some subjects were told that they would be getting information about friendly, sociable men. Other subjects were informed that the men were achievement-oriented intellectuals. Both groups were then given the same information about 50 men and asked to say how many of the men were friendly and how many were intellectual. The subjects who had expected to hear about friendly men dramatically overestimated the number of friendly men, and those who had expected to hear about intellectual men greatly overestimated the number of intellectual men. Moreover, each group of subjects forgot many of the details that were inconsistent with their expectations (Rothbart, Evans, & Fulero, 1979). In short, the subjects tended to hear and remember what they expected to hear.

Schemas can also lure us into "remembering" things about people that we never actually observed. For most of us, shyness, quietness, and preoccupation with one's own thoughts, for example, are all traits associated with the schema *introvert*. If we notice that Marjorie is shy, we are likely to categorize her as an introvert. Later, we may "remember" that she also seemed preoccupied with her own thoughts. In other words, thinking of Marjorie as an introvert saves us the trouble of taking into account all the subtle shadings of her personality. But this can easily lead to errors if we attribute to Marjorie qualities that belong to the schema but not to her.

Now that you've had a chance to read about how impressions are formed, consider some information about a young man named Jim:

> Jim left the house to get some stationery. He walked out into the sun-filled street with two of his friends. . . . Jim entered the stationery store, which was full of people. Jim talked with an acquaintance while he waited for the clerk to catch his eye. On his way out, he met the girl to whom he had been introduced the night before. They talked for a short while, and then Jim left for school.

> After school, Jim left the classroom alone. . . . The street was brilliantly filled with sunshine. Jim walked down the street on the shady side. Coming down the street toward him, he saw the pretty girl whom he had met the previous evening. Jim crossed the street and entered a candy store. . . . Jim waited quietly until the counterman caught his eye and then gave his order. Taking his drink, he sat down at a side table. When he had finished his drink, he went home.

What do you think of Jim? Would you say that he is introverted or extroverted? Luchins (1957) used these two descriptions to study the **primacy effect** in impression formation: the extent to which the first information we receive about someone influences our impression of that person more heavily than later information. Ninety-five percent of the

Primacy effect The extent to which early information about someone weighs more heavily than later information in influencing one's impression of that person.

To avoid the *primacy effect*, interviewers must take care to interpret information about others slowly and carefully.

Self-fulfilling prophecy The process in which a person's expectation about another elicits behavior from the second person that confirms the expectation.

Stereotype A set of characteristics presumed to be shared by all members of a social category.

people who read only the first paragraph described Jim as an extrovert, while 86 percent of those who read only the second paragraph described him as an introvert. When people were asked to read both paragraphs in the order given here, 78 percent described Jim as an extrovert (as you probably did). When the order of the paragraphs was reversed, 63 percent called him introverted. Apparently in each case, the first paragraph "primed" a certain schema—a way of thinking about Jim. The subjects then reinterpreted, explained away, or ignored facts in the second paragraph that were inconsistent with the schema suggested by the first.

If people are specifically warned to beware of first impressions, or if they are encouraged to interpret information about others slowly and carefully, the primacy effect can be weakened or even nullified (Luchins, 1957; Stewart, 1965). Generally, however, the first impression is the lasting impression, and it can affect our behavior even when it is not entirely accurate. In one study, Snyder and Swann (1978) asked pairs of subjects to play a competitive game. They told one member of each pair that the partner was either hostile or friendly. Players who were led to believe that their partners were hostile behaved differently from players led to believe that their partners were friendly. In turn, the supposedly hostile partners actually began to display hostility. Later on, the partners continued to show hostility, even though they were now paired with new players who had no expectations about them at all. The expectation of hostility on the player's part therefore produced actual aggressiveness in the other partner, and this behavior persisted with another player. When we bring about expected behavior in another person in this way, our impression has become a **self-fulfilling prophecy.**

STEREOTYPES. A **stereotype** is a set of characteristics believed to be shared by all members of a social category. In effect, a stereotype is a special kind of schema that is based on almost any distinguishing feature, including sex, race, occupation, physical appearance, place of residence, and membership in a group or organization (Hansen, 1984). When our first impressions of people are governed by a stereotype, we tend to infer things about them solely on the basis of their social category and to ignore facts that are inconsistent with the stereotype. As a result, we may remember things about them selectively or inaccurately, thereby perpetuating the initial stereotype.

Like schemas in general, stereotypes can easily become the basis for self-fulfilling prophecies. Snyder, Tanke, and Berscheid (1976) paired college-age men and women who were strangers to each other and arranged for each pair to talk by phone. Before the call, each male was given a snapshot, presumably of the woman whom he was about to call. In fact, however, the snapshot was a randomly selected photo of either an attractive or an unattractive woman. Attractiveness carries with it a stereotype that includes sociability and social adeptness (see Box on pg. 606). The males in the experiment therefore expected attractive partners to display these qualities and expected the unattractive females to be unsociable, awkward, and serious. These expectations produced radically different behavior. The men who believed that they were talking to an attractive woman were warm, friendly, and animated; in response, the women acted in a friendly, animated way. The other men spoke to their partners in a cold, reserved manner. In response, the women reacted in a cool, distant manner. In other words, the stereotype took on a life of its own, subtly forcing the women to play appropriate roles.

So far, we have seen how people form impressions of other people and how those impressions affect subsequent behavior. But social perception goes beyond simple impression formation. We also try to make sense out of people's behavior, to uncover the reasons why they act as they do. This is the subject of the next section.

Attribution

Suppose you run into a friend at the supermarket. You greet him warmly, but he barely acknowledges you, mumbles "Hi," and walks away. You feel snubbed and try to explain his behavior. Did he behave that way because of something in the situation? Perhaps you said something that offended him; perhaps he was having no luck finding the groceries he wanted; or perhaps someone had just blocked his way by leaving a cart in the middle of an aisle. Or did something within him, some personal trait such as moodiness or arrogance, lead him to behave that way? Clearly, it makes quite a difference which of these explanations is correct.

Social interaction is filled with occasions like this one that invite us to make judgments about the causes of behavior. And social psychologists have discovered that we go about this process of judgment in predictable ways. These findings and the principles derived from them can be summarized under the heading **attribution theory.** One of the most influential of these attribution theories was developed by Harold Kelley (1967). According to Kelley, we rely on three kinds of information about behavior in an effort to draw conclusions about its cause.

The first piece of information is **distinctiveness.** If Joan laughs during a particular movie but not very often at movies in general, we would tend to assume that the movie was funny, not that Joan has a tendency to laugh. To the extent that a behavior (laughing) occurs only when a particular event also occurs (the movie), we tend to attribute the behavior to that event.

Second, we consider **consensus**—the degree to which other people in the situation are behaving in the same way. If everyone in the theater is laughing, we tend to attribute Joan's laughter to the film. But if she alone is laughing, we would tend to attribute her behavior to some aspect of her personality, such as an unusual sense of humor. Thus, high consensus points to the environment as a cause, while low consensus suggests a cause that is unique to the person.

Finally, we consider **consistency** of behavior, or the extent to which the behavior is the same whenever the presumed cause is present. If behavior is inconsistent, it is probably due to some temporary feature of the environment. If Joan saw the movie last week but did not laugh then, we cannot confidently explain her mirth either in terms of her personality or the movie. Instead, we would tend to assume that a passing mood, a good day at work, or some other momentary circumstance is operating.

Research has generally confirmed the predictions of Kelley's model. However, it has become increasingly clear that his model does not take into account all aspects of the attribution process. In particular, our attributions appear to be open to a number of intriguing biases.

Probably the most important bias is our general tendency to attribute

Attribution theory Theory that addresses the question of how people make judgments about the causes of behavior.

Distinctiveness The extent to which a behavior is present only when a particular stimulus is also present.

Consensus The extent to which everyone in a given situation is behaving in the same way.

Consistency The extent to which a particular event produces the same behavior each time it is present.

Fundamental attribution error The tendency of people to overemphasize personal causes for other people's behavior and to underemphasize those causes for their own behavior.

Defensive attribution Tendency to attribute success to our own efforts or qualities and failure to external factors.

our own actions to situational factors and the behavior of others to internal or personal factors (Jones & Nisbett, 1972). In your view, the unforeseen bump and icy conditions caused your fall as you zoomed down the ski hill. A companion, however, might be more inclined to relate your mishap to your inexperience as a skier or to your carelessness or awkwardness. The prosecutor in a trial may try to convince the jury that the defendant "did it on purpose and deserves to be blamed," while the defense attorney may respond by pointing out that her client was "a victim of circumstances and shouldn't be blamed." The tendency to give too much emphasis to personal factors when accounting for other people's actions is so common that one psychologist has termed it the **fundamental attribution error** (Ross, 1977).

A related bias is called **defensive attribution.** A number of studies have shown that we tend to explain our successes according to our personal abilities while attributing our failures to forces beyond our control (Zuckerman, 1979). For example, students tend to regard exams on which they do well as good indicators of their abilities, and exams on which they do poorly as defective indicators (Davis & Stephan, 1980). By the same token, studies also show that when students do well, teachers are more

■ People Do Judge Books—and People—by Their Covers

Appearance does make a difference. Physical attractiveness, clothing, hairstyle, and eyeglasses can powerfully influence the conclusions that other people reach about your character. Moreover, while you may not be able to buy groceries with your good looks, your appearance can have a real impact on your chances for success in life.

Attractive people are generally given credit for more than their beauty. They are presumed to be more intelligent, interesting, happy, kind, sensitive, and successful than are people who are not perceived as attractive. They are also thought to make better spouses and to be more sexually responsive (Dion, Berscheid, & Walster, 1972). People also tend to assume that handsome or beautiful strangers more closely resemble them in terms of personality traits than do less attractive individuals (Marks & Miller, 1980). If this weren't distressing enough, positive assumptions also attach themselves to the *partner* of an attractive person: Subjects rate a male more positively if a woman described as his girlfriend is attractive than if she is not (Meiners & Sheposh, 1977). However, being beautiful carries with it a few negative preconceptions: Attractive women are more likely to be seen as vain and apt to cheat on their husbands (Dermer & Thiel, 1975).

Aspects of appearance other than attractiveness also affect our judgments of others. People who wear glasses are thought at first to be more intelligent, reliable, and persevering than people who do not (Argyle & McHenry, 1971). And, as dress-for-success handbooks have been quick to point out, clothes make the man, or woman. A black raincoat, penny-loafers, or a shirt with a floral pattern does not reflect favorably on the credentials of a young man eager to enter banking.

Appearance can also have material consequences. Attractive people are often more persuasive when they communicate with others. In addition, other people try harder to please good-looking individuals (Sigall, Page, & Brown, 1971). Another study found that even in nursery school, children are more responsive to attractive than to less attractive peers. Moreover, teachers tend to be more lenient toward the undesirable behavior of an exceptionally attractive child and to have higher expectations about his or her intelligence and grades. These reactions can eventually give attractive people substantial advantages in life.

This almost universally favorable attitude toward physical attractiveness can become a self-fulfilling prophecy. Physically attractive people may come to think of themselves as good or lovable because they are continually treated that way. Conversely, unattractive people may begin to see themselves as bad or unlovable because they have always been regarded that way—even as children (Aronson, 1984).

likely to assume responsibility for their performance than when students perform poorly (Arkin, Cooper, & Kolditz, 1980).

Another kind of attribution error arises from the assumption that the world is just: Bad things happen to bad people and good things happen to good people. This is called the **just world hypothesis** (Lerner, 1980). Thus, when misfortune strikes someone, we often assume that the person deserved it rather than give full weight to situational factors that may have been responsible. One explanation for this attribution error is that we defend ourselves against the implied possibility that such a thing could happen to us. For example, by relocating the cause of a major accident from a chance event (something that could happen to us) to the victim's own negligence (a trait that we, of course, do not share), we defend ourselves against realizing that we could ever suffer such a misfortune (Chaikin & Darley, 1973).

Attraction and Liking

So far, we have seen how people form impressions of one another and judge the causes of their behavior. When people meet, what determines if they will like each other? This is the subject of much speculation and not a little mystification, with popular explanations running the gamut from fate to compatible astrological signs. Romantics believe that irresistible forces propel them toward an inevitable meeting with their beloved, but social psychologists take a more hardheaded view of the matter. They have found that attraction and liking are closely linked to such things as *proximity, similarity of attitudes and interests, attractiveness, rewardingness,* and *reciprocity.*

PROXIMITY. **Proximity** is probably the most important factor in determining attraction. The closer two people live to each other, the more they like each other.

Festinger, Schachter, and Back (1950) investigated the effects of proximity on friendship in a housing project for married students at MIT.

Just world hypothesis An attribution error based on the assumption that bad things happen to bad people and good things happen to good people.

Proximity How close two people live to each other.

By attributing the cause of a major accident to someone's negligence rather than to chance, we lessen the implication that something similar could happen to us.

Students taking exams may practice a bias called *defensive attribution error*—they may regard exams on which they do well as valid indicators of their abilities, while regarding exams on which they do poorly as defective indicators.

Figure 16-1
The relationship between proximity and liking "Units of approximate physical distance" means how many doors apart the people lived—2S means two doors and a stairway apart. The closer together people lived, the more likely they were to become friends.

Reprinted from *Social Pressures in Informal Groups* by Festinger, Schachter, and Back, 1950. Copyright © 1950 by the authors, used with permission of the publishers, Stanford University Press. Copyright renewed.

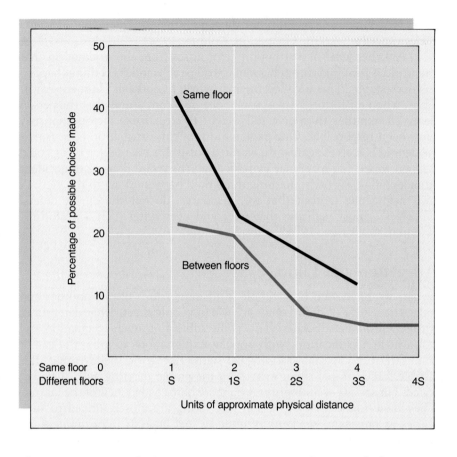

The project consisted of two-story apartment complexes, with five apartments to a floor. The investigators found that 44 percent of the residents were most friendly with their next-door neighbors, while only 10 percent said their best friends lived down the hall. An even smaller number were best friends with an upstairs or downstairs neighbor (see Figure 16-1). Similarly, Nahemow and Lawton (1975) found that 93 percent of the residents of an inner-city housing project chose their best friends from the same building.

SIMILARITY. Similarity of attitudes, interests, values, backgrounds, and beliefs is a powerful determinant of interpersonal attractiveness (Gonzales et al., 1983; Buss, 1985). When we know that a person shares our attitudes and interests, we tend to have more positive feelings toward that person (Byrne, 1961); the higher the proportion of attitudes that two people share, the stronger the attraction between them (Byrne & Nelson, 1965). This relationship between similarity and attraction holds true only up to a point, however. Some bases of similarity are clearly more important than others. A shared taste for bran muffins is not as consequential for friendship as a common interest in sports or religion. And the true degree of similarity may not be as important as *perceived* similarity (Marsden, 1966). We often assume that we share attitudes with people who attract us in other ways. Some research indicates that marriage may rest in part on the *illusion* of similarity. Spouses tend to perceive more similarity in their partner's attitudes than in fact exists (Byrne & Blaylock, 1963).

If similarity is such an important determinant of attractiveness, what about the notion that opposites attract? Aren't people sometimes attracted to others who are completely different from them? Extensive research has failed to confirm this notion: While it may be exciting and interesting to meet and get to know another person who is quite different from yourself, it is highly unlikely that you will be strongly attracted to each other. In long-term relationships, where attraction plays an especially important role, people overwhelmingly prefer to associate with other people who are similar to them (Buss, 1985).

PHYSICAL ATTRACTIVENESS. Not only do we tend to credit physically attractive people with a wealth of positive qualities, but we also tend to like them more than we do less attractive people. In a classic experiment, Hatfield and her colleagues (Walster et al., 1966) randomly paired male and female subjects at a dance. During a break in the dance, participants were asked how much they liked their partners. The only predictor of liking that the researchers could uncover was physical attractiveness. The better-looking the partner, the more he or she was liked. This relationship has been found to hold among members of the same sex as well: The physically attractive are more popular than less attractive people (Byrne, London, & Reeves, 1968).

REWARDINGNESS. According to the *reward theory of attraction*, we tend to like people whom we associate with rewards—with behavior that appeals to our own values and beliefs. But the relationship between attraction and rewardingness is complex. For example, Aronson's (1984) gain-loss theory of attraction suggests that *increases* in rewarding behavior influence attractiveness more than constant rewarding behavior does. In other words, if you were to meet and talk with the same person at three successive parties, and if, during these conversations, that person's behavior toward you changed from polite indifference to overt flattery, you would be inclined to like this person more than if he or she had immediately started to praise you during the first conversation and continued the praise each time you met. The reverse is also true: We tend to dislike people

Attraction and liking are closely linked to such factors as *proximity*, *similar interests*, *attractiveness*, *rewardingness*, and *reciprocity*. Men and women with common social characteristics are more likely to meet, develop relationships, and marry.

whose opinion of us changes from good to bad even more than we dislike those who consistently display a low opinion of us from the start.

Attitudes

The phrase "I don't like his attitude" is a telling one. People are often told to "change your attitude." What does this mean? Just what are attitudes? How are they formed? How can they be changed?

The Nature of Attitudes

An **attitude** toward something has three major components: *evaluative beliefs* about the object, *feelings* about the object, and *behavior tendencies* toward the object. Beliefs include facts, opinions, and our general knowledge about the object. Feelings include love, hate, like, dislike, and similar sentiments. Behavior tendencies include our inclinations to act in certain ways toward the object—to approach it, avoid it, and so on. For example, our attitude toward a political candidate includes our beliefs about the candidate: his or her qualifications and positions on crucial issues, expectations about how the candidate will vote on those issues, and the like. We also have feelings about the candidate—liking or disliking, trust or mistrust—and we are inclined to behave in certain ways toward the candidate—to vote for or against the candidate, to contribute

How to Win Friends the Hard Way

You don't necessarily have to be a nice person to get people to like you. Psychologists have discovered that insults and blunders can win friends too—under the right conditions (Worchel & Cooper, 1983). In one study, people who insulted other people before commencing a series of compliments were liked much more than those who delivered nothing but compliments. Apparently, people who begin with insults establish their credibility by doing so. Their subsequent compliments are more rewarding than still another good word from a person who has nothing but good words (Aronson & Linder, 1965).

Blunders can also endear you to others if you are perceived generally as being highly competent. In one experiment, some subjects listened to a taped interview with a highly competent person who was being interviewed for a chance to compete on a college quiz show. He answered 92 percent of the sample questions correctly and was described as an achiever in high school. Other subjects heard another tape

of an interview with a candidate who sounded much less competent. For each tape, half of the subjects heard a version of the tape that also included the sound of the candidate spilling coffee all over his suit. The other half of the subjects did not hear this blunder. Afterward, subjects were asked whether they liked the person being interviewed. Competent persons were more popular than less competent ones, but the most popular of all were the competent people who committed clumsy blunders (Aronson, Willerman, & Floyd, 1966). The blunder seemed to reduce the distance between the average person and those who were perceived as highly competent, making the latter more attractive.

Thus, if similarity of interests and attractiveness fail to lay the groundwork for a desired relationship, do not despair. You may be able to make good use of some of your usually less than charming qualities to achieve your goal.

time or money to the candidate's campaign, to attend or avoid rallies for the candidate, and so forth.

As we will see shortly, these three aspects of an attitude are very often consistent with one another. For example, if we have positive feelings toward something, we tend to have positive beliefs about it and to behave positively toward it. This does not mean, however, that our *actual* behavior will accurately reflect our attitude. Let's look more closely at the relation between attitudes and behavior.

Attitudes and Behavior

The relationship between attitudes and behavior is not always straight-forward. In one noted study done in the early 1930s, LaPiere (1934) traveled through the United States with an Oriental couple—at a time when prejudice against Orientals was still running high in this country. LaPiere discovered that they were refused service at only one of the 250 hotels and restaurants that they visited. Six months later, LaPiere sent a questionnaire to each of these establishments and asked if they would serve Chinese people. Most said they would not. LaPiere therefore concluded that attitudes are not reliable predictors of actual behavior. Subsequent research on the relationship between attitudes and behavior has often supported LaPiere's conclusion, particularly with respect to behavior in nonlaboratory settings (Wicker, 1969; Hanson, 1980).

But Fishbein and Ajzen (1975) point out that the weak relationship between attitudes and behavior may be due to improper measurement of either attitudes or behavior or both. For example, LaPiere measured attitudes toward Chinese people in general and then used that to predict specific behavior. If LaPiere had asked about attitudes toward the particular Chinese people who traveled with him rather than about Chinese people in general, the correlation between attitudes and behavior probably would have been higher.

Other researchers have pointed out that behavior is influenced by many factors besides attitudes. For instance, Ajzen and Fishbein (1980) have argued that behavior is closely linked to a person's intentions. Intentions, in turn, are only partly a product of the person's attitudes; they also reflect his or her acceptance of norms, including social pressures to perform or not to perform the behavior.

Personality traits are also important. Some people consistently match their actions to their attitudes (Norman, 1975). Others have a tendency to override their own attitudes in order to behave properly in a given situation. As a result, attitudes do not predict behavior as well among some people as among others (Snyder & Tanke, 1976).

Attitudes, then, can predict behavior, but psychologists have learned that many other variables affect the relationship between the two (Chaiken & Stangor, 1987). Intentions, social norms, and willingness to override one's attitudes are just a few of these other factors.

The Development of Attitudes

How do we acquire our attitudes? Where do they come from? Many of our most basic attitudes derive from early, direct personal experience. Children are rewarded with positive encouragement when they please

Our attitude toward a political candidate includes our beliefs, feelings, and behavioral tendencies toward that person. These three factors tend to be consistent with one another.

Attitudes can result from imitating other people. Children often adopt their parents' attitudes on issues, even when no attempt is made to influence their beliefs.

© Copyright 1983 S. Gross

S. GROSS

their parents, and they are punished through disapproval when they displease them. These early experiences give the child enduring positive and negative attitudes toward objects (Oskamp, 1977). Attitudes are also formed by imitation. Children mimic the behavior of their parents and peers and thus acquire attitudes even when no one is trying to influence their beliefs.

But parents are not the only source of attitudes, and often they are not even the most lasting influence in our lives. Our teachers, friends, and even famous people can be more important. If a young man joins a fraternity, for example, he may model his behavior and attitudes on those of the members. If a young woman idolizes one of her teachers, she may adopt many of the teacher's attitudes toward controversial subjects, even if they run counter to attitudes expressed by her parents.

Television and newspapers also have a great impact on the formation of attitudes in our society. Television bombards us with messages—not merely through commercials, but in more subtle ways: Violence is commonplace in life . . . women are dependent on men . . . without possessions your life is empty, and so on. Similarly, Hartmann and Husband (1971) have shown that without experience of their own, children are particularly reliant on television in forming their social attitudes. They found that white children in England who had little contact with nonwhites tended to associate race relations with conflicts and hostility more often than white children who lived in integrated neighborhoods. The first group of children was informed exclusively by TV news reports that focused on the problems caused by integration.

Attitude Change

A man watching TV on Sunday afternoon ignores scores of beer commercials but makes a note of an overnight delivery service that he sees advertised. A political speech convinces one woman to vote one way and her next-door neighbor to vote another. What makes one attempt to change attitudes fail and another succeed? More generally, just how and why do attitudes change? When do we resist change? And how successful is our resistance likely to be?

The answers to these questions depend in part on the technique used to influence our attitudes. We will look first at attempts to change attitudes with various kinds of persuasive messages.

THE INFORMATIONAL APPROACH. Although we are all bombarded with attempts to change our attitudes on subjects ranging from abortion to toothpaste, few of the methods used by interest groups and advertising agencies succeed (Costanzo et al., 1986). One of the major reasons for this is our ability to tune out what we do not want to hear. Brock and Balloun (1967) found that subjects were more likely to attend to *supportive* messages than *nonsupportive* ones. Kleinhesselink and Edwards (1975) took this a step further. They found that people listen to even nonsupportive messages as long as they are easy to refute but block out nonsupportive messages that are hard to refute.

Even if we do attend to a message, several factors determine how likely it is change our attitudes. In part, the effectiveness of the message depends upon its *source*. The *credibility* of the source is especially important

(McGuire, 1985). One source may have greater expertise or be more trustworthy than the other and thus be more credible (Hass, 1981). For example, we are less likely to change our attitude toward the oil industry's antipollution efforts if the president of a major refining company tells us about them than if we hear the same information from an impartial commission appointed to study the situation.

Recent research indicates that the credibility of the source is most important when we are not inclined to pay attention to the message itself (Petty & Cacioppo, 1981, 1986a; Cooper & Croyle, 1984). In cases where we have some interest in the message, the message itself plays a greater role in determining whether we change our attitudes (Petty & Cacioppo, 1986b). For example, the more arguments the message makes in favor of a position, the more effective the message (Calder, Insko, & Yandell, 1974). Also, audiences who are familiar with a subject seem to respond better to moderately novel arguments than to old standbys that they have heard many times before.

Another important aspect of the message is *fear*. Research has found that fear is an effective persuader in efforts to convince people to get tetanus shots (Dabbs & Leventhal, 1966), to drive safely (Leventhal & Niles, 1965), and to take care of their teeth (Evans et al., 1970). But too much fear can scare an audience to such an extent that the message has little effect (Worchel & Cooper, 1983).

Whether to include both sides of an argument is another well-researched question. The data indicate that one-sided and two-sided arguments are equally persuasive. But a two-sided presentation generally makes the speaker seem less biased and thus adds to his or her credibility.

The organization of a message and the medium in which it is presented also affects its impact. In presenting two sides of a question, for example, it is generally better to put forth your own side first. But if a long time elapses between presentation of the first and second positions, the audience tends to recall best what it heard last. In this situation, present your own view second (Miller & Campbell, 1959). As to the choice of medium, writing appears to be best suited to getting others to understand complex arguments. Videotaped or live media presentations are more effective in persuading an audience once it has understood an argument (Chaiken & Eagly, 1976).

Overall, the most important factors in changing attitudes are those that have to do with the audience, although these factors are often the most difficult to control. *Commitment* of the audience to its present attitudes is critical. A person who had just gone on a speaking tour publicly advocating more liberal abortion laws is less likely to change his or her attitudes toward the subject than someone who has never openly expressed an opinion one way or the other. Likewise, a person whose attitudes are shared with other people is less susceptible to attitude change. Moreover, if the attitude has been instilled during early childhood by important groups such as the family, even massive assaults on the attitude can be ineffective.

Another audience factor is the *discrepancy* between the contents of the message and the present attitudes of the audience. Up to a point, the greater the difference between the two, the greater the likelihood of attitude change. However, if the discrepancy is too great, the audience may reject the new information altogether. The expertise of the com-

Cognitive dissonance Perceived inconsistency between two cognitions.

municator is also important in this context. Influence increases with the size of the discrepancy only when the speaker is considered an expert.

A number of personal characteristics, including aspects of personality, also tend to make some people more susceptible to attitude change than others. People with low self-esteem are more easily influenced, especially when the message is complex and hard to understand. Highly intelligent people tend to resist persuasion because they can think of counterarguments more easily. When the message is complex, however, only highly intelligent people may be able to understand it and hence be influenced by it.

Traditionally, women have been considered easier to influence than men. A review of the relevant research, however, shows that this is only true when men conduct the research; otherwise, there are no sex differences in persuasibility (Eagly, 1978). Eagly accounts for this discrepancy by noting that male experimenters tend to use materials unfamiliar to women, making them seem more subject to attitude change in general.

In theory, then, attitudes are open to change. But in fact, they are very difficult to change. Fortunately for advertisers, politicians, and others, attitude change is often not as important as a change in behavior—buying Brand X, voting for Jane Smith. In fact, in many cases it is possible to change behavior directly and then obtain attitude change as a result. We will now look in more detail at how behavior can affect attitudes.

THE COGNITIVE CONSISTENCY APPROACH. One of the more fascinating approaches to understanding attitude change is the theory of **cognitive dissonance** developed by Leon Festinger (1957). Cognitive dissonance exists whenever a person has two contradictory cognitions at the same time. In this theory, a *cognition* is a piece of knowledge about something. "I do not like gory movies" is a cognition; so is "Yesterday I went to see *The Texas Chainsaw Massacre*." These two cognitions are dissonant—each one implies the opposite of the other. According to Festinger, cognitive dissonance creates unpleasant psychological tension, and this tension motivates the individual to try to resolve the dissonance in some way.

Sometimes, changing one's attitude is the easiest way to reduce the discomfort of dissonance. I cannot easily change the fact that I have gone to a gory movie. Therefore, it is easier to change my attitude about such movies. My new attitude now fits my behavior.

It is important to point out that discrepant behavior does not necessarily bring about attitude change. There are other ways a person can reduce cognitive dissonance. One alternative is to *increase the number of consonant elements*—the thoughts that support one or the other dissonant cognitions. For example, I might note that the movie was a bargain since it was "dollar night" at the theater, that I really needed to get out by myself for a while, and that the movie would probably teach me something about abnormal psychology. Now my action is less discrepant with my attitude about gory films. Another option is to *reduce the importance of one or both cognitive elements*. "I just wanted to check and be sure that I really don't like that sort of movie. And I was right, I don't." By reducing the significance of my behavior, I reduce the dissonance that I experience.

So far, we have ignored an important question: Why would someone engage in attitude-discrepant behavior in the first place? One answer is that cognitive dissonance is a part of everyday life. For example, simply choosing between two or more desirable alternatives leads inevitably to dissonance. Suppose you are in the market for a computer but can't decide between an IBM and a Macintosh. If you choose the IBM, all of its bad features and all of the good aspects of the Macintosh contribute to dissonance. After you have chosen the IBM you can reduce the dissonance by changing your attitude: You might decide that the Macintosh keyboard wasn't "quite right" and that some of the "bad" features of the IBM are actually desirable. You may also engage in attitude-discrepant behavior because you are enticed to do so. Perhaps someone offers you a small bribe or reward: "I will pay you 25 cents just to try my product." Curiously, the larger the reward, the smaller the change in attitude that is likely to result. When rewards are large, dissonance is at a minimum, and attitude change is small, if it happens at all. Apparently, when people are convinced that there is a good reason to perform a discrepant act, they experience little dissonance and their attitudes are not likely to change, although their behavior may shift for a time. However, if the reward is small, just barely enough to induce behavior that conflicts with one's attitude, dissonance will be great, maximizing the chances for attitude change. The trick is to get the discrepant behavior to happen while leaving people feeling personally responsible for the dissonant act. That way they are more likely to change their attitudes than if they feel they were forced to act in a way that contradicts their beliefs (Cooper, 1971; Kelman, 1974).

Social influence Any actions performed by one or more persons to change the attitudes, behavior, or feelings of one or more others.

Conformity Voluntarily yielding to social norms, even at the expense of one's own preferences.

■ Social Influence

To social psychologists, **social influence** refers to "any actions performed by one or more persons to change the attitudes, behavior, or feelings of one or more others" (Baron & Byrne, 1981, p. 229). In the previous section, we studied one form of social influence: attitude change. In the following discussion, we'll focus on the direct control of behavior by others without regard to underlying attitudes.

Conformity

To conform is to choose to yield to *social norms*, which are shared ideas and expectations about how members of a group should behave. Some norms are written into law, while many more are unwritten expectations enforced by teasing, frowns, ostracism, and other informal means of punishment. Without norms, social life would be chaotic. With them, the behavior of other people becomes fairly predictable despite great differences in underlying attitudes and preferences.

Most cases of uniformity are not cases of **conformity.** For instance, millions of Americans drink coffee in the morning, but they do not do so to conform. They drink coffee because they have learned to like and desire it. Conformity implies a conflict between the individual and the group—a conflict that the individual resolves by yielding his or her own preferences or beliefs to the norms or expectations of a larger group.

Figure 16-2
In Asch's experiment on *conformity*, subjects were shown a comparison card like the one on the left, and were asked to indicate which of the three lines on the card on the right was the most similar.

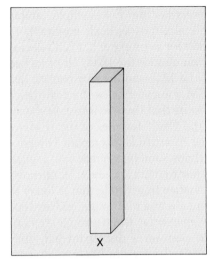
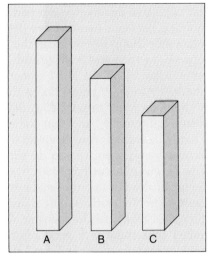

Since the early 1950s, when Solomon Asch conducted the first careful study of the subject, conformity has been a major subject of research in social psychology. In a series of experiments Asch demonstrated that under some circumstances, people conform to group pressures even when this results in the denial of physical evidence. His studies ostensibly tested visual judgment. People were asked to choose from a card with several lines of differing lengths the line most similar to the line on a comparison card (see Figure 16-2). The lines were deliberately drawn so that the comparison was obvious and the correct choice was clear. All but one of the subjects were planted by the experimenter. On certain trials these people deliberately gave the same wrong answer. This put the subject on the spot. Should he conform to what he knew to be a wrong decision and agree with the group, thereby denying the evidence of his own senses, or should he disagree with the group and not conform?

Overall, the subjects conformed on about 35 percent of the trials. There were large individual differences, however, and in subsequent research experimenters discovered that two kinds of factors influence the likelihood that a person will conform: characteristics of the situation and characteristics of the individual. The size of the group is one situational variable that has been studied extensively. Asch (1951) found that the likelihood of conformity increased with group size until four confederates were present. After that point, the number of others made no difference in the subjects' tendency to ignore the evidence of his own eyes. Another important factor is the degree of unanimity in the group. If just one confederate broke the perfect agreements of the majority by giving the correct answers, conformity among the subjects in the Asch experiments fell from an average of 35 percent to about 25 percent (Asch, 1956). Apparently, having just one "ally" eases the pressure on the subject to conform. The ally need not even share the subject's viewpoint. Just breaking the unanimity of the majority is enough to reduce conformity (Allen & Levine, 1971).

The nature of the task is still another situational variable that affects conformity. For instance, conformity has been shown to vary with the difficulty and the ambiguity of a task. When the task is difficult or poorly defined, conformity tends to be higher (Blake, Helson, & Mouton, 1956).

In an ambiguous situation, individuals are less sure of their own view and are more willing to conform to that of the majority.

Personal characteristics also influence conforming behavior. The more an individual is attracted to the group, expects to interact with it in the future, is of relatively low status in the group, and does not feel completely accepted by the group, the more he or she tends to conform. The fear of rejection apparently motivates conformity when a person scores high on one or more of these variables.

Compliance

Conformity is a response to pressure exerted by norms that are generally left unstated. In contrast, **compliance** is a change of behavior in response to the explicit request of someone else. The demand may reflect a social norm, as when a doorman of a nightclub informs a customer that proper attire is required. Or the request may be intended to satisfy the needs of the person making it: "Please help me fold the sheets."

Social psychologists have studied several techniques by which people can get others to comply with their requests. One procedure is based on the so-called *foot-in-the-door effect*. Any seller knows that the moment a person allows the sales pitch to begin, the chances of making a sale improve greatly. In general, once a person has granted a small request, he or she is more likely to comply with a larger one too.

A new-car dealer using the *lowball procedure* tries to get the customer to comply with one proposal and then raises the cost of the compliance once the commitment has been made.

In the most famous study of this phenomenon, Freedman and Fraser (1966) approached certain residents of Palo Alto, California, posing as members of a Committee for Safe Driving. Residents were asked to place a large, ugly sign reading "Drive Carefully" in their front yards. Only 17 percent agreed to do it. Then other residents were asked to sign a petition calling for more safe-driving laws. When these same people were later asked to place the ugly "Drive Carefully" sign in their yards, an amazing 55 percent agreed to do so. Compliance with the initial small request more than tripled the rate of compliance with the larger request.

The reason why this technique works so well is not clear. One possibility is that agreeing to the token act (signing the petition) changes the subject's self-perception slightly to that of the person favoring the cause. When presented with the larger request, the person then feels obligated to comply (Snyder & Cunningham, 1975). Another explanation is that the subject becomes more comfortable in helping situations in general after being asked for a small commitment.

Another trick from the salesperson's bag is the *lowball prodecure* (Cialdini et al., 1978). The first step of this procedure is to induce a person to agree to do something. The second step is to raise the cost of compliance after the commitment to the behavior has been made. Among new-car dealers, lowballing works as follows: The dealer persuades the customer to buy a new car by reducing the price well below that of competitors. Once the customer has agreed to buy the car, however, the terms of the sale shift abruptly, making the car even more costly than the market rate. One technique is to reduce the trade-in value promised by the used-car manager. Despite the added costs, many customers follow through on their commitment to buy.

Under certain circumstances, a person who has refused to comply with one request may be more likely to comply with a second. This phenomenon has been labeled the *door-in-the-face effect* (Cialdini et al., 1975). In one study, researchers approached students and asked them to make an unreasonably large commitment: Would they counsel delinquent youths at a detention center for two years? Nearly everyone declined, thus effectively "slamming the door" in the face of the researcher making the request. Upon then being asked to make a much smaller commitment—supervising children during a trip to the zoo—many of the same subjects quickly agreed. The door-in-the-face effect may work because subjects interpret the smaller request as a concession by the experimenter, and they feel pressured to comply in return.

Obedience

Compliance involves agreeing to change behavior in response to a request. **Obedience** is compliance with a command. Like compliance, it is a response to an explicit message; but in this case the message is a direct order, generally from a person in authority, such as a police officer, principal, or parent, who can back up the command if necessary. Obedience is social influence in its most direct and powerful form.

Several studies by Stanley Milgram that were mentioned in Chapter 1 showed how far many people will go in order to obey someone in authority (Milgram, 1963). Milgram informed his subjects that they would be participating in an experiment designed to test the effects of punishment on learning. Their job was to administer an electric shock to another subject, actually a confederate, every time he or she made an error in a learning trial. The shocks were to be increased in voltage for each error, up to a potentially fatal 450 volts. In fact, the learner received no real shock whatsoever. Each time a subject balked, the experimenter pointed out that he was expected to continue. An astounding 65 percent of Milgram's subjects proceeded to administer the entire series of shocks, up to the maximum.

What factors influence the degree to which people will do what they are told? Studies in which people were asked to put a dime in a parking meter by people wearing uniforms showed that one important factor is the amount of power vested in the person giving the orders. A guard whose uniform looked like a police officer's was obeyed more often than a man dressed either as a milkman or as a civilian. Another factor

The tragic mass suicide of the members of People's Temple in Jonestown, Guyana is an extreme example of *obedience*, the response to direct orders from someone in authority.

is surveillance. If we are ordered to do something and then left alone, we are less likely to obey than when we are being watched. This seems to be true especially when the order involves an unethical act. Most of the subjects still put a dime in the meter when the policeman-impersonator was out of sight, but Milgram found that his "teachers" were less willing to give severe shocks when the experimenter was out of the room.

Milgram's experiments revealed other factors that influence a person's willingness to follow orders. When the victim was in the same room as the teacher, obedience dropped sharply. When another "teacher" was present who refused to give shocks, obedience also dropped. But when responsibility for an act was shared, so that the person was only one of many doing it, obedience was much greater. Executions by firing squads illustrate this principle.

What makes people willing to obey an authority figure, even if it means violating their own principles? Milgram (1974) thinks that people feel obligated to those in power: first, because they respect their credentials and assume that they know what they are doing; and second, because often they have established trust with the people in authority by agreeing to do whatever they ask. Once this happens, subjects may feel conflict about what they are doing but through rationalization can "forget" about it and thus minimize the conflict.

Helping Behavior

Attitude change, conformity, compliance, and obedience are not the only ways in which we are influenced by other people. Our willingness to help others is another behavior that is sensitive to social influence. Our treatment of others is often motivated by our own self-interest. We offer our boss a ride home from the office because we know that our next promotion depends on how much he or she likes us. We volunteer to water our neighbors' lawn while they are away because we want to use their pool. But if this kind of behavior is not linked to personal gain, it is called **altruistic behavior.** A person who acts in an altruistic way does not expect any recognition or reward in return, except perhaps the good feeling that comes from helping the needy. Many altruistic acts, including many charitable contributions, are directed at strangers and are made anonymously (Hoffman, 1977).

Under what conditions is helping behavior most likely to occur? Like other social-psychological phenomena, helping is influenced by two sets of variables: those pertaining to the situation and those relevant to the individual.

Probably the most important situational variable is the presence of other people. As the number of passive bystanders increases, the likelihood decreases that any one of them will help someone in trouble. In one experiment, subjects completing a questionnaire heard a taped "emergency" in the next room, complete with a crash and screams. Of those who were alone, 70 percent offered help, but of those who were with an experimenter who did nothing, only 7 percent offered help (Latané & Rodin, 1969).

Another key aspect of the situation is its ambiguity. Any factors that make it harder for others to recognize a genuine emergency reduce the probability of helping. Clark and Word (1974) had a "workman"

Altruism and the Holocaust

In 1939, when the German army occupied the city of Warsaw, Poland, they segregated the city's Jews in a barbwire ghetto. Deeply concerned about the fate of her Jewish friends, a 16-year-old Catholic girl named Stefania Podgórska made secret expeditions into the ghetto with gifts of food, clothing, and medicine. When the Jewish son of her former landlord escaped from the ghetto in a desperate flight to avoid being deported to a concentration camp, Stefania agreed to hide him in her apartment. Throughout Nazi-occupied Europe, only a few thousand non-Jews like Stefania risked their lives to rescue Jews from persecution, deportation, and death. Why did they do what so many millions of others did not do? What qualities of Stefania's personality enabled her to behave so altruistically, bravely, and competently?

In 1981, several researchers set out to find answers to questions like these and combined their efforts two years later in the Altruistic Personality Project. By 1985, the project had published findings based on interviews with 25 rescuers and 50 survivors, as well as historical documents about the activities of others (Fogelman & Wiener, 1985). The people with whom the researchers spoke came from several countries and differed widely in education and vocation. The rescuers did, however, share one characteristic: They preferred not to see themselves as heroes or heroines, and considered their behavior to be quite natural.

While no single personality characteristic emerged, researchers could identify some common trends. For example, rescuers tended to fall into one of two groups: those who were motivated by deeply rooted moral values and felt ethically bound to rescue victims, and those who were attached personally to the victims and sometimes identified with them emotionally. These findings support the contention of social psychologist Carol Gilligan (1982) that there are fundamentally two forms of moral reasoning: one based on a sense of justice, the other based on a sense of responsibility and care.

Morally motivated rescuers often harbored intense anti-Nazi attitudes, and for some, religious belief was an important influence on their lives. Morally motivated rescuers also tended to help victims regardless of whether they liked or disliked them. On the other hand, emotionally motivated rescuers frequently had strong personal attachments to the people whom they helped—neighbors, for instance. Some helped people whom they scarcely knew but with whom they identified. In some cases, the empathy sprang from the rescuer's belief that he or she was also vulnerable to persecution. "It is easy to understand what the Jews felt," explained one Ukrainian rescuer, "because Jews and the Ukrainians were in similar positions everywhere" (Fogelman & Wiener, 1985, p. 63).

During World War II, a Swede named Raoul Wallenberg helped thousands of Jews to escape from German-controlled Hungary. Arrested by the Soviets at war's end, Wallenberg has not been heard from since.

Despite their differences in motivation, the rescuers shared a number of characteristics. Many of them belonged to families with traditions of concern for others outside the family, and many stated that their behavior was strongly influenced by their parents' values. Stefania Podgórska cited her parents' insistence on religious tolerance. Most rescuers had uncommon capacities for perseverance and unusually strong beliefs in their competence to risk and survive danger. Stefania and her sister managed to shelter 13 Jews for two and a half years in the attic of their small apartment—and for seven months while two German nurses and two German soldiers were bivouacked in the apartment!

carry a ladder and a venetian blind past a waiting room in which subjects were sitting. A loud crash soon followed. In this ambiguous situation, the fewer the bystanders, the more likely the workman was to receive help. When he clarified matters by calling out that he was hurt, however, all subjects without exception went to his aid.

The personal characteristics of bystanders also affect helping behavior. Not all bystanders are equally likely to help a stranger. According to Moriarty (1975), increasing the amount of personal responsibility that one person feels for another increases the likelihood of helpful support. In his experiment, subjects were more likely to try to stop the theft of a stranger's property if they had promised to watch the property while the stranger was away than if they had had no contact with the stranger. The amount of empathy that we feel with another person also affects our willingness to act in a helpful way. Krebs (1975) found that when subjects felt that their values and personalities were similar to a victim's, they were more likely to help, even if their own safety was jeopardized.

Mood also makes a difference. A person in a good mood is more likely to help another in need than is someone who is in a neutral or bad mood. Isen & Levin (1972) demonstrated this by leaving a dime in the scoop of a pay phone in order to put the finder in a good mood. These subjects were much more likely than other subjects to help a confederate who dropped a folder full of papers on the sidewalk near the phone booth. Other research suggests that individuals who fear embarrassment are less likely to help (McGovern, 1976). Mistakenly offering help to someone who does not really need it can be highly embarrassing. Finally, when others are watching, people who score high on the need for approval are more likely to help than are low scorers (Satow, 1975).

Altruistic behavior When a jetliner crashed in Washington in 1982, numerous onlookers hurried to help passengers without expecting reward or recognition in return.

Deindividuation Loss of personal sense of responsibility in a group.

Deindividuation

We have seen several cases of social influence in which people act differently in the presence of others than they would by themselves. Perhaps the most striking and frightening instance of this is *mob behavior*. Some well-known violent examples are the beatings and lynchings of blacks, the looting that sometimes accompanies urban rioting, and the wanton destruction of property that occurs during otherwise peaceful protests and demonstrations. After a power blackout in New York City in 1977, during which considerable looting took place, some of the looters were interviewed. These interviews indicated that many people would never have thought of looting had they been alone and that others were later shocked by their own behavior.

One reason for such behavior is that people lose their personal sense of responsibility in a group, especially in a group subjected to intense pressures and anxiety. This is called **deindividuation,** because people respond not as individuals, but as anonymous parts of a larger group. In general, the more anonymous people feel in a group, the less responsible they feel as individuals.

Groups of four women were recruited to take part in a study supposedly involving responses to strangers (Zimbardo, 1969). In one group, the women were greeted by name, wore name tags, and were easily identifiable. In another group, they wore oversized white lab coats and hoods over their heads; they resembled members of the Ku Klux Klan and were not identifiable at all. The groups were given an opportunity to deliver electric shocks to a woman not in the group. The subjects who were "deindividuated" gave almost twice as many electric shocks as did the subjects who were clearly identifiable. Apparently, being "deindividuated" produced more aggressive and more hostile behavior. This hypothesis supports the idea that the loss of a feeling of individuality may be a major cause of the violent, antisocial behavior sometimes shown by groups.

Deindividuation partly explains mob behavior. Another factor is that, in a group, one strongly dominant and persuasive person can convince people to act through a *snowball effect*: If he or she convinces a few people, those few will convince others. Moreover, large groups provide *protection*. Anonymity makes it difficult to press charges. If 2, or even 10, people start smashing windows, they will probably be arrested. If a thousand people do it, very few of them may be caught or punished.

■ Group Processes

The various kinds of social influence that we have just discussed can take place between two people, in groups of three or more, or even when no one else is physically present. We refrain from walking our dog on our neighbor's lawn, comply with jury duty notices that we receive in the mail, and obey traffic signals even when no one else is present to enforce the social norms that dictate these actions. We now turn our attention to processes that do depend on the presence of other people. Specifically,

One of the most studied group processes is *group decision-making*.

we will examine processes that occur when people interact in small groups. One of the most thoroughly studied group processes is decision-making.

Group Decision-Making

There is a tendency in our society to turn important decisions over to groups. In the business world, most important decisions are made around a conference table rather than behind one person's desk. In politics, major policy decisions are seldom vested in just one person. Groups of advisers, cabinet officers, committee members, or aides meet to deliberate and decide. In the courts, a defendant may request a trial by jury, and for some serious crimes a jury trial is required by law. And of course, the U.S. Supreme Court renders group decisions on issues of major importance.

When a group of advisers meet to make a decision, they frequently wait for a consensus before acting. It is possible that this sort of group decision making is what caused oil company officials to delay in taking action to contain the oil leaking from the crippled tanker, *Valdez*.

Why are so many decisions entrusted to groups rather than to individuals? One reason is that we tend to assume that individuals acting alone are more likely to take greater risks than a group considering the same issue. We assume that a corporate board, a cabinet, or a jury will be more judicious and cautious than any single individual.

The assumption that groups make more conservative decisons than individuals remained unchallenged until the early 1960s. At that time, James Stoner (1961) designed an experiment to test this idea. He asked subjects individually to counsel imaginary persons who had to choose between a risky but potentially rewarding course of action and a conservative and less rewarding alternative. Next, the advisers met in small groups to discuss each decision until they reached unanimous agreement. Stoner and many other social psychologists were surprised to find that the groups consistently proposed a riskier course of action than that counseled by the group members working alone. This phenomenon is known as the **risky shift.**

Subsequent research suggests that the risky shift is simply one aspect of a more general group phenomenon called **polarization**—the tendency for individuals to become more extreme in their attitudes as a result of group discussion. Groups that start out fairly risky will become more so during discussion, but groups that tend to be cautious will grow even more cautious during their deliberations (Fraser, 1971).

What causes polarization in decision-making groups? In part, people discover during discussion that the other group members share their views to a greater degree than they realized. In an effort to be seen positively by the others, at least some group members become strong advocates for what appears to be the dominant sentiment in the group. Thus, the group discussion shifts to a more extreme position, as new and more persuasive arguments begin to emerge. As group participants listen to these arguments and find themselves in general agreement, their own positions become more extreme. In other words, initially popular positions attract the most persuasive arguments. In turn, these arguments not only reassure people that their initial attitudes are correct, but also intensify those attitudes so that the group as a whole becomes more extreme in its position. Thus, if you refer a problem to a group in order to ensure that it will be resolved in a cautious, conservative direction, you should make sure that the members of the group are cautious and conservative in the first place.

The Effectiveness of the Group

Another reason for assigning so many important problems to groups is the assumption that the members of the group will pool their skills and expertise and therefore solve the problem more effectively than would any individual member working alone. "Two heads are better than one" reflects this way of thinking about groups.

In fact, groups are more effective than individuals only under some circumstances. According to Steiner (1972), the effectiveness of a group depends on three factors: (1) the nature of the task, (2) the resources of the group members, and (3) the interaction among group members. There are many different kinds of tasks, each of which demands certain kinds of skills. If the requirements of the task match the skills of the group members, the group is likely to be more effective than any single individual. To build the first atom bomb, for example, the directors of the Manhattan Project assembled a team of specialists in various subfields of physics and engineering. For one scientist working alone, the task would have been impossible.

Even if the task and personnel are matched perfectly, the ways in which the people interact in the group can sometimes reduce its efficiency. For example, high-status individuals tend to exert more influence in groups, regardless of those individuals' problem-solving ability. If high-status members are not the most qualified group members to solve the problem, the group may well settle on the wrong answer, even though one or more of the participants could have found the right answer working alone. In one experiment with bomber crews, Torrance (1954) found that the low-status gunners who correctly solved a problem were about six times less likely than the high-status pilots to convince the group that their answer was correct.

Another factor is group *size*. The larger the group, the more likely it is to include someone who has the skills needed to solve a difficult problem. On the other hand, it is much harder to coordinate the activities of a large group than those of a small group.

Still another variable is the *cohesiveness* of a group. When the people in the group like one another and feel committed to the goals of the group, cohesiveness is high. Under these conditions, members may work hard for the group, spurred on by high morale. But cohesiveness can also cause serious problems that undermine the quality of group decision-making. Janis (1972) has called this phenomenon *groupthink*. Strong pressure to conform, he believes, prevents people from expressing critical ideas. In a group, amiability and morale take precedence over judgment. As group cohesiveness increases, self-criticism decreases, and members seem more willing to act at the expense of nonmembers. Members with doubts may hesitate to express them. The result may be bad decisions—such as the Bay of Pigs invasion, the Watergate coverup, or the *Challenger* disaster (Kruglanski, 1986).

Leadership

A group may be formal or informal, task-oriented or purely social, but it is sure to have a leader. The leader may be a formal leader—the chairman of the board, for instance—or merely the member who exerts the strongest influence on the group. Group leadership can be self-perpetuating, or it may change, as in a parliamentary system when a vote of "no confidence" causes the government to fall.

There are many theories about the emergence of group leaders. The dominant theory for many years was the *great person theory*. This theory states that leaders are extraordinary people who assume positions of influence and then shape events around them. In this view, Washington, Napoleon, and even Hitler were "born leaders" who would have led any nation at any time in history.

Most historians and psychologists now regard this theory as naive because it ignores social and economic factors. For instance, had Germany not lost World War I and suffered a crippling depression, its people might not have been open to the nationalistic fervor that Hitler preached. Moreover, had Hitler been born in America, his chances of becoming a world leader in the 1930s would have been significantly lower.

An alternative theory suggests that leadership is the result of the right person being in the right place at the right time. For instance, in the late 1950s and early 1960s, Dr. Martin Luther King, Jr., emerged as the leader of the black civil rights movement. Dr. King was clearly a "great person"—intelligent, dynamic, eloquent, and highly motivated. Yet, had the times not been right, according to this theory, it is doubtful that he would have been as successful as he was.

Recently, social scientists have argued that there is more to leadership than either the great person theory or the right-place-at-the-right-time theory implies. According to the *transactional view*, a number of factors interact to determine who becomes the leader of a group. The leader's traits, certain aspects of the situation in wich the group finds itself, and the response of the group and the leader to each other are all important considerations. Fred Fiedler's contingency model of leader effectiveness is based on such a transactional view of leadership (Fiedler, 1967, 1981). According to Fiedler, a number of factors affect the success of a leader. Personal characteristics are important, and Fiedler thinks of them in terms of two contrasting *leadership styles*. One kind of leader is task-oriented, concerned with doing the task well even at the expense of poor relationships among members of the group. Other leaders are just the reverse. Which style is most effective depends on three sets of factors.

One theory holds that the particularly effective leader is the right person in the right place at the right time—as in the case of Martin Luther King's leadership of the civil rights movement in the 1950s and 1960s.

One is the nature of the *task*: Some problems are clearly structured, while others are ambiguous. The second consideration is the *relationship* between leader and group—whether the leader has good or bad personal relations with the group members. The third consideration is the leader's ability to exercise great or little *power* over the group. Fiedler has shown that if conditions are either very favorable (good leader-member relations, structured task, high leader power) or very unfavorable (poor leader-member relations, unstructured task, low leader power) for the leader, the most effective leader is the one who is task-oriented and concerned with completing the task successfully. However, when conditions within the group are only moderately favorable for the leader, the most effective leader is one who is concerned about maintaining good interpersonal relations. Fiedler's view of leadership, which has received a great deal of support from research conducted in the laboratory as well as in real-life settings, clearly indicates that there is no such thing as an ideal leader for all situations. "Except perhaps for the unusual case," he says, "it is simply not meaningful to speak of an effective or of an ineffective leader; we can only speak of a leader who tends to be effective in one situation and ineffective in another" (Fiedler, 1967, p. 261).

Organizational Systems and Influences

Since one of the major ways in which people think about themselves is in terms of their professional roles, it is not surprising that their work experiences influence their attitudes toward themselves and toward others (Simmons & Mares, 1983). Furthermore, most people develop patterns of professional behavior within the organizations for which they work. The study of this behavior is the field of the industrial/organizational psychologist. Of course, most people are involved in a wide variety of organizations outside the workplace. If you belong to a church or play on a softball team, your behavior in those contexts is influenced by the organizational goals and functions of your church or athletic league. **Industrial/organizational (I/O) psychology** is thus concerned with a wide variety of behavior in organizational situations, but as the term implies, its main focus has become the study of behavior in the workplace. Whereas the study of groups is aimed in general at small-group behavior, I/O psychology is concerned with the effect of larger, more complex organizational systems on human interaction.

In a practical sense, the industrial psychologist tries to find out what works in a given workplace and applies those findings to the solution of various problems that the organization is encountering. For example, what role do psychological factors play in employee turnover and absenteeism? Are "happier" workers more productive workers? Are "unhappy" workers necessarily less productive? What makes a worker "happy" or "unhappy"?

One of the first studies of the relationship between productivity and working conditions was conducted in the late 1920s at the Western Electric Hawthorne plant in Cicero, Illinois. Elton Mayo and his colleagues experimented by installing increasingly improved lighting in the workplace, and workers' output increased, apparently confirming the prevailing assumption that good working conditions were a key factor in motivating workers. But then the researchers found that productivity continued to improve even when the illumination was increased above a comfortable level. Moreover, productivity rose slightly even when the lighting was systematically worsened! In addition, workers in a control group whose lighting was not tampered with at all also improved their output! The study clearly demonstrated that there is not a simple, direct relationship between working conditions and worker productivity. More importantly, the study demonstrated that psychological factors can have a profound effect on productivity. In the Hawthorne plant, workers' behavior changed simply because they were aware that they were receiving the special attention of the investigators (Mayo, 1933). The principle that people will modify their behavior because of researchers' attention and not necessarily because of any specific manipulations on the researchers' part has since become known as the **Hawthorne effect.**

The methods of Mayo's team have since been criticized (Parsons, 1974), but their study was one of the first to highlight the general importance of psychological and social factors on behavior in the workplace. Since the 1930s, I/O psychologists have attempted to analyze that relationship in more specific terms. For example, recent studies have demonstrated that the psychological requirements of a job are just as important to understanding productivity as the physical activities that it requires (Katzell & Guzzo, 1983). For example, a worker whose job requires a greater variety of skills is more likely to perceive his or her job as meaningful and to exhibit increased motivation and satisfaction; a worker whose job affords more autonomous activity is more likely to perceive his or her job as responsible and to produce work of a higher quality (Hackman & Oldham, 1976). Job changes can thus be used as a means of improving motivation, satisfaction, and productivity in the workplace.

The work unit itself can also have a significant effect on productivity. People tend to work better in smaller, more cohesive groups than in larger, more impersonal ones. Workers who perform repetitive tasks on long assembly lines may not feel that they are functioning as part of an identifiable group, and I/O psychologists have found that increasing a worker's sense of group membership helps to increase his or her productivity. One innovation in this area is called the *autonomous work group*: The assembly line is replaced by small groups of workers who produce an entire unit (a whole car, for instance), and workers periodically alternate tasks. The group is assigned a quota, but the group members themselves decide how that quota can best be met. Evidence indicates that this system contributes to greater work satisfaction and higher quality work while decreasing absenteeism and turnover (Jenkins & Gupta, 1983).

The communication and decision-making systems of an organization can also have an important effect on both the organization's efficiency and the attitudes of its members. For instance, in a group in which the members are all responsible for communicating with just one person, that person will normally become a leader and the communications system will become centralized. All communications flow to and from one central person. Such centralized systems are typically efficient at solving simple problems that require little more than the assembly and transmission of information. But complex problems that require exchanges of ideas and modifications of proposed solutions are generally handled more effectively by decentralized systems in which all group members communicate freely with each other (Porter & Roberts, 1976).

Hawthorne effect Principle that subjects will alter their behavior because of researchers' attention and not necessarily because of any specific experimentation.

People often work better in smaller, more cohesive groups. In many companies *autonomous work groups* are replacing the assembly line. Evidence indicates that employees in these groups are more satisfied and produce higher-quality goods

Environmental psychology The study of how the environment influences individuals and their relationships with others.

Personal space The psychological space surrounding a person.

I/O psychologists have also examined the value of having work groups be responsible for important decisions. As you will recall from our earlier discussion of decision-making groups, it is not always the case that groups will make better decisions than individuals. Locke and Schweiger (1979) reviewed the evidence bearing on group decision-making in the workplace and found that in 22 percent of the cases, the groups made better decisions, while in another 22 percent of the cases, the groups made worse decisions; there was no significant effect at all in 56 percent of the cases. However, group decision-making had a positive effect on membership satisfaction in 60 percent of the cases analyzed. There is more satisfaction among members of an organization who have opportunities to discuss important decisions with one another, even if their decisions are no better as a result.

Worker satisfaction also varies according to the position that the person occupies in the organization: The more a position allows its occupant to communicate with others, the more satisfied the person is likely to be. In addition, patterns of communication become more satisfying as group members become more comfortable with their positions in the work group. Thus, communications systems tend to become less rigid as the members get to know one another better. Less formal patterns of communication—and hence of influence and leadership—develop over the course of time. Even where, as in many large organizations, the communications system is defined by a formal organizational chart, there are often informal systems of communication that bypass the formal pattern. In almost every academic department, the chairperson's secretary has more to say about what goes on than do most of the instructors. The secretary is at the center of the network of communication and controls access to the chair. The secretary may not exercise it but may well have considerable informal power by virtue of holding a strategic position in the communication network.

■ Environmental Psychology

In recent years, more attention has been paid to how our environment influences us and our relationships with others. Because we accept our environment as a given, we are often unaware of the effects of such factors as crowding, noise, isolation, and urban tension. **Environmental psychology** studies how these factors contribute to the complex ways in which we relate to our world.

Personal Space

Personal space is a phrase coined by the anthropologist Edward T. Hall (1959). It refers to the amount of physical space between people, how they relate to this space, and how they manipulate it in their relationships with others. In one experiment, a student posed as a policeman and interviewed other students about the contents of their wallets. As the interview progressed, the "policeman" edged closer to the students. When the "policeman" moved as close as 8 inches to a student, the student usually grew tense, uncomfortable, and suspicious. When the distance was kept at about 2 feet, the interviews went smoothly, with no sign of discomfort from the students (Insel & Lindgren, 1978).

In general, the more intimate we are with people, the more likely we are to sit or stand closer to them. Similarly, the more friendly people are with one another, the less they notice how close to one another they are standing or sitting. Indeed, the distance that you put between yourself and others is one way of showing interest or liking, especially with someone you have just met or want to get to know. If we do not want to meet people—for instance, while studying at the library—we are inclined to view any attempt to "enter" our space as an invasion. Robert Sommer (1959) tested this principle by having women approach other women who were studying alone at a library table. If the confederate sat down a few chairs away, she was ignored. But if she sat next to the subject, the subject often expressed discomfort, irritation, and even anger.

In follow-up studies, Fisher and Byrne (1975) discovered some interesting differences in the way men and women react to strangers who invade their personal space, again at library tables. The experimenters had confederates approach students sitting alone and sit either directly across the table or in the chair next to the student on the same side of the table. Regardless of the invader's sex, males were most disturbed by a person sitting across from them, while females were bothered more by someone sitting beside them. Another study revealed that even when no intruder was present, men tended to guard their personal space by placing books or other objects in *front* of them, while women built barriers on either *side*.

The circumstances in which we find ourselves also affect our perception of personal space. When a stranger has no other choice but to stand close to us, we tend to ignore the intrusion of our personal turf. At rush hour, for instance, buses and trains in some cities are so jammed that it is often impossible to preserve even a trace of personal space. Thus people who would otherwise be repelled by the closeness of strangers seem to pay no heed to their proximity during these hours. On the other hand, if we sense that some strange person is deliberately invading our personal space, even in a crowded setting, we are likely to be offended (Russell & Ward, 1982).

The ways in which we behave with regard to our sense of personal space are very significant forms of nonverbal behavior. Research has shown that children are sensitive to violations of personal space within months of becoming mobile, and the extent to which people require or tolerate spatial contact seems to be fairly standard regardless of culture (Hayduk, 1983).

Environmental Stress

DENSITY AND CROWDING. In New York City, as many as 70,000 people live and work within a single square mile. One of New York's larger apartment complexes could house the entire population of many small towns. Sidewalks are so jammed at certain hours of the day that even walking from one place to another becomes a challenge, and traffic maneuvers such as passing, weaving, and dodging become as important to people walking on the sidewalk as to the cars on the street. Although

A baseball manager will often violate an umpire's *personal space* in order to underscore his verbal argument with a powerful form of nonverbal behavior.

Density In environmental psychology, the number of people per unit of area.

Crowding In environmental psychology, the subjective experience of being crowded, regardless of actual population density.

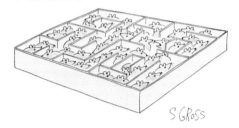

"I just hate the rush hour. Don't you?"
© 1987 S. Gross

Crowding can become stressful when people feel that they have lost control over their surroundings.

many suburban towns were originally built to avoid this sort of crowding, they, too, have become densely populated, and it is becoming increasingly rare—especially in the older, more developed areas of the country—for Americans to have the kind of "elbow room" that they have been brought up to value and expect.

Because of increased crowding in urban and suburban areas, more attention has been paid recently to how human beings react to crowding and to the invasion of their personal space (Holahan, 1986). Researchers in this area often distinguish between **density,** the number of people per square foot, and **crowding,** which is the subjective experience of being crowded (Stokols, 1972). It is possible to feel crowded even when density is low. If, for example, you go to a secluded beach to swim with a friend and discover that there are five or six other people there, you may *feel* crowded even though there is no lack of physical space.

Many studies have examined how animals react to high population density. Calhoun (1962) created rat colonies in which the population was far denser than normal. He found that rats developed "abnormal" traits under these conditions that had not been present before: Maternal behavior was disturbed, and cannibalism and homosexuality developed. In general, the rats behaved as if their social bonds had been dissolved (see Figure 16-3).

Although similar reactions to high population density have been observed in mice, lemmings, and hares, it is not entirely clear how these findings apply to human behavior. Some studies have found strong positive correlations between density and various forms of social pathology, such as juvenile delinquency, mental illness, and the infant death rate (Schmitt, 1966). Others have failed to find a link between density and pathology.

Among humans, the distinction between density and crowding is critical—it's the *experience* of being crowded that produces psychological stress. In part, the stress may be due to sensory overload: Sights and sounds multiply so fast that they soon overload the sensory circuits of people in crowds (Stokols, 1978). In part, the stress of crowding may also be due to lack of privacy (Altman, 1975). Individuals who cannot withdraw from contact with others or prevent them from intruding on their personal space experience stress. In addition, when many people surround us, it is more difficult to control our interactions with them. The loss of control over one's surroundings can be stressful. Baum and Valins (1977), for example, discovered that students living in long-corridor dorms felt more crowded than students living in short-corridor residences, even though actual density was the same. The reason appeared to be that the heavier traffic in the halls and lounges of long-corridor dorms led to feelings of greater crowding. Students who lived in the long-corridor dorms were also more likely to feel powerless to control their environment.

Not everyone reacts to crowding in the same way. Individualistic persons tend to experience more stress from crowding than do those who work easily in cooperation with others. Compatibility is also more important. Being enclosed in tight quarters with others whose company one does not enjoy is a perfect recipe for stress, as we have all learned. Some evidence suggests that men suffer more stress from high-density conditions than do women (Penrod, 1986).

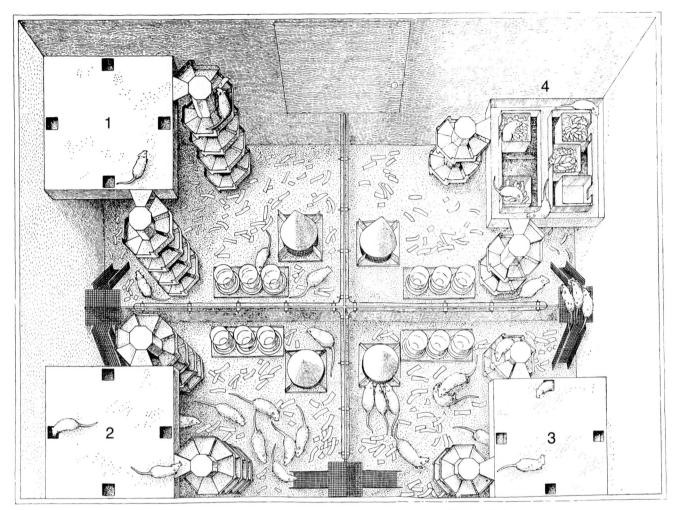

NOISE. Noise can have a powerful impact on mental functioning. In a classroom in a large city several years ago, hundreds of students had just begun to work on the Graduate Record Examination when the sound of an electric guitar pierced the walls. In a park a quarter of a mile away, a young man had set up a pair of loudspeakers so powerful that the examinees could hear every mistake he made on his guitar. Because it was impossible for most of the students to concentrate on the examination under these distracting conditions, the proctors had to collect the exam booklets and move everyone to a room on the other side of the building.

But noise affects more than concentration. It also affects interpersonal interaction, including the tendency to help others who are in need. In one study, subjects exposed to different levels of noise saw a stranger drop a stack of books and magazines. The greater the noise, the less likely subjects were to help pick up the books (Matthews & Cannon, 1975). Noise also seems to impair our ability to notice cues in social situations and in the environment in general. In one experiment, subjects watching a videotape while exposed to noise were less able to distinguish victims from harm-doers than were other subjects who were not exposed to noise (Siegel & Steele, 1979). Finally, noise facilitates aggressive responses. In one experiment, a group of college students heard loud random bursts

Figure 16-3
Calhoun's study of crowding among rats A room divided into four pens connected by ramps housed 80 rats. Because Pens 1 and 4 were not connected by a ramp, the rats tended to congregate in Pens 2 and 3, where deviant behavior became most noticeable. In Pens 1 and 4, a dominant male was able to establish a harem, but in Pens 2 and 3, where males outnumbered females, such forms of deviant behavior as cannibalism and homosexuality developed more readily. In Pens 1 and 4, where the females were protected by dominant males and were able to take care of their young, the infant mortality rate was only about 50 percent; in Pens 2 and 3, the infant mortality rate escalated to 96 percent.

Adapted from *Population Density and Social Pathology* by John B. Calhoun (1962). Copyright © 1962 by Scientific American, Inc. All rights reserved.

Noise can be a major source of environmental stress.

of noise and then were angered by a confederate. Next, they had the chance to "shock" another person. These subjects delivered more intense shocks than did students who had heard only soft noise (Donnerstein & Wilson, 1976). Noise, then, is more than a distraction: Under certain conditions, it can also reduce altruism, attention to social cues, and self-restraint in interaction with others.

 APPLICATION

Prejudice and Discrimination

Although we often use the terms *prejudice* and *discrimination* interchangeably, they are, in fact, different. Prejudice is an unfair, intolerant, or unfavorable *attitude* toward another group of people. Discrimination is an *act* or a series of acts taken toward another group—or toward people who belong to that group—that are unfair when compared with our behavior toward other groups. You should not be surprised to learn by now that prejudice (an attitude) and discrimination (a behavior) do not always occur together. A motel owner who is prejudiced against blacks may nonetheless manage to be polite as he or she rents a room to a black family. He or she is prejudiced but does not discriminate. Conversely, the personnel manager of a conservative bank may refuse to hire a woman whom he has interviewed for a management job, not because he is sexist himself, but because bank policy discourages the hiring of women managers. In this case, discrimination is present without prejudice.

PREJUDICE.   Like attitudes in general, prejudice has three components: beliefs, feelings, and behavior tendencies. Prejudicial beliefs are virtually always stereotypes, and as we mentioned earlier in this chapter, the use of stereotypes leads to certain kinds of errors in thinking about other people. When a prejudiced employer interviews a black, for instance, the employer attributes to the job candidate all of the traits associated with the black stereotype. To make matters worse, qualities of the individual that are inconsistent with the stereotype are ignored or quickly forgotten. In his classic study *The Nature of Prejudice*, Gordon Allport (1954) recorded the following dialogue:

Mr. X: The trouble with the Jews is that they only take care of their own group.
Mr. Y: But the record of the Community Chest campaign shows that they gave more generously in proportion to

their numbers to the general charities of the communities than did non-Jews.

Mr. X: That shows that they are always trying to buy favor and intrude into Christian affairs. They think of nothing but money; that is why there are so many Jewish bankers.

Mr. Y: But a recent study shows that the percentage of Jews in the banking business is negligible, far smaller than the percentage of non-Jews.

Mr. X: That's just it; they don't go in for respectable business; they are only in the movie business or run night clubs.

Along with stereotyped beliefs, prejudicial attitudes are usually marked by strong emotions, such as dislike, fear, hatred, or loathing. Understandably, such attitudes also lead the individual to discriminate against the group in question.

SOURCES OF PREJUDICE.   There have been many studies of the sources of prejudice, and an extraordinary number of theories have been advanced about its causes.

Frustration-Aggression.   One of the most popular theories explains prejudice in terms of the submerged frustrations of the prejudiced group (Allport, 1954; Hovland & Sears, 1940). The *scapegoat theory* asserts that prejudice and discrimination result from displaced aggression. Historically, for example, violence against Jews has often followed periods of economic unrest or natural catastrophe. Similarly, blacks in this country have been scapegoats for the economic frustrations of lower income white Americans who are essentially powerless. Poor whites who feel exploited and oppressed cannot vent their anger against the proper target, so they displace their hostility by directing it against those who are even "lower" on the social scale than they are—blacks.

Authoritarian Personality.   Another theory explains prejudice in terms of the psychological characteristics of the bigot. Adorno and his colleagues (1950) linked prejudice to a complex cluster of personality traits termed *authoritarianism*. Authoritarians tend to be rigidly conventional, submissive to authority, hostile toward people who violate conventional values, inclined to think about the world according to rigid categories, preoccupied with power and toughness, and both destructive and cynical. Such individuals fear, suspect, and reject all groups other than the ones to which they belong.

Conformity.   Conformity is also important in forming and sustaining prejudice and discrimination.

If we associate with people who also have clearly expressed prejudices, we are more likely to go along with their prejudices than we are to resist them. During the 1960s in the South, for example, many restaurant owners maintained that they themselves did not mind serving blacks but that their customers would not tolerate it (Deaux & Wrightsman, 1984). Children are especially likely to conform to the attitudes of their peers, which is partly why it has often been so hard to integrate schools. Those white children who are willing to go to school with black children are subjected to immense peer-group pressure to conform to the hostile behavior—based on stereotypes—displayed by their friends and classmates.

REDUCING PREJUDICE.   We noted earlier that people tend to like others who are similar to them. How important is racial similarity to people's liking for others? In a series of studies (Byrne & Wong, 1962; Rokeach & Mezei, 1966; Stein, Hardyck, & Smith, 1965), some subjects were given a description of a person of another race whose attitudes were similar to their own, while other subjects received descriptions of a person of their own race whose attitudes were very different from their own. The results showed that, in general, similarity of attitudes was more important than belonging to the same racial group in determining who was liked.

It would indeed be pleasant to believe that these findings bear directly on real contacts between people. If this were so, it would indicate—as many educators and activists believed—that simply *educating* people about the similarities between themselves and others might reduce racial tensions. These studies, however, apply primarily to nonintimate relationships—working or studying together, for example. Racial similarity is far more important in intimate relationships such as dating or marriage.

It is also wise to remember that the subjects in these studies were presented with hypothetical people and situations and that there was a subtle pressure to be objective and nonbiased. In real life, biases are often more important. Silverman (1974) described various people as roommates to incoming college students. Some subjects were told that these choices would actually *be* their assigned roommates. Other subjects were told that these were merely hypothetical roommates. Racial discrimination was far more important to the choice of *actual* roommates than to the choice of *imagined* roommates. But similarity in attitude and belief was important in both groups. Thus, although it is somewhat discouraging to see the difference between our "lip service" to racial equality and our practice of it, these studies offer some hope that people will weigh attitude similarity fairly under the right conditions.

During the late 1950s, when school desegregation was given massive attention, many people believed that it too would change prejudicial attitudes. This belief has proved to be only partly true. Moreover, the attempt to educate the public with films and literature designed to explode racial myths has been a dismal failure (Aronson, 1984). As we have seen, people are quite adept at ignoring what clashes with their own deep-seated beliefs.

There has, however, been some progress. We now know that when blacks and whites share the same goals and cooperate to reach them, prejudice lessens. The important point here is that mere *contact* between groups is not enough to lessen prejudice. The contact must be *interdependent* and *cooperative*, not competitive. Interracial groups organized to solve specific problems cooperatively—a student council, a working team, a study group—can reduce prejudice. Unfortunately, these situations are rare in society, although studies among residents of housing projects, department store workers, and police officers all show the same thing: When racial groups work or live together in noncompetitive, nonthreatening situations, racial animosities decrease (Clore et al., 1978).

One interesting series of studies by Elliot Aronson and his colleagues (Aronson et al., 1978) seems to point the way for future efforts at reducing racial prejudice. Each student in a class was given a different

When blacks and whites share the same goals and work together to achieve them, prejudice lessens.

section of material to learn and report on to his or her fellow students—it was called the *jigsaw method* because the pieces fit together to form a whole. The students were left on their own, but were told that they would be tested on the material. Thus, it was to their advantage to learn from one another, to coax those who needed it, and to cooperate in assembling the "whole picture." The results were remarkable. While it took some students longer than others to realize the value of cooperation, most of the groups adapted well, and students of all races found themselves cooperating and learning from one another.

This method, however, works best with young children. It is also hard to implement such a program on any but a small scale. Still, it offers some hope for those who believe that education is the best way to change people's preconceived racial prejudices.

■ Summary

- *Social psychology* is the scientific study of the way in which the thoughts, feelings, and behaviors of one individual are influenced by the real, imagined, or implied behavior or characteristics of other people.

- **How do we form first impressions?** Social perception involves forming impressions of other people. When we first meet someone, we use cues to fit him or her into preexisting categories called *schemas*. Schemas allow us to make inferences about other people and to recall facts about them. They can also lead to selective or inaccurate recall.

- **If a friend says, "Sam is a lot of fun," is it likely** that you will like him when you meet him? A *primacy effect* exists when the first information that we receive about someone weighs more heavily than later information in the formation of impressions. Under certain conditions, the primacy effect can be overcome.

- A *stereotype* is a special kind of schema in which we believe a set of characteristics is shared by all the people who belong to a particular social group. As with all schemas, stereotypes can affect what we remember about people and become *self-fulfilling prophecies.*

- **You run into a friend at the supermarket and greet**

him warmly, but he barely acknowledges you, mumbling "Hi" and walking away. **What affects how you interpret his reaction?** The study of the inferences we make about the behavior of other people is called *attribution theory.* An attribution is an inference that one draws about the actions of another—or oneself—on the basis of observing overt behavior. In making attributions we tend to consider such things as *distinctiveness, consensus,* and *consistency* of behavior.

- The attribution process is subject to a number of biases, of which the most important is the *fundamental attribution error:* the tendency to overemphasize personal causes for the behavior of others and to underemphasize those causes for our own behavior. Another attribution bias is the tendency to attribute catastrophes to personal rather than situational factors; to assume that if people behave differently from us in a situation, it is because of personal factors; and to take personal credit for good events and deny responsibility for bad things (*defensive attribution*).

- **When it comes to love, do opposites attract?** Many factors propel us toward liking another person. Some of the major factors are: *proximity,* similarity, physical attractiveness, and rewardingness. Similarity, having shared attitudes, beliefs and interests, is especially important.

- An *attitude* is a fairly stable organization of evaluative beliefs, feelings, and behavior tendencies directed toward some object such as a person or group. Some attitudes derive from our personal experience and from the information we received from our parents when we were children. Admired individuals, as well as social groups, may also have a lasting influence on attitudes. Studies also show that television is a major source of societal attitudes. Children, especially, rely on television to form their social attitudes.

- Various factors contribute to the success of an attempt to change an attitude by providing information. Credibility of the source, the content of the message (number of arguments presented, use of fear), and the organization of the message all affect the amount of attitude change. Also important are characteristics of the audience, such as its commitment to its present attitudes, the discrepancy between the message and present attitudes, and personality characteristics.

- **If someone who has never particularly liked the city accepts a great job in Manhattan, are their feelings about city life likely to change?** Changes of behavior sometimes lead to changes of attitude. *Cognitive dissonance* theory maintains that a state of unpleasant tension follows from the clashing of two incompatible cognitions. We are motivated to try to reduce dissonance in one way or another. When the discrepancy is between behavior and attitude, it is often easiest to reduce dissonance by changing the attitude.

- Attitude change is a common result of cognitive dissonance, because changing one's attitude is an easier means of reducing dissonance than the other two alternatives, which are (1) increasing the number of consonant elements, and (2) reducing the importance of one or both cognitive elements.

- *Social influence* refers to any actions performed by one or more persons to change the attitudes, behavior, or feelings of one or more others. Attitude change is one form of social influence. Conformity, compliance, and obedience are the results of successful attempts to exert social influence on behavior.

- *Conformity* is the voluntary yielding to social norms, even at the expense of one's own preferences. *Compliance* is a change of behavior in response to an explicit request from another person. Like compliance, *obedience* is a change in behavior in response to an explicit statement by another person, in this case a command from an authority figure.

- **If you're in a crowded shopping mall and you see someone sitting on the floor crying, possibly because they've fallen, why is it unlikely that you will walk over and ask if they need help?** *Altruistic behavior* is helping behavior that is not linked to personal gain. The likelihood of helping behavior is determined by situational variables and variables related to the bystander. The greater the number of bystanders and the greater the ambiguity of the situation, the less likely bystanders are to help a stranger in need. In addition, the mood of the bystander and other personal qualities affect the likelihood of helping behavior.

- The effectiveness of group decision-making depends on three factors: (1) the nature of the task, (2) the resources of the group members, and (3) the interaction among group members. If the requirements of the task match the skills of group members, groups are likely to be more effective than the same number of individuals working alone. However, the social status of group members, group size, and cohesiveness also determine how effective a group will actually be.

- **What makes a person a leader?** All groups have a leader, whether a formal one or an informal one. Some theorists argue that leaders are "great persons" who could lead no matter what the historical conditions. Another theory stresses that leaders happen to appear in the right place at the right time. The transactional viewpoint argues that both personal traits and situational factors are important. Also important is the relation between the leader and the group.

- *Industrial/organizational (I/O) psychology* is concerned with behavior in a wide variety of organizational environments, including the workplace. Industrial psychologists examine the role of psychological factors in such problems as employee turnover and absenteeism. Studies have confirmed that the psychological requirements of a job are as important as its physical activities. Productivity can be increased when a worker is encouraged to employ a greater variety of skills or is afforded more autonomous activity.

- The communications and decision-making systems of an organization also affect both its efficiency and its members' attitudes. Centralized communications systems, in which most communications flow to and from one person, are more suitable for solving problems involving the assembly of information, while problems requiring the exchange and examination of ideas are often better handled by decentralized systems in which all the members regularly communicate with one another. In addition, the more freely his or her position allows a worker to communicate with others, the more satisfied he or she is likely to be with that position.

- **How does the environment in which we live and work affect our relations with others?** *Environmental psychology* studies the way in which such things as personal space, crowding, and noise affect the way we relate to the world around us and to other people. *Personal space* refers to the psychological space surrounding a person. There are differences in the way national groups, ethnic and cultural groups, and even the two sexes relate to personal space. In general, the degree of intimacy or liking of other people determines our willingness to stand or be seated close to them. Circumstances also dictate perception of personal space. Forced proximity is more readily tolerated than what is perceived as a deliberate invasion of personal space.

- Several sources of environmental stress are high population *density, crowding,* and *noise.* Density refers to the number of persons per unit of area. While animals appear to be greatly affected by high density, in humans it seems that the experience of feeling crowded is more stressful. Noise also affects people profoundly, especially when it is unpredictable and uncontrollable. Noise not only distracts, it also affects interpersonal interaction, ability to notice social cues, and self-restraint.

▪ Review Questions

1. The scientific study of the way in which the thoughts, feelings, and behaviors of one individual are influenced by the real, imagined, or implied behavior or characteristic of other people is _____ psychology.

2. When we first meet someone, we use cues to fit that person into preexisting categories called _____ . Sometimes we think and behave in accordance with a _____ , a set of characteristics thought to be shared by all of the people who belong to a particular social group.

3. A _____ effect exists to the extent that the first information that we receive about someone weighs more heavily than later information in the formation of impressions.

4. The study of the inferences we make about the behavior of other people is
   a. psychology.
   b. social psychology.
   c. attribution theory.
   d. cognitive dissonance.

5. Which of the following has NOT been established as a factor that promotes liking between two persons?
   a. proximity
   b. complementary needs
   c. complementary attitudes and interests
   d. rewardingness

6. A/an _____ is a fairly stable organization of beliefs, feelings, and behavioral tendencies directed toward some object such as a person or group.

7. The best way to predict behavior is to measure attitudes. T / F

8. Which of the following decreases the likelihood that a message will change the attitude of an audience?
   a. credible sources
   b. attitudes shared with other people
   c. inclusion of numerous arguments of the desired attitude
   d. moderate appeal to fear

9. _____ _____ theory maintains that a state

of unpleasant tension follows the clashing of two incompatible cognitions.

10. According to cognitive dissonance theory, when a discrepancy between behavior and attitudes exists, it is often easiest to change _____ to reduce the dissonance.
    a. attitudes   c. neither attitudes nor behavior
    b. behavior   d. intentions

11. Match each of the following terms with its definition:
    ____ social influence
    ____ compliance
    ____ obedience
    ____ conformity

    a. voluntarily yielding to social norms, even at the expense of one's own preferences
    b. a change of behavior in response to a command from another person
    c. a change of behavior in response to an explicit request from another person or from a group
    d. any actions performed by one or more persons to change the attitudes, behavior, or feelings of others

12. If group members are inclined to take risks, then the group decision is likely to be risker than individual decisions. This phenomenon is termed the _____ _____.

13. A shift in attitudes by members of a group toward more extreme positions than the one held before group discussion is termed _____.

14. The effectiveness of a group depends on three factors: (1) the nature of the _____, (2) the resources of the group members, and (3) the _____ among group members.

15. All groups have a leader, whether a formal one or an informal one.   T / F

16. _____ psychology concerns the way in which such things as personal space, crowding, and noise affect the way we relate to the world around us and to other people.

17. Density, crowding, and noise are all sources of environmental _____.

18. The way in which different kinds of people—men and women, national groups, and ethnic groups—relate to personal space does not vary much.   T / F

Appendix: Measurement and Statistical Methods

■ Thinking Critically

Are there different ways of measuring behavior?

If there is a high correlation between income and voting—for example, that wealthy people are more likely to vote—why is it not also true that voting makes people wealthy?

Would polling people at a shopping mall be a good way to get a random sample?

How do psychologists know that the differences uncovered in the results of their studies are not just due to chance?

The answers to these and other questions about how psychologists measure and analyze data about behavior appear in this appendix.

■ Outline

Most of the experiments described in this book involve measuring one or more variables and then analyzing the data statistically. The design and scoring of all the tests we have discussed are also based on statistical methods. **Statistics** is a branch of mathematics. It provides techniques for sorting out quantitative facts and ways of drawing conclusions from them. Statistics let us organize and describe data quickly, guide the conclusions we draw, and help us make inferences.

Statistical analysis is essential to conducting an experiment or designing a test, but statistics can only handle numbers—groups of them. To use statistics, the psychologist first must measure things—count and express them in quantities.

Scales of Measurement

No matter what we are measuring—height, noise, intelligence, attitudes, and so on—we have to use a scale. The data we want to collect determine the scale we will use and, in turn, the scale we use helps determine the conclusions we can draw from our data.

NOMINAL SCALES. If we decide to classify a group of people by the color of their eyes, we are using a **nominal scale.** We can count how many people have blue eyes, how many have green eyes, how many have brown eyes, and so on, but we cannot say that one group has more or less eye color than the other. The colors are simply different.

A nominal scale is a set of arbitrarily named or numbered categories. If we look up how many Republican, Democratic, and Independent voters registered in a certain congressional district in the last election year, we are using a nominal scale. Since a nominal scale is more of a way of classifying than of measuring, it is the least informative kind of scale. If we want to compare our data more precisely, we will have to use a scale that tells us more.

ORDINAL SCALES. If we list horses in the order in which they finish a race, we are using an **ordinal scale.** On an ordinal scale, data are ranked from first to last according to some criterion. An ordinal scale tells the order, but nothing about the distances between what is ranked first and second or ninth and tenth. It does not tell us how much faster the winning horse ran than the horses that placed or showed. If a person ranks her preferences for various kinds of soup—pea soup first, then tomato, then onion, and so on—we know what soup she likes most and what soup she likes least, but we have no idea how much better she likes tomato than onion, or if pea soup is far more favored than either one of them.

Since we do not know the distances between the items ranked on an ordinal scale, we cannot add or substract ordinal data. If mathematical operations are necessary, we need a still more informative scale.

INTERVAL SCALES. An **interval scale** is often compared to a ruler that has been broken off at the bottom—it only goes from, say, $5\frac{1}{2}$ to

12. The intervals between 6 and 7, 7 and 8, 8 and 9, and so forth are equal, but there is no zero. A thermometer is an interval scale—even though a certain degree registered on a Fahrenheit or centigrade thermometer specifies a certain state of cold or heat, there is no such thing as no temperature at all. One day is never twice as hot as another; it is only so many equal degrees hotter.

An interval scale tells us how many equal-size units one thing lies above or below another thing of the same kind, but it does not tell us how many times bigger, smaller, taller, or fatter one thing is than another. An intelligence test cannot tell us that one person is three times as intelligent as another, only that he or she scored so many points above or below someone else.

RATIO SCALES. We can only say that a measurement is two times as long as another or three times as high when we use a **ratio scale,** one that has a true zero. For instance, if we measure the snowfall in a certain area over several winters, we can say that six times as much snow fell during a winter in which we measured a total of 12 feet as during a winter in which only 2 feet fell. This scale has a zero—there may be no snow.

▨ Measurements of Central Tendency

Usually, when we measure a number of instances of anything—from the popularity of TV shows to the weights of eight-year-old boys to the number of times a person's optic nerve fires in response to electrical stimulation—we get a distribution of measurements that range from smallest to largest or lowest to highest. The measurements will usually cluster around some value near the middle. This value is the **central tendency** of the distribution of the measurements.

Suppose, for example, you want to keep 10 children busy tossing rings around a bottle. You give them three rings to toss each turn, the game has six rounds, and each player scores one point every time he or she gets the ring around the neck of the bottle. The highest possible score is 18. The distribution of scores might end up like this: 11, 8, 13, 6, 12, 10, 16, 9, 12, 3.

What could you quickly say about the ring-tossing talent of the group? First, you could arrange the scores from lowest to highest: 3, 6, 8, 9, 10, 11, 12, 12, 13, 16. In this order, the central tendency of the distribution of scores becomes clear. Many of the scores cluster around the values between 8 and 12. There are three ways to describe the central tendency of a distribution. We usually refer to all three as the *average*.

The arithmetical average is called the **mean**—the sum of all the scores in the group, divided by the number of scores. If you add up all the scores and divide by 10, the total number of scores in this group of ring tossers, you find that the mean for the group is 10.

The **median** is the point that divides a distribution in half—50 percent of the scores fall above the median, and 50 percent fall below. In the ring-tossing scores, five scores fall at 10 or below, five at 11 or above. The median is thus halfway between 10 and 11—10.5.

The point at which the largest number of scores occurs is called the

Ratio scale Scale with equal distances between the points or values and with a true zero.

Central tendency Tendency of scores to congregate around some middle value.

Mean Arithmetical average calculated by dividing a sum of values by the total number of cases.

Median Point that divides a set of scores in half.

Mode Point at which the largest number of scores occurs.

Frequency distribution A count of the number of scores that fall within each of a series of intervals.

mode. In our example, the mode is 12. More people scored 12 than any other.

Differences between the Mean, Median, and Mode

If we take many measurements of anything, we are likely to get a distribution of scores in which the mean, median, and mode are all about the same—the score that occurs most often (the mode) will also be the point that half the scores are below and half above (the median). And the same point will be the arithmetical average (the mean). This is not always true, of course, and small samples rarely come out so symmetrically. In these cases, we often have to decide which of the three measures of central tendency—the mean, the median, or mode—will tell us what we want to know.

For example, a shopkeeper wants to know the general incomes of passersby so he can stock the right merchandise. He might conduct a rough survey by standing outside his store for a few days from 12:00 to 2:00 and asking every tenth person who walks by to check a card showing the general range of his or her income. Suppose most of the people checked the ranges between $15,000 and $25,000 a year. However, a couple of the people made a lot of money—one checked $100,000–$150,000, one checked the $200,000-or-above box. The mean for the set of income figures would be pushed higher by those two large figures and would not really tell the shopkeeper what he wants to know about his potential customers. In this case, he would be wiser to use the median or the mode.

Suppose instead of meeting two people whose incomes were so great, he noticed that people from two distinct income groups walked by his store—several people checked the box for $15,000–$17,000, and several others checked $23,000–$25,000. The shopkeeper would find that his distribution was bimodal. It has two modes—$16,000 and $24,000. This might be more useful to him than the mean, which could lead him to think his customers were a unit with an average income of about $20,000.

Another way of approaching a set of scores is to arrange them into a **frequency distribution**—that is, to select a set of intervals and count how many scores fall into each interval. A frequency distribution is useful for large groups of numbers; it puts the number of individual scores into more manageable groups.

Suppose a psychologist tests memory. She asks 50 college students to learn 18 nonsense syllables, then records how many syllables each student can recall two hours later. She arranges her raw scores from lowest to highest in a rank distribution:

2	6	8	10	11	14
3	7	9	10	12	14
4	7	9	10	12	15
4	7	9	10	12	16
5	7	9	10	13	17
5	7	9	11	13	
6	8	9	11	13	
6	8	9	11	13	
6	8	10	11	13	

The scores range from 2 to 17, but 50 individual scores are too cumbersome to work with. So she chooses a set of two-point intervals and tallies the number of scores in each interval:

Frequency histogram Type of bar graph that shows frequency distributions.

Frequency polygon Type of line graph that shows frequency distributions.

Interval	Tally	Frequency (f)
1–2	|	1
3–4	|||	3
5–6	ⅢⅢ |	6
7–8	ⅢⅢ ||||	9
9–10	ⅢⅢ ⅢⅢ |||	13
11–12	ⅢⅢ |||	8
13–14	ⅢⅢ ||	7
15–16	||	2
17–18	|	1

Now she can tell at a glance what the results of her experiment were. Most of the students had scores near the middle of the range, and very few had scores in the high or low intervals. She can see these results even better if she uses the frequency distribution to construct a bar graph—a **frequency histogram.** Marking the intervals along the horizontal axis and the frequencies along the vertical axis would give her the graph shown in Figure A-1. Another way is to construct a **frequency polygon,** a line graph. A frequency polygon drawn from the same set of data is shown in Figure A-2. Note that the figure is not a smooth curve, since the points are connected by straight lines. With many scores, however, and with

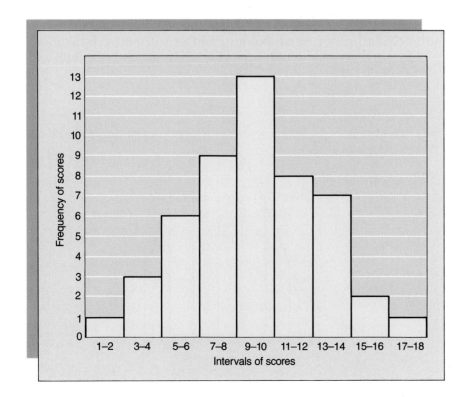

Figure A-1
A frequency histogram for a memory experiment The bars indicate the frequency of scores within each interval.

Figure A-2
A frequency polygon drawn from data used in Figure A-1 The dots, representing the frequency of scores in each interval, are connected by straight lines.

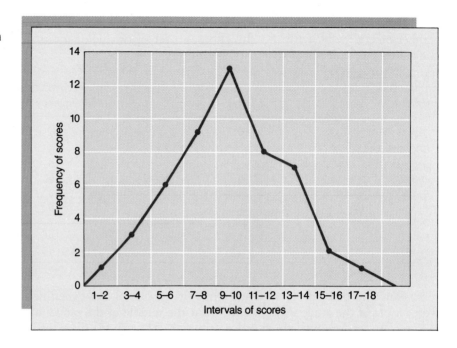

small intervals, the angles would smooth out, and the figure would resemble a rounded curve.

The Normal Curve

Ordinarily, if we take enough measurements of almost anything, we get a *normal distribution*. Tossing coins is a favorite example of statisticians. If you tossed 10 coins into the air 1,000 times and recorded the heads and tails on each toss, your tabulations would reveal a normal distribution. Five heads and five tails would occur most often, six heads/four tails and

Figure A-3
A normal curve, based on measurements of the heights of 1,000 adult males. From Hill, 1966.

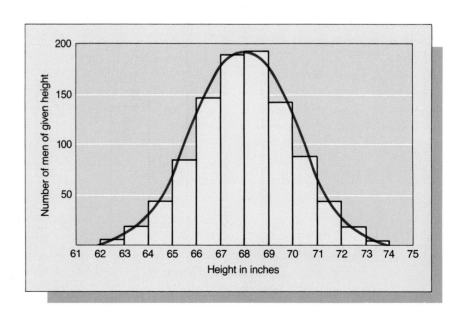

four heads/six tails would be the next most frequent, and so on down to the rare all heads or all tails.

Plotting a normal distribution on a graph yields a particular kind of frequency polygon, called a **normal curve.** Figure A-3 shows data on the heights of 1,000 men. Superimposed over the gray bars that reflect the actual data is an "ideal" normal curve for the same data. Note that the curve is absolutely symmetrical—the left slope parallels the right slope exactly. Moreover, the mean, median, and mode all fall on the highest point on the curve.

The normal curve is a hypothetical entity. No set of real measurements show such a smooth gradation from one interval to the next, or so purely symmetrical a shape. But because so many things do approximate the normal curve so closely, the curve is a useful model for much that we measure.

Normal curve Hypothetical, bell-shaped distribution curve that occurs when a normal distribution is plotted as a frequency polygon.

Skewed Distributions

If a frequency distribution is asymmetrical—if most of the scores are gathered at either the high end or the low end—the frequency polygon will be *skewed.* The hump will sit to one side or the other, and one of the curve's tails will be disproportionately long.

If a high-school mathematics instructor, for example, gives her students a sixth-grade arithmetic test, we would expect nearly all the scores to be quite high. The frequency polygon would probably look like the one in Figure A-4. But if a sixth-grade class is asked to do advanced algebra, the scores would probably be quite low. The frequency polygon would be very similar to the one shown in Figure A-5.

Note, too, that the mean, median, and mode fall at different points in a skewed distribution, unlike in the normal curve, where they coincide. Usually, if you know that the mean is greater than the median of a distribution, you can predict that the frequency polygon will be skewed to the right. If the median is greater than the mean, the curve will be skewed to the left.

Bimodal Distributions

We have already mentioned a bimodal distribution in our description of the shopkeeper's survey of his customers' incomes. The frequency polygon for a bimodal distribution has two humps—one for each mode. The mean and the median may be the same (Figure A-6) or different (Figure A-7).

■ Measures of Variation

Sometimes, it is not enough to know the distribution of a set of data and what their mean, median, and mode are. Suppose an automotive safety expert feels that too much damage occurs in tail-end accidents because automobile bumpers are not all the same height. It is not enough to know what the average height of an automobile bumper is. He or she also wants

Figure A-4
A skewed distribution Most of the scores are gathered at the high end of the distribution, causing the hump to shift to the right. Since the tail on the left is longer, we say that the curve is skewed to the left. Note that the *mean, median,* and *mode* are different.

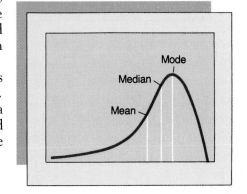

Figure A-5
In this distribution, most of the scores are gathered at the low end, so the curve is skewed to the right. The *mean, median,* and *mode* do not coincide.

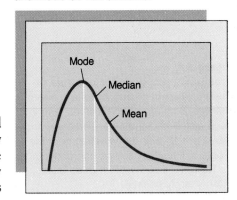

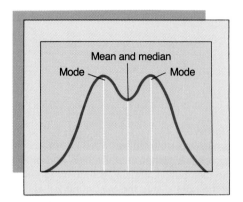

Figure A-6
A bimodal distribution in which the *mean* and the *median* are the same.

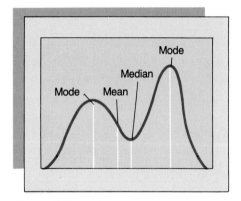

Figure A-7
In this bimodal distribution, the *mean* and *median* are different.

Figure A-8
Frequency polygons for two sets of measurements of automobile bumper heights Both are normal curves, and in each distribution the *mean, median,* and *mode* are 15. But the variation from the mean is different, causing one curve to be flattened and the other to be much more sharply peaked.

to know about the variation in bumper heights: How much higher is the highest bumper than the mean? How do bumpers of all cars vary from the mean? Are the latest bumpers closer to the same height?

Range

The simplest measure of variation is the **range**—the difference between the largest and smallest measurements. Perhaps the safety expert measured the bumpers of 1,000 cars two years ago and found that the highest bumper was 18 inches from the ground, the lowest only 12 inches from the ground. The range was thus 6 inches—18 minus 12. This year the highest bumper is still 18 inches high, the lowest still 12 inches from the ground. The range is still 6 inches. Moreover, he or she finds that the means of the two distributions are the same—15 inches off the ground. But look at the two frequency polygons in Figure A-8—there is still something he or she needs to know, since how the measurements cluster around the mean is drastically different. To find out how the measurements are distributed around the mean, our safety expert has to turn to a slightly more complicated measure of variation—the standard deviation.

The Standard Deviation

The **standard deviation,** in a single number, tells us much about how the scores in any frequency distribution are dispersed around the mean. Calculating the standard deviation is one of the most useful and widely used statistical tools.

To find the standard deviation of a set of scores, we first find the mean. Then we take the first score in the distribution, subtract it from the mean, square the difference, and jot it down in a column to be added up later. We do the same for all the scores in the distribution. Then we add up the column of squared differences, divide the total by the number of scores in the distribution, and find the square root of that number. Figure A-9 shows the calculation of the standard deviation for a small distribution of scores.

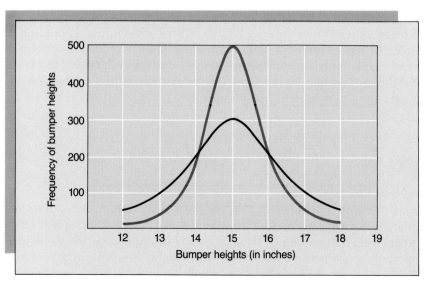

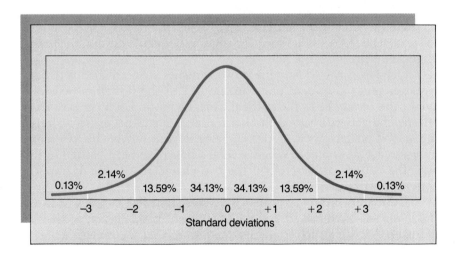

Number of scores = 10		Mean = 7

Scores	Difference from mean	Difference squared
4	7 − 4 = 3	$3^2 = 9$
5	7 − 5 = 2	$2^2 = 4$
6	7 − 6 = 1	$1^2 = 1$
6	7 − 6 = 1	$1^2 = 1$
7	7 − 7 = 0	$0^2 = 0$
7	7 − 7 = 0	$0^2 = 0$
8	7 − 8 = − 1	$− 1^2 = 1$
8	7 − 8 = − 1	$− 1^2 = 1$
9	7 − 9 = − 2	$− 2^2 = 4$
10	7 − 10 = − 3	$− 3^2 = 9$

Sum of squares = 30
÷
Number of scores = 10
Variance = 3
Standard deviation = $\sqrt{3}$ = 1.73

Figure A-9
Step-by-step calculation of the *standard deviation* for a group of 10 scores with a mean of 7.

Figure A-10
A normal curve, divided to show the percentage of scores that fall within each *standard deviation* from the *mean*.

In a normal distribution, however peaked or flattened the curve, about 68 percent of the scores fall between one standard deviation above the mean and one standard deviation below the mean (see Figure A-10). Another 27 percent fall between one standard deviation and two standard deviations on either side of the mean, and 4 percent more between the second and third standard deviations on either side. More than 99 percent of the scores fall between three standard deviations above and three standard deviations below the mean. This makes the standard deviation useful for comparing two different normal distributions.

Now let us see what the standard deviation can tell our automotive safety expert about the variations from the mean in the two sets of data. The standard deviation for the cars measured two years ago is about 1.4. A car with a bumper height of 16.4 is one standard deviation above the mean of 15; one with a bumper height of 13.6 is one standard deviation

Scatter plot Diagram showing the association between scores on two variables.

Correlation coefficient Statistical measure of the strength of association between two variables.

below the mean. Since the engineer knows that the data fall into a normal distribution, he or she can figure that about 68 percent of the 1,000 cars he measured will fall somewhere between these two heights: 680 cars will have bumpers between 13.6 and 16.4 inches high. For the more recent set of data, the standard deviation is just slightly less than 1. A car with a bumper height of about 14 inches is one standard deviation below the mean; a car with a bumper height of about 16 is one standard deviation above the mean. Thus, in this distribution, 680 cars have bumpers between 14 and 16 inches high. This tells the safety expert that car bumpers are becoming more similar, although the range of heights is still the same (6 inches), and the mean height of bumpers is still 15.

■ Measures of Correlation

Measures of central tendency and measures of variation are used to describe a single set of measurements—like the children's ring-tossing scores—or to compare two or more sets of measurements—like the two sets of bumper heights. Sometimes, however, we need to know if two sets of measurements are in any way associated with one another—if they are correlated. Is parental IQ related to children's IQ? Does the need for achievement relate to the need for power? Is watching violence on TV related to aggressive behavior?

One fast way to determine if two variables are correlated is to draw a **scatter plot.** We assign one variable (X) to the horizontal axis of a graph, the other (Y) to the vertical axis. Then we plot a person's score on one characteristic along the horizontal axis and his or her score on the second characteristic along the vertical axis. Where the two scores intersect, we draw a dot. When several scores have been plotted in this way, the pattern of dots tells if the two characteristics are in any way correlated with each other.

If the dots on a scatter plot form a straight line running between the lower left-hand corner and the upper right-hand corner, as they do in Figure A-11a, we have a perfect *positive correlation*—a high score on one of the characteristics is always associated with a high score on the other one. A straight line running between the upper left-hand corner and the lower right-hand corner, as in Figure A-11b, is the sign of a perfect *negative correlation*—a high score on one of the characteristics is always associated with a low score on the other one. If the pattern formed by the dots is cigar-shaped in either of these directions, as in Figure A-11c, we have a modest correlation—the two characteristics are related, but not highly correlated. If the dots spread out over the whole graph, forming a circle or a random pattern, as they do in Figure A-11d, there is no correlation between the two characteristics.

A scatter plot can give us a general idea if a correlation exists and how strong it is. To describe the relation between two variables more precisely, we need a **correlation coefficient**—a statistical measure of the degree to which two variables are associated. The correlation coefficient tells us the degree of association between two sets of matched scores— that is, to what extent high or low scores on one variable tend to be

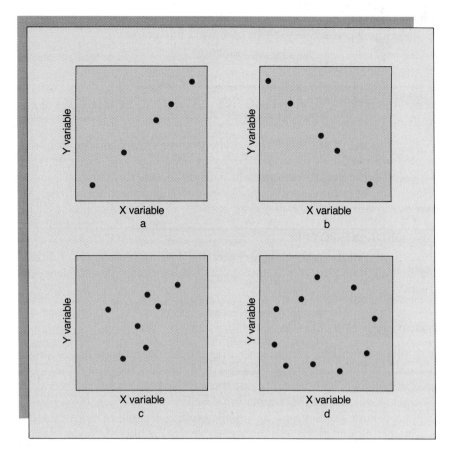

Figure A-11
Scatter plots can be used to give a rough idea of the strength and direction of correlation. Plot *a* shows a perfect *positive correlation*; plot *b* shows a perfect *negative correlation*. Plot *c* shows a moderate positive correlation, but in plot *d* there is no correlation at all.

associated with high or low scores on another variable. It also provides an estimate of how well we would be able to predict from a person's score on one characteristic how high he or she will score on another characteristic. If we know, for example, that a test of mechanical ability is highly correlated with success in engineering courses, we could predict that success on the test would also mean success as an engineering major.

Correlation coefficients can run from $+1.0$ to -1.0. The highest possible value ($+1.0$) indicates a perfect positive correlation—high scores on one variable are always and systematically related to high scores on a second variable. The lowest possible value (-1.0) means a perfect negative correlation—high scores on one variable are always and regularly related to low scores on the second variable. In life, most things are far from perfect, of course, so most correlation coefficients fall somewhere between $+1.0$ and -1.0. A correlation smaller than $\pm.20$ is considered insignificant, from $\pm.20$ to $\pm.40$ is low, from $\pm.40$ to $\pm.60$ is moderate, from $\pm.60$ to $\pm.80$ is high, and from $\pm.80$ to ±1.0 is very high. A correlation of zero indicates that there is no correlation between two sets of scores—no regular relation between them at all.

Correlation tells us nothing about causality. If we found a high positive correlation between participation in elections and income levels, for example, we still could not say that being wealthy made people vote or that voting made people wealthy. We would still not know which came first, or if some third variable explained both income levels and voting behavior. Correlation only tells us that we have found some association between scores on two specified characteristics.

■ Using Statistics to Make Predictions

Behind the use of statistics is the hope that we can generalize from our results and use them to predict behavior. We hope, for example, that we can use the record of how well a group of rats run through a maze today to predict how another group of rats will do tomorrow, that we can use a person's scores on a sales aptitude test to predict how well he or she will sell life insurance, that we can measure the attitudes of a relatively small group of people about pollution control to indicate what the attitudes of the whole country are. But first we have to determine if our measurements are representative and if we can have confidence in them.

Sampling

It is often impossible, or at least impractical, to measure every single occurrence of a characteristic. No one could expect to measure the memory of every human being, or test all the rats or pigeons in the world in Skinner boxes, or record the maternal behavior of all female monkeys.

In a large population, we usually study a **sample** of cases of some reasonable, practical size and then generalize our results to the population as a whole. One way to guarantee that the results of our measurements are accurate for the whole population is to make sure that the sample is truly a random one.

Suppose, for example, that each household in a neighborhood is sold one chance on door prizes at a local raffle. After all the stubs are put into a big drum and churned around, a blindfolded person is asked to reach into the drum and pull out the winning numbers. The prize-winners would then constitute a **random sample** from that neighborhood because, in theory, every single household is likely to win a prize—chance determines which households are selected.

A **biased sample** does not truly represent the population in question. If we want to find out if a town's garbage is being collected adequately, we could not just stand outside the best department store in town at 3:00 in the afternoon and ask everyone who happened by how many times his or her garbage had been collected that week and at what time. The people who shop at that department store in the middle of the afternoon on a workday are unlikely to represent the town's population. We would have to figure out how to make sure that all the town's neighborhoods will be presented proportionally in our sample.

Generalizations based on biased samples can lead to erroneous conclusions. If the advertising manager of a bank wanted to test a few potential campaigns designed to persuade all middle-aged people with incomes over $100,000 to set up trust funds for their children, she would be unwise to base her decisions on interviews with migrant workers. The classic sampling story involves a national magazine that predicted the election

"Young man, I am no random sample."
© Punch/Rothco

of a certain candidate, who then lost the election. The magazine had based its prediction on a telephone survey. The editors forgot, however, that many voters did not have telephones at that time, and it turned out that many people without phones voted for the other candidate.

Probability

Errors based on inadequate sampling procedures are somebody's fault. Other kinds of errors occur randomly. In the simplest kind of experiment, a psychologist will gather a representative sample, split it randomly into two groups, and then apply some experimental manipulation to one of the groups. Afterward, he or she will measure both groups and determine if the experimental group's score is now different from the score of the control group. But even if there is a large difference between the scores of the two groups, the psychologist may still be wrong to attribute the difference to the manipulation. Random effects might influence the results and introduce error.

Statistics give the psychologist many ways to determine precisely if the difference between the two groups is really significant, if something other than chance produced the results, and if the same results would be obtained with different subjects. These probabilities are expressed as measures of **significance.** If the psychologist computes the significance level for the results as .05, he or she knows that there are 19 chances out of 20 that the results are not due to chance. But there is still 1 chance in 20—or a .05 likelihood—that the results are due to chance. A .01 significance level would mean that there is only 1 chance in 100 that the results are due to chance.

Significance Probability that results obtained were due to chance.

Answers to Review Questions

CHAPTER 1

1. scientific; 2. Galton; 3. b—Wundt and Titchener; 4. _E_ structuralism, _A_ functionalism, _D_ behaviorism, _H_ psychoanalysis, _C_ existential psychology, _F_ humanistic psychology, _B_ Gestalt psychology, _G_ cognitive psychology; 5. reinforcement; 6. behavior _and_ mental processes; 7. describe, explain, predict, _and_ control; 8. naturalistic observation; 9. laboratory; 10. independent—dependent; 11. c—experimenter bias; 12. correlational; 13. basic—applied; 14. d—failure to follow federal regulations can result in penalties; 15. b—results can add to our understanding of human behavior.

CHAPTER 2

1. _D_ neuron, _A_ nerve, _C_ axon, _B_ dendrite; 2. positive—negative; 3. _B_ relative refractory; 4. F; 5. neurotransmitters; 6. peripheral; 7. d—parathyroid; 8. cerebral cortex; 9. _B_ sensory projection areas, _C_ association areas, _A_ motor projection areas; 10. B—reticular formation; 11. F; 12. c—corpus callosum; 13. _C_ pancreas, _D_ gonads, _B_ thyroid, _A_ anterior pituitary; 14. hormones; 15. c—the adrenal cortex and the adrenal medulla; 16. _B_ strain studies, _C_ family studies, _A_ selection studies.

CHAPTER 3

1. B—difference; 2. _D_ cornea, _H_ pupil, _A_ iris, _F_ lens, _B_ fovea, _E_ retina, _G_ rod, _C_ cone; 3. A—dark adaptation; 4. b—blind spot; 5. hue, saturation, _and_ brightness; 6. B-subtractive; 7. _2_ oval window, _1_ anvil, _4_ cochlea, _5_ auditory nerve, _3_ round window; 8. _B_ frequency theory, _A_ volley principle, _C_ place theory; 9. vestibular; 10. taste buds—sweet, sour, salty, _and_ bitter; 11. perception; 12. figure—ground; 13. _D_ similarity, _C_ continuity, _B_ common fate, _E_ proximity, _A_ closure; 14. _B_ retinal disparity, _M_ texture gradient, _M_ shadowing, _B_ convergence, _M_ motion parallax, _M_ accommodation, _B_ stereoscopic vision, _M_ linear perspective, _M_ superposition; 15. A—monaural; 16. apparent.

CHAPTER 4

1. altered states of; 2. attention; 3. sexual and aggressive; 4. F; 5. paradoxical; 6. REM rebound; 7. _C_ insomnia, _B_ apnea, _A_ narcolepsy; 8. hallucinations; 9. sympathetic nervous; 10. suggestibility; 11. depressant—stimulant; 12. barbiturates; 13. c—crack; 14. _D_ alcohol, _A_ amphetamines, _F_ barbiturates, _B_ opiates, _C_ cocaine, _E_ hallucinogens.

CHAPTER 5

1. conditioning; 2. before; 3. a—CS and CR; 4. spontaneous recovery; 5. stimulus generalization; 6. operant (or instrumental) conditioning; 7. shaping; 8. a—negative reinforcement; 9. _1_ food, _2_ diploma, _2_ money, _1_ sex; 10. _FI_ , _FR_ , _VR_ , _VI_ ; 11. cognitive map; 12. a—insight; 13. c—blocking; 14. c—both a and b.

CHAPTER 6

1. sensory registers; 2. attention; 3. "cocktail party"; 4. short-term; 5. decay—interference; 6. elaborative; 7. rote; 8. semantic—episodic; 9. retrieval cues; 10. proactive; 11. eidetic; 12. c—using carefully developed memory techniques; 13. survey, question, read, recite, review; 14. T.

CHAPTER 7

1. cognition; 2. images _and_ concepts; 3. a—concepts; 4. T; 5. T; 6. language; 7. phonemes—morphemes—sentences; 8. linguistic relativity; 9. transformations; 10. _C_ algorithm, _A_ heuristics, _B_ hill climbing, _E_ means-end analysis, _D_ working backward; 11. d—hill climbing; 12. compensatory; 13. set; 14. functional fixedness; 15. F; 16. noncompensatory; 17. b—the stakes are high.

CHAPTER 8

1. _D_ Cattell, _C_ Spearman, _A_ Sternberg, _B_ Thurstone, _E_ Guilford; 2. componential—experiential—contextual; 3. IQ—100—Binet-Simon Scale; 4. T; 5. Wechsler Adult Intelligence Scale—Revised (WAIS—R); 6. group tests, c—Wechsler Adult Intelligence Scale; 7. performance—culture-fair; 8. d—a and b; 9. reliable; 10. a—correlation coefficient; 11. validity; 12. school—career; 13. c—racial differences in IQ are largely due to genetic factors; 14. F; 15. a—creativity.

CHAPTER 9

1. cross-sectional; 2. prenatal; 3. F; 4. _C_ rooting reflex, _A_ grasping reflex, _B_ sucking reflex; 5. maturation; 6. developmental norms; 7. _B_ perceptual ability, _D_ depth perception, _A_ visual acuity, _C_ object permanence; 8. visual cliff; 9. language; 10. _D_ sensory-motor stage, _A_ preoperational thought; _B_ concrete operations, _C_ formal operations; 11. schemes; 12. attachment; 13. social.

CHAPTER 10

1. puberty; 2. menarche; 3. _A_ moratorium, _D_ identity achievement, _B_ identity diffusion, _C_ foreclosure; 4. d—10; 5. friendship groups; 6. formal operations; 7. c—5,000; 8. climacteric; 9. mid-life transition; 10. F; 11. social; 12. proper exercise; 13. Alzheimer's disease; 14. F.

CHAPTER 11

1. motives _and_ emotions; 2. c—stimulus; 3. homeostasis; 4. F; 5. hunger—satiety; 6. d—fluids; 7. testosterone; 8. stimulus; 9. _U_ sex, _U_ curiosity, _L_ affiliation, _U_ activity, _L_ power, _L_ aggression, _U_ manipulation, _L_ achievement, _U_ contact; 10. aggression; 11. achievement; 12. affiliation; 13. T; 14. Yerkes-Dodson; 15. intensity; 16. _B_ Cannon-Bard, _C_ cognitive theory, _A_ James-Lange; 17. B—expressive behavior; 18. facial expressions _and_ body language.

CHAPTER 12

1. time _and_ situations; 2. _E_ unconscious, _C_ id, _F_ supergo, _B_ ego, _D_ ego ideal, _A_ libido; 3. ego—id; 4. A—primary; 5. _C_ persona, _D_ animus, _B_ collective unconscious, _A_ archetype; 6. _C_ style of life, _A_ inferiority complex, _B_ compensation, _D_ fictional finalism; 7. anxiety; 8. _C_ industry versus inferiority, _A_ trust versus mistrust, _G_ generativity versus stagnation, _F_ intimacy versus isolation, _E_ identity versus role confusion, _B_ autonomy versus shame and doubt, _C_ initiative versus guilt, _H_ integrity versus despair; 9. self-actualizing; 10. A—situationists; 11. expectancies; 12. learning; 13. objective; 14. projective.

CHAPTER 13

1. adjustment; 2. stress; 3. T; 4. pressure; 5. frustration; 6. conflict; 7. _C_ approach/approach; _A_ avoidance/avoidance, _B_ approach/avoidance, _D_ double approach/avoidance; 8. anxiety; 9. direct _and_ defensive; 10. direct; 11. defensive; 12. _F_ denial, _A_ repression, _G_ projection, _I_ identification, _C_ regression, _B_ intellectualization, _D_ reaction formation, _E_ displacement, _H_ sublimation; 13. alarm—resistance; 14. F.

CHAPTER 14

1. F; 2. _D_ cognitive, _A_ psychoanalytical, _B_ biological, _C_ behavioral; 3. b—physicians; 4. anxiety; 5. A—panic attacks; 6. A—somatization disorder; 7. T; 8. B—dissociative; 9. A—affective; 10. T; 11. bipolar; 12. _C_ sexual dysfunction, _D_ paraphilias, _B_ fetishism, _F_ pedophilia, _A_ exhibitionism, _E_ sadomasochism; 13. _C_ schizoid personality disorder, _A_ paranoid personality disorder, _D_ narcissistic personality disorder, _B_ antisocial personality disorder; 14. schizophrenic.

CHAPTER 15

1. d—insight; 2. _B_ psychoanalysis, _C_ client-centered therapy, _D_ cognitive behavior therapy, _A_ rational-emotive therapy; 3. unconditional positive; 4. insight—behavior; 5. A—desensitization; 6. aversive conditioning; 7. _C_ Gestalt, _B_ large-group awareness training, _A_ est, _D_ interpersonal therapy; 8. F; 9. F; 10. d—antipsychotics; 11. institutionalization; 12. T; 13. deinstitutionalization; 14. prevention.

CHAPTER 16

1. social; 2. schemas—stereotype; 3. primacy; 4. c—attribution theory; 5. c—complementary attitudes and interests; 6. attitude; 7. F; 8. b—attitudes shared with other people; 9. cognitive dissonance; 10. a—attitudes; 11. _D_ social influence, _C_ compliance, _B_ obedience, _A_ conformity; 12. risky shift; 13. polarization; 14. task—interaction; 15. T; 16. environmental; 17. stress; 18. F.

Glossary

Absolute refractory period A period after firing when the neuron will not fire again no matter how strong the incoming messages may be.

Absolute threshold The least amount of energy that can be detected as a stimulation 50 percent of the time.

Acetylcholine (ACh) A neurotransmitter that plays an excitatory role where neurons meet skeletal muscles.

Achievement motive The need to excel, to overcome obstacles; a social motive.

ACTH Hormone released by the anterior pituitary that stimulates hormone production of the adrenal cortex.

Actualizing tendency According to Rogers, the drive of every organism to fulfill its biological potential and become what it is inherently capable of becoming.

Adaptation Adjustment of the senses to stimulation.

Additive color mixing The process of mixing lights of different wavelengths to create new hues.

Adjustment Any effort to cope with stress.

Adoption studies Research carried out on children adopted at birth by parents not related to them with the object of determining environmental effects on human behavior.

Adrenal cortex Outer covering of the two adrenal glands that releases hormones important for dealing with stress.

Adrenal glands Two endocrine glands located just above the kidneys.

Adrenal medulla Inner core of the adrenal glands that also releases hormones to deal with stress.

Aerial perspective Monocular cue to distance and depth based on the fact that more distance objects are likely to appear hazy and blurred.

Affective disorders Conditions in which there is a disturbance of affect or emotional state.

Affiliation motive The need to be with others.

Afterimage Sense experience that occurs after a visual stimulus has been removed.

Aggression Behavior aimed at doing harm to others; also the motive to behave aggressively.

Aggressive type According to Horney, the individual who customarily relates to others aggressively.

Agoraphobia Excessive fear of being alone and, in severe cases, of leaving home and being in open spaces.

Alcohol Depressant that is the intoxicating ingredient in whiskey, beer, wine, and other fermented or distilled liquors.

Algorithm A step-by-step method of problem-solving that guarantees a correct solution.

Altered state of consciousness (ASC) State of awareness that differs noticeably from states that we experience when awake and alert.

Altruistic behavior Helping behavior that is not linked to personal gain.

Amnesia Loss of memory for past events.

Amniocentesis Technique that involves collecting cells cast off by the fetus into the fluid of the womb and testing them for genetic abnormalities.

Amphetamines Stimulant drugs that initially produce "rushes" of euphoria often followed by sudden "crashes" and, sometimes, severe depression.

Amplitude The magnitude of a wave; in sound, the primary determinant of loudness.

Anal stage Second stage in Freud's theory of personality development, when a child's erotic feelings center on the anus and on elimination.

Anima In Jung's theory, the feminine side of masculine personality.

Animus The masculine side of feminine personality.

Anterior pituitary Part of the pituitary known as the "master gland" because it produces numerous hormones that trigger the action of other glands; one of these hormones regulates body growth.

Antisocial personality disorder Disorder that involves a pattern of violent, criminal, or unethical and exploitative behavior and an inability to feel affection for others.

Anxiety A feeling like fear without an identifiable source.

Anxiety disorders Disorders in which anxiety is a characteristic feature or the avoidance of anxiety seems to motivate abnormal behavior.

Apnea Sleep disorder characterized by breathing difficulty during the night and feelings of exhaustion during the day.

Applied psychology Direct study of social problems, often with the intent to change human behavior.

Approach/approach conflict Result of simultaneous attraction to two appealing possibilities.

Approach/avoidance conflict Result of being simultaneously attracted to and repelled by the same thing.

Archetypes In Jung's theory of personality, thought forms common to all human beings, carried in the collective unconscious.

Artificial intelligence Use of computers to simulate human cognitive processes.

Association areas Areas in the cerebral cortex where incoming messages from the separate senses are combined into meaningful impressions and outgoing messages from the motor areas are integrated.

Attachment Social bond that develops between an infant and its primary caregiver.

Attention Selection of some incoming information for further processing.

Attitude A fairly stable organization of beliefs, feelings, and behavior tendencies directed toward some object such as a person or group.

Attribution theory Theory that addresses the question of how people make judgments about the causes of behavior.

Auditory nerve The bundle of neurons that carries signals from the ear to the brain.

Autokinetic illusion Perception that a stationary object is actually moving.

Autonomic nervous system The part of the peripheral nervous system that carries messages between the central nervous system and the internal organs.

Autonomy A sense of independence and trust in one's own abilities and powers.

Availability A heuristic by which a judgment or decision is based on information that is most easily retrieved from memory.

Aversive conditioning Behavior therapy techniques that aim at eliminating undesirable behavior patterns by teaching the person to associate them with pain and discomfort.

Avoidance/avoidance conflict Result of facing a choice between two undesirable possibilities.

Avoidance training Learning a desirable behavior in order to prevent an unpleasant condition such as punishment from occurring.

Axon Single long fiber extending from the cell body that carries outgoing messages.

Axon terminal or **synaptic knob** Knob that forms the end of an axon terminal branch.

Barbiturates Potentially deadly depressants, first used for their sedative and anticonvulsant effects, now used only to treat such conditions as epilepsy and arthritis.

Basic research Research for its own sake, usually done to test a theory or to follow up on other research rather than to solve practical problems.

Basilar membrane Vibrating membrane in the cochlea of the inner ear that contains sense receptors for sound.

Behavior genetics Study of the relationship between heredity and behavior.

Behavior therapies Therapeutic approaches aimed at teaching new behavior and based primarily on applying the principles of conditioning.

Behavioral contracting A form of operant conditioning therapy in which client and therapist set reinforcements for reaching behavioral goals.

Behavioral model of abnormal behavior View that abnormal behavior is the result of faulty learning.

Behaviorism School of psychology that studies only observable and measurable behavior.

Beta endorphin One of the endorphins, a natural painkiller released by the body.

Biased sample Sample that does not truly represent a whole population.

Binaural cue Cue to sound location that involves both ears working together.

Binet-Simon Scale The first test of intelligence, developed for testing children.

Binocular cues Visual cues requiring the use of both eyes.

Binocular depth inversion Tendency to create three-dimensional perceptual experiences that agree with past experience, despite sensory information to the contrary.

Biographical approach Method of research that tries to reconstruct an individual's past.

Biological model of abnormal behavior View that abnormal behavior has a biochemical or physiological basis.

Biological treatment Treatment of behavior disorders with such methods as electroconvulsive therapy, insulin shock treatment, psychosurgery, and drug therapy.

Bipolar disorder Affective disorder in which a person experiences periods of both depression and mania.

Bipolar neurons Neurons that have only one axon and one dendrite; in the eye these neurons connect the receptors on the retina to the ganglion cells.

Blind spot Place on the retina where the axons of all the ganglion cells leave the eye and where there are no receptors.

Blocking Prior conditioning prevents conditioning to a second stimulus even when the two stimuli are presented simultaneously.

Brain stem The top end of the spinal column that widens out to form the lower part of the brain.

Brainstorming A problem-solving strategy in which an individual or a group collects numerous ideas and evaluates them only after all ideas have been collected.

Brightness The nearness of a color to white as opposed to black.

Brightness constancy Perception of brightness as the same, even though the amount of light reaching the retina changes.

Cannon-Bard theory of emotion States that the experience of emotion occurs simultaneously with biological changes.

Catatonic schizophrenia Type of schizophrenia in which disturbed motor behavior is prominent.

Cell body Part of the neuron that contains the nucleus and is the site where metabolism and respiration take place.

Central nervous system Division of the nervous system that consists of the brain and the spinal cord.

Central tendency Tendency of scores to congregate around some middle value.

Cerebellum Two hemispheres in the hindbrain that control certain reflexes and coordinate the body's movements.

Cerebral cortex The two hemispheres of the forebrain that regulate most complex behavior.

Chromosomes Pairs of threadlike bodies within the cell nucleus that contain the genes.

Chunking Grouping of information into meaningful units for easier handling by short-term memory.

Classical conditioning Type of learning in which an organism learns to transfer a response from one stimulus to another, previously neutral stimulus.

Classical view of adolescence The theory, held by Freud and others, that adolescence is inevitably a period of great conflict, anxiety, and tension.

Client-centered or **person-centered therapy** A nondirective form of therapy developed by Carl Rogers that calls for unconditional positive regard on the part of the therapist; the aim of treatment is to help clients become fully functioning.

Climacteric Major physical change in middle age resulting in the decline in function of the reproductive organs.

Cocaine Drug that, while producing a sense of euphoria by stimulating the sympathetic nervous system, also produces anxiety, depression, and addictive cravings.

Cochlea Part of the inner ear containing fluid that vibrates, which in turn causes the basilar membrane to vibrate.

Cognition The processes of thinking.

Cognitive behavior therapy A type of psychotherapy that emphasizes changing the client's perceptions of his or her life situation as a way of modifying behavior.

Cognitive dissonance Perceived inconsistency between two cognitions.

Cognitive learning Learning that depends on mental processes that are not able to be observed directly.

Cognitive map A learned mental image of a spatial environment that may be called on to solve problems when stimuli in the environment change.

Cognitive model of abnormal behavior View that abnormal behavior is the result of maladaptive ways of thinking.

Cognitive psychology School of psychology devoted to the study of mental processes generally.

Cognitive theory of emotion States that emotional experience depends on one's perception or judgment of the situation one is in.

Cohort Total population of individuals born during the same period of historical time.

Collective unconscious In Jung's theory of personality, the part of the unconscious that is inherited and common to all members of a species.

Color blindness Partial or total inability to perceive colors.

Color constancy Inclination to perceive familiar objects as retaining their color despite changes in sensory information.

Compensation According to Adler, the person's effort to effect or overcome imagined or real personal weaknesses.

Compensatory model A rational decision-making model in which choices are systematically evaluated on various criteria.

Complementary colors Two hues, far apart on the spectrum, that when added together in equal intensities produce a neutral gray rather than a third hue.

Compliance A change of behavior in response to an explicit request from another person or group.

Compliant type In Horney's theory, a person whose relations to others are marked by deference and submission.

Compromise Deciding on a more realistic solution or goal when an ideal solution or goal is not practical.

Concept A mental category for classifying objects, people, or experiences.

Conditional positive regard The acceptance and love for another person that depends on that person's behavior.

Conditioned food aversion Animals' conditioned avoidance of poisonous food even after a lengthy interval and only one pairing of conditioned and unconditioned stimuli.

Conditioned response (CR) Response an organism learns to produce when a conditioned stimulus is presented.

Conditioned stimulus (CS) Originally neutral stimulus that is paired with an unconditioned stimulus and eventually produces the desired response in an organism when presented alone.

Conditioning The acquiring of fairly specific patterns of behavior in the presence of well-defined stimuli.

Cones Receptor cells in the retina responsible for color vision.

Conflict Simultaneous existence of incompatible demands, opportunities, needs, or goals.

Conformity Voluntarily yielding to social norms, even at the expense of one's own preferences.

Confrontation Acknowledging a stressful situation directly and attempting to find a solution or attain a goal.

Consciousness Our awareness of such cognitive processes as sleeping, dreaming, concentrating, and making decisions, among many others.

Consensus The extent to which everyone in a given situation is behaving in the same way.

Consistency The extent to which a particular event produces the same behavior each time it is present.

Constitutional theory A personality theory that proposes a relationship between a person's body type and his or her behavior.

Content validity Refers to a test's having an adequate sample of the skills or knowledge it is supposed to measure.

Contents According to Guilford, the terms we use in thinking, such as words or symbols.

Contingency theory Proposes that for learning to take place, the stimulus must provide the learner with information about the likelihood of other events occurring.

Control group In a controlled experiment, the group not subjected to a change in the independent variable; used for comparison with the experimental group.

Convergence Binocular distance cue based on sensations from the muscles that turn the eyes toward or away from each other.

Convergent thinking Thinking that is directed toward one correct solution to a problem.

Conversion disorder Disorder in which a dramatic specific disability has no physical cause and instead seems related to psychological problems.

Convolutions Folds in the cerebral cortex that allow its mass to fit inside the skull.

Cornea The transparent protective coating over the front part of the eye.

Corpus callosum Band that connects the two hemispheres of the brain and coordinates their activities.

Correlation Degree of relationship between two or more variables.

Correlation coefficient Statistical measure of the strength of association between two variables.

Correlation coefficients Statistical measures of the degree of association between two variables.

Correlational method Research technique based on the naturally occurring relationship between two or more variables.

Countertransference A therapist's projecting of his or her own emotions onto the client.

Creativity The ability to produce novel and unique ideas or objects.

Criterion-related validity Validity of a test as measured by a comparison of the test score and independent measures of that which the test is designed to measure.

Cross-sectional study Study of the different comparisons between people of different ages at just one point in time.

Crowding In environmental psychology, the subjective experience of being crowded, regardless of actual population density.

Culture-fair tests Intelligence tests designed to eliminate cultural bias by minimizing skills and values that vary from one culture to another.

Dark adaptation Increased sensitivity of rods and cones in darkness.

Daydreaming Alteration in consciousness that occurs seemingly without effort and, typically, when we would prefer to escape momentarily the demands of the real world.

Death instincts In Freud's theory of personality, the group of instincts that lead toward aggression, destruction, and death.

Decay theory Holds that the passage of time itself causes forgetting.

Decibel Unit of measurement for the loudness of sounds.

Deep structure The underlying meaning conveyed by verbal information.

Defense mechanisms Self-deceptive techniques for reducing stress, including denial, repression, projection, identification, intellectualization, reaction formation, displacement, and sublimation.

Defensive attribution Tendency to attribute success to our own efforts or qualities and failure to external factors.

Deindividuation Loss of personal sense of responsibility in a group.

Deinstitutionalization The practice of providing patients with continued mental health care in the local community rather than keeping them in institutions.

Delusions False beliefs about reality with no basis in fact.

Dendrites Short fibers that branch out from the cell body and pick up incoming messages.

Denial Refusing to acknowledge a painful or threatening reality.

Density In environmental psychology, the number of people per unit of area.

Deoxyribonucleic acid (DNA) Complex molecule that is the main ingredient of chromosomes and genes and forms the code for all genetic information.

Dependence Strong physical need for a substance, such as some drug.

Dependent variable In an experiment, the variable that is measured to see how it is changed by manipulations in the independent variable.

Depersonalization disorder Condition in which a person feels unreal and unconnected to his or her body.

Depressants Chemicals that slow down behavior or cognitive processes.

Depression Disorder in which a person is overwhelmed by feelings of sadness, apathy, guilt, and self-reproach.

Desensitization Behavior therapy technique designed to gradually reduce anxiety about a particular object or situation.

Desensitization therapy Conditioning technique designed to gradually reduce anxiety about a particular object or situation.

Detached type According to Horney, a person who relates to others in a basically detached manner.

Developmental norms Ages when the average individual reaches various milestones of development.

Developmental psychology Study of the psychological and physical changes that take place throughout life.

Diathesis-stress model of abnormal behavior View that people biologically predisposed to a disorder will exhibit that disorder when particularly affected by stress.

Dichromats People who are blind to either red-green or yellow-blue.

Difference threshold or **just noticeable difference (jnd)** The smallest change in stimulation that can be detected 50 percent of the time.

Disorganized schizophrenia Type of schizophrenia in which bizarre and childlike behaviors are common.

Displacement Conversion of a vague anxiety resulting from threatening unconscious impulses into a fear of something specific.

Displacement Shifting repressed motives and emotions from an original object to a substitute object.

Dissociative disorders Disorders in which some aspect of the personality seems fragmented from the rest, as in amnesia or multiple personality.

Distinctiveness The extent to which a behavior is present only when a particular stimulus is also present.

Divergent thinking Thinking that meets the criteria of originality, inventiveness, and flexibility.

Dominant gene Member of a gene pair that controls the appearance of a certain trait.

Dopamine A prevalent inhibitory neurotransmitter.

Double-blind procedure Experimental design useful in studies on the effects of drugs in which neither subject nor researcher knows, at the time of administration, which subjects are receiving an active drug or an inactive substitute.

Double standard Expectation that females, but not males, will postpone the expression of sexual needs until they are married.

Dreams Vivid images or experiences that occur primarily during REM periods of sleep.

Drive reduction theory The theory that motivated behavior moves the organism toward a reduction of arousal.

Ego According to Freud, the part of the personality that mediates between environmental demands (reality), conscience (superego), and instinctual needs (id); now often used as a synonym for "self."

Ego ideal That part of the superego that consists of standards of what one would like to be.

Eidetic imagery Ability to reproduce unusually sharp and detailed images of something that has been seen.

Elaborative rehearsal The linking of new information in short-term memory to familiar material stored in long-term memory.

Electroconvulsive therapy (ECT) A physical therapy in which a mild electrical current is passed through the brain for a short period, often producing convulsions and temporary coma; used to alleviate sudden and severe depression.

Elevation Monocular cue to distance and depth based on the fact that the higher on the horizontal plane an object is, the farther away it appears.

Emotion A feeling such as fear, joy, or surprise, that energizes and directs behavior.

Endocrine glands Glands of the endocrine system that release hormones into the bloodstream.

Endocrine system Internal network of glands that release hormones directly into the bloodstream to regulate body functions.

Enkephalins and **endorphins** Chemical substances involved with the reduction of pain.

Environmental psychology The study of how the environment influences individuals and their relationships with others.

Epinephrine Adrenal hormone that is released mainly in response to fear and causes the heart to beat faster.

Episodic memory Portion of long-term memory that stores more specific information that has personal meaning.

est A form of large-group awareness training that emphasizes the direct experience of reality.

Exhibitionism The compulsion to expose one's genitals in public in order to achieve sexual arousal.

Existential psychology School of psychology that sees the meaninglessness and alienation of modern life as leading to apathy and psychological problems.

Expectancies In Mischel's view, what a person anticipates in a situation or as a result of behaving in certain ways.

Experimental group In a controlled experiment, the group subjected to a change in the independent variable.

Experimenter bias Expectations by the experimenter that might influence the results of an experiment or their interpretation.

Extinction Decrease in the strength or frequency of a learned response due to withholding of reinforcement (operant conditioning) or to failure to continue pairing the US and CS (classical conditioning).

Extrovert According to Jung, a person who usually focuses on social life and the external world instead of his or her internal experience.

Factor analysis A statistical technique used by Cattell to identify a set of basic personality traits.

Family studies Studies of heritability in humans based on the assumption that if genes influence a certain trait, close relatives should be more similar on that trait than distant relatives.

Family therapy A therapeutic approach that sees the family as a unit and as a part of the problem in an individual's treatment.

Fantasy period Ginsberg's first stage of vocational choice, during which pre-adolescents play out various occupational roles.

Fetishism The reliance on nonhuman objects as the preferred or exclusive method of achieving sexual excitement.

Fetus An unborn infant at least eight weeks old.

Fictional finalism According to Adler, motivating goals that people establish to guide their behavior even though such goals might not be actually attainable.

Figure Object perceived to stand apart from the background.

Fixation According to Freud, a partial or complete halt at some point in a person's psychosexual development.

Fixed-interval schedule Reinforcement schedule that calls for reinforcement of a correct response after a fixed length of time.

Fixed-ratio schedule Reinforcement of the correct response after a fixed number of correct responses.

Forebrain Top part of the brain, including the thalamus, hypothalamus, and cerebral cortex.

Foreclosure According to Marcia, accepting an identity provided by others rather than one chosen by oneself.

Formal operations Fourth and final stage in Piaget's theory of cognitive development, characterized by the transition from concrete to abstract thinking.

Fovea Area of the retina that is the center of the visual field.

Fraternal twins Twins developed from two separate fertilized ova, and therefore different in genetic makeup.

Free association In psychoanalysis, the uninhibited disclosure of thoughts and fantasies as they occur to the client.

Free nerve endings Finely branched nerve endings in the skin that serve as receptors for pain, pressure, and temperature.

Frequency The number of cycles per second in a wave; in sound, the primary determinant of pitch.

Frequency distribution A count of the number of scores that fall within each of a series of intervals.

Frequency histogram Type of bar graph that shows frequency distributions.

Frequency polygon Type of line graph that shows frequency distributions.

Frequency theory of hearing Theory that pitch is determined by the frequency with which hair cells in the cochlea fire.

Frigidity In women, the inability to become sexually aroused or reach orgasm.

Frontal lobes Largest of the association areas; the site of such uniquely human activities as self-awareness, initiative, and planning.

Frustration Source of stress that occurs when a person is prevented from reaching a goal.

Fully functioning person According to Rogers, individuals whose self-concepts closely resemble their inborn capacities or potentials.

Functional fixedness The tendency to perceive only a limited number of uses for an object, which interferes with the process of problem-solving.

Functionalist theory Theory of mental life and behavior that is concerned with how an organism uses its perceptual abilities to function in its environment.

Fundamental attribution error The tendency of people to overemphasize personal causes for other people's behavior and to underemphasize those causes for their own behavior.

Ganglion cells Neurons that connect the bipolar neurons in the eyes to the brain.

Gate control theory of pain Theory that the pain-signaling system consists of a pattern of nerve impulses transmitted to the brain through a "neurological gate" in the spinal cord.

Genes Elements found on the chromosomes that control the transmission of traits.

Genetics Study of how traits are passed from one generation to the next.

Genital stage In Freud's theory of personality development, the final stage of normal adult sexual development.

Gestalt psychology School of psychology that studies how people perceive and experience objects as whole patterns.

Gestalt therapy Form of therapy, either individual or group, that emphasizes the wholeness of the personality and attempts to reawaken people to their emotions and sensations in the here-and-now.

Giftedness Refers to superior IQ combined with demonstrated or potential ability in such areas as academic aptitude, or creativity, or leadership.

Glucose A simple sugar that is the main source of body energy.

Gonads The reproductive glandstestes in males and ovaries in females.

Graded potential A shift in the electrical charge in a tiny area of the neuron caused by an incoming message too weak to stimulate the neuron to fire.

Grammar The language rules that determine the meaning and form of words and sentences.

Grasping reflex A reflex in newborns that causes them to clasp their fingers around anything that is put in their hands.

Ground Background against which the figure appears.

Group tests Written intelligence tests administered by one examiner to many people at one time.

Group therapy Form of psychotherapy in which clients meet regularly in a group.

Growth spurt Rapid increase in height and weight that begins at about age 8 or 9 in girls and 10 or 11 in boys.

Hallucinations Sensory experiences in the absence of external stimulation.

Hallucinogens Any of a number of drugs, such as LSD and mescaline, that distort visual and auditory perception.

Hammer, anvil, stirrup The three small bones in the middle ear that relay vibrations of the eardrum to the inner ear.

Hawthorne effect Principle that subjects will alter their behavior because of researchers' attention and not necessarily because of any specific experimentation.

Hertz (Hz) Cycles per second; unit of measurement for the frequency of waves.

Heuristics Rules of thumb that help in simplifying and solving problems, though they do not guarantee a correct solution.

Higher-order conditioning Conditioning based on previous learning; the conditioned stimulus is used as an unconditioned stimulus in further training.

Hill-climbing A heuristic problem-solving strategy in which each step moves you progressively closer to the final goal.

Hindbrain Brain area containing the medulla, pons, and cerebellum.

Hippocampus Part of the limbic system that is vital to memory formation.

Homeostasis State of balance and stability in which the organism functions effectively.

Hormones Chemical substances released by the endocrine glands that help regulate bodily activities.

Hue The aspect of color that corresponds to names such as red, green, blue.

Humanistic personality theory Any personality theory that asserts the fundamental goodness of people and their striving toward higher levels of functioning.

Humanistic psychology School of psychology that emphasizes nonverbal experience and altered states of consciousness as a means of realizing one's full human potential.

Hypnosis Trancelike state in which the subject responds readily to suggestions.

Hypochondriasis A condition in which a person interprets small and insignificant symptoms as signs of serious illness in the absence of any organic symptoms of such illness.

Hypothalamus Forebrain region that governs motivation and emotional responses.

Hypothesis Tentative assumption that is tested empirically.

Id In Freud's theory of personality, the collection of unconscious urges and desires that continually seek expression.

Identical twins Twins developed from a single fertilized ovum, and therefore identical in genetic makeup.

Identification Taking on the characteristics of someone else to avoid feeling incompetent.

Identity achievers According to Marcia, adolescents who achieve identity by making personal decisions about goals.

Identity Erikson's term for the stable sense of self necessary to make the transition from dependence on others to dependence on oneself.

Identity diffusion According to Marcia, failure to develop a clear sense of one's own identity.

Image A mental recollection of a sensory experience.

Impotence In men, the inability to achieve or keep an erection.

Imprinting Rapid formation by a young animal of a strong bond to the first moving object with which it comes into contact, generally its mother.

Incentive An external stimulus that prompts goal-directed behavior.

Independent variable In an experiment, the variable that is manipulated to test its effects on the other, dependent variables.

Industrial/organizational (I/O) psychology Area of psychology concerned with behavior in such organizational environments as the workplace.

Inferiority complex In Adler's theory, the condition by which an individual is emotionally paralyzed by feelings of inferiority.

Information retrieval A problem-solving strategy that requires only the recovery of information from long-term memory.

Inhibited orgasm Psychosexual dysfunction characterized by an inability to achieve orgasm even when aroused and adequately stimulated.

Inhibited sexual desire Psychosexual dysfunction involving lack of sexual interest.

Inhibited sexual excitement Psychosexual dysfunction characterized by an inability to achieve or sustain arousal during sexual activity.

Insight An awareness of how and why we feel and act as we do.

Insight Learning that occurs rapidly as a result of understanding all the ingredients of a problem.

Insight therapy Type of psychotherapy aimed at having the client achieve greater self-understanding of his or her motives, expectations, means of coping, and so on.

Insomnia Sleep disorder characterized by difficulty in falling asleep or remaining asleep throughout the night.

Instinct Inborn, goal-directed behavior tendency that fulfills specific biological needs and contributes to an organism's survival.

Insulin and **glucagon** Hormones that work in opposite ways to regulate the level of sugar in the blood.

Intellectualization Thinking abstractly about stressful problems as a way of detaching oneself from them.

Intelligence A general term referring to the ability to learn and to behave adaptively.

Intelligence quotient (IQ) A numerical value given to intelligence that is determined from the scores on an intelligence test; based on a score of 100 for average intelligence.

Intelligence tests Tests designed to measure a person's general mental abilities.

Interference theory Holds that interference from other information causes forgetting.

Intermittent pairing Pairing the conditioned stimulus and the unconditioned stimulus on only a portion of the learning trials.

Interneurons or **association neurons** Neurons that carry messages from one neuron to another and do most of the work of the nervous system.

Interpersonal theory Theory of behavior emphasizing the effects of a person's characteristic relationships with others.

Interstimulus interval Time lapse between the presentation of the conditioned stimulus and the unconditioned stimulus.

Interval scale Scale with equal distances between the points or values, but without a true zero.

Introvert In Jung's theory, a person who usually focuses on his or her own inner thoughts and feelings.

Ions Electrically charged particles found both inside and outside of the neuron.

Iris Colored part of the eye.

Irrational people According to Jung, those people who base their decisions on perception, either through the senses (sensation) or through unconscious processes (intuition).

James-Lange theory of emotion States that physical reactions precede experienced emotions.

Just world hypothesis An attribution error based on the assumption that bad things happen to bad people and good things happen to good people.

Krause bulb Skin receptor believed to be responsive to coldness.

Latency period In Freud's theory of personality, a period after the phallic stage in which the child appears to have no interest in the opposite sex.

Latent learning Learning that is not immediately reflected in behavior change.

Law of effect The theory that behavior which consistently results in a reward will be "stamped in" as learned behavior.

Learned helplessness Apathy and passivity learned in a situation where one's behavior has no effect on reward and punishment.

Learning The process by which experience or practice results in a relatively permanent change of behavior.

Learning set Ability to become increasingly more effective in solving problems as more problems are solved.

Lens Transparent part of the eye that focuses light onto the retina.

Libido According to Freud, the energy generated by the sexual instinct.

Life instincts In Freud's theory of personality, all those instincts involved in the survival of the individual and the species, including hunger, self-preservation, and sex.

Light adaptation Decreased sensitivity of rods and cones in bright light.

Limbic system Ring of structures around the thalamus that plays a role in learning and emotional behavior.

Linear perspective Monocular cue to distance and depth based on the fact that two parallel lines seem to converge at the horizon.

Linguistic relativity hypothesis Whorf's idea that patterns of thinking are determined by the specific language one speaks.

Locus of control According to Rotter, an expectancy about whether reinforcements are under internal or external control.

Long-term memory (LTM) Portion of memory that is more or less permanent and that corresponds to everything we "know."

Longitudinal study Study of a fixed group of people at selected intervals over an extended period of time.

LSD (lysergic acid diethylamide) Hallucinogen or "psychedelic" drug that produces hallucinations and delusions similar to those occurring in a psychotic state.

Mania Disorder in which a person is overly excited and hyperactive.

Marijuana Plant containing a mild hallucinogen and producing a "high" often characterized by feelings of euphoria, a sense of well-being, and swings in mood from gaiety to relaxation.

Marital therapy A form of therapy aimed at helping couples improve communication and interaction.

Maturation Automatic unfolding of development in an organism over time.

Mean Arithmetical average calculated by dividing a sum of values by the total number of cases.

Means-end analysis A heuristic strategy that aims to reduce the discrepancy between the current situation and the desired goal at a number of intermediate points.

Median Point that divides a set of scores in half.

Meditation Any of various methods of concentration, reflection, or focusing of thoughts that reduce the activity of the sympathetic nervous system.

Medulla Part of the hindbrain that controls such functions as breathing, heart rate, and blood pressure.

Meissner corpuscle Skin receptor believed to be sensitive to pressure.

Menarche Onset of menstruation.

Menopause Cessation of menstruation.

Mental retardation Condition of significantly subaverage intelligence combined with deficiencies in adaptive behavior.

Mid-life transition According to Levinson, process whereby adults assess the past and formulate new goals for the future.

Midbrain Region between the hindbrain and the forebrain; it is important for hearing and sight and is one of several places in the brain where pain is registered.

Minnesota Multiphasic Personality Inventory (MMPI) The most widely used objective personality test, originally intended for psychiatric diagnosis.

Mnemonics Techniques that make material easier to remember.

Mnemonist Someone with highly developed memory skills.

Mode Point at which the largest number of scores occurs.

Modeling Type of learning in which a person learns by observing someone else perform a desired behavior.

Monaural cue Cue to sound location that requires just one ear alone.

Monochromats Persons who are totally color blind.

Monocular cues Visual cues that require one eye.

Moratorium According to Marcia, period during which an adolescent delays developing an identity while exploring alternatives and choices.

Morphemes The smallest meaningful unit of speech such as simple words, prefixes, and suffixes.

Motion parallax Monocular distance cue in which objects closer than the point of visual focus seem to move in the direction opposite to the viewer's moving head, and objects beyond the focus point seem to move in the same direction as the viewer's head.

Motive A specific need, desire, or want such as hunger, thirst, or achievement, that energizes and directs goal-oriented behavior.

Motor or efferent neurons Neurons that carry messages from the spinal cord or brain to the muscles and glands.

Motor projection areas Areas of the cerebral cortex where response messages from the brain to the muscles and glands begin.

Multiple personality disorder Condition in which more than one personality seems present in a single person.

Myelin sheath Fatty covering found on some axons.

Narcissistic personality disorder Disorder in which a person has an exaggerated sense of self-importance and needs constant admiration.

Narcolepsy Hereditary sleep disorder characterized by sudden nodding off during the day and sudden loss of muscle tone following moments of emotional excitement.

Naturalistic observation Research method involving the systematic study of animal or human behavior in natural settings rather than in the laboratory.

Negative reinforcer Any event whose reduction or termination increases the likelihood that ongoing behavior will recur.

Negative transference Displacement of hostility felt for a parent or other authority figure to one's therapist.

Neonate A newborn baby.

Nerve Group of axons bundled together.

Nervous system The brain, the spinal cord, and the network of nerve cells that transmit messages throughout the body.

Neural impulse or **action potential** The firing of a nerve cell caused by depolarization of the neuron.

Neuron Individual cell that is the smallest unit of the nervous system.

Neurotic trends In Horney's view, irrational strategies for coping with emotional problems and minimizing anxiety.

Neurotransmitters Chemicals released by the synaptic vesicles that travel across the synaptic space and affect the next neuron.

Nodes Pinched intervals on the myelin sheaths of some axons that help speed the passage of neural impulses.

Nominal scale A set of categories for classifying objects.

Non-REM (or NREM) sleep Non-rapid-eye-movement stages of sleep that alternate with REM stages during the sleep cycle.

Noncompensatory model A decision-making model that does not try to systematically weigh comparisons among alternatives.

Nonspectral color A hue, such as purple, that is not found in the spectrum.

Norepinephrine An adrenal hormone that causes blood pressure to rise; also, an excitatory neurotransmitter that carries nerve impulses across the synaptic gaps.

Normal curve Hypothetical, bell-shaped distribution curve that occurs when a normal distribution is plotted as a frequency polygon.

Obedience A change of behavior in response to a command from another person, typically an authority figure.

Object permanence Realization that objects hidden from view nonetheless still exist.

Objective tests Personality tests that are administered and scored in a standard way, such as the Minnesota Multiphasic Personality Inventory.

Observational or **vicarious learning** Learning by observing other people's behavior.

Obsessive-compulsive disorder A disorder in which a person feels compelled to think disturbing thoughts and perform senseless rituals.

Occipital lobe Part of the cerebral cortex that receives and interprets visual information.

Oedipus complex According to Freud, a child's sexual attachment to the parent of the opposite sex and jealousy toward the parent of the same sex.

Olfactory bulb Either of the two smell centers in the brain.

Olfactory epithelium Nasal membranes containing receptor cells sensitive to odors.

Operant behavior Behavior designed to operate on the environment in a way that will gain something desired or avoid something unpleasant.

Operant or **instrumental conditioning** Type of learning in which the likelihood of a behavior is increased or decreased by the use of reinforcement or punishment.

Operations According to Guilford, the act of thinking.

Opiates Addictive drugs, such as opium and heroin, that dull the senses and induce feelings of euphoria, well-being, and relaxation.

Opponent-process theory Theory of color vision that holds that three sets of color receptors (yellow-blue, red-green, black-white) respond in an either/or fashion to determine the color you experience.

Optic chiasm Point near the base of the brain where some fibers in the optic nerve from each eye cross to the other side of the brain.

Optic nerve The bundle of axons of ganglion cells that carries neural messages from each eye to the brain.

Oral stage First stage in Freud's theory of personality development, in which the infant's erotic feelings center on the mouth, lips, and tongue.

Ordinal scale Scale indicating order or relative position of items according to some criterion.

Organ of Corti Structure on the surface of the basilar membrane that contains the receptor cells for hearing.

Orgasm Peaking of sexual pleasure and release of sexual tension.

Oval window Membrane across the opening between the middle ear and inner ear that conducts vibrations to the cochlea.

Overtones Tones that result from sound waves that are multiples of the basic tone; primary determinant of timbre.

Pacinian corpuscle Skin receptor believed to be sensitive to pressures between internal organs.

Pancreas Organ lying between the stomach and small intestine that secretes insulin and glucagon.

Panic attack A sudden unpredictable feeling of intense fear or terror.

Papillae Small bumps on the tongue that contain taste buds.

Paranoid personality disorder Disorder in which a person is inappropriately suspicious and mistrustful of others.

Paranoid schizophrenia Type of schizophrenia characterized by extreme suspiciousness and complex, bizarre delusions.

Paraphilias Unconventional objects or situations that cause sexual arousal in some people.

Parasympathetic division The branch of the autonomic nervous system that calms the body after stress.

Parathormone Hormone that controls the levels of calcium and phosphate in the blood and tissue fluids.

Parathyroids Four tiny glands embedded in the thyroid that secrete parathormone.

Parietal lobe Part of the cerebral cortex that responds to sensations of touch and bodily position and informs the brain of events worthy of special attention.

Pedophilia Desire to have sexual relations with children as the preferred or exclusive method of achieving sexual excitement.

Peer group Age-mates who provide a supportive network for the adolescent.

Perception Process of creating meaningful patterns from raw sensory information.

Perceptual constancy Tendency to perceive objects as stable and unchanging despite changes in sensory stimulation.

Perceptual illusion Illusion which is due to misleading cues in stimuli and which causes us to create perceptions that are inaccurate or impossible.

Performance standards In Bandura's theory, standards that people develop to rate the adequacy of their own behavior in a variety of situations.

Performance tests Intelligence tests that do not involve language.

Peripheral nervous system Division of the nervous system that connects the central nervous system to the rest of the body.

Person variables According to Mischel, cognitive processes that influence behavior in different situations.

Persona According to Jung, our public self, the mask we put on to represent ourselves to others.

Personal space The psychological space surrounding a person.

Personal unconscious According to Jung, one of the two levels of the unconscious; the personal unconscious contains the individual's repressed thoughts, forgotten experiences, and undeveloped ideas.

Personality A person's unique pattern of thoughts, feelings, and behaviors that persists over time and situations.

Personality disorders Disorders in which inflexible and mal-adaptive ways of thinking and behaving cause distress and conflicts.

Personality traits Enduring dispositions within the individual that cause the person to think, feel, and act in characteristic ways.

Phallic stage Third stage in Freud's theory of personality development, when erotic feelings center on the genitals.

Pheromones Substances secreted by some animals that, when scented, enhance the sexual readiness of the opposite sex.

Phi phenomenon Apparent movement caused by flashing lights in sequence, as on theater marquees.

Phobia Excessive unreasonable fear attached to an apparently harmless stimulus.

Phobic disorder A condition characterized by intense phobias and compulsive avoidance behavior.

Phonemes The basic sounds that make up any language.

Physical illusion Illusion due to distortion of information reaching receptor cells.

Pitch Auditory experience corresponding primarily to frequency of sound vibrations, resulting in a higher or lower tone.

Pituitary gland Gland located on the underside of the brain that produces the largest number of the body's hormones; composed of the posterior and anterior pituitary.

Place theory of hearing Theory that the pitch of a sound is determined by the location of greatest vibration of the basilar membrane.

Placebo Chemically inactive substance used for comparison with active drugs in experiments on the effects of drugs.

Placenta Organ that connects the developing fetus to the mother's body, providing nourishment to it and filtering out some harmful substances.

Pleasure principle According to Freud, the way in which the id seeks immediate gratification of an instinct.

Polarization A shift in attitudes by members of a group toward more extreme positions than the ones held before group discussion.

Polarization Condition of a neuron at rest when most positive ions are on the outside and most negative ions are on the inside of the cell membrane.

Polygenic inheritance Process in which several genes interact to produce a certain trait; responsible for our most important traits.

Pons Connects the cerebral cortex at the top of the brain to the cerebellum.

Positive reinforcer Any event whose presence increases the likelihood that ongoing behavior will recur.

Positive transference Development of warm feelings toward one's therapist.

Posterior pituitary Separately functioning part of the pituitary that is controlled by the nervous system.

Posttraumatic stress disorder A condition in which episodes of anxiety, sleeplessness, and nightmares are the result of some disturbing event in the past.

Power motive The need to win recognition or to influence or control other people or groups; a social motive.

Prenatal development Physical and psychological changes in an organism before birth.

Pressure A feeling that one must speed up, intensify, or change the direction of behavior or live up to a higher standard of performance.

Primacy effect The extent to which early information about someone weighs more heavily than later information in influencing one's impression of that person.

Primary colors A set of three colors, such as red, green, and blue, that when mixed in unequal amounts can produce any visible hue.

Primary drive A physiologically based unlearned motive (e.g., hunger).

Primary prevention Techniques and programs for preventing or reducing the occurrence of mental illness by promoting mental health.

Primary-process thinking In Freud's theory, the process by which the id achieves immediate partial satisfaction of an instinct through mental images such as dreams and daydreams.

Primary reinforcer Reinforcer that is rewarding in itself, such as food, water, and sex.

Proactive interference Process by which old material already in memory interferes with new information.

Problem representation Defining or interpreting a problem.

Procedural memory Portion of long-term memory that contains learned associations between stimuli and responses.

Products According to Guilford, the ideas that result from thinking.

Projection Attributing one's own repressed motives, feelings, or wishes to others.

Projective tests Personality tests consisting of ambiguous or unstructured material that do not limit the response to be given, such as the Rorschach inkblot test.

Prototype According to Rosch, a mental model containing the most typical features of a concept.

Proximity How close two people live to each other.

Psychoanalysis Both Freud's personality theory and his form of therapy.

Psychoanalysis Therapeutic technique created by Freud, based on uncovering people's unconscious motives, feelings, and desires.

Psychoanalytic model of abnormal behavior View that abnormal behavior is the result of unconscious internal conflicts.

Psychology The scientific study of behavior and mental processes.

Psychophysiological disorder Disorder in which a genuine physical disorder has a psychological cause.

Psychosurgery Brain surgery used in the treatment of severe mental disorders.

Psychotherapy Treatment of behavioral and emotional disorders using psychological techniques.

Psychotherapy Use of psychological techniques to treat personality and behavior disorders.

Puberty Onset of sexual maturation, with accompanying physical development.

Punishment Any event whose presence decreases the likelihood that ongoing behavior will recur.

Pupil Small opening in the iris through which light enters the eye.

Random sample Sample in which each potential subject has an equal chance of being selected.

Range Difference between the largest and smallest measurements in a distribution.

Ratio scale Scale with equal distances between the points or values and with a true zero.

Rational-emotive therapy (RET) A highly directive therapeutic approach based on the idea that an individual's problems have been caused by his or her misinterpretations of events and goals.

Rational people According to Jung, those people who regulate their actions by the psychological functions of thinking and feeling.

Reaction formation Expression of exaggerated ideas and emotions that are the opposite of one's repressed beliefs or feelings.

Realistic choice period Ginsberg's third stage of vocational choice, during which young adults actively explore various kinds of work and make a commitment to a career.

Reality principle According to Freud, satisfaction of instincts safely and effectively in the real world, characteristic of the ego.

Receptor cell Specialized cell that responds to particular type of energy.

Receptor site A site on the other side of the synaptic space that matches a neurotransmitter, which locks into it.

Recessive gene Member of a gene pair that can control the appearance of a certain trait only if it is paired with another recessive gene.

Reciprocal determinism In Bandura's model, proposal that the person influences the environment and is in turn influenced by the environment.

Regression Reverting to childlike behavior and defenses.

Reinforce To present a stimulus that increases the probability that the preceding response will recur in the future.

Reinforcement Anything that follows a response, making that response more likely to recur.

Reinforcement contingencies The particular pattern of reinforcement that a person has received as part of his or her life history.

Relative refractory period A period when the neuron is returning to its normal polarized state and may refire if the incoming message is much stronger than usual.

Reliability Ability of a test to produce consistent and stable scores.

REM (or paradoxical) sleep Sleep stage characterized by rapid eye movement and during which most vivid dreaming occurs.

Representativeness A heuristic by which a new situation is judged on the basis of its resemblance to a stereotypical model.

Repression Excluding uncomfortable thoughts from consciousness.

Response generalization Giving a response that is somewhat different from the response originally learned to that stimulus.

Reticular formation (RF) Network of neurons in the hindbrain, midbrain, and part of the forebrain whose primary function is to filter incoming messages and alert the higher parts of the brain to those that are important.

Retina Lining of the eye containing receptor cells that are sensitive to light.

Retinal disparity Binocular distance cue based on the difference between the images cast on the two retinas when both eyes are focused on the same object.

Retroactive interference Process by which new information interferes with old information already in memory.

Retrograde amnesia Inability to recall events immediately preceding an accident or injury, but without loss of earlier memory.

Risky shift Greater willingness to take risks in decision-making in a group than as independent individuals.

Rods Receptor cells in the retina responsible for night vision and perception of brightness.

Rooting reflex A reflex in newborn babies that causes them to turn their heads and search for a nipple when they are picked up.

Rorschach test A projective test composed of ambiguous inkblots; the way a person interprets the blots is thought to reveal aspects of his or her personality.

Rote rehearsal Retaining information in STM simply by repeating it over and over.

Round window Membrane between the middle ear and inner ear that equalizes pressure in the inner ear.

Ruffini ending Skin receptor believed to be responsive to warmth.

Saccule Organ in the inner ear that provides information about vertical movement of the body and gravitation.

Sadomasochism Obtaining sexual gratification from aggression.

Sample Selection of cases from a larger population.

Saturation The purity of a hue.

Scatter plot Diagram showing the association between scores on two variables.

Schedule of reinforcement In partial reinforcement, the program for choosing which responses to reinforce.

Schema Set of beliefs or expectations about something that is based on past experience.

Schemes Piaget's term for the frameworks one uses to organize experience, which change as one develops.

Schizoid personality disorder Disorder in which a person is withdrawn and lacks feelings for others.

Schizophrenic disorders Disorders in which there are disturbances of thoughts, communication, and emotions, including delusions and hallucinations.

Scientific method Approach to knowledge characterized by collecting data, formulating a hypothesis, and testing the hypothesis empirically.

Secondary prevention Techniques and programs emphasizing early detection of maladaptive behavior and prompt treatment in high risk groups.

Secondary-process thinking In Freud's theory, the process by which the ego uses intelligent reasoning to find safe and effective ways to gratify id instincts in the real world.

Secondary reinforcer Reinforcer whose value is learned through association with primary reinforcers.

Selection studies Studies that estimate the heritability of a trait by looking at successive generations of animals bred with one another.

Self-actualizing tendency According to Rogers, the drive of human beings to fulfill their self-concepts, or the images they have formed of themselves.

Self According to James, anything that the person can empirically claim to be part of his or her own person as distinct from all others.

Self-efficacy According to Bandura, the expectancy that one's efforts will be successful.

Self-fulfilling prophecy The process in which a person's expectation about another elicits behavior from the second person that confirms the expectation.

Semantic memory Portion of long-term memory that stores general facts and information.

Semantics The criteria for meaning in a language.

Semicircular canals Structures in the inner ear particularly sensitive to body rotation.

Senility Mental and physical deterioration brought on by disease that occurs in some older adults.

Sensation Experience of sensory stimulation.

Sensory or **afferent neurons** Neurons that carry messages from sense organs to the spinal cord or brain.

Sensory deprivation Extreme reduction of sensory stimuli.

Sensory projection areas Areas of the cerebral cortex where messages from the sense receptors are registered.

Sensory registers Entry points for raw information from the senses.

Serotonin Neurotransmitter that inhibits virtually all behavior, including emotions.

Set Tendency to perceive and to approach problems in certain ways.

Sexual dysfunction The loss or impairment of the ordinary physical responses of sexual function.

Shadowing Monocular cue to distance and depth based on the fact that shadows often appear on the parts of objects that are more distant.

Shape constancy Tendency to see an object as the same shape no matter what angle it is viewed from.

Shaping Reinforcing successive approximations to a desired behavior.

Short-term memory (STM) Working memory; briefly stores and processes selected information from the sensory registers.

Significance Probability that results obtained were due to chance.

Simple phobia Phobia directed at a specific situation (such as being in the dark) or a specific object (such as snakes).

Situationism The theory that views behavior solely as a response to external stimuli.

Sixteen Personality Factor Questionnaire Objective test designed by Cattell to provide scores on his 16 basic personality traits.

Size constancy Perception of an object as the same size regardless of the distance from which it is viewed.

Skinner box Box equipped with a bar, in which an animal is placed during operant conditioning; pressing the bar releases food, which reinforces the bar-pressing behavior.

Social cognition A mental understanding of the social world and one's place in it.

Social influence Any actions performed by one or more persons to change the attitudes, behavior, or feelings of one or more others.

Social learning theory View of learning that emphasizes the ability to learn by observing a model or receiving instructions, without firsthand experience by the learner.

Social motive Learned motive associated with relationships among people, such as needs for affiliation, achievement, and power.

Social phobia Phobia centered on the fear of being with other people.

Social psychology The scientific study of the way in which the thoughts, feelings, and behaviors of one individual are influenced by the real, imagined, or implied behavior or characteristics of other people.

Socialization Process by which children learn the behavior and attitudes appropriate to their family and culture.

Somatic nervous system The part of the peripheral nervous system that carries messages from the senses to the central nervous system and between the central nervous system and the skeletal muscles.

Somatization disorder Disorder characterized by recurrent vague somatic complaints without a physical cause.

Somatoform disorders Disorders in which there is an apparent physical disorder for which there is no organic basis.

Somatotypes According to Sheldon, three basic body types endomorphic, mesomorphic, and ectomorphic that are believed to influence personality.

Sound localization Ability to determine where a sound originates.

Spinal cord Complex cable of nerves that runs down the spine, connecting the brain to most of the rest of the body.

Split-half reliability A method of determining test reliability by dividing the test into two parts and checking the agreement of scores on both parts.

Spontaneous recovery The reappearance of an extinguished response after the passage of time, without further training.

Standard deviation Statistical measure of variability in a group of scores or other values.

Stanford-Binet Intelligence Scale Terman's adaptation of the Binet-Simon Scale.

Statistics A branch of mathematics that psychologists use to organize and analyze data.

Stereoscopic vision Combination of two retinal images to give a three-dimensional perceptual experience.

Stereotype A set of characteristics presumed to be shared by all members of a social category.

Stimulants Drugs, including amphetamines and cocaine, that stimulate the sympathetic nervous system and produce feelings of optimism and boundless energy.

Stimulus discrimination Learning to respond to only one stimulus and inhibit the response to all other stimuli.

Stimulus generalization Transfer of a learned response to different but similar stimuli.

Stimulus motive An unlearned motive, such as curiosity or activity, that depends more on external stimuli than on internal physiological states.

Strain studies Studies of the heritability of behavioral traits using animals that have been inbred to produce strains that are genetically very similar to one another.

Stress Any adjustment demand that creates a state of tension or threat and that requires change or adaptation.

Stress-inoculation therapy Form of cognitive behavior therapy that trains clients to cope with stressful situations by understanding their misconceptions about them.

Stroboscopic motion Apparent movement that results from flashing a series of still pictures in rapid succession, as in a motion picture.

Structuralism School of psychology that stresses the basic units of experience and the combinations in which they occur.

Style of life According to Adler, each individual's development of a particular set of meanings and beliefs.

Subgoals Intermediate, more manageable goals used in one heuristic strategy to make it easier to reach the final goal.

Subjects Individuals whose reactions or responses are observed in an experiment.

Sublimation Redirecting repressed motives and feelings into more socially acceptable channels.

Subtractive color mixing The process of mixing pigments, each of which absorbs some wavelengths of light and reflects others.

Sucking reflex A reflex in newborns that causes them to suck on anything that touches their faces.

Superego According to Freud, the social and parental standards the individual has internalized; the conscience and the ego ideal.

Superposition Monocular distance cue in which one object, by partly blocking a second object, is perceived as being closer.

Surface structure The particular arrangement of verbal information, such as words in a sentence.

Sympathetic division Branch of the autonomic nervous system that prepares the body for quick action in an emergency.

Synapse Area composed of the axon terminal of one neuron, the synaptic space, and the dendrite or cell body of the next neuron.

Synaptic space or **synaptic cleft** Tiny gap between the axon terminal of one neuron and the dendrites or cell body of the next neuron.

Synaptic vesicles Tiny sacs in a synaptic knob that release chemicals into the synapse.

Syntax The rules for the structure of word forms and sentences.

Tactic of elimination A problem-solving strategy in which possible solutions are evaluated according to appropriate criteria and discarded as they fail to contribute to a solution.

Taste buds Structures on the tongue that contain the receptor cells for taste.

Temporal lobe Part of the cerebral cortex that controls hearing and some processing of visual information.

Tentative choice period Ginsberg's second stage of vocational choice, during which adolescents begin to match interests, abilities, and values with opportunities.

Tertiary prevention Techniques and programs for reducing the long-term consequences of mental illness by facilitating an individual's readjustment to family and community life.

Testosterone Hormone that is the primary determinant of the sex drive in both men and women.

Texture gradient Monocular cue to distance and depth based on the fact that objects seen at greater distances appear to be smoother and less textured.

Thalamus Area of the forebrain that relays and translates incoming messages from the sense receptors, except those for smell.

Thematic Apperception Test (TAT) A projective test composed of ambiguous pictures about which a person writes stories.

Thyroid Gland Endocrine gland located below the voice box that produces the hormone thyroxin.

Thyroxin Hormone that regulates the rate of metabolism.

Timbre Quality or texture of a sound caused by overtones.

Token economies A means of behavioral change whereby members of an institution receive tokens, which may be exchanged for tangible reinforcements, for adaptive behaviors.

Token economy Form of behavior therapy in which patients earn tokens (reinforcers) for desired behavior and exchange them for desired items or privileges.

Tolerance Phenomenon whereby higher doses of a drug are required to produce its original effects or to prevent withdrawal symptoms.

Traditional standard Expectation that adolescents will postpone the expression of sexual needs until they are responsible married adults.

Transvestism Dressing in the clothing of the opposite sex to achieve sexual gratification.

Trial and error A problem-solving strategy based on successive elimination of incorrect solutions until the correct one is found.

Triarchic theory of intelligence Sternberg's theory that intelligence involves mental skills (componential aspect), insight and creative adaptability (experiential aspect), and environmental responsiveness (contextual aspect).

Trichromatic theory Theory of color vision that holds that all color perception derives from three different color receptors in the retina (usually red, green, and blue receptors).

Trichromats people who have normal color vision.

Twin studies Studies of identical and fraternal twins to determine the separate influences of heredity and environment on human behavior.

Unconditional positive regard The acceptance and love for another person regardless of that person's behavior.

Unconditioned response (UR) Response that takes place in an organism whenever an unconditioned stimulus occurs.

Unconditioned stimulus (US) Stimulus that invariably causes an organism to respond in a specific way.

Unconscious In Freud's theory, all the ideas, thoughts, and feelings of which we are not and cannot normally become aware.

Undifferentiated schizophrenia Type of schizophrenia in which there are clear schizophrenic symptoms that don't meet the criteria for another type.

Utricle Organ in the inner ear that provides information about horizontal movement of the body.

Validity Ability of a test to measure what it has been designed to measure.

Variable-interval schedule Reinforcement schedule in which the first correct response is reinforced after various lengths of time.

Variable-ratio schedule Reinforcement schedule in which a varying number of correct responses must occur before reinforcement is presented.

Vestibular sacs Sacs in the inner ear that are responsible for sensing gravitation, and forward, backward, and vertical movement.

Vestibular senses Senses of equilibrium and body movement and position.

Visual acuity Ability to distinguish fine details.

Visual acuity The ability to distinguish fine details.

Visualizing A problem-solving strategy in which principles or concepts are drawn, diagrammed, or charted so that they can be better understood.

Volley principle Modification of frequency theory that suggests that receptors in the ear fire in sequence, with one group responding, then a second, then a third, and so on, so that the complete pattern of firing corresponds to the frequency of the sound wave.

Voyeurism The desire to watch others having sexual relations or to spy on nude people.

Waking consciousness State of consciousness that includes the thoughts and feelings that occur when we are awake and reasonably alert.

Wechsler Adult Intelligence ScaleRevised (WAIS-R) Individual intelligence test developed especially for adults; measures both verbal and performance abilities.

Wechsler Intelligence Scale for Children-Revised (WISC-R) Individual intelligence test developed especially for school-aged children; measures verbal and performance abilities and also yields an overall IQ score.

Withdrawal Avoiding a situation when other forms of coping are not practical.

Withdrawal Unpleasant physical or psychological effects that follow the discontinuance of a dependence-producing substance.

Working backward A heuristic strategy in which one works backward from the desired goal to the given conditions.

Yerkes-Dodson law States that there is an optimal level of arousal for the best performance on any task; the more complex the task, the lower the level of arousal that can be tolerated before performance deteriorates.

References

Aaronson, B., & Osmond, H. (1970). *Psychedelics*. Garden City, New York: Doubleday.

Aaronson, D., & Scarborough, H. S. (1976). Performance theories for sentence coding: Some quantiative evidence. *Journal of Experimental Psychology: Human Perception and Performance, 2*, 56–70.

Aaronson, D., & Scarborough, H. S. (1977). Performance theories for sentence coding: Some quantitative models. *Journal of Verbal Learning and Verbal Behavior, 16*, 277–304.

Acredolo, L. P., & Hake, J. L. (1982). Infant perception. In B. B. Wolman (Ed.), *Handbook of developmental psychology* (pp. 244–283). Englewood Cliffs, NJ: Prentice-Hall.

Adams, G. R., & Gullota, T. (1983). *Adolescent life experiences*. Monterey, CA: Brooks/Cole.

Adams, J. L. (1980). *Conceptual blockbusting: A guide to better ideas* (2nd ed.). New York: Norton.

Adorno, T. W., Frenkel-Brunswick, E., Levinson, D. J., & Sanford, R. N. (1950). *The authoritarian personality*. New York: Harper & Row.

Agras, W. S., & Kraemer, H. (1983). The treatment of anorexia nervosa: Do different treatments have different outcomes? *Psychiatric Annuals, 13*, 928–935.

Ainslie, G. (1975). Specious reward: A behavioral theory of impulsiveness and impulse control. *Psychological Bulletin, 82*, 463–496.

Ainsworth, M. D., Blehar, M. C., Waters, E., & Wall, S. (1979). *Patterns of attachment*. New York: Halstead Press.

Ajzen, I., & Fishbein, M. (1980). *Understanding attitudes and predicting behavior*. Englewood Cliffs, NJ: Prentice-Hall.

Albee, G. W. (1982). Preventing psychopathology and promoting human potential. *American Psychologist, 37*, 1043–1050.

Allan, C., & Brotman, H. (1981). *Chart book on aging in America*. Washington, DC: White House Conference on Aging.

Allen, V. L., & Levine, J. M. (1971). Social support and conformity: The role of independent assessment of reality. *Journal of Experimental Social Psychology, 7*, 48–58.

Allgeier, E. R., & Allgeier, A. R. (1984). *Sexual interactions*. Lexington, MA: D. C. Heath.

Allport, G. W. (1954). *The nature of prejudice*. New York: Anchor.

Allport, G. W., & Odbert, H. S. (1936). Trait-names: A psycholexical study. *Psychological Monographs, 47* (1, Whole No. 211).

Altman, I. (1975). *The environment and social behavior*. Monterey, CA: Brooks/Cole.

Amabile, T. M. (1983). The social psychology of creativity: A comparative conceptualization. *Journal of Personality and Social Psychology, 45*, 357–376.

American Psychiatric Association (1980). *Diagnostic and statistical manual of mental disorders* (3rd ed.). Washington, DC: American Psychiatric Association.

American Psychiatric Association (1987). *Diagnostic and statistical manual of mental disorders* (3rd ed., rev.). Washington, DC: American Psychiatric Association.

American Psychological Association (1953). *Ethical standards of psychologists*. Washington, DC: American Psychological Association.

American Psychological Association (1973, 1982, 1985). *Ethical principles in the conduct of research with human participants*. Washington, DC: American Psychological Association.

American Psychological Association (1975). Report of the task force on sex bias and sex-role stereotyping in psychotherapeutic practice. *American Psychologist, 30*, 1169–1175.

American Psychological Association (1978). Guidelines for therapy with women. *American Psychologist, 33*, 1122–1123.

Anastasi, A. (1982). *Psychological testing* (5th ed). New York: Macmillan.

Anastasi, A. (1988). *Psychological testing* (6th ed.). New York: Macmillan.

Anch, A. M., Browman, C. P., Mitler, M. M., & Walsh, J. K. (1987). *Sleep, A Scientific Perspective*. Englewood Cliffs, NJ: Prentice-Hall.

Anderson, B. L. (1983). Primary orgasmic dysfunction: Diagnostic considerations and review of treatment. *Psychological Bulletin, 93*, 105–136.

Anderson, R. C., & Pichert, J. W. (1978). Recall of previously unrecallable information following a shift in perspective. *Journal of Verbal Learning and Verbal Behavior, 17*, 1–12.

Angoff, W. H. (1988). The nature-nurture debate, aptitudes, and group differences. *American Psychologist, 43*, 713–720.

Aranya, N., Kushnir, T., & Valency, A. (1986). Organizational commitment in a male dominated profession. *Human Relations, 39*, 433–438. New York: Basic Books.

Argyle, M., & Furnham, A. (1983). Sources of satisfaction and conflict in long-term relationships. *Journal of Marriage and Family Counseling, 45*, 481–493.

Argyle, M., & McHenry, R. (1971). Do spectacles really affect judgments of intelligence? *British Journal of Social and Clinical Psychology, 10*, 27–29.

Arieti, S. (Ed.) (1975). *American handbook of psychiatry* (Vol. 6). New York: Basic Books.

Arkema, P. H. (1981). The borderline personality and transitional relatedness. *American Journal of Psychiatry, 138*, 172–177.

Arkin, R. M., Cooper, H., & Kolditz, T. (1980). A statistical review of literature concerning the self-serving attribution bias in interpersonal influence situations. *Journal of Personality, 48*, 435–448.

Armor, D. J., Polach, J. M., & Stambul, H. B. (1978). *Alcoholism and treatment.* New York: Wiley.

Arnold, M. B. (1960). *Emotion and personality* (2 Vols.). New York: Columbia University Press.

Aronson, E. (1984). *The social animal* (4th ed.). New York: Freeman.

Aronson, E., Cookie, S., Sikes, J., Blaney, N., & Snapp, M. (1978). *The jigsaw classroom.* Beverly Hills, CA: Sage.

Aronson, E., & Lindner, D. E. (1965). Gain and loss of esteem as determinants of interpersonal attractiveness. *Journal of Experimental Social Psychology, 1*, 156–171.

Aronson, E., Willerman, B., & Floyd, J. (1966). The effect of a pratfall on increasing interpersonal attractiveness. *Psychonomic Science, 4*, 227–228.

Asch, S. E. (1946). Forming impressions of personality. *Journal of Abnormal and Social Psychology, 41*, 258–290.

Asch, S. E. (1951). Effects of group pressure upon the modification and distortion of judgments. In H. Guetzkow (Ed.), *Groups, leadership, and men.* Pittsburgh: Carnegie Press.

Asch, S. E. (1956). Studies of independence and conformity: I. A minority of one against a unanimous majority. *Psychological Monographs, 70* (9, Whole No. 416).

Asher, J. (1975, April). Sex bias found in therapy. *APA Monitor, 1*, 5.

Asher, S. R., & Renshaw, P. D. (1981). Children without friends: Social knowledge and social-skill training. In S. R. Asher & J. M. Gottman (Eds.), *The development of children's friendships.* Cambridge: Cambridge University Press.

Aston, R. (1972). Barbiturates, alcohol and tranquilizers. In S. J. Mule & H. Brill (Eds.), *The chemical and biological aspects of drug dependence.* Cleveland: CRC Press.

Atchley, R. C. (1976). *The sociology of retirement.* Cambridge, MA: Schenkman.

Atkinson, J. W., & Birch, D. (1970). *The dynamics of action.* New York: Wiley.

Atkinson, J. W., & Raynor, J. O. (1975). *Motivation and achievement.* Washington, DC: Winston.

Ayllon, T., & Azrin, N. H. (1965). The measurement and reinforcement of behavior of psychotics. *Journal of the Experimental Analysis of Behavior, 8*, 357–383.

Azzi, R., Fix, D. S. R., Keller, R. S., & Rocha e Silva, M. I. (1964). Exteroceptive control of response under delayed reinforcement. *Journal of the Experimental Analysis of Behavior, 7*, 159–162.

Bachtold, L. M., & Werner, E. E. (1973). Personality characteristics of creative women. *Perception and Motor Skills, 36*, 311–319.

Baddeley, A. D. (1986). *Working Memory.* Oxford: Clarendon Press.

Baddeley, A. D., & Hitch, G. (1974). Working memory. In G. H. Bower (Ed.), *The psychology of learning and motivation* (Vol. 8). New York: Academic Press.

Bahrick, H. P., Bahrick, P. O., & Wittlinger, R. P. (1974, December). Those unforgettable high school days. *Psychology Today*, pp. 50–56.

Balagura, S. (1973). *Hunger: A biopsychological analysis.* New York: Basic Books.

Baldassare, M., Rosenfield, S., & Rook, K. (1984). The types of social relations for predicting elderly well-being. *Research on Aging, 6*, 549–559.

Baldwin, A. Y. (1985). Programs for the gifted and talented: Issues concerning minority populations. In F. D. Horowitz & M. O'Brien (Eds.), *The gifted and talented: Developmental perspectives.* Washington, DC: American Psychological Association.

Bandura, A. (1962). Social learning through imitation. In M. R. Jones (Ed.), *Nebraska symposium on motivation.* Lincoln: University of Nebraska Press.

Bandura, A. (1965). Influence of models' reinforcement contingencies on the acquisition of imitative responses. *Journal of Personality and Social Psychology, 1*, 589–595.

Bandura, A. (1973). *Aggression: A social learning analysis.* Englewood Cliffs, NJ: Prentice-Hall.

Bandura, A. (1977). *Social learning theory.* Englewood Cliffs, NJ: Prentice-Hall.

Bandura, A., Blanchard, E. B., & Ritter, B. (1969). Relative efficacy of desensitization and modeling approaches for inducing behavioral, affective, and attitudinal changes. *Journal of Personality and Social Psychology, 13*, 173–199.

Banyai, E. I., & Hilgard, E. R. (1976). A comparison of active-alert hypnotic induction with traditional relaxation induction. *Journal of Abnormal Psychology, 85*, 218–224.

Barron, F. (1963). *Creativity and psychological health.* Princeton, NJ: Van Nostrand.

Barron, F., & Harrington, D. M. (1981). Creativity, intelligence, and personality. *Annual Review of Psychology, 32*, 439–76.

Bartlett, F. C. (1932). *Remembering: A study in experimental and social psychology.* New York: Macmillan.

Bartoshuk, L. M. (1974). Taste illusions: Some demonstrations. *Annals of the New York Academy of Sciences, 237*, 279–285.

Baruch, F., & Barnett, R. (1986). Role quality, multiple role involvement, and psychological well-being in mid-life women. *Journal of Personality and Social Psychology, 51*, 578–585.

Basow, S. A. (1986). *Gender stereotypes: Traditions and alternatives* (2nd ed.). Pacific Grove, CA: Brooks/Cole.

Baum, A., & Valins, S. (1977). *Architecture and social behavior: Psychological studies of social density.* Hillsdale, NJ: Erlbaum.

Baumeister, A. A. (1987). Mental retardation, some conceptions and dilemmas. *American Psychologist, 42*, 796–800.

Baumrind, D. (1972). Socialization and instrumental competence in young children. In W. W. Hartup (Ed.), *The young child: Reviews of research* (Vol. 2). Washington, DC: National Association for the Education of Young Children.

Baumrind, D. (1978). A dialectical materialist's perspective on knowing social reality. *New Directions for Child Development, 2.*

Baumrind, D. (1985). Research using intentional deception. *American Psychologist, 40*, 165–174.

Baxter, D. W., & Olszewski, J. (1960). Congenital insensitivity to pain. *Brain, 83*, 381.

Bayley, N. (1956). Individual patterns of development. *Child Development, 27*, 45–74.

Bazelon, D. L. (1980, March). Eyewitless news. *Psychology Today*, pp. 102–106.

Bazelon, D. L. (1982). Veils, values, and social responsibility. *American Psychologist, 37*, 115–121.

Beaubier, J. (1980). Biological factors in aging. In C. L. Fry (Ed.), *Aging in culture and society.* Brooklyn, NY: J. F. Bergin.

Beck, A. T. (1967). *Depression: Clinical, experimental and theoretical aspects.* New York: Hoeber.

Beck, A. T. (1976). *Cognitive therapy and emotional disorders.* New York: International Universities Press.

Beck, R. (1983). *Motivation: Theories and principles* (2nd ed.). Englewood Cliffs, NJ: Prentice-Hall.

Beier, E. G. (1974, October). Nonverbal communication: How we send emotional messages. *Psychology Today,* pp. 53–56.

Bellack, A. S. Hersen, M., & Turner, S. M. (1976). Generalization effects of social skills training in chronic schizophrenics: An experimental analysis. *Behavior Research and Therapy, 14,* 391–398.

Belmont, L., & Marolla, F. A. (1973). Birth order, family size, and intelligence. *Science, 182,* 1096–1101.

Belsky, J., Lang, M. E., & Roving, M. (1985). Stability and change in marriage across the transition to parenthood: A second study. *Journal of Marriage and the Family, 97,* 855–865.

Belsky, J., & Rovine, M. (1988). Nonmaternal care in the first year of life and infant parent attachment security. *Child Development, 59,* 157–167.

Bem, D. J., & Allen, A. (1974). On predicting some of the people some of the time: The search for cross-situational consistencies in behavior. *Psychological Review, 81,* 506–520.

Bem, S. L. (1974). The measurement of psychological androgyny. *Journal of Consulting and Clinical Psychology, 42,* 155–162.

Bem, S. L. (1975). Sex-role adaptability: One consequence of psychological androgyny. *Journal of Personality and Social Psychology, 31,* 634–643.

Benjamin, L. S. (1982). Use of structural analysis of social behavior (SASB) to guide intervention in psychotherapy. In J. C. Anchin & D. L. Kiesler (Eds.), *Handbook of interpersonal psychotherapy.* New York: Pergamon.

Benson, H. (1975). *The relaxation response.* New York: William Morrow.

Benson, H., Alexander, S., & Feldman, E. L. (1975). Decreased premature ventricular contractions through use of the relaxation response in patients with stable ischemic heart disease. *Lancet, 2,* 380–382.

Benson, H., Kotch, J. B., Crassweller, K. D., & Greenwood, M. M. (1979). The relaxation response. In D. Goleman & R. Davidson (Eds.), *Consciousness: Brain, states of awareness and mysticism.* New York: Harper & Row.

Benson, H., & Wallace, R. K. (1972). Decreased drug abuse with transcendental meditation—a study of 1,862 subjects. In C. J. D. Zarafonetis (Ed.), *Drug abuse proceedings of the international conference.* Philadelphia: Lea and Febiger.

Berger, P. A. (1978). Medical treatment of mental illness. *Science, 200,* 974–981.

Berger, R. J. (1969). The sleep and dream cycle. In A. Kales (Ed.), *Sleep: Physiology and pathology.* Philadelphia: Lippincott.

Bergin, A. E., & Lambert, M. J. (1978). The evaluation of therapeutic outcomes. In S. L. Garfield & A. E. Bergin (Eds.), *Handbook of psychotherapy and behavior change: An empirical analysis.* New York: Wiley.

Bergman, J. (1974). Are little girls being harmed by Sesame Street? In J. Stacey, S. Bereaud, & J. Daniels (Eds.), *And Jill came tumbling after: Sexism in American education.* New York: Dell.

Berkowitz, L. (1983). Aversively stimulated aggression. *American Psychologist, 38,* 1135–1144.

Berkowitz, M. W., & Gibbs, J. C. (1983). Measuring the developmental features of moral discussion. *Merrill-Palmer Quarterly, 29,* 399–410.

Berlin, B., & Kay, P. (1969). *Basic color terms: Their universality and evolution.* Berkeley: University of California Press.

Bernard, L. L. (1924). *Instinct.* New York: Holt.

Bernstein, I. L. (1978). Learned taste aversions in children receiving chemotherapy. *Science, 200,* 1302–1303.

Bersoff, D. N. (1981). Testing and the law. *American Psychologist, 36,* 1047–1056.

Bertenthal, B. I., & Fischer, K. W. (1978). Development of self-recognition in the infant. *Developmental Psychology, 14,* 44–50.

Bertrand, S., & Masling, J. (1969). Oral imagery and alcoholism. *Journal of Abnormal Psychology, 74,* 50–53.

Best, J. B. (1989). *Cognitive psychology* (2nd ed.). St. Paul, MN: West Publishing Co.

Bettelheim, B. (1943). Individual and mass behavior in extreme situations. *Journal of Abnormal and Social Psychology, 38,* 417–452.

Bettelheim, B. (1960). *The informed heart.* New York: Free Press.

Bewley, T. H. (1974). Treatment of opiate addiction in Great Britain. In S. Fisher & A. M. Freeman (Eds.), *Opiate addiction: Origins and treatment.* New York: Wiley.

Bhatt, R. S., Wasserman, E. A., Reynolds, W. F., & Knauss, K. S. (1988). Conceptual behavior in pigeons: Categorization of both familiar and novel examples from four classes of natural and artificial stimuli. *Journal of Experimental Psychology: Animal Behavior Processes, 14,* 219–324.

Bieber, I., et al. (1962). *Homosexuality: A psychoanalytic study.* New York: Basic Books.

Birch, H. G., & Rabinowitz, H. S. (1951). The negative effect of previous experience on productive thinking. *Journal of Experimental Psychology, 41,* 121–125.

Birdwhistell, R. L. (1952). *Introduction to kinesics.* Louisville, KY: University of Louisville Press.

Birdwhistell, R. L. (1974). Toward analyzing American movement. In S. Weitz (Ed.), *Nonverbal communication: Readings with commentary.* New York: Oxford University Press.

Birnbaum, I. M., Parker, E. S., Hartley, J. T., & Noble, E. P. (1978). Alcohol and memory: Retrieval process. *Journal of Verbal Learning and Verbal Behavior, 17,* 325–335.

Birren, J. E. (1983). Aging in America: Role for psychology. *American Psychologist, 38,* 298–299.

Bitter, R. G. (1986). Late marriage and marital instability: the effects of heterogeneity and inflexibility. *Journal of Marriage and the Family, 48,* 631–640.

Bjorklund, D. F. (1989). *Children's thinking, developmental function and individual differences.* Pacific Grove: Brooks/Cole.

Blake, R. R., Helson, H., & Mouton, J. (1956). The generality of conformity behavior as a function of factual anchorage, difficulty of task and amount of social pressure. *Journal of Personality, 25,* 294–305.

Blakemore, C., & Cooper, G. F. (1970). Development of the brain depends on the visual environment. *Nature, 228,* 477–478.

Blasi, A. (1980). Bridging moral cognition and moral action: A critical review of the literature. *Psychological Bulletin, 88*(1), 1–45.

Block, H. H., Block, J., & Harrington, D. M. (1974). The relationship of parental teaching strategies to ego-resiliency in preschool children. Paper presented at the meeting of the Western Psychological Association, San Francisco.

Block, J. (1971). *Lives through time.* Berkeley, CA: Bancroft.

Block, J. (1976). Issues, problems, and pitfalls in assessing sex differences: A critical review of the psychology of sex differences. *Merrill-Palmer Quarterly, 22,* 283–308.

Block, J. (1978). Rorschach. In O. K. Buros (Ed.), *The eighth mental measurements yearbook.* Highland Park, NJ: Gryphon.

Block, J. (1979). Another look at sex differentiation in the socialization behaviors of mothers and fathers. In F. Denmark & J. Sherman (Eds.), *Psychology of women: Future directions of research.* New York: Psychological Dimensions.

Bloom, L. (1970). *Language development: Form and function in emerging grammar.* Cambridge, MA: M.I.T. Press.

Blum, J. M. (1979). *Pseudoscience and mental ability: The origins and fallacies of the IQ controversy.* New York: Monthly Review Press.

Bokert, E. (1970). The effects of thirst and related auditory stimulation on dream reports. Paper presented to the Association for the Physiological Study of Sleep, Washington, DC.

Bolles, R., & Fanselow, M. (1982). Endorphins and behavior. *Annual Review of Psychology, 33,* 87–101.

Bolles, R. C. (1972). Reinforcement, expectancy, and learning. *Psychological Review, 79,* 394–409.

Bolton, B. F. (1978). Sixteen personality factor questionnaire. In O. K. Burios (Ed.), *The eighth mental measurements yearbook.* Highland Park, NJ: Gryphon.

Bonham, M., Cloninger, C. R., Sigvardsson, S., von Knorring, A. L. (1982). Predisposition to petty criminality in Swedish adoptees: I. Genetic and Rh environmental heterogeneity. *Archives of General Psychiatry, 39,* 1233–1241.

Borgatta, E. F. (1964). The structure of personality characteristics. *Behavioral Science, 9,* 8–17.

Boring, E. G., Langfeld, H. S., Weld, H. P. (1976). *Foundations of psychology.* New York: Wiley.

Bornstein, M.H., & Lamb, M.E. (1988). *Developmental psychology: An advanced textbook* (2nd ed.). Hillsdale, NJ: Lawrence Erlbaum Associates.

Botwin, M.D., & Buss, D. M. (in press). The structure of act report data: Is the five factor model of personality recaptured? *Journal of Personality and Social Psychology.*

Bourne, L. E., Dominowski, R. L., Loftus, E. F., & Healy, A. F. (1986). *Cognitive processes* (2nd ed.). Englewood Cliffs, NJ: Prentice-Hall.

Bower, G. H. (1973, October). How to . . . uh . . . remember. *Psychology Today,* 63–70.

Bower, G. H., Black J., & Turner, T. (1979). Scripts in text comprehension and memory. *Cognitive Psychology, 11,* 177–220.

Bower, T. G. R. (1971). The object in the world of the infant. *Scientific American, 226,* 20–38.

Bower, T. G. R. (1972). Object perception in infants. *Perception, 1,* 15–30.

Bower, T. G. R. (1976). Repetitive processes in child development. *Scientific American, 235,* 38–47.

Bower, T. G. R. (1977). Comment on Yonas et al., Development of sensitivity to information for impending collision. *Perception and Psychophysics, 21,* 281–282.

Bowers, K. S. (1973). Situationism in psychology: An analysis and a critique. *Psychological Review, 80,* 307–336.

Bramel, D. (1962). A dissonance theory approach to defensive projection. *Journal of Abnormal and Social Psychology, 64,* 121–129.

Bransford, J. D., Stein, B. S., Vye, N. J., Franks, J. J., Aubel, P. M., Mezynsky, K. J., & Perfetto, G. A. (1982). Differences in approaches in learning: An overview. *Journal of Experimental Psychology: General, 111,* 390–398.

Braveman, N. S., & Bronstein, P. (Eds.) (1985). *Experimental assessments and clinical applications of conditioned food aversions. Annals of the New York Academy of Sciences, 443.* New York: New York Academy of Sciences.

Brazelton, T. B. (1969). *Infants and mothers: Differences in development.* New York: Dell.

Brazelton, T. B. (1973). *Neonatal behavioral assessment scale.* London: Heinemann.

Bredemeier, B., & Shields, D. (1985, October). Values and violence in sports today. *Psychology Today,* pp. 23–32.

Brehony, K. A., & Geller, E. S. (1981). Agoraphobia: Appraisal of research and a proposal for an integrative model. In M. Hersen, R. M. Eisler, & P. M. Miller (Eds.), *Progress in behavior modification* (Vol. 12). New York: Academic Press.

Breier, A., Kelsoe, J. R., Kirwen, P. D., Beller, S. A., et al., (1988). Early parental loss and development of adult psychopathology. *Archives of General Psychiatry, 45,* 987–993.

Breland, K., & Breland, M. (1972). The misbehavior of organisms. In M. E. P. Seligman & J. L. Hager (Eds.), *Biological boundaries of learning.* Englewood Cliffs, NJ: Prentice-Hall.

Brenneis, B. (1970). Male and female modalities in manifest dream content. *Journal of Abnormal Psychology, 76,* 434–442.

Brenner, M. H. (1973). *Mental illness and the economy.* Cambridge, MA: Harvard University Press.

Brenner, M. H. (1979). Influence of the social environment on psychopathology: The historic perspective. In J. E. Barrett (Ed.), *Stress and mental disorder.* New York: Raven Press.

Brewer, W. F., & Nakamura, G. V. (1984). The nature and function of schemas. In R. S. Wyer and T. K. Srull (Eds.), *Handbook of Social Cognition.* Hillsdale, NJ: Erlbaum.

Brill, N. Q., & Christie, R. L. (1974). Marihuana and psycho-social adjustment. *Archives of General Psychiatry, 31,* 713–719.

Broadbent, D. E. (1958). *Perception and communication.* New York: Pergamon.

Brock, T. C., & Balloun, J. L. (1967). Behavioral receptivity to dissonant information. *Journal of Personality and Social Psychology, 6,* 413–428.

Broderick, C. B. (1982). Adult sexual development. In B. B. Wolman (Ed.), *Handbook of developmental psychology* (pp. 726–733). Englewood Cliffs, NJ: Prentice-Hall.

Brody, L. (1985). Gender differences in emotional development: A review of theories and research. In A. J. Stewart & M. B. Lykes (Eds.), *Gender and personality: Current perspectives on theory and research* (pp. 14–61). Durham, NC: Duke University Press.

Brody, N. (1980). Social motivation. *Annual Review of Psychology, 31,* 143–168.

Bronfenbrenner, U. (1977). Toward an experimental ecology of human development. *American Psychologist, 32,* 513–531.

Bronfenbrenner, U. (1986). Ecology of the family as a context for human development: Research perspectives. *Developmental Psychology, 22,* 723–742.

Brooks, A. D. (1974). *Law, psychiatry, and the mental health system.* Boston: Little, Brown.

Brooks-Gunn, J., & Furstenberg, F. F., Jr. (1989). Adolescent Sexual Behavior. *American Psychologist, 44,* 249–257.

Brown, B., & Grotberg, J. J. (1981). "Head Start: A successful experiment." *Courrier* (Paris: International Children's Centre).

Brown, E. L., & Deffenbacher, K. (1979). *Perception and the senses.* Oxford: Oxford University Press.

Brown, P. L., & Jenkins, H. M. (1968). Autoshaping of the pigeon's key peck. *Journal of Experimental and Analytical Behavior, 11,* 1–8.

Brown, R. (1958). *Words and things.* New York: Free Press/Macmillan.

Brown, R., & Kulik, J. (1977). Flashbulb memories. *Cognition, 5,* 73–99.

Brown, R. W., & Lenneberg, E. H. (1954). A study in language and cognition. *Journal of Abnormal and Social Psychology, 49,* 454–462.

Browning, D. (1982, February). Waiting for mommy. *Texas Monthly,* pp. 124–131, 183–192, 197.

Bruch, C. B. (1971). Modification of procedures for identification of the disadvantaged gifted. *Gifted Child Quarterly, 15,* 267–272.

Bruch, H. (1980). *The golden cage: The enigma of anorexia nervosa.* New York: Random House.

Buckley, P. (1982). Identifying schizophrenic patients who should not receive medication. *Schizophrenia Bulletin, 8,* 429–432.

Budzynski, T., Stoyva, J., & Adler, C. (1970). Feedback-induced muscle relaxation: Application to tension headache. *Journal of Behavior Therapy and Experimental Psychiatry, 1,* 205–211.

Buhrich, N., Theile, N., Yaw, A., & Crawford, A. (1979). Plasma testosterone, serum FSH, and serum LH levels in transvestism. *Archives of Sexual Behavior, 8,* 49–54.

Bunney, W. E., Pert, A., Rosenblatt, J., Pert, C. B., & Gallaper, D. (1979). Mode of action of lithium: Some biological considerations. *Archives of General Psychiatry, 36,* 898–901.

Burchinal, L. G. (1965). Trends and prospects for young marriages in the U.S. *Journal of Marriage and the Family, 27,* 243–254.

Buss, A. H. (1980). *Self-consciousness and social anxiety.* San Francisco: Freeman.

Buss, A. H., Plomin, R., & Willerman, L. (1973). The inheritance of temperaments. *Journal of Personality, 41,* 513–524.

Buss, D. M. (1985). Human mate selection. *American Scientist, 73,* 47–51.

Butler, R. N. (1963). The life review: An interpretation of reminiscence in the aged. *Psychiatry, 26,* 63–76.

Butler, R. N., & Lewis, M. I. (1982). *Aging and mental health: Positive psychological and biomedical approaches.* St. Louis: Mosby.

Byrne, D. (1961). Interpersonal attraction and attitude similarity. *Journal of Abnormal and Social Psychology, 62,* 713–715.

Byrne, D. (1977). The imagery of sex. J. Money & H. Masaph (Eds.), *Handbook of sexology.* New York: Elsevier/North Holland.

Byrne, D., & Blaylock, B. (1963). Similarity and assumed similarity of attitudes between husbands and wives. *Journal of Abnormal and Social Psychology, 67,* 636–640.

Byrne, D., London, O., & Reeves, K. (1968). The effects of physical attractiveness, sex, and attitude similarity on interpersonal attraction. *Journal of Personality, 36,* 259–271.

Byrne, D., & Nelson, D. (1965). Attraction as a linear function of properties of positive reinforcements. *Journal of Personality and Social Psychology, 1,* 659–663.

Byrne, D., & Wong, T. J. (1962). Racial prejudice, interpersonal attraction, and assumed dissimilarity of attitudes. *Journal of Abnormal and Social Psychology, 65,* 246–253.

Cain, W. S. (1981, July). Educating your nose. *Psychology Today,* pp. 48–56.

Calder, B. J., Insko, C. A., & Yandell, B. (1974). The relation of cognitive and memorial processes to persuasion in simulated jury trial. *Journal of Applied Social Psychology, 4,* 62–92.

Calhoun, J. B. (1962). Population density and social pathology. *Scientific American, 206,* 139–148.

Campbell, A. (1975, May). The American way of mating: Marriage si, children only maybe. *Psychology Today,* pp. 39–42.

Campbell, A. (1976). Subjective measures of well-being. *American Psychologist, 31,* 117–124.

Campos, J. L., Langer, A., & Krowitz, A. (1970). Cardiac responses on the visual cliff in prelocomotor human infants. *Science, 170,* 196–197.

Canavan-Gumpert, D., Garner, K., & Gumpert, P. (1978). *The success-fearing personality.* Lexington, MA: D. C. Heath.

Caplan, P. J., MacPherson, G. M., & Tobin, P. (1985). Do sex-related differences in spatial abilities exist? A multilevel critique with new data. *American Psychologist, 40,* 786–799.

Carey, G., & Gottesman, I. I. (1981). Twin and family studies of anxiety, phobic, and obsessive disorders. In D. F. Klein & J. Rabkin (Eds.), *Anxiety: New research and changing concepts.* New York: Raven Press.

Carlson, N. R. (1977). *Physiology of behavior.* Boston: Allyn and Bacon.

Carmen, E. H., Russo, N. F., & Miller, J. B. (1981). Inequality and women's mental health: An overview. *American Journal of Psychiatry, 138,* 1319–1330.

Carroll, J. B., & Horn, J. L. (1981). On the scientific basis of ability testing. *American Psychologist, 36,* 1012–1020.

Carroll, J. L. & Rest, J. R. (1982). Moral development. In B. B. Wolman (Ed.), *Handbook of developmental psychology* (pp. 434–451). Englewood Cliffs, NJ: Prentice-Hall.

Carroll, J. M., Thomas, J. C., & Malhotra, A. (1980). Presentation and representation in design problem solving. *British Journal of Psychology, 71,* 143–153.

Carson, R. C., Butcher, J. N. & Coleman, J. C. (1988). *Abnormal psychology and modern life* (8th ed.). Glenview, IL: Scott, Foresman.

Caspi, A., & Elder, G. H., Jr. (1986). Life satisfaction in old age: Linking social psychology and history. *Journal of Psychology and Aging, 1,* 18–26.

Catania, A. C., & Cutts, D. (1963). Experimental control of superstitious responding in humans. *Journal of the Experimental Analysis of Behavior, 6,* 203–208.

Cates, W., Jr., & Rauh, J. L. (1985). Adolescent and sexually transmitted diseases: An expanding problem. *Journal of Adolescent Health Care, 6,* 1–5.

Cattell, R. B. (1965). *The scientific analysis of personality.* Baltimore: Penguin.

Cattell, R. B. (1971). *Abilities: Their structure, growth, and action.* Boston: Houghton-Mifflin.

Cattell, R. B., & Kline, P. (1977). *The specific analysis of personality and motivation.* New York: Academic Press.

Chaiken, S., & Eagly, A. H. (1976). Communication modality as a determinant of message persuasiveness and message comprehensibility. *Journal of Personality and Social Psychology, 34,* 605–614.

Chaiken, S., & Stangor, C. (1987). Attitudes and attitude change. *Annual Review of Psychology, 38,* 575–630.

Chaikin, A. L., & Darley, J. M. (1973). Victim or perpetrator?: Defensive attribution of responsibility and the need for order and justice. *Journal of Personality and Social Psychology, 25,* 268–275.

Chase, W. G., & Ericsson, K. A. (1981). Skilled memory. In J. Anderson (Ed.), *Cognitive skills and their acquisition.* Hillsdale, NJ: Erlbaum.

Chase, W. G., & Simon, H. A. (1973). Perception in chess. *Cognitive Psychology, 4,* 55–81.

Chavis, D. M., Stucky, P. E., & Wandersman, A. (1983). Returning basic research to the community. *American Psychologist, 38,* 424–434.

Cherry, C. (1966). *On human communication: A review, a survey, and a criticism* (2nd ed). Cambridge, MA: M.I.T. Press.

Chomsky, N. (1957). *Syntactic structures.* The Hague: Mouton.

Chomsky, N. (1965). *Aspects of the theory of syntax.* Cambridge, MA: M.I.T. Press.

Christensen, F. (1986). Pornography: The other side. Unpublished paper, University of Alberta.

Chumlea, W. C. (1982). Physical growth in adolescence. In B. B. Wolman (Ed.), *Handbook of developmental psychology* (pp. 471–485). Englewood Cliffs, NJ: Prentice-Hall.

Cialdini, R. B., Cacioppo, J. T., Bassett, R., & Miller, J. A. (1978). Lowball procedure for producing compliance: Commitment then cost. *Journal of Personality and Social Psychology, 36,* 463–476.

Cialdini, R. B., Vincent, J. E., Lewis, S. K., Catalan, J., Wheeler, D., & Darby, B. L. (1975). A reciprocal concessions procedure for inducing compliance: The door-in-the-face technique. *Journal of Personality and Social Psychology, 21,* 206–215.

Clanan, A. D. (1966). Sexual difficulties after 50, a panel discussion. *Canadian Medical Association Journal,* 207–219

Clark, R. D., & Word, L. E. (1974). Where is the apathetic bystander? Situational characteristics of the emergency. *Journal of Personality and Social Psychology, 29,* 279–287.

Clarke-Stewart, K. A. (1989). Infant day care, maligned or malignant? *American Psychologist, 44*, 266–273.

Clarren, S. K., & Smith, D. (1978). The fetal alcohol syndrome. *New England Journal of Medicine, 298*, 1063–1067.

Cleary, P. D. (1987). Gender differences in stress-related disorders. In R. C. Barnett, L. Biener, & G. K. Baruch (Eds.), *Gender and stress* (pp. 39–71). New York: The Free Press.

Clore, G. L., Bray, R. B., Atkin, S. M., & Murphy, P. (1978). Interracial attitudes and behavior at a summer camp. *Journal of Personality and Social Psychology, 36*, 107–116.

Cobb, S., & Rose, R. M. (1973). Hypertension, peptic ulcer, and diabetes in air traffic controllers. *Journal of the American Medical Association, 224*, 489–493.

Cohen, D. B. (1973). Sex, role orientation and dream recall. *Journal of Abnormal Psychology, 82*, 246–252.

Cohen, D. B. (1974, May). Repression is not the demon who conceals and hoards our forgotten dreams. *Psychology Today*, pp. 50–54.

Cohen, D. B. (1976). Dreaming: Experimental investigation of representation and adaptive properties. In G. Schwartz & D. Shapiro (Eds.), *Consciousness and self-regulation*. New York: Plenum.

Cohen, L. B. (1979). Our developing knowledge of infant perception and cognition. *American Psychologist, 34*, 894–899.

Cohen, M. L., Seghorn, T., & Calmas, W. (1969). Sociometric study of the sex offender. *Journal of Abnormal Psychology, 74*, 249–255.

Cohen, R. A. (1969). Conceptual styles, culture conflict, and nonverbal tests. *American Anthropologist, 71*, 828–856.

Cole, J., & Davis, J. M. (1975). Anti-anxiety drugs. In S. Arieti (Ed.), *American handbook of psychiatry* (Vol. 5). New York: Basic Books.

Cole, N. S. (1981). Bias in testing. *American Psychologist, 36*, 1067–1077.

Colegrove, F. W. (1982; orig. pub. 1899). Individual memories. *American Journal of Psychology, 10*, 228–255. Reprinted in U. Neisser. (Ed.), *Memory observed: Remembering in natural contexts*. San Francisco: Freeman.

Coleman, J. C. (1979). *Contemporary psychology and effective behavior* (4th ed.). Glenview, IL: Scott, Foresman.

Comfort, A. (1976). *A good age*. New York: Crown.

Condry, J., & Condry, S. (1976). Sex differences: A study in the eye of the beholder. *Child Development, 47*, 812–819.

Conger, J. J. (1977). *Adolescence and youth: Psychological development in a changing world* (2nd ed.). New York: Harper & Row.

Conger, J. J. (1985). Adolescence: A time for becoming. In National Mental Health Association, *The prevention of mental-emotional disabilities*. Alexandria, VA: NMHA.

Conger, J. J., & Petersen, A. C. (1984). *Adolescence and youth* (3rd ed.). New York: Harper & Row.

Conrad, R. (1972). Short-term memory in the deaf: A test for speech coding. *British Journal of Psychology, 63*, 173–180.

Conway, F., & Siegelman, J. (1980). *Snapping*. New York: Dell.

Cook, M., Mineka, S., Wolkenstein, B., & Laitsch, K. (1985). Observational conditioning of snake fear in unrelated rhesus monkeys. *Journal of Abnormal Psychology, 94*, 591–610.

Cook, S. W. (1976). Ethical issues in the conduct of research in social relations. In P. Nejelski (Ed.), *Social research in conflict with law and ethics*. Cambridge, MA: Ballinger.

Cookerly, J. R. (1980). Does marital therapy do any lasting good? *Journal of Marital and Family Therapy, 6*, 393–397.

Coombs, C. H., Coombs, L. C., & McClelland, G. H. (1975). Preference scales for number and sex of children. *Population Studies, 29*, 273–298.

Cooper, A. J. (1969). A clinical study of coital anxiety in male potency disorders. *Journal of Psychosomatic Research, 13*, 143–147.

Cooper, J. (1971). Personal responsibility and dissonance. *Journal of Personality and Social Psychology, 18*, 354–363.

Cooper, J., & Croyle, R. T. (1984). Attitudes and attitude change. *Annual Review of Psychology, 35*, 395–426.

Cooper, R., & Zubek, J. (1958). Effects of enriched and restricted early environments on the learning ability of bright and dull rats. *Canadian Journal of Psychology, 12*, 159–164.

Coren, S., Porac, C., & Ward, L. M. (1984). *Sensation and perception* (2nd ed.). Orlando, FL: Academic Press.

Costa, P. T., & McCrae, R. R. (1980). Still stable after all these years: Personality as a key to some issues in adulthood and old age. In P. B. Baltes & O. G. Brim (Eds.), *Lifespan development and behavior* (Vol. 3). New York: Academic Press.

Costanzo, M., Archer, D., Aronson, E., & Pettigrew, T. (1986). Energy conservation behavior: The difficult path from information to action. *American Psychologist, 41*, 521–528.

Cowen, E. L. (1982). Help is where you find it: Four informal helping groups. *American Psychologist, 37*, 385–395.

Coyne, J. C. (1976). Depression and the responses of others. *Journal of Abnormal Psychology, 85*, 186–193.

Coyne, J. C. (1982). A critique of cognitions as causal entities with particular reference to depression. *Cognitive Therapy and Research, 6*, 3–13.

Craig, G. J. (1989). *Human development* (5th ed.). Englewood Cliffs, NJ: Prentice-Hall.

Craik, F. I. M., & Watkins, M. J. (1973). The role of rehearsal in short-term memory. *Journal of Verbal Learning and Verbal Behavior, 12*, 599–607.

Crick, F., & Mitchison, G. (1983). The function of dream sleep. *Nature, 304* (5922), 111–114.

Crockenberg, S. B. (1980). Creativity tests: A boon or boon-doggle for education? *Review of Educational Research, 42*, 27–44.

Crockenberg, S. B. (1985). Professional support and care of infants by adolescent mothers in England and the United States. *Journal of Pediatric Psychology, 20*, 413–428.

Cronbach, L. J. (1970). *Essentials of psychological testing*. New York: Harper & Row.

Crook, T., & Eliot, J. (1980). Parental death during childhood and adult depression: A critical review of the literature. *Psychological Bulletin, 87*, 252–259.

Crutchfield, R. A. (1955). Conformity and character. *American Psychologist, 10*, 191–198.

Cruz-Coke, R. (1971). Genetic aspects of alcoholism. In Y. Israel & J. Mardones (Eds.), *Biological basis of alcoholism*. New York: Wiley.

Cumming, E., & Henry, W. E. (1961). *Growing old: The process of disengagement*. New York: Basic Books.

Cunningham, S. (1983, June). Animal activists rally in streets, urge Congress to tighten laws. *APA Monitor*, pp. 1, 27.

Curran, J. W., Jaffe, H. W., Hardy, A. M., Morgan, W. M., Selik, R. M., & Dondero, T. J. (1988). Epidemiology of HIV infection and AIDS in the United States. *Science, 239*, 610–616.

Cutler, B. L., & Penrod, S. D. (1988). Improving the reliability of eyewitness identification: Lineup construction and presentation. *Journal of Applied Psychology, 73*, 281–290.

Cutrona, C., Russell, D., & Rose, J. (1986). Social support and adaptation to stress in the elderly. *Journal of Psychology and Aging, 1*, 47–54.

Dabbs, J. M., & Leventhal, H. (1966). Effects of varying the recommendations in a fear-arousing communication. *Journal of Personality and Social Psychology, 4*, 525–531.

Damasio, Tranel, Damasio (May 1988). *Neurology*, as reported by S. Blakeslee in the *New York Times*, May 4, 1988.

D'Amato, M. R. (1974). Derived motives. *Annual Review of Psychology, 25*, 83–106.

Daniel, W. F., & Crovitz, H. F. (1983). Acute memory impairment following electroconvulsive therapy: 2. Effects of electrode placement. *Acta Psychiatrica Scandinavica, 67,* 57–68.

Daniell, H. W. (1971). Smokers' wrinkles: A study in the epidemiology of "Crow's feet." *Annals of Internal Medicine, 75,* 873–880.

Darwin, Charles. (1872). *The expression of the emotions in man and animals.* London: John Murray.

Datan, N., Rodeheaver, D., & Hughes, F. (1987). Adult development and aging. *Annual Review of Psychology, 38,* 153–180.

Davis, D. L. (1962). Normal drinking in recovered alcohol addicts. *Quarterly Journal of Studies of Alcohol, 23,* 94–104.

Davis, M. H., & Stephan, W. G. (1980). Attributions for exam performance. *Journal of Applied Social Psychology, 10,* 235–248.

Davitz, J. (1952). The effects of previous training on postfrustration behavior. *Journal of Abnormal and Social Psychology, 47,* 309–315.

Dean, S. R. (1970). Is there an ultraconscious? *Canadian Psychiatric Association Journal, 15,* 57–61.

Deaux, K. (1985). Sex and gender. *Annual Review of Psychology, 36,* 49–81.

Deaux, K., & Wrightsman, L. (1984). *Social psychology in the 80s* (4th ed.). Monterey, CA: Brooks/Cole.

de Beauvoir, S. (1972). *The coming of age* (Patrick O'Brian, trans.). New York: Putnam.

DeCasper, A. J., & Spence, M. J. (1986). Prenatal maternal speech influences newborns' perception of speech sounds. *Infant Behavior and Development, 9,* 133–150.

deCharms, R. (1968). *Personal causation.* New York: Academic Press.

DeFreitas, B., & Schwartz, G. (1979). Effects of caffeine in chronic psychiatric patients. *American Journal of Psychiatry, 136,* 1337–1338.

de Groot, A. D. (1965). Perception and memory versus thought: Some old ideas and recent findings. In B. Kleinmuntz (Ed.), *Problem solving: Research, method, and theory.* New York: Wiley.

de Groot, A. D. (1965). *Thought and choice in chess.* The Hague: Mouton.

Deikman, A. J. (1973). Deautomatization and the mystic experience. In R. E. Ornstein (Ed.), *The nature of human consciousness.* San Francisco: Freeman.

Dekker, E., Pelser, H. E., & Groen, J. (1957). Conditioning as a cause of asthmatic attacks. *Journal of Psychosomatic Research, 2,* 97–108.

DeLong, F., & Levy, B. I. (1974). A model of attention describing the cognitive effects of marihuana. In L. L. Miller (Ed.), *Marijuana: Effects on human behavior.* New York: Academic Press.

Dember, W. N. (1965). The new look in motivation. *American Scientist, 53,* 409–427.

Dember, W. N., Earl, R. W., & Paradise, N. (1957). Response by rats to differential stimulus complexity. *Journal of Comparative and Physiological Psychology, 50,* 514–518.

Dement, W. C., (1965). An essay on dreams: The role of physiology in understanding their nature. In F. Barron (Ed.), *New directions in psychology* (Vol. 2). New York: Holt, Rinehart and Winston.

Dement, W. C. (1974). *Some must watch while some must sleep.* San Francisco: Freeman.

Dement, W. C., Cohen, H., Ferguson, J., & Zarcone, V. (1970). A sleep researcher's odyssey: The function and clinical significance of REM sleep. In L. Madow and L. H. Snow (Eds.), *The psychodynamic implications of the physiological studies of dreams.* Springfield, IL: Charles C. Thomas.

Dement, W. C., & Wolpert, E. (1958). Relation of eye movements, body motility, and external stimuli to dream content. *Journal of Experimental Psychology, 55,* 543–553.

Denney, N. W. (1982). Aging and cognitive changes. In B. B. Wolman (Ed.), *Handbook of developmental psychology* (pp. 807–827). Englewood Cliffs, NJ: Prentice-Hall.

Dennis, W., & Dennis, M. G. (1940). The effect of cradling practices upon the onset of walking in Hopi children. *Journal of Genetic Psychology, 56,* 77–86.

Dermer, M., & Thiel, D. J. (1975). When beauty may fail. *Journal of Personality and Social Psychology, 31,* 1168–1176.

DeValois, R. L., & DeValois, K. K. (1975). Neural coding of color. In E. C. Carterette & M. P. Friedman (Eds.), *Handbook of perception: Seeing* (Vol. 5). New York: Academic Press.

deVries, H. A. (1986). *Fitness after 50.* New York: Scribner's.

Diamond, S. (1977). Francis Galton and American psychology. *Annals of the New York Academy of Sciences, 291,* 47–45.

Dickinson, A., & Mackintosh, N. J. (1978). Classical conditioning in animals. *Annual Review of Psychology, 29,* 587–612.

DiFranco, D., Muir, D. W., & Dodwell, P. C. (1978). Reaching in very young infants. *Perception, 7,* 385–392.

Digman, J. M., & Takemoto-Chock, N. K. (1981). Factors in the natural language of personality: Re-analysis, comparison, and interpretation of six major studies. *Multivariate Behavioral Research, 16,* 149–170.

DiMatteo, M. R., & Friedman, H. S. (1982). *Social psychology and medicine.* Cambridge, MA: Oelgeschlager, Gunn, & Hain.

Dion, K. K., Berscheid, E., & Walster, E. (1972). What is beautiful is good. *Journal of Personality and Social Psychology, 24,* 285–290.

Dirks, J., & Gibson, E. (1977). Infants' perception of similarity between live people and their photographs. *Child Development, 48,* 124–130.

Dobzhansky, T. (1973, December). Differences are not deficits. *Psychology Today,* pp. 97–101.

Doherty, W. J., & Jacobson, N. S. (1982). Marriage and the family. In B. B. Wolman (Ed.), *Handbook of developmental psychology* (pp. 667–680). Englewood Cliffs, NJ: Prentice-Hall.

Dohrenwend, B. P., & Dohrenwend, B. S. (1982). Perspectives on the past and future of psychiatric epidemiology: The 1981 Rema Lapouse Lecture. *American Journal of Public Health, 72,* 1271–1279.

Dohrenwend, B. P., Dohrenwend, B. S., Gould, M. S., Link, B., Neugebauer, R., & Wunsch-Hitzig, R. (1980). *Mental illness in the United States: Epidemiological estimates.* New York: Praeger.

Dollard, J., & Miller, N. E. (1950). *Personality and psychotherapy.* New York: McGraw-Hill.

Domjan, M. (1987). Animal learning comes of age. *American Psychologist, 42,* 556–564.

Donchin, E. (1987). Can the mind be read in the brain waves? In F. Farley & C. Null (Eds.), *Using psychological science: Making the public case,* pp. 25–42. Washington, DC: The Federation of Behavioral, Psychological, and Cognitive Sciences.

Donnerstein, E., & Wilson, D. W. (1976). The effects of noise and perceived control upon ongoing and subsequent aggressive behavior. *Journal of Personality and Social Psychology, 34,* 774–781.

Doob, A. N., & Wood, L. (1972). Catharsis and aggression: The effects of annoyance and retaliation on aggressive behavior. *Journal of Personality and Social Psychology, 22,* 156–162.

Doty, R. L., Shaman, P., Applebaum, S. L., Giberson, R., Siksorski, L., & Rosenberg, L. (1984). Smell identification ability: Changes with age. *Science, 226,* 1441–1443.

Douvan, E., & Adelson, J. (1966). *The adolescent experience,* New York: Wiley.

Dreyfus, H. L., & Dreyfus, S. E. (1986). *Mind over machine.* New York: Free Press.

Dreyer, P. H. (1982). Sexuality during adolescence. In B. B. Wolman (Ed.), *Handbook of developmental psychology* (pp. 559–601). Englewood Cliffs, NJ: Prentice-Hall.

Dubois, P. M. (1981). *The hospice way of death.* New York: Human Sciences Press.

Dunkle, T. (1982, April). The sound of silence. *Science '82,* pp. 30–33.

Dunphy, D. C. (1963). The social structure of urban adolescent peer groups. *Sociometry, 26,* 230–246.

Dweck, C. S., & Reppucci, N. D. (1973). Learned helplessness and reinforcement responsibility in children. *Journal of Personality and Social Psychology, 25,* 109–116.

Eagly, A. H. (1978). Sex differences in influenceability. *Psychological Bulletin, 85,* 86–116.

Eagly, A. H. (1983). Gender and social influence: A social psychological analysis. *American Psychologist, 38,* 971–981.

Eagly, A. H. (1987). Reporting sex differences. *American Psychologist, 42,* 756–757.

Eagly, A. H., & Carli, L. L. (1981). Sex researchers and sex-typed communications as determinants of sex differences in influenceability: A meta-analysis of social influence studies. *Psychological Bulletin, 90,* 1–20.

Ebbinghaus, H. (1913). *Memory* (H. A. Ruger & C. E. Bussenius, trans.). New York: Teachers College/Columbia University.

Eccles, J. C. (1983). Attributional processes as mediators of sex differences in achievement. *Journal of Educational Equality and Leadership, 3,* 19–27.

Eccles, J. S., & Jacobs, J. E. (1986). Social forces shape math attitudes and performance. *Signs, 11,* 367–389.

Eimas, P. D., & Tartter, V. C. (1979). The development of speech perception. In H. W. Reese & L. P. Lipsitt (Eds.), *Advances in child development and behavior* (Vol. 13). New York: Academic Press.

Einhorn, H. J. (1980). Learning from experience and suboptimal rules in decision making. In T. S. Wallsten (Ed.), *Cognitive processes in choice and decision behavior.* Hillsdale, NJ: Erlbaum.

Eisdorfer, C. (1983). Conceptual models of aging: The challenge of a new frontier. *American Psychologist, 38,* 197–202.

Eisenberg, N., & Lennon, R. (1983). Sex differences in empathy and related capacities. *Psychological Bulletin, 94,* 100–131.

Elkind, D. (1968). Cognitive development in adolescence. In J. F. Adams (Ed.), *Understanding adolescence.* Boston: Allyn & Bacon.

Elkind, D. (1969). Egocentrism in adolescence. In R. E. Grinder (Ed.), *Studies in adolescence* (2nd ed.). New York: Macmillan.

Ellis, A. (1973). *Humanistic psychotherapy: The rational emotive approach.* New York: Julian Press.

Ellis, A., & Harper, R. A. (1975). *A new guide to rational living.* No. Hollywood, CA: Wilshire Book Co.

Ellsworth, P. C. (1977). From abstract ideas to concrete instances: Some guidelines for choosing natural research settings. *American Psychologist, 32,* 604–615.

Elstein, A. A., Shulman, L. S., & Sprafka, S. A. (1978). *Medical problem solving.* Cambridge, MA: Harvard University Press.

Engen, T. (1973). The sense of smell. *Annual Review of Psychology, 24,* 187–206.

Engen, T. (1982). *The perception of odors.* New York: Academic Press.

Entwisle, D. R., & Hayduk, L. A. (1978). *Too great expectations.* Baltimore: Johns Hopkins University Press.

Epstein, A. N., Fitzsimmons, J. T. & Simons, B. (1969). Drinking caused by the intracranial injection of angiotensin into the rat. *Journal of Physiology, 200,* 98–100.

Epstein, R., Kirshnit, C. E., Lanza, R. P., & Rubin, L. C. (1984). "Insight" in the pigeon: Antecedents and determinants of an intelligent performance. *Nature, 308,* 61–62.

Epstein, S. (1962). The measurement of drive and conflict in humans: Theory and experiment. In M. R. Jones (Ed.), *Nebraska symposium on motivation.* Lincoln: University of Nebraska Press.

Ericsson, K. A., & Chase, W. G. (1982). Exceptional memory. *American Scientist, 70,* 607–615.

Erikson, E. H. (1963). *Childhood and society* (2nd ed.). New York: Norton.

Erikson, E. H. (1968). *Identity: Youth in crisis.* New York: Norton.

Erikson, E. H. (1982). *The life cycle completed: A review.* New York: Norton.

Eron, L. D. (1982). Parent-child interaction, television violence, and aggression of children. *American Psychologist, 37,* 197–211.

Evans, D. R., Newcombe, R. G., & Campbell, H. (1979). Maternal smoking habits and congenital malformations: A population study. *British Medical Journal, 2,* 171–173.

Evans, L. I., Rozelle, R. M., Lasater, T. M., Dembroski, R. M., & Allen, B. P. (1970). Fear arousal, persuasion and actual vs. implied behavioral change: New perspective utilizing a real-life dental hygiene program. *Journal of Personality and Social Psychology, 16,* 220–227.

Exner, J. E., & Weiner, I. B. (1982). *The Rorschach: A comprehensive system.* New York: Wiley.

Eyer, J. (1977). Prosperity as a cause of death. *International Journal of Health Services, 7,* 125–150.

Eysenck, H. J. (1952). The effects of psychotherapy: An evaluation. *Journal of Consulting and Clinical Psychology, 16,* 319–324.

Eysenck, H. J. (1970). *The structure of human personality* (3rd ed.). London: Methuen.

Eysenck, H. J. (1985). *The decline and fall of the Freudian empire.* London: Pelican.

Eysenck, H. J., Wakefield, J. A., Jr., & Friedman, A. F. (1983). Diagnosis and clinical assessment: The DSM-III. *Annual Review of Psychology, 34,* 167–193.

Fagan, J. F., III (1973). Infant's delayed recognition: Memory and forgetting. *Journal of Experimental Child Psychology, 16,* 424–450.

Fagot, B. I. (1974). Sex differences in toddler's behavior and parental reactions. *Developmental Psychology, 10,* 554–558.

Fairweather, G. W., Sanders, D. H., Maynard, H., & Cressler, D. L. (1969). *Community life for the mentally ill: An alternative to institutional care.* Chicago: Aldine.

Fallon, A., & Rozin, P. (1985). Sex differences in perceptions of desirable body states. *Journal of Abnormal Psychology, 84,* 102–105.

Fantz, R. L. (1961). The origin of form perception. *Scientific American, 205,* 450–463.

Fantz, R. L. (1965). Visual perception from birth as shown by pattern selectivity. *Annals of the New York Academy of Sciences, 118,* 793–814.

Farber, Susan. (1981, January). Telltale behavior of twins. *Psychology Today,* pp. 58–62, 79–80.

Fast, J. (1970). *Body language.* New York: M. Evans.

Federal Bureau of Investigation (FBI) (1984). *Crime in the United States (Uniform crime reports).* Washington, DC.

Feingold, A. (1988). Cognitive gender differences are disappearing. *American Psychologist, 43,* 95–103.

Feinson, M. C. (1986). Aging widows and widowers: Are there mental health differences? *International Journal of Aging and Human Development, 23,* 244–255.

Fengler, A. P. (1976). Productivity and representation: The elderly legislator in state politics. Paper presented at the meeting of the Gerontological Society, New York.

Ferguson, C. A., & Macken, M. A. (1983). The role of play in phonological development. In K. E. Nelson (Ed.), *Children's language* (Vol. 4). Hillsdale, NJ: Erlbaum.

Feshbach, S., & Weiner, B. (1982). *Personality.* Lexington, MA: D. C. Heath.

Festinger, L. (1957). *A theory of cognitive dissonance.* Evanston, IL: Row, Peterson.

Festinger, L., Schachter, S., & Back, K. (1950). *Social pressures in informal groups: A study of human factors in housing.* New York: Harper & Row.

Fiedler, F. E. (1967). *A theory of leadership effectiveness.* New York: McGraw-Hill.

Fiedler, F. E. (1981). Leadership effectiveness. *Behavioral Scientist, 24,* 619–623.

Finkelstein, P., Wenegrat, B., & Yalom, I. (1982). Large group awareness training. *Annual Review of Psychology, 33,* 515–539.

Fischman, J. (1985, September). Mapping the mind. *Psychology Today,* pp. 18–19.

Fishbein, M., & Ajzen, I. (1975). *Belief, attitude, intention and behavior: An introduction to theory and research.* Reading, MA: Addison-Wesley.

Fisher, J. D., & Byrne, D. (1975). Too close for comfort: Sex differences in response to invasions of personal space. *Journal of Personality and Social Psychology, 32,* 15–21.

Fisher, S., & Greenberg, R. P. (1985). *The scientific credibility of Freud's theories and therapy.* New York: Columbia University Press.

Fishman, D. B. & Neigher, W. D. (1982). American psychology in the eighties. *American Psychologist, 37,* 533–546.

Fitch, J. H. (1962). Men convicted of sexual offenses against children. *British Journal of Criminology, 3,* 18–37.

Flavell, J. F. (1986). The development of children's knowledge about the appearance-reality distinction. *American Psychologist, 41,* 418–425.

Fletcher, C. & Doll, R. (1969). A survey of doctor's attitudes to smoking. *British Journal of Social and Preventive Medicine, 23,* 145–153.

Flexser, A. J., & Tulving, E. (1978). Retrieval independence in recognition and recall. *Psychological Review, 85,* 153–171.

Fliegler, L. A., & Bish, C. E. (1959). The gifted and talented. *Review of Educational Research, 29,* 408–450.

Flynn, J. R. (1988). The decline and rise of scholastic aptitude scores. *American Psychologist, 43,* 479–480.

Foa, E. B., Steketke, G., & Young, M. C. (1984). Agoraphobia: Phenomenological aspects, associated characteristics, and theoretical considerations. *Clinical Psychology Review, 4,* 431–457.

Fogelman, E., & Wiener, V. L. (1985, August). The few, the brave, the noble. *Psychology Today,* pp. 60–65.

Fontana, A. (1966). Familial etiology of schizophrenia: Is a scientific methodology possible? *Psychological Bulletin, 66,* 214–228.

Fouts, R. S. (1973). Acquisition and testing of gestural signs in four young chimpanzees. *Science, 180,* 978–980.

Fox, A. J., & Adelstein, A. M. (1978). Occupational mortality: Work or way of life. *Journal of Epidemiology and Community Health, 32,* 73–78.

Fox, B. (1983). Current theory of psychogenic effects on cancer incidence and prognosis. *Journal of Psychosocial Oncology, 1,* 17–32.

Fox, L. H. (1981). Identification of the academically gifted. *American Psychologist, 36,* 1103–1111.

Fraser, C. (1971). Group risk-taking and group polarization. *European Journal of Social Psychology, 1,* 7–30.

Frederickson, N. (1986). Toward a broader conception of human intelligence. *American Psychologist, 41,* 445–452.

Freed, W. J., Morihisa, J. M., Spoor, E., Hoffer, B. J., Olson, L., Seiger, A., & Wyatt, R. J. (1981). Transplanted adrenal chromaffin cells in rat brain reduce lesion-induced rotational behavior. *Nature, 292,* 351–352.

Freedman, J. L. & Fraser, S. C. (1966). Compliance without pressure: The foot-in-the-door technique. *Journal of Personality and Social Psychology, 4,* 195–202.

Freize, I., Parsons, J., Johnson, P., Ruble, D., & Zellman, G. (1978). *Women and sex roles: A social-psychological perspective.* New York: Norton.

Frenzel, L. E., Jr. (1987). *Crash course in artificial intelligence and expert systems.* Indianapolis, IN: Howard W. Sams & Co.

Freud, S. (1900). *The interpretation of dreams.* In J. Strachey (Ed.), *The standard edition of the complete psychological works of Sigmund Freud* (Vol. 5). London: Hogarth Press.

Freudenberger, H. J. (1983). The public lectures. *APA Monitor,* p. 24.

Freudenberger, H. J., & Richelson, G. (1980). *Burnout: The high cost of high achievement.* New York: Bantam.

Friedan, B. (1963). *The feminine mystique.* New York: Norton.

Friedman, H. S., & DiMatteo, M. R. (1989). *Health psychology.* Englewood Cliffs, NJ: Prentice-Hall.

Friedman, M., & Rosenman, R. H. (1974). *Type A behavior and your heart.* New York: Knopf.

Frieze, I., Fisher, J., Hanusa, B., McHugh, M., & Valle, V. (1979). Attributions of success and failure in internal and external barriers to achievement in women. In J. Sherman & F. Denmark (Eds.), *Psychology of women: Future of research.* New York: Psychological Dimensions.

Fromm, E. (1970). Age regression with unexpected reappearance of a repressed childhood language. *International Journal of Clinical and Experimental Hypnosis, 18,* 79–88.

Frumkin, B., & Ainsfield, M. (1977). Semantic and surface codes in the memory of deaf children. *Cognitive Psychology, 9,* 475–493.

Funkenstein, D. H., King, S. H., & Drolette, M. (1953). The experimental evocation of stress. In *Symposium on stress.* Division of Medical Sciences of the National Research Council and Army Medical Services Graduate School of Walter Reed Army Medical Center. Washington, DC: Government Printing Office.

Furstenberg, F. F. (1983). *Unplanned parenthood: The social consequences of teenage child rearing.* New York: Free Press.

Furstenberg, F. F., & Brooks-Gunn, J. (1987). *Adolescent mothers in later life.* New York: Cambridge University Press.

Furstenberg, F. F., Jr., Brooks-Gunn, J., & Chase-Lansdale, L. (1989). Teenaged pregnancy and childbearing. *American Psychologist, 44,* 313–320.

Gager, N., & Schurr, C. (1976). *Sexual assault: Confronting rape in America.* New York: Grosset & Dunlap.

Galanter, M. (1984). Self-help large-group therapy for alcoholism: A controlled study. *Alcoholism: Clinical and Experimental Research, 8,* 16–23.

Gallistel, C. R. (1981). Bell, Magendie, and the proposals to restrict the use of animals in neurobehavioral research. *American Psychologist, 36,* 357–360.

Garcia, J., Hankins, W. G., & Rusiniak, K. W. (1974). Behavioral regulation of the milieu interne in man and rat. *Science, 185,* 824–831.

Garcia, J., Kimeldorf, D. J., Hunt, E. L., & Davies, B. P. (1956). Food and water consumption of rats during exposure to gamma radiation. *Radiation Research, 4,* 33–41.

Garcia, J., & Koelling, R. A. (1966). Relation of cue to consequence in avoidance learning. *Psychonomic Science, 4,* 123–124.

Gardner, H. (1981, February). How the split brain gets a joke. *Psychology Today,* pp. 74–78.

Gardner, H. (1982). *Developmental psychology* (2nd Ed.). Boston: Little, Brown.

Gardner, H. (1983, May). Prodigies' progress. *Psychology Today,* pp. 75–79.

Gardner, R. A., & Gardner, B. T. (1969). Teaching sign language to a chimpanzee. *Science, 165,* 664–672.

Gardner, R. A., & Gardner, B. T. (1975). Evidence for sentence constituents in the early utterances of child and chimpanzee. *Journal of Experimental Psychology: General, 3,* 244–267.

Gardner, R. A., & Gardner, B. T. (1977). Comparative psychology and language acquisition. In K. Salzinger & R. Denmark (Eds.), *Psychology: The state of the art. Annals of the New York Academy of Sciences.*

Garfield, S. L. (1981). Psychotherapy: A 40-year appraisal. *American Psychologist, 36,* 174–183.

Garfield, S. L. (Ed.) (1983). Special section: Meta-analysis and psychotherapy. *Journal of Consulting and Clinical Psychology, 51,* 3–75.

Garfinkel, P. E., & Garner, D. M. (1982). *Anorexia nervosa: A multidimensional perspective.* New York: Brunner/Mazel.

Garner, D. M., Garfinkel, P. E., & Bemis, K. M. (1982). A multidimensional psychotherapy for anorexia nervosa. *International Journal of Eating Disorders, 1,* 3–64.

Garrett, C. J., & Langer, P. (1983). Effects of instructions at encoding on constructive memory processes: A small-n approach. *Psychological Reports, 52,* 435–444.

Gazzaniga, M. S. (1983). Right hemisphere language following brain bisection. *American Psychologist, 38,* 525–537.

Gazzangia, M. S. (1985). The social brain. *Psychology Today,* (November), 29–38.

Geldard, F. A. (1972). *The human senses* (2nd ed.). New York: Wiley.

Gelman, R. (1979). Preschool thought. *American Psychologist, 34,* 900–905.

Gentner, D., & Stevens, A. L. (1983). *Mental models.* Hillsdale, NJ: Erlbaum.

Gergen, K. J. (1973). The codification of research ethics—views of a Doubting Thomas. *American Psychologist, 28,* 907–912.

Getzels, J. W., & Jackson, P. (1962). *Creativity and intelligence.* New York: Wiley.

Giambra, L. (1974, December). Daydreams: The backburner of the mind. *Psychology Today,* pp. 66–68.

Gibson, E. J., Shurcliff, A., & Yonas, A. (1970). Utilization of spelling patterns by deaf and hearing subjects. In H. Levin & J. P. Williams (Eds.), *Basic studies on reading.* New York: Basic Books.

Gilbert, E. H., & DeBlassie, R. R. (1984). Anorexia nervosa: Adolescent starvation by choice. *Adolescence, 19,* 839–853.

Gilligan, C. (1982). *In a different voice: Psychological theory and women's development.* Cambridge, MA: Harvard University Press.

Ginsberg, E. (1972). Toward a theory of occupational choice: A restatement. *Vocational Guidance Quarterly, 20,* 169–176.

Ginsberg, H. (1972). *The myth of the deprived child.* Englewood Cliffs, NJ: Prentice-Hall.

Gist, R., & Stolz, S. (1982). Mental health promotion and the media. *American Psychologist, 37,* 1136–1139.

Glaser, R., & Kiecolt-Glaser, J. (1988). Stress-associated immune suppression and Acquired Immune Deficiency Syndrome (AIDS). In T. P. Bridge, A. F. Mirsky, & F. K. Goodwin (Eds.), *Psychological, neuropsychiatric, and substance abuse aspects of AIDS* (pp. 203–215). New York: Raven Press.

Glass, D. C. (1977). *Behavior patterns, stress and coronary disease.* New York: Wiley.

Glenberg, A., Smith, S. M., & Green, C. (1977). Type 1 rehearsal: Maintenance and more. *Journal of Verbal Learning and Verbal Behavior, 16,* 339–352.

Glucksberg, S., & King, L. J. (1967). Motivated forgetting mediated by implicit verbal chaining: A laboratory analog of repression. *Science, 158,* 517–519.

Gold, P. E., & Delaney, R. L. (1981). ACTH modulation of memory storage processing. In J. L. Martinez, Jr., R. A. Jensen, R. B. Messing, H. Rigter, & J. L. McGaugh (Eds.), *Endogenous peptides and learning and memory processes.* New York: Academic Press.

Goldberg, L. R. (1981). Language and individual differences: The search for universals in personality lexicons. In L. Wheeler (Ed.), *Review of personality and social psychology* (Vol. 2, pp. 141–165). Beverly Hills, CA: Sage.

Goldberg, L. R. (1982). From ace to zombie: Some explorations in the language of personality. In C. D. Spielberger & J. N. Butcher (Eds.), *Advances in personality assessment* (Vol. 1, pp. 203–234). Hillsdale, NJ: Erlbaum.

Golden, G. (1982). Coping with aging: Denial and avoidance in middle-aged care-givers. Unpublished doctoral dissertation, University of California, Berkeley.

Goldenberg, H. (1973). *Contemporary clinical psychology.* Monterey, CA: Brooks/Cole.

Goldsmith, H. H. (1983). Genetic influences on personality from infancy to childhood. *Child Development, 54,* 331–355.

Goldstein, M., & Rodnick, E. (1975). The family's contribution to the etiology of schizophrenia: Current status. *Schizophrenia Bulletin, 14,* 48–63.

Gonzales, M. H., Davis, J. M., Loney, G. L., Lukens, C. K., & Junghans, C. M. (1983). Interactional approach to interpersonal attraction. *Journal of Personality and Social Psychology, 44,* 1192–1197.

Goodwin, D. W., & Guze, S. B. (1984). *Psychiatric diagnosis* (3rd ed.). New York: Oxford University Press.

Gorn, G. J. (1982). The effects of music in advertising on choice behavior: A classical conditioning approach. *Journal of Marketing, 46*(1), 94–101.

Gottesman, I. I., & Shields, J. (1982). *The schizophrenic puzzle.* New York: Cambridge University Press.

Gould, J. L., & Gould, C. G. (1981, May). The instinct to learn. *Science, '81,* pp. 44–50.

Gould, R. L. (1972). The phases of adult life: A study in developmental psychology. *American Journal of Psychiatry, 129,* 521–531.

Gould, R. L. (1978). *Transformations: Growth and change in adult life.* New York: Simon & Schuster.

Graham, J. R., & Lilly, R. S. (1984). *Psychological testing.* Englewood Cliffs, NJ: Prentice-Hall.

Graziadei, P. P. C., Levine, R. R., & Graziadei, G. A. M. (1979). Plasticity of connections of the olfactory sensory neuron: Regeneration into the forebrain following bulbectomy in the neonatal mouse. *Neuroscience, 4,* 713–728.

Greaves, G. B. (1980). Psychosocial aspects of amphetamine and related substance abuse. In J. Caldwell (Ed.), *Amphetamines and related stimulants: Chemical, biological, clinical and sociological aspects.* Boca Raton, FL: CRC Press.

Greenberg, R., & Pearlman, C. (1967). Delirium tremens and dreaming. *American Journal of Psychiatry, 124,* 133–42.

Greenberger, E. (1983). The case of child labor. *American Psychologist, 38,* 104–111.

Greenfield, P. M., & Savage-Rumbaugh, E. S. (1984). Perceived variability and symbol usage: A common language-cognition interface in children and chimpanzees (Pan Troglodytes). *Journal of Comparative Psychology, 98,* 201–218.

Greenfield, P. M., & Smith, J. H. (1976). *The structure of communication in early language development.* New York: Academic Press.

Gregory, R. L. (1978). *Eye and brain: The psychology of seeing* (3rd ed.). New York: McGraw-Hill.

Grief, E. B., & Ulman. K. J. (1982). The psychological impact of menarche on early adolescent females: A review of the literature. *Child Development, 53,* 1413–1430.

Griffiths, R. R., Bigelow, G. E., & Henningfield, J. E. (1980). Similarities in animal and human drug-taking behavior. In N. K. Mello (Ed.), *Advances in substance abuse* (Vol. 1). Greenwich, CT: JAI Press.

Grinker, R. R., & Spiegel, J. P. (1945). *War neurosis.* Philadelphia: Blakiston.

Grinspoon, L. (1977). *Marihuana reconsidered.* Cambridge, MA: Harvard University Press.

Grinspoon, L. (Ed.) (1985). Borderline personality disorder: Part I. The *Harvard Medical School Mental Health Letter, 2*(6), 1–3.

Grinspoon, L., Ewalt, J. R., & Shader, R. I. (1972). *Schizophrenia: Pharmacotherapy and psychotherapy.* Baltimore: Williams & Wilkins.

Grossman, H. J. (Ed.) (1983). *Classification in mental retardation.* Washington, DC: American Association on Mental Deficiency.

Groth, A. N., & Birnbaum, J. J. (1979). *Men who rape: The psychology of the offender.* New York: Plenum.

Groth, A. N., Burgess, A. W., & Holmstrom, L. L. (1977). Rape: Power, anger and sexuality. *American Journal of Psychiatry, 134,* 1239–1243.

Guilford, J. P. (1961). Factorial angles to psychology. *Psychological Review, 68,* 1–20.

Guilford, J. P. (1967). *The nature of human intelligence.* New York: McGraw-Hill.

Gunderson, J. G. (1984). *Borderline personality disorder.* Washington, DC: American Psychiatric Press.

Gundlach, H. U. K. (1986). Ebbinghaus, nonsense syllables, and three-letter words. *Contemporary Psychology, 31,* 469–470.

Gunne, L. M., & Anggard, E. (1972). Pharmical kinetic studies with amphetamines—relationship to neuropsychiatric disorders. *International Symposium on Pharmical Kinetics.* Washington, DC.

Gurman, A. S., & Kniskern, D. P. (1978). Research on marital and family therapy: Progress, perspective, and prospect. In S. L. Garfield & A. E. Bergin (Eds.), *Handbook of psychotherapy and behavior change: An empirical analysis* (2nd ed.). New York: Wiley.

Gustavson, C. R., & Gustavson, J. C. (1985). Predation control using conditioned food aversion methodology: Theory, practice, and implications. *Annals of the New York Academy of Sciences, 443,* 348–356.

Gwirtsman, H. E. (1984). Bulimia in men: Report of three cases with neuro-endocrine findings. *Journal of Clinical Psychiatry, 45,* 78–81.

Haber, R. N. (1969, April). Eidetic images. *Scientific American,* pp. 36–44.

Hackman, J. R., & Oldham, G. R. (1976). Motivation through the design of work: Test of a theory. *Organizational Behavior and Human Performance, 16,* 250–279.

Haefele, J. W. (1962). *Creativity and innovation.* New York: Reinhold.

Haith, M. M., & Campos, J. J. (1977). Human infancy. *Annual Review of Psychology, 28,* 251–293.

Hall, C. S., & Lindzey, G. (1978). *Theories of personality* (3rd ed.). New York: Wiley.

Hall, E. (1982). *Child psychology today.* New York: Random House.

Hall, E. T. (1959). *The silent language.* Garden City, NY: Doubleday.

Hall, G. S. (1904). *Adolescence: Its psychology and its relations to physiology, anthropology, sex, crime, religion and education* (Vol. 1). New York: Appleton-Century-Crofts.

Hall, W. S. (1986). Some recent developments in the study of children's language. A transcript of a *Science and Public Policy Seminar,* given on July 25, 1986. Sponsored by the Federation of Behavioral, Psychological and Cognitive Sciences.

Hallahan, D., Kauffman, J., & Lloyd, J. (1985). *Introduction to learning disabilities* (2nd ed.). Englewood Cliffs, NJ: Prentice-Hall.

Hammen, C. L. (1985). Predicting depression: A cognitive-behavioral perspective. In P. Kendall (Ed.), *Advances in cognitive-behavioral research and therapy* (Vol. 4). New York: Academic Press.

Hanback, J. W., & Revelle, W. (1978). Arousal and perceptual sensitivity in hypochondriacs. *Journal of Abnormal Psychology, 87,* 523–530.

Hann, N., Millsap, R., & Hartke, E. (1986). As time goes by: Change and stability in personality over 50 years. *Journal of Psychology and Aging, 1,* 220–232.

Hansen, R. D. (1984). Person perception. In A. S. Kahn (Ed.), *Social psychology.* Dubuque, IA: Wm. C. Brown.

Hanson, D. J., (1980). Relationship between methods and findings in attitude-behavior research. *Psychology, 17,* 11–13.

Hardy, J. B. (1985). Adolescent pregnancy and parenting. In National Mental Health Association, *Prevention of mental–emotional disabilities.* Alexandria, VA: NMHA.

Hare, R. D. (1983). Diagnosis of antisocial personality disorder in two prison populations. *American Journal of Psychiatry, 140,* 887–890.

Harlow, H. F. (1949). The formation of learning sets. *Psychological Review, 56,* 51–65.

Harlow, H. F. (1958). The nature of love. *American Psychologist, 13,* 673–685.

Harlow, H. F. (1959). Love in infant monkeys. *Scientific American,* 68–74.

Harlow, H. F., & Zimmerman, R. R. (1959). Affectional responses in the infant monkey. *Science, 130,* 421–432.

Harmatz, M. G. (1978). *Abnormal psychology.* Englewood Cliffs, NJ: Prentice-Hall.

Harrell, R. F., Woodyard, E., & Gates, A. I. (1955). *The effect of mother's diet on the intelligence of the offspring.* New York: Teacher's College, Columbia Bureau of Publications.

Harrington, A., & Sutton-Simon, K. (1977). Rape. In A. P. Goldstein, P. J. Monti, T. J. Sardino, & D. J. Green (Eds.), *Police crisis intervention.* Kalamazoo, MI: Behaviordelia.

Hart, J., Jr., Berndt, R. S., & Caramazza, A. (1985). Category-specific naming deficit following cerebral infarction. *Nature, 316,* 439–440.

Hartmann, P., & Husband, C. (1971). The mass media and racial conflict. *Race, 12,* 267–282.

Hartup, W. W. (1989). Social relationships and their developmental significance. *American Psychologist, 44,* 120–126.

Haskins, R. (1989). Beyond metaphor, the efficacy of early childhood education. *American Psychologist, 44,* 274–282.

Hass, R. G. (1981). Effects of source characteristics on cognitive responses in persuasion. In R. E. Petty and J. T. Cacioppo (Eds.), *Attitudes and persuasion: Classic and contemporary approaches.* Dubuque, IA: Wm. C. Brown.

Hatch, O. G. (1982). Psychology, society, and politics. *American Psychologist, 37,* 1031–1037.

Hathaway, S. R., & McKinley, J. C. (1942). A multiphasic personality schedule (Minnesota): Ill. The measurement of symptomatic depression. *Journal of Psychology, 14,* 73–84.

Hauri, P. (1970). Evening activity, sleep mentation, and subjective sleep quality. *Journal of Abnormal Psychology, 76,* 270–275.

Hauri, P. (1982). *Sleep disorders.* Kalamazoo, MI: Upjohn.

Hauser, S. T. (1976). Loevinger's model and measure of ego development: A critical review. *Psychological Bulletin, 83,* 928–955.

Havinghurst, R. J. (1982). The world of work. In B. B. Wolman (Ed.), *Handbook of developmental psychology.* Englewood Cliffs, NJ: Prentice-Hall.

Hawkins, R. D., & Kandel, E. R. (1984). Is there a cell-biological alphabet for simple forms of learning? *Psychological Review, 91,* 375–391.

Hay, D. F. (1986). Infancy. *Annual Review of Psychology, 37,* 135–161.

Hayden, T., & Mischel, W. (1976). Maintaining trait consistency in the resolution of behavioral inconsistency: The wolf in sheep's clothing? *Journal of Personality, 44,* 109–132.

Hayduk, L. A. (1983). Personal space: Where we now stand. *Psychological Bulletin, 94,* 293–335.

Hayes, C., & Hayes, K. (1951). The intellectual development of a home-raised chimpanzee. *Proceedings of the American Philosophical Society, 95,* 105–109.

Hearst, E. (1975). The classical-instrumental distinction: Reflexes, voluntary behavior, and categories of associative learning. In W. K. Estes (Ed.), *Handbook of learning and cognitive processes* (Vol. 2). *Conditioning and behavior theory.* Hillsdale, NJ: Erlbaum.

Heath, R. C. (1972). Pleasure and brain activity in man. *Journal of Nervous and Mental Disease, 154,* 3–18.

Hebb, D. O. (1955). Drives and the CNS (conceptual nervous system). *Psychological Review, 62,* 243–254.

Heider, E. R. (1972). Universals in color naming and memory. *Journal of Experimental Psychology, 93,* 10–20.

Heider, E. R., & Oliver, D. C. (1972). The structure of the color space in naming and memory in two languages. *Cognitive Psychology, 3,* 337–354.

Heilbrun, A. B., Jr. (1981). Gender differences in the functional linkage between androgyny, social cognition, and competence. *Journal of Personality and Social Psychology, 41,* 1106–1118.

Heiman, J. R. (1977). A psychophysiological exploration of sexual arousal patterns in females and males. *Psychophysiology, 14,* 266–274.

Held, R., & Hein, A. (1963). Movement-produced stimulation in the development of visually guided behavior. *Journal of Comparative and Physiological Psychology, 56,* 872–876.

Helmreich, R., & Spence, J. (1978). The Work and Family Orientation Questionnaire: An objective instrument to assess components of achievement motivation and scientific attainment. *Personality and Social Psychology Bulletin, 4,* 222–226.

Helson, R. (1971). Women mathematicians and the creative personality. *Journal of Consulting and Clinical Psychology, 36,* 210–220.

Henderson, N. D. (1982). Human behavior genetics. *Annual Review of Psychology, 33,* 403–440.

Hendricks, J., & Hendricks, C. D. (1977). *Aging in mass society: Myths and realities.* Cambridge, MA: Winthrop.

Henry, W. E. (1956). *The analysis of fantasy.* New York: Wiley.

Herman, C. P., Polivy, J., & Silver, R. (1979). Effects of an observer on eating behavior: The induction of sensible eating. *Journal of Personality, 47,* 85–99.

Herman, J., & Hirschman, L. (1981). Families at risk for father-daughter incest. *American Journal of Psychiatry, 38,* 967–970.

Heron, W. (1957). The pathology of boredom. *Scientific American, 199,* 52–56.

Heron, W. (1961). Cognitive and physiological effects of perceptual isolation. In P. Solomon et al. (Eds.) *Sensory deprivation.* Cambridge, MA: Harvard University Press.

Herrnstein, R. J., & Mazur, J. E. (1987). Making up our minds: A new model of economic behavior. *The Sciences, 27,* 40–47.

Hersher, L. (Ed.) (1970). *Four psychotherapies.* New York: Appleton-Century-Crofts.

Heston, L. L. (1966). Psychiatric disorders in foster-home-reared children of schizophrenic mothers. *British Journal of Psychiatry, 112,* 819–825.

Hilgard, E. R. (1974, November). Hypnosis is no mirage. *Psychology Today,* pp. 121–128.

Hilgard, E. R. (1965). *Hypnotic susceptibility.* New York: Harcourt Brace Jovanovich.

Hilgard, E. R. (1977). *Divided consciousness: Multiple controls in human thought and action.* New York: Wiley-Interscience.

Hilgard, E. R. (1980). Consciousness in contemporary psychology. *Annual Review of Psychology, 1980, 31,* 1–26.

Hilgard, E. R., Hilgard, J. R., & Kaufmann, W. (1983). *Hypnosis in the relief of pain* (2nd ed.). Los Altos, CA: Kaufmann.

Hill, A. B. (1966). *Principles of medical statistics* (8th ed.). London: Oxford University Press.

Hill, D. (1952). EEG in episodic psychotic and psychopathic behavior: A classification of data. *EEG and Clinical Neurophysiology, 4,* 419–422.

Hill, J. (1980). The family. In M. Johnson (Ed.), *Toward adolescence: The middle school years. The 79th yearbook of the National Society for the Study of Education: Part I.* Chicago: University of Chicago Press.

Hill, W. F. (1956). Activity as an autonomous drive. *Journal of Comparative and Physiological Psychology, 49,* 15–19.

Hobbs, N., & Robinson, S. (1982). Adolescent development and public policy. *American Psychologist, 37,* 212–223.

Hobson, J. A. (1988). *The Dreaming Brain.* New York: Basic Books.

Hobson, J. A., & McCarley, R. (1977). The brain as a dream state generator: An activation-synthesis hypothesis of the dream process. *American Journal of Psychiatry, 134,* 1335–1348.

Hoch, Z., Safir, M. P., Peres, Y., & Stepler, J. (1981). An evaluation of sexual performance—comparison between sexually dysfunctional and functional couples. *Journal of Sex and Marital Therapy, 7,* 195–206.

Hochberg, J. (1978). *Perception* (2nd ed.). Englewood Cliffs, NJ: Prentice-Hall.

Hodapp, R., & Mueller, E. (1982). Early social development. In B. B. Wolman (Ed.), *Handbook of developmental psychology* (pp. 284–300). Englewood Cliffs, NJ: Prentice-Hall.

Hoepfner, R. (1975). *Castro Valley Unified School District Title III: Parents as partners summative evaluation report.* Castro Valley Unified School District, Castro Valley, CA.

Hofferth, S. L., & Hayes, C. D. (Eds.) (1987). *Risking the future: Adolescent sexuality, pregnancy, and childbearing: Vol. 2. Working papers and statistical reports.* Washington, DC: National Academy Press.

Hoffman, H. S., & DePaulo, P. (1977). Behavioral control by an imprinting stimulus. *American Scientist, 65,* 58–66.

Hoffman, L. W. (1977). Changes in family roles, socialization, and sex differences. *American Psychologist, 32,* 644–657.

Hoffman, L. W. (1983). The study of employed mothers over half a century. In M. Lewis (Ed.), *In the shadow of the past: Psychology portrays the sexes.* New York: Columbia University Press.

Hoffman, L. (1989). Effects of maternal employment in the two-parent family. *American Psychologist, 44,* 283–292.

Hoffman, M. L. (1977). Personality and social development. *Annual Review of Psychology, 28,* 295–321.

Hogan, R., & Schroeder, D. (1981, July). Seven biases in psychology. *Psychology Today,* pp. 8–14.

Holahan, C. J. (1986). Environmental psychology. *Annual Review of Psychology, 37,* 381–407.

Holden, C. (1985). A guarded endorsement for shock therapy. *Science, 228,* 1510–1511.

Hollingshead, A. B., & Redlich, F. C. (1958). *Social class and mental illness: A community study.* New York: Wiley.

Holmes, D. S. (1984). Meditation and somatic arousal reduction: A review of the experimental evidence. *American Psychologist, 39,* 1–12.

Holmes, T. H., & Rahe, R. H. (1967). The social readjustment rating scale. *Journal of Psychosomatic Research, 11,* 213.

Horn, J. (1975, March). Family therapy—a quick fix for juvenile delinquency. *Psychology Today,* pp. 80–81.

Horn, J. (1983). The Texas Adoption Project: Adopted children and their intellectual resemblance to biological and adoptive parents. *Child Development, 54,* 268–275.

Horn, J. L. (1976). Human abilities: A review of research and theory in the early 1970s. *Annual Review of Psychology, 27,* 437–485.

Horner, M. (1969, November). A bright woman is caught in a double bind. *Psychology Today,* pp. 36–38, 62.

Horney, K. (1937). *The neurotic personality of our time.* New York: Norton.

Horowitz, F. D., & O'Brien, M. (Eds.) (1985). *The gifted and talented: Developmental perspectives.* Washington, DC: American Psychological Association.

Horowitz, F. D., & O'Brien, M. (1986). Gifted and talented children: State of knowledge and directions for research. *American Psychologist, 41,* 1147–1152.

Horvath, F. S. (1977). The effect of selected variables on interpretation of polygraph records. *Journal of Applied Psychology, 62,* 127–136.

Hosford, R. E., Moss, C. S., Cavior, H., & Kevish, B. (1980). *Research on erhard seminar training in a correctional institution.* Federal Correctional Institution, Lompoc, CA.

Hovland, C. I., & Sears, R. R. (1940). Minor studies in aggression: VI.

Correlation of lynchings with economic indices. *Journal of Abnormal and Social Psychology, 9,* 301–310.

Howard, K. I., Kopta, S. M., Krause, M. S., & Orlinsky, D. E. (1986). The dose-effect relationship in psychotherapy. *American Psychologist, 41,* 159–164.

Hubel, D. H. (1963). The visual cortex of the brain. *Scientific American, 209,* 54–62.

Hubel, D. H., & Wiesel, T. N. (1959). Receptive fields of single neurons in the cat's striate cortex. *Journal of Physiology, 148,* 574–591.

Hubel, D. H., & Wiesel, T. N. (1979). Brain mechanisms of vision. *Scientific American, 241,* 150–162.

Hudspeth, A. J. (1983). The hair cells of the inner ear. *Scientific American, 248,* 54–64.

Hull, R. H. (1982). The impact of hearing impairment on aging persons: A dialogue. In R. H. Hull (Ed.), *Rehabilitation audiology.* New York: Grune & Stratton.

Husain, S. A., & Vandiver, M. S. (1984). *Suicide in children and adolescents.* New York: SP Medical & Scientific Books.

Huston, A. C., Watkins, B. A., & Kunkel, D. (1989). Public policy and children's television. *American Psychologist, 44,* 424–433.

Hutchings, B., & Mednick, S. A. (1977). Criminality in adoptees and their adoptive and biological parents: A pilot study. In S. A. Mednick & K. O. Christensen (Eds.), *Biosocial bases of criminal behavior.* New York: Gorner.

Huttenlocher, J., Smiley, P., & Charney, R. (1983). Emergence of action categories in the child: Evidence from verb meanings. *Psychological Review, 90,* 72–93.

Hyde, J. S. (1981). How large are cognitive gender differences? *American Psychologist, 36,* 892–901.

Hyde, J. S. (1982). *Understanding human sexuality* (2nd ed.). New York: McGraw-Hill.

Inhelder, B., & Piaget, J. (1958). *The growth of logical thinking from childhood to adolescence* (A. Parson & S. Milgram, trans.). New York: Basic Books.

Insel, P. M., & Lindgren, H. C. (1978). *Two close for comfort: The psychology of crowding behavior.* Englewood Cliffs, NJ: Prentice-Hall.

Isen, A. M., & Levin, P. F. (1972). The effect of feeling good on helping: Cookies and kindness. *Journal of Personality and Social Psychology, 21,* 384–388.

Izard, C. E. (1971). *The face of emotion.* New York: Appleton-Century-Crofts.

Izard, C. E. (1982). The psychology of emotion comes of age on the coattails of Darwin. *Contemporary Psychology, 27,* 426–429.

Jacklin, C. N. (1989). Female and male: Issues of gender. *American Psychologist, 44,* 127–133.

Jackson, C. W. (1928). Some aspects of form and growth. In W. J. Robbins (Ed.), *Growth.* New Haven, CT: Yale University Press.

Jacobs, M. K., & Goodman, G. (1988). Psychology and self-help groups: Predictions on a partnership. *American Psychologist, 44,* 536–545.

Jaffe, A. C., Dynaeson, L., & Tenbensel, R. W. (1975). Sexual abuse of children: An epidemiological study. *American Journal of Diseases of Children, 129,* 689–692.

James, W. (1890). *The principles of psychology.* New York: Holt.

Janis, I. L. (1972). *Victims of groupthink: A psychological study of foreign-policy decisions and fiascos.* Boston: Houghton Mifflin.

Janis, I. L., Mahl, G. G., & Holt, R. R. (1969). *Personality: Dynamics, development and assessment.* New York: Harcourt Brace Jovanovich.

Jarvik, L. F., Mintz, J., Steuer, J., & Gerner, R. (1982). Treating geriatric depression: A 26-week interim analysis. *Journal of the American Geriatrics Society, 30,* 713–717.

Jemott, J. B., III, & Locke, S. E. (1984). Psychosocial factors, immunologic mediation, and human susceptibility to infectious disease: How much do we know? *Psychological Bulletin, 95,* 78–108.

Jenkins, G. D., Jr., & Gupta, N. (1983, August). Successes and tensions in a "new design" organization. Paper presented at the meeting of the American Psychological Association, Anaheim, CA.

Jensen, A. R. (1969). How much can we boost IQ and scholastic achievement? *Harvard Educational Review, 39,* 1–123.

John, O. P. (1988). Personality assessment in the 1990ies: Issues and challenges. Paper presented at the meeting on *Emerging issues in personality psychology,* University of Michigan, April, 1988.

Johnson, C., Lewis, C., Love, S., Lewis, S., & Stuckey, M. (1984). Incidence and correlates of bulimic behavior in a female high school population. *Journal of Youth and Adolescence, 13,* 15–26.

Johnson, R. C., & Brown, C. (1988). *Cognizers: Neural networks and machines that think.* New York: Wiley.

Johnston, W. A., & Dark, V. J., (1986). Selective attention. *Annual Review of Psychology, 37,* 43–75.

Jones, E., Forrest, J. D., Henshaw, S. K., Silverman, J., & Torres, A. (1988). Unintended pregnancy, contraceptive practice and family planning services in developed countries. *Family Planning Perspectives, 20*(2), 53–67.

Jones, E. E., & Nisbett, R. E. (1972). The actor and the observer: Divergent perceptions of the causes of behavior. In E. E. Jones, D. E. Kanouse, H. H. Kelley, R. E. Nisbett, S. Valins, & B. Weiner (Eds.), *Attribution: Perceiving the causes of behavior.* Morristown, NJ: General Learning Press.

Jones, M. C. (1924). Elimination of children's fears. *Journal of Experimental Psychology, 7,* 381–390.

Jones, M. C. (1958). A study of socialization patterns at the high school level. *Journal of Genetic Psychology, 93,* 87–111.

Jones, M. C. (1965). Psychological correlates of somatic development. *Child Development, 36,* 899–911.

Jones, M. C., & Bayley, N. (1950). Physical maturing among boys as related to behavior. *Journal of Educational Psychology, 41,* 129–148.

Jones, R. (1978). Marihuana: Human effects. In L. L. Iverson, S. Iverson, & S. H. Snyder (Eds.), *Handbook of Psychopharmacology* (Vol. 12). New York: Plenum.

Jones, R. T., & Benowitz, N. (1976). The 30-day trip: Clinical studies of cannabis tolerance and dependence. In M. C. Braude & S. Szara (Eds.), *Pharmacology of marijuana* (Vol. 2). New York: Academic Press.

Jones, W., Chernovertz, M. E., & Hansson, R. O. (1978). The enigma of androgyny: Differential implications for males and females? *Journal of Consulting and Clinical Psychology, 46,* 298–313.

Kagan, J. (1976). Emergent themes in human development. *American Scientist, 64,* 186–196.

Kagan, J. (1989). Temperamental contributions to social behavior. *American Psychologist, 44,* 668–674.

Kahana, B. (1982). Social behavior and aging. In B. B. Wolman (Ed.), *Handbook of developmental psychology* (pp. 871–889). Englewood Cliffs, NJ: Prentice-Hall.

Kahn, M. L., & Schooler, C. (1983). *Work and personality: An inquiry into the impact of social stratification.* Norwood, NJ: Ablex Press.

Kail, R. (1984). *The development of memory in children* (2nd ed.). New York: Freeman.

Kales, A., Wilson, T., Kales, J. D., Jacobson, A., Paulson, M. J., Kollar, E., & Walter, R. D. (1976). Measurements of all night sleep in normal elderly persons: Effects of aging. *Journal of the American Geriatrics Society, 15,* 405–414.

Kamin, L. J. (1969). Selective association and conditioning. In N. J. Mackintosh & W. K. Honig (Eds.), *Fundamental issues in associative learning.* Halifax: Dalhousie University Press.

Kaplan, H. S. (1974). No nonsense therapy for six sexual malfunctions. *Psychology Today*, pp. 76–80, 83, 86.

Kastenbaum, R. (1977). *Death, society, and human behavior*. St. Louis: Mosby.

Kastenbaum, R., & Costa, P. T., Jr. (1977). Psychological perspectives on death. *Annual Review of Psychology, 28*, 225–249.

Katz, A. H. (1981). "Self-help and mutual aid: An emerging social movement?" *American Review of Sociology, 7*, 129–155.

Katzell, R. A., & Guzzo, R. A. (1983). Psychological approaches to productivity improvements. *American Psychologist, 38*, 468–472.

Kaufman, L. (1979). *Perception: The world transformed*. New York: Oxford University Press.

Kazdin, A. E. (1976, October). The rich rewards of rewards. *Psychology Today*, pp. 98, 101–102.

Kelley, E. L. (1955). Consistency of the adult personality. *American Psychologist, 10*, 659–681.

Kelley, H. H. (1967). Attribution theory in social psychology. In D. Levine (Ed.), *Nebraska symposium on motivation*. Lincoln: University of Nebraska Press.

Kellogg, W. N. (1968). Communication and language in the home-raised chimpanzee. *Science, 162*, 423–427.

Kellogg, W. N., & Kellogg, L. A. (1933). *The ape and the child*. New York: McGraw-Hill.

Kelly, J. B. (1982). Divorce: The adult perspective. In B. B. Wolman (Ed.), *Handbook of developmental psychology* (pp. 734–750). Englewood Cliffs, NJ: Prentice-Hall.

Kelman, H. C. (1974). Attitudes are alive and well and gainfully employed in the sphere of action. *American Psychologist, 230*, 310–324.

Kershner, J. R., & Ledger, G. (1985). Effect of sex, intelligence, and style of thinking on creativity: A comparison of gifted and average IQ children. *Journal of Personality and Social Psychology, 48*, 1033–1040.

Kessler, R. C. (1979). Stress, social status, and psychological distress. *Journal of Health and Social Behavior, 20*, 259–272.

Kessler, R. C., Price, R. H., & Wortman, C. B. (1985). Social factors in psychopathology: Stress, social support, and coping processes. *Annual Review of Psychology, 36*, 531–572.

Kety, S. S. (1979). Disorders of the human brain. *Scientific American, 241*, 202–214.

Kiecolt-Glaser, J., & Glaser, R. (1988). Major life changes, chronic stress, and immunity. In T. P. Bridge, A. F. Mirsky, & F. K. Goodwin (Eds.), *Psychological, neuropsychiatric, and substance abuse aspects of AIDS* (pp. 217–224). New York: Raven Press.

Kiesler, C. A. (1982a). Mental hospitals and alternative care: Noninstitutionalization as potential public policy for mental patients. *American Psychologist, 37*, 349–360.

Kiesler, C. A. (1982b). Public and professional myths about mental hospitalization, *American Psychologist, 37*, 1323–1339.

Kihlstrom, J. F. (1985). Hypnosis. *Annual Review of Psychology, 36*, 385–418.

Kihlstrom, J. F. (1987). The cognitive unconscious. *Science, 237*, 1445–1452.

Kimmel, D. C. (1974). *Adulthood and aging*. New York: Wiley.

King, F. A. (1987). Importance and benefits of animal research to human health. In F. Farley & C. H. Null (Eds.), *Using psychological science: Making the public case*, (pp. 5–12). Washington, DC: Federation of Behavioral, Psychological and Cognitive Sciences.

Kinsey, A. C., Pomeroy, W. B., & Martin, C. E. (1948). *Sexual behavior in the human male*. Philadelphia: Saunders.

Kinsey, A. C., Pomeroy, W. B., Martin, C. E., & Gebhard, P. H. (1953). *Sexual behavior in the human female*. Philadelphia: Saunders.

Klatzky, R. L. (1980). *Human memory: Structures and processes* (2nd ed.). San Francisco: Freeman.

Klatzky, R. L., Lederman, S. J., & Metzger, V. A. (1985). Identifying objects by touch: An 'expert system.' *Perception & Psychophysics, 37*(4), 299–302.

Klein, G. S. (1951). The personal world through perception. In R. R. Blake & G. V. Ramsey (Eds.), *Perception: An approach to personality*. New York: Ronald Press.

Kleinhesselink, R. R., & Edwards, R. E. (1975). Seeking and avoiding belief-discrepant information as a function of its perceived refutability. *Journal of Personality and Social Psychology, 31*, 787–790.

Kobasa, S. C. (1979). Stressful life events, personality, and health: An inquiry into hardiness. *Journal of Personality and Social Psychology, 37*, 1–11.

Kohlberg, L. (1976). Moral stages and moralization: The cognitive-developmental approach. In T. Lickona (Ed.), *Moral development and behavior*. New York: Holt, Rinehart and Winston.

Kohlberg, L. (1979). *The meaning and measurement of moral development*. Clark Lectures, Clark University.

Kohlberg, L. (1981). *The philosophy of moral development* (Vol. 1). San Francisco: Harper & Row.

Köhler, W. (1927). *The mentality of apes*. New York: Liveright.

Kolodny, R. C., Masters, W. H., & Johnson, V. E. (1979). *Textbook of sexual medicine*. Boston: Little, Brown.

Koulack, D., & Goodenough, D. R. (1976). Dream recall and dream recall failure: An arousal-retrieval model. *Psychological Bulletin, 83*, 975–984.

Kovacs, M., Rush, A. J., Beck, A. T., & Hollon, S. D. (1981). Depressed outpatients treated with cognitive therapy or pharmacotherapy: A one-year follow-up. *Archives of General Psychiatry, 38*, 33–39.

Krebs, D. (1975). Empathy and altruism. *Journal of Personality and Social Psychology, 32*, 1134–1140.

Kringlen, E. (1981). Stress and coronary heart disease. *Twin Research 3: Epidemiological and clinical studies*. New York: Alan R. Liss.

Kripke, D. F., & Gillin, J. C. (1985). Sleep disorders. In G. L. Klerman, M. M. Weissman, P. S. Applebaum, & L. N. Roth (Eds.), *Psychiatry* (Vol. 3). Philadelphia: Lippincott.

Kruglanski, A. W. (1986, August). Freeze-think and the Challenger. *Psychology Today*, pp. 48–49.

Ktsanes, V. (1980). The teenager and family planning experience. In C. S. Chilman (Ed.), *Adolescent pregnancy and childbearing: Findings from research*. Washington, DC, Department of Health and Human Services (NIH Publication No. 81–2077).

Kübler-Ross, E. (1969). *On death and dying*. New York: Macmillan.

Kübler-Ross, E. (1975). *Death: The final stage of growth*. Englewood Cliffs, NJ: Prentice-Hall.

Kulik, J., & Brown, R. (1979). Frustration, attribution of blame, and aggression. *Journal of Experimental Social Psychology, 15*, 183–194.

Kunkel, D. (1988). Children and host-selling television commercials. *Communication Research, 15*, 71–92.

LaBerge, S. (1986). *Lucid dreaming*. New York: Ballantine.

Labouvie-Vief, G. (1986). Modes of knowledge and the organization of development. In M. L. Commons, L. Kohlberg, F. A. Richards, & J. Sinott (Eds.), *Beyond formal operations 3: Models and methods in the study of adult and adolescent thoughts*. New York: Praeger.

Lachman, S. J. (1984). Processes in visual misperception: Illusions for highly structured stimulus material. Paper presented at the 92nd annual convention of the American Psychological Association. Toronto, Canada.

LaGreca, A. M., Stone, W. L., & Bell, C. R., III. (1983). Facilitating the vocational-interpersonal skills of mentally retarded individuals. *American Journal of Mental Deficiency, 88*, 270–278.

Lamb, M. E. (Ed.) (1976). *The role of the father in child development*. New York: Wiley.

Lamb, M. E. (1979). Paternal influences and the father's role. *American Psychologist, 34*, 938–943.

Lambert, W. W., Solomon, R. L., & Watson, P. D. (1949). Reinforcement and extinction as factors in size estimation. *Journal of Experimental Psychology, 39*, 637–641.

Landesman, S., & Butterfield, E. C. (1987). Normalization and deinstitutionalization of mentally retarded individuals, controversy and facts. *American Psychologist, 42*, 809–816.

Landman, J. C., & Dawes, R. M. (1982). Psychotherapy outcome: Smith and Glass' conclusions stand up under scrutiny. *American Psychologist, 37*, 504–516.

Landy, F. (1985). *The psychology of work behavior.* Homewood, IL: Dorsey Press.

Lang, E. L., & Reifman, A. (1988). Reestimating Zajonc's confluence effects on the SAT. *American Psychologist, 43*, 477–478.

LaPiere, R. T. (1934). Attitudes versus actions. *Social Forces, 13*, 230–237.

Larson, R., Mannell, R., & Zuzank, J. (1986). Daily wellbeing of older adults with friends and family. *Psychology and Aging, 1*, 117–126.

LaRue, A., & Jarvik, L. (1982). Old age and biobehavioral changes. In B. B. Wolman (Ed.), *Handbook of developmental psychology* (pp. 791–806). Englewood Cliffs, NJ: Prentice-Hall.

Lasch, C. (1979). *The culture of narcissism.* New York: Norton.

Lashley, K. S. (1950). In search of the engram. *Symposia of the Society for Experimental Biology, 4*, 454–482.

Latané, B., & Rodin, J. (1969). A lady in distress: Inhibiting effects of friends and strangers on bystander intervention. *Journal of Experimental Social Psychology, 5*, 189–202.

Lazarus, R. S. (1969). *Patterns of adjustment and human effectiveness.* New York: McGraw-Hill.

Lazarus, R. S. (1981, July). Little hassles can be hazardous to health. *Psychology Today*, pp. 58–62.

Lazarus, R. S. (1982). Thoughts on the relations between emotion and cognition. *American Psychologist, 37*, 1019–1024.

Lazarus, R. S., & De Longis, A. (1983). Psychological stress and coping in aging. *American Psychologist, 38*, 245–254.

Lazarus, R. S., De Longis, A., Folkman, S., & Gruen, R. (1985). Stress and adaptational outcomes. *American Psychologist, 40*, 770–779.

Lazarus, R. S., & Monat, A. (1979). *Personality* (3rd ed.). Englewood Cliffs, NJ: Prentice-Hall.

Leeper, R. W. (1935). A study of a neglected portion of the field of learning: The development of sensory organization. *Pedagogical Seminary and Journal of Genetic Psychology, 46*, 41–75.

Leff, J. P. (1976). Schizophrenia and sensitivity to the family environment. *Schizophrenia Bulletin, 2*, 566–574.

Lefkowitz, M. M., Eron, L. D., Walder, L. O., & Huesmann, L. R. (1972). Television violence and child aggression: A follow-up study. In G. A. Comstock & E. A. Rubinstein (Eds.), *Television and social behavior.* Vol. 3: *Television and adolescent aggressiveness.* Washington, DC: Government Printing Office.

Lefrancois, G. R. (1986). *Of children: An introduction to child development.* Belmont, CA: Wadsworth.

Leibowitz, H. W., & Owens, D. A. (1977). Nighttime driving accidents and selective visual degradation. *Science, 197*, 422–423.

LeMagnen, J. (1952). Les pheromones olfactosexuals chez le rat blanc. *Archives des Sciences Physiologiques, 6*, 295–332.

Lemish, D., & Rice, M. L. (1986, June). Television as a talking picture book: A prop for language acquisition. *Journal of Child Language, 13*, 251–274.

Leonard, J. M., & Whitten, W. B. (1983). Information stored when expecting recall or recognition. *Journal of Experimental Psychology: Learning, Memory, and Cognition, 9*, 440–455.

Lerner, M. J. (1980). *The belief in a just world: A fundamental delusion.* New York: Plenum.

Lerner, R. M., & Karabenick, S. A. (1974). Physical attractiveness, body attitudes, and self-concept in late adolescents. *Journal of Youth and Adolescence, 3*, 307–316.

Lerner, R. M., & Shea, J. A. (1982). Social behavior in adolescence. In B. B. Wolman (Ed.), *Handbook of developmental psychology* (pp. 503–525). Englewood Cliffs, NJ: Prentice-Hall.

Leventhal, H., & Niles, P. (1965). Persistence of influence for varying duration of exposure to threat stimuli. *Psychological Reports, 16*, 223–233.

Levinson, B. M. (1959). Traditional Jewish cultural values and performance on the Wechsler tests. *Journal of Educational Psychology, 50*, 177–181.

Levinson, D. J. (1978). *The seasons of a man's life.* New York: Knopf.

Levinson, D. J. (1986). A conception of adult development. *American Psychologist, 41*, 3–13.

Levinson, D. J. (1987). *The seasons of a woman's life.* New York: Knopf.

Levinthal, C. (1979). *The physiological approach in psychology.* Englewood Cliffs, NJ: Prentice-Hall.

Levy, B. A. (1978). Speech processing during reading. In A. M. Lesgold, J. W. Pellegrino, S. D. Fckhema, & R. Glaser (Eds.), *Cognitive psychology and instruction.* New York: Plenum.

Levy, S. M. (Ed.) (1982). *Biological mediators of behavior and disease.* Neoplasia, NY: Elsevier Biomedical.

Lewin, K. A. (1935). *A dynamic theory of personality* (K. E. Zener & D. K. Adams, trans.). New York: McGraw-Hill.

Lewinsohn, P. M. (1974). A behavioral approach to depression. In R. J. Friedmann & M. M. Katz (Eds.), *The psychology of depression: Contemporary theory and research.* Washington, DC: V. H. Winston.

Lewinsohn, P. M., & Arconad, M. (1981). Behavioral treatment in depression: A social learning approach. In J. Clarkin & H. Glazer (Eds.), *Behavioral and directive treatment strategies.* New York: Garland.

Lewinsohn, P. M., & Hoberman, H. M. (1982). Depression. In A. S. Bellack, M. Hersen, & A. E. Kazdin (Eds.), *International handbook of behavior modification and therapy.* New York: Plenum.

Lewis, J. W., Cannon, J. T., & Liebeskind, J. C. (1980). Opiod and nonopiod mechanisms of stress analgesia. *Science, 208*, 623–625.

Lewis, R. A., & Spanier, G. B. (1979). Theorizing about the quality and stability of marriage. In W. Burr, R. Hull, F. Nye, & I. Reiss (Eds.), *Contemporary theories about the family.* New York: Free Press.

Liben, L. (1974). Operative understanding of horizontality and its relation to long-term memory. *Child Development, 45*, 416–424.

Liberman, M. A., & Tobin, S. S. (1983). *The experience of old age: Stress, coping, and survival.* New York: Basic Books.

Libet, B. (1985). Unconscious cerebral initiative and the role of conscious will in voluntary action. *The Behavioral and Brain Sciences, 8*, 529–539.

Lieberman, M. (1986). Self-help groups and psychiatry. *American Psychiatric Association Annual Review, 5*, 744–760.

Liem, R., Liem, J. V. (1978). Social class and mental illness reconsidered: The role of economic stress and social support. *Journal of Health and Social Behavior, 19*, 139–156.

Lifton, R. L. (1961). *Thought reform and the psychology of totalism.* New York: Norton.

Limber, J. (1977). Language in child and chimp. *American Psychologist, 32*, 280–295.

Lindsay, P. H., & Norman, D. A. (1977). *Human information processing* (2nd ed.). New York: Academic Press.

Lingjaerde, O. (1983). The biochemistry of depression. *Acta Psychiatrica Scandanavica Supplementum, 302, 69*, 36–51.

Linn, R. L. (1982). Admissions testing on trial. *American Psychologist, 37*, 279–291.

Lipsitt, L. P. (1971, December). Babies: They're a lot smarter than they look. *Psychology Today*, pp. 70–72, 88–89.

Locke, E. A., & Schweiger, D. M. (1979). Participation in decision-making: One more look. In B. Staw (Ed.), *Research in organizational behavior* (Vol. 1). Greenwich, CT: JAI Press.

Locksley, A., & Colten, M. E. (1979). Psychological androgyny: A case of mistaken identity? *Journal of Personality and Social Psychology, 37,* 1017–1031.

Loehlin, J. C., & Nichols, R. C. (1976). *Heredity, environment, and personality.* Austin: University of Texas Press.

Loftus, E. F. (1980). *Memory.* Reading, MA: Addison-Wesley.

Loftus, E. F. (1983). Silence is not golden. *American Psychologist, 38,* 564–572.

Loftus, E. F. (1984, August). Eyewitness: Essential but unreliable. *Psychology Today,* pp. 22–26.

Loftus, E. F., Miller, D. G., & Burns, H. J. (1978). Semantic integration of verbal information into a visual memory. *Journal of Experimental Psychology: Human Learning and Memory, 4,* 19–31.

Logue, A. W., Ophir, I., & Strauss, K. E. (1981). The acquisition of taste aversions in humans. *Behavior Research and Therapy, 19,* 319–333.

Loranger, A. W., Oldham, J. W., & Tulis, E. H. (1983). Familial transmission of DSM-III borderline personality disorder. *Archives of General Psychiatry, 40,* 795–799.

Lorenz, K. (1935). Der Kumpan in der Umwelt des Vobels. *Journal of Ornithology, 83,* 137–213, 289–413.

Lorenz, K. (1968). *On aggression.* New York: Harcourt.

Lott, B. (1985). The potential enrichment of social/personality psychology through feminist research and vice versa. *American Psychologist, 40,* 155–164.

Lowenstein, J. M., & Sihlman, A. L. (1985). Human evolution and molecular biology. In E. D. Garber (Ed.), *Genetic perspective in biology and medicine.* Chicago; University of Chicago Press.

Lowenthal, M. F., & Haven, C. (1968). Interaction and adaptation: Intimacy as a critical variable. *American Sociological Review, 33,* 20–30.

Lubin, B., Larsen, R. M., & Matarazzo, J. D. (1984). Patterns of psychological test usage in the United States: 1935–1982. *American Psychologist, 39,* 451–454.

Lubin, B., Larsen, R. M., Matarazzo, J. D., & Seever, M. (1985). Psychological test usage patterns in five professional settings. *American Psychologist, 40,* 857–861.

Lucas, O. N. (1975). The use of hypnosis in hemophilia dental care. *Annals of the New York Academy of Science, 240,* 263–266.

Luce, G., & Segal, J. (1966). *Sleep.* New York: Coward, McCann & Geoghegan.

Luchins, A. (1957). Primacy-recency in impression formation. In C. Hovland, W. Mandell, E. Campbell, T. Brock, A. Luchins, A. Cohen, W. McGuire, I. Janis, R. Feierbend, & N. Anderson (Eds.), *The order of presentation in persuasion.* New Haven, CT: Yale University Press.

Lundin, R. W. (1974). *Personality: A behavioral analysis* (2nd ed.). New York: Macmillan.

Luria, A. R. (1968). *The mind of a mnemonist* (L. Solotaroff, trans.). New York: Basic Books.

Lykken, D. T. (1975, March). Guilty knowledge test: The right way to use a lie detector. *Psychology Today,* pp. 56–60.

Lynn, S. J., & Rhue, J. W. (1988). Fantasy proneness, hypnosis, developmental antecedents, and psychopathology. *American Psychologist, 43,* 35–44.

Maccoby, E., & Jacklin, C. N. (1974). *The psychology of sex differences.* Stanford, CA: Stanford University Press.

MacKay, D. G. (1973). Aspects of the theory of comprehension, memory, and attention. *Quarterly Journal of Experimental Psychology, 25,* 22–40.

MacKinnon, D. W. (1962). The nature and nurture of creative talent. *American Psychologist, 17,* 484–495.

MacLeod, D. I. A. (1978). Visual sensitivity. *Annual Review of Psychology, 29,* 613–645.

Maddi, S. R. (1989). *Personality theories: A comparative approach* (5th ed.). Homewood, IL: Dorsey.

Maier, S. (1987). Stress: Depression, disease, and the immune system. In F. Farley & C. N. Hull (Eds.), *Using psychological science: Making the public case* (pp. 13–24). Washington, DC: The Federation of Behavioral, Psychological, and Cognitive Sciences.

Maier, S. F., & Seligman, M. E. P. (1976). Learned helplessness: Theory and evidence. *Journal of Experimental Psychology: General, 105,* 3–46.

Main, M. (1973). Exploration, play and cognitive functioning as related to child-mother attachment. Unpublished dissertation, Johns Hopkins University.

Major, B., Carnevale, P. J. D., & Deaux, K. (1981). A different perspective on androgyny: Evaluations of masculine and feminine personality characteristics. *Journal of Personality and Social Psychology, 41,* 988–1001.

Makstein, N. K., McLaughlin, A. M., & Rogers, C. M. (1979, September). Sexual abuse and the pediatric setting: Treatment and research implications. Paper presented at the meeting of the American Psychological Association, New York.

Malamuth, N. M. (1981). Rape fantasies as a function of exposure to violent sexual stimuli. *Archives of Sexual Behavior, 10,* 33–48.

Malamuth, N. M., & Check, J. V. P. (1980). Penile tumescence and perceptual responses to rape as a function of victim's perceived reactions. *Journal of Applied Social Psychology, 10,* 528–547.

Malamuth, N. M., & Donnerstein, E. (Eds.) (1984). *Pornography and sexual aggression.* Orlando, FL: Academic Press.

Maloney, M. P., & Ward, M. P. (1976). *Psychological assessment: A conceptual approach.* New York: Academic Press.

Manfredi, M., Bini, G., Cruccu, G., Accornero, N., Beradelli, A., & Medolago, L. (1981). Congenital absence of pain. *Archives of Neurology, 38,* 507–511.

Maratsos, M. P. (1973). Nonegocentric communication abilities in preschool children. *Child Development, 44,* 697–700.

Marcia, J. E. (1976). Identify six years after: A follow-up study. *Journal of Youth and Adolescence, 5,* 145–160.

Marcia, J. E. (1980). Identify in adolescence. In J. Adelson (Ed.), *Handbook of adolescent psychology.* New York: Wiley.

Marks, G., & Miller, N. (1980). The effect of physical attractiveness on perception of similarity. Unpublished manuscript, University of Southern California, Los Angeles.

Marlatt, G. A., & Rohsenow, D. J. (1981, December). The think-drink effect. *Psychology Today,* pp. 60–69, 93.

Marlin, N. A. (1983). Second-order conditioning using a contextual stimulus as S1. *Animal Learning and Behavior, 11,* 290–294.

Marmot, M. G., & Syme, S. L. (1976). Acculturation and coronary heart disease in Japanese-Americans. *Journal of Epidemiology, 104,* 225–247.

Marsden, E. N. (1966). Values as determinants of friendship choice. *Connecticut College Psychological Journal, 3,* 3–13.

Marshall, W. A. (1973). The body. In R. R. Sears & S. S. Feldman (Eds.), *The seven ages of man.* Los Altos, CA: Kaufmann.

Marvin, R. S. (1975). Aspects of the pre-school child's changing conception of his mother. Unpublished.

Maslach, C. (1982). *Burnout.* Englewood Cliffs, NJ: Prentice-Hall.

Masling, J., Rabie, L., & Blondheim, S. H. (1967). Obesity, level of aspiration, and Rorschach and TAT measures of oral dependence. *Journal of Consulting Psychology, 31,* 233–239.

Maslow, A. H. (1954). *Motivation and personality*. New York: Harper & Row.

Maslow, A. H. (1970). *Motivation and personality* (2nd ed.). New York: Harper & Row.

Mason, W. A., & Lott, D. F. (1976). Ethnology and comparative psychology. *Annual Review of Psychology, 27,* 129–154.

Masters, W. H. & Johnson, V. E. (1970). *Human sexual inadequacy.* Boston: Little, Brown.

Masters, W. H., Johnson, V. E., & Kolodny, R. C. (1982). *Human sexuality.* Boston: Little, Brown.

Matas, L., Arend, R., & Sroufe, L. (1978). Continuity in adaptation in the second year: The relationships between quality of attachment and later competence. *Child Development, 49,* 547–556.

Matthews, K. E., & Cannon, L. K. (1975). Environmental noise level as a determinant of helping behavior. *Journal of Personality and Social Psychology, 32,* 571–577.

Mayer, R. E. (1983). *Thinking, problem solving, cognition.* San Francisco: Freeman.

Mayer, W. (1983). Alcohol abuse and alcoholism: The psychologist's role in prevention, research, and treatment. *American Psychologist, 38,* 1116–1121.

Mayo, E. (1933). *The human problems of an industrial civilization.* New York: Macmillan.

Mayr, E. (1982). *The growth of biological thought.* Cambridge, MA: Belknap Press.

Mazel, J. (1981). *The Beverly Hills diet.* New York: Macmillan.

Mazur, J. E. (1986). *Learning and behavior.* Englewood Cliffs, NJ: Prentice Hall.

McBurney, D. H., & Collings, V. B. (1984). *Introduction to sensation/perception* (2nd ed.). Englewood Cliffs, NJ: Prentice-Hall.

McClelland, D. C. (1958). Methods of measuring human motivation. In J. W. Atkinson, (Ed.), *Motives in fantasy, action and society: A method of assessment and study.* New York: Van Nostrand.

McClelland, D. C. (1973). Testing for competence rather than for "intelligence." *American Psychologist, 28,* 1–4.

McClelland, D. C., & Atkinson, J. W. (1948). The projective expression of needs: I. The effect of different intensities of the hunger drive on perception. *Journal of Psychology, 25,* 205–222.

McClelland, D. C., Atkinson, J. W., Clark, R. A., & Lowell, E. L. (1953). *The achievement motive.* New York: Appleton.

McCloskey, M., & Egeth, H. E. (1983). Eyewitness identification: What can a psychologist tell a jury? *American Psychologist, 38,* 550–563.

McCord, J. (1972). Some differences in the backgrounds of alcoholics and criminals. *Annals of the New York Academy of Science, 197,* 183–187.

McCormick, D. A., Clark, G. A., Lavond, D. G., & Thompson, R. F. (1982). Initial localization of the memory trace for a basic form of learning. *Proceedings, National Academy of Sciences, 79,* 2731–2735.

McCrae, R. R., & Costa, P. T. (1984). *Emerging lives, enduring dispositions: Personality in adulthood.* Boston: Little, Brown.

McCrae, R. R., & Costa, P. T., Jr. (1985). Updating Norman's "adequate taxonomy": Intelligence and personality dimensions in natural language and in questionnaires. *Journal of Personality and Social Psychology, 49,* 710–721.

McCrae, R. R., & Costa, P. T., Jr. (1987). Validation of the five-factor model of personality across instruments and observers. *Journal of Personality and Social Psychology, 52,* 81–90.

McCrae, R. R., & Costa, P. T., Jr. (1989). More reasons to adopt the five-factor model. *American Psychologist, 44,* 451–452.

McGaugh, J. L. (1983). Preserving the presence of the past. *American Psychologist, 38,* 161–174.

McGeer, P. L., & McGeer, E. G. (1980). Chemistry of mood and emotion. *Annual Review of Psychology, 31,* 273–307.

McGlashan, T. M. (1983). The borderline syndrome: I. Testing three diagnostic systems. *Archives of General Psychiatry, 40,* 1311–1318.

McGothlin, W. H., & West, L. J. (1968). The marijuana problem: An overview. *American Journal of Psychiatry, 125,* 370–378.

McGovern, L. P. (1976). Dispositional social anxiety and helping behavior under three conditions of threat. *Journal of Personality, 44,* 84–97.

McGuffin, P., Reveley, A., & Holland, A. (1982). Identical triplets: Non-identical psychosis? *British Journal of Psychiatry, 140,* 1–6.

McGuire, F. H., & Dohavio, F. C. (1986–87). Outdoor recreation participation across the lifespan: Abandonment, continuity, or liberation? *International Journal of Aging and Human Development, 24,* 87–100.

McGuire, W. J. (1985). Attitudes and attitude change. In G. Lindzey & E. Aronson (Eds.), *Handbook of social psychology.* Reading, MA: Addison-Wesley.

McHugh, M. C., Koeske, R. D., & Frieze, I. H. (1986). Issues to consider in conducting nonsexist psychological research: A guide for researchers. *American Psychologist, 41,* 879–890.

McKean, K. (1985, April). Of two minds: Selling the right brain. *Discover,* pp. 30–41, 60.

McKim, W. A. (1986). *Drugs and behavior: An introduction to behavioral pharmacology.* Englewood Cliffs, NJ: Prentice-Hall.

McLaughlin, C. L., Peikin, S., & Boile, C. (1984). Decreased pancreatic CCK receptor binding and CCK-stimulated amylase release in Jucker obese rats. *Physiology and Behavior, 32,* 961–965.

McLemore, C. W., & Benjamin, L. S. (1979). Whatever happened to interpersonal diagnosis: A psychological alternative to DSM III. *American Psychologist, 34,* 17–34.

McMurray, G. A. (1950). Experimental study of a case of insensitivity to pain. *Archives of Neurology and Psychiatry, 64,* 650.

McNamara, H. J., Long, J. B., & Wike, E. L. (1956). Learning without response under two conditions of external cues. *Journal of Comparative and Physiological Psychology, 49,* 477–480.

McNeill, D. (1972). *The acquisition of language: The study of developmental psycholinguistics.* New York: Harper and Row.

Mead, M. (1928). *Coming of age in Samoa.* New York: Morrow.

Mead, M. (1930). *Growing up in New Guinea.* New York: Morrow.

Mednick, S. A. (1962). The associative basis of creativity. *Psychological Review, 69,* 220–232.

Meichenbaum, D. (1974). *Cognitive behavior modification.* Morristown, NJ: General Learning Press.

Meichenbaum, D., & Cameron, R. (1982). Cognitive-behavior therapy. In G. T. Wilson & C. M. Franks (Eds.), *Contemporary behavior therapy: Conceptual and empirical foundations.* New York: Guilford.

Meiners, M. L., & Sheposh, J. P. (1977). Beauty or brains: Which image for your mate? *Personality and Social Psychology Bulletin, 3,* 262–265.

Melamed, B. G., Hawes, R. R., Heiby, E., & Glick, J. (1975). Use of filmed modeling to reduce uncooperative behavior of children during dental treatment. *Journal of Dental Research, 54,* 797–801.

Meltzoff, A. N. (1988). Imitation of televised models by infants. *Child Development, 59(5),* 1221–1229.

Meltzoff, A. N., & Moore, M. K. (1985). Cognitive foundations and social functions of imitation and intermodal representation in infancy. In J. Mehler & R. Fox (Eds.), *Neonate cognition: Beyond the blooming, fuzzing confusion.* Hillsdale, NJ: Erlbaum.

Meltzoff, J., & Kornreich, M. (1971, July). It works. *Psychology Today,* pp. 57–61.

Melzack, R. (1980). Psychological aspects of pain. In J. J. Bonica (Ed.), *Pain.* New York: Raven.

Mendelsohn, E., Robinson, S., Gardner, H., & Winner, E. (1984). Are preschoolers' renamings intentional category violations? *Developmental Psychology, 20,* 187–192.

Mendleson, H. H., Kuehnle, J. C., Greenberg, I., & Mello, N. K. (1976).

The effects of marijuana use on human operant behavior: Individual data. In M. C. Broude & S. Szara (Eds.), *Pharmacology of marihuana* (Vol. 2). New York: Academic Press.

Mercer, T. B., & Lewis, J. G. (1978). Using the system of multicultural assessment (SOMPA) to identify the gifted minority child. In A. Y. Baldwin, G. H. Gear, & L. J. Lucito (Eds.), *Educational planning for the gifted: Overcoming cultural, geographic, and socioeconomic barriers.* Reston, VA: Council for Exceptional Children.

Meyer, A. (1982, June). Do lie detectors lie? *Science 82*, pp. 24–27.

Meyer, R. E., & Mirin, S. M. (1979). *The brain stimulus.* New York: Plenum.

Michael, R. P., Bonsall, R. W., & Warner, P. (1974). Human vaginal secretions: Volatile fatty acid content. *Science, 186*, 1217–1219.

Michelson, L. (Ed.) (1985). Meta-analysis and clinical psychology. [Special issue.] *Clinical Psychology Review, 5*(1).

Milgram, S. (1963). Behavioral study of obedience. *Journal of Abnormal and Social Psychology, 67*, 371–378.

Milgram, S. (1974). *Obedience to authority: An experimental view.* New York: Harper & Row.

Miller, B. C. (1976). A multivariate developmental model of marital satisfaction. *Journal of Marriage and the Family, 38*, 643–657.

Miller, G. A. (1956). The magical number seven, plus or minus two: Some limits on our capacity for processing information. *Psychological Review, 63*, 81–96.

Miller, J. A. (1984, April 21). Looking out for animal research. *Science News*, p. 247.

Miller, N., & Campbell, D. (1959). Recency and primacy in persuasion as a function of the timing of speeches and measurements. *Journal of Abnormal and Social Psychology, 59*, 1–9.

Milner, B. (1959). The memory defect in bilateral hippocampal lesions. *Psychiatric Research Reports, 11*, 43–52.

Minton, H. L., & Schneider, F. W. (1980). *Differential psychology.* Monterey, CA: Brooks/Cole.

Mintz, A. (1951). Nonadaptive group behavior. *Journal of Abnormal and Social Psychology, 46*, 150–159.

Mischel, W. (1968). *Personality and assessment.* New York: Wiley.

Mischel, W. (1969). Continuity and change in personality. *American Psychologist, 24*, 1012–1018.

Mischel, W. (1977). The interaction of person and situation. In D. Magnusson & N. S. Endler (Eds.), *Personality at the crossroads: Current issues in international psychology.* Hillsdale, NJ: Erlbaum.

Mischel, W. (1979). On the interface of cognition and personality: Beyond the person-situation debate. *American Psychologist, 34*, 740–754.

Mischel, W. (1981). *Introduction to personality.* New York: Holt, Rinehart & Winston.

Mohr, J. W., Turner, R. E., & Jerry, M. B. (1964). *Pedophilia and exhibitionism.* Toronto: University of Toronto Press.

Molineux, J. B. (1985). *Family therapy: A practical manual.* Springfield, IL: Charles C. Thomas.

Mollon, J. D. (1982). Color vision. *Annual Review of Psychology, 33*, 41–85.

Monahan, L, Kuhn, D., & Shaver, P. (1974). Intrapsychic versus cultural explanations of the "fear of success" motive. *Journal of Personality and Social Psychology, 29*, 60–64.

Moncrieff, R. W. (1951). *The chemical senses.* London: Leonard Hill.

Moore, K. A. (1978). Teenage childbirth and welfare dependency. *Family Planning Perspectives, 10*, 233.

Moray, N. (1959). Attention in dichotic listening: Affective cues and the influence of instructions. *Quarterly Journal of Experimental Psychology, 11*, 56–60.

Moriarty, T. (1975). Crime, commitment and the responsive bystander:

Two field experiments. *Journal of Personality and Social Psychology, 31*, 370–376.

Morris, C. (1990). *Contemporary psychology and effective behavior* (7th ed.). Glenview, IL: Scott, Foresman.

Morris, N. M., & Udry, J. R. (1978). Pheromonal influences on human sexual behavior. *Journal of Biosocial Science, 10*, 147–159.

Morrison, A. (1983). A window on the sleeping brain. *Scientific American, 249*, 94–102.

Mortimer, J. T., Lorence, J., & Kumka, D. (1986). *Work, family and personality: Transition to adulthood.* Norwood, NJ: Ablex.

Moskowitz, B. A. (1978). The acquisition of language. *Scientific American, 239*, 92–108.

Munjack, D. J., & Kanno, P. H. (1979). Retarded ejaculation: A review. *Archives of Sexual Behavior, 8*, 139–150.

Murray, H. A. (1938). *Explorations in personality.* New York: Oxford University Press.

Murray, H. G., & Denny, J. P. (1969). Interaction of ability level and interpolated activity in human problem solving. *Psychological Reports, 24*, 271–276.

Mussen, P. H., & Jones, M. C. (1957). Self-conceptions, motivations, and interpersonal attitude of late and early maturing boys. *Child Development, 28*, 243–256.

Mussen, P. H., & Jones, M. C. (1958). The behavior-inferred motivations of late and early maturing boys. *Child Development, 29*, 61–67.

Myers, J. K., Weissman, M. M., Tischler, G. L., Holzer, C. E., III, Leaf, P. J., Orvaschel, H., Anthony, J. C., Boyd, J. H., Burke, J. D., Jr., Kramer, M., & Stoltzman, R. (1984). Six-month prevalence of psychiatric disorders in three communities. *Archives of General Psychiatry, 41*, 959–967.

Nagler, S. H. (1957). Fetishism. *Psychiatric Quarterly, 31*, 713–741.

Nahemow, L., & Lawton, M. P. (1975). Similarity and propinquity in friendship formation. *Journal of Personality and Social Psychology, 32*, 205–213.

National Center for Health Statistics (1984, December). *Monthly vital statistics report.* Hyattsville, MD: Public Health Service.

National Commission on Marijuana and Drug Abuse. (1973a). *Drug use in America: Problem in perspective.* Washington, DC: Government Printing Office.

National Commission on Marijuana and Drug Abuse. (1973b). *Drug use in America: Problem in perspective. Technical papers—appendix.* Washington, DC: Government Printing Office.

National Institute of Mental Health (1982). *Television and behavior: Ten years of scientific progress and implications for the eighties* (Vol. I. Summary Report). Rockville, MD: National Institute of Mental Health.

National Institute of Mental Health (1982). *Television and behavior: Ten years of scientific progress and implications for the eighties* (Vol. II. Technical Reviews). Rockville, MD: National Institute of Mental Health.

Neisser, U. (1982). *Memory observed: Remembering in natural contexts.* San Francisco: Freeman.

Newman, B. M. (1982). Mid-life development. In B. B. Wolman (Ed.), *Handbook of developmental psychology* (pp. 617–635). Englewood Cliffs, NJ: Prentice-Hall.

Newman, P. R. (1982). The peer group. In B. B. Wolman (Ed.), *Handbook of developmental psychology* (pp. 526–536). Englewood Cliffs, NJ: Prentice-Hall.

Nickerson, R. S., & Adams, M. J. (1979). Long-term memory for a common object. *Cognitive Psychology, 11*, 287–307.

Nielsen, G. D. & Smith, E. E. (1973). Imaginal and verbal representations in short-term recognition of visual forms. *Journal of Experimental Psychology, 101*, 375–378.

Nisbett, R. E., Fong, G. T., Lehman, D. R., & Cheng, P. W. (1987). Teaching reasoning. *Science, 238*, 625–631.

Norman, D. A. (1969). *Memory and attention*. New York: Wiley.

Norman, R. (1975). Affective-cognitive consistency, attitudes, conformity, and behavior. *Journal of Personality and Social Psychology, 32,* 83–91.

Norman, W. T. (1963). Toward an adequate taxonomy of personality attributes: Replicated factor structure in peer nomination personality ratings. *Journal of Abnormal and Social Psychology, 66,* 574–583.

Norris, P. A. (1986). On the status of biofeedback and clinical practice. *American Psychologist, 41,* 1009–1010.

Offer, D., & Offer, J. (1975). *From teenager to young manhood*. New York: Basic Books.

O'Keefe, J., & Nadel, L. (1978). *The hippocampus as a cognitive map*. London: Oxford University Press.

O'Leary, V. E., & Smith, D. (1988, August). *Sex makes a difference: Attributions for emotional cause*. Paper presented at the meeting of the American Psychological Association, Atlanta, GA.

Olson, G., Olson, R., Kastin, A., & Coy, D. (1979). Endogenous opiates: Through 1978. *Neuroscience and Biobehavioral Reviews, 3,* 285–299.

Olton, D. S., Becker, J. T., & Handelmann, G. E. (1980). Hippocampal function: Working memory or cognitive mapping. *Physiological Psychology, 8,* 239–246.

Olton, D. S., & Noonberg, A. R. (1980). *Biofeedback: Clinical applications in behavioral science*. Englewood Cliffs, NJ: Prentice-Hall.

Olton, D. S., & Samuelson, R. J. (1976). Remembrance of places passed: Spatial memory in rats. *Journal of Experimental Psychology, 2,* 97–115.

Orlofsky, J. L. (1978). Identity formation, *N* achievement, and fear of success in college men and women. *Journal of Youth and Adolescence, 7,* 49–62.

Orlofsky, J. L., Marcia, J. E., & Lesser, I. M. (1973). Ego identity status and the intimacy versus isolation crisis of young adulthood. *Journal of Personality and Social Psychology, 27,* 211–219.

Ortar, G. (1963). Is a verbal test cross-cultural? *Scripta Hierosolymitana, 13,* 219–235.

Oskamp, S. (1977). *Attitudes and opinions*. Englewood Cliffs, NJ: Prentice-Hall.

Osmond, H. (1957). A review of the clinical effects of psychotomemetic agents. *Annals of the New York Academy of Science, 66,* 418–434.

Oswald, I. (1973). Is sleep related to synthetic purpose? In W. P. Koella & P. Levin (Eds.), *Sleep: Physiology, biology, psychology, psychopharmacology, clinical implications*. Basel, Switzerland: Karger.

Oswald, I. (1974). Pharmacology of sleep. In O. Petre-Quadens & J. D. Schlag (Eds.), *Basic sleep mechanism*. New York: Academic Press.

Overmier, J. B., & Seligman, M. E. P. (1967). Effects of inescapable shock upon subsequent escape and avoidance responding. *Journal of Comparative and Physiological Psychology, 63,* 23–33.

Packard, R. G. (1970). The control of "classroom attention": A group contingency for complex behavior. *Journal of Applied Behavior Analysis, 3,* 13–28.

Palmer, J. O. (1979). *The psychological assessment of children*. New York: Wiley.

Panksepp, J. (1986). The neurochemistry of behavior. *Annual Review of Psychology, 37,* 77–107.

Paris, S. G., & Weissberg, J. A. (1986). Young children's remembering in different contexts: A reinterpretation of Istomina's study. *Child Development, 57,* 1123–1129.

Parke, R. D., & Asher, S. R. (1983). Social and personality development. *Annual Review of Psychology, 34,* 465–509.

Parker, J. G., & Asher, S. R. (1987). Peer relations and later personal adjustment: Are low-accepted children at risk? *Psychological Bulletin, 102,* 357–389.

Parkes, C. M. (1976). Components of the reaction to loss of limb, spouse, a home. *Journal of Psychosomatic Research, 16,* 343–349.

Parsons, H. M. (1974). What happened to Hawthorne? *Science, 183,* 922–932.

Patterson, F. (1978). The gestures of a gorilla: Language acquisition in another pongid. *Brain and Language, 5,* 72–97.

Patterson, F. (1980). Innovative uses of language by a gorilla: A case study. In K. E. Nelson (Ed.), *Children's language* (Vol. 2). New York: Gardner Press.

Patterson, F. (1981). *The education of Koko*. New York: Holt, Rinehart & Winston.

Pattison, E. M. (1977). *The experience of dying*. Englewood Cliffs, NJ: Prentice-Hall.

Paul, G. L. (1982). The development of a "transportable" system of behavioral assessment for chronic patients. Invited address. University of Minnesota, Minneapolis, MN.

Paul, G. L., & Lentz, R. J. (1977). *Psychosocial treatment of chronic mental patients: Milieu versus social learning programs*. Cambridge, MA: Harvard University Press.

Pavlov, I. P. (1927). *Conditioned reflexes* (G. V. Anrep, trans.). London: Oxford University Press.

Pearlin, L. I., Schooler, C. (1978). The structure of coping. *Journal of Health and Social Behavior, 19,* 2–21.

Penfield, W., & Jasper, H. H. (1954). *Epilepsy and the functional anatomy of the human brain*. Boston: Little, Brown.

Penland, J. G. Trace elements, nutrition, and sleep behavior in healthy adult women. Under review for publication in *Sleep*.

Pennebaker, J. W., & Skelton, J. A. (1981). Selective monitoring of physical sensations. *Journal of Personality and Social Psychology, 41,* 213–223.

Penrod, S. (1986). *Social psychology* (2nd ed.). Englewood Cliffs, NJ: Prentice-Hall.

Perlmutter, M., & Hall, E. (1985). *Adult development and aging*. New York: John Wiley.

Perls, F. S. (1979). *Gestalt theory verbatim*. Lafayette, CA: People Press.

Peskin, H. (1967). Pubertal onset and ego functioning. *Journal of Abnormal Psychology, 72,* 1–15.

Peskin, H. (1973). Influence on the developmental schedule of puberty on learning and ego functioning. *Journal of Youth and Adolescence, 2,* 273–290.

Petersen, A., & Taylor, B. (1980). The biological approach to adolescence: Biological change and psychological adaptation. In J. Adelson (Ed.), *Handbook of adolescent psychology*. New York: Wiley.

Peterson, L. R., & Peterson, M. J. (1959). Short-term retention of individual verbal items. *Journal of Experimental Psychology, 58,* 193–198.

Peterson, R. A. (1978). Rorschach. In O. K. Buros (Ed.), *The eighth mental measurements yearbook*. Highland Park, NJ: Gryphon.

Petty, R. E., & Cacioppo, J. T. (1981). *Attitudes and persuasion: Classic and contemporary approaches*. Dubuque, IA: Wm. C. Brown.

Petty, R. E., & Cacioppo, J. T. (1986a). The elaboration likelihood model of persuasion. In L. Berkowitz (Ed.), *Advances in experimental social psychology*, Vol. 19.

Petty, R. E., & Cacioppo, J. T. (1986b). *Communication and persuasion: Central and peripheral routes to attitude change*. New York: Springer-Verlag.

Pevnick, J., Jasinski, D. R., & Haertzen, C. A. (1978). Abrupt withdrawal from therapeutically administered diazepam. *Archives of General Psychiatry, 35,* 995–998.

Pfeiffer, E. (1977). Sexual behavior in old age. In E. W. Busse & E. Pfeiffer (Eds.), *Behavior and adaptation in late life*. Boston: Little, Brown.

Phares, E. J. (1978). Locus of control. In H. London & J. E. Exner (Eds.), *Dimensions of personality* (pp. 263–304). New York: Wiley Interscience.

Phares, E. J. (1984). *Introduction to personality*. Columbus, OH: Charles E. Merrill.

Piaget, J. (1932). *The moral development of the child.* New York: Harcourt Brace.

Piaget, J. (1967). *Six psychological studies.* New York: Random House.

Piaget, J. (1969). The intellectual development of the adolescent. In G. Caplan & S. Lebovici (Eds.), *Adolescence: Psychosocial perspectives.* New York: Basic Books.

Piaget, J., & Szeminska, A. (1952; orig. French ed. 1941). *The child's conception of number* (C. Gattegno & F. M. Hodgson, trans.). New York: Humanities Press.

Pines, Maya. (1982, September). The human difference. *Psychology Today,* pp. 62–68.

Piroleau, L., Murdock, M., & Brody, N. (1983). An analysis of psychotherapy versus placebo studies. *Behavioral and Brain Sciences, 6,* 275–310.

Plomin, R. (1989). Environment and genes, determinants of behavior. *American Psychologist, 44,* 105–111.

Plomin, R., DeFries, J. C., & McClearn, G. E. (1980). *Behavioral genetics: A primer.* San Francisco: Freeman.

Plutchik, R. (1980). *Emotion: A psychoevolutionary synthesis.* New York: Harper & Row.

Poincaré, H. (1924). *The foundations of science* (G. B. Halstead, trans.). London: Science Press.

Polivy, J., & Herman, P. (1985). Dieting and binging: A causal analysis. *American Psychologist, 40,* 193–201.

Polivy, J., Herman, C. P., Hackett, R., & Kuleshnyk, I. (1983). The effects of personal and public monitoring of consumption on eating in restrained and unrestrained subjects. Unpublished manuscript, University of Toronto.

Pope, H. G., Jonas, J. M., Hudson, J. I., Cohen, B. M., & Gunderson, J. G. (1983). The validity of DSM-III borderline personality disorder. *Archives of General Psychiatry, 40,* 23–30.

Porter, L. W., & Roberts, K. H. (1976). Communication in organizations. In M. D. Dunnette (Ed.), *Handbook of industrial and organizational psychology.* Chicago: Rand McNally.

Postman, L. (1975). Verbal learning and memory. *Annual Review of Psychology, 26,* 291–335.

Powell, D. H., & Driscoll, P. F. (1973). Middle class professionals face unemployment. *Society, 10(2),* 18–26.

Premack, D. (1971). Language in chimpanzees. *Science, 172,* 808–822.

Premack, D. (1976). *Intelligence in ape and man.* Hillsdale, NJ: Erlbaum.

Premack, D. (1983). Animal cognition. *Annuel Review of Psychology, 34,* 351–362.

Prien, R. F., Kupfer, D. J., Mansky, P. A., Small, J. G., Tuason, V. B., Voss, C. B., & Johnson, W. E. (1984). Drug therapy in the prevention of recurrences in unipolar and bipolar affective disorders. *Archives of General Psychiatry, 41,* 1096–1104.

Prince, V., & Bentler, P. M. (1972). Survey of 504 cases of transvestism. *Psychological Reports, 31,* 903–917.

Prociuk, T. J., & Breen, L. J. (1975). Defensive externality and its relation to academic performance. *Journal of Personality and Social Psychology, 31,* 549–556.

Prociuk, T. J., & Breen, L. J. (1977). Internal-external locus of control and information-seeking in a college academic situation. *Journal of Social Psychology, 101,* 309–310.

Pryor, K. (1981, April). The rhino likes violets. *Psychology Today,* pp. 92–98.

Pulaski, M. A. S. (1974, January). The rich rewards of make believe. *Psychology Today,* pp. 68–74.

Putnam, F. W. (1982, October). Traces of Eve's faces. *Psychology Today,* p. 88.

Quill, T. E. (1985). Somatization disorder: One of medicine's blind spots. *Journal of American Medical Association, 254,* 3075–3079.

Ramey, C. T., MacPhee, D., & Yeates, K. O. (1982). Preventing developmental retardation: A general systems model. In L. Bond & J. Joffe (Eds.), *Facilitating infant and early childhood development* (pp. 343–401). Hanover, NH: University Press of New England.

Rayman, P., & Bluestone, B. (1982). The private and social response to job loss: A metropolitan study. Final Report of Research sponsored by the Center for Work and Mental Health, National Institute of Mental Health.

Reder, L. M., & Anderson, J. R. (1980). A comparison of texts and their summaries: Memorial consequences. *Journal of Verbal Learning and Verbal Behavior, 19,* 121–134.

Reed, S. F., Ernst, G. W., & Banerji, R. (1974). The role of analogy in transfer between similar problem states. *Cognitive Psychology, 6,* 435–450.

Reed, S. K. (1988). *Cognition: Theory and applications.* Monterey, CA: Brooks/Cole.

Regier, D. A., Boyd, J. H., Burke, J. D., Jr., Rae, D. S., Myers, J. K., Kramer, M., Robins, L. N., George, L. K., Karno, M., & Locke, B. Z. (1988). One-month prevalence of mental disorders in United States based on 5 epidemiologic catchment area sites. *Archives of General Psychiatry, 45,* 977–986.

Reis, S. M. (1989). Reflections on policy affecting the education of gifted and talented students, past and future perspectives. *American Psychologist, 44,* 399–408.

Reisberg, B. (Ed.) (1983). *Alzheimer's disease: The standard reference.* New York: Free Press.

Reitman, J. S. (1974). Without surreptitious rehearsal, information in short-term memory decays. *Journal of Verbal Learning and Verbal Behavior, 13,* 365–377.

Renzulli, J. S. (1978). What makes giftedness? Reexamining a definition. *Phi Delta Kappan, 60,* 180–184, 216.

Reschly, D. J. (1981). Psychology testing in educational classification and placement. *American Psychologist, 36,* 1094–1102.

Rescorla, R. A. (1967). Pavlovian conditioning and its proper control procedures. *Psychological Review, 74,* 71–80.

Rescorla, R. A. (1988). Pavlovian Conditioning: It's not what you think. *American Psychologist, 43,* 151–160.

Rescorla, R. A., & Holland, P. C. (1982). Behavioral studies of associative learning in animals. *Annual Review of Psychology, 33,* 265–308.

Rescorla, R. A., & Solomon, R. L. (1967). Two-process learning theory: Relationships between Pavlovian conditioning and instrumental learning. *Psychological Review, 74,* 151–182.

Rettig, K. D., & Bubolz, M. M. (1983). Interpersonal resource exchanges as indicators of quality of marriage. *Journal of Marriage and the Family, 45,* 497–509.

Rice, B. (1979, September). Brave new world of intelligence testing. *Psychology Today,* pp. 27–38.

Rice, M. L., & Woodsmall, L. (1988, April). Lessons from television: Children's word learning when viewing. *Child Development, 59(2),* 420–429.

Riesen, A. H. (1947). The development of visual perception in man and chimpanzee. *Science, 106,* 107–108.

Riesen, A. H. (1950). Arrested vision. *Scientific American, 186,* 16–19.

Riordan, R. J., & Beggs, M. S. (1987). Counselors and self-help groups. *Journal of Counseling and Development, 65,* 427–429.

Ritchie, E., & Phares, E. J. (1969). Attitude change as a function of internal-external control and communication status. *Journal of Personality, 37,* 429–443.

Roberts, A. H. (1985). Biofeedback: Research, training, and clinical roles. *American Psychologist, 40,* 938–941.

Robins, L. N. (1966). *Deviant children grown up: A sociological and psychiatric study of sociopathic personality.* Baltimore: Williams and Wilkins.

Robins, L. N., Schoenberg, S. P., Holmes, S. J., Ratcliff, K. S., Benham, A., & Works, J. (1985). Early home environment and retrospective recall: A test for concordance between siblings with and without psychiatric disorders. *American Journal of Orthopsychiatry, 55,* 27–41.

Robinson, D. (1977). Factors influencing alcohol consumption. In G. Edwards & M. Grant (Eds.), *The pharmacological basis of therapeutics.* London: Collier Macmillan.

Robitscher, J., & Williams, R. (1977, December). Should psychiatrists get out of the courtroom? *Psychology Today,* p. 85.

Rodgers, J. L. (1988). Birth order, SAT and confluence: Spurious correlations and no causality. *American Psychologist, 43,* 476–477.

Rodgers, L. J. (1983). Family configuration and adolescent sexual behavior. *Population and Environment, 62,* 73–83.

Rodin, J. (1981a). Current status of the internal-external hypothesis for obesity. *American Psychologist, 36,* 361–371.

Rodin, J. (1981b). Understanding obesity: Defining the samples. *Personality and Social Psychology Bulletin, 7,* 147–151.

Rodin, J. (1985). Insulin levels, hunger, and food intake: An example of feedback loops in body weight regulation. *Health Psychology, 4,* 1–24.

Rodin, J., Striegel-Moore, R. H., & Silberstein, L. R. (1985, July). A prospective study of bulimia among college students on three U.S. campuses. First unpublished progress report, Yale University, New Haven, CT.

Rodon, J. (1980). Managing the stress of aging: The role of control and coping. In S. Levine & H. Ursin (Eds.), *Coping and health.* New York: Plenum.

Rofe, Y. (1984). Stress and affiliation: A utility theory. *Psychological Review, 91,* 251–268.

Rofe, Y., Hoffman, M., & Lewin, I. (1985). Patient affiliation in major illness. *Psychological Medicine, 15,* 895–896.

Rogers, C. R. (1961). *On becoming a person: A therapist's view of psychotherapy.* Boston: Houghton Mifflin.

Rogers, D. (1980). *The adult years: An introduction to aging.* Englewood Cliffs, NJ: Prentice-Hall.

Rokeach, M., & Mezei, L. (1966). Race and shared belief as factors in social choice. *Science, 151,* 167–172.

Rollins, B. C., & Feldman, H. (1970). Marital satisfaction over the life cycle. *Journal of Marriage and the Family, 32,* 20–28.

Rolls, B. J., Wood, R. J., & Rolls, E. T. (1980). The initiation, maintenance and termination of drinking. In J. M. Sprague & A. N. Epstein (Eds.), *Progress in psychobiology and physiological psychology* (Vol. 9). New York: Academic Press.

Romeo, F. (1984): Adolescence, sexual conflict, and anorexia nervosa. *Adolescence, 19,* 551–557.

Ronch, J. L. (1982). Who are these aging persons? In R. H. Hull (Ed.), *Rehabilitation audiology.* New York: Grune & Stratton.

Rosch, E. H. (1973). Natural categories. *Cognitive Psychology, 4,* 328–350.

Rosch, E. H. (1978). Principles of categorization. In E. H. Rosch & B. B. Lloyd (Eds.), *Cognition and categorization.* Hillsdale, NJ: Erlbaum.

Rosen, R. C., & Rosen, L. (1981). *Human sexuality.* New York: Knopf.

Rosenthal, D. (1970). *Genetic theory and abnormal behavior.* New York: McGraw-Hill.

Rosenthal, R., Archer, D., DiMatteo, M. R., Koivumaki, J. H., & Rogers, P. L. (1974, September). Body talk and tone of voice: The language without words. *Psychology Today,* pp. 64–68.

Rosenthal, R., Hall, J. A., Archer, D., DiMatteo, M. R., & Rogers, P. L. (1979). The PONS test: Measuring sensitivity to nonverbal cues. In S. Weitz (Ed.), *Nonverbal communication* (2nd ed.). New York: Oxford University Press.

Rosenzweig, M. R., & Leiman, A. L. (1982). *Physiological psychology.* Lexington, MA: D. C. Heath.

Ross, L. (1977). The intuitive psychologist and his shortcomings: Distortions in the attribution process. In L. Berkowitz (Ed.), *Advances in experimental social psychology* (Vol. 10). New York: Academic Press.

Rossi, E. I. (1973). The dream protein hypothesis. *American Journal of Psychiatry, 130,* 1094–1097.

Roth, D., & Rehm, L. P. (1980). Relationships among self-monitoring processes, memory, and depression. *Cognitive Therapy and Research, 4,* 149–157.

Rothbart, M., Evans, M., & Fulero, S. (1979). Recall for confirming events: Memory processes and the maintenance of social stereotypes. *Journal of Experimental Social Psychology, 15,* 343–355.

Rotter, J. B. (1954). *Social learning and clinical psychology.* Englewood Cliffs, NJ: Prentice-Hall.

Rotter, J. B. (1966). Generalized expectancies for internal versus external control of reinforcement. *Psychological Monographs, 80* (Whole No. 609).

Roznowski, M. (1988). A comment on Zajonc. *American Psychologist, 43,* 478–479.

Ruberman, J. W., Weinblatt, E., Goldberg, J. D., & Chaudhary, B. S. (1984). Psychological influences on mortality after myocardial infarction. *New England Journal of Medicine, 311,* 552–559.

Rubin, J. A., Provenzano, F. J., & Luria, A. (1974). The eye of the beholder: Parents' views on sex of newborns. *American Journal of Orthopsychiatry, 44,* 512–519.

Rubin, Z. (1983, March). Taking deception for granted. *Psychology Today,* pp. 74–75.

Rubinstein, E. (1983). Television and behavior: Research conclusions of the 1982 NIMH report and their policy implications. *American Psychologist, 38,* 820–825.

Ruble, D. N., Parsons, J. E., & Ross, J. (1976). Self-evaluative responses of children in an achievement setting. *Child Development, 47,* 990–997.

Rudd, N. M., & McKenry, P. C. (1986). Family influences on the job satisfaction of employed mothers. *Psychology of Women Quarterly, 10,* 363–372.

Rumbaugh, D. M. (1977). *Language learning by a chimpanzee.* New York: Academic Press.

Rumbaugh, D. M., von Glaserfeld, E., Warner, H., Pisani, P., & Gill, T. V. (1974). Lana (Chimpanzee) learning language: A progress report. *Brain and Language, 1,* 205–212.

Rumbaugh, D. M., & Savage-Rumbaugh, E. S. (1978). Chimpanzee language research: Status and potential. *Behavior Research Methods and Instrumentation, 10,* 119–131.

Rumelhart, D. E., & McClelland, J. L. (Eds.) (1986). *Parallel distributed processing: Explorations in the neurostructure of cognition.* Cambridge, MA: M.I.T.

Rush, A. J., Beck, A. T., Kovacs, M., & Hollon, S. D. (1977). Comparative efficacy of cognitive therapy and pharmacotherapy in the treatment of depressed outpatients. *Cognitive Therapy and Research, 1,* 17–39.

Rushton, J. P., & Endler, N. S. (1977). Person by situation interactions in academic achievement. *Journal of Personality, 45,* 297–309.

Russell, J. A., & Ward, L. M. (1982). Environmental psychology. *Annual Review of Psychology, 83,* 651–88.

Russell, M. H. A. (1976). Tobacco smoking and nicotine dependence. In R. J. Gibbins, Y. Israel, H. Kalant, R. E. Popham, W. Schmidt, & R. G. Smart, (Eds.), *Research advances in alcohol and drug problems.* New York: Wiley.

Russo, N. F. (1985). *A woman's mental health agenda.* Washington, DC: American Psychological Association.

Russo, N. F., & Sobel, S. B. (1981). Sex differences in the utilization of mental health facilities. *Professional Psychology, 12,* 7–19.

Rutter, M. (1982). Social-emotional consequences of day care for preschool children. In E. F. Zigler, & E. W. Gordon, (Eds.), *Day care: Scientific and social policy issues.* Boston: Auburn House.

Ryan, S. (1974). *A report on longitudinal evaluations of preschool programs: Vol. 1: Longitudinal evaluations* (DHEW Publications No. OHD 74–24). Washington, DC: Office of Human Development.

Rylander, G. (1969). Clinical and medico-criminological aspects of addiction to central stimulating drugs. In F. Sjoquist & M. Tottie (Eds.), *Abuse of central stimulants.* Stockholm: Almqvist & Wiksell.

Saccuzzo, D. P. (1975). What patients want from counseling and psychotherapy. *Journal of Clinical Psychology, 31,* 471–475.

Sacks, O. (1987). *The man who mistook his wife for a hat and other clinical tales.* New York: Harper & Row.

Sameroff, A. J., & Chandler, M. J. (1975). Reproductive risk and the continuum of caretaking casuality. In F. D. Horowitz (Ed.), *Review of child development research* (Vol. 4). Chicago: University of Chicago Press.

Sanford, R. N. (1937). The effects of abstinence from food upon imaginal processes: A further experiment. *Journal of Psychology, 3,* 145–159.

Sarason, I. G., & Sarason, B. R. (1987). *Abnormal psychology: The problem of maladaptive behavior* (5th ed.). Englewood Cliffs, NJ: Prentice-Hall.

Sarason, I. G., & Sarason, B. R. (1989). *Abnormal psychology: The problem of maladaptive behavior* (6th ed.). Englewood Cliffs, NJ: Prentice-Hall.

Sarason, I. G., Sarason, B. R., Potter, E. H., & Antoni, M. H. (1985). Life events, social support, and illness. *Psychosomatic Medicine, 47,* 156–163.

Satow, K. K. (1975). Social approval and helping. *Journal of Experimental Social Psychology, 11,* 501–509.

Sattler, J. M. (1975). *Assessment of children's intelligence.* New York: Holt, Rinehart, & Winston.

Sattler, J. M. (1982). *Assessment of children's intelligence and special abilities* (2nd ed.). Boston: Allyn & Bacon.

Sattler, J. M. (1988). *Assessment of children* (3rd ed.). San Diego, CA: J. M. Sattler.

Savage-Rumbaugh, S., McDonald, K., Sevcik, R. A., Hopkins, W. D., & Rubert, E. (1986). Spontaneous symbol acquisition and communicative use by pygmy chimpanzees (Pan paniscus). *Journal of Experimental Psychology: General, 115,* 211–235.

Scarr, S. (1984, May). What's a parent to do? *Psychology Today,* pp. 58–63.

Scarr, S., & Weinberg, R. (1983). The Minnesota Adoption Study: Genetic differences and malleability. *Child Development, 54,* 260–267.

Scarr-Salapatek, S., & Weinberg, R. A. (1976). IQ test performance of black children adopted by white families. *American Psychologist, 31,* 726–739.

Schachter, S. (1959). *The psychology of affiliation: Experimental studies of the sources of gregariousness.* Stanford, CA: Stanford University Press.

Schachter, S. (1971a). Some extraordinary facts about obese humans and rats. *American Psychologist, 26,* 129–144.

Schachter, S. (1971b, April). Eat, eat. *Psychology Today,* pp. 44–47, 78–79.

Schaefer, H. H., & Martin, P. L. (1966). Behavioral therapy for "apathy" of hospitalized patients. *Psychological Reports, 19,* 1147–1158.

Schaie, K. W. (1984). Midlife influences upon intellectual functioning in old age. *International Journal of Behavioral Development, 7,* 463–478.

Schally, A. V., Kastin, A. J., & Arimura, A. (1977). Hypothalamic hormones: The link between brain and body. *American Scientist, 65,* 712–719.

Schantz, C. (1975). The development of social cognition. In E. M. Hetherington (Ed.), *Review of child development* (Vol. 5). Chicago: University of Chicago Press.

Schiffman, H. R. (1982). *Sensation and perception: An integrated approach* (2nd ed.). New York: Wiley.

Schmitt, R. C. (1966). Density, health and social disorganization. *Journal of the American Institute of Planners, 32,* 39–40.

Schreiber, J. (1978). *The ultimate weapon: Terrorists and world order.* New York: Morrow.

Schroeder, S. R., Schroeder, C. S., & Landesman, S. (1987). Psychological services in educational setting to persons with mental retardation. *American Psychologist, 42,* 805–808.

Schulz, D. A. (1984). *Human sexuality* (2nd ed.). Englewood Cliffs, NJ: Prentice-Hall.

Schwartz, B. (1984). *Psychology of learning and behavior* (2nd ed.). New York: Norton.

Schwartz, G. E. (1974, April). TM relaxes some people and makes them feel better. *Psychology Today,* pp. 39–44.

Schweinhart, L. J., & Weikart, D. P. (1980). Young children grow up: The effects of the Perry Preschool Program on youths through age 15. *Monographs of the High/Scope Educational Research Foundation* (Series No. 7).

Scott, K. G., & Carran, D. T. (1987). The epidemiology and prevention of mental retardation. *American Psychologist, 42,* 801–804.

Scovern, A. W., & Kilmann, P. R. (1980). Status of electroconvulsive therapy: A review of the outcome literature. *Psychological Bulletin, 87,* 260–303.

Sears, R. R., Maccoby, E. E., & Levin, H. (1957). *Patterns of child rearing.* New York: Harper & Row.

Sejnowski, T. J., & Rosenberg, C. R. (1986). NET-talk: A parallel network that learns to read aloud. *The Johns Hopkins E. E. and C. S. Tech. Report.* JHV/EECS 86/01.

Seligman, M. E. P. (1972). Phobias and preparedness. In M. E. P. Seligman & J. L. Hager (Eds.), *Biological boundaries of learning.* Englewood Cliffs, NJ: Prentice-Hall.

Seligman, M. E. P. (1975). *Helplessness.* San Francisco: Freeman.

Selye, H. (1976). *The stress of life* (rev. ed.). New York: McGraw-Hill.

Shapiro, B. A. (1985). Recent applications of meta-analysis in clinical research. *Clinical Psychology Review, 5,* 13–34.

Shaw, J. S. (1982). Psychological androgyny and stressful life events. *Journal of Personality and Social Psychology, 43,* 145–153.

Sheldon, W. H. (1942). *The varieties of termperament.* New York: Harper & Row.

Sheldon, W. H., Stevens, S. S., & Tucker, W. B. (1970). *The varieties of human physique: An introduction to constitutional psychology.* Darien, CT: Hafner.

Shepard, R. N. (1978). Externalization of mental images and the act of creation. In B. S. Randhawa & W. E. Coffman (Eds.), *Visual learning, thinking, and communicating.* New York: Academic Press.

Shepard, R. N., & Metzler, J. (1971). Mental rotation of three-dimensional objects. *Science, 171,* 701–703.

Shields, J. (1977). Genetics and alcoholism. In G. Edwards & M. Grant (Eds.), *Alcoholism: New knowledge and new responses.* London: Croon Helm.

Shiffrin, R. M., & Cook, J. R. (1978). Short-term forgetting of item and order information. *Journal of Verbal Reasoning and Verbal Behavior, 17,* 189–218.

Shortliffe, E. H. (1976). *Computer-based medical consultations: MYCIN.* New York: American Elsevier.

Shover, L. R., Friedman, J. M., Weiler, S. J., Heiman, J. R., & LoPiccolo, J. (1982). Multiaxial problem-oriented system for sexual dysfunctions. *Archives of General Psychiatry, 39,* 614–619.

Siegel, J. M., & Steele, C. M. (1979). Noise level and social discrimination. *Personality and Social Psychology Bulletin, 5*, 95–99.

Siegel, O. (1982). Personality development in adolescence. In B. B. Wolman (Ed.), *Handbook of developmental psychology* (pp. 537–548). Englewood Cliffs, NJ: Prentice-Hall.

Siegel, R. K. (1977). Hallucinations. *Scientific American, 237*, 132–140.

Siegel, R. K. (1982). Cocaine smoking. *Journal of Psychoactive Drugs, 14*, 271–359.

Sigall, H., Page, R., & Brown, A. C. (1971). Effect of expenditure as a function of evaluation and evaluator attractiveness. *Representative Research in Social Psychology, 2*, 19–25.

Silverman, B. I. (1974). Consequences, racial discrimination, and the principle of belief congruence. *Journal of Personality and Social Psychology, 29*, 497–508.

Simmons, J., & Mares, W. (1983). *Working together: Employee participation in action.* New York: Knopf.

Simon, H. A. (1974). How big is a chunk? *Science, 165*, 482–488.

Sims, J. H., & Baumann, D. D. (1972). The tornado threat: Coping styles of the north and south. *Science, 176*, 1386–1391.

Singer, J. L. (1975). *The inner world of daydreaming.* New York: Harper Colophon.

Singer, J. L., & Singer, D. G. (1983). Psychologists look at television: Cognitive, developmental, personality, and social policy implications. *American Psychologist, 38*, 826–834.

Singular, S. (1982, October). A memory for all seasonings. *Psychology Today*, pp. 54–63.

Skeels, H. M. (1938). Mental development of children in foster homes. *Journal of Consulting Psychology, 2*, 33–43.

Skeels, H. M. (1942). The study of the effects of differential stimulation on mentally retarded children: A follow-up report. *American Journal of Mental Deficiencies, 46*, 340–350.

Skeels, H. M. (1966). Adult status of children with contrasting early life experiences. *Monographs of the Society for Research in Child Development, 31*(3), 1–65.

Skinner, B. F. (1948). "Superstition" in pigeons. *Journal of Experimental Psychology, 38*, 168–172.

Skinner, B. F. (1953). *Science and human behavior.* New York: Macmillan.

Skinner, B. F. (1957). *Verbal behavior.* Englewood Cliffs, NJ: Prentice-Hall.

Skinner, B. F. (1961). Teaching machines. *Scientific American, 223*, 9–11.

Sloane, R. B., Staples, F. R., Cristol, A. H., Yorkston, N. J., & Whipple, K. (1975). Short-term analytically oriented psychotherapy versus behavior therapy. *American Journal of Psychiatry, 132*, 373–377.

Smith, D., & Kraft, W. A. (1983). DSM-III: Do psychologists really want an alternative? *American Psychologist, 38*, 777–784.

Smith, G. P., & Gibbs, J. (1976). Cholecystokinan and satiety: Theoretic and therapeutic implications. In D. Novin, W. Wyrwicka, & G. Bray (Eds.), *Hunger: Basic mechanics and clinical implications.* New York: Raven Press.

Smith, M. L., & Glass, G. V. (1977). Meta-anaylsis of psychotherapy outcome studies. *American Psychologist, 32*, 752–760.

Smith, M. L., Glass, G. V., & Miller, T. I. (1980). *The benefits of psychotherapy.* Baltimore: Johns Hopkins University Press.

Smyser, A. A. (1982). Hospices: Their humanistic and economic value. *American Psychologist, 37*, 1260–1262.

Snyder, M., & Cunningham, M. R. (1975). To comply or not comply: Testing the self-perception explanation of the "foot-in-the-door" phenomenon. *Journal of Personality and Social Psychology, 31*, 64–67.

Snyder, M., & Swann, W. B., Jr. (1978). Behavioral confirmation in social interaction: From social perception to social reality. *Journal of Experimental Social Psychology, 14*, 148–162.

Snyder, M., & Tanke, E. D. (1976). Behavior and attitude: Some people are more consistent than others. *Journal of Personality, 44*, 501–517.

Snyder, M., Tanke, E. D., & Berscheid, E. (1976). Social perception and interpersonal behavior: On the self-fulfilling nature of social stereotypes. *Journal of Personality and Social Psychology, 35*, 656–666.

Snyder, S. H. (1977). Opiate receptors and internal opiates. *Scientific American, 236*, 44–56.

Snyderman, M., & Rothman, S. (1987). Survey of expert opinion on intelligence and aptitude testing. *American Psychologist, 42*, 137–144.

Sodano, A. G., & Baleris, G. (1983). Accommodation to contrast: Being different in the organization. In S. L. White (Ed.), *Advances in occupational mental health: New directions for mental health services.* San Francisco: Jossey-Bass.

Sommer, R. (1959). Studies in personal space. *Sociometry, 22*, 247–260.

Sontag, L. W. (1964). Implications of fetal behavior and environment for adult personalities. *Annals of the New York Academy of Science, 134*, 782–786.

Southern, S., & Gayle, R. (1982). A cognitive behavioral model of hypoactive sexual desire. *Behavioral Counselor, 2*, 31–48.

Sorensen, R. C. (1973). *Adolescent sexuality in contemporary America.* New York: World.

Spence, J. T., & Helmreich, R. L. (1983). Achievement-related motives and behaviors. In J. T. Spence (Ed.), *Achievement and achievement motives: Psychological and sociological approaches.* San Francisco: Freeman.

Sperling, G. (1960). The information available in brief visual presentations. *Psychological Monographs, 74*, 1–29.

Spero, M. (1978). Thoughts on computerized psychotherapy. *Psychiatry, 41*, 279–288.

Sperry, R. W. (1964). The great cerebral commissure. *Scientific American, 210*, 42–52.

Sperry, R. W. (1968). Hemisphere disconnection and unity in conscious awareness. *American Psychologist, 23*, 723–733.

Sperry, R. W. (1970). Perception in the absence of neocortical commissures. In *Perception and its disorders* (Res. Publ. A. R. N. M. D., Vol. 48). New York: The Association for Research in Nervous and Mental Disease.

Spettle, C. M., & Liebert, R. M. (1986). Training for safety in automated person-machine systems. *American Psychologist, 41*, 545–550.

Spezzano, C. (1981, May). Prenatal psychology: Pregnant with questions. *Psychology Today*, pp. 49–57.

Spiesman, J. C. (1965). Autonomic monitoring of ego defense process. In N. S. Greenfield & W. C. Lewis (Eds.), *Psychoanalysis and current biological thought.* Madison: University of Wisconsin Press.

Spitzer, R. L., Endicott, J., & Gibbon, M. (1979). Crossing the border into borderline personality and borderline schizophrenia. *Archives of General Psychiatry, 36*, 17–24.

Spitzer, R. L., Skodal, A. E., Gibbon, M., & Williams, J. B. W. (1981). *DSM-III case book.* Washington, DC: American Psychiatric Association.

Spitzer, R. L., Skodal, A. E., Gibbon, M., Williams, J. B. W. (1983). *Psychopathology: A casebook.* New York: McGraw-Hill.

Squire, S. (1983). *The slender balance: Causes and cures for bulimia, anorexia, and the weight-loss/weight gain seesaw.* New York: Putnam.

Stechler, G., & Halton, A. (1982). Prenatal influences on human development. In B. B. Wolman (Ed.), *Handbook of developmental psychology* (pp. 175–189). Englewood Cliffs, NJ: Prentice-Hall.

Stein, D. D., Hardyck, J. A., & Smith, M. B. (1965). Race and belief: An open and shut case. *Journal of Personality and Social Psychology, 1*, 281–289.

Steinberg, L. D., & Silverberg, S. (1986). The viscissitudes of autonomy in adolescence. *Child Development, 57*, 841–851.

Steiner, J. A. (1972). A questionnaire study of risk-taking in psychiatric patients. *British Journal of Medical Psychology, 45,* 365–374.

Steiner, J. E. (1979). Facial expressions in response to taste and smell stimulation. In H. W. Reese & L. P. Lipsitt (Eds.), *Advances in child development and behavior* (Vol. 13). New York: Academic Press.

Stellar, E. (1982). Brain mechanisms in hedonic processes. In D. W. Pfaff (Ed.), *The physiological mechanisms of motivation* (pp. 377–407). New York: Springer-Verlag.

Stern, R. M., Breen, J. P., Watanabe, T., & Perry, B. S. (1981). Effect of feedback of physiological information on responses to innocent associations and guilty knowledge. *Journal of Applied Psychology, 66,* 677–681.

Sternberg, R. J. (1981). Testing and cognitive psychology. *American Psychologist, 36,* 1081–1089.

Sternberg, R. J. (1982, April). Who's intelligent? *Psychology Today,* pp. 30–39.

Sternberg, R. J. (1985). *Beyond IQ: A triarchic theory of human intelligence.* New York: Cambridge University Pres.

Sternberg, R. J. (1986). *Intelligence applied.* Orlando, FL: Harcourt Brace Jovanovich.

Sternberg, R. J., Conway, B. E., Ketron, J. L., & Bernstein, M. (1981). People's conceptions of intelligence. *Journal of Personal and Social Psychology, 41,* 37–55.

Sternberg, R. J., & Davidson, J. E. (1985). Cognitive development in the gifted and talented. In F. D. Horowitz & M. O'Brien (Eds.), *The gifted and talented: Developmental perspectives.* Washington, DC: American Psychological Association.

Steuer, J. L., & Hammen, C. L. (1983). Cognitive-behavioral group therapy for the depressed elderly: Issues and adaptations. *Cognitive Therapy and Research, 7,* 285–296.

Stewart, R. H. (1965). Effect of continuous responding on the order effect in personality impression formation. *Journal of Personality and Social Psychology, 1,* 161–165.

Stinnett, M., Carter, L. M., & Montgomery, J. E. (1972). Older persons' perceptions of their marriages. *Journal of Marriage and the Family, 34,* 665–670.

Stock, M. B., & Smythe, P. M. (1963). Does undernutrition during infancy inhibit brain growth and subsequent intellectual development? *Archives of Disorders in Childhood, 38,* 546–552.

Stokols, D. (1972). On the distinction between density and crowding. Some implications for future research. *Psychological Review, 79,* 275–279.

Stokols, D. (1978). A typology of crowding experiences. In A. Baum & Y. Epstein (Eds.), *Human response to crowding.* Hillsdale, NJ: Erlbaum.

Stone, L. J., & Church, J. (1984). *Childhood and adolescence: A psychology of the growing person* (5th ed.). New York: Random House.

Stone, R. A., & Deleo, J. (1976). Psychotherapeutic control of hypertension. *New England Journal of Medicine, 294,* 80–84.

Stoner, J. A. F. (1961). A comparison of individual and group decisions involving risk. Unpublished master's thesis, School of Industrial Management, MIT.

Straub, R. O., Seidenberg, M. S., Bever, T. G., & Terrace, H. S. (1979). Serial learning in the pigeon. *Journal of the Experimental Analysis of Behavior, 32,* 137–148.

Straus, M. A. (1977, March). Normative and behavioral aspects of violence between spouses. Paper presented at the Symposium on Violence, Simon Fraser University.

Strickland, B. R. (1979). Internal-external expectancies and cardiovascular functioning. In L. C. Permutter & R. A. Monty (Eds.), *Choice and perceived control.* Hillsdale, NJ: Erlbaum.

Strommen, E. A., Mckinney, J. P., & Fitzgerald, H. E. (1983). *Developmental psychology: The school-aged child.* Homewood, IL: Dorsey.

Strupp, H. H., & Hadley, S. W. (1977). A tripartite model of mental health and therapeutic outcomes: With special reference to negative effects on psychotherapy. *American Psychologist, 32,* 187–196.

Strupp, H. H., & Hadley, S. W. (1979). Specific versus non-specific factors in psychotherapy: A controlled study of outcome. *Archives of General Psychiatry, 36,* 1125–1136.

Suedfeld, P. E. (1975). The benefits of boredom: Sensory deprivation reconsidered. *American Scientist, 63,* 60–69.

Suedfeld, P. E., & Borrie, R. A. (1978). Altering states of consciousness through sensory deprivation. In A. Sugerman & R. Tarter (Eds.), *Expanding dimensions of consciousness.* New York: Springer.

Sullivan, H. S. (1953). *The interpersonal theory of psychiatry.* H. S. Perry & M. L. Gawel (Eds.). New York: Norton.

Sulser, F. (1979). Pharmacology: New cellular mechanisms of antidepressant drugs. In S. Fielding & R. C. Effland (Eds.), *New frontiers in psychotropic drug research.* Mount Kisco, NY: Futura.

Suomi, S. J., & Harlow, H. F. (1977). Production and alleviation of depressive behaviors in monkeys. In J. D. Maser and M. E. P. Seligman (Eds.), *Psychopathology: Experimental models.* San Francisco: Freeman.

Swartz, J. D. (1978). Thematic apperception test (Review). In O. K. Buros (Ed.), *The eighth mental measurements yearbook* (Vol. 1). Highland Park, NJ: Gryphon.

Swensen, C. H., & Trahaug, G. (1985). Commitment and the long-term marriage relationship. *Journal of Marriage and the Family, 47,* 939–945.

Tanner, J. M. (1973). Growing up. *Scientific American, 235,* 34–43.

Taylor, S. E. (1983). Adjustment to threatening events. *American Psychologist, 38,* 1161–1173.

Terman, L. M. (1925). *Mental and physical traits of a thousand gifted children: Genetic studies of genius* (Vol. 1). Stanford, CA: Stanford University Press.

Terrace, H. S. (1979). *Nim: A chimpanzee who learned sign language.* New York: Knopf.

Thibaut, J. W., & Kelley, H. H. (1959). *The social psychology of groups.* New York: Wiley.

Thigpen, C. H., & Cleckley, H. (1954). *The three faces of Eve.* Kingsport, TN: Kingsport Press.

Thomas, A., & Chess, S. (1977). *Temperament and development.* New York: Brunner-Mazel.

Thomas, A., Chess, S., & Birch, H. G. (1970). The origin of personality. *Scientific American, 224,* 102–109.

Thompson, A. P. (1984). Emotional and sexual components of extramarital relations. *Journal of Marriage and the Family, 46,* 35–42.

Thompson, D. F., & Meltzer, L. (1964). Communication of emotional intent by facial expression. *Journal of Abnormal and Social Psychology, 68,* 129–135.

Thompson, J. K., Winnik-Berland, N., Linton, P., & Weinsier, R. (1986). Utilization of a self-adjusting light beam in assessment of body distortion in seven eating disorder groups. *International Journal of Eating Disorders, 5,* 113–120.

Thompson, R. F. (1986). The neurobiology of learning and memory. *Science, 233,* 941–947.

Thorndike, E. L. (1898). *Animal intelligence.* Psychological Review Monograph, *2* (4, Whole No. 8).

Thurstone, L. L. (1938). Primary mental abilities. *Psychometric Monographs, 1.*

Tierney, J. (1982, June). Doctor, is this man dangerous? *Science '82,* pp. 28–31.

Timiras, P. S. (1972). *Developmental physiology and aging.* New York: Macmillan.

Timiras, P. S. (1978). Biological perspectives on aging. *American Scientist, 66,* 605–613.

Tollison, C. D., & Adams, H. E. (1979). *Sexual disorders: Treatment, theory, and research.* New York: Gardner Press.

Tolman, E. C. (1938). The determiners of behavior at a choice point. *Psychological Review, 45,* 1–41.

Tolman, E. C., & Honzik, C. H. (1930). Introduction and removal of reward, and maze performance in rats. *University of California Publications in Psychology, 4,* 257–275.

Tomkins, S. S., & McCarter, R. (1964). What and where are the primary affects: Some evidence for a theory. *Perceptual and Motor Skills, 18,* 119–158.

Torgersen, S. (1983). Genetic factors in anxiety disorders. *Archives of General Psychiatry, 40,* 1085–1089.

Torrance, E. P. (1954). Leadership training to improve air-crew group performance. *USAF ATC Instructor's Journal, 5,* 25–35.

Treisman, A. M. (1960). Contextual cues in selective listening. *Quarterly Journal of Experimental Psychology, 12,* 242–248.

Treisman, A. M. (1964). Verbal cues, language and meaning in selective attention. *American Journal of Psychology, 77,* 206–219.

Tresemer, D. W. (1977). *Fear of success.* New York: Plenum.

Trice, A. D. (1986). Ethical variables? *American Psychologist, 41,* 482–483.

Trotter, R. J. (1983, August). Baby face. *Psychology Today,* pp. 12–20.

Trotter, R. J. (1986, August). Three heads are better than one. *Psychology Today,* pp. 56–62.

Tryk, H. E. (1968). Assessment in the study of creativity. In P. McReynolds (Ed.), *Advances in psychological assessment* (Vol. 1). Palo Alto, CA: Science and Behavior Books.

Tryon, R. C. (1940). Genetic differences in maze-learning abilities in rats. In *39th Yearbook, Part I.* National Society for the Study of Education. Chicago: University of Chicago Press.

Tucker, D. M. (1981). Lateral brain function, emotion, and conceptualization. *Psychological Bulletin, 86,* 1322–1338.

Tulving, E. (1972). Episodic and semantic memory. In E. Tulving & W. Donaldson (Eds.), *Organization and memory.* New York: Academic Press.

Tulving, E. (1985). How many memory systems are there? *American Psychologist, 40,* 385–398.

Tulving, E., & Patkau, J. E. (1962). Concurrent effects of contextual constraint and word frequency on immediate recall and learning of verbal material. *Canadian Journal of Psychology, 69,* 344–354.

Tupes, E. C., & Christal, R. E. (1961). Recurrent personality factors based on trait ratings. *USAF ASD Technical Report* (No. 61–97).

Turk, D. C., & Salovey, P. (1985). Cognitive structures, cognitive processes, and cognitive behavior modification: II. Judgments and inferences of the clinician. *Cognitive Therapy and Research, 9,* 19–34.

Turnbull, C. M. (1961). Observations. *American Journal of Psychology, 1,* 304–308.

Tversky, A., & Kahneman, D. (1973). Availability: A heuristic for judging frequency and probability. *Cognitive Psychology, 5,* 207–232.

Tyler, L. E. (1980). The next twenty years. *The Counseling Psychologist, 8,* 19–21.

Tyrer, P., Lee, I., & Alexander, J. (1980). Awareness of cardiac function in anxious, phobic, and hypochondriacal patients. *Psychological Medicine, 10,* 171–174.

Ullman, L. P., & Krasner, L. (1975). *A psychological approach to abnormal behavior* (2nd. ed.). Englewood Cliffs, NJ: Prentice-Hall.

Ulrich, R., & Azrin, N. (1962). Reflexive fighting in response to aversive stimulation. *Journal of Experimental Analysis of Behavior, 5,* 511–520.

Ungerer, J. A., Brody, L. R., & Zelazo, P. R. (1978). Long-term memory for speech in 2- to 4-week old infants. *Infant Behavior and Development, 1,* 177–186.

U.S. Bureau of the Census (1980). *Statistical abstract of the United States.* Washington, DC: Government Printing Office.

U.S. Bureau of the Census (1981). *Statistical abstract of the United States.* Washington, DC: Government Printing Office.

U.S. Bureau of the Census (1983). *Statistical abstract of the United States.* Washington, DC: Government Printing Office.

U.S. Bureau of the Census (1984). *Statistical abstract of the United States, 1984.* Washington, DC: Government Printing Office.

Vaillant, G. E. (1977). *Adaptation to life.* Boston: Little, Brown.

Vandenbos, G. R., DeLeon, P. H., & Pallak, M. S. (1982). An alternative to traditional medical care for the terminally ill: Humanitarian policy, and political issues in hospice care. *American Psychologist, 37,* 1245–1248.

Van Ornum, W., & Mordock, J. B. (1983). *Crisis counseling of children and adolescents.* New York: Crossroads/Continuum.

Van Putten, T., May, P. R. A., Marder, S. R., & Wittman, L. A. (1981). Subjective response to antipsychotic drugs. *Archives of General Psychiatry, 38,* 187–190.

Vaughan, E. D. (1977). Misconceptions about psychology among introductory psychology students. *Teaching of Psychology, 4,* 138–140.

Videka-Sherman, L. (1982). Effects of participation in a self-help group for bereaved parents: Compassionate friends. *Prevention in Human Services, 1*(3), 69–77.

Virkkunen, M. (1983). Insulin secretion during the glucose tolerance test in antisocial personality. *British Journal of Psychiatry, 142,* 598–604.

Vogel-Sprott, M. (1967). Alcohol effects on human behavior under reward and punishment. *Psychopharmacologia, 11,* 337–344.

Vogel-Sprott, M. (1984). Response measures of social drinking: Research implications and applications. *Journal of Studies on Alcohol, 44,* 817–836.

Vokey, J. R., & Read, J. D. (November, 1985). Subliminal messages: Between the devil and the media. *American Psychologist, 40,* 1231–1239.

Vondracek, F. W., & Lerner, R. M. (1982). Vocational role development in adolescence. In B. B. Wolman (Ed.), *Handbook of developmental psychology* (pp. 602–614). Englewood Cliffs, NJ: Prentice-Hall.

Von Frisch, K. (1974). Decoding the language of the bee. *Science, 185,* 663–668.

Wadja, I. J. (1979). Comparison between the effects of ethanol and those of opioid drugs on the metabolism of biogenic amines. In E. Majcvhrowitz & E. P. Noble (Eds.), *Biochemistry and Pharmacology of Ethanol. 1.* New York: Plenum.

Wahba, N. A., & Bridwell, L. G. (1976). Maslow reconsidered: A review of research on the need of hierarchy theory. *Organizational Behavior and Human Performance, 15,* 212–240.

Waid, W. M., & Orne, M. T. (1981). Cognitive, social, and personality processes in the physiological detection of deception. In L. Berkowitz (Ed.), *Advances in experimental social psychology* (Vol. 14). New York: Academic Press.

Waid, W. M., & Orne, M. T. (1982). The physiological detection of deception. *American Scientist, 70,* 402–409.

Waid, W. M., Orne, E. C., & Orne, M. T. (1981). Selective memory for social information, alertness, and physiological arousal in the detection of deception. *Journal of Applied Psychology, 66,* 224–232.

Walk, R. D., & Gibson, E. J. (1961). A comparative and analytical study of visual depth perception. *Psychological Monographs,* No. 75.

Walker, L. J., & Richards, B. S. (1979). Stimulating transitions in moral reasoning as a function of state of cognitive development. *Developmental Psychology, 15,* 95–103.

Walker, L. S., & Green, J. W. (1986). The social context of adolescent self-esteem. *Journal of Youth and Adolescence, 15,* 315–322.

Walker, N., Jones, J. P., & Mar, H. H. (1983). Encoding processes and recall of text. *Memory and Cognition, 11,* 275–282.

Walker, P. C., & Johnson, R. F. Q. (1974). The influence of presleep suggestions on dream content: Evidence and methodological problems. *Psychological Bulletin, 81,* 362–370.

Wallace, R. K., & Benson, H. (1972). The physiology of meditation. *Scientific American, 227,* 84–90.

Wallach, M. A., & Wing, C. W., Jr. (1969). *The talented student.* New York: Holt, Rinehart & Winston.

Walster, E., Aronson, V., Abrahams, D., & Rottmann, L. (1966). Importance of physical attractiveness in dating behavior. *Journal of Personality and Social Psychology, 4,* 508–516.

Wang, G. H. (1923). The relation between spontaneous activity and oestrous cycle in the white rat. *Comparative Psychology Monographs, 49,* 15–19.

Warr, P., & Parry, G. (1982). Paid employment and women's psychological well-being. *Psychological Bulletin, 91,* 498–516.

Wasserman, E. A., Kledinger, R. E., & Bhatt, R. S. (1988). Conceptual behavior in pigeons: Categories, subcategories, and pseudocategories. *Journal of Experimental Psychology: Animal Behavior Processes, 14,* 219–324.

Wasson, R. G. (1972). The divine mushroom of immortality. In P. T. Furst (Ed.), *Flesh of the gods.* New York: Praeger.

Waterman, C. K., Buebel, M. E., & Waterman, A. S. (1970). Relationship between resolution of the identity crisis and outcomes of previous psychosocial crises. *Proceedings for the Annual Convention of the American Psychological Association, 5* (Pt. I), 467–468.

Waters, E., Wippman, J., & Sroufe, L. (1979). Attachment, positive affect, and competence in the peer group: Two studies in construct validation. *Child Development, 50,* 821–829.

Watkins, L. R., & Mayer, D. J. (1982). Organization of opiate and non-opiate pain control systems. *Science, 216,* 1185–1192.

Watson, D. L., & Tharp, R. G. (1985). *Self-directed behavior* (4th ed.). New York: Norton.

Watson, J. B. (1919). *Psychology from the standpoint of a behaviorist.* Philadelphia: Lippincott.

Watson, J. B. (1930). *Behaviorism.* New York: Norton.

Watson, J. B., & Rayner, R. (1920). Conditioned emotional reactions. *Journal of Experimental Psychology, 3,* 1–14.

Watson, J. S. (1971). Cognitive-perceptual development in infancy: Setting for the seventies. *Merrill-Palmer Quarterly, 12,* 139–152.

Weil, A. (1972, October). The open mind. *Psychology Today,* pp. 51–56.

Weil, A., & Zinberg, N. E. (1969). Acute effects of marihuana on speech. *Nature, 222,* 434–437.

Weiner, I. B. (1982). *Child and adolescent psychopathology.* New York: Wiley.

Weinstein, S. (1968). Intensive and extensive aspects of tactile sensitivity as a function of body part, sex, and laterality. In D. R. Kenshalo (Ed.), *The skin senses.* Springfield, IL: Charles C Thomas.

Weiss, J. M., Glazer, H. I., & Pohorecky, L. A. (1975). Coping behavior and neurochemical changes: Alternative explanation for the original "learned helplessness" experiments. In G. Serban & A. Ling (Eds.), *Relevance of the animal model to the human.* New York: Plenum.

Weissberg, J. A., & Paris, S. G. (1986). Young children's remembering in different contexts: A reinterpretation of Istomina's study. *Child Development, 57,* 1123–1129.

Werker, J. F. (1989). Becoming a native listener. *American Scientist, 77,* 54–59.

Wexler, D. B. (1973). Token and taboo: Behavior modification, token economies, and the law. *California Law Review, 61,* 81–109.

White, J., Davison, G. C., & White, M. (1985). Cognitive distortions in the articulate thoughts of depressed patients. Unpublished manuscript, University of Southern California, Los Angeles, CA.

Whitehurst, G. J. (1982). Language development. In B. B. Wolman (Ed.), *Handbook of developmental psychology* (pp. 367–386). Englewood Cliffs, NJ: Prentice-Hall.

Whyte, W. H. (1956). *The organization man.* New York: Simon & Schuster.

Whorf, B. L. (1956). *Language, thought, and reality.* New York: M.I.T. Press-Wiley.

Wickelgren, W. A. (1974). *How to solve problems: Elements of a theory of problems and problem solving.* San Francisco: Freeman.

Wickelgren, W. A. (1977). *Learning and memory.* Englewood Cliffs, NJ: Prentice-Hall.

Wickelgren, W. A. (1979). *Cognitive psychology.* Englewood Cliffs, NJ: Prentice-Hall.

Wicker, A. (1969). Attitudes versus actions: The relationship of verbal and overt behavioral responses to attitude objects. *The Journal of Social Issues, 25,* 1–78.

Widom, C. S. (1978). A methodology for studying noninstitutionalized psychopaths. In R. D. Hare & D. A. Schalling (Eds.), *Psychopathic behavior: Approaches to research.* Chichester, Eng.: Wiley.

Wielkiewicz, R. M., & Calvert, C. R. X. (1989). *Training and Habilitating Developmentally Disabled People: An Introduction.* Newbury Park, CA: Sage Publications.

Wiens, A. N., & Menustik, C. E. (1983). Treatment outcome and patient characteristics in an aversion therapy program for alcoholism. *American Psychologist, 38,* 1089–1096.

Wiesel, T. N., & Hubel, D. H. (1963). Effects of visual deprivation on morphology and physiology of cells in the cat's geniculate body. *Journal of Neurophysiology, 26,* 978–993.

Wilcoxon, H. C., Dragoin, W. B., & Kral, P. A. (1971). Illness-induced aversions in rat and quail: Relative salience of visual and gustatory cues. *Science, 171,* 826–828.

Wilks, J. (1986). The relative importance of parents and friends in adolescent decision making. *Journal of Youth and Adolescence, 15,* 323–334.

Williams, J. H. (1977). *Psychology of women: Behavior in a biosocial context.* New York: W. W. Norton.

Williams, J. H. (1987). *Psychology of women: Behavior in a biosocial context* (3rd ed.). New York: W. W. Norton.

Williams, M. D. (1976). Retrieval from very long-term memory. Unpublished doctoral dissertation, University of California, San Diego.

Willis, S. L. (1985). Towards an educational psychology of the elder adult learner: Intellectual and cognitive bases. In J. E. Birren & K. W. Schaie (Eds.), *Handbook of the psychology of aging* (2nd ed.). New York: Van Nostrand.

Willis, S. L., & Schaie, K. W. (1986). Training the elderly on the ability factors of spatial orientation and inductive reasoning. *Psychology and Aging, 1,* 239–247.

Wilson, D. W., & Donnerstein, E. (1976). Legal and ethical aspects of nonreactive social psychological research: An excursion into the public mind. *American Psychologist, 31,* 765–773.

Wilson, G. T., & O'Leary, K. D. (1980). *Principles of behavior therapy.* Englewood Cliffs, NJ: Prentice-Hall.

Wilson, R. S. (1983). The Louisville Twin Study: Developmental synchronies in behavior. *Child Development, 54,* 298–316.

Wilson, T. D., Goldin, J. C., & Charbonneau-Powis, M. (1983). Comparative efficacy of behavioral and cognitive treatments of depression. *Cognitive Therapy and Research, 7,* 111–124.

Wimer, R. E., & Wimer, C. C. (1985). Animal behavior genetics: A search for the biological foundations of behavior. *Annual Review of Psychology, 36,* 171–218.

Wincze, J. P., Hoon, E. F., & Hoon, P. W. (1978). Multiple measure analysis of women experiencing low sexual arousal. *Behavior Research and Therapy, 16,* 43–49.

Winograd, T. (1972). *Understanding natural langugage.* New York: Academic Press.

Winter, D. G. (1973). *The power motive.* New York: Free Press.

Winter, D. G. (1976, July). What makes the candidates run? *Psychology Today,* pp. 45–49, 92.

Witkin, A. H., Dyk, R. B., Faterson, H. F., Goodenough, D. R., & Karp, S. A. (1962). *Psychological differentiation.* New York: Wiley.

Wolberg, L. R. (1977). *The technique of psychotherapy* (3rd ed.). New York: Grune and Stratton.

Wolf, M., Mees, H., & Risley, T. (1964). Application of operant conditioning procedures to the behavior problems of an autistic child. *Behavior Research Therapy, 1,* 305–312.

Wolfe, L. (1978, June). Why some people can't love. *Psychology Today,* p. 55.

Wolff, C. T., Friedman, S. B., Hofer, M. A., & Mason, J. W. (1964). Relationship between psychological defenses and mean urinary 17-hydroxycorticosteroid excretion rates: I. A study of parents of fatally ill children. *Psychosomatic Medicine, 26,* 576–591.

Wolman, B. B. (Ed.) (1978). *Psychological aspects of gynecology and obstetrics.* Oradell, NJ: Medical Economics.

Wolpe, J. (1973). *The practice of behavior therapy* (2nd ed.). New York: Pergamon.

Wolpe, J. (1982). *The practice of behavior therapy* (3rd ed.). New York: Pergamon.

Wolpe, J., & Rachman, S. (1960). Psychoanalytic evidence: A critique of Freud's case of little Hans. *Journal of Nervous and Mental Diseases, 130,* 198–220.

Wood, P. B. (1962). Dreaming and social isolation. Unpublished doctoral dissertation, University of South Carolina.

Woodhead, M. (1988). When psychology informs public policy, the case of early childhood intervention. *American Psychologist, 43,* 443–454.

Worchel, S., & Cooper, J. (1983). *Understanding social psychology* (2nd ed.). Homewood, IL: Dorsey Press.

Yamamoto, K., & Chimbidis, M. E. (1966). Achievement, intelligence, and creative thinking in fifth grade children: A correlational study. *Merrill-Palmer Quarterly, 12,* 233–241.

Young, P. (1983, August). A conversation with Richard Jed Wyatt. *Psychology Today,* pp. 36–41.

Zabin, L. S., Kanter, J. F., & Zelnik, M. (1979). The risk of adolescent pregnancy in the first months of intercourse. *Family Planning Perspectives, 10,* 205.

Zabrucky, K., Moore, D., & Schultz, N. R., Jr. (1987). Evaluation of comprehension in young and old adults. *Developmental Psychology, 22,* 39–43.

Zacks, R. T., Hasher, L., Sanft, H., & Rose, K. C. (1983). Encoding effort and recall: A cautionary note. *Journal of Experimental Psychology: Learning, Memory, and Cognition, 9,* 747–756.

Zaidel, E. (1983). A response to Gazzaniga: Language in the right hemisphere, convergent perspectives. *American Psychologist, 38,* 542–546.

Zajonc, R. B. (1980). Feeling and thinking: Preferences need no inferences. *American Psychologist, 35,* 151–175.

Zajonc, R. B. (1984). On the primacy of affect. *American Psychologist, 39,* 117–129.

Zajonc, R. B. (1986). The decline and rise of scholastic aptitude scores: A prediction derived from the confluence model. *American Psychologist, 41,* 862–867.

Zajonc, R. B., & Markus, G. B. (1975). Birth order and intellectual development. *Psychological Review, 82,* 74–88.

Zajonc, R. B., Murphy, S. T., & Inglehart, M. (1989). Feeling and facial efference: Implications of the vascular theory of emotion. *Psychological Review, 96.*

Zamansky, H. S., & Bartis, S. P. (1985). The dissociation of an experience: The hidden observer observed. *Journal of Abnormal Psychology, 94,* 243–248.

Zelnick, M., & Kantner, J. F. (1978). First pregnancies to women 15–19; 1976 and 1981. *Family Planning Perspectives, 10,* 11–20.

Zerbin-Rüdin, E. (1972). Genetic research and the theory of schizophrenia. *International Journal of Mental Health, 1,* 42–62.

Zigler, E., & Berman, W. (1983). Discerning the future of early childhood intervention. *American Psychologist, 38,* 894–901.

Zimbardo, P. G. (1969). The human choice: Individuation, reason, and order versus deindividuation, impulse, and chaos. In N. J. Arnold & D. Levine (Eds.), *Nebraska symposium on motivation.* Lincoln: University of Nebraska Press.

Zuckerman, M. (1979). Attribution of success and failure revisited, or: The motivational bias is alive and well in attribution theory. *Journal of Personality, 47,* 245–287.

Zuckerman, M., & Wheeler, L. (1975). To dispel fantasies about the fantasy-based measure of fear of success. *Psychological Bulletin, 82,* 932–946.

Zwislocki, J. J. (1981). Sound analysis in the ear: A history of discoveries. *American Scientist, 245,* 184–192.

Photo Credits

The Seattle Post Intelligencer, 545; James Kamp/Black Star, 549; Irene Springer, 553; Bettmann Newsphotos, 557.

CHAPTER 15

Dan McCoy/Rainbow, 562; Photo by Edmund Engelman, 565; Picture collection, the Branch Libraries, New York Public Library, 565; The Bettmann Archive, 569; American Cancer Society, 573; Courtesy Dr. Albert Bandura, 575 Courtesy of Aaron T. Beck, 575; Jim Pickerell/FPG International, 577; Joseph Nettis/Photo Researchers, 577; Courtesy the William Alanson White Institute, 578; Richard Hutchings/Photo Researchers, 582; Photo C. Andy Freeberg, 584; Louis Fernandez/Black Star, 585; Eric Roth/The Picture Cube, 588; Laima Druskis, 589; Mark Antman/The Image Works, 590.

CHAPTER 16

Lynn Johnson/Black Star, 600; The Picture Cube, 602; Michal Heron/Woodfin Camp & Associates, 603; Gail Greig/ Monkmeyer Press, 607; Mimi Forsyth/Monkmeyer Press, 607; Laima Druskis, 609; Lawrence Migdale/Photo Researchers, 609; Stan Wakefield, 611; Jacques M. Chenet/Woodfin Camp & Associates, 611; Laima Druskis, 617; Jim Chasmen/Black Star, 618; UPI/Bettmann Newsphotos, 620; AP/Wide World Photos, 621; Frank Siteman/Stock, Boston, 623; AP/Wide World Photos, 623; UPI/Bettmann Newsphotos, 625; Ray Ellis/Photo Researchers, 627; UPI/Bettmann Newsphotos, 629; Four By Five, 630; L. Fisher/Custom Medical Stock Photo, 632; Bill Stanton/ International Stock Photo, 634.

Glossary Index

Extinction, 185
Extrovert, 455

Factor analysis, 465
Family studies (genetic), 66
Family therapy, 577
Fantasy period, 386
Fetishism, 545
Fetus, 336
Fictional finalism, 457
Figure, 108
Fixation, 452
Fixed-interval schedule, 196
Fixed-ratio schedule, 197
Forebrain, 44
Foreclosure, 376
Formal operations, 377
Fovea, 80
Fraternal twins, 67
Free association, 565
Free nerve endings, 103
Frequency (of sound), 92
Frequency distribution, 642
Frequency histogram, 643
Frequency polygon, 643
Frequency theory of hearing, 98
Frigidity, 544
Frontal lobes, 45
Frustration, 495
Fully functioning person, 463
Functional fixedness, 268
Functionalist theory, 5
Fundamental attribution error, 606

Ganglion cells, 84
Gate control theory of pain, 106
Genes, 63
Genetics, 63
Genital stage, 455
Gestalt psychology, 7
Gestalt therapy, 579
Giftedness, 321
Glucagon, 60
Glucose, 411
Gonads, 61
Graded potential, 35
Grammar, 278
Grasping reflex, 338
Ground, 108
Group tests, 304
Group therapy, 577
Growth spurt, 371

Hallucinations, 551
Hallucinogens, 167
Hammer (middle ear), 94
Hawthorne effect, 627
Hertz (Hz), 92
Heuristics, 264
Higher-order conditioning, 187
Hill-climbing, 264
Hindbrain, 43
Hippocampus, 54
Homeostasis, 409
Hormones, 58
Hue, 86
Humanistic personality theory, 462
Humanistic psychology, 8
Hypnosis, 152
Hypochondriasis, 535
Hypothalamus, 44
Hypothesis, 15

Icon, 221
Id, 451

Identical twins, 67
Identification, 504
Identity, 375
Identity achievers, 375
Identity diffusion, 376
Image, 256
Impotence, 544
Imprinting, 354
Incentive, 410
Independent variable, 16
Industrial/organizational (I/O) psychology, 626
Inferiority complex, 457
Information retrieval, 263
Inhibited orgasm, 544
Inhibited sexual desire, 544
Inhibited sexual excitement, 544
Insight, 205, 566
Insight therapy, 564
Insomnia, 148
Instinct, 409
Instrumental conditioning, 188
Insulin, 60
Intellectualization, 505
Intelligence, 295
Intelligence quotient (IQ), 301
Intelligence tests, 295
Interference theory, 230
Intermittent pairing, 184
Interneurons, 34
Interpersonal theory, 578
Interstimulus interval, 183
Interval scale, 641
Introvert, 455
Ions, 34
Iris, 79
Irrational people, 456

James-Lange theory of emotion, 435
Just noticeable difference (jnd), 78
Just world hypothesis, 607

Krause bulb, 103

Latency period, 454
Latent learning, 203
Law of effect, 191
Learned helplessness, 208
Learning, 178
Learning set, 207
Lens, 80
Libido, 452
Life instincts, 451
Light adaptation, 83
Limbic system, 53
Linear perspective, 116
Linguistic relativity hypothesis, 285
Locus of control, 469
Longitudinal method, 335
Long-term memory (LTM), 234
LSD (lysergic acid diethylamide), 167

Mania, 540
Marijuana, 169
Marital therapy, 577
Maturation, 339
Mean, 641
Means-end analysis, 266
Median, 641
Meditation, 151
Medulla, 43
Meissner corpuscle, 103
Menarche, 372
Menopause, 385

Mental retardation, 319
Midbrain, 44
Mid-life transition, 387
Minnesota Multiphasic Personality Inventory (MMPI), 476
Mnemonics, 245
Mnemonist, 244
Mode, 642
Modeling, 574
Monaural cue, 120
Monochromats, 90
Monocular cues, 116
Moratorium, 376
Morphemes, 277
Motion parallax, 119
Motive, 408
Motor neurons, 34
Motor projection areas, 44
Multiple personality disorder, 537
Myelin sheath, 33

Narcissistic personality disorder, 547
Narcolepsy, 149
Naturalistic observation, 14
Negative reinforcer, 193
Negative transference, 566
Neonate, 337
Nerve, 33
Nervous system, 32
Neural impulse, 35
Neuron, 33
Neurotic trends, 458
Neurotransmitters, 38
Nodes, 36
Nominal scale, 640
Noncompensatory model, 274
Non-REM sleep, 142
Nonspectral color, 88
Norepinephrine, 38
Normal curve, 644

Obedience, 618
Objective tests, 476
Object permanence, 347
Observational learning, 210
Obsessive-compulsive disorder, 531
Occipital lobe, 47
Oedipus complex, 453
Olfactory bulb, 99
Olfactory epithelium, 99
Operant behavior, 188
Operant conditioning, 188
Operations, 298
Opiates, 162
Opponent-process theory, 90
Optic chiasm, 85
Optic nerve, 84
Oral stage, 452
Ordinal scale, 640
Organ of Corti, 95
Orgasm, 544
Oval window, 95
Overtones, 93

Pacinian corpuscle, 103
Pancreas, 60
Panic attack, 531
Papillae, 100
Paradoxical heat, 104
Paradoxical sleep, 142
Paranoid personality disorder, 547
Paranoid schizophrenia, 551
Paraphilias, 545
Parasympathetic division, 58
Parathormone, 60

Parathyroids, 60
Parietal lobe, 47
Pedophilia, 546
Peer group, 376
Perception, 76
Perceptual constancy, 110
Perceptual illusion, 123
Performance standards, 472
Performance tests, 304
Peripheral nervous system, 42
Persona, 455
Personality, 450
Personality disorders, 546
Personality traits, 464
Personal space, 630
Personal unconscious, 455
Person-centered therapy, 568
Person variables, 473
Phallic stage, 453
Pheromones, 417
Phi phenomenon, 123
Phobia, 532
Phobic disorder, 532
Phonemes, 277
Physical illusion, 123
Pitch, 92
Pituitary gland, 60
Placebo, 156
Placenta, 336
Place theory, 98
Pleasure principle, 451
Polarization, 34, 623
Polygenic inheritance, 64
Pons, 43
Positive reinforcer, 193
Positive transference, 566
Posterior pituitary, 60
Posttraumatic stress disorder, 531
Power motive, 428
Prenatal development, 336
Pressure, 495
Primacy effect, 603
Primary colors, 89
Primary drive, 410
Primary prevention, 590
Primary-process thinking, 451
Primary reinforcer, 193
Proactive interference, 238
Problem representation, 261
Procedural memory, 234
Products, 298
Projection, 504
Projective tests, 479
Prototype, 259
Proximity, 607
Psychoanalysis, 7, 451, 564
Psychoanalytic model of abnormal behavior, 528
Psychology, 2
Psychophysiological disorder, 536
Psychosurgery, 584
Psychotherapy, 564
Puberty, 372
Punishment, 197
Pupil, 79

Random sample, 651
Range, 646
Rational-emotive therapy (RET), 569
Rational people, 455
Ratio scale, 641
Reaction formation, 505
Realistic choice period, 387
Reality principle, 451
Receptor cell, 80
Receptor site, 38
Recessive gene, 64

Subject Index